HUMAN DEVELOPMENT

THE SPAN OF LIFE

HUMAN DEVELOPMENT

THE SPAN OF LIFE

GEORGE KALUGER, Ph.D.
Shippensburg University,
Shippensburg, Pennsylvania

MERIEM FAIR KALUGER, Litt.M.
Psychologist and Educational Consultant,
Shippensburg, Pennsylvania

THIRD EDITION
with 260 illustrations

Merrill Publishing Company
A Bell & Howell Company
Columbus Toronto London Sydney

Assistant editor: Catherine H. Converse
Manuscript editors: Mary Gleason, Sylvia B. Kluth
Design: Nancy Steinmeyer
Production: Teresa Breckwoldt, Jeanne A. Gulledge
Cover Art: *Spectrum,* Courtesy of Paul Jenkins

THIRD EDITION

Library of Congress Catalog Card Number: 83-13241
International Standard Book Number: 0-675-20604-9
Printed in the United States of America

2 3 4 5 6 7 8 9 10 - 91 90 89 88 87 86

To

our parents

who, by precepts and examples,
taught us the joy of living, the goodness
of man, and the love of God.

PREFACE

Every so often, in our personal and professional lives, we have a need to grow. We feel a need to venture out into the world in order to get a significant perspective concerning human development. For us, growth comes through travel, study, and writing. If we do nothing more than read what others have said, we are stifled in our own creativity and growth because we can only reflect the thinking of others. To be on the fine edge of knowledge, we must constantly be involved. We know we cannot be on the leading edge of research in all areas of human development, but we believe we should be able to recognize the trends, report them, and in some respects contribute to them. We travel in order to observe people in various cultures so we can extend our horizons; we read and study so we can be aware of what others are developing in the field; we write because in so doing we are forced to digest, condense, and internalize new information so that we will be able to report it in a meaningful, understanding way to our readers.

According to the reviewers, this third edition is substantially different from the previous editions and definitely upgraded. The first edition, written 10 years ago, was intended for the students and their cohorts of the seventies. The second edition, in which major changes were made, had a somewhat "transitional" growth and development look. The third edition is for today's approach to human development; it has a stronger conceptual format than the second edition, more social and developmental issues, and some of the new research. As a simple illustration of the changes that have occurred in human development, this third edition has a reference list of over 1,200 entries, which represents an increase of more than 60% in the number of additional references, as compared to the second edition. There is a tremendous change in the quality and quantity of references.

We continue to use the chronological age-stage format, being careful to note the limitations of such an approach. It is our intent to humanize and personalize the content of the growth and development topics presented in this introductory life-span book. A prime observation in the teaching of a life-span development course is that students want to learn about themselves and about people they know. Older students say, "I can see my children in that chapter"; younger students comment, "I now can understand my parents or grandparents better"; all students say "I see myself in the information in the book." Many students indicate that they plan to keep the book for future reference.

Our goal has been to be responsive to student interest without sacrificing the data-based information and scholarship so important to the discriminating instructor. There are only occasional descriptive comments, fewer generalizations, and much more conceptual-based material than was presented previously. The book has been enhanced for both student and instructor without losing the "charm" of the individual. We care about both the individual and the ideas. The content is professional and neutral. Eclecticism is used because we believe that no one paradigm or theoretical approach is comprehensive enough to cover the vast area of life-span psychology.

This book is intended for those individuals who need or want to understand the unique characteristics of individuals at different stages of life. The text has been used in human development and related courses in the fields of psychology, home and family life, home economics, the health services—especially nursing and practical nursing, social sciences and social work, teacher education, family studies and services, counseling, occupational therapy, and physical therapy. The book is written especially for the student who will probably take only one course in human development or the individual in society.

There are two approaches to the study of human development, topical and chronological. The topical approach provides a format for presenting in a chapter or so a single major topic of development behavior. Some instructors prefer the topical structure. This book is not for them. Our chronological approach does provide depth—but as threads that flow through each age stage of the life span. We prefer this type of organization because it does not fragment or lose sight of the individual.

The first two chapters present principles, theories, and determinants that provide a preliminary foundation. Then these ideas are expanded where they are relevant to a specific age stage. For example, the cognitive theory of Piaget is introduced in Chapter 2. It is then developed in depth in the chapters on infancy (sensorimotor stage), early childhood (preoperational stage), middle childhood (concrete stage), adolescence (formal operations), and adulthood (new views on Piagetian theory for adults). The same type of theoretical threads are used to elaborate other major theories. The fundamental context core that runs throughout the book is based on the five domains of development: physical, cognitive, social, emotional (including personality), and moral, with an accent on the continuity of threads from one age stage to the next. There is better balance of physiological and psychological material than there was in the second edition.

The chronological approach permits the inclusion of a wider variety of topics, including relevant social, health, and contemporary issues. The reader will find a comprehensiveness of coverage with an even balance across the life span. More details have been provided in the chapters on prenatal development, birth, infancy, and early childhood. The middle and late childhood and adolescent chapters have been given stronger support by introducing material from several disciplines, such as psychology, sociology, anthropology, biology, genetics, and medicine, as well as cross-cultural observation. The five chapters on adulthood have been enhanced by current material. Life span is not just the span of an individual life but the life span of a family. Family interaction is presented at all age levels.

Specific changes in the third edition

1. A better structure in Chapter 1 has been provided for the theoretical approaches to human development based on the theories of physiological maturation, the cognitive developmental view, behaviorism and social learning, psychoanalytical theory, and humanism. A critique is presented for each theory. The critique concept is used throughout the text. The metaphysical section in Chapter 2 has been given support from the literature.
2. A readable section on the significance of life-span research methods, the interpretation of statistics, and cohort differences and their research application has been added to Chapter 1.
3. There is expanded coverage on influences on prenatal development, including influence of the father. New material on prenatal medical technology is presented in the chapter on prenatal development.
4. A section on preparing for birth and "prepared childbirth," with expanded coverage of the Lamaze method, the use of anesthetics, and perinatal assessment techniques, is given in the chapter on birth.
5. The developmental tasks presented in all of the age-stage chapters include not only those of Havighurst but also, where appropriate, those of Erikson, White, Peck, Levinson, and others.
6. Presentation of the theories of Piaget, Erikson, and Kohlberg has been expanded at all age levels. The theories of Bruner, Selman, Hoffman, Gilman, Levinson, and Gould have been added as deemed appropriate.
7. Major additions, including the information-processing model and the mental-operations model, have been made in Chapters 7 and 8. The presentation of learning, of memory, and of learning disabilities has been improved.
8. The psychoanalytic, humanistic, and behavioristic-social learning theories as they relate to personality development are presented in greater depth in Chapter 6 on infancy.
9. Theories of attachment, language, and moral development have been added to infancy and early childhood chapters.
10. Patterns of parenting have been included; material

on the one-parent family and birth-order research as it relates to childhood has been revised. Throughout the book the focus is on the family.

11. The chapters on adolescence have been restructured, presenting a better data-based balance and less stereotyping. Contemporary issues of teenage childbearing, chemical substance use and abuse, adolescent aggression, psychopathology (including personality disorders, suicide, and anorexia nervosa) have been added. The material relating to morality, spirituality, and religion has been either eliminated or given a data base.
12. The chapter on emerging adulthood has been completely rewritten, laying a foundation for the study of adulthood with such topical threads as theories of adulthood, career and vocational development, moral development, concepts of adult maturity, and phases of adulthood.
13. A major section has been added to early adulthood on parenting, divorce, and life crisis and stress. The section on the choice to remain single has been expanded. There is new material on women in all of the chapters on adulthood.
14. Major changes in middle adulthood include personality changes and midlife, cognition and achievement, parenting and grandparenting at midlife, and vocational status. There is a flow of vocational and work issues throughout adulthood.
15. The chapters on later adulthood have either been added to or expanded in the areas of health maintenance, educational pursuits, diseases and causes of death, the time of retirement, growing old while never married, housing and living arrangements, and hospice care.
16. The Appendix includes an extensive table on birth defects.

Learning aids and features

Many who take the life-span human development course are students who have little or no background in psychology. With this observation in mind, we have included several learning features and aids to help the student. We operate on the principle that a *good* teacher (or writer) is one who can present difficult material in a way that students find easy to learn.

Writing style. We made an effort to present the material so that it would be clear, smooth, and easy to read. Attention should be paid to the main headings and subheadings; they indicate which topics will be discussed. Chapters are introduced with a vignette to help the student focus on the reading. Then a short overview is presented to provide a mind-set of what is coming.

Key words. The most important part of any course is the vocabulary of the subject. We have treated this element in the most comprehensive way possible. *First,* these key words are presented in boldface italics in the text. They are also highlighted and defined in a separate area on the page where they are first used. *Second,* many are explained or illustrated by examples. *Third,* they are identified in the Chapter Review along with the appropriate material. *Fourth,* these key words, as well as others, are presented in the Glossary. This emphasis on vocabulary assimilation will also assist the student in identifying essential concepts.

Chapter review. Each chapter has an extensive review section. The facts and principles are numbered instead of being presented in summary paragraphs. The key words are in italics.

Review questions. A complete list of questions and learning activities is presented at the end of each chapter, identifying what should have been learned from the chapter. Some of the answers to the questions may be long because many of the items are written as essay questions.

Thought questions and activities. This additional section is intended to expand the thinking of the student and the class concerning the information from the chapter. These questions or activities should challenge the students to do more thinking and investigating.

Further readings. Several types of readings are suggested. Some are articles, others are chapters, and some are books. All are annotated. There are always two or three recent research articles to help the students become more data-base oriented in their thinking.

Vignettes and profiles. Each chapter begins with a vignette, which is set off in a distinctive type and is easily identifiable. Except for Chapters 1 and 2, *these vignettes have all been written by students.* The reason for including them is that, in addition to being interesting, they either illustrate the material studied or help make it relevant and meaningful. A number of chapters also include a profile from the book *Pacific Profiles* so that the students can extend their thinking with a cross-cultural view of a common occurrence. These profiles from the South Pacific are a reminder that there are other cultures in the world and that the textbook, for the most part, presents only a view of Western society.

Instructor's manual. A manual is provided for the instructor as an educational aid. It contains suggestions for teaching, a list of visual aids, and, most important, an extensive collection of multiple-choice questions for objective tests. Also included in the Instructor's Manual is a set of printed masters from which transparencies can be made. This visual aid material is developed from the material in the text and can be used as an effective teaching aid. The Instructor's Manual is available either through the sales representative or directly from Times Mirror/Mosby College Publishing.

Acknowledgments

Many people participated in the third edition of *Human Development: The Span Of Life*. First, there were a large number of students who were gracious enough to fill out evaluative forms on each section of each chapter of the second edition. Over a period of 2 years a number of forms were turned in, giving us a student perspective of what was good or bad, interesting or not, significant or not. Second, we had a number of comments sent to us from instructors and students from other colleges and universities. These unsolicited letters were very meaningful and appreciated. We learned much about what appeals to people and what doesn't—and we learned about the diversity of background and orientation that our readers have. Out of this exchange of letters came an invitation to be a speaker at a "capping" ceremony for student nurses who used the book.

Third, we want to acknowledge how much we have appreciated the help and understanding of our college editor at Times Mirror/Mosby, Catherine H. Converse. She worked along with us, doing research, making contacts, providing suggestions and insights, and setting up time schedules by which the work could be reasonably done. She was tremendously valuable. Fourth, we appreciate the help of our typist, Margaret Baker, who has worked with us on at least five of our eight books. It's nice to have someone who can type from rough copy, correct our spelling and grammar, and who can understand the language of psychology.

Fifth, we owe a special thanks to Robert A.C. Stewart of the University of the South Pacific, Suva, Fiji. Dr. Stewart was kind enough to permit us to use a number of profiles from the book he edited, *Pacific Profiles*. We share a common interest with Dr. Stewart in the use of profiles written by students to illustrate a cross-cultural perspective of the human experience. Sixth, we want to express our appreciation to Mr. and Mrs. Jack Polk and their daughter Alexa for permitting us to photograph her development during the first 12 months after birth.

Finally, we acknowledge with sincere gratitude the work of our professional peers who were reviewers of the second edition and of the new manuscript. They represent a diversity of background, some with orientations quite different from ours. They were thorough, they were conscientious, they were honest. We appreciate their knowledge and professionalism. They, along with the reviews of the students, gave us some very important things to consider. We took their suggestions seriously, making the final judgment of what, how, and how much should be written. We are grateful to them for helping us "grow." We acknowledge:

Leann Birch
University of Illinois

Robert Brummett
Towson State University

Janet Fritz
Colorado State University

Linda Harris
University of Connecticut

Susan Kontos
University of Northern Colorado

Murray Krantz
Florida State University

Ruth Gouner
Nicholls State University

Hugh Oxford
San Bernardino Valley Community College

Neil J. Salkind
University of Kansas

To all of our readers, we invite you to write us if you have any questions, corrections, or comments. We appreciate and endorse the personalized approach. May your days be bright and shining, filled with a love for all humankind.

GEORGE KALUGER
MERIEM FAIR KALUGER

CONTENTS

CHAPTER 11

MIDDLE AND LATER ADOLESCENCE: 15 TO 18 YEARS OF AGE, 385

CHAPTER 12

EMERGING ADULTHOOD: THE AWAKENING YEARS, 429

CHAPTER 13

EARLY ADULTHOOD: THE DEVELOPING YEARS, 471

CHAPTER 14

MIDDLE ADULTHOOD: THE YEARS OF CONTINUITY, 519

CHAPTER 15

LATER ADULTHOOD: THE AGED AND AGING, 565

CHAPTER 1

LIFE-SPAN DEVELOPMENT

INDIVIDUALITY AND UNIVERSALITY

An ancient philosopher observed that one of the most significant questions one person can ask of another is "What do you see when you see a human being?" The answer to this question will reflect the person's degree of understanding and insight, as well as faith and acceptance, concerning the dignity of nature and human worthiness.

As a seed develops, changes, and matures into a tree by following a specified direction of growth, so does an infant change and mature into an adult in accordance to principles pertaining to growth and development. Thus this maturational sequence can be identified, observed, and recorded.

The developmental process is not limited to one aspect of growth, however, since each individual grows in five ways—physically, intellectually, emotionally, socially, and morally. The environment makes an impact on this growth mechanism, but the initial step-by-step process remains virtually the same. Adults ascribe positive or negative values to the developing personality. Your insights concerning human growth and development largely determine what you *do* see when you see a human being.

IN THIS CHAPTER . . .

You will read about

1 The concepts of individuality and universality and how they pertain to human development.
2 The theoretical goals of human development, the definitions of age stages and their relationship to cultural variations, and the life-span perspective.
3 General and specific principles of human development and the issue of continuity versus discontinuity in development.
4 The basic processes of homeostasis, motivation, and learning and the way in which they affect behavior.
5 The issue of nature versus nurture and the five theoretical approaches or views of human development.
6 The concept of developmental tasks and its limitations in regard to age stages in different societies.
7 Methods available for the study of growth and development and the cautions that must be exercised.

A Vermont farmer is quoted as having said, "People are mostly alike, but what difference they are can be powerful important." In one statement is the general concept of individuality and universality. "People are mostly alike . . ." reflects a sameness, a universal likeness of humans in their development. ". . . But what difference they are can be powerful important" suggests the magnitude and depth of individual differences that can be found in people.

The facts of human individuality are astounding. Each one of us is built in a highly distinctive way in every particular, and these differences form the bases of *individuality*. It is well known that each individual has distinctive fingerprints and a natural odor, distinctive enough for a bloodhound to follow. It has also been determined that people have unique voice prints, lip prints, and footprints.

More startling are the physical differences that are inside people. There are variations in the size, shape, and operations of stomachs of normal people. There are also large differences in hearts and endocrine glands. Diversity of the structure of the brain and nervous system is as great between individuals as is diversity between related species of animals. Each individual is extraordinary. Although the illustrations given all pertain to physical growth, they could have been equally given to any aspect of growth.

Universality refers to the commonality of human beings. Everyone can give examples of ways in which men and women the world over are alike. Behind the facade of cultural influences people are pretty much the same physically, intellectually, emotionally, socially, and morally. The five ways of growing up are purposely being emphasized so that the total developmental pattern can be realized.

The universality of human beings is deeply ingrained within the developmental processes. Babies are conceived and born the same way the world over. They go through the same stages in learning to walk and to talk. Children develop their self-concept, their processes of learning, and their adjustive patterns of behavior in much the same way. Puberty is a universal experience. In other words, there are some fundamental principles governing growth and development to which human beings are subjected, whether they know about them or not, whether they agree with them or not, and whether they are ready for them or not.

The implications of individuality and universality are manifold. For one thing they state that people are like others in very basic ways. Yet they are different enough in other ways to make each person a unique being. The ultimate implication is to recognize the individual worth of each human being, understanding and accepting that person, and at the same time understanding and accepting ourselves, seeking to make the most of ourselves with whatever traits we may have.

The one thing that is consistent in the world is the fact that everything changes all the time. Our life is a dizzy succession of changes for which we rarely seem prepared. Like the flowers that bloom and fade, like the grass that sprouts and withers, permanence is at best a dream. Yet it all works out. Through it all, indeed behind it all, there is an element of stability and structure that serves as a basic foundation on which a body, a mind, and a life will evolve. There is an essence of universality within the frame of reference called growth and development. In spite of the modifications, transitions, and transformations that emerge, there is continuity with change.

A LOOK AT DEVELOPMENTAL PSYCHOLOGY

As life advances and experiences increase, both internal and external phases of behavior and growth change constantly. The aim of developmental psychology, of which the study of the span of life is a part, is to learn about the changes that take place. By definition, ***developmental psychology*** is the study of the development of activity, growth, and behavior, including both its internal and external phases.

Developmental psychologists attempt to determine the characteristic changes from one developmental period to another. They are interested in learning why these changes come about, when they come about, how they come about, and what factors influence the changes for better or for worse. It is important to learn if the changes are universal and cross-cultural (found in all societies) or if they are found only in certain individuals and cultures.

developmental psychology a division of psychology that investigates the growth, maturation, and aging processes of the human organism and personality, as well as cognitive, social, and other functions, throughout the span of life.

Goals of development

There is some interest in determining if there is an ultimate goal of development and whether or not it is the same for all individuals. Admittedly, speculation on this topic is metaphysical in nature. At this point in time, abstract reasoning has the edge in investigating the nature, principles, and problems of the ultimate reality of the meaning of life and of being. Many psychologists relate to the principle that the goal of development is to enable the individual to adapt to the conditions of life and to make the most of one's human (physical and psychological) potential. However, not all developmental theories and psychologists assume that there is a goal of development nor that changes have to be orderly and goal-oriented. Abraham Maslow (1968)* refers to this impetus toward "becoming" as self-actualization. He believes that life with a commitment to the highest values that human beings can envision brings self-fulfillment and self-actualization.

Erik Erikson (1974) believes that the standard of maturity is the development of a strong ego and a capacity for intimacy. Erikson's final stage in life is integrity. However, B.F. Skinner (1971) says that

*Any time a name and a date are presented, reference is made to a documentation that can be found in the Bibliography section in the back of this textbook. If you look there for the name *Maslow* and a 1968 publication date, you will find the citation. This approach to indicating references of a study or an idea is recommended by the American Psychological Association.

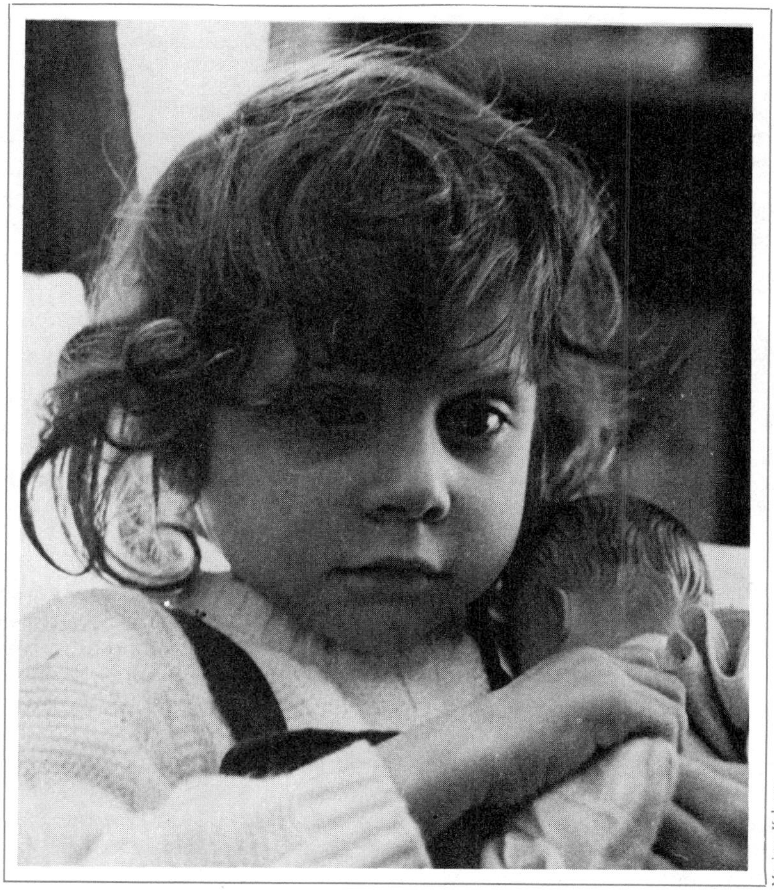

Meriem Kaluger

For Beauty is an idea,
And ideas are the province of the mind,
And the mind is the sign of human life.
The first beauty therefore that must be known
Is the beauty,
The wonder,
The marvel of life.

John E. Valusek
Jottings

TABLE 1-1 Age-related phases of the life span in complex societies

Life stage	*Age approximations*	*Descriptive phase*
I. Prenatal		
Conception	—	Genetic foundation is set
Zygote	7 to 10 days	Conception to implantation
Embryo	10 days to week 8	Implantation to recognizable human
Fetus	Week 8 to birth	Fetal period to birth
II. Infancy*		
Neonate	First 2 weeks	Period of physiological stabilization
Infant	To 2 years	Basic attachment, motor, perceptual, and language development
III. Childhood*		
Early	3 to 5 years	Preschool and readiness years
Middle	6 to 8 years	Learning basic skills in reading, writing, arithmetic
Late	9 to 11 years	Same sex groups; preadolescence
IV. Adolescence		
Early	12 to 15 years	Transitional; puberty to heterosexuality
Middle-late	16 to 18 years	Building personal and sexual identity
Emerging adulthood	19 to 21-23 years	Transitional; youth to young adult
V. Adulthood		
Early adulthood	23 to 40-45 years	Expanding and developing adult roles
Middle adulthood	43 to 60-65 years	Years of stability and maintenance
Early old age	65 to 75-80 years	Retirement to senescence
Late old age	80 and over	Senescence and decline

*Many pediatric textbooks present the following age divisions for early development: (1) neonate, the first 28 days of life, (2) infancy, newborn to 1 year of age, (3) toddler, 1 year of age to 3 years, (4) preschooler, 3 years of age to 6 years. A definitive conclusion has not been reached by developmental psychologists and others as to what the ages of the various divisions should be. As a result, writers may differ as to the ages included in the various periods or stages of the life span. Always check for the definitions of the terms used.

human behavior is determined by external (environmental) factors, so the standard of maturity would be an anxiety-free set of responses to external stimuli. Different views and theories on development are presented later in this chapter. But, as you can suspect, it is not easy to get a common consensus of the goal of development or of the nature of humankind.

Concept of age stages

Each stage of growth and development has an encompassing relationship to other periods of life, yet it also has its own unique characteristics, needs, and demands. Life-span psychology considers growth and development, in its major components, from the event of conception to the incident of death and slightly beyond.

Traditional divisions of the life span include (1) prenatal, (2) infancy, (3) childhood, (4) adolescence, and (5) adulthood. Certainly the stages of life can be grossly delineated along those lines. But, as the amount of research on growth and development increases, psychologists find it desirable to expand some of these stages. Table 1-1 presents such an expansion, especially in terms of the age levels as they are treated in this book. Within certain periods, such as adulthood, there are wide differences in the adult at 25, 55, and 75 years of age. There is also a difference between the early adolescent, just passing through puberty, and the late adolescent who is ready for adulthood. What a preschool child of 4 can do intellectually and physically is quite different from that of the child of 7 who, in turn, cannot perform like the child of 11!

An interesting sidelight on the existence of an adolescent stage is that certain primitive societies, such as the Masai of East Africa and the natives of the Sepik and Karawari River areas in Papua New Guinea, do not have a distinctive adolescent period. These individuals move from childhood directly into adulthood through the practice of puberty rites, a series of ceremonies that induct the young into manhood or womanhood.

The designation *complex* (or *sophisticated*) *society* refers to a culture that is industrially and technologically oriented in terms of people working and making a living. A *simple* (or *primitive*) *society* is one in which the people primarily work the land, forests, or waters for subsistence. The implication of this difference for age stages is that a longer period of time is needed between childhood and adulthood for an individual in a complex society to learn the skills of handling the work and responsibilities of an adult. Thus an extended period of learning is needed to get ready for adulthood. That stage, coming after childhood and before adulthood, is called adolescence.

Another note should be made. The concept of age stages is beginning to lose some of its appeal as developmental psychologists learn more about the nature of human change. Age, as an independent variable, is a simple and somewhat rough explanation for human change. Age alone does not produce change; other factors, such as maturation, learning, or growth, also bring about change. However, age levels have provided guidelines for researchers, allowing them to indirectly account for the influence of experience. Age can be readily identified, along with observable characteristics of the age level, and stated in statistical terms—for example, "Two thirds of all infants are toilet trained by the age of 2 years" and "The average age of puberty in girls is 12½ years." The information is precise and uncluttered, but it is also simplistic because it does not tell the whole story. Your attention is called to the section presented later in this chapter, entitled "Critique of stage approach." It indicates some of the limitations of the age-stage concept in explaining changes. There are more sophisticated and advanced ways of describing human change that take into account the biases produced by the inherent effects of the influence of the social sciences on the people they describe and explain and about whom they make predictions (Gergen, 1982; Palazzoli, 1978; Watzlawick et al., 1974).

Why do we consider the age-stage approach if it has restrictions? Because, as beginning students in the field of human development, it may be helpful to be aware of both the ***descriptive data*** that are available and the process of ***conceptualization.*** The age-stage concept can provide descriptive and/or normative (statistical) information that is easy to grasp and understand. It is our hope that such information is neither misleading nor limiting. Our major responsibility is to avoid applying the normative findings unquestionably and indiscriminately. A conceptual basis is also needed. Knowledge in human development is in the process of building. We must be alert to new ideas; we must keep our minds flexible and open. We must be ready to grow with the field as new concepts and new methods of research to study human development emerge. Conceptualization is the process of thinking or imagining to form new concepts or modify existing ones. The age-stage level of understanding is only a beginning step.

conceptualization the process of concept formation in which various items are grouped into units on the basis of commensurable characteristics.

descriptive data numerical statistics assembled, classified, and tabulated to describe and summarize the characteristics of the data.

Cultural variations and norms

Although an effort is made to apply research findings to culturally diverse and different segments of our Western society, there are times when the material in this text will *appear* to be primarily related to the white, middle-class group. There is no bias intended or omission by design. It is just that most of the research has been done on the largest and most common segment of the population. That segment is not exclusively white, nor is it exclusively middle class. It is a conglomerate of people who happen to be mostly white, coming from an upper-lower and a lower-middle socioeconomic group. These individuals constitute a large majority of the total population and, thereby, suggest the most common practices and levels of development in Western society. Child-rearing practices, school demands, and adult expectations in any society are made significant by the sheer number of people engaged in them. They set somewhat of a norm.

Because of the nature of our diverse population, it will be important for those interested in culturally different populations such as the blacks, Appalachian whites, Mexican Americans, Puerto Ricans, rural whites, lower socioeconomic groups, Asians, migrant workers, Indians, Eskimos, and other minority groups to recognize that some of the information included is not complete. In addition, recognize that customs and expectations in non-Western societies may differ in significant ways from those in Western countries. A series of vignettes, such as "The Bulubulu Ceremony," is presented in various chapters to illustrate cross-cultural variations. Those profiles were written by students at the University of The South Pacific at Suva, Fiji.

The point to be remembered is that babies, children, adolescents, and adults, in any social or cultural milieu, are more like other babies, children, adolescents, or adults than they are different. They are all to be respected, revered, and esteemed because they are all "children of the universe ." We are all born. We live a life in which we seek to survive in as pleasant a manner as we can in our environment. We all eventually die. We come, we go. What we do in between contributes to individual differences.

THE BULUBULU CEREMONY*

The Fijian custom of *i Lakovi*† has been performed and accepted by my parents. Thus my sister's engagement was being traditionally recognised and we were all delighted at home. For the *i Lakovi* was an elaborate affair and had consisted of many *vulos*‡ *of tabua*§. That was a good sign, for it meant that my sister would be well looked after by her future in-laws. It also indicated that they were well off.

Plans for a huge traditional wedding ceremony began. Relatives from both sides enthusiastically carried out their preparations, each eager to outdo the other. This was going to be a big occasion. A day in the month of May was set for the event.

Late in April, five months after the *i Lakovi* had taken place, it was discovered that my sister was three months pregnant. This was a big blow to my parents, and preparations were immediately called off. Our relatives were informed that the wedding was going to be only a small affair after all. It was an even bigger blow to my sister's future in-laws, for it meant that they would have to perform the *Bulubulu*‖ ceremony. This custom—*Bulubulu*—had to be done in order to pacify my father and ask for his forgiveness, and also to strengthen the ties between the two groups. The bonds would most certainly weaken because the couple hadn't complied with the unwritten rules. It was the boy who had made the girl pregnant; as such, the girl was the victim, and compensation was called for. This is how the Fijian society operates.

On the day of the *Bulubulu*, all of our immediate relatives were present to help prepare the *magiti* [ceremonial feast] and to witness the ceremony. In most cases there would be no feast prepared, but since the *i Lakovi* had been granted, it was only befitting to prepare a *magiti*.

In the early afternoon two busloads of people arrived, together with two trucks loaded with goods. The visitors gathered on one side of the lawn and my relatives on the opposite side. Then a spokesman from the other party, looking solemn and humble, made a speech and presented several *vulos of tabua* to my father. By accepting the gifts my father showed that there was goodwill and understanding, and that my sister's future in-laws were welcome.

Then my sister, who had accompanied the other party and who was elaborately dressed in the traditional barkcloth costume of *kumi* and *masi*, moved toward my father and presented her *tabua* to him. She then took off her outer costume and laid it in front of my father. After that she returned to her in-laws to be dressed again. This time she moved toward my mother and presented her *tabua;* but before she could take off her second costume, my mother gave her a big hug and both cried silently in each other's arms. Feelings are never displayed easily, least of all publicly; both were trying their hardest to control their emotions. Looking around, I saw several heads bowed and tears silently shed by many. It was a moving moment.

Then my father spoke, and the spell was broken. He talked about how he respected the visiting party for still upholding some important aspects of tradition, thanked them for coming and bringing so much wealth, and invited them to stay and join in the *magiti*. Plans for a big wedding ceremony were underway again. We were all delighted that the wonderful occasion was going to be held after all—thanks to the *Bulubulu* ceremony.

*From Stewart, R.A.C. (Ed.). *Pacific profiles*. Suva, Fiji: University of The South Pacific Extension Services, 1982.

†*i Lakovi*—custom of formally asking for the girl's hand in marriage. The boy's relatives would bring *tabua* with them to ask permission from the girl's father.

‡*vulo*—one *vulo* means ten whale's teeth. Many *vulos* means many tens of whale's teeth.

§tabua—whale's tooth—a symbol of wealth, valued above all gifts.

‖*Bulubulu*—the custom of asking for forgiveness of any kind, especially in the case of elopement, illegitimate pregnancies, etc.

Life-span perspective

The concept of life-span developmental approaches to the study of human behavior is not particularly new. However, these approaches have not been used extensively until recent years. Most of the developmental research has been done on a short-term, experimental basis. As a result, short-term age-specific data have been collected. The short-term approach gives information only on the age level studied but not on the long-term, or life-span, development of the characteristic under investigation. For example, the reasoning and learning processes of 4-year-olds can be studied. We can learn a lot about how 4-year-olds do problem solving, but that approach tells us very little about how these 4-year-olds will reason and learn when they are 10 years old.

Of course, we could study the reasoning and learning processes of 10-year-olds, 20-year-olds, and 60-year-olds, but that still gives us only age-specific data. It will not present a picture of *how* the reasoning and learning processes develop over the span of life. It only says what happens for the ages studied. It should be noted that age-specific studies do not become life-span oriented by merely including a wider range of ages in the research design (Weimer, 1979).

Life-span oriented views of human development deal with the study of long-term sequences and patterns of change in human behavior. The long-term sequences and patterns may be studied for intraindividual (within the individual) changes or for interindividual (between persons) changes (Labouvie, 1982). Development over the span of life may have patterns of change that differ in terms of onset, direction, duration, and termination (Baltes et al., 1980).

In a study of life-span developmental psychology there is a need for both the short-term and the long-term approaches. Age-specific (short-term) studies provide immediate information. Long-term life-span oriented studies may add to that information by correcting parts that are distorted or underdeveloped by age limitations, by demonstrating that the facts do not hold up over the life span, or by providing information that would only emerge when the total picture (life-span) is studied.

A look at Table 1-2, a Life-cycle Calendar developed by the editors of *The Futurist* (Selim, 1979), illustrates the broad range of development in the life span. The age stages indicate the types of behavior and development found in six areas of growth or involvement. Follow through any one of the areas, from age to age, and note the changes that take place. Growth and development are implied for the age level as a whole, even though individual differences will exist. According to this table, the picture of the total life cycle is one of movement from one phase of development to another.

DEVELOPMENTAL PRINCIPLES

The principles of growth and development that follow reflect the universality of the laws by which human beings grow and develop. The maturational process, the sequential stages of development, and the directions of growth are fundamental to human life everywhere and at any point in time in history.

Although the physical principles of maturational development unfold naturally because of their innate origin, they are subject to changes in rate of development and often to the extent to which they do develop. For example, under normal conditions, the sequential pattern of development in the prenatal state follows a predictable pattern. However, if the uterine environment of the mother should change because of the introduction of an adverse chemical or drug, such as thalidomide, this unusual or unexpected change in the blood chemistry could affect the typical manner of development of the arms and legs of the embryo. Another example is that of a child raised in an environment that is lacking in sensory-stimulating experiences or that is deficient in the proper nutritional values important to neural growth. As a result this child develops an ineffective or inefficient intellectual processing system. Never underestimate the importance of the environment in the developmental process. It is not the only influential factor, but it is quite significant in the part it does play.

Direction of growth changes

Human growth and development bring about changes in the physical, intellectual, emotional, social, and moral components of being. Growth is used by some developmental psychologists to refer to the gradual increase in magnitude (size) of an organism or its parts. It may also refer to an incremental increase in the magnitude or range of a function, such as growth in reading skills. Growth is basically quantitative.

Development generally refers to a sequence of continuous changes in a system over a considerable time, with the changes following one another until maturity or death. These changes lead to a higher degree of

TABLE 1-2 The stages of life: a life-cycle calendar

	Infancy and early childhood (0-5)	*Late childhood (5-12)*	*Adolescence (12-18)*
Family	Mother is the center of universe. Child's behavior varies from complete devotion to unpredictability to outright rebellion. Dramatic changes in child's behavior can occur in only 6 months.	Still very dependent on mother, but goes to extremes of affection or dislike. Proud of father, family, and home. Generally good with siblings.	Family gradually becomes less important . . . Sometimes adolescents feel the need to break away from family. Occasional embarrassment over parents or siblings.
Education and employment	Children are just entering school. Children show a wide range of skills and interest in letters and numbers.	Children most often like school, sometimes devoted to teacher. Increasingly comfortable with the three R's. Behavior varies from studiousness to boredom to explosive activity.	Adolescents vary in opinion of school and teacher. . . . Many students concerned about college. Beginning to get part-time jobs after school and full-time jobs in the summer.
Entertainment	Infant's first activity is simple sight—then interest in toys and objects, crawling, throwing, exploring, toddling, eventually leading to the crayons and puzzles of nursery school and kindergarten.	Swimming, roller skating, climbing, swinging, bicycling, simple ball games, jigsaw puzzles. Children this age collect anything and everything. Growing interest in organized sports and activities.	Some of the same activities as in childhood but more emphasis on organized sports. Growing interest in individual sports such as tennis and golf. Countless activities after school. Movies, parties, drug use.
Friends	Children make friends easily at about age 3 and grow more social, with occasional lapses, from then on. By age 5 many children are sure of themselves and at ease with amost everyone.	Considerable quarreling among friends, but some moments of good cooperation. Children this age begin to feel the importance of peer groups. Opinion of family members may be less valued than that of peers.	Friends become almost all-important. Prefer friends to family. Dating begins. Both sexes tend to socialize with large groups of friends. First sexual experience and increasing sexual activities.
Personal growth	Children speed through the developmental stages at a dizzying pace. Growth is marked by alternating stages of equilibrium and disequilibrium.	Children go through stages of introversion and extroversion. Steadily becoming more self-assured and independent.	Important physical and psychological changes. Puberty. Extended periods of self-analysis and withdrawal give adolescents a firmer grip on themselves.

From Selim, R., and the editors of *The Futurist*, February 1979, published by the World Future Society, 4916 St. Elmo Ave., Washington, DC 20014.

Young adulthood (18-25)	*Adulthood (25-40)*	*Middle age (40-65)*	*Retirement years (65 and over)*
Most people have left home. Many begin their own families.	Most people are married. . . . Many divorces occur in this stage. Single people often finally get married. Married couples may choose to have children before child-bearing years end.	Family size may decrease as children leave home. Parents of middle-aged people are dying. Some middle-aged couples become grandparents.	Many will be grandparents. Many may find themselves alone due to the death of a spouse. Women, especially, may spend many years alone.
Many young adults are in college; some continue education after college. Most begin working. Many unemployed or underemployed. Career choices assume special importance for some.	Some adults go back to school. Many change jobs. Married women may re-enter the work force. Increased emphasis on furthering career for breadwinners, who now have growing financial responsibilities.	Most workers are at the height of their careers. This is the stage of the most power and prestige at the work-place. For many, it brings the realization that their career can go no further. Some pick second careers.	Workers begin to retire. They may travel, resume education, develop new hobbies. For women who have stayed in the home, the job continues. Income will probably shrink.
Some organized athletics. Less recreation and more entertainment. Continued drug use, especially alcohol.	Spectator sports, travel, entertaining. Many start new hobbies such as pottery, painting, or photography.	Entertaining, travel, more expensive vacations. Hobbies may develop into second careers.	Increased opportunities to travel, entertain, spend time with relatives, concentrate on avocations, do volunteer work, etc., if money and health permit.
Friends and peer groups still very important. Single men and women searching for partners. Continuing emphasis on sexual activity.	Importance of friends declines as family size increases. Adults depend less on the opinions of peers to judge themselves.	As children leave home, friends may become somewhat more important. Sexual activity may decline.	Friends and peers are dying. There is more time to spend with those that remain. Old acquaintances are renewed.
The developmental pace slows and stages become less obvious. Psychologist Erik Erikson calls this the "intimacy vs. isolation" stage—a time for testing one's identity and growing further or hiding it and stagnating.	A stage of creation and production, often accompanied by dissatisfaction with past choices and an urge to change directions in order to build a new and more solid life.	A mid-life [adjustment] may come as individuals confront their own morality and the consequences of choices already made.	The individual comes to accept his past, his life, and the approach of death, or grows bitter and despairing.

cephalocaudal sequence the progression of physical and motor development from head to foot. For example, a baby's head develops and grows before the torso, arms, and legs.

proximodistal sequence the progressive growth of the body parts in a center-to-periphery direction. See also **cephalocaudal sequence.** For example, a baby learns to control the movements of the shoulders before the direction of arms or fingers.

differentiation and complexity in the system. Development is usually considered to be a life-long process.

Present usage of the terms growth and development has distorted their intended meanings so that the two terms are most often used interchangeably and synonymously. Growth is frequently used to indicate a change to a more developed or mature state. Development frequently includes the concept of growth. Some psychologists like to reserve the use of growth to organic changes and the use of development to functional or nonorganic changes. We will use that term which seems appropriate to better explain the point or fact under discussion.

Since the words growth and development imply change that is constructive in nature, it should be noted that change can also take place in the direction of deterioration. Atrophy, the emaciation or wasting of tissues and organs, also appears. Although atrophy is more predominant in the latter stages of life, it can occur during the embryonic period when the secondary yolk sac disintegrates.

There are four principles related to directions of growth and development. The first direction of growth is the ***cephalocaudal sequence.*** Cephalocaudal sequence is the hypothesis that physical growth tends to begin in the head end and to progress to the tail end. The development of the major aspects of physical growth takes place in the head first, the trunk next, and the legs last. In Fig. 1-1 the letter C indicates that maturation and development start initially in the brain and head area and then proceed with maturational progress into the trunk area and, finally, into the feet.

This direction is vividly illustrated in both prenatal and postnatal stages of development. In the embryonic state the brain and the central nervous system start to develop first, followed by features of the head, then the region of the trunk with its organs. The development of the head proceeds more rapidly than that of any other part of the body because of the importance of the brain and central nervous system to the operation of the rest of the body. This change results from the unfolding of the maturational sequential process and is independent of learning or training. At birth the head constitutes 20% of the body length. After the rest of the body grows to maturity the head will be only 8% of the body length. After birth babies first gain control of their head, eyes, mouth, and neck; then they gain control over the trunk. Babies can sit before they can stand, and they can stand before they can walk.

The second direction of growth is the ***proximodistal sequence.*** It also is related to physical growth. Proximal refers to that portion of the body that lies closest to the body center; distal refers to the part of that body portion most remote from the central part of the body. Thus a thigh is proximal, the foot is distal. A shoulder is proximal, the hand is distal. In Fig. 1-1 the letter P indicates that the areas of the shoulders and the thighs begin to develop toward maturity before the hands and feet. Progression is from the central parts of the body maturing earlier and functioning before

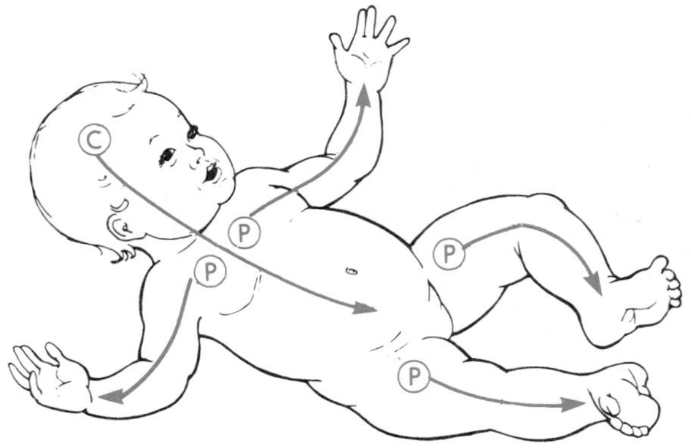

FIG. 1-1 *Direction of cephalocaudal sequence, Ⓒ, is from development and control of head movement to trunk, to legs, and to feet. Direction of growth of proximodistal sequence, Ⓟ, is from the development and maturation closest to the center of the body to later development of peripheral parts of the body. The changes that take place are a result of the maturational process.*

those located nearer the periphery. Babies gain control of their shoulders before their hands. They can control their thighs before they can control their feet. The central nervous system develops more rapidly than the peripheral nervous system.

The third direction of growth is expressed by the principle of ***differentiation.*** This principle states that the trend of the direction of growth proceeds from general to specific responses. In other words development is from simple operations to more complex performances. It is characterized by increasing differentiation and complex performance by a developing central nervous system. There will be a development of gross muscle usage before fine muscle control can take place. Babies learn to grasp with their whole hand before making use of their thumb and forefinger. They crawl before they creep, and they creep before they walk. Control of grown body parts is a result of maturation, not of the growth of the limb. Development in all areas—intellectually, socially, emotionally, physically, and morally—proceeds from general to specific.

The fourth direction of growth is one of ***integration.*** It would appear from the other three principles that all of the directions of growth are fragmentary or

differentiation the process by means of which structure, function, or forms of behavior become more complex or specialized; the change from homogeneity to heterogeneity.

integration (hierarchic) the developmental trend of combining simple, differentiated skills into more complex skills.

Harold Geyer

Developmental principles are most evident in early infancy. The cephalocaudal direction of growth can be detected as the baby learns to control the head and upper part of the body before being able to control the lower half.

readiness the combination of growth development and experience that prepares an individual to acquire a skill or understanding with facility.

isolated in that they have their own purpose, going from top to bottom, center to outer, or gross to fine. However, as the developmental process takes place, there is a blending of the directions into a whole pattern, an incorporation of the growth processes into a larger unit to be known as the person. Not only do the physical elements evolve into a coordinated being, but also the intellectual, social, emotional, and moral components of development merge into an integrated personality. An integrated individual is the ultimate outcome of the total growth and developmental processes at work.

Specific principles

There are several significant facts about development that are fundamental and predictable and thus important to the understanding of growth and development. The first principle indicates that maturational, physical, motor, speech, and cognitive development, especially in the early stages of life, follow a definite, orderly, sequential, predictable pattern. Growth is a continuous process following an unfolding maturational pattern. It is directional. Normally, each child passes through each stage in the developmental process. Although individual differences exist within the developmental pattern, they do not appreciably influence the general trend of development. Individual cases that are exceptions because of environmental influences may result in irregular short-term growth. As a child grows older and is exposed to increasingly varied environments and experiences, the pattern of development becomes less predictable.

A second principle is that development comes from a combination of maturation, learning, and influences of the environment. The maturational pattern is genetically programmed so that certain aspects of physiological growth take place innately. Learning refers to changes that are primarily the result of experience. The environment provides opportunities for learning that may hinder or aid in the development of organic elements to their maximum. The maturational process is, in turn, influential in determining when and if certain types of learning can take place. For example, a child will not be ready to be toilet trained or to walk, read, or respond to conceptual development until the "teachable moment," as established by physiological maturation, has arrived.

The concept of readiness is implied. ***Readiness*** is a state or condition of the person that makes it possible for the individual to engage profitably in a given learning activity. It depends on (1) physiological maturity, (2) relevant preparatory training, and (3) an aroused interest or motive. Readiness is a composite of many personal qualities and conditions and differs from one learning task to another. Parents and teachers should be happy to know that certain undesirable behavior patterns can or will be changed by maturation and learning but only if the child learns the new behavior pattern.

A third principle states that although all individuals follow a definite pattern of growth and development, they do so in their own style. Some children develop smoothly, others develop in spurts. Individual differences in rate of growth and development result partly from differences in hereditary endowment, the manner or rate in which the maturational process manifests itself, environmental influences, and the type of learning that has taken place.

Factors that may be responsible for producing differences in rate of development include innate sex differences (male or female), appropriateness of glandular functions, adequacy of nutrition, genetic endowment, rate of intellectual development, nature of health, amount of fresh air and sunshine, position of the child within the family as regards siblings, incentive and motivational drive, and parental attitudes, interest, and support. The rate of growth is not the same for all children, nor is it consistent for a specific child. There is some correlation between different types of growth; for example, a heavy child may be a late walker.

A fourth developmental principle suggests that each phase or stage of life has characteristic traits that are typical of that phase. The phases of life in chronological order are as follows: zygote, embryo, and fetus before birth, neonate, infancy (0 to 2 years), early childhood (3 to 5 years), middle childhood (6 to 8 years), late childhood (9 to 11 years), early adolescence (12 to 15 years), middle to late adolescence (16 to 18 years), late adolescence to emerging adulthood (19 to 21-23 years), early adulthood (23 to 40-45 years), middle adulthood (43 to 60-65 years), early old age (65 to 75-80 years), and late old age (80 years and older).

Each stage has its own psychology, distinguishing traits and features, and developmental tasks to be achieved. Please note the comments on age-related phases of the life span at the bottom of Table 1-1.

The fifth principle stresses that it is during infancy and early childhood that basic attitudes, traits, life-styles, behaviors, and patterns of growth are formed. These factors determine how the individual will develop as he or she grows older. Different physical and psychological traits have their roots in the earlier stages of life. Basic personality patterns may be set during the first 5 years of life. The patterns are not irreversible, but they are foundational; future growth builds on them. The role that children play in the family and in the peer group will determine whether they develop into leaders, followers, or nonresponders. Because of the plasticity of the central nervous system of early childhood, children are capable of being molded into a wide variety of developmental patterns by environmental and psychological influences.

A sixth principle is a little less definite because it has not been supported adequately by research. It is the concept of critical periods in development. A ***critical period*** is a point or stage in early development when a child is unusually receptive to influences by environmental events, objects, or persons. The term is used in different ways. It is used to imply a time period in development when an aspect of growth is most susceptible to damage by abnormal conditions. For example, the second to eighth weeks after conception are most critical in terms of the embryo being adversely affected by a change in the mother's blood chemistry brought on by a case of rubella (German measles).

A second interpretation of the critical period principle seeks to suggest that there are periods when some forms of development can benefit the most from certain types of training. In other words, there is a point in time when a baby can best develop a muscle structure suitable for sports or a socialized responsiveness to others; or, more specifically, a time to develop eye and hand motor match or perceptual development. This definition of critical period still needs to be explored.

The third usage relates to the concept of imprinting that is found in animals and birds. It is known that there is a sensitive period when a newly born animal or bird can form a strong social attachment to either the mother or a mother substitute. The mother substitute can even be a human being or, for that matter, any moving object. The question is whether or not such a sensitive or critical period exists in human babies.

continuity/discontinuity a concept in developmental psychology referring to the way in which changes in growth and development occur. Continuity states that the changes take place in a gradual, continuous, methodical manner. Discontinuity states that changes emerge in a series of distinct, quantitative changes reflecting structural or functional reorganization.

critical periods specific times in development during which a child is best able to learn a specific lesson; also, in fetal development, crucial times at which various specific physical features and organs develop; detrimental environmental influences during those periods can adversely affect organic development.

Issue of continuity versus discontinuity

The idea of continuity versus discontinuity in the growth progress is an important concept to remember when studying life-span theories of development. The topic has to do with the way in which changes in growth, development, and behavior occur. Are the changes gradual and continuous (continuity), or are they sudden and separate or distinct from other levels of change (discontinuity)?

The principle of ***continuity*** states that growth is a gradual, continuous, methodical change that occurs over a period of time. The continuity model describes development in terms of quantitative changes, with the elaboration of function increasing in complexity by small degrees. The whole notion of continuity is that development and behavior are continuous in the sense that the same underlying principle, construct, or mechanism is present to direct the patterns of growth in smooth, uninterrupted transition from simple to increasingly complex levels. Developmental continuity of structure and function is somewhat similar to the biological continuity of evolution. Some psychologists, such as B.F. Skinner, Daniel Berlyne, Sidney Bijou, and Robert Sears, maintain that the psychological processes that direct human functioning do not undergo fundamental changes during their development but instead change gradually in their efficiency or functioning capacity. If the progress of continuous development were to be put on a graph, a smooth curve, such as , would be drawn to show the continuity of development. For example, when children first begin to speak, they use only short sentences of two or three words. Later the sentences become longer, the sentence structure becomes more complex. The continuity model states that these changes reflect gradual increases in the child's ability to remember words and to use them in sentences; there is no fundamental change in the child's knowledge of language.

The principle of ***discontinuity*** states that growth and development emerge in a series of somewhat distinct changes that reflect structural and functional reorganizations of the organism. The discontinuity model of development reflects qualitative changes that tend to occur in a segmented manner as separate entities; the basic elements or structures are unrelated to each other. Discontinuity models are often described as a sequence of stages, with the emergence of each successive stage dependent on the appearance of the preceding stage level. The assumed changes are not gradual nor accumulations of growth but rather the appearance of new kinds of elements and reorganizations. Psychologists such as Jean Piaget, Erik Erikson, and Roger Brown maintain that the changes we observe in development reflect fundamental changes in the psychological processes that mediate functioning. A graph illustrating discontinuous development would show separate states or a wavy line 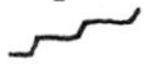 indicating both plateaus and change.

Most, if not all, theorists agree that there are continuities and discontinuities in development. The question is one of which processes take place in a continuous fashion and which ones occur by stages or plateaus. The human being reflects a complexity of organic and psychological phenomena. Just because one behavioral system may suggest developmental continuity does not mean that all behavioral systems develop in the same way. Even Piaget, a strong advocate of discontinuity with his stages of cognitive development, does not deny the existence of continuity phenomena. The issue is one of identifying which growth processes are governed by continuous underlying constructs or mechanisms (continuity) and which growth processes are influenced only when experiential circumstances, events, or environmental forces enter the picture (discontinuity).

According to Kagan (1979) there is some question concerning the assumptions about the long-term effects of early experiences on future behavior. He is skeptical about a strong form of the continuity assumption over the life span. The Fels study (Kagan and Moss, 1962), a longitudinal study of 15 years, provides fragile support for the notion that certain traits in infants predict relevant dispositions in adolescence and adulthood. Kagan did find, however, that there was consistent predictive validity of traits found during preadolescence with dispositions in adulthood. His observation is that there is an increasing acceptance of the influential nature of the interaction of biological and experiential variables. Physiological factors are predominant up to or through childhood (continuity); experiences determine when certain competencies will appear in adolescence and adulthood (discontinuity). However, there is much to be determined concerning the research in continuity and discontinuity before any valid conclusions can be reached.

BASIC PROCESSES RELATED TO BEHAVIOR

There are many processes at work within the human body, but none of them are as fundamental as homeostasis, motivation, and learning. These are responsible for an individual's physical and psychological well-being and are instrumental in initiating behavior for a variety of purposes. They are crucial for survival. Many other functions take place as a result of these three processes. For a person's body and mind to operate at a high level of efficiency and effectiveness it is necessary for homeostasis, maturation, and learning to function at peak levels of performance. These processes all respond to the aims of the life-force.

The *life-force* is that basic element that focuses on the meaning and purpose of life and provides the innate energy by which organisms survive and perform their prescribed functions. The meaning of life is a philosophical concept, but the dynamics (force and energy) of life have a scientific (i.e., a measurable basis) foundation. What is this thing called life? What's it all about? What are the dynamics involved? There are no ready answers but, as indicated in Table 1-3, there appear to be three basic aims or objectives of life. First, there is the aim of self-maintenance, the care and protection of the body and mind. Its purpose is personal survival. Second, there is the objective of the propagation of the species through the process of reproduction. This aim has as its purpose the survival of the species as a group. Third, there is the aim of self-actualization and self-realization so that the potential of human beings can be realized. Human potential and motivational capacity for growth, development, and behavior are inherent in each person. How the capability is used differs according to what an individual can and does do with it.

An extension of the life-force is found in the principle of homeostasis and in the processes of motivation and learning. Together these three basic processes seek to enhance life and to provide it with the most effective means of living. If any of these processes are deficient because of genetic, psychological, or environmental limitations, the pursuit of life will be less efficient because of those deficiencies.

Homeostasis

The scientific laws that govern the physical universe, including the human body, operate in precise and specific ways. As long as these laws operate as they were intended to, all will be well. However, whenever anything interferes with their effectiveness, unpleasant, even dire, consequences result. Natural forces then seek to bring about conditions that will restore the initial balance so that the principles once again can function normally. To maintain an equilibrium, to restore a balance, to be in harmony with the underlying principles and laws by which the universe operates is fundamental to the very essence of life and the universe itself.

Homeostasis is a principle stating that there is a tendency for the body to seek to maintain a relatively stable, constant state of equilibrium of its internal environment, even under changing external or internal circumstances. Any departure from that equilibrium sets in motion activities that tend to restore it. The purpose of this equilibrium is to maintain a state of constancy of the physiological processes so that all of the "laws" governing the body will work in harmony and permit the individual to survive and perform at an efficient and effective level of being. For example, normal body temperature is 98.6° F. It is interesting to note that the body maintains that temperature rather well, whether the air temperature is 120° or 32° F. In general, rapid adjustments are made by the autonomic nervous system to restore or maintain the balance, while slower adjustments occur through chemical and hormonal influences.

This demand for a steady, balanced internal consti-

homeostasis **the tendency to preserve a stable or constant internal state, despite fluctuations of bodily conditions and external stimulations. Cannon's term for the relative constancy—for example, in temperature, blood pressure, and pulse rate—that the body must maintain to function properly.**

TABLE 1-3 Basic processes related to behavior and development

Concept/process	*Definition*	*Basic aims*
Life-force	A philosophical concept related to the meaning and purpose of life; the innate force or energy that is a manifestation of life.	To attain self-maintenance; propagation of the species; actualization of the human potential.
Homeostasis	A scientific principle that demands the maintenance of a constancy, balance, or equilibrium in the functions of the bodily processes. An imbalance results in unmet needs.	To alert the body or mind that an imbalance exists and to seek a restoration of the balance.
Motivation	A psychological process that initiates, directs, and sustains the behavior necessary to achieve a goal that fulfills the unmet needs.	To mobilize the energy needed to activate and direct behavior designed to attain the goals that will satisfy unmet needs.
Learning	The possession of knowledge and critical judgment, obtained from the environment, that can be used in response to a demand for goal-seeking behavior or rational thought.	To provide information for the motivational process as to the identification of a desired goal and how to reach it.

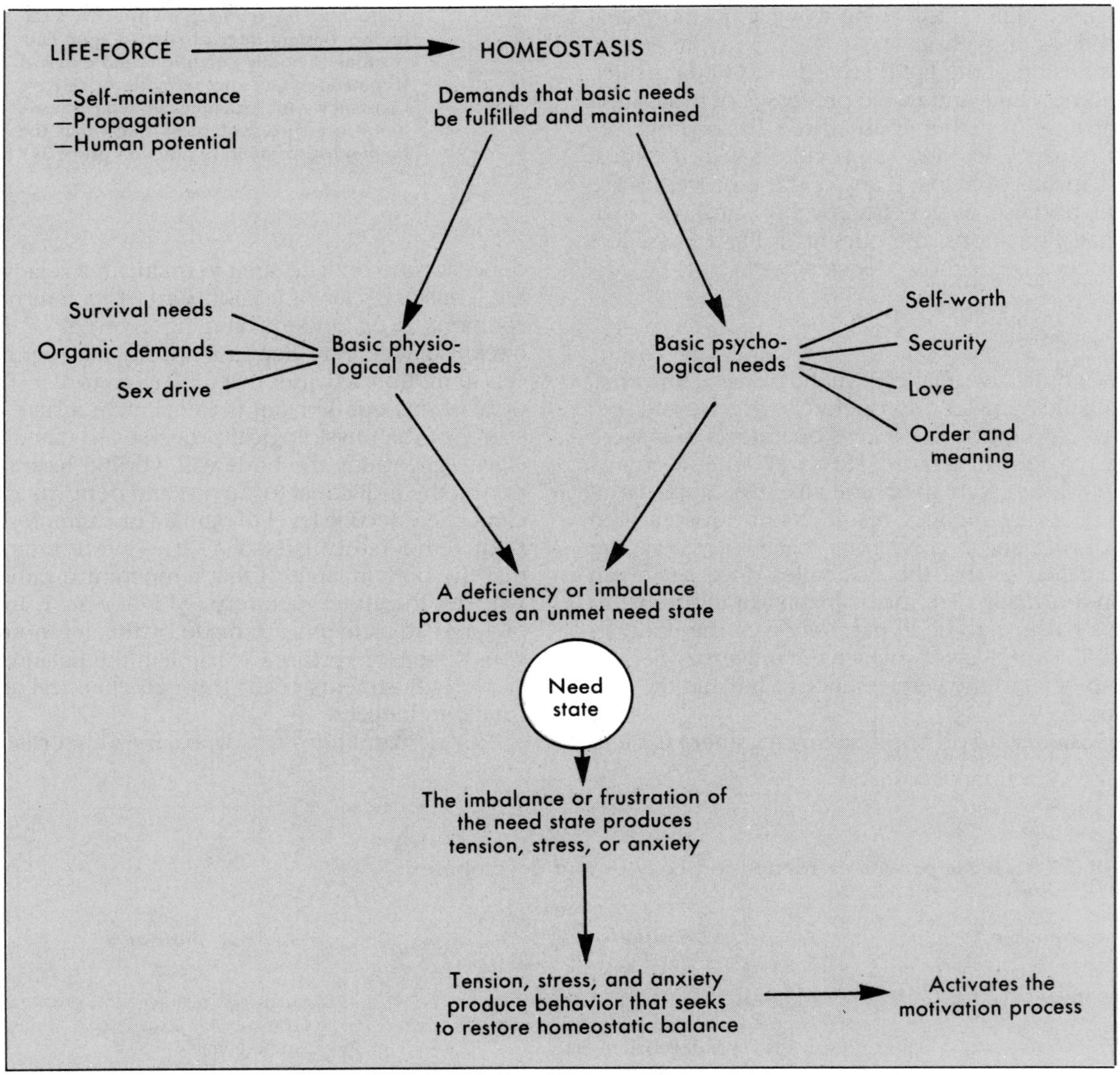

FIG. 1-2 ***The principle of homeostasis and how it operates to provide a relatively stable, constant state of physiological and psychological balance.***

tution allows for necessary responses of the body to meet the daily needs of tissues. The principle of homeostasis operates to keep the body in good working order on a long-term basis and a short-term basis. To illustrate, the tissues of the body require food, almost daily, to function. A person cannot eat enough food at one sitting to last for a lifetime. In fact, a person cannot eat enough food to last for a whole month or even a whole week. So on the one hand there is a need to maintain a stable, constant, long-term balance, and, on the other hand, there is a built-in process by which tissue needs regularly go out of equilibrium. In both cases behavior is initiated that can restore the balance.

Fig. 1-2 explains how the homeostatic principle operates. It must be said that we are taking some liberties with the technical definition of homeostasis by including psychological processes in its coverage. Actually, there is a seeking of balance in promoting psychological well-being, just as there is in achieving physical well-being.

The physiological and psychological conditions that must be satisfied may be *innate,* ones with which a person is born, or they may be *acquired* by learning or experiencing within the environment. Most physiological demands are innate, but the body may learn to desire some substances, such as alcohol or drugs, that develop physiological cravings. Innate needs or genetically programmed behavior are within themselves a necessary and sufficient condition for survival.

Some psychological needs, such as a need for love, security, self-worth, and structure (order and meaning), are considered by many psychologists to be innate. However, many emotional needs are acquired by interacting with people and conditions in the environment. In either area, physical or psychological, when conditions are not as they should be (according to the laws that indicate what is needed to maintain a state of well-being), an imbalance occurs, indicating that there is a deficiency of something needed for an equilibrium to exist. Whenever this "need-state" occurs, stress or anxieties are created. These, in turn, bring about energy mobilization, which activates the organism to action or behavior. Behavior is actually initiated by the process of motivation.

G. Spensor Brown (1973) in *Laws of Form* indicates that a homeostatic notion of organization in reference to human systems may be a controversial issue. Research is inconclusive as to whether systems, per se, can ever go back to a previous state. Homeostasis may explain how hunger may be satisfied, but the homeostatic concept may be misleading when considered as a systems theory.

Motivation

There is a reason or cause responsible for everything that a person does. Behind each action is an explanation, and included in that explanation will be an element of the motivation process. The term ***motivation*** is used to refer to the process by which behavior is initiated in response to a need, a deficiency, or an imbalance in the organism or person. This need-instigated behavior is goal-oriented in the sense that the behavior initiated is directed toward a goal or objective that, when attained, will satisfy the need by overcoming the deficiency and restoring the balance.

motivation **a general term referring to factors within an organism that arouse and maintain behaviors directed toward satisfying some need or drive or toward accomplishing a goal.**

The type of behavior initiated depends on the type of need encountered, physiological or psychological (Fig. 1-3). If the need is physiological, the behavior becomes task-oriented in the sense of "I have a task to fulfill; I must get some food" (or water, sleep, release of bowel or bladder tension, or whatever the biological need may be). If the need is psychological, a defense mechanism is used. Such behavior may be (1) an aggressive action to get what one needs, (2) a withdrawal reaction to get away from the problem, or (3) compromise behavior, which is a willingness to accept secondary goals if the primary goal is difficult to attain. Defense mechanisms are identifiable forms of normal behavior, utilized consciously or unconsciously, to meet psychological needs. An action that enables the individual to adjust to environmental circumstances in order to get something done is considered coping behavior.

In any case if the goal is reached and it is a proper goal (in the sense of providing what it was intended to provide), the deficiency is overcome, balance is restored, and the individual no longer has any stress or anxiety on that account. If the goal is not appropriate or if the individual is prevented from attaining the goal for some reason, such as use of the wrong behavior, obstacles that have not been overcome, or personal limitations that restrict the use of appropriate behavior, then the inability to gain the needed goal produces a frustration. The frustration, in turn, produces more stress and anxiety, since the need has not been relieved, and more behavior is produced.

Learning

Learning is fundamental to the good life. There is a need to learn the knowledge, skills, and attitudes that will help a person to survive and to actualize in his or her culture and society. The more complex the society or culture, the more facts and skills the individual must learn to maintain a comfortable level of physical and psychological balance.

The reason for presenting the concepts of homeostasis, motivation, and learning is to help the student understand some of the processes responsible for behavior and decision making. These processes may be functional and individualistic, but they are not intended to explain how development takes place. As will be noted later, learning and motivation are involved in making life choices, but they do not suggest what must be done to "develop" smoothly.

The process of learning is perhaps the most crucial basic process related to effective behavior because it is the one process in which the individual must be actively involved. Homeostasis is just a principle that pertains to laws that seek the maintenance of an equilibrium in functions related to physical and psychological

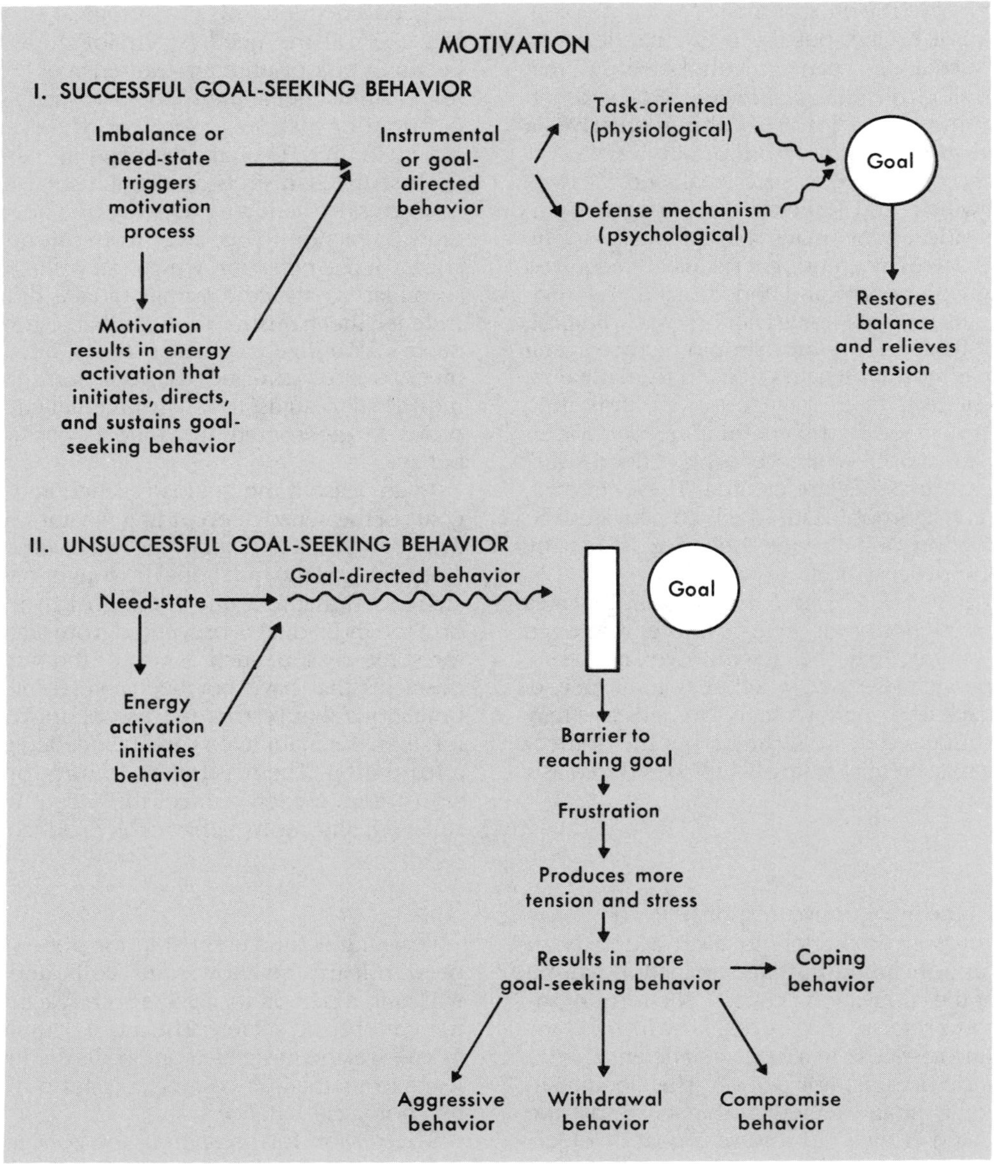

FIG. 1-3 *Motivation process and behavior produced.*

learning a relatively permanent modification of behavior resulting from experience.

well-being. Motivation is just the process that initiates, directs, and sustains the behavior necessary to reach a goal that will restore the equilibrium. Now the question is, how does the individual know which goal will produce the response or information necessary to provide relief from the need-state? Just as important, how does the individual know what behavior should be used to reach the goal? The answer to both questions is that the person must *learn* which goals and behavior are appropriate. ***Learning*** provides the cognitive insight and knowledge necessary to determine the proper behavior for reaching a desired goal.

Behavioral responses can be learned, or they can be innate. *Reflexes* are an example of innate or unlearned behavior. An infant is born with simple reflexes. Some reflexes, such as the sucking reflex, are directly related to survival. All other types of goal-seeking behavior must be learned. In fact, most behavior is learned; behavior is initiated on the basis of learned elements. For example, a person learns to identify the signs indicating that the fluid content of the body cells is getting low and that water is needed to restore the balance: "My mouth is dry and my lips are parched. I know from past experience that these signs mean that I need some liquids. I am thirsty. Where is the nearest fountain where I can get some water?" This person has learned the symptoms of a need for water and the place to get some relief. An Australian aborigine or an African bushman who has never been out of the wilds of his native bush country could suffer from the lack of water if, by some magic, he were to be transported and trapped in a room in a modern building, even if a drinking foutain were in that room. He may never have learned what a drinking fountain was or how to operate it to get water.

Follow Fig. 1-4 for a discussion of the elements of learning. The learning process for information gathering must be developed and learned. The sensory systems are the means by which stimuli are sensed and

Meriem Kaluger

Hands-on experiences, making use of the motor and sensory processes, help to facilitate learning "how to learn."

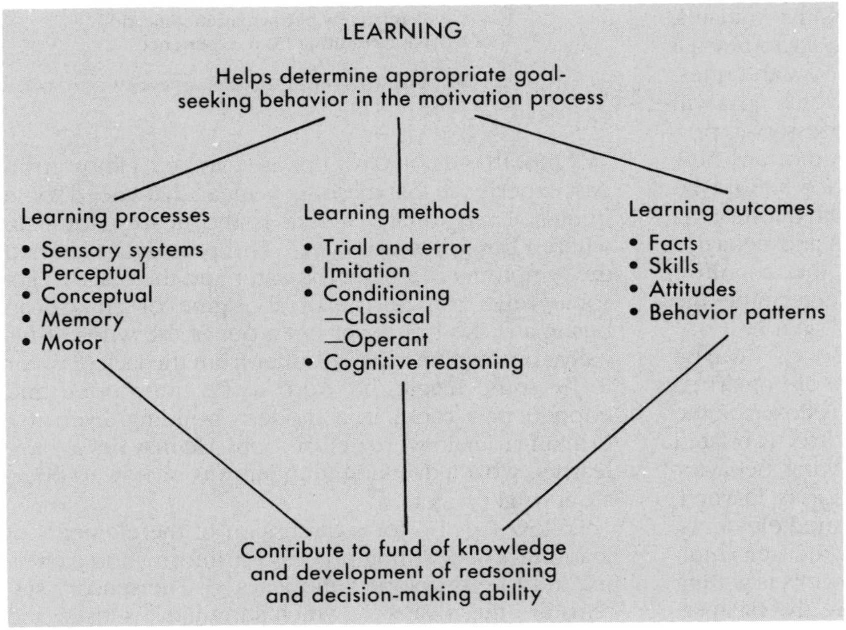

FIG. 1-4 ***Component parts of learning process that influence quality of goal-seeking behavior.***

sent to the brain to be identified. Each of the senses—visual, auditory, tactile, smell, and taste—has its own *perceptual system* that processes and organizes the incoming stimuli. Each perceptual process must be developed. The *conceptual process* consists of skills in the use of problem solving, interpretation, and reasoning ability. These also must be developed. All aspects of sensory and verbal stimulation, the development of language usage, and the acquisition of socialization skills contribute to the learning process.

What is learned are called *learning outcomes*. Learning outcomes are (1) facts, knowledge, or information, (2) skills or habits, (3) attitudes, interests, or values, and (4) patterns or styles of behavior. The facts, skills, and attitudes are stored in memory banks for future reference. The methods by which the outcomes are learned are by (1) trial and error (hit or miss), (2) imitation, (3) conditioning, or (4) cognitive reasoning. The learned data become the fund of knowledge from which the motivation process, with the help of the thinking and reasoning parts of the brain, decides which behaviors and goals are appropriate to satisfy physical and psychological needs. Sometimes the right information is available; sometimes it is not.

A person has a freedom of choice in initiating behavior and in making decisions. The individual can choose an action that will be correct or one that will be wrong. The outcomes of many actions can be predicted if one could only know all the principles and laws involved. Once a behavior is initiated, however, its actions are taken over by the cause-and-effect element inherent within all physical and psychological laws.

It is important for an individual to develop a value judgment system, a life philosophy of what is considered good or bad, better or worse, desirable or undesirable, to enable that person to make decisions in keeping with what is considered to be most important. Learning will contribute, positively or negatively, to the decision-making process. A psychological behaviorist would ask that a person learn to stress behavioral controls and to manipulate factors in the environment to bring about desired results by the use of reinforcement, rewards, or punishment. A psychological humanist would suggest that the individual learn how to achieve self-actualization by fulfilling the inner self and by seeking to develop one's human potential.

THEORETICAL VIEWS OF HUMAN DEVELOPMENT

What is the basic nature of human development? There are a number of different views. None appears

TABLE 1-4 Theoretical approaches to development

	Physiological	*Cognitive*	*Behavioristic*	*Psychoanalytic*	*Humanistic*
Basic concepts	Maturation: orderly sequential unfolding of physiological changes	Cognitive stages: intellectual adaptation to environmental demands develops cognitive structures by stages	Conditioning: development is related to learning based on classical and operant conditioning	Freudian: biological instincts in the unconscious are forces of development	Phenomenology: self-concept as a unified theme through personal precepts of conscious experience
	Ethology: animal development reflects formation and evolution of human development	Information processing: development of the perceptual, conceptual, and memory systems by use of symbolic representation	Social learning: development is influenced by imitation, vicarious learning, and reinforcement	Eriksonian: development results from resolving psychosocial crisis	Humanism: emphasizes uniqueness of human beings, subjective feelings, and human values
Sources of development	Biogenetic predisposition to development	Interaction of mental potentials with verbal and sensory stimulation and problem-solving situations in the environment	Drives respond to environmental stimuli, incentives, and reinforcement	Freud: energy of the libido, id, superego, and ego Erikson: resolution of conflict between opposing psychosocial forces	Inner qualities of self-realization and self-actualization
Goals	The emergence of physical structures, organic systems, and motor behavior	Qualitative improvement of the cognitive structures to process information	Socially acceptable behavior based on environmental learning	Freud: psycho-sexual and resolving conflicts originating in the unconscious Erikson: sense of identity and psycho-social development	Personal growth through fulfillment of human potentials
Limitations	Minor emphasis on importance of environmental influences	Stress is basically on intellectual development and its usages but very little stress on physical growth	Emphasis is only on behavior that can be learned and measured	Focus is largely limited to personality development	Elements of humanistic theory are subjective and difficult to measure
Theorists	Maturation Arnold Gesell Ilg and Ames Ethology Konrad Lorenz	Cognitive Stages Jean Piaget Lawrence Kohlberg Information processing D.E. Broadbent Jerome Bruner	Conditioning B.F. Skinner Social learning Albert Bandura Miller and Dollard	Psychoananlysis Sigmund Freud Carl Jung Neopsychoanalysis Erik Erikson Harry Stacks Sullivan	Phenomenology Carl Rogers Humanism Abraham Maslow

nature the genetic-biological determinants used to explain developmental changes.

nurture the impact of environmental factors on child growth and development. Nurture is usually contrasted with nature in describing development.

to answer all the questions raised concerning growth and development, but all offer a rationale that should be considered for the contribution they make toward a systematic understanding of human development.

The various developmental theories differ in at least four general characteristics. First, some theories stress a sequence of age-related stages of development; others stress a continuous topical growth pattern without reference to age levels. Second, the theories differ as to the type of growth, development, and behavior studied; none of the theories presents a rationale for all five domains of development (physical, intellectual, social, emotional, and moral). Third, the theories vary as to the age levels studied. Some only consider development in adulthood; others do not consider that age level at all. Fourth, theories differ as to the basic determinants of growth and development that are emphasized. Some stress biological and genetic determinants; others emphasize social and cultural determinants; only a few attempt to include all of these determinants. In this chapter the theoretical approaches are presented in a very general, descriptive form. In those chapters where they have application they are presented in greater detail. Table 1-4 summarizes the theoretical approaches to growth and development.

Issue of nature versus nurture

A side issue, but not a theoretical approach to development, is the question of which is more important in growth and development—heredity or environment. In the past many major debates have been held on the "heredity versus environment" or "nature versus nurture" issue. Each side could make some positive points, but neither side won the debate. It was like asking, "When you clap your hands, which hand makes the loudest noise, the right one or the left one?" They both make a major contribution to the noise! The current position on the importance of heredity and environment is that both are in a continual process of interaction (they act on each other). There are exceptions in which the influences of one of these factors take over to the virtual exclusion of the other, but these situations are not common. The typical course of development is characterized by a continuous interplay of hereditary and environmental forces, even during pregnancy. The interplay of ***nature*** and ***nurture*** is unique to the individual. The "either-or" view of heredity or environment is not tenable. They both have major contributions to make (Miller, 1983).

Physiological approach

The physiological approach most pertinent to human growth and development is the maturational approach. The *maturational view* emphasizes the emergence of patterns of development of organic systems, physical structures, and motor capabilities under the influence of genetic and maturational forces. Physiological development and motor development occur in an almost inevitable, orderly, sequential pattern in children the world over. The changes are initiated by the inherent predisposition of the organism to spontaneously develop the neurological, muscular, and hormonal systems of the body. This spontaneous development may be inhibited by severe environmental deprivation, but it does follow a normal course if the individual is not unduly influenced by inhibiting environmental factors.

The individual who has done much, if not the most, to pioneer the exploration of the importance of maturational determinants in shaping human development was *Arnold Gesell.* Along with Francis Ilg and Louise Bates Ames, Gesell did extensive longitudinal studies of the developing human from birth to age 16 (Gesell et al., 1956). They stated that growth of the mind and of physical functions was profoundly bound up with the growth of the nervous system. Only when the nervous system was developed enough for the performance of a particular function would the child be ready to perform that function. Gesell believed that the pattern of human development, particularly physical, followed certain laws of maturation that evolved and unfolded in very specific, predetermined ways if they were not interfered with adversely by environmental factors. He placed great stress on observable growth, development, and behavior of the child or adolescent and on the role of the environmental variables in adolescent development. Some of his findings, including his work on developmental schedules, are presented in Chapter 5.

According to the physiological theoretical approach to human development, unimpeded physiological maturation will, at its own pace and in its own time, unfold the physical readiness needed to learn to walk, to ride a bicycle, or to climb to the top of a jungle gym. From that vantage point you get another perspective of your life space.

cognition the process of gaining knowledge about the world through sensing, perceiving, using symbols, and reasoning; the actual knowledge that an individual has about the world. Knowing the world through the use of one's perceptual and conceptual abilities.

Gesell's works are well documented with films and recorded observations. His principles and sequences of physical development are generally well recognized and accepted although a little outdated as to the timing of certain motor sequences. A limitation of his work is that he did not stress environmental influences as much as later researchers thought he should have. Gesell tended to overemphasize the importance of maturation and did not stress the influence of learning. He assumed that the physiological developmental quotient, based on maturational levels, reflected the child's rate of growth in all domains of development at the moment of testing. It was as if he considered physiological development to reflect the development of the total child, cognitively, socially, and emotionally.

Cognitive approach

Cognitive theories emphasize the active role played by the child in his or her own development. ***Cognition*** is a general term referring to mental processes, such as awareness, perception, recognizing, reasoning, and assessing, by which knowledge is gained. Cognitive development refers to the way in which cognitive ability (cognition) is acquired. Cognitive theorists view the child as continually striving to function more effectively in his or her world. Through this effort the child develops more efficient cognitive ways of exploring the environment, thinking about experiences, and learning to make appropriate responses. Foremost among cognitive theorists is *Jean Piaget.*

The *cognitive approach* recognizes the importance of the relationship between the developing person and the environment. At any one moment the level of cognitive development depends on the maturation of the nervous system plus the experience and materials encountered in the environment. A simple formula might be: *Maturation + Experience = Level of cognitive development.* As a result cognitive development is not a steady, continuous, uninterrupted process; rather it is one that is marked by stages, involving shifts in ways of thinking and behaving. The emphasis is on processes and not on end results. The environment is involved in the extent to which it slows down, speeds up, or contributes to the process of development.

Jean Piaget's theory (1970) covers the development of intelligence over the life span. It has influenced much of the research in the fields of perceptual and intellectual growth. All knowledge, according to Piaget, comes from interaction with the environment. Newborn infants have certain reflex behaviors and random movements that can be used in interacting with objects and events in the environment. Knowledge comes as babies make a link or connection between their actions and the objects with which they come into contact. The link becomes a construction of reality, as the baby sees it. With an accumulation of understanding, stages of intellectual development are created. This understanding will filter into other areas, such as social, language, and moral development. Aspects of Piaget's theory of cognitive development are presented in Chapters 2, 5, 7, 8, and 10.

Piaget and his followers are students of the structure of cognitive thought and its orderly sequence of development. They believe that cognitive structures provide the basis for other complex behavior, such as the use of language. One important controversy concerns the extent to which the learning of language determines the structure of thought or vice versa (Chomsky, 1972). Not all theorists, especially behaviorists, accept Piaget's description of the processes that underlie developmental changes or his assumption that a child must progress through an unchanging series of four unique stages in the course of cognitive development. Piaget's developmental stages stop at about the age of 16. Other theorists, such as Pascual-Leone (1980), Arlin (1975, 1980) and Neimark (1982), are investigating adult levels of cognitive development. If there is another limitation to Piaget's theory, it is a lack of in-depth discussion after infancy of the social, emotional, and neurological development of the child and the influence of these elements on cognitive development (Miller, 1983).

Behaviorism—learning approach

In *behavior-learning* theories the primary motivator of development and behavior is the environment, which manipulates basic biological and psychological drives and needs by offering incentives or rewards for "good" or "correct" behavior and punishment for undesirable behavior. We are what our environment makes us. Changes within the individual are quantitative and therefore are measurable, providing scientists with "proofs" that learning (change in behavior) is taking place.

Conditioning. The two basic conditioning processes by which learning takes place are classical conditioning and operant or instrumental conditioning. ***Classical conditioning*** establishes a relationship among a stimulus, a natural response, and a conditioned stimulus that is developed to bring out the response. The stimulus can be the presentation of dry cat food like Friskies. The natural response is the saliva beginning to flow in the cat's mouth. Soon the cat responds to the conditioned stimulus alone, the shaking of the box. Before classical conditioning, the unconditioned stimulus (food) brings about the unconditioned response (saliva). During conditioning, the conditional stimulus (the shaking of the box) is related to food and the salivation. After conditioning, the conditioned stimulus (shaking of box) is enough to bring about the salivation (conditioned response).

Operant conditioning involves the giving of a reward immediately after desired behavior is performed. No stimulus is provided to initiate a behavior. In this case, children (or animals) receive a reward like something to eat or social approval ("That's good!") after they have performed the desired behavior. It may be necessary to build by reinforcing small behavioral steps to the complete desired behavior. This approach is called ***shaping behavior.*** Afterwards, the behavior is maintained by periodic reinforcement. The procedure is much more complex than presented here. *B.F. Skinner* (1974) has developed elaborate designs whereby all types of animal and human behavior can be instrumentally influenced and changed.

Social learning theory. The application of behavior learning theory plus cognitive processes to the development of learning and thinking is known as *social learning theory* (Bandura, 1977; Rosenthal and Zimmerman, 1978). This approach focuses on patterns of behavior the individual learns in coping with the environment. It emphasizes the reciprocal interaction between behavior and environment. The type of behavior learned is partly determined by the ***reinforcement*** received. Social learning theory differs from a strict behaviorist position (conditioned learning) by stressing the importance of cognitive processes. Because we think, we are able to foresee the probable consequences of our actions and alter our behavior accordingly in order to achieve the desired outcome (reward or reinforcement). In freezing weather we don't have to wait until we experience shivering and numbness in order to know that we should be wearing warm clothing and gloves.

classical conditioning an experimental method in which a conditioned stimulus is paired with an unconditioned stimulus to condition a particular response.

modeling a principle and a process by which an individual learns by observing the behavior of others.

operant conditioning a type of conditioning in which an organism's responses change as a result of the application of reinforcement or reward. It is based on the principle that organisms tend to engage in behavior that succeeds in producing desirable outcomes. Associated with B. F. Skinner, it is also called instrumental conditioning.

reinforcement in operant conditioning, the presentation or withdrawal of an event following a response, which increases or decreases the likelihood of that response occurring again.

shaping behavior applying reinforcement to every increment of behavior that approximates one's goal or target behavior.

Learning may come vicariously from observation—that is, watching the behavior of others and noting its consequences for them. Social learning theorists emphasize the role of *models* in transmitting specific behaviors and emotional responses. ***Modeling*** is a form of learning from observing a model. This type of learning goes much further than copying or imitating. Children especially may generalize from the model's behavior to a wide range of similar behaviors of their own.

Another aspect of social learning theory is the importance of *self-regulatory processes.* People set their own standards of conduct or performance and respond to their behavior in self-satisfied or self-critical ways. Thus reinforcement has two sources: external and self-evaluative. Sometimes the feedback from these sources coincides, and sometimes it is contradictory. An adolescent may be reinforced by the peer group for certain behaviors even though, in terms of personal standards, he or she may not approve of that behavior.

Meriem Kaluger

Social learning theory states that learning may come from observing a model, as well as from receiving reinforcement. These children in Bali are being exposed to the religious practices of their mothers. Note the sashes worn around the waists and the small woven baskets that will be filled with flowers and presented to Buddha.

In behaviorism and social learning theories, the focus is on the external behavior of the individual, although social learning theorists acknowledge the importance of cognitive processes in developing behavior. However, both approaches are environmentally oriented. A criticism of the behavioristic theories, according to Hogan (1974), is that they do not recognize any natural goals for development and do not propose that behavior undergoes qualitative changes over time. Therefore, says Hogan, these are not theories of development but only theories of change. They assume a different model of human nature, one that ignores patterns of growth and development that cannot be measured, and one that rejects concepts such as the unconscious, innate predispositions (maturation), and inner dynamics. A discussion of social learning theory and behaviorism is also presented in Chapters 6 and 7.

Psychoanalytic approach

The *psychoanalytic approach* emphasizes the role of internal factors in development, especially in personality and emotional development. Psychoanalytic theories view the process of development as dynamic interaction between (1) internal needs, drives, and forces of energy, and (2) environmental forces, including significant others, that impose constraints in the form of societal norms. These norms indicate the boundaries within which an individual's drives may be expressed and needs satisfied.

Freud. Sigmund Freud (1953), in his classic psychoanalytic theory, suggests that children must pass five stages of psychosexual development before reaching maturity. Each stage is defined by the dominant source of gratification for the instinctual needs of the individual. These stages are (1) oral stage, receiving pleasure from sucking and the use of the mouth, (2) anal stage, during which the child receives pleasure from controlling (or using) the bowels and bladder, (3) phallic stage, focusing on physical contact with the opposite-sex parent as a love object, (4) latency stage, a calming period in which the intense needs for pleasure are suppressed, and (5) genital stage, during which the sexual drive and interest in heterosexual relationships with others (not the parents) is once again kindled.

The end product of development, according to traditional psychoanalysts, is dependent on the extent to which gratification is frustrated at any one of the stages by factors in the child's environment and by the responses of the child to the frustrations. Theoretically, conflicts or frustrations causing an emotional fixation at any stage result in a need to continue seeking the pleasure that was characteristic at that stage. For example, an individual frustrated at the oral period may, as an older person, emphasize smoking, overeating, or the biting of fingernails. Frustration at the anal stage may result in seeking pleasure by controlling one's own behavior (compulsive or perfectionistic) or the behavior of others (domineering). Psychoanalytic theory of personality is presented in Chapter 6..

Erikson. A sociopsychoanalytic view is presented by Erik Erikson (1963). He places less emphasis on Freud's theory of psychosexual development as fundamental to human development. Erikson postulates that the inherent drives in humans lead them to confront a series of psychosocial personal conflicts at different stages of life. For Erikson, the personality of an individual is a reflection of the way in which each conflict is resolved. Compared to Freud's theory, Erikson's approach places greater emphasis on adaptive behavior.

Erikson describes eight stages of an individual's development, beginning at birth and infancy and culminating in old age. Each stage has a psychosocial crisis or task to master. For example, the psychosocial crisis at birth to age 1 is *trust* versus *mistrust:* "Can I or can I not trust others?" At middle childhood the crisis is one of *industry* versus *inferiority:* "Can I do some things well, or am I a failure?" In early adulthood, the psychosocial crisis is one of *intimacy* versus *isolation:* "Can I share myself intimately with others, or must I remain alone?"

There is possibility of a conflict at each stage. The conflict or crisis must be successfully resolved so a positive quality can be built into the personality structure in order for further development to take place. The overall task is to acquire a positive ego identity while moving from one stage to another. The eight stages are discussed in Chapters 2, 10, and 12.

• • •

Psychoanalytic theory is difficult to subject to scientific inquiry. Some psychologists, mostly behaviorists, do not completely accept Freud's view of the unconscious. They prefer to speak to degrees of awareness rather than to assume a sharp distinction between conscious and unconscious thoughts. Humanists consider Freud's view of instincts a negative view of life. There is criticism of Freud's emphasis on the powerful force

dynamic refers to forces and potent influences that are capable of producing changes within the organism or personality.

developmental task a specific learning problem that arises at a particular stage of life and that individuals must accomplish to meet the demands of their culture. Developmental tasks vary with one's age and persist as objectives throughout life. The nature of the developmental task is such that one learning is related to, merges into, and forms the basis for the next learning.

of the id. Some prefer to emphasize the importance of the ego or of the self in personality (Miller, 1983).

Humanistic approach

Humanistic psychology emphasizes the qualities that differentiate human beings from animals, particularly feelings, creativity, humor, human potential, and psychological growth. It focuses on subjective experiences together with the individual's own perception and interpretation of these events. This is the idea behind the statement, "Get in touch with your own feelings."

Like psychoanalytic theory, some humanistic theories emphasize dynamics. *Psychodynamic theories* are concerned with motivation and the ***dynamics*** of behavior and development in all their ramifications. *Gestalt psychology* is an example of dynamic psychology. Other humanistic theories cluster around the terms *humanistic, existential, phenomenology,* and *self-theory psychology*. They all emphasize the positive aspects of human potential. Humanistic theories of personality are presented in Chapter 6.

Rogers. The basic motive for each individual is self-realization, a tendency toward growth and fulfillment as a human being. Carl Rogers (1961) speaks of personal growth toward the goal of self-acceptance. He introduces the ideas of the innate goodness of the self, its natural potential, and its desire for knowledge and healthy growth. What is important is that the individual becomes aware of potential for personal growth. Awareness of the various aspects of current external situations is also important.

Maslow. Abraham Maslow (1968) has contributed heavily to the theory of human growth with two concepts. First, he speaks of nested motivation, the idea that human motives are nested in a hierarchical order and that a person is always motivated to higher-order motives as lower-order motives are satisfied. Once the motives of survival (food, water, and so on) are satisfied, the individual seeks higher-order motives, such as security, belongingness, esteem, and cognitive, aesthetic, and altruistic needs.

The second concept is that of self-actualization, which is attained when individuals make real the breadth and depth of their human potentialities. Competent human beings not only fulfill their needs, but they cope, resolve conflicts, give support to others, and contribute to their societies. The psychoanalyst emphasizes the importance of resolving conflicts originating in the unconscious; the behaviorist stresses interaction with the environment for the purpose of learning desired behaviors; the self-actualization theory concentrates on inner qualities that enhance the personal growth of the individual. Maslow's concepts are presented in depth in Chapter 12.

The limitations of the humanistic approach to development and behavior are found in its emphasis on many elements that cannot be measured. The humanists make a valuable point when they emphasize the need to focus attention on solving problems relevant to human welfare and personal development rather than studying isolated bits of behavior in the laboratory. But to assume, as some liberal humanists do, that the methods of scientific psychology can contribute nothing worthwhile to an understanding of human nature is to invite a relativistic, subjective approach to the study of growth and development. Both Rogers and Maslow have approached most of their studies on a data base. Other humanists have not been as scientifically oriented.

DEVELOPMENTAL TASKS

Robert Havighurst (1979) primarily addresses human growth and development in Western societies and is interested in stages of growth, predicated somewhat on an age basis. At each stage, he presents some major developmental tasks that must be mastered or achieved in order to meet the developmental needs of that age level. His developmental task theory is an eclectic one combining previously developed concepts into one theory.

Concept: Developmental tasks

Havighurst states that "A developmental task is a task which arises at or about a certain period in the life of the individual, successful achievement of which leads to his happiness and to success with later tasks, while failure leads to unhappiness in the individual, disapproval by the society, and difficulty with later tasks" (1972, p. 2). ***Developmental tasks*** may arise from physical maturation, from expectations of the surrounding society, and from the desires and values of the emerging personality (Havighurst, 1982). Examples of developmental tasks in infancy and early childhood are learning to take solid food, to achieve physiological stability, and to form simple concepts of social and physical reality. In middle childhood some tasks are to learn physical skills necessary for games and to learn appropriate sex roles. In adolescence, tasks include developing new relations with age mates of both sexes and developing intellectual skills necessary for duties of citizenship. Early adulthood tasks may include selecting a mate and getting started in an occupation. Some middle adulthood tasks are establishing and maintaining an economic standard of living and, for those who are married, relating to the spouse as a person. In later maturity, tasks include adjusting to retirement and reduced income and establishing satisfactory physical living arrangements. In this book developmental tasks will be presented for each age level discussed.

In general, Havighurst seeks to combine the age-level needs of the individual with the demands of society—or the culture—for that stage of development. What the individual needs and what society demands comprise the developmental tasks. The tasks are the skills, knowledge, behaviors, and attitudes that an individual has to acquire through physical maturation, social learning, and personal effort.

The developmental tasks may differ from culture to culture, depending on biological, psychological, and cultural expectations of the group. Tasks that are determined primarily by biological factors may be almost universal in nature. Tasks determined by cultural elements may differ greatly, not only from culture to culture, but also according to the demands of socioeconomic classes or "caste" systems existing within a culture. The behavior patterns learned are essential to personal and social adjustments; indeed, some of the tasks to be learned are vital to survival, especially in the earlier years. Each phase or stage of development has a number of tasks or organizational (intellectual) patterns that must be learned if the individual is to achieve the level of maturity expected by the cultural group. The expectations change at each stage of development.

stage (in development) a concept used to explain the orderly relationship among developmental changes in behavior and indicating that the organization of behavior is qualitatively different from one stage to the next.

Havighurst's theory has both strong and weak points. It helps place the life span of development in perspective and underscores the importance of society's expectations and the teachable moment. However, some people purposely choose to deviate from the developmental tasks proposed by Havighurst, such as choosing to remain single and being a career person rather than a family person. The proposed tasks do not need to apply to all individuals. Kenkel (1977) prefers to change the concept from tasks to developmental strivings so that the need for defining what is successful completion of the task can be eliminated. It is also important to note that Havighurst's developmental tasks primarily pertain to a Western society and, more specifically, to the societies of the United States of America and of Canada.

Critique of stage approach

Mention should be made of the *stage approach* in development and of its limitations. The ***stage concept*** refers to developmental age-level stages that are found in various theories. (The age-stage concept is presented earlier in this chapter.) Society tends to organize life tasks and roles by age stages. It makes assumptions and assignments of what people should do or how they should act at different times in their lives.

Piaget, Freud, Erikson, Havighurst, and others have ascribed developmental levels according to ages. For instance, Piaget presents four levels of cognitive development: sensorimotor stage, ages 0-2; preoperational stage, ages 2-7; concrete operations stage, ages 7 to 11; and formal operations stage, ages 11 to 16. Freud predicates personality development on an age-stage format consisting of the oral period, the anal period, the phallic period, the latency period, and the genital period. Each has an age-level designation. Erikson has a series of psychosocial crises extending over the life span of an individual. Each stage is indicated by an age. Havighurst has identified developmental tasks that become appropriate at different times of life. The concept of stage is basic to each of these theories.

A major characteristic attributed to stages is that distinctive stages emerge in development in an unchanging and constant order. Furthermore, the stages occur at rather specific age levels. Some authorities question stage theories that portray an individual as having life stages that unfold, somewhat automatically, according to some inner psychological plan. As pointed out by the cohorts concept, individuals change according to a changing society, and the effects of such events will vary with generations and with life cycles. Lacy and Hendricks (1980) report that research failed to produce any consistent support for developmental stage models. They conclude that stage models of the life span are not compatible with the daily problems of living in specific societies.

The implications of the critique of stage models are that not everyone goes through all of the stages and not everyone experiences stages at the same age. The developmental tasks model of Havighurst is especially vulnerable because the tasks place much emphasis on society's prescription of behaviors and tasks to be learned. Society in the Western nations is becoming far less rigid and life-styles are becoming more fluid. Society no longer provides a consistent clock that says when a child should go to school, when a person should marry, or how old a person must be before holding a major executive position. However, if handled with care and some mental reservations, the concept of developmental tasks, as well as the other theories, has something to offer in terms of providing a structure or a framework from which discussion and interpretation may begin.

LIFE-SPAN RESEARCH

Every so often there are students in a developmental course who do poorly in class work because of misconceptions they have concerning their depth of understanding of human development and behavior. Consider these three statements: "I know about young children because I am the oldest in a family of seven kids and I had to help rear them." "When I was in high school, I was involved in many activities where I interacted with teenagers on a personal basis. I got to know a lot about adolescent behavior and problems." "In my profession (ministry) I deal with people all the time. I teach children in Sunday School, I counsel adults, I visit the elderly, and I've raised a family on my own. I thought I knew enough about growth and development to get me through this course." These comments were made by three persons who had failed a major test in a developmental psychology course. Life-span psychology as a field of study is not that simple or naive.

Human behavior and human development are aspects of life in which we are constantly immersed. We are living the development, we are experiencing the behavior, and we are constantly observing what is happening within ourselves and in others. No wonder it is so easy to be mistaken about how much we really know. Yet who has not had the experience of thinking: "I don't understand what's happening to me [or to him or her]. I'm confused"? Or who has not made an observation concerning a phase of development or behavior based on preconceived ideas? "Oh, it's just a stage he's going through" or "That's what you have to expect when you're that age." Are you beginning to see the point that we're trying to make? The point is that, in spite of our involvement in growth and development, we all have bits of information that are false because they are based on half-truths, stereotyped notions, bias and prejudices, myths, or mistaken ideas. We cannot afford to assume that we know it all because "we've been there." The study and science of developmental psychology must be data based inasmuch as possible. Statements of principles or facts must be predicated on verifiable information. Findings and observations are not accepted by scientists unless they can be substantiated by corroborating evidence. In the pursuit of psychological knowledge and understanding, we should do the same. Theories are not facts; they are considered judgments based on the best observations available to the theorist. It is important to determine if the concept is based on a fact, theory, myth, bias, or on unsubstantiated information. At the same time we must also recognize the limitations of science in being able to give all the answers. Science cannot "prove" what love, friendship, and religious feelings are. As human beings we must acknowledge the input of experiential knowing in our search for total knowledge.

Research considerations

dependent variable some facet of a child's functioning that is measured in an experiment and presumed to be under the control of one or more manipulated factors. See also **independent variable.**

experimental method the method of investigation of natural events that seeks to control the variables involved so as to more precisely define cause and effect relationships. Most frequently done in a laboratory, but need not be.

independent variable the variable that is controlled by the experimenter to determine its effect on the dependent variable.

naturalistic observation a form of study in which there is observation of behavior without any interference from the investigator.

As age advances and experiences increase, the internal and the external phases of development constantly change. Developmental psychology seeks to study the internal and external phases of developmental changes. The *aims of developmental psychology* are to learn how these changes take place, how to describe and explain them, how to predict them, and how (when necessary or possible) to control them. The individual interested in the application of research findings needs to know the degree of validity of those findings just as much as does the researcher. The quality and the degree of scientific rigor must be recognized. Since our approach is from a life-span perspective, it is also important to know how a piece of research was conducted. For example, does the research sample consist of different individuals of different ages (cross-sectional study), or does it consist of the same individuals studied at different ages in their lives (longitudinal study)? The dissimilarity of these two approaches could provide a difference in their findings because of the time factor involved.

An initial consideration is whether the research approach is experimental or ***naturalistic observation.*** Both approaches have their place, depending on the problem being investigated and the degree to which the research setting can be controlled. An ***experimental method*** is one in which the variables (factors or conditions capable of being changed) relating to the research problem can be controlled or manipulated. The research setting is usually a laboratory where factors can be highly regulated so that only one condition (variable) will be treated or manipulated differently for the experimental group. The same variable within the control group is not manipulated. If a difference in the ultimate performance of the two groups occurs, it is assumed to result from the one condition that was changed. The way the variable was treated differently is known as the ***independent variable.*** The change(s) that occurred in the factor that was treated in a different way is referred to as the ***dependent variable.*** Refer to Fig. 1-5 for a diagram of the experimental approach.

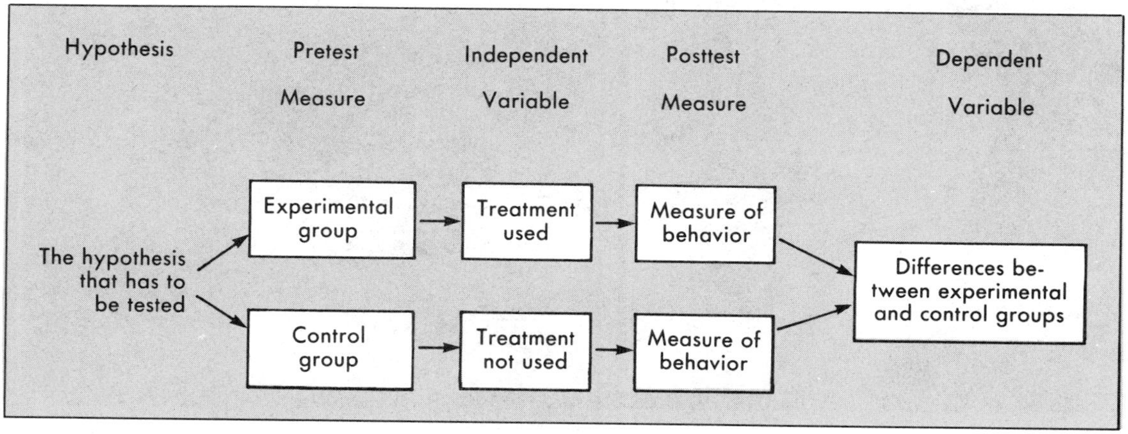

FIG. 1-5 *A simple experimental design.*

cohorts the members of a certain age group; a group of people of the same age.

Methods of developmental research

Developmental psychologists are primarily interested in changes that take place in an individual. These changes can be studied by the cross-sectional method, the longitudinal method, or a combination of the two, the cross-sectional/longitudinal sequential method. The reason for having more than one approach is related to an age available, a time factor, and the complication of cohort differences. It is possible to study a number of different age groups at one time (*cross-sectional method*), to study the same group of individuals as they reach different ages over a longer time span (*longitudinal method*), or to study the data obtained from studies involving the successions of two or more groups studied at different times of measurement *(sequential strategies)*.

Cohorts and cohort differences

Before we present the developmental methods of research, it is important to consider the concept of cohorts and cohort differences. ***Cohorts*** are a group of people all born and living during the same period of time, experiencing the same historical, social, economic, and political conditions. A *cohort group* may extend over an age range of 5 to 7 years. The individ-

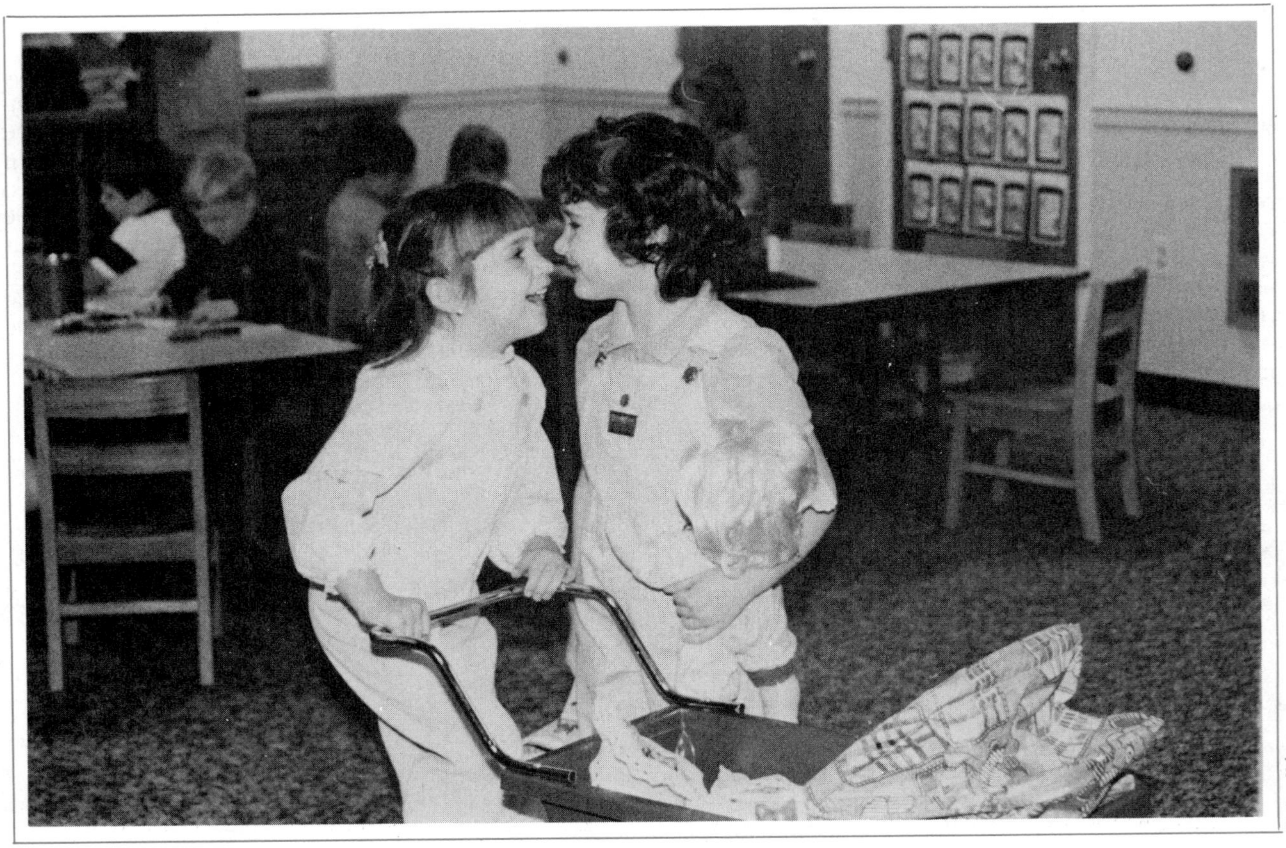

Meriem Kaluger

Isn't this picture typical of 3-year-old girls, playing with dolls and a baby buggy? Don't be too quick to stereotype little girls. At the same time this picture was taken, there were four other little girls playing with trucks.

uals within a cohort group would be living during the same time frame. These cohorts would also be experiencing personal life events—such as beginning school, graduating from high school, getting married, rearing a family, reaching retirement and social security age—at about the same time.

The implication is that cohorts would be exposed to major influences that may be unique to them and affect their lives and development in special ways. Consider the following two cohort groups. Think of the people who were in their preadolescence and adolescence during the depression years of the middle 1930s and in their early twenties during World War II. They would have been exposed to a considerably different historical period than the cohorts born in 1960 who were in preadolescence and adolescence during the middle 1970s and in their twenties during the early 1980s. The social, economic, political, and emotional climates were quite different. The members of the latter cohort group were born in an affluent economy, had better health care and more educational opportunities, were exposed to television, space travel, and computers, and were aware of, but not involved in, a war effort in Vietnam. What impressions or effects did their different time spans have on their growth, development, and behavior? A simple but significant illustration is to think of all the young men and women whose lives were destroyed during World War II, making that age cohort group smaller than usual. The members of that cohort group are now in their early 60s. They are a unique sample of 60-year-olds. They are not like the people who were in their 60s during 1930, nor are they like those who will be in their 60s in 2020.

Cohort differences are differences that exist between people of different age-groups. These differences are attributable to changing social, cultural, historical, or environmental conditions and experiences.

The cohort factor affects life-span research methods. Age-groups who are faced with a different set of life conditions during important, impressionable periods in their lives will develop, and perhaps behave, in ways that are not found in other age-groups. Table 1-5 illustrates prominent events that occurred at different ages for cohort groups. Each cohort group has its own historical period, economic climate, definition of maturity, and sense of responsibility.

Cross-sectional method

The most common research method in developmental research is the ***cross-sectional method.*** The cross-sectional method consists of research that selects and compares individuals of different ages at one time of testing. For example, a psychologist is interested in examining speaking vocabulary development in children from 1 to 6 years of age. Using the cross-sectional approach, the psychologist will select children of different age levels (maybe groups at every 6 months) and do a spoken vocabulary word count. The study of the different age-groups would be done only once and within a short time frame. A comparison of the percentage change in vocabulary size would provide normative or descriptive data. A norm chart for development would describe the vocabulary size found at different age levels.

cross-sectional research **studies that compare different age groups at some specific point in time.**

The advantage of the cross-sectional method is that the psychologist can collect much data quickly without having to wait for children to pass through all of the age levels. This method can be used to study the behavior or development that characterizes the different age-groups. It is an economical way to obtain normative data.

The disadvantage of the cross-sectional method is that it cannot be used to examine the stability of a behavior over a long period of time nor to examine the impact of life experiences on subsequent development and behavior. This method does not observe the same child at different ages; it can only compare the development or behavior of different age-level children. As a result, cohort differences may occur. This method cannot establish whether the differences are due to age changes or to cohort differences.

The normative data provided by cross-sectional methods provide a scale or guideline to which other children can be compared. However, a limitation is that the group in the study that provided the norms may be quite different from the children who are being compared to those norms. The study may have been based on white, middle-class, suburban children while the group (or child) compared to the norms may consist of black, inner city-children from a lower economic class.

Longitudinal method

The ***longitudinal research*** design is a method in which the same individuals are tested periodically

longitudinal research a study technique in which the same individual is examined over a long period or over a complete developmental stage.

over a length of time, sometimes even a lifetime. The results of the testing at the different ages are then compared and attempts are made to account for the observed changes. For example, a psychologist wants to study the rate at which changes take place in vocab-

TABLE 1-5 Cohorts and generational events*

Decades of cohorts	*Historical events*	*Business and technology*	*Social and media events*	*Music and dancing*	*Famous people*
Older adults					
1900-1909	Turn of century Spanish-American War McKinley assassinated	Severe unemployment Trolley cars Model T Ford Electric light bulb	First airplane flight First radio message First world series Yellow fever epidemic	"Let Me Call You Sweetheart" "Home on the Range" "Sweet Adeline" The turkey trot	William McKinley Teddy Roosevelt W.H. Taft Henry Ford Orville and Frank Wright Charlie Chaplin
1910-1919	First woman in Congress World War I Communism started	Federal income tax Telephone invented Vitamins discovered Use of electricity	Panama Canal opens Haley's comet Titanic sinks	"Alexander's Ragtime Band" "When Irish Eyes Are Smiling" "Over There" The fox-trot	W.H. Taft Woodrow Wilson Thomas Edison Buffalo Bill Jack Dempsey Susan B. Anthony
Midlife adults					
1920-1929	Prohibition Act Harding's Teapot Dome Scandal League of Nations	Child labor laws Oil replacing coal Mechanical cotton picker Wall Street collapse	Bootlegging Lindbergh's Atlantic flight Empire State Building	Vaudeville "Yes, We Have No Bananas" "Old Man River" The Charleston	Woodrow Wilson Warren Harding Calvin Coolidge Herbert Hoover Babe Ruth Andrew Carnegie
1930-1939	Great Depression New Deal Social Security Act	Bank panic WPA—public works Color movies	Amelia Earhart solo across the Atlantic John Dillinger: public enemy no. 1 Hindenburg explosion	WPA orchestras "Brother, Can You Spare a Dime?" "I've Got You Under My Skin" The big apple	New York Yankees Bing Crosby Mickey Mouse
Early adults					
1940-1949	World War II United Nations GI Bill of Rights	Taft-Hartley Act 40-hour week First electric locomotive First atomic bomb	Pearl Harbor attack First black major league baseball player—Jackie Robinson Country of Israel	Big band sounds "In the Mood" "White Christmas" "When You Wish Upon a Star" Jitterbug	Franklin D. Roosevelt Harry Truman Winston Churchill Joseph Stalin Bob Hope Frank Sinatra

*Cohort differences are influenced by the major events that occurred during significant periods in a person's life,,such as 15 years to 25 years of age.

ulary size in children. Using the longitudinal method, this psychologist would get a group of children, all the same age (let's say, 12 months of age) and determine the number of words in the children's speaking vocabulary at that age. Then every 6 months the psychologist would test the *same* children to learn how much the size of their vocabulary had changed. The research with the same children could be continued on a less frequent basis for the rest of their lives.

The advantages of the longitudinal method are its

TABLE 1-5 Cohorts and generational events—cont'd

Decades of cohorts	*Historical events*	*Business and technology*	*Social and media events*	*Music and dancing*	*Famous people*
Early adults—cont'd					
1950-1959	Korean War Cold war Truman fired MacArthur	Minimum wage 75¢ per hour AFL-CIO merger First earth-circling satellite Salk antipolio vaccine	Racial segregation banned School desegregation Development of television Two monkeys in space	Hit Parade "Rock Around the Clock" "My Fair Lady" Twist; rock and roll Elvis Presley	Harry Truman Dwight Eisenhower George Meany Grace Kelly Perry Como
Youth and children					
1960-1969	Civil Rights Act Assassinations of J.F. Kennedy Robert Kennedy Martin Luther King, Jr. Vietnam War	Minimum wage $1.25 per hour Affluent economy Men on the moon Birth-control pill	Fifty-star flag Beatniks, hippies, Woodstock Student demonstrations Drug culture	Beatles "Hello, Dolly" "Moon River" Rock	J.F. Kennedy Lyndon Johnson Richard Nixon Warren Burger Martin Luther King, Jr. Neil Armstrong
1970-1979	End of Vietnam War Watergate scandal 18-year-olds vote Israel-Egypt accord	Minimum wage $2.65 Oil embargo Inflation increases Test-tube baby	Nixon resigns Women's lib Two popes die within 40 days	Rolling Stones Country western Punk rock Disco dancing "You Light Up My Life"	Richard Nixon Gerald Ford Jimmy Carter Muhammad Ali Hank Aaron Pittsburgh Steelers
Preschool children					
1980-	Hostage crisis in Iran President Reagan shot Israel-PLO war in Lebanon	Major recession Energy crunch subsides Inflation slows down Industry and business in transition	Prince Charles marries Princess Grace dies Home computers are big items *E.T.: The Extra-Terrestial* *Star Wars* series	Rock subsiding Country rock Barry Manilow Dolly Parton Flashdance "Gloria"	Ronald Reagan Pope John Paul Sally Ride Jesse Jackson John McEnroe

sequential strategies complex descriptive research designs that permit the separation of within- and between-cohort changes and differences.

ability to determine the evolution of change within an individual, to examine the stability of behavior for an individual as he or she grows older, and to examine the impact of early life experiences and events, within or outside the child, on subsequent developmental or behavioral patterns. Longitudinal studies eliminate cohort differences because only one cohort group is studied at a time. It is reasonable to assume that, if changes occur over a time period, the changes are due to age factors.

There are several disadvantages of using the longitudinal method. First, a long period of time is involved. This may result in extra expenses and other time-related problems. Second, there is the problem of trying to keep the initial group intact. People move, die, or are lost in one way or another. This factor raises the question of whether the later groups are the same as the initial groups. Third, there is the question of whether the results from longitudinal studies can provide information applicable to a time frame quite different from the one in which the individuals in the study grew up. For example, suppose the speaking vocabulary study was done originally with a group reared before television sets became a common household product (before 1950). Would the content and size of vocabulary of those children reared without exposure to children's television programs be the same as for children who listened to Mr. Rogers and "Sesame Street"? Would the content and size of vocabulary of adolescents and adults be different for individuals raised before and during the television era?

Sequential strategy method

To eliminate the problems created by the limitations of cohort differences and intrapersonal changes inherent in other methods, Schaie and Parham (1965) developed the ***sequential strategies*** research model for use in developmental research. The term sequential refers to the fact that the sampling frame for these strategies requires that a sequence of samples must be used at different times for the purpose of measurement (Schaie & Hertzog, 1982). In other words, there must be a replication or a second study in addition to the original study, using different individuals. There may be either a cross-sectional sequence or a longitudinal sequence. The sequential strategy method considers development and behavior to be functions of (1) the age of the individual, (2) the cohort group to which the individual belongs, and (3) the historical time at which the measurement was taken.

Cross-sectional sequential strategy. A *cross-sectional sequential strategy* involves the replication of a cross-sectional study in the same age range of interest, assessed at two or more different time periods. For example, a cross-sectional vocabulary size study could be done for ages 1 to 6 in 1980; then 5 or 10 years later a similar study would be done again. In this way norms could be obtained for more than one cohort group. Interindividual variability could be detected. Similarities or differences that appear would confirm or deny the stability of the norms.

Longitudinal sequential strategy. A *longitudinal sequential strategy* would involve two or more longitudinal studies, begun at the same age, but several years apart. This approach considers development as a process dependent on a length of time. As such, Schaie and Hertzog (1982) consider the longitudinal sequential approach to be a better indicator of both intraindividual differences and interindividual changes.

Critique of sequential strategy approach. The advantages of the sequential strategy approach are (1) the advantages of a cross-sectional or a longitudinal design are obtained and (2) it is possible to draw better conclusions concerning the continuity of development and behavior. The major difficulty is in resolving differences that may be found between the first study and the second. Are the differences age related or environmental-time related? There is also the disadvantage of working with a more sophisticated, complex research design that is still in the process of having its "bugs" worked out. Fig. 1-6 presents a summary of the various research methods in developmental psychology.

Myths, stereotypes, and statistics

A caution must be mentioned. Remember that developmental psychology is a science and all information must be data based. Being a relatively young science, there will be topics on which the research is limited or inconsistent. Recognize the need to be careful about placing too much stress on concepts that do not have adequate scientific foundations.

Beware of myths about development and behavior.

I. CROSS-SECTIONAL METHOD

Tested in 1980	Age 5	Age 10	Age 15	Age 20	Age 25	Age 30	Age 35	Age 40	For as many age levels as desired

Groups at different age levels are studied at the same time.

II. LONGITUDINAL METHOD

1970 Age 5	1975 Age 10	1980 Age 15	1985 Age 20	1990 Age 25	For as many years as desired

The same individuals are studied periodically at different time intervals.

III. CROSS-SECTIONAL SEQUENCE METHOD

Tested in 1980	Age 5	Age 10	Age 15	Age 20	Age 25	Age 30	Age 35	Age 40

The first group of different age levels was studied in 1980.

Tested in 1985	Age 5	Age 10	Age 15	Age 20	Age 25	Age 30	Age 35	Age 40

A second group of different age levels will be studied in 1985. Then the two groups will be compared.

IV. LONGITUDINAL SEQUENCE METHOD

1970 Age 5	1975 Age 10	1980 Age 15	1985 Age 20	1990 Age 25	— — —

Group 1: The same individuals are studied periodically. This group began in 1970.

1980 Age 5	1985 Age 10	1990 Age 15	1995 Age 20	2000 Age 25	— — —

Group 2: A different group began in 1980. The same individuals are studied periodically. The two groups are then compared.

FIG. 1-6 *Methods of developmental research.*

central tendency a statistical term that represents the central point on a scale of scores. The mean, median, and mode are such measures.

stereotype an overgeneralized, often false, belief about a group of people that lets one assume that every member of the group possesses a particular trait; for example, the false stereotyped belief that all male homosexuals are effeminate.

Myths are ill-founded beliefs that are held uncritically. Just because "everybody says so" doesn't make it right. Fifty million Frenchmen *can* be wrong! There are myths concerning almost all phases of the life cycle. For example, consider the following statements. "Pregnant women will lose a tooth for every fetus they carry because the unborn child needs calcium to build bones." "Spare the rod and you spoil the child." "Sow your wild oats before marriage and you will have a stable marriage." "Most women have hot flushes and misery during menopause." "The elderly become senile and enter a second childhood." The statements are all false. They are common beliefs, but they are ill-founded.

Beware of stereotypes in development and behavior. A ***stereotype*** is a preconceived mental picture or idea of people that is held in common by members of a group. It is usually based on an oversimplified opinion, an affective (emotional) attitude, or an unquestioning attitude. A stereotype is usually directed at a race, ethnic group, occupation, or subcultural group. For example, "The British have only one sauce for their food but many meat dishes. The French, however, have many sauces but only one meat dish." False. "Germans are methodical, Italians are gregarious, and the Russians are boorish." False. Stereotypes are usually based on limited information, outdated studies, and samples or comments beginning with "on the average. . . ." Stereotyping is sometimes difficult to identify, but it should be avoided if at all possible. Development and behavior characteristics are easy targets for stereotyping.

Beware of how statistics are used and interpreted. Don't place undue emphasis on them. Know what they mean and what they represent. Recognize that even statistics have to be interpreted—and not everyone would interpret them the same way. For example, the average IQ is 100. Does that mean that an IQ of 101 is above average and an IQ of 99 is below average? No! An average is a ***central tendency***—more or less the midpoint—of a distribution. Statistically, the average range would include plus or minus one standard deviation. In other words the range of average IQ is between 90 and 110, with 100 being the midpoint, the

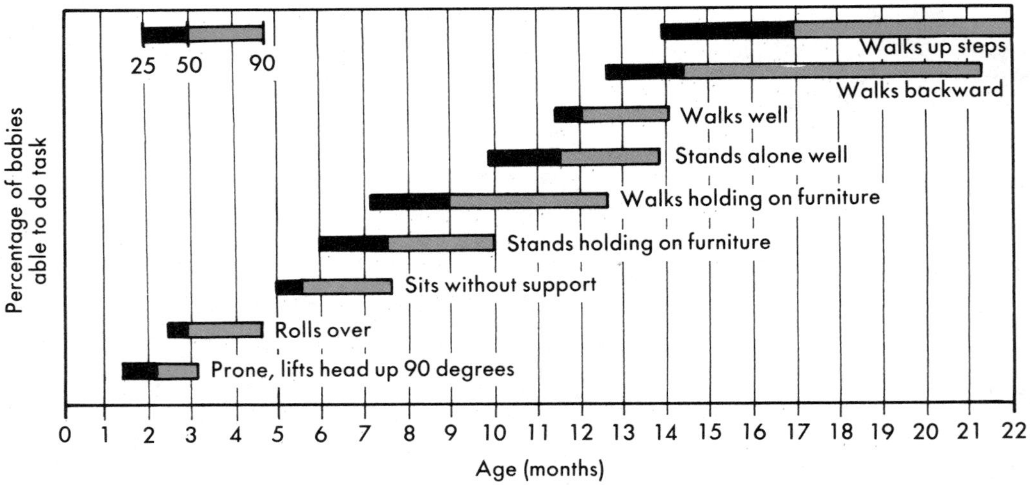

FIG. 1-7 ***Development of gross motor skills.***
Modified from Frankenburg, W.K., & Dodds, J.B. Journal of Pediatrics, *1967,* 71, *181-191.*

statistical "average." This point will come up often in developmental psychology. Developmentalists like to talk about such things as the average age at which an infant walks or the vocabulary level of a 4-year-old. But in each case there is an average range within which a developmental activity (e.g., age of walking) may fall or the size of a characteristic (e.g., vocabulary level) may extend. Fig. 1-7 illustrates how the statistical average and the normal (average) range must be perceived.

A special point must be made about the use and interpretation of a ***coefficient of correlation.*** A *correlation* is a statistical figure that indicates the measure of the degree to which two variables are related. For example, the degree of relationship between academic success in college and a person's high school grade average is a correlation of about .70 to .75. This means that the correlation is highly positive—but not perfect. (A correlation of +1.0 would be a perfect positive one and a correlation of −1.0 would be a perfect negative or opposite one.) The closer the coefficient of correlation is to .00 the less the degree of relationship. Correlation figures are frequently used because they do show the degree of relationship and they are convenient and easy to calculate.

coefficient of correlation a numerical index used to indicate the degree of correspondence between two sets of paired measurements. The most common kind is the product-moment coefficient designated by Pearson.

However, there is a major point that must be kept in mind. Correlation figures *do not* show a cause and effect relationship. They have a predictive value but it can be wrong. A high average of high school grades does not guarantee academic success in college. That approach would assume a cause and effect relationship, which correlations cannot do. A high average of high school grades would predict—but not guaran-

PSYCHOLOGY JOURNALS

Adolescence
American Journal of Mental Deficiency
American Journal of Orthopsychiatry
Annual Review of Psychology
Child Care, Health & Development

Child Care Quarterly
Child Development
Child Development Abstracts
Child Psychiatry & Human Development
Child Study Journal

Cognitive Psychology
Developmental Psychology
Developmental Review
Exceptional Children
Family Therapy

Genetic Psychology Monographs
Human Development
Infant Behavior & Development
International Journal of Behavioral Development
Journal of Abnormal Child Psychology

Journal of Applied Developmental Psychology
Journal of Autism & Developmental Disorders
Journal of Behavioral Analysis

Journal of Child Development
Journal of Child Language

Journal of Child Psychology & Psychiatry & Allied Disciplines
Journal of Clinical Child Psychology
Journal of Clinical Psychology
Journal of Developmental & Behavioral Pediatrics
Journal of Educational Psychology

Journal of Experimental Child Psychology
Journal of Family Counseling
Journal of Genetic Psychology
Journal of Gerontology
Journal of Learning Disabilities

Journal of Marriage and Family
Journal of Pediatric Psychology
Merrill-Palmer Quarterly
Monography of the Society for Research in Child Development
Psychological Abstracts

Psychological Bulletin
Psychological Review
Psychology Today

tee—academic success in college. Beware of the fallacy of cause and effect in correlation figures.

The box on p. 39 lists professional journals that may be useful to you for readings in developmental psychology. The magazine *Psychology Today,* sponsored by the American Psychological Association, is written for popular consumption.

CHAPTER REVIEW

1. *Universality* refers to human characteristics of growth, development, and behavior that are common to people the world over. *Individuality* refers to individual differences that people have because of genetic, cultural, or psychological differences or experiences.
2. *Developmental psychology* is the study of the development of activity, growth, and behavior, including internal and external phases. The goals of developmental psychology in general are (a) to accurately describe the behavior, development, or phenomenon, (b) to explain and report the scientific principles by which the conditions occurred, (c) to verify the principles involved so that predictions of future development can be made, and (d) to understand the principles involved so that appropriate control or direction of development can be promoted. (These four goals are not developed in the chapter.) The ultimate goals of developmental psychologists are to help an individual (a) to adapt to the conditions of life so that the best possible growth, development, and behavior can take place and (b) to utilize most of his or her physical and psychological human potential.
3. The *traditional divisions of the life span* are (a) prenatal, (b) infancy, (c) childhood, (d) adolescence, and (e) adulthood. Developmental psychologists subdivide these divisions into areas of study that are more narrow and descriptive of a stage of life. Not all cultures of the world have the same divisions. In some less complex, primitive cultures, adolescence is practically nonexistent and the stages of adulthood are compressed because of decreased longevity.
4. *Cross-cultural psychology* is a comparative study of the same phenomena of growth, development, or behavior in different cultures to determine if universal principles are involved or if cultural influences create differences.
5. The concept of a *life-span perspective* is being studied to provide a greater understanding of the development process over the span of life. Short-term research approaches and long-term research approaches frequently provide different answers. There is a need to develop a methodology that can consider both approaches so that a firmer perspective of life-span development can be obtained.
6. *Directions of growth* include (a) *cephalocaudal* sequence, from head to tailbone, (b) *proximodistal,* from central body joints to extremities of arms and feet, (c) *differentiation* of growth from general development of systems and behaviors to specific details of development, and (d) *integration* of parts into a coordinated whole. A fifth direction, not mentioned in the text, is the principle of *bilateral development,* with each side of the body developing at the same rate in a symmetrical fashion.
7. *Specific principles of development* include the following concepts: (a) maturational growth follows and orderly, sequential, predictable pattern; (b) development is an interaction of the forces of maturation, environment, and learning experiences; (c) the rate of growth and development differs from child to child; (d) each phase of life has its own physical and psychological characteristics; (e) physical and psychological traits have their roots in infancy and childhood, but environmental factors can cause changes in direction as the child gets older; and (f) there are *critical periods* of development at which certain traits or characteristics can be best developed.
8. Continuity versus discontinuity refers to psychological discussion as to whether growth and development are gradual, continuing, and even (*continuity*) or whether they occur in stages, with starts and stops (*discontinuity*).
9. There are three basic processes related to behavior and development—homeostasis, motivation, and learning. The proper and adequate functioning of these processes will lead to a more efficient and effective level of development and performance. In some ways these processes interact with one another.
10. *Homeostasis* is a scientific principle stating that there is a tendency for the body to seek to maintain a relatively stable, constant balance in the functioning of the physiological systems. If something is not working correctly, an action will be initiated to seek to make it right so that an equilibrium or balance can be maintained. Homeostatic concepts have been expanded to include psychological as well as physiological needs.
11. *Motivation* is the process by which behavior is initiated, directed, and sustained until a goal is reached. Motivational activity may be initiated by a homeostatic need, a learned behavior response based on an incentive or reinforcement activity, or by personality or cognitive factors. (These activators have not all been mentioned in the text.) If the behavior initiated during the motivational process does not reach the intended goal, the need or the imbalance continues to exist and frustration takes place, leading to additional behavior that seeks to satisfy the motivational need.

12. *Learning* is the process by which knowledge, skills, and affective (values) characteristics are acquired. These cognitive components become part of one's memory system. Learning provides the "know how" and the "know why" of doing things. It is essential for helping the individual know what goals and behaviors would be needed in the motivational process to meet the demands of a homeostatic imbalance or need.
13. The views or theoretical approaches to an understanding of human development or behavior can be grouped as follows: (a) physiological approach, (b) cognitive approach, (c) behaviorism/social learning approach, (d) psychoanalytic approach, and (e) humanistic approach. None of the approaches covers all aspects of the life span. Some differ in their views on the same topic.
14. The *physiological approach*, as presented in the text, stresses the physiological maturation view of Arnold Gesell. The *genetic-oriented views* of ethology and social biology are not included because they relate to animal biology, with only presumed implications for human behavior. Gesell's concept of physiological maturation is based on a long-time study (1922 to 1946) of the growth and development of infants. He and his co-workers have determined the sequence of physical development in infants. A limitation in his study is that he was not able to identify the major influences that environmental factors have on the otherwise orderly, sequential development.
15. *The cognitive approach* to growth and development stresses the development of the intellectual processes that will eventually make major contributions to overall development. The child plays an active role in his or her development by becoming aware of stimulating activity in the surroundings, absorbing them, and eventually making use of the newfound knowledge in problem-solving situations. The cognitive approach is used in the Kohlberg moral development theory as well as in the cognitive development theory of Piaget.
16. *Behaviorism* is an approach that stresses learning by the process of *classical or operant conditioning* or by the *social learning theory.* The primary motivator of behavior and development is the reinforcement or incentive than an individual receives from agents or forces in the environment. The responses made become learned responses if they are reinforced often enough.
17. The *psychoanalytic approach* of Freud is based on the biological instinct of the libido that seeks to direct behavior. The child learns to control the motivational actions of the unconscious, where the driving energy of the *libido* is located, by developing an ego structure made up of the *id* (unconscious), the *ego* (the conscious), and the *superego* (moral conscience). As the individual interacts with reality (the environment), these three forces develop differing degrees of strength, thereby affecting the nature of behavioral responses. *Psychosexual development* occurs by five stages, beginning at birth. Personality becomes based on the strengths and weaknesses of the ego structure and the experiences encountered through psychosexual development. Psychoanalysts, such as Erikson, have modified Freud's theory to fit their own areas of emphasis or points of view.
18. The *humanistic approach* to development and behavior is somewhat nebulous or "fuzzy." The word is used in different ways and includes a variety of theories that have different approaches to rationalizing behavior and development. What they all have in common is that they emphasize those characteristics that are uniquely human as opposed to animal. Thoughts, perceptions, and, sometimes, values are based on feelings and emotions. In addition psychologists such as Rogers and Maslow stress human potentials and qualities that are available only to humans. Maslow refers to the self-actualization process. Rogers refers to self-realization and self-acceptance.
19. *Developmental tasks*, according to Havighurst, refer to tasks that arise at various stages of an individual's life, with their attainment being necessary to the satisfactory growth, development, and comfort of the individual. The nature of the tasks differs from culture to culture and from time to time. The tasks are part of the stage concept of life-span development.
20. The concept of *stage theories* has limitations that must be recognized. Stages assume age-level characteristics and a continuity of development. People vary too much to be able to make specific statements about individuals and stages.
21. As a science, the principles of developmental psychology are based on the findings of research. As a relatively young science, the tools and methodology of developmental research are still in the process of being refined. However, a research design format is followed. One of the major questions to be resolved in life-span psychology is how much can be revealed by short-term research (cross-sectional) and by long-term research (longitudinal). In addition, what is the effect of cohorts and cohort differences? *Cohorts* are individuals of the same age level who experience the same historical, social, economic, and political periods.
22. The *cross-sectional method* of research (a) examines several age levels simultaneously, (b) requires little time, little money, and few researchers, (c) collects and interprets much data in a short time peri-

od, but (d) provides only representative samples of age-groups and controls, losing sight of individual changes.

23. The *longitudinal method* of research (a) examines and reexamines the same group of individuals repeatedly over the years or decades, (b) requires much time, more money, and many people, (c) collects much data but requires more time for collection and interpretation, (d) provides data that allow for individual growth and developmental change but (e) loses some subjects by death, moving away, etc., making the final sample more selective.
24. The *sequential strategy method* seeks to eliminate the problems of cohort difference and intrapersonal change by having two or more studies done in a step-sequence. Cross-sectional studies would retain their original features, but there would be two or more such studies done about 5 years apart. Two or more longitudinal studies would be conducted, starting several years apart.
25. Myths, stereotypes, popular opinions, and unscientific ideas have major limitations when applied to human growth, development, and behavior. Even statistics derived from research have to be understood and properly interpreted. For example, the use of a *coefficient of correlation* can demonstrate the degree of a relationship between two variables (such as a home condition and a personality trait), but the correlation does not, and cannot, prove a cause and effect relationship (that a home condition *caused* a personality trait to develop).

REVIEW QUESTIONS

1. What do universality and individuality mean in regard to developmental psychology?
2. Define developmental psychology. What are its goals?
3. How and why do divisions of the life span differ according to complex versus simplistic societies and cultures?
4. What is meant by the life-span perspective? Why do research methods differ in their implications for life-span development?
5. How do the terms *growth* and *development* differ in meaning? Why are they used interchangeably?
6. Define the cephalocaudal sequence of development. Give an example.
7. Define the proximodistal sequence of development. Give an example.
8. Define differentiation of development. Give an example.
9. List six specific principles of development. What does each one mean?
10. What is the difference between the concepts of continuity and discontinuity as they relate to development?
11. Describe the life-force. Why is an understanding of it important?
12. Look at Table 1-3. Begin at the left and follow the arrows in the designated direction. These arrows identify the basic processes of life, homeostasis, motivation, and learning. Identify the components of each basic process. How do the major processes interact? What are their relationships?
13. Define homeostasis. Study Fig. 1-2 to determine how the homeostatic principle works.
14. Define motivation. Study Fig. 1-3 to determine how the motivational process works. Why is the motivational process successful sometimes and other times not?
15. What is the importance of learning? Why is it called a basic process of development? Don't guess or generalize. Be specific. Look at Fig. 1-4 for ideas.
16. List the five major categories of theories or approaches to human development. What are the basic tenets or points of view of each category? What theorist(s) is a major exponent of the view? What are the limitations of each category of theories? Study Table 1-4 for help.
17. Define developmental task. Give some examples. Name the major theorist for developmental tasks.
18. In general, what are the limitations of the stage approach to developmental theories?
19. How much can your judgments or ideas concerning growth and development be based on common sense? What are the limitations of the common sense approach?
20. Define cohorts. Why are cohort differences important in research?
21. Discuss the cross-sectional method of research, its approach, its strengths, its weaknesses.
22. Discuss the longitudinal method of research, its approach, its strengths, its weaknesses.
23. What is the sequential strategy method? Why is it needed in addition to the cross-sectional and longitudinal approaches? How is the sequential strategy approach conducted?
24. Why is it important to beware of statistics?
25. Define correlation of coefficient. What does it mean? What is a common error that people make when considering correlation figures?

THOUGHT QUESTIONS AND ACTIVITIES

1. Make a list of ways in which the developmental characteristics of men, women, and children are universal in nature. Make a second list of characteristics that are subject to cultural influences. Are people more alike or more different? Can you really tell? Is cross-cultural psychology a necessary part of a study of developmental psychology? Why or why not?
2. Consider the basic processes of homeostasis, motivation, and learning. How are they interrelated? How do they fit into a study of human development?
3. The five approaches to human development are presented in a brief fashion in this chapter and elaborated on in other chapters. From this chapter you should be able to

prepare a descriptive definition of each theory and gain a suggestion of the limitations of each approach. What do you see as strengths and weaknesses in each theoretical approach? Offhand, which approach appeals to you?

4. Can all questions in human development be answered by a scientific study? What areas might be less amenable to scientific inquiry? How much emphasis should be placed on scientific data-based knowledge?

FURTHER READINGS

Achenbach, T. *Research in developmental psychology: Concepts, strategies, methods.* New York: The Free Press, 1978. An easy-to-read introduction to how research is done in the field of developmental psychology is presented in this text.

Carwin, W.C. *Theories of development: Concepts and applications.* Englewood Cliffs, N.J.: Prentice-Hall, 1980. More than a dozen of the major developmental theories of current interest in human development are summarized and critiqued.

Ethical principles of psychologists. *American Psychologist,* 1981, *36*(6), 633-638. This article presents the latest thinking of the American Psychology Association concerning what should be the ethical practices of psychologists in providing services and in doing research with human beings and animals. The preamble begins: "Psychologists respect the dignity and worth of the individual and strive for the preservation and protection of fundamental human rights."

Kagan, J. Overview: Perspective on human development. In J. Osofsky (Ed.), *Handbook of infant development.* New York: John Wiley & Sons, 1979. Chapter 1 in this book gives a broad view of the historical perspective of research approaches to the study of human nature. You can detect the problems and struggles of developmental psychologists in coming to grips with the study of infancy.

Larossa, R., Bennett, L.A., & Gelles, R.J. Ethical dilemmas in qualitative family research. *Journal of Marriage and the Family,* 1981, *43*(2), 303-313. The basic ethical research questions of informed consent and the risk-benefit equation are evaluated as they relate to qualitative family research.

Selim, R. (Ed.). The stages of life: A life-cycle calendar. *The Futurist*, February 1979. This article develops the information presented in this book in Table 1-2. A perspective of the life-span is suggested.

CHAPTER 2

DETERMINANTS OF DEVELOPMENT

LAYING A FOUNDATION

Bedrock! That is what a builder looks for when laying a foundation to support a large building. Bedrock is the solid rock underlying loosely arranged surface material such as soil. To build a house with its foundation upon soft earth is to invite disaster. "For when the rains came and the winds blew, the battered house built upon the sands fell with a great crash." A house built upon bedrock has no such problems; its foundations are firm.

In building the house of human development it is also necessary to build upon a firm foundation. The bedrock of the study of human development is composed of determinants, theories, and research. The determinants are the elements and conditions that determine how, when, where, and if the house is to be built. The theories offer a variety of blueprints suggesting how the house should be built. The findings of research will provide the construction materials that will actually be used in building the house. Once built, the house of human development will require maintenance and even occasional renovation if it is to last over the life span. Yet the firmer the foundation, the better it will stand.

Chapters 1 and 2 are designed to provide a firm foundation for the study of life-span human development, based on the best blueprints and research materials available. The groundwork is being laid in these two chapters. The rest of the chapters will build upon this information. By the time you get to the end of the book, you will have constructed a fairly good concept of the total growth and development of an individual. By learning and remembering the building elements in the first two chapters, you will be able to deal with "the rains that came and the winds that blew." Your knowledge will stand, even though revised at times, for it has been built upon a strong foundation.

IN THIS CHAPTER . . .

You will read about

1 A composite look at the factors that influence growth and development.
2 The physiological determinants that influence development. These include genetic foundations of DNA and RNA, the divisions and functions of the nervous system, the endocrine glandular system, and the process of physical maturation.
3 The major environmental determinants, including the influence of the socialization process, society, culture, and the physical environment.
4 The psychological determinants, with an introduction to personality self-structure, psychosocial development, and cognitive (intellectual) development.
5 Metaphysical determinants, which are philosophical considerations that may or may not affect life and human development.

The study of life-span development is a complex, multidimensional continuum that requires a multidisciplinary effort. There is a need to examine all the biomedical and psychosocial aspects of human development in the context of a person's total environment. It is necessary to consider the individual's physiology, psychological makeup, family, home, community, culture, education, religion, race, sex, and economic status, as well as those outside events that impinge upon an individual's life. In other words, to study growth and development you must be concerned with anything and everything that can affect or influence the full spectrum of human life.

FACTORS INFLUENCING DEVELOPMENT

Robert Aldrich (1977) made up a diagram listing the broad factors involved in the development of the life-span continuum. Because of the diagram's shape (Fig. 2-1) the concept has been labeled the "watermelon theory." The top half of the "watermelon" acknowledges the biological aspects of development; the bottom half acknowledges the psychosocial aspects. The biomedical aspects are the cardiovascular, central nervous, musculoskeletal, and endocrine systems and the skin. The psychosocial factors include cognitive, personality, social, and ekistic development. Ekistic refers to a study of human settlements, symbolizing the context of the environment.

The implication of the diagram is that if you want to

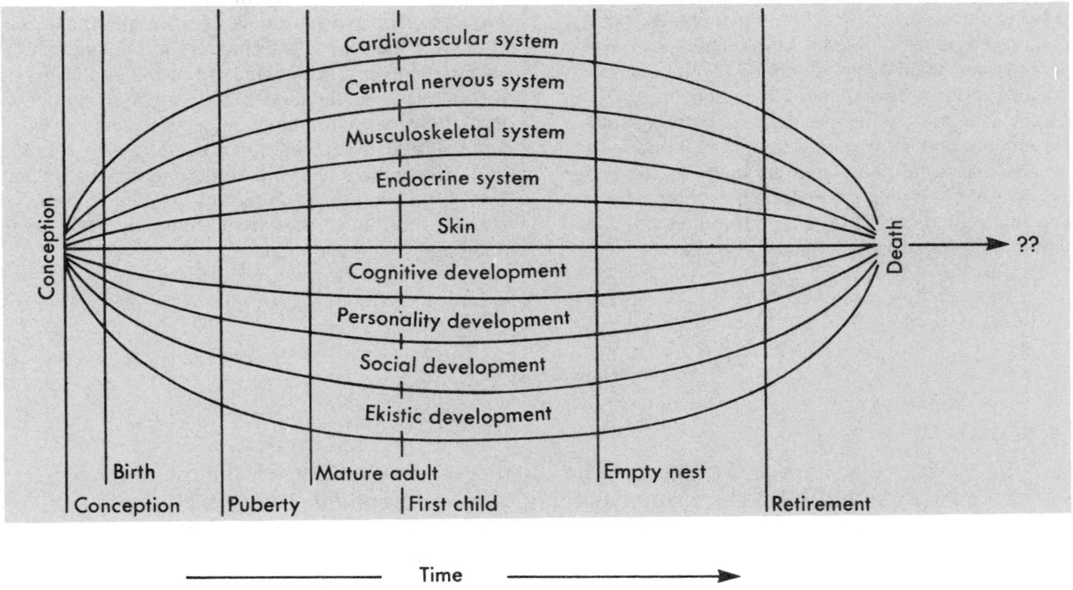

FIG. 2-1 ***The top half of Robert A. Aldrich's "watermelon model" represents biological factors, and the lower half represents psychosocial factors in the individual's life. The word*** **ekistic*****—coined by the late Constantine Doxiadis—refers to the study of human settlements, here symbolizing the environmental context. Milestones along the way (bottom) indicate possible critical points in the life span. ("Empty nest," for example, refers to that time of life when the children grow up and leave home.)***

From Aldrich, R.A. Major transitions in the human life cycle. *New York: Academy for Educational Development, Inc., 1977.*

understand or know a person at any particular point in time, you must slice through the entire "watermelon"—at that moment—to be aware of the many factors that are part of the individual's makeup. By looking at the part of the "watermelon" that has developed since conception, it is possible to learn a great deal about the developmental level of the individual. By knowing the present and the past, it is possible to gain a glimpse of future development, although it is recognized that the future is modifiable.

Look at Fig. 2-1. There are several implications of this diagram for the life-span perspective. First is the recognition that life-span development is a "total package" made up of a variety of physiological systems that are growing and functioning at the same moment and a series of psychosocial areas that are being developed or changing at the same time. A human being is not a bundle of fragmented dimensions that develop and operate in isolation but rather a total being with many systems working as a global unit. Second, the growth elements, as separate entities, have a progression from beginning (conception) to end (death). It is important not only to know the present level of development but also to recognize that there was growth in the past and that there will be changes in the future.

Third, there is an implication that an individual has horizontal growth as well as vertical growth. Vertical growth refers to reaching a level of maturity. Horizontal growth suggests that changes can continue to take place by expanding or broadening—or by decreasing—even after vertical maturity has taken place. It may be that as far as life is concerned the melon is

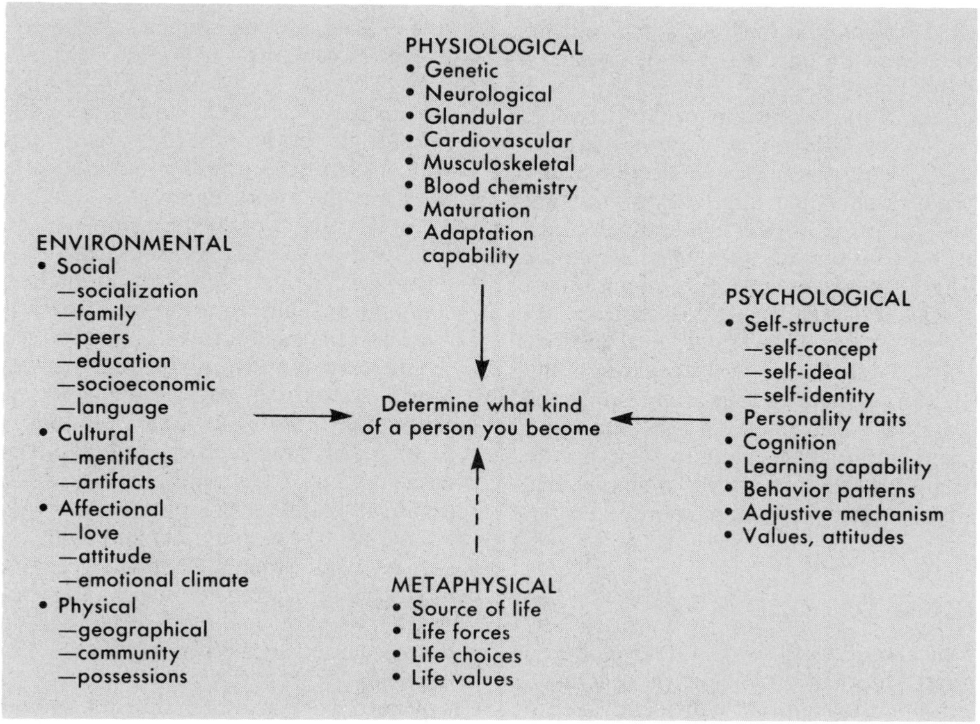

FIG. 2-2 ***Determinants of human growth and development. In various ways these elements influence the way in which an individual develops. The metaphysical determinant is philosophical and speculative. It may or may not be influential. Yet it should not be ignored because there just may be an underlying force that affects life. This possibility has been considered since the time of the ancient Greeks.***

genetics the branch of biology concerned with the transmission of hereditary characteristics.

germ cell a sex cell that has the capability of being fertilized.

somatic cells the cells of the body that compose the tissues, organs, and other parts of the individual, other than the germ cells.

sweeter in the middle when it is at its height of functional maturity rather than at either end.

Another observation from the diagram relates to the periods listed at the bottom along the time line. These are critical periods in the life span. They refer to life events that will occur to most people. They are milestones. Finally, a casual thought—could it be that life is not a bowl of cherries, as the song says? It is really more like a watermelon with some ripe, red, mouth-watering sections, as well as some unripe, green parts. And, even though it is full of unwanted seeds, it still tastes good!

We like to speak of the "determinants" of development. The word *determinant* means factors that have an influencing effect on conditions or events: in this case, factors that influence growth, development, and behavior. For our purpose, we will divide the determinants into four groups—physiological, environmental, psychological, and metaphysical. The metaphysical determinant is purely speculative and abstract. We note a number of articles in psychological journals dealing with metaphysical questions regarding life, so we feel it is appropriate to call attention to this area of discussion. Fig. 2-2 presents the four major determinants and influential categories or factors in each group; the broken line above "metaphysical" indicates that this category is seldom mentioned as a determinant.

PHYSIOLOGICAL DETERMINANTS

The physiological basis for growth and development includes the genetic foundation, the neural system, the glandular system, and the maturation process. The presentations given here will be short and slanted toward the way in which they influence growth and development. The mechanics of these influences are discussed in a cursory way. Readers seeking more extensive physiological details are encouraged to seek other texts dealing specifically with these topics.

Genetic foundations

Genetics is the biology of heredity. It especially studies (1) the mechanism of hereditary transmission from one generation to another and (2) the variations of organismal characteristics and the factors that cause those differences. Involved in the study of genetics are the chromosomes and genes, which are in every cell of an organism. A *gene* is a basic unit of heredity found within a chromosome. Genes determine the specific characteristics of an organism. Since genes are subject to influences, outside or inside the organism, they can be changed so that they produce *mutations*. This means that genes can be altered or changed so that they do not produce the characteristic appearance originally intended. For example, genes that are altered by radiation, drugs, or "accidents" in the transmission of genetic material will produce a characteristic different from the one the genes were supposed to create. Malfunctions, weaknesses, or undesirable characteristics can result from defective genes.

Two categories of cells are found in the human organism: somatic cells and germ cells. The ***somatic cells*** are the body cells. They make up the organs, the brain, the muscles, the skin—the body itself. The ***germ cells*** are the reproductive sex cells. Although both types of cells contain the same structural pattern or combination of chromosomes, only the germ cells are transmitted from the mother and father at the time of conception. These are the cells that carry and determine the hereditary traits passed on to the child.

The somatic cells are the ones that can "learn" how to do something. Muscle cells learn coordination skills; the brain cells learn thinking processes. An infant learns how to use thumb and forefinger to pick up a small object; a child learns how to read or play a piano; an adult learns how to work with mathematical equations. These are traits and skills acquired by the somatic cells. Since the somatic cells are not transmitted in the reproductive process, the acquired learning is not passed on to the offspring. Only the characteristics contained in the germ cells will be passed on by heredity.

Some of the qualities subject to inheritance include physical features, sensitivity of the sense organs, vigor and strength of tissues, early or late puberty, a vulnerability to certain diseases such as heart disease and diabetes due to inherited bodily weaknesses, level of maintenance function in the storage of energy, the rate at which energy can be released and restored, and the

Similarities of hereditary characteristics are evident in a family group. However, the diversity of genetic combinations allows for some individuality in appearance and development.

chromosomal aberration a typical development or growth caused by extra chromosomal material or insufficient chromosomal material on one of the chromosome pairs.

DNA deoxyribonucleic acid molecule, containing the genetic code—"the molecule of life." Each cell in its nucleus contains DNAs arranged in the form of a double helix.

mitosis the process of ordinary cell division that results in two cells identical to the parent cell.

ribonucleic acid (RNA) RNA molecules playing the role of a messenger or transfer agent for vital DNA functions by lining up amino acids in ribosomes to form proteins according to a particular sequence.

degree of femaleness or maleness that an individual exhibits. Although intellectual ability per se is not inherited, the physical characteristics of the brain and the nervous system that respond to cognitive development are inherited.

DNA and RNA. The elements of heredity constitute a highly complicated process. In humans, each cell of the body contains 23 pairs of chromosomes. Each pair is made up of one chromosome from the mother ovum cell and one chromosome from the father sperm cell. A *chromosome* is a complex structure composed of many chemical packets called genes. Genes are threaded together to look like a string of beads that has been twisted. This twisted string of beads is called a double *helix*.

Each gene contains the chemical substance known as ***DNA*** (deoxyribonucleic acid). The DNA makes up the *genetic code*. The code indicates which hereditary characteristics will be developed in the offspring. DNA directs growth according to its blueprint. Since there are thousands of genes in each chromosome, there are many possible arrangements of the maternal and paternal chromosomes. As a result, the large variety of combinations makes it possible for individuals to develop many unique physical and biomedical characteristics. As McClearn and DeFries (1973) state, "With 4 billion people alive today, this represents an incredible genetic diversity." What is just as interesting is to note that in spite of the vast array of genetic differences that people have, they all have but one nose, two eyes, two ears, one head, two legs, and two arms, if there are no mutations.

An individual begins as one fertilized egg created at the moment of conception. This egg will divide. When the fertilized egg divides, the DNA genetic code double helix (the string of beads in the 23 pairs of chromosomes) unzips like a long zipper. Then each side of the helix attracts compatible chemical compounds that are floating freely in the cell.

Eventually, two new, complete sets of 23 pairs of chromosomes are developed within the cell. Each set then moves to opposite sides of the cell, and the cell divides in half, making two new cells, each with a complete set of chromosomes. This special method of cell division or replication of chromosomes is known as ***mitosis.*** These two cells go through the same process, creating four cells. This division process continues to take place as the fertilized egg moves toward and attaches itself to the wall of the uterus. At that point, protein and cell development, guided by the genetic code, begin to form the shape, organs, and physical characteristics of the new embryo.

DNA is located only within the nucleus of a cell. For development to occur, the vital message concerning what tissue or organ is to be built must be delivered to the site of growth. This information is transmitted by ribonucleic acid ***(RNA).*** Basically there are two kinds of RNA molecules. One is called the *messenger RNA*. Produced by DNA, this molecule moves out of the nucleus and into the cytoplasm, carrying with it the code for protein (tissue) development.

A second kind of RNA is the *transfer RNA*. Its function is to bring together different amino acids in the proper code sequence. The building blocks of the protein molecule are *amino acids*. Transfer RNA delivers the sequential amino acids to the coded templates formed by messenger RNA so that the correct tissues and organs can be built. A change in a characteristic or organ may occur if only one amino acid within the pattern is out of order. For example, sickle cell anemia (characterized by the presence of an abnormal red blood cell of crescent shape) is the result of only one change in the 574 amino acid sequence that makes up the protein hemoglobin. A summary of the protein-building process is presented in Fig. 2-3.

Chromosomal deviations. In considering genetic characteristics, two terms that often appear are chromosomal aberration and gene mutation. These processes are responsible for most of the abnormal organic development in humans. ***Chromosomal aberration*** merely means a deviation from the expected genetic code. ***Gene mutation*** refers to a change in the gene's chemical structure, which can produce (1) chemical dysfunction, (2) cell destruction, or (3) alteration in the base coding of DNA. One of the most frequent causes of mutations is exposure to high-energy radiation. Another cause of gene mutation is the use of certain drugs such as LSD.

Certain chemicals can cause abnormalities in a child's development. Chemicals that produce mutations are formaldehyde, nitrous acid, peroxide, and mustard gas. One particular drug that had a drastic effect on normal development in children was thalidomide. In 1961 and 1962 European physicians were reporting the births of a large number of deformed children. After searching the past records of the mothers, almost all reportedly had taken thalidomide during pregnancy. Thalidomide had been prescribed by physicians as a tranquilizer for women who had just learned they were pregnant and who had a high anxiety level about their new condition. There were numerous deformities of limbs, absence of fingers, arms, and legs, webbed fingers, undersized ears, dislocation of hips, absence of kidneys or gallbladders, and abnormal livers in these babies.

In chromosomal aberrations there is an alteration in the structure of the chromosome or in the number of chromosomes. For example, Down's syndrome, a type of clinical mental retardation, is produced when three molecules instead of two get together to form a pair (Fig. 2-4). ***Down's syndrome*** is characterized by a short stature, slightly slanted eyes, and moderate to severe mental retardation. It occurs with greater frequency in children born to older women than to younger women, which may be due to a different type of chemical balance and hormonal secretion in older women. According to Nagle (1979), 30% of all Down's syndrome births occur in women over 40 years of age.

Other aberrations include Turner's syndrome and Klinefelter's syndrome, each produced by an abnormal number of sex chromosomes. In Turner's syndrome there is only one sex chromosome, whereas in Klinefelter's syndrome there are three instead of the normal two sex chromosomes. *Turner's syndrome* is characterized by short stature, infantile sexual development, and variable abnormalities that may include webbing of the neck, low posterior hairline, and car-

Down's syndrome a congenital physical condition associated with mental retardation, characterized by thick, fissured tongue, flat face, and slanted eyes. Formerly called mongolism.

mutation any change of a gene, usually from one allele to another.

1
DNA code contains the genetic instructions for forming proteins (cell tissues).

2
DNA produces messenger RNA in its nucleus to carry out the protein construction orders of the DNA blueprint.

3
Messenger RNAs travel from nucleus to cytoplasm where transfer RNAs and 20 different amino acids are found.

4
Transfer RNAs are coded to attract specific kinds of amino acids. Messenger RNAs activate the appropriate transfer RNAs.

5
Transfer RNAs, with proper amino acids attached, approach and match the sequential code pattern set up by messenger RNAs.

6
Amino acids, now in correct sequence, produce proteins at that site as requested by the DNA initially.

FIG. 2-3 *How the genetic code produces body cell proteins from amino acids by means of DNA and RNA molecules.*

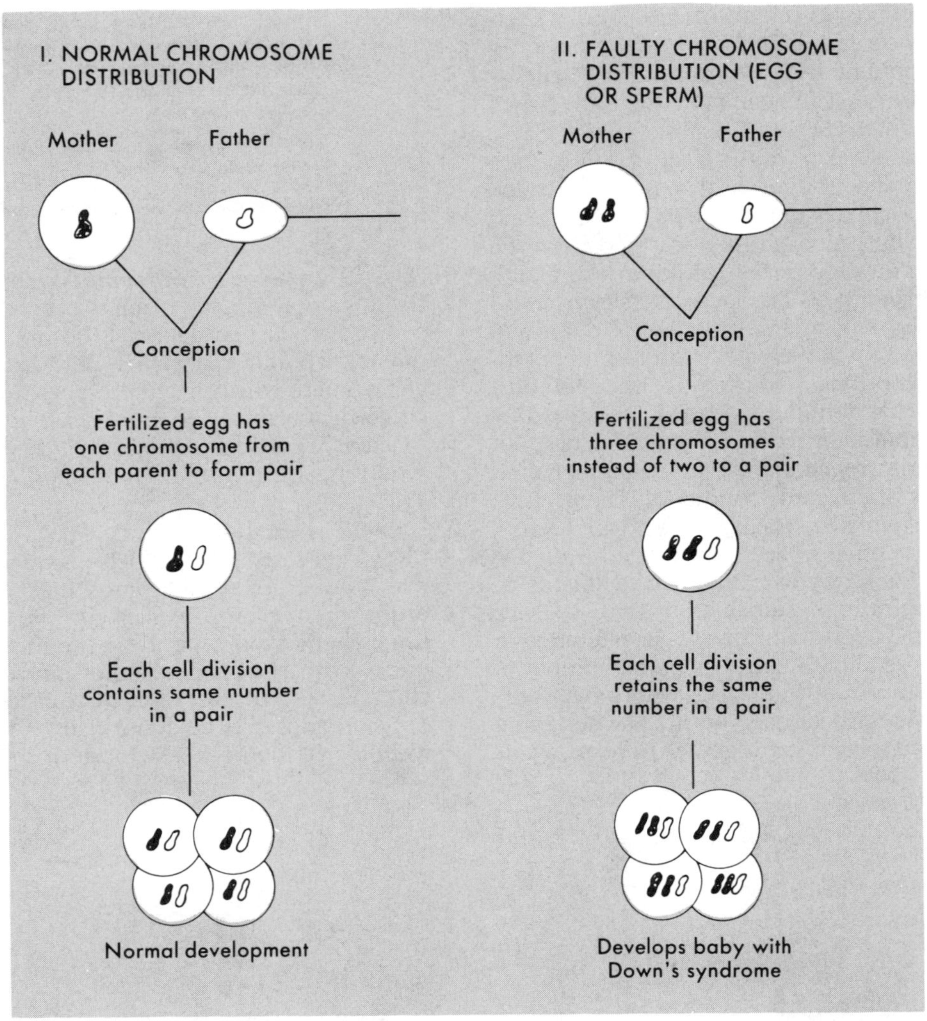

FIG. 2-4 *Normal distribution of a set of chromosomes is shown in* I. *Down's syndrome, as caused by a chromosomal aberration, is shown in* II. *The egg in* II *has an extra set of chromosomes, and the extra set is transmitted in cell division.*

diac defects. *Klinefelter's syndrome* is a condition characterized by the presence of small testes, sparse sexual hair, sterility, and sometimes, excessive development of the male mammary glands (breasts), even to the functional state.

• • •

There are reasons for knowing more about DNA, RNA, and the genetic code. First, DNA, RNA, and enzymes are related in some ways to intelligence and memory. It may be possible eventually to determine how to improve intelligence and memory chemically. Second, we should know about chromosomal aberrations and the fact that some of these aberrations become hereditary in nature. If aberrations exist in a family, it may be desirable for the children, at the time of marriage or adulthood, to have genetic counseling to determine if they are carriers of the chromosomal deviation. Genetic counseling is explained in Chapter 3.

Third, we should be aware of the genetic code and the social implications of seeking to change, influence, or tamper with it. This approach is called *genetic engineering*. Changing the genetic code to bring about desirable characteristics and eliminate undesirable ones may be significant, but where and how to draw the line at influencing the genetic code for social or political purposes must be considered. An ethical question is involved.

Nervous system

Of all of the systems of the body the nervous system is one of the most important. Everything that takes place, consciously or unconsciously, voluntarily or automatically, has its primary beginning within the nervous system. Growth, development, and behavior all depend on the efficient functioning of the nervous system. The effectiveness of a response is greatly influenced by the quality and capability of the nervous system and the brain. It is important to know the parts of the nervous system and how they function. It is equally important to know how the nervous system reacts to stimuli, what it does to interpret those stimuli, and how it makes appropriate responses.

Neural divisions. The nervous system has two major divisions: a ***central nervous system (CNS),*** consisting of the spinal cord and the brain, and a ***peripheral nervous system (PNS),*** made up of (1) the nerves related to the skin and muscles (somatic or voluntary) and (2) the nerves found in the organs and glands (visceral or autonomic).

Look at the main subdivisions of the central nervous system and their functions as presented in Table 2-1. Note that the forebrain, including the cerebrum, thalamus, and hypothalamus, is concerned with complex physiological functions, such as metabolism and endocrine balance, and with cognitive processes, such as learning, thinking, and remembering. The midbrain has a wide variety of complicated functions, mostly involving systems of transmission and consciousness. The hindbrain, containing the cerebellum, medulla, and pons, is primarily concerned with less complex physiological functions, such as balance, breathing, and digestion. A defect, disease, or hindrance in any part of the brain would affect the function related to that section of the brain. Even a chemical change in the blood that feeds the brain could hamper the efficient use of the brain. Growth, development, and behavior can be affected.

autonomic nervous system the division of the peripheral nervous system that regulates smooth muscle; i.e., organ and glandular activities. It is divided into the sympathetic and parasympathetic divisions.

central nervous system (CNS) the brain and spinal cord.

parasympathetic nervous system a division of the autonomic nervous system.

peripheral nervous system (PNS) that part of the nervous system outside the brain and spinal cord; it includes the autonomic nervous system and the somatic nervous system.

sympathetic nervous division the part of the nervous system that regulates vital body functions in response to emergency.

The peripheral nervous system, as seen in Table 2-1, consists of the autonomic nervous system and the craniosacral nerves. The ***autonomic nervous system*** is concerned chiefly with the largely automatic regulation of the smooth muscles of the internal organs, such as the heart, the liver, and the lungs, and of the endocrine glands. The activities of the autonomic nervous system are seldom subject to voluntary control, that is, to purposeful, conscious control by the individual. The autonomic nervous system can be controlled to some degree by yoga or relaxation activities, but generally the organs operate automatically. The *spinal nerves* are the group of nerves that originate in the spinal cord and viscerals of the trunk and limbs. The *cranial nerves* emerge from the brain stem and connect receptors and effectors of the head and face to the brain. The cranial nerves also include the vagus.

The ***parasympathetic division*** of the PNS operates at a normal level when there is no danger or stress situation present. The ***sympathetic division*** takes over the vital functions whenever the body or the mind is under great stress or is in physical or psychological danger. It does so in order to help the body or mind survive as best it can by enabling it to perform more effectively to overcome the emergency threat. Operations unnecessary to survival are slowed down or stopped. Body functions that can help are speeded up. The nostrils of the nose enlarge, and the person breathes more quickly to take in more oxygen. Epinephrine and sugar are secreted into the bloodstream.

left hemisphere the left cerebral hemisphere. Controls the right side of the body and, for most people, speech and other logical, sequential activities (syn. *major hemisphere*).

right hemisphere the right cerebral hemisphere. Controls the left side of the body and, for most people, spatial and patterned activities (syn. *minor hemisphere*). See also **left hemisphere.**

The heart beats faster to pump blood, with its additional fuel, to all parts of the body. The body is geared to meet the threat. When the emergency is over, the body functions settle down, and the normal parasympathetic division takes over again. The manner by which the body responds to emergencies is known as the general adaptation syndrome and was hypothesized by Hans Selye (1973).

Left-right hemispheric functions. Interesting pioneer work by Roger Sperry and his associates (1968, 1982) has demonstrated that each hemisphere of the brain has cognitive functions in which it specializes. Working with split-brain patients (individuals whose hemispheres were disconnected at the corpus callosum by an accident or the need for drastic surgery), Sperry learned that the ***right hemisphere*** and the ***left hemisphere*** perform different kinds of functions.

TABLE 2-1 Major structures of the nervous system

	I. Central nervous system (the brain and the spinal cord)	
	A. Brain	
Forebrain	1. Cerebrum (Cerebral cortex)	Sense perception; voluntary movements; learning, remembering, thinking; emotion; consciousness; personality integration
	2. Thalamus	Sensory relay station on way to cerebral cortex
	3. Hypothalamus	Control of visceral and somatic function, such as temperature, metabolism, and endocrine balance
Midbrain	4. Corpus callosum	Fibers connecting two cerebral hemispheres
	5. Midbrain	Conduction and switching center; pupillary light reflex, etc.
	6. Reticular formation	Arousal system that activates wide regions of cerebral cortex; involves attention and perceptual discrimination
	7. Limbic system	Active in functions of attention, emotion, motivation, and memory
Hindbrain	8. Cerebellum	Muscle tone; body balance; coordination of voluntary movement, as of fingers and thumb
	9. Medulla	Via cranial nerves exerts important control over breathing, swallowing, digestion, heartbeat
	10. Pons	Fibers connecting two hemispheres of cerebellum
	B. Spinal cord	Conduction paths for motor and sensory impulses; local reflexes
	II. Peripheral nervous system (all outlying nerve structures)	
	A. Autonomic nervous system	Autonomous or self-regulating mechanism
	1. Parasympathetic division	Operates and controls vital life functions at normal level
	2. Sympathetic division	Takes over vital life functions in stress or emergency situation; increases function of those necessary to meet threat and decreases function of those not necessary for survival
	B. Cranial nerves	Control sensory nerves, motor and somatic nerves of the face and head, and vagus nerve
	C. Spinal nerves	Respond to the nerves of the skin, muscles, viscerals, and sensory systems of the trunk and limbs.

For example, the left hemisphere specializes in verbal activities. It is the main language center where speech, writing, and calculations take place. It handles the verbal-intellectual-analytical-symbolic business of life.

The right hemisphere is predominantly nonverbal in nature. As Robert Ornstein (1977) states, it has a different mode of consciousness. Performing with a mechanical kind of information processing, it excels in spatial construction, perceptual tasks of spatial orientation, recognition of shapes and textures, the use of touch, and musical and artistic ability. It handles the more spontaneous, intuitive, experiential aspects of information processing.

The significance of left and right hemisphere specialization becomes evident when we recognize that some people become left hemisphere dominant, others right hemisphere dominant, and a few do not develop any cerebral dominance. They are not split-brain individuals. The implication is that a person's cognitive strength (or weakness) depends on which hemisphere is dominant. By dominant hemisphere we mean the one that operates more efficiently and tends to take over whenever some type of cognition is involved. For example, a left-hemisphere-dominant individual would be able to work or learn well in a situation that is verbally oriented or based on logic. Schools basically emphasize verbal content. A left-hemisphere-dominant student would be able to make better use of his or her intellectual capacity than a student who is right hemisphere dominant.

A right-hemisphere-dominant person would do better in activities involving space relationships, such as learning how a motor operates or how to read a map or blueprint. This person could also do better in musical or artistic activities. There is some language function in the right hemisphere, but it is simple and elementary in nature.

An individual who has not established cerebral dominance would probably have problems learning verbal material, such as reading, and would also be confused in learning situations where a directional orientation, such as left to right, is involved (Kaluger and Kolson, 1978). Letters, numbers, and even designs may be perceived backward.

Endocrine glandular system

Within the human body there exists a group of small capsules of tissue, the endocrine glands. These glands are distributed widely throughout the body; they differ from one another in their structure and in the nature of their secretions. The endocrine glands secrete directly into the bloodstream and are therefore called ductless glands or glands of internal secretion. They include the pituitary, thyroid, parathyroids, adrenals, pancreas, ovaries, testes, and pineal body.

hormone **a specific chemical substance produced by an endocrine gland, which brings about certain somatic and functional changes within the organism.**

The endocrine glands are innate regulators of development. They affect health and development through the secretion of complicated chemical substances called ***hormones.*** Hormones are secreted directly into the bloodstream and are carried to all parts of the body, where they have the special function of regulating some of the activities of organs and tissues. Although the amount of the secretions of these glands may be almost imperceptible, they have incredible potency.

The functions of these hormones are diversified. They range from influencing the rate and pattern of physical growth and maturation to regulating the amount of water excreted by the kidneys. They control the processes by which humans digest foods and rebuild them into blood, bone, muscle, and brain tissue. They largely determine the length of bones, the distribution of fat, and whether an individual will be short, stout, tall, or thin. They pace the beating of the heart and supervise the working of the liver and kidneys. They time the onset of puberty and control the menstrual cycle. They govern the many-staged processes of reproduction, from the first ripenings of an egg cell to the final muscle contractions that propel an infant toward independent life (Leukel, 1976). They even regulate one another. The activity of one gland is affected by the secretion of another, and thus the performance of one gland reflects the activity of another. (See Table 2-2 for their functions.)

When the endocrine glands function correctly, the individual is well and happy. When their delicate balance is upset, the individual may suffer from a host of disease processes or emotional disturbances. They are as indispensable to physical welfare as are food, air, and water. Diseases of the endocrine glands are usually associated with their hyperactivity (oversecretion) or hypoactivity (undersecretion). These changes from normal activity may even exist before the birth of a child. In some cases glandular dysfunction of women during pregnancy may retard fetal development.

The endocrine glands appear to be the bridge between the organic constitution of the body and the cognitive capacities of the individual. The importance of these glands as major forces influencing both the outer form and inner experience of every individual is becoming ever more manifest and irrefutable.

Physiological maturation

There are several reasons why it is important to know about the physical maturation process. First, it suggests the sequence of physiological maturity and its behavior. By knowing the sequence, the level of development a child has achieved can be determined. By comparing this level to the proper norms, it is possible to tell if development is at a normal rate (Eichorn, 1979). Second, knowledge of physiological maturation enables detection if a child is skipping any stages of development or moving through them too quickly or too slowly. These factors are deemed to have some significance in the development of the perceptual learning processes of the child (Kaluger and Heil, 1970). Third, approximately one fourth of all children ages 5 to 8 years have a maturational lag in neurolog-

TABLE 2-2 Principal endocrine glands*

Gland	*Hormones secreted*	*Function*	*Oversecretion*	*Undersecretion*
Pituitary				
Anterior lobe Posterior lobe	Growth hormone Gonadotropic Antidiuretic Oxytocin	Growth; regulates other glands; water metabolism	Acromegaly; gigantism	Dwarfism; Simmonds' disease; diabetes insipidus
Thyroid	Thyroxine	Regulates basal metabolic rate, activity, fatigue, body weight	Toxic goiter; Graves' disease	Cretinism; simple goiter; Gull's disease; myxedema
Parathyroid	Parathormone	Regulates calcium and phosphorus; normal excitability of nervous system	Osteitis fibrosa; sluggishness; loss of weight	Splitting headaches; tetany
Adrenals				
Cortex Medulla	Cortisone Epinephrine	Salt, water balance; body changes in emotions; carbohydrate metabolism	Virilism; sexual precocity; Cushing's syndrome	Addison's disease; anemia; low blood pressure
Pancreas (islets of Langerhans)	Insulin Glucagon	Controls blood sugar level and carbohydrate	Hyperinsulinism stupor	Diabetes mellitus
Gonads				
Ovaries Testes	Androgens Estrogens Progesterone	Regulate sexual development and functioning	Menstrual disturbance	Failure of sexual maturation; menopause symptoms
Pineal	Melatonin Serotonin Norepinephrine	Influences sex hormones; regulates day and night cycles; affects brain chemistry; blanches skin	Delayed sexual development; alters body chemistry	Very early puberty; alters emotions and behavior

*The thymus was once considered to be an endocrine gland but is now thought to be a lymphoid body.

ical development of the perceptual processes (Kaluger and Kolson, 1978). It would behoove parents and teachers to be aware of this lag and its implications.

Maturation is the emergence of personal and behavioral characteristics through growth processes. Physiological maturation is the unfolding of innate organic patterns in an ordered sequence through the growth of the organisms (Lewis and Starr, 1979). Prenatal and some postnatal developments of behavior result from the unfolding of potentialities resident within the genes and are thus inherited. However, in light of the great amount of work in experimental embryology, development cannot be regarded as potential within the genes alone; neither can it be regarded as essentially determined by environment (Kagan, 1979). It is a product of these two sets of conditions. The universality of the reflex responses is presumptive evidence for the generalization that early fetal behavior is dependent on maturation of sensory, neural, and motor structures. Once the structures have attained a certain degree of functional maturity, exercise may determine some part of further development. As Ashley Montagu (1970) has stressed, "Where we control the environment, we to some extent control heredity. Heredity, it has been said, determines what we *can* do, and environment what we *do* do."

Implicit in the principle of maturation is the ***principle of readiness.*** It is impossible to teach a child, in spite of any amount of practice, any task for which the innate disposition or readiness for learning is not already present. Capacities such as walking, talking, and even doing multiplication depend on natural, innate aptitudes that have reached their "teachable moment" and not on early training. However, although these capacities are innate and will inevitably emerge, practice and training can make all the difference between developing a skilled or a clumsy performance (Suyur, 1976). For some activities there is an optimum time for development that, if it could be determined, is the best time for giving training and practice. For example, it appears that the age for establishing the foundations for a good muscle structure and motor coordination system is about 2½ or 3 years of age.

Environmental conditions play an important part in encouraging or retarding the process of maturation (Kagan, 1979). The environment is the arena in which a child's potentialities are expressed. The more suitable the environment, the better will be the development. The child learns to walk, but he or she walks "somewhere." What the infant finds and experiences in the places where he or she walks will have much to do with the development of other attributes. The environment determines which of a child's native potentialities are developed and which ones are left undeveloped. It is unlikely that a child born and raised in the Sahara desert will ever learn to be a great swimmer.

maturation developmental changes manifested in physiological functioning primarily due to heredity and constitution; organismic developments leading to further behavioral differentiation.

readiness, principle of refers to the neurological and psychological disposition to attend to and assimilate a category of stimuli to which sensitivity and learning responses were previously lacking.

socialization a progressive development in relating and integrating oneself with others, especially parents, peers, and groups; the process of psychologically growing into a society, in which an individual acquires the behaviors, attitudes, values, and roles expected of him.

ENVIRONMENTAL DETERMINANTS

No child is born with a ready-made "human behavior." All children learn to behave like human beings through associating with other humans. All babies are pretty much alike when they are born. They have the same needs, go through the same sequence in developing locomotion and speech, and have a need to relate to people. Children become different because of the culture in which they grow, the experiences that they have, the genetic uniqueness of their individual differences, and the physical, geographical, and political conditions under which they live. The process of socialization teaches them how to be like their compatriots.

Socialization

All human beings experience ***socialization.*** A child is born in a specific culture and is thus subjected to the socializing forces found in that culture. The brief period of childhood, during which human beings are most malleable, is the period when the whole process of socialization, the shaping of the person into a socially

social role a set of expectations or evaluative standards associated with an individual or a position.

acceptable form, must occur. The perpetuation of a heritage and a culture requires that each new generation acquire the patterns of living inherent in their culture.

Becoming socialized means that the person behaves in such a way so as to be acceptable to the social group with which the individual wishes to identify. The infant develops the social attitudes common to that particular social group and will consciously employ these attitudes so as to regulate and control his or her behavior. It should be noted that the evidence concerning the importance of early childhood experiences in the shaping of the individual has been challenged (Gergen and Gergen, 1981). The influence of early experiences may not be as great as once thought. Socialization factors will be presented in appropriate places in ensuing chapters.

A ***social role*** is a pattern of behavior expected of fellow members by the members of a social group. For example, there are roles for teachers, students, and parents. Their behavior or role is prescribed to them by the other members of their social group, and they must generally act in accordance with these specified patterns of behavior. Every social group has its own recognized patterns of behavior for its members.

Socialization imposes the attitudes, appreciations, social roles, and skills of a culture on the individual.

George Kaluger

The family unit is the primary socializing force in the lives of children. The culture, however, influences the direction of attitudinal growth. This family in New Guinea will have much to say about ancestral worship. Note the wooden art form the woman is holding; it is a representation of the ancestral heritage of her village.

Societies vary in the means used to achieve these goals. Much of the socialization process is implemented by agents—people (or groups) who interpret the culture to the child. They guide and reinforce the learning of the appropriate behavior patterns for the child's sex, age, and social class, and they inhibit the learning of inappropriate behavior. Fig. 2-5 from McNeil (1969) shows the overall effect that these social agents have on the process of socialization.

Family. The family is the socializing agent most directly responsible for the transmission of the cultural content of the society to the growing child. The socialization process begins in the home. The family passes on its attitudes, prejudices, and points of view to the child. The family also determines the social class, ethnic origin, race, and usually the religion of the child. The family, through the experiences they offer the child, will teach him concepts concerning the world—real and unreal. This information is given to the child through the use of words. Therefore one of the most important roles of the family is to teach the child language.

How the parents interact with the child is important in the development of personality traits and self-esteem. The classic work of Schaefer (1961) suggested that there were four types of family atmospheres: love and control of the child's behavior, love and autonomy or permissiveness of the child's behavior, hostility or hate and control of the child's behavior, and hostility or hate and permissiveness of the child's behavior (Table 2-3). The types of personality traits, temperament, or behavior that developed in children raised in these

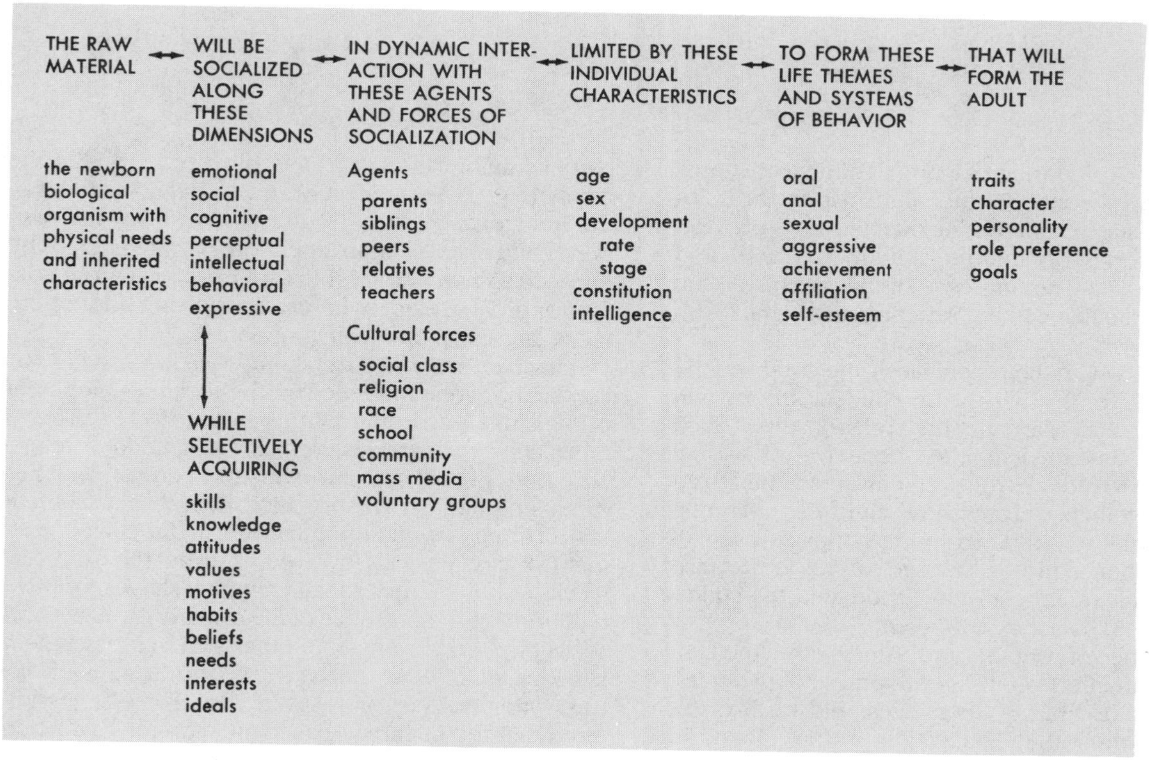

FIG. 2-5 ***Process and components of socialization.***
From McNeil, E.B. Human socialization. *Copyright 1969 by Wadsworth Publishing Co. Reprinted by permission of the publisher, Brooks/Cole Publishing Co., Monterey, Calif.*

TABLE 2-3 Children's personality traits resulting from love or hostility and control or autonomy in the home

Love and control	*Love and autonomy*	*Hostility and control*	*Hostility and autonomy*
Submissive, dependent, polite, neat, obedient Minimal aggression Dependent, not friendly, not creative Maximal compliance Maximal rule enforcement, boys	Active, socially outgoing, creative, successfully aggressive Minimal rule enforcement, boys Facilitates adult role taking Minimal self-aggression, boys Independent, friendly, creative, low projective hostility	"Neurotic" problems More quarreling and shyness with peers Socially withdrawn Low in adult role taking Maximal self-aggression, boys	Delinquency Noncompliance Maximal aggression

Modified from Schaefer, E.S. Converging models for maternal behavior and child behavior. In J. Gildewell (Ed.), *Parental attitudes and child behavior,* Springfield, Ill.: Charles C Thomas, Publisher, 1961.

four different categories of parent-child home environments vary greatly. Further information on influence of the pattern of parenting on children is presented in Chapter 8 on middle childhood (Lamb and Baumrind, 1978). The influence of the parents on the child is a theme that will be presented in several forthcoming chapters.

The way in which the parent views the child and the circumstances under which the child was born will also affect the parent-child relationship. Such circumstances as, for example, the arrival of a long-awaited baby to older parents, an unwanted child to an unmarried woman, an unwanted child to quarreling parents, or the first child of a young, happy couple will surely have some effect on how the parents feel toward the child, their treatment of the child, and the child's adjustment and social development.

The presence of brothers and sisters within the family also has an effect on the development of the child. The number of siblings, their ages, and birth order help to determine the socialization practices found in the home. For example, a study done by Elder and Bowerman (1963) reveals that in large families the mechanics of managing several children dictates parental authoritarianism. The birth order within the family may have an effect on the social adjustment of the individual. Booth (1981) has found that the first-born child receives more attention, is more likely to be exposed to psychological discipline, and is more anxious and dependent, whereas later-born children are more aggressive and self-confident.

Attachment. The parent-child relationship is a factor that has great influence on the social development of the child. According to Ainsworth (1973) a process of attachment occurs whereby a young child develops an emotional relationship with the parents or other caretaking figures. The first indication that attachment is occurring is when the infant seeks out contact with the primary person involved. During the first few weeks of life the infant simply shows positive responses in the presence of the primary caretaker and seeks physical closeness. Another sign that attachment is taking place is when the infant shows signs of distress when that person is absent. Bronson (1973) indicated that the infant is relaxed and comfortable when the primary caretaker (usually the mother) is around and less relaxed or anxious in the presence of others. Successful early attachment somehow "proves" to a child that he or she is capable of loving and receiving love and provides a prototype for the development of later successful interpersonal relationships (Maccoby & Feldman, 1972). The concept of attachment is presented in greater detail in Chapter 5.

Peer group. The peer group consists of individuals who are approximately of the same age and of the same social class. In childhood the peer group is more like a play group, whereas in adolescence the peer group takes on the appearance of a clique, gang, or close social group.

The peer group projects a pattern of conformity. The members reinforce responses that conform to their expectations. These responses will be reinforced, adopted, and strengthened by the peer group. Responses that are nonconforming will be discouraged.

The concept of impersonal authority is introduced to the child through the peer group. Even though in the childhood peer group no one child is the leader, there are certain unwritten rules of the game to which the child must conform (Hartup, 1970). Through his peers the child comes in contact with various attitudes toward himself, toward adults, and toward those things that are to be valued or disregarded.

The child soon learns how to secure the recognition of the group, how to participate as one of its members, and how to avoid the group's displeasure. The child learns patterns of behavior from the peer group that cannot be learned from adults (Vogel et al., 1970). Concepts of cooperation, sharing, and participation are also transmitted by the peer group to the individual. The child's peer group is one way by which he can become independent of his parents and other authorities. This is particularly apparent during adolescence, when the child identifies with new models and develops new emotional ties.

Society

In the society of today there are numerous opportunities to interact. Mass transportation and mass media have provided the ability to reach out and communicate beyond the community. By broadening one's environment, the individual perceives and learns about differences in customs and mores.

The community is a large social structure that provides a framework for socioeconomic life. The community is involved with the individual at every level of development. In comparing one community with another vast differences in their characteristics can be recognized. In some large cities there are neighborhoods where the population is constantly on the move. There are few ties between the people. The morale of the people is negligible and disorganized; cultural values and expectations appear confused (Milgram, 1970). In more stable communities there is more interaction between the family and school, business people, civic leaders, and clergy, helping to provide a basis for community concern.

The school is the first socializing agent within the community that the child usually encounters outside of the family. One of the aims of education is to extend the socialization process begun in the family. Educational institutions transmit the knowledge, beliefs, customs, and skills of the society. Organized education is the tool that society employs to civilize its young citizens.

In general, contemporary societies affect individuals across the entire spectrum of the life span. Rapid technological and social changes tend to make the past less relevant and the future less secure. Gaps sometimes develop between the generations because their experiences and exposures differ greatly. The cohort effect is at work. As a result, communication between the generations can become difficult. Cultural confusion and difficulty in establishing values and beliefs also result when rapid changes take place in a pluralistic society (Braungart, 1980).

Urbanization and bigness make personal relationships more difficult. There is no question but that growing up within an urban complex is complicated. Bigness is conducive to the creation of alternative life-styles. The observance of a variety of ways of living and the values associated with them can create some confusion as to what is desirable or "best for me." The bigness of urban centers makes it difficult for a growing child or an adolescent to perceive reality (Rutter, 1981).

Mass communication media bring all kinds of conditions to the attention of the public. Ninety-eight percent of all homes in the United States have at least one television set. Not only is the public subjected to instant news but often to manipulated or distorted news coverage, so that it is difficult at times to put "what's happening" within a proper perspective. The hard-sell approach of some mass media makes it difficult for some people to know what is "for real."

Cultural expectations

The study of growth and development in the life cycle is sometimes approached from an understanding of the cultural expectations, obligations, and responsibilities that are thought to produce satisfactory growth in a society. Since societies and cultures differ, it is reasonable to assume that the expectations would vary from culture to culture.

Cultural anthropologists, such as Margaret Mead (1970) and Ruth Benedict (1954), stress the role of culture in personality development and socialization. In their studies they contrasted primitive cultures with those of Western societies and found distinct cultural differences that influence growth and development patterns. The basic premise of their observations is best illustrated by the principle of continuity versus discontinuity in cultural conditioning.

Mead and Benedict view growth as a continuous process begun at birth. The more that the culture instills in the children the type of behavior and beliefs they must exhibit as adults, the more continuous and less disruptive will be their growth. Mead discovered, for example, that the children of Samoa and the Arapesh of New Guinea follow a relatively continual growth pattern, with no abrupt changes from one age to another. The individuals are not expected to behave one way as a child, another way as an adolescent, and yet another way as an adult. They do not have to change or unlearn as an adult what they learned as a child. There is no sudden change or transition from one pattern of behavior to another. As children, boys play with a bow and arrow at hunting games. As adults, this hunting "play" becomes hunting "work." There is no discontinuity. Social patterns of behavior, such as dominance over younger siblings and sex roles, are also continuous, merging into adult behavior.

THIN IS ALSO BEAUTIFUL*

Being plump is considered by my society on Cook Island as the ideal standard of beauty, the symbol of attractiveness and health. To be on the thin side is regarded as inappropriate, and not matching up to society's expectation. Thus as a child and right through to the age of twenty-one, I regarded my thinness as a curse.

Moreover, the fact that I wasn't plump like the rest of the girls my age was of great concern to my parents. Mum would cook all sorts of food just to make me eat; and on top of this, I was given a tablespoon of cod-liver-oil with an iron tablet every morning. I loathed those doses after breakfast but more often than not I was told: "Be a good girl and swallow it, if you want to be fat and beautiful." The desire to be beautiful, accepted and loved by my parents forced me to go through that every morning.

Every day, while dressing for school, I used to stand in front of the mirror to see if I had gained any weight. On the way, I'd stop at the nearest shop and weigh myself. But every time I was disappointed. At school I faced all sorts of names, such as 'bony', 'stick' and 'skinny'. To avoid being ridiculed, I buried myself in my work and kept away from the other children. Many times I desperately wanted to play basketball and tennis but the thought of being laughed at held me back. So I slowly became an isolate.

A year later I was admitted to secondary school. I thought everything would be different, but I was mistaken. The second week I was there, the names were flung at me again. It was at this stage that I decided to try to gain some weight. Every cent I saved was spent on sweets, biscuits and chocolates. On top of this I ate whatever was laid in front of me. But because I walked to school, which was about three miles away from home, I never managed to put on an ounce! I simply noticed that my legs were getting longer than ever. At the age of fourteen I was 5 foot 8 inches and weighed only eight stone. Moreover, I earned a new name—*kuea roroa* (long legs).

My height combined with my thinness disturbed me a lot. I yearned for the softness and curves that I saw in other girls. I even dreamed of it and prayed that God would help me gain some weight. I blamed God for creating me with long legs, long arms and a thin body. Over the years when my dream didn't come true and my prayers were not answered, I decided to play a different tune altogether.

When they called me 'bony,' I laughed in their faces and told them I like the name. I pretended the names didn't hurt. I also joined the games and the netball team at school, because I knew that isolation wouldn't solve my problems. After the first few weeks in netball, my height became an advantage and I seemed to be getting all the goals. The others noticed this and started to appreciate me, so I started to develop some pride in my height. Moreover, as most of them couldn't run because

*From Stewart, R.A.C. (Ed.). *Pacific profiles.* Suva, Fiji: University of The South Pacific Extension Services, 1982.

of their weight, I again had an advantage over them. This led me to like netball.

I also decided to join the dance team. Here I found that I looked better in a hula skirt than the rest of them! They started to comment on how nice I looked in my skirt. As for them, I could see their bulges and I had no hesitation in pointing it out to them! Perhaps the knowledge that I looked better in a hula skirt made me a better dancer than the rest of them. After a while I noticed that they hated being seen in one. But, as dancing is our culture, they had to wear their hula skirts and dance. During the performance, the thin girl really stood out well. I ended up being the leader of the team.

Thus, although plumpness is still considered by my society as beauty, I have learned to accept my own physique. Furthermore I have proved to my age mates that there are advantages also in being thin!

By contrast, in Western cultures children have few responsibilities. As they grow up, they must assume drastically different roles. There is a shift from nonresponsible play to responsible work. The child in Western cultures must drop his or her childhood submissive behavior and adopt its opposite, dominance, as he or she becomes an adult.

By showing that there is continuity of development in some cultures and not in others, some doubt is cast upon the universality of the concept of stages of growth and development. However, we were interested to note that the continuity versus discontinuity format can exist within the same country. For example, as recently as 1978 we observed the continuity pattern among the primitive cultures of the Sepik and Karawari River areas in Papua, New Guinea. There appeared to be no adolescent stage of development. The skin-cutting ceremonies and the puberty rites marked the transition from childhood into adulthood, not only with "all the rights and privileges thereof," but also with the skills, knowledge, and responsibilities of adulthood.

In the same country, in Port Moresby, their largest city, there was a distinct adolescent group, as evidenced by the young people attending high schools and colleges. They exhibited characteristics of individuals in transition from childhood to adulthood. Cultural anthropologists see the continuous growth process as a cultural phenomenon, with individuals reacting to the social expectations of their culture. Only those societies that emphasize discontinuity of behavior—one type of behavior as a child and another as an adult—can be described as "age-grade societies" or as having stages of growth.

Physical factors

It would be easy, but dangerous, to surmise generalizations concerning the influence of climatic and geographical features on the growth and development of children. Wide differences do exist. Do children who are raised in rural areas or small villages and towns have the same experiential opportunities for social and educational development as those raised in large urban cities? How are youngsters raised in isolated regions such as mountains, plains, or deserts affected? Think of such areas as they exist around the world. Does it make a difference if a child is raised in a tropical climate where food such as fruits and vegetables grows profusely as compared to being raised in a frigid, desolate area where food is difficult to come by? To what extent do physical and geographical factors make a difference in the development of language, cognition, and attitudinal patterns? People do adapt to living in almost any kind of climate or topography, but at what developmental price?

The altoplano region of Bolivia, in the area of Lake Titicaca, is at an altitude above 3,656 m (12,000 ft.). Half of all the oxygen in the atmosphere is found below 3,000 m (10,000 ft.). How do the thousands of people living in the altoplano survive? Physically, their bodies have adapted to the environmental setting by producing more than the normal amount of red blood cells to transport oxygen to various parts of the body. These people have a "barrel-chest" appearance; the chest and lungs are expanded so that more air and oxygen can be taken in with each breath. We have seen children in this area run and play just as vigorously as do children in the lowlands.

Physical adaptation can take place, but what about language and social development? As with any semi-isolated area, the language and social patterns developed will be affected by whatever restrictive factors are present (Shatz and Gelman, 1977). This inhibition of development could occur in a large urban area if the child is secluded within a home and not permitted to associate with other children or adults. There are known cases of children who have been isolated in attics or upstairs rooms and never sent to school.

Meriem Kaluger

This mother and daughter live on the shore of Lake Titicaca, in Bolivia, at an altitude of over 12,000 feet. Their bodies have adapted to the thin atmosphere. Human beings can adapt to living in a variety of harsh physical environments.

Invariably these children are severely restricted in language development. On the other hand, some children living in isolated areas have good language development because they have access to television and have a supply of books and other reading materials in the home that they are encouraged to use.

What is important to verbal and cognitive development is the nature of the materials present and what use is made of them. A child in a primitive culture plays with materials found in the environment such as sticks, seedpods, and shells. A child in another culture may have toys that can be explored and manipulated, visual materials and books that introduce written language, and access to cultural, social, and educational facilities that can be visited. The child in the primitive culture may become jungle or tribal "wise": the other child can become book or school "wise." The elastic mind theory of Kagan (1978), however, postulates that the child in a primitive culture need not be forever stymied by impoverished cognitive development because of his early childhood setting. An intellectually enriched environment later in childhood or adolescence can stimulate cognitive growth and improve abstract reasoning ability. Either way, it is somewhat evident that the materials, as well as the people, of the environment can influence growth and development.

Certainly the quality of nutrition available to the

individual influences physical growth and central nervous system development, especially of the brain. Diets do differ according to the locale. In some parts of the world, rice is the staple diet. In other places, diets can be found that consist primarily of fish, sago palm, fruits and vegetables, beef or lamb, or just eggs and dairy products. The lack of a balanced diet can make a difference in total development.

Winick (1976) studied the adverse influence of malnutrition on development. A project in Uganda revealed that close to 50% of the children up to 4 years of age in the districts studied showed either biochemical signs of protein imbalance or growth retardation or both. Winick indicated that these findings were consistent in many developing countries throughout the world. The children with severe malnutrition typically belong to poor families living in crowded, unsanitary, slum sections in the cities or in poor rural areas of Latin America, Africa, and Asia. Evidence of extensive malnutrition has also been found in the United States, particularly among Native American populations, such as the Navajo Indian children in Arizona (Moore et al., 1972).

In summary, personal possessions, available artifacts, the ease of making a living and the accessibility of food, the degree of geographical or physical isolation, and the consciousness of the neighborhood, community, or social unit all have an influence on total development. The effects of this influence need not be irreversible, however.

PSYCHOLOGICAL DETERMINANTS

Psychology views a human being as a physiological being, an environmental being, and a psychological being. Growth and development is a total process involving all three views. The psychological view is more complex than the other two because there are more abstractions involved, making it more difficult to research.

Personality self-structure

The newborn child is not born with a ready-made personality pattern, an established intellect, or even a concept of what he or she is like. Certainly a new baby does not think, "Hey, how about that. I'm a girl!" Conscious awareness in the newborn is on a primitive functional level. Self-awareness, personality development, and cognitive growth are all yet to come. A "self-structure" is yet to emerge. The self-structure is the personality of the individual.

According to the psychodynamic theories of psychoanalysts, phenomenologists, humanists, and others, an infant must develop an inner sense by which the self is somehow revealed or becomes known to the child. Psychoanalysts refer to the self as the ego. The self or the ego is that aspect of the person that carries out psychic, cognitive, or psychological acts through a complex organization of characteristics and dynamic forces that make up the individual. The organization is the self-structure around which a self-concept, a value judgment system, and a pattern of behavioral response and control are built. Through this organizational structure, the self becomes the agent for behavior.

Each individual develops a *self-structure,* a pattern of interacting inner forces that serve as reference points around which experiences are organized and behavior patterns formed. The inner forces are psychophysical systems that will provide dynamics that will influence the direction and the intensity that behavior responses take. Since psychophysical systems differ somewhat from individual to individual, behavioral responses will tend to differ.

Erikson: Ego identity

Erik Erikson modified Freud's psychoanalytic theory in order to include a greater emphasis on social context in the development of personality. Erikson (1972) has developed an elaborate stage theory that describes emotional and personality development across the life span. The central theme of his theory is that life is constant change.

Erikson's theory of psychosocial development, including ego identity, describes eight stages of psychosocial development. Each stage has a psychosocial task to be mastered. The overall purpose for the individual is to acquire a positive ego identity by the time the individual reaches early adulthood. Confronting and learning to solve the problems at one stage of life, however, does not guarantee that they will not reappear and have to be solved again. Nevertheless, contrary to Freud's theory, adolescent or adult crises need not be traced to childhood frustrations as the basic cause of failure. Table 2-4 presents a summary of Erikson's eight stages of psychosocial development.

Infancy and childhood. Identity formation neither begins nor ends with adolescence. Its roots go back in childhood to the experience of mothering and being mothered. The initial psychosocial task to be achieved is that of trust; failure to achieve it leads to mistrust. Trust of people and of the world depends on the quality of care and love the infant receives. The issue is not entirely resolved at this time, but a beginning toward learning trust can be made.

During the second stage, children are to gain a sense of autonomy, implying that they learn they can do some things for themselves. Children build on new motor and mental skills and must learn to feel capable of being in control. Overprotective parents, ones who do too much for their children, can induce failure to get the feeling of autonomy. Complete autonomy is not gained at this time, but children should, at least, not have a fear of going beyond their present capabilities.

From the third through the fifth year of life, children are exposed to environmental invitations and even demands to assume some responsibilities and to master certain tasks. The psychosocial task situation is one of initiative versus guilt. Parents must reinforce intellectual and motor initiatives rather than making children feel like nuisances. Freedom to pursue initiatives without a feeling of guilt is very important.

From 6 years to the onset of puberty, children are to learn how things are made and how they work. They should be encouraged by their family and school to do so, and they should receive praise for their industry. The neighborhood and the school can encourage or discourage their work. If their efforts are viewed as mischief, they can develop feelings of inferiority.

Adolescence. Adolescence is a time for the integration of the roles an individual follows. For example, a boy may see himself in the roles of a son, a student, a scout, and an aspiring athlete. He should be able to integrate these various views he sees of himself into an ego identity. Having learned trust, autonomy, initiative, and industry in the past will help toward the development and integration of identity roles. The peer group and models of leadership, the social milieu, help or hurt the continuity of development of ego identity. Role confusion (identity diffusion) leads to a fragmented ego or to a negative identity. The identity formed now is not the final identity of an individual; it will be

TABLE 2-4 Eight stages of psychosocial development

Stages (ages are approximate)	*Psychosocial crises*	*Significant social relations*	*Favorable outcomes*
1. First year	Trust versus mistrust	Maternal person	Trust and optimism
2. Second year	Autonomy versus doubt	Parental persons	Sense of self-control and adequacy
3. Third year through fifth year	Initiative versus guilt	Basic family	Direction and purpose; can initiate own activities
4. Sixth year to puberty	Industry versus inferiority	Neighborhood; school	Competence in intellectual, social, and physical skills
5. Adolescence	Identity versus identity diffusion	Peer groups and outgroups; models of leadership	Integrated image of oneself
6. Early adulthood	Intimacy versus isolation	Partners in friendships, sex, competition, cooperation	Ability to form close and lasting relationships; career commitments
7. Middle adulthood	Generativity versus self-absorption	Divided labor and shared household	Concern for family, society, and future generations
8. Later adulthood	Integrity versus despair	"Mankind" "My kind"	Sense of fulfillment and satisfaction with one's life; willingness to face death

Modified from Erikson, E.H. *Childhood and society* (2nd ed.). New York: W.W. Norton & Co., 1963.

challenged by changes that occur later in life. Identity formation is discussed in Chapter 10.

Adulthood. Early adulthood is the period of courtship and early family life. Intimacy refers to the ability to share and to care about others. The concept of intimacy is presented in Chapter 12 on emerging adulthood. Early adulthood changes to middle adulthood, and concern for others beyond the family must be extended to future generations and worlds. The children must be raised as a contribution to humankind and to society. Generativity is a concern with productivity in work and with the welfare and care of others. Self-absorption merely leads to stagnation.

In later adulthood the major efforts of life are nearing completion, with the result that the time becomes one of reflection. Integrity is being able to look back on life with some satisfaction. A person at this stage who feels despair fears death in an ironic way that those with ego integrity do not. Although the despairing person expresses disgust over his life, he yearns for another chance. The person with integrity accepts death as another step in a meaningful life.

Piaget: Cognitive development

Another psychological determinant is the development of cognition. *Cognition* is a general term for any mental process whereby an individual becomes aware of or obtains knowledge. It includes perceiving, recognizing, conceiving, judging, reasoning, and the various perceptual-conceptual processes. Cognition is another word for intelligence or mental abilities, the means by

According to Erikson, the psychosocial crisis during the second year is one of autonomy versus doubt. This child is developing a sense of adequacy by imitating his mother mowing the lawn. He believes he is "helping mother."

cognitive development the development of a logical method of looking at the world, utilizing one's perceptual and conceptual powers.

schema or schemes Piaget's term for action patterns that are built up and coordinated throughout the course of cognitive development. In the infant, they are like concepts without words. Throughout development, such schemes are presumed to be involved in the acquisition and structuring of knowledge.

which human beings can think. There are several theories relating to cognitive development, such as the social learning approach, Bruner's theory of instruction, and the information-processing approach. We choose to present a general overview of Piaget's theory of cognitive development as an example of a construct of a psychological determinant. His theory is presented in greater detail in the appropriate age-stage chapters.

Piaget (1952) postulates that human beings inherit two basic tendencies. One is that of *organization,* the tendency to systematize and organize mental processes and the content of knowledge into coherent systems. The other tendency is that of *adaptation* or adjustment to the environment. Piaget believes that a child, or any individual, can use intellectual processes to change experiences into a cognitive form that can later be used in dealing with new situations.

The tendencies of organization and adaptation combine to produce cognitive structures that Piaget calls a schema. The ***schema*** is the organization of a number of ideas or concepts combined into a coherent plan or outline that indicates the essential or important relations between concepts. The child can use this framework to differentiate between experiences and to generalize from one experience to another. In the newborn the schema, or cognitive network, is based on a primitive level of development, dependent almost completely, if not totally, on the use of reflexes. As reflexive behavior develops and the infant gains bodily control or "learns" behavioral responses that are beneficial, the quality of the schema rises to a higher level of cognitive function. ***Cognitive development,*** therefore, consists of the growth of successive stages of schema derived logically, starting on a physiological maturational format and maturing to higher levels of schematic cognition by interacting with forces in the environment.

Piaget's theory divides the cognitive developmental process into four main chronological stages, which are further divided into phases. The order of succession of these steplike patterns is constant, although the ages at which different stages are attained may vary somewhat, depending on the child's rate of maturation, innate capacity, practice, and environmental influences. The four stages are (1) sensorimotor stage, ages 0 to 2 years; (2) preoperational stage, ages 3 to 7 years; (3) concrete operations stage, 7 to 11 years; and (4) formal operations stage, ages 11 to 15 or 16 years. The stages and their characteristics can be studied in Table 2-5. They are elaborated upon in the age-related chapters.

METAPHYSICAL DETERMINANTS

If a person has been in an accident that left that individual with irreversible, total paralysis, in a deep coma, with no detectable brain wave activity, and completely

Meriem Kaluger

By using eye-level coordination and observing what happens as the tower gets taller, this girl is learning something about stability and height. She may not know how to explain the relationship, but she will learn what she must do in order to be able to build a taller tower.

dependent on life support systems for survival, should the plug be pulled and the person left to natural forces to determine whether the person lives or dies? If this individual were 85 years old, should heroic efforts be made to keep the person alive or should "comfort" therapy be used? Suppose this individual were only 18 years old? Or 2 years old? Would the age of the person make a difference? Answers to these questions cannot be determined or proven correct by science. Science can only deal with questions that involve something concrete that can be detected and measured by the senses. If "it" cannot be seen, heard, touched, smelled, or tasted, "it" cannot be scientifically proven. The only approach to the question is through thoughtful consideration of metaphysical determinants (Haan, 1982; Koch, 1981).

If developmental psychologists are to discuss questions pertaining to issues such as ethics on human research, questions related to life or death, the use of genetic engineering to eliminate genetic defects, the mind-body problem, or the approach to the care and concern for the general welfare of individuals and society, then a step beyond scientific inquiry is a viable consideration (Ethical principles of psychologists, 1981). Physicists could apply scientific laws to determine how to build the first atomic bomb. However, they had no scientific laws to indicate whether the atomic bomb should have been dropped on Hiroshima and Nagasaki. It was dropped with the hope that it would bring World War II to an end before more lives of men and women in the armed forces of both countries were lost. The moral issue was based on human judgment. The strict scientists would say, "That is not our field of study." The flexible scientist would say, "We are dealing with human lives. Let's at least think about it." The study of metaphysics offers a philosophical basis to begin that consideration (Royce, 1982). Our position is simply that we cannot afford to close our eyes, ears, and mind to anything that might give us a better perspective, insight, or concept concerning human growth, development, and behavior. We can always set aside or eliminate ideas that do not seem to fit or to make sense at our level of understanding. But, at least, let's be receptive to new ideas.

TABLE 2-5 Piaget's stages of cognitive development

Stage	*Approximate ages*	*Characterization*
I. Sensorimotor period	Birth to 2 years	Infant differentiates himself from objects; seeks stimulation and makes interesting spectacles last; prior to language, meanings defined by manipulations; with object permanence the object remains "the same object" with changes in location and point of view.
II. Preoperational thought period		
Preconceptual phase	2 to 4 years	Child is egocentric, unable to take viewpoint of other people; classifies by single salient features: if A is like B in one respect, then A must be like B in other respects.
Intuitive phase	4 to 7 years	Child is now able to think in terms of classes, to see relationships, to handle number concepts, but is "intuitive" because the child may be unaware of the true basis for the classification.
III. Period of concrete operations	7 to 11 years	Child is able now to use logical operations such as *reversibility* (in arithmetic), *classification* (organizing objects into hierarchies of classes), and *seriation* (organizing objects into ordered series, such as increasing size). Gradual development of *conservation* in this order: mass (age 6 or 7), weight (age 9 or 10), and volume (age 11 or 12).
IV. Period of formal operations	11 to 15 years	Final steps toward abstract thinking and conceptualization; capable of hypothesis testing.

Modified from Piaget, J. *The origins of intelligence in children.* New York: International Universities Press, 1952.

metaphysics the system of principles underlying a particular study or subject; the nature of first principles and the problems of ultimate reality.

This section is admittedly included for speculative and discussion purposes. The term ***metaphysics*** refers to the system of principles underlying a particular study or subject. It is a division of philosophy that relates to the nature of being or kinds of existence (ontology) and to the study of the universe as an orderly system (cosmology). Since the particular subject involved in this text is the development of the human being, it would seem reasonable to at least acknowledge the possibility of the existence of principles that underlie the study of the nature of humankind and its place in the universal scheme of things.

Sources of life

What is life? What is humankind? In terms of theoretical approaches, there are three points of view. First is the approach that considers life as being the *planned genesis* of a creator of the universe. The natural universe, including outer space as well as the internal functions of planets, animals, and human beings, is predicated on precise scientific and mathematical principles. The thought is that the universal nature of these exact laws could not have happened by accident but rather was the result of a planned design, probably guided by a divine being.

The second approach is one that considers that the universe and the life therein is a *cosmic happenstance* that somehow set into motion forces and chemical combinations, resulting in life particles that could reproduce themselves. Through the process of adaptation and survival, higher forms of life evolved. The physical features of the universe evolved to the form that we know them today by natural changes, dynamic forces, and time.

A third approach is one that combines elements of the two views mentioned above. It could be that the universe, the cosmic force, the chemical elements, and the scientific principles always did exist. It is possible, in the view of some theologians and scientists, that evolution could have been part of a universal design that was initiated by some divine (or cosmic) intervention. As such, the source of life was planned, but it was planned to develop along evolutionary lines.

To study developmental psychology, it is not necessary to pursue these ideas. We can approach a study of many aspects of human development without resolving the question of the source and significance of life. However, if we wish to consider the question of the basic nature of life, then there are some implications for development and behavior. If life is the result of a planned design, then there may be a meaning behind that plan that indicates a universal direction or purpose for human beings. If life is the consequence of a cosmic accident, then there is no meaning, direction, or purpose. Human beings are to develop their own meaning and direction (Paull, 1980).

Some developmental theories, directly or indirectly, suggest a position. For example, Maslow postulates a hierarchy of needs that must be met before an individual can attain the upper levels of one's potential as a human being. The higher needs go beyond basic physiological and social demands to making use of one's potential to reach out for intellectual truth, creative beauty, and the common good of others. In Erikson's theory of psychosocial crisis the movement toward identity achievement and adult psychosocial striving is from personal, self-seeking development to generativity for the good of others. Kohlberg's theory of moral development emphasizes development of moral thinking from a hedonistic or punishment-obedience orientation to a higher law-and-conscience orientation.

On the other hand, ethologists such as Eibl-Eibesfeldt (1970) and Jones (1972) believe that there is a remarkable likeness between animals and human beings and that the similarities stem from a biological source. The suggestion is that genetic factors control human behavior to a greater degree than we think. If that is true, then the concept of unique potentials and idealism as human beings is diminished because behavior is subject to physiological and (indirectly) to evolutionary forces. A person's position on metaphysical issues is often reflected in their theoretical rationale.

Life-forces

Life-forces refer to innate inner dynamics or motivating drives that impel an individual to certain behaviors. Philosophers and psychologists have considered this topic down through the ages. Epicurus and Aristippus considered this driving force to be pursuit of pleasure of the senses and of the mind (hedonism). The utilitarians under John Stuart Mill said that the greatest pleasure has as its primary concern the welfare and happiness of others. Arthur Schopenhauer was not so altruistic. He said that the driving force in human beings was the "will to live," a biological drive inherent in life itself. Friedrich Nietzsche spoke of the "will to power" to conquer and control; William James cited the "will to believe" in something so there would be order and meaning in the structure of life.

Psychologists have spoken of the inner driving life-forces. Sigmund Freud emphasized the "libido," which is psychic energy in pursuit of pleasure or erotic desire. Alfred Adler stressed the individual's desire to gain "mastery" as the main driving force. Carl Jung spoke of the "collective unconscious," which acts as the background of all human thought and emotion. The "will to love" has been advanced by Rollo May. Carl Rogers considers the central force to be "self-acceptance," and Abraham Maslow makes a case for "self-actualization" of the human potential.

In summary, it appears to us that the life force has two thrusts: (1) survival values, for both the individual and the species, and (2) personal values, in humanization and self-realization. If there is such a thing as a life-force, might it not have something to say about the direction of or reason for human growth, development, and behavior?

Life choices

Another consideration is the matter of making *life choices*. Does an individual have the freedom to make a free-will choice or are all choices predetermined? This question is appearing frequently in academic journals in psychology (Bandura, 1982). The answer to the question has much to say about the nature and responsibility of decision making. The source of behavioral outcomes is involved.

We consider three possible positions. First, the position of ***free-will*** choices states that an individual determines his or her own destiny and direction in life by being free to choose and to decide what behavior the person wishes to initiate. Regardless of past experiences, or in spite of them, when the moment comes to make a behavioral decision, it can be done on the basis of one's own judgment and volition.

The second position, ***determinism,*** states that what appears to be a free choice is actually predetermined by factors and causes beyond the control of the individual. The pattern for life direction is set, and if you know the pattern, you can even predict what the outcome will be.

determinism a philosophical doctrine stating that all decisions of the mind or acts of the will, all social and psychological phenomena, and all acts of nature are determined by prior causes.

free will the ability to choose between alternatives so that the choice or the behavior is freely determined by the individual.

A third possibility is that both of the previous conditions exist. A presupposition is that the universe is predicated on set principles of governance; these principles have a "cause and effect" element about them. An individual has the freedom to decide what behavior he or she wishes to initiate, but once the decision is made and the behavior is started, then the deterministic "cause and effect" principle takes over and will decide the outcome. Individuals are free to choose what they want to do, but they cannot change what the outcome will be. If individuals knew the cause and effect principles involved, then, of course, they could choose to initiate the proper behavior to bring about the desired result. The implication for human growth and development is that the more we know about the principles underlying growth and development, the more we can understand what behavior should be initiated and the better we can predict the outcomes.

Theories with a humanistic orientation, especially the concept of existentialism, would emphasize the free-will approach to making choices. Existentialism stresses the importance of making your own choices and providing your own meaning and direction to life. The essence of life is of your own choosing; furthermore, if it is *your* choice, then it is correct regardless of what others may do or say.

The determinism approach is exemplified by the theories of ethology, physiological maturation, and genetic-oriented concepts. The plan for development is in the biological mechanism; it is determined. The maturational process simply unfolds. Even psychoanalytic theory is somewhat deterministic because it stresses the innate biological foundations of the libido, which includes the instincts of the sex drive (life) and of aggression (death). According to Freud these drives *will* be expressed because they are instincts.

Harold Geyer

You may give them your love
but not your thoughts.
For they have their own thoughts.
You may house their bodies
but not their souls,
For their souls dwell
in the house of tomorrow,
which you cannot visit,
not even in your dreams.

Kahlil Gibran
The Prophet

Life values

Life values or *value-judgment* involves decision-making choices. Anytime that an individual makes a choice or expresses a preference, that person is indicating a value. "I choose this one because it is better than, or as good as, the other one."

One view of values is that behavioral standards are *relative*. They vary for people according to circumstances, and in different periods of time. As a result there is no stabilized "truth." It changes or "depends upon the situation."

A second view is that behavioral standards and developmental principles have a *universal basis* and, as such, are true, correct, or best for all people at all times, under all circumstances, whether they are known, accepted, or not. These values or behavioral principles are fundamental and carry a "cause and effect" relationship with them. They are predicated on a universal fact. There is no way you can get around or away from them.

A third view is a combination of the previous two. It states that the nature of life values depends upon whether the decision-making topic or subject is in the realm of human-made values or in the domain of inherent universal principles. If the behavior involved is based on situational or changeable conditions, then a relative-type decision may be in order. However, if the circumstance is basic to humankind, then the universal principle applies.

Developmental theories of values include those of Kohlberg, Piaget, and Bandura. Both Kohlberg and Piaget stress a stage-theory approach, suggesting that moral development, which is also the development of a value-judgment system, emerges as the cognitive domain of the individual matures. In both theories the direction of growth is from being self-centered to being a responsible, law-abiding member of society. Kohlberg's theory continues in development to a level of universal morality beyond human interaction. What is interesting are the number of cross-cultural studies that have been done using Kohlberg's theory and demonstrating a universal moral development at least to the level of human interaction.

The social learning theory of Bandura takes another direction. It says that the development of a value system depends on the experiences an individual has had and the rewards and reinforcements that were received because of the behavioral responses made. In this way the individual learns which behaviors bring rewards and should be continued and which behaviors should be avoided because they result in punishment or neglect.

Metaphysical determinants are interesting to study. However, their abstract nature makes it difficult to pin down or even to prove their existence. As the horizons of knowledge are extended, however, sooner or later those of us interested in human nature must come to grips with questions that relate to the meaning of life (Sampson, 1981). As of this moment, there is still so much to be learned about the objective facts of life. There is still so much to be discovered about what men, women, children, and their relationships are really like. Some concepts that we considered as "facts" just a few short years ago are now being demolished by new research, greater perspectives, and deeper insight. We must continually be open-minded and flexible in our search for the truth.

CHAPTER REVIEW

1. The watermelon theory presents a total look at the life-span continuum. It presents biological aspects of development in the upper half of the melon and psychosocial aspects in the lower half. The whole watermelon shows the life span as a total unit, with many functions and processes occurring at the same time.
2. *Determinants* are categories of forces or factors that have an influence on growth, development, and behavior. The three major categories are physiological, environmental, and psychological. A fourth determinant, metaphysical, is not part of the scientific realm of study. It is philosophical in nature and, therefore, considered by some psychologists not to be part of the developmental psychology field of study. The concept of metaphysics is included because there are some aspects of life that cannot be measured scientifically.
3. *Genetics* is the biology of heredity. The two kinds of cells found in the human organism are somatic cells and germ cells. The *somatic cells* are the body tissue cells; they are capable of learning responses and skills. The *germ cells* are the reproductive cells that are passed on from parents to offspring. Although all types of cells contain the same chromosomes, only the germ cells pass on hereditary characteristics.
4. Chromosomes are found in each cell. *Chromosomes* contain strings of chemical packages called genes. The genes contain the *DNA molecule*, which has the genetic code of physical development, indicating which tissues and structures will be built and where. The DNA genetic code does not move out of the nucleus of the cell. It does send out into the cell a *messenger RNA* that carries with it a part of the genetic code, indicating which protein (tissue) is to be built. *Transfer RNA*, located within the body of the cell, picks up the message of the genetic code, selects the appropriate *amino acids* (which are the building blocks of protein), and arranges the amino acid compounds in proper order.
5. Occasionally *chromosomal aberrations* or mutations will occur. This means that the genetic code is distorted or disarranged and the appropriate tissue or protein will not be built. Changes in blood chemistry, high-energy radiation, certain drugs, and "accidents" in genetic code transmissions can create unwanted physical growth or changes during prenatal development.
6. The nervous system is central to all growth, development, and behavior. It is the system that determines how well the body will develop, function, and learn. The *central nervous system* (CNS) consists of the brain and the spinal cord. It is this area in which efficient and effective progress is most crucial for overall development. The *peripheral nervous system* (PNS) is made up of the network of nerves that go to the various parts of the body beyond the brain and spinal cord. The *parasympathetic division* of the PNS operates during normal conditions. The *sympathetic division* takes over the functions of the PNS whenever there is a physiological or psychological stress or an emergency threat to the body or mind.
7. The left and right hemispheres of the brain have different primary functions. The *left hemisphere* has the primary verbal or language function. It handles logical, systematic, and symbolic operations of intellect. The *right hemisphere* has the nonverbal, spatial, and tactile operations of intellect. It is concerned with intuitive, spontaneous, and experiential expressions of information processing. An individual who has not developed good left hemisphere dominance or control could experience difficulty with such verbal activities as learning to read with comprehension, learning how to spell with phonetic input, and learning how to reason out mathematical problems.
8. The *hormones* secreted by the glands have much to say about physical factors, such as the rate and pattern of physical growth and the functions of various bodily systems. Hormones also affect blood chemistry, with the result that psychological reactions such as moodiness, irritability, temperament, and level of intellectual functions can be unduly influenced.
9. *Physical maturation* is the emergence of physiological structures and functions according to an innate growth and development plan. The plan is orderly and sequential. Under normal conditions the organic pattern unfolds with regularity. This situation is especially true during the prenatal period and in the postnatal period for the first 18 months or so. It is possible for environmental factors to influence the maturational flow in utero or after birth. Environmental influences cannot hasten the process but can delay or distort the process.

10. To say that the "environment" affects growth is a gross distortion and an inappropriate way to refer to the influence of the environmental determinants. The environment is a vast category, almost an abstraction. Specifics within the environment must be mentioned if environment is used as a determinant. Don't say, "It's due to the person's environment." Be specific: "It's due to the home situation where there is only one parent and that person is at work much of the time when the child is awake."
11. *Socialization* is the process by which an individual becomes civilized and inducted into the social pattern of the environment. Socialization imposes the attitudes, appreciations, social roles, and the culture of the group on the individual by social forces such as the family, peer group, significant others, social institutions, and the media.
12. The psychological, social, and emotional climate of the family will be instrumental in the development of a child. The degree of love or hostility found in the home along with the degree of behavior control or freedom (autonomy) will have much to do with the direction in which the child's personality will progress.
13. *Attachment* is a process whereby an infant develops an emotional relationship with parents or other caretaking figures. Successful attachment establishes a good foundation of emotional support and love.
14. The peer group projects a pattern of conformity by "teaching" the child which interpeer behavior responses are acceptable and which ones are not. Peer group exposures also reveal alternative attitudes, behavior patterns, and ways of living that the individual may not have known before.
15. The physical and social aspects of society provide conditions and situations that will probably direct the social thinking and behavior of individuals into channels related to or similar to what they are experiencing and observing. The makeup of society and its subgroups varies according to types of communities.
16. *Environmental physical determinants* refer to geographical locations, landscape features, material objects found in the life space of the individual, climatic factors, and the availability of food.
17. *Psychological determinants* primarily include the development of a personality system, known as a *self-structure* or *ego-structure*, and of an intellectual or cognitive pattern of operations. There are various theories as to the way in which both types of determinants develop.
18. *Erikson's psychosocial crisis approach* is an eight-stage theory covering the life span. At each stage a psychosocial crisis or task must be accomplished in order for the individual to develop a personality structure that includes a sense of personality identity, a willingness to share intimacy with others, and a sense of life satisfaction that permits reaching out and helping others and being content with one's life.
19. *Piaget's theory of cognition* suggests how intelligence and the use of the intellect develop. The theory has a four-stage approach, with subphases. Cognitive development begins with the use of reflexes. The process of adaptation organizes mental activities until a schema is developed. The schema represent the level of cognitive thought and processing at which the individual can function. The level of the schema gets higher through intuitive thinking and the acquisition of concepts and skills by learning. A level of concrete reasoning is reached when the child can put together ideas of a tangible nature to answer problems. Formal operations, the highest level of cognitive development, consists of the use of logic and insights to do abstract reasoning.
20. *Metaphysical determinants* refer to the study of philosophical considerations related to the nature of existence and the study of the universe and its component parts, including humanity. In particular, questions are raised about the source of life, life forces, life choices, and life values. The *source of life* will suggest whether there is a direction or meaning of life, implying that the underlying purpose of life should serve as a guiding force. If there is no basic meaning to life, the direction of life can be anything that humans, individually or in groups, decide the direction should be. *Life forces* refer to the basic driving dynamics of life. Is it the libido, as Freud claims, or is it some other driving need that provides the energy that makes life go? *Life choices* are concerned with the existence of free will versus determinism in making life decisions. Existentialism says individuals are free to decide and to choose what the nature (essence) of their lives should be. Geneticists and psychoanalytic theorists are not so sure that life choices can be made that freely. *Life values* have either a social base or a universal base. It may be that the specific situation would determine which of the two sources is pertinent for that specific condition.

REVIEW QUESTIONS

1. What are the implications of the watermelon theory of Robert Aldrich? Does it make sense?
2. List the four categories of determinants of development and briefly describe some of the component parts of each category. Fig. 2-2 would be helpful. Why is the metaphysical determinant a questionable one to be included?
3. In a general way, how are the characteristics of heredity transmitted from parents to child? What are some of the characteristics that can be transmitted?
4. What are the functions of DNA and RNA molecules? How do they perform their work? (Study Fig. 2-3 for a summary.)
5. In respect to genetic deviations, why is a knowledge of DNA and RNA functions important in a study of developmental psychology? What are some of the aberrations or mutations that can occur? Describe them. Look at Fig. 2-4 for an example.
6. If you want to truly understand how development, behavior, and learning take place, you must understand how the brain and the nervous system operate. Do you agree with that statement? Explain why or why not.
7. What is the difference between the central nervous system (CNS) and the peripheral nervous system (PNS) in their purpose and basic functions?
8. Look at Table 2-1. Number I represents the *central nervous system* (CNS). Can you imagine all those functions taking place in the brain? Think of a picture or drawing you have seen of the human body with a nerve network going to the arms, legs, and various organs. That network is the peripheral nervous system (PNS).
9. What is the difference in the function of the parasympathetic division and the sympathetic division of the autonomic nervous system? What is the function of the autonomic nervous system as a whole?
10. List the primary functions that take place in the left hemisphere of the brain. Do the same for the right hemisphere. What is the implication of these divisions for growth and development?
11. Glands secrete chemical hormones into the blood so that various bodily and cognitive functions can take place according to schedule (growth, puberty, menstruation, basal metabolism, etc.). Look at Table 2-2. Don't try to memorize it. But take each gland and express in your own words what that gland is supposed to do and what happens when it does not secrete the right amount of the hormone. You may have to look up some of the words and diseases.
12. Describe the meaning and implication of physiological maturation.
13. Look at Fig. 2-5; carefully work your way through the figure. Look at the top line first so that you will understand the topics to be developed. Then look under each heading to see the types of dimensions, forces, or characteristics involved. Under Life Themes and Systems of Behavior, oral, anal, sexual, and aggressive refer to parts of psychoanalytic theory.
14. You know that the family is important in the development of a child's behavior and personality. Take specific note of Table 2-3; observe exactly what kinds of characteristics are developed in each of the four models of maternal behavior. Remember love means a positive response and regard for the child, and hostility means hate or a negative regard. Autonomy means permissiveness or freedom to do what the child wants to do, and control implies supervision and direction of behavior.
15. Discuss the effects of peer groups, society, and physical factors on growth and development. Give examples if you can.
16. What is the meaning of metaphysics? Make a chart with three columns. In the first column list Source of life, Life forces, Life choices, and Life values. In the second column indicate the different philosophical positions. In the third column give examples of developmental theories, positions, or conditions that may have some relationship to the metaphysical alternatives mentioned in the second column.

THOUGHT QUESTIONS AND ACTIVITIES

1. Consider the four determinants related to human development. Which determinant is the most important? Does one group of determinants seem to be more significant than the other groups? Is it possible that the determinants each assume a level of importance at different stages of a life span? Elaborate on your opinion.
2. What other major influences of growth and development can you think of that have not been in this chapter?
3. What do you suppose would happen to a preschool child if he or she should suddenly be deprived of all human contacts? Could this child survive? Could it be raised by animals? How would this person be as an adult if he or she could somehow survive? Does the concept of socialization have a meaning?
4. Expand, by discussion, the meaning of *psychological* determinants for growth and development. Do animals have psychological determinants? Are human beings animals?
5. You can discuss metaphysical determinants without discussing religion. Philosophy is not religion, but religion can be philosophy. Do you agree or disagree?

6. Is an understanding of the alleged determinants of human development necessary before you can have in-depth insights concerning the nature of growth and development? Wouldn't a solid knowledge of the findings of research be enough to give in-depth understanding of human beings?

FURTHER READINGS

Bandura, A. The psychology of chance encounters and life paths. *American Psychologist,* 1982, *37*(7), 747-755. This well-known social learning theorist and researcher examines the fundamental issue of what determines people's life paths. He says that chance encounters play a prominent role in shaping the course of human lives.

Bohman, M. The interaction of heredity and childhood environment: Some adoption studies. *Journal of Child Psychology and Psychiatry,* 1981, *22*, 195-200. Various hypotheses regarding the relative impact of hereditary and environmental factors are tested by a review of adoption studies.

Haan, N. Can research on morality be "scientific"? *American Psychologist,* 1982, *37*(10), 1096-1104. Norma Haan takes a look at the question of scientific inquiry into moral development. She states that moral meaning in people's lives can no longer be ignored if social science is to be complete and competent.

Juhasz, A. M. Youth, identity and values: Erikson's historical perspective. *Adolescence,* 1982, *17* (66), 443-450. Erikson's ideas on the importance of historical perspective in identity formation provide the basis for a discussion of values.

The new age of genetic screening. *Science 81*, 1981, *1, 2*(1), 32-34. Three articles, "Who Should Be Born?" "Pregnant Pauses," and "Wrongful Life" are presented, dealing with prenatal checks for defects and the quality control of unborn children.

Rowe, D. C. Environmental and genetic influences on dimensions of perceived parenting: A twin study. *Developmental Psychology,* 1981, *17*(2), 203-208. Identical and fraternal twins and their parents are studied to determine if environmental factors were primarily responsible for a resemblance of the perception of the twins regarding parenting behavior.

Rutter, M. The city and the child. *American Journal of Orthopsychiatry,* 1981, *51*(4), 610-625. The data presented by Rutter points out that the incidence of psychosocial problems of various kinds tends to be much higher in the inner cities than in small towns or in rural areas.

CHAPTER 3

PRENATAL DEVELOPMENT

A NEW LIFE—AND A NEW LIFE

December 27 was the big day . . . Amy L. Baker walked up the aisle and became my wife. We had waited for this moment for six years, and now we were joined as one. We spent our honeymoon in the Poconos and arrived back home late on New Year's Day. Then it happened. On a beautiful, snow-covered winter evening in January, Amy and I decided to start a family. We thought everything would be beautiful, but it wasn't completely.

You see, we live on a farm that my former college roommate bought last summer. My friend, Reed, decided to rent the two floors of the farm house. My wife and I rented the upstairs, and a social worker and his family rented the downstairs. Reed was really without a place to stay until he and his father could finish renovating the garage into a bachelor flat. So, only five weeks after we had returned from our honeymoon, Reed asked if he could move in with us for "only a couple of days." Things were fine the first two weeks, but during the third week, Amy thought she had the flu and was quite ill. Although Amy refused to believe me, she was going through the first stages of pregnancy.

The days turned into weeks. Amy and I were getting quite upset but couldn't bring ourselves around to asking our landlord to move out because, underneath it all, we both really liked him. This continued until Reed had been living with us seven weeks out of our twelve weeks of married life. Then it happened. I teased Amy one morning about living with two men for more than half her married life. She lost her temper and went into a frenzied rage. Reed moved out entirely within an hour!

March and April were a joyous time for Amy and me. She got an appointment with one of the obstetricians in town who confirmed that she was indeed pregnant. Of course, I had told her so all along. Baby books were obtained at the county library by the armloads, and many nights were spent in diligent reading.

May was a beautiful month. Amy and I were so very happy. One night, around the twentieth of May, Amy and I went to the movies. It was very dark as we drove back to the farm. When we reached the driveway entrance, Amy let out a gasp. She thought she felt some movement within her but then dismissed the thought. However, around 3:00 a.m. the following morning I was awakened by the delighted shouts of "Ted! Ted! He moved! He moved!" My response to this middle-of-the-night statement was "Huh? Good, Honey. ZZZZZZZZZZZ" The little one had begun to make his presence felt as well as known.

Perhaps at this point I should discuss my wife's "magic belly," as we have come to call it. Most men, I presume, would say that their wives had good figures when they were first married. I am no exception. When we got married, my wife had a figure that would make any woman envious. As the months progressed, things happened and Amy's magic belly began doing magical things. The magic belly made Amy's skin very smooth and silky. The magic belly also made Amy's breasts swell and harden, which is a magic trick that I have thoroughly enjoyed. And the magic belly has even grown itself. Being a woman, Amy is quite upset with her figure these days. But, being her husband, I am quite proud of her physique and still think that she has a beautiful figure. In my estimation, she is the most beautiful pregnant woman in the world.

Meanwhile, back at the ranch . . . or perhaps I should say back in the womb, the little one is doing just fine, kicking about seventy-five to eighty percent of the time. It is such a joyous feeling to place my hand on the magic belly and feel those kicks of life. Amy and I have even obtained a stethoscope with which to hear the little one's heartbeat.

Amy is almost seven months pregnant now, and she and I are eagerly looking forward to the next two months. The doctor is very strict with Amy about her weight. Since my wife is a nurse, she does know better than to eat the wrong kinds of food and get overweight. Our big concern is that she has a small pelvis that was broken five years ago by a fall from a horse. Because of the doctor's strictness and very high professional competency, I am confident that my wife is receiving and will continue to receive the best of everything when the time comes to bring a new life into the world. Amy and I are both hoping and praying that we will have a healthy child.

IN THIS CHAPTER . . .

You will read about

1 The female and male gametes and how fertilization occurs. Modified or alternative modes of reproduction are also explained.
2 How tests for pregnancy are conducted; how the sex of the newly conceived baby is determined; and how multiple births (twins) are created.
3 A monthly report of the development of the unborn child throughout the entire prenatal period.
4 A wide variety of factors, such as diet and drugs, that can affect the growth and development of the fetus.
5 Techniques of medical technology that can be used to preserve the well-being of the mother and the unborn child.
6 The methods of abortion and reactions to the termination of pregnancy.

uterus the female organ in which the prenatal organism develops and is nourished prior to birth.

The greatest miracle of this age, or of any age, is not the knowledge explosion brought on by electronic technology, or the transplanting of organs from one human being to another, or the landing of men on the moon. The greatest miracle of all is the creation and birth of a new life. When one considers the intricate and complex processes involved in creating, developing, and maintaining life, how a human being is formed from a ball-shaped cell smaller than the period at the end of this sentence, and how human development takes place in such an orderly, sequential manner, one has to be impressed by the wonder and marvel of it all.

LIFE BEGINS

Living things have the power to reproduce themselves. The simplest kinds of animals and plants reproduce by the splitting of one cell in half, thus making two separate organisms. Animals and plants that are more complex in development have special cells designated for the purpose of reproduction. In human beings, as in other vertebrates, the union of two of these distinctive cells called ***gametes,*** the sperm from the male and the egg or ovum from the female, is necessary to create new life.

The sex cells

The sex cells (gametes or germ cells) are the egg, or *ovum* (plural, ova), in the female and the sperm, or *spermatozoon* (plural, spermatozoa), in the male. The ovum is one of the largest cells in the human body, whereas the spermatozoon is one of the smallest. The spermatozoon is approximately 0.05 mm (1/6,000 in.) in diameter. It has either an oval-shaped head or a smaller, round-shaped head, plus a fine, hairlike tail about ten times as long as its head. The oval-shaped-head sperm carries the male or Y sex cell, and the round-shaped-head sperm carries the female or X sex cell. The tail lashes back and forth, enabling the spermatozoon to swim through the semen in which it is found. The ovum is a single, ball-shaped cell approximately 0.1 mm (1/200 in.) in diameter and has no means of locomotion within itself. Its movement is dependent on the contractions of the tissues by which it is surrounded. The ovum is a tiny speck barely visible to the naked eye. However, it is still some 85,000 times greater in volume than the sperm (Hellman and Pritchard, 1976).

Female gametes and organs

The human female has in her ovaries at birth over 400,000 rudimentary ova. Many of these will atrophy before she reaches puberty. Of the 150,000 ova remaining at puberty, approximately 400 will mature at monthly intervals, one at a time usually, prior to the menopause. The ovum is yellowish in color because it contains yolk that will be used to nourish a new individual should the ovum be fertilized.

In its nucleus the ovum contains 46 chromosomes in 23 pairs. One of the 23 chromosomes is the X sex cell. Chromosomes direct the cells they occupy to grow in certain ways, perform certain functions, and transmit hereditary traits. When the ovum is ready to be fertilized, the pairs of chromosomes split. Half the chromosomes remain at the center of the ovum; the other half migrate to the outer portion of the ovum and eventually disintegrate. When the ovum is fertilized, it will receive 23 chromosomes from the sperm, thus again having a total of 46.

Female organs. The ***uterus*** (womb) is a hollow, pear-shaped organ with strong but elastic muscular walls. It is within the uterus that the baby will develop (Fig. 3-1). The lower end of the uterus, which extends to the vagina, is called the *cervix.* The cervix has an opening through which the sperm will make their way from the vagina into the uterus. When the baby is being born, the cervix will dilate and the baby will pass through this enlarged opening into the vagina and be delivered into the external world.

Menstrual cycle. During a woman's childbearing years the uterus is normally prepared each month for fertilization and pregnancy. If no pregnancy occurs, menstruation takes place. The menstrual "cycle" begins with the flow of mucus and blood that had accumulated during the previous cycle. The discharge will continue for 4 or 5 days. At the end of this time the uterine wall is relatively thin. In the postmenstrual phase the uterus will come under the influence of an

estrogens female sex hormones, produced primarily in the ovaries.

ovulation expulsion of an ovum from the ovary, which occurs once about every 28 days from puberty to menopause.

progesterone a female sex hormone produced by the ovaries; it helps prepare the uterus for pregnancy and the breasts for lactation.

estrogen hormone that seeks to increase sexual excitability—and also influences thickening of the *endometrium* (uterus wall lining). This period is the follicular phase (Fig. 3-2). At the time of ovulation, when the ovum is released from the ovary, the hormone ***progesterone*** takes over and prepares the endometrium with thin layers of cells for the reception and development of the fertilized ovum. The lining inside the uterus continues to thicken. If fertilization of the ovum does not take place, the level of progesterone begins to drop about the twenty-fifth day, during the luteal phase, resulting in a degeneration of the thickened uterine lining. The surface layer of cells passes out with the flow of mucus and blood during the next menstrual phase. The content is normally about 90 to 120 ml (6 to 8 tbsp.). A menstrual cycle lasts for an average of 28 days, paralleling the time of a lunar month.

Ovulation process. ***Ovulation*** is the process by which a mature ovum is discharged from one of the two ovaries. The *ovaries* are glands about the size and shape of almonds that lie about 7.5 cm (3 in.) on either side of the midway point between the vaginal opening and the navel. They are located on each side of the outer uterine wall at the end of the fallopian tubes.

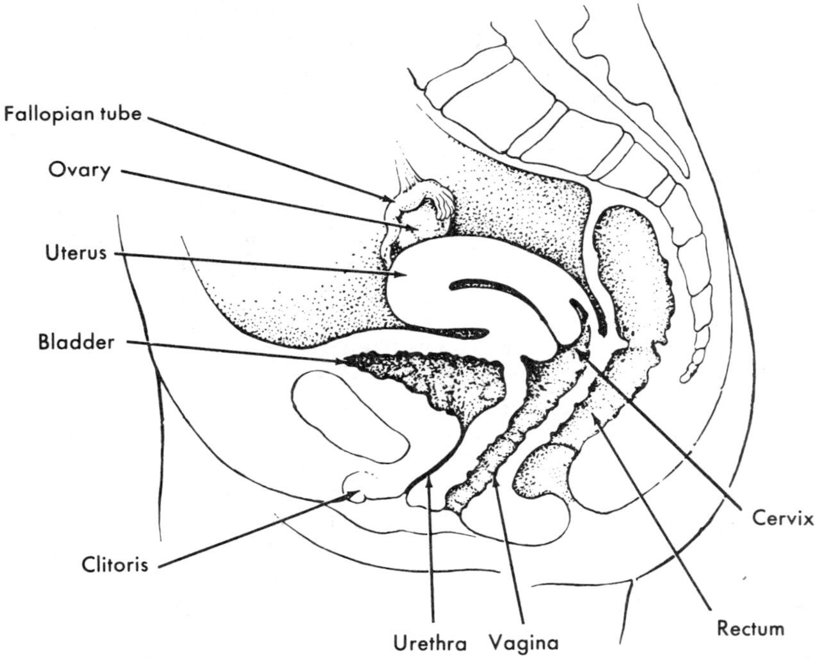

FIG. 3-1 *Internal female sex organs. The ovary releases one ovum (egg) a month. The egg travels through the fallopian tube, where fertilization occurs if sperm are present. If the egg is not fertilized, the wall of the uterus breaks down, and blood cells and disintegrated egg are discharged through the vagina by the process of menstruation. The female system prepares itself for motherhood each month.*

Modified from Iorio, J. Childbirth: family-centered nursing *[3rd ed.]. St. Louis: The C.V. Mosby Co., 1975.*

There is a tube for each ovary. Generally the ovaries alternate in releasing one mature ovum on or about the fourteenth day of the menstrual cycle. The usual cycle is counted from the beginning of one menstrual flow to the beginning of the next. Therefore the period of ovulation—the time when pregnancy can most likely take place in a woman with a normal menstrual cycle—occurs for about 48 hours just about midway between the periods of menstrual flow.

The ovum within the ovary is surrounded by a small sac known as a graafian follicle. The follicle holding the ovum works its way to the surface of the ovary and there forms a blisterlike swelling. This blister, containing estrogen fluid, ruptures and releases the ovum at the open end of the nearest fallopian tube. The tiny round egg finds its way into the tube and is propelled through the tube by hairlike cilia cells on the sides of the tube, by the estrogen fluid, and by rhythmic contractions of the walls of the tube. The fallopian tube is about 10 cm (4 in.) long and connects to the uterus.

The ovum will survive for 3 or 4 days or longer, although it is generally capable of being fertilized only during the first 24 hours. If the ovum is not fertilized, it deteriorates, and its remains will then be discharged along with other menstrual materials and blood from the uterine lining.

Male gametes and organs

Whereas only one ovum is ripened every menstrual cycle, several hundred million sperm are developed every 4 or 5 days. The implication is that the man is capable of providing sperm for the purpose of conception at almost anytime, whereas the woman produces a mature ovum on the average of only once every 28 days. Furthermore, sperm are formed well into old

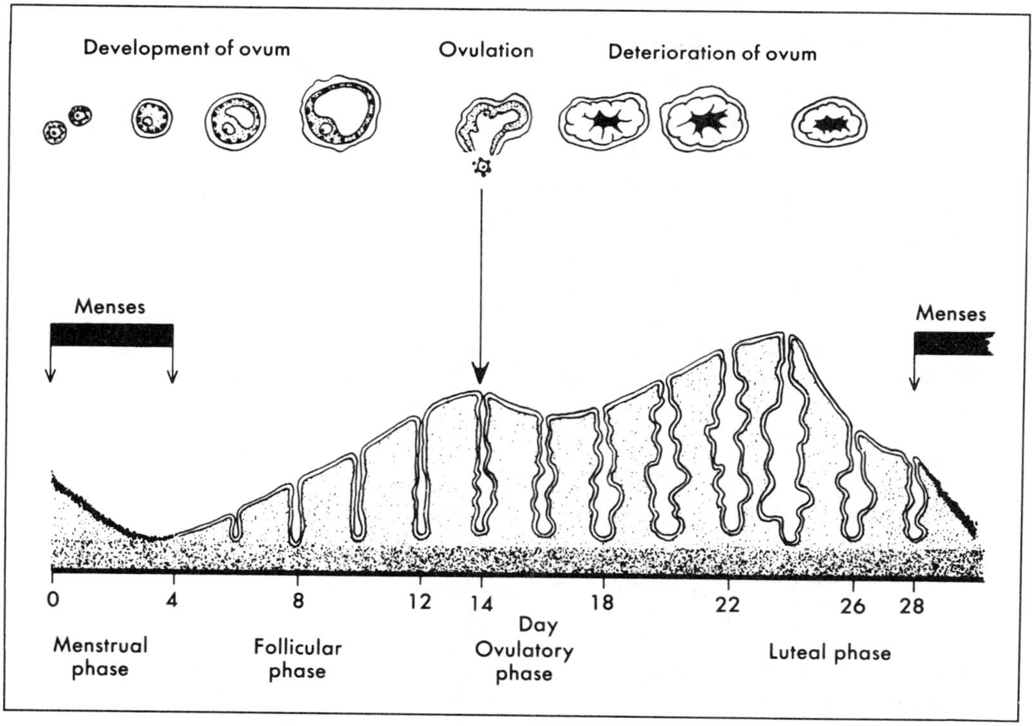

FIG. 3-2 ***Menstrual cycle.***

Modified from Iorio, J. Childbirth: family-centered nursing *[3rd ed.]. St. Louis: The C.V. Mosby Co., 1975.*

age, even though the sperm may not always be capable of fertilizing an egg. In the woman, production of the sex cells will cease with the completion of menopause.

Sperm are formed in the two *testes* (testicles or male gonads) suspended in the scrotum, a thin-walled sac of skin (Fig. 3-3). The sperm-making cells within the testicles are extremely sensitive to heat. They must have a temperature several degrees below that of the interior of the body; otherwise they rapidly deteriorate and cease producing the male sex cells. The scrotum has a large area of skin surface for the purpose of heat evaporation. The sac will pull close to the body when cold to get more heat and will hang loose when warm to become cooler (Smith, 1975).

The sperm cell will reduce the 46 chromosomes to only half that number. The mature sperm has 22 chromosomes plus a sex determination chromosome (X or Y). These 23 chromosomes will pair with the 23 chromosomes found in the female sex cell at the time of conception.

From the testes the mature sperm will pass through a long, narrow, much coiled tube called the *epididymis,* where they mix with a fluid. The sperm will then move through other long tubes called the *vas deferens* to the seminal vesicles, where the sperm is temporarily stored. Located near the seminal vesicles is the prostate gland. At the time of ejaculation the fluid carrying the sex cells passes the prostate gland, where a milky secretion is added to make semen. Up to the time of ejaculation the sperm have been relatively motionless. With the addition of the fluids from the prostate gland they become very vigorous.

After ejaculation, sperm remain actively mobile in the seminal fluid for 36 to 48 hours, on the average, if secreted into the vagina and the upper portions of the female reproductive tract (Crouch, 1972). Since sperm can live as long as 2 or 3 days within the uterus of the woman, the depositing of sperm in the vagina as much as 72 hours prior to ovulation can lead to pregnancy. Sperm that do not enter the uterus from the vagina usually die within a few hours because of the toxic environment of the vagina.

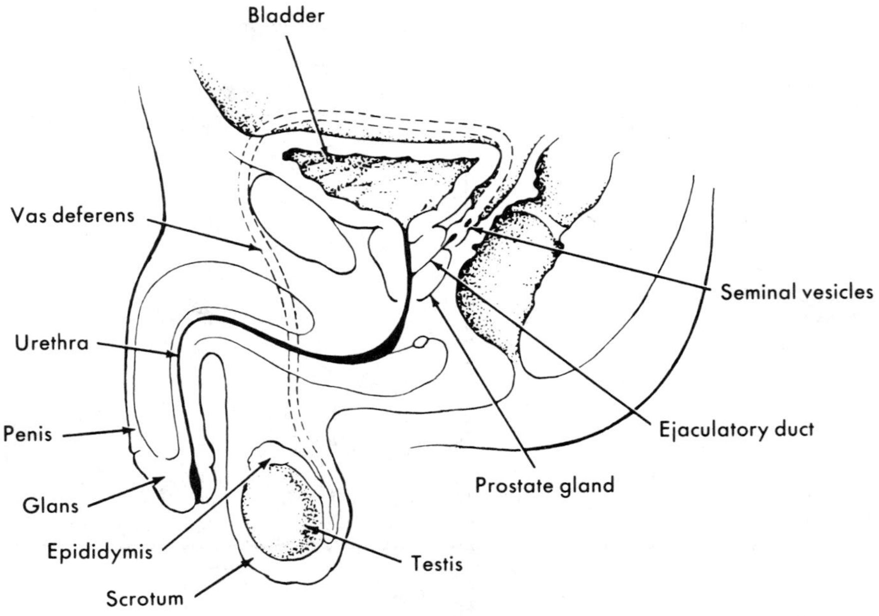

FIG. 3-3 ***Male sex organs and gamete production. The sperm cells are produced in the testes and are temporarily stored in the seminal vesicles. Male sex organs constantly make and deliver active sperm cells capable of fertilizing the ovum in the body of the female.***
Modified from Iorio, J. Childbirth: family-centered nursing *[3rd ed.]. St. Louis: The C.V. Mosby Co., 1975.*

How fertilization occurs

fertilization the union of an egg cell with a sperm.

It is the act of mating, or sexual intercourse, that brings the sperm cells and ovum together and makes it possible for ***fertilization*** to occur. The stimulating effect of intercourse on the penis causes the male to ejaculate about 5 ml (1 tsp.) of semen containing about 300 to 400 million sperm into the vagina near the cervix. Only about 20 million of the sperm succeed in working their way through the cervical opening into the uterus (Kaiser, 1977). Even fewer find their way into the fallopian tubes. The journey takes about 1 to 2 hours.

If a viable ovum is present in the tube, the sperm that have made their way into the tube will be drawn to the egg and will cover it. Sperm cells make an enzyme that helps to break down the rather tough outer membrane of the egg cell. Once a sperm does pierce the cell wall, it still has to find its way to the nucleus of the egg. Considering that the ovum is 85,000 times larger than the sperm, the little sperm still has a comparatively long way to go. When a sperm does reach the nucleus, the other sperm cease their activities.

Meriem Kaluger

Take twin mounds of clay
Mold them as you may
Shape one after me,
Another after thee.
Then quickly break them both.
Remix, remake them both—
One formed after thee,
The other after me.
Part of my clay is thine;
Part of thy clay is mine.

Kwan Tao-Shing
13th Century

in vitro fertilization fertilization of an ovum in a laboratory setting, outside the woman's body. The egg is later implanted in the woman's uterus. Commonly referred to as "test-tube" fertilization.

The nucleus of the sperm and the nucleus of the ovum will merge, and their contents will combine. The 23 chromosomes of the ovum's nucleus will pair off with the 23 chromosomes from the nucleus of the sperm to make 23 pairs of chromosomes with thousands of genes. In that fraction of a second when the chromosomes form pairs, the sex of the new child will be determined, hereditary characteristics received from each parent will be set, and a new life will have been created.

Infertility

There are couples who would like to conceive and have children but cannot. *Infertility* refers to a condition in which a couple fails to achieve pregnancy after 1 year of having engaged in sexual relations with normal frequency and without contraception. The American Medical Association estimates that about 15% of all married couples are unable to have children. Another 10% have fewer children than they would like to have because one or both members are subfertile (Kolata, 1977).

Causes of infertility. Several conditions might exist to prevent conception from taking place. In the male the problem may be (1) an inability to produce healthy sperm or enough sperm, (2) an inability of the male to transfer the sperm to the genital tract because of a physiological obstacle or the inability to achieve erection, or (3) a psychological, drug-, or alcohol-related condition. In the female the problem may be (1) a poor uterine environment for the fertilized egg, (2) hormonal failure of ovulation due to endocrine or metabolic imbalance, (3) blockage in the fallopian tubes, (4) physiological obstacles to conceiving or carrying a fetus to term because of congenital or infectious disease (such as gonorrhea), or (5) psychological, drug-, or alcohol-related problems (Jensen et al., 1981). Current figures suggest that the male is found to be the primary source of the infertility about 40% of the time because of a low sperm count or poor quality of the sperm (Kolata, 1977). Zorgniotti and associates (1982) have reported that hypothermia (subnormal temperature) of the testes produces poor semen, causing infertility. Toth and Lesser (1982) determined that T-mycoplasma infections and other bacterial infections in the urogenital tract could cause infertility. However, treatment of these infections resulted in restored fertility in a significant number of cases.

Modified modes of reproduction. There are three major modes of modified reproduction that have potential: (1) artificial insemination or artificial inovulation, (2) in vitro fertilization and embryo transplantation, and (3) asexual reproduction, known as cloning.

Artificial insemination involves the collection of semen, usually through masturbation. It is then introduced directly through the vagina to the cervix of the uterus by a syringe. This method is used if the husband is subfertile and needs more sperm to gain access to the egg. If the husband is infertile, however, then a donor is required. Fresh semen can either be used within 30 minutes after it is ejaculated, or it can be frozen and placed in a sperm bank.

Artificial inovulation is a possibility for women who have blocked oviducts. By means of a simple surgical procedure, eggs can be removed and transferred to lower portions of the oviduct, detouring the blockage. Fertilization can then occur by normal intercourse or artificial insemination.

In vitro fertilization refers to the union of the egg and sperm outside the body in a laboratory. The procedure is more complicated than it may seem. However, some successful human fertilizations have occurred. On July 26, 1978, a 2608 g (5 lb. 12 oz.) girl believed to be the world's first baby conceived in vitro was born in Oldham, England. Mother and child were in excellent condition. Since then a number of other such pregnancies have been reported. The first successful birth of an in vitro fertilized child in the United States was in 1982.

Cloning represents a radical departure from traditional reproduction. Cloning is the process of duplicating living things from an individual cell. It has been used to create plants since 1963. Dr. J. B. Gurdon of Oxford University reported the production of cloned frogs in 1966. As far as we know, it has not been attempted on humans. Rumors of such attempts are heard every now and then, even to the point of stating that at least one human was created that way. The problem with human cloning appears to be one of technique. The microsurgical technique used with the cell of the frog to bring about a clone would be totally inadequate with the more refined, delicate, complex human cell. A cell-fusion technique is said by supporters of the idea to be able to overcome cell damage and offers a better technique of cloning. No scientific evidence has been revealed at this point.

ASPECTS OF PREGNANCY

The moment that a new life is conceived is not immediately evident to the woman. The fertilized egg, however, will probably begin within the hour of conception to divide and to start its development toward becoming a baby. The woman may not learn of her pregnancy for some days to come.

Diagnosis of pregnancy

A diagnosis of pregnancy can be determined from three types of information: the symptoms of the woman, specific laboratory tests, and certain bodily changes found by the physician on his physical examination of the woman. Failure to menstruate is usually the earliest evidence of pregnancy. However, failure to menstruate may also result from illness or anxiety. Likewise, occasionally a woman may be pregnant and still have signs of menstruation for a month or more. As a result, laboratory tests for pregnancy provide more definite information. Most laboratory tests seek to determine whether a substance known as human chorionic gonadotropin (HCG) is present in the urine. This hormone is secreted by the trophoblasts and is always present 9 to 10 days after the first missed menstrual period. The HCG reaches a peak between the sixtieth and seventieth days of pregnancy. The new life is now in the embryonic period of development.

Aschheim and Zondek did the original research that led to the first methods by which pregnancy could be indicated with at least 95% accuracy. A small quantity of the woman's urine is injected into a female mouse or rabbit. If the woman is pregnant, a hormone in her urine will cause changes in the animal's ovaries within 48 hours in rabbits and 96 hours in mice. Another test using frogs provides results in 2 to 6 hours.

More recently, tests have been devised that can give results in a shorter period of time. One test consists of a chemical analysis for color change of the woman's urine when mixed with a special reagent. This sensitive hemagglutination-inhibition test gives results in 2 hours. In another test two preparations are placed on a glass slide, and a drop of urine is put on the preparations. If the preparations do not clump together in particles, the urine contains HCG and the woman is pregnant. (Iorio, 1975). This latex-inhibition test is completed in 3 minutes. Pregnancy frequently can be confirmed as early as 4 weeks after conception, although 6 weeks is generally required for certainty. The sixth week would be about a month after the missed menstrual period.

A "do-it-yourself" pregnancy kit became available in 1976. The E.P.T. In-home Pregnancy Test (E.P.T. stands for Early Pregnancy Test) is now distributed nationally in the United States. It has been available in Europe since 1970 under the name of Predictor. The test makes use of the principle that the pregnant body begins to produce HCG on the ninth day after the date that the menstrual period was to begin. Instructions are simple: after the ninth day put 3 drops of urine into the test tube provided. Add the contents of the plastic vial in the E.P.T. kit, shake for 10 seconds, and place the test tube in the holder. It must remain undisturbed for 2 hours. If a dark brown ring is visible in the mirror that comes with the holder after 2 hours, an active pregnancy is indicated.

Studies by the producing company claim that positive readings are 97% accurate. However, suggestions are that negative readings indicate a second test should be taken a week later. If the second test is also negative, then the results are considered to be 91% accurate. E.P.T. information points out that the first 60 days are critical in fetal development and suggests that improper use of cigarettes, alcohol, household medications, or poor nutrition can be harmful to the developing fetus.

The most positive signs of pregnancy include hearing and counting of fetal heart tones after the eighteenth to twentieth week of pregnancy, spontaneous fetal movement as felt by the physician, and evidence of fetal bones after the fourth month of pregnancy. Commonly experienced physical signs in a woman include (1) cessation of menstruation, (2) nausea and vomiting (morning sickness) from shortly after the first missed period to the end of the first trimester, (3) fatigue, requiring 10 to 12 hours of sleep, (4) tenderness and gradual enlargement of breasts and deeper color in the area around the nipples about the third month, (5) increased frequency of urination, and (6) the feeling of fetal movements (quickening) about the seventeenth or eighteenth week of pregnancy (Jensen et al., 1981).

TEN SHORT MINUTES

"Miss Ellison, your tests show positive. Will you be coming for monthly checkups?"

Positive! Oh, no! It is really happening. Don't kid yourself, Jean. I mean, weren't you expecting it? Isn't that why you came here in the first place?

"Miss Ellison, will you be coming back?"

"No! I don't think so. Thank you."

I wonder what my facial expression must be telling that nurse. I'm sure she has seen hundreds of such cases, so mine shouldn't upset her in the least. Don't gaze at me with that pathetic look either.

Me, simple little me! Here I was, waking each morning and sleeping each night, pretending to be busily attending to the duties of life, to give others the impression that I knew what life was all about. Here I am now, realizing what I didn't know before, that *this* is what sex is all about—the creation of new life.

Positive, it's still ringing in my ears like vibrating cymbals. Instead of fading, it's increasing in pitch and intensity as if to remind me of all the changes taking place within me at this very moment. Jean, get out of this office. Be careful of those steps, little mother. Now, plant your feet firmly on the sidewalk and walk, one foot up while the other foot is down.

It almost seems mechanical. But the doctor said I was pregnant; he was positive of that. That makes me something more than a machine. I'm participating in one of the marvels of time and, for some reason. I want to tell the whole world about it.

Hey, Jean, you can't do that. It's wonderful, the creation of life and all that; but don't shout too loud. People might hear, turn away from you, and shake their righteous heads. You realize that you aren't married; so that makes the growing embryo somewhat taboo in the minds of some people.

I shouldn't have to think of a thing like that now, not at such an eventful moment in my life. No one has the right to look upon me with pity or scorn for the joyous event happening. They should be envious that I am doing something that perhaps their age or circumstance will not permit. They should feel deep respect for this living being soon to become a part of their world.

A part of their world! How can you think a thing like that when you know your own moral parents will reject it, and you as well? How can you look into the eyes of your mother and say: "Mom, I'm fulfilling my role as a woman. I'm pregnant." Have you thought about the gossiping neighbors who will plague your grandmother? At least your proud sister will not have the honor of bearing the first grandchild. That will be a blow to her ego. And, Dave—what do you do about Dave? Certainly the father of the child should know so he can take his credit. Remember, dear one, you haven't met Dave's parents yet. You're going to make quite an impression on them by the time you see them in July. The crosswalk sign says: "Walk, Don't Run." Can you manage that, Jean?

Yes, I can. I can walk into the situation, but now I must be careful not to run through the solution. If only time could be slowed down to give me a chance to think it through. Instead, it rushes along like a babbling brook. While I was having fun at the shore a few short weeks ago, a fertilized egg implanted itself in the wall of my uterus. Already the embryo is differentiating the tissues to form all the major systems and organs of the body.

Chestnut Street, that's the wrong street. You turned the wrong corner. Retrace your steps, you silly girl—or is it woman now?

Retrace steps. If only I could retrace the past two months. That would be foolish too: Dave and I conceived that child in love, and I wouldn't want to blot out that moment. True, the conception was unintentional, but I'm not sorry for what we did. I wonder if that man notices. I'd love to tell him, but he'd notice the missing wedding band. I don't even have an engagement ring. Dave and I discussed it and decided we both needed more time to get settled in life. His job means we would have to move around a lot and I'm not sure I can cope with that. For a while it may be all right, but not after a family gets started.

It's started. It's here right now. Except I'm still not ready for marriage and, financially, not ready for a child. There are still so many things I want to do before worrying about washing diapers and warming bottles. My whole routine will have to change; regular meals, plenty of sleep, doctor appointments. All of this will require money.

Go straight on Vine, then two more blocks and you'll be in the privacy of your own car. Privacy, what privacy have I now? I can't expect to return to my teaching job in the fall and I'll have to move out of the house. It will make it easier on Mom and Dad if they don't have to look at my growing condition each day. Just bring the newborn infant to them and try to make your peace. But where to now, Jean?

I know Dave will marry me, but I'm not sure that it would be the right thing. We both agreed to wait a year to let our feelings solidify. I don't want the child to bring together a relationship that may not work. The environment, under the present conditions, may not be the best for the child; but why increase the problems?

It's not too late to have a miscarriage, Jean. You could involve yourself in active sports and try to dislodge the embryo from the uterus. It certainly seems like the easy way out of your predicament. How about an abortion? No one would know.

I'd know. And I do want that child. I want to see nature's handiwork in which I have been an instrument.

A telephone booth? I could call Dave at the plant; but that may upset the rest of his day, or cheer it up tremendously. I'd better wait till he gets up from Delaware this weekend.

Well, . . . 327-555-7902. Hurry, before I chicken out!

"Hello."

"Hello, Dave?"

"Yes."

Boy or girl?

autosomes the chromosomes of a cell, excluding those that determine sex.

meiosis the process of cell division in which the daughter cells receive half the normal number of chromosomes, thus becoming gametes.

Of the 46 chromosomes found in germ cells, two are sex determination chromosomes. In the female these two sex determination chromosomes are identical and so are given the letter designation of X and X. In the male, however, these chromosomes are different and so are designated as X and Y. By the process of ***meiosis,*** a special method of sex cell division, the ovum will always have 22 nonsex chromosomes (called ***autosomes***) plus an X sex determination cell. The sperm will also have 22 autosomes plus a sex determination cell, but that cell may be either an X cell or a Y cell. Should it be an X cell from the male that pairs with the X cell from the female, the result will be a girl. A Y cell from the male that pairs with an X cell from the female will produce a boy. It is from the germ cells of the father that the sex of the child is determined. Fig. 3-4 illustrates how the determination of the sex of the baby takes place.

There have been numerous theories and methods advocated throughout the ages in an effort to choose the sex of a child. The research of Shettles (Shettles and Vande Weile, 1974) indicates that some basic principles regarding sex selection may have been found. Using a phase-contrast microscope and carbon dioxide gas to slow down the movement of living sperm cells, Shettles noticed that sperm came in two distinct sizes and shapes. He eventually concluded that the small, round-headed sperm carry the male-producing Y chromosomes. The larger, oval-shaped type carry the female-producing X chromosomes. The male-producing type he calls *androsperm* and the female-producing type he calls *gynosperm.* He further postulated that the male sperm are weaker and less viable than those carrying the trait for a female. The male sperm are also highly sensitive to the type of acid found in the vaginal tract and do not survive long in that environment. In the female, alkaline secretions generally appear only during the 24 hours before ovulation. It also appeared the the relative percentage of androsperm to gynosperm decreases after repeated intercourse and ejaculations.

Donald and Locky Schuster of Iowa State University hypothesize that the less-stressed parent tends to produce his own or her own gender. Wittels and Bornstein (1974) provided support for this idea based on a study of the sex of children born as a result of rape. In such situations it was reasoned that the mother was probably under greater stress than the father. If the Schusters' hypothesis is true, more than half the children born should be boys. Working with a religious organization, the researchers found 10 rape-conceived children out of a total of 349 babies handled by the organization during a 30-month period. Of the 349 babies, 191 were boys and 158 girls. Of the 10 rape-caused births, nine were boys. They found that the one rape victim who gave birth to a girl admitted to having a relationship with the alleged father previous to the alleged rape. Further investigation of this theory warrants attention.

dizygotic (DZ) twins twins who develop from two separate eggs; fraternal twins. See also **monozygotic (MZ) twins.**

monozygotic (MZ) twins twins who develop from the same fertilized ovum; identical twins. See also **dizygotic (DZ) twins.**

Twins or more

Normally the human female produces only one mature ovum every menstrual cycle. Sometimes the one egg released is fertilized, but certain conditions exist that cause that egg to split, thus producing two embryos. Occasionally, however, some women will release two or more mature ova at the same time. If more than one ovum are in the fallopian tube at the same time, there is a good chance that more than one will be fertilized. Either way more than one life has been conceived.

Twins may be of two types, identical or fraternal. The term *identical* is misleading because no two people are alike in every way. For this reason geneticists prefer to use other terms that refer to the origin of the twin types. Identical twins are referred to as ***monozygotic*** (MZ), or one-egg twins, and fraternal twins are ***dizygotic*** (DZ), or two-egg twins (Fig. 3-5). MZ twins originate from a single fertilized ovum that divided into two or more parts at an early stage of development. MZ twins will always be of the same sex. One third of all twins are MZ twins.

DZ twins occur when two or more eggs are present in the fallopian tubes (oviducts) and two or more are fertilized by different sperm cells. Since DZ twins originate from different ova as well as different sperm cells, the genetic relationship between the twins is only slightly greater than that of ordinary siblings (Bouchard and McGue, 1981). Thus DZ twins can be two girls, two boys, or one girl and one boy. Twins

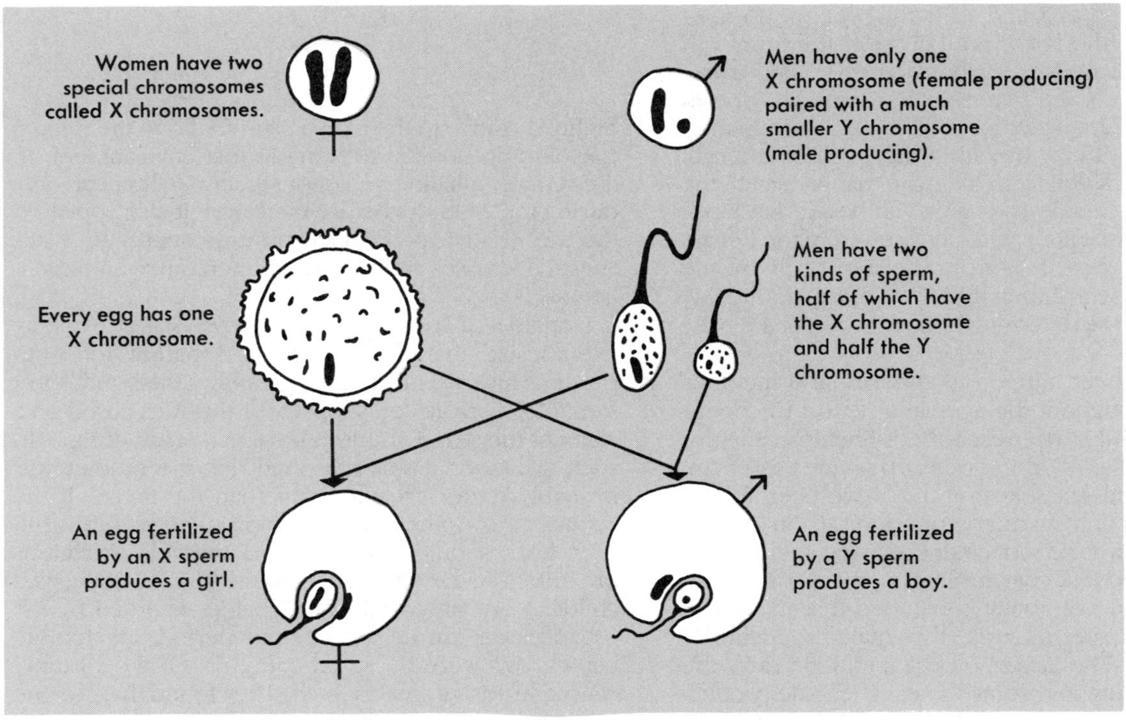

FIG. 3-4 *Sex determination. If the X (female producing) sperm of the male unites with the X chromosome from the egg, a girl is produced. If the Y (male producing) sperm unites with the X chromosome from the egg, a boy is created.*

Lisa and Linda are monozygotic twins (identical), originating from a single fertilized egg and having the same DNA coding.

Andrew and Julie are dizygotic twins (fraternal), originating from two ova, fertilized at the same time. Their DNA coding will be different.

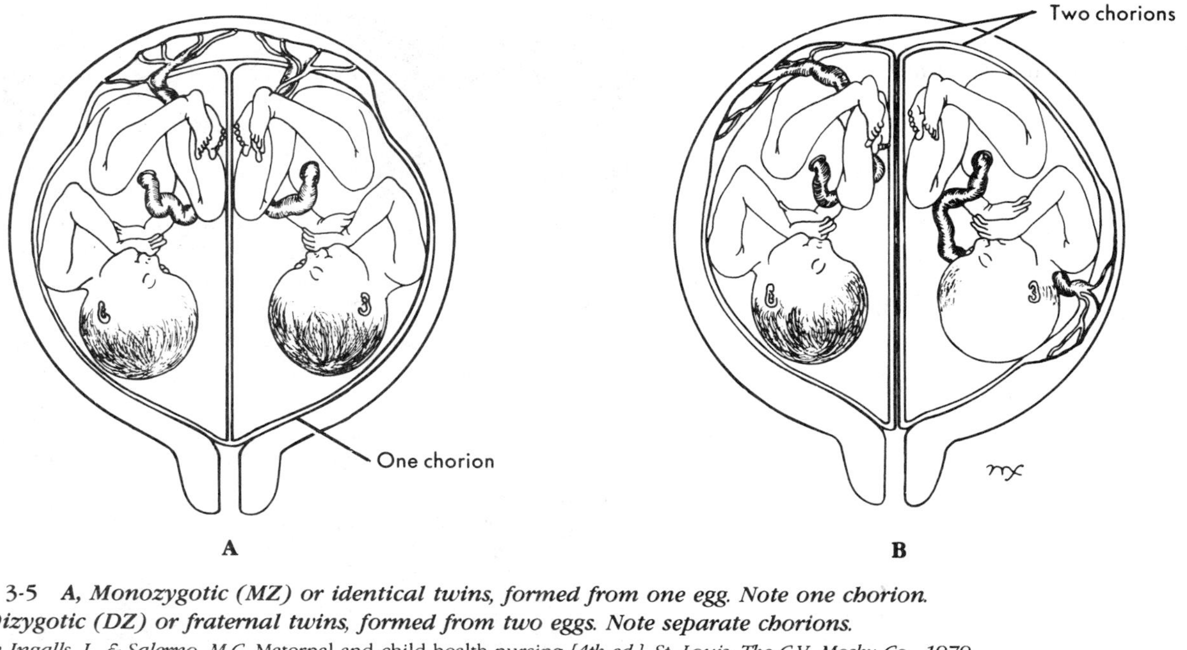

FIG. 3-5 ***A,** Monozygotic (MZ) or identical twins, formed from one egg. Note one chorion.*
***B,** Dizygotic (DZ) or fraternal twins, formed from two eggs. Note separate chorions.*
From Ingalls, J., & Salerno, M.C. Maternal and child health nursing *[4th ed.]. St. Louis: The C.V. Mosby Co., 1979.*

Meriem Kaluger

The Heindel girls, at 19 years of age, are a combination of fraternal and identical triplets. Michelle, at the left, is a fraternal triplet, originating in an egg separate from the other two girls. Melissa and Melinda (right) originated from one egg.

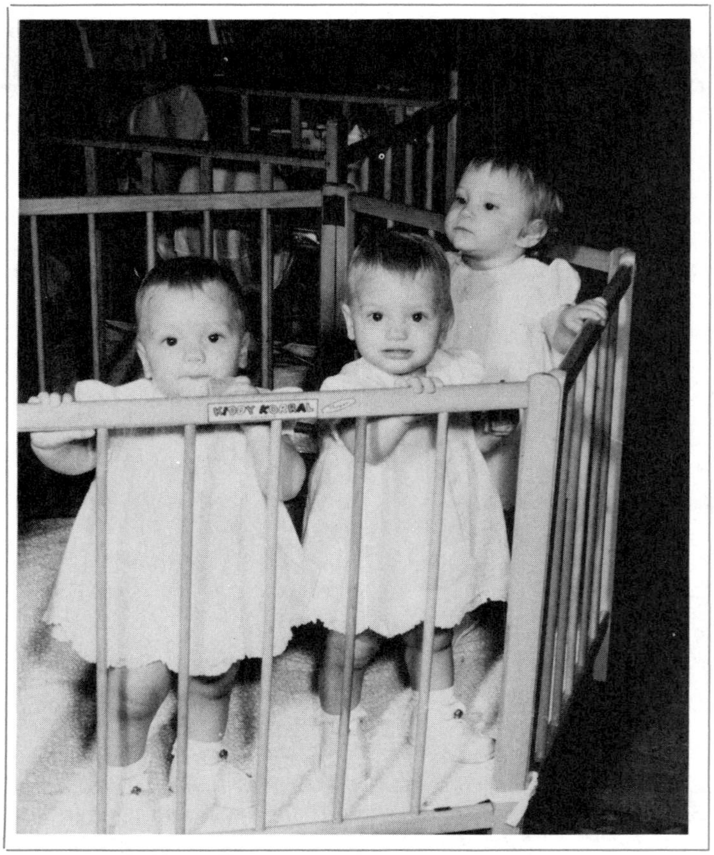

The Heindel triplets at 1 year of age. Can you tell which is which? From left to right, they are Melissa, Melinda, and Michelle.

occur in 1 out of 88 births; triplets occur in 1 out of 7,564 births (Timiras, 1972).

During the development of twins, several factors are present that are not as common in single-child pregnancies. Both DZ and MZ conceptions must deal with crowding factors, especially if they have a common chorion. In MZ twins the fertilized egg had enough food stored within it for only one baby. Of course, when the egg splits, the food is divided. Food may be lacking for the zygotes to survive. The chance of a premature birth is greater among multiple births than for single births. A study of 62 sets of twins found (1) the incidence of prematurity was about 5% higher for twins, (2) most early births occurred in the lowest class families, (3) prematurity rate is higher for girl twins, (4) prematurity rate is higher for MZ twins, (5) chances for American black mothers to have twins are one-third higher than for whites, but for Japanese and Chinese mothers it is one-third less, and (6) chances for twins increase with the age of the mother and the number of previous births (Vaughan et al., 1979).

Whatever is true about twins applies in extended ways to triplets, quadruplets, and other "twin-plus" sets. These multiple pregnancies are produced by basically the same process as twins. Formerly only five or six sets of quadruplets were born in the United States every year.

Since the mid-1960s certain hormones have been administered to previously sterile women to induce ovulation and conception. These procedures often trigger the release of more than one egg at a time and have resulted in twins and "twins plus." Using hormones, four women conceived quadruplets; three sets are surviving and healthy. Two sets of quintuplets were born, with all five surviving in one set but only one surviving in the other. Sextuplets were born in Denver, Colorado, in 1973 and all have survived to this time. In 1971 nine children were born to a woman in South America, but all of them died within 10 days. All of these were fraternal fertilizations, since they resulted from more than one egg. The statistics on the number of multiple pregnancies produced may be upset by a wider use of the hormone procedures with sterile women.

PRENATAL DEVELOPMENT AND BEHAVIOR

Once the fertilization of an ovum has taken place, nature appears to be in a fantastic hurry to move on with the developmental processes. Within an hour or two the fertilized egg will divide to form new cells. Cell division continues until the young embryo is implanted in the uterus; then structures begin to appear. By the time the woman misses her first menstrual period, the baby's heart, nervous system, and intestines are already developing. The woman at this point may not even know she is pregnant.

prenatal before birth; the stage of human development lasting from conception to birth.

zygote a new individual formed by the union of male and female gametes; the resultant globule of cells during the first phase of prenatal development after conception and lasting approximately 2 weeks.

Embryologists usually divide ***prenatal*** development into three periods. Each period has its own growth characteristics. First is the period of the zygote, also called the period of the ovum or the germinal period, during which the fertilized egg makes its way to the uterus. Second is the embryonic period, at which time the round ball, the fertilized egg, changes to a recognizable human fetus. The third stage is the fetal period, during which the fetus enhances and refines the structures developed during the previous period. The miracle of growth, the wonder of life, and the marvel of the laws of nature are perhaps most perfectly illustrated during these three periods in which a child develops from two minute cells that came together into a baby boy or girl, the newest member of humankind.

Period of the zygote

Once conception has taken place, two things occur simultaneously: the fertilized egg ***(zygote)*** begins to divide, and at the same time it makes its way down the fallopian tube to the uterus. The zygote will divide, perhaps within 30 minutes, certainly within an hour or two after conception. Ten hours later these 2 cells divide to make 4 cells, then the 4 to make 8 cells, then 16 cells, and so on. The cells are related to one another in accordance to the genetic code plan as prescribed for the total organic structure in the DNA molecules. The entire sphere made up of cells is called a *blastocyst,* or a zygote. Although the cells increase in number, they do not increase the overall size of the zygote. Fig. 3-6 illustrates the process of fertilization, cell division, and implantation.

Formation of cells. During the first 2 weeks after fertilization the important job is not the development of the actual form of the child but the making of clusters of cells that have special functions. Not all the cells become the human being. Imagine a drawing of the fertilized egg. The outer surface of the fertilized egg does not change into the shape of the child but eventually becomes part of the chorion (an extraembryonic membrane) and, later, the placenta. The formation of the child comes from the interior cells being formed.

Cells begin to form within the cell wall of the fertilized egg. An inner mass of cells will develop at one end or side of the interior of the sphere. Within this inner cell mass two hollow areas will be formed with a wall of cells separating the two. (This part is not shown in Fig. 3-6.) The hollow area next to the outer wall will eventually become the amnion (water sac), and the other cavity will become the yolk sac. The thick wall of cells between the two cavities is called the embryonic, or germinal, disk. This disk becomes the child. The

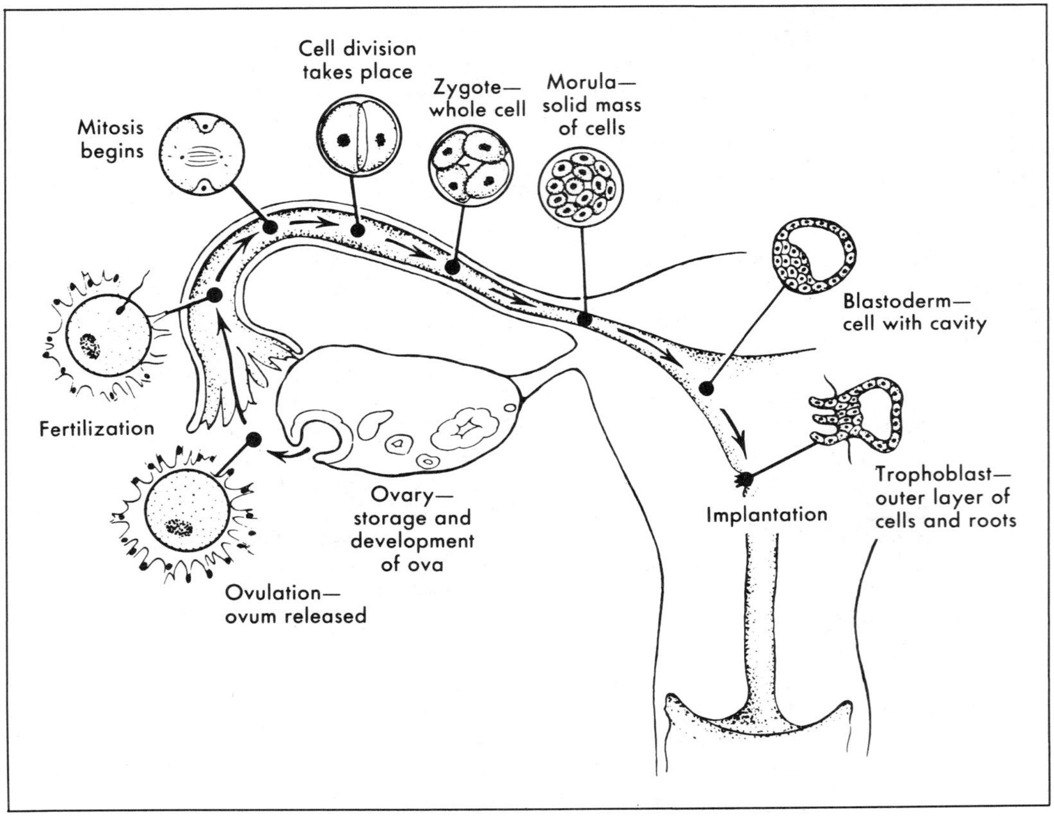

FIG. 3-6 *Process of fertilization, cell division, and implantation. Sperm cells enter the uterus and fallopian tube about the time the ovum is released from the ovary and enters the fallopian tube. The sperm and egg cell meet and unite in the tube. The sperm fertilizes the egg by entering its nucleus. The fertilized egg cell begins to divide as it travels to the uterus, where it attaches itself to the uterine wall and begins to form into an embryo.*

Modified from Iorio, J. Childbirth: family-centered nursing *[3rd ed.]. St. Louis: The C.V. Mosby Co., 1975.*

outer layer of cells of the zygote is known as the *trophoblast* (Fig. 3-6). It will develop roots with which to attach itself to the uterus and will eventually become the chorion.

Implantation of zygote. The journey down the fallopian tube to the uterus takes 3 to 5 days. Once in the uterus (womb), the fertilized ovum floats in a fluid for a few days before it attaches itself to the uterus. Meanwhile the uterus has prepared itself—as it does every month—for the reception of the fertilized egg. At this time its lining is at its thickest state and has considerable nourishment in its cells.

The free zygote begins to attach itself to the uterine wall about the sixth or seventh day after conception. By the tenth day it will usually be completely covered, and implantation will have taken place. Implantation marks the end of the period of the zygote. During this time the zygote remains at about the size of a pin head.

The trophoblast of the zygote has roots that will act on the uterine lining once the zygote comes to rest. Enzymes enable the trophoblast to digest or liquefy the tissue of the uterus. At implantation it will burrow into the uterine lining and form a nest for the zygote. Now the ***chorion*** begins to develop a network of fine roots, called *villi,* which spread into the lining of the uterus. They are the sole means by which oxygen and nourishment are received from the mother. The placenta will not be completely developed until the third month of pregnancy.

Survival hazards. There are certain hazards to the survival of the fertilized egg during the period of the zygote. The ovum must survive largely on its own food until it is implanted. If it does not receive enough nourishment, either because of the minimal amount of food supply or because the zygote takes too long to become implanted, it dies. It will be shed during the next menstrual period without the woman's ever realizing that conception had taken place. Occasionally there will be interference with the migration of the ovum down the fallopian tubes. Again, the ovum will die if it does not reach the uterus in time to become implanted. The ovum degenerates in the tube. An ectopic pregnancy, or a tubular pregnancy, takes place when the fertilized egg is implanted in the tube rather than in the uterus.

Period of the embryo

The ***embryonic period*** is one of rapid change. It covers that period of pregnancy from the time of implantation of the ball-shaped zygote in the uterine wall to the time the embryo becomes a recognizable human fetus. Embryologists say that this time span extends to the eighth week after conception. It is difficult to be precise about the time span because knowledge of this growth period is limited.

Tissue development. During the early part of the embryonic period the placenta, the amniotic sac, the yolk sac, and the umbilical cord are developed to the point where they can protect and nourish the embryo.

At maturity the pancakelike ***placenta*** will measure about 20 cm (8 in.) in diameter and 2.5 cm (1 in.) in thickness and will weigh about 450 g (1 lb.). Although the developing placenta is much too small to be seen at the time of implantation, it does begin to alter the hormonal pattern of the mother. Fig. 3-7 presents the development of various fetal membranes after the embryo begins to develop.

The ***amniotic sac*** (amnion) will enclose the embryo in a protective bag of fluid. The fetus will be able to move in this fluid and also to swallow it. This sac will serve to cushion the fetus against possible bumps, shocks, and injuries and will help to regulate its temperature.

The yolk sac has a temporary function of making blood cells for the embryo; however, it will soon shrink and gradually disappear when the liver takes over this function. The amniotic sac, the yolk sac, and the ***embryonic disk*** will become separated from the

amniotic sac fluid-filled membrane encasing the embryo/fetus.

chorion the protective and nutrient cover of the amnion, which contains the developing organism in the womb.

embryonic disk during the germinal period, the part of the prenatal organism that will eventually become the embryo.

embryonic period the period of prenatal growth that follows the germinal period, lasting from the second to the eighth week after conception; marked by development of a primitive human form and life-support system.

placenta the organ that forms in the uterine lining and through which the developing prenatal organism receives nourishment and discharges waste.

outer layer of cells by the formation of a short connecting stalk that becomes the umbilical cord (Moore, 1974).

The umbilical cord is developed from the body stalk that connects the placenta to the embryo. Nourishment in the form of minerals, proteins, and oxygen from the mother is passed through the placenta to the embryo by way of the umbilical cord, and waste products from the embryo are filtered back. The cord contains two arteries and one vein but no nerves. It eventually becomes about 2 cm (3/4 in.) thick, about 55 cm (22 in.) in length, and looks like a whitish, rubbery tube. It is filled with a substance called Wharton's jelly. The jelly and the pressure of the blood rushing through the blood vessels keep the umbilical cord somewhat stiff, like a soft garden hose. The cord tends to straighten itself automatically when bent. Because of these factors the danger of the umbilical cord's choking a baby are slim, even though it is not uncommon for it to pass around the baby's neck. The baby is enclosed in the double-walled membrane of the chorion and the amniotic sac. The sac contains a fluid in which the baby floats and moves around, thus giving the umbilical cord a chance to straighten out.

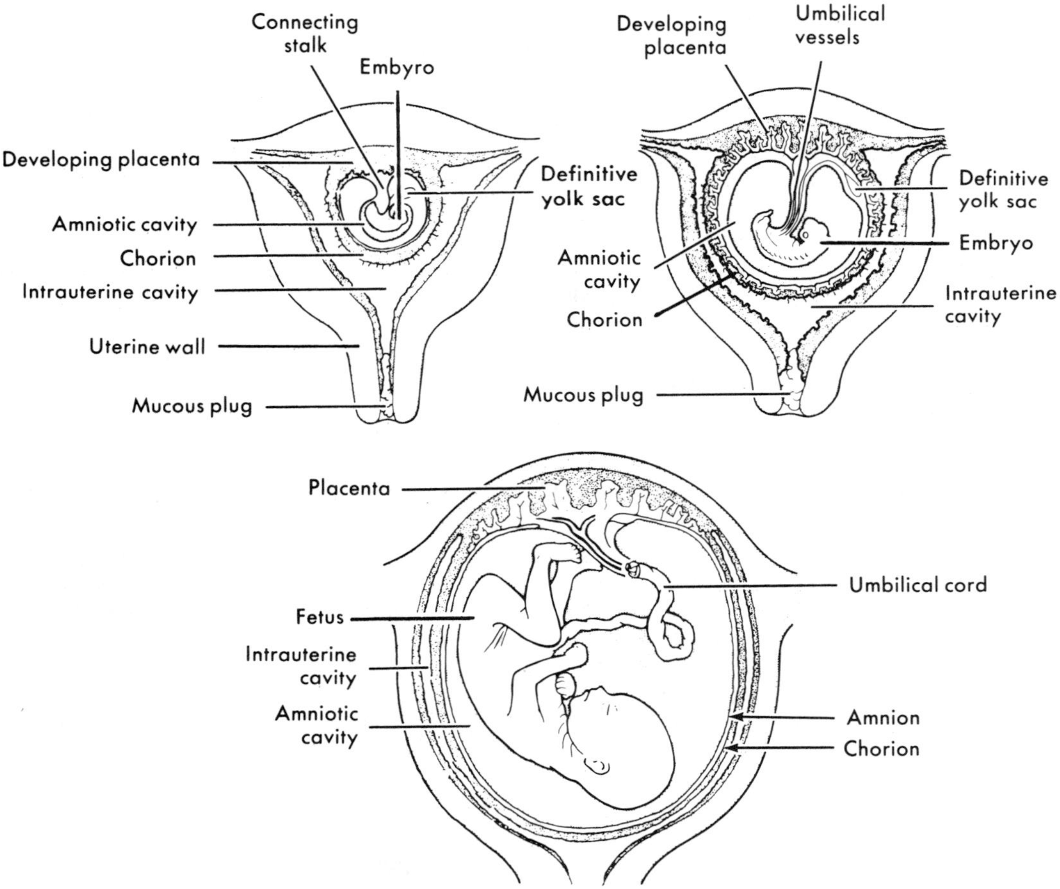

FIG. 3-7 ***Development of fetal membranes. Note thinning of uterine wall. Chorionic and amniotic membranes are adjacent to each other but may be peeled apart.***
Modified from Jensen, M.D., Benson, R.C., & Bobak, I.M. Maternity care: the nurse and family. *St. Louis: The C.V. Mosby Co., 1977.*

First month. By 2½ weeks the ***embryo*** has already begun to take shape. Its head-to-feet and top-to-bottom directions have been determined. The nervous system has begun to develop with the start of a longitudinal neural plate and a groove that will eventually form into a tube with two protrusions for the brain at the upper end.

embryo the form of prenatal life from the second to the eighth week. The period of the embryo follows the germinal period and is succeeded by that of the fetus.

In the beginning the brain and spinal cord grow more quickly than the other structures. Development starts with the brain and head area and then works down the body, the feet developing last. This progression is the cephalocaudal direction of growth.

The 28-day embryo still does not look like a baby, but it does have an oval body, a differentiated head region that takes up one third of its length, and at the lower end of the body, a short, slim, tail-like protrusion that will become the last bone in the spine. The heart is becoming developed, although it is still only a C-shaped bulge in the body wall. The heart, at first a single tube, may beat haltingly as early as the eighteenth day, even though there is no blood for it to circulate. The heart will pump more confidently by 3½ weeks, but it will not be regular for some weeks to come.

The embryo has developed simple kidneys, a primitive liver, and a simple digestive tract extending from the mouth area to the lower end. The first limb buds of the arms and legs appear about this time. Although all these body systems are being developed, the embryo is only about 0.5 cm (⅕ in.) long—about half the size of a pea. The mother is 2 weeks overdue for her menstrual cycle. She may not realize she is pregnant as yet because the embryo is so small and causes her no discomfort. (See Box for a summary of changes in the developing baby and the mother during the first 3 months.)

Second month. During the second month the main features of the human form rapidly appear. The nose, mouth, and tongue emerge more clearly. The developing eye appears as a dark circle. The limbs grow longer; webbed saddles and ridges appear on the end of them, later forming fingers and toes. The stomach, intestines, pharynx, lungs, and rudiments of the rectum, bladder, and external genital organs all grow from enlargements of the digestive tract. The endocrine system takes shape, the adrenal medulla secretes epinephrine, and the testes in the male begin to secrete androgens. Fig. 3-8 presents the critical periods of development of specific organs.

At the end of the second month the embryo will measure about 2.5 cm (1 in.) from the top of its head to

FIRST TRIMESTER DEVELOPMENT

FIRST 4 WEEKS

The baby: Spinal canal and brains forming.
Heart has first pulsations.
Digestive system begins to form.
Small buds form for arms and legs.
No eyes, nose, or ears visible.

The mother: May experience some morning nausea.
May have to urinate more frequently.
Breasts may swell and be tender.
First missed menstrual period.

END OF SECOND MONTH

The baby: About 2.5 cm (1 in.) long by eighth week.
Weighs about 18 g (⅔ oz.).
Brain, spinal cord, and nervous system are developed.
Heart pumps some blood, irregularly.
Limbs begin to show distinct arms and webbed hands; legs and webbed feet.
Face and features forming; eyelids fused.
Distinct umbilical cord formed.
Eighth week, has human likeness.

The mother: Breasts enlarge and are tender.
May notice changes in sense of taste and smell.
May crave certain kinds of food.

END OF THIRD MONTH

The baby: About 7.5 cm (3 in.) long.
Weighs about 28 g (1 oz.).
Arms, hands, legs, feet are formed.
Bone replacing cartilage.
External ears appear.
Tooth sockets and buds forming.

The mother: A yellowish fluid may ooze from nipples.
Blood supply increases to provide nutrients to fetus.
Center of gravity seems to shift.
Nausea usually subsides.

the buttocks. It will weigh approximately 18 g (⅔ oz.). The embryo now represents a miniature individual in its development. The two factors indicating the completion of the embryonic period are the formation of the first real bone cells that begin to replace the cartilage and the completion of features that resemble a human being. The embryo looks like a human being and not a monkey, a puppy, or a cat. Human likeness is clearly imprinted on it.

Survival hazards. The most crucial time, when the embryo's development can be most seriously affected, is the first 8 to 9 weeks of pregnancy, which is precisely the time when most women pay little attention to their new condition. There is a sequence of physical development taking place during the embryonic stage that is systematic and regular. There is a particular time for the emergence of each of the organs and their systems. Any disturbance or interruption with this sequence can be disastrous. If the delicate chemical balance of the mother is upset seriously, permanent damage can occur. Rubella (German measles) and certain drugs are especially serious during the first 3 months of pregnancy, since they can cause damage to whatever structures are being formed at the time. The brain too is susceptible to damage.

It has been estimated that 1 out of every 10 fertilized ova does not survive, the most critical time being the embryonic period (Willson and Carrington, 1979). Miscarriages are nature's way of getting rid of an abnormally developing embryo or fetus. It could mean that the uterine environment was not conducive to survival. About 75% of all miscarriages occur by the third or fourth month. Defective germ plasma, maternal disease, abnormalities of reproductive organs, blood group incompatibilities, malnutrition, and hormone imbalance are among the causes of spontaneous abortion. There are three boy miscarriages for every two girl miscarriages (160 to 100), indicating that in some respects the female has better survival capability than the male. This point will also be noted at other stages in the developmental process.

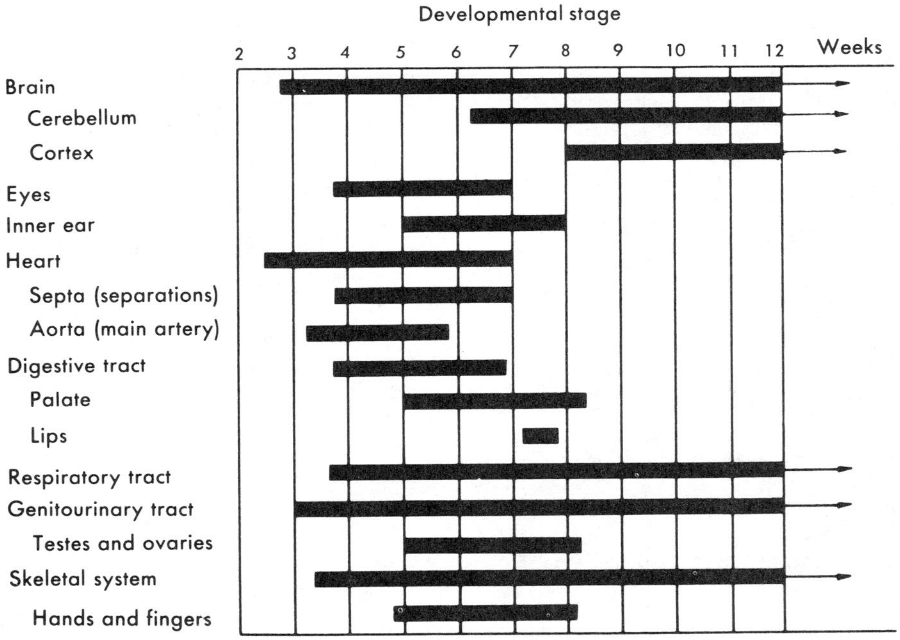

FIG. 3-8 ***Approximate periods of critical differentiation for some specific organs.***
From Whaley, L. Understanding inherited disorders. *St. Louis: The C.V. Mosby Co., 1974.*

Period of the fetus

fetal period the period of prenatal growth lasting from about the eighth week until birth.

fetus the prenatal human organism from approximately 8 weeks after conception to birth. See also **embryo.**

vernix caseosa a sebaceous deposit covering the fetus due to secretions of skin glands.

The ***fetal period*** of development is from about the eighth week, when the embryo becomes a recognizable human being, to the time of birth. Once the critical embryonic stage has passed, the chances of survival for the ***fetus*** are greatly increased. The organs, which have all been started by now, continue to develop and become functional. It is about this time that women usually make an appointment with their physician to find out if they are pregnant. Many expectant mothers would be surprised to learn that by the time they first see their physician their child has already been completely formed and is simply growing and preparing for his entrance into this world.

Third month. During the ninth week the eyelids grow rapidly, and their gluey edges soon fuse and seal the eyes shut. The eyes will now be protected during the final, more delicate stages of their formation and will stay shut until the sixth or seventh lunar month. The first muscle movements of the baby probably occur in the mouth and jaw muscles because they are the first ones to develop.

By the ninth week the muscles of the arms and legs are capable of responding to tactile (touch) stimulation. During the tenth week the genitals are clearly defined, and it is possible for the first time to determine the sex of the baby by external inspection. By the end of the third month, bones are beginning to replace the cartilage around the cheek, jaw, and nose, giving a more definite shape to the head.

Although the fetus gets its oxygen through the umbilical cord from the chorion, it will swallow, inhale, and exhale the fluid in the amniotic sac, as if it were practicing breathing. The fetus becomes more active and vigorous, with much smoother movements than before. It can turn its head, bend its elbows, make a fist, move its hips, and fan its toes. However, these movements are too minute and weak to be felt by the mother. It may even get the hiccups. If it does, the mother will feel every one. For most women the experience of feeling life for the first time is an unforgettable moment. The fetus is now 7.5 cm (3 in.) long and weighs about 28 g (1 oz.).

Fourth month. The fourth month is a growth month. The fetus will increase its length two or three times and its weight five or six times. By the end of the month it will be 15 cm (6 in.) long and will weigh about 112 g (4 oz.). As a result the fetus is more crowded than before, and the placenta becomes stretched tightly. The toes and fingers have separated, and fingerprint patterns emerge on the fingertips. Uniqueness and individuality are established at this early age. The baby gains in strength, and movements become stronger.

About the middle of the month the mother begins to feel the baby stirring. At first it is very soft, like the fluttering of butterfly wings. As the baby develops, the movements become more strenuous, and the mother begins to feel the sharp kicks and thrusts of the arms and legs. As the fourth month comes to a close, the mother's abdomen begins to protrude, and she begins to gain weight. Her pregnancy will be noticed by others at about 4½ months, the midpoint of pregnancy. Any morning sickness will probably be past, and she will be in the most comfortable period of pregnancy. (See Box for developmental characteristics of baby and mother during the second trimester.)

Fifth month. Movements of the fetus continue to get stronger during the fifth month. The baby can turn all the way around from side to side and even turn somersaults. He or she gives the impression of being an astronaut moving weightlessly in space. The fetus sleeps and wakes at regular times. When sleeping, the baby has a favorite resting position called a *lie.* He or she may put a thumb in the mouth as if to suck it. The sucking reflex is present. Fingernails reach the tips of the fingers. The heartbeat becomes regular between the fourteenth and sixteenth weeks. By the middle of the fifth month the heartbeat is strong enough for a physician to hear it through a stethoscope placed on the abdomen of the mother, maybe even hearing two beats if there are twins. By the end of the fifth calendar month the fetus weighs almost 450 g (1 lb.) and is about 20 to 30 cm (8 to 12 in.) long.

Sixth month. The sixth month of pregnancy is the time when the skin changes from a thin, transparent layer through which blood vessels can be seen to one that has a layer of fat and some accumulation of hair. In addition the skin becomes covered with a whitish, oily, fatty substance, ***vernix caseosa,*** that protects the skin

viability capability for maintaining life. A fetus is viable after 28 weeks, since it can then usually be kept alive if born prematurely.

from the long immersion in fluid. During the previous month a soft, fine hair called *lanugo* began to grow on the body. During the sixth month there is an accumulation of this hair above the eyes and on the upper lip. The vernix caseosa accumulates on the lanugo and gives the fetus an aged appearance. Hair on the scalp begins to grow heavier and longer than in other places. The eyes are developed, and the eyelids may separate so that the fetus can now open and close its eyes. If the baby should be born at the end of this month, he or she would probably breathe for a few minutes to a few hours but seldom would survive. The fetus is now 27.5 to 35 cm (11 to 14 in.) long and weighs about 900 g (2 lb.).

Seventh month. An interesting theory regarding when a fetus is considered to be viable (capable of living) is presented by Dr. Dominick Purpura, a neuroscientist at the Albert Einstein College of Medicine. He says that if "brain life" is used as a determinant, then life begins between the seventh and eighth months of gestation (Purpura, 1975). He defines brain life as the ability of the cerebral cortex, the thinking part of the brain, to develop consciousness, self-awareness, and other functions normally associated with the formation of nerve cell circuits (cognition). He says if "brain death" is the chief standard for deciding when a person is dead, then "brain life," when brain waves can be detected, should determine ***viability.*** The generally accepted 24-week standard at which the fetus is considered viable would then have to be lengthened to 28 weeks. Purpura studied the brain wave responses to light of 30 infants delivered prematurely between the twenty-fourth and thirty-second weeks of pregnancy.

The chance for survival of a baby born after 28 weeks of pregnancy is fairly good. It actually depends on the capability of the nervous system to effectively operate the organs and vital functions of the body. If born during the seventh month, the infant will need special care in terms of oxygen, prevention of blindness associated with retrolental fibroplasia (treatment nowadays is good), and protection against infections. Some time will have to be spent in an incubator. The fetus is about 40 cm (16 in.) long and weighs about 1125 g (2½ lb.). (See Box for characteristics of the third trimester.)

Eighth and ninth months. The eighth and ninth months are "fattening-up" months. The fetus gains about 225 g (½ lb.) a week for a total of 2250 g (5 lb.) on the average. The body is becoming more rounded, and fatty layers are developing that will help to nourish

SECOND TRIMESTER DEVELOPMENT

FOURTH MONTH

The baby: About 15 cm (6 in.) long.
Weighs about 112 g (4 oz.).
Toes and fingers separated; fingerprints emerge.
Movements become stronger.

The mother: Begins to gain weight and notices abdomen enlarging.
Feels first stirring of the baby.
Usually experiences a sense of physical well-being.
Darker skin pigmentation may occur on face, breasts, and abdomen.

FIFTH MONTH

The baby: About 20 to 30 cm (8 to 12 in.) long.
Weighs about 450 g (1 lb.).
Has fairly regular heart beat.
Sleeps and wakes at regular times.
May put thumb in mouth.

The mother: Can really feel life inside the body.
Abdominal skin stretches, increasing pressure on rectum.
May be some constipation, varicose veins, or hemorrhoids.

SIXTH MONTH

The baby: About 27.5 to 35 cm (11 to 14 in.) long.
Weighs about 900 g (2 lb.).
Skin layer no longer transparent.
Soft, fine hair begins to grow.
Outline of the fetus can be felt.
Eyes are developed, and eyelids may separate.

The mother: Month of greatest weight gain.
Feels vigorous movements of the body.
Linea nigra, dark line, may extend from pubic hair to navel.

the baby and keep him warm after he is born. The rapid growth of the baby may cause stretch marks on the mother's abdomen. The finer lanugo hair is being shed and has largely disappeared. The skin is less reddish looking than before, becoming lighter or pinkish in color, no matter what the racial heritage is.

Fingernails are firm and protrude beyond the end of the fingers. Sometimes nails are so long at birth that the nurse will need to trim them. The baby still moves, but the living quarters are getting more and more crowded. The mother's abdomen stops enlarging about the end of the eighth month, and there is a slowing down of fetal movements. About 2 weeks before birth the fetus will settle or "drop" into the pelvic cavity.

gestation period the amount of time the prenatal organism spends in the uterus; the total period of prenatal development calculated from the beginning of the mother's last menstruation (280 days, 40 weeks, or 9 calendar months).

teratogen any agent that causes birth defects.

THIRD TRIMESTER DEVELOPMENT

SEVENTH MONTH

The baby: About 37.5 cm (15 in.) long.
Weighs about 1100 to 1350 g (2½ to 3 lb.).
Body is filling out.
Internal organs formed and almost functional.

The mother: Weight of baby causes increased stress on body systems.
Backaches, muscle strains, stretch marks may occur.

EIGHTH MONTH

The baby: About 40 to 45 cm (16 to 18 in.) long.
Weighs about 1800 to 2250 g (4 to 5 lb.).
Settles into a favorite position.
Fat deposits increase.

The mother: Feels strong movements from baby.
Experiences mild to moderately strong contractions.
May have muscle cramps or spasms.
Heavy demand for calcium and iron.
Abdomen stops enlarging.

NINTH MONTH

The baby: About 45 cm (18 in.) long.
Weighs 3100 to 3600 g (7 to 8 lb.).
Gains 225 g (½ lb.) a week.
Bones of head are soft and flexible.
Skin becomes pinkish.

The mother: Feels less fetal movement.
Fetus settles into pelvic cavity—"lightening."
Contractions begin to signal the approach of labor and delivery.

When the fetus stops its frequent movements and lightening occurs, it will usually take up a more-or-less fixed position. Frequently this position is with the head down, as has been its most common position during much of the pregnancy. However, the lie assumed could be with feet or bottom downward, or it could be across the opening of the uterus in a transverse lie. A *transverse lie* is one in which the fetus lies across the birth canal horizontally, instead of with the head or one or more of the limbs in the birth canal. Birth through the vagina from a transverse lie is impossible unless there is a shoulder within the uterine cavity; the baby's position should be changed. The most advantageous presentation is head first.

The total ***gestation period*** is 266 days on the average. Since it is difficult, if not impossible, to date conception exactly, pregnancy is generally reckoned from the *beginning* of the last menstrual period. The normal term is then set at 280 days, or 10 lunar months. About 75% of all babies are born within 1 week, either way, of this date.

Up to this point babies the world over develop the same way. All human beings have this part of their growth processes in common. The stage has now been set. The drama of birth is ready to begin—that magic moment when life begets life.

INFLUENCES ON PRENATAL DEVELOPMENT

There are a variety of conditions that can affect the normal development of an unborn baby. An agent that can cause a birth defect or kill the fetus is called a ***teratogen.*** The field of study that focuses on birth defects is called *teratology.* Fortunately, 97% of all babies are born without any serious defect. Of the other 3%, there is a wide range in type and severity of defects; not all defects are serious ones.

optimal weight gain the most desirable or satisfactory weight gain in pregnancy.

Diet of the pregnant woman

Nutrition has long been considered in prenatal care. However, it is now becoming apparent to an ever-increasing number of health professionals and psychologists that diet is not only important but is crucial in determining the health of the childbearing woman and her offspring as well as in the development of the cognitive aspects of the brain. The brain develops in two major spurts, the first during the fifteenth and twentieth weeks of pregnancy, the second from late pregnancy to 1 year of life. Shortage of food during either period stunts growth and intelligence (Stein and Susser, 1976).

Mother's milk from birth is basic to normal brain development. Ironically, mothers in low-income groups, for whom breast-feeding recommends itself as economical, are less likely to nurse their babies than are economically secure, better educated mothers. Studies show that inadequate diet is probably the most frequently encountered hazard of intrauterine life. It is awesome to consider the effect of undernourishment on the development of the brain and intellect when one recognizes the worldwide incidence of malnutrition. The "junk food" diets of many Westerners and the inadequate diets of many adolescent mothers suggest that poor nutrition is not limited to the people of poor, developing countries. The incidence of stillbirth, prematurity, rickets, severe anemia, and tuberculosis is somewhat higher for babies whose mothers are malnourished.

It is what the mother eats, not how much, that is crucial to the baby's proper development. The most important foodstuff, so far as mental development is concerned, is protein (McKay et al., 1978). In a nationwide study of 50,000 expectant mothers, those who had protein-deficient diets during pregnancy produced children whose IQs at age 4 averaged 16 points below those of children of well-nourished mothers (Winick, 1976). The average pregnant woman should eat a 2,300-calorie diet every day of foods recommended by her physician.

The idea that a woman should not gain more than 4.5 or 7.5 kg (10 or 15 lb.) during pregnancy has been dispelled (Winick, 1981). The National Academy of Sciences and the National Research Council published a report stating that limiting weight gain may be contributing to the high infant mortality rate in the United States. United Nations figures show that many European countries, where women gain up to 10 to 13.5 kg (25 to 30 lb.), have lower infant death rates.

According to a study by Dr. R.L. Naeye of the Milton S. Hershey Medical Center (1981) the ***optimal weight gain*** should largely depend upon the mother's weight at the start of the pregnancy. Women who are overweight to begin with have the fewest fetal losses and losses at or soon after delivery when they gain only 7 kg (15 lb.) by delivery time. For women underweight to begin with, the optimal gain is 13.5 kg (30 lb.) or a little more. For women who start the pregnancy with normal weight a 9 to 11.5 kg (20 to 26 lb.) gain is best. Naeye indicates that child loss increases with weight gains of either less or more than the optimal values.

According to Naeye (Brody, 1982) the implications of inadequate weight gain or malnutrition are tied in with a reduced blood supply to the fetus from the mother. Mother's blood carries oxygen, water and electrolytes, nutrients, hormones, antibodies, drugs, and viruses, which are taken in by the baby through the placenta. Baby's blood carries carbon dioxide, water and urea, waste products, and hormones, which pass through the placenta and are diffused in the mother's bloodstream. Anything that interferes with the blood flow between mother and baby reduces the blood supply the fetus needs. A fetus that receives less blood would get fewer nutrients and less oxygen to grow on, resulting in a baby that is smaller and more at risk of survival than normal. Reduced blood flow could also lead to placental defects and intrauterine infections.

Weight gain programs produce a 5% to 7% increase in birth weight; raising the mother's blood pressure by hormone prescription produced an 18% increase (Naeye, 1981). In an analysis of 11,082 pregnancies, Naeye reported that inadequate maternal nutrition jeopardized fetal and neonatal survival by increasing the risk of a variety of disorders, such as infections. Naeye cautions especially against fasting or eating infrequently during pregnancy because pregnant women develop an acidic condition in their blood when deprived of food for as little as 24 hours. This condition contributes to a higher risk of fetal death.

Other factors that reduced the blood flow to the fetus as determined by Naeye were (1) stand-up work (on the job) after the thirty-second week of pregnancy and especially after the thirty-seventh week; (2) maternal exercise over a period of many hours (the effects of mild to moderate exercise were not determined); (3) mother being over the age of 39, resulting in the uterine blood vessels being stiffer and less flexible than at a younger age; and (4) cigarette smoking, because it increases the risk of placental lesions, the hardening of uterine blood vessels, and the premature separation of the placenta or an abnormal placement of the placenta.

Infections during pregnancy

One of the prime functions of the placenta is to safeguard the embryo by keeping out bacteria and bringing in antibodies that produce an immunity to a variety of diseases. The placenta, however, cannot screen out everything that might be injurious. Certain viruses, drugs, and chemical agents manage to slip through the barrier and cause defects (Heinonen et al., 1977).

German measles, or ***rubella,*** if contracted by the mother in the first 8 to 10 weeks of pregnancy will cause visual, auditory, mental, or heart abnormalities in one out of three babies (Behrman, 1977). From 1963 to 1965 an epidemic of rubella centered on the eastern seaboard of the United States approached the level of a national disaster. Fifty thousand women were infected during the first trimester of pregnancy. The total result was 30,000 miscarriages and stillbirths. Even more disturbing were the 20,000 rubella children who were born with defects ranging from mental retardation and heart disorders to blindness and deafness. The most common birth defect is a loss of hearing. Affected children may also develop cataracts. Many of these children will be small for their age.

Rubella is characterized by a rash the first few days but no pronounced cold symptoms. Within 24 hours, pink spots appear, which tend to fade and run together. The overall appearance is a flushed effect. Other noticeable symptoms of rubella are swollen lymph glands in the neck, a slight body temperature rise to 100° F., and a scratchy throat. The incubation period is 14 to 21 days, and the disease is contagious. The mother gets over the effects of rubella in 3 days. Her unborn child, however, may never get over them.

A vaccine has been developed for preventing rubella. Public health officials hope to stamp out rubella by giving the vaccine to the reservoir of susceptible subjects who can spread the infection. Mass inoculation programs have been conducted in many countries.

rubella German measles. Rubella in a pregnant woman can cause damage to the developing child if she contracts it during the first 3 months of pregnancy.

Immunization is usually started in the earliest grades of school, since this age group is the main source of virus dissemination in a community. The main purpose of vaccination, however, is to protect pregnant women for the sake of their unborn children. If a woman wants the vaccine, she should be tested first to be certain she is not pregnant, and then she should carefully avoid pregnancy for at least 2 months following vaccination.

Other viral infections are also suspect. Herpes 2, a cold-sore-like blister in the genital area, can severely damage the fetus, especially if the mother's genital organs are infected, which in turn can infect the child during the birth process (Babson et al., 1980). Viral diseases such as mumps, polio, smallpox, chicken pox, infectious hepatitis, and regular measles can cause some fetal damage when they occur during pregnancy. There is no evidence, as yet, that the common cold viruses cause any damage, but the influenza virus is suspected of increasing the possibility of some slight damage to the infant. In our study of inefficient learners (children with learning disabilities) we found a larger than usual number of mothers reporting having had the "flu" during early pregnancy (Kaluger and Kolson, 1978). The problems created were not irreversible nor severe, but they did cause some concern for the child during the first 3 years of schooling.

Undetected syphilis in the mother frequently attacks the nervous system of the fetus and may result in congenital weakness. Syphilis may cause stillbirth, miscarriage, deafness, blindness, or congenital mental deficiency. In some cases the child may not show any signs of syphilitic symptoms until several years later. One known case in which a child was born with syphilis resulted in senility at the age of 14 years because the syphilitic spirochetes had destroyed so many of the brain cells.

Mother and Rh blood factor

Human blood is not interchangeable. Blood from a donor must be matched with the blood of the recipient to ensure that they are compatible. Although the blood

Rh factor an agglutinizing factor present in the blood of most humans; when introduced into blood lacking the factor, antibodies form. Such a situation occurs when an organism with Rh-positive blood inherited from its father resides within a mother whose blood is Rh negative. A first-born child is rarely affected, but subsequent children may require transfusions.

of the mother does not mix profusely with that of the fetus, a problem of compatibility could arise if both the mother and the father have a blood type from the Rh blood group. If both parents are Rh negative or if both are Rh positive, there is no problem, because the fetus will inherit a blood type that will be compatible with that of the mother. If the parents differ in their ***Rh blood factor*** and the baby inherits an Rh-positive blood type from the father, there could be a problem if the mother is Rh negative.

In about 10% of the cases some blood from the fetus can be diffused through the placenta into the bloodstream of the mother. If the blood does pass through, it is likely to occur at the time of labor or delivery rather than earlier in the pregnancy (Gorbach and Feinbloom, 1979). Since the blood types are incompatible, the Rh-negative mother will produce antibodies to resist the "invasion of foreign bodies." If the antibodies are passed back to the fetus by diffusion, the antibodies will attack the fetal red cells, causing the fetus to become anemic. Usually the fetus can make red cells fast enough for its needs, but if it cannot, it will either die or be born with a severe anemic condition called *erythroblastosis fetalis*. If the child lives, it is highly susceptible to jaundice, which in severe cases can cause some brain damage. Successive pregnancies of the

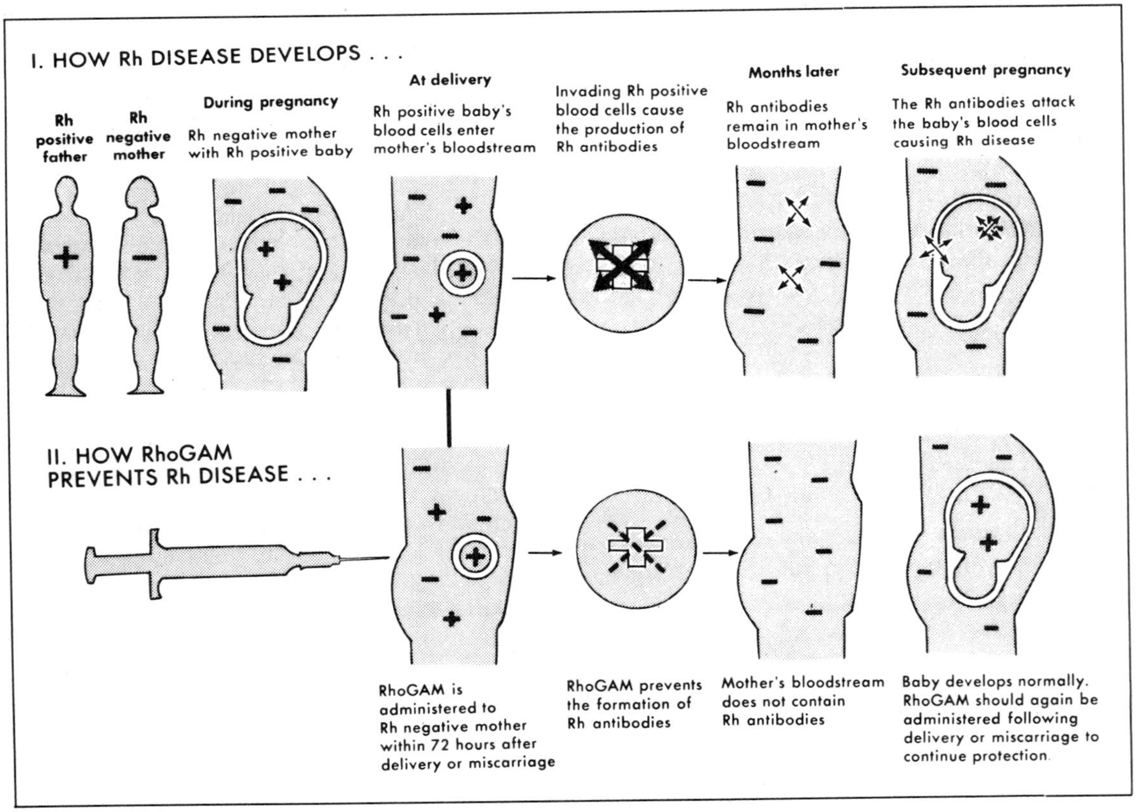

FIG. 3-9 ***How Rh disease develops and how it can be prevented.***
Reprinted by permission of Ortho Diagnostics, Inc., Raritan, N.J.

mother with fetuses having Rh-positive blood will raise the level of antibodies in the mother's blood to a critical level and will be more dangerous to these fetuses. Only Rh-negative mothers are affected. Review Fig. 3-9.

The following outline provides the reaction of Rh blood factors.

1. Rh compatibility (no problems)
   Father Rh+ and mother Rh+ = baby Rh+
   Father Rh− and mother Rh− = baby Rh−
   Father Rh+ and mother Rh− = baby Rh−
2. Rh incompatibility (possibility of problems)
   If father Rh+ and mother Rh− = baby Rh+, then Rh− mother and Rh+ baby are incompatible.
   a. Blood antigens from Rh+ baby enter mother's Rh− blood.
   b. Mother's Rh− blood produces antibodies to fight off foreign antigens.
   c. Some of mother's antibodies enter baby's blood by diffusion.
   d. Mother's antibodies in baby's blood attack red corpuscles, causing anemia, edema, or jaundice.
   e. With successive pregnancies mother's supply of antibodies can increase to a level dangerous for the fetus.

Seventeen percent of mothers in Western societies are Rh negative. Striking advances have taken place in the treatment of Rh incompatibility. A serum, RhoGAM, has been developed to prevent the production of antibodies in mothers who have not already formed antibodies. Fig. 3-9 shows how RhoGAM can be used to prevent Rh disease. If a child with Rh factors is born anemic, an exchange transfusion can be given to remove sensitized blood. In 1963 the first intrauterine transfusion was attempted with considerable success by a New Zealand physician. This treatment is used if the fetus is in danger of death and is too immature to risk premature delivery.

Drugs and medication

According to current medical opinion, pregnant women should not take drugs except when they have conditions that seriously threaten their health, and then *only* under the supervision of a physician. This statement is especially true during the first 3 months of pregnancy, the period when the embryo is most vulnerable. Some medical specialists even advise against taking extra vitamins unless they are prescribed by a physician.

The effect of drugs on the unborn baby can be most pronounced (Heinonen et al., 1977). The category "drugs" includes medicines that physicians prescribe such as antibiotics; over-the-counter remedies like

TABLE 3-1 Some substances that may harm the fetus*

Danger established (definite evidence of harm)	*Danger suspected (appear to increase the chances of death or disability)*	*Possible danger (animal data are suggestive, but human data are limited)*
Alcohol	Anesthetic gases	Caffeine
Antibiotics (some)	Narcotics	Carbon disulfide
Antitumor drugs	Appetite depressants that work on the nervous system	Chlordane
Cadmium	Anticonvulsive drugs (Dilantin)	Insulin
DES	Quinine	Lithium
Lead	Drugs for heart disease or high blood pressure (thiazides, reserpine)	Aspirin
Mercury		Tranquilizers (Valium, Librium, meprobamate, phenothiazines)
Oral contraceptives		
Cigarettes		
Thalidomide		

Modified from Babson, S.G., Pernoll, M.L., Benda, G.I., & Simpson, K. *Diagnosis and management of the fetus and neonate at risk: A guide for team care* (ed. 4). St. Louis: The C.V. Mosby Co., 1980, pp. 26-27.

*This sampling from the growing list of harmful substances reinforces the wisdom of the obstetrician's advice to take as little medication during pregnancy as possible.

toxemia blood poisoning; the presence of poisonous or infective matters in the bloodstream.

aspirin, cold tablets, vitamins, and nose drops; and abused or illegal drugs such as heroin, LSD, cocaine, amphetamines, and marijuana. The full meaning of the influence of medication and drugs on prenatal development is still being investigated. The evidence, however, appears to indicate that women of reproductive age should be cautious about taking medications that are not prescribed. Aspirin is included in this point. Table 3-1 presents a sample of substances that can be harmful to the fetus.

In the early 1960s a sedative drug named thalidomide appeared on the European market. Not realizing the consequences of its effects on pregnant women, physicians prescribed it for those who were tense because of their new condition. Many babies born to these women had flipperlike arms or no arms or legs at all. Deafness of some children can be traced to the mother's use of quinine.

Addictive narcotics are carried in the bloodstream of the mother and are transmitted to the fetus. Less than a day after birth the baby shows the classic signs of withdrawal, which may be so violent that the infant may die (Fricker and Segal, 1978). Premature births are higher among women addicted to narcotics than among the general population.

Although there is still much to be learned about the relationship of drugs and narcotics to birth defects, there is more known about the effects on newborn babies of sedative medication given to mothers during the birth process. These drugs do affect the baby, although only temporarily. The more anesthetic given to the mother, the longer the adjustment period of the newborn baby to postnatal life. Babies of mothers who were heavily medicated showed disorganized behavior for 3 to 4 days after birth as compared to 1 or 2 days for babies of nonmedicated mothers. What is significant in these cases is that at the time of birth, just when a baby's systems have to be at the peak level of performance to make a smooth transition to the outer world, they are in a state of sedation and may not have that extra push needed to overcome difficulties that may arise.

Toxemia of pregnancy

Toxemia refers to a large group of undesirable physical conditions that may occur in the mother after the twenty-fourth week of pregnancy or soon after giving birth. The signs or symptoms that these conditions have in common are (1) edema, a rapid or excessive weight gain during the third trimester owing to an accumulation of fluid in the body, (2) hypertension, a rise in blood pressure, and (3) the presence of albumin, a protein product, in the urine (Ferris, 1975). Acute toxemia is known as preeclampsia. Treatment of preeclampsia is usually effective. If the toxemia becomes severe (eclampsia), convulsions and finally coma will occur. It is estimated that 6% to 10% of all pregnancies are complicated by one of the many toxemias of pregnancy—mostly preeclampsia. With the inception of blood banks and antibiotics, toxemia of pregnancy has replaced hemorrhage and infection as the leading cause of maternal mortality. Infant mortality in all toxemias is about 10% to 25%.

The pill, hormones, and DES

Consumption of sex hormones, such as are found in oral contraceptives (the pill), has been linked to birth defects when taken within 1 month of or during the early period of pregnancy. Sex hormone usage during early pregnancy occurred in three forms: (1) continuing to take birth-control pills after fertilization has unknowingly occurred, (2) using estrogen or progesterone hormones for the treatment of reproductive system disorders, or (3) taking pregnancy tests that use hormones, such as are found in some home kits. The exact effect of hormones introduced into the body in the fetus is not completely known, but some effects have been noted.

Heinonen et al. (1977) examined data on 50,282 pregnancies within the United States and found a difference between users and nonusers of hormones in the percentage of babies born with congenital heart defects. Mothers who took hormones had a rate of 18.2 per 1,000 of their children born with serious heart abnormalities. Women who did not receive hormones had a rate of only 7.8 per 1,000 with congenital heart defects.

In comparing 1,370 infants born with various malformations with 2,968 healthy infants, Bracken et al. (1978) checked their mothers' use or nonuse of oral contraceptives. They found a slight risk factor in the babies for some specific diagnoses, such as certain cardiovascular defects, when the women had taken oral contraceptives after becoming pregnant. The risk was much greater for women who were heavy smokers and who also took the pill while pregnant. But, overall, they concluded that the mothers' use of the pill was generally unrelated to the development of malformations.

The findings appear to be unclear. The problem of the discrepancies may be one of research methods and procedures. A major limitation of both studies cited is that they only examined survivors and did not take into account the number of conceptions that were spontaneously aborted. It is clear, however, that more research is needed on the effects of sex hormones on the unborn child.

Between 1945 and 1970 the hormone DES *(diethylstilbestrol)* was prescribed during the first trimester of pregnancy with the hope that it would prevent miscarriage and other complications. The effect of the hormone on the fetus was not known. By the time DES was found to be ineffective in preventing spontaneous abortions, an untold number of individuals had been exposed to it in the wombs of their mothers.

In 1971, DES appeared to be responsible for the development of vaginal or cervical cancer in the daughters of mothers who had been prescribed DES (Herbst et al., 1971). Since then a number of studies have been conducted seeking to establish the effect of DES on the daughters. A study commissioned by the National Cancer Institute found no cancer among a group of 1,275 DES daughters, although 34% of the young women did show changes in vaginal tissue or in vaginal or cervical structure (O'Brien et al., 1979). However, a study by Herbst and co-workers (1978) of 292 cases of this rare cancer determined that 182 were exposed to DES prenatally, 27 to an unknown drug, 7 to another hormone, and 75 were not exposed to any hormone. Males exposed to DES prenatally also have abnormalities of the reproductive organs (Bibbo et al., 1977).

A 1980 report indicates that structural abnormalities in young women due to DES tended to decrease and even disappear over a 5-year period (Antonioli et al., 1980). The time of exposure and dosage were important. The likelihood of vaginal adenosis (disease) was highest when exposure to DES was at 21 days gestational age or less and when the dosage was large (Johnson et al., 1979). The risk of genital cancer does not seem to be as great as originally feared. However, the DES task force of the Department of Health and Human Services still recommends that the daughters of women who took DES during pregnancy be examined regularly. It seems that DES daughters may encounter an increased risk of miscarriage or premature delivery (Barnes et al., 1980).

A DAUGHTER OF DES

I suppose I shall remember that day in February forever. My mother felt it necessary to call me at work to tell me the results of her inquiries. The medical records showed that she had been given diethylstilbesterol (DES) during the first trimester of her pregnancy with me. I was extremely upset but not surprised. You see, my doctor had explained to me that I had many of the physical signs of DES exposure.

Since my mother had five miscarriages before I was conceived, her doctors began giving her DES toward the end of our second month and increased the dosage during the third and fourth months. At that time my mother was not given any information about DES. She only knew that her doctors were trying everything possible to help her have a much wanted child. My mother's activities were minimal; she spent 75% of her pregnancy in bed. But for her the rewards were worth it all. On a rainy March day her miracle baby was born—healthy and beautiful!

It is quite ironic how I learned about my exposure to DES. I had been married for almost a year; we had been trying to conceive for seven months. I knew that I would have problems because I had lost an ovary and fallopian tube several years earlier. We decided that I should begin the process of fertility testing, so I made an appointment at a very fine university hospital with some highly recommended gynecologists. I was excited about my first visit because I felt certain that I'd soon be getting pregnant. During my examination the doctor asked my permission to consult one of his colleagues. I agreed and soon found myself (specifically my cervix) being discussed by two total strangers. The doctors asked me if I had any idea whether my mother had been given a hormone called DES during her pregnancy. I immediately said no and that I doubted that she would have taken anything like that. As I look back, my initial response was more of a reaction to an article I had read just the day before in *Newsweek*. The article was about DES and its "victims." It described a young woman who had lost all her reproductive organs to cancer as a result of DES exposure and had her vagina reconstructed through plastic surgery. Needless to say, this was terrifying to a young newlywed! At the doctor's mere mention of DES I felt despair. As I told my husband about the examination, I began to sob uncontrollably. He was very understanding and optimistic, but I also sensed his fears.

The process of finding out for certain was very involved. We were living in a different state from my parents, and my mother's doctor had retired. It took about ten days for my mother to locate the records of her pregnancy. The confirmation call from my mother was a very emotional time for both of us. I tried not to show my despair, assuring my mother that everything would be fine. But as I hung up the receiver, I lost control completely. I left work in tears, and by the time I got home I had my grave dug and my eulogy practically read. I felt doom, gloom, and despair in the strongest sense. When I called my doctor to tell him, he suggested that I come in right away to discuss treatment. The next day I entered the office in much the same emotional state. Upon seeing my despair, my doctor very calmly explained to me the medical facts concerning DES. He informed me that only one in 10,000 "daughters of DES" suffers any real problems as a result of DES. He explained exactly what DES does and assured me that treatment would be successful in my case. He also suggested that, although DES exposure is serious and demands attention, many of the "lay " articles I had read were written for sensationalism. He made me feel hopeful, suggesting that treatment begin at once. Treatment consisted of vaginal cream inserted twice daily for six months, with extensive pap tests every month. At the end of six months the pap test indicated normal cells. IT HAD WORKED! Now on with living.

Well, all of that was seven years ago. I'm fine and healthy, but the DES exposure is still a part of my life. Every six months I must go in for an extensive pap smear to check for irregular cells. Last December I had to begin treatment again but only for a month. Another lasting effect is that when I take antibiotics I must also use the vaginal cream to prevent cell mutation and cervical infection. It's strange how something given to my mother all those years ago can so affect me now.

I feel extremely lucky to be here, to be living. I honestly think that with her track record my mother would have lost me, too, without the prescribed DES. I certainly do not blame my mother; all she wanted was a child to love. I suppose the lasting impact that DES has had on me is that I am very aware of anything unnatural that I put into my body.

Other factors influencing prenatal development

Age. The age of the mother when she gives birth to a child appears to have some bearing on the ease of the birth process, the mental ability level of the child, and the physical well-being of the child. Mothers under 18 and over 40 years of age tend to have a higher proportion of retarded children than do mothers who are between these ages. Women who have their first baby when they are 35 years old or over are more likely than younger women to experience illnesses during pregnancy and have a more difficult labor. The optimum age for childbearing appears to be between 20 and 28 years of age. However, advances in obstetrics have made pregnancy and birth at any age much less dangerous and complicated than previously.

Smoking. A relationship between the weight of a newborn baby and the amount of smoking done by the mother is suggested by several studies. The U.S. Department of Health, Education, and Welfare (1979b) states that the size of a newborn baby is affected by the mother's smoking somewhat in proportion to the number of cigarettes she smokes per day. Six or more cigarettes a day was considered very harmful. The heavy cigarette smoker will have smaller babies (on the average 225 g (8 oz.) lighter) than a nonsmoker. In addition, there will also be a significantly greater number of premature deliveries among heavy smokers (Butler and Goldstein, 1973; Babson et al., 1980). However, new evidence from the U.S. Department of Health and Human Services (1981) suggests that a woman who gives up smoking by her fourth month of pregnancy has no greater risk of delivering a low-birthweight infant than a nonsmoker has.

Alcohol. The National Institute of Alcohol and Alcoholism reports that at least 9 million Americans are alcoholics and that only about one tenth of these are receiving treatment. The rate of alcoholism in Europe equals or, in most cases, exceeds that of the United States. Alcohol usage among young people is said to have reached epidemic proportions. What effect does alcohol or alcoholism have on pregnancy? To begin with, alcohol can affect gamete development in an individual even before pregnancy takes place (Rosett and Sander, 1979). The use of alcohol can produce cadmium sulfide in increased amounts in the kidneys of hypertensive women. In men it produces busulfan, which acts directly on gamete-producing tissue.

Alcohol can have serious effects on the fetus or neonate (Streissguth et al., 1980). If the blood level of the fetus or neonate is equal to that of the alcoholic mother, convulsions, withdrawal symptoms, low birth weight, small size for age, poor sucking reflex, poor mental performance, and malformations of various types can occur. *Fetal alcohol syndrome* is a syndrome suffered by some infants ingesting alcohol during the prenatal period. The characteristics are often facial, limb, or organ defects; small physical size; and reduced intellectual ability. The risk rate is about 10 % if the mother drinks 30 to 60 ml (1 to 2 oz.) of alcohol a day. The rate approaches 74% for chronic drinkers (Hanson et al., 1978). Alcohol readily passes through the placenta to the developing child. A pregnant woman who drinks to excess increases the likelihood of not eating properly and of possibly injuring herself as well as the fetus. Women who were moderate drinkers, one to three drinks a day, have a higher risk of spontaneous abortions than nondrinkers (Harlap and Schiono, 1980; Kline et al., 1980).

Anxiety and stress. Some anxiety in a pregnant woman is inevitable and seldom harmful. However, excessive emotional stress is known to be transferred to the developing fetus by hormones and chemical factors in the bloodstream (Willensen, 1979). As a result the infant may be born with a physiological defect or weakness, a slight decrease in bodily weight, or undesirable behavior characteristics. The infant's behavior pattern after birth may take the form of excessive crying, irritability, difficulties in digestion, vomiting, and sometimes diarrhea. Before birth there is increased movement by the fetus whenever the mother is undergoing emotional stress. The longer the period of stress, the greater will be the increase of the baby's activity.

A case illustrating the efffect of great emotional stress on prenatal development is that of an 11-year-old girl who developed ulcerative colitis (ulcer of the colon), which is an uncommon condition in persons so young. The prenatal developmental history revealed that during the second month of pregnancy the girl's mother was subjected to intense emotional stress when both her parents were in a serious accident and were not expected to live. The medical report on the 11-year-old reasoned that this event occurred at the time when the digestive system, including the colon, was being formed. It was assumed that the stress of the moment produced a chemical change in the mother's blood and affected the development of the colon in the fetus, producing a weakness that made it more susceptible to colitis.

Diabetes. Diabetes is a medical condition characterized by a deficiency in the supply of insulin, which is secreted by the pancreas. Insulin controls the processing of sugar in the body. If the level of insulin is low, the condition leads to high levels of sugar in the blood and urine. Before the method of manufacturing insulin was discovered, it was rare for a woman with a moderate to severe case of diabetes to have a successful pregnancy. The complication of diabetic pregnancies is miscarriage. Now the majority of diabetics can have successful pregnancies if their condition is controlled.

A classification system of pregnant diabetic women takes into account when the diabetes began, how long the woman has had the condition, and what complications she may have (Silvian, 1977). Women who know they have diabetes should bring that condition under control before pregnancy starts. The methods of control are either diet or a combination of insulin and diet. Women who developed diabetes after the age of 19 and have had the condition less than 10 years have the same chance of miscarriage as nondiabetic women—about a 10% chance. They usually have a normal delivery.

Women who developed diabetes between the ages of 13 and 19 and have had the condition for 10 to 19 years have about a 24% chance of miscarriage, especially if they have hypertension (Silvian, 1977). The younger the age of onset, the greater the duration, and the more physical complications there are because of the diabetes, the greater the chance of a miscarriage. Women who are in the categories mentioned in this

genetic counseling analysis and communication of a couple's chances of producing a child with birth defects.

karyotype picture of the chromosomes, in a tiny photograph, created with a high-powered microscope and a stain.

paragraph usually have induced labor or a cesarean delivery. The survival rate of infants born to diabetic women who are in good health and who have received good prenatal care is close to 95%.

Father's role in transmitting defects

A number of studies have shown that genetic abnormalities or mutations occur more frequently as a man ages. Older fathers may be responsible for the occurrence of certain unborn disorders. Advanced age of the father is associated with several rare, dominantly inherited diseases. These include *achondroplasia,* a type of dwarfism; *Apert's syndrome,* related to facial and limb deformities; and *fibrodysplasia ossificans progressiva,* a deformity of bones. Advanced age of the father also seems to be a factor in one out of four cases of Down's syndrome (Abroms and Bennett, 1979).

Chemicals that may have no harmful effects on adults may cause birth defects and behavioral abnormalities in prenatally exposed organisms. The testes of the male appear to be sensitive to noxious chemicals. Exposure to lead, radiation, and certain pesticides may result in production of abnormal sperm. Hudec et al. (1981) found the flame retardant chemical Tris in the seminal fluid in 25% of the college men in their sample. Tris is capable of producing mutations in the genetic material of the sperm cells.

PRENATAL MEDICAL TECHNOLOGY

In recent years medical technology has made tremendous advances in terms of monitoring the fetus while it is still in the mother's womb. Most pregnancies do not require technological intervention because there is no risk involved. However, if the risk of a genetic disorder or an abnormality is involved, the use of technological medical intervention may be in order.

Genetic counseling

Genetic counseling is of special interest to prospective parents who have a family history of hereditary illnesses or genetic defects or who, because of age or other extenuating factors, suspect the possibility of a chromosomal aberration that may produce a defective fetus.

A genetic counselor usually begins by collecting information about the couple's families, going back as many generations as possible, tracing the marriages and the children produced. Questions will be raised about the family history of particular diseases, the occurrence of abortions, babies born with abnormalities, and so forth. A second step is to do a physical examination, including urine and blood samples, which can provide information about the presence of certain abnormalities. A sample of skin tissue is often taken, from which chromosome patterns of the man and the woman can be prepared and photographed. The chromosome patterns are arranged on a chart called a ***karyotype.*** See Fig. 3-10 for a sample karyotype.

The karyotype chart consists of the 22 pairs or sets of chromosomes plus the sex chromosome. The individual chromosome pairs are studied to determine if any abnormalities are present in the genetic makeup of the couple. More research needs to be done before all the signs can be read, but some things can already be determined. For example, if any set of a pair has only one or more than two chromosomes, an aberration exists because there should be only two chromosomes in each pair. *Down's syndrome,* a clinical type of mental retardation, is caused by an extra chromosome in the twenty-first pair of chromosomes. That is why Down's syndrome is called "trisomy 21." *Trisomy 21* means there is an additional chromosome in pair 21. *Klinefelter's syndrome,* which gives female breast characteristics to a male, is detected by an extra X chromosome in the sex cell, making an XXY sex chromosome. In *Turner's syndrome,* producing a short stature, a webbed neck, and the hindering of the development of secondary sexual characteristics, women have only one chromosome in the sex cell (XO). *Tay-Sachs disease* and *sickle cell anemia* carriers can also be determined.

We have been involved in working with two women for whom we suggested genetic counseling. The first was a young, married woman who was experiencing difficulty in sexual activities with her husband because

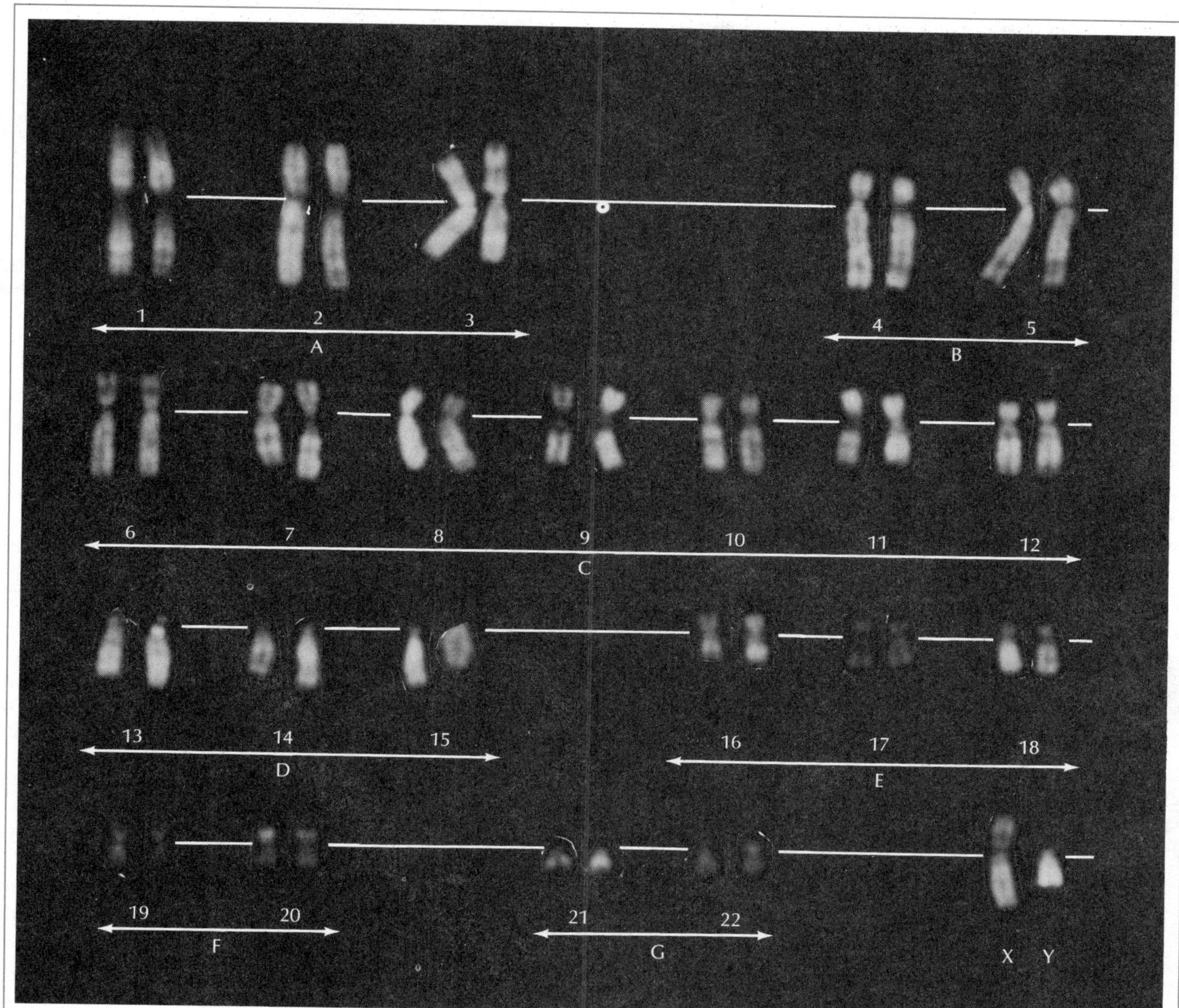

FIG. 3-10 ***Male chromosomes. The 46 chromosomes are arranged according to a standard pattern (karyotype).***

Courtesy L.R. Emmons, Washington and Lee University; from Hickman, C.P., Sr., Hickman, C.P., Jr., Hickman, F.M., & Roberts, L.S. Integrated principles of zoology *(ed. 6). St. Louis: The C.V. Mosby Co., 1979.*

amniocentesis a means of detecting fetal abnormality by the insertion of a hollow needle through the maternal abdomen and the drawing out of a sample of amniotic fluid on which chromosomal analyses can be performed.

she had a strong fear of becoming pregnant. Yet she indicated that she wanted children. It turned out that she had a sister who had Down's syndrome; the young woman was afraid that she would also bear a child with Down's syndrome. She was given the name of a medical center where she could receive genetic counseling. She had a karyotype done; it was discovered that she was a carrier of the abnormal chromosome, indicating that the chances were one in three in each pregnancy that the child would have Down's syndrome. She learned about the use of amniocentesis to determine if a fetus had received the defective sex cell. When the woman became pregnant, she had the amniocentesis done and learned that the fetus did indeed have Down's syndrome. There was an abortion. Later she conceived again. This time the karyotype of the fetus was normal. She gave birth to a beautiful girl.

The other case involved a pregnant woman who was 39 years old; she was concerned about having a child born with birth defects because of her age. She was advised about genetic counseling and amniocentesis. She followed through with the processes, having the amniocentesis done at the proper time. Everything was normal except for one pair of chromosomes. She and her husband were told that the deviation suggested a family trait of some type, but the genetic counselors could not determine what it was. Since no gross deviation was implied, the couple decided to complete the pregnancy. A delightful child was born. There is no evidence to indicate what the familial trait may be; the child is growing normally.

In both the cases described above the couples were aware that the sex of the child was also described on the karyotype. In the one case the couple wanted to know the sex of the unborn child. In the other case they wanted to be surprised. Everything worked out well for both couples. For information on places that offer genetic counseling contact The National Clearinghouse for Human Genetic Diseases, 805 15th St. NW, Washington, DC 20005, or any of the chapters of the March of Dimes Birth Defects Foundation.

Amniocentesis

Amniocentesis is a procedure by which some fetal abnormality and hereditary defects can be detected through an analysis of fetal cells obtained from fluid in the amniotic sac in which the fetus is being carried. Sometime during the second trimester a hollow, sterile needle is inserted through the mother's abdomen into the amniotic cavity. (Little or no pain is involved.) A small amount of fluid is withdrawn. The amniotic fluid contains cells discarded from the fetus. This sample is put into a centrifuge to separate the fetal cells from the fluid. The cells are grown in a laboratory culture and then analyzed for chromosomal and genetic abnormalities. A karyotype of the chromosomes can be photographed for further analysis.

These cells contain the chromosomes of the genetic code and can be analyzed for genetic abnormalities such as Down's syndrome and Tay-Sachs disease. About 70 inherited biochemical disorders can be detected. There are 20,000 children in the United States and 700,000 worldwide born with detectable abnormalities each year. Results from large surveys show that about 5% of the women tested have a fetus with abnormalities. The test is also useful for women over 45 years of age who have 1 chance in 50 that the fetus will have Down's syndrome. For the woman who is 40 to 44 years of age, the chances are 1 in 100.

Is it safe? Research was done at nine major medical centers by Dr. Aubrey Milunsky (1975). The study compared 1,040 amniocentesis cases to 992 match control cases that did not have it done. There were no significant differences in the rate of fetal deaths, prematurity, infant health, birth defects, or developmental status at 1 year of age. In the 1,040 cases, 34 fetuses had chromosomal metabolic disorders and 11 were in danger of sex-linked diseases. Of the 45 mothers, 35 had abortions. The diagnosis of the 1,040 was 99% accurate, with only six errors in the entire group. Sex determination of the fetus by examination of the sex chromosome was 100% accurate. A study by Golbus and colleagues (1979) terms amniocentesis safe, reliable, and extremely accurate, following their survey of 3,000 women.

Ultrasound

High-frequency sound waves, referred to as ***ultrasound,*** can be directed into the abdomen of a pregnant woman to produce an "echo-visual" picture of the inner structures of the uterus, the fetus, and the placenta. No surgical opening or invasion is made into the mother's body. Ultrasound can be used (1) to detect the presence of twins, (2) to measure the size of the baby's head and determine its gestation age, (3) to detect and evaluate uterine abnormality that might complicate the birth, and (4) to diagnose abnormalities of the fetal skeleton and other major organ systems (NIH Consensus Development Conference, 1979).

Birnholz (Biomedicine, 1982) makes use of ultrasound to visualize and document normal eye movements of the human fetus. He can also spot abnormal eye movements that may indicate developmental problems. Birnholz used ultrasound to visualize the eyes of 57 human fetuses at various stages of development. He found there was slow eye movement present at 16 weeks gestation, rapid eye movements between 23 and 35 weeks, but few eye movements after 36 weeks. Birnholz was successful in determining the eye movements in 93% of the cases. He theorizes that abnormal eye movements may be indications of brain malformations or at least a fetus at high risk during birth.

Fetoscopy

Fetoscopy is the use of a tiny telescope to view the inside of the uterus. Guided by ultrasound to determine the fetal outline, an endoscope tube with fiber optic bundles to transmit light is inserted directly into the uterus. The endoscope permits direct visual examination of the surface of the fetal anatomy. It is possible to detect such abnormal conditions as spina bifida, anencephaly (abnormal fetus due to absence of brain or spinal cord), or a placenta previa that blocks the passageway out of the womb. Fetoscopy also makes use of a small hypodermic needle to draw blood samples from the fetal vein in the placenta so that sickle cell anemia, hemophilia, muscular dystrophy, and possibly Tay-Sachs disease can be detected (Perry et al., 1979).

Fetoscopy findings have been 98% correct (NIH Consensus Development Conference, 1979). However, fetoscopy carries a greater risk to the fetus than does amniocentesis. Miscarriages occur in about 5% of pregnancies in which fetoscopy has been used.

fetoscopy method used with ultrasound to visually inspect part of the fetus while it is still in the uterus.

induced abortion the premature removal of the fetus by deliberate interference.

spontaneous abortion the expulsion from the uterus of a fetus older than 28 weeks.

ultrasound method of scanning the womb for detection of fetal outline to determine whether the pregnancy is progressing normally.

TERMINATION OF PREGNANCY

It is interesting to note that abortion is an ancient practice and that it has always provoked differences of opinion. Plato and Aristotle approved of it under certain conditions. Seneca and Cicero condemned abortions on ethical grounds, and the Justinian code prohibited it. Since 1973 when the U.S. Supreme Court ruled that a woman had the right to elect an abortion within 14 weeks after the last menstrual period, provided it was performed by a licensed physician, confirmed abortions have increased dramatically. Legal abortions are replacing self-induced abortion or termination of pregnancy by unskilled persons.

Definitional perspective

The term *abortion* is the termination of pregnancy before viability of the fetus. Viability is considered to be reached at about the twenty-fourth week of gestation when the fetus weighs 600 g (1 lb. 6 oz.) or more. A ***spontaneous abortion*** is one that results from natural causes and is usually called a miscarriage. An early spontaneous abortion is one that occurs prior to 16 weeks' gestation, and a late one occurs between 16 and 24 weeks' gestation. About three fourths of abortions occur before the sixteenth week of pregnancy, with the majority of these taking place prior to the eighth week (Gordon, 1975). If a woman has three or more spontaneous abortions, she is considered to be a habitual aborter. (Less than three are said to be incidental.) Habitual abortions are usually due to endocrine imbalance or an abnormality in the reproductive tract or are psychogenic. Spontaneous abortions may be due to abnormalities of the ovum or sperm or severe maternal disease, infection, or malnutrition (Danforth and Holly, 1977). Physical trauma usually does not produce an abortion.

Induced abortion is an intentionally produced loss of pregnancy by the mother or by others. It is considered to be a therapeutic or legal abortion if appropriate interference is used by a licensed practitioner because of a grave or hazardous condition of the mother or any other just cause, such as a known genetic defect. *A criminal abortion* is one that is performed without medical or legal consultation. Indications for induced abortion are chronic hypertension or chronic nephritis, cancer of female organs, advanced diabetes, rubella (German or 3-day measles), and psychiatric considerations.

The abortion has different clinical stages. It is classified as a *threatened abortion* if the eventual outcome is uncertain, as implied by slight bleeding or spotting and slight cramping pain. If the cramps become more severe and bleeding increases, the abortion is inevitable. A *complete abortion* is one in which the uterus empties itself completely of the embryo or fetus and its membranes. If some placental tissue remains within the uterus, the abortion is incomplete. A *missed abortion* is one where the products of conception are retained within the uterus for about 6 weeks after the embryo or fetus has died.

Methods of induced abortion

There are four common methods of induced abortion: vacuum aspiration, dilation and curettage (D & C), saline injection, and hysterotomy.

Vacuum aspiration is performed during the first 12 weeks of pregnancy on an outpatient basis. The cervix is dilated, and a small hollow tube attached to a suction is inserted into the uterus, resulting in the product of the conception being suctioned. The uterine lining is then curettaged to remove all fetal tissue. Suction abortion done beyond 12 weeks' gestation carries an increased rate of uterine perforation.

Dilation and curettage (D & C) are performed when the pregnancy is of 12 to 14 weeks' duration. A local or general anesthetic is used. The cervix is dilated, and a cigar-shaped metal dilator of increasing diameter is introduced into the uterus. The fetal substance is scraped loose with a curettage and removed with ovum forceps. It is safer for the patient to be admitted to the hospital for an overnight stay. Not all D & Cs are performed for the purpose of abortion. Most D & Cs are done because there is a problem in the uterus that must be medically corrected.

Saline injection (salting) is done when the pregnancy is from 14 to 24 weeks' duration. An amniocentesis is done after a local anesthetic is administered. Using a large needle, the physician withdraws about 180 ml (6 oz.) of amniotic fluid and replaces it with an equal amount of saline solution. A safer method is to instill the saline via drip infusion since there is better control and placement of the flow. Labor commences within 18 to 36 hours, and the patient expels the placenta and the fetus. A short hospital stay is in order.

Hysterotomy is a miniature cesarean section. A small longitudinal incision is made in the middle of the lower abdomen, the uterus is opened, and the fetus is removed. If sterilization is desired, the fallopian tubes are ligated at the same time. Hysterotomy is performed after 16 weeks' gestation. It requires a few days of hospitalization. It is the type of abortion procedure that is used least.

Personal reactions to abortions

A therapeutic abortion will leave women with different kinds of feelings. Most psychiatrists agree that it will not cause lasting psychological damage. In one study mentioned in *Medicine Today,* 22% had moderate guilt feelings and 13% had marked guilt feelings after their abortions. However, these feelings subsided with the passage of time. Most of the women experienced an immediate sense of relief, followed by a period of grief lasting up to 6 months, followed by adjustment in most cases.

Little is written about how fathers, including unwed fathers, feel about the abortion of their child. A general assumption is that they usually leave the matter up to the mother. Unwed fathers are supposed to "heave a sigh of relief" or indicate they couldn't care less. Not so, say some fathers. Not only do some claim that they care, but they also feel hurt if they are left out of the decision-making process. Of course, there will be all types of reactions. But no one will know for certain how the majority of the fathers feel about abortions until well-designed studies are conducted.

CHAPTER REVIEW

1. The sex cells are called *gametes*. The female sex cell is the *ovum* or egg. The male sex cell is the sperm. The ovum is much larger than the sperm. There are two types of sperm: one that carries the X chromosome, the female-producing sperm, and the other that carries the Y chromosome, the male-producing sperm.
2. Each developing ovum has 46 individual *chromosomes*, combined into 23 pairs. The sex cell has a pair of X chromosomes. As the ovum matures in the ovary, the 23 pairs are split in half so that the

mature ovum has only 23 chromosomes (not 46) as it migrates into the fallopian tube.

3. The female reproductive organs consist of the ovary, the fallopian tube, and the uterus, with an opening called the cervix. The cervix opens into the vagina. In the female of childbearing age the uterus is prepared each month for a pregnancy. One ovum is usually released from the ovary into the fallopian tube each 25 days. If the egg (ovum) is not fertilized, the prepared lining of the uterus and the unfertilized egg are discharged from the body of the woman by the normal menstrual cycle.
4. Sperm are produced in the testes. The 46 chromosomes are reduced to 23. The sex cells, which as a pair had one X and one Y chromosome, will contribute only one of these chromosomes to the sperm. The male reproductive organs consist of the testes, which produce the sperm; the vas deferens, a tube through which the sperm travel to the storage area in the seminal vesicles; the prostate gland, which provides semen for the sperm; and the penis, through which the sperm and semen are ejaculated.
5. *Fertilization* occurs when a sperm penetrates the nucleus of the ovum. The 23 chromosomes from the female and the 23 from the male combine into 23 pairs. The sex cell chromosomes will form either an X-X pair (female) or an X-Y pair (male).
6. Infertility occurs in about 15% of all married couples. Another 10% have fewer children than they want to have because of subfertility conditions. About 40% of the time the male is the primary source of infertility. Major factors relating to infertility have been located in both partners in about 40% of the cases. Modified modes of reproduction are (a) artificial insemination or artificial placement of the ovum or both, (b) in vitro fertilization, and (c) asexual reproduction or cloning.
7. The laboratory diagnosis of pregnancy is made by injecting rabbits, mice, or frogs with the urine of the woman. The hormone in the urine would produce changes in the ovaries of the animals. Newer tests, which can be done in the doctor's office or at home, seek to detect the *human chorionic gonadotropin* (HCG) in the urine by chemical analysis.
8. Twins may be identical, *dizygotic* (DZ), or fraternal, *monozygotic* (MZ). Identical twins come from the same fertilized egg with the same chromosomal structure. Fraternal twins come from separate fertilized eggs with different chromosomal structures.
9. Prenatal development has three stages: the *period of the zygote* (ovum or germinal), which is from conception to implantation, about 6 to 10 days; the *period of the embryo*, from implantation to the development of a recognizable human being (eighth week); and the *period of the fetus*, from the eighth week to the moment of birth.
10. The period of the zygote is characterized by a free moving fertilized egg within which cell division takes place. The cells are forming the layers of cells, which will eventually become the chorion, the amniotic sac, the fetus, and the umbilical cord.
11. The period of the embryo is a time of rapid growth, with all the structures, the organs, and the shape of the human individual being formed. Most of the organic systems become at least partially functional. The nervous system develops the fastest during this period.
12. The period of the fetus is a time of growth and refinement of the organs, structures, and functional systems. As the fetus approaches the moment of birth, it develops fatty tissue and becomes more viable. At least 7 months of prenatal development are needed. The closer the fetus approaches the ninth month of development, the better are its chances of survival.
13. Prenatal development can be influenced by chemical changes made in the blood of the uterine environment. Inadequate nutrition of the mother can affect the growth of brain cells and the cardiac system and make the fetus at greater risk at birth. Maternal infections of many types can affect the growth of physical structures and produce mental retardation. Incompatible Rh blood factors between the mother and the fetus place the child at great risk. Drugs of all types, as well as infections, can change the chemical composition of the blood and in turn create all kinds of problems for the fetus. Toxemia indicates that things are not right in the mother's blood; it can place the unborn child, and especially the mother, in grave danger. The chemical ingestion of tobacco and alcohol places the fetus at risk in development by causing a low birth weight.
14. Weight gain programs for pregnant women improve the survival chances of unborn babies. Optimal weight gain for overweight women is 7 kg (16 lb.); underweight women should gain at least 13.5 kg (30 lb.); women with normal weight should gain 9 to 11.5 kg (20 to 26 lb.). The increase in weight gain improves the blood flow from the mother to the fetus, providing more nutrients, oxygen, hormones, electrolytes, and antibodies.
15. *Genetic counseling* is recommended for couples with family histories of hereditary illnesses and genetic defects. Genetic counseling studies the chromosomal makeup of each individual to determine if any distortion, defects, or damaging indicators are present. The chromosome pattern is pictured on a karyotype picture.
16. *Amniocentesis* is a procedure whereby a hollow needle is inserted through the abdomen into the uterus

and the amniotic sac. Fluid containing fetal cells is withdrawn. The cells are studied for abnormalities.

17. *Ultrasound* medical technology makes use of high-frequency sound waves to produce an "echo-visual" picture of the fetus and internal organs. It has been used successfully to guide surgeons in performing surgery on the fetus in the womb. In one instance a catheter was placed in the defective bladder of a twin fetus so urine could be drained into the amniotic sac. (This was not mentioned in the text.)
18. *Fetoscopy* is a technique using a tiny telescope and light to examine the fetus while it is still in the amniotic sac. Body structure can be examined, and blood samples can be drawn from the fetal body.
19. The text does not mention this point, but ethical questions are being raised about medical invasion of the body of a pregnant mother and the fetus. Should surgery be done in the womb? Should defective genes and structures be removed or replaced? Should genetic engineering be done to obtain the physical results someone desires for the fetus? Suppose the fetus was found to be seriously defective; should an abortion be performed? Metaphysical considerations do enter the picture of developmental psychology as research findings and technological advances provide more options for the direction of development.
20. A *spontaneous abortion* is one that happens without any intent or interference on the part of the mother. This type of abortion is called a miscarriage. An *induced abortion* is intentionally produced. A *therapeutic abortion* is done to protect the life of the mother or for some other just cause, such as rape or a known fetal abnormality. A *criminal abortion* is one done illegally. Not all abortions performed are complete; sometimes parts of the fetal membrane remain, only to be expelled later. The four most common methods of induced abortions are (a) vacuum aspiration, (b) dilation and curettage (D & C), (c) saline injection, and (d) hysterotomy.

REVIEW QUESTIONS

1. What are the names of the female and male sex cells? Describe each one.
2. Explain the reason why the ovum and the sperm as germ cells carry only 23 chromosomes into reproduction rather than all 46 chromosomes, which the cells normally have.
3. What are the uses of the uterus, the cervix, and the vagina?
4. Describe the menstrual cycle from beginning to end (28 days). What happens at the beginning, in the middle, and at the end?
5. At what phase of the menstrual cycle is pregnancy most likely to take place?
6. Discuss the ovulation process from the development of the ovum until it disintegrates or is fertilized.
7. How are sperm formed, stored, and released? Why are there two types of sperm but only one type of ovum?
8. What is meant by a fertilized egg? How does it become fertilized?
9. List some causes of infertility in males and in females.
10. Describe each of the following modified modes of reproduction: (a) artificial insemination, (b) artificial inovulation, (c) in vitro fertilization, and (d) cloning.
11. What is the chemical hormone that appears after pregnancy has taken place? It is used in the diagnosis of pregnancy.
12. Describe the hemagglutination-inhibition test for pregnancy. Describe the E.P.T. in-home test for pregnancy. Which one is more accurate?
13. Study Fig. 3-4 on sex determination. What decides if the conceived child is a boy or a girl?
14. What are monozygotic (MZ) twins? How would they appear in the amniotic sac? (See Fig. 3-5.)
15. What are dizygotic (DZ) twins? How would they appear in the amniotic sac?
16. Describe what happens during the period of the zygote. What hazards are there?
17. The period of the embryo ends about the eighth week after conception. When does it begin? Why is it so important to the health and well-being of the unborn child? Look at Fig. 3-8 on the periods of critical development.
18. What is the purpose or function of the period of the fetus? How long does it last?
19. Review the boxed information on developmental features of the three trimesters.
20. Discuss the specific importance of the nutrition of the pregnant woman and the significance of weight gain.
21. How do infections, especially rubella and venereal disease, affect the unborn child? Be specific.
22. Look at Fig. 3-9 on the Rh blood factor and disease. Also look at the outline on the Rh factor. Follow both of them through to see how incompatible Rh factors can affect a fetus. Remember, in Fig. 3-9, RhoGAM is a means by which Rh incompatibility can be eliminated.
23. How do prescription drugs, nonprescription drugs, and illegal drugs affect a fetus?
24. What is toxemia? What is preeclampsia? Why are they dangerous?
25. How do age, smoking, drinking, and worrying affect a fetus?
26. Discuss the meaning of genetic counseling. What is a karyotype?
27. How is amniocentesis done? What use does it have?
28. How is ultrasound used? What does it tell?
29. What is fetoscopy? What can it do?
30. Look in the Chapter Review at number 19. Do you agree or disagree that there are ethical questions involved in

the medical technological invasion of the amniotic sac and the fetus? Discuss your reasons. Is there an ethical difference between surgery to remove cancerous growth and surgery to ensure the life of a fetus? What about surgery to implant an artificial heart? Where do you draw the line—or do you draw a line?

31. What is the difference between a spontaneous and an induced abortion? Are all abortions complete?
32. Define the following methods of abortion: (a) vacuum aspiration, (b) dilation and curettage (D & C), (c) saline injection, (d) hysterotomy. At what point in time in a pregnancy may they be used?

THOUGHT QUESTIONS AND ACTIVITIES

1. The mention of the use of modified modes of reproduction, such as artificial insemination, artificial placement of the ovum, and in vitro fertilization, appears frequently in newspapers and magazines. What do you and your classmates think of these alternative approaches to creating a new life? What do you think of surrogate mothering as an alternative to traditional adoption by a barren couple? The circumstances are such that the wife cannot conceive but she wants to rear a child. Another woman, the surrogate mother, is artificially inseminated with the husband's semen. The surrogate mother bears the child and gives birth to it. At that time the child is turned over to the barren couple. The surrogate mother is paid well for her services.
2. Consider prenatal development. Why are the first 8 weeks after conception so special and so important? What is happening and what could happen?
3. Research on smoking, drinking, and drug use during pregnancy is taking place at a rapid pace. Consult the library, especially the *Psychological Abstracts* and *Index Medicus,* for the latest findings on the ways in which chemical substances can affect the unborn child. From a research point of view, how do you account for discrepancies in the findings?
4. Maternal influences on prenatal development are always being mentioned. But, what about the father? In what ways can he contribute to fetal abnormalities? See what you can find in the literature.
5. Medical science and medical technology are moving at a rapid pace in dealing with the unborn. Consider amniocentesis, ultrasound, fetoscopy, surgery in utero, and other medical invasions that have not been mentioned. What considerations must be given to these actions? What are the hard ethical questions?
6. We would suggest a debate on the pros and cons of abortion, but this issue is too emotionally loaded to permit free interchange of ideas. Read what you can about the topic if you are interested. Should a person's point of view on abortion be respected even if it is an obviously biased opinion? If you say "no," why shouldn't it be respected?
7. If possible, arrange a visit and interview with any of the following: a pregnant mother, a genetic counselor, or an instructor for a course on prepared birth.

FURTHER READINGS

Brody, J.E. Fetal health: A new view emerges. *New York Times,* Science Times, May 16, 1982, C1-2. Brody discusses the new medical technology and use of microsurgery on the fetus while still in the uterus. See also "Biomedicine, Eyeball to eyeball with the human fetus," in *Science News,* 1982, *120,* p. 142.

Falkner, F., & Macy, C. Pregnancy and birth. New York: Harper & Row, Publishers, 1980. An easy-to-read description of the experiences that mothers have during pregnancy and childbearing is presented in this book.

McAuliffe, K., & McAuliffe, S. The gene trust. *Omni,* March 1980, 62-66 and 120-122. This article examines genetic engineering and the feats it can perform. Genetic engineering appears to hold considerable significance for life in the years ahead.

Naeye, R.L. Pregnancy weight gain. *American Journal of Obstetrics and Gynecology,* 1981, *135,* 3. Naeye reviews the latest research on how much weight women should gain during pregnancy.

Nilsson, L., Furuhjelm, M., Ingelman-Sundberg, A., & Wirsen, C. A child is born (ed. 2). New York: Delacorte Press, 1977. This is a beautiful photographic record of prenatal development from conception to birth. The text is straightforward.

prepared childbirth method of childbirth in which the woman is prepared for delivery by knowledge about the physiological processes involved and by learning a series of exercises that make the delivery easier.

No woman should have to go through the experience of pregnancy alone. It is such a special time for an individual that this personal life event should include a social network of family, friends, and well-wishers for the purpose of caring, sharing, and loving—as well as preparation for birth. The first trimester will be one of getting used to pregnancy and to the thought that things are really going to change. Identification with the idea of becoming a parent begins. The second trimester is a rather happy, placid, comfortable time, with excitement building as the first movements of the baby are felt. The third trimester usually brings on some apprehension as the moment "we've all been waiting for" approaches. Uncertainties arise, parental concerns emerge, and the wondering and waiting begin. How wonderful it can be! No pregnancy or childbirth is completely free from some anxiety or pain. But the process can be made more pleasant, and even relaxing, with professional preparation and psychological support.

PREPARING FOR BIRTH

The first preparation for birth occurs soon after conception. It is the visit to the doctor's office to determine if pregnancy has occurred. Once the answer is "yes," a physical examination is in order.

Medical examination

A family history is taken because it is essential in assessing a pregnant woman's needs. Such a history includes medical, surgical, gynecological, and obstetrical data. The physician will perform a complete physical examination, including palpation (exploring by touching) of the thyroid; an examination of the mouth, teeth, eyes, ears, and nose; listening to the lungs to ensure that there is sufficient oxygen intake; taking a blood pressure reading and listening to heart functions; palpation of the abdomen (which will then be measured regularly); and an internal examination of the pelvic area, including the vagina, the cervix, and the uterus. The mother is weighed, a urinalysis is done, and a blood sample is drawn. Regular office visits will then be scheduled.

An *estimated date of delivery* (EDD) is determined, usually by counting back 3 months from the first day of the last menstrual period and adding 7 days plus 1 year. Duration of a pregnancy is approximately 280 days, counting 10 lunar months of 28 days each, or 276 days, based on 9 calendar months of 30 days. It is normal for a baby to arrive 2 or 3 weeks before the estimated due date, but it is rare for the pregnancy to go more than 3 weeks past term. About 10% of all pregnancies continue for at least 2 weeks beyond the EDD. If the last menstrual date is not known, other physical conditions can be used to determine the EDD. These conditions are the date of quickening, the height of the fundus (enlarged abdomen), or changes in the size of the opening of the cervix. Ultrasonography and amniocentesis can also be used to determine gestation age.

In addition to making plans for the new baby's living arrangements and clothing needs, many women are aware of the importance of education in preparation for childbearing. They take advantage of programs offered by the American Red Cross, hospitals, adult education departments, family life agencies, and other agencies in the community that provide instruction and information on childbearing and birth.

These programs usually teach the expectant parents simple anatomy, the psychology of pregnancy, labor, and delivery, a program of exercises and breathing, and ways by which the father and mother can help each other during pregnancy and birth. Programs for prepared birth usually center around modified versions of natural childbirth. The site for delivery may be a hospital delivery room, a special birthing room, which many hospitals now have, or at home with a midwife doing the delivering.

Natural childbirth

Natural childbirth is considered to be *prepared childbirth*. ***Prepared childbirth*** refers to the preparation of the mother and father for the labor and delivery and includes their active involvement in the childbirth process. It implies that the use of drugs or anesthetics is to be avoided or minimized. Exercises to strengthen the appropriate muscles, breathing techniques to aid during labor and delivery, and psychological mind-set, imagery, or relaxation procedures are taught to lessen birth pains and to permit a spontaneous birth to occur.

The use of anesthesia in childbirth is widely practiced in Western societies (Brackbill and Broman, 1979). The intent of its use is to eliminate or lessen pain and fear. General anesthesia puts the mother to sleep; many times, under this condition, the baby is also anesthetized through the blood of the mother. The mother misses the joys of childbirth. The father also misses the joy of seeing his child born because he is seldom permitted in the delivery room if the mother is completely sedated. The partially anesthetized baby is also deprived, but in a different sense. Under these conditions the baby is not at peak capability of responding to the demands of a new environment. The anesthetized fetus becomes a survival risk (Brazelton, 1970).

Grantly Dick-Read (1972) of England believes the anesthetic or medical birth approach is wrong. Mother should be awake, aware, and undrugged. Father should be present to share the experience and provide support to his wife. Baby should be given every opportunity to survive and to make contact with mother and father at the time of birth. During the 1930s and 1940s Dick-Read began to expound the view that pain and fear in childbirth could be greatly reduced if the mothers understood the birth process and learned to relax properly. He developed a natural childbirth training program that included (1) prenatal health care, (2) a childbearing and birth education program, and (3) a series of techniques for proper breathing, physical fitness, and relaxation. He wanted to prepare the mother for the delivery of her child. Much emphasis is placed on positive thinking, passive relaxation, and the performance of the woman. Dick-Read made natural childbirth a team effort that includes the mother, father, and a family-centered maternity hospital health care unit. A variety of other programs and methods have been developed on these basic premises.

The Lamaze method

One of the more widely known programs of "prepared childbirth" is that of the French physician, Fernand Lamaze (Lamaze, 1972; Parfitt, 1977). Lamaze classes and courses are quite standard. Parents begin the course about 2 months before the expected birth. The first session acquaints the couple with the Lamaze philosophy and goals. The next lesson provides a thorough insight into the woman's physiological and mental processes. Wide use is made of films, diagrams, and anatomical models to teach how the baby develops from conception to birth and how the baby can cope with growth and the actual birth. The parents are shown how tensed muscles can cause discomfort and how, by relaxing these muscles, a woman can alleviate pain.

Other classes teach the mechanics of birth: how labor begins, the role and nature of contractions, the different phases of labor, and the birth itself. The mother and father are taught how to respond with an effective type of breathing during each phase of labor. Relaxation and breathing exercises are taught and practiced during class time. Finally the parents are taught how, as a team, they can aid in the expulsion of the baby (Ewy and Ewy, 1982).

Much of the fear felt by mothers-to-be is caused by a lack of knowledge of what is really happening; as a result, a feeling of helplessness sets in. Fear builds tension and tension eventually produces pain. The Lamaze program seeks to use relaxation techniques to control pain. The relaxation technique is based on the principle that the brain can efficiently process only one stimulus at a time. By concentrating on a new focal point, such as an object that is interesting and colorful, a person can increase tolerance to pain and thereby decrease the perception of the intensity of a contraction.

Breathing techniques and relaxation concentration are used together at the time of *contraction*. A contraction is the shortening and thickening of a muscle, producing a pain. The breathing technique used differs with the degree or intensity of the pain. A contraction generally lasts 40 to 60 seconds. The mother is taught how to identify (1) the beginning of the contraction, (2) the point at which it reaches its apex of intensity, and (3) the end of the contraction. In the first stage of labor when mild contractions occur, the woman is to do slow, regular, and deep chest breathing. As the contractions do their work of dilating the cervix, they become stronger, longer, and harder to manage, lasting 1 to 3 minutes over a period of several hours. Breathing is kept regular as long as possible. At the apex of intensity, breathing becomes shallow and accelerated, then slows down as the contraction passes.

At the time of delivery, contractions are extremely strong, 60 to 90 seconds in duration, and occur at shorter intervals. At this time, shallow, light breathing or sustained bursts of shallow panting are used during the contraction, with strong, forced blowing out (like blowing out a candle) in the intervals between contractions. Since the mother-to-be often tries to breathe too fast, too hard, and too loud, her husband (or coach) should be prepared to help her slow down, calm down, and be more quiet. Some methods, such as the Bradley method (1981), do not use the panting and strong, forced blowing because of the danger of hyperventilation.

The Lamaze method (or other methods) does not guarantee a painless labor. If a small dose of analgesic or anesthetic is needed, it can be given without denying the experiences of an educated birth. All of the modern obstetrical techniques are available in a delivery room, should there be complications. The primary concern is to deliver a healthy baby, regardless of what it takes to do so.

The role of the husband in the Lamaze method is of great importance. A husband and wife team is the best combination at the time of pregnancy. It starts the parents off with a sense of partnership that has long-lasting benefits. By both attending Lamaze classes they develop a common approach in attitudes and expectations. They provide psychological support to each other. The husband can be of help during the daily practice sessions and in the hospital during the actual labor and delivery. He learns how and when to apply light massage and stroking to reduce discomfort. He learns how to be a "coach." Talking together and experiencing together make a relationship that strengthens the husband-wife bond. They are better prepared to handle changes from the delivery and birth pattern that they have been taught to expect. They learn that if things do not happen the way they were told, they should react to their own sensations because every labor is different. If some anesthetic is necessary, such as meperidine (Demerol) to help the mother relax or a paracervical block to relax the cervical area in order to reduce the pain and speed up the dilation, that is acceptable.

The father can be with the expectant mother in the delivery room. He times the interval between the contractions and gives comfort to the mother. He puts on a gown and special sandals and goes into the delivery room with his wife. There, he is by her side as she lies on the delivery table with her legs lifted and usually spread apart by metal braces. A sterile sheet covers the mother's abdomen. He holds her hand; she grips it hard. The doctor takes over and directs the event to take place. When a contraction starts, she is to bear down with effort and concentration. The doctor gives reassurances and directions, explaining what is happening. "There's the head." "Give me one more good push, one for the shoulders." "It's a girl!"

The baby, still wet from the womb, is held up for the mother and father to see. Mother and father look at each other, their eyes usually brimming with tears. They kiss. "I love you." "I love *you*." Both of them have a sense of pride in the bringing forth of *their* child into the world.*

*More information regarding facts about childbirth may be obtained from the American Society for Psychoprophylaxis in Obstetrics, Inc., 36 W. 96th St., New York, NY 10025, or the International Childbirth Education Association, ICEA Secretary, P. O. Box 5852, Milwaukee, WI 53220.

JOYS OF NATURAL CHILDBIRTH

When my wife, Meg, became pregnant, we decided to look into the method of natural childbirth. We read as much information as we could find and took advantage of special films and lectures given in our city. We became very well acquainted with Dr. Lamaze's method, especially as explained by Margery Karmel in her book, *Painless Childbirth*.

Without too much trouble we found an obstetrician who had been using this method for some time. In her seventh month, Meg and I began private instructions on the Lamaze method from a registered nurse who was well trained in the use of this technique.

The first thing presented was a detailed description of the bodily functions during labor and delivery. We learned how and why the uterus contracted and the different positions of the baby during delivery. A basic concept of the method is that if the woman knows what is taking place, then she can cooperate with nature. The less the person knows about the prenatal process and delivery, the more apt she is to interfere with it.

Interference with the natural processes causes pain. The patient, knowing what is happening, can usually relax and do specific breathings that help alleviate certain pain impulses. No anesthetics are used: therefore, the mother remains awake throughout labor and delivery. The gratifying moment comes when the mother sees her child being born. Since no drugs are used, the baby is born alert and ready for the oxygen that is needed to begin life.

Meg was x-rayed because there was a suspicion that she might be having twins. The x-ray revealed two fetuses in a vertical position. The next morning she was admitted to the hospital and, later that day, her labor was induced. During the long hours that she was in labor I stayed with her and helped her as I had been taught. I reminded her to stay relaxed, to do her breathing at the proper time, and to use the proper type breathing. I massaged her back and kept her alert and ready for her contractions. A problem developed in that the babies had intertwined themselves in such a manner that neither could give way to the other to be born. I overheard the doctors and nurses talking in the hallway about a cesarean. Immediately I got hold of a telephone and called the nurse who had trained us. I wanted to know if we would have to give up the Lamaze method at this point in view of what was happening. She wasn't very encouraging except to say that it should not be given up until it became absolutely necessary. Following that conversation I had a moment of prayer.

A number of hours into labor the doctor finally took Meg into the delivery room. I was asked to go with the doctor into the dressing room. There I was supplied with the proper garments for the delivery room. I was asked to scrub and out we went. Once in the delivery room I took my place next to Meg and continued to proceed with the instructions that I had been given for this phase of delivery.

At 5:20 PM my first son was born, and thirteen minutes later my second son arrived. They both were crying before they were completely born. This was the moment when I was most proud. While the doctor was delivering the babies, I felt a real part of the team.

It was the experience of a lifetime to have participated together with my wife in such an important event. It was exciting to see my children right from the start and to have been of moral support and encouragment for my wife. I would have missed a great deal had I been pacing the floor in the waiting room.

When the babies were taken to the incubators, a nurse, mistaking me for a doctor, asked me to come into the nursery to see the boys. I went in but when she asked me to pick up the babies, I was afraid to do so since I had never picked a baby up before. The nurse, noticing my hesitation, asked me if I was a doctor. When I said "No," she sent me packing!

I then took off my gown and cap and went to be with my wife until she was taken to her room. She and I paused to give thanks to God for such a wonderful experience. We cried with happiness, not only because everything had gone all right but also because we were both there and able to be part of it all.

Leboyer method a method of childbirth proposed by a French physician, Leboyer. The newborn is not spanked or held by the feet after birth but is placed on the abdomen of the mother, and a peaceful and calm post-delivery environment is maintained to minimize the shock of childbirth for the infant.

Leboyer delivery room practices

Dr. Frederick Leboyer (1975) of France has introduced a different approach to delivery room practices. Whereas Lamaze focuses on the mother, Leboyer focuses on the baby. For instance, Lamaze techniques help to lessen the pain of childbirth for the mother by eliminating the fear of that pain. Leboyer's techniques seek to remove the fear of childbirth for the infant. At least, he believes that the delivery process can be made less traumatic for the baby by making the transition from the uterine environment to the delivery room environment less harsh; this is accomplished by making the differences between the two more similar and less abrupt. Leboyer likes to emphasize that he is seeking to put across an attitude rather than developing a method; the procedures are less important than the feelings behind them. A modified Lamaze technique of natural childbirth is often used in conjunction with Leboyer's approach.

The ***Leboyer method*** proposes the following procedure to lessen the trauma of normal birth: delivery in a room with soft or subtle lights instead of bright glaring lights; an absolute minimum of sound, with the doctor

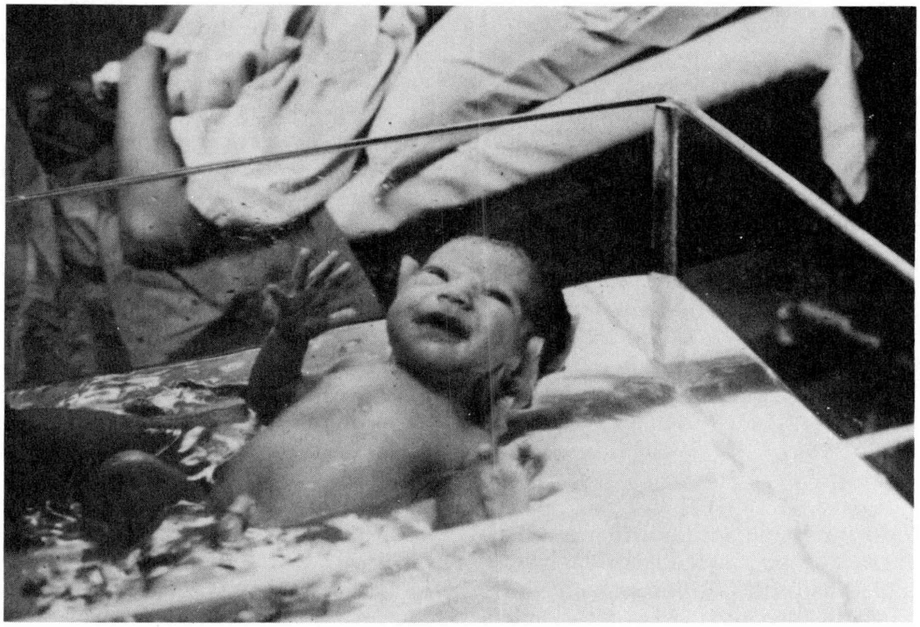

In the Leboyer delivery room approach the baby is placed in body-temperature water soon after birth to reduce the trauma of the transition from uterine weightlessness to the feel of gravitational pull on the body.
From Jensen, M.D., Bensen, R.C., & Bobak, I.M., Maternity care: The nurse and family. *St. Louis: The C.V. Mosby Co., 1977.*

saying "push, push" in a lowered voice; immediately after birth, placing the baby on the mother's stomach and encouraging her to stroke it; delay in cutting the umbilical cord until it stops pulsating, usually about 6 minutes, unless there is an indication that something might be wrong; and placing the baby in a body-temperature, warm bath where it becomes weightless again after feeling the new sensation of the weight of its body. The transition from uterine weightlessness to gravitational pull, then back to weightlessness is reassuring to the infant.

Leboyer is critical of physicians who dangle the baby by its heels and slap it to stimulate breathing. Such tactics may have been necessary when mothers and babies were both anesthetized, but that seldom occurs now that newer techniques are used. To make certain that the proper perspective is recognized, let it be known that Leboyer is not rigid in insisting on these procedures. The baby's survival and well-being come first. If there is any hint of trouble, he is the first to say, "Turn on the lights, use suction, use oxygen, follow standard medical procedures."

A point made by researchers and observers concerning Leboyer-delivered children is that they are noticeably different in their overall attitude and behavior, in their unusual avid interest in the world around them, in a greater sense of calmness, and in more graceful movements. "They seem to be reaching out instead of protecting themselves." Leboyer feels that a more gentle birth might produce happier children. The report of the Parisian psychologist, Danielle Rapaport (Horn, 1977), of 120 Leboyer babies, from birth to the age of 3, found them all to be significantly alert, able to concentrate longer on play, extremely clever with their hands, good in psychomotor tests, and having fewer sleeping and eating problems (Leboyer, 1975). Since the babies are more relaxed and agreeable, the mothers are more relaxed, establishing a relationship relatively free of anguish and worry.

A study by Nelson and his colleagues (1980), how-

cervix the narrow canal connecting the vagina and the uterus.

ever, did not find an advantage for a group of Leboyer-delivered babies when compared to a group of conventionally delivered babies. There were no differences in infant mortality or in infant behavior at the first hour of life, at 24 and 72 hours, or at 3 months of age. The only difference, determined 8 months after delivery, was that the Leboyer mothers had a feeling that somehow the Leboyer approach had influenced the behavior of their children. These mothers felt better about having taken this approach at the time of delivery.

BIRTH PROCESS

The last few weeks before a baby is born are spent by the baby and the mother getting ready for the birth. The baby has assumed its birth position, usually with the head pushing against the cervix. The uterus sinks downward and forward. The mother's profile changes, making her clothes fit differently. The pressure against her upper abdomen is eased, and she breathes more freely. These changes are called the "lightening" by some; others say that the baby has "dropped." The indications are that the baby is getting ready to be born. Lightening may occur as early as 4 weeks before birth or as late as the onset of labor. The usual time for lightening to occur is 10 to 14 days before delivery. It may be accompanied by some discomfort and intermittent pain. When this occurs, first-time anxious mothers may think that labor has started and call the physician, only to learn later that nothing eventful is about to happen.

Signs of true labor

True labor is characterized by one or more of the following. The most usual sign of real labor is the onset of contractions, which have a definite rhythm, gradually increasing in frequency, duration, and intensity. They may be 10, 15, or 20 minutes apart at first, lasting about 40 to 60 seconds each. Within an hour or two the contractions occur closer together. A characteristic of the true contractions is that they begin in the lower back and then travel to the front of the abdomen. The muscles of the abdomen become stiffer with subsequent contractions. The sharpness of the contractions increases as the uterine muscles prepare to ease the baby out of the uterus.

False labor is characterized by contractions that are far apart, with no rhythmic regularity, and with no muscular hardening of the abdomen. Nevertheless, occasionally false labor is difficult to distinguish from real labor. Many a would-be mother has rushed to the hospital only to return home.

A second sign of real labor is the appearance of a blood-tinged mucuslike discharge called *show*. During pregnancy the opening of the uterus is sealed shut by mucus, which acts like a plug. When labor is about to begin, the mucus is eased out and discharged.

A third sign of labor is the bursting of the water bag. The amniotic fluid that has been cushioning the baby is released before the baby is born, and either a gush of clear fluid or a slow leaking of clear fluid from the vagina may occur. Usually the bag ruptures toward the end of labor. However, it is not unusual for a bag to break a day or so before the child is delivered.

Stages of labor and birth

First stage. Obstetricians generally recognize three stages of labor in the birth process. The first and longest phase is the period of rhythmic and regular labor contractions. During this time, the ***cervix*** will dilate or "ripen" so that the birth canal can be stretched or widened enough for the baby to pass through. The contractions help to widen the opening of the cervix. Physicians usually prefer to be called when the contractions are 10 to 15 minutes apart or when the water bag has ruptured, regardless of "show" or contractions. Contractions come closer together as the cervix dilates to its full width of about 10 cm (4 in.) in diameter.

The length of this first stage of labor can vary considerably in time. For a first baby the average length of total labor is about 14 hours. For later babies labor lasts an average of 8 hours. Ideally, the labor should not last too long or take place too quickly, since a slow delivery will exhaust both the mother and the baby and a fast delivery may mean that the baby is unable to make the quick physiological adjustment required. Many such children have marginal perceptual problems in learning when they enter school (Kaluger and Kolson, 1978).

Second stage. When contractions are about 2 or 3 minutes apart and last 60 to 70 seconds, the second stage of labor begins. The baby is born during this

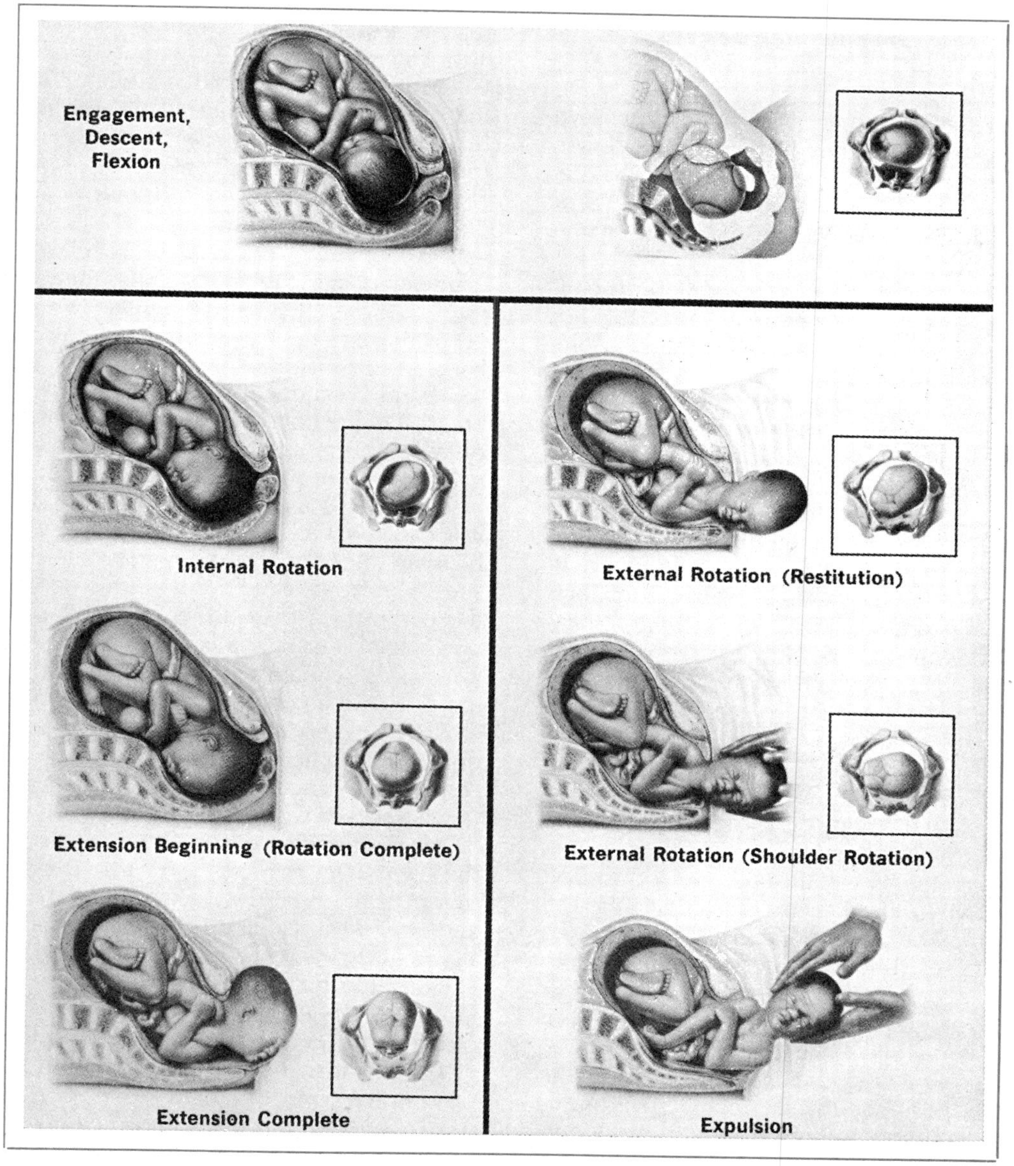

FIG. 4-1 ***Mechanism of normal labor. Left occipito-anterior (L.O.A.) position.***
From Mechanism of normal labor, Nursing education aid *No. 13, Ross Laboratories, Columbus, Ohio,* *1978.*

episiotomy surgical incision of the vulva for obstetrical purposes to prevent uneven laceration during delivery.

period. The actual birth may take about 20 to 70 minutes. With each contraction the baby moves downward through the cervix, through the vagina, and out. The mother can "bear down" (push) to help these movements once the head has passed between the bones forming the pelvic outlet.

A woman who has participated in a childbirth education program, such as the Lamaze, will probably not be given an analgesic or anesthetic unless needed. She wants to feel the thrill of helping push the baby out. She wants to be conscious the minute the baby is born and to hear its first cry. However, there are some women who have a low threshold for pain; they do not want to be hurt. Some want several children and don't want a painful or uncomfortable first-time experience to deter them from having another child.

If needed or desired, an *analgesic,* which is a medication like Demerol, can be used to reduce pain. *Anesthetics* are used to produce a tissue insensibility to pain or touch, such as the use of Novocain by a dentist. Anesthetics may be local or general. A *local anesthetic* affects only the area where the anesthetic is injected. One type of local is the *saddle block*. Anesthetics are injected in the lumbar region of the back while the woman is in a sitting position. The anesthetic affects that regional area of the body that ordinarily contacts a saddle when one is riding a horse. A local *caudal anesthetic* is injected at the base of the tailbone. It will affect the regional nerve trunks that emerge in that area. The caudal method can be used to eliminate labor pains as well as birth pains, but it is more complicated to administer.

Another widely used local procedure, the *pudendal block,* is simply to inject the perineum, the space between the rectum and the vagina, numbing the pudendal nerves peripherally. This technique is one of choice for the mother who desires to participate during delivery. This technique allows for as natural a childbirth as possible while also providing pain relief if there is danger of the vaginal or surrounding tissues being torn (Jensen et al., 1981). If this is the case, a small incision, called an ***episiotomy,*** can be made to relieve the strain on the tissues and to make a larger opening. Stitches, which will later dissolve, are made after the delivery.

A *general anesthesia* puts the individual to sleep. The deeper the sleep, the more likely that the baby will be anesthetized. General anesthesia is usually done by injection of thiopental sodium (Pentothal) into the arm. A *spinal anesthesia* is commonly used for a cesarean section, during which the mother is still alert. Mention should also be made of the use of hypnosis or hypnoanesthesia. Hypnosis does minimize the need for drugs to provide relief from pain; however, hypnosis can be used effectively with only one of four mothers (Iorio, 1975).

The "crowning" of the head occurs when the widest diameter of the baby's head is at the mother's vulva, the outer entrance to her vagina. The physician will grasp the emerged head beneath the chin with one hand and gently draw on the baby, helping it out. The head and shoulder rotate as they emerge (Fig. 4-1). The rest of the body will usually be delivered with one or two more contractions after the head is out. The baby, as he or she now appears, has a whitish look from the protective vernix coating with which the fetus was covered while in the amniotic sac. There may also be some blood on the body from the mucus and tissues. The head may be a little misshapen because of the contraction pressure exerted on it while in the birth canal, but it is pliable and quickly resumes its normal shape. Nature wisely sees to it that the bones of the head are among the last ones to be formed.

When delivery is completed, a head-downward position is maintained to facilitate drainage of mucus and respiration. Mucus and other amniotic residue are quickly sucked from the mouth and nose by the obstetrician or attending nurse. The buttocks or the soles of the baby's feet may be given a mild tap, or the back may be rubbed gently to get the baby to inhale enough air to unfold and inflate all the tiny air sacs in the lungs, which have never been used before. As the baby exhales, the first audible wail is uttered. The crying forces the breath through faster. As the baby takes in oxygen, the body color changes to a pinkish hue.

The umbilical cord is tied off, cut, and kept clean to prevent infection. The baby is now completely on his or her own in terms of bodily functions. Drops are put in each of the baby's eyes to prevent eye infection or blindness, which could be caused by a gonorrheal infection of the mother. The baby is cleaned, identified with a name bracelet or band, usually footprinted or thumbprinted, weighed, measured, and put to bed in a warm blanket. The baby is fine.

Third stage. The final stage of labor consists of the delivery of the *afterbirth*—the placenta with the

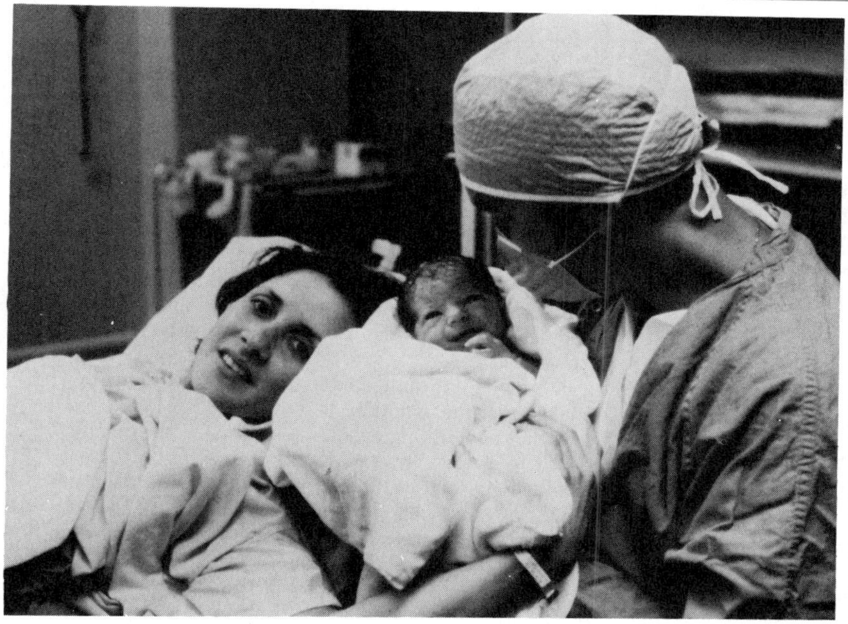

My mother groan'd! my father wept.
Into the dangerous world I leapt:
Helpless naked, piping loud:
Like a fiend hid in a cloud.

William Blake
Songs of Experience

attached amniotic and chorionic membranes and the remainder of the cord. This process takes about 20 minutes and is virtually painless. The physician will quickly examine the mother and the afterbirth to make certain that no abnormalities exist. The mother will lose a pint of blood, more or less, in giving birth. The physician may knead her abdomen to help restore tone to the uterine muscles. For the next 10 to 14 days the uterine lining will disintegrate and will be shed in a process resembling menstruation.

MY SISTER'S BIRTH*

Prior to the birth, my mother's state of mind began to deteriorate. In many ways this affected her attitude to the life that she was carrying at that time. My father's drinking habits did not help at all, and at one stage we watched in fear during a bitter argument when we thought they would separate. Thank God, this did not happen. The thought of not having my parents together to live with was so frightening that I remember crying at night.

Mum grew in her pregnancy and began to become irritated and annoyed at small mistakes that we made. It was about 4.30 PM on the 11th of January while she was hanging up the washing that her water broke. Seeing my mother kneeling with her hands on her stomach in pain gave me no thought of an emergency, for I was only twelve years old at that time.

She was crying as she called me to fetch Dad home from work. In no time my father was home and with the help of my brother took Mum inside into my room. Then Dad went up the village to get two very old women to assist in the birth. All this time I was in my room watching my mother as she sat on the floor, weeping and screaming between grimaces of pain that she did not want to give birth to the baby inside her so that she could die. Being brought up in a family where a girl was

*From Stewart, R.A.C. (Ed.). *Pacific profiles*. Suva, Fiji: University of The South Pacific Extension Services, 1982.

expected to be passive, all I could do was share the thought with her. Those few hours while she laboured I prayed, I really did, that she would realize how much we needed her.

By now the old women had arrived. In soft tones they were telling her to bear down, to help push the baby out, but still her stubbornness prevailed. This was too much for me. I pushed past the two old women, grabbed my mother's hand, and cried, "Mum, you can't do this to us, you can't leave us. Please, Mum, please!" She must have been trying hard to concentrate through the pain because, as I watched her, I saw a change in her face: the look of understanding that only a daughter can share in such moments as this. She continued to hold and squeeze my hand, and she began to push. Dad came and stood behind her to support her.

As the minutes passed she showed signs of intense pain; it became an effort for my father to keep her still. She gasped twice in pain, and I saw the head of my sister appear. As the rest of her appeared, a warm feeling came over me. Describing it now I would say it was an intense love, for my mother and my new sister—a female who would one day give birth to another life. Then my sister opened her mouth to assure us that she was very much alive and wanted someone to please pay attention to her, as she was tired and wanted to sleep before meeting the world. The midwives took care of that. Dad and I finally left Mum fast sleep beside a beautiful daughter.

Coming from a Polynesian society on Cook Island where old customs are still treasured we had one more task to perform—to plant the afterbirth under a young sprouting coconut tree. This tree would be my sister's, and her progress in years would be compared with the tree's as it grew.

All that is left to be said is that if one ever gets the chance to witness a birth, take it; it can be a very beautiful and moving experience. For me, it has made me more aware of myself as a female and of the role of childbearing that I will perform one day. As for my sister, I love her very much, a love I doubt I would have felt so deeply if I had not seen her being born. My sister's birth brought a change in my parents. Slowly they began to repair the breaks in their marriage, and ever so slowly but surely our home became a happy one once more.

cesarean section a surgical operation through the walls of the abdomen and uterus for the purpose of delivering a child.

vertex presentation the birth of a baby in which the head appears first.

Kinds of birth deliveries

Vertex presentation. Ninety-five percent of all babies are born with their heads emerging first in what is called a ***vertex presentation*** (McLennan and Sandberg, 1974). This type of birth is the normal spontaneous delivery. No instruments are necessary. Things progress according to the plans prescribed by nature in its wonderful wisdom for the birth of a baby. Fig. 4-2 illustrates various forms of presentation at birth.

Breech birth presentation. About 3% of all babies assume a lie just before birth in which the buttocks instead of the head are positioned in the lower pelvic area. As a result, the buttocks and feet emerge first in birth, with the head appearing last. This type of delivery is a *breech presentation* (Fig. 4-2). Such births, which physicians can usually detect before they happen, may require special attention because they are generally more difficult. However, in most cases there is a satisfactory delivery.

Cesarean delivery. In cases in which the baby is disproportionately large or where the head is larger than the mother's pelvic opening, the physician may advise a cesarean birth. More than 15% of all deliveries in the United States are cesarean (National Institutes of Health, 1981). Such a birth is especially necessary if the fetus has assumed a transverse lie and the position cannot be changed. A ***cesarean section*** is a surgical delivery through an incision in the abdominal wall and the uterus. The child is removed through the slits, and then both incisions are carefully sewn. This delivery is considered major surgery, but the risks are minimal with modern medical technique. It used to be a common belief that once a woman had a cesarean section, the uterus and abdominal wall were weakened. It is now known that a woman may have several cesarean births satisfactorily.

Use of forceps. A forceps or instrument delivery is suggested if the uterine contractions weaken or stop

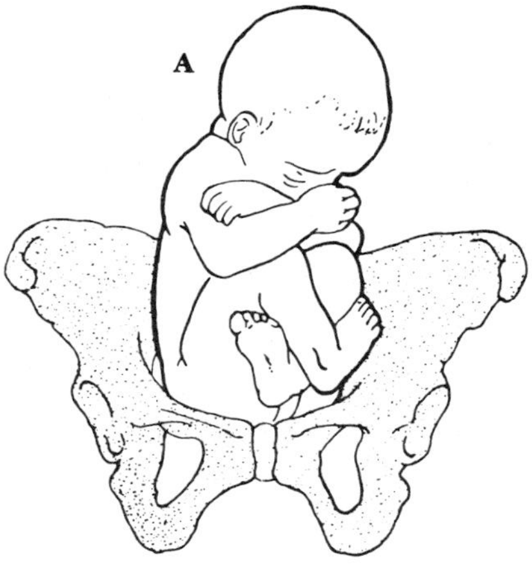

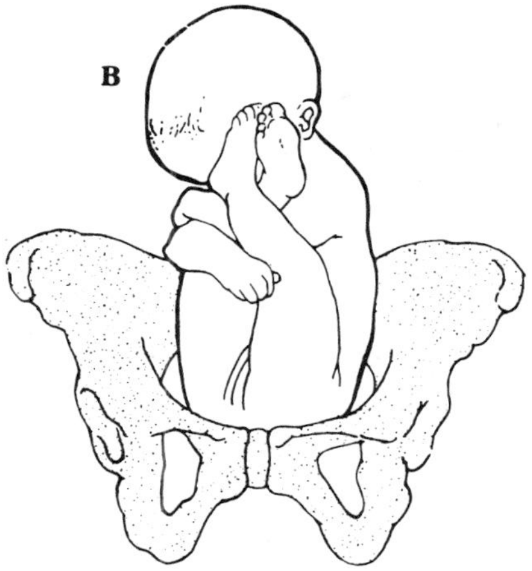

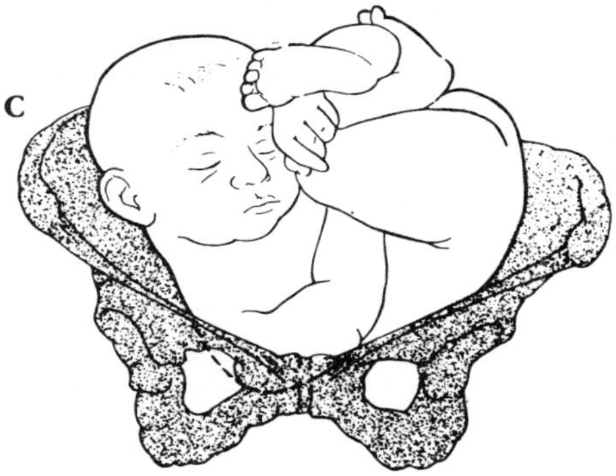

FIG. 4-2 ***Forms of presentation. A fetus will usually assume a head-down attitude or lie (cephalic presentation) within the uterine cavity. At times, the baby will make a breech presentation (buttocks and/or feet first) or a shoulder presentation if there is a transverse lie. A and B are breech presentations; C is a shoulder presentation; D is a vertex (head) or occiput presentation, which is the most common; and E is a face presentation.***

From Iorio, J. Childbirth: family centered nursing *[3rd ed.]. St. Louis: The C.V. Mosby Co., 1975.*

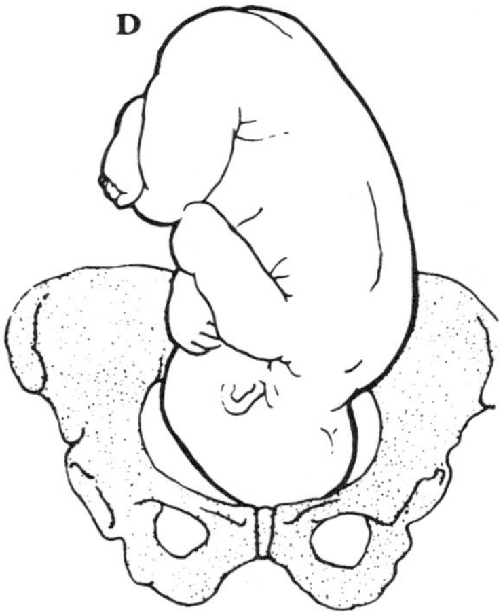

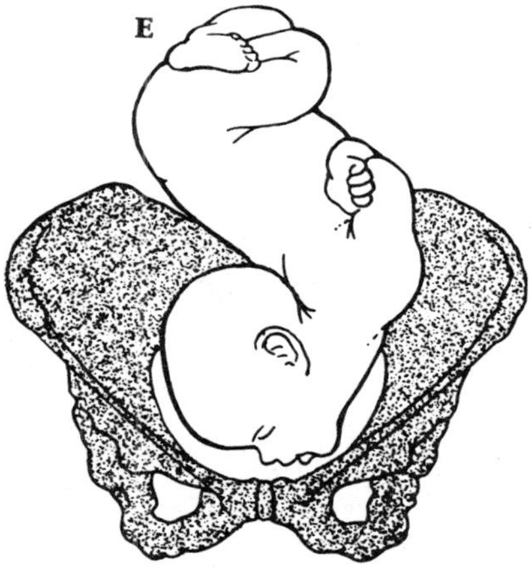

Apgar scale developed by Apgar and James in 1962, a much-used and practical scoring system for assessing, on a scale from 0 to 2, color, heart rate, reflex irritability, muscle tone, and respiratory effort in newborns. The totaled score may vary from 0 to 10 (10 being best).

during delivery or when some physiological condition makes it difficult for the baby to push through the birth canal. Forceps are curved, tonglike instruments shaped to fit on each side of the baby's head. As an emergency procedure, *a high-forceps delivery* may be made during the first stage of labor or early in the second stage. This procedure is somewhat uncertain because an accurate placement of the forceps may be difficult. A *low-forceps delivery* is made at the stage of actual delivery and involves less risk. The forceps will occasionally make a bluish mark on each side of the infant's head where the tongs touched, but these disappear after several days. Although the technique of using forceps has improved tremendously because of better training, there is a wide variance in the use of forceps from hospital to hospital and physician to physician.

Induced delivery. A growing number of obstetricians believe in inducing labor when a woman is at the end of term. The end of term is determined by a drop in the level of progesterone in the mother's blood. Medical indications for induction of labor include: prolonged pregnancy (42 to 43 weeks); prolonged rupture of the membranes; preterm delivery in diabetic mother; severe preeclampsia, placenta abruptio, or fetal death; and uterine inertia. Elective indications are multiple pregnancy with a history of precipitate (quick) labor and patients who live long distances from the hospital. The hormone oxytocin is injected intravenously into the patient. Ninety-two percent of the women give birth on the day they receive the oxytocin. The advantage of induced labor is that a woman can have her baby on a chosen day when the hospital is fully staffed.

Assessment of newborn

Apgar scale. The normalcy of the baby's condition and survival chances at birth have been systematized in the ***Apgar scale*** (Table 4-1), developed by Virginia Apgar (Apgar and James, 1962). The scale gives a sum of ratings, scored from 0 to 10, in five conditions: breathing effort, heart rate, muscle tone, reflex irritability, and skin color. Large-scale research studies show that the scores are good gross predictors in identifying babies who need special care. Scores are given by the physican or anesthetist 60 seconds after complete birth. Ninety percent of the infants score 7 or better (Self and Horowitz, 1980). A score of 5 to 10

TABLE 4-1 Apgar score for condition of the newborn baby

Sign	*0*	*1*	*2*	*Score*
Heart rate (pulse)	Absent	Slow, below 100	Over 100 beats per minute	______
Breathing effort	Absent	Slow, irregular	Good, strong cry	______
Muscle tone	Limp	Some flexion of extremities	Active motion, well flexed	______
Reflex irritability (response to catheter in nostril)	No response	Grimace	Cough, sneeze, or cry	______
Skin color	Blue, pale	Body pink, extremities blue	Completely pink	______
			Total	______

Modified from Apgar, V. *Journal of the American Medical Association,* 1958, *168,* 1958.

usually indicates no need for treatment; a score of 4 or below indicates need for prompt diagnosis and treatment. A second assessment is done 5 minutes after birth.

Brazelton scales. The Apgar Scale (Apgar, 1967) is used to measure the degree of gross abnormalities of the physical systems of a newborn baby. The Brazelton Behavioral Assessment Scale (Brazelton, 1973) has been devised to detect milder dysfunctions of the central nervous system (CNS) and the development of behavioral responses during the neonatal period. This scale is first given 2 or 3 days after the child is born, when the immediate stresses of delivery and some of the medication effects have begun to wear off. It is given again on day 9 or 10, when the baby has been at home and has adjusted to the home environment. The

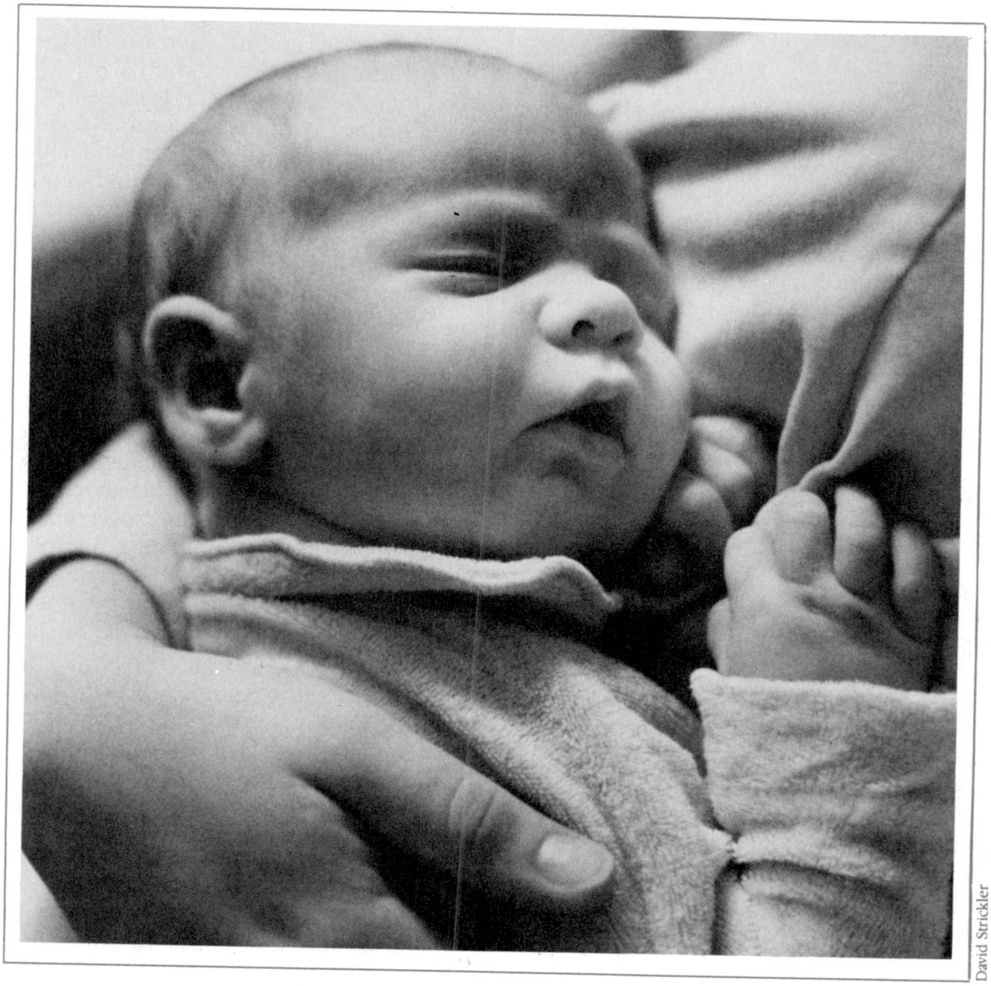

David Strickler

The Brazelton Behavioral Assessment Scale is unique in that it provides an assessment 2 or 3 days after the baby is born, then another assessment on day 9 or 10 when the baby is home from the hospital. The mother, father, and baby have an opportunity to relax from the stress of delivery.

anoxia a severe deficiency in the supply of oxygen to the tissues, especially the brain, causing damage to their structural integrity.

phenylketonuria (PKU) an error of metabolism caused by a recessive gene that gives rise to a deficiency in a certain enzyme. It can cause mental retardation if it is not caught in time. The inherited inability to metabolize phenylalanine, a component of some foods. It occurs when the two recessive genes for PKU are paired.

intent is to determine the curve of recovery of the neurological system and of behavioral responses by ascertaining the full-term neonate's capacity to organize responses to social stimuli as it moves from sleep to crying and to alert states of consciousness.

The examination assesses the neonate's neurological intactness of 20 reflex items, such as rooting, sucking, the Moro, the Babinski, and so on. The neonate's behavior repertoire is assessed on 26 behavioral items related to (1) capacity to attend to environmental events (such as responding to light, a rattle, or a bell), (2) ability to control motor behavior, (3) maintenance of a calm, alert state despite increased stimulation, and (4) ability of the infant to inhibit startle responses, tremors, and interfering movements. The curve of recovery of overall organization becomes the most important measure of prediction. (Tronick and Brazelton, 1975). Als et al. (1979) conclude that the Brazelton Scale has a place in the early assessment of neonates whenever there is any question of neurological integrity in the child.

CONDITIONS AT BIRTH AFFECTING DEVELOPMENT

There are prenatal and perinatal factors that affect the growth and development of an infant. We will consider four of the major areas: phenylketonuria (PKU), anoxia, certain birth defects, and premature deliveries. A summary of conditions that can cause a newborn to be at high risk for survival are listed in the box.

Phenylketonuria

Phenylketonuria, known as PKU, is a hereditary defect in an enzyme of the liver. The child needs the enzyme to metabolize the common protein food product phenylalanine. If the enzyme abnormality is not found and treated soon after birth, certain substances accumulate in the blood and bring about mental retardation by causing damage to the brain.

The infant born with PKU looks normal and acts as expected for a month or two after birth (Kopp and Parmelee, 1979). Then a pattern of listless behavior, apathy, and delayed development is apparent. Toward the end of the first year of life a drop in developmental abilities is noted. By the time the child is 3 years of age, severe retardation is often observed. PKU appears about once in 10,000 births.

The condition can often be detected by a simple blood test given before the baby leaves the hospital. The infant's heel is pricked, and a few drops of blood are obtained on filter paper and then tested. A urine test should also be done after the infant is 2 weeks old (Holtzman et al., 1974). Treatment consists of a scientifically controlled diet, which is begun within the first few weeks of life. If the diet is continued, the child will grow and develop normally. In some cases children with PKU can be given normal diets after a few years.

Anoxia: Lack of oxygen

Anoxia is a deficiency or an absence of oxygen to the tissues. The ease or difficulty with which the newborn infant starts to breathe after birth is critical. If breathing is not established soon, enabling oxygen to reach the brain, serious consequences may occur. If oxygen deprivation is severe, the infant may die. Less severe deprivation may result in enough damage to brain cells to cause cerebral palsy or similar conditions (Towbin, 1978). A lesser degree of anoxia may cause disturbances in cognitive functioning, such as in mental processes related to verbal, conceptual, and perceptual development.

Oxygen deprivation may result from a prolonged or difficult birth or by birth in the breech position. Occasionally, infants born by cesarean section will develop a *hyaline membrane,* a glossylike condition in the lungs, shortly after birth that causes difficulty in breathing and possibly death. Babies born with a congenital heart defect that bars normal circulation of blood can also be oxygen starved. These so-called blue babies are placed in incubators to enable them to survive without producing any damage to the brain. Once their problem has been corrected, they respond adequately.

HIGH-RISK INFANTS

FAMILY HISTORY
Presence of mutant genes
Central nervous system disorders
Low socioeconomic group
Previous defective sibling
Parental consanguinity
Intrafamilial emotional disorder

MEDICAL HISTORY OF MOTHER
Diabetes
Hypertension
Radiation
Cardiovascular or renal disease
Thyroid disease
Unknown cause of hemorrhage

PREVIOUS OBSTETRICAL HISTORY OF MOTHER
Toxemia
Miscarriage immediately preceding pregnancy
Size of infants
Many children
Prolonged infertility

PRESENT PREGNANCY
Maternal age <16 or >35
Multiple births
Excessive amnionic fluid
Inflammation of kidney
Out-of-wedlock pregnancy
Small amount of amnionic fluid
Medications
Radiation

PRESENT PREGNANCY—CONT'D
Anesthesia
Maternal rubella in first trimester
Diabetes
Toxemia
Fetal-maternal blood group incompatibility

LABOR AND DELIVERY
Absence of prenatal care
Prematurity
Postmaturity or dysmaturity
Precipitate, prolonged, or complicated delivery
Low Apgar score—5 minutes

PLACENTA
Massive stoppage in canal
Amnion nodosum (multiple lesions)
Inflammation of placenta

NEONATE
Single umbilical artery
Jaundice
Head size
Infection
Anoxia
Severe dehydration
Convulsions
Failure to regain birth weight by 10 days
Manifest congenital defects
Disproportion between weight or length and gestational age
Survival following meningitides, encephalopathies, and traumatic intracranial episodes

Modified from *Proceedings of the White House Conference on Mental Retardation,* Washington, D.C., 1963; and from the American Medical Association. Mental retardation—a handbook for the primary physician. *Journal of the American Medical Association,* 1965, *191,* 183.

Major birth defects

An understandable concern of parents is whether the baby is born free from congenital defects. Fortunately, the large majority of babies are born without serious abnormalities that cause disfigurement or a physical or mental handicap. Yet some children are born with defects. A table of birth defects is located in Appendix A. About 20% of birth defects result from heredity; another 20% are caused by environmental factors, such as drugs, medicine, viral infections, and vitamin deficiencies. The remaining 60% result from an interaction of some environmental factor and a genetic predisposition (Korones, 1976).

One child in 500 will be born with *spina bifida,* which is an open spine. Failure of the spinal column (neural groove) to close permits some nerves of the spinal cord to protrude. Sometimes surgery in the first 3 months of the child's life can correct the condition so that other complications do not occur. Clinical cases of mental retardation appear as Down's syndrome (trisomy 21) once in 600 births (one in

50 for women over 45 years of age) and as hydrocephaly (water on the brain) in 1 in 500 births. Down's syndrome is caused by a chromosomal error, whereas hydrocephaly usually is caused by an obstruction of the flow of cerebrospinal fluid. Fibrocystic disease, cystic fibrosis, occurs once in 1,000 births. Children with this condition have chronic respiratory problems and persistent intestinal difficulties. The cause is usually hereditary and involves a metabolic error.

The significant point to be remembered is that most births, 97 out of 100, produce normal, healthy babies. If the mother takes care of herself, especially during the first 3 months of pregnancy, chances are considerably greater that the baby will be normal.

Donnie

Throughout my nine months of pregnancy I felt no pain, suffered no diseases, encountered no accidents. All precautions were taken for a healthy baby, including vitamins, proper diet, plenty of rest, proper exercise, and avoidance of alcohol and cigarettes. Blood types were checked since my mother has the Rh-negative blood factor and because I received several transfusions as an Rh-negative baby: however, my blood proved to be O positive. The obstetrician informed me that my neonatal condition would have no effect whatsoever on my baby. There are no cases of deformity or mental deficiencies in either my family or my husband's family. During birth there were no complications, so the question still remains: Why did I give birth to a hydrocephalic child?

The question was asked of me whether or not to permit the surgeon to perform a ventriculovenous shunt soon after my son Donnie was born. My only thought was that I wanted my baby alive, so I consented. Little did I know to what extent the "alive" would be.

Donnie is now fourteen months old and very far behind the average child. The extent of brain damage has not yet been determined, but simple observation shows a noticeable degree of deficiency. Donnie has been further handicapped by the fact that his thumbs have never extended themselves from his palms.

For the first four months of Donnie's life there was no activity from him at all. He lived in an immobile and silent world. He ate, slept, and watched things, void of expression. He made no attempts at self-mobility or at expression. No object seemed familiar to him, yet he cried when he was hungry or uncomfortable. He jerked at loud sounds and sudden movements but showed no advancement from the neonatal stage. Donnie received special attention from everyone but was given no ray of hope from the doctors. He spent his first four months in and out of hospitals.

When Donnie was four months old, I had to resume my career. It was also the turning point in Donnie's behavior. Even though much of his first four months was spent away from his family, he seemed to object to being separated again. His first discernible changes were facial. He seeemed to cry with more feeling than before. For the first time, a smile was noticed. He grimaced at certain foods and began some bodily movements. It seemed that Donnie was acting like a newborn infant. His features took new form. His red hair seemed to look like hair, and his blue eyes began sparkling with recognition.

Within days Donnie was busy making funny noises and waving his arms around wildly. His enlarged head seemed, for the first time, cumbersome to him. He began noticing toys, colors, sounds, and people all at once. He was suddenly really alive and aware, and each new moment became precious for him and for us. On his next visit to the doctor, Donnie decided to show off. He kicked, cooed, cried, laughed, and pointed with his right forefinger extended for the first time. He seemed to be showing everyone that he really wanted to live and to learn. He seemed so fascinated with himself. Life had once again begun.

In the ensuing months many new things were noticed. He began trying to pick things up but could not because of the immobile thumbs. Then the plans went into action for surgery to correct this situation by inserting muscles and tendons into the thumbs to provide movement. While in his playpen, he began to raise himself with his arms, never really getting very far. Most of his wasted effort seemed due to his heavy unbalanced weight, but some of the cause was his thumbs. Donnie began sitting with support and was then firmly placed into a high chair. In his chair he became aware of more objects and wanted a chance to feel them. Usually his attempts to grab things and pick them up were futile, since they fell to the floor. Then he began to enjoy pushing everything onto the floor. We actually encouraged such behavior, for it afforded him more and more exposure to his environment. When Donnie was ten months old, he worked his two hands together to pick up items. Some he could hold for quite a while, but others were too heavy for him.

At ten and one-half months Donnie's first thumb operation was performed. It failed to provide for him the proper use of his thumb and also seemed to set him back again emotionally. Soon after, a second attempt was made, with supposed success. Even though success was claimed, at thirteen months there was still no sign of movement in the thumb. Plans are now in the making for an operation on the second thumb.

At thirteen months Donnie's life had once again reached a lull. No new activities were observed, only an increase in nonsensical noise-making. He still could not sit by himself, nor stand, nor creep, all attributed to his head size and his thumbs. He had improved in picking things up; he managed to pick up objects, even small ones, by using both index fingers together. We were waiting for some true signs of communication to form but until this time none was made.

Last Tuesday Donnie was fourteen months old. On this same day two new and wonderful acquisitions were noticed. He was lying in his playpen when I got home. I went over to him and he, as usual, rolled over to his back and reached out to be held. After picking him up, I began to talk to him. When we went into the kitchen, I reached for a cup to get him some water. Donnie pointed and said: "Water." His pronunciation was clear; I was so stunned that I couldn't move. Donnie started squirming in my arms and insisted: "Water, Mommy." Needless to say, he got all the water he wanted. I think I sat and stared at this remarkable boy for some time. Despite all the odds, he wanted to learn. Later, during his nap I approached his crib to discover him asleep. There was something different about him, but I didn't notice it at first. Then it hit me; he had his thumb in his mouth! It was his first self-extension of that thumb.

I know now that there are many new days of excitement ahead for Donnie. When the second thumb surgery is completed, we will have a son who may be able to really advance. We are also aware of the drawbacks that will continue to plague Donnie forever, but he seems happy now. For us that is the apex of life.

Prematurity and low birth weight

low birth weight any neonate weighing less than 2500 g (5½ lb.) with limited fat deposits, poor temperature and muscle control, and other frailties.

premature, or preterm baby baby born before the 37th week of pregnancy, dated from the mother's last menstrual period.

The term ***premature*** relates to the length of the gestation period and applies to an infant born before thirty-seven completed weeks of pregnancy. Due date is usually 40 weeks. The term ***low birth weight*** is applied to any newborn, regardless of gestation age, who weighs less than 2,500 grams (about 5½ pounds) at birth. Recognition of the different groups of premature babies is important because they differ greatly in terms of the kind of care they may need.

Premature birth is the biggest single problem facing those responsible for the care of the newborn. Although most body organs can function fairly adequately by the twenty-eighth week, the brain is still insufficiently developed to control behavior. The cerebral cortex has little, if any, control over the behavior patterns of either a 7- or an 8-month-old term baby (Kopp and Parmelee, 1979). Special attention must be given to the physical needs of the newborn infant. The premature infant requires nearly three times as much oxygen as a full-term infant, is often anemic, and may require a blood transfusion. Furthermore, this infant is more subject to infection and will require careful medical supervision. The use of an incubator (Isolette) helps with these problems while at the same time providing a temperature and humidity climate designed to duplicate conditions of the intrauterine environment. Fig. 4-3 illustrates the difference between a premature and a normal infant in motor control shortly after birth.

There are many reasons why a mother may have a baby of low birth weight or a premature delivery. Some of the factors are toxemia, a multiple birth, accidental hemorrhage during pregnancy, a placenta previa (a misplaced placenta covering the opening of the womb instead of lying in the proper place), hypertensive cardiovascular disease, diabetes, glandular disturbance, nutritional deficiency, undue emotional stress, heavy smoking, overwork, or a number of other reasons. About 7% of all births are premature. Prematurity is more common among first-born babies and among boys than among girls. It is more frequent in the lower socioeconomic class and more frequent among nonwhites than among whites (Kopp and Parmelee, 1979).

Of the babies who die within 4 weeks of birth, over half are born prematurely, which is the greatest cause of neonatal death in the United States; respiratory distress is second, and congenital anomalies are third as causes of death.

Studies of the development of premature children reveal that these infants do differ from the normal, at least up to about the ages of 7, 8, or 9 years (Taub et al., 1977). By then most premature children catch up in weight, height, and functional mental ability. At the beginning of school a greater percentage of premature children are distractible and excessively active or restless. They obtain slightly lower scores on test of motor and cognitive development. More premature children have difficulty in learning to read than do other children (Kaluger and Kolson, 1978).

The extent of the lag in maturation and functional ability is related to the degree of deviation in low birth weight or prematurity of birth. Most children, however, have an amazing ability to adapt or compensate for any deficiencies they may have (Kagan, 1978). One should look for positive attributes in children rather than focus or dwell on limitations or deficiencies. Children progress to the degree that they are free to do so, and that includes freedom from overprotectiveness by parents, who frequently underestimate the capabilities of children who are born prematurely.

Preventing birth defects

Apgar and Beck (1972) in their book *Is My Baby All Right?* make a number of suggestions that could help to prevent birth defects. Some of their suggestions follow:

1. If a close relative has a disorder that might be hereditary, take advantage of genetic counseling.
2. From a statistical point of view, avoid pregnancy before age 18 or after age 40. The ideal age to have children is between 20 and 35 (elsewhere we say 20 to 28).
3. Men should beget their children before they reach the age 45, although this is not as statistically significant as it is for women.

A

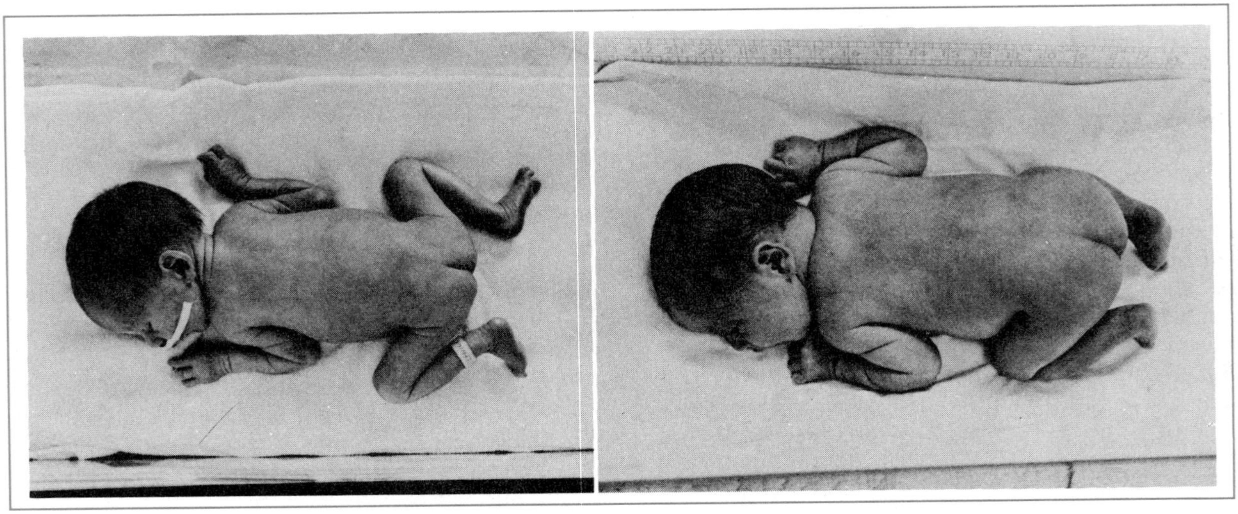

B

FIG. 4-3 ***Motor control of a premature and a full-term newborn infant. A, In prone position premature infant lies with pelvis flat and legs splayed out sideways like a frog. B, Normal infant lies with limbs flexed, pelvis raised, and knees usually drawn under abdomen.***

Courtesy Mead Johnson & Co., Evansville, Ind.

4. There should be an interval of at least 2 years between the end of one pregnancy and the beginning of another.
5. After the second birth, statistical chances increase somewhat for stillbirth, congenital malformation, and prematurity.
6. When a couple is trying to conceive, intercourse should be at intervals of not more than 24 hours for several days, just preceding and during the estimated time of ovulation. The sperms and eggs are fresher and stronger.
7. Have good prenatal care checkups and good obstetrical care and delivery.
8. Be immunized against rubella. Avoid exposure to contagious disease.
9. During pregnancy, avoid eating uncooked meat that might be a source of toxoplasmosis infection. Another source of toxoplasmosis infection is the feces of cats; care should be taken in cleaning litter boxes.
10. Do not take any drugs or medication unless prescribed.
11. Avoid x-ray examinations, especially during the first 3 months of pregnancy.
12. Do not smoke cigarettes.
13. Eat a nourishing diet, high in proteins, vitamins, and minerals.
14. A prospective mother with Rh-negative blood should have her physician take the necessary steps to protect her and the baby.
15. Take every precaution to prevent a baby from being born prematurely in less than 266 days or under 5½ pounds.

THE NEONATE

The newborn baby is not really new at all. By the day of birth the infant is already a distinct and accomplished person with characteristics that are peculiarly unique. About 280 days old, the baby carries the developmental traits that will influence future growth characteristics. Birth does not alter the basic patterns of the nervous system. Although weight has increased 2 billion times from what it was at conception, the newborn baby is still small enough to curl comfortably in a shoebox. When the time comes to leave the hospital the infant has a name and a life history that is well underway.

Although being born is a natural process, it is not always an easy one. The infant will usually require a few days just to overcome the birth experience. The more difficult the birth, the longer is the period for stabilization or recovery. Since so many features of this stage of life are different from the other stages, a special name is given to the newborn child: ***neonate***. According to many developmental psychologists, the neonatal period generally lasts for about 2 weeks; however, some pediatric textbooks specify the neonatal period as the first 28 days of life. By either definition the infant is a newborn.

neonate a newborn infant.

Physical characteristics of the neonate

Even the fondest of mothers may be somewhat shocked at the sight of her newborn infant, especially if it is her first child. The infant is tiny, the skin wrinkled or shriveled looking, and the body seems out of proportion. Fat cheeks, a short flat nose, and a receding chin give the newborn a useful facial profile for the purpose of sucking but do not always make the baby attractive initially. The wobbly head is about one fourth the body size and may be strangely lopsided as a result of pressures caused by passage through the birth canal. The shape of the head will soon become normal in appearance however.

The neck seems to be no more than a fold of skin separating head from narrow shoulders. The milky blue eyes of most new arrivals are about one half their adult size. Since the body is only about one twentieth of its adult size, the baby appears to have an unusually large head and eyes. The legs are extremely short in relation to the trunk. Fig. 4-4 presents an overall view of what the newborn baby looks like at 1 week of age.

The average weight of a newborn is about 3.5 kg (7½ lb.) and the average height is 50 to 51 cm (20 to 20½ in.). Girl babies, on the average, weigh slightly less than boy babies and are not quite as tall. During the first 4 or 5 days, the neonate may lose 170 to 198 g (6 to 7 oz.). This loss of weight results from inadequate nutrition while the process of digestion is being established and from the evaporation of moisture from the tissues. Once the body is stabilized, usually in 7 to 9 days, the child begins to gain weight. The weight will generally double in 6 months and triple to about 9.5 kg (21 lb.) in 12 months. The height increases by 30% to

HEAD usually strikes you as being too big for the body. (Immediately after birth it may be temporarily out of shape—lopsided or elongated—due to pressure before or during birth.)

ON THE SKULL you will see or feel the two most obvious soft spots, or fontanels. One is above the brow, the other close to crown of head in back.

EYES appear dark blue, have a blank stary gaze. You may catch one or both turning or turned to crossed or wall-eyed position.

A DEEP FLUSH spreads over the entire body if baby cries hard. Veins on head swell and throb. You will notice no tears because tear ducts do not function as yet.

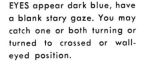

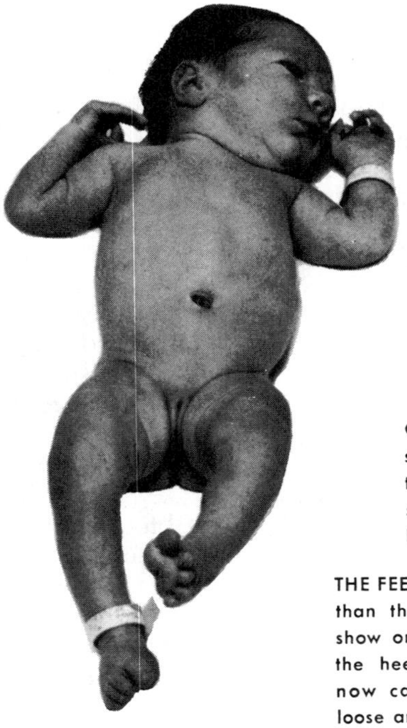

THE FACE will disappoint you unless you expect to see pudgy cheeks, a broad, flat nose with mere hint of a bridge, receding chin, undersized lower jaw.

THE HANDS, if you open them out flat from their characteristic fist position, have finely lined palms, tissue-paper thin nails, dry, loose-fitting skin, and deep bracelet creases at wrist.

THE TRUNK may startle you in some normal detail: short neck, small sloping shoulders, swollen breasts, large rounded abdomen, umbilical stump (future navel), slender, narrow pelvis and hips.

GENITALS of both sexes will seem large (especially scrotum) in comparison with the scale of, for example, the hands to adult size.

THE LEGS are most often seen drawn up against the abdomen in prebirth position. Extended legs measure shorter than you would expect compared to the arms. The knees stay slightly bent, and legs are more or less bowed.

THE FEET look more complete than they are. X-ray would show only one real bone of the heel. Other bones are now cartilage. Skin often loose and wrinkly.

WEIGHT unless well above the average of 6 or 7 pounds will not prepare you for how really tiny newborn is. Top-to-toe measure: anywhere between 18 and 21 inches.

THE SKIN is thin and dry. You may see veins through it. Fair skin may be rosy red temporarily. Downy hair is not unusual.

FIG. 4-4 ***What a healthy week-old baby looks like.***
Photograph from Ingalls, A.J., & Salerno, M.C. Maternal and child health nursing *[2nd ed.]. St. Louis: The C.V. Mosby Co., 1971; description from Birch, W.G.* A doctor discusses pregnancy. *Chicago: Budlong Press Co., 1963.*

50% to about 75 cm (30 in.) in 12 months.

The newborn baby has a coating or protective layer of vernix over the skin that dries and rubs off in a few days; peeling hands and feet are therefore usual. Rose pink or purplish, mottled skin is common with the new baby. The fingers and toes often look blue and will be cold until the baby's circulation pattern is regulated. The bones are soft and cartilaginous, and the total muscular equipment of the newborn infant weighs less than one fourth of its entire body (Latham et al., 1977).

Behavioral characteristics of the neonate

The most common behavior noted in newborn babies is sleep. For the first few days they seem to exist in a nearly continuous twilight state of being. The neonate sleeps, dozes, or cries approximately 90% of the time. By the fourth week this figure drops to about 79% (Wolff, 1973). Neonatal sleep is broken by short waking periods, which occur every 2 or 3 hours, with fewer and shorter waking periods during the night than during the day. As an infant, the child will sleep as much as is necessary and when necessary. Later, the child will learn the culturally approved patterns of sleep and wakefulness.

A new baby sleeps best directly after eating. Although quickly adjusting to familiar household noises, the infant should have either a special room or an undisturbed corner away from family traffic. A flat firm mattress without a pillow is best. New babies generally waken once or twice during the night for a feeding, but they grow and mature so quickly that they can soon sleep until breakfast time.

During the neonatal period, stimulation of any part of the body tends to activate the entire body. Stimuli such as pain, hunger, or physical discomfort seem to arouse the greatest activity. A wide-awake, hungry neonate is capable of making as many as 50 movements per minute (Tanner, 1970). Newborns need exercise to strengthen their muscles. In their brief wakeful periods they will wave their arms and legs, and before a feeding they become exceedingly active.

Although there is little control of the head movements at birth, early movements of the head and shoulders are basic to the later development of manipulation, posture, perception. Placed on their abdomens on a flat surface, newborns quickly learn to lift their heads and turn them from side to side. Supported in water, they will make swimminglike movements.

Neonates make throaty sounds and can purse their lips. They have an amazing variety of grunts, mews, and sighs. They cry but have no tears at this age. They sneeze to clear the nose of lint, and they yawn when they need extra oxygen. Accomplished young babies can scowl, grimace, and "smile" in a funny uncertain way.

At birth the child has a ready-made capability for learning. This condition is evident in the way an infant can adapt to a feeding schedule. The healthy newborn averages seven to eight feedings in 24 hours and takes 20 to 30 minutes to complete a meal (Caplan, 1981). The interrelationship established between the mother and the child during the first weeks after birth will often determine the type of response the child will have toward eating. The infant who feels maternal impatience or hostility will have more anxiety than the child whose mother is patient. The newborn who is held lovingly every feeding, and especially one who is breastfed, will have a better psychological and physiological start in life. The satisfactions and pleasures a baby gets from feeding affect his or her sense of well-being. Frequent changes in the type of food or manner in which it is given may create problems in learning because the newborn benefits most from some structure, similarity, and routine. It takes the infant 2 or 3 weeks to form a hunger rhythm and to adjust to a regular feeding schedule (Laupres, 1975).

Sensory abilities of the neonate

During the embryonic and fetal stages of life, the sensory mechanisms gradually develop. By the time of birth the senses can function to the extent that they possess survival value. The infant can use the senses to enhance physiological and cognitive well-being.

Vision. At birth the neonate can see. It is not known, however, how clearly. Researchers had assumed that the newborn could not focus the eyes until 3 or 4 weeks of age. Until then, the baby would only see things as a blur. Recently, studies on the vision of neonates have discredited this assumption (Macfarlane, 1977). It is known that soon after birth a baby can respond visually to a moving light. Even on the first day of life a momentary fixation on a near object can be observed. The length of the fixation depends on how awake the infant is.

Sustained fixation on a near object, at about 23 cm (9 in.), is noted by the end of the first week. This is about the same distance the mother's face is from her baby's when she is breast-feeding. There is some suggestion that the baby may be able to look at objects that are between 25 to 50 cm (10 to 20 in.) away, but no nearer or farther. By the end of the month the baby can sustain fixation on more distant objects.

Tom Bower (1976) of the University of Edinburgh filmed the reactions of babies less than 2 weeks old while an object moved toward them at different speeds. As the objects approached, the babies pulled back their heads and put their hands between themselves and the object. He also found that if the object was moving to one side or away from the baby, the child did not react. Another study by Bower involved an optical illusion of an object within reach of the infant. An attempt was made to grasp it. Bower concluded that at least one aspect of the coordination between eye and hand is present at birth. The newborn baby expects to be able to touch objects seen. This observation may have important meaning, as noted later, for the development of the cognitive processes.

A major item related to the beginnings of cognition was studied by Robert Fantz of Case Western Reserve University (Fantz, 1974). He showed a series of babies three flat objects the size and shape of a head. On the first, there was a stylized face, on the second a scrambled face, and on the third a half-white, half-black patch (Fig. 4-5). The babies, regardless of age from 4 days to 6 months, looked the most at the real face and the least at the patch. However, the face may not be the main attraction but rather the complex pattern (Acredolo and Hake, 1982). Development of the ability of the infant to differentiate faces is now a major research concern.

The very young infant is also sensitive to perceiving color. Peeples and Teller (1975) conclude that not only do infants see color but also that brightly colored objects are highly attractive to them. The pupillary reflex, in which the size of the opening of the pupil of the eye reacts to the brightness of light, is well established shortly after birth, as are the protective responses of moving the head, closing the eyelids, and crying. Eye movements generally make use of the gross muscular patterns but not the finer ones. Some children have immature eye muscle development so that one or both eyes may rotate outwardly or inwardly. Eye muscle control is usually gained by 4 weeks of age. Vision improves rapidly. By 6 months most babies can see as clearly as adults (Banks and Salapatek, 1981).

Hearing. While still in the womb, normal babies have been known to respond to musical tones by a

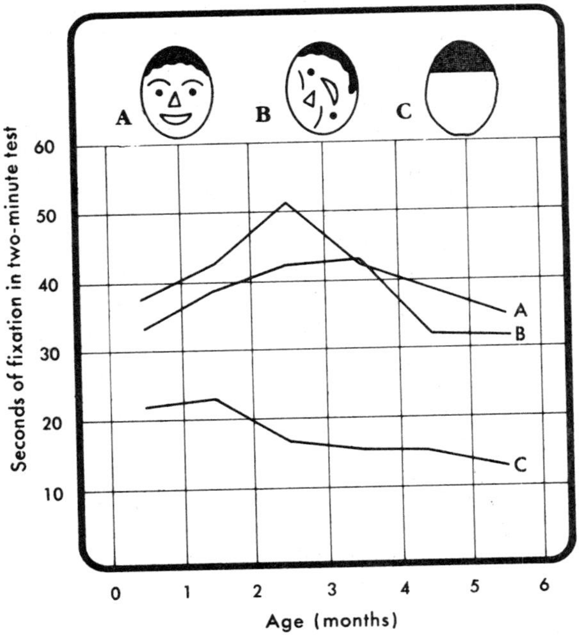

FIG. 4-5 ***These three stimuli were shown to babies from 2 weeks to 6 months of age. All babies preferred to look at the face, A, and scrambled features, B, rather than the black-patched oval, C.***

From Frantz, R.L. The origin of form perception. Scientific American, *1961, 204, 66. Copyright © (1961) by Scientific American, Inc. All rights reserved.*

speeding up of their heartbeats (Macfarlane, 1977). Of all the senses at birth, however, hearing is the least functional because the passages of the ear are not completely open. In some infants hearing acuity is completely lacking because the middle ear is filled with amniotic fluid. It may take several hours to several days for the fluid to drain out. Only then can hearing function normally. With normal hearing the neonate can discriminate between loud and soft sounds but does not respond to variations in pitch (Bench, 1978). The newborn is startled by loud noises but is soothed by a soft, gentle voice or low auditory stimuli.

Eimas (1978) has conducted research to assess an infant's ability to perceive sound differentiations that are important in speech. He concluded that infants are able to discriminate important distinctions in speech signals and are receptive to speech. This ability to respond to fine differences in sound is crucial if the infant is going to respond to speech.

Mendelson and Haith (1976) have attempted to demonstrate a relationship between the visual and auditory capabilities of the newborn infant. They conclude that the infant has the appropriate sensory capabilities and tendencies to begin forming concepts about sight and sound very early in life. They see the infant's tendency to respond to sound by visual scanning as an indication that the young infant is ready to start gathering and processing information from the environment.

Smell, taste, touch. The senses of smell, taste, and touch are all better developed at birth than is sight or hearing. Once the passages of the head are dry, after having been submerged in the prenatal liquid environment, the senses of smell and taste respond fairly well to gross differences in stimuli. Infants can distinguish between different odors such as acetic acid, phenylethyl alcohol, and anise oil and may even try to escape from unpleasant odors by turning their bodies (Sarnat, 1978). Six days after birth, they even are capable of spending more time with their heads turned to a pad that had been placed inside the mother's bra so the baby could become familiar with her odor (Macfarlane, 1975). Two breast pads, one clean and the other from the bra of the infant's mother, were suspended on either side of the infant's head. The neonates spent significantly more time turned toward their own mother's breast pads than toward the clean breast pads.

Most infants react with a feeling of satisfaction to the taste of milk. A sugar solution will cause a sucking that is maintained. The neonate will usually react negatively to unpleasant taste stimuli such as sour, bitter, and salt solutions (Steiner, 1979). It requires a much greater amount of bitterness or sweetness to elicit a discriminatory response in infants than is the case with adults.

The skin of the newborn infant is sensitive to touch, pressure, temperature, and some pain. At the time of

TABLE 4-2 Reflexes of the newborn baby

Effective stimulus	*Reflex*
Tap upper lip sharply	Lips protrude
Tap bridge of nose	Eyes close tightly
Show bright light suddenly to eyes	Eyes close
Clap hands about 45 cm (18 in.) from infant's head	Eyelids close
Touch cornea with light piece of cotton	Eyes close
With baby held on back turn face slowly to right side	Jaw and right arm extend out; left arm flexes
Extend forearms at elbow	Arms flex briskly
Put fingers into infant's hand and press child's palms	Infant's fingers flex and enclose finger
Press thumbs against the ball of infant's feet	Toes flex
Stroke sole of foot starting from toes toward the heels	Big toe bends upward and small toes spread (Babinski's reflex)
Prick soles of feet with pin	Infant's knee and foot flex
Tickle area of corner of mouth	Head turns toward side of stimulation (rooting reflex)
Put index finger into mouth	Sucks
Hold infant in air, stomach down	Infant attempts to lift head and extends legs

Modified from Caplan, F. *The first twelve months of life.* Princeton, N.J.: The Princeton Center for Infancy and Early Childhood, 1981.

rooting reflex a reflex that is most easily elicited during the baby's first 2 weeks of life, consisting of the baby turning the head in the direction of any object that gently stimulates the corner of the mouth; the newborn infant's involuntary movement of the mouth toward any source of stimulation in the mouth area.

birth, sensitivity to pain is lessened so that the baby will not feel its effects while passing through the birth canal. Responses to pain increase about 2 days after birth. Certain parts of the body, namely the lips, eyelashes, soles of the feet, skin of the forehead, and the mucous membrane of the nose are more sensitive than are other parts. The neonate can react to differences in temperature, as is shown by differentiated sucking reactions to changes of temperature of its milk. Cold stimuli produce quicker and more pronounced reactions than do heat stimuli (Yang and Douthitt, 1974). Infants also respond with signs of discomfort to temperatures above or below normal and especially to extremes of cold.

Body movements and reflexes of neonates

Motor development is not a process that begins at the time of birth, but rather, it has its origins in the prenatal period. During the second month of prenatal development, the muscles begin to take shape. By the end of the third month they are developed to the degree that spontaneous movements of arms, legs, shoulders, and fingers are possible. By the fourteenth week the human fetus is capable of producing almost all the reflex responses of a newborn infant. Some reflexes will be vital for survival; other reflexes will function merely as general protective measures. The remainder of the prenatal period is spent in perfecting these movements. Initial diffused mass activities of the organism become more integrated and specific with maturation. Reflexes of the newborn baby are listed in Table 4-2.

Just as with the fetus during prenatal life, the development of the neonate during postnatal life largely follows the cephalocaudal and proximodistal directions of growth. Functions appear and develop earliest in the infant's head and neck, then in the shoulders and upper trunk, and later in the lower trunk and legs. The direction of this sequence is obvious to the observer and is a result of maturation. The newborn baby lacks voluntary coordinated motor control (Caplan, 1981). Neonatal reflex activity is subcortical in origin and so is not voluntary.

Mouth and throat response. From birth the neonate is capable of opening and closing the mouth. One of the earliest of the various lip movements is sucking. The sucking response can be elicited by light pressure on the cheeks or by touching above or below the side of the lips. This response is the ***rooting reflex*** shown in Fig. 4-6. Swallowing usually follows the sucking movements. Infants less than 2 weeks old show that they are able to discriminate between the intake of milk or air (Crook, 1979). When sucking milk, the neonate swallows it; when sucking air, there is no swallowing movement.

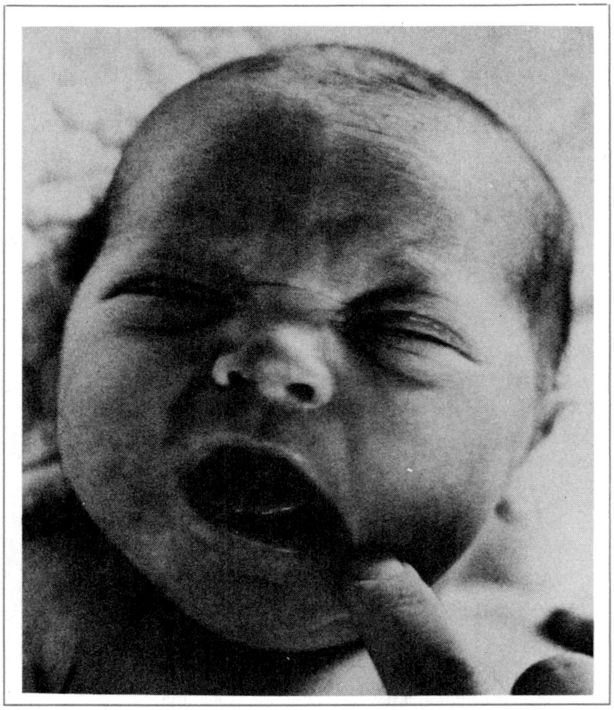

FIG. 4-6 *Rooting reflex. Rooting reflex is apparent when corner of newborn infant's mouth is touched. Bottom lip lowers on same side; tongue moves toward stimulus.*
Courtesy Mead Johnson & Co., Evansville, Ind.

When the newborn infant cries, there is much mass body activity such as rolling the head, opening the mouth wide, jerking and twisting the body, throwing the arms about, and kicking the legs. Other mouth and throat responses present in the neonate are sneezing, coughing, yawning, thumb-sucking, hiccoughing, vomiting, holding the breath, and rejecting things from the mouth.

Head and arm movements. Neonates have the ability to move the head up and down as well as to the left and right. They cannot hold the head in midposition, however. They move their arms a great deal. They flex them, extend them, randomly move them about in different directions, throw them over their chest, and move the hands and fingers. The newborn baby can also grasp a rod or a finger placed in the hand and hold onto it. Many babies are able to support their weight by the grasping reflex when holding onto a rod. This grasping reflex, also known as the *Darwinian reflex,* later diminishes and is replaced in about 3 months by the voluntary grasp (Caplan, 1981).

Moro's reflex the newborn infant's involuntary response to having the head fall backward—arms are stretched outward and brought together over the chest in a grasp gesture. A reflex that is most easily elicited during the infant's first 3 months of life.

startle response a reaction to stimuli in infants outwardly characterized by eye widening, jaw dropping, cooing, squealing, or crying and inwardly characterized by changes in heart rate, respiration, and galvanic skin potential.

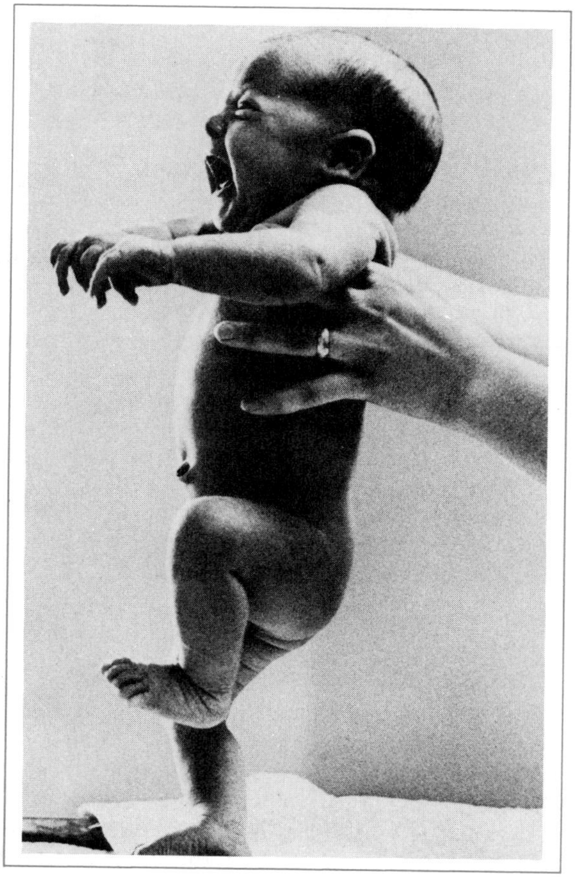

FIG. 4-7 ***Walking reflex. Walking reflex is phase of neuromuscular maturity from which infant normally graduates after 3 or 4 weeks. If infant is held so that sole of foot touches table, reciprocal flexion and extension of leg occur, simulating walking.***
Courtesy Mead Johnson & Co., Evansville, Ind.

Trunk and leg movements. Newborns are capable of only a few trunk movements, since the back is lacking in muscular support. They are able to arch the back and twist the body, but only to a slight degree. The movements in the neonate's legs, feet, and toes are characterized by flexing, extending, kicking, jerking, rotating, rolling, or trembling. The *Babinski reflex,* the upward and fanning movement of the toes, is observed when the bottoms of the neonate's feet are stroked. When the neonate is held upright so that the feet barely touch a flat surface, the infant will lift one leg. This is the *walking reflex,* as shown in Fig. 4-7.

When in a resting or sleeping position, the infant will usually have legs flexed, fists closed, upper arms out straight from the shoulders with forearms flexed at right angles parallel to the head. The infant who is frightened by a loud noise, such as that caused by someone's hand hitting a table top, will throw arms apart, spread fingers, extend legs, and throw the head back. This reaction is the ***Moro's reflex*** or ***startle response*** (Fig. 4-8). The response is basically symmetrical. It will disappear by the age of 3 or 4 months. Persistence of the entire Moro response beyond 3 or 4

A B C

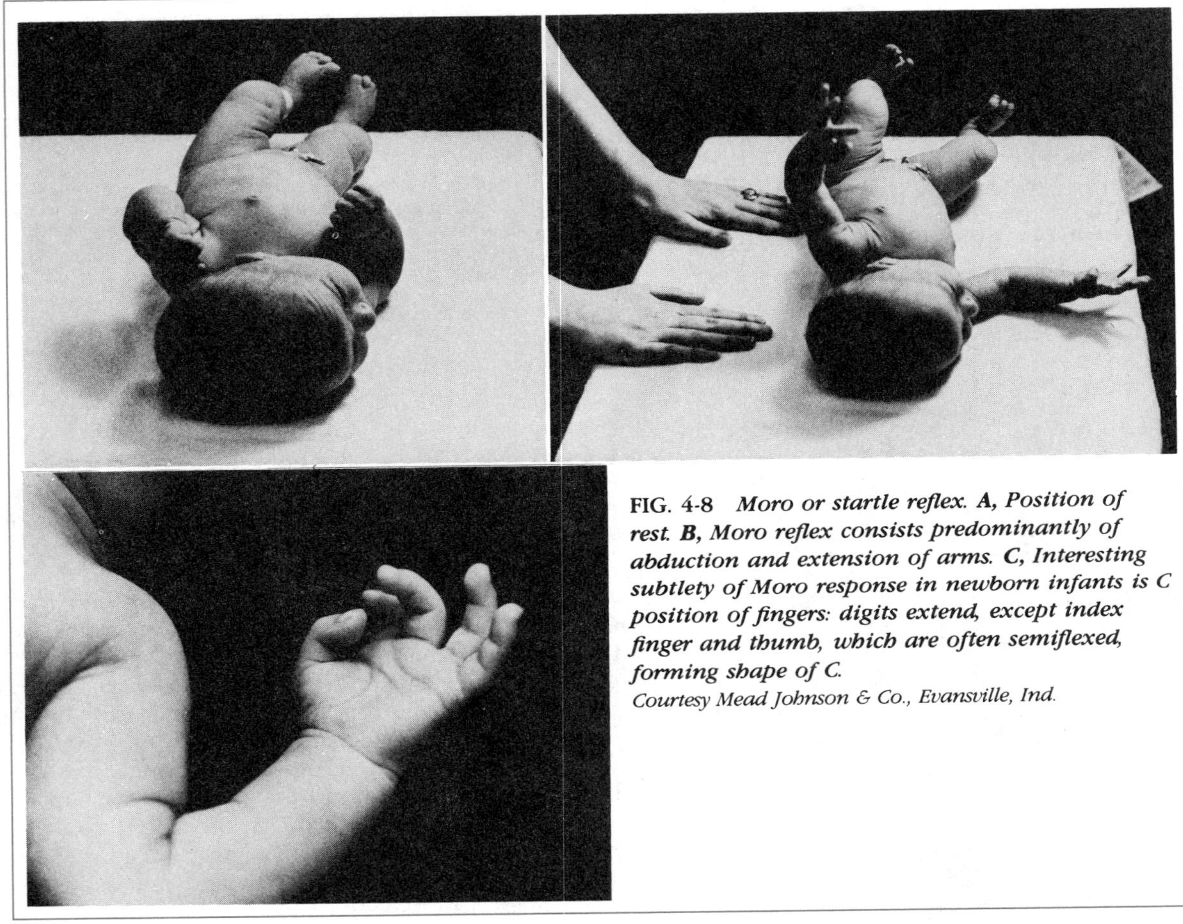

FIG. 4-8 ***Moro or startle reflex. A, Position of rest. B, Moro reflex consists predominantly of abduction and extension of arms. C, Interesting subtlety of Moro response in newborn infants is C position of fingers: digits extend, except index finger and thumb, which are often semiflexed, forming shape of C.***
Courtesy Mead Johnson & Co., Evansville, Ind.

months is considered a sign of delay in neurological development.

In conclusion, it is evident that the neonate has the foundations, although very primitive, for the development of many sensory and motor activities that will need to be performed in the growth and cognitive processes. This new baby—so fresh, so recently from the mother's womb—already has some capacity to see, hear, smell, taste, feel a touch, and respond with reflexive motor behavior. It is truly amazing when one considers the potentialities with which this neonate comes into the outside world. May those potentialities develop to their utmost. And may there be caretakers present who will nourish this child with tender, loving care and with verbal, sensory, and motor stimulation so that the human potentials present may be realized to their fullest. Most of all, may this child grow surrounded by love, beauty, and a sense of excitement, anticipation, and learning.

CHAPTER REVIEW

1. In preparing for birth, the first step is a complete physical examination of the mother to make certain that her circulatory and respiratory systems can provide the blood and oxygen the developing fetus will need and that no other physical abnormalities exist that could interfere with the pregnancy and the birth process.
2. The *estimated date of delivery* (EDD) is determined by counting back 3 months from the first day of the last menstrual period and adding 7 days plus 1 year.
3. According to Grantly Dick-Read, *natural childbirth* refers to the preparation of the mother and father for labor and delivery and includes their active involvement in the childbirth process. His program includes prenatal health care, a childbearing and birth education program, and the teaching of breathing techniques, exercises, and passive relaxation images in order to reduce fear and pain. Giving birth is a natural process for the mother. She should have no fear.
4. The *Lamaze method* is a widely known program of prepared childbirth. It is similar to the Dick-Read natural childbirth program in that it stresses education in the pregnancy and birth process, breathing and relaxation techniques, and exercises to tighten the abdominal muscles. It differs from Dick-Read in that Lamaze recognizes the possible need for anesthesia. The emphasis is on the needs and well-being of the body, not on the performance of the mother.
5. The *Leboyer approach* to delivery room practices seeks to make the transition from the womb to the outside world as gentle as possible by controlling conditions outside the mother's body so that they approximate conditions inside the body. Temperature, sound, and light intensity are controlled; there is no hurry to cut the unbilical cord; and the baby is bathed in water close to 37° C (98.7° F). The results are supposed to be a more tranquil, serene, and calm baby and child. Although the research does not support that contention, mothers who experience it believe the Leboyer approach made a difference in them and in the child.
6. The signs of *labor* are (a) rhythmic contractions that grow in intensity, (b) the appearance of a blood-tinged discharge, and (c) usually, the rupture of the amniotic sac, releasing a clear fluid.
7. The *first stage of labor* is the period of rhythmic and regular labor contractions that increase in intensity. The contractions dilate the cervix, making the opening about 10 cm (4 in.) so the baby can pass through. The *second stage of labor* is the actual delivery. The *third stage*, about 20 minutes after delivery, is the expulsion of the afterbirth.
8. Anesthetics used at birth may be general or local. General anesthesia puts the mother to sleep. A local will only anesthetize a particular spot or region. A *saddle block* and a *caudal block* are regional. A *pudendal block* is very local. The pudendal block is preferred by mothers who want to fully participate in the delivery of the child.
9. A *vertex* or head presentation is the most common type of delivery. A *breech birth* is the appearance of the buttocks first. There are also shoulder, legs, and face-first deliveries. A *cesarean delivery* is an operation involving an incision in the abdomen and the uterine wall. Forceps are instruments that may be used to aid with a vaginal delivery. An *induced delivery* is one in which medication, usually oxytocin, is given the mother so that the delivery process will take place.
10. The *Apgar scale* is used to assess the well-being of the infant at birth. Five factors are measured for a total of 10 points. The assessment is done at the end of 1 minute and at 5 minutes. A score of 7 to 10 points is good, 5 or 6 points is marginal, and 4 points or lower requires immediate special attention.
11. *Phenylketonuria (PKU)* is a defect in an enzyme that will affect the metabolism of food proteins. If not detected, it will cause severe mental retardation. It can be corrected and, many times, outgrown if a proper diet is started early enough. *Anoxia* is a deficiency of oxygen to the body and the brain. Brain cells will be affected if oxygen is not supplied regularly. There are a wide variety of mental and physical defects that can be present at birth. The table in Appendix A presents many of these. The important thing to remember, however, is that 97 out of every 100 babies born have no disfiguring or disabling defects.
12. The *premature* or *low birth weight* baby is at higher risk for survival than a full-term baby. About 7% of all births are premature. With good care the majority of premature and low birth weight babies live and become free of any limitation the prematurity may have imposed at birth.
13. *Neonate* is the name given to the newborn babies for the first weeks after birth. Circumstances and conditions exist that make this period a difficult and a very special time in life. Particular care and attention are needed for the baby. The weight of the newborn baby is about 3 to 3.5 kg (7 to 7½ lb) on the average and the length is 50 to 51 cm (20 to 20½ in.). Boy babies are slightly larger than girls. The head for both sexes seems too large for the size of the body. The neonate sleeps about 90% of the time at first, dropping off to 79% by the fourth week. There is very little motor control when the infant is awake.

14. At the time of birth the neonate has a capacity to learn. By the end of the first week the baby is conditioned to feeding times. Mother-infant interaction is very important at this time to establish a good psychological and physiological start in life.
15. The neonate can respond to visual stimuli soon after birth, can sustain some fixation by 1 week, and responds to distinct faces rather than scrambled faces. After the channels of the head are freed from the amniotic fluid, the neonate can discriminate between a loud sound and a soft sound, between a high-pitch and a low-pitch sound. Smell, taste, and response to touch are developed in the neonate but only to the point of being able to differentiate between gross degrees of stimuli rather than fine discriminations.
16. There are a number of motor reflex actions present in the newborn. The *sucking reflex* is most important because the neonate needs to be able to suck in order to eat. The *rooting reflex* enables the baby to turn its head in the direction of a touch on the face in order to find a nipple. The purpose of the *Babinski reflex* (fanning of the toes when the sole of the foot is stroked), the *Moro or startle reflex* when a loud noise is made, or the *walking reflex* when baby's feet touch a flat surface, is not well documented. However, their absence, as well as the absence of any of the reflexes, has serious neurological implications.

REVIEW QUESTIONS

1. What is included in a physical examination of a pregnant woman? Give the purpose of each part of the examination.
2. How is the estimated date of delivery determined? Why does one approach give 280 days and another 276 days for the duration of the pregnancy?
3. Why is a prepared or educated birth program important for the mother?
4. Describe Grantly Dick-Read's natural childbirth program. What is meant by an "emphasis on the performance of the mother"?
5. Describe the Lamaze method of prepared childbirth. How is relaxation obtained? What are the different types of breathing techniques and at what points in the labor process are they used? What part does the father play in the Lamaze method? Does the Lamaze approach advocate anesthesia? Under what conditions?
6. In anesthesia, what is the difference between a general and a local anesthetic?
7. Describe a saddle block, a caudal block, and a pudendal block.
8. List the three signs of labor.
9. Describe the types of contractions that occur during the first stage of true labor. What is the purpose of the contractions? According to Lamaze, what are the mother and her coach (the father) supposed to do during the contractions?
10. What happens during the second stage of labor?
11. What happens during the third stage of labor? How long does the entire labor and birth process usually take?
12. Define each of the following: a vertex presentation, a breech birth, a cesarean birth, the use of forceps, and induced labor.
13. What are the five parts of the Apgar Scale? What do the scores of 9, 6, and 3 mean?
14. What is PKU?
15. Why is anoxia dangerous?
16. Describe spina bifida, Down's syndrome, and cystic fibrosis. Look at the table of birth defects in Appendix A. Pay special attention to how many children out of every 100 are born with these defects.
17. Discuss the significance of premature birth and a low birth weight. What is the meaning of each one? What conditions exist because of them? Are the conditions permanent?
18. What is a neonate?
19. Describe what a newborn baby looks like. Review Fig. 4-4.
20. List at least five physical characteristics of a newborn.
21. List at least five behavioral characteristics of a newborn.
22. What can the newborn see? How well can the newborn see?
23. How good is a newborn's hearing, sense of smell, taste, and touch? What do all of these sensory capabilities say to you about a newborn baby's ability to respond to environmental factors?
24. Look at Table 4-3 on the reflexes of the newborn baby. How many of these reflexes does a person of your age have? How do you explain the difference between the reflexes you have and the ones the neonate has?

THOUGHT QUESTIONS AND ACTIVITIES

1. Consider natural childbirth, the Lamaze method, the Leboyer approach, and other "prepared childbirth" programs. What is to be gained by the use of these approaches? Talk to mothers and fathers who have had babies delivered under any of these conditions. Better yet, invite them to talk to the class. How do you feel about what they experienced? Do they tend to agree on the feelings?
2. If possible, arrange to visit a "prepared childbirth class," a maternity ward, or "birthing room" in a hospital. (The last two places may be "off limits" to visitors.) Perhaps one or two students may have the opportunity to visit someone who just had a baby. What are your observations and impressions?
3. What educational, social, economic, physical, and material preparations should a mother and father make for the

coming of a new baby?

4. Should mentally retarded adults, social criminals, or handicapped people have children?
5. Imagine a newborn baby before being brought home from the hospital. How helpless is this infant? After 2 or 3 weeks, is there anything at all that this baby can do for or by himself or herself? Consider self-care, feedings, body movements, communication, speech and language, emotional responses, socializing gestures, intellectual responses, and personality characteristics.
6. Talk about the type of research procedure that a professional might use to study the capabilities of newborn babies. How would you know if they can see, hear, smell, taste or sense a touch?

FURTHER READINGS

Caplan, F. *The first twelve months of life.* New York: Bantam Books, 1981. Caplan makes good use of the research findings in his easy-to-read, well-illustrated, and well-written account of each of the first 12 months of life.

Fischel, J. E. The organization of human newborn sucking and movement during auditory stimulation. *Infant Behavior and Development,* 1982, *5*(1), 45-61. This is one of the more recent research studies on the nature of neonatal behavior during sucking and during pausing (not sucking). The two activities respond in different ways to auditory stimulation.

Leboyer, F. *Birth without violence.* New York: Alfred A. Knopf, 1975. This book describes the procedures advocated by Leboyer for reducing the shock of birth for the baby.

Ragozin, A. S., et al. Effects of maternal age on parenting role. *Developmental Psychology,* 1982, *18*:4, 627-634. This study examines the proposition that maternal age (young or old) influences parental role performance and satisfaction.

Siegel, L. S., et al. Predictors of development in preterm and full-term infants: A model for detecting the at risk child. *Journal of Pediatric Psychology,* 1982, *7*(2), 135-148. This model appears promising for the detection of infants at risk for developmental problems. Factors predicting developmental delay include socioeconomic status and parental education, maternal cigarette smoking, number of previous pregnancies, and degree of anoxia or respiratory distress.

von Hofsten, C. Eye-hand coordination in the newborn. *Developmental Psychology,* 1982, *18*(3), 450-461. This research concluded that there exists in the newborn a rudimentary eye-hand coordination, the primary function of which is attentional rather than manipulative.

CHAPTER 5

INFANCY: MOTOR DEVELOPMENT AND COGNITION

"SHE'S WALKING!"

Observing my daughter Audrey learning to walk was a most fascinating experience. The process of "locomotion" actually started when she was in her crib. She would crawl from one end to the other. Soon she yearned for more room and tried to crawl through the posts of the crib. Eventually she was allowed to crawl on the living-room floor. With much struggle and strain she could sometimes traverse the living room in the amazing time of two minutes. She started out by using a method that made her look like a frog in water. It was a completely uncoordinated attempt at locomotion. Soon she graduated to kneeling and leaning on her palms, and thus she would creep. This seemed like a most efficacious way to get across the room and pleased her greatly. After each successful venture I tried to give her some kind of reinforcement, be it a kiss or some other type of reinforcer.

Eventually her creeping became a means to an end. Before, she was content to creep for the sake of creeping, but now her creeping was goal directed. When she set out on an expedition, her purpose was usually to crawl over to a small coffee table that she could grasp onto. Like an acrobat she would, without hesitation, pull herself up until she was standing. Of course, once she got up she did not know what to do for an encore. She just stood there for a few moments and then realized that she was in trouble. She was too scared to leave the table, but she did not know how to get back down. In a few moments she would summon our help by a loud wail.

After a few weeks she simply let herself drop to the floor. On hitting the floor, she immediately began to laugh. Often I wanted to stop her, but my wife always intervened. She thought that this was natural and that we should not stop her. Of course, there were no injuries, and she soon graduated to her next level of development. Instead of dropping down when she would get adjacent to the table, she would gradually descend. Slowly her knees would bend, and she would lower herself onto the floor.

This up-and-down activity lasted for about a month; then something happened. On certain occasions she would get herself up and then release her grip on the table. With great timidity she would stand about six inches away from the table. After about 30 seconds of this she grabbed the table and descended. In no time at all she was taking a step or two away from the table. After a few steps she would lower herself to the floor. The next great achievement occurred when she would take a few additional steps and then fall down. All these precursors of actual walking lasted until about the thirteenth month.

Then it happened! Without any fanfare she just started to walk. It was one of life's greatest moments for me—one that is indelibly marked in my mind. I was talking on the telephone while Audrey was holding onto a chair in the kitchen. Always liking telephones, she apparently wanted to play with the telephone that I was using. Without any hesitation she let go of her support and started to cross the kitchen, a distance of about 20 feet. At first I thought that she would take a few steps and fall to the ground as she had been doing. Holding her hands out for balance, like an acrobat on a high wire, she started to cross the room. Wavering from side to side, but regaining her balance each time, she actually crossed the room. I must have been in a state of shock as I saw her walking for the first time because no words came out of my mouth. The person to whom I was talking on the phone must have thought that I had dropped dead because my silence lasted at least 30 seconds. Finally I was able to shout, "She's walking, Audrey is walking!" In about another month she began to walk freely. As walking ability increased, so did her confidence.

IN THIS CHAPTER . . .

You will read about

1. The developmental tasks of infancy as presented by Havighurst and Erikson.
2. The tests and assessment instruments that are used to measure the progress that infants are making in growth and development.
3. Three of the basic routines that must be established during infancy: stabilizing a sleep pattern, developing a feeding schedule, and creating a schedule for toilet training.
4. The way in which control of motor functions, such as sitting, walking, and grasping, takes place.
5. The growth of the intellectual (cognitive) processes in infancy, from responding only by reflexes to showing signs of intellectual thinking.
6. The ways the infant learns.

autonomy versus shame and doubt according to Eriksonian theory, the second nuclear conflict of personality development.

trust versus mistrust the first stage in Erikson's eight-stage theory of development, in which the infant develops either the comfortable feeling that those around him care for his needs or the worry that his needs will not be taken care of.

There is a very fine line between the time when neonatal development is completed and infant development begins. The neonatal period is a very special period of development but, in truth, it is basically a transitional period from the time of birth until the child's physiological systems are sufficiently stabilized so that they can operate effectively and efficiently. The point at which physiological stability arrives differs for each child. The average time is about 2 weeks. It is at this time that the growth and development of infancy begins in earnest. However, it must be kept in mind that the physiological and perceptual systems that had their beginnings during the neonatal period keep right on developing. The only difference is that the child's neurological system has matured to the point that the other systems can function with a better degree of certainty.

DEVELOPMENTAL TASKS

In the initial stages of life, much of the development will be physical and maturational in nature. This means that the rate of the sequential, unfolding of the species-specific patterns of development—physical and motor in particular—will be greatly dependent on the relative speed with which the central nervous system (CNS) develops. Motor functions are greatly dependent on the functional level of the CNS for readiness to perform motor control. The direction of growth will be cephalocaudal and proximodistal (see Chapter 1). The infant will learn to control the head and eyes before the trunk. The child will be able to point to objects before he or she can grasp them with thumb and forefinger.

Havighurst: Developmental tasks

There are several developmental tasks that the child must achieve before reaching the *second* birthday. With the accomplishment of each task, the infant becomes a more competent individual, preparing for independent living. According to Havighurst (1972), the developmental tasks for infancy are (1) to achieve physiological stability, especially in the coordination of eyes, sleep rhythm, and hunger rhythm, (2) to walk and to control the use of fine muscles, (3) to gain at least partial control of bowel and bladder functions, (4) to acquire the foundations of speech and language, to begin to communicate, and to understand language, (5) to learn to eat solid foods, and (6) to begin to relate emotionally to parents and siblings.

Considering how physically helpless this little infant is at birth and recognizing how much most children can do by the time they are 2 years of age, we submit that a tremendous amount of learning will have taken place in such a short time. There is probably more learning taking place in the first 2 years of life than at any other time period.

Erikson: Psychosocial tasks

Erikson (1963a) also presents some tasks that must be faced during infancy. He refers to them as *psychosocial crises.* He postulates that the inherent drives in humans lead them to confront a series of personal conflicts. The way in which the conflicts are resolved will have an influence on the developing personality. The psychosocial crisis faced during the first year of life is that of ***trust versus mistrust.*** The issue is one of the infant developing trust in the caretaker(s). Trust of people depends on the quality of care and love received during this age. Failure to achieve trust leads to mistrust. The question that the infant has to answer is, "Can I or can I not trust others?"

The second of Erikson's psychosocial crises comes during the second year of life. It is the issue of ***autonomy versus shame and doubt.*** Autonomy implies being able to do things for oneself or "being in charge of my actions." During this stage the infant is learning to do things independently. New motor and cognitive skills are being developed. If the child is restricted in learning by an overprotective parent who rushes to do everything for the child, anticipating every need and desire, or if the parent is constantly shaming the child by stressing the mess that was made by saying, "Don't touch that!" shame and doubt result. The child won-

TABLE 5-1 Representative items from the fiftieth percentile for each month

4 months Turns head toward sound of bell Complete thumb apposition Defensive hand motions to paper placed lightly on face	6 months Exploratory manipulation of spoon Looks for fallen object Reacts to mirror image
9 months Lifts inverted cup and secures cube placed under it Releases cube in cup Holding two cubes, accepts a third (without dropping any)	12 months Builds tower of three cubes Spontaneously scribbles when given paper and pencil Walks unsupported
18 months Builds tower of four cubes Points to two or more parts of body Asks for things by words	24 months Imitatively builds a three-block bridge Uses color names Gives full name and sex

ders, "Can I do things for myself?" or "Should I feel ashamed of some of my newfound skills?"

INFANT ASSESSMENT

Arnold Gesell was a pioneer in the research of infant development. He considered the formative preschool time of life to be the most consequential period of development. The infant learns to see, to hear, to handle objects, to walk, to comprehend, and to talk. The child acquires a number of habits fundamental to the complex art of living. Gesell was interested in determining and assessing those processes of growth.

Gesell Developmental Schedules

The Gesell Developmental Schedules (Gesell, 1940) cover the ages of 4 weeks to 6 years, with special emphasis on the period of infancy. Four general fields are measured: (1) *motor behavior,* including postural control, locomotion, prehension, and others, (2) *language behavior,* assessing vocabulary, word comprehension, conversation, and reproduction, (3) *adaptive behavior,* comprising a number of items such as eye-hand coordination, imitation, comprehension, and number conception, and (4) *personal and social behavior,* involving reactions to persons and such matters as personal habits and play responses. Sample items are given in Table 5-1. All of the items were standardized in the Yale Child Development Clinic, but with only a sample of 107 infants, primarily middle class and of northern European ancestry (Yang, 1979).

In 1966 Knoblock and Pasamanick (1966) reported high correlations between the Gesell scales and scores on the Stanford-Binet Intelligence Scale. However, the scales do *not* measure intelligence; they measure total development (Yang, 1979). Gesell was aware of the interplay of genetic and environmental influences, but he saw development to be primarily the result of a maturational unfolding process; the learning process was not considered to be a major factor in the early months or years. Clinical judgment becomes important. As such, the scales are somewhat subjective.

Bayley Scales of Infant Development

Bayley's infant scales (Bayley, 1969) were developed and improved over a long period of time. Initially, she relied heavily on Gesell's items, but she strengthened her scales by standardizing the scores on a large normative group. Her population sample of 1,262 term and normal infants was stratified by sex, color, rural or urban residence, and education of the head of the household. However, she also used a sizable number of infants whose fathers were professional individuals or college students.

The Bayley scales have a mental scale and a motor

A dreary place would be this earth
Were there no little people in it;
The song of life would lose it mirth
Were there no babies to begin it.

scale. The mental scale ranges from 2 months to 30 months; performance is expressed as a mental development index. The motor scale also covers the same age range and produces a psychomotor development index. Bayley notes, however, that intelligence is an emergent function, taking different forms at different periods of development. Bayley considered the development of intelligence to come about as a natural or logical consequence of the interaction of genetic and environmental factors.

Denver Developmental Screening Test

A very widely used screening device for infants and preschool children is the Denver Developmental Screening Test (Frankenburg and Dodds, 1967). The Denver test does not try to measure intelligence. It is a screening device that seeks to detect those children who are not developing normally. There are four categories of items: (1) personal social, (2) fine motor adaptive, (3) language, and (4) gross motor. The age range covered is from 1 month to 6 years.

normative data based on averages, standards, values, or norms.

standard deviation a statistical technique for expressing the extent of variation of a group of scores from the mean. It is a distance on a curve of probability, of which the first unit in both directions from the mean includes 68.3% of the total group of scores. About 99.7% of the scores are within three standard deviations in each direction from the mean.

A child must pass a specific test at an age when 90% of children of the same age ordinarily pass. If the child fails, this is considered to be a developmental delay. A child who has two or more delays in two or more categories is considered to be in need of special attention. Personal social items at 9 months include resisting the pulling away of a toy, playing peek-a-boo, and working to reach a toy that is out of range; only about 50% can play pat-a-cake. On the language test, 90% of 11-month-olds are supposed to be able to say dada or mama (with meaning); not quite 25% of 9-month-olds can do so. A limitation of the Denver Developmental Screening Test is that its norms are based only on white, middle-class children.

Uzgiris and Hunt scales

A Piagetian approach to infant assessment was developed by Uzgiris and Hunt (1975). Piaget believed that the traditional approach to infant scales was largely in error because of an emphasis on how much an infant could do on a particular task. According to Piaget, development was not just a matter of maturation. Although the initial stages of growth were based on reflex actions, later growth was an integration of internal processes and physical coordination, bound definitely to an involvement with the environment. Growth was both horizontal and vertical and, essentially, a method employed in problem solving.

The Uzgiris and Hunt assessment procedure makes use of six scales based on Piaget's theory of cognitive development. The scales include (1) visual pursuit and permanence of objects, (2) development of means for obtaining desired actions or events, (3) development of imitation, (4) development of anticipatory behavior, (5) appreciation of three-dimensional space, and (6) development of ways of relating to objects (toys) in the environment. The scales reflect cognitive development, even though cognitive growth may be uneven. Although some impressive results have been claimed for these Piaget-based scales (Wachs, 1975), the research is too limited, compared to the work done by Gesell and Bayley, to warrant major comparative conclusions. The impact of the Uzgiris and Hunt scales is that they introduce a different approach to the assessment of infant development.

Conclusions on infant assessment

The general conclusion of the effectiveness of infancy assessment techniques is that, although the assessment results may be somewhat appropriate for the age when the infant was tested, the results, for the most part, have little predictive value for later in life (Yang, 1979). The basic question answered is "How is the infant developing at this moment?" The assessment instrument used indicates what was measured.

Gesell, Bayley, and the Denver scales survey development based more or less on maturational factors. Bayley did at least conceive of intelligence as being emergent and functionally unique at different periods. The Uzgiris and Hunt scales were constructed from the viewpoint that qualitative changes in intelligence, and not maturation, characterize growth. The different approaches suggest the many-sided aspects of human growth and development that must be considered. Is growth based on maturation, cognitive development, or both?

An important observation must be made in the use of any kind of assessment of development. Most scales, such as the Gesell, Bayley, and Denver Developmental Scales, present ***normative data.*** These figures indicate the average development for the population of children (or adults) measured. These norms do not attempt to describe an individual child's development but rather the average development of a group of children. The norm given is for the middle of the group. The concept of "average" in a normal distribution of the population would include 34% of the individuals to each side of the norm given as average. This statistical measure is called a ***standard deviation.*** This means that the 34% to the left of the norm and the 34% to the right of the norm are part of the average group. Therefore, if a chart indicates that the average infant begins to crawl at 5 months, that norm represents only the middle score of the group. The range of the average age of crawling must cover a period earlier and later than 5 months in order to include 68% of the group. (See Chapter 1 on Myths, stereotypes, and statistics.) If a child deviates from the normal range covering the 68%, something may be interfering with the usual development.

Uzgiris and Hunt (1975) suggest that ordinal scales may be more useful than normative scales if what we want to know is how much the child has developed. ***Ordinal scales*** assess where the child is in the sequence of development; they are not based on age. The rationale is that children develop at different rates but that the sequence is basically the same. If you know where a child is in the sequential pattern, you know what should come next. This knowledge is useful in working with children who may have physical, mental, or environmental handicaps interfering with development. Educational or stimulation programs can be provided to help the child progress to the next phase in the sequence of development.

ordinal scale a ranking device that indicates the order of development in a series.

DEVELOPMENT OF BASIC ROUTINES

Developing physiological stability is the first order of business for the neonate. Then comes the task of regulating the daily routine. The schedule to which the baby gets accustomed after delivery in the hospital usually changes somewhat after the homecoming. A period of transition from one routine to another usually takes a while. Some babies adjust within a few days; others may take as long as a month to adapt to a new environment and life-style.

Sleep patterns

Sleep patterns change as the neonate and infant gets older, probably reflecting changes in the developing neural organization (Salamy and McKean, 1976). Newborn infants sleep approximately 18 out of each 24 hours (Berg et al., 1973). The neonate usually drifts in and out of sleep around the clock, with the longest sleep averaging about 4½ hours. Some neonates do sleep a little more at night than during the day.

A month-old baby will sleep more than anything else, will cry more than be active, and will divide the small amount of time awake between being drowsy and being alert. While the eyes may be shut, the infant will actually be awake and can receive and respond to stimulation (Clifton and Nelson, 1976).

The various states of sleep and arousal and the infant's general behavior during these states have been classified by researchers. Apparently, the young infant has periods of quiet sleep and active sleep. Anders et al. (1971) suggest that these states are the beginnings of dreaming. Anders and his co-workers have record-

TABLE 5-2 States of arousal

State or degree of arousal	*Characteristic behavior*
Regular sleep	Regular breathing. Very little body movement present. Will not respond to mild stimulation.
Irregular sleep	Breathing becomes irregular and body movement increases as infant makes the transition from regular sleep. More easily aroused by external stimuli.
Drowsiness	Infant shows little motor activity but is sensitive to external stimulation.
Alert inactivity	After basic needs are catered to, the infant seems alert, relaxed, and may become attentive toward specific stimuli.
Waking activity	Diffuse activity provoked by a mild state of physiological need. Soft whimperings and gentle movements gradually becoming louder and more spastic.
Crying	Thrashing about. Loud crying or screeching because of noxious stimuli or a cycle of motility, suggesting that the more sensitive infants become, the more they'll cry, and the more they cry, the more sensitive they become.

Modified from Wolff, P.H. The causes, controls, and organization of behavior in the neonate. *Psychological Issues,* 1966, 5:1, 1-105.

rapid eye movement (REM) a type of eye movement that occurs during a certain period of sleep and that is accompanied by changes in respiratory, muscle, and brain-wave activity.

ed the distinctive brain-wave pattern associated with dreaming. Wolff (1973) has classified the various states of sleep and arousal as (1) regular sleep, (2) irregular sleep, (3) drowsiness, (4) alert inactivity, (5) waking activity, and (6) crying. Generalizations concerning the characteristics of these states of sleep and arousal are presented in Table 5-2.

As the weeks go by, infants increase the time they spend being quiet, although awake. It is during these hours of alert inactivity that infants seem to be most receptive to stimuli from the environment. Infants, from the time of birth, display ***rapid eye movement (REM)*** during sleep states (Schulte et al., 1977). Thus, asleep or awake, the early infant has a mind that is very active.

By 5 weeks the baby has naps that are longer, taking 2 to 4 of them each day and combining one or two of them into a 5- or 6-hour nighttime sleep. By the third month, the infant's daily patterns of sleeping, eating, and being alert are clearly regulated. The baby sleeps better and more predictably. However, bedtime may be difficult. The baby may resist going to sleep because of awareness that bedtime means the end of socializing, play, and attention. What started as a brief period of fussing and whimpering a month or so earlier may now become an intermittent period of crying out and wailing, then waiting and listening for a parental reaction. However, once asleep, the baby is likely to sleep for 10 or 11 hours. On awakening, the 3-month-old baby may lie quietly, sucking a fist or looking at the toys hanging about the crib.

By 5 months, sleeping and waking become sharply defined. The baby sleeps 12 to 14 hours and may take one or two naps during the day. The problem of "games babies play" at bedtime in order to stay up becomes more pronounced with time. A nightly routine may need to be established and firmly enforced to prevent a parent-child crisis from developing. Some play at bedtime, followed by a cuddle, a kiss, and a "nighty-night," may bring a pleasant ending to the day. If needed, a soft light can be left on in the baby's room so that visual contact with familiar surroundings can be maintained. The 5-month-old, however, is usually an early riser, quickly awakening to practice new muscular and social skills. Eventually, the need for attention will result in crying or calling out, which will arouse the entire household.

Feeding the infant

Babies spend a lot of time eating. It is a very important part of the day because of the closeness of the parent-child relationship. The specific feeding practice—breast or bottle, schedule or demand—matters less emotionally than the personal contact involved (Caplan, 1981). The warmth or rejection of the mother is more important than the style of feeding. The baby needs the sensory and social stimulation—the comfort contact—that a mother can give while holding or feeding the baby.

Breast-feeding. There are both advantages and disadvantages to breast-feeding an infant. It is a case where the decision of the parents should be respected. With regard to advantages, breast-feeding is a more convenient method, and for most women it provides great emotional satisfaction. In 1976 more than half of all American infants and almost half of all Canadian babies were breast-fed (American Academy of Pediatrics, 1980). Nursing also helps the uterus return to its normal shape more quickly. The composition of breast milk is ideal for most infants' needs; it is superior to a formula, even with vitamin supplements. The protein of human milk is easily digested, aseptic, and delivered at the proper temperature. Holding and cuddling the baby while breast-feeding aids in maternal-infant bonding (Jensen et al., 1981). Of course, maternal-infant bonding can also occur with bottle feeding.

The disadvantages relate more to the restrictive nature of breast-feeding than to any pathology that may occur. Mothers who have to return to work may not want to be involved in the weaning process. Some women and men are repelled by the idea of breast-feeding. If a woman feels strange or unsure of herself concerning the idea, it may be reason enough to begin using a formula. Every care should be taken to help a mother feel comfortable and secure in her child-caring ability. If breast-feeding causes concern, then another approach should be taken.

Information about breast-feeding may be obtained from the La Leche League Information, Inc., 9616 Minneapolis Ave., Franklin Park, IL 60131, and the Nursing Mothers Council, 2817 Carlson Circle, Palo Alto, CA 94306.

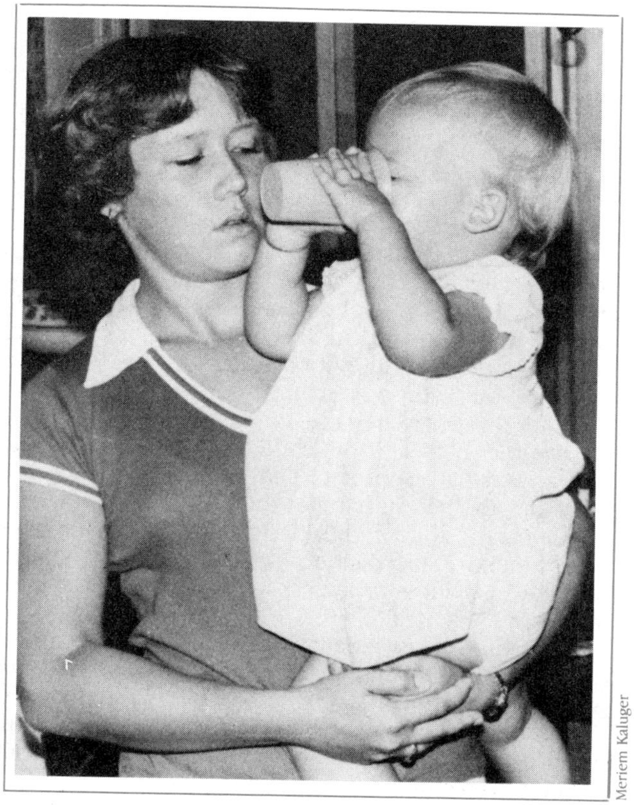
Meriem Kaluger

The progression of motor development and feeding is such that by 12 months of age, the infant can usually hold a cup with both hands and drink from it.

The infant's formula or breast milk will be the major source of nutrients in the early months of infancy. The formula composition is calculated on the basis of protein, calorie, and fluid needs, which are determined by the infant's body weight. As the infant grows, the stomach capacity increases, and the baby is able to take a larger amount of formula at each feeding. Supplements to the formula may include some ascorbic acid about the second to the fourth week of life to provide for bone and teeth formation. Some supplements of vitamin D may be needed. Of course, all of this should only be done at the recommendation of the physician.

Feeding schedule. The 2-month-old may be on a fairly regular feeding schedule, drinking as much as 35 ounces of milk a day at about 4-hour intervals, although babies usually set their own time pattern. Some parents may want to introduce solid foods during the second month, but Foman et al. (1979) and many pediatric nutritionists disagree with this practice because there is no way the 2-month-old can tell a caretaker when he or she is satisfied and full. A more mature intestinal tract is also better able to digest and react to foods (Caplan, 1981).

By the middle of the third month the baby may begin to eat solids. Solids should be introduced carefully and gradually, presenting one food at a time at about 3- or 5-day intervals. The transition to three meals and three milk feedings instead of four can be made during the fourth month. Besides the milk, the infant may consume as much as half a jar each of two baby foods. A 6-month-old may enjoy starting to drink from a cup but may also enjoy holding a bottle of milk. After the baby begins to creep, and especially after beginning to walk, interest in eating may decrease significantly. Breast-feeding can continue into the tenth month or even the eighteenth month (Foman et al., 1979), with other foods being introduced. It would be important, however, to teach the infant to drink from a cup before the first birthday.

Feeding and attachment. The psychological significance of feeding has to do with being wanted (Erikson, 1963a) and with attachment between parent and child (Ainsworth, 1979). Ainsworth describes how the mother's style of feeding her baby may relate to later behavior. The mothers in the Ainsworth study who paced the feedings to the wishes of their babies responded quickly to signs of hunger or satisfaction in their infants. They allowed their babies to participate actively in the feeding, developing a smooth and mutually gratifying relationship. At the end of a year, these babies showed a healthy attachment to their mothers. Babies whose mothers were relatively insensitive and unresponsive to them in feeding situations lacked interest in keeping in touch with their mothers or were ambivalent about making contacts. There is more information on attachment in Chapter 6.

Toilet training

Toilet training depends in part on the maturation process and in part on learning. In early infancy, eliminating the body wastes from the bladder and bowel is an involuntary reflex. When these organs are full, the sphincter muscles open automatically. The young child has to learn to recognize the feeling of fullness and learn how to tighten the sphincter muscles to prevent elimination. When the child can stand alone, the nerve pathways have developed to the extent that the infant can have some control over the anal and urethral sphincters. Very good control is usually achieved at about 20 months of age (Latham et al., 1977). The age for beginning toilet training is a matter of individual development. Usually, by the end of the first year, the infant is physiologically and psychologically ready for some training. However, if the child does not understand what is expected, the parents should wait until later to start. Recognize that the child is faced with a conflict when unexpectedly asked to give up a usual pattern of behavior in order to gain the approval of mother or father.

Training schedule. According to Latham et al. (1977), bowel training should begin before bladder training since the number of stools a day is fewer than the number of times the child urinates. Usually, it is wise to wait at least a month after bowel training has been established to begin bladder training. Generally, the later that toilet training is begun, the faster a child learns. The maturational process enables the infant to have better voluntary control of the sphincters. According to the classical study of Sears et al. (1957), it takes about 7 months to achieve control when training begins at about 12 months of age but only 5 months when training is not begun until the child is about 20 months of age. Recently, some operant conditioning methods have been promoted to "toilet train your child in 1 day" (Azren and Fox, 1976). Needless to say, the child must still be physiologically mature enough to control elimination.

With training beginning at 11 months, bowel control is frequently established by one third of the infants at 18 months of age (Sears et al., 1957). According to research by Oppel and co-workers (1968), of 859 children studied in Baltimore, 8% of the 1-year-olds stayed dry during the day and night. Over 50% of the 2-year-olds were dry through the day and 40% at night. By 3 years of age, 84% had daytime dryness and 66% were dry at night. It was not until after the age of 5 that 95% maintained daytime dryness. Girls become dry day and night earlier than boys.

After some continence has been learned, problems in maintaining elimination control may still be encountered and should not be upsetting to parents. Children revert to daytime or nighttime wetting for a variety of reasons. Sometimes children do not want to interrupt their play and do not allow enough time to get to the toilet. Teething, illness, and excessive intake of liquids are reasons for wetting. An emotional strain or upset may cause a relapse (Rutter et al., 1973). The arrival of a new baby in the family and the beginning of school are situations that commonly cause strain, resulting in nighttime wetting.

Effects of type of toilet training. What are the effects of severe or lax toilet training on the child? According to psychoanalytic theory, later infancy corresponds to the anal stage of psychosexual development. Freud suggests that the child's greatest pleasure is derived from the anal area and its products. It would not be unusual for a child to manipulate fecal matter and to smear it on the floor. According to Freud, the parent should not show strong disapproval but should, instead, provide clay, sand, or finger paints as a more acceptable means for the child to gratify this desire to smear. What is important, states Freud, is to recognize that how the parent handles the problem will eventually affect the child's adult personality. In fact, he states that the entire approach to toilet training—harshness or laxity, earliness or lateness—will have an effect on the child.

According to psychoanalytic theory (Freud, 1940), if toilet training is begun too early before the child can gain control, the infant will become frustrated and insecure. The child may develop an ambivalent feeling toward the mother, loving her on the one hand but feeling antagonistic on the other because of being forced to comply with her wishes. Severe pressure during toilet training can cause the child to be tight-lipped, perfectionistic (compulsive), and even punitive (rebellious) in adult life. No pressure to control at all, however, may cause the child to develop a lax, permissive attitude toward any kind of control (hedonistic and self-seeking).

Longitudinal studies are not available, as far as we know, to indicate whether psychoanalytical theory concerning toilet training is correct or not. The rationale of the theory is inconsistent, however. For example, it states that harsh toilet training can lead to either a compliant, compulsive personality (to get approval) or to a rebellious personality (to gain autonomy). Something more than toilet training is involved (Shaffer, 1981).

MOTOR DEVELOPMENT DURING INFANCY

The period of infancy is one of tremendous motor development. The word *motor* refers to muscular movements. The general mass activity and reflex actions of the neonate gradually change to specific muscle control, permitting voluntary, coordinated motor responses to take place. In addition to muscle development, motor control also makes use of sensory acuity and awareness, perceptual discrimination ability, and sensorimotor integration and coordination. Accurate perception of sensory stimuli is needed to perfect the use of motor skills.

During the first year of life, maturational forces are important in the development of motor coordination. Maturation determines the rate, the level of readiness, and the pattern of the early motor responses (Bayley, 1969; Robertson and Halverson, 1977). Progress in motor development can be influenced, however, by factors such as a lack of opportunity to practice the motor skills, the child's attitude toward learning the skills, and psychological and physiological inhibitions to learning. The process of development is sequential in nature unless interfered with by unusual conditions within or outside the infant. The foundations begun during the prenatal stage are basic to the later development of posture, locomotion, prehension, and cognition.

The following two complex motor tasks must be learned during infancy: (1) upright postural (body) control and locomotion and (2) manipulation skills and prehension—the ability to reach with the hand, to grasp, and to manipulate objects.

Body control and locomotion

There is a basic sequence that leads to walking. This sequence will vary as to time of occurrence from infant

TABLE 5-3 Developmental progression of motor behavior when prescribed testing procedures are followed

Motor behavior	*Average age achieved (in months)*	*Expected normal variation (in months)*
Lateral head movements	0.1	—
Arm and leg thrusts	0.8	0.3-2
Head erect and steady	1.6	0.7-4
Turns from side to back	1.8	0.7-5
Elevates self by arms	2.1	0.7-5
Sits with support	2.3	1-5
Turns from back to side	4.4	2-7
Makes effort to sit	4.8	3-8
Pulls to sitting position	5.3	4-8
Sits alone momentarily	5.3	4-8
Rolls from back to stomach	6.4	4-10
Sits alone, steadily	6.6	5-9
Early stepping movements	7.4	5-11
Pulls to standing position	8.1	5-12
Raises self to sitting posture	8.3	6-11
Stands up by furniture	8.6	6-12
Stepping movements	8.8	6-12
Walks with help	9.6	7-12
Sits down	9.6	7-14
Stands alone	11.0	9-16
Walks alone	11.7	9-17
Walks backward	14.6	11-20
Jumps off floor, both feet	23.4	17-30+
Jumps from bottom step	24.8	19-30+
Walks upstairs alone: both feet on each step	25.1	18-30+
Walks downstairs alone: both feet on each step	25.8	19-30+

Adapted and reproduced by permission from the Bayley Scales of Infant Development.

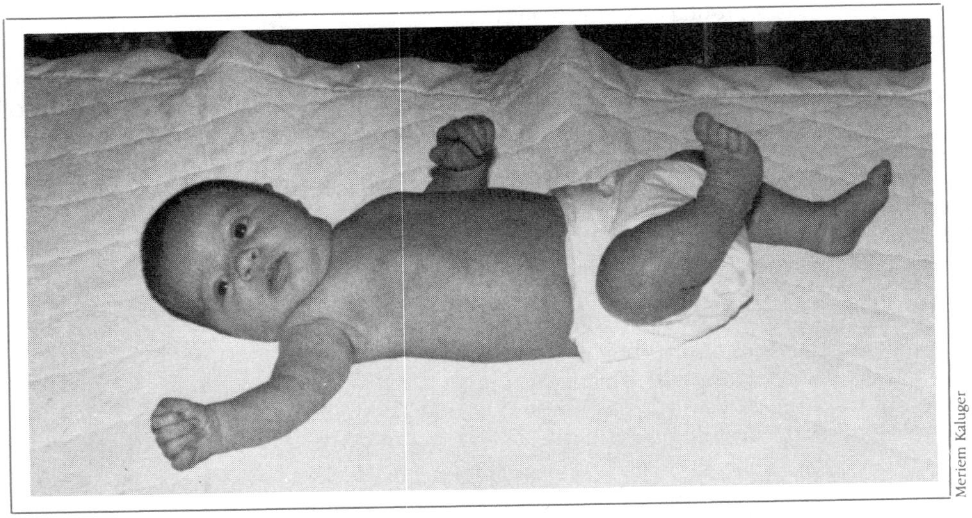

Newborn infant. *Tonic neck posture is readily assumed (fencer's position).*

to infant, but there is a progressive regularity in the development. The five basic stages are (1) body control as in sitting with support, (2) body control as in sitting alone, (3) active efforts toward locomotion, (4) creeping and walking with support, and (5) walking alone (Vaughan et al., 1979).

Remember that normative data must be thought of in terms of a normal range and not just the figure quoted as "average." The norm is an approximation. Also, keep in mind that the population samples used by different studies differ, resulting in some discrepancies from table to table. Cross-cultural research, especially, reveals that variations occur in different cultures in the timing of motor development (Le Vine, 1970). The degree of parent-infant stimulation may be a factor producing differences (Ainsworth, 1967). The following norms in Table 5-3 are taken from the Bayley Scale of Infant Development (1969).

The newborn infant is normally unable to hold the head erect when lying prone or when being held in a sitting position. However, there can be lateral head movement. Michel (1981) states that the lateral direction in which a newborn turns the head significantly predicts later handedness. At the age of 1 month the infant can hold its head straight out in a horizontal plane when supported in the prone (lying on the stomach) position. By the age of 2 months the infant can lift his or her head above the horizontal plane at an angle of as much as 30 degrees. By the time an infant is 4 months old, the child nearly always lifts the head and upper trunk when placed prone on a table. The child is now no longer content to lie on his or her back. However, the infant must develop a certain amount of rigidity of the spine before being able to sit up unsupported. This rigidity is usually developed about the seventh month; then the infant sits alone.

Prewalking motions are attained about the seventh month. *Crawling* refers to various forms of progression in which the infant does not lift the stomach from the floor while moving all four limbs. In *hitching* or *scooting,* the infant may even move about in a sitting position, using one leg to push the body along. A child may pull himself or herself to a standing position during the eighth month. In *creeping* the infant's body is lifted off the floor and moved along on all four limbs. Creeping happens at about 10 months (Vaughan et al., 1979). The child may stand alone at 11 months and take several steps shortly thereafter.

When a child first begins to walk, the movements are awkward. The infant walks in a stiff-legged manner, with the legs far apart, toes turned outward, and arms close to the body or held out like a tightrope walker. If the infant watches the floor, balance cannot be maintained. To keep from falling the child holds the head erect and slightly forward. The steps are high off the floor and uneven. At first he or she may move one foot

Text continued on p. 167.

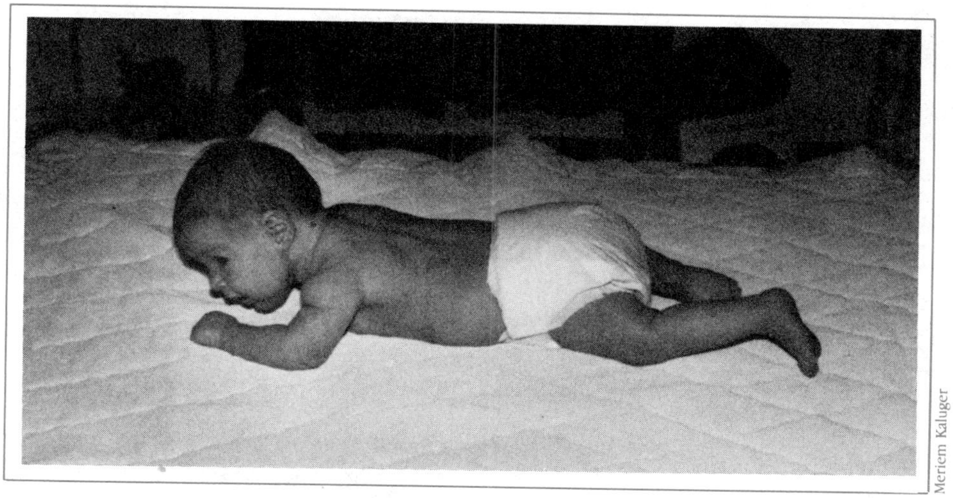

Meriem Kaluger

Infant at 1 month. *Lifts and turns head when prone.*

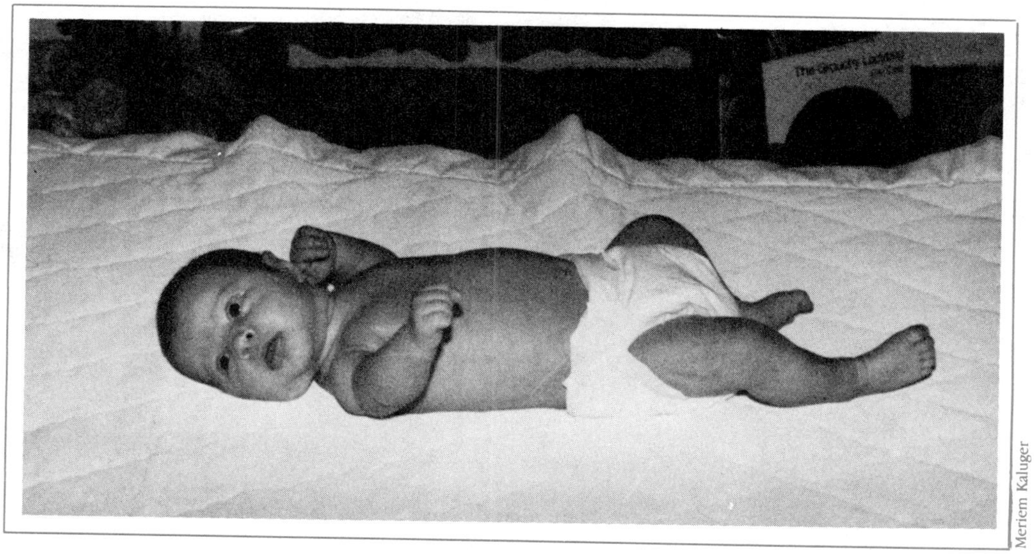

Meriem Kaluger

Lying on back, turns head 45 degrees and looks.

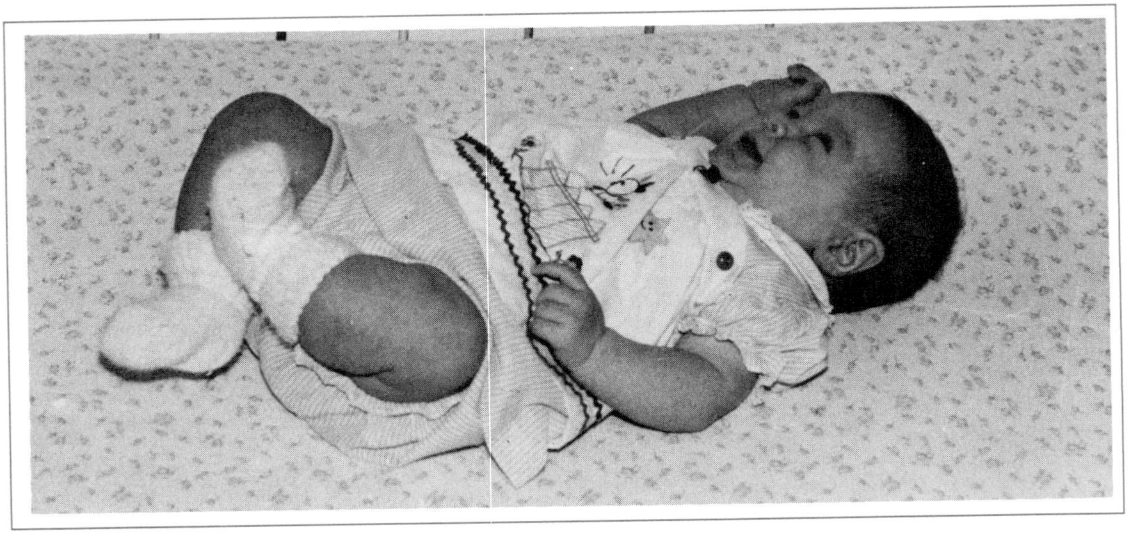

Meriem Kaluger

Infant at 2 months. *A sociable smile appears.*

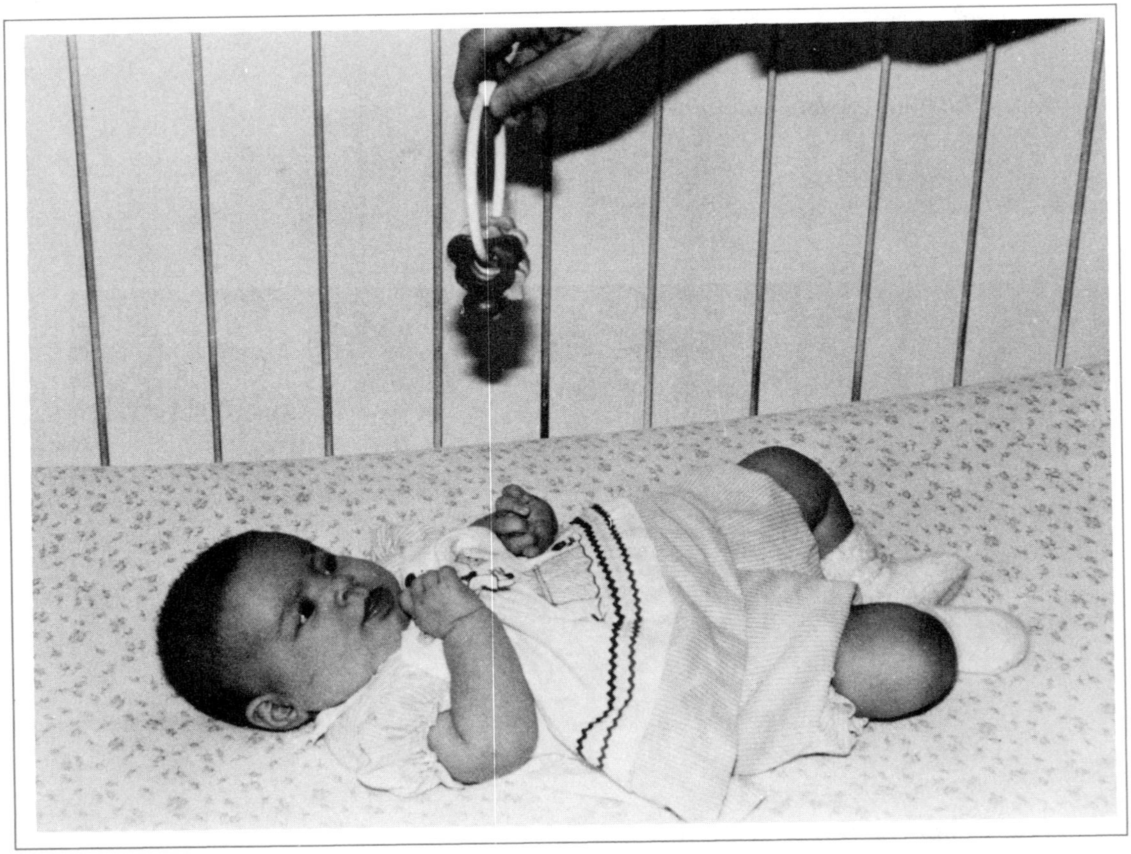

Meriem Kaluger

Eyes will follow an object.

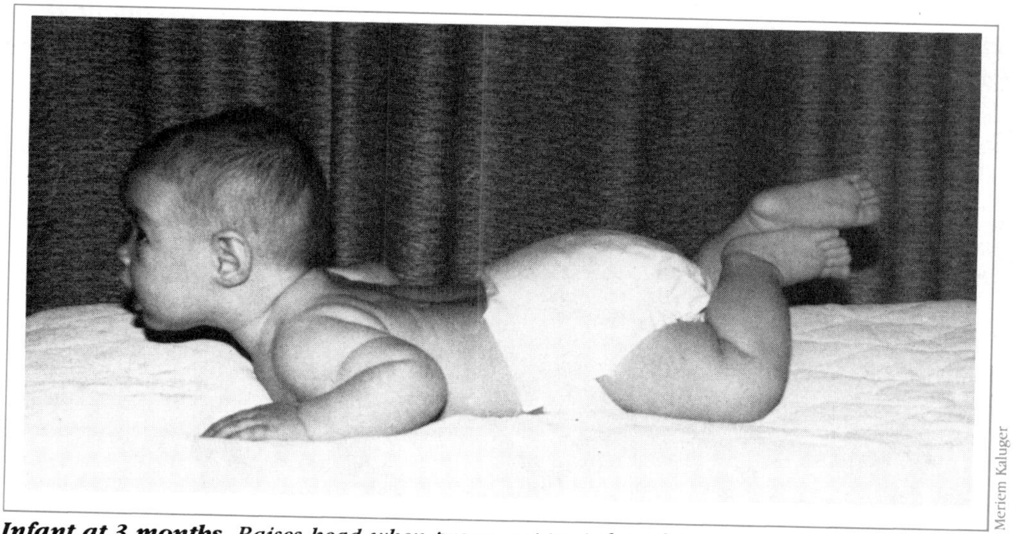

Infant at 3 months. *Raises head when prone, supported on forearms.*

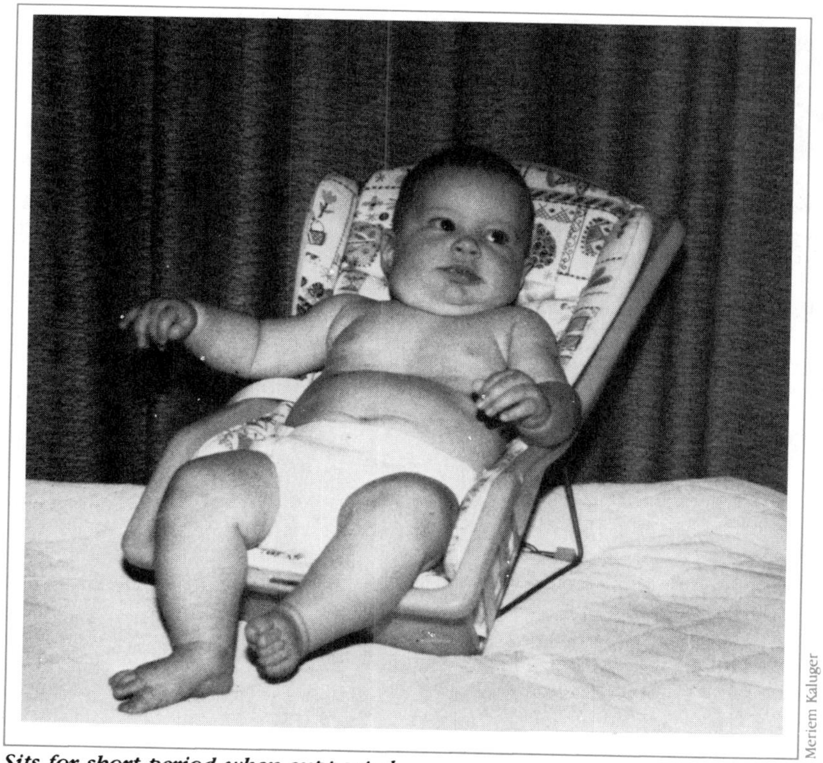

Sits for short period when supported.

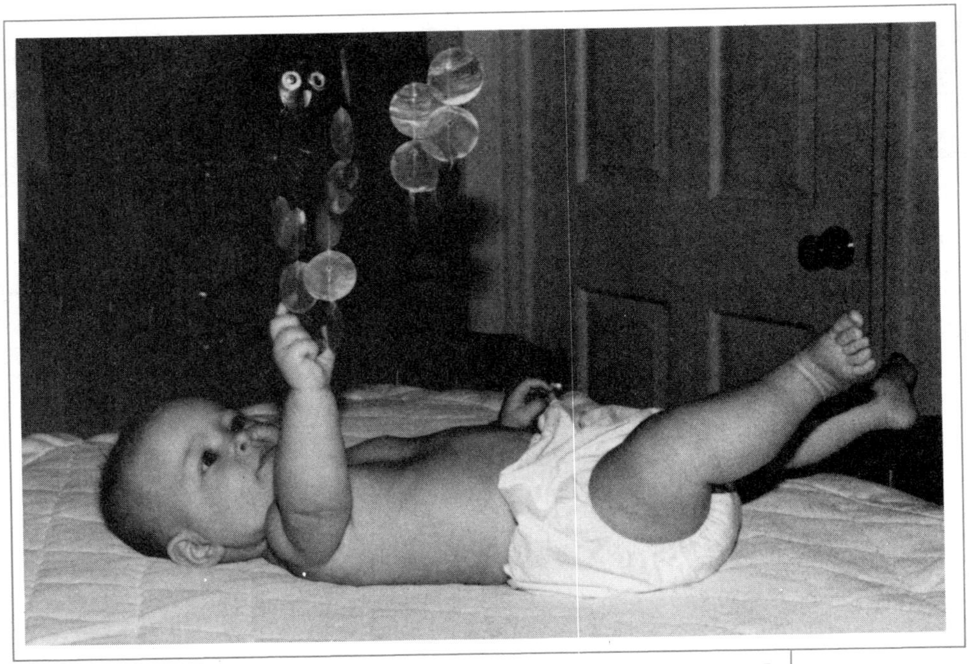

Meriem Kaluger

Infant at 4 months.
Reaches and grasps at objects.

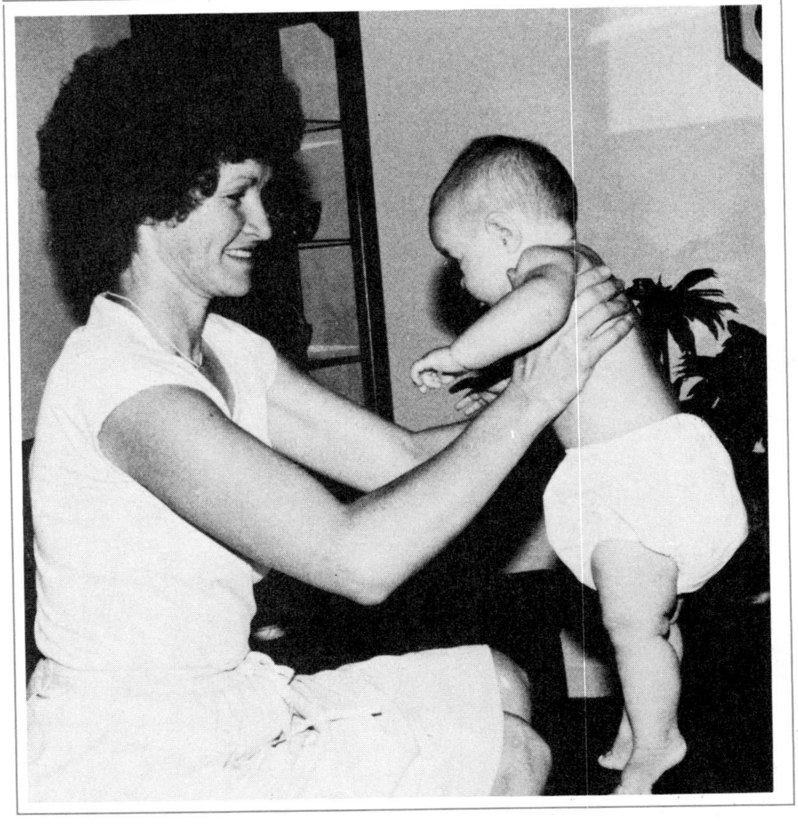

Meriem Kaluger

Pushes with feet when held erect.

forward, shift the weight to it, and then bring the second foot about even with the front foot. Next the child may shift the weight back to the second foot and move the first foot forward again. Gradually, as the movements become coordinated, the infant begins stepping forward by alternating the feet.

By 14 months of age two thirds of the babies can walk without support, and by the age of 18 months the average baby walks like an adult.

The infant will be able to creep up stairs about the thirteenth month. At 16 months the child will be able to walk up the stairs if his or her hand is held, climb into an adult chair, and throw a ball but not with much accuracy. When the infant reaches the twenty-first or twenty-second month, he or she will squat while playing, walk upstairs while holding the railing, and kick a large ball. By 25 months of age the child can run well without falling and walk up and down the steps alone, putting both feet on each step.

kinesthesis the muscle, tendon, and joint senses, yielding discrimination of position and movement of parts of the body.

prehension the ability to pick up a small object using thumb and index finger.

Prehension or grasping

The infant's grasping reflex and uncoordinated arm movements are the starting points for a sequence that eventually leads to highly skilled manual activities of the adult. ***Prehension,*** the act of taking hold, seizing or grasping, is not merely a function of motor control but, rather, a function of eye-hand coordination. Kinesthesis and vision are the two chief sensory activities involved in the coordination of arm-hand movements. ***Kinesthesis*** refers to the sense of movement involved

Text continued on p. 174.

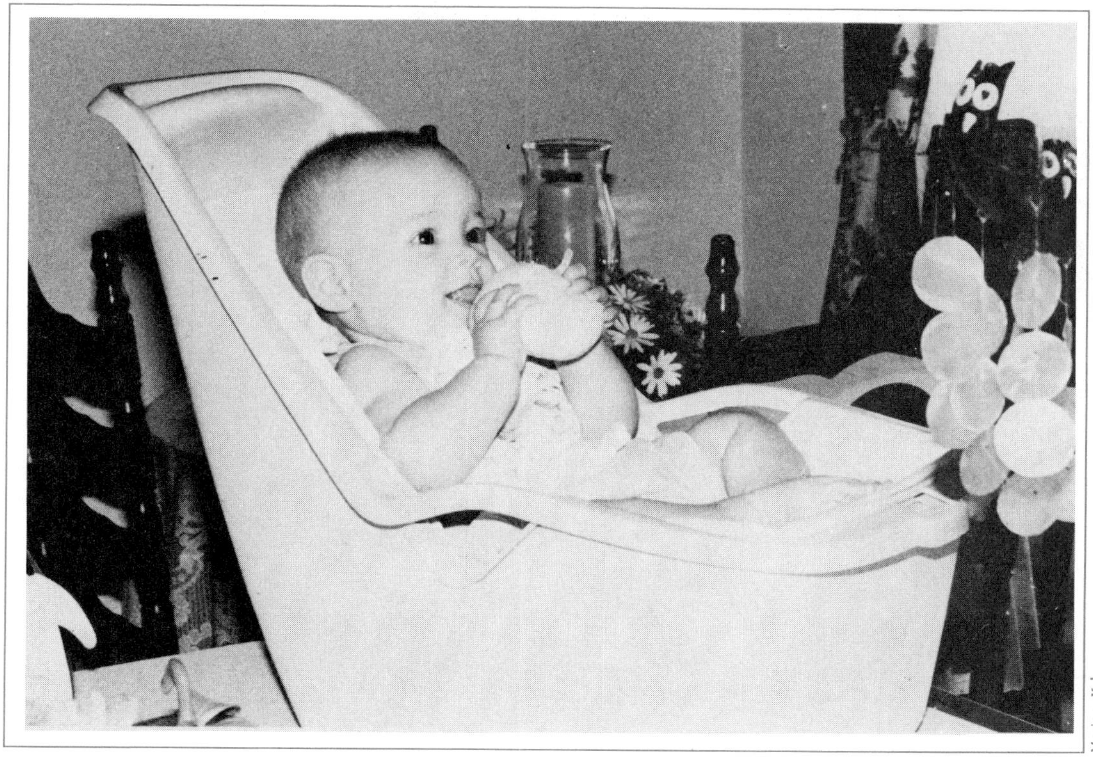

Meriem Kaluger

Infant at 5 months. *Manipulates and chews small objects. Is alert to surroundings.*

Meriem Kaluger

Infant at 6 months. *Sits alone with slight support; balances well.*

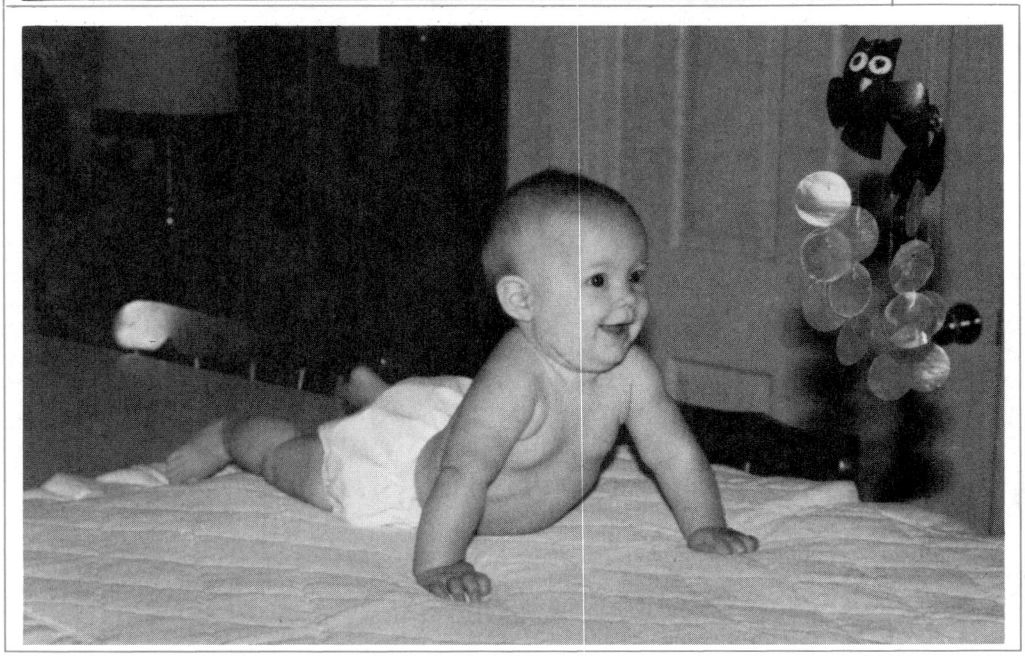

Meriem Kaluger

Rises on wrists and assumes a symmetrical posture.

Meriem Kaluger

Infant at 7 months. *Propels self forward on belly (crawling).*

Meriem Kaluger

Can grasp cracker or biscuit to chew on.

Meriem Kaluger

Sits alone without support.

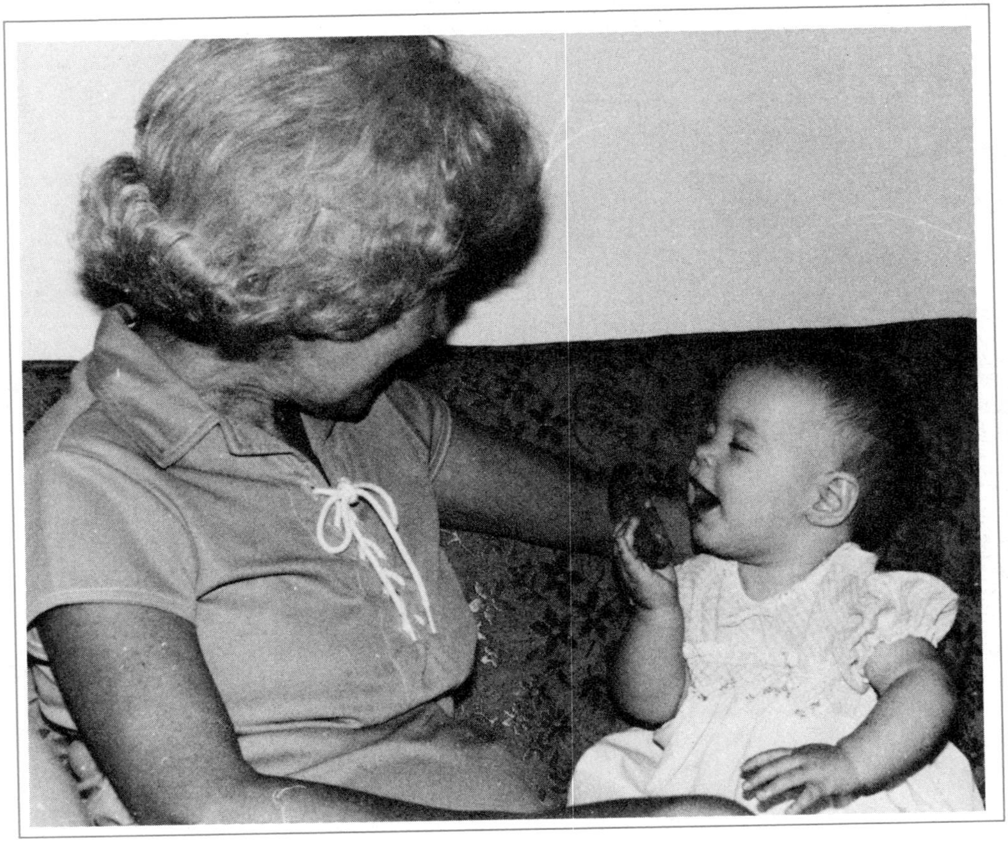

Meriem Kaluger

Infant at 8 months.
Loves to play with adults who are not strangers.

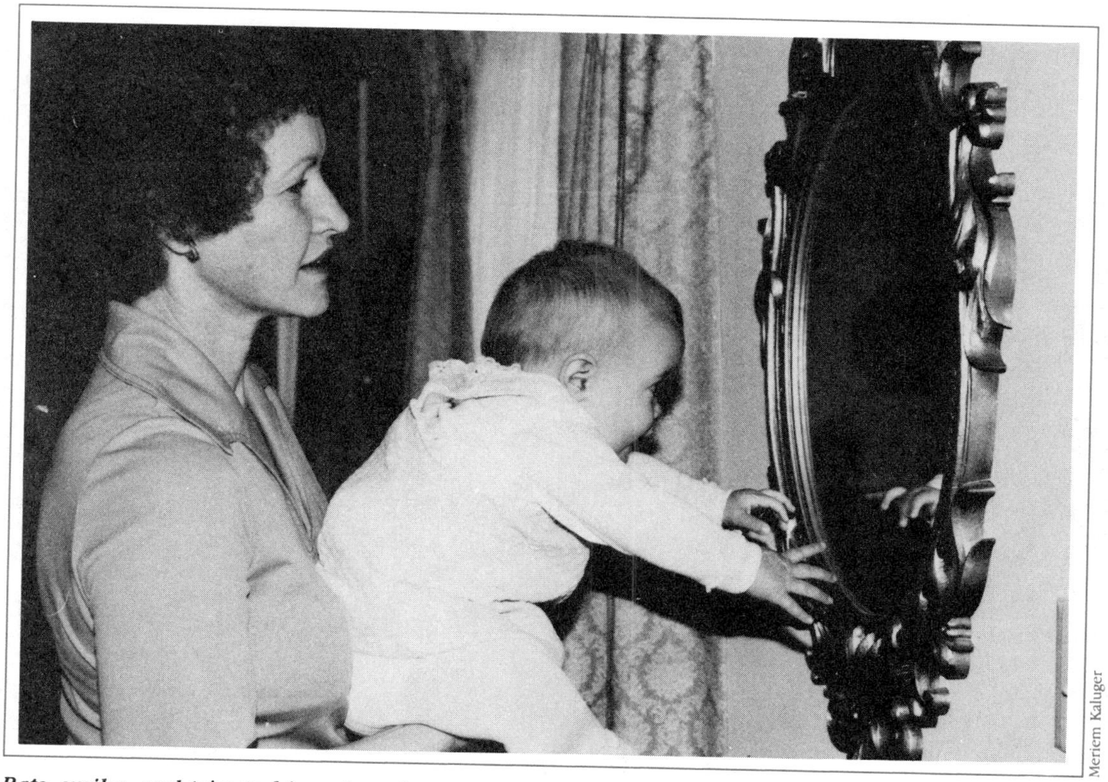

Meriem Kaluger

Pats, smiles, and tries to kiss mirror image.

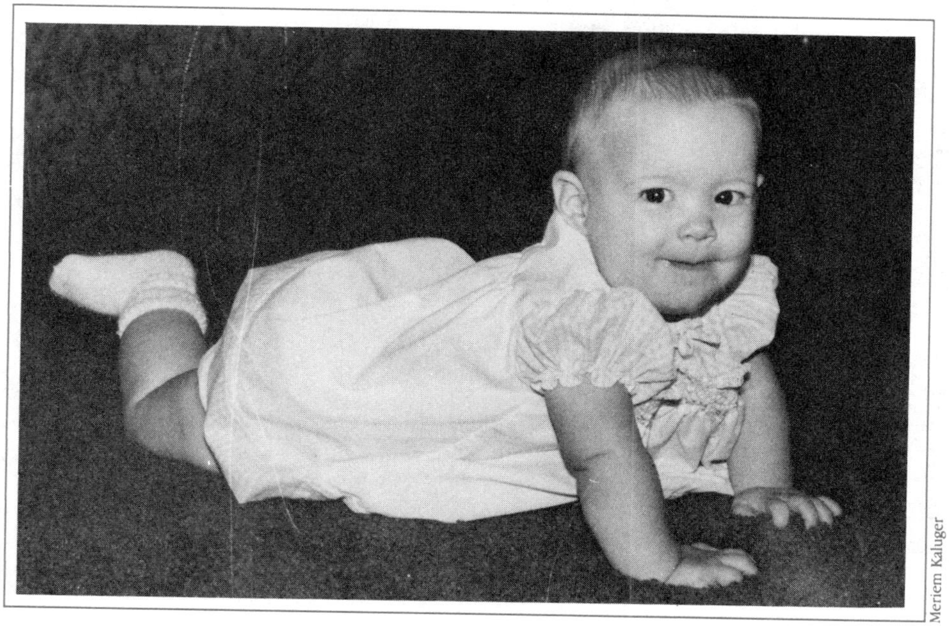

Meriem Kaluger

Infant at 9 months.
Propels self forward on all fours, trunk not touching floor (creeping).

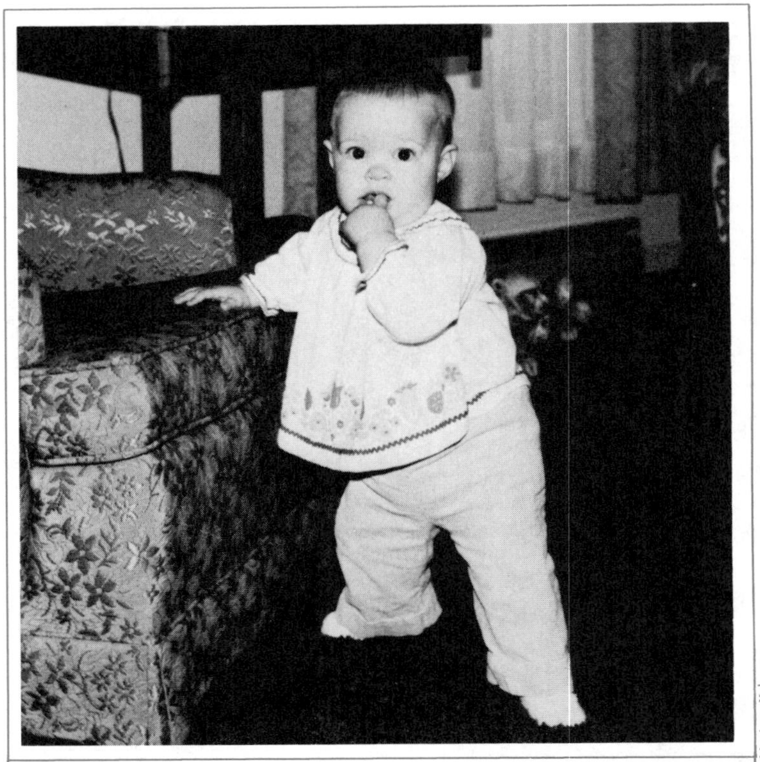

Meriem Kaluger

Can pull self up to standing position.

Meriem Kaluger

Picks up a small pellet with thumb and forefinger.

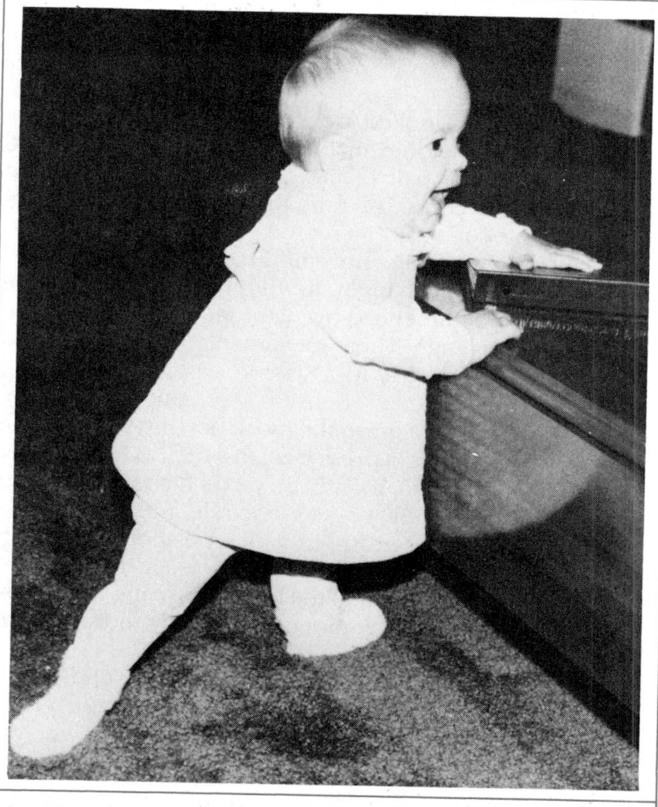

Meriem Kaluger

Infant at 10 months. *Sidesteps by holding on to furniture.*

Meriem Kaluger

Infant at 11 months. *Stands alone on wide base; balances with arms.*

TABLE 5-4 Advances in prehension

Motor performance	*Age placement in months*
Retains red ring (retains a ring, designed for the test, when placed in his hand)	0.8
Hands predominantly open (hands predominantly open even though not grasping an object)	2.7
Palms the cube, perhaps briefly, without thumb opposition (beginning evidence of use of fingers to hold cube in the palm)	3.7
Partial thumb opposition (touches thumb to fingers in a partial, but not complete, manner, using the palm of the hand, as well as thumb and fingers in picking up the cube)	4.9
Unilateral reaching (tends to reach and manipulate with one hand more often than bimanually)	5.4
Rotates wrist (rotates wrist in manipulating toys)	5.7
Complete thumb opposition (picks up the cube with thumb and fingers completely opposed, and without the use of the palm)	6.9
Partial finger prehension (picks up a small pellet with several fingers opposed to thumb and not with a scooping into the palm with the fingers)	7.4
Fine prehension with pellet (picks up a small pellet precisely with thumb and forefinger)	8.9

Adapted and reproduced by permission from the Gesell Developmental Schedules Scale.

in muscles, joints, and tendons. Table 5-4 illustrates the development of prehension.

The reflex grasp that is present at birth is different from the voluntary grasp of later life in that the reflex grasp is a palm grasp rather than a finger and thumb grasp. The reflex grasp begins to decline about the second month, and the voluntary grasp, which becomes well established by the ninth month, begins to develop.

According to a study by Ausubel and Sullivan (1980), very young infants made no effort to grasp a cube placed before them on the table. At 3 to 4 months of age the infants looked at the cube for approximately 5 seconds but seldom made an effort to grasp it. By 6 months of age half of the children reached for and touched the cube. The time that the infants spent gazing at the cube also increased.

Infants' grasping movements undergo a series of developmental changes as they grow older. These changes are influenced by maturation and experimentation (learning). Their movements progress from a whole hand closure to a scissors-type of closure and finally to a pincer prehension. At about 4 months of age infants do not grasp the block but, instead, corral it with their hand and press it against their body or other hand. By the fifth month they reach the palm-grasp stage where their fingers encircle the block. The thumb-and-finger grasp, in which position the thumb and fingers cooperate in picking up and holding the cube against the palm of the hand, is usually evident by 7 months of age. By 9 months of age the more mature pincer movement is well established. The child can grip a pellet between the thumb and the end of the forefinger.

SUDDEN INFANT DEATH SYNDROME (SIDS)

Sudden unexpected death in a previously normal 2- to 4-month-old infant constitutes a major health concern, even though it occurs in only 16 out of every 1,000 babies. SIDS or "crib death" is still a mysterious occurrence. Although families at all socioeconomic levels have been affected, several studies point to an increased incidence in the lower strata. It appears more likely to occur in premature babies and babies of teenage mothers who received little or no prenatal care. However, many babies with these characteristics are not affected. Infants who are usually well-nourished and free of any evidence of illness are found dead in their crib or carriage several hours after having been fed.

So far, none of the research has been able to reveal the cause of crib deaths. The most commonly proposed theories are (1) overwhelming infection with an unknown virus, (2) unknown errors in metabolism, (3) abnormalities in the central nervous system that might lead to a spasmodic closure of the larynx or failure of cardiac conduction, and (4) apnea, a cessation of breathing for brief periods during sleep.

A point of interest is the work of pediatricians Harvey Kravitz and Robert G. Scherz, which was reported

Meriem Kaluger

Infant at 12 months. *Walks alone but still prefers creeping.*

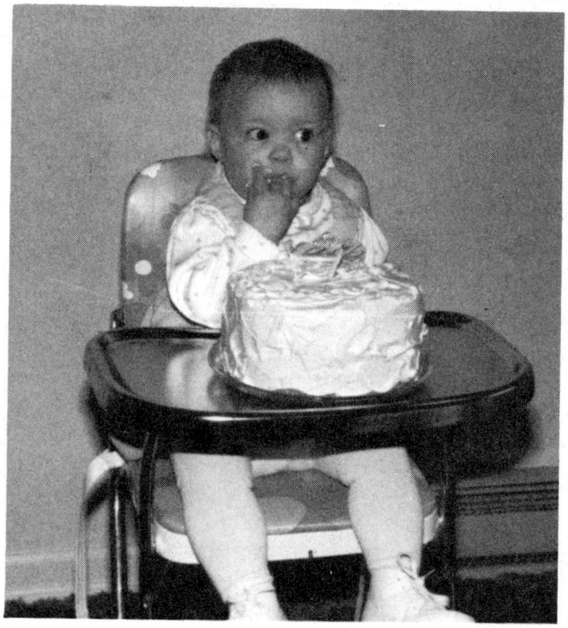

Meriem Kaluger

Enjoys icing from birthday cake.

in the Journal of the American Medical Association (Kravitz and Scherz, 1976). They noted from published reports that crib-death victims almost invariably are found in a horizontal position on their stomachs or backs. They surmised that in this position the baby's air supply might be cut off by a blockage of the lower jaw or tongue, a soft palate, or regurgitated food, milk, or saliva. Of 438 reported victims, the doctors learned that 435 died in a horizontal position. Not one crib-death victim was found in an infant carrier. They offer this advice: (1) raise the head of the baby's crib up to 2 inches (about a 10-degree angle elevation) by placing a wedge of wood under the mattress; (2) for at least 20 minutes after feeding, put the baby in an infant carrier rather than directly into the crib.

It is important to remember that these deaths are not caused by parental negligence. The parents should be supported emotionally to make them feel that they could not in any way have been responsible, that there was nothing they could have done to prevent the event, and that greater care would not have made a difference. There is a society of parents who have had infants die from SIDS; it would be well for parents who lose a baby in this manner to be in touch with this society for supportive and counseling purposes. Contact National SIDS Foundation, 310 South Michigan Avenue, Chicago, IL 60604.

DEVELOPMENT OF INFANT COGNITION

Consider newborn babies at birth. How much "intelligence" do they have? What is their "intellectual potential"? These questions are difficult to answer because the true nature of intelligence is not yet known. Most of the definitions of intelligence tell what intelligence "does" rather than what intelligence "is." Generally, the definitions center on (1) the ability to deal effectively with tasks involving abstractions, (2) the ability to learn, and/or (3) the ability to deal with new situations.

Neural development and cognition

The origins of intelligence are to be found in the central nervous system and in its capability to perceive, retain, recall, integrate, and reorganize cognitive components. Both the maturational process and the functioning of the sensing and perceiving (perceptual) processes in a stimulating and responsive environment aid in intellectual development. The word *cognition* refers to any process whereby an organism (the brain) becomes aware of or obtains knowledge of an object or a situation. It includes sensing, perceiving, recognizing, conceiving, conceptualizing, judging, reasoning, and problem solving.

The implications of intellectual growth are as follows. First, the infant is born with certain innate physical characteristics that operate in accordance with principles and laws of nature related to how the intellect is to develop. Second, intellectual attributes will develop only to the extent or limit to which these innate elements have the potential to develop. Third, the potentiality of intellectual growth can be influenced by factors or forces outside the child, such as nutritional adequacy, sensory stimulation, perceptual activities, verbal and language development, learning experiences, and opportunity to learn.

Fourth, some kind of change must take place within the neurological system when the intellect is developing. Fifth, since the intellect "develops," it must start from a meager "reflexive-cognitive" beginning and grow to an accumulative, integrated, cognitive pattern or "mental computer" kind of process that can be used for abstracting, learning, and problem solving in new situations.

Piaget: Adaptation

Jean Piaget, the noted Swiss child psychologist, developed a significant theory concerning cognitive development. Piaget believes that cognitive development is a coherent process whereby the individual develops incremental levels of cognitive structures called *schemes*. Originally, Piaget used the terms schema and schemata (plural). The trend today is to use scheme and schemes. Each successive scheme is derived logically and inevitably from the adaptation processes of assimilation and accommodation.

Assimilation describes the capability of the individual to meet and absorb new situations and new information. In so doing the person "assimilates" new knowledge, skills, and insights from interaction with the world.

Accommodation describes the process of change through which the individual becomes able to handle situations that were too difficult to handle before. It is a method by which the cognitive process, because of the new knowledge assimilated, has matured to the point that it can now "accommodate" or solve a more difficult task than it could before. Fig. 5-1 illustrates how assimilation and accommodation operate to improve an individual's cognitive ability (scheme) by adaptation.

Adaptation occurs when the person has improved his or her ability to meet new environmental demands through the processes of assimilation and accommodation. One form of adaptation is coping with the environment by organizing and reorganizing thought patterns to the extent that this new cognitive capability becomes a higher level scheme.

Intelligence, according to Piaget, is a process of adaptation by which higher cognitive levels are attained. Piaget tries to identify the characteristic structures of the scheme of each age-group and seeks to show how individuals adapt to environmental demands and to one another (Piaget and Inhelder, 1969).

Piaget's theory divides the intellectual development process into four main chronological stages, which are further divided into substages. The order of succession of these steplike patterns is constant, although the ages at which different stages are attained may vary somewhat, depending on the child's maturation, innate capacity, practice, and environmental differences. The four stages are (1) sensorimotor stage covering ages 0 to 2 years, (2) preoperational stage, ages 3 to 7 years, (3) concrete operations stage, 7 to 11 or 12 years of age, and (4) formal operations stage, ages 11 to 15 or 16 years. A general overview of Piaget's theory of cognitive development is presented in Chapter 1. The four stages are presented separately in those chapters dealing with the relevant age levels. Only the sensorimotor stage is discussed in this chapter.

accommodation the tendency to change one's schema or operations or to make new ones to include new objects or experiences enabling a higher level of thinking. Term is used by Piaget in his theory on cognitive development. See also **assimilation.**

adaptation a key principle in ethological theories referring to the way that behavior changes or develops to meet environmental demands and to ensure survival and reproduction.

assimilation the incorporation of new objects and experiences into a structure or schema in the mind to be used later in problem-solving situations. See also **accommodation.**

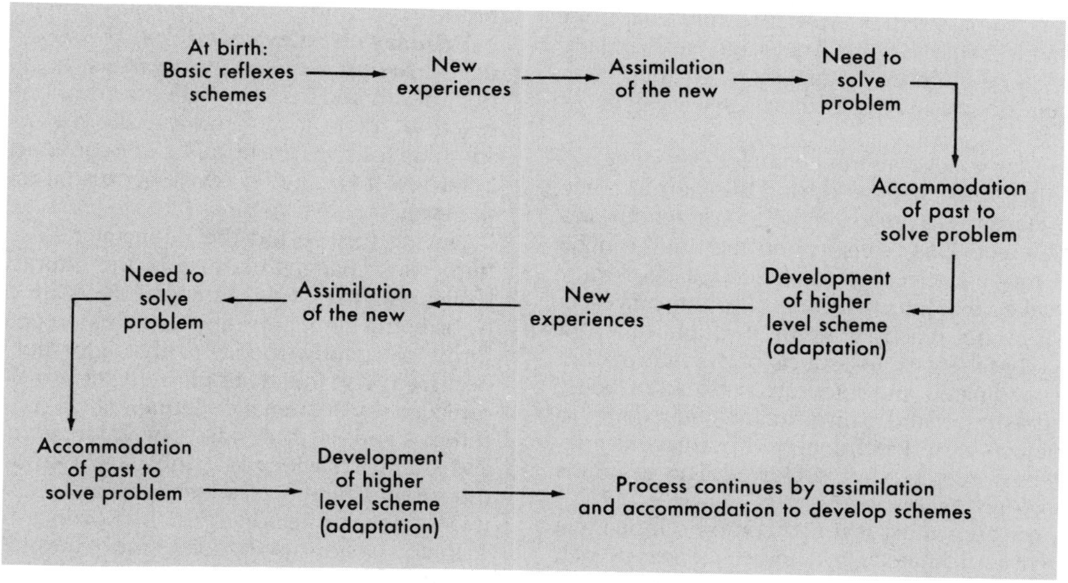

FIG. 5-1 *Piaget's development of schemes by the adaptation process of using assimilation and accommodation.*

object permanence in cognitive development, the ability to recognize the continuing existence of an object that is no longer visible or audible. It is achieved at about 11 months by the majority of infants.

primary circular reactions a reaction, generally occurring between 1 and 4 months of age, in which the infant attempts to repeat a pleasurable event that first happened by chance; for example, sucking the fingers when they accidentally come close to the mouth.

sensorimotor stage according to Jean Piaget, the stage in cognitive development during which the child is essentially involved in perfecting contact with the objects that surround him or her. It generally occurs from birth to 2 years of age. It is characterized by the development of sensory and motor functions and by the infant's coming to know the world as a result of interacting with and affecting it. See also **concrete operational stage; formal operational stage; preoperational stage.**

Piaget: Sensorimotor stage of cognitive development

The ***sensorimotor stage*** of development, according to Piaget, encompasses the period in a child's life from birth to about 2 years of age. This stage is essentially preverbal, since children's adaptations to their new environment do not involve extensive use of symbols or language.

Children have several intellectual developmental tasks that they must achieve during this period. First, they must learn to organize simple motor actions and incoming perceptions (sensory) so that they can be converted into adaptive behavior. Second, they must come to realize that information concerning an object or event can be reaching them through different senses and that the various aspects of the information must be coordinated and integrated instead of being considered as unrelated. Third, infants must come to think of objects as independent and permanent entities that exist even when not perceived. This insight is known as ***object permanence.***

Fourth, children must learn to combine individual actions into a coordinated effort and sequence to reach a goal. By the end of the sensorimotor period children should be able to use simple tools to obtain what they want by anticipating the consequences of their actions (Inhelder and Piaget, 1964). Although the cause-and-effect principle is not comprehended during infancy, its recognition is enhanced by repeating certain actions and observing the results.

Piaget has divided the sensorimotor period into six substages (1) the use of reflexes, (2) primary circular reactions, (3) secondary circular reactions, (4) coordination of secondary circular reactions, (5) tertiary circular reactions, and (6) invention of new means by mental combinations. Table 5-5 presents each substage.

Use of reflexes. The first substage, the use of reflexes, begins at birth and lasts until the end of the first month. Children use the reflexes with which they were endowed. The *reflex behaviors* that Piaget believes are most important are sucking, grasping, eye movements and visual accommodations, and reflexes associated with hearing and phonation. The reflexes mostly used shortly after birth include sucking, tongue movements, swallowing, crying, and gross bodily movements.

Infants do not perceive their actions because, as babies, they are in a state of complete bodily self-absorption, unaffected by their contacts with a nebulous, outer reality. There is an absence of genuine intelligent behavior. Nonetheless, this phase is an extremely important one, since it is from behavior patterns established during this period that subsequent intelligence will emerge. The reflexes are the building blocks of cognitive development.

Primary circular reactions. The second substage, that of ***primary circular reactions,*** begins after the first month and lasts until the fourth month. *Circular reaction* refers to a behavior that provides its own stimulus for the repetition or the continuation of that behavior. It is called *primary* because it involves only the body.

During this period the neonatal reflexes undergo numerous changes because of the interaction of the babies with their environment. Infants are continuously bringing about, prolonging, and repeating some forms of adaptive behavior that have not previously occurred. The initial simple reflexes are slowly being replaced by systematic, sequential combinations of reflexes and, in some cases, by voluntary movements. For example, sucking is an innate reflex, but systematic thumb and finger sucking is learned or acquired as infants develop hand-to-mouth coordination.

Infants' vision also becomes more developed during the second and third months. They begin to "look" at objects within their visual field; they learn to focus on stationary objects; then they learn to follow moving objects. During this substage a differentiation is noted in the cries of infants in that they begin to cry in different ways for different needs. They also begin to differentiate other vocalizations and to repeat some sounds for their own sake. By the end of the second developmental substage, children are beginning to lose some of their body egocentrism and to respond to the world around them.

Secondary circular reactions. The behavior patterns of the third substage of sensorimotor development, ages 4 to 8 months, consist of repetitive actions that are concerned with the external environment rather than with the infants' bodies, as was true in primary reactions. ***Secondary circular reactions*** focus on objects and events in the environment. The *beginnings* of "intentional" adaptations are noted; that is, a desire, intention, or a purpose can be associated to the behavior. Thus children kick their legs to shake their crib and make a hanging mobile or toy move. They will shake a rattle to produce a sound. They enjoy noticing or hearing what happens when they move or do something. They begin to show a greater awareness of the world surrounding them.

Babies also begin to recognize objects and people that are familiar to them. Their conception of a stable external world has begun. They still do not have an idea of object permanence—that an object exists even when it is out of sight. Nor do they have enough intelligence to reverse a feeding bottle that has been presented to them the wrong way. However, when an object vanishes, they will wonder where it may be.

coordination of secondary schemes Piaget's fourth substage in the period of sensorimotor development.

secondary circular reactions between 4 and 8 months of age, actions that the infant attempts for more than personal need satisfaction; for example, shaking a rattle or imitating baby talk or physical gestures.

Coordination of secondary schemes. There are two principal areas of intellectual accomplishment during the ***coordination of secondary schemes*** substage, from the eighth to the twelfth month. First, the behaviors initiated are now unquestionably intentional. Children also begin to exhibit anticipatory behavior by using actions to indicate that they anticipate coming events. They indulge in such activities as removing a lid from a box to find a ball inside. They can now reverse a feeding bottle that has been given to them the wrong way. Second, they can use new schemes in different situations to solve problems. For the first time children's actions correspond to a definition of intelligence from a functional point of view. This substage

TABLE 5-5 Piaget's sensorimotor stage of cognitive development

Substages	*Behavior*	*Examples*
1. Reflexive schemes (0 to 1 month)	Reliance on reflexes	Sucking is most salient reflex
2. Primary circular reactions (1 to 4 months)	Extension of reflexes; focus on own body	Sucks fingers; puts out tongue; repeats hand-to-mouth action
3. Secondary circular reactions (4 to 8 months)	Earliest stage at which "intention" in environment is distinguished	Moves in crib to make toys on crib shake
4. Coordination of secondary schemes (8 to 12 months)	Application of familiar means to new situations	Holds a block in each hand and drops one, picking up a third one just presented
5. Tertiary circular reactions (12 to 18 months)	Discovery through active experimentation	Devises different ways of making something fall or slide "to see what happens"
6. Invention of new means through mental combinations (18 to 24 months)	Emergence of capacity to respond to or think about things not immediately observable	Uses a stick to reach out beyond arm length to pull something closer

tertiary circular reactions schemes in which the infant (between ages 12 to 18 months) explores new possibilities with the same object, changing what is done and examining the results. This is the first reaction that is not imitation; marking the beginnings of curiosity.

marks the beginning of understanding the permanence of objects and of objective spatial groups.

Tertiary circular reactions. The fifth substage, 12 to 18 months of age, deals with ***tertiary circular reactions*** and the discovery of new means. *Tertiary* refers to the third circular reaction cycle. During this time the infant displays exploratory behavior. These reactions refer to the repetitive behavior that fascinates children of about 1 year of age when they repeat an action many times but do not necessarily repeat it the same way. Children not only act on the objects in their environment but also vary their action on them. They try out

David Strickler

During Piaget's secondary circular reaction phase, an infant will take objects, such as leaves, from the environment and repeat the same action with them several times in succession.

new responses to reach the same goal. This behavior is the beginning of trial-and-error experimentation and problem solving.

Children also become extremely interested in pursuing new experiences. They try to produce new actions that create a pleasing effect for themselves. Every situation has numerous possibilities that seem to need further exploration, explanation, or modification. The adaptive reactions of this phase have all the characteristics of true intelligence.

Invention of new means. The final substage begins about the eighteenth month and continues to the twenty-fourth month. The most significant cognitive skill developed during this substage involves the children's ability to solve problems without having to physically explore their possibilities or solutions as they did in substage five. This approach is called the ***invention of new means*** through mental deduction or mental combinations. It is the beginning of thought: the beginning use of representation and foresight.

Children are now able, by ***representation,*** to use symbolic or visual imagining, to "invent" or "figure out" the solutions mentally. They can solve simple problems, can remember, can plan, and can imagine. For example, children playing next to a fence take hold of an object on the other side. The object is too big to be brought in between the slats. At this stage of development they know enough to raise the object to the top of the fence (if not too high) and bring it over the top. The children are able to picture the events to themselves and follow them through mentally as they lift the object up and over the fence. They are thinking and doing primitive problem solving.

invention of new means an infant's discovery and first use of new combinations of mental thoughts to initiate intentional means-to-an-end behavior in order to achieve a goal; early intentional accommodation.

representational level the level of cognitive development at which the child begins to use symbols as well as images.

Reaction to Piaget's theory

Piaget's theory of cognitive development has encouraged much research in the United States. Barely known in the 1950s, Piaget's theory received a great deal of recognition in the 1960s and 1970s. As a result, some of his concepts have been verified, others have been modified, and a few have been reinterpreted.

In an interesting study, Uzgiris (1972) observed infants from 4 weeks of age to about 2 years and confirmed Piaget's order for the progressive substages of the sensorimotor period. The study resulted in the development of the Uzgiris and Hunt Infant Psychological Development Scales (IPDS) (1975). Wachs (1975) used the scales to test the sensorimotor development of 23 babies. When the babies were 31 months old, they were given the Stanford-Binet Intelligence Scale, which has norms and items for individuals 24 months and older. Wachs, finding a positive relationship between the IPDS and the Stanford-Binet, concluded that, by observing the development of object permanence in an infant, it was possible to predict later performance on intelligence tests.

However, Bower (1976) has found that cognitive development does not always follow the orderly sequence described by Piaget. Some abilities show up at an earlier age, only to disappear and to reappear later. Bower demonstrated that an 18-month-old infant may have a concept of weight conservation; the infant may not respond to that concept at about age 3 or 4, only to have the concept reappear about the age of 6 or 7. However, at this age level the child is solving the same concept problems by using a higher level cognitive process. Training and practice in certain skills can make a permanent difference. Unevenness may be the rule of development (Fisher, 1980). Thus Piaget's emphasis on maturation and strict stages of development may not credit infants with being able to learn more than was expected (Flavell, 1977).

Object permanence refers to the understanding that objects do not cease to exist when they cannot be seen. A memory of the object is implied. For the very young infant, under 4 months of age, an object placed out of sight means out of existence. Between the ages of 4 to 8 months, infants do not search for an object hidden under a cover. They may search manually if a familiar object is only partially hidden. According to Piaget, it is not until 8 to 12 months of age that infants begin to search persistently for objects they saw as they were being hidden. This behavior implies that infants are now able to represent objects and events in terms of visual images and memories. However, Kagan and associates (1978) observed that these stages are not consistent for all infants. This study found that some younger infants seem to have an understanding of

enactive a Bruner term meaning that the mode of thinking is one that responds through motor actions, as is done in infancy.

iconic a sensory image.

symbolic representation a Bruner term referring to the use of abstract and logical thought to employ symbols as the representation of things or ideas.

object permanence. There is some question as to whether the object permanence phenomenon pertains to the baby's perception of his or her parents. For example, infants as young as 2 or 3 months may cry when their parents leave the room, implying that the infant is responding to the absence of an object.

On the theoretical front, there is a difference between the thinking of Jerome Bruner and Jean Piaget, although both are concerned with stages of cognitive development. Bruner is a distinguished developmental psychologist in his own right. The difference between the two theorists concerns the roots and nature of intellectual growth. Piaget holds to a rather vigorous stage approach in which knowledge can be gained only when the schemes are ready to receive and deal with that knowledge (the adaptation process). Bruner's view is that the foundations of any subject could be taught in some form to anyone at any age (Bruner, 1972). Thus Bruner stresses the educational process rather than the maturation-environment interaction of Piaget. Bruner speaks of favored modes for thinking about the world (reality). The favored mode for infants, says Bruner, is ***enactive,*** whereby infants respond through motor actions. In preschool and kindergarten years, the favored mode is ***iconic,*** the use of mental images or pictures. In the middle school years (ages 10 to 13), the favored mode shifts to ***symbolic representation,*** the use of abstract and logical thought to internally manipulate symbols as the representations of things (Bruner et al., 1966).

Piaget's theory still remains a major force. But there is some moving away from what is perceived by many to be a rather strict adherence to the stage process. Other theories and considerations are suggesting that too much emphasis may have been placed on Piaget's thinking as the primary or only approach to cognitive development during the past decade.

LEARNING IN INFANCY

Cognition refers to the process of acquiring, storing, and using knowledge. During the first 2 years of life, infants acquire a wealth of information regarding how to control motor movements and bodily functions, how to concentrate and attend to stimulating factors in the environment, how to produce speech sounds and to use language, how to interact with people, and a host of other types of learning. How does a newborn baby learn to do all of these things? To answer the question, we must first look at the capabilities with which an infant is born.

Learning is a general term for a relatively permanent change in response or thinking that is made to a task-demand as the result of experience. In other words, learning is the process by which a change is brought about in thinking or behaving as a result of interacting with the environment and practice. It should be noted that, in addition to motor reflexes and gross sensory (perceptual) capabilities, the infant also has a maturational capability, a memory capability, and the capability to imitate. Fig. 5-2 summarizes these capabilities.

Basic capabilities

By basic capabilities we are referring to a developing neurological structure and the innate potentialities for learning with which a child is born. At birth a neonate responds almost completely on the basis of physiological reflexes (mostly motor), gross sensory responses, and a few random behavioral movements. Piaget calls infancy the sensorimotor stage of cognitive development because apparently during this age knowledge is acquired through the child's sensory and motor interactions with sources of stimulation in the environment.

Reflexive capability. Reflexes are the newborn's predetermined systematic motor responses to specific stimulations. Reflexes are important because they provide some information concerning the soundness or strength of the neurological system of the newborn; some of the reflexes provide the neonate with a means of responding to a stimulus, a person, or an object in the environment. Modifications of these reflexes are the infant's first attempt to accommodate to the environment. The changes in reflexive actions to accommodate can be considered an aspect of learning. It should be noted that, in addition to the motor reflexes of the arms, legs, and body, there are also motor reflex

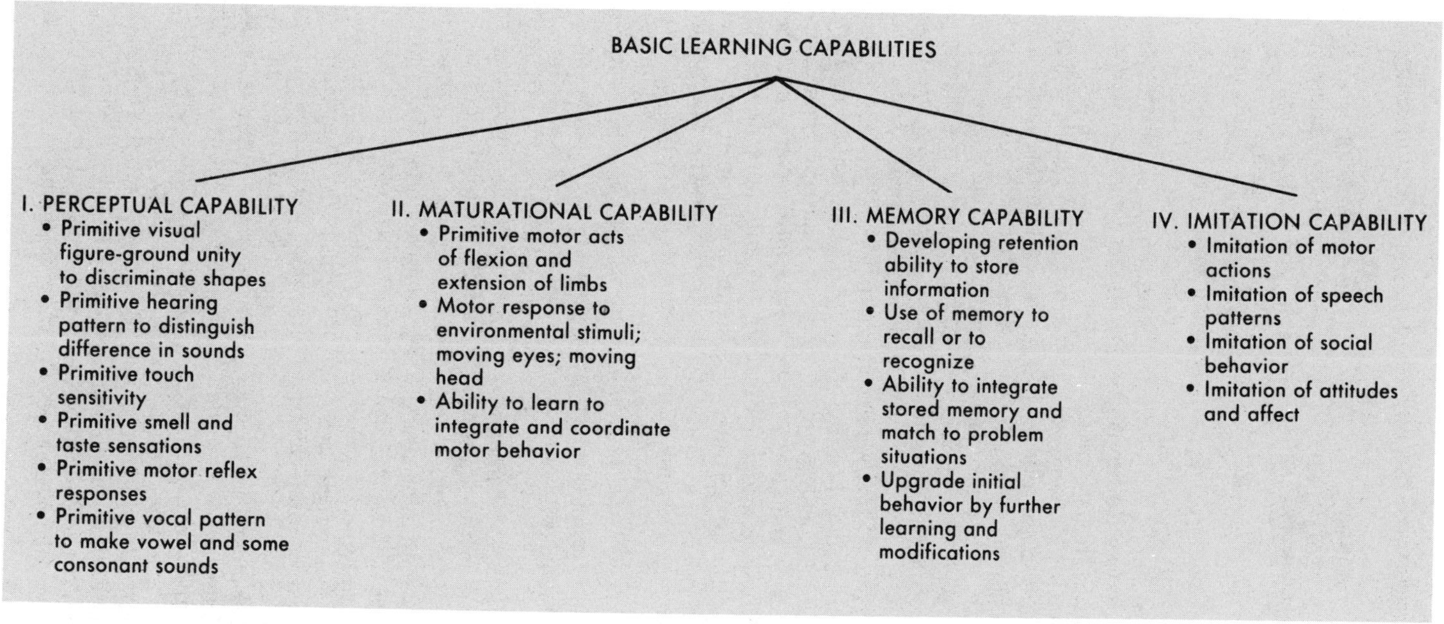

FIG. 5-2 *What a baby has at birth to facilitate "learning how to learn." These behaviors are not mature at birth, of course, but the foundations for their development are present.*

perception the awareness of one's environment obtained through interpreting sensory data.

perceptual pertains to the process or the data of perception.

responses in the throat to permit vocal production of vowels and some consonant sounds.

Sooner or later, the reflexive responses are supplemented by voluntary motor responses that are more appropriate for meeting the demands of personal needs or the environment. In fact some major reflexes, such as the tonic neck reaction, disappear. When the tonic neck reaction fades, the arms and legs of the infant are free to move together instead of the body moving onesidedly. The baby, as a result, will not twist to one side or flip over as often.

Perceptual capabilities. *Perceptual capabilities* refer to the sensory responses of seeing, hearing, smelling, tasting, and feeding through touching with which an infant is born. Awareness of muscles and joint movements, a kinesthetic response, is also a sensory response. At the time of birth or shortly thereafter, a neonate can make use of all of these senses. That is important because it is through the sense organs that the infant becomes aware of stimulation (stimuli) from the environment.

Perception is a cognitive process by means of which the sensory systems make a person aware of stimuli within or outside the body. The central nervous system, the brain in particular, provides a meaningful interpretation of those stimuli. To be aware of a stimulus, one must get that stimulus into the nervous system by seeing, hearing, touching, smelling, or tasting the stimulus. An infant first makes use of the senses in a gross manner and then, through learning and development, refines the use of the perceptual process to the point where finer details regarding the stimuli can be noted.

The term ***perceptual*** refers to the mental activity by which the brain processes the information that the senses have given it. Visual stimuli must be organized; sounds must be received in sequence and discriminated. Thus the concept of perception has two aspects. First, there must be a stimulation of a sense, providing a neural sensation that travels with the stimuli information to the brain. Second, a perceptual process takes place by which the information from the stimuli is organized into a meaningful package for the brain to interpret.

The research appears to be inconclusive in regard to the development of depth perception in infancy (Acredolo and Hake, 1982), although Gibson and Walk (1960) thought they detected it with their famous "visual cliff" experiments. There is some agreement that dichromatic (two color) vision is present as early as 2 months of age (Bornstein, 1978), that shape constancy is present in a rudimentary way in some infants as young as 3 months, and that 1-month-old infants can discriminate pictures from the objects they depict (Acredolo and Hake, 1982). Data also exist that infants, quite early in life, are sensitive to the acoustical patterns characterizing human speech. Auditory discrimination of speech sounds is present (Eisenberg, 1979). Although this presentation on perceptual capabilities is brief, do not underestimate the infant's perceptual foundation or the amount of research available in this field.

Maturational capabilities. The maturational process has already been discussed. Suffice it to say that *maturation* refers to those developmental changes that occur spontaneously in an individual, as long as there are no extenuating circumstances to interfere with that growth. The significant element for learning is that as long as the neurological system is maturing in accordance to its genetic plans, the infant will gradually be able to control, retain, and respond with more proficiency.

Memory capabilities. When an infant responds with a smile and a reaching out to be picked up, this means that the child at least remembers the pleasure of being held by a person. A young infant is observed making sucking movements with the lips when mother is approaching. The baby probably remembers the experience of being fed by her. Infants have the capacity for developing retention ability to store information (Fagan, 1973). They learn how to use different types of memory to recall or to recognize. They can integrate stored memory and match it to problem situations. Furthermore, infants can upgrade the quality of memory storage and usage by further learning and modifications (Foreman and Sigel, 1979).

Imitation capabilities. A marvel of growth and development is the infant's ability to imitate. How does this little baby know how to jabber when someone baby-talks with him or her? How does the infant know how to imitate faces that are made and sounds that are

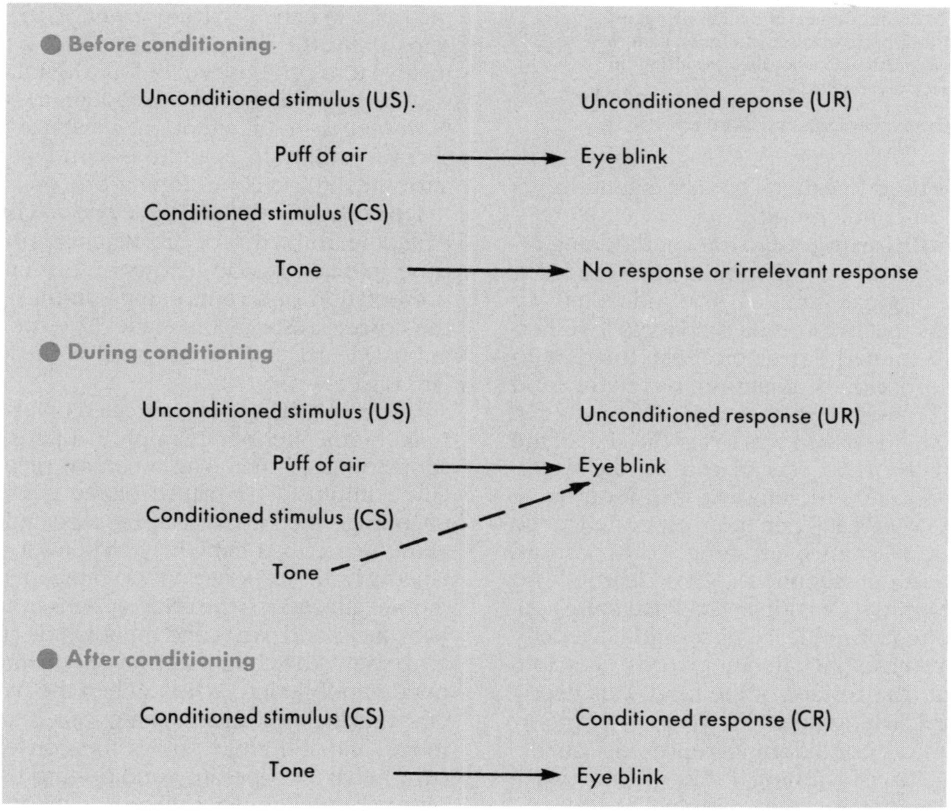

FIG. 5-3 ***Diagram of classical conditioning. The association between the puff of air and the eye blink exists at the start of the experiment and does not have to be learned. The association between the tone and eye blink is learned. The individual learns that the two stimuli (puff of air and the tone) tend to go together.***

produced? Somehow, that little brain knows how to do all of these things—in time. Kaye (1978) demonstrated that 6-month-old infants increase their mouth movements when held by adults who are making such movements. Meltzoff and Moore (1977) had similar findings with newborns. There is some question, however, about whether these movements are imitation or merely social facilitation. It is known that at 7 months an infant shows imitative behavior initiated by the mother. By the end of the second year, an infant begins to imitate new behavior (McCall et al., 1977). The child will imitate motor actions, speech and language patterns, social behavior, and attitudes and affect.

Conditioning and habituation

Certainly much learning in infancy occurs as a result of classical conditioning or operant conditioning. As the infant gets past the 1-year mark, some learning occurs because of social learning. The average infant is also capable of using cognitive insight through observation and adaptation (Piaget) to solve simple problems and needs. Social learning theory is a combination of conditioning through reinforcement and vicarious learning aspects of cognition. The infant comes to consciously anticipate consequences, even though they may not have been directly experienced. As the child grows older, social learning and cognitive learn-

habituation the process of becoming accustomed to a particular set of circumstances or to a particular stimulus, resulting in decreased awareness.

ing are probably used to a much greater extent than is learning based on conditioning.

Classical conditioning. Classical conditioning refers to learning that a second stimulus has the same meaning as the original stimulus. The individual (or the animal) learns that two stimuli tend to go together. For example, we trained our tropical fish to come to the right-hand corner of the aquarium by putting food in that corner. The usual response was to come to that corner and eat. The next step was to tap the side of the aquarium when the food was placed on the water. Soon the fish associated the tapping with food being supplied so they could eat. Then they responded to the tapping on the aquarium by coming to the corner, even if food was not supplied. They "learned" to respond to the tapping. Of course, food had to be supplied every so often or the learning would have deteriorated and become extinct. In other words, occasional reinforcement (the reward of the food) was necessary to keep the learning intact.

Although classical conditioning represents an extremely simple form of learning, it has specific provisions that must be met. A major point in classical conditioning is that the unconditioned response to the original stimulus must be a natural or reflexive response. For example, when a puff of air is blown on the eye, the natural response is to blink If a tone is sounded immediately before the air puff, an individual soon learns to associate the tone with the air puff and blinks on hearing the tone alone. This procedure has been used in studying learning in very young infants, 5 to 7 days old. The conditioned stimulus (CS) is a tone, and the unconditioned stimulus (US) is a mild puff of air. The response is an eye-blink that is soon conditioned to the onset of the tone. In our illustration of the tropical fish the assumption is made that a natural response of the fish is to come to the surface of the water to get the food floating there. Fig. 5-3 illustrates the classical conditioning method.

Can newborn infants be conditioned? The research is inconclusive. Some studies have been done, but the methodology was flawed. What is known is that older infants can be conditioned if they have developed an orienting response (Fitzgerald and Brackbill, 1976). The orienting response is an alerting response indicating that the baby is paying attention to some stimulus. Apparently, the neurological system of the infant must mature to a certain level before the infant can interact with the environment long enough to be conditioned. Orienting arousal, attention, a state of consciousness, and the ability to select the stimulus are important attributes in the conditioning process.

Operant conditioning. *Operant conditioning* is a type of learning that occurs when an operant behavior (one initiated by the learner) is strengthened by the presentation of a reinforcing stimulus if, and only if, the correct response is made. The individual (or the animal) learns that certain behavior leads to a particular consequence.

Operant behavior is controlled by its consequences. Initially, the behavior simply happens, or at least is spontaneous rather than a natural response to a specific stimulus. The nature of the consequences may encourage the behavior to be repeated. For example, alone in a crib, a baby may kick, twist, and coo spontaneously in response to nothing in particular. If a mobile attached to the crib happens to move when the baby kicks and twists and the infant is attracted by that movement, the child may move some more in order to put the mobile into action. When the baby has learned that the kicking and twisting can make the mobile move, and the child enjoys the consequences of its own behavior, operant conditioning has taken place. The baby will purposely move in order to get the mobile going.

Operant conditioning can be effected with newborns. Butterfield and Siperstein (1972) found that neonates would respond to music as a reinforcement. The babies would suck on a nipple (bottle without milk) for a long time when music was being played. They did not suck as long when the music was turned off. Watson and Ramey (1972) used operant conditioning to teach 10-week-old infants to turn their heads to make a crib mobile move.

Although conditioning cannot fully explain all development and learning in infancy, some psychologists attribute many infant responses to this form of learning.

Habituation. Infancy is a time when certain behaviors, such as feeding, bathing, and diapering the child, are done over and over by the mother or father. These events are stimuli. If the same event (or object) is presented repeatedly, the infant soon gets used to the repeated event, and attention and interest in it decline. If infants responded to every stimulus to which they were subjected, they would become overwhelmed!

This process of becoming accustomed to a sound, a sight, an object, or some other kind of stimulus is a type of learning known as ***habituation.*** It represents an early form of memory and an early adaptive response to the environment. However, if the stimulus is then withheld for a short period of time, the infant recovers the reflex response that it stopped making (Haith and Campos, 1977).

CHAPTER REVIEW

1. Most of the growth and development of the infant after birth is a result of physical maturation.
2. According to Havighurst, the *developmental tasks of infancy* center around motor development and control, development of speech and language, and the beginnings of socialization.
3. According to Erikson, the psychosocial crises of infancy are (1) *trust versus mistrust* and (2) autonomy versus shame and doubt.
4. *Assessment in infancy* can be conducted with the Gesell Developmental Schedules, Bayley Scales of Infant Development, Denver Developmental Screening Test, and the Uzgiris and Hunt scales. The Uzgiris and Hunt scales are ordinal scales, based on Piaget's cognitive approach. The first three assessment instruments focus on motor, language, and social development based on normative scores.
5. Newborn infants sleep approximately 18 hours a day. At 1 month the infant will have various *states of arousal*, such as regular sleep, irregular sleep, drowsiness, alert inactivity, waking activity, and crying. The infant appears to be most receptive to stimuli during the alert inactivity state. Bedtime for the 3-month-old may be more difficult but, once asleep, the child may sleep 10 or 11 hours. By 5 months, the periods of sleeping and waking are sharply divided.
6. The *advantages of breast-feeding* are (a) the ideal composition of breast milk, (b) the convenience of providing nutritious, digestible milk of the right temperature, and (c) the emotional satisfaction that generally leads to healthy mother-infant attachment. *Disadvantages* are (a) mother may not be able, for a variety of reasons, to breast-feed the infant; (b) mother may feel uncomfortable with the idea of breast-feeding and may transmit the feeling to the infant; and (c) some mothers are uncertain about going through the process of weaning the baby from breast-feeding and, later, from bottle feeding.
7. The *feeding schedule* of a 2-month-old infant may be fairly regular, although babies set their own time patterns. It is recommended by most pediatricians that solid food not be introduced until the middle of the third month.
8. The time to begin *toilet training* is after the sphincter, bladder, and bowel muscles have matured enough for the infant to be able to control them to prevent or induce elimination. That time is usually when the child can stand without help, about the end of the first year. The training schedule should begin with bowel training. One third of the infants have bowel control by 18 months of age. Girls become dry day and night earlier than boys.
9. The effects of severe or lax toilet training on an infant's personality development are not known. Psychoanalytical theory postulates that strict toilet training may produce either a compulsive or a rebellious personality. Lax toilet training may produce a self-seeking, hedonistic personality.
10. *Sudden infant death syndrome* (SIDS) is a mysterious occurrence that happens to about 16 out of every 1,000 infants between the ages of 2 to 4 months. Several theories are suggested, with one of the more prominent ones suggesting that *apnea* (stoppage of breath during sleep) may be responsible for many cases of SIDS.
11. *Motor* refers to muscular movements, whether they be muscles in the trunk, legs, arms, hands, or throat (for speaking). Body or postural control develops in the cephalocaudal direction, head to seat. Normative data are presented, but they must be interpreted cautiously because these norms refer to groups of children for whom the extreme scores have been averaged out, not to an individual child.
12. The average 4-month-old infant can nearly always lift the head and chest when placed prone on a flat surface. *Prewalking motions*, such as crawling, hitching, scooting, or creeping, occur about the seventh or eighth month. By 14 months, two thirds of the babies can walk without support.
13. *Prehension* is the act of taking hold, seizing, or grasping with the thumb and fingers. It is an eye-hand coordination function. By 6 months of age, half of the infants will reach out and touch a cube. By 9 months of age, fairly well-developed pincer movement of finger and thumb has occurred.
14. Intelligence is usually defined by what it does rather than what it is. What *intelligence* does is basically attend to and solve problems encountered.
15. The origins of intelligence are found in the central nervous system. The faster the system matures, the sooner the infant is ready to use its capabilities for learning and memory.
16. *Piaget's theory of cognitive development* is based on the concept of *adaptation*, which occurs when an individual has improved his or her ability to do more problem solving of situations encountered in the environment. *Assimilation* is the process of gathering new knowledge and skills. *Accommodation* is the process by which the individual uses assimilated

information to solve new problem situations. Together they make up adaptation. Each time adaptation occurs, the *scheme*, which is the ability level of intellectual activity, increases.

17. According to Piaget, the *sensorimotor stage* is the first stage of cognitive development. It occurs during infancy and has six substages: (1) the use of reflexes in responding to the environment, (2) the primary circular reaction substage wherein the infant is stimulated by its own bodily (primary) motor actions, (3) the secondary circular reaction substage, where the baby is stimulated by objects and events (secondary) in the environment, (4) the coordination of secondary scheme substages, where intentional behavior is readily identified and the concept of object permanence begins to be evident in the infant, (5) the tertiary circular reaction substage, where exploratory, reaching out into the environment (tertiary) behavior is practiced, and (6) the intervention of a new means substage, where the infant begins to think through a solution to a simple problem before acting on it.
18. Research findings related to Piaget's theory of cognitive development are definitely positive but contain some reservations. A relationship has been determined between age of development of object permanence and intelligence as determined by the Stanford-Binet Intelligence Scales. However, cognitive development apparently does not always follow the even, orderly, sequence described by Piaget.
19. Bruner, a distinguished developmental psychologist, differs with Piaget on the roots of cognitive growth. *Piaget* emphasizes the adaptation process based on maturation and environmental interaction. *Bruner* stresses the importance of an educational process in developing *modes of thinking*, such as *enactive* (motor activity), *iconic* (mental pictures), and *symbolic* representation.
20. Infants are born with basic (innate) capabilities for learning. These include (a) *reflex capabilities* for developing motor actions, (b) *perceptual capabilities* for the development of sensory input and organization, (c) *maturational capabilities* that promote physiological growth, (d) *memory capabilities* related to the ability to retain, recall, recognize, and retrieve information, and (e) *imitation capabilities* to copy sounds and actions.
21. *Habituation* is a process of learning whereby an infant gets accustomed to behaviors, objects, or people that are experienced fairly frequently in its life.
22. *Classical conditioning* is the kind of learning that occurs when a stimulus, other than the original one, can be developed to elicit a response.
23. *Operant conditioning* is the kind of learning that occurs when a behavior is reinforced. The infant repeats the behavior so that a reinforcement will be forthcoming.
24. *Shaping behavior* is a technique whereby the infant is trained to make a response (behavior), not previously made, by reinforcing the child for actions that are progressively more and more like the act to be learned, until that act finally occurs and is reinforced. From then on, only the completed action is reinforced.
25. Conditioning appears to be the basic approach by which learning takes place in infancy. Social learning approach and the cognitive approach are apparently not the primary ways by which infants learn.

REVIEW QUESTIONS

1. List the Havighurst developmental tasks for infants. List the psychosocial crises suggested by Erikson for infancy. How do the two sets supplement each other?
2. How are the Gesell Developmental Schedules, the Bayley Scales of Infant Development, and the Denver Developmental Screening Tests similar in their approaches to assessing growth and development in infancy? Cite some examples. How do the Uzgiris and Hunt scales differ from the others just mentioned?
3. Indicate, by age levels, the development and change in the sleeping patterns of an infant.
4. Discuss the pros and cons of breast-feeding a baby. What nutritional values are needed in a formula?
5. What is the progressive pattern of a feeding schedule for baby?
6. How does feeding influence mother-infant attachment?
7. When is a child ready to be toilet trained? What would be a reasonable training schedule? How did Freud suggest that toilet training might affect an infant's personality as an adult? Do you agree with Freud on this last point?
8. What is the sudden infant death syndrome? What are some possible causes?
9. Describe the sequence by which an infant develops body control and learns to walk. What does postural control mean?
10. What is prehension? What are the steps in developing prehension? Look at Table 5-4 on prehension.
11. Define assimilation, accommodation, and adaptation. How are they all related?
12. Look at Table 5-5 on Piaget's sensorimotor stage. Take each of the six substages and explain each one in a sentence or two.
13. Evaluate Piaget's sensorimotor stage. What do the research and others say about Piaget's approach?
14. There are five capabilities that an infant has for use in learning. What are they? Describe each one.
15. Define habituation, classical conditioning, and operant conditioning. Illustrate each one.

THOUGHT QUESTIONS AND ACTIVITIES

1. If you decided to design a "good" assessment instrument to measure the overall developmental level of infants, ages 2 weeks of age to 2 years of age, what would you include in the instrument? Would you follow Bayley's approach or Uzgiris and Hunt's? Why?
2. If a mother is physically and psychologically healthy, she should breast-feed her newborn baby. Do you agree or disagree?
3. If indeed there were any personality characteristics developed because of a toilet-training regime, which would you consider to be most important: (a) the way the mother (or caretaker) handled the toilet training program; (b) the personality characteristics of the mother (or caretaker) at the time that toilet training was being taught; or (c) some other factor at the time of toilet training?
4. Invite a mother and an infant to class (or visit in the home). Observe the motor behavior development of the child; compare it to the norms presented in the text (tables or otherwise). Do the norms seem to fit? What might be some limitations of using norms to indicate a standard? Does "average" always imply "good"?
5. Using infants aged 4 months, 8 months, and 12 months, set up an experiment to determine the degree to which each infant has developed the concept of object permanence. Some studies have already been done on the topic. Perhaps you could replicate one of them or at least use the procedure involved.
6. Review Piaget and Bruner's positions on cognitive development. Which one makes more sense to you? Why?
7. The section on conditioning and learning is brief. Look into the literature and make some notes on the type of research done or the experimental approach used in investigating conditioned learning theory as compared to the cognitive theory of development in infants.

FURTHER READINGS

Caplan, F. *The first twelve months of life.* New York: Bantam Books, 1981. This book is written for the general public. It is well-written and well-illustrated. It is based on the findings of research.

Caplan, F. *The second twelve months of life.* New York: Bantam Books, 1982. This book follows *The first twelve months of life,* with the same format of illustrations, tables, and well-written accounts.

Frankel, D.G., & Roer-Bornstein, D. Traditional and modern contributions to changing infant-rearing ideologies of two ethnic communities. *Monographs of the Society for Research in Child Development,* 1982, *47* (4), 1-51. This cross-cultural study investigates the modernization of birth practices and infant-rearing ideologies of grandmother and granddaughter generations of two ethnic communities: Yemenite and Kurdish Jews.

Ginsburg, H., & Opper, S. *Piaget's theory of intellectual development* (2nd ed.). Englewood Cliffs, N.J.: Prentice-Hall, 1979. This text has one of the better descriptions and explanations of Piaget's theory of cognitive development. It is clear and easy to read.

Goodwin, R.S., & Michel, G.F. Head orientation position during birth and in infant neonatal period, and hand preference at nineteen weeks. *Child Development,* 1981, *52*(3), 819-826. This study of lateral preference hypothesized that the way the baby's head was turned when it emerged at birth would indicate a hand preference at 19 weeks of age.

Lamb, M.E., Garn, S.M., & Keating, M.T. Correlations between sociability and motor performance scores in 8-month-olds. *Infant Behavior and Development,* 1982, *5*(1), 97-101. Correlations between measures of social responsiveness, social class, social intensity, and motor development were computed.

Osofsky, J.D. *Handbook of infant development.* New York: John Wiley & Sons, 1979. This rather large volume is a comprehensive collection of articles about the major areas of infant development. Each article, written by experts, reviews the research in the various areas.

Stevens, J.H., Jr., & Baxter, D.H. Malnutrition in children's development. *Young Children,* April 1981, *36*(4), 60-71. The research of the last 15 years on malnutrition and its impact on child development is reviewed, summarized, and its implications discussed.

CHAPTER 6

INFANCY: LANGUAGE, SOCIAL, AND PERSONALITY DEVELOPMENT

LORDY, LORDY

The first word, if it was a word, that my daughter learned was "Lordy." One has to wonder how a child would ever learn such a word as her first word. I think it was probably due to the fact that I sang "la, la, la" to her when she was younger. That's the only word she said for quite a while: "Lordy, lordy." I thought for a long time that would be the only word she would ever say. But she was only one year old at the time and had plenty of time to learn other words.

My worries soon came to an end. After learning the motion of waving bye-bye, she soon formed her lips to roll out the phoneme of "bye." It is interesting to note that she never said "bye-bye" as such. "Hi" was a word that was relatively easy for Stephanie to learn. When I added the motion to the word, however, she seemed to get "hi" and "bye" confused. She would say "hi" when she meant "bye" and vice versa.

Next in her vocabulary came the names of animals. Stephanie learned about animals from her books and from seeing the live animals. The latter seemed to be the more educational. The first animal word Stephanie tried to say was "cow," although it didn't sound like it was supposed to. It came out "keeeee" and sounded that way for nearly a month. I, as a first-time mother, was worried that that was the way she would say cow for the rest of her life.

Soon she came to call all four-legged creatures cows, or in her language, "kees." It wasn't until her grandmother got her a kitten that she learned the correct pronunciation of the word cow. I would say over and over to her, "nice kitty-cat." Soon she came out with "kitty-cat." The kitten had one sound of her own which, as everyone knows, is "meow." When rough treatment of the kitten takes place, naturally the kitten says "meow" and tries to get away. When saying "meow," this kitten really meant "ow!" Soon "meow" was added to the broadening vocabulary of my little one. Driving into the country one day gave me the opportunity to say to Stephanie, "Look at all the cows." And Stephanie said "cow" just as plain as could be. I was so proud of her that I almost ran off the road. I came to the conclusion that she rhymed "meow" and "cow" and ended with the correct pronunciation.

All parents want their children to learn good manners. Like some, I believe this should be taught while a child is young. So when my daughter wants anything, she has been taught to say "please." Of course, it doesn't quite come out like that; she says "peas." It sounds so cute and innocent that everybody makes a big thing out of it. I even heard an adult saying "peas" back to her. Now the problem is to get her to say "peas" meaning the vegetable and not "please." At the table when she says, "Peas, I want some," I always say, "Some what?" and then follow up with "peas?" Stephanie thinks I want her to say "please" and she says "peas." If only she would say, "Peas, some peas," I would be very happy. Of course, time works everything out. She does say "thank you," but it comes out "tank tu." Thank heavens, there is no homonym for "tank tu"!

Then there are always those expressions I wish my child had never heard. When I once took liver out of the freezer to thaw for supper, my sister-in-law said, "Whew! are you having that for supper?" Of course, my two-year-old echoed, "Whew." I did not reprimand her for saying that word, but an incident soon occurred for her to use it.

We were shopping at the grocery store, and one of my selections was a container of liver. Stephanie always places the grocery items in the cart. She put the liver in the cart without saying a word. When I took the liver out of the cart at the check-out counter, Stephanie said as loudly as she could, "Whew." She selected the exact moment when there was a line of customers waiting to be checked out. I was very embarrassed. The lady behind me said, "That's all right; I can't stand liver either."

I guess the word that touches most mothers' hearts is "Mommy" said for the first time. Stephanie says this with no trouble at all. There's one thing that puzzles me, however. I've tried to teach her the word "Grandma"; she always says, "Mom-Mom." I don't know what made her say this, but she calls both of the grandmothers Mom-Mom. So I call them Mom-Mom to her when talking about one or both of them.

No matter what she says, it's always interesting to observe her trying to say different sounds. Sometimes she tries so hard, but they just come out all wrong. I'm sure she thinks they're right. If they're right to her, they're right to me. I know from listening to her she'll soon acquire the correct pronunciation of words.

IN THIS CHAPTER . . .

You will read about

1. The stages of the development of speech in infancy.
2. The theories of language development and factors that influence language usage.
3. Emotional behavior in infancy and the effect of parenting.
4. The concepts of parent-infant bonding and attachment in early social development.
5. The psychoanalytic, humanistic, and behavioristic theories of the development of personality.
6. A concept of the emergence of personality based on developmental characteristics.

Although the emergence of motor and cognitive skills is the most noted element of development in infancy, there are other aspects of growth that are just as important. Psychosocial development is fundamental to the mental well-being of each person throughout life. Speech and language, social and emotional characteristics, and the origins of personality all have their beginnings in infancy.

EARLY SPEECH PRODUCTION

The foundations of speech development begin as soon as the infant is born. When babies cry and their mothers respond to this cry, the first step in communication has been taken.

Infants make their needs and feelings known by using simple forms of communication consisting of body movements, facial expressions, and emotionally charged vocalizations such as whimpers, urgent screams, gentle coos, attention-seeking calls, and laughter. A mother quickly learns to interpret these prelinguistic communications and reinforces them by responding to their calls (Murray, 1979). As mother and child interact, speech, language, and thought are developed. Prelinguistic communication usually reaches a peak at about 16 to 18 months of age. As children's spoken language and vocabulary improve, they have less need to communicate in nonverbal ways.

True language development, that is, interpersonal linguistic communication with understanding, begins when the infant is about 2 years old. Much speech development must have taken place in the meanwhile. According to McClinton and Meier (1978), infants must progress through five essential prelinguistic stages before they can speak conventional, adult words. These stages are (1) reflexive vocalization, (2) cooing, (3) babbling, (4) lalling, and (5) echolalia. Finally, true speech occurs.

Reflexive vocalization

The first sound a newborn baby makes is the birth cry. It is produced by a reflexive inhalation and exhalation of air across the vocal cords, which have been tightened by the trauma associated with the air pressure and temperature changes of the extrauterine environment. Almost no noncrying vocalization is heard until after breathing, sucking, and swallowing are well established. The *reflexive period* of speech development is one of nondescript sounds or speechlessness. It involves undifferentiated crying.

By the end of the first month mothers can usually detect differences in the cries of their babies. The infants have matured enough, physically and mentally, to react with differentiation to varying stimuli and conditions. Babies have one kind of cry that they make when they are hungry, another kind when they have a sharp pain, and still another kind when they have a dull, aching pain or a fever. They have different cries to indicate when they are uncomfortable, wet, tired, or want attention. At this early age children are seeking to communicate to others to make their needs known (Goldberg, 1977). Baby now has differentiated crying.

The shrill cries of hunger or discomfort are quite different from sounds made when the baby is comfortable and happy. This is due to the contractions of the facial muscles when a child is experiencing discomfort and to the more relaxed muscle tone when the baby is comfortable. It is with these shrill cries and comfort sounds that the infant begins to form many consonant and vowel sounds. A child makes vowel sounds before making consonant sounds because when the mouth is opened and air is expelled, a vowel sound is made. To make a consonant sound the lips or the tongue must be used.

Cooing

At about 6 or 7 weeks of age infants show by their behavior that they are aware they are making sounds. Thus reflexive vocalization becomes cooing. In *cooing,* babies make squealing, gurgling sounds, lasting about 15 to 20 seconds. They usually make sounds when they are enjoying themselves, and one can tell that they delight in producing or repeating sounds. These sounds are different from the comfort sounds or the discomfort cries. Although they may only be making about seven different phonemes (the smallest unit of speech sounds), the sounds are phonetically diversified. The cooing sounds made most often are open vowel sounds, such as "oooo" or "aaah." It is usually around the third or fourth month that infants learn to manipulate their tongue and lips along with their throat and voice. At that time they may experiment with the sounds they can make.

echolalia a speech pattern in which the child repeats rather than responds to spoken communications; characteristic of autistic children.

Babbling

The early babbling period is a transition period. It begins about the third or fourth month and usually lasts until about the sixth month. The sounds produced are still mainly reflexive in nature. In *early babbling* the sounds are an extension of the cooing vowel sounds, with an occasional consonant sound. As a result all babies everywhere, the Occidental babies as well as the Oriental babies, make the same sounds. (Sachs, 1976). For the same reason babies who are born deaf often can babble and make the same sounds that are made by children with normal hearing. However, Gilbert (1982) questions the often stated assertion that deaf babies start to babble at the same age as hearing children. Gilbert could find no data to back that claim.

Babbling is the vocalization that babies make for their own pleasure. While lying in their cribs, they are practicing self-initiated sounds that they will need to use in the more advanced stages of articulation and speech development.

The earliest signs of children's response to language are their responses to their mothers' voice. Mothers are the center of children's lives. They satisfy their needs, so their voices become part of the whole experience. As young as 4 or 5 weeks old, infants can be comforted solely by the sound of their mothers' voice. A little later they may smile on hearing her voice, and soon after that they may smile and make comfort sounds and excited bodily movements. At about 4 or 5 months of age infants usually begin to differentiate their responses on the basis of the tone or manner of the voice. They still do not understand specific words, but they can respond to intonation of voice (Dale, 1976). This is shown by babies who respond differently to the same word spoken in different tones of voice.

Lalling or imperfect imitation

About the sixth or seventh month it becomes apparent that babies are beginning to repeat sounds they have picked up from their environment. Some psychologists refer to this period as the late babbling stage or *lallation* stage. In *lalling* there is a repetition of sounds or sound combinations that the child has heard. For the first time hearing and sound production are associated. Hearing comprehension is taking place. Vocalization also becomes more socialized as babies begin making squeals or shouts of delight at the approach of a familiar person.

At about 6 or 7 months of age babies begin to join their vocalized syllables into repetitive sequences of consonant and vowel syllables, such as ma-ma-ma or ba-ba-ba-ba. It is usually about this time that the mother or father says that the baby first said "ma-ma" or "da-da" (Caplan, 1981). As the parents constantly work with the children to bring about more words, the babies will increasingly use the words of their culture and will drop from their repertoire sounds not used in their environment. Children who are born deaf may increase the number of sound combinations they make, but these sounds will be mostly of the reflexive type that they were making earlier in life.

Echolalia and imitation of sounds

At about 9 or 10 months of age infants begin to repeat, by imitation, sounds they have heard around them. There is a definite acoustic awareness of the sounds made by others. Frequently the sounds just made by the babies are repeated by someone near them. This repetition by others and the consequent ***echolalia*** (imitative repetition or "echoing" of sounds or words just spoken by another) by the babies stimulate even more speech activity (Lenneberg, 1967). In other words, language and speech development go along at a faster pace if the parents repeat the baby's sounds. Babies in turn will echo the parents' sounds.

The feel of their tongue, lips, and throat, the sounds they make and hear, the association of other people's voices with lip and facial movements all play an important part in the development of speech. Soon they will be producing elaborate reduplication of two or more syllable combinations. Although there is no comprehension of the sounds, the babies are developing a repertoire of sounds of the language they are to learn. Children who have a remarkable ability to echo sound combinations and speech inflections may develop an expressive "jargon" that has all the mannerisms of conversational adult speech. *Jargon* is a series of utterances expressed like sentences, with pauses, inflections, and rhythm. However, it is no more than meaningless sounds that seem to imitate an adult's manner of speaking.

True speech

When the children are 10 to 12 months of age, they begin to pay attention to a few familiar words. They also seem to have more interest in some words than in others. By their first birthday they can stop when told "no" and, sometimes, can follow very simple directions. The infants are demonstrating a passive understanding of the language. The active use of it will come later. They recognize their name and usually those of their family and household pets. They will turn to look for them if they are mentioned.

True speech takes place when children intentionally and correctly use a conventional sound pattern (a word) and anticipate a response appropriate to the word they have just uttered. The term ***holophrase*** is used to refer to one-word phrases that convey meanings, such as naming the object being acted upon, saying "ball." Verbal understanding is necessary on the part of children for them to use and to respond to true speech. Average children begin to use true speech between 12 and 18 months of age, although the first word spoken may have been said at the age of 10 or 11 months. By 15 months of age they usually speak 10 intelligible words even though their *understanding* vocabulary is more than 50 words (Nelson et al., 1978).

holophrase the single-word utterance of a child who is just learning to talk; from the child's point of view, the single word may be an entire phrase or message.

At about 18 months of age their average *speaking* vocabulary consists of about 50 spoken words. They can respond to "give me that" and can point to their nose or eyes on command. Children understand the language of others before they are able to use the same words. Average children of 2 years of age use more than 50 words, and they can put two distinct words together into a sentence. Language comes when children can use differentiated speech communication in sentences with grammatical structure.

EARLY LANGUAGE DEVELOPMENT

It is necessary to point out that the terms *language development* and *speech development* have different meanings to the professional. Language development refers to the words, their pronunciation, and the methods of combining them for use and understanding by others. As a form of communication, language may be verbal, through the use of words or sounds, or it may be nonverbal, as in the use of gestures, motor responses, facial expressions, or "body language." Eventually language development concerns itself with the length and patterns of sentence structure, grammatical construction, and syntax—the way in which words are put together to form phrases, clauses, or sentences.

Speech development primarily concerns itself with the development of units of speech sounds, the phonemes, and with the maturation and proper articulation of these sounds. In a sense, speech development refers to vocalization, the earliest vocal form of which is crying. The development of vocalization was described in the last section, indicating how a child goes from reflexive vocalization to cooing, babbling, lalling, echolalia and jargon, to true speech. True speech is the appropriate usage of a word. At this point, speech and language usage begin to merge.

Theories of language development

By the age of 2 years the initial steps to the acquisition of language are well under way. The child has, in most cases, learned to combine words into simple two-word sentences. The time has come to make use of the rules of language. Three theories are presented to describe the growth of language development. Table 6-1 presents a summary of theoretical views.

Behavioristic view. Behaviorists believe that language is learned through operant conditioning (Skinner, 1957). Since parents and others selectively reinforce speech and words, they shape language behavior and development. Words are learned because the child receives a tangible reward for producing the word. For example, a child will get a cookie if he or she says "cookie." However, Skinner notes that shaping and rewarding of language takes time; this could not account for all of language development.

He points out that infants and young children generalize rules learned as a result of reinforcement.

generalization (1) in concept formation, problem solving, and transfer of learning, the detection by the learner of a characteristic or principle common to a class of objects, events, or problems; (2) in conditioning, the principle that once a conditioned response has been established to a given stimulus, similar stimuli will also evoke that response.

Generalization is a concept in learning theory whereby an individual takes the main features of one object or concept and relates them to other similar objects or concepts. For example, if a child learns the plural of one word, he or she may generalize the rule for plural endings of other words. Language acquisition, according to behaviorists, is an extension of learned language structure by inferences, analogies, generalization, and differentiation.

Social learning theorists would add that imitation and modeling play a major role in the acquisition of language (Dale, 1976). For example, parents serve as models for their children in language development. As

TABLE 6-1 Theoretical positions on language development

Behavioristic view	*Nativistic view*	*Cognitive view*
1. Environmental orientation. 2. All learning is based on a few basic principles.	1. Hereditary orientation. 2. Concern with generative linguistics. Distinction between deep and surface structure. Determination of ways sentences are formed and related to one another.	1. Developmental orientation. 2. Rooted in European psychological and developmental thought.
3. Language development is part of a universal learning system. Anything that anyone learns is learned the same way.	3. Emphasis on similarity of languages.	3. Concern with development of perceptions and relation between language and cognition. Language development takes place through organism's adaptation to environment and organization of conceptual schemes.
4. Language mechanisms are simple. Stimulus-response. Operant behavior.	4. Goal of language study is development of language theory.	4. Continuous interaction between hereditary structure of organism and input from environment.
5. Language is an acquired function. Only innate aspect is ability to deal with stimulus-response.	5. Linguistic structuring and acquisition are innate.	5. Concern with linguistic ontogeny. Language develops along with capacity for logical thought.
6. Interest in language as an observable behavior.	6. Concern with question of internalized competence. Syntactic structures. Biological foundations.	6. Belief that language and thought influence and reflect each other.

Modified from Shigaki, I., and Zorn, V. Leadership program in the care of infants and toddlers: A training model, Washington D.C.: National Institutes of Health, 1978 their children imitate their language and speech, the parents reinforce their utterances. Children also learn by forms of adult speech. They may not use them immediately but will use them on a later occasion when appropriate. Bandura (1977) suggests that both language comprehension and its use are based on observational learning. According to Whitehurst and Vastra (1975), delayed selective imitation explains the way children acquire language. Whitehurst reinforced 4-year-olds each time they used direct and indirect objects correctly, such as, "The girl gave me a drawing of a clown." The 4-year-olds later used similar constructions in their own speech.

An evaluation of the behaviorist position on language development reveals that the reinforcement theory of Skinner has not provided any clear-cut answers. The assumption of behaviorism is that particular experiences will lead to novel and grammatical utterances. But, with the exception of the principle that reinforcement and imitation are important, few details on the

David Strickler

According to social learning theory, imitation and modeling play a major role in the acquisition of language. Usually we think of the mother or father as the model. However, it is possible that a playful, responsive sibling could also be a model.

language acquisition device (LAD) inborn mental structure that enables children to build a system of language rules.

transformations syntactical rules that explain how a common deep structure can assume alternative surface forms, such as active and passive, positive and negative, statement and question.

acquisition of language are present (Whitehurst, 1982). Furthermore an examination of when and how parents reinforce language reveals that parents pay more attention to speech and language patterns that are factually correct than to those that are grammatically correct. If a child says, "Debbie cookie," mother responds to the request of her little girl for a cookie, reinforcing that word, but not correcting the grammar (Brown and Hanlon, 1970). When children do imitate adult speech, they reformulate the sentence using their own grammar.

Nativistic or innate view. Chomsky (1957, 1965, 1968) maintains that the ability and use of language is biologically innate or native to the infant. He postulates that the human brain is programmed to enable individuals to create and understand language through a ***language acquisition device*** (LAD) (Chomsky, 1975). As the brain cells of the cerebral cortex mature, the LAD allows the brain to perform cognitive functions upon the sounds received, enabling infants and preschoolers to produce grammar and invent totally new sentences. As they develop speech, children produce as well as receive and imitate. The implication is that the child learns so much in such a short time that the source of language and grammar must already be present and not acquired. This rationale supports the concept of language acquisition device.

Lenneberg (1967) also attributes language development to innate mechanisms. His rationale is that language seems to develop in much the same sequence and at the same rate in all cultures. The first words appear about the age of 12 months, two-word sentences with a rudimentary understanding of grammar between 18 and 24 months, and a substantive use of grammar between the ages of 4 and 5 years. There is also an asumption that there is a set of principles common to *all* languages. For example, the subject-verb relationship is found in sentences in the various languages. In Chomsky's analysis, called *transformational grammar,* classes such as subject, predicate, object, verb, and modifier are innate. ***Transformation*** refers to the relationship that exists between *surface structure* (the rules of grammar) and *deep structure* (the deeper meaning of a sentence).

In reference to Chomsky's claim that certain aspects of language structure are universal, Dale (1976) believes that some evidence exists in its favor. However, whether the entire deep structure of language is universal is still a question not resolved by research. For example, even if a child begins with an innate concept of the structure of language, he or she must still learn how that structure is substantiated in the language of the parents. After all, Swahili is different from Chinese.

Cognitive development view. Cognitive theorists believe that language grows out of intellectual development. Piagetian theory states that a child must first be capable of mental representations before utterances can be considered language (Clark, 1978). Such images do not occur until the period between 18 and 24 months. In Piaget's view language does not influence cognitive development during infancy and early childhood but, rather, emerges out of cognitive development. Language is initially related to the infant's sensorimotor knowledge of how to organize the world (Sinclair, 1971).

Bruner (Bruner et al., 1966) describes language development as emerging from three ways of representing the world: through action *(enactive),* through images *(iconic),* and through *symbolism* (the predominant form being language). Bruner believes that language as symbolic representation follows the infant's representation of the world—first by action and then by image. Action (enactive) is based on memory. Image (iconic) is based on imitation. For some time, image memories are still tied to representation through action. Words and language are used by a child by the age of 2, but symbolic representation is just beginning to form. The infant has only an incomplete understanding of the concepts represented by the words. Although the child may know many words and some grammatical structure, the understanding of what language stands for is as yet undeveloped and naive. With time the development of language and thought blend together and become interdependent, helping each other.

A review of cognitive theory and language development suggests that the idea of an underlying cognitive structure that accounts for language is an overly simplistic account of the complexities involved. According to Cromer (1981), cognition can be shown to account for the acquisition of formal linguistic rules. There is the question of how nonlinguistic and linguistic knowledge match or interact. Children know far more nonlinguistically than they do linguistically. How do they figure out which distinctions are important for language? There is general agreement that while there are strong parallels between cognition and grammar, more is involved in learning formal linguistic structure than general conceptual growth alone (Rice, 1982).

Language gradation

Language apparently has a sequential pattern of development (Dale, 1976). Language recognition may occur as early as the third or fourth week when baby responds or attends to a speaking voice, usually that of the mother. Between the third and fourth months baby begins to vocalize in response to social stimulation. During the babbling stage, vocal activity occurs frequently, especially if a mother talks much to the baby.

By 6 months an infant can usually discriminate between friendly and angry talking. Between the ninth and tenth months baby understands gestures and responds to "bye-bye" (if so inclined). It is about this time that babies utter their first word. Response to simple commands occurs between the tenth and twelfth months, when baby begins to understand simple sentences. By 18 months the infant understands and may respond to a simple request, such as "Put your finger on your nose." Baby begins to name animals in a book when about 19 or 20 months of age and, about this time, begins to utter two-word sentences (Nelson, 1973). Full sentences are initiated at about 24 months of age. Prepositions such as "in" and "under" are understood by the 2-year-old. Grammatically correct utterances are common by the age of 3 years. The foundation of language development is now set, and giant strides will be made in the next 2 years.

Motherese

motherese the speech and language interaction between the mother and the infant.

According to Molfese and associates (1982), early in life the infant possesses many of the speech discrimination abilities that characterize adult language. The infant can discriminate between speech sounds, perceive the sounds categorically, and respond to some speech sound contrasts. The context in which the speech sounds are heard, as well as the intonation and the quality of the speaker's voice, has some influence on the perception of speech sounds. Language acquisition apparently occurs within the context of social interactions with caretakers. It also appears to be the result of receptive cognitive ability on the part of the infant.

Motherese and fatherese refer to speech and language interaction between the infant and the mother or father. You can imagine how the parents like to talk to the baby while feeding, bathing, dressing, or playing with him or her. Since the research conducted comparing fathers' and mothers' speech to their young children has reported fathers' input to be very similar to mothers' (Gleason, 1975), we will just use the term motherese or mother here for convenience. Mother is the primary source of interaction with an infant in language and social development.

Snow (1978) has shown that the intent of the questions asked by mother change over a period of time. When the mother of a 3-month-old infant asks the child, "Where is it?" or "What can you see?" both mother and infant focus attention on the same object. At 7 to 12 months these same questions are used to direct the attention of the infant to what the mother is interested in. At 18 months the questions are used to get an information response or to teach something. By asking questions mothers create situations within which their children can function as conversational partners. Questioning also aids in cognitive development. The area of motherese is being researched; more definitive findings should emerge in the not too distant future.

Snow (1977) points out that language acquisition is the result of interplay between mother and child. It begins early in infancy. The contribution made by the child is considered as important as that of the mother. Mother's language with the infant is simple, redundant, contains many questions, is higher pitched, and has an exaggerated intonation pattern (Garnica, 1977).

Benedict (1975) notes that mothers talk differently to very young children than they do to adults. For example, they use shorter sentences, fewer words, simpler grammar, slower speech, and a lot of repetition. Babies paid much more attention and were more likely to carry out simple commands when the moth-

early intervention programs programs for lower-class, educationally deprived mothers, designed to improve their child-rearing skills and enhance the cognitive and personality development of their children.

ers repeated their commands. Strain and Vietze (1975) found that infants did much more vocalizing when mothers talked to them; mothers were more likely to continue talking if the infants kept making sounds. Baby would talk to inanimate objects if mother happened to be out of the room.

Early intervention

According to Tulkin and Kagan (1972), social class differences are evident at a very early age in the way mothers talk to their offspring. Middle-class mothers talk much more to their babies than do working-class or lower socioeconomic class mothers. This difference exists in spite of the fact that both groups of mothers love and care for their babies equally well and spend the same amount of time with them. Working-class mothers apparently do not recognize how early babies can respond to parental involvement with them.

The Milwaukee Project of Richard Heber (Falender and Heber, 1975; Heber, 1976) has special significance concerning the verbal interaction between low-socioeconomic-status mothers and their infants. The purpose of the study was to determine if intellectual deficits in "high-risk" infants could be prevented by ***early intervention programs.***

Heber and his associates gathered a group of mothers whose IQs were 80 or lower and brought them into a maternal rehabilitation program. A control group was also part of the study, but they did not participate in the training program. The intent of the program was to provide an environment and a set of experiences that would allow the children to develop normally. For the first year, children were brought to a center on a daily basis. The specific focus of the program was to prevent language, problem-solving, and motivation deficits that are associated with mild mental retardation and severe disadvantagedness.

Although the program was cognitive-language oriented, vocational training, remedial education, and training in homemaking and child-care skills were offered to the mothers. The mothers improved in mother-child interaction. They were encouraged to talk to their babies; they were taught how to initiate problem-solving behavior in the infants by the use of verbal clues or suggestions. The mothers learned to use verbal reinforcement and more verbal responses.

The results were exciting! The experimental group of children gained scores of 20 to 30 points higher on standardized IQ tests than the control group (Falender and Heber, 1977). What's more, they maintained that advantage after the third grade in school. The children in the experimental group raised their IQ level from 75-80 to 88-120, with a 20-point IQ advantage over the others, mostly because of better language development, in conjunction with an emphasis on verbal inquiry and discovery.

Some doubts have been raised concerning the validity of the results of the Heber Milwaukee study (Beller, 1979; Sommer and Sommer, 1983). Apparently, technical details of the study have not been made available to other investigators for analysis nor have they been presented in any scholarly journals. The study is yet to be replicated. Although the reported results are interesting, caution is in order until the findings have been verified by qualified investigators.

EMOTIONAL DEVELOPMENT

The word *emotion* is sometimes used to describe certain behavior, such as fear, anger, joy, disgust, affection, or pity. It is also used, however, to imply a system of feelings, such as sentiment. Most psychologists agree that (1) emotion is affective and there is a feeling or awareness present; (2) the central nervous system and the autonomic system are involved in producing facial, motor, glandular, and visceral activities; (3) emotion is related in some way to motivation as an energizer of behavior; and (4) emotions can be classified into types of phenomena such as fear, anger, and affection. The problem in applying all these factors of emotions to young infants is in knowing how to determine if they do have such a complex feeling state and, if so, how they manifest this state into a behavior.

Infant emotional behavior

A baby's emotional life is relatively simple and spontaneous. Children place no restraint on a free expression of their emotions, which come and go depending on the extent to which their desires and needs are satisfied or frustrated and on the amount of understanding they possess of their relationship to others

Infants are egocentric little human beings with most of their needs and desires coming from within. However, by the age of 8 to 10 months, they are aware of another child close by and may have empathy with the other child's emotional behavior.

and to their environmental makeup. The baby's emotions are brief and transitory, although expressed more frequently than in adults (Gesell et al., 1974). As soon as the emotion is past, it is forgotten and the baby is free from stress and strain until new conditions arise that require an emotional response.

Infants are egocentric little human beings with most of their desires and needs coming from within. There is a definite relationship between emotional states and personal organismic needs. Needs are simple at birth and so are emotions. When babies have a strong need, such as for food, their emotional response will be one of crying and fairly intense physical movements. If children are hungry and their mothers make them wait beyond the point of endurance, their whole body will reflect their displeasure. Likewise, when they have been fed and are satisfied, their movements will subside and they appear to no longer have an emotional condition.

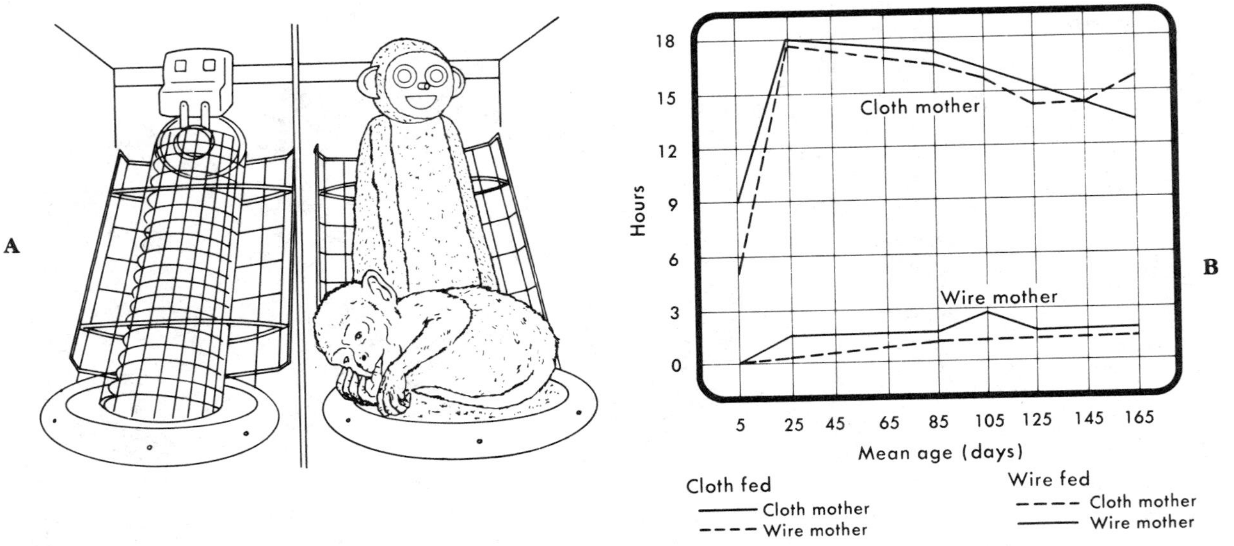

FIG. 6-1 ***A,*** ***Wire and cloth mother surrogates. B, Comparison of time spent on cloth and wire mother surrogates. Long-term effects show that infant monkeys spend their time on the terrycloth mother surrogate no matter which surrogate feeds them—a clear rejection of the reinforcement-theory explanation of infant-mother attachment.***

From Harlow, H.F. American Psychologist, *1958,* **13,** *673-685. Copyright (1958) by the American Psychological Association. Reprinted by permission of the publisher and author.*

Emotions and parenting

The mother is the first emotional climate to which the infant is exposed. The way in which the mother feels about the baby is consequently extremely important. Warmth, softness, and bodily satisfaction become the equivalent of love of the mother for the baby. If the mother is gentle and loving and makes the infant comfortable while being fed, the infant feels physically (and possibly psychologically) secure and develops a positive, friendly response to people (Klaus and Kennell, 1981).

The reward value of a mother's touch was demonstrated by Harlow (1971) in his experimentation with newborn monkeys (Fig. 6-1). He placed each monkey into a booth with two surrogate mothers. One mother substitute was made of wire mesh, which gave it a hard surface. The other surrogate, made of wire mesh also, was covered with foam and terry cloth and made soft. The monkeys consistently preferred the soft mother, even when the only food given to the monkeys was placed by the hard mother. When frightened, the monkeys would run to the terry cloth mother for security. Similar studies done with babies reflect the same types of preferences.

Early mother-child relationships influence both immediate behavior and long-term adjustment (Kennel et al., 1982). Changes that occur in the emotional responses of the infant during middle infancy and the beginning of late infancy are products of complex interactions of maturation and learning. Maturation of the nervous system and muscles provides the potential for differentiated reactions, whereas learning has a determining effect on the manner in which the emotion will be expressed. Learning by conditioning seems to occur easily during the early years, although this question has not been resolved by research (Hirschman et al., 1982).

Emergence of emotions

There is a question among developmental psychologists as to when the first emotions emerge in infancy. The classic work of Bridges (1932) suggested that there are no emotions in the early weeks of life. The

Text continued on p. 207.

Meriem Kaluger

Infant at 15 months. *Climbs the stairs, holding on to the rail.*

Meriem Kaluger

Uses a spoon to feed self, but may spill some food.

Meriem Kaluger

Infant at 18 months. *Curious about his or her environment; needs supervision.*

Meriem Kaluger

Loves to pull and push toys.

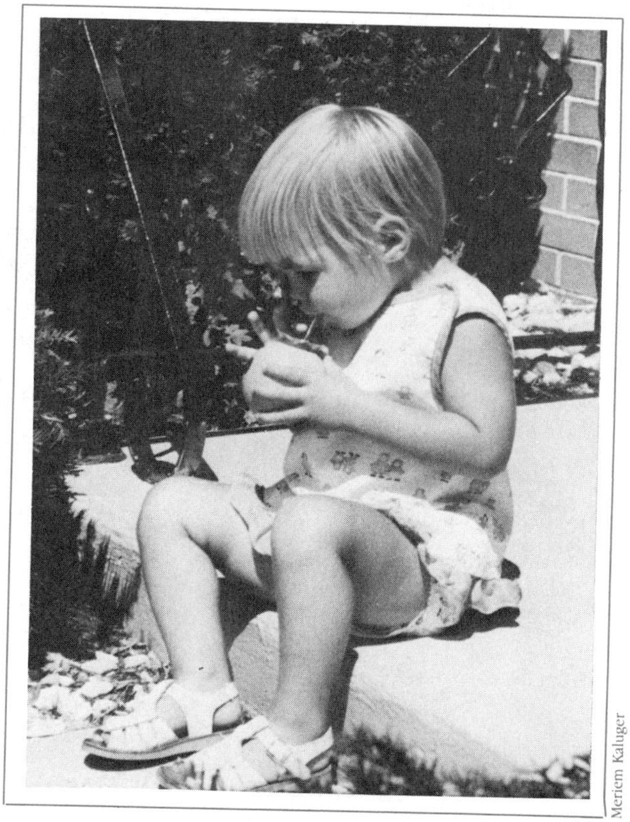

Meriem Kaluger

Infant at 24 months. *Can sip juices through a straw.*

Meriem Kaluger

Begins to emulate a sex role.

Meriem Kaluger

Infant at 30 months. *Enjoys a swing.*

Meriem Kaluger

Plays with stuffed animals; imitates social behavior.

first emotion evident in infancy, according to Bridges, is a general, gross behavior response that can best be described by the term *general excitement*. This undifferentiated behavior soon changes by the end of the first month to the emotion of distress. Subsequently other emotions, such as delight and anger, emerge.

The question posed by researchers is whether a true emotion is present before the infant has at least a rudimentary consciousness of self (Yarrow, 1979). Lewis and Brooks (1978) believe that children are not aware of their own emotional states until about one year of age. However, Sroufe (1979) suggests that 2- to 3-month-old infants are actively involved with their surroundings and thus are able to feel emotions. Sroufe provides a developmental chart based on available empirical literature to illustrate the emergence of three basic human emotions (Table 6-2).

SOCIAL BEHAVIOR IN INFANCY

Every infant, like every adult, depends on other people for existence. The social group not only provides support to the child but also helps to determine what kind of individual the child will become. There is research suggesting that the infant is genetically pro-

TABLE 6-2 The development of three basic human emotions*

Month	*Pleasure-joy*	*Wariness-fear*	*Rage-anger*	*Periods of emotional development*
0	Endogenous smile	Startle/pain	Distress due to: covering the face, physical restraint, extreme discomfort	Absolute stimulus barrier
1	Turning toward	Obligatory attention		Turning toward
2				
3	Pleasure		Rage (disappointment)	Positive affect
4	Delight Active laughter	Wariness		
5				
6				Active participation
7	Joy		Anger	
8				
9		Fear (stranger aversion)		Attachment
10				
11				
12	Elation	Anxiety Immediate fear	Angry mood, rude	Practicing
18	Positive valuation of self-affection	Shame	Defiance	Emergence of self
24		Intentional hurting		
36	Pride, love		Guilt	Play and fantasy

Modified from Sroufe, L.A. Socioemotional Development. In J.D. Osofsky (Ed.), *Handbook of Infant Development.* Copyright 1979 by John Wiley & Sons. Reprinted by permission.

*The age specified is neither the first appearance of the affect in question nor its peak occurrence; it is the age when the literature suggests that the reaction is common.

attachment the primary social bond that develops between an infant and its caretaker.

parent-infant bonding an attachment between neonate and parent that occurs in the first few hours after birth under conditions of close physical contact.

grammed to be responsive to perceptual features of the caretaker. From the earliest weeks of life the infant is inclined to behave in ways to promote contact with other humans (Ainsworth, 1973). The baby glances, smiles, or cries to bring about an interaction. Social-emotional adaptations and cognitive development derive from the process of the infant acting upon humans in the environment (Beckwith, 1979). A positive parent-infant interaction pattern may be established as early as a few days after birth.

Parent-infant bonding

Parent-infant bonding is the process by which the mother or the father becomes attached to the infant. Apparently there is a sensitive period during which this bonding is best made. A study by Kennell et al. (1974) emphasizes the importance of the first few minutes and hours of maternal-infant contact. Twenty-eight mothers of full-term infants were divided into two groups. The first group were given their nude babies in bed for 1 hour in the first 2 hours after delivery and for an extra 5 hours on each of the next three days. The second group were given routine contact, a glimpse of the baby at birth, a contact at 6 to 8 hours, and then 20 to 30 minutes for feeding every 4 hours.

When the mothers and infants returned to the hospital at 1 month, there were significant differences in the behavior of the mothers. During an intense physical examination of the baby, the "early contact" mothers usually stood near their infants, soothed their crying infant significantly more, and engaged in more eye-to-eye contact and fondling during feeding. They were also more reluctant to share their infants with someone else than were the other mothers. It should be noted that a review by Hodapp and Mueller (1982) states that the claim for a sensitive period for mother-infant relations directly following birth may be overly strong. It may be that *any* contact with the infant in the alert, awake state in the first few days after birth can get the mother-infant—or even the father-infant—interaction established in a positive manner.

Studies of father-infant interaction indicate that fathers can become attached to their infants in the early period following delivery if they are allowed contact with them (Lamb, 1977). Lind et al. (1973) found the paternal caregiving in the first 3 months was increased when the father was asked to undress his infant twice and to establish eye-to-eye contact with the child for 1 hour during the first 3 days of life.

There are few differences in the way a child attaches to father and to mother. Men have the potential of being at least as good as women in the capacity of caretakers (Parke, 1979). Although mothers smile at their babies more, fathers touch, look at, hold, and kiss their babies much in the same way that mothers do.

Attachment

Attachment refers to the tendency of an infant to seek and attempt to maintain a close physical relationship with another person. According to the organizational view of attachment, it is conceived to be an enduring affective bond between infant and caretaker (Ainsworth, 1973; Sroufe, 1979; Sroufe and Walters, 1977). Social learning theorists, however, state that attachment is really nothing more than the interaction between infant and caretaker (Cairns, 1972; Rosenthal, 1973). Both approaches agree that interaction does take place.

According to Yarrow (1972) there are four prerequisites for the development of attachment to take place. First, the infants must establish that they are distinct from the environment around them. Since infants respond to objects in their environment within 4 weeks after birth, the concept of a separate self seems to be developed by that time. Second, infants must discriminate the person or persons to whom they will become attached from others. Since 3- to 4-month-old infants stare at strangers rather than smiling, discrimination of unfamiliar faces must have taken place (Kreutzer and Charlesworth, 1973). Third, infants must develop specific expectations for those to whom attachment will develop. Regularity of behavior is necessary, as well as some cognitive ability on the part of the infant to anticipate events based on past experiences. Finally, infants must develop trust and confidence in those with whom attachment will develop (Erikson, 1963). It is around 7 months of age that the infant begins to develop attachments to specific individuals, typically the mother, but also the father if he has been actively involved with the caretaking of the child. It is about this time that an infant develops the cognitive ability of object permanence. In most children, attachment to a number of people will emerge a few months after specific attachment has taken place.

Outgrowths of attachment. Two phenomena appear as outgrowths of attachment: stranger anxiety and separation anxiety. Stranger anxiety appears about the age of 7 or 8 months after specific attachment to a caretaker emerges. The 1-month-old child responds much the same way to strangers and familiar people or just has a blank stare for strangers while making positive responses to persons the child recognizes. The 8- to 12-month-old child often exhibits crying and agitation when confronted by a stranger (Kagan, 1979). This response is ***stranger anxiety.***

However, not all infants fear strangers. Some children get very upset for a long time, some only mildly and briefly, and some do not react at all negatively to strangers. The baby's own ***temperament*** is an important determinant. Easy children show little or no negative reactions. Difficult and hesitant children become more disturbed (Thomas and Chess, 1977). Infants also tend to be more afraid when their attachments to their own caretakers are insecure (Lamb, 1977b). Babies who are raised by many adults, such as in a kibbutz, do not show stranger anxiety at all as compared to those raised by few adults (Schaffer and Emerson, 1964).

Separation anxiety refers to the anxiety and crying that occur when children are separated, or anticipate being separated, from the individual to whom they have become attached. Separation anxiety often emerges at about 10 months of age, reaches a high point between 13 and 18 months, then diminishes gradually after the age of 2 (Ainsworth and Bell, 1970). Greater anxiety is aroused if the infant is left in a strange place or if the parent leaves by an exit unfamiliar to the child.

separation anxiety the distinctly negative reaction of an infant to separation and his attempts to regain contact with his attachment figure.

stranger anxiety the negative response and withdrawal that occurs in reaction to strangers, usually developing a month or two after specific attachments begin.

temperament the general nature, behavioral style, or characteristic mood of the individual; usually thought to have a physical or constitutional basis.

Infant social patterns

Social development follows a pattern. Every child usually passes through certain phases of becoming socialized at about the same age that other children do. Children must learn social skills and how to make adjustments to others.

At birth babies have a lack of interest in people. They do not demand the companionship of others as long as their bodily needs are taken care of. They will stop crying when they are lifted or touched. Table 6-3 summarizes the social interaction pattern of the infant.

Social behavior begins when the baby first distinguishes between objects and persons. The first social responses of the baby are to adults. Smiling in the alert awake state occurs in the third week (Hodapp and Mueller, 1982). Although at 4 weeks of age the baby is not ready for real social stimulation, behavior patterns are undergoing organization. The baby stares at faces that are close by and seems to enjoy following the movements of objects and people.

In the second month infants give evidence that they are actively aware of adults who care for them but make fewer or no responses to other babies in the same room (Field et al., 1982). They gradually begin to respond to smiles of those around them and also to differentiate among the individuals in their home. They begin to coo.

By the end of the third month babies may turn their head or eyes in response to a voice and may follow their mother's movements (Caplan, 1981). Their social presence is beginning to be felt. A smile can be evoked by an adult, using any facial expression. Incidentally, a child born blind knows how to smile. A baby's first response to people is a positive one.

There is an increased demand for sociability at 4 months of age. Infants now like to have people pay attention to them by talking or singing to them or just moving them about. Usually this demand for social attention is stronger toward the end of the day. Beginning at the age of 5 months they may even begin to cry when people leave the room or their presence.

At 5 months of age children smile in reply to another's smile, and they may cry at other social stimuli. Their powers of perception are developing rapidly,

TABLE 6-3 Social interaction in infancy

Age zone	*Social pattern*
Birth	Lack of social interest
3 to 4 weeks	Smiling when alert; stares at faces; may follow movements
4 to 8 weeks	Aware of caretaker; gradually begins to respond to smiles; some differentiation of caretakers
3 months	Turns head in response to a voice; a smile can be evoked by adults
4 months	Increased demand for sociability; likes attention
5 months	May cry when people leave the room; smiles in response to a smile
7 months	May respond to "peek-a-boo" game; can respond to more than one person at a time; is doubtful of strangers
8 to 10 months	More aggressive behavior toward adults, pulling their hair, nose, or clothing; awareness of another child close by
10 months	Does not like to play alone for long periods; likes to be with others in family
12 months	Social give and take; likes others beyond the family
15 months	Likes to get into everything; cooperative in being dressed
18 months	Likes to move and explore; conscious of social approval

Compiled from Bayley (1969) and Caplan (1981).

and they begin to interact with the various forces of their immediate environment. Their interest in their father and siblings increases.

At 7 months of age children may join in a game of peek-a-boo or "hide your face." They follow any object that is placed in motion and will smile when a person uses his hands to cut off the view from their face. Their interest in people and things is increasing. They can respond to more than one person at a time. They enjoy the attention of others but are becoming a little doubtful of strangers; they prefer familiar faces (Caplan, 1981).

Babies display more aggressive behavior toward adults between the eighth and tenth months. They will pull an adult's hair, grab his or her nose, tug at clothes or other personal features. They are also able to imitate some vocal sounds. They now show an awareness of another child placed close by them, although they are not able to share toys at this point.

At 10 months of age babies will not play by themselves for long periods of time and are quick to show their desire for a shift of company or toys. When shown a mirror, they make a sort of playful response to it. Although they stay in the crib for specific periods of time, they like to be with the family group.

One-year-olds. Social give and take is greatly enjoyed at the 1-year-age level. If children have been alone in their playpen during the morning, their sociality occurs in the afternoon. They learn that others besides their family are friendly. Their attention is no longer held by playthings because they now love being chased while they are creeping. They throw things to the floor with the hope that they will be restored to them.

It seems that at the 15-month level children are getting into everything. They seem to enjoy pulling things out of place and, less often, putting them back. At this age children want to be attending to their own business of walking, bending, and stooping, instead of bothering with people. They do, however, cooperate in being dressed.

At 18 months children are still getting into everything, never seeming to stay in one place for any period of time. Now they like to be on their feet to go exploring. They are beginning to know where things are kept because of their interest in the activities of the household, and they know what belongs to different people. At this age they are more responsive to adults and are conscious of social approval.

Two-year-olds. Two-year-old children are egocentric persons. At this stage they take, others give. They will become concerned with others, learn their own limitations, and develop into socialized persons, but only after they have received some training and have had more social experiences with other children.

Children's companions at this time are usually adults of the family, brothers and sisters, and a few children from the immediate neighborhood. Because the first social group for children is their family, that group plays an important role in establishing their attitudes and habits. It also influences their approach to the other groups with which they will come in contact as they grow older. With each succeeding year their interest in playmates of their own age increases, and with this comes a decrease in interest in adult associations.

negativism a primary mode of expressing one's own will by persistent refusal to respond to suggestions from parental and authority figures.

Negativism is a form of behavior by which children show their resistance to adult authority by being self-assertive and independent. This behavior reaches a peak at 2½ to 3 years. It is so common at this age that it may be regarded as normal. ***Negativism*** may result from aggressive use of discipline, intolerant attitudes on the part of adults, or aggressive behavior by children who have not learned to curb their primitive, self-assertive impulses.

Two-year-olds also become increasingly aware of people and at the same time go through a period of being shy with strangers, especially adults. There is the desire to hide from them by burying the head in the mother's lap, hiding behind a piece of furniture, or refusing to speak. How pronounced this will be depends on the opportunities that the children have had to come into contact with different people and environments.

Play. At the beginning of the second year children may prefer solitary play to parallel play (playing alongside another child) and seldom play cooperatively. They are in the precooperative stage, watching what others are doing rather than participating. By the age of 2½ years, however, most children enjoy playing in the company of other children. They may go directly from isolated play to group play (Smith, 1978). Parallel play is not an inevitable step in social play development, especially if the children are friends (Doyle et al., 1980).

Two-year-olds have not learned to share or take turns yet, and problems arise when two children want to play with the same toy. This is the period of everything being "mine" and little understanding of "yours." It is a good idea for an adult to stay close by when the children are playing because kicking, pulling hair, and snatching of toys from one another may take place.

CROSS-CULTURAL ANALYSIS

Cross-cultural analysis helps us to see which principles of growth, development, and behavior are universal in nature and which ones are "man-made" or culturally influenced. By *cross-cultural analysis,* we mean a comparison of the special features, artifacts, and mentifacts of different societies and their groupings of people. All parents, in all societies, want things for and from their children. There appears to be much universality in what parents want for their children. Le Vine (1974) has suggested three goals that all parents have for their children:

1. The physical survival and health of the child, including normal development and change during puberty.
2. The development of the child's capacity for economic self-maintenance during adulthood (maturity)
3. The development of the child's ability to achieve cultural values and status as considered important by that culture

As noted, physical survival and growth are paramount, followed by providing for self-maintenance, and finally, the perpetuation of the culture and enhancement of one's self within that culture. Le Vine's reviews of studies done in African, Latin American, and Indonesian communities with high infant mortality rates show that child-rearing practices in these societies are very responsive to environmental conditions. Our observations in these countries, as well as in primitive societies of New Guinea, the Solomon Islands, and other South Pacific islands, support his conclusions. The more life-threatening an environment is, in terms of food or physical dangers, the more the practice is to leave the baby on or near the mother's body at all times. Whenever the babies cried, the mothers responded quickly by feeding them.

In societies where infant mortality is not high but food and subsistence items are scarce, the emphasis is on the development of behavior that would ensure physical self-maintenance later (Langman, 1973). The emphasis in subsistence societies is on producing children who are obedient to the task. Obedience produces the self-discipline needed to work at making a living. These, and other cultural factors, influence the nature of the socialization process. Western societies, with their subcultural groups, also produce variations of socialization practices within their countries. Working-class homes have different priorities than do affluent home environments. Liebert and associates (1977) do an excellent job in their text of showing how cross-cultural patterns make a difference in developmental and behavioral practices.

libido according to Freud, a basic psychological energy inherent in every individual; this energy supplies the sexual drive, whose goal is to obtain pleasure.

THEORIES OF PERSONALITY DEVELOPMENT

The distinctness of a human being as a "person" includes the concept of an individual who performs both physiological and psychological functions. This individual, although unique, self-contained, and striving for goals, is also receptive to the world around him and is capable of having experiences. The physiological part of a person is readily observed and accepted. The psychological side is not as easily known or observable. Thus personality, which is basically psychological in nature, is difficult to ascertain with any degree of accuracy or ease.

Definitions of personality

The term *personality* embodies two root ideas in definitions. First, it may refer to the outer distinguishing qualities or characteristics of the individual that can be observed by others. Second, personality may also refer to the inner being, which is made up of psychophysical systems and forces that are part of a dynamic intrapersonal organization. The inner self is usually considered to have conscious and unconscious elements of being. Both outer and inner manifestations of personality must develop.

Many psychologists and psychiatrists believe that in addition to the individual's organic systems, such as the cardiovascular, neuromuscular, haptic, cerebral, and endocrinal systems, a person also possesses a psyche system. The psyche is that part of a person that is the performer of psychological functions and activities. It is the mind, yet more than the mind—it is the personification of the life principle.

Many psychologists accept a schematization of the psyche, such as the one postulated by Freud and various psychoanalytical theorists. Behaviorists believe it neither necessary nor desirable to apply terms to psychological abstractions that are, for all intents and purposes, unknowable and possibly nonexistent.

There is no general theory of personality on which psychologists agree. This point alone should make a person careful as to how much stress should be placed on any one theory as the explanation of personality development. In other words, it would be unwise to proceed on the basis of a theory and to act as if it were fact. Too many wrong notions have been held and too many wrong decisions have been made because someone treated a theoretical concept as a truth.

In general there are three major contemporary approaches to theories of personality development. These are (1) psychoanalytic theory and its modifications, (2) humanistic theories, and (3) behavioral theories.

Psychoanalytic theory

Psychoanalytic theory, as developed by Sigmund Freud, was the first of the major contemporary theories on personality development. Although many of Freud's original thoughts have been modified, he is still highly regarded as the founder of psychoanalysis (Freud, 1953). His basic principles and views are still strongly supported even though new interpretations or additions have been made by his followers. The theory of psychoanalysis has three themes: a theory of a psychic energy called the libido, a theory of personality structure, and a theory of personality development.

The libido. According to Freud the ***libido*** is the basic energy force of life. It is made up of the life instincts and the death instincts, which are the prime motivators of behavior. Since the libidinal energy is in the unconscious, an individual may or may not be aware of its existence or its motivating force. The libido initiates behavior that seeks physical or sensual pleasure through human contact. At times it is destructive in its behavior.

The *life instincts* are related to pleasure seeking and erotic desire. The intent of the life instincts is self-gratification. Lack of gratification will interfere with the person's psychosexual development. Freud gave no systematic scheme for the death instincts, but the concept of the death instincts has been interpreted by some psychologists to explain the source of aggressive behavior in humans. The energy of the death instincts builds up within an individual until it must be discharged, either outwardly through aggressive actions or inwardly in the form of self-destruction.

Personality structure. Freud's theory includes a schematic representation of a personality structure that must be developed by each individual. Fig. 6-2 is an illustration of that representation. The structure is made up of three major systems: the id, the ego, and the superego.

The ***id*** is the source of an individual's impulses and drives. The impulses of the id operate on the pleasure principle. The id is the depository for all the physiological and psychological drives with which a person is born. The newborn baby is considered to be all id, governed exclusively by self-seeking needs for gratification. The id also contains all the individual's experiences, learned behaviors, and feelings. In some ways the id is like a vast secret warehouse where all innate drives and impulses are stored and all desires and memories are kept. The id constantly wants to make its "wants" known and fulfilled and uses internal dynamics to pursue its desires. Since the id operates on the unconscious level of the human mind, it has to make its demands known to the ego indirectly through physical or psychological signs.

The ***ego*** is the conscious part of the personality structure. The ego comes into existence because the individual needs some type of conscious element to serve as a go-between for the objective world of reality and the unconscious, impulse-driven world of the id. It is that part of the mind which seeks to operate on the reality principle. On one hand, it may become conscious of signals and signs from the unconscious demanding that certain behaviors be pursued. On the other hand, the individual (through the ego) is also conscious of the reality of the situation. The role of the ego is to decide how to fulfill the demands of the id, while still being realistic about what can or cannot be done. The ego adapts to reality by making use of processes such as perception, cognition, and interpersonal behavior. Since the psyche is at first dominated

ego the conscious core of personality that exercises control demanded by the superego and directs drives and impulses of the id in accordance with the demands of reality; guides a person's realistic coping behavior and mediates the eternal conflicts between what one wants to do (id) and what one must or must not do (superego).

id according to Freud, that part of the personality consisting of primitive instincts toward sexuality and aggression; an aspect of personality in which all unconscious impulses reside. The id seeks immediate gratification regardless of the consequences but is held in check by the superego. See also **ego; superego.**

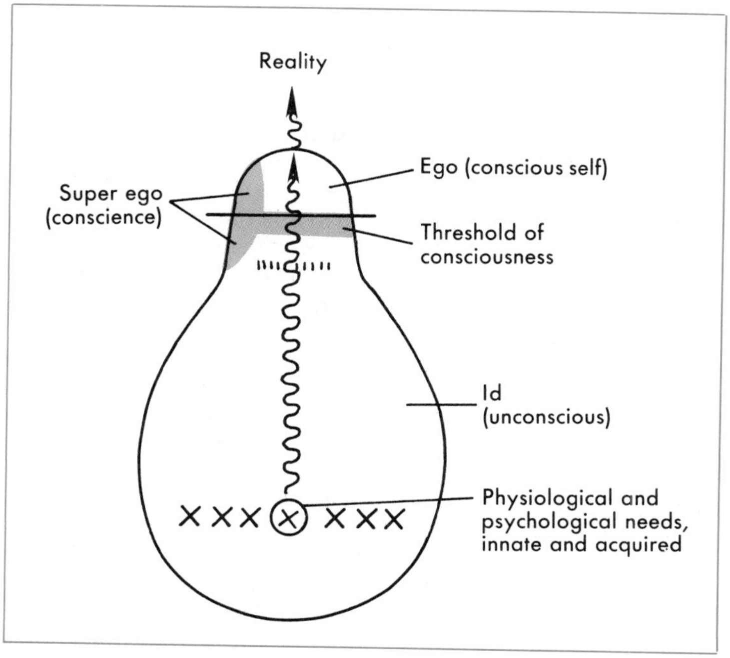

FIG. 6-2 ***The psychic forces as postulated by Freud. The id, which is a "storage area" of past memories, learnings, and so on, as well as a depository for all human needs, must send signals (symptoms) to the ego to tell it what it wants. The superego, on the unconscious level, makes a moral, or value, judgment on whether the signal should be permitted to reach the ego. The ego is the only psychic force that can initiate behavior. The ego is subject to the demands of the id, the superego, and reality.***

psychosexual development in Freudian theory, the sequence of stages through which the child passes, each characterized by the different erogenous zones from which the primary pleasure of the stage is derived. See also **anal stage; genital stage; oral stage; phallic stage.**

superego a psychoanalytic term that refers to the part of the personality structure that is built up by early parent-child relationships and helps the ego to enforce the control of primitive instinctual urges of the id; later functions as a moral force; analogous to an early form of conscience. An aspect of personality, in Freud's theory, defined as the conscience.

wholly by the instinctual process of the id, the reality-perceiving ego must gradually differentiate itself from the id. The term "self" is used by some psychologists to refer to this differentiation and to the development of awareness in the infant.

Through interaction with the environment the ego eventually differentiates itself into the third major system of the personality structure, the superego. The ***superego*** judges whether an action is right or wrong. It develops in response to parental rewards and punishment. The functions of the superego are to inhibit the impulses of the id, to persuade the ego to use moralistic goals, and to strive for perfection.

The superego has two parts, the ego ideal and the conscience. The *ego ideal* is the internalized representation of the positive values and morals of society as taught to the child by the parents and others. The ego ideal includes those actions for which the child is rewarded, making the individual feel proud. The *conscience* incorporates all the things for which the child is punished or reprimanded and makes the individual feel guilty. A superego is not differentiated until the child learns to value certain behaviors or objects as being more desirable than others. The superego arises out of the relations of the id to the ego and their interaction with the environment.

Sometimes the three systems of personality are at odds. The ego, in recognition of reality, postpones or denies the gratification that the id wants immediately. The superego may battle both the ego and the id if the behavior decided upon falls short of the moral code the ego ideal represents. The superego may develop into a strict one with high standards and demands or a weak or loose one with marginal standards. The influence of factors in the environment will determine the strength of the superego.

Personality development. ***Psychosexual development,*** founded on a biologically based sequence of libido progress, is considered by Freud to be the genesis of personality development. The libido, or human energy, flows to and from erogenous zones of the body. In the course of development, different zones of the body take on erogenous qualities. As the intensity of the libido changes its location, gratification in that area is necessary for emotional well-being. The theory of psychosexual stages is based on the bodily location of libidinal energy at different times of life.

The first of the psychosexual stages is the *oral stage.* It is present from birth until some time between the twelfth and the eighteenth month; during this period the mouth is the principal region of activity. Most of the infant's pleasure at this time comes through the mouth as food is eaten while the baby is held. This stage is at a peak during the first year when the feelings of dependency are great. These feelings of dependency tend to persist throughout life and are apt to come to the front whenever the person feels anxious and insecure. Freud believed that the most extreme symptom of dependency is the desire to return to the womb. People with "oral personalities" are ones who were fixated during this period. They derive much satisfaction from activities involving the mouth, such as smoking, overeating, drinking, nailbiting, or sucking on objects such as lollipops or ice.

The *anal stage* is most prominent during the second and third years of life when the main channel of gratification becomes the digestive tract, the movement of the bowels, and the anus. It is during this period that baby gains some control over anal and bladder sphincter muscles, and supposedly the infant becomes preoccupied with anal function. The fact that this period is also the time during which the child is being toilet trained only intensifies the stage. The manner in which toilet training is handled determines if fixation will occur at this stage. Freud believed that the anal period was a time of inevitable conflict between parent and child as to who should regulate the time and place of defecation. If toilet training is too strict and if anxiety is aroused about these activities, the individual could become fixated at this stage. The anal personality, as a result of strict toilet training, may become either (1) obsessively clean and neat, obsessively precise, and rigidly tied to routine if the infant tries diligently to please the parent (anal retention) or (2) defiantly messy, destructive, and disorderly if the infant rebels at being made to conform by harsh parental demands (anal expulsion). If few or no demands are made for control in toilet training, the person may grow up making no attempt at self-discipline or control and may be very uninhibited in his or her actions.

The *phallic* or *early genital stage* takes place about the ages of 3 or 4 years when the child becomes interested in or conscious of the genital area. About the ages of 4 and 5 the Oedipus complex period (for boys) and the Electra complex period (for girls) emerge. The boy and the girl lavish love and affection on the parent of the opposite sex, competing with the parent of the same sex for the love of the other parent. Conflicting feelings usually merge during this period, according to the theory. There are feelings of genuine affection for one parent and rivalry, jealousy, and hostility for the other. How these conflicting feelings are resolved is supposed to affect the personality development of the individual.

The *latency stage* begins at approximately the sixth year and extends to the twelfth year. Earlier pleasures with oral, anal, and genital activities are variously subdued. During this period the child learns to identify with the parents and other adults and may become conscious of the opposite sex but avoids them in activities. Identification of the boy with his father or other male figures and of the girl with her mother becomes intensified. During this time sexual interests are dormant and sexuality is repressed. Oedipal strivings are repressed out of fear of parental disapproval.

The *genital stage* usually lasts from the twelfth to the eighteenth or nineteenth year. The sexuality that was repressed now reasserts itself with force. The adolescent must continue to control sexual strivings. However, there is less repression and more inhibition than in the latency period. Kissing, fondling, and related forms of erotic behavior are adopted. Masturbation is common, and attachment to members of the same sex is not uncommon. The younger adolescent's need to satisfy sexual urges is still highly self-seeking and is not governed by consideration for a love object.

During the infancy stages the individual tends to center interest on himself. When he or she enters the genital stage and normal heterosexual interests emerge, interest is focused more and more on others and on playing the normal roles of the adult in society.

The term fixation should be explained. According to Freud a ***fixation*** occurs when there is an incomplete or inhibited development of the libido at one of the stages. The implication is that the child received either insufficient or too lavish pleasure or gratification. The stage at which the inadequacy of gratification occurred would be the stage at which personality development was fixated. As an adult the individual will, under stress or anxiety, revert to the level of the fixation and manifest a preoccupation with activities associated with that stage.

fixation **the persistence of infantile, childish, pubertal, or adolescent response patterns, habits, and modes of adjustment throughout successive phases of development.**

Evaluation of psychoanalytic theory. There is no question that Freud and his theory made quite an impact on the study of personality and behavior. Perhaps one of the most significant contributions was the introduction and rationale of the unconscious, the internal dynamics, and the energy force. That same point, however, provides a stumbling block to behaviorists and others who want to "prove" the existence of an unconscious. "How can you prove there is an unconscious if it is unconscious and untouchable?" they ask. Regardless, the concept has opened up the field of psychology at a time when so much emphasis was being placed on laboratory experiments, learning studies, and observable phenomena.

In spite of the contributions, some questions and issues remain. Is the emphasis that Freud placed on pleasure seeking and the sex drive justified and accurate? Freud's later writings seem to downplay the force of the sex drive. A look at Freud's early historical period and the people with whom he worked may provide some insight. Freud did his initial work at the height of the Victorian era when there was a strong social emphasis on morality and manners. Sex was "taboo."

Freud did much of his initial work with the mentally ill. Sexual problems were common among his patients. The question to be answered is, Are sexual conflicts the only cause of personality disturbance? It is possible that other causes exist. Freud may have drawn his conclusions on behavior (sexual conflict) that he associated with a social or cohort difference of his time (Victorian morality).

What remains is the question of research backing the theory of psychoanalysis. The rationale sounds

holistic emphasizing the need to study people as a whole, as opposed to looking at fragments of their behavior; stressing the unified, integrated organization of behavior.

self-realization the lifelong process of unhampered development marked by self-direction and responses in terms of one's capabilities or potentialities.

good; to many people it is plausible or at least interesting and inviting; yet there is no psychological research to back up the main stages of the psychosexual development theory. Aspects of the dynamics of the personality structure appear to have more support, but how much of what is observed can be contributed to the unconscious? Freud placed much emphasis on instinctive and biological aspects that are unverifiable. He failed to recognize the importance of society and the environment in the development of personality. Neopsychoanalysis does state that a function of the ego is to deal with objects in the real world and to make sense out of experiences by exploration, manipulation, and competence in behavioral performance.

Other psychoanalytically oriented, post-Freudian psychologists are Alfred Adler, Carl Jung, Erik Erikson, Eric Fromm, Karen Horney, and Harry Stack Sullivan. Each makes a contribution to the psychoanalytical theory. You may want to look up their themes and note what differences they propose as compared to Freud.

Humanistic theories

The humanistic or ***holistic*** approach to personality development is not a systematic theory but more a way of looking at the developing individual as a totality and as what a human being can become. Personality is viewed as the central fact of development and the source of all unity in human behavior. The individual basically does not seek pleasure or the gratification of physical desires (although these are part of his or her makeup), but rather he or she seeks the satisfaction that comes from the attainment of wholeness and unity of self.

Maslow. Abraham Maslow (1954) stressed the growth and self-actualizing features in the development of the personality. He conceived personality as the organized striving of a person to achieve the highest level of one's human potential. This striving is inhibited by forces of socialization and by needs of survival that are inherent within the physiological being. However, as a person gains control over the environment to satisfy basic needs, the individual is free to move up the hierarchy of values and needs to become the person or gain the potential that is ascribed to all human beings. The *hierarchical order* of development from survival needs to self-actualization is from physiological needs, safety or security needs, belongingness and love needs, self-esteem needs, cognitive needs, aesthetic needs, to self-fulfillment of one's potentials. The highest form of satisfaction, a peak experience, involves a sense of complete self-actualization.

Rogers. Carl Rogers speaks of ***self-realization*** and self-concept. He states that the self exists as it is perceived by the individual. The term *phenomenology* is often used to indicate the perception one has of self. The growth and development of the self are influenced by the values of the environment and the persons who constitute it as perceived by the individual. An individual tends to incorporate into the self-concept the ideas that are being expressed. In order to maintain a constant self-concept, we regulate our behavior to match what we perceive ourselves to be. If we have a negative self-concept, we will have low self-esteem. A positive view produces confidence. Rogers believes that each person has an ideal self that represents the goals and aims of the individual. The individual wants to attain this ideal self in order to become a "fully functioning person."

Self-theory. *Self-theories* stress that learning about oneself is a basis for personal growth and feelings of well-being. In the self-theories of Maslow and Rogers it is postulated that a person is born with an innate tendency to move in the direction of growth, maturity, and positive change. A concept of oneself—the self—emerges as various elements unite to form the individuality and identity of the person. The *self* consists of all the ideas, perceptions, and values that characterize "I" and "me" and gives the awareness of "what I am" and "what I can do." The composite, perceived self is the *self-concept.* The perception may be of a strong or weak self.

The development of personality and the self is influenced by significant others in the environment. The child's behavior is evaluated by the parents. The child learns to discriminate between what is deemed worthy by the parents and what is not. Unworthy thoughts and behavior are to be excluded from the self-concept. The child must integrate "proper" feelings and behavior

Behavioral theories of development suggest that environmental experiences involving reinforcement factors strongly influence social learning.

into the self-concept. The more that a person has to deny his or her own true feelings and take on the values of others, the more uncomfortable that individual becomes. There must be psychological congruence between what we do and what we really want to do.

The individual compares his or her experiences in living with their self-ideal. The *self-ideal* is one's image of the person we would like to be and think we should be. If there is an inconsistency between how one acts or lives (the perceived self) and how one would like to be (the self-ideal), the person must psychologically defend the self by distorting or denying his or her authentic feelings. If a major gap is perceived, much anxiety is encountered.

Evaluation of humanistic theory. The emphasis of the humanistic and phenomenological approach to personality is on the whole healthy person; this is a holistic view. It is a positive, optimistic view of human nature. The criticism of this approach is that it is difficult to validate its concepts through research. Self-actualization is really difficult to pinpoint and to define. There is also a need to investigate the conditions that influence the self-concept. It is difficult to distinguish between the self as a causal agent (a doer of behavior) and the self-concept (attitudes and feelings about the self) as a causal agent.

Behavioral theories

The behavioral approach to personality is based on the psychology of learning. Personality characteristics are learned in much the same manner that other things are learned. Behaviorists concentrate on the environment as a teaching arena. Learning comes as an individual responds to rewards and punishment actions resulting from his or her own behavior. Learning comes from either classical or operant conditioning situations. Personality is the structure that results from learned behavior. The emphasis is on environmental or situational factors.

Reinforcement. Dollard and Miller (1950) emphasize the role of drives and drive reduction in human behavior. They emphasize learned or acquired drives rather than innate drives. They concentrate on motivation and reinforcement. According to their theory, four childhood situations play a significant role in shaping personality: (1) feeding, (2) cleanliness training, (3) early sex training, and (4) training in the control of anger and aggression. The feeding situation, for example, can be a setting where an infant finds satisfaction and pleasure in the presence of other people, or it can be a time of turmoil and tension if feeding is carried out in a detrimental fashion. Dollard and Miller use the principle of reinforcement to substitute for Freud's concept of the pleasure principle; they also use other principles of behavior modification to explain why a child adopts certain ideas and behavior for himself or herself and rejects others.

A classical behaviorist, such as B. F. Skinner (1953), does not make a major distinction between behavior and personality. An individual's personality consists of the responses he or she makes. There is no reference made to concepts such as motivation or drives. The behavior of an individual is made up of functionally unified sets of responses that differ from one situation to another. A person may act one way in front of peers, another way in front of parents, and another way in school. It can be said that the personality "changes according to the specific stimulus context in which the behavior occurs." There is, according to this theory, more than one self.

Behavior modification of a one-year-old

Sammy, age one year, was well versed in modifying behavior. Of course, he did not understand what it was all about when he modified my behavior three months earlier, but he had been responsible for an attitude I had to adopt or suffer the consequences to my emotional health.

Most babies of nine months are adept at twisting, turning over, and grabbing for things. For parents this is an exciting time—until it comes to changing a diaper. What used to be a simple task becomes a challenge. At first I rebelled against all this activity while removing and replacing the diaper. I had always been careful about putting the pins out of reach, strapping him on the table, and chatting with him during the diaper changes. Then Sammy began turning over and grabbing for things. Reaching for things did not bother me very much; the turning over was my main concern, since he could fall off the changing table so quickly. At first I would talk to him in a stern tone of voice, reminding him that I might stick the pin into him even though I tried to be very careful. I told him that he might fall and that I was worried that he might hurt himself. Still he persisted in kicking and wiggling and trying to turn over. I figured that I could get the message across with a quick pat on his bottom. He was startled the first time and cried. Subsequent changings produced the same cry after the paddling, but the fussing continued.

The changing routine occurred so often during the day that I felt frustrated much of the time. It did not take me long to realize that he was not being affected by the changing trauma since he had few carry-over feelings once it was over. I was the one who was upset and angry; my feelings held on longer than his did. In the middle of a diaper change it finally dawned on me that my attitude was incongruent with what I value. Here I was, getting upset because Sam, who was acting like any normal nine-month-old child, would not conform to the way I thought he should behave. In a hierarchy of things to become upset over, lying on the changing table ranked very low. Yet I was about to get angry because Sam was acting curious and happy, completely oblivious to diapers and pins. It was then that I decided that I would intentionally decide when a situation was important enought to warrant anger. Once I came to this decision, diaper changing became enjoyable again. I learned how to change a diaper upside down, backward, and sideways with little effort. Sammy certainly had much to do with modifying my behavior.

Within three months the tables were turned. Sammy was now crawling around very well. He was also pulling himself up to a standing position and walking as he held on to the furniture. It was at this point that we began to notice Sammy's fascination with the knobs and dials on the television set. This was our new piece of furniture and much of our entertainment. In the winter, only a few months away, static electricity built up in the nylon carpeting, and a shock would be produced each time we touched the set. Knowing this, we felt that the television should be off limits to Sam. We began the discipline process. At first we said in a stern tone of voice, "No, Sammy, you may not touch that!" He persisted, so we picked him up and put him in a different location in the living room. He crawled back over to the television set immediately. Our next step was to say "No!" and give him a paddling. Soon he became immune to the paddling. He would cry and become upset for a few minutes and then crawl right back to the set.

About this time my husband was taking a class in behavior modification, so we discussed using this technique on Sammy. We decided to institute a "time-out" procedure. One of the few things Sammy disliked was to be confined and held when there was so much to explore. He would start crying to indicate to us that he had been held long enough and wanted to get down and explore. We decided that each time he touched the television set we would hold him for two minutes or until he stopped crying. The first day he was held about eight times. He looked surprised the first time we initiated our plan. He then began to cry and squirm, trying to get away. He looked confused about the silence on our part. There were no angry words or spankings, just neutral silence. During subsequent holdings he would cry hard and push our hands, trying to force them open. After the first few times he gave up the struggling but continued to cry. The second day he touched the television set only four times. The next two days he tried to get the knobs twice a day. The following three days he only attempted his feat once a day. For the next few weeks it was necessary only to hold him once a week. Then about once a month he would test us to see if we were still emphatic about his boundary. We continued to enforce it.

We were happy that our system of "time-out" had worked. It was due to the conscious effort on our part and to the fact that it was consistently enforced, regardless of the inconvenience to us. This was perhaps one of the most efficient and effective ways of extinguishing a particular behavior that we had tried. It was a calm approach to what could have been a trying and hectic experience for the three of us. Sammy learned rapidly that there were some objects in the house he could not touch. This lesson was learned without the usual spanking and scolding often associated with the exploration stage of the one-year-old. One other side benefit for my husband and me was that we were able to keep our tempers, since there was no yelling involved. It was a beneficial experience for all of us.

Social learning. A social learning theory that recognizes the role of cognition—such as perceiving, thinking, and expecting in the development of personality—is one developed by Rotter (1966). His theory is based on the concept of expectation and the perceived value of rewards. We learn to expect certain consequences as a result of what we do. Some of the consequences are positive; others are negative. They influence us by encouraging or limiting our behavior. The more often we experience positive results, the more likely it is that we will make the behavior that brought about the rewarding experience part of our regular behavior pattern. We anticipate and desire reinforcement.

Whereas Rotter speaks of perceived consequences influencing our behavior, Bandura (1973) states that people learn by observing and modeling others. Reinforcement helps to determine whether we will do what we have learned. Observation, according to Bandura, is the major factor in learning. Patterns of behavior are developed as the individual interacts and learns to cope with the environment. In both approaches, however, social learning is involved.

Evaluation of behaviorism. The social learning approach to personality development has made some valuable contributions to understanding. It points out why and how human actions are reactions to specifics in the environment. Behaviorism shows how environment can influence behavior and how environment can be changed to modify behavior. However, there is an overemphasis on situational and environmental factors and not enough attention given to individual differences. A major limitation is that neither the behaviorists nor the social learning theorists have been able to show how various learned behaviors are integrated to form the total personality.

Table 6-4 presents a summary of basic concepts in the major approach to personality.

TABLE 6-4 A comparison of basic concepts in four major approaches to personality

	Freudian psychoanalytic	*Post-Freudian*	*Humanistic*	*Behavioral*
Basic unit of study	Life history of individual (based on psychoanalytic interviews)	Life history of individual; emphasizes interpersonal relations	Perception of self	Responses to stimuli
Basic concepts	Unconscious	Inner mental processes	Unawareness, particularly of self	Unawareness; unlabeled behavior
	Libido	Biological needs (rejects libido concept of Freud)	Self-actualization (Maslow refers to "hierarchy of needs")	Basic drives; also includes acquired drives
	Id	Instinctual aspects of personality	Individual's natural impulses	Principle of reinforcement
	Ego	Mechanisms of perception, memory, thinking; interaction of person with environment	Self	The individual's pattern of learned responses and learned ways of perceiving
	Superego	Acceptance of moral standards; formation of ideals	Guiding principles of conduct; usually conscious	One's moral code, acquired through learning

From Silverman, R.E. *Psychology* (3rd ed.). Englewood Cliffs, N.J.: Prentice-Hall, 1978, p. 351.

DEVELOPMENTAL PERSONALITY THEORY

All children are born with certain basic, innate processes, drives, and demands necessary for self-maintenance and survival. These forces are universal in nature. Babies the world over have the same needs for food, water, air, sleep, comfortable temperature, release of bowel and bladder tension, rest, and avoidance of pain. In addition, they also have certain psychological needs such as those provided for by comfort contact, assertiveness, curiosity, affection, and security. Whenever any of the biological or psychological needs are not fulfilled to a satisfactory degree (satisfactory for physical or mental survival), the infant will try in every way it can to make its survival wants known. The behavior pattern developed in making his or her wants known becomes identified as part of the personality.

Basic premises

The following account of the development of personality in infancy and the preschool years is based on a compilation of growth and development characteristics that can be observed in a growing child. That is why this section is headed Developmental Personality. The characteristics referred to have general acceptance by enough psychologists to provide a basis for this theoretical construct. The sequence presented was initially suggested by Hadfield (1962), a British child psychologist. He based some of his thinking on the developmental concepts of Gesell and Bayley and some on modified psychoanalytic theory. What follows is a developmental personality construct predicated on what appears to be taking place in the growth and development patterns of infants and preschoolers. Table 6-5 presents a summary of the phases.

We believe the initial part of an infant's early development of personality is related to behavioral elements that emerge as part of an unfolding maturational process. These behaviors have physical, psychological, and social survival values. They become the foundation of personality growth. Uniqueness and deviations in personality come from differences in the way in

TABLE 6-5 Emerging behavioral characteristics and personality development

Age level	*Characteristic phase*	*Main emphasis*
0 to 14 months	Control of motor movements Sensorimotor satisfaction	Vital life systems stabilize Sitting, reaching, locomotion Oral and motor pleasures
15 to 30 months	Attention seeking Exploration and curiosity Verbal development Self-assertiveness	Calls attention to self Investigates surroundings Speech and language development Exerts his or her will
31 to 48 months	Behavior imitation Suggestibility to feelings Identification prone Emerging self-ideal	Copies actions of others Reflects attitudes and moods Personality identification Start of self-judgment

which the primary caretakers handle or influence these behavioral expressions.

Newborn and very young infants are not considered to have a differentiated conscious awareness of self or even of existence. The stimuli of the external world will force themselves on the infant. As the maturing central nervous system, memory, and perceptual systems absorb and accumulate more and more of these experiences, an organized psychic structure called the ego, or self, is formed.

The ego, or self, is the conscious part of the psychic structure. The prime functions of the self are the perception of reality and the learning to deal rationally and effectively with reality. Eventually, the tasks of the mature self will include such cognitive processes as perception, adaptation to reality, use of the reality principle and the mechanism of anxiety to ensure safety and self-preservation, motor control, reason and making judgments, storing knowledge, and solving problems. The self seeks to overcome the egocentric demands of the primary physiological drives and impulses of the self by using the secondary cognitive processes of judgment, logic, and intellect to regulate and control them. These abilities only develop with time.

For the first 2 years or so of life, primary biological urges necessary for survival and development emerge. These urges are survival-reaction oriented and egocentric in nature. After the child has achieved the first developmental tasks necessary for stability, the secondary processes of cognition and socialization begin to emerge and develop. They will seek to control the intense demands of the physiological impulses so the child can become less egocentric.

Development of the self begins to take place as the cognitive system gains some control over the primary urges. The foundations of personality will form as the primary and secondary forces work out a compromise and establish behavior patterns. The first 2 years are spent in permitting the primary physiological forces to express themselves so that these forces can promote a survival drive for the child. Then for the next 2 years or so the secondary cognitive processes seek to gain control by developing a socially acceptable behavior control pattern. This pattern comes to be recognized as part of the child's unique personality.

The infant and the child, then, do go through phases of development. Each phase has a special learning task, purpose, or function that needs to be accomplished during that phase. If the task is not learned, the demands of that task continue into the next phase and cause some confusion and conflicts. The environment, especially the one involving the parents and siblings, will have a great influence on the nature, direction, and type of personality that a baby develops by determining how well the developmental tasks are accomplished.

Dependency and bodily stability

Consider the newborn child. The only responses made are reflexes and gross motor reactions. The child needs care and help to survive. The first dominant characteristic behavior of the newborn is one of achieving physiological stability and physical dependency. The infant is dependent on others for food, warmth, protection, and security and is so egocentric that he or she is not even aware at first of the fact that others are tending to him or her. This concern for developing stability is shown during the first month by the fact that the baby sleeps for 60% to 80% of the time and dozes much of the rest of the time.

The baby has a need to have close contact with the mother; he or she will snuggle close and wants to be nursed and cuddled. This contact gives the infant a sense of protection and security. This feeling of dependence never completely disappears. It does, however, later in life change its form from physical to psychological, to social dependency, and finally, to interdependency.

Control of motor movements

Developing body and motor control is another dominant feature of the first year of life. At about the third month the infant will have sufficiently matured neurologically so that he or she can now coordinate some of the reflexes and movements. The child now has some motor control. Body control will start with the eyes, moving down the body from head to foot in sequential order, according to the cephalocaudal direction of growth principle. During the first year the infant will kick, twist, jerk the head, move the arms, and make many motions that appear to have no purpose. Actually this period is one of physical preparedness (Mahler, 1979). The baby is getting ready for the time when he or she will put his or her muscles to good use. The maturational process is still at work. Motor development, in conjunction with perceptual development, is thought to provide a foundation for the development of the cognitive processes.

Sensorimotor satisfaction

During the latter half of the first year the infant appears to be performing several sensorimotor actions for the fun he or she gets out of them. Pleasure is derived from shaking things, touching things, and reaching for and trying to grasp objects. And, of course, anything that can be picked up is brought to the mouth, which has been a major source of pleasure. So many of a child's satisfactions and pleasures up to this time have come through the mouth. For instance, consider the number of times the baby has been fed during the first year alone. Eating gives the child pleasure. The baby has pleasure in moving the limbs. The infant is thrilled with his or her accomplishments in learning to move about. During this phase the baby is experiencing pleasure in physiological activities and bodily function. The child seeks to enhance those activities that give him or her pleasure. The child who is permitted to find pleasure in these early physical activities by not being unduly restricted tends to develop a joyous attitude toward life.

Attention seeking

Once the child begins to walk or to get around fairly well, he or she is now ready to move out of the egocentric shell and take a more active interest in the world. The child has had a year of protectiveness and close watching. But now he or she has accomplished some of the personal developmental tasks necessary for autonomy, and the child is ready to begin emphasizing some of the other primary innate behavioral responses necessary for the pursuit of independent living.

The infant is ready to explore the environment but does not have the confidence to feel secure enough to move freely into the environment. So the baby seeks to call attention to himself or herself to make sure others are watching out after him or her. This phase of self-display is often brought about because the child is left alone in a room more frequently than before. The mother is now used to the baby, and she does have a "million" things to do around the house. The baby, however, wants to make sure that mother is still near, so he or she calls out to her. The infant is reassured when her voice answers.

At this age of 12 to 14 months the baby does enjoy being the center of attention. Everybody loves a baby who is socially responsive. The baby of this age can jibber-jabber, wave bye-bye, play peek-a-boo, and enjoy having someone play "this little piggy went to market" with his or her toes. The baby is developing social contacts and is discovering what behavior pleases people. All of this attention, plus the recognition that mother is still around even when she cannot be seen, helps the infant move from the strong need for direct care and protection of the first year to a freedom to explore in the second year.

Meriem Kaluger

Have you noticed how often an infant shows as much curiosity—or more—about the box in which a gift is given as in the actual toy? A box provides a source of sensory and perceptual exploration activity.

Exploration and curiosity

As the baby feels more secure, he or she begins to roam around. Use is made of innate curiosity, exploring at first close to the mother, then moving further away (Mahler, 1979). The child learns to discriminate between various objects. Soon the infant is going into other rooms and getting into things. This is about the time the baby discovers the bottom cabinets and drawers in the kitchen where mother keeps her pots and pans. Sooner or later the baby wants to see what mother keeps in these cabinets, and so he or she takes out all the pots and pans and puts them in the middle of the kitchen floor. Soon the baby wonders how mother got all of those pots and pans into that small cabinet. When mother tries to get all of them back into the cabinet, she wonders the same thing! Most parents can recall some similar experience that their child had at this phase of life.

Verbal development

Speech and language are the major adaptive behaviors being emphasized during the second year. With speech the child takes a major step in the direction of personal independency and adaptation to life. Verbal communication not only permits the child to make his or her needs known more readily but also will serve as a mediator for thought processes. Thinking usually involves the use of words. Thus the greater the comprehension vocabulary a child has, the further afield the child can go by way of his or her cognitive processes. As the baby responds to mother or father, direct learning takes place in behavior, attitudes, and the social graces in addition to language.

Self-assertiveness

By the age of 2 or 2½ years the toddler has learned to do the basic developmental tasks needed for survival. The child can eat solid food, can communicate, can comprehend verbal responses, can walk and make coordinated movements of all sorts, and can generally exercise some control of bodily processes. What else is left for the child to do but seek to assert his or her will upon the world? Assertiveness and aggressiveness become characteristic behavior of this age. The time of the "terrible twos" and temper tantrums has arrived for many children.

As the child pushes to make his or her wants known, he or she is not trying to be a "bad" child. The child is only emphasizing a concept and behavior pattern that was learned in the first 2 years of life. During the first year of life any time that he or she needed or wanted something, someone provided it. The pattern did not change much during the second year. Whenever the child wanted anything, he or she simply cried or asked for it. Sometimes the child had to be persistent, but he or she usually got what was wanted.

However, the parents have now reached the point where they have decided that their child must learn that he or she cannot always have what is asked for, and certainly the child must learn that the crying "has got to stop"! Unfortunately the parents do not fully realize just how embedded the baby's idea is of how he or she is supposed to let the parents know when something is wanted. The child has always cried or made some kind of fuss when he or she wanted something. This was standard procedure.

All of a sudden this approach no longer works because the parents have decided to put a stop to it, but the baby does not know how else to make his or her needs known. So the child intensifies the crying and fussing, begins to bang the head on the floor, or holds his or her breath to let the parents know how desperately something is wanted. The child does not realize, as yet, that he or she is going to have to curb these "pleasure-seeking" impulses and that one's wishes are not "commands." Temper-tantrum behavior will continue until the child realizes that this approach no longer works. It is at this point that the child is ready to seek new ways of getting what is wanted.

Temper tantrums can be considered as ways by which a child is practicing asserting himself or herself. In life there are times when a person must be assertive for his or her own good. However, one cannot or should not be assertive in all situations. The give and take of social interaction and of compromise must also be learned. Parents can help a child who is having a temper tantrum by diverting attention from what he or she is crying about to something else that is interesting, such as looking out a window, or introducing a new object, toy, or idea.

The golden rules for the parent are calmness, fairness, firmness, and consistency. A quiet firmness on the part of the parent may enable the child to be quiet and firm with himself or herself. An occasional "that's enough of that—it's time for you to learn that there are better ways of asking for what you want and also to realize that no one can ever get everything he or she asks for." The child needs to learn more acceptable behavior patterns and control. The parents should set good examples by their actions and attitudes. The child will learn by imitation and identification. The secondary psychological processes are now ready to be developed. The remainder of this developmental approach to personality will be presented in Chapter 7.

Summary and evaluations

A basic premise is made that in the early years of life the progression of a child's development of personality can be identified by noting the growth and behavioristic characteristics that emerge during that period. Whether that is a correct assumption is not known. Another premise is that an infant is born with certain innate predispositions to development that have survival values. That is to say, the infant has some inborn characteristics that will emerge as the central nervous system matures through the maturational process and the child gains control over bodily movements. As motor control improves, the infant interacts with persons and objects in the environment, and cognition develops. As cognition improves, the infant begins to make use of innate capabilities such as attention seeking, curiosity, imitation, and assertiveness to relate to the world around him or her. These innate potentialities have survival values for life, not only as a child but also as an adult.

Once these characteristics have been practiced and are in place, the child is ready for social training. This moment is some time around 30 to 36 months of age. A

David Strickler

His whole picture of his father's world—the world in which his father moved—as he built it in his brain with all the naive but passionate intensity of childhood was not unlike a Currier and Ives drawing, except that here the canvas was more crowded and the scale more large. It was a world that was drawn in very bright and very innocent and very thrilling colors.

Thomas Wolfe
The Web and the Rock

final comment has to do with whether a description of a child's growth and development pattern can be said to be representative of personality development. This approach is also limited to development of personality during the early years of life; nothing is indicated for personality development in adolescence or adulthood.

CHAPTER REVIEW

1. Early speech production evolves through a series of stages: (a) *reflexive vocalization*, birth to about 6 weeks of age, (b) *cooing*, 6 weeks to almost 4 months of age, (c) *babbling*, 4 to 6 months of age, (d) *lalling*, 6 to about 9 months of age, and (e) *echolalia*, 9 to 10 or 12 months of age. *True speech* develops between 12 and 18 months of age when a child intentionally and correctly uses a word.
2. Three theoretical approaches to language development are those of behaviorism, nativism, and cognitive development. *Behaviorism* stresses the importance of environment in reinforcing a child's language patterns. The *nativistic* view is based on a biological or innate predisposition to language development. The *cognitive view* is a model stating that language grows out of intellectual development.
3. The sequence of early language development is tied in with speech production and social responses. The infant first recognizes or responds to a speaking voice, usually mother's. Vocalization then occurs in response to social stimulation. Later the infant learns to discriminate between friendly and angry voices. About the ninth or tenth month, baby understands gestures. By the first birthday most babies can understand simple commands. At a year and a half, they may respond to simple requests and by 20 months of age utter two-word sentences.
4. *Motherese* is the way mothers talk to their babies. It is simple, redundant, asks many questions, is higher pitched, and has an exaggerated intonation pattern.
5. Social differences exist in language development. Mothers talk differently to infants than to adults. Middle-class mothers talk more to babies than do lower socioeconomic class mothers. Using early intervention, Heber found that lower socioeconomic class mothers could be taught how to converse with their infants in order to make a difference in cognitive development.
6. The emotional climate and response of the mother and the father to the infant will have an influence on the child's psychological development. Harlow's study with newborn monkeys and surrogate mothers shows the importance of soft *"comfort contact"* to develop a feeling of security. Emotions may emerge from general, gross responses shortly after birth to more differential emotions as the child matures. The average 2- or 3-year-old appears to respond emotionally to his or her environment.
7. *Parent-infant bonding* is the psychological, and perhaps physical, process by which a mother or a father becomes attached to a newborn infant.
8. *Attachment* is the tendency of an infant to develop an enduring, affective, close physical relationship with another person. Attachments to specific individuals occur around 7 months of age, after the infant can differentiate between familiar and nonfamiliar persons. At this time the infant also develops a sense of object permanence. Two phenomena occur in less secure infants at the time of attachment—stranger anxiety and separation anxiety.
9. Social development in infancy follows the gross to specific developmental principle. The *social interaction* pattern begins when the baby can distinguish between objects and persons. A 1-year-old will enjoy social give and take. Negativism is not unusual in a 2-year-old. In a social play group a 2-year-old usually prefers solitary play.
10. *Cross-cultural analysis* of infant development and care reveals similarities in what parents want for their children. In cultures where survival is at a greater risk, mothers are quicker to feed infants when they cry, and they keep the babies closer to their bodies.
11. Psychoanalytic theory of personality development stresses the existence of a dynamic unconscious and an energy force called the *libido*. The libidinal energy seeks pleasure gratification. The theory also postulates a *personality structure* made up of the id, ego, and superego. Personality development occurs by a sequence of *psychosexual stages:* oral, anal, phallic, latency, and genital. Freud's theory stresses biological aspects and instincts. It does not stress environment and social influences on personality development.

12. Humanistic theories are basically *holistic self-theories*, stressing the inherent possibilities of growth, maturity, and positive change in the total person. Maslow postulates a hierarchy of needs, reflecting the potentials of human development and the capability of fulfilling those needs to the point of self-actualization. Rogers stresses the recognition and fulfillment of an ideal self, which is to be found in each individual. Self, self-concept, and self-ideal emerge and interact. A conflict among these structures may result in maladjustment. The humanistic approach to personality development is difficult to research.
13. The *behavioral approach* to personality development does not stress a personality structure but does emphasize the changes that can occur in an individual as a result of learning. The personality pattern, as evident by outer behavior and observable characteristics, is developed by interaction with social forces of the environment. According to Skinner, behavior that is approved is continued, especially if the behavior continues to receive reinforcement. *Social learning theory* of Bandura, Rotter, and others suggests that learning may come incidentally or vicariously through observation and cognitive recognition of the worthiness of the behavior. Behaviorism has a limitation in that it does not demonstrate how learned behaviors are integrated into a personality structure.
14. *Developmental personality* is an approach by the authors which suggests that the early personality of a child, up to the age of 4 or 5, is an outgrowth of observable growth and development characteristics based on the innate aspects of survival needs. Maturation is involved in the early stages, to about 7 months of age, when social and cognitive factors begin to have a more prominent influence than previously. *Survival behavior* is developed during the first 2 to 3 years of life. During the third and fourth years of life the child learns socially acceptable patterns of behavior and is enculturated. Whether this concept is a valid approach to personality development and structure has not been ascertained.

REVIEW QUESTIONS

1. List the five stages of early speech production and give a brief description of each one.
2. Study Table 6-1 on the theories of language development. How do the three theories differ? Which one do you think is more sensible? Why? Don't forget to consider the evaluations of each theoretical approach.
3. What is motherese? Describe it.
4. What social differences are there between the way in which mothers of different socioeconomic classes talk to infants?
5. Does early intervention in language development help? If yes, how?
6. What is the relationship between parenting and emotional development?
7. Why is it so difficult to study emotional development in infants? What does Sroufe have to say about the emergence of emotions during infancy?
8. What is parent-infant bonding? Is infant bonding different for fathers than for mothers?
9. Discuss attachment: what it is, what the prerequisites are, and when it takes place.
10. What is stranger anxiety?
11. What is separation anxiety?
12. Study Table 6-3 on the social developmental patterns of infants.
13. What does the cross-cultural analysis of infant development and care mean to you?
14. What is the meaning and the purpose of the libido?
15. Describe the id, ego, and superego. How do they interact?
16. List the five stages of psychosexual personality development. What happens at each stage? What is fixation? Make up and describe a fixated personality.
17. What is the basis of the humanistic approach of personality development? How do Maslow and Rogers differ? How are they the same?
18. Consider behavioral theories. What does Skinner say influences personality development? How does social learning differ from traditional behaviorism?
19. Review Table 6-4 on a comparison of the basic theoretical approaches to personality.
20. What are the major limitations of the psychoanalytic, humanistic, and behavioral approaches to personality development?
21. Summarize the developmental personality approach. What is the major thrust of development during the first 2½ years? What is the major thrust in the third and fourth years?

THOUGHT QUESTIONS AND ACTIVITIES

1. Imagine a baby seeing a cat for the first time. Consider the cognitive understanding that this infant gains as it sees, hears, touches, and maybe smells the cat. Could the infant learn as much about a cat if only one of these senses was used? Think of the words that could be used for cat: kitty, kitten, pussy cat, tom cat, feline, or a pet's name such as Smoky. What does all of this discussion tell you about how children learn and how language is developed?
2. Observe and record the behavior, social and otherwise, of several infants for a period of 1 to 2 hours. What impresses you about them?
3. Assign three debate teams the topic of theories of language development. One team argues for the behavioristic view, another team for the nativistic view, and the third for the cognitive view.
4. The theory of parent-infant bonding seems to be changing. Its early promises do not seem to be coming true. What does this state of flux tell you about research in developmental psychology?
5. Is it possible to spoil a 1-year-old or a 2-year-old? What would the parents have to do in order to spoil an infant? Would it really hurt the baby to be spoiled?
6. Pick a personality theory. Read about it in depth. Come to class prepared to discuss—and perhaps defend—the theory.

FURTHER READINGS

Brown, H.D. *Principles of language learning and teaching.* Englewood Cliffs, N.J.: Prentice-Hall, 1980. This elementary text on language acquisition presents some good techniques for language development in preschool and school settings. The reading is easy.

Emde, R., & Harmon, R. (Eds.). *Attachment and affiliative systems: Neurobiological and psychological aspects.* New York: Plenum Press, 1981. Outstanding researchers in the field of attachment write about their studies and views. The reading is moderately difficult.

Herbert, M., Sluckin, W., & Sluckin, A. Mother-to-infant "bonding." *Journal of Child Psychology and Psychiatry and Allied Disciplines,* 1982, *23*(3), 205-221. A review of the literature leads to the conclusion that the use of the term *bonding* is often misleading because of a tendency to simplify attachment phenomena.

Hunter, M.A., Ross, H.S., & Arnes, E.W. Preferences for familiar or novel toys: Effect of familiarization time in 1-year-olds. *Developmental Psychology,* 1982, *18*(4), 519-529. The habituation process seens to be involved in the preference for novel or familiar stimuli.

Melson, G.F., & Fogel, A. Young children's interest in unfamiliar infants. *Child Development,* 1982, *53*(3), 693-700. Two-year-olds and 4-year-olds were observed in 10-minute encounters with 26 unfamiliar 7-month-old infants and their mothers.

Nelson, K. Individual differences in language development: Implications for development and language. *Developmental Psychology,* 1981, *17*(2), 170-187. Nelson reviews the recent research in an effort to explain differences in children's styles of language acquisition and usage.

Osofsky, J.D., *Handbook of Infant Development,* New York: John Wiley & Sons, 1979. The following articles from this book are recommended:

Gerald Gratch: The development of thought and language in infancy, 439-458.

Ross D. Parke: Perspectives on father-infant interaction, 549-583.

J.H. Kennel, D.K. Voos, and M.H. Klaus: Parent-infant bonding, 786-797.

E. Kuno Beller: Early intervention programs, 852-891.

Smith, P.K., Eaton, L., & Gubdmarch, A. How one-year-olds respond to strangers: A two-person situation. *Journal of Genetic Psychology,* March 1982, *140*:1, 147-148. This study investigated whether positive stranger-infant relationships would be maintained over four visits if the stranger behaved naturally and the mother remained present.

CHAPTER 7

EARLY CHILDHOOD

3 TO 5 YEARS OF AGE

"CONCEPTS OF A FOUR-YEAR-OLD"

It is about the age of four and five years that a child no longer completely relies on sensory equipment to learn about things but can now use language to satisfy curiosity by asking question upon question. Sometimes the questions may be asked to get attention, but soon enough the child really wants to know.

Questions about life and death are frequent. Although the youngster cannot fully understand the meaning of death, it is necessary to try and answer questions within his or her experience and level of understanding. Four-year old Joey accepted the death of his pet goldfish easily because he accepted the idea that the fish was old and ready to die. When it comes to the thought of himself dying or someone close to him dying, he becomes disturbed. The sooner he is given short and practical answers that he can understand, the less disturbed he is.

Joey reacts to those things that have meaning for him. However, he needs an experience to develop realistic concepts. Since his experiences are limited, he will create experiences to relate to a realistic concept. Apparently Joey feels the need to create an experience in his imaginary play dealing with birth. He has a toy horse that he can ride and crawl under. He loves to pretend the horse is his mother and that he is the baby horse that came from the mother's belly. While he is trying to provide a realistic experience about birth to gain a realistic concept, he may also be relieving some of the tension he must be feeling because he cannot understand the whole complicated idea of birth. His reasoning tends to explain things by "magical" or mysterious forces.

His spatial relationships are just now beginning to have meaning for him. He understands that adults are taller than he. He knows he cannot reach the sky. He likes to make himself bigger by standing on a chair or sitting on an adult's shoulders. Touching the ceiling is a great feat.

Although he can say his numbers up to nine and recognize their symbols, he still cannot relate a number to a set of objects consisting of that number. He does not understand the sixness of six or the fiveness of five. In fact, he cannot count to nine while touching successive objects up to nine.

Another interesting factor about the four- and five-year-old's intellectual development is sense of time. At this particular age time sense is just beginning to develop. Joey knows that after he eats lunch he must rest. He knows that during suppertime "Lassie" is on the television. He can tell you that he was born on the eighth of March. He does not know how long he will rest or how long the "Lassie" program will last. He does not make any connection between his birthday and other happenings or holidays in the year. Any important event, such as a tonsillectomy in Joey's case, that occurred in the past week or so may seem ages ago to him. In fact, when we asked him how long ago it was that he was in the hospital, he said it was not a real long time ago, only three months ago. Actually, it was only one week ago.

IN THIS CHAPTER . . .

You will read about

1. The developmental tasks of early childhood.
2. The physical growth curve and the physical and motor characteristics of 3- to 5-year-olds.
3. The second stage of Piaget's theory of cognitive development: preoperational stage, with the substages of preconceptual thought and intuitive thought.
4. The information-processing model, which is presented as an alternative approach to cognitive processing.
5. The structure of language, preschool language development, and nonstandard English.
6. The social development and play of 3- to 5-year-olds.
7. The concept of sex-role differentiation and the Maccoby and Jacklin findings on differences between the sexes.
8. The emotional development of preschool children.
9. The second stage of the developmental personality growth theory.

In early childhood children are complex individuals with important tasks to accomplish. Developmentally they are about to begin the steepest ascent of their lives. Between the ages of 2½ and 5 years children will be transformed from babies who are just beginning to be aware of the concrete world around them to individuals who are ready to delve into the abstract world of books. Life at this age moves extremely rapidly. Many significant events and achievements take place. The adult of the future is truly being formed. In this chapter some references are made to the 2-year-old level of development. This is done so that the reader can picture the transition of development from infancy into early childhood.

Infants of the first 2 years matured and enhanced their physical selves to accomplish the developmental tasks for their age. Preschool children will need to make a more solid contact with the world of people and objects to accomplish their goals. Basically most of the developmental tasks of early childhood are extensions of tasks that were being learned in infancy. Certain tasks must now be developed to a higher level of proficiency or sophistication. Some new tasks will be added. Life is a combination of continuity and change.

Developmental tasks emphasized during early childhood include the following: (1) achieving integrated motor and perceptual control, (2) completing control of the elimination of bodily wastes, (3) achieving physiological stability, (4) improving ability to communicate and to comprehend what others say, (5) achieving independence in self-care areas such as eating, dressing, and bathing, (6) learning sex differences and sexual modesty, (7) forming simple concepts of social and physical reality and learning how to behave toward persons and things, (8) learning to relate oneself emotionally to parents, siblings, and other people, and (9) learning to distinguish right and wrong and developing a conscience (value judgment system).

According to Erikson (1963) the psychosocial task or crisis to be resolved in early childhood, ages 3 to 5, is that of ***initiative versus guilt***. Young children are eager to explore new territory and to master new skills. During this stage their motor and mental abilities expand. Parents who give their children the freedom to attempt new skills and to have new experiences are permitting them to learn how to plan and carry out activities. These children will gain confidence and initiative; they will be active participants in their world. Parents who unduly restrict the freedom to pursue activities may be giving the children the sense that they are being nuisances, and as a result these youngsters will develop a sense of guilt about wanting to do so many things. These children become passive spectators to whatever the environment offers. The question the child must answer at this stage is, Can I initiate roles and activities for myself, or must I do only what others want me to do?

initiative versus guilt Erikson's third crisis of psychological development, occurring during the preschool years; the child may develop a desire for achievement, or he may be held back by self-criticism.

PHYSICAL CHARACTERISTICS AND MOTOR SKILLS

Stages of physical maturational development always follow a particular order. Children do not stand before they sit, nor can they draw a square before they can draw a circle. However, this orderly progression of events moves forward at different rates of speed, some children growing and developing at a faster rate than others.

Therefore some 3-year-olds may be able to do certain tasks normally expected of 5-year-olds, and some 5-year-olds can do only the tasks usually expected of 3-year-olds. There is a wide range of individual differences, and each child must be treated as a unique person. It is established, however, that girls pass through the periods of development more rapidly than boys. Adults, as well as the children themselves, should realize that many different patterns of growth are normal.

Growth curves

The following paragraphs are an analysis of Fig. 7-1 on the growth curves. The growth rates of four major types of organs and tissues do change. General body tissue, including most of the internal organs, muscles, and bones, grows rapidly during the first 2 years of life. After the third birthday, body growth increases at a slow but steady pace until the age of puberty, when a growth spurt takes place.

Neural development takes place so rapidly in the early years that by the age of 2 years, neurological development is 60% complete, and by the age of 6 years the brain is close to 90% complete. Nature has provided for this rapid neural growth because it is so important and fundamental to all other aspects of growth. Genital development, however, is slow because reproductive organs need not be functional until after puberty.

Lymphoid development is interesting. It has the second most rapid rate of growth. By the age of 4 years it is 60% complete; by the age of 8 years it is 90% complete. Note the rapid increase in the next 3 years to a peak at the age of 11 years, of 195% (almost double) of what will be development of the lymphoid masses at maturity. Lymphoid masses fight infections and help ward off illnesses. As compared to any other age level, fewer 11-year-olds die of diseases, and more 11-year-olds die from accidents.

Physical development

The typical 3-year-old weighs between 14.5 and 16 kg (32 and 35 lb.). Over the next two years the child will gain 1.5 to 2.5 kg (3 to 5 lb.) a year in weight. The average 5-year-old weighs between 18 and 19.5 kg (40 to 43 lb.). There is no significant difference in weight between boys and girls, although boys do tend to be slightly heavier (Vaughan, 1979).

The height for a 3-year-old is, on the average, approximately 92.5 to 97.5 cm (37 to 39 in.). There will be a steady increase of 5 to 7.5 cm (2 to 3 in.) in height

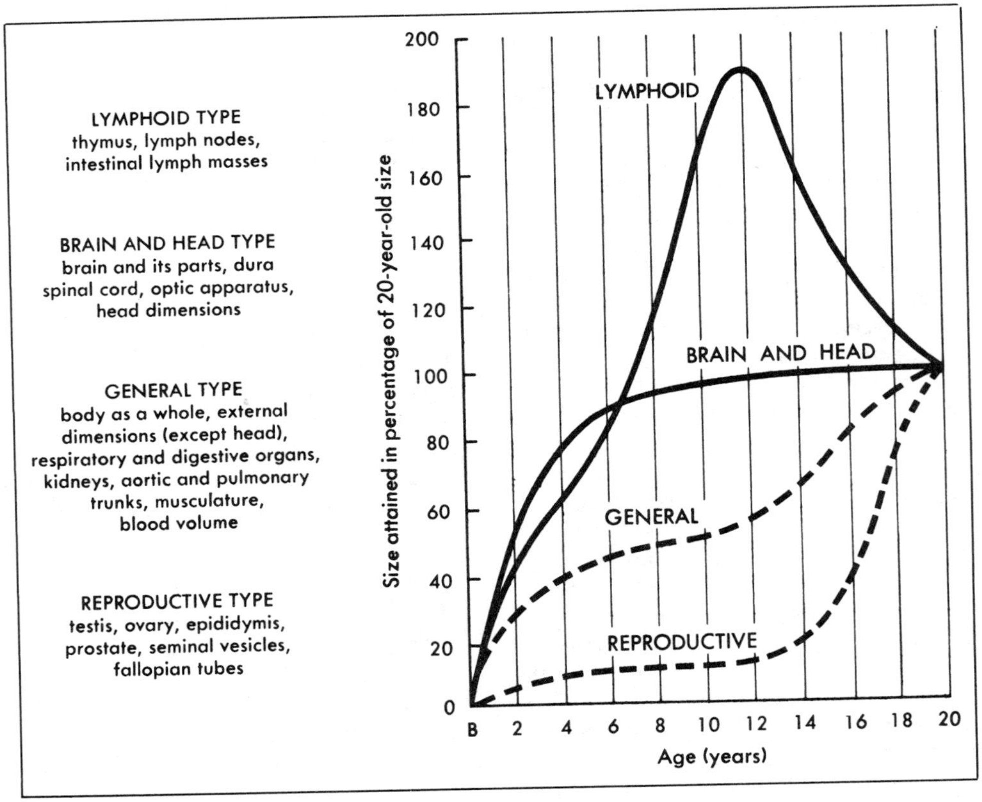

FIG. 7-1 *Growth curves of different parts and tissues of the body, showing the four chief types. All curves are of size attained and plotted to that size at age 20, which is 100 on the vertical scale. Redrawn after Tanner, J.M. Growth at adolescence (2nd. ed.). Oxford, England: Blackwell Scientific Publications, 1962.*

a year for the next 4 years. The typical child of 5 is 107 to 112 cm (42 to 44 in.) tall. The differences in height between boys and girls is slight. The child's stature at the age of 5 years is a moderately good predictor of adult height since the correlation between heights at these two ages is close to .70.

One major change that all children go through is the "lengthening out" process, during which the child's build changes from a baby look to a proportioned "little adult" look. The child gradually becomes slimmer, taller, and more solid looking. The protruding abdomen flattens, and the shoulders become broader. These changes in baby proportions are due mainly to an increase in the length of the legs. By the second year the length of the arms and legs has increased 60% to 75% from what they were at birth.

Up to the age of 4 years, growth in the muscular system is roughly proportional to the growth of the body as a whole. Thereafter the muscles develop at a faster pace. During the fifth year, 75% of the child's weight can be attributed to muscular development (Tanner, 1970). Throughout this period the larger muscles remain better developed than the small fine muscles. For this reason the young child is more skillful in activities involving large movements than in those involving fine coordination.

For children to develop normally they must have adequate nutrition, exercise, rest, and sleep. Children inherit their potential for growth from their parents and grandparents, but environmental factors such as physical care, nutritional adequacy, and parents' attitude toward health and safety have a great bearing on the physical growth of the children. Children who are undernourished and lack good sleeping habits are low in energy and will not be mentally alert. Four- or 5-year-olds cannot develop their physical being and motor skills to their fullest potential if they are the victims of poor health (Hildebrand, 1976).

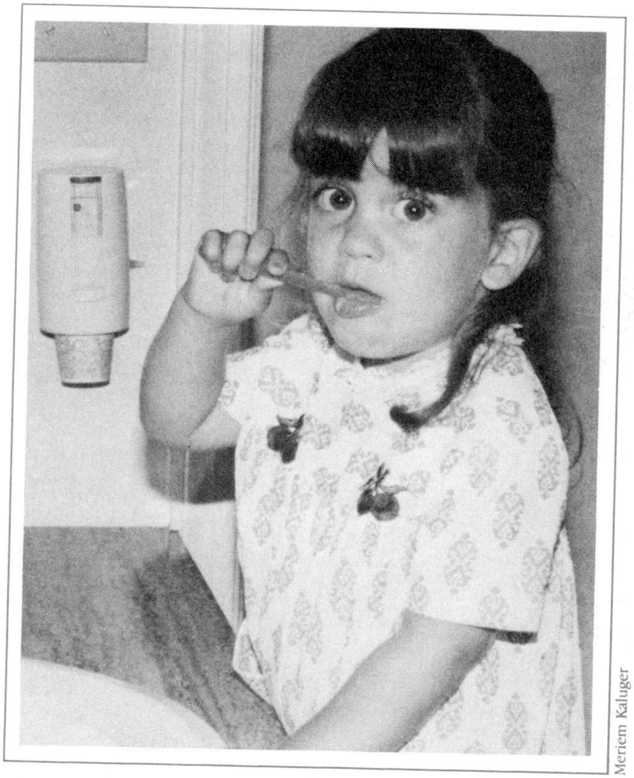

Meriem Kaluger

***Early childhood at 3 years.** Can brush teeth and wash hands.*

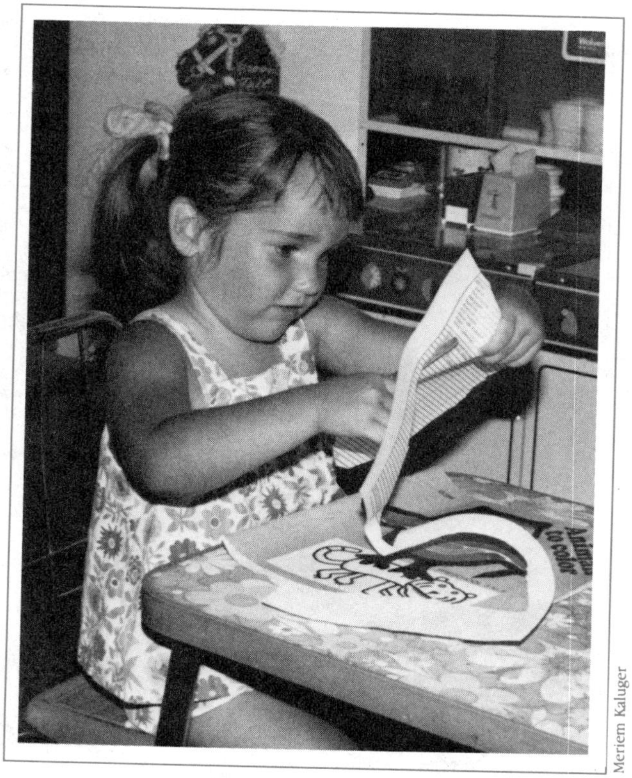

Meriem Kaluger

Can use blunt end scissors to cut paper.

Meriem Kaluger

Early childhood at 4 years. *Enjoys playing in the sand and experimenting.*

Meriem Kaluger

Begins to control crayon for coloring pictures.

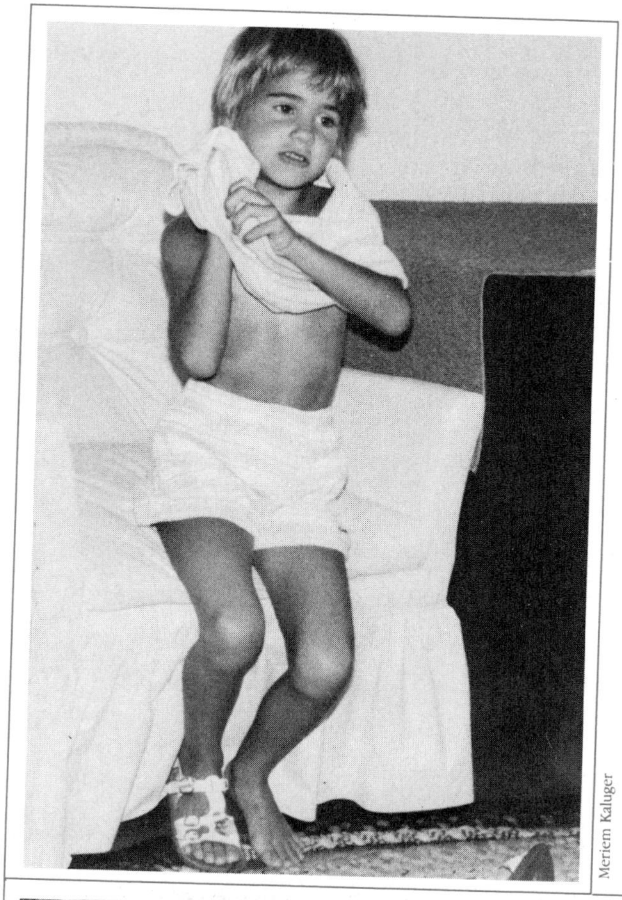

Meriem Kaluger

***Early childhood at 5 years.** Dresses and undresses with a minimum of help.*

Meriem Kaluger

Enjoys sharing in group activities.

TABLE 7-1 Gross and fine motor and perceptual-motor attributes in ages 2 to 5 years

Approximate time of appearance in years	*Selected gross motor and perceptual-motor behaviors*	*Selected fine motor and perceptual-motor behaviors*
2	Walking in even rhythm, up and down stairs, backward and sideward; true running; picks up object without falling; throws a small ball 1.2 to 1.5 m (4 to 5 ft.).	Puts on shoes, socks; turns doorknob, unscrews lid; with pencil imitates circular stroke.
3	Can walk line, heel to toe, 3 m (10 ft.) long; can throw a ball about 3 m; rides tricycle.	Copies circle; unbuttons front and side buttons; builds tower with 9 cubes; variety of scribbling patterns.
4	Goes down stairs one foot per step; running with good form and leg-arm coordination; can walk balance beam; skillful jumping apparent.	Can button clothes fully; copies cross and later square; crudely drawn human figures and houses.
5	Can catch large ball bounced to him; skips on both feet; can hop about 15 m (50 ft.) in 11 seconds; stands on one foot 4 to 6 seconds.	Can tie shoelaces; copies triangle; refinement of animal and house drawings.

Compiled from Cratty (1979) and Illingworth (1971).

Motor characteristics

Because of their limited physical development, most 2-year-olds are still geared to gross motor activity. They like to run and romp, but their coordination is still slow in improving. Two-and-a-half-year-olds are at the crossroads stage in the growth of their action system. Their capacity for determining the proper amount of muscle control to use in a certain action is poor because their nerve cell organization is still immature and incompletely developed. This limitation shows itself in such actions as grasping and releasing. They tend to grasp too strongly and to release with overextension. They have not learned to let go. Table 7-1 indicates the types of motor activities usually performed by children ages 2 to 5 years.

By the time children are 3 years old they have much more motor control. They are more sure on their feet, walk erect, and can stand on one foot. They can go upstairs alternating feet. They like to hurry up and down stairs, but they also enjoy sedentary pastimes that involve finer motor coordination. They can build a block tower of 9 or 10 blocks. This is also the year when sphincter muscles of bladder and bowel come under rather complete voluntary control.

Children in the middle phase of early childhood, such as 4-year-olds, are able to run smoothly and quickly with confidence. They can swerve to avoid obstacles and turn corners at an angle. They can gallop, but not well. They can steer their tricycle at full speed. They can wash their hands and face, brush their teeth (fairly well), dress themselves, button their front buttons, and comb their hair. Although they will work at it, tying their shoelaces is still a difficult task (Lefrancois, 1973). Most 4-year-olds draw objects with few details. They enjoy painting, but they shift their ideas frequently. They like to copy their name but usually copy only the first few letters, making marks for the rest of the letters in their name. They attempt to use scissors and can cut a crude straight line.

In the latter phase of early childhood, children are more agile than they were earlier and in greater control of their bodily activities. They are closely knit. Their arms are held near their bodies. Their stance is more narrow. They still have more control over their large muscles than over their small ones. They are beginning to use their hands more in catching a ball, but they still have some trouble catching it. Their alternating mechanism is put to practice in much of their behavior. They alternate their feet when descending stairs. They can march to music with good rhythm. Five-year-old girls usually do better than boys at hopping, catching a ball, or balancing on one foot (Cratty,

1979). Five-year-olds are active children but without the restlessness that they may have at the age of 4 years. They play in one location for longer periods of time. They respond to their growth needs by enjoying games in which there is plenty of action. Their activity has definite direction.

Handedness is frequently identifiable at 4 years of age; 5-year-olds can indicate the hand they want to use for writing. Their initial approach is with the dominant hand; they do not transfer a pencil or crayon to the free hand. The hand and eye do not yet work with complete coordination. They may still have difficulty when they try to reach for things beyond arm's length and may sometimes spill or knock them over.

centration tendency to focus on one aspect of a situation and to neglect the importance of other aspects; characteristic of preoperational thought in Piaget's theory.

egocentrism failure to appreciate that another person's perceptions of a situation may differ from one's own; a characteristic of preoperational thought.

handedness the tendency to use either the right or the left hand predominantly.

preoperational stage according to Jean Piaget, the stage in a child's development occurring from 18 months to 7 years of age, during which he begins to encounter reality on the representational level. A subperiod of the representational period, which begins when children start to record experiences symbolically; involves the use of language to record experiences, and involves the appearance of the ability to think in terms of classes, numbers, and relationships. See also **concrete operational stage; formal operational stage; sensorimotor stage.**

PIAGET: PREOPERATIONAL STAGE

During the sensorimotor stage of Piaget's theory of cognitive development the dominant mental activity of infants is one of outward behavior and direct interaction with the environment. Apparently little internal intellectualizing is done until close to the end of this stage. (The sensorimotor stage may be reviewed in Chapter 4.)

During the second stage of Piaget's theory of cognitive development, the ***preoperational stage,*** the dominant mental activities of the child change from overt actions to the use of symbolic representations of objects or events. During this preoperational stage there will be an increasing cognitive differentiation of verbal and nonverbal symbols. The child will be able to have mental thoughts and use language (mediations) to represent objects or events, even if they are not present. However, the emphasis will be on concreteness, not abstractions.

The stage of preoperational thought begins at approximately 2 years of age. There are several characteristics of cognitive function noted by Piaget during this period that are considered to be obstacles to logical thinking. One of these characteristics is ***egocentrism,*** which refers to the child's inability to imagine or realize that another person may be viewing the same problem or situation from another perspective or angle. This child thinks, "What I see is what everybody sees." A child between the ages of 2 and 5 does not understand that a person sitting in a different part of the room from the child would see the room in a different way.

A second characteristic is centered thought, *centering,* or ***centration.*** The child's attention is centered on one detail of an event and is unable to take into account other features that are also important. The child cannot see variations; the focus is on a single, salient part (such as the height but not the width of a glass), leading to illogical reasoning.

A third characteristic is irreversible thought or *nonreversibility*. The child is unable to change the direction of his thinking to return to its point of origin. If taken on a short walk, the preoperational child would not be able to retrace the walk accurately. If you add three objects to a group, this child would not consider that you can then take three objects away.

Substages of preoperational thought

There are two substages of preoperational thought. The first 2 years (until about the age of 4 years) are known as the *preconceptual substage*. During this phase children begin to think of certain objects as representing other objects. They begin to indulge in symbolic play. They think of their toy gun or even a stick as a real gun and of their tricycle as a racing car or fire engine. They frequently talk to themselves or to their toys, even in the presence of others. Their conversations are associated with their immediate activity, such as asking their truck, "Did you haul in that load of logs that you were supposed to bring?" Physical cause-and-

animism a characteristic of preoperational thought in which human qualities are inappropriately attributed to inanimate objects.

effect relationships or conceptions of the world and nature are of little interest to them at this age (Piaget and Inhelder, 1969).

From approximately 4 to 7 years of age children progress through the second substage of preoperational thought, which is known as the period of *intuitive thought.* During this time they begin to think more complexly, and they elaborate their concepts more. Their egocentrism tends to be replaced by social interaction and social signs (Flarell, 1973). They become more flexible in the use of language and begin to use the word "because" spontaneously, thus making simple associations between ideas. They are now able to group objects together into classes according to their own perception of their aspects of similarity. This cognitive ability is known as *classification.*

They refrain from talking aloud to themselves to any degree and, instead, resort to covert speech while manipulating an object or a toy. The function of language begins to take on the purpose of communicating their thoughts to other people as they strive to make their hearers listen.

As for their perception of the world about them, Piaget noticed that in earlier stages infants had no image either of themselves or of the external world as such. However, with the emergence of symbolic thinking, their egocentricity induces them to draw for themselves highly specific images of themselves and of environmental objects (Phillips, 1975). They are likely to ask many questions concerning various phenomena. They begin to have definite perceptions of various situations but can only take into account one idea or dimension at a time. These children cannot cope intellectually with problems concerning time, space, causality, measurement, numbers, quantity, movement, and velocity. They merely understand these things in simple, concrete situations. They are certain that everything is just as it appears.

Preoperational thought tends to be ***animistic.*** Consequently, children of this age think of inanimate objects as having human powers such as thinking, feeling with emotion, and desiring. Thus a tree, a rock, and the child's doll can see, have feelings, and think in the same way the child can. The child's observations are allied somewhat in terms of movement. Hence any object that seems to have movement is considered to be conscious or alive. In this respect the sun, moon, stars, clouds, rivers, winds, fire, carts, and so on are all regarded as conscious (Wadsworth, 1971). The words "because" and "since" increase in their vocabulary. If they are asked to give a reason for a certain happening, they will give some coincidentally occurring characteristic, such as "The sun sets because people want to go to bed." This example illustrates *intuitive thought.* The child is becoming aware of the cause-and-effect relationship principle.

Concept formations

The concepts used by children ages 3 to 5 have four characteristics. These properties are more evident in a 3-year-old than in the 5- and 6-year-old. First, the concepts are usually defined in terms of one or two characteristics, not all the characteristics. Since father is a man, all men are fathers. Second, the meaning of concepts are often unique to the child and not easily evident or understood by others. The child understands what he or she means, but no one else is quite certain. Third, the concepts utilized may be changeable or poorly defined by the child, resulting in unreliability. For example, a child may classify cars by color one time and by size the next time. Fourth, concepts that are used by the child become absolutes. The younger child will have trouble with the concepts of bigger and smaller. To this child, objects are either absolutely big or small. Once an object is "big," there is no such thing as bigger or smaller.

According to Piaget's theory of cognitive development, children do not begin to internalize verbal images until sometime after the age of 2 years. After that age their language development provides them with words that will represent objects and events in their environment. At first these words apparently have no other use than merely to provide a means or way of indicating "What is that?" Children are learning the labels (words) by asking, "How do you call that?" Later, about the age of 4 years, they are more interested in "What makes it go?" and "Why?" Thus they indicate that they are beginning to use words as agents or mediators for reasoning. As a result of this gradual development of understanding, many concepts learned by children before the age of 5 years have only "surface" meanings, with no depth of insight or relationships to other concepts.

According to Piaget, preoperational thought tends to be animistic, projecting human feelings and emotions to objects: "The car has to be washed because it likes to feel clean."

Concepts of time are rather vague in early childhood. Children cannot tell time by a clock much before the age of 6 or 7 years, and they have no idea of the length of time in terms of minutes, hours, days, or weeks. By associating specific activities such as "Daddy comes home after my TV program," they can make some estimates if they have been told the time involved. By the age of 4 or 5 years most children can learn what day of the week it is. They will not know the month, season, or year before the age of 6 years unless they were specifically taught that concept.

Numbers mean little to young children. At first they learn the concept "one." For a good while afterward any amount or quantity more than one is always "two." A person can usually tell when children have learned "half" because when asked their age, they will often say, "Four and a half" if they are past their fourth birthday. Children ages 3 to 5 years can be taught the meanings of the numbers one to five, but they will have only vague concepts about numbers above that.

Concepts of space and size develop more readily. At a mental age of 3 years children can select the largest and the smallest objects from a group of objects of varying sizes. Selecting middle-sized objects or in-

classification ability to sort stimuli into categories according to characteristics (for example, color or shape); occurs in Piaget's concrete operations stage.

conservation the realization that one aspect of something (for example, quantity) remains the same, while another aspect is changed (for example, shape, position). Used by Piaget. For example, rearranging a row of objects does not affect their number.

seriation ability to sort stimuli into categories according to characteristics (for example, color or shape).

transformation a Piagetian term referring to the ability to tell how one state or appearance of a substance is changed into another state or appearance.

between variations of size in sequential order does not occur until the age of 5 years. When shown two lines of different length, 3-year-olds can also select correctly in answer to, "Which one is shorter?" These children can also answer the question, "Which one has more?" but they cannot do such a simple intellectual task as realizing that the liquid poured from a wide, squatty glass into a narrow tall glass is the same amount. Until children learn that different materials have different weights, they are likely to estimate weight in terms of size. Five-year-olds can make some differentiations.

Classification, seriation, conservation

We would like to mention three concepts that Piaget has studied in the developing cognitive ability of children as they grow from the preoperational level of thinking and reasoning to concrete operations at the age of 7. These concepts are classification, seriation, and conservation.

Classification is the ability to sort stimuli, such as colors, shapes, or sizes, into categories according to their characteristics. Not only is the ability to sort significant but so is the ability to verbalize and understand the basis of the categorization. The 2½ to 4½-year-olds make figural designs, representative of people or animals. They do not sort out the shapes, such as placing all the circles in one pile (or whatever the scheme for the classification is). From 4½ to 6 or 7 years, children make quasi-classifications, sometimes moving freely from one basis of classification to another, such as classifying by color, then by shape. They work with only one dimension at a time. Children 7 or 8 years and older are able to deal with several dimensions or classes.

Seriation is the ability to arrange objects in a sequence according to one or more relevant dimensions, such as increasing or decreasing size, weight, or volume. Most children can pick the longest and the smallest sticks by ages 4 or 5. However, it takes a child of 5 or 6 to put them in sequential order, and then it is usually done only with some degree of difficulty. To be able to insert sticks of varying lengths into a sequence that had empty slots, the child had to be about 7 years of age. Seriation of weight is usually not attained until age 9. Seriation of volume is not arrived at until age 12 or so.

Conservation is the Piagetian term for the awareness that the amount or quantity of a matter remains the same (in substance, weight, length, number, volume, or area) regardless of any changes in shape or position, so long as nothing has been added to or taken away. For example, if we have a row of eight pennies and we move the pennies farther apart in the row, we still have eight pennies. A 4- or 5-year-old would probably say there are *more* pennies in the row where the pennies are spread out. It isn't until age 6 or 7 that the child learns to conserve numbers.

In the *conservation of substance* a child is shown two equal balls of clay. If one ball is rolled into a log shape, the child of 4 or 5 will say it has more substance "because it is longer." Children usually cannot conserve substance until they are 6 or 7; at 9 or 10 they can *conserve weight;* and at 11 or 12 they can *conserve volume.*

The hallmark of preoperational thought is the inability of the child of that age to conserve. The child learns to conserve only when he can decenter his perceptions, reverse operations, and attend to the transformations. In Piaget's developmental theory, ***transformation*** is the ability to tell how one state or appearance (of a liquid, for example) is changed into another state or appearance. The preoperational child pays attention only to the initial and final states of the object, not to the transformation from one state or position to another.

INFORMATION-PROCESSING MODEL

The vast amount of research that has been conducted on Piaget's theory of cognitive development has led to modifications of some aspects of his theory. For example, Gelman in the *Annual Review of Psychology* (1978) cites a number of studies suggesting that there is a subtle shift in emphasis from the Piagetian view that the preschooler is cognitively incompetent to one that grants the preschooler at least some reasoning capability. The preschoolers simply must have more competence than earlier research has revealed (Fodor, 1975). An alternative approach to the study of cognitive development is the information-processing model.

Gelman's review indicates that under certain circumstances, such as the specific teaching of how to do reasoning, children in early childhood can do some operational thought. Rather than discarding Piaget's theory, this research actually enriches the work of Piaget by making some positive modifications.

Most critics are still highly respectful of Piaget's work. However, the emphasis of the research on the topic of cognitive development has generated some new ideas and approaches. The information-processing model is one such approach. It seeks to extend the knowledge of the field of cognition by describing what takes place when a person reacts to stimuli. Piaget provides the foundation or springboard for other ideas. We view the information-processing model as a complementary adjunct to Piaget's theory of cognitive development. For example, the scheme of Piaget may be related to the level of performance competency of the perceptual-conceptual (information-processing) function; assimilation, which in part is information gathering, resembles the memory bank; accommodation, which is using the information, is the problem-solving and learning aspect of conceptual processing; and, operations is the conceptual process at work in thinking and reasoning. Piaget provides the "what" of cognition and its development; the information-processing model provides more details into "how" cognition works. In our clinical work we find that we can make use of both models very nicely.

Definition: Information processing

The information-processing model views the human being as a receiver and processor of sensory information, not unlike a computer. By definition, ***information processing*** is an approach to cognitive psychology by which the process of task execution or problem solving is broken down into a series of steps. Each step entails much greater detail of cognitive processing than is ordinarily provided in accounts of cognitive development (Keating, 1979; Schwantes, 1979).

information processing approach **a theoretical view of cognition that analyzes cognitive activity in terms of successive stages of information processing such as attention, perception, memory, thinking, and problem solving.**

There seem to be two major approaches to the development of information-processing models in psychology. The first involves the use of models based on computer simulations. The second involves the development of simple experimental systems based on fundamental mental operations that produce the performance to be described (Posner and McLeod, 1982). These two approaches should not be seen as opposed but rather as complementary. *Computer modeling* tends to encourage attention to process, while the *mental operations* approach states the functional relationships between experimental conditions and outcomes (Simon, 1981). We will present examples of both approaches.

Perceptual-conceptual model

Although newborn children have about all the brain cells they will ever have, their central nervous systems are not developed or organized to the point that they can provide meaning to stimuli. In fact the neonate will have only the grossest type of awareness of stimuli outside the body. Children need to develop a perceptual-conceptual process by which they can receive stimuli, get meaning from them, develop concepts, and make appropriate responses. The perceptual-conceptual model is an example of an information-processing system.

Perception is the cognitive process by which the various senses (1) become aware of stimuli, within or outside the body, and (2) refer the stimuli to the central nervous system (CNS), where a meaningful interpretation is attached to them. The CNS then seeks to make an appropriate response. The word *perceptual* pertains to the process and the function of perception. *Conceptual* refers to concept, idea, or general meaning that has evolved from perception. The *perceptual-conceptual process* refers to the means by which an individual becomes aware of something, attaches

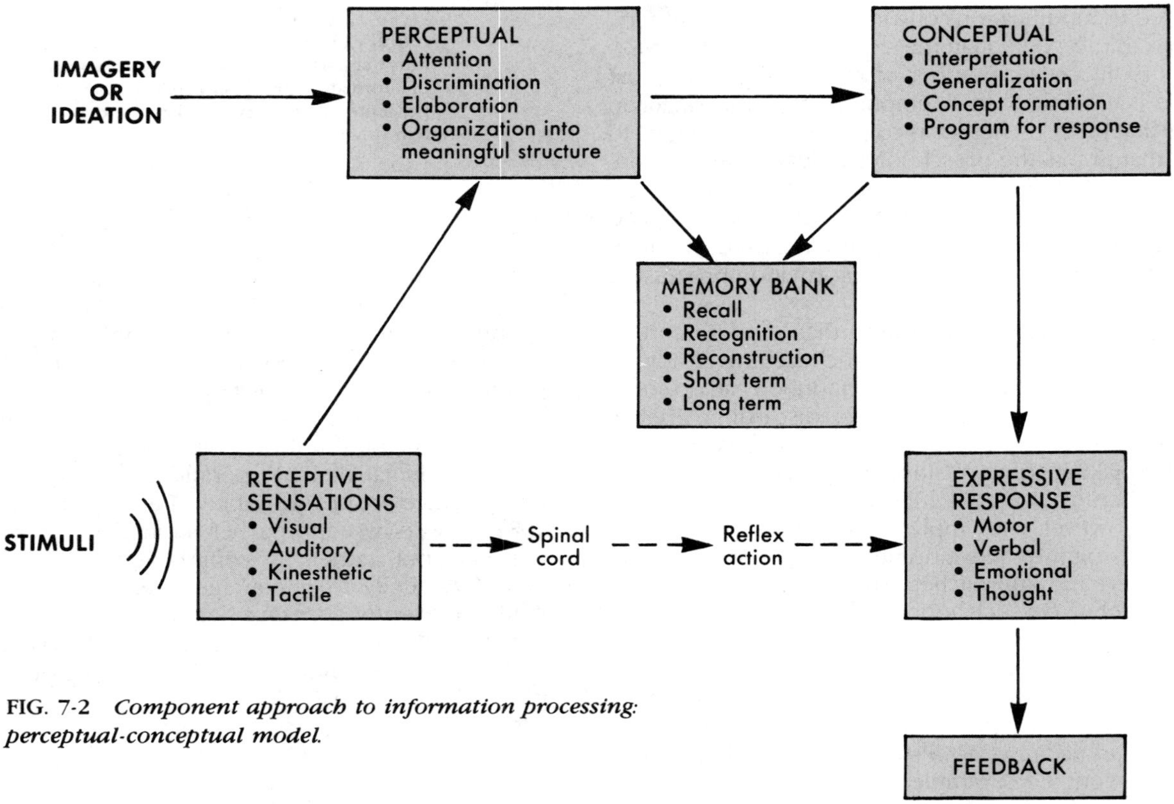

FIG. 7-2 *Component approach to information processing: perceptual-conceptual model.*

meaning to it, and changes the meaning into a "memory bit" or knowledge that can be used at another time. Learning and the cognitive processes are involved in the perceptual-conceptual process (Kaluger and Kolson, 1978). The development of intelligence, it is believed, hinges on the nature and development of the perceptual-conceptual process.

Fig. 7-2 illustrates the components of the perceptual-conceptual model as an information-processing system. There are six aspects of this model: (1) receptive, (2) perceptual, (3) conceptual, (4) expressive, (5) memory storage, and (6) feedback.

Step 1: Receptive. The stimuli are detected by sense organs as sensations and translated into neural impulses. These impulses are transmitted to the brain by the central nervous system. If the impulse that is triggered is viewed as having need for a quick response, the impulse message will only travel to the spinal cord and be sent back out as a reflex. Another type of input would be a thought (*ideation*) or an *imagery* that has its source in the brain and does not have to be detected by the sensory system.

Step 2: Perceptual. The neural impulses are transmitted to the perceptual areas in the brain for organization. A decoding process will take place. The brain will transform the stimuli (neural signals) into messages. This process seeks to organize, elaborate, and integrate all the sensory inputs being received. A variety of perceptual processes, such as attention to the stimuli, discrimination of stimuli, retrieval recall or recognition, scanning, and sequentialization of stimuli may be involved.

Step 3: Conceptual. Once the stimuli have been organized into a meaningful pattern, the message is sent to another part of the brain where it is interpreted, given conceptual meaning, or encoded. Problem solving or concept formation takes place. Once meaningfulness has been given to the stimuli, a deci-

Kit Luce/Image, Inc.

The quality of expressive responses, motor or verbal, will depend on the maturational level of development of the child. The drawings of preschoolers may consist of only a series of lines or curves, but this development is the beginning of control for handwriting.

mental operations model an approach to the information processing model that studies the specific elements of processing, such as attention, memory, and problem solving.

sion must be made as to what to do with the information. It may be stored in the memory bank for further use or utilized for a response. If a response is in order, the brain will program for the appropriate response.

Step 4: Expressive. The expressive response will be an action of some sort. It may be a motor movement, a verbal response, a physiological change, or an affective condition. The output varies according to the decision-making process and programming commitment in the conceptual phase.

Step 5: Memory. Memory is a component and not necessarily a step in the process. There are various types of memory: immediate, short-term, long-term, sensory, primary, secondary, and so on. The memory bank can be used to help the perceptual step organize the incoming stimuli into meaningful patterns or to store the new information learned.

Step 6: Feedback. Feedback is the process by which the brain evaluates the outcome of the response and makes a value judgement about the appropriateness of the behavior. It also makes a judgment as to where there may be an error or inadequacy in the information-processing system. The brain will not provide feedback unless the individual seeks to or can utilize this function.

• • •

This information-processing model merely describes the steps a thought process goes through in order to gain meaning from the stimuli being received and to enable learning to take place. It does not describe the way in which the subtleties, such as perception, attention, memory, and problem solving, take place.

In early childhood the perceptual-conceptual process will operate on a lower level of efficiency than it will in an older person. A primary factor causing less effectiveness in information processing in children is the maturational level of the central nervous system. Since it is still in the process of maturing, it is not capable of operating at full capacity. In some children there is a maturational delay or lag in the development of the neurological system because of prenatal or perinatal factors. The infant at high risk because of a premature birth or prenatal trauma may be a prime candidate for some delay in neurological development. The lack of information in the memory bank is another factor to be considered. So much has to be learned, and up to this point in the young child's life there has been so little time in which to learn. Time will make a difference.

Mental operations model

The research in the ***mental operations model*** approach to information processing is concerned with the specific elements of processing, such as perceptual development, attention, memory, and problem solving. In infancy, consideration is focused on the perceptual development of visual attention and auditory attention and the development of memory or habituation.

A quick review of mental processing in infancy reveals that very young infants can notice brightness, movement, color, and pattern. By the age of 10 weeks, infant can perceive colors ranging over a fairly large portion of the visible spectrum (Oster, 1975). Also newborn babies do not look at a pattern in a random fashion. Their attention becomes attracted to a point of high contrast, such as a corner of a pattern where black and white contrast is greatest; they will focus on that area rather than look around the pattern (Banks and Salapatek, 1981). Babies respond differently to sounds of contrasting frequencies or pitch. Low tones tend to quiet them, whereas high-frequency sounds are likely to distress them (Eisenberg, 1970). Although the newborn's sensory systems do function, the ability to discriminate among stimuli is limited. They tune some things in and tune other things out. The newborn's perceptual world is relatively simple, even though somewhat orderly. Memory of a stimulus and its retrieval is possible, but the early infant can soon become weary of the stimulus, as shown in the habituation process.

Perception. In early childhood, development of the cognitive processes proceeds rapidly in perception, attention, and memory functions. As the perceptual skills of vision and hearing improve, preschool children can obtain information more efficiently, can attend to important features more readily than previously, and can gain more precise information from sensory stimulation (Gibson, 1974). Intersensory coordination, such as between visual and auditory perception or tactile and visual perception, improves dramatically between the ages of 3 and 5. Children can coordinate the information they gather through their separate senses into a more complex perceptual field (Vlietstra and Wright, 1971).

Attention. As children get older, their visual scanning of a pattern or a picture becomes more systematic. A 4-year-old will generally focus on the center of interest first, then scan downward from that point. A 5-year-old, generally ignoring the center of interest, will scan the picture or pattern by beginning at the top and working downward (Day, 1975). However, the scanning is still not completely systematic, and they tend to stop before they have all the information. Children 2 and 3 years of age generally prefer color to form, whereas those 4 to 6 tend to pay greater ***attention*** to the form of an object rather than its color (Stevenson, 1979). According to Wright and Vlietstra (1975), between the ages of 3 and 6 a major shift occurs in the salient points that attract children's attention. Before the age of 3, children respond to the prominent feature of a stimulus. As they get older, they become more systematic in their approach; they are guided more by logic and the need for information than by curiosity or attention-getting features.

Memory. Recognition, reconstruction, and recall are functions of ***memory***. *Recognition* is the form of

attention the focusing of perception on a certain stimulus while ignoring others; needed for learning to take place.

memory the mental activity of reliving past events. It can be considered as having two functions: the storage of experience for a period of time and the revival of that information at a later time.

Elaine Ward

After all, it doesn't amuse me very much to make mudpies, to scribble, to perform my natural functions; in order for these to have value in my eyes, at least one grown-up must go into raptures over my products.

Jean-Paul Sartre
The Words

Brodmann's areas Brodmann made a map of the cerebral cortex of the brain and identified each small area by number. Neurologists have a common basis for identifying the locations in the brain.

memory in which the previously learned material is identified or remembered as having been seen, heard, and so on before. *Reconstruction* refers to the ability to put together or reproduce a symbol or pattern from memory when asked to do so. *Revisualization* and *reauditorization* refer to remembering how to reconstruct the stimulus visually or auditorially in the mind. *Recall* is the form of memory in which previously learned material can be remembered. Recall is more difficult than recognition because there are usually no concrete clues to prod the memory.

Recognition skills have been detected in young infants. They have the ability to match a present perception (what they see or hear) with a representation in their memory. Daehler and O'Conner (1980) found that 2- and 3-year-olds can recognize objects to which they have been exposed. Four-year-olds are capable of recognizing familiar objects. Reconstructive memory has been determined to exist in young children when they intentionally reproduce an action or a pattern (Piaget and Inhelder, 1973). By the time children are 3 and 4 years old they are capable of accurate recall. Preschoolers can remember jingles from TV commercials and nursery rhymes. They never forget a promise that a parent has made! By the time they are 5, however, they overestimate their ability to recall, thinking that they can remember almost anything (Wellman et al., 1981).

According to information-processing theorists, there are two views of memory. The first view is a *multistore* model, with memory being a series of structures. Information may be stored as *immediate or sensory memory*, where memory begins to disappear after 3 seconds; *short-term memory*, where active memory is stored for as long as it is being used; and *long-term memory*, where information is stored indefinitely. The second view is a *levels of processing* model. Information is analyzed at different stages of depth, from initial levels of perception to deeper levels of understanding. Information not analyzed at deeper levels of meaning is soon forgotten (Ornstein and Corsale, 1979). As children get older, they improve in their ability to interpret and analyze material at deeper levels.

Problem solving. Some psychologists propose that most young children learn a conditioning process that associates a response with a stimulus. The reinforcement factor strengthens the response to the stimulus. Kendall (1979) states that since preschoolers learn to choose behavior that has previously been reinforced, they find it difficult to attempt a problem-solving approach that requires them to respond in ways for which they have not been previously reinforced. However, Cantor and Spiker (1979) found that about a fourth of the 5-year-olds and a third of the 6-year-olds could be taught to use hypothesis testing when given direct instructions. There are other psychologists, however, who suggest that the reason preschool children cannot do efficient problem solving is because of the limitations of the preoperational mind, as indicated by Piaget (Gholson, 1980).

Schematic representation

Fig. 7-3 is a diagram of the brain and some of its known cognitive functional areas. The intent of Fig. 7-3 is to illustrate brain functions and processes by which stimuli are detected, organized, conceptualized, and acted upon. This figure is predicated on components of the perceptual-conceptual process presented in Fig. 7-2. Fig. 7-2 presented an overall picture; Fig. 7-3 presents the specific elements of mental processing.

Fig. 7-3 is also a schematic representation of the perceptual-conceptual information-processing system. Note that there are four circled numbers in the drawing. These represent the four components of the information-processing system. The smaller numbers in the brain are referred to as Brodmann's areas. ***Brodmann's areas*** serve as a guide or a map to sites and functions in the brain. The numbers are used universally by neurologists and psychologists to specify locations in the brain. When a researcher identifies a certain portion of the brain as performing a function, the area is usually indicated by numbers. For example, areas 17, 18, and 19 have visual functions; areas 37, 39, 41, and 42 collectively have to do with verbal understanding and reading. Broca's area deals with speech formulation, while area 44 is involved in the motor production of speech. Thought association, reasoning, and idea formation usually take place in the front of the brain in areas 9, 10, and 11. Damage to any of the areas of the brain cited in these examples would affect the intended function(s) of that area.

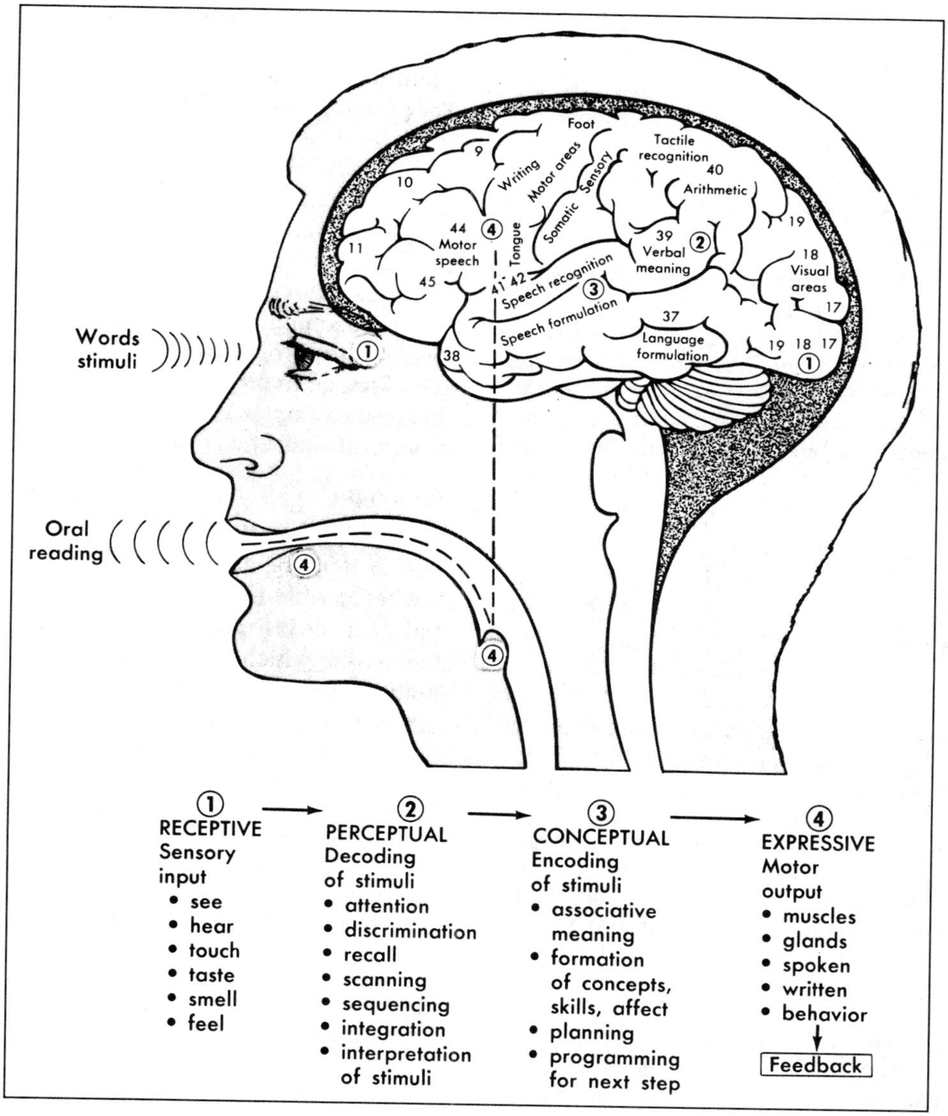

FIG. 7-3 *The perceptual pattern for receiving, interpreting, learning, and responding. The drawing illustrates the processes and neural areas involved in oral reading:* ***1****, receives stimuli and transmits to visual area;* ***2*** *and* ***3****, interpret and prepare responses;* ***4****, produces the responses.*

pragmatics rules concerned with the appropriate use of language in social contexts.

semantics the study of meaning conveyed in language.

syntax the rules for combining morphemes to form words and sentences.

Summary statement of information processing

The information-processing model seeks to describe what is happening cognitively when an individual is alerted by a stimulus and thinking takes place. The model, as pictured in Fig. 7-2, states that in the receptive phase something must trigger a neural impulse that can be transmitted to the central nervous system. The "trigger" may be a stimulus, a thought, or a visual picture in the mind (imagery). The incoming information is first handled by the perceptual system (process), which seeks to organize all the stimuli into a meaningful (sensible, understandable, or distinctive) pattern before sending the impulses on to the conceptual system. A simile might be the way you can see all the information typed into the computer being organized—perhaps in graphic form—on the computer screen.

The conceptual system takes over and makes use of the information by adding something new to its existing fund of information or knowledge, making an interpretation of the meaning of the stimuli and planning a response, or doing with the information whatever seems apropos. If a response is in order, the brain will program for the appropriate expressive action. If new learning has occurred, it will be stored in the memory bank. How well it will be stored will be determined by the type of memory that has been "created."

The mental operations model is concerned more with the specifics of cognition than with the entire cognitive process. This model will focus on aspects of cognition, such as how perception takes place, what attention is and how it develops, what happens when a person tries to think or reason through a problem, and what the different forms of memory are and how they are used. One memory model considers memory to be made up of different types of memory; another memory model considers memory to be one component but having different depths.

PRESCHOOL LANGUAGE

During the early childhood years the development of language and thought is one of the child's most important accomplishments. The development of true language ability begins when children are about 2 years old. By the time they are 5 years old they are usually proficient in their speech and are capable of using an amazing number of words. This time of life can be a bit trying for parents, since children seem to ask an inexhaustible number of questions; they want to know "what?" and "why?" about everything. Later development of language is related, almost inseparably, to children's ability to think. Language makes it possible for children to put thoughts and feelings into words. The better their language ability, the better they can make clear to themselves what they know.

Components of children's language

In language, ***semantics*** refers to meaning or meaningfulness. Words are symbolic representations of people, objects, ideas, and events. When words are used purposefully and correctly, they convey meaning. Meaning expressed in language is semantics. In early childhood, children learn words at an amazing speed. Researchers state that the rate of increase among children of average intelligence may be more than 20 words a day (Miller, 1978).

Syntax is a part of grammar, the rules or ways in which words are put together to form phrases and sentences. The syntax of a language is what makes it productive, capable of combining individual words into an unlimited number of sentences. The rules of syntax may vary from language to language. Near the second year, children convey their intentions by applying syntactic devices of intonation, inflection, and word order to their store of words.

Pragmatics refers to a speaker's knowledge of the way in which to adjust language to suit the social context. An important part of a child's language learning involves knowing the social conventions and rules for the use of language, such as how to make requests, to address someone, to initiate a conversation, to say thank you, or to adjust one's comments to the perspective of the listener. This kind of knowledge is known as sociolinguistics or pragmatics. Children talk differently to parents, to peers, to younger siblings, and to teachers. (Dunn and Kendrick, 1982). By the time children are 5, their grammar and vocabulary have become flexible enough to choose from their various speech styles

Sociolinguistics or pragmatics is language that is adjusted to suit the social context. These girls may conceivably be talking differently to each other than they would talk to their nursery school teacher.

the appropriate language for the situation (deVilliers and deVilliers, 1978).

Learning how to use semantics, syntax, and pragmatics constitutes the set of skills referred to as "communicative competence" (Hymes, 1972). The trend in child language study has broadened from the initial, relatively narrow focus on the formal structure of language, to a consideration of the meanings expressed in word combinations, to a concern with rules for the social use of linguistic knowledge (Rice, 1982). The findings reveal an often surprisingly sophisticated grasp of the rules of communication by very young children, even though the words are not always pronounced correctly.

Preschool language development

By 2 years of age children may know more than 100 words. By 2½ years most children use twice as many words as they did at 2 years, and by 3 years they can generally use twice as many as at 2½ years. Although this rate of learning does slow down somewhat, children often learn 50 new words a month until they are 4½ years old (Brown, 1973). Children may spend a good amount of time whispering words to themselves. They seem to do this for the pure enjoyment of making and using the sounds they have just learned. Table 7-2 presents the pattern of normal language development for children from 1 to 6 years of age.

By the time they are 3 years of age children start

using the vocabulary and language skills that they have been developing. The 3-year-old may often seem to talk continuously with hardly a pause for a breath! This gives the child practice, and usually by 3½ years of age articulation has greatly improved. The mispronunciations used in baby talk are generally gone; however, grammatical constructions still leave much to be desired. A sentence such as, "I'm busy, I'm the mostest busy" is typical of this age.

Initially children's vocabulary consists mainly of nouns, although they will use a few verbs, adjectives, or adverbs. In the beginning children hardly ever use pronouns, conjunctions, and prepositions. The relativism of pronouns may cause problems for young children. They may call themselves "you" and someone else "I." Much of their vocabulary is learned by hearing words in context. Along with an increase in vocabulary they are also learning grammar and syntax. Their grammar is anything but flawless, however. It is not uncommon to hear them say things like "I bringed" or "I walk homed."

Children's language at age 4 is now a social skill. They learn how to communicate their complex feelings and motivations to others. They use language to solve problems they formerly solved by physical means. They remember, generalize, and reproduce former experiences through words and apply them in the context of the present situation.

Questions at 5 years of age are fewer and more relevant than they were at 4 years. Children now ask questions for information and not merely for practice in the art of speaking. Parents tend to be less annoyed by their questions because they are more meaningful than they were at the age of 4 years.

TABLE 7-2 Pattern of normal language development in expressive speech and comprehension of speech from 1 to 6 years of age

Age	*Expression*	*Comprehension*
1 to 2 years	Uses 1 to 3 words at 12 months, 10 to 15 at 15 months, 15 to 20 at 18 months, about 100 to 200 by 2 years. Knows names of most objects he uses. Names few people, uses verbs but not correctly with subjects. Jargon and echolalia. Names 1 to 3 pictures.	Begins to relate symbol and object meaning. Adjusts to comments. Inhibits on command. Responds correctly to "give me that," "sit down," "stand up," with gestures. Puts watch to ear on command. Understands simple questions. Recognizes 120 to 275 words.
2 to 3 years	Vocabulary increases to 300 to 500 words. Says "where kitty," "ball all gone," "want cookie," "go bye bye car." Jargon mostly gone, vocalizing increases. Has fluency trouble. Speech not adequate for communication needs.	Rapid increase in comprehension vocabulary to 400 at 2½ years. 800 at 3 years. Responds to commands using "on," "under," "up," "down," "over there," "bye," "run," "walk," "jump up," "throw," "run fast," "be quiet," and commands containing two related actions.
3 to 4 years	Uses 600 to 1,000 words; becomes conscious of speech. Uses 3 to 4 words per speech response. Personal pronouns, some adjectives, adverbs, and prepositions appear. Mostly simple sentences, but some complex. Speech more useful.	Understands up to 1,500 words by age 4 years. Recognizes plurals, sex difference, pronouns, adjectives. Comprehends complex and compound sentences. Answers simple questions.
4 to 5 years	Increase in vocabulary to 1,100 to 1,600 words. More 3- to 4-syllable words, more adjectives, adverbs, prepositions, and conjunctions. Articles appear. Uses 4-, 5-, and 6-word sentences; syntax quite good. Uses plurals. Fluency improves. Proper nouns decrease, pronouns increase.	Comprehends from 1,500 to 2,000 words. Carries out more complex commands, with 2 to 3 actions. Understands dependent clause, "if," "because," "when," "why."
5 to 6 years	Increase in vocabulary to 1,500 to 2,100 words. Complete 5- to 6-word sentences, compound, complex, with some dependent clauses. Syntax near normal. Quite fluent. More multisyllable words.	Understands vocabulary of 2,500 to 2,800 words. Responds correctly to more complicated sentences but is still confused at times by involved sentences.

Modified from Miller, G.A. *Language and communication.* New York: McGraw-Hill Book Co., 1951, pp. 140-157.

Non-Standard English

Variations within a language are called dialects; they often result in non-Standard English. The major difference between formal and informal English usage is the carefulness or the casualness of the communication. There are several nonstandard dialects in the United States. A blend of Spanish and English is found in the Southwest, Florida, and New York City. In some areas of the West a mixture of English and American Indian languages has produced a distinctive dialect. The most widespread non-Standard English dialect in the United States is black English.

From a linguistic point of view the differences between Standard English and black English are small. The basic structure of sentences and the formal representation of utterances are similar (Munsinger, 1975). A major difference, however, is that agreement between a subject and verb in person and number is not necessary. Examples are "I gone home now" or "He be coming soon." These differences, plus the dropping of some letter sounds ("bof" for "both") and the merging of some sounds ("gimmedat" for "give me that"), have led some authorities to speculate that academic failure among some black children is due to impoverished or inadequate language development (Baratz, 1973). The sounds for doing phonetic analysis in reading, for example, were not part of the child's everyday vocabulary.

Some school personnel assumed that children from culturally different backgrounds would not have the vocabulary or verbal concepts necessary for traditional school learning. This assumption was especially true for Spanish-speaking children. Teaching English as a second language to both black and Spanish-speaking children seemed to help (Wilson, 1978). In New York City, "downtown English" was taught so the students could get jobs in the stores and offices. They could continue to use their dialect when they were back in their neighborhoods.

SOCIAL DEVELOPMENT AND PLAY

As with the other aspects of growth and development in early childhood, social and emotional maturity are still in a beginning budding stage. Two-year-olds receive considerable attention from those around them. However, they have been so busy learning how to control their motor processes and how to make their needs known that they have not had time to learn the social and emotional skills necessary for smooth interaction with others.

IMAGINE THAT

To me, the imagination of a three-and-a-half-year-old boy is limitless. I have a son, Nino, who never ceases to amaze me with his imagination. At about the age of twenty-eight months Nino was able to talk, using sentences with four to seven words. This was the time when his imagination began to blossom. At first he would carry on conversations between two of his trucks with which he usually played. Sometimes he would have the trucks talking, and sometimes the people who were supposed to be inside the cab talked.

As he grew older, he began to talk to all types of objects as if they were alive. Whenever we would go for a ride out in the country, he would say, "Hi, Mr. Cow." "Hi, Mr. Corn." "What are you doing, Mr. Silo?" The other day my wife bought some blueberries. She gave Nino a few of them to eat. He took one look at them and came running over to me, excitedly shouting: "Look, Daddy, Mr. Blueberry only has one eye. Can't he see?" I told him that Mr. Blueberry doesn't have to see because he just grows big so people can put him in a pie to eat. Nino accepted this explanation but examined each blueberry carefully before putting it into his mouth.

There is also an imaginary friend, a bug, with which he plays. He keeps him in his pocket and takes him out only to pet him, talk to him, or put him in his mouth. I am allowed to pet the bug only if I promise not to eat it.

All of the above experiences are not really out of the ordinary. However, he told me something a few weeks ago that really surprised me. He said he was going to build four buttons on the floor; when he would push a certain one, he would grow big; push another one, and I would grow little; push a third one, and Maria, our second child, would grow big; push the last one, and Mommy would grow little. I asked him how he was going to make the buttons, and he said, "I will go to school with you and learn!"

TABLE 7-3 Developmental sequences of play activities from 15 months to 5 years

Age	Play activities
15 months	Endless exercise of walking activities Throws and picks up objects Puts objects in and out of receptacles
18 months	Rapid shifts in attention; moves actively and "gets into" everything Pulls toy Carries or hugs doll or teddy bear Imitates many things as reading paper, dusting, and so on Solitary or onlooker play
2 years	Less rapid attention shifts; manipulates play material by patting, pounding Interest in dolls and teddy bears (domestic mimicry), strings beads, transports blocks in wagon Imitates things and events present to senses Parallel play although obviously enjoys being with other children Little social give-and-take Does not ask for help; adult must be constantly watchful and ready to assist without waiting to be asked
3 years	Dramatization and imagination begin to enter into play Interest in combining playthings such as blocks and cars Increasing interest in playing with other children; may play in groups of two or three, but these are always shifting in makeup and activity Will put away toys with some supervision
4 years	Considerable increase in constructive use of materials and in manipulation and dramatization of play Has complicated ideas but is unable to carry them out in detail and has no carry-over from day to day Prefers to play in groups of two or three Suggests turns but is often bossy Puts away toys alone Likes to dress up
5 years	Fond of cutting out and pasting Likes to work on specific project that is carried over from day to day Plays in groups of two to five Friendships are becoming stronger Spurred on in activity by rivalry

Modified from Gesell, A., et al. *The first five years of life.* New York: Harper & Row, Publishers, 1940, p. 251.

Social interaction and play

In the beginning phase of early childhood, children become a bit more mature in their play activity. There is an increase in social play because these children have increased their ability to control their body movements, to handle objects, and to talk (Garvey, 1977). They are now beginning to understand what it means to take turns, and they like to play simple games with others. By the end of this year children begin to impersonate adults near and dear to them.

When children reach 4 years of age, most of them want to become involved in associative play. They are more mature mentally and physically and can participate in cooperative activities. Furthermore they are ready to learn social patterns. They get satisfaction from playing with other children and in many cases are rewarded for having friendly and outgoing responses. Four-year-olds will play with others for about half their playtime. Table 7-3 presents the developmental sequence of play in infancy and early childhood.

When children encounter frustrating experiences with one another, they will argue. Boys tend to be more violent and participate in more physical attacks than girls (Maccoby, 1976). On the whole, however, 4- and 5-year-olds are more friendly and cooperative than uncooperative. Competitiveness appears around the age of 3 to 4 years. By the time children are 5 years

Meriem Kaluger

Four-year-olds begin to associate together and to play in small groups. They enjoy playground activities, conversation, and simple projects.

old they are competing vigorously with other children.

Young children who have no real playmates will often create an imaginary playmate or pet. Children derive much pleasure from playing with their imaginary playmates, since this relationship fills a gap in their social development. Parents may have to go along with this imaginary playmate even to the extent of setting an extra plate at the table "for my friend, Charlie." This interest in imaginative playmates can begin as early as 2½ years of age. Imagination and imaginary play reach a peak at about 3½ or 4 years, but it is not unusual for a 5-year-old to have an imaginary playmate (Singer and Singer, 1981). Probably all imaginative life in children satisfies some inner need for companionship, someone to look up to, or someone to boss (Manosevitz et al., 1973).

Later in early childhood, children are good at playing. It is one of the things they can do best. Their imagination is still used as much as it was previously (Singer and Singer, 1979). They will want to play with others about 80% of the time. Five-year-olds are greatly interested in their home and act out this interest by playing "house," being mother or father, playing "doctor," or "going to the store." Both boys and girls enter into this home-centered dramatic play. Most 5-year-old boys do not mind this type of activity. They will be willing to be mother, baby, or any other character.

sex roles patterns of behavior deemed appropriate to each sex by society.

sex typing the learning of behavior patterns appropriate to the sex of the person; for example, acquisition of masculine behavior traits for a boy.

The age of 5 years is that delightful stage when one takes life as it comes. Children's life problems are restricted in scope and easy for them to handle. Their parents find them a joy to have around the house. They are extremely helpful; they are usually within earshot; and they keep their parents posted about their activities by asking permission.

Under normal circumstances a 5-year-old boy will display a particularly warm attachment to his mother. He is most concerned if he cannot find her when he comes in from play. He wants a close working relationship with her and constant assurance of her approval. When things go wrong, he wants her physical and psychological attention. He likes her to talk with him, to explain things, and to tell him about the exciting and mysterious things in life.

All this may be disturbing to a father, but it is only a characteristic of the age. The attachment to the mother will lessen in a year or so. The love of a 5-year-old son for his father can be perfectly normal, and still he will call on his mother when trouble arises. A girl will also depend rather heavily on her mother at this age, but she will also display a warm attachment to her father.

Sex-role differentiation

Although an individual's biological sexuality is determined at conception by the combination of an ovum and a chance sperm, from that moment on intrauterine and extrauterine environmental influences do much to shape each human's development of a lifetime ***sex-role*** pattern of behavior and emotions. Biochemical factors, such as the circulating level of androgen, influence the intrauterine environment to the extent that the development of genital organs and the glandular system can be affected (Petersen, 1979). The extrauterine environment, made up of the significant persons in the child's life and the nature of the sex-role patterns prescribed by that culture or society, will influence the individual during many years of life.

Kagan (1964) suggests that a sex role standard is acquired by three processes: (1) identification with models, (2) expectation of affection and acceptance for possession of sex-appropriate attributes, and (3) expectation that possession of such attributes will prevent social rejection. Once sex role standards are acquired, individuals become less dependent on external sources of reinforcement and rely more on self-monitoring and self-evaluation (Shepherd-Look, 1982). From a social learning point of view, theorists are in considerable agreement as to the central importance of two major processes: differential reinforcement of the sexes and identification by the boy or the girl (Mussen, 1969; Mischel, 1973).

There are a variety of factors that may influence sex differentiation and the development of sex roles. Biological factors, such as the circulating levels of hormones and hemispheric lateralization, have more influence on sex differentiation than has been usually mentioned in the literature. Hemispheric lateralization and hemispheric specialization may produce sex differences in such areas as verbal, manual, visual, auditory, and cortical activity (Bryden, 1979).

Social factors that have been related to sex-role differentiation include (1) differential treatment of boys and girls on the first day they were born, (2) learned ***sex-typed behavior*** by imitation of same-sex parents and peers, (3) absence of a parent from the home, (4) sex roles in television programming and in printed matter, and (5) the influence of the school system.

In general, differential treatment of boys and girls has been found in terms of how the children are treated and what the expectations are. It is clear that boys and girls show definite sex-typed interests from the early preschool years onward (Shepherd-Look, 1982). Separation of the father from the home environment, either temporarily or permanently, has a definite negative effect on male children (Drake and McDougall, 1977), especially if the separation occurred at or before the age of 5. In general the effects of an absent father on girls is minimal in sex-typing, although their sex-role development in later life may be affected. A study of television influence on sex-role socialization revealed that children who view a great amount of television have higher traditional sex-role identities than those who do not. Boys had higher scores than girls (Freuh and McGhee, 1975).

Gender labeling begins early in most cases (Werner, 1979). "Blue" means it's a boy; "pink" means it's a girl. Of course, the babies don't know the significance of

Meriem Kaluger

A variety of factors influence sex differentiation and the development of sex roles. These young boys in China can relate to the Panda doll with no implication of sex role.

Meriem Kaluger

The young girls in Bali are already carrying the baby in traditional fashion and using a head rest to carry produce.

Meriem Kaluger

The boys on the Karawari River in Papua New Guinea paint their faces as their elders do; they play at hunting game and shooting arrows.

gender identity an individual's sense of being a boy or a girl, a male or a female.

the colors, but the adults do. "Look at him. He's all boy. See how tight he can hold on to my finger!" "Isn't she a doll! A real picturebook baby—so dainty and pretty." From the time the infant is viewed in the maternity ward, the infant is exposed to comments such as, "She's such a good girl" and "He is getting to be a big boy" (Rubin et al., 1974). By 2 or 3 years of age the child can correctly identify his or her own sex.

Gender labeling can help bring about ***gender identity*** and sex-role identification (Travis and Offir, 1977). Sex-role standards are subject to cultural and societal influences and, as such, are prone to sex-role stereotyping. Rheingold and Cook (1975) found a distinct difference between the contents of boys' and girls' rooms in terms of decorations and toys present, showing that sex-role stereotypes exist in the minds of adults. It is not until school age, and more frequently adolescence, that the parentally defined sex roles are openly questioned.

Maccoby and Jacklin (1974) have reviewed many studies on assumed differences between males and females. They stress caution in interpreting their findings because the details of the studies and the variables differed so greatly. In summary, they presented the following findings in regard to beliefs concerning differences between the sexes.

These beliefs are apparently unfounded.

1. Girls are more socially oriented than boys.
2. Girls are more receptive to suggestions.
3. Boys and girls differ in learning ability.
4. Boys are naturally more analytical than girls.

These differences appear to be real.

1. Girls are more proficient at verbal skills.
2. Boys are more capable at making visual-spatial judgments.
3. Boys are better in mathematical areas.
4. Boys are basically more aggressive.

The following questions are considered debatable.

1. Are girls naturally more anxious than boys?
2. Is there an overall difference in activity level?
3. Is one sex more competitive and dominant than the other?
4. Are girls more nurturant and compliant than boys?

Maccoby and Jacklin indicate that some of the differences just mentioned do not appear until middle childhood or adolescence.

EMOTIONS AND BEHAVIOR

Emotions seen in a simple form in infants change by the age of 2 years, when significant conditioning begins to take place. The infant is egocentric, but the early childhood child shows more responsiveness to the environment. With this involvement comes a change of emphasis from the child's inner world, with its sensations and desires, to an outer world. The eventual outcome is a transfiguration in personality. New contacts and experiences increase children's chances of emotional stimulation. As the children's awareness of their surroundings increases, so does their capacity for emotional response (Lewis and Brooks, 1978). Not only are children influenced by their immediate environment but also by their anticipation of future events. Even though emotional development of the 3- to 5-year-old has extended far beyond infancy, it is important to remember that these children are still babies in many respects. They still depend highly on their parents for emotional support.

At the preschool level children's fears are associated more with imaginary, anticipated, and supernatural dangers than with fears of actual objects or unusual stimuli, as is the case in infants (Bauer, 1976). For the most part the frequency and intensity of overt signs of fear decrease with age. Crying reactions diminish, although characteristic facial expressions remain.

Early childhood is the time when personal-social experience, such as the addition of a member to the family, begins to have an influence on the child's emotional responses (Thomas and Chess, 1977). When a new baby comes, jealousy may build up in preschoolers if they feel deprived of attention and affection. This reaction does not always occur, but it is a common characteristic when the children are the firstborn and have been accustomed to having the full attention of their parents (Kendrick and Dunn, 1980). Because the new baby is showered with so much attention, older children feel neglected. Young children are too immature to comprehend the need for the changes in their lives that the arrival of a new baby will bring. It must be realized that a certain amount of jealousy in any child is normal, whether it is jealousy of the baby, of older brothers or sisters, or even of the mother or father. Love and affection freely given to the 4- and 5-year-old can go far in counteracting the negative effects of deep-seated jealousy.

Aggression is a complex emotion that takes different forms at different age levels (Maccoby, 1980). Children of 4 and 5 outgrow the tantrums of kicking, pounding, and screaming because they can now translate their anger and frustration into words. They often begin to threaten and yell at other children at this age (Hartup, 1974). Many 4-year-olds direct their anger to the object causing the frustration. For example, a boy may blame a chair for causing him to trip and spill his milk rather than put the blame on his own clumsiness. Children of this age tend to remain frustrated and aggressive for longer periods of time now, but they begin to find ways to keep from showing their anger to other persons. Two of the best ways for children to get rid of frustration, fear, anger, and guilty feelings is by creative art work such as painting, using clay, or pounding wood and by playing out the fears that are real and imaginary.

"IMAGINARY MONSTERS"

Fear does strange things to people. Many of our childhood fears are forgotten when we grow up; we look back and laugh at how silly we were. However, these fears will never leave some people. This seems to be my problem.

Many small children imagine seeing things in the dark, especially before falling asleep at night. Well, my imaginary monsters were chickens. Every night as I lay in bed, I remember feeling sure there were chickens all around my bed. The worst part was that I was certain one of them would jump up on the bed and start flapping its wings. Just when I knew one was about to get on the bed, I would scream for my mother. Thinking back now, I realize my mother remained quite patient through this stage. I would explain to her about the chickens surrounding my bed. It was funny that the chickens never seemed to be there when the light was turned on. After a thorough search on all sides of my bed and, of course, under it, I could finally fall asleep.

My grandmother had a pet canary at this time. Often when we went to visit she would let it out of the cage to fly around in the house. This was usually to please my brothers, who were delighted when the bird would land on their heads. At first I would make excuses to go outside or try to get the boys interested in something else so that my grandmother would put the bird back in the cage. After what seemed an eternity the canary died. To my relief, it was never replaced!

Even walking outside, I remember constantly keeping a lookout for birds that might be nearby. Everywhere I went there seemed to be birds that wanted to fly at me. I even suspected my mother of putting pieces of dead chicken in my food. Chocolate milk was my favorite drink, but for a while I could never finish the whole glass because I thought there was a piece of chicken floating in it.

When I decided to write about this fear, I wanted to find reasons that could possibly be the cause of this fear. There are several incidents that I remember that I'm sure helped to develop it.

One of these is being chased by my brothers with a dead sparrow. We had been outside playing when they found it. The first thing they did was throw it in my direction, and I jumped. This was their cue to have some fun. They picked it up and chased me with it until, sobbing and terrified, I ran to Mother.

Looking back on these things I still remember the thoughts and feelings I had. Even today I don't eat chicken or any other fowl. I try to tell myself that it is because I don't like the taste, although I'm sure it's a carry-over from this fear. The worst part of having this fear was keeping it a secret. I was ashamed and dreaded the ridicule and teasing I would get if I admitted to being afraid of birds. I was a victim of fear that I created in my own mind. How long it took me to allow myself to forget about this, I can't remember. I haven't lost the fear, but I now realize how it developed and can understand it. No longer does it completely overshadow everything I do. Perhaps the best part is now I can tell people about it. Will I ever be able to lose this fear entirely? I'm not sure, but I do know I'm better equipped to cope with it.

DEVELOPMENTAL ORGANIZATION OF PERSONALITY

Up to the age of 2½ years the personality of infants has been a natural development with the emergence of behavior characteristics that are innately provided for children to help them promote their own well-being and survival. Infants developed through stages where they sequentially emphasized physical dependence, control of body movements, physiological pleasures, self-display, curiosity and exploration, imitation of verbalisms, and by 2½ years, self-assertiveness.

During the phase of self-assertiveness infants are reminded in many ways by their parents that "this is not the way you are supposed to act." Children become amenable and are willing to learn new ways of behaving. Between the ages of 2½ to 4 years or so children learn to control their primary nature forces, drives, and impulses. They also develop a behavior pattern that will reflect the influence of secondary external elements on their personality development. The social and emotional atmosphere and environment of 3- to 5-year-olds are extremely important because both overt and covert aspects of personality are being crystallized.

Imitation of behavior

The temper tantrums of the twos and the general conflict that exists between parents and children at this time give way to children who now say, "Maybe I really wasn't ready to be on my own yet. I guess there is more to be learned." So, as they approach being 3-year-olds, they revert to a learning technique that they had used earlier. They make use of imitation again. This time they replicate the behavior and actions of others. In a way they are saying, "If my behavior wasn't correct when I was 2, then I'll copy yours so I can learn the right way to behave." They are taking over the behavior of others, especially of their parents. The actions of their parents, for better or worse, will become their actions. They are developing standards of behavior that will be based on the actions of others who are important to them.

Suggestibility of feelings

As children move into the "trusting threes," they allow themselves not only to imitate the behavior of others but also to begin to reflect their moods, attitudes, and ideas. Children are in the phase of suggestibility. In some ways they are becoming dependent on others for the development of their mental and emotional responses. They are unconsciously absorbing their feelings and outlooks. Children tend to copy their mothers or fathers. If their mothers are calm, cheerful, and happy, the children can become the same way; if the children respond more to the fathers, let us hope that he is not irritable, cynical, or selfish. Politeness, friendliness, consideration for others, patience, and moral conduct in general are all suggestible traits.

Children are not aware that they are taking over the moods and feelings of others because suggestibility is an unconscious process. If the suggestions were to be made openly and deliberately taught, children would probably reject them. To illustrate: At a state park the swimming area was away from the bathhouses where swimmers could change clothes. To get to the lake it was necessary to walk across a road covered with gravel. A father and his boy started barefooted across the road. As he stepped on the small bits of gravel, the boy winced and said, "That hurts." "Yes, it does," replied the father and kept on walking. The little boy made a real effort to be brave like his daddy as he walked across. Another father and his boy started across the graveled road. "That hurts," cried the boy. "Oh, nonsense," said the father, "it doesn't hurt at all." As this boy stepped gingerly over the stones, you could tell by the expression on his face that he was thinking. "That does *so* hurt!" Which father provided a better example for his son? You can imagine the second boy thinking about his father, "He's either lying or else he's some kind of a superman. Either way, can I ever hope to be like him? Can I really trust him to know how I feel?"

Identification of personality

The phase of suggestibility gives way to identification, in which children take over the entire personality of another, with all its strengths and attributes. Personality identification is the process of accepting another person emotionally so completely that his or her characteristics and abilities are adopted as a person's own. Children no longer are just pretending that they are doing things "like my daddy [or my mommy] does," but for all intents and purposes they act as if their parents' traits and abilities are also their own traits and abilities. Children impersonate another so completely that for the moment they are that person.

We know of children who identified so completely with "Superman" or "Batman" in their play that when they received costumes of these characters, the children believed that they could do what Superman and Batman did. Two children, playing in Batman costumes, jumped from the railing of a porch as they pretended to be chasing the "bad guys." Each child broke his right arm. One 4-year-old, pretending he was the "Bionic Man," stepped out into a street and raised his arms as if to stop a truck. Identification is a behavior mechanism used by people of all ages. Have you ever cried during a movie or felt "choked up inside" while reading a story or observing an event? You were identifying with an individual or a situation, and for the moment his or her circumstances were yours.

During the identification phase, children generally respond to people whom they love or who possess some trait or power that they admire. Children gain a sense of security by identifying with an older person whom they love, in whom they have complete confidence and trust. The older person is loved because he or she is lovable to the child. There is no hesitancy on the part of children to become like that person.

When children identify with a person or a characterization because of the traits that individual or character possesses, they are beginning to reach out into the world for personal characteristics that they wish to make their own. They like the idea of the power or ability implicit in the brave act or performance of another, and they do not mind becoming that way.

With the identification motive of either love or power the children are developing characteristic behaviors or attitudes that can be instrumental in setting the direction their personality development will take. They are on the threshold of developing their own character, with behavior and attitudes that will have a tremendous influence on all their future actions.

Beginnings of a value judgment system

As children mature, the impact of the identification process as a motivator of behavior is lessened to the degree that the children will eliminate the personal attachment to the individual as an object of identification, although still retaining the characteristics of that person. It is no longer, "I want to be brave like my daddy," Now it is simply, "I want to be a brave person." The traits and ideals of the person become part of the child's emerging self-ideal. A *self-ideal* is an integration of the values that one holds for oneself and that one seeks to realize. The self-ideal becomes sort of an inner standard of behavior that is considered important enough to strive for and live by.

The self-ideal is also called the superego, the ego ideal, and the conscience. We like to consider it as a value judgment system that will eventually be highly instrumental in influencing the decisions that an individual makes as well as regulating his behavior. "I want to be brave. Brave boys don't cry, so I'll try very hard not to cry." We can imagine a 4-year-old boy with his eyes filled with tears, biting his lips as he tries so hard not to cry.

As children incorporate a self-ideal into their personality, several things happen. They now have an "other self," which they can consider when they are making decisions about what is good or bad, important or unimportant, of interest or of no interest. They become more conscious and critical of their behavior in terms of its appropriateness and, as a result, seek to control their behavior so it will be more acceptable. This function of self-evaluation concerning one's behavior constitutes the essence of a conscience and a self-esteem. It should be realized that not all children develop an adequate value system. Some children will identify with adults who have values and ideals that are too strict and severe, others with adults who tend to be too easygoing and undisciplined. Either way, these models can induce unhealthy mental patterns in children who identify with them.

The self-ideal should be such that it (1) can control the innate survival drives and impulses of the early years of life while still enabling use of their energy output and (2) makes use of an integrated, well-developed value judgment system to give direction to one's behavior. It will take many years before individuals will have an effective, competent value system, but when they do develop it, they will be considered "mature persons."

With the beginnings of a self-ideal 4-year-olds develop more self-assurance and independence. They feel more capable because they are acting more like "little adults." After all, they are copying their behavior; they have an organized personality that, along with their budding intellect, is enabling them to ask better questions and to make better decisions than before. They feel more independent. They like to show off, and they ask others to watch them while they demonstrate how capable they are. They are noisy at times and constantly into something. At Christmas time, several years ago, a mother became aware of an unusual quietness in her house. She decided she had better check on her 4-year-old to see what he was up to. She found him sitting in a chair in the living room. "What are you doing?" she asked. "Nothing," he replied. "What can I do, what with you, God, and Santa Claus watching me all the time!"

CHAPTER REVIEW

1. *Developmental tasks* include a rapid extension of motor, language, self-care, social, and cognitive skills begun in infancy. Erikson's psychosocial crisis in early childhood is one of *initiative versus guilt.*
2. The general curve for brain and head development accelerates rapidly from birth to the age of 6. General body and lymphoid growth are also rapid, but their growth is not as rapid as the brain and head. There is only slight development of the reproductive organs.
3. Physical growth is one of "lengthening out," developing a proportional look more like that of an adult.
4. Two-year-olds have little fine-motor control. Three-year-olds are more adept at running and walking up stairs. They are beginning to make use of fine motor coordination in building block towers. Four-year-olds have smoother gross motor movements than they had previously and can generally dress themselves except for tying shoelaces. Five-year-olds often do well at alternating movements. Motor development in girls is usually faster than in boys.
5. The *preoperational stage* of Piaget's theory of cognitive development has two substages: preconceptual (ages 2 to 4) and intuitive (ages 5 to 7). During the *preconceptual* substage there is an extension of

symbolic thought, but only on a concrete level. During the *intuitive* stage the child is beginning to be aware of a cause-and-effect relationship. Preoperational thought tends to be *animistic*.

6. *Concept formations* begin in earnest after the child can grasp the idea that words (verbal images) stand for something. The questions of young children evolve from "what" to "why" or "how." Concepts of time are vague in childhood. Concepts of space and size develop more readily.
7. *Classification* ability in early childhood is generally restricted to the use of one item of similarity. *Seriation* of long and short is developed in most 4- or 5-year-olds. *Conservation of substance* is not usually developed in 4- or 5-year-olds.
8. There are two approaches to the information processing model of cognition. One approach is a sequential step-by-step process based on computer simulation models. The other approach stresses specific mental operations.
9. The perceptual-conceptual *information-processing* model is based on the computer analogy. The major steps are (1) receptive, (2) perceptual, (3) conceptual, and (4) expressive. In addition there are the components of memory and feedback. Each element has its several specifics of operation.
10. Fig. 7-3 is a representation of the brain and some of its known areas for cognitive functioning. The information-processing scheme involved is the perceptual-conceptual model, which has four parts: receptive phase, perceptual phase, conceptual phase, and expressive phase. Difficulty in thought processing at any place in the sequence will produce inefficient learning or reasoning or both.
11. The *mental operations* model stresses specific entities of cognition rather than the step-by-step process. In particular the processes of perception, attention, memory, and problem solving are studied.
12. Three components of language are semantics, syntax, and pragmatics. *Semantics* refers to knowing the meaningfulness of words or word phrases. *Syntax* is the way by which words are put together to form sentences. *Pragmatics* is the ability to adjust one's language to suit a particular social situation.
13. Two-year-olds are busy learning a vocabulary. Three-year-olds are developing elementary syntax skills. Four-year-olds usually ask many questions and are more social in the use of language than previously. Five-year-olds ask questions that are more relevant and meaningful than those asked by four-year olds.
14. Non-Standard English is spoken English that differs from the traditional dialect used in schools and the communication media.
15. Play in early childhood may be *isolated or solitary play*, *parallel play* beside others, or *associative or group play* with varying degrees of cooperation. Children may go directly from solitary play to group play.
16. *Sex-role differentiation* may be acquired by (a) identification with models, (b) reinforcement for sex-appropriate behavior, and (c) behavior that leads to social acceptance rather than rejection. *Sex-roles* may be influenced by biological factors, such as hormones or hemispheric lateralization, social factors related to differential treatment, learned sex type behavior, or the expectations and influences of the family structure in the home. Maccoby and Jacklin have a list of findings related to which beliefs of sex differences are real, which ones are unfounded, and which ones are debatable.
17. Emotional development in early childhood starts on a strong egocentric basis and gradually becomes responsive to the environment. The more a child becomes aware of the surroundings, the more the capacity for emotional response increases.
18. The developmental approach to the organization of personality in early childhood includes the following phases: *imitation* of behavior, *suggestibility* of feelings and emotions, *identification* with a personality, and the discarding of the idea of the person in identification but the retaining of the characteristics and values of that person. A *value judgment system* emerges based on the personality structure of a self-ideal. The self-ideal leads to self-evaluation and self-esteem.

REVIEW QUESTIONS

1. Review the developmental tasks of early childhood.
2. Look at the growth curves in Fig. 7-1. Why is the growth curve for the brain and head so sharp in infancy and early childhood? The growth curve for lymphoid development indicates that development goes beyond 100%, then decreases to that of the level of an adult. Why is that so?
3. Compare the height and weight of a 3-year-old to that of a 5-year-old.
4. Look at Table 7-1 on gross and fine motor development. What growth do you note in motor control and coordination?
5. List the principal characteristics of the preconceptual and the intuitive substages. Why are they considered preoperational? What does animistic mean?
6. What are the four characteristics of concepts that 3- to 5-year-olds have? How do these relate to the preoperational stage of cognitive development?
7. What level of understanding do children in early childhood have of time, numbers, space, and size?

8. Define classification, seriation, conservation, and transformation. What is the developmental level of each of these in early childhood?
9. What is the theoretical position of the information-processing model? How does it differ from Piaget's model of cognitive development?
10. In your own words, define and describe the steps and procedures in the perceptual-conceptual model of information processing. You may use Fig. 7-2 as a guide.
11. Look at Fig. 7-3. Review the four component parts of the perceptual-conceptual model of information processing at the bottom of the figure. Then trace the flow of the process through the brain by looking at the four numbers that are circled. What do the other numbers mean?
12. What is meant by a mental operations model of information processing?
13. Briefly discuss perception and attention in early childhood.
14. What are the three types of functions of memory? Define each one.
15. According to information processing theorists, what are the two views of memory? Describe each view.
16. Why is problem solving difficult for children in early childhood?
17. Define semantics, syntax, and pragmatics. How do they relate to language development in early childhood?
18. Describe and give examples of non-Standard English.
19. How does the play of children differ between 2-year-olds and 4-year-olds? Why the difference?
20. What is meant by sex-role differentiation? What influences sex-role development and gender labeling?
21. Look at the findings of Maccoby and Jacklin on assumed differences between males and females. Are they more than assumptions or stereotypes?
22. Discuss emotional development characteristics in early childhood.
23. List the four phases of the developmental organization of personality in early childhood. Briefly describe each phase. Analyze the beginnings of a value judgment system. What is the significance of a self-ideal? What does it have to do with self-esteem?

THOUGHT QUESTIONS AND ACTIVITIES

1. Imagine yourself having had your fourth birthday. As a 4-year-old, how does the world (life) look to you? How capable are you in terms of competent self-help skills and independent living? In other words, how much do you know and what will you have to learn in order to be capable of purposeful action and reasoning? The class may want to discuss this question. After the discussion, observe several 4-year-olds to determine how correct your insights concerning this age level were. In groups of two or three you may want to observe children in a nursery school, on a playground, or at a place like McDonald's.
2. Form a story-telling group, perhaps at a nearby library or day school nursery. Arrange to tell a story or two to a group of preschoolers once or twice a week for about 6 weeks. Record, mentally or graphically, the characteristics of the children.
3. With a pad, pencil, and stopwatch, follow the activities of a 2-, 3-, 4-, or 5-year-old for 2 hours. Record the types of behavior and the length of time spent on each activity. Compare your notes with someone else's. What did you find in common?
4. Discuss: How does a child learn *how* to learn?
5. Discuss: How much love should a preschool child be given? Does the child need anything else beyond tender loving care (TLC) to grow into a nice, pleasant person with some intellectual competency?
6. Investigate the prevalence—or meaning—of non-Standard English, be it black, Spanish, Navajo, Vietnamese, or other.
7. Do you perceive the Piaget model of cognition and the information processing model to be related, unrelated, completely opposite, different—or what?
8. There has been some interesting work done on sex-role differentiation that goes beyond the book. Look it up in *Psychological Abstracts.* What is the new research saying?
9. Does the developmental organization of the personality model make sense to you? Does it have an appeal?

FURTHER READINGS

Curtis, S. *Genie: A psycholinguistic study of a modern day "wild child."* New York: Academic Press, 1981. This is an exciting account of a girl who, from the age of 20 months until she was a little over 13 years of age, lived in almost total isolation. Easy reading.

Earls, F. Temperament characteristics and behavior problems in three-year-olds. In J. S. Chess and A. Thomas (Eds.), *Annual progress in child psychiatry and child development.* New York: Brunner/Mazel, 1982. This paper examines the relationship of temperamental characteristics to behavioral adjustment in preschool children. Three characteristics—low distractibility, high intensity, and low adaptability—were found to be closely linked to poor behavioral adjustment.

Garvey, C. *Play.* Cambridge, Mass.: Harvard University Press, 1977. Videotapes were made of children's play. Anecdotal illustrations and examples are used to show how the changing forms of play help the child cope with a physical and social environment.

Maccoby, E. E. *Social development: Psychological growth and the parent-child relationship.* New York: Harcourt Brace Jovanovich, 1980. The child's social development in the context of the family is presented for the early and middle childhood years.

Nye, R.D. *What is B. F. Skinner really saying?* Englewood Cliffs, N.J.: Prentice-Hall, 1979. The basic concepts and underlying assumptions behind Skinner's view of behaviorism are presented. The text considers some controversies and misunderstandings of Skinner's work.

Parke, R. D., & Asher, S. R. Social and personality development. In M. R. Rosenzweig and L. W. Porter (Eds.), *Annual review of psychology* (Vol. 34). Palo Alto, Calif.: Annual Reviews, 1983. A review of recent research is conducted in the field of social and personality development. Reading is moderately difficult.

Rice, M.L., Child language: What children know and how. In T.M. Field, A. Huston, H.C. Quay, L. Troll, & Y.E. Finley (Eds.), *Review of human development.* New York: John Wiley & Sons, 1982. Mabel Rice seeks to capture the sense of excitement that is current in the study of children's language. New models of what children know linguistically are presented, a great amount of research is reviewed, and new explanations of how children come to acquire language are developed. Moderately difficult reading.

Siegler, R. S. Information-processing approaches to development. In W. Kessen (Ed.), *Carmichael's manual of child psychology* (Vol. 1). New York: John Wiley & Sons, 1982. The chapter on information processing presents a description and perspective of the development of this model. Moderately difficult reading level.

Wilson, A. N. *The developmental psychology of the black child.* New York: African Research Publications, 1978. This paperback, written for African Research Publications, covers many of the developmental topics, but the information is related to the black child. The book is aimed at the professional, but it is also written for black parents.

CHAPTER 8

MIDDLE CHILDHOOD

6 to 8 YEARS OF AGE

WHAT IS A FIRST GRADER?

What do you see when you look at a first grader? You may see a front-toothless, squirmy six- or seven-year-old jumping rope, swinging, or tumbling on the grass. You may see a clean pair of trousers become grass stained before the blink of an eye. You may see imagination and personality bubbling forth as in no other time in life. But to be sure, you will see a group of individuals unique and yet unbelievably alike.

As a first-grade teacher, I never cease to marvel at my "charges." They come to school knowing so little, and they leave, having acquired a vast amount of information ranging from reading, to social relationships with others, to a discovery of what school is really all about.

A first grader usually has fairly well-developed large muscle movements. Small muscle coordination is another story. A pencil surely is a strange and horrible creation during those first few weeks, and to have to sit still for more than ten minutes at a time! Unheard of! Often it takes a whole year before some first graders learn to control their small muscles and their huge bursts of energy.

Cognitive development during this age is truly amazing. Imagine seeing all those strange-looking symbols called the alphabet, being told that each symbol is a letter, that each has its own sound, and that combinations of these funny-looking things will form something called words. How frightening and overwhelming it must seem in those first few weeks of school. Often I am amazed at how fast these little bundles of energy can learn—not only reading but arithmetic as well. More strange symbols with unique meanings! I feel that in no other grade do the children begin with so little and learn so much. So much progress can be seen in all pupils. Yet some youngsters encounter a sense of frustration when others begin to pull away, leaving them behind. Learning is harder for some, and these children come to know that "Steve is a good reader" but that "I can't read so good."

Individual differences begin to show through in other areas as well. Social relationships concern every first grader. Whereas some children have companions and best friends, others become isolates and encounter social problems. No one wants to be friends with a child who always wants his or her own way, who does not play fairly, or who cannot keep up in games because of intellectual or physical limitations. Here children must learn to cope with the "different" children and help them to become accepted and adjusted.

Influence by peers increases greatly in first grade. Previously, ideas fostered at home were supreme. Now the realization begins that other ideas and beliefs might not be so bad after all. Maybe everything Mommy and Daddy say isn't right! "But my friend Jimmy said . . . " becomes a new phrase. First graders want to go to their friends' homes. They want to call them on the telephone. They delight in seeing each other in the grocery store or at the shopping center. They desire to have the toys their friends have and to wear the same types of clothing. One coloring book is shown and is followed by ten more like it the next day. Interests truly are dictated by peer-group influence.

Emotional developments are great in six- to seven-year-olds. Many first graders are quick to cry, whereas others brood and pout. The first day of school is an emotional trauma—the strange bus ride, meeting a new teacher, and just being taken away from Mommy is enough to set the tears in motion, not to mention being thrown in with 26 other children undergoing similar trauma. But luckily, fears and tears soon disappear as the days go on. Emotional adjustment continues throughout the year, and vast improvements can be seen by the end of school.

First graders love competition. Whether they are racing on the playground or trying to see who will get their work done first, these children are in their glory when competing. They delight in playing games, as long as they do not lose all the time. Spelling bees and arithmetic competitions are a source of enjoyment, even for the slower pupils who manage to win often enough to keep them interested.

A typical day might begin with two children forgetting their lunch money, a common problem. ("My mother forgot to give it to me!") The day continues with a few tattles ("Donnie pulled my hair," "Mark is copying from my paper") and some comments by the teacher: "Michele, put that away," "Robert, don't you ever stop talking?" As an aside, first graders love to talk. They begin when they come in the morning and are still talking as they walk up the hall to their buses when school is over for the day. Recess is enjoyed, since it is a time for running and playing. After lunch the afternoon begins with settling an argument about whose turn it really was to take the ball out at noon recess or determining whose superball Roger really has—his or David's! The afternoon concludes with the usual race of the children riding Bus 51 to see who can get into line first.

Working with first graders is interesting and rewarding. This age-group is dependent, yet independent; serious, yet comical; aggravating, yet satisfying. The first graders' teacher is their mother away from home, their helper, referee, friend, and aid to learning. If one were to look at a first grader, just what *would* that person see?

IN THIS CHAPTER . . .

You will read about

1 The body growth and physical skills of 6- to-8-year-olds.
2 Piaget's concrete operational stage and what kinds of thinking, reasoning, and problem solving can take place during this age level.
3 The way in which the neuropsychological organization model of information processing develops and functions. Also, the reason children with learning disabilities cannot make as efficient use of information processing as others can.
4 Language and thought in middle childhood.
5 Social interaction with peers and patterns of parenting.
6 The one-parent family and its effect on the child.
7 Self-concepts and sex roles in middle childhood.
8 Emotional characteristics of the age-group.
9 The moral development views of Piaget and of social learning theory.

industry versus inferiority Erikson's fourth crisis of psychological development; the school-aged child may develop a capacity for work and task-directedness, or he may view himself as inadequate.

Six- to 8-year-old children are fascinating little people. For the parent they are full of surprises, new and different each day; for their siblings they are someone to love, someone to tolerate, or someone to have nothing to do with; for their teacher they are individuals, eager to learn in any way they can. As children go through these years, different growth characteristics appear. There is no clear-cut line or age at which one stage of development ends and the next begins. Generally, children go from one phase to another without any earth-shattering experience to announce the change. Most of the time they proceed without any trouble. Parents, teachers, and friends will be able to see differences, however, between children at 6 years of age and at 8 years.

Up to the age of 5 or 6 years children all over the world grow, develop, and act similarly. Throughout the ages, babies everywhere have been much the same. The principles of growth and development are eternal and universal in nature. By the age of 5 or 6 years, however, the distinctive cultures of each society are imprinted on its children. Little Ivan, little Joe, and little Wang-Ti start the same, but the human-made influences of their respective cultures begin to have a different impact on the growth and development of each child, creating differences in attitudes, behavior, and even in certain physical characteristics that are unique to the culture.

The developmental tasks of middle childhood are centered about "three great outward pushes." Socially, children make their way out of their family environs into a peer-group society. Physically, they move into a world of games and activities requiring neuromuscular skill. Mentally, there is a thrust into school and the world of concepts, symbols, logics, and communication. Specifically, the developmental tasks are as follows: (1) acquiring social and physical skills necessary for ordinary games, (2) learning to get along with peers, (3) building a wholesome concept of self, (4) learning an appropriate sex role, (5) developing fundamental skills in reading, writing, and arithmetic, (6) breaking family ties and developing a growing independence by entering school, and (7) developing conscience, morality, and a value judgment system (Havighurst, 1979). These developmental tasks will be paramount in importance until the child reaches puberty and adolescence.

During the years of 6 to puberty, children learn the skills valued by society. These include not only reading, writing and arithmetic but also physical skills, the ability to share responsibility, and the social skills needed to get along with people. To the extent that efforts in these areas are successful, children develop feelings of competence; unsuccessful efforts result in feelings of inferiority. Erikson (1963) suggests that the psychosocial crisis that must be met during this age period is one of ***industry versus inferiority.*** "Can I do things well, or am I a failure?" are the questions to be answered. The task outcome is one of competence in intellectual, social, and physical skills. Children can discover that they are capable of producing something and that they can achieve social acceptance and a feeling of self-worth.

PHYSICAL DEVELOPMENT

The middle childhood years are characterized by a relatively slow but steady growth rate as compared to the years of infancy or puberty. This age level is one of the most comfortable periods of physical adjustment. The developmental pace is sufficiently slow so that under normal conditions children can meet the physical and psychological demands made on them.

Body growth

By 6 years of age children have usually lost most of their baby contours. Their legs and arms are lengthening, and they are gaining in height and weight, although growth is less rapid than before. Girls at this age are generally more physically mature than boys in terms of ultimate level of physical development. However, boys do tend to be slightly taller and heavier than girls up to the age of 10 years. The average child of 6 years in North America stands 117 cm (46 in. tall) and weighs about 22 kg (48 lb.) The annual expected growth is 5 to 7.5 cm (2 to 3 in.) in height and 1.5 to 3 kg (3 to 6 lb.) in weight (Latham et al., 1977). All children have their own growth rate, however, and there are a few 6-year-olds who are as tall and heavy as some 10-year-olds.

Meriem Kaluger

Middle childhood at 6 years.
Has increased interest in games.

Meriem Kaluger

Can use a knife to spread peanut butter on bread.

Meriem Kaluger

Middle childhood at 7 and 8 years.
A 7-year-old likes to help with simple chores.

Meriem Kaluger

An 8-year-old relates to a younger sibling as an "older" brother or sister, teaching, directing, demonstrating.

There is a change in the structure of the face that is noticeable in comparing a 4-year-old with a 6-year-old. The face begins to look more slim and lean because the children are beginning to lose their "baby fat." It is during this sixth year, also, that they lose their first tooth. Being more physiologically mature, girls shed their teeth a bit earlier than boys. As permanent teeth replace baby teeth and as new molars come in, the jaw lengthens and the face changes in shape. The "toothless gap era" declines at about the age of 8 years, when the permanent teeth appear, starting at the front and developing to the back. Permanent teeth will continue to arrive until about the age of 11 or 12 years.

The eyes of a 6-year-old are still immature in size and shape. There is a strong tendency to farsightedness, a situation usually corrected naturally between the ages of 8 and 10 years when the child's eyes attain adult size and shape. The younger child should be provided with books that have larger than normal print. At this age it is important for the child to be tested for near-point vision. Most visual screening charts test a child's vision at far point, but it is near-point vision that a child must use in reading.

Girls have somewhat poorer visual acuity than boys, but their color discrimination is superior on the average to that of boys. Auditory acuity is as good at 7 years of age as it will ever be. The ability to discriminate pitch, however, will continue to improve for the next 3 or 4 years (Graham et al., 1980). Nervous physical habits begin to appear in 7-year-olds. The most common habits are nail biting, tongue sucking, or scratching and pulling at the ear. These are more frequently found among girls than among boys. Some of these habits may disappear within a matter of months whereas others, such as nail biting, may persist into adulthood.

TABLE 8-1 Motor development in middle childhood

Age	*Selected behaviors*
6 years	Girls superior in movement accuracy; boys superior in forceful, less complex acts
	Skipping acquired
	Throwing with proper weight shift and step
7 years	One-footed balancing without vision becomes possible
	Can walk 5 cm-(2-in.) wide balance beams
	Can hop and jump accurately into small squares
	Can execute accurate jumping-jack exercise
8 years	5.4 kg (12-lb.) pressure on grip strength by both sexes
	The number of games participated in by both sexes is greatest at this age
	Can engage in alternate rhythmical hopping in a 2-2, 2-3, or 3-3 pattern
	Girls can throw a small ball 131 m (40 ft.)

From Cratty, B. *Perceptual and Motor Development in Infants and Children,* 2nd ed. ©1979, p. 222. Reprinted by permission of Prentice-Hall, Inc., Englewood Cliffs, N.J.

Motor skills development

When motor development is viewed from an ordinal perspective, it can be observed that motor characteristics develop from the use of fine-motor activities in a rather gross manner to a much greater control of fine-motor movements. *Ordinal* refers to an order or rank in a series—in this case, the order of the development of motor control. Development is a series of hierarchical, qualitatively different stages, containing horizontal and vertical movement. In some ways it is bound to environmental exchange and interaction (Yang, 1979). Although in this presentation of motor characteristics there will be some references to age levels, the major consideration should be given to the flow of development, with age levels having secondary meaning. Not every child develops or advances at the same pace. Yet enough children develop at about the same rate so that some normative data can be provided. The ordinal approach is also used in this chapter to describe mental, social, and emotional development.

Children at the early stages of middle childhood—at 6 years of age—can usually hop, skip, jump, dress and undress, tie a bow, and use scissors. However, their larger muscles are more advanced in development than their smaller ones. Because of this condition, their small muscles do not permit them to do precise writing, sewing, or drawing. Tying shoelaces will still be an effort for some at this age. They still become frustrated by their lack of fine motor skill development. Table 8-1 presents some of the motor skills achieved in middle childhood.

Six years is an age of activity. Running, jumping, climbing, bike riding, and "clean-up" jobs at school make use of the child's large muscles. Although they enjoy finer motor activities, children become restless after sitting for a short period of time. They wriggle on a chair and sit on the edge.

Frequent bangs or thumps can be heard in the classroom—they have fallen off their chairs. There is a good deal of oral activity such as blowing through the lips, extending the tongue, and making all kinds of mouthing noises. These children are easily distracted by the environment.

Although their large muscles are still better developed than their small ones, seven-year-olds are gradually becoming more skillful in using their small muscles in eye-hand coordination activities. Indication of improved small muscle control is shown by the Stanford-Binet test of tying a bowknot. Only 35% of the 6-year-olds could pass this test as compared to 69% of the 7-year-olds and 94% of the 9-year-olds (Terman and Merrill, 1960). It is during the second grade in the United States that most children learn to do cursive writing, which requires a different kind of control over their hand motions than was needed for manuscript writing.

Advancing from the gross activities approach, many 7-year-olds combine thought with activity. They are more inclined to "think before jumping." They are more cautious in new performances and show a new awareness of heights. They will play vigorously in one activity but will quickly drop it for another, although they do not change from loud to quiet types of activities as frequently as was done earlier.

The older middle-childhood individuals are continuing to develop steadily and slowly. Active play is most characteristic of this period. Most 8-year-olds have achieved equilibrium in body balance and can move freely with fluidity because of improved small muscle development. They do not drop their pencil as frequently as they did earlier nor lose it as often as when they were beginning school. In writing they space words and sentences well and can control their hand movements so that slanting letters can be achieved easily.

Since nearsightedness may develop in middle childhood, visual care must be maintained. These children are quicker in their responses, mentally and physically. Their attention span is longer, which is helpful to the teacher, who will not have to cope with the multitude of distractions that face the first-grade teacher.

In summary, with the development of large muscles to the point that they can be used effectively in producing alternating movements, the 6- to 8-year-olds now seek to try out a variety of physical skills that they could not do before. They delight in doing the physically unusual or different, such as walking on ledges or balancing on fences rather than walking on the sidewalks. A ball becomes an indispensable toy because children can now take aim and make the ball go where or do what they want it to. Kicking skills become important because the repertoire of games in middle childhood includes many involving kicking, running, and jumping. Children in this age-group will kick cans, rocks, anything that can be moved. A favorite playground game is kick ball.

A significant developmental point to be noted at this time is that making one's way into the peer group begins to depend on the child's skills for playing the approved games of the group. The importance of these skills increases as the child reaches the ages of 10 to 12 years. This factor is more important for boys than for girls because their sex role includes more physical activities. Some children, boys in particular, become misfits when unfortunate circumstances make them meagerly equipped to play games with their peers. A large number of delinquent boys have been found to be unskilled in playing games of the group. Generally, children learn the skills needed for games without help from the school. It is the wise teacher or parent who tries to find ways for children to learn the skills if they do not possess them.

CONCRETE OPERATIONAL STAGE

Children who are 6 to 8 years old are on the threshold of a new world. They can control their muscle movements so that they can do more precise physical activities than ever before. Socially, they are becoming members of a society consisting largely of others of their own age. Intellectually, they are on the verge of answering their own "why" questions. It is important to understand that children are only at the starting point of all of these ventures, but they are at that point, and the school will seek to help them make the most of their newly developed abilities and interests.

Brief review of Piaget's cognitive theory

Piaget's theory of cognitive development embraces four stages: sensorimotor, preoperational, concrete operational, and formal operational. The *sensorimotor stage* covers the ages of birth to 2 years. During this period the baby learns to coordinate sensory experi-

concrete operational stage the stage of cognitive development that occurs from about 7 to 12 years of age and during which the child develops the operations of conservation, class inclusion, and serialization. This stage begins when children understand new kinds of logical operations involving reversible transformations of concrete objects and events.

reversibility the mental operation or understanding, according to Piaget's theory of cognitive development, in which one can think of a transformation that would reverse a sequence of events or restore the original condition.

ence with motor activity. The child explores new objects and events, but the infant focuses on salient characteristics that appeal to the senses. Soon exploration becomes linked with intention, and improvement in the ability to accommodate to new situations occurs. Toward the end of this period, there emerges the ability to represent objects, events, and actions in the mind as mental images. Object permanence has occurred when the child can retain the mental images.

During the *preoperational stage,* there is an improvement in the ability to represent objects symbolically and to understand that action on objects produces results. The child begins to know things without being directly involved. Reasoning is from salient point (the particular) to salient point without any generalizations or logical association between the objects. Problem solving becomes intuitive and is limited by egocentrism, centering, and irreversibility. Concepts that are formed are limited by what is perceptually obvious.

Characteristics of the concrete operational stage

The ***concrete operational stage*** covers the approximate ages of 7 to 11 or 12 years. During this time the child acquires basic logical ways of reasoning (operations) but only on the concrete level. The implication is that the child depends on what can be seen, touched, or heard (concrete) to base thinking—rather than reasoning abstractly with ideas. The child can reason about things but not about verbal propositions.

The child's thinking becomes reversible. ***Reversibility*** is the ability to conceptualize the way in which a transition occurs from one state to another and the way things return to their original state. This means that the child can be aware that an operation can be reversed to bring back the original situation. For example, the child can not only trace the way to school but can also tell the way back home from school. Further, the child with reversibility skill knows that a clay ball rolled into a sausage can be rolled back into a ball.

Play becomes focused on the representation of objects and events and is more strongly rule-governed. There is an improvement in the ability to mentally represent classes of objects and to establish relationships between classes.

As a result, the child improves in the ability to do classification, to serially order objects on some continuum such as size, weight, or volume (seriation), and to conserve some property of an object even when other properties of the object have been changed (transformed) in some way.

Conservation. Children who can *conserve* are those who understand that irrelevant changes in the external appearance of an object have no effect on the object's weight, length, mass, or volume. The famous experiment with a short but wide glass, a high but narrow glass, and colored water can illustrate this point. The child is shown the high narrow glass with the water in it. The researcher pours the liquid into the short wide glass and asks, "Which glass contained more water?" The nonconserver says, "The high glass because it is taller." The conserver will say, "They both have the same amount of water because the short glass is wider. If you pour the water back into the high glass, it will go to the same level as before." The conserver can *decenter* by focusing on more than one feature at a time. That is, this child can focus simultaneously on both the width and the height of the containers. Furthermore, this child can attend to *transformation* of the liquid from one height to another by being able to conceptualize the states through which one moves in getting from one situation to another and the processes that allow these changes to take place.

Research now suggests that perhaps not all of the variables have been covered in the traditional approach to the experiment. For example, the researcher pours the water into the second container and says, "Now watch what I do," implying that something is going to change or happen (Donaldson, 1979). It appears that the experimenter can influence the results. Changing the way in which a test is presented may make a difference for some children as to how they perceive conservation. By approaching the conservation task in a different way, Rosenthal and Zimmerman (1978) were able to teach 3- and 4-year-old children to pass the conservation tests. Piaget maintained that children can apply cognitive structures already acquired only to new cognitive situations. Social learning theorists raise a question about that statement. Developmental psychologists are still far from understanding exactly how children acquire conservation concepts.

Classification. *Classification* is the operation of grouping objects into a class or dimension. When a child achieves the cognitive ability to do true classification, he or she is able to differentiate and use two important properties of class, intention and extension. Class inclusion or *intention* is the criterion or the quality that defines the class. Examples of intention are characteristics, such as shapes or colors. The grouping task would be "Put all the square pieces in one pile and all the round ones in another" or "The black buttons go in one box and the white ones in the other."

Extension is the number of all the objects meeting that criterion. For example, suppose there are two white squares and two black squares. If the intention criterion is white square, the extension answer is two. If the intention criterion is the number of squares (white or black), the extension answer is four. The child who is in the early preoperational stage cannot perform this classification grouping task; the youngster, easily distracted because of centering on one aspect of the objects, may include objects that do not meet the classification criterion. The child may put both round and square black pieces in a pile when directed to put only round pieces there. The child who is capable of concrete operations works from a class idea that is stable and permanent—one that will not change under any condition.

Time and speed. Piaget contends that children do not understand the relationship among time, speed, and distance until ages 10 or 11 (Piaget and Inhelder, 1969). Before this age an object is considered to travel faster than another object only if the second overtakes the first while moving. In addition, the child in the preoperational stage considers only the point of arrival and not the starting points or the paths that were followed. If two cars arrive at the same point, even if one took a circular path and the other traveled in a straight line, this youngster will say that both cars traveled at the same speed. Another illustration is the child's explanation: "If I walk slow, it's far; if I run, it's closer."

The child in the concrete operations stage has a better concept of movement, speed (velocity), and time than the younger child because the older one can decenter and focus on a transformation rather than concentrating on only one salient point (Phillips, 1975).

Seriation. *Seriation* is the ability to mentally arrange elements or objects according to increasing or decreasing size. If a child in the preoperational stage is shown two sticks (A and B) of different lengths, he or she can compare them and determine that stick A is longer than stick B. If the longer stick (A) is taken away and hidden, and a shorter stick (C) is brought out, the child can still tell that stick B is longer than stick C. However, if asked which was the longest stick (A or C), this child could not mentally order the events in a series to say A is longer than B; B is longer than C; therefore, A is longer than C. The 7-year-old in the operational stage could probably tell that A was longer.

Seriation of objects of the same size but different weights is usually understood at about age 9. Seriation of volume is a concept acquired at approximately age 12. The ability to seriate or order objects along a certain dimension usually occurs at the same time that conservation skills with respect to the same dimension emerge.

Conceptual development. During the concrete operations stage, children reach a level where they understand equality relations, use arithmetic and measurements, understand the notion of right and left as applied to objects themselves, and understand the concept of number. Piaget hypothesizes that children's conception of numbers goes hand in hand with the development of logic (Piaget, 1965).

It is during this stage that children realize that other people see things differently from the way they do. The child is moving away from egocentrism. Through repeated and often frustrating interchanges with their peers, they have come to cognitive grips with viewpoints and perspectives that differ from their own. At the same time the necessity of maintaining an original premise in an argument is also being developed.

During the concrete operations period, children's conception of the world definitely changes. The idea that nature is made by humans disappears entirely toward the age of 9 or 10 years. By this time all of nature is imbued with purpose (i.e., the sun has been made for the purpose of giving us warmth and light and the clouds for the purpose of bringing us rain). This stage of cognitive development—conception of

Conceptual development during the concrete operations period is enhanced by first-hand experiences. These children visited a Pizza Hut and learned how pizzas are made. Then they put together their own pan pizza, later enjoying the fruits of their labor.

Meriem Kaluger

Meriem Kaluger

physical causality—produces a new parallelism between logic and the real categories. In other words, at approximately the age of 10 years, when logical thought becomes deductive, interpretation of reality breaks away from forms of primitive realism, such as "seeing is believing," and becomes a logical or reasoning necessity (Piaget, 1966).

Descriptive mental characteristics

Most 6-year-olds operate on a precausal level of reasoning. These children have not firmly established a concept of "cause and effect" or the idea that a person can sometimes reason what the cause or the result might be. However, children do ask "Why?" and "What for?" and "How?" They begin to realize that objects and events serve certain purposes that they want to know. The average 6-year-olds are still in the preoperational stage of conceptual development, however. Therefore their reasoning process will be largely governed by the appearance of things, and they can form only rudimentary generalizations.

When given two objects, 6-year-olds can more easily see the differences that exist between the objects than the similarities. Differences can be seen or experienced directly, but similarities must be abstracted from generalizations, an ability not developed until about 9 years of age. Most 6-year-olds also have difficulty in making decisions, even about such things as what flavor of ice cream they would like to have or what color of a balloon to buy. Their memory is such that they can repeat sentences of 10 or 12 words or repeat four digits in order. They know number combinations up to 10.

The experience of school has helped most 7-year-olds in developing their mental powers. Their activities are becoming more specialized. They now have the mental ability that enables them to count by ones, twos, fives, and tens. They now grasp the basic idea of addition and subtraction. However, many times the work done along these lines is the result of memorizing addition and subtraction tables. Modern math seeks to teach how to reason by sets and groups.

Operationally, 7-year-olds do little abstract thinking.

Meriem Kaluger

cognitive style an individual's characteristic style of processing information. For example, some people are deliberate, reflective, and analytical; others are impulsive, inflexible, and intolerant of ambiguity.

They learn best in concrete terms and when they can be active while learning. They prefer to participate rather than to be just spectators. Their speech is no longer egocentric but is now sociocentric—others centered.

They have a rudimentary understanding of time and monetary values. They can tell time and make some small purchases. Allowing children to make these purchases on their own gives them a feeling that their parents trust them to handle money, even if they are standing by and watching.

At this age curiosity begins to arise as to the difference between the sexes and where babies come from. These ideas show an interest in reality and indicate the importance of giving truthful information. Sex information may well be given at this age—not to be taught in great detail but enough to satisfy the child's curiosity.

Children in middle childhood are entering Piaget's stage of concrete operations. They now begin to use elementary logic and to reason about size, space, weight, volume, number, and time. They can group objects according to a given attribute, such as color, and still realize that they can be regrouped according to another attribute, such as size. They can also order things into a series, such as from larger to smaller. They are able to apply the principle of conservation, which states that certain properties remain constant and invariant regardless of changes in their appearance. For example, they understand that the water from a beaker remains the same when poured into a shallow dish.

Almy and associates (1966) investigated children's ability to apply the principle of conservation. They used a longitudinal approach to test and retest youngsters on conservational ability in three tasks, two involving number and one involving quantity of liquid. One of their findings was that 76% of the 7-year-olds from a middle-class socioeconomic background conserved on all three tasks. This was in agreement with Piaget's theory.

Children in the latter part of middle childhood show an interest in causal relationships. They are curious about all types of changes and happenings and want to know about cause and effects. This level of thinking represents the scientific dimension of recognition and is proceeding from concrete to abstract and metaphysical relations.

The 8-year-old's memory span is increasing. Memory span for words will, of course, vary greatly according to the familiarity, interest, and meaning of words for the child. Most 8-year-olds can answer five out of six simple questions on a story about 100 words long and can repeat without errors a sentence of about 16 words after hearing it once.

Mentally, 8-year-olds are still developing through experience. They like to take field trips and question all they see. They still see the teacher as the authority. Children are much interested in the past. They like to talk about Indians and their ways. They can now tell the day of the month and the year. Far-off places and ways of communication now have real meaning. As a result of all this experience the children are starting to use some abstract thinking.

Cognitive style

As might be expected, there are individual differences to be found in the way children (and adults) process information and solve problems, regardless of their level of intelligence or development. In dealing with various aspects of our environment, each one of us has our own way of thinking and problem solving. This unique manner of thinking is known as cognitive style. ***Cognitive style*** refers to individual variations in modes of attending, perceiving, remembering, and thinking. Kogan (1982) refers to four cognitive styles: (1) reflection-impulsivity, (2) field-dependence–independence, (3) constricted versus flexible control, and (4) conceptualizing styles. Differences in cognitive styles of processing information can be related to level of maturation, memory, attentiveness, personality, social class, and age.

The reflection-impulsivity cognitive style refers to the speed with which an individual responds in thinking. A *reflective cognitive style* is one where the individual's thinking is deliberate and accurate. The *impulsive cognitive style* is noticed in children who are impulsive, tending to respond quickly and with many inaccuracies. Reflective individuals generate more hypotheses, take more time to solve a problem, and pay more attention to details. They do better than impulsive thinkers on the Piagetian tasks of reasoning (Pascual-Leone, 1973). Impulsive thinkers generally excel at

Meriem Kaluger

Cognitive style refers to individual variations in modes of attending, perceiving, remembering, and thinking. A teacher should be able to identify individual differences in learning style and cognition.

intellectual tasks requiring broad analyses (Zelniker and Jeffrey, 1976). The results of some studies have shown that children who tend to be impulsive in problem solving can be trained to be more reflective (Messer, 1976; Zelniker and Oppenheimer, 1976).

Field-dependence–independence cognitive style refers to the capacity to identify embedded contexts in perception; that is, to separate a part from an organized whole. This characteristic shows up in tests where a person is asked to find simple figures camouflaged within more complex figures. An example would be puzzles with the question, "How many faces can you find in this picture of trees, shrubs, and clouds?" A typical simple task would be to locate the outline of a fish drawn in a rectangle with a number of diagonal lines superimposed on it. *Field-independent* thinkers tend to analyze the elements of a scene. They excel in concentrating on tasks under distracting circumstances. They also tend to excel in the solution of analytical restructuring tasks. *Field-dependent* thinkers tend to look at the scene as a whole and usually overlook the individual details that compose it. In general, they think in the opposite fashion from field-independent individuals.

Cognitive *styles of conceptualization* refer to the bases for grouping. The grouping of objects or ideas may be done by perceptual similarities, names of the objects, rational-thematic (complementary), or categorical-inferential (similarities of categories). The rational-thematic style of grouping of geometrical forms or common objects is most common among 5-to 7-year-olds (Cicirelli, 1976). The *constricted versus flexible cognitive style* refers to the freedom of cognitive processing that the individual has in being able to move from one thought pattern or idea to another. A *constricted cognitive style* finds it difficult to change direction or areas of emphasis. A *flexible cognitive style* is one in which the person can set an idea aside and move on to another one, break one train of thought and introduce another one, or change from one approach of problem solving to another.

The concept of cognitive style has much meaning for adults as well as children. Each individual has a cognitive style that operates well for him or her; different strategies work with different individuals (Cronbach and Snow, 1977). For example, field-independent college students tend to respond well to subjects that require a high level of analytical thinking, such as the natural sciences, mathematics, and engineering. Field-dependent students tend to major in the social sciences, humanities, education, and fields that involve a global perspective. Many students whose first choice of a college major is inconsistent with their cognitive style change their majors to more compatible programs (Witkin et al., 1977).

NEUROPSYCHOLOGICAL DEVELOPMENT AND INFORMATION PROCESSING

What happens internally when children are learning *how* to learn? Something has to occur in the neurological processes because it is only there that any kind of cognitive consciousness can take place. As the advertisement used to say, "If it hasn't got it there, it hasn't got it." According to Piaget, young infants are busy maturing their motor areas so they can begin to make coordinated movements that will enhance their survival level. Soon their sensory systems combine with the motor systems to develop the perceptual-motor processes. Eventually, children reach a point when they must develop their skills for learning so that they can make better use of their potential intellect.

Although infants are born with all the brain cells and nerves that they will ever have, they are not born with an innate, ready-made neuropsychological organization for processing information received as stimuli from the environment. For a child to be able to do problem solving and learn through cognition, an information-processing system that includes perceptual organization and conceptualization must be developed. The classical, pioneer works of de-

COLOR ME HAPPY

Five-line poetry written by third graders. The Harper and Row Reading Series book, *Trouble and Turnips,* gives these instructions: "The first line of the poem usually has one word and names something. The second line tells in two words what the thing might do. The third line uses three words to describe the thing, and the fourth line is a four-word phrase. The last line names the thing again."

Owl
Sleeping, hooting
Soft, brown, scary
Flying in the night
Owl

by Glenn

Hermit crabs
Crawl, sleep
Shelled, hard, ugly
Sleeping all the time
Hermit crabs

by Linda

Ducks
Quack, wobble
White, soft, wonderful
Swim in the pond
Ducks

by John

Bat
Flies, bites
Ugly, furry, strong
Flies through the sky
Bat

by Stacey

Snakes
Sliver, crawl
Spiney, spring, long
Sneak through the meadow
Snakes

by Donnie

Mouse
Squeaks, scampers
Soft, gray, funny
Squeaking across the floor
Mouse

by Michelle

velopmental specialists and neurologists such as Gesell and Ilg (1949), Piaget (1952), Penfield and Roberts (1958), Hebb (1967), Smith and Henry (1967), Gibson (1969), and Kephart (1970) leave little doubt concerning the importance of developing a neuropsychological organization that can receive, retain, recall, and respond.

It may be helpful at this point to define a few words because they will appear frequently in the discussion of neuropsychological organization as it relates to perceptual processing. Each of the following terms may be used in conjunction with any of the perceptual processes—visual, auditory, or tactile.

attention the act or state of attending to a task, object, or thought. Attention consists of four components: awareness of or alertness to a task, selection of the significant stimulus, focusing on the stimulus for an appropriate length of time, and vigilance or concentration by avoiding distracting stimuli.

memory the process of reproducing or recalling what has been learned and retained. Memory is an aspect of each perceptual modality. Memory span is the length of time something is remembered. There are immediate, short-term, and long-term memory.

sequentialization the ability to recall or relate learned information in a specific order.

figure-ground perception the ability to focus on one or more parts of a stimulus while the remaining parts become background.

closure the process of obtaining or achieving a perception or an idea from a presentation that is incomplete or provides only partial information.

Concept of neuropsychology

The term neuropsychology is enough to frighten anyone, including professors, psychologists, occupational therapists, nurses, and even physicians who do not understand the basic meaning of the word. It sounds so "technical." Actually, it can be easily understood if you know its components. ***Neuropsychology*** is simply the study of how the nervous system processes psychological information. The primary neuropsychological processes related to the perceptual process are (1) sensorimotor functions, (2) visual perception, (3) auditory perception, (4) tactile perception, and (5) memory. If we look at the way in which the individual makes use of these processes, we can understand something about neuropsychology. We are *not* going to study neurology. We study how the person performs these activities.

neuropsychology **the study of the organic and the perceptual-conceptual processes involved in cognition.**

Each perceptual system is made up of such processes as (1) attention, (2) discrimination, (3) memory, (4) sequentialization, and (5) various sensorimotor combinations. Each sensory system makes use of these processes. In other words, there are auditory discrimination, visual discrimination, and tactile discrimination. The same is true with the other perceptual elements. There are other perceptual processes, such as figure-ground, closure, and spatial relationships, but we will not deal with these functions. The conceptual cognitive skills include the ability to make associations, to reason, to do problem solving, to imagine, and to be able to think verbally. Memory and attention are factors in conceptual processing as well as in perceptual processing.

The reasons why it is important to know about the neuropsychological systems are that (1) they are vital to information processing and learning, (2) they help us understand how and what should be happening during learning and thinking, and (3) they tell us when a process is not operating as it should. Piaget's cognitive theory of development can be related to the maturational levels of the neuropsychological systems. Infants have some perceptual capabilities early in life, but time and development are needed for the systems to mature to more refined, efficient, functional levels. Eventually, all of the perceptual systems should become interrelated so that stimuli in one system can be utilized by another system.

One last point as to why it's important to know about neuropsychological functions and development: If anything, physical or psychological, interferes with the smooth functioning of the neuropsychological system, the operational efficiency of that system will be affected. The hindering factor may be nothing more than a delay in neurological development (a maturational lag), but it will lower the functional level of the system affected as compared to what might have been expected in terms of chronological age or mental age.

Difficulty in processing the stimuli may occur at any point in the perceptual-conceptual process because of such factors as lesions, scar tissues, tumors, poor synaptic transmission, cerebral hemorrhage, or an under-

perceptual constancy the tendency for perceptions of objects, symbols, and sounds to remain relatively unchanged in spite of changes in the way the stimuli are received.

developed information-processing system resulting from a maturational delay in the neurological development of the areas involved in receiving, transmitting, perceiving, retrieving, conceiving, or responding (Kaluger and Kolson, 1978).

Rationale of neuropsychological development

We believe that the neuropsychological processes must be adequately developed if children are to be able to learn to read, work with symbols, or develop abstract concepts. The only means by which individuals can pick up information from their environment is through their senses (the receptors). The more abstract, intricate, and complex the stimuli, the more efficient must the perceptual processes be in order to perceive complicated stimuli, discriminate differences, and attach meanings to them.

According to Kaluger and Kolson (1978), there are four adaptive or neuropsychological processes related to the perceptual pattern for learning that are developing within children. Although all four processes are operating and developing at the same time, they differ as to the degree to which they are emphasized at any age level. The *neuropsychological organization* related to the perceptual processing system for learning are (1) neural and motor organization, including laterality and directionality, (2) auditory perception, (3) fine visual-motor organization, and (4) related cognitive processes.

Neural and motor organization

Of all the processes the gross sensorimotor processes receive the most developmental emphasis during the first 2 years of life. Infants first learn to control their eyes, then to hold their heads in the midline position. The sequential maturation process of motor development soon has them sitting up, reaching out, and grasping as prehension develops. After creeping and crawling, infants are walking. These are the more obvious gross perceptual-motor tasks learned.

In a more subtle way infants are actually developing a sensorimotor organization that will enable them eventually to control and to work better with incoming stimuli and outgoing responses. One of the goals of motor organization is to establish a balanced, stable base or body platform. From this base children can perceptually receive stimuli in such a way that they can depend on perceiving the stimulus as it actually is. What is needed is the development of ***perceptual constancy*** and certainty in terms of the perceptual input of symbols. Children should be able to reach a point where they can count on their perceptual system telling them every time they look at a "b" that it is a "b" and not a "d," "p," or "q."

If children are to accurately receive and organize information from the world about them, they must develop an organized, internal neuropsychological structure. Evidence of this internal structure is noted when children can perform integrated motor movements and retain their postural balance in so doing (Cratty, 1979; Kephart, 1970). This ability may not be reached until the children are about 5 or 6 years old. Constancy (accurate perception) of sensory input is needed if children are to build a memory bank that has any degree of accuracy. In addition, a perceptual-motor match is needed to be able to do the motor movement that they perceptually realize they should do. *Perceptual-motor match* refers to combining the input to the motor system with the input from the perceptual system so that contact between the two can be made at some point in space. For example, when reaching for a pencil, the motor pattern should enable the child to move the arm, hand, and fingers to the exact spot where the eyes see the pencil.

Refer to the two columns to the right in Fig. 8-1. It is our belief that basic body symmetry in terms of postural control is usually acquired by the age of 6 months. Symmetry and postural weight-shift balance are fundamental to developing an adequate motor base on which perceptual input and information can be structured.

Symmetry refers to the ability to maintain the body, the head, and the limbs in a balanced or matching position on each side of the midline of the body.

Postural weight shift balance means being able to move the body to one side, out of symmetry, and still maintain a balance. For example, 6-month-old infants lying on their stomach should be able to raise the upper part of their body and support it on one hand, while reaching for an object with the other hand.

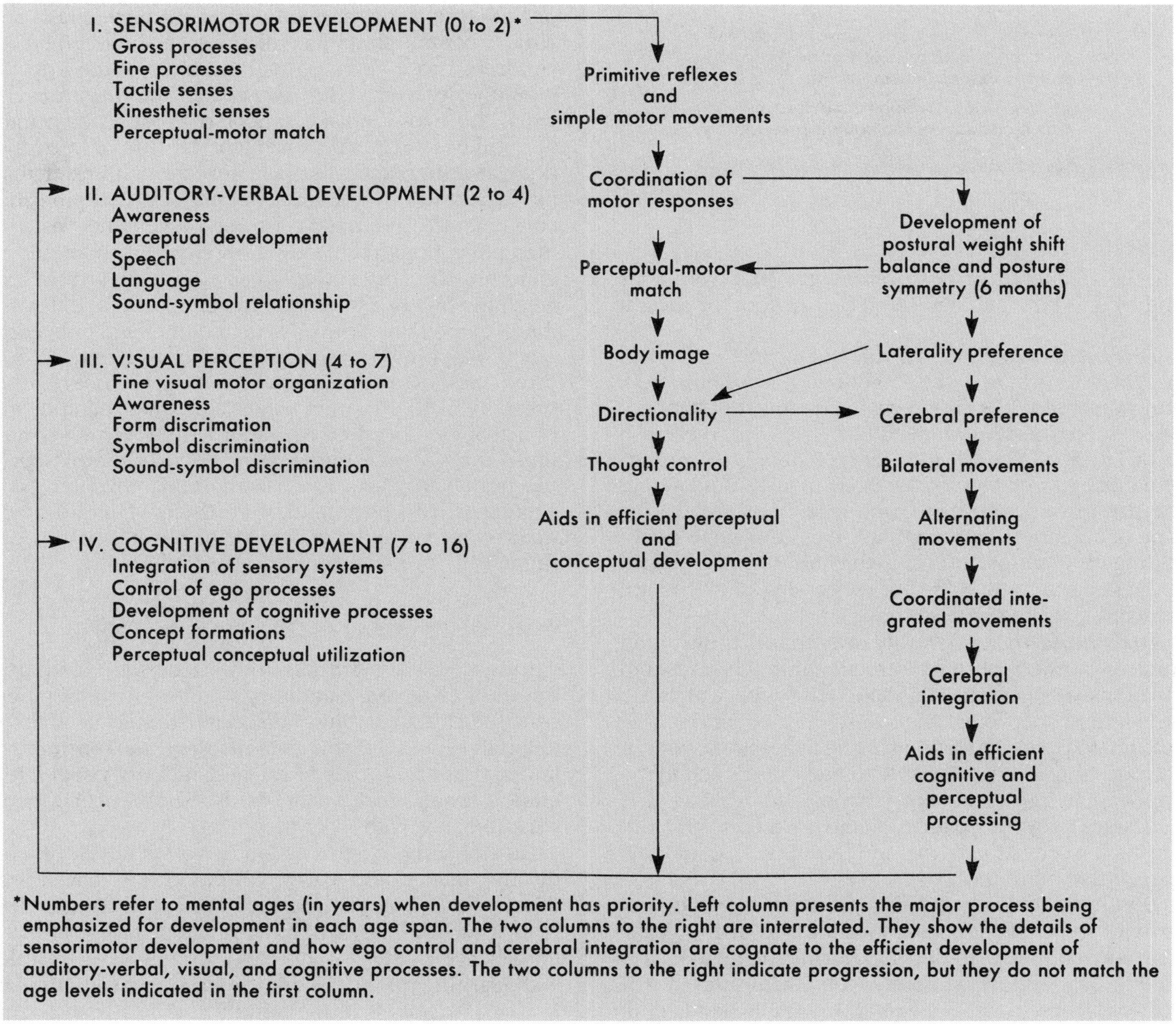

FIG. 8-1 *Theoretical concept of neuropsychological development of motor and perceptual processes. Numbers refer to mental ages (in years) when development has priority. Left column presents the major process being emphasized for development in each age span. The two columns to the right are interrelated. They show the details of sensorimotor development and how ego control and cerebral integration are cognate to the efficient development of auditory-verbal, visual, and cognitive processes. The two columns to the right indicate progression, but they do not match the age levels indicated in the first column.*

auditory perception ability to hear sounds accurately and to be able to organize them into meaningful units.

directionality an inner sense of left and right, or directions, that can be projected into the external environment.

laterality the developmental process in which one side of the body is preferred.

Another example of postural weight shift, for older children, is being able to stand on one foot for several seconds.

Laterality refers to the neurologically preferred sidedness, such as being right-handed, right-footed, and right-eyed. It is an internal preference of handedness, footedness, and eyedness and not merely a knowledge of "rights" and "lefts." It entails the preferential use of one side of the body in tasks demanding the use of only one hand, one foot, or one eye. This type of sidedness is thought to be conducive to establishing cerebral preference, which, in turn, is thought to be needed for an efficient processing of the neural structures related to cognition.

Directionality, or *left-right orientation* ability, is an inner awareness of outer directional movements and locations in space. It is also the ease with which the individual can project the conscious self into space, relating to rights and lefts and other directional cues. It includes the ability to be able to move one's self in the appropriate direction. For example, in reading it is necessary to develop directionality to keep from reading such words as *was, on,* and *but* backward and saying *saw, no,* and *tub.*

Body image, the identification of size, shape, and parts of the body, comes about the age of 2½ years. Laterality continues to develop during the next 3 years so that handedness is usually well established in a 5-year-old. Directionality stems from established laterality. Most children 6 years of age are able to tell their left and right sides of the body. Seven-year-olds should be able to cross the midline of their body and perform in the proper manner when directed to "touch your left knee with your right hand." Being able to discern lefts and rights on another person or object usually appears about the age of 8.

The first level of gross motor coordination is the *bilateral level,* where both sides of the body do approximately the same thing at the same time. This movement can be seen in babies who move both arms or both legs at the same time in a coordinated fashion. A more complicated bilateral movement performed by children 3 to 4 years old is the side-straddle hop or jumping-jacks exercise. *Alternating laterality* occurs when the two-sided movement is broken down into the ability to control movement on one side of the body at a time and, also, to alternate or transfer that movement to the other side of the body. Creeping and crawling are alternating lateral movements, as are marching, hopscotch, and hopping games in older children. The *integrated laterality* level is reached when the two sides of the body can either do different things at the same time or work together and help each other. Skipping is an integrated movement, as are using scissors to cut out a pattern on paper held by the opposite hand, stringing beads, and other manipulatory activities. Coordinated integrated movements may imply that cerebral integration of sensorimotor activities has taken place. If it has, then cognitive and perceptual processing should be enhanced. This last statement is a theoretical assumption, but it is based on Cratty (1979), Kephart (1970), and others.

Auditory perception

It is necessary for children to develop auditory attention (listening), auditory memory to remember what they heard, auditory discrimination to be able to tell differences in sounds, ***auditory perception*** to know what the sounds mean, and auditory-visual integration (sounds and symbols) to be able to connect what they see with what they hear.

Lack of auditory stimulation or verbal development during infancy and early childhood will have dire effects on children when they seek to learn how to read at school. They will have difficulty in discriminating between letter sounds and so will have trouble with learning phonics. Faulty hearing, even a marginal loss of 15 decibels in the middle and higher frequencies, can also cause a deficiency in learning to hear and use phonics. Lack of auditory awareness, perhaps a result of the auditory perceptual process being dormant, is occasionally found in 6-year-olds.

We worked with a 6-year-old girl who was having difficulty detecting differences in phonetic sounds. Her hearing acuity was good, so the problem had to be related to something else. We learned that she was a monotone singer, singing every word on the same

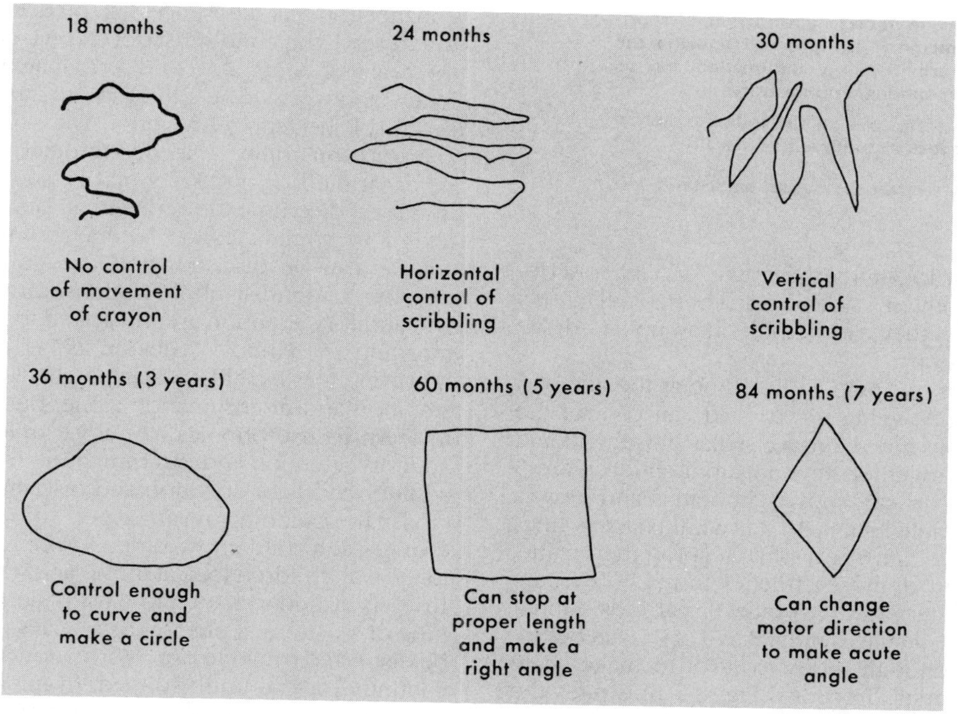

FIG. 8-2 *Development of perceptual-motor control in children. Ages refer to mental ages.*

note; she could not imitate the teacher's voice as the teacher sang the musical scale. About the third week after the teacher started working with her individually to teach her the scale, the little girl suddenly looked puzzled and said, "Sing that note again." The teacher did—and the girl imitated the pitch correctly. Another note, and again another correct pitch. The girl said, "I didn't know you were making your voice go up and down when you sang!" The girl's auditory system had been dormant to pitch; she had not developed awareness. The same problem existed in being aware of differences in phonetic sounds. From that moment on, she improved in her ability to identify sounds in phonics.

Fine visual-motor organization

By the age of 2 years children have fairly good gross control, but their finer visual-motor coordination patterns still need to be developed. Between the ages of 3½ and 7 years children emphasize the development of visual perception and visual-motor coordination.

Most 2-year-olds have the visual perceptual ability to match a circle, square, and triangle to similar holes in a form board, provided the shapes are lined up with the holes in the form board. The average child of 3 years should easily match the forms to the holes, even if the form board has been turned around. The 4-year-old should be able to discriminate among a larger number of shapes, and the 5-year-old should have little difficulty picking out the item that is different in a series of pictures or symbols, such as letters.

Finer visual-motor coordination begins to develop when infants learn to make use of their finger and thumb to pick up a small object that they are observing. They can do this at about 10 months of age. When it comes to controlling and guiding a crayon over paper, however, they still have much maturing to do before they can make effective use of it. At the age of 18 months the average infant will just make a haphazard line or mark on the paper—there is no rhyme or reason to it. The marking is mostly accidental. By 2 years

rehearsal to recycle information in short-term memory. The process facilitates the short-term recall of information and its transfer to long-term memory.

visual discrimination the ability to discern similarities and differences visually.

of age children can control the crayon enough to scribble predominantly in a side-to-side (horizontal) direction. At 2½ years they can scribble in an up-and-down (vertical) direction.

They can copy a single vertical line at the age of 3 years. In fact the average 3-year-old can control the crayon enough to move it in a circular movement and bring the ends together. It is not until children are 5 years old that they can copy right angles and draw a square. They should be able to stay within narrow lines with a pencil. Average 5-year-olds can print their name, but they usually "draw" each letter instead of writing or printing it smoothly. Average 6-year-olds cannot copy a diamond; it takes a mental age of 7 years before children have enough motor control to make acute angles and reverse directions. Fig. 8-2 illustrates the development of perceptual and fine motor control in young children. Children who have difficulty controlling handwriting after the age of 7 may have moderate to severe delay in the development of fine motor coordination.

Attention, memory, and problem solving

As the child matures into middle childhood, so does information processing improve. Because of increased neurological development, the child learns new, more efficient ways to process attention, to develop memory, and to do problem solving.

Attention. *Attention* is the focusing of perception on a task or object so that it leads to heightened awareness of a limited range of stimuli. Attention involves the implication that the child learns to avoid visual or auditory distractions in order to be able to attend. In other words, with the ability to attend, the child is not distracted by nonessential stimuli. There is an inner perceptual control that must be achieved in order to be able to focus in on the stimulus long enough to pick up the details.

As attention improves from infancy and early childhood, the ability to attend to sensory stimuli is enhanced so that differences can be detected. In learning to read, the child must develop visual attention to the point of being able to discriminate differences in letters and words. The child can "attend" to important details of the letters or words. The same ***visual discrimination*** ability is needed to detect differences in other printed or written symbols, such as numbers. Auditory discrimination depends on the ability to attend to sounds. Once letters and their phonetic sounds can be discriminated, the child is ready to develop a sound-symbol relationship whereby visual and auditory attention are integrated to provide verbal meaning to symbols (Gibson, 1974). It is possible, however, for a child to learn sight words by visual attention and discrimination alone. But, if the child is to learn to use phonics to unlock unfamiliar words, auditory attention and discrimination must be used in addition to visual attention and discrimination.

Visual scanning, as an aspect of attention, also changes as a child grows older. *Visual scanning* refers to the way children look at things and what they notice. In early childhood, a child who is doing visual scanning of a pattern, a picture, or a series of symbols will be distracted by irrelevant information and will usually continue to scan until stopped. In middle childhood, the child is likely to scan more systematically from the top of a picture, pattern, or page until the relevant information is found and then stop (Day, 1975). This older child has usually learned to scan more rapidly than in preschool years and can process information faster because of the ability to pick up more information with each fixation of the eyes (Day, 1975).

Memory. Memory improves throughout childhood as children gradually develop strategies for putting information into memory (input) and getting it back out again (retrieval). As children enter and progress in school, they become aware of the need to develop strategies, which are plans or approaches by which they can better remember and learn the information taught. The more they interact with their environment, the more they will remember. The development of memory also improves as the child increases his or her fund of information (Lindberg, 1980). Material that is meaningful is more easily remembered.

The strategies most frequently studied are rehearsal, imagery, and organization. ***Rehearsal*** is a strategy whereby a child repeats the material that is to be remembered. The teacher will use drill or rote memory as a technique for teaching a list of words or a poem by the rehearsal strategy. At some point in time

How much does it cost?
How much change should you receive?
DO YOU NEED PRACTICE?
PENNIES
DIME

David Strickler

With increased development of neuropsychological processes, children improve in their problem-solving ability. What is needed, however, are opportunities to learn and to practice problem-solving skills.

children need to be instructed how to use this recall and repeat technique. Older children, preadolescent or older, are more likely than younger children to be aware of the helpfulness of rote memory and generally make more use of rehearsal time (Waters, 1982).

Imagery is the strategy by which a person associates visual images in the mind with the items to be remembered. If a list of words, such as dog, chair, cloud, and happy, are to be remembered, the person tries to visualize the items as pictures or feelings. Children, aged 6, who were instructed to use imagery in learning paired words did better than those who did not (Pressley and Levin, 1980). However, a child has to be about the age of 9 to show a marked improvement in memory by using imagery. When pictures are presented to provide a clue to the visual image to be used, even 5- and 6-year-olds show improvement (Reese, 1977).

Organization is the strategy in memory development by which a person groups items to be remembered around a common element or theme. If a visual memory task is to recall as many displayed items as possible, the person may organize the items according to location, color, size, usage, classification, or whatever seems appropriate. This approach is not deliberately used by 6-year-olds or even some 8-year-olds. However, if asked to recall items by category, they do remember items they did not recall spontaneously (Corsale and Ornstein, 1980).

A final comment on memory in middle childhood is to recognize that in learning there are visual memory, auditory memory, tactile memory, or memory of any of the senses. As the child learns to read, visual memory is important for learning sight words. In phonetic analysis of words, auditory memory of sound-symbol relationships is important. Memory ability may be different for immediate rote memory, short-term memory (a few seconds delay), or long-term memory (memory of items when an unrelated thought or action has intervened). In addition, random recall permits the recollection of items in any order. However, there are times

maturational lag a delay in the normal or usual rate of development of the central nervous system structure and its perceptual functions.

when sequential memory is important—times when items must be presented in a specific order, such as reciting the alphabet or a poem. Ability in one form of memory does not ensure ability in other forms or styles of memory (Kaluger and Kolson, 1978).

Problem solving. As with age-related development in attention and memory, so does problem-solving ability generally improve with age and the maturing of the neurological areas of the brain related to learning. Six-year-olds use much trial and error in problem solving rather than a systematic approach based on a hypothesis (Gholson, 1980). Older children appear to use hypothesis testing and so are more orderly in their problem-solving approach.

Most 6-year-olds find it difficult to reverse or retrace their thinking and rework a problem in another way. They will either keep giving the same answer or will revert to random guessing unless a hypothesis is presented (Tumblin et al., 1979). Piaget refers to this difficulty as lack of reversibility. The older child apparently has the ability of reversibility and can retrace the steps and locate an error in thinking. Being able to do reversibility is one of the criteria of having attained operational thinking.

Individual differences in the use of cognitive processes appear to arise from differences in the speed and efficiency with which individuals process information. Children and adults differ in the rate at which they can retrieve information, shift it from one form of memory to another, and manipulate the information in the working memory (Hunt, 1976).

Children with learning disabilities

There are some children who, in spite of a good intellect, have difficulties in learning. The children we are referring to are those who have a central nervous system dysfunction in neuropsychological processing and whose condition is called learning disabilities. They make up about 30% of the 5- and 6-year-olds, about 20% of the 7- and 8-year-olds, and about 10% of those age 9 and older, including adults.

The definition of *learning disabilities* is still a little tenuous because the field is too new and all the variables have not been worked out. There are, however, four areas of agreement in all the definitions of learning disabilities (Kaluger and Kolson, 1978). They are:

1. Intellectual capacity is average or better.
2. There is a major discrepancy between expected and actual achievement.
3. There is a disorder in one or more of the neuropsychological processes involved in using spoken or written language.
4. The deficiencies are not caused by visual, hearing, or motor handicaps; by mental retardation; by emotional disturbance; or by environmental disadvantage or differences.

By implication, the problem of the learning disabled children results from *central nervous system dysfunctions* in perceptual and conceptual processing. The causes of the dysfunction may be organic or biochemical in nature. The large percentage of 5- and 6-year-olds who are identified as learning disabled have a ***maturational lag*** or delay in neurological development of the perceptual-conceptual adaptive organizations involved in the learning process. They usually mature and outgrow their problems.

The largest percentage of children with learning disabilities (LD) have mild disturbances. There are, however, some moderate, severe, and profound cases as well. Most LD children have difficulty in learning to read, especially in learning how to use phonetic analysis. Surprisingly, most of the LD children who are poor readers have average to above-average achievement in arithmetic and math. About 10% of LD children do very poorly in arithmetic and math but do well in reading. A goodly number of the LD cases, about 35% to 40%, have difficulty with handwriting. The implication is that LD children differ as to the areas of their academic deficiencies because of differences in the location and nature of their central nervous system dysfunction.

According to Kaluger and Kaluger (1978), LD children may have characteristics that can be classified under five headings: (1) difficulties in academic learning, (2) perceptual-motor problems, (3) language and speech disorders, (4) difficulties with thought processes, and (5) behavior and affective characteristics. One of the more common characteristics is distractibility, either visual or auditory, causing the child to have a short attention span. Perceptual processing difficulty, especially of auditory stimuli, is another common symptom. Excessive restlessness, sometimes miscalled hyperactivity, is found in about 30% of the children.

Such factors, plus about 50 other observed characteristics, make these children inefficient learners in some academic areas and, as a result, they get behind in their work.

Treatment of learning disabilities is usually based on a *diagnostic-prescriptive* plan. LD children vary in terms of what causes their learning problem. As a result, a thorough diagnosis must be made first. An educational prescription is written, based on what has been found to be deficient in learning skills and in academic skills. A ***multisensory*** approach is frequently used to get information to the brain. The LD child is to see it, hear it, and touch it—all at the same time. Academic and perceptual skills are taught in this manner. Because of the varied problems, many professionals may be required to work with the child—a classroom teacher, a language and speech therapist, a psychologist, an occupational therapist, and/or a physical therapist.

multisensory relating to or involving several physiological senses.

One contributor to learning disabilities is a central nervous system allergy caused by certain foods (Feingold, 1974). Not all individuals are affected; of those that are affected, not all react to the same food product. In general, the principle is that LD children appear to be more susceptible than other children to artificial food coloring, artificial food flavoring, food preservatives, and to foods that contain salicylates. Salicylates are salts from salicylic acid. They produce an analgesic action on tissue but also have irritant qualities. The individual, child or adult, susceptible to salicylates will be more restless, will find it difficult to concentrate or settle down, or will get physical symptoms such as headaches or a dull feeling. Some adults do not drink coffee at night because it keeps them awake. Some children get "wound up" when they drink artificially colored and artificially flavored fruit punch (usually red in color). In general, "junk food" such as soft drinks, sugar-coated cereals, hot dogs, potato chips, some lunch meats, ice cream, candy, and similar foods are suspect. However, natural salicylates are found in apples, strawberries, tomatoes, cucumbers, and other vegetables and fruits. The remedy is to avoid the food or foods causing the restlessness and distractibility. Remember, not all children are affected by the same foods. One child may be able to eat apples; another may be affected by them.

LANGUAGE AND THOUGHT

During the elementary school years, children refine and extend the language they have developed up to that point. Their speech becomes more socialized. They begin to put their thoughts and feelings into words more easily and soon begin logical thought. They begin to understand more abstract forms of language such as puns and figures of speech.

Language development

By the time children are 6 years old they have an oral vocabulary of approximately 2,500 words. They use sentences averaging about five words in length, and they make use of all the various parts of speech and syntax (Gardner, 1982.) However, Whitehurst (1982) claims this achievement is not true of all 6-year-olds. They know most of the letters of the alphabet and can give their names on seeing their visual form.

Two- to 3-year-olds ask the question "What is that?" They want to increase their vocabulary by asking for a word or a name for an object. Four- to 5-year-olds ask "Who is that?" "What is he doing?" "Why does . . .?" and other similar questions. Children are reflecting their awareness of the world around them, especially of the actions of humans. They are usually satisfied by almost any positive response, as compared to one which merely suggests that they be quiet. The implication is that the children are reflecting their curious and inquisitive natures, but they are not yet aware of logic and reasoning. To some degree their questioning may also indicate the type of communicative skill they have developed for carrying on a conversation with adults. They may not know of any other way by which they can talk to older people.

Most 6- to 7-year-olds, however, have reached the precausal level of reasoning, and so their questions of "Why?" and "What for?" and "How?" indicate that they are beginning to know that objects, actions, and events serve certain purposes; they want to know what they are.

Verbal understanding increases, and the children can now communicate their own thoughts more objectively. Seven- to 8-year-olds are more likely than younger children to be able to arrange stories of explanations logically. Eight-year-olds' growth in vocabulary is shown not only in an increased number of words but also in their ability to give more precise definitions

egocentric speech speech that fails to take into consideration the needs of the listener and thus is not appropriate for communication.

socialized speech speech intended to communicate.

than previously. Six-year-olds will define an orange as "You eat it," and a puddle as "You step in it." Eight-year-olds respond with "It's a color or a fruit" and "A little pool of water made by rain."

Piaget and language

During the preschool years, language is mainly ***egocentric*** in the forms of (1) repetition of words, syllables, or rhythmic phrases that children enjoy saying, (2) a monologue whereby children converse with themselves as if they were thinking out loud, or (3) a dual or collective monologue that concerns another person or persons but in which the children do not make a strong effort to communicate with them. One child may be talking about one thing, while the other children—in answering—may be talking about something entirely different. It's like listening to two intertwining monologues. By the time children enter school, however, their language is proceeding toward more socialized speech.

Piaget (1959) divides ***socialized speech*** into (1) *adaptive information* that involves an exchange of information between two or more people, (2) *criticism,* by which the child is making some sort of a subjective value judgment, not just stating a fact as in adaptive information, (3) *commands,* requests, and threats, representing the minimum interchange of speech necessary for communication, and (4) *questions and answers*. Socialization of thought and speech comes to children between their seventh and eighth year, partly because they now have a more extensive social life as they begin to work and play with a larger, more stable peer group.

Vygotsky (1962) has a view different from Piaget on the early development of language. Piaget says that the infant first uses language as a means of representing sensorimotor schemes already developed. Vygotsky supposes that development of speech and thought in the first 2 years are parallel but unrelated; only after age 2 do they fuse. Vygotsky believes that higher forms of human intelligence and thought are achieved because language is developed. Language rules are more sophisticated and abstract than is early thought.

SOCIAL GROWTH

The ages of 6 to 8 are years when the children's social environment expands rapidly. Children's lives begin to center around the school and the children and activities found there. Youngsters now have authority figures other than the mother and father who seek to guide them. Peers take on greater importance, and group phenomena begin to influence children's behavior and growth. Family influences lessen as the external socialization process makes its impact (Bronfenbrenner, 1970). Since their whole beings evolve around their friends and peers, children must learn social skills and communication skills that will enable them to maintain successful relationships. Learning to get along well with others is often difficult, and lack of social experiences or of good teaching models (mothers, fathers, and other acceptable adults) can be handicapping.

Descriptive social characteristics

Social behavior in middle childhood develops more rapidly than previously because children are away from home more and are with others their own age. Social maturity and stability are highly inconsistent, however. Behavior often regresses in maturity, especially when the children are tired. Group activities help to develop social maturity. Children learn new ascribed roles for their age, develop social interaction and communicative skills, and begin to understand the needs and rights of others. Through maturation and learning, youngsters acquire the more refined social behavior of adults.

Many 6-year-olds are often trying to their parents. One minute they are agreeable and loving, and the next minute they dislike everybody and everything. Six years is just not old enough to be reliable and stable. The children crave help but refuse to accept it. They want to play with others, but if things do not go their way, they may threaten to go home or engage in name calling. Six-year-olds cannot handle a younger brother or sister well without considerable direction and attention from the parent. At times they can be bossy with a younger sibling. Despite all of these problems, there are times when they have a very close relationship with

A PRESCHOOL PARENT GROWS UP

Our eight-year-old slammed the front door, dropped his book bag, and exploded, "Well, Mom, you weren't there to see it!" He was very upset. "See what?" I asked, wiping my dishpan hands and wondering why I must go through all these parental growing pains so quickly. "It's recess again, Mom!"

At that moment our second grader charged through the back door. "Boy, am I hungry! Don't ask me; I can't remember what we did in school today. . . . Mom, where is the peanut butter? Oh, I have to do a picture about my vacation, and Mom, you can't help."

My husband and I had felt great changes going on. Now I knew what it was! We had graduated from preschool parenthood! We were in a new world. It's a world of "hold my hand, but not too tight." A world of "let me fly—but catch me" and "help me only when I can't figure it out all by myself." These are all new to a parent who has been used to a preschooler's world of "block logic" and "your turn–my turn" psychology. We didn't have all the answers at two and we have fewer at seven and eight! Can we grow as fast as our children?

Not long ago, as parents, my husband and I taught walking, eating, and dressing. Now we learn together as a family to communicate about much higher and more abstract meanings and values in life. Indeed, this is a grave but most challenging and exciting time with our "little people."

As a family we share the many experiences that have happened to show us that the controlled world of preschool is far behind. For example, as preschool parents, we were always concerned about the language our children heard. We had made a special effort to control our own speech patterns. We talked with the boys when they had heard a "bad word" used by adult friends or relatives. At that time we discussed the fact that they might hear "bad language" but that it was not necessary for them to say "those words." My husband and I emphasized to the boys that, if they heard a word they did not understand or thought was wrong to use, they could always come and talk to us about it. This seemed to help the boys, so my husband and I felt things were under control.

However, now away from the preschool world, the exposure to bad language seems to be happening daily either during school time or play. To help our own children, we have used a plan that seems to be maintaining the quality of language, at least during after-school playtime. When certain neighborhood children come to play with the boys, we always have the group decide a penalty that will take place if bad language is used. They have made some very harsh punishments. It was very gratifying for me to overhear this remark as they stood in the "huddle" deciding on the punishment for the day. The comment was, "You don't play any better when you call other people those names, and it ruins the game because people feel like quitting. Now, everybody knows you're out five plays if you call people those names."

A parent has to constantly maintain open lines of communication to help the child learn that cursing, swearing, and the use of slang sex terms may be a part of the world but need not be a part of his or her personal world.

Another experience that confronts the older child has to do with peer problems. As a child grows to school age and is placed in a group situation with limited adult supervision, we hear ourselves say, "Don't pick fights, but defend yourself." This is quite a different statement from the preschool idea of "We don't hit our friends" and "Now it is Susie's turn." Most peer problems must be handled by the child or they will never be solved in his or her own mind but will grow to be much bigger problems.

Through a peer problem on the playground which developed in my older son's class, the teacher taught me a very valuable technique that has even worked at times when our two boys have had to work out brotherly problems. It was a typical recess where there was much shouting, chasing, skipping, jumping, laughing, and climbing. Each child was glimpsing the real world, and each was surviving in his or her own way. Most were even enjoying it! But then the supervising teacher noticed a growing group of children and some very upset voices. She went over, pulled two small boys away from one another, and said, "You two have five minutes of *Together Time*."

The other children dispersed and went about their play. The two boys disappeared into the school building. The teacher allowed them five minutes on their own, sitting in the quiet classroom together, to see if they could find a solution to the problem that had started the fight. If no solution could be decided, then she would become the intermediary. As she explained to me, 98% of all misunderstandings were straightened out with much less hard feelings than when she had to determine the outcome.

My husband and I have been through at least five academic graduations. We find that graduation always taught us that there is more learning to be done; often it has sparked thoughts of the future. We are now graduates from *preschool parenthood*. That gives us good cause for contemplation. We realize now that we are mere "graduate assistants" preparing for a real lesson soon to come: . . . *adolescence!*

their parents (Bigner, 1979). Six-year-olds are sensitive to parental moods and tensions, and they can be most sympathetic when their mother is sick. Not only may children show anxieties concerning the well-being of the mother and father but of their teacher as well.

A highly important aspect of social development at this age pertains to *ethnic identification*. Six-year-old white children are unaware of ethnic identification of the children with whom they play although they can tell the difference in color. (Williams and Moreland, 1976). They pick their playmates more on qualities of age and size rather than sex and color. As children mature, they respond more to the prejudice of others, often as a result of the influence of their home atmosphere. Children view the opinions and ideas of their parents and teachers as most important because to them they are the smartest people in the world.

Comer and Poussaint (1975) in their book *Black Child Care* state that ethnic identification for black children is usually different from that of white children. The average 4-year-old black child barely understands racial difference. However, the 7- or 8-year-olds do understand and may respond with anger or hostile racial feelings if they feel rejected or uncertain (Lessing, 1977). This age is the time when children do or do not "sign a contract" with society. They are being exposed to the attitudes, values, and ways of the larger society. These attitudes and values may or may not be what the children's family accepts or believes. Children are mature enough to sense feelings of social conflicts in their parents, and this affects their own attitudes toward society. They may choose not to sign the contract. Comer and Poussaint (1975) suggest that black parents teach their children to develop attitudes that will enable them to be prepared to handle the realities of living black in a white-controlled America. Their obligation is to bring about personal skill development in their children that will help them to develop realistic ways of bringing about a better society. The existing system need not be accepted, but it is necessary to have some obligation to themselves instead of only being against something.

A social concern both at home and at school is manners. Children in early middle childhood have considerable difficulty in formal social situations because they have not yet learned the social skills. They do not know how to speak or act properly. They are not good at shaking hands with strangers and saying "How do you do" or "Good-bye"; likewise they have difficulty in responding to "How are you?" They often forget to say "Please," "Thank you," and "Good-bye." Children will open the door to people they know and say with enthusiasm "Come in," but it is a different situation with strangers. If parents give children the exact words to use in a social situation, they may be able to repeat them; but on their own they may be at a loss to know what to say or do.

All of the ups and downs of 6-year-olds are a part of their growing up and their search for autonomy. They thought they were ready for independence when they were 2 years old and had learned all of the developmental tasks that were necessary for their basic survival. Again, when they were 4 years old, they thought that they were ready for the world because they were developing a consciousness of good and bad actions. Now, at 6 years of age they are in a new world; surely they must be ready for independence. Their past experiences and their intellectual insights, however, raise some uncertainties in their minds.

Most 7-year-olds are becoming more aware of the social differences around them but not to any great extent that will change their thinking. The choice of friends at this level is still uninfluenced by the social and economic status of the children or their home. However, the awareness of differences between their home and that of their friends is increasing.

Children of 7 years are learning to be self-critical; they like to do things well. This self-insight is leading toward a state of autonomy. They like to assume some responsibility. These children are also very talkative, often fighting verbally rather than physically. Frequently, when they are angry at their parents, they toy with the idea that they are not their child or get a notion about running away from home. Stealing is not unusual at this age.

They can now greet people with "Hello" while looking straight at them, but "Good-bye" may not be as easy. They may be able to shake hands but not comfortably. Many 7-year-olds will say "Excuse me" spontaneously if things go wrong. One point difficult for many older people, especially grandparents, to understand is that children may initially behave well when company is present, but they are likely to withdraw to their own activities before too long. Oftentimes one hears "Why won't Jimmy stay in the room with us when he comes for a visit?" Frequently it is because he does not understand what is going on and wants to do something that is of interest to him.

At home 7-year-olds are usually more cooperative members of the family than they were at 6 years.

Although they like to help around the house, their performance does not always match their good intentions. They do get along better with their mothers and are developing a closer relationship with their fathers. They will play with their younger brothers and sisters and will look after them, although jealousy will still occur at times.

At play most 7-year-olds do fairly well with others, but they will spend some time in solitary activity as well. There is less chance that they will use direct physical and verbal attack if things go badly in play. They are more concerned than previously about their place in the group and about being well liked. It is not unusual for some 7-year-olds to develop "love affairs." In fact, boys may have more than one girl friend, and girls may like more than one boy. If one friend stops liking you, you simply find another. The loss of a boy or girl friend is usually taken as a matter of course, although some children cannot move this readily from one friend to another. This kind of a child can become upset, and tears may result when they have lost their "one and only." In spite of these relationships, the peer culture is beginning to separate the sexes in play activities.

Most 8-year-olds will have completed the transition to their peer culture. They now accept and prefer the activities, fads, and associations of their peers rather than those of adults (Hartup, 1978). They generally give their allegiance to other children instead of to adults in case of a conflict.

Eight-year-olds generally gain security from being accepted by the group. They are responsive to group activities, and they hate playing alone. Whatever they do they want to do with other persons. Eight-year-olds are fond of team games, comics, television, movies, adventure stories, and collections. Their best friends are usually those of the same sex.

They are often careless and argumentative, but at the same time they are alert, friendly, and interested in people. Their self-concept is affected as they learn what other people are like and how they behave. Eight-year-olds are sensitive to criticism. However, they are growing individuals, and their contacts with others will modify their personality for better or for worse.

Most 8-year-olds recognize property rights if their training has been sound. There is increasing modesty and self-control. Social pressures, especially by their peers, are influential in this respect. The children have a new awareness of individual differences and of what to do about them.

The social manners of most 8-year-olds are better than they were, but they still need some improvement. Most 8-year-olds verbalize proper greetings and goodbyes. Some can carry on excellent social conversations with adults; many have good company and table manners—away from home (Ilg and Ames, 1962). Eight-year-olds get along well with their parents, but they get along better with their friends. Their relationship with their mothers can be demanding, complicated, and subtle. They expect her to do certain things and are annoyed when she does not do them. They often demand her complete attention and companionship. Although they express a preference for their mother, father is coming in for an increased share of affection if he is available and reachable. It is not unusual for 8-year-olds to be strict with younger siblings; they may become upset if forced to follow the same home rules as are required of the younger children, such as the time they have to go to bed. In terms of chores and work around the house they like to be paid for their help; often parents become dismayed by this sudden "money-mad interest."

Peer and play culture

There is something both universal and eternal about the nature, purpose, and semblance of play in children. Children have been playing as long as there has been history. Toys, play materials, and drawings of children playing games have been found in the pyramids of Egypt and in the ruins of Pompeii. Blindman's buff, hide-and-seek, and tug-of-war were enjoyed by children in Plato's Greece (Opie and Opie, 1969). Ancient Rome knew the finger-flashing game of paper-scissors-stone, still played around the world and not only by youngsters. We were "taught" the game at a geisha party in Kyoto, Japan, on a visit there. There are drawings in the ancient tombs of noblemen and pharaohs buried in Luxor showing children at play, and on the pavements of old Jerusalem there are stone carvings that were used by the Roman soldiers to play adult games. The interesting observation is the similarity of the types of games played by children throughout the ages in all types of cultures.

The nature, and perhaps the purpose, of play changes as the child gets older. Table 8-2 illustrates changes in play interests. The central ingredient of play undergoes three separate, although somewhat overlapping, stages of evolution (Pickard, 1965). During the first 2 or 3 years of life, the most noticeable feature

Harold Geyer

Peer association makes group games favorites of 6- and 7-year-olds.

of play is physical activity involving sensorimotor recognition of objects and happenings. At about the ages of 3 or 4 years to about 6 or 7 years, fantasy is added to physical activity, thereby permitting certain gestures, objects, or behavior to indicate or "stand for" other things or situations. Emotions are experienced more intensely at these ages than at any other time in life. The third stage involves much physical activity and fantasy but now includes a greater emphasis on being with children of the same age-group. The children begin to see the need for rules. They may make up their own rules, and once agreed on, the demand to abide by them is vigorous.

At all age levels the play of children can be divided into four categories: imitative, exploratory, testing, and model-building play (Sutton-Smith, 1972). *Imitative play* reaches a peak when 4- to 6-year-olds play "house," "police officer," "school," or circular group singing and rhythmic games such as "ring-around-the-rosy," "mulberry bush," or "Sally Waters." *Exploratory play* increases with cognitive development and the discovery of manipulative objects, such as blocks, clay,

TABLE 8-2 General play interests from ages 5 to 10 years

Age zone	*General play interests*
5 years	More independent play
	Much play centers around a house
	Plays with dolls
	Runs, climbs, swings, skips, dances
	Rides tricycle or bicycle
	Uses sand in making roads
	Imitative play: house, store, hospital
	Paints, draws, colors, cuts, pastes
	Copies letters and numbers
	Builds with blocks
6 years	Games of tag, hide-and-seek
	Ball playing: tossing, bouncing
	Rough-and-tumble play
	Roller skates, ice skates
	Simple carpentry
	Table games with cards
	Paints, colors, draws, uses clay
	Collects odds and ends
	Imaginative play
	Builds with blocks
7 years	More intense interest in some activities, fewer new ventures
	Bicycles
	Puzzles, magic, tricks
	Collecting and swapping
	Swimming
	Rudiments of ball play
8 years	Variety of play interests; prefers companionship in play
	Games of all kinds
	Dramatic play of giving shows
	Collecting and arranging of collections
	Beginning interest in group games
	Unorganized group play of wild running, chasing
	Boys and girls begin to separate in play
9 years	Variety of play interests
	Works hard at his play
	Individual differences become stronger
	Baseball, skating, swimming, sports
	Collecting of stamps, minerals, etc.
	Hikes
	Complicated table games

Compiled from Garvey (1977); Sutton-Smith (1972); and Tauber (1979).

and toy models. Riddles can be an aspect of exploratory play. Most children 6 to 12 years of age engage in *testing play,* whereby a child tests personal ability, agility, and capability. Physical contests such as dodge ball, kick ball, or jumping rope become important. Games involving memory, impulse and physical control, choice, or decision are also popular.

Five- to 6-year-olds play "hide-and-seek" or tag games, which will continue for many years. Seven- to 8-year-olds play "release," "relievo," and "kick the can," which involve some harassment of the person who is "it" (or "he" in Great Britain). On rainy days or in the evenings 8-year-olds and older childern can be enthusiastic about table games such as Monopoly, Parcheesi, rummy, and hearts. Red Rover and run-sheep-run are popular with 9- to 10-year-olds, whereas 11- to 12-year-olds play the more complex game of prisoner's base.

Model building in a primitive way becomes explicit by about the age of 4 years when youngsters like to play with cars or doll houses and reaches a peak at 10 to 12 years of age. The commercial world of today provides so many video games and model toys such as trains, dolls, cars, and even monsters that they may be interfering with the advantages gained by some of the constructive, solitary play of children who used to make their own models. By the same token, at many schools playground or recess time is a period of free or unstructured play, with the result that these children may not learn games like Red Rover.

As children of 6 years and older grow, individual differences become stronger. Some children read more and enjoy sedentary activities, whereas others head for the out-of-doors at the first chance. The sex role as emphasized by the family, neighborhood, and culture will have some influence on games played and types of interests displayed. A 5-year-old boy will not particularly hesitate to play the part of the mother in playing house; a 9-year-old boy would not be "caught dead" playing that part. Sex differences vary slightly in games and activities for the 5- to 7-year-old, but as the children grow older they tend to drift apart more in interests and play activities.

At all ages girls generally like to play with boys. Their advanced physical maturity enables them to hold their own in games. But the influence of what it is "to be a man" begins to show in boys. The mores of the peer culture take over, and the gulf between boys and girls begins to widen. As an illustration, at the age of 5 years the girl tells the boy what games they will play

authoritarian parenting a style of childrearing that focuses on parental power and strict obedience to rules.

authoritative parenting a childrearing pattern that places moderate restrictions on the range of acceptable behaviors but also incorporates nurturance and sensitivity to the child's needs.

permissive parenting parenting with few demands about rules and regulations and lax control.

and the boy plays them. At 6 years of age the girl tells the boy what games they will play and the boy says, "No, I want to play this game," and the girl plays it. At the age of 7 years the boy tells the girl what games they will play, and she plays them. At the age of 8 years the boy says, "I don't know if I want to play with you; you're a girl." The 9-year-old boy is likely to say to the girl, "Get out of here!"

PATTERNS OF PARENTING

Every parent would like to know the "correct" way to rear a child, but realistically there is no one "best" way. How effective any technique will be depends a great deal on four factors: (1) the personality and social characteristics of the parents, (2) the characteristics of the child, (3) the kind of child the parents wish to raise, and (4) the resulting interaction between the child and parents and its impact on both. Research by Baumrind (1972) and Lamb and Baumrind (1978), who have been studying the interaction of parents and children for 20 years, suggests that parental styles fall into one of three categories. Parents may be authoritarian, authoritative, or permissive, and each style has a particular effect on the growing child.

Authoritarian parent

The ***authoritarian parent*** is a controlling and unconcerned parent. He or she tends to establish rigid standards of conduct that do not take into consideration the needs of the child. Discipline is firm; infractions of the rules are seldom overlooked. Obedience is seen as a virtue. Verbal give-and-take is discouraged, rules are not explained, no alternatives are offered, and the child's opinion is unsolicited. The child is expected to accept without question the parent's word on matters of right or wrong. While expecting conformity to parental standards of conduct, the parent tends to minimize the amount of love, care, and praise given to the child.

The children of authoritarian parents usually exhibit self-control and some self-reliance. However, they seem somewhat withdrawn, obedient, apprehensive about their own actions, and often lacking in curiosity and display of affection (Baumrind, 1967). Daughters tend to set low goals for themselves and to withdraw in the face of frustration. Sons tend to be hostile and resistive to adults.

Authoritative parent

The ***authoritative parent*** controls his or her children but is also a concerned parent. This parent is confident as a parent and is loving and caring toward the children, although not overly so. Behavioral standards are established and communicated to the children. The standards are explained, alternatives are offered, and the children's opinions are solicited. These rules take into consideration the needs of the children as well as the needs of the parents and society. Children are disciplined when the standards are broken, but control is not rigid or unnecessarily restrictive. Usually, the reason for the discipline is given. The children are encouraged to be independent and to respond appropriately to people around them. When the children do so, they are praised by the authoritative parent. The aim is the child's responsible conformity to group standards without loss of independence. This parent seeks to present a model of a mature, well-socialized adult.

The children of authoritative parents tend to be competent, self-controlled, assertive, self-reliant, and explorative. They are content with themselves. They tend to be friendly with other children and with adults. They are highly achievement oriented. Daughters tend to be independent and socially responsible, at least until age 9. Sons are also socially responsible but no more independent than average.

Permissive parent

The ***permissive parent*** tends to exert little firm control over his or her children and insists on little in the way of mature behavior from them. There are few demands to take on household responsibilities. No annoyance is shown, impatience is hidden, and negative reactions are inhibited. These children can get their own way because rules are not enforced and disobedience is not confronted. These parents are caring, at least more so than the authoritarian parent. When it is time for the children to go to bed, they will usually request them to do so. However, if the children ask to stay up to see one more television program, the permissive parents usually back down and grant the children their wish.

The children of permissive parents usually reflect the nondemanding characteristics of their parents. They tend to be the least self-reliant and self-controlled and the most dependent and immature of the three categories presented. Daughters of permissive parents tend to be somewhat achievement oriented and domineering. The sons are usually not achievement oriented, tending to be more aimless in their approach to life.

There is another category of parents but one that has not been researched to any great extent. This group would consist of the *nonconformist* parents. This parent is against authority and authoritarianism but will exert more outright control than the permissive parent. There may also be a demand for high performance in some areas. Daughters of nonconformist parents tend to be dependent and to cope with frustration by withdrawing. However, sons tend to be more independent than the sons of permissive and authoritarian parents, and they usually set higher goals for themselves.

Baumrind (1972) has determined several parental practices and attitudes that seem to bring about the development of socially responsible and independent behavior in children. First, it helps when the parents are models of socially responsible and self-assertive people. Second, parents need to have firm discipline policies geared to encourage socially responsible and independent behavior; deviant behavior should not be ignored. Third, parents should be accepting, reinforcing individuals but not overprotective. Fourth, parents need to encourage self-expression, initiative, individuality, and socially appropriate assertiveness. And fifth, parents must provide their children with a stimulating environment that offers challenge, excitement, and enrichment.

THE ONE-PARENT FAMILY

So far not enough research has been done to prove that the one-parent family is inherently pathological or is not as good as the two parent (Maccoby, 1980). The two-parent system has its own pathology—both parents may be equally competent but unable to work together as a team in raising a family; one parent may be more competent than the other but afraid to express this competence for fear of ruining the team effort; one parent may be competent but have his/her efforts overwhelmed by the incompetent parent; the two parents may be in serious conflict as to how their parental roles should be performed, which may cause the children to be caught in the middle between the two parents.

Parental roles

Identification, defined as the process by which one person tries to become like another, usually with the parent of the same sex, is an important factor in the development of personality in children 6 to 8 years old. If two parents are living at home, it is very rare that a child would identify with only one parent and exclude the other. This identification is not limited to a certain period of time. Children react most to the expectations that the most prominent people in their lives have of them, even though these people do not exhibit the behavior themselves. For example, Joel learns to obey his father because his father expects it, although his father does not obey Joel. Both Joel and his father have expectations of the other and each knows what the other expects of him. Even though Joel has never himself played the father's role, he is learning it through this type of experience.

The roles played by the mother and father are very different and can usually be considered as *expressive* (being sensitive to the feelings, thoughts, and needs of others) or *instrumental* (being responsible for solving the problems of the group and making decisions on their behalf). Although both men and women play both expressive and instrumental roles, usually women are the more expressive leaders and men the more instrumental leaders.

Most sources tended to agree on this description of a two-parent family. Both boys and girls are more closely attached to their mothers than their fathers during infancy through early pre-school years (Rebelsky and Hanks, 1971). Thus children of both sexes first relate to the person playing the expressive role. This is when boys and girls first learn to be expressive, are first exposed to love-oriented discipline, and take basic steps toward internalizing conscience.

The next step is to identify with the father and outgrow some of the dependence on the mother. However, the father reacts differently with his sons and daughters. With his daughters he acts very expressively, praising and enjoying their feminine acts, while he is usually more demanding and applies more discipline to his sons (Yarrow et al., 1971). The father plays boisterously with the boy, stimulating vigorous play, discouraging tears, and acting very casual about bumps and bruises. The mother is usually appreciative when her son is aggressive, active, and courageous and when her daughter is sensitive, charming, and delightful (Minton et al., 1971). The felt presence of the father in the family was proved to have an important effect on the boy's assumption of his sex role. A boy will be a great deal more masculine the more he interacts with a powerful father, one who does both rewarding and punishing. Sons conformed more to the expectations their fathers had of them when the fathers took part in raising the children (Smart and Russell, 1972).

Every child needs both a mother and father figure to act as models for the child's social and emotional development. When the children are living with only one parent, this parent must play a dual role, that of the mother and father. This dual role is hard to play, but it is especially more difficult when it is only played at intervals—for instance, if the parents are divorced and the children spend time with both parents and see conflicting ideas.

In addition to the following material on one-parent families, more information is presented on families in Chapter 13 on early adulthood.

Divorced families

One basic question parents contemplating divorce ask themselves is: Is it better for the children if we remain together in an unhappy marriage, or should we end the marriage and therefore end many personal frustrations? Society in the United States holds two conflicting beliefs. One is that the couple's first concern should be with their parental roles and that they should try to put aside their marital problems, which implies that marriage roles are secondary to parental roles. Yet in a society that places great emphasis on personal ego-need satisfaction in marriage, the placing of marriage in a secondary position may be difficult for the married person to accept.

Within 5 years of being divorced, three quarters of all divorced people are remarried. There are approximately 1 million children under 18 years of age living in one-parent homes following the divorce of their parents. In most cases the mother has custody of the children (Bell, 1971). As the head of a family, most women will eventually conquer the difficult process of taking over the role of the father. During the time the woman is the head of the family, she no longer has to consult with the other parent or worry about what the other parent thinks. However, if she remarries, she must undertake an even more difficult process of relinquishing the father role that she had previously assumed. Divorced mothers, as well as all other parents without partners, feel that not having to share daily parental decisions with a partner who might not agree with his/her strategy is an advantage. They feel that the parental partner can be a great asset if the two parents agree, but if this is not usually true, one parent can probably do a better job alone.

Mother—only parent

Approximately 20% of American families have only one parent (Glick, 1979b). Since most one-parent families are ones in which the father is absent, it is only natural that mother-only parent families are those studied most. It is the boys in such families that have been usually researched. Most of the research studies seem to focus on personality and cognitive development.

Types. Mothers without husbands fall into five categories: divorced, separated, deserted, widowed, and never married. If the mother has a job outside of the home, there are other factors that create added strain, along with having to fill the role of both parents. Children leave too late for school, get home too early, and have too many vacations to fit into the schedule of the working mother.

Psychologically, desertion may cause more trauma than divorce. This affects both men and women. It is less planned. The parent does not know whether to accept the other parent's role. They are not free to remarry or to go out with other people since they are still technically married. These problems are basically the same for separated parents. Although the widowed mother faces the same problems of being the head of a household, she has one advantage that gives her added emotional support. Her family, friends, and community have a more favorable attitude toward her, as compared to the less desirable attitudes held toward unmarried, separated, deserted, and divorced mothers. The unmarried mother, who keeps her children as opposed to having an abortion or giving her children up for adoption, faces the problems other women as heads of families face. However, she may believe that society disapproves of her. She may have to deal with conflicting public opinion about her status.

IQ. Researchers at the Institute for Developmental Studies (IDS) in New York City studied a sample of 543 black and white children who were selected from various socioeconomic levels. For children in first and fifth grades, they found that IQ was definitely related to the presence of a father in the home (Henderson and Bergan, 1976). Other studies also suggest that IQ as well as academic performance may be negatively affected by paternal absence. The IDS found that the association between IQ and father absence was higher for fifth graders than for first graders. This finding seems inconsistent with previous research cited, postulating that paternal influence decreased as the child got older. However, what is clear is that the effect of father absence is definitely interwoven to varying degrees with factors such as community, economics, and family.

Maturity and sex typing. Lacking a father supposedly affects the development of boys mainly because the resolution of the Oedipal situation, as cited in psychoanalytic theory, is supposed to be of major importance in developing emotional maturity and appropriate sex-role identification. Thomes did a study that examined the impact of mother-only families on sons and daughters. She found that the assumption that boys would be more affected than girls by the absence of the father was not true. "On the contrary, the differences that were found between the two groups of children tended to differentiate between girls whose fathers were absent and those whose fathers lived in the home" (Thomes, 1968).

However, since Thomes' study was the only one giving evidence to the fact that fathers may influence their daughters more than their sons, we should still work on the assumption that fathers serve as the chief model for the development of appropriate sex typing in boys, and if the father is absent, they will develop less appropriate sex typing (Drake and McDougall, 1977). Freudian theories imply that if the father is absent from the home, the child will be more mother-identified and is more likely to develop latent or overt homosexual tendencies or feminine characteristics.

The results of studies done by Mischel (1973) suggest that father absence may indicate an overall inadequate home environment, one in which the children may not learn appropriate heterosexual social behavior. This study also included older children between 11 and 14 years of age. For this age-group it was found that as the children get more experience outside of the home, their behavior is influenced more by extrafamilial sources. They become less dependent on influences in the home and more dependent on influences from peers.

Masculinity. It is very important that the mother give her son positive descriptions of the father's masculinity in characteristics such as strength, physical ability, and competence for a normal, healthy, masculine development in her boy (Hetherington et al., 1979). This positive action is essential because the mother's interpretation of the father, whether he is absent or present, has a direct influence on the personality development of the children, especially the boys. The mother's feelings about the father, men, and masculinity in general are significant in social relationships. A boy raised in a fatherless home may be unsure about his masculinity and may overcompensate for this in order to prove it to himself and his peers. One should consider this theory in regard to black children who come from homes where there is a higher ratio of father absence.

Father—only parent

There has been little research done on these father-only families, but one must remember that in most of the divorce cases, custody of minor children is awarded to the mother. This seems to indicate that most of these father-only families represent either desertion or death of the mother. However, a great number of these fathers remarry, in which case they experience the same problems of role changes as mothers who remarry.

Fathers of father-only families experience the same problems as mothers as heads of families. They experience role conflicts with their jobs, their social life, and their parental responsibilities. However, these fathers do feel that it is better for the children to have one parent make the rules and decisions rather than have a conflicting opinion of the other partner.

Black—only parent

Most black families are headed by men as are other American families. However, the proportion of fami-

David Strickler

Father–only parent families have many of the same role conflicts with their jobs, social life, and parental responsibilities as mother–only parent families. Fathers can provide the psychological support and sex-role direction that their children need.

lies with female heads is greater at all levels of income among blacks than among whites. This difference is greatest among those families in the lowest income bracket—families most likely to live in disadvantaged big-city neighborhoods.

The problem of fatherless families among black families is compounded by the fact that blacks in many places are in a low-income bracket. The only parent may have to strive to make ends meet. As a result both money and parental care suffer as the parent struggles to perform both parental roles (Wilson, 1978).

A view from a juvenile court

Children from broken homes are more likely to be charged and committed for delinquent acts than are children from two-parent homes. The family's socioeconomic status plays an important role because blacks and children from the lower socioeconomic levels are more likely to be tried and convicted for juvenile offenses than are white and middle-class children (Herzog and Leurs, 1971).

The Juvenile Court of Franklin County, Chambersburg, Pennsylvania, published the following set of suggestions on how to raise a child. The recommendations are based on what the judges were observing in working with children and their families who were being brought into their courtroom or chambers.

1. Give your child religious and spiritual training; at any rate, help the child develop a moral backbone.
2. Setting a good example yourself in all things is the most direct and effective manner of bringing up a child of whom you can always be proud.
3. To prevent untruthfulness in your child, avoid deceptions in your own relations with him or her or with others. Be frank and honest with your child. If he or she is untruthful, try to find the real cause and do something to eliminate it.
4. Avoid humiliating your child in the presence of his or her friends. It lessens the child's respect for you.
5. Be consistent in giving orders or instructions to your child. If you forbid something today, apply the same rule tomorrow and next week. If you promise a licking for disobedience, be sure to give it. Do not promise or threaten something you do not intend to accomplish.
6. Grave harm results when both parents are not agreed on discipline of the child. It is essential that, outside the child's presence, parents reach agreement on methods of training and that afterward they avoid interfering with each other in requiring obedient conduct on the part of the child. When obedience is not taught in the playpen, it often becomes necessary that it be taught at the federal or state pen.
7. Do your level best to answer the endless "whys" and "hows" of your children.
8. If a conflict of wills arises between you and your child, don't just knock the child down; explain the reasons for your decisions.
9. Use constructive discipline, rewarding the child for little acts "above and beyond the call of duty." Do not, however, try to buy your child's love, respect, or obedience by means of gifts or privileges. These wholesome attitudes of the child should come as a by-product of your whole manner of living and of all your actions toward him or her.
10. Keep in mind that educational and emotional development is first and foremost a parental responsibility. Schools can neither teach nor apply discipline as well as parents can.
11. Encourage the child to discuss plans, problems, or pleasures with you. Never be too busy.
12. In the child's presence and elsewhere always be respectful of womanhood, of humankind, of law, and of elders.
13. Always speak respectfully of all races, creeds, and colors.
14. Open your home to his or her companions; they won't mess up the place if given a little supervision.
15. If possible, give the child a modest allowance. Let the child learn early how to save or spend.
16. Keep yourself from being shocked and exploding when your child tells you of a wrong doing. Try to understand what motivated the child. Think and speak *with,* not *at,* the child.
17. Do things *with* the child, not *for* him or her. Let the child have a share in earning what he or she receives.

PERSONALITY, SELF-CONCEPT, AND SEX ROLE

A major influence on children's developing personality and self-concept is their entrance into a school

self-concept the individual's awareness of and identification with his or her organism, cognitive powers, and modes of conduct and performance, accompanied by specific attitudes toward them.

situation that stresses learning of the basic academic skills. There is a cultural significance attached to "going to school" that may make children see themselves differently in terms of their capabilities (or lack of them) and of what they perceive is expected of them by others.

Personality development

Individual differences in basic personality attributes are fairly well established by the age of 6 years. However, the basic traits are not completely formed by this age, and three significant changes in personal makeup usually occur. *First,* children learn some degree of self-control. As such, they are beginning to learn to live and cope with frustrations. They find ways of avoiding trouble and of achieving success through their own decisions.

Second, there is an increase in the independence of children between the ages of 6 and 9 years. They make friends away from home, become interested in external events and experiences, and begin to demand decision-making prerogatives in keeping with what they learn other children have. *Third,* a feeling of self-worth is either enhanced or decreased. An influence on self-worth is the ease with which children acquire the basic skills of reading, writing, and arithmetic. The way in which youngsters react to specific situations greatly affects their future personality characteristics, patterns of adjustment, and degree of self-acceptance.

During middle childhood, children's social and communicative skills must expand rapidly or they risk the possible rejection or aggression of their peers. The teacher becomes a major socializing agent. At least in the initial school environment the teacher assumes the role of the surrogate parent. In this role teachers are in a position to influence both the social and the personality development of children. They can teach social and communicative skills as they are needed. By their actions, attitudes, and words they are instrumental in shaping the pliable, developing self-image of children (Hogan and Green, 1971).

For the first time the children are away from the constant supervision of their mother. As a result, they are in a position where they can make some value judgments and simple decisions of their own, such as which way to walk home from school and whom to talk and play with in the meanwhile. With this increase in freedom a more realistic self-concept develops. Instead of relying on their parents and family for an appraisal of their behavior, they can now look to their teacher and peers for such impressions.

As they get older, more and more will the peer group be influential in determining which personality traits they will develop. The personality of children is affected by people and how they respond to them. They are especially vulnerable to labels or characteristics that others apply to them, such as lazy, stupid, happy, friendly, neat, or careless. As children strive for an identity that they can recognize and accept, they will often feel insecure and lonely. Parents and teachers need to show their confidence in children until they gain a satisfactory self-impression.

Self-concept

When children recognize and identify with their ways of growing, behaving, and thinking, they are strengthening their awareness of themselves. This awareness of self-attributes, as they see and believe them to be, constitutes their ***self-concept.*** It is their appraisal or evaluation of themselves. The self-concept is developed from comments made by others and from inferences from experiences the children have had in their life space. Only as cognitive ability increases to the stage that children are able to conceptualize will they have a concept of self and their particular physical, social, and emotional characteristics (Maccoby, 1980). Their reasoning ability has to develop to the concrete operations stage, as conceived by Piaget, before they have an opportunity to ascertain a more realistic concept of self. Harter's developmental model of self-perception corresponds roughly to the Piagetian stages (1982).

Children reach middle childhood with a self-concept derived through their parents, immediate family, and a limited number of peers. Their self-concept is likely to be distorted or incomplete. As they are subject to the approval or disapproval of teachers, other adults, and peers, they may begin to question the validity of their view of their attributes and abilities. Between the ages of 6 and 9 years children will be concerned about their capability and acceptibility.

Far from wanting to shine, I laughed in chorus with the others, I repeated their catchwords and phrases, I kept quiet, I obeyed, I imitated my neighbors' gestures, I had only one desire; to be integrated.

Jean-Paul Sartre
The Words

TABLE 8-3 Relationships between parental attitude and child behavior

Parental attitude	*Child behavior associated with it*
Rejective	Submissive, aggressive, adjustment difficulties, feelings of insecurity, sadistic, nervous, shy, stubborn, noncompliant
Overprotective, "babying"	Infantile and withdrawing, submissive, feelings of insecurity, aggressive, jealous, difficult adjustment, nervous
Dominating parent	Dependable, shy, submissive, polite, self-conscious, uncooperative, tense, bold, quarrelsome, disinterested
Submissive parent	Aggressive, careless, disobedient, independent, self-confident, forward in making friends, noncompliant
Inharmonious	Aggressive, neurotic, jealous, delinquent, uncooperative
Defective discipline	Poor adjustment, aggressive, rebellious, jealous, delinquent, neurotic
Harmonious, well adjusted	Submissive, good adjustment
Calm, happy, compatible	Cooperative, superior adjustment, independent
Child accepted	Socially acceptable, faces future confidently
Parents play with child	Security feelings, self-reliant
Logical, scientific approach	Self-reliant, cooperative, responsible
Consistent, strict discipline	Good adjustment
Giving child responsibilities	Good adjustment, self-reliant, security feelings

From Radke, M.J. *The relation of parental authority to children's behavior and attitudes.* Child Welfare Monograph No. 22. Minneapolis: University of Minnesota Press. Copyright 1964 by the publisher.

Negative concerns such as "I'm no good" and "Nobody cares about me" may arise. These thoughts will not be easily dispelled. As children grow more insightful, they are more likely to wonder about themselves.

Unfortunately, some children get little or no support or direction from others they consider important to help them keep negative thoughts in proper perspective. In fact some parents unknowingly nurture a negative self-concept in children by (1) teasing or never being satisfied, (2) usually doing for the children what the children could do for themselves, thus making them feel inadequate and helpless, (3) being so dominant that children feel that they are not being completely trusted and loved, or (4) being more concerned with something other than the children and thus neglecting them. A negative self-concept may also come from a type of discipline by parents or teachers that embarrasses and humiliates. Table 8-3 illustrates some of the attitudes and behaviors that may develop because of parental attitudes.

A positive self-concept enables a person to feel adequate, likeable, intrinsically worthy, and free. These feelings lead to self-respect, self-confidence, and, eventually, happiness. Children must be considered as individuals with characteristics all their own. They must be brought up in an atmosphere of trust, respect, and good regard if they are to emerge as happy, well-adjusted persons. The middle years are a time when the self-concept needs to be carefully nurtured and developed into a stable, acceptable image.

Sex roles

Sex role development refers to the identification of the individual with culturally assigned physiological, sociological, and psychological characteristics and concepts of what constitutes maleness and femaleness. The implication is that a boy should take on and aspire to the male characteristics and girls to the female characteristics. However, there is some evidence to indicate that boys and girls are beginning to show more flexibility; they see that stereotypes are not absolute and that alternatives are feasible (Huston, 1982).

Until children reach the middle childhood years, there is no extensive striving or concern for assuming the appropriate sex role (Block, 1978). As mentioned previously, at the age of 5 years a boy will play the part of either the father or the mother in a make-believe situation. However, by the age of 9 years the boy would absolutely reject the idea of playing a female part. This change suggests the degree to which sex roles are strengthened during middle childhood.

According to social learning theory, the sex role phenomenon is one that generally takes place in the home and family setting (Mischel, 1973). Boys find it natural to pattern themselves after their fathers and girls after their mothers. The parents find this responsiveness gratifying. When chronic antagonism and disharmony exist between the parents, problems arise. The boy may find it hard to identify with his father because he is afraid of losing his mother's love. Likewise, he is also fearful of identifying with his mother because he may incur his father's anger. However, if emotional circumstances are such that the boy rejects the father completely, he may overidentify with the mother.

A case in point regards a boy in a kindergarten class who was brought to our attention. When the boy was 3 years old, his baby brother died. He witnessed his mother's hysteria and his father's sternness in trying to help his wife gain control of herself by slapping her. Unfortunately, for a long period of time afterward the father showed no love for his wife or for the surviving son. The boy only remembered that his father slapped his mother and that during that period of life his father was rather mean and short-tempered with him. The mother was the child's only adult source of love and protection. He became afraid to go near his father and began to identify with his mother and his two sisters, who were nice to him. The boy became obsessed with the idea of being a girl. He had gone as far as asking the other children to call him Janie. During playtime, he preferred to play house, at times dressing up in women's clothes and pretending to do the shopping or take care of the baby. It was only through skillful handling by his teacher that he began to work at a workbench and finally became interested in working with tools.

If the mother or father is missing from the home and no model is there with whom to identify, the child may identify with the teacher at school. In the case of boys, researchers have concluded that some male teachers are needed in elementary schools (Lee and Wolinsky, 1973). One study of the effects of a male teacher showed an improvement in the behavior of hostile boys; mothers of boys in the study reported that their sons were easier to handle at home. In another study it was determined that the male elementary school teacher was especially significant in the inner city. The conclusion was that boys from low-income families needed an effective male figure with whom they could associate and identify to learn their appropriate sex role (Wilson, 1978).

In the past, sex roles were rather clearly defined. Today the characteristics of the sex roles are not as readily ascertained: in fact the nature of the roles is changing. It was also determined that girls from modern families were the most likely to depart from sex-typed expectations. Traditional families produced the most highly aggressive boys and the most highly dependent girls (Lamb and Baumrind, 1978). The study indicated that sex typing was more the result of family experiences than school experiences.

EMOTIONAL GROWTH

The innate excitement of the newborn is the beginning of emotions. Gradually, distress and delight appear and, eventually, other emotions, most of which are learned through experience. During the preschool years children display their emotions rather openly. As they enter school and get older, they tend to use more subtle expressions of emotions. Emotional development is shaped by the experiences of the children and the forms of emotional expression or behavior they have learned to apply to the affective experience. Moral development also partly depends on the types of events, attitudes, and verbal experiences to which children have been exposed. Unlike emotional development that is related to affective responses, moral development depends on cognitive development, knowledge, and awareness.

Descriptive emotional characteristics

Although there is a decrease in the number of emotional explosions during the age of 6 years, children are still in a more-or-less constant state of emotional tension and agitation. In some respects 5-year-olds seem to be more emotionally stable than 6-year-olds. The intense activity of 6-year-olds is partly a result of new social and scholastic demands and their desire to take a giant step forward in asserting independence. In a sense they are now trying to act on their own even though they are beset with uncertainties and fearfulness. Sibling jealousy may still persist, especially if there are younger siblings at home that the children believe may be getting more attention now that they are away at school all day. At 6 years of age many children are very fearful, especially of sounds such as thunder, rain, and wind. Environmental noises, such as static, telephone, or flushing of toilet may induce fear until they are identified. There exists some fear of ghosts and witches. Fears of someone hiding under their beds or of someone in the closet are common.

Most 7-year-olds are less stubborn and more polite, responsive, and sensitive than they were at 6 years. They show less aggression and have fewer outbursts. Many children 7 years of age are their own main concern. They worry that things will be too difficult for them, that second grade may be too hard, that people may not like them, that something might happen to them. These children have a tendency to withdraw from situations or at least are hesitant before acting. They often lack confidence to the point of not wanting even to try. Six-year-olds jump right in only to find they cannot handle the situation.

Most 7-year-olds are more protective of themselves, possibly because their cognitive development has reached a point where they are just a little more aware of consequences and cause and effect than they were previously. They accept some form of discipline, although grudgingly. They are conscientious and try to take their responsibilities seriously, although they are not old enough to be completely reliable.

They are beginning to be able to put themselves in another's place, so much so that they are moved by sad stories. Thus fears can be stimulated by television programs, movies, or reading. They still have fears of ghosts and of "someone hiding in the cellar" but are learning to control some fears such as swimming with their face under water and having their hair washed. There is a more common understanding regarding fear between children and their peers than between most children and their parents. Parents are likely to recognize and agree with fears related to objective conditions but may be ignorant of subjective situations. For example, some 7-year-olds report a fear of being an adopted child, whereas most mothers are not aware of this fear in their child.

Most 8-year-olds are less likely to withdraw than 7-year-olds. In fact they may be full of impatience and wanting to get things done at once. They seek to display courage and often will not admit their fears even to themselves. However, they may still be afraid of fighting, failing in school, or of others finding fault with them. Often they may attack a feared experience, directly or indirectly, or compulsively dwell on it to resolve it. Children who tend to cling to the past and who have difficulty coming smoothly into the future may become worriers.

Generally, 8-year-olds cry less than others from inner confusion, but they may burst into tears, especially when tired, for reasons such as having their feelings hurt by being criticized or not receiving or being able to do something that they wanted. Sometimes these children begin to think of themselves as martyrs and rationalize to themselves: "They'll be sorry they treated me so mean when they see how bad I've been hurt (or am gone or when I'm sick in bed because of what they did)."

A number of 8-year-olds are often bossy, rude, and argumentative, even with their mother, but they are also affectionate and friendly. These children think of giving something to their mother and father. They are developing a feeling of being able to create love by initiating an activity on their own.

MORAL DEVELOPMENT

Children develop their basic philosophical orientation to life at home. The family is the workshop, where for better or for worse children develop an internal pattern of attitudes and beliefs that shape their character and influence their behavior. The community exerts a major modifying influence, to be sure. However, the home determines the initial strength and nature of the moral character of the children, and this strength, in turn, determines the degree to which the influences of the community can change the character.

Descriptive moral characteristics

Children learn early in childhood that there are some forms of behavior that are acceptable and some that are not. They come to associate "good" with a reward for approved behavior and "bad" with a punishment for unacceptable behavior. Eventually, children conceptualize the thought that there are certain rules and regulations that must be followed to receive the acceptance and approval of others (society). By the age of 6 or 7 years children have internalized the concept of rules and the idea of right and wrong.

As 6-year-olds enter the classroom world, they usually become aware of forces outside the home that relate to their concepts of "good," "bad," "right," and "wrong." For the next few years they consider making adjustments to their moral consciousness that they now recognize must be more extensive, insightful, and judgmental than the family-oriented code of conduct that they had developed up to this time. Turner, Peck, and Havighurst, as cited by Rains and Morris (1969), suggest that there is little reason to expect significant changes in a person's basic character after the ages of 9 or 10 years. It could be, then, that the primary teacher may be the last person who could help make a major impact on the basic character of children.

Six- to 8-year-olds are still somewhat egocentric, a characteristic that greatly affects their own concept of moral behavior. As a result, their inclination is to justify their behavior by some rationalization that, to them, is perfectly logical and acceptable. If this approach does not work, they may seek to protect themselves by lying or cheating. Most 7-year-olds are quick to demand honesty from others and recognize the moral implications of not lying to their friends. Many 8-year-olds become conscious of the effect of their wrongdoing on their status among their peers. Older primary children have a strong sense of fair play for themselves. The cry "That's not fair!" is often heard. Children may be right, but sometimes they are trying to avoid the fact that they are in the wrong. By the age of 9 years "being fair" tends to apply to all who are playing the game.

Taking things that belong to others is rather common among 6- and 7-year-olds. Six-year-olds do this openly, and if confronted with the fact, will deny the stealing or will say, "But he gave it to me." Seven-year-olds are more subtle, and 8-year-olds are more careful.

A conscience, or a moral judgment, is slowly developing in the child. This development started at the age of 4 years, when the child began to develop a self-ideal. By the age of 8 years the conscience will serve as a source of self-control or, if overdeveloped, as a cause for feelings of guilt. However, the conscience of an 8-year-old will tolerate some stretching of the truth but will have some control over impulses of the moment, for example to steal. The 8-year-old may become proficient at alibiing or at placing the blame for a misconduct on something or someone else. Predicting a child's social behavior from his or her reasoning is a risky affair (Damon, 1977). A third grader who wanted to stay at a friend's house longer to play turned his watch back an hour. When he got home late, he acted surprised, saying that something must be wrong with his watch.

There is an expanding awareness of moral conduct in society as children mature. As they get older, they differentiate between what is acceptable conduct within their peer group and what is acceptable to the adult world. They recognize, but do not necessarily understand, the ambiguities that they observe between what adults tell them is the "right" thing to do and what the adults themselves do under the same circumstances.

heteronomous morality in Piaget, the moral thinking of children up to age 10, in which rules are sacred and consequences of an act determine guilt regardless of a person's intentions.

Piaget: Moral development

Piaget studied the moral development of children and concluded that, in many respects, moral judgment was related to level of cognitive development and to the degree of interaction with other children, especially in learning rules of games.

Piaget's book on the growth of moral development remains one of the most influential works on the topic (Piaget, 1955). His conceptualization of moral development and his research directions are more important than the specific findings of his research (Carroll and Rest, 1982). His major directions might be summarized under four points. *First,* an individual has an underlying cognitive framework with which to interpret moral situations. Piaget believes that we cannot assume that social situations are perceived in the same way by all persons. This approach differs from the behaviorists who look at the external factors rather than the internal organization of concepts.

Second, Piaget believes that the child's first experience of social rules is that of commands handed down by respected authority figures. He refers to this initial unilateral respect for authority as a ***heteronomous***

autonomous morality in Piaget, the moral thinking of children 11 or older; rules are flexible and considered to be mutual agreements among equals; intentions are considered in evaluating guilt.

extinction a process in which a conditioned response is reduced to its preconditioned level. Previously reinforced responses are no longer reinforced.

reinforcement schedule a well-defined procedure for reinforcing a given response.

morality (morality is subject to external controls). At first the child attends to the letter of the law without question because he or she does not have the understanding that social rules are the way by which social cooperation is structured. After understanding the rationale behind the rules, the child develops an ***autonomous morality*** (morality can be carried on without external control). Piaget, therefore, studied cognitive development to understand how a child developed the concept of cooperation in play and with peers.

A *third* point of Piaget is the concept of justice in moral development. Justice indicates how social systems of cooperation attempt to be "fair" so that a balance can be obtained in regard to the concerns and the varying interests of the individuals involved. In one way or another, conflicts of interest must be worked out and accepted on a rational basis. The *fourth* major characteristic of Piaget's approach to morality is that development involves a fundamental reorganization of a person's behavior and thinking, starting with heteronomous morality, which is a morality of constraint imposed by others, and developing into an autonomous morality, which is a morality based on the spirit of cooperation. A restructuring of cognitive organization is involved, not just a progressive socialization process as social learning theorists would imply. (Piaget's theory of moral development is presented more fully in Chapter 10.)

To study children's moral judgments Piaget used pairs of stories in which children were involved in misdeeds of various kinds (Elkind, 1970). The children between 6 and 8 years of age had to decide which story depicted the worst misdeed. In one pair of stories the first was about a boy who broke 15 cups while helping his mother set the table, whereas the second story was about a boy who broke one cup while trying to get some jam that he had been forbidden to have. Up to the age of 10, the children judged the boy who broke the 15 cups to have been the most at fault. Children at this age judge actions on a quantitative basis rather than on intentions.

Another story involved the telling of falsehoods. A boy came home from school and told his mother, to amuse her, that he had seen an elephant in the street. Another boy tried to deceive his mother and stated that he had received a better grade than he had actually received. In this case the children stated that the boy who told the elephant story was most at fault.

Piaget also studied the games of children to discover their "natural morality." He believed that in simple childhood games the morality or rules are taught by older children to the younger. In this manner the rules are passed down from generation to generation with little or no influence or change by adults. Based on his studies Piaget divides children's morality into (1) the practice of the rules and (2) the consciousness of rules.

The *practice of the rules* evolved through four stages from (1) a purely motor and individual character in which children were learning to play the game, to (2) the egocentric stage, beginning anytime from 2 to 5 years of age, in which children play largely by themselves but know that rules exist, to (3) the cooperation on the rules for the games in which children play together, beginning about ages 7 or 8, to (4) the codification of the rules, in which the rules are fixed and everyone knows them, beginning about ages 11 or 12.

Consciousness of the rules develops at the same time that the practice of the rules evolves. Consciousness evolves from the level (1) at which the rules are not coercive in nature or believed to be mandatory, ages 4 to 7, to (2) at which the rules are sacred and must not be broken, ages 7 to 10, to the last stage (3) at which the rules must be respected but may be changed by common consent, ages 10 and over.

Social learning and moral development

Piaget is challenged by social learning researchers on his theory concerning development of moral judgment (Bandura and McDonald, 1963). In general, two observations are made. First, although moral judgment of children is affected somewhat by age, it is more strongly affected by sociocultural influences. Piaget did not place enough emphasis on this point, say the dissident researchers. Second, although Piaget believed that reactions at one given stage tend to be uniform, others found that there seem to be different levels and types of development within a given stage. The researchers challenging Piaget believe that learning experiences are more important than maturational processes in forming character. Significant learning experiences encompass such areas as social class attitudes and learning conditions, cultural and traditional behavior, parental emphasis and attitudes, and type of disciplinary measures to which the child was subjected.

Social learning theory stresses that moral development is growth of behavioral conformity to moral rules rather than cognitive-structural change. According to this theory, the basic motivation for morality at every point of moral development is rooted in biological needs or the pursuit of social reward and the avoidance of social punishment (Lickona, 1976). Therefore, basic moral norms are the internalization of external cultural rules, based on the reinforcement system or the modeling influence of conforming behavior by parents and other socializing models.

To these general statements must be added the following qualifiers. For example, the effectiveness of rewards and punishment depends on (1) the consistency with which they are administered and (2) the nature of the reinforcement schedule, continuous or partial. Consistency of reinforcement is needed until a behavior has been established. After that, a ***reinforcement schedule***—a matter of how often the behavior is reinforced—is needed. Partial reinforcement illustrates the orderliness of operant behavior; once a particular behavior has been established, it can be sustained by occasional reinforcement. ***Extinction,*** the deterioration of a behavior, occurs much more slowly after partial reinforcement than after continuous reinforcement.

Each child develops a unique moral pattern because social learning experiences differ. There is no reason to expect that a child's behavior will be the same in each realm of social behavior. The socialization forces that contribute to one behavioral domain may ignore another. For this reason, a slightly different pattern of moral development emerges in each area.

CHAPTER REVIEW

1. The middle childhood developmental years feature three thrusts or "pushes": *a physical thrust* into the world of games and neuromuscular skills; *a mental thrust* into school and the world of symbols and concepts; and a *social thrust* from the family environs into the peer group. Erikson's psychosocial crisis is one of industry versus inferiority.
2. Physically, the body assumes more adult-like proportions. Girls are generally more physically advanced than boys, but the boys are slightly taller and heavier. Gross motor skills are better developed than fine motor skills for 6-year-olds. Although 8-year-olds have more fine motor skills than they had at 6, they still have some developing to do.
3. The Piagetian *concrete operations stage* of cognitive development covers ages 7 to 11 or 12. During this stage the child becomes less egocentric in thought, can decenter, can do reversibility of thought, and can attend to transformation of matter. These characteristics are aspects of operational thought. Improvement is made in the ability to do classification, seriation, and conservation. Some research suggests that conservation may be handled at an earlier age than Piaget predicts if the child is taught what to think about.
4. The mental characteristics of middle childhood operate on a concrete level. The child can learn to reason about things (concrete) but not about verbal propositions (abstractions). Eight-year-olds show an interest in causal relationships.
5. The cognitive task of *classification* involves the grouping of objects or ideas into a class or dimension. *Intention* refers to the criterion for grouping, such as "Pick out all of the brown beads." *Extension* refers to the ability to determine how many objects meet the criterion. Children who are efficient on the concrete operational level can do both intention and extension in classification.
6. Children at the preoperational stage have difficulty reasoning about the relationship between *time* and *speed*. The toy car that arrives first at the designated point of arrival is the fastest car, even if it traveled the shortest distance. Children at the concrete operations stage can focus on more than one dimension—the arrival point and the longest distance to get there.
7. *Seriation* is the ability to mentally and physically arrange elements or objects according to increasing or decreasing size, whether it be length, weight, or volume. The child at the preoperational stage has difficulty with weight and volume but not with length, providing all the sticks can be seen. Children at the concrete operational level can do weights at age 9 and volume at age 12.

8. *Cognitive style* refers to the different ways in which an individual thinks, remembers, perceives, or attends. *Reflection-impulsivity* refers to the speed and accuracy with which a person responds in thinking. *Field-dependent—independent cognitive style* refers to whether a person takes a global view of a situation, object, or task (field dependent) or can separate the parts or details from the whole. *Styles of conceptualization* relate to the bases that an individual uses for grouping. The *constrictive versus flexible cognitive style* indicates the ease of thinking in going from one thought or plan to another.
9. *Neuropsychology* is the study of how the nervous system processes information. The perceptual system is that part of neuropsychology that deals with sensorimotor functions, visual perception, auditory perception, and tactile perception. Perception is further subdivided into *attention*, *discrimination*, *memory*, *sequentialization*, *figure-ground* and *closure* processing. The neuropsychology of the conceptual system has to do with the process of reasoning, thinking, problem solving, and imagining.
10. Development of the perceptual processing phase involves four adaptive neuropsychological organizations: (1) neural and motor organization, including laterality and directionality, (2) auditory perceptual processes involving attention, discrimination, memory, and the ability to integrate sound-symbol relationships, (3) fine visual-motor organization, including visual attention, discrimination and memory, and ability to integrate fine visual-motor actions such as copying, and (4) the general cognitive processes of attention, memory, and problem solving.
11. *Attention*, also known as *attending*, involves alertness and a lack of distractibility. Alertness must take place so the stimuli can be detected. Distractibility is a factor that hinders the child from being able to focus on (attend to) the stimuli. Attention is necessary for visual or auditory discrimination of stimuli to take place.
12. A child may develop strategies to improve visual, auditory, or tactile memory. The strategies commonly studied in memory are *rehearsal*, *imagery*, and *organization*.
13. Problem solving in middle childhood is restricted to concrete thinking. Trial and error is used much of the time. The strategy of a *systematic approach* based on a hypothesis in problem solving appears to require more cognitive development than the average youngster in middle childhood possesses.
14. A child with *learning disabilities* is an inefficient learner because of a central nervous system dysfunction in neuropsychological processing rather than a lack of mental ability. This child may have poor development of any of the adaptive processes of motor organization, auditory perception, fine visual-motor organization and perception, or one or more of the processes of attention, memory, or problem-solving ability.
15. Language development in terms of syntax is said to be developed by the age of 6, but some researchers question this statement. The middle-childhood youngster is able to use sentences and to ask questions of a personal nature and appears to have reached the point of *socialized speech*, as defined by Piaget. Vocabulary increases rapidly as the child is exposed to a school and peer environment.
16. The social characteristics of middle childhood reveal children who are aware of their peers. However, at the age of 6, they are observers of the behavior of older children rather than active participants in the older peer group. By the age of 8, the children are rather strongly involved in their own peer group. Social courtesy and manners are just in the beginning stages of development in middle childhood.
17. *Play culture* is strongly based on the use of activities involving gross motor skills and much energy. Sit-down games become more popular as the child approaches the age of 8. Play of childhood can be categorized as imitative, exploratory, testing, or model building.
18. According to Baumrind (1972), patterns of parenting fall into three categories—authoritarian, authoritative, or permissive— and each has a particular effect on the child. The *authoritarian* parent controls and disciplines the child but shows little concern for the needs (and rights) of the child: "You just do what I tell you because I am your parent." The *authoritative* parent controls and disciplines the child but does so with concern and a regard for the child: "You broke the rules we agreed on; you know you'll have to pay the consequences that were established." The *permissive* parent exerts little or no firm discipline and demands little in terms of mature behavior: "I wish you wouldn't do that."
19. The roles played by mothers and fathers have an effect on their children because youngsters usually identify with their parents. Mothers tend to play a role that is *expressive*, demonstrating a sensitivity to the feelings, needs, and thoughts of others. Fathers usually play a role that is *instrumental*, one that is responsible for making decisions and doing what has to be done. Children can develop both expressive and instrumental characteristics from their parents. They will benefit from having both a mother and a father figure.

20. In families where mother is the only parent, boys need not be affected more than girls because of the absence of a father. However, the mother needs to give her son some positive descriptions of masculinity such as strength, physical ability, and competence. Mother's attitude about the father, and men in general, is significant for the development of acceptable social relationships by both boys and girls.
21. Individual differences in basic *personality attributes* are fairly well established but not completed by the age of 6 years. More must be learned about self-control, independent behavior, a feeling of self-worth, and value judgments and decisions. *Self-concept* develops as a result of social interaction and an assessment of self-adequacy in that interaction. The characteristics of *sex role* behavior are changing in today's society in the direction of similarity and equality between the sexes as compared to rather sharply defined sex roles of 20 years ago.
22. Emotional characteristics in middle childhood can be described as changing and developing according to the cognitive insight, social learning, and self-control that a child gains. There is still much room for growth toward emotional stability.
23. Moral characteristics in middle childhood appear to be related to the level of cognitive development and the type of social learning the child has encountered. Piaget's theory of moral development is based on cognitive development involving the practice of rules and conscious awareness of the rules.

REVIEW QUESTIONS

1. Review the developmental tasks of middle childhood. How does Erikson's psychosocial crisis relate to the tasks?
2. How do the motor skills of a 6-year-old differ from those of an 8-year-old?
3. In a few sentences, describe the main feature or characteristic(s) of cognitive development during the sensorimotor stage and the preoperations stage. Then use a sentence or two to relate the main characteristic of cognitive development during the concrete operations stage. What do you see happening as cognitive development improves?
4. Define reversibility, classification, seriation, conservation, and transformation, according to Piaget's theory.
5. What is the difference between children who are conservers and those who are not?
6. What is meant by a cognitive style? Describe the reflection-impulsivity cognitive style. What kind of thinking does a field-independent person do best?
7. Make three columns with the following headings: 6-year-old, 7-year-old, and 8-year-old. Then give a short summary of the mental characteristics of each age level.
8. List the four adaptive or neuropsychological processes of the perceptual pattern for learning. In a sentence or two, tell how each process relates to learning.
9. Discuss attention in terms of awareness, distractibility, discrimination, and scanning.
10. List three strategies used in improving memory. Define each one.
11. How much and what kind of problem solving can be done by a child in middle childhood?
12. Define learning disabilities, using the four areas of agreement. Why, or in what way, is a learning disabled individual an inefficient learner?
13. Describe Piaget's concept of egocentric speech and socialized speech.
14. Summarize the main feature(s) of the social characteristics of 6-year-olds, 7-year-olds, and 8-year-olds.
15. Review Table 8-2 on play interests of middle childhood.
16. Make two columns. In one, define the authoritarian, authoritative, and permissive patterns of parenting. In the second column, describe the kinds of characteristics developed in the children of these different kinds of parents.
17. What is the difference between expressive and instrumental roles of parenting?
18. How do boys fare in mother-only-parent families?
19. How do father-only-parent families compare to mother-only families? Although the information presented appears meager, compare the two.
20. Speculate on how low income can affect one-parent families.
21. Do you agree or disagree with the suggestions made by judges on how to raise children? Do judges have credentials to make such statements?
22. What personality changes are characteristic of middle-childhood personality development?
23. Define self-concept. How is it developed during middle childhood?
24. What is meant by sex role? In principle, how does today's concept of sex role differ from that of the past?
25. Emotionally, how do 6-year-olds differ from 8-year olds?
26. Outline the main points of Piaget's theory of moral development.

THOUGHT QUESTIONS AND ACTIVITIES

1. When a child matures from the preoperational level of cognition to concrete operations, some major differences in thinking can be noted. Piaget says that the capacity for concrete operations does not occur until age 7. Does this mean that the average first grader, a 6-year-old, cannot do reasoning? Might there be such a thing as a transition period from one stage to the other? With the right kind of teaching, could a 4- or 5-year-old be taught some types of concrete reasoning? What does the research indicate?
2. Set up a series of experiments of conservation, classification, seriation, and/or time and speed. Administer the experiments to children of preschool age, children in the first three grades, and children in grades 4 to 6.
3. The term *neuropsychology* has been in vogue in recent years. Is it a new concept, or is it simply a new name for a concept that has been around awhile? See if you can find the term neuropsychological or psychoneurological in some of the literature of 10 or more years ago.
4. Do the styles of patterning change from generation to generation? Is there a cohort effect in parenting styles? Or do they merely reappear under new labels?
5. Is a child with specific learning disabilities a candidate for special education? Discuss.
6. Are children who go to school in urban areas, perhaps inner city, any different from those who go to school in a suburban area? A rural area? Do they have different types of experiences? Does it matter? Would it make a difference?
7. Talk to elementary teachers; ask what content and basic skills are taught in first, second, third, and fourth grade. Do you note a progression of skill learning?
8. Visit an elementary school playground—with permission of the principal, of course. Observe the children. Can you tell the difference between second and third graders? What kinds of games do they play? Talk to some of the children.
9. What differences might you find in one-parent families as compared to two-parent families? In what ways is a two-parent family better for the child? Couldn't the one-parent family provide the same qualities?

FURTHER READINGS

Fincher, J. Lefties. New York: Perigee Books, 1980. This comprehensive study of handedness tells all you ever wanted to know about left-handedness—and more. It explores theories, examines customs, and delves into historical attitudes and implications for left-handed people.

Haywood, H.C., Meyers, C.E., & Switzky, H.N. Mental retardation. In M.R. Rosenzweig & L.W. Porter (Eds.), *Annual Review of Psychology*, (Vol. 33). Palo Alto, Calif.: Annual Reviews, Inc., 1982. This chapter reviews the behavioral research on severely and profoundly retarded persons and presents some contemporary developmental problems.

Hope, K., & Young, H. (Eds.). *Momma: The sourcebook for single mothers.* New York: The New American Library, 1976. A number of short articles, written by single parents, give a composite picture of what their lives are like. Practical information is offered on divorce, working, and helping children adjust to parental separation.

Kail, R. *The development of memory in children*. San Francisco: W. H. Freeman & Co., 1979. This book is an easy-to-read review of memory and research on children's memory.

Manual, L. Rules in children's moral judgments: Integration of intent, damage, and rational information. *Developmental Psychology*, 1982, 18(6), 835-842. Six- and 7-year-olds responded to stories about boys who interfered with workmen painting a house.

Mussen, P., & Eisenberg-Berg, N. *Roots of caring, sharing and helping*. San Francisco: W. H. Freeman & Co., 1977. Research on prosocial behavior is presented in an interesting, easy-to-read fashion.

Tant, J.L. & Douglas, V.I. Problem solving in hyperactive, normal, and reading-disabled boys. *Journal of Abnormal Child Psychology*, 1982, 10(3), 285-306. The results of this research suggest that the attentional difficulties of hyperactive boys retard the development of strategies for complex problems.

CHAPTER 9

LATE CHILDHOOD

9 TO 11 YEARS OF AGE

THAT FIRST CIGARETTE

All through elementary school my best girlfriend lived across the street from me. Sally was a year younger than I, but we were inseparable. We played Cowboys and Indians, played marbles, rode our bikes, spent nights at each other's houses, and walked to school together. We both had vivid imaginations, and because of this we were quite active and experimental in trying new experiences. We would try things out just for fun, even though we knew we might get punished for doing them. One might say we were very curious.

On this particular Saturday my parents and sister had gone away. My neighbor was babysitting for me, but Sally and I were out playing. While we were playing, Sally suggested smoking a cigarette to see what it was like. So we decided to try it. We knew it was wrong and that if we were caught we would be punished, but my parents were out of town and we decided to hide from her parents. I do not remember where we got the money, but we bought the cigarettes at the grocery store two doors away from her house. The lady thought nothing about a fourth and fifth grader buying cigarettes because Sally often bought them for her father. I got the matches from my father's pipe stand, and we were ready for a new experience.

The junior high school was on a hill a block from our houses. Behind the school was a dense growth of trees, bushes, and shrubs, so we decided to go there and hide while we smoked. We were pretty brave after a while, so we moved to a small clearing on the hill where we could look down at the cars going by on the street. A few people saw us, but that was all right because we didn't know them. But the next thing we knew, Sally's father went by and happened to look up. We thought he saw us, but when he didn't stop, we assumed he didn't see us after all. As it turned out, he *did* see us. At the time we didn't know that, so feeling quite brave, we decided to stop hiding and walk along the street. We were laughing, talking, showing off, and feeling very grownup. We were completely pleased with ourselves.

After we had smoked all we wanted, we discarded the rest of the pack and went to my house where we gargled with mouthwash to get rid of the cigarette smell. Then we decided to go over to Sally's house. When we got there, her mother informed us that her father had seen us smoking and that Sally was not allowed to play anymore. She also said that she was going to tell my parents. Feeling very safe, I thought to myself "ha-ha"; then I told her my parents were out of town and would not be back until time for supper. But she said she would come over then. When I left, I began to worry—should I tell my parents when they got home or should I just wait? I knew it was better to tell them myself, but I just could not do it, so I waited, hoping Sally's mother would forget.

It was not long before my parents and sister came home; by then I was really worried. Just as we were ready to sit down to eat, the doorbell rang. When Mother answered the door and I saw who it was, I started to go upstairs to my room. Mother knew something must be pretty important to have a visitor at mealtime. I got halfway upstairs when I heard, "Mary Anne, I think you ought to stay and hear this." My parents shot a startled, shocked look at me, and I sat down with my head bowed, waiting for the lead ball to fall. Then it came. I knew by my parents' expressions that they could not believe I would do such a thing. Then they sent me to bed without any supper! And I was so hungry! I could not believe it. I had never been punished like this before.

After what seemed to be hours, actually only about fifteen minutes, my parents came up to my room and, sitting down on my bed, asked me why I did it. When I said I had smoked just to see what it was like and promised never to do it again, I was allowed to go downstairs and finish eating my meal with them.

I will never forget how ashamed I was! I sat at the end of the table, with my sister at the other end and our parents in between us. While I ate, there were three pairs of eyes just staring at me, and no one said a word. I just looked at my plate and tried to eat between tears. I was ashamed because I had disappointed by parents, but I was especially ashamed for my sister to know what I had done. She was eighteen, in college, and she did not smoke. I tried very hard to imitate her—she was my ideal.

I don't smoke today because I don't want to smoke. I tried once again in college because it seemed to be the thing to do, but I remembered my mother telling me that if I started to smoke, then she would also (and I detested the thought of my mother's smoking). I also felt as if three pairs of eyes were watching me every time I puffed a cigarette, and I decided it was not worth feeling guilty about!

IN THIS CHAPTER . . .

You will read about

1. The physical characteristics and health of children ages 9 to 11. You will also read about the physical prelude to puberty.
2. Sexual awareness and the need for sex information by this age group. Sexuality and sexual learning are explored.
3. The cognition characteristics of children in late childhood as they apply to the type of learning done in school.
4. The social structure of preadolescence as it is related to peer groups, friendships, and family relationships.
5. Birth order and the general meaning that it has for personality characteristics of individuals.
6. The emotional behavior pattern, fears, and worries of late childhood.
7. The social role-taking theory of Selman and how it relates to moral judgment.

The ages of 9 to 11 years are interesting because they depict childhood at its highest form of development. Soon the youngsters will leave childhood and move on to the next major phase of growth and development—adolescence. They will never be children again. There is no universal rule as to when children take on the characteristics of late childhood or preadolescence. (We use the two terms interchangeably in this text.) Generally the first psychological signs are detected in 9-year-olds; the signs are clearly evident in the 11- and 12-year-olds.

Preadolescence can be a trying period for parents and teachers as well as for children. The children are trying to grow out of their dependence on their parents for guidance and direction. They enjoy separating themselves from the family in their interests and activities, so family relationships and interactions change from what they used to be. They may challenge their parents and other authority, although their judgment is often erroneous and immature. The children's interest in acquiring knowledge is a wholesome development, but it also creates problems at times. Children can no longer be "fooled" by their parents or teachers. Yet many do not have enough information and insight to produce good perspectives on their own. Preadolescents are highly competent as children, but they still lack the development necessary to make them completely reliable, effective, and resourceful.

The developmental tasks of late childhood are somewhat clouded because there is such a strong continuum of life experiences that pass on from middle childhood into the adolescent period. The developmental tasks begun in middle childhood continue to be faced in late childhood. The difference is that in late childhood the tasks require a higher level of proficiency for attainment. The developmental tasks for preadolescence are (1) gaining freedom from a primary identification with adults by learning to become self-reliant, (2) developing social competency in forming and maintaining friendships with peers, (3) learning to live in the adult world by getting a clearer perspective of one's peer group role or place in that world, (4) developing a moral code of conduct based on principles rather than specifics, (5) consolidating the identification made with one's sex role, (6) integrating and refining motor patterns to a higher level of efficiency, (7) learning realistic ways of studying and controlling the physical world, (8) developing appropriate symbol systems and conceptual abilities for learning, communicating, and reasoning, and (9) evolving an understanding of self and the world (society and cosmos) (Havighurst, 1979).

preadolescence **the period of human development just preceding adolescence, usually between the ages of 9 and 12 years.**

PHYSICAL GROWTH AND MOTOR DEVELOPMENT

The preadolescent years are transitional years. For some children, particularly girls, this period is the beginning of pubescence. For others, particularly boys, it is a time of steady growth in height and weight. For all it is the most healthy period of their lives. During these few short years they will enjoy a pause between childhood diseases and the diseases of adulthood. However, it is important to watch out for accidents because these are "daring" years.

Physical characteristics

Physical growth during late childhood is characterized by a gradual, steady gain in bodily measurements. The various parts of the body not only increase in size but also become more functional. In other words, physical development improves in quality as well as quantity. The skeletal frame becomes larger, the trunk increases moderately in length, and the extremities become proportionately longer. The trunk broadens and deepens, with shoulders and hips developing similarly in each sex. The muscles accelerate their rate of growth, and the ligamentous structures become firmer and stronger. As a result, body posture is improved over that found in the young child. Body stance and balance are more appropriate for efficient erectness, for locomotion, and for strength in the use of arms and trunk. At 12 or 13 years of age girls are about a year ahead of boys in the development of the bones of the wrist (carpal bones), which is one of the best single measurements of physical maturity (Latham et al., 1977).

Boys at the age of 9 years will have an average *height* of 132.5 cm (53 in.) and at 11 years, 142.5 cm (57 in.).

David Strickler

Motor ability and gracefulness of movement emerge in late childhood as sensorimotor control and coordination are developed.

There is an increase in height of a little over 2.5 cm (1 in.) per year. Nine-year-old girls will have an average height of 130 cm (52 in.), and 11-year-olds, 145 cm (58 in.). There is an average increase of about 5 cm (2 in.) a year. From third to fifth grade, boys are slightly taller than girls, but in sixth grade the average girl is taller than the boy. Progress in height is closely correlated with approaching sexual maturity. The most rapid growth period in height for girls precedes menarche, usually by 1 or 2 years. Growth in height for boys appears linked to genital development.

Boys at 9 years of age will have an average *weight* of 30 kg (66 lb.), and at 11 years, 35 kg (77 lb.). Increase in weight for boys per year is almost 2 kg (4 lb.). Girls will weigh an average of 29 kg (64 lb.) at 9 years of age and 35.5 kg (78 lb.) at 11 years. The increase in weight for girls is almost 2.5 kg (5 lb.) per year. Weight, like height, seems related to advent of sexual maturity. The greatest increase in weight for girls occurs about 3 months before menarche, around 12 years of age. The greatest growing period for weight for boys is around the age of 14 years.

Late childhood is the time when the permanent teeth appear. Girls are more advanced than boys in dentition at any age in childhood. In the following statements the sequence of the appearance of teeth is more significant than the age at which they are said to appear. Major individual differences occur in the age of appearance. At 8 years of age the first permanent back teeth (first molars) and the center front teeth (central incisors) appear. Between 8 and 9 years of age the eye teeth on the lower jaw (canines) emerge. The upper canines may not appear for at least 2 more years. Between the ages of 10 and 12 years the two teeth (bicuspids) on the sides behind each canine appear. Most children have all their permanent teeth except wisdom teeth by the age of 12 or 13 years (Latham et al., 1977).

TABLE 9-1 Motor development in late childhood

Age (years)	*Selected behaviors*
9	Girls can vertical-jump 21.25 cm (8½ in.) and boys 25 cm (10 in.) over their standing height-plus-reach
	Boys can run 4.9 m (16½ ft.) per second
	Boys can throw a small ball 21 m (70 ft.)
10	Can judge and intercept pathways of small balls thrown from a distance
	Girls can run 5.1 m (17 ft.) per second
11	Standing broad jump of 1.5 m (5 ft.) possible for boys; 15 cm (6 in.) less for girls
12	Standing high jump of 0.9 m (3 ft.) possible

Modified from Cratty, B. ***Perceptual and motor development in infants and children*** (2nd ed.). Englewood Cliffs, N.J.: Prentice-Hall, © 1979, p. 222. Reprinted by permission of Prentice-Hall, Inc.

Health in late childhood

The ages from 9 to 12 are usually the healthiest years of a child's life. A major reason is that the *lymphoid masses,* which help to fight infections, are at their highest point of development in quantity. Average 11-year-olds have almost twice the lymphoid masses that they will have as adults, and before and after the age of 11 years their bodies will have well above the amount of 20-year-olds. (See Fig. 7-1.) Mother Nature must have known how difficult it would be to keep preadolescents out of the rain and to have them button their coats to keep warm in the winter, so she wisely gave this age group some extra protection to ward off colds and other diseases. A more likely explanation for the extra lymphoid masses is that if the child has survived to this stage in life, nature wanted to do what it could to increase survival potential to adulthood when the individual can help to perpetuate the species, which is one of the basic aims of life.

Another reason for the good health of this age group is that most children have already been exposed to the communicable diseases of childhood or have in some manner become immune. They have an interest in outdoor games that gives them sufficient physical exercise to maintain good muscle tone and good intake of oxygen. For the most part they get 9 to 10 hours of sleep a night. They are not as tempted to stay up late as they will be when they are older. They have enormous appetites so that they generally get enough food. Fresh air, rest, exercise, good nutrition, plus an innate ability to ward off diseases all contribute to a healthy life.

Motor ability and activities

During late childhood, children gain in vigor and balance in sensorimotor control and coordination. They generally improve in manual dexterity, increase their resistance to fatigue, and develop greater muscular strength. These factors allow for finer motor usage of small muscles over longer periods of time, resulting in a rapid improvement in the ability of these children to control their bodies and to manipulate objects with which they play. They improve in agility, accuracy, and endurance. They run faster, throw and catch much better, and can jump and climb with ease and assurance. By the age of 9 years eye-hand coordination is good. Children are ready for crafts and shop work. Their eyes are almost adult size, and they are ready to do close work with less strain. Table 9-1 illustrates certain motor skills achieved in late childhood (Cratty, 1979).

This is a period when children have so much energy that they often do not know when to stop. Their con-

puberty the period of life during which an individual's reproductive organs become functional and secondary sexual characteristics appear; the period characterized by rapid somatic growth and the assumption of adult traits or features.

stant drive, inability to be quiet, and concentration on the game are enough to drive the most understanding adult supervisor to distraction. Parents often become concerned with so much physical play and roughhousing. Popular physical activities at this stage are playing ball, riding a bicycle, jumping rope, ice and roller skating, hiking in the woods, hopscotch, swimming, and running. Team games are popular. Vigorous bodily activities are preferred to finer motor skills (Galton, 1980). Children usually devote more time to the use of their body than to tools or toys. There are few sex differences until the age of 11 when boys tend to improve their coordination more than girls do (Espenschade and Eckert, 1967). Unhappy are the youngsters who do not possess the physical skills needed to play the games of their peer group.

At this age children, boys especially, are constantly pushing themselves into new activities that require new skills or courage. "I dare you" is an often-used phrase. Playing follow-the-leader or taking a dare to walk along the top of a narrow fence improves motor skills and balance. Thus children develop more versatility, speed of movement, physical strength, and control of their bodies.

Lack of success is rarely frustrating to the young preschool child. However, elementary grade youngsters become easily frustrated when they fail to grasp immediately the technique of an activity such as dribbling a large rubber ball. They need freedom from overdemanding standards of control while learning simple coordinations. Exposure to fellow classmates and the scrutiny of the teacher when learning a new skill can be particularly upsetting. If at all possible, a teacher should arrange a time or way for the child to experiment and practice motor skills in an accepting atmosphere. It is unwise to push children into a game or test situation until they have an adequate chance to learn the particular skill or skills needed.

Prelude to puberty

The onset of ***puberty*** usually occurs at about 10 years for girls and 12 years for boys (Tanner, 1978). As will be noted in the next chapter, there are indications that there is an increase in the number of girls who begin puberty at 9 years of age. In general the average age of the peak of puberty for girls is a little over 12 years, and for boys it is about 14 years (Tanner, 1973). Before puberty occurs, however, there are some physiological changes that take place in both sexes, in girls before boys.

With the approach of puberty general body proportions change in both sexes. In girls an overall rounding and softening of the body features begins. At 11 years of age noticeable individual differences are apparent between slow and fast physically maturing girls. Heavier, taller girls generally begin the pubertal period before thinner, shorter girls. The pelvic area of the prepubescent girl broadens, whereas the shoulder width remains about the same. An adipose (fatty) tissue is formed on the hips and chest. The face is fuller. The legs become more shapely as they lose their long, thin, toothpick look. The breast buds appear, and the nipples begin to darken. Nine- to 10-year-old girls are usually aware of breast development and may be concerned if there is no evidence of this (Tanner, 1973). The spurt in height growth starts a year or two before the climax of puberty. For girls the fastest growth in height and weight, on the average, is during the twelfth year. They may gain 5 to 10 cm (2 to 4 in.) in height and 3.5 to 4.5 kg (8 to 10 lb.) in weight during their peak year.

Boys do little sexual maturing until the end of late childhood, when the genital organs begin to grow. At the age of 10 years a smaller proportion of adult height is achieved than in previous years. At 11 years of age there is usually a general overall adding of fatty tissues. Body proportions of the boys become more solid, and rounding of the contours around the neck and chin becomes noticeable. There is an increase in the bone structure, bringing the skeletal structure into prominence, especially in the chest area. The peak year for gains in height and weight, on the average, is 13 or 14 years of age, when boys gain 10 to 12.5 cm (4 to 5 in.) in height and 5.5 to 6.5 kg (12 to 14 lb.) in weight. At about 11 or 12 years of age boys usually begin to show the first signs of sexual development (Root, 1973).

There is a change in *body chemistry* in prepubescence. The pituitary gland pours hormones into the bloodstream that have potent effects on growth. Other hormones have emotional effects on the children. In some cases personality traits change or behavior patterns become different. Children may withdraw temporarily from their family, they may react with irritation over little things that never bothered them before, and they have some strong rebellious feelings that manifest themselves in unexpected ways. They have a growing awareness of sex and sex differences. They are concerned about the appearance of their changing bodies. Natural developments may alarm some youngsters if they do not understand what is happening. They need information and reassurance from a competent adult they can trust.

E BERO . . . E BERO

Walking slowly along the road, I heard many voices calling from behind, "*Bubeeroo e kanimomi tabona* . . . [an uncircumcised boy]." Puzzled, I turned around, and saw a number of boys of my own age standing naked and pointing at their circumcised *kabanga* [penis]. I began to ask myself, "How long should I remain uncircumcised?" By the age of ten, there was a general feeling that all boys should be circumcised. Yet I remained the only one left.

How unfortunate I was. If only I was not born to be a boy, I would have not encountered such mocking remarks. However, it was really my fault since I had once been told to present myself to the local doctor. Instead I had fled away defiantly, thinking that a whole part of my penis would be cut off. I remained strong and firm in my decision that I should remain uncircumcised.

Then one evening there was a social gathering in the village *maneaba* [meeting hall] in which everyone in the village participated. It so happened that I was there with those boys who had previously teased me for being uncircumcised. A number of pretty young girls were present; therefore it promised to be an enjoyable evening. But for me it turned out to be one of my worst! A middle-aged man came up to me and commanded me to stand up in front of those who were present. I did not know what he had in mind until he grabbed hold of the *lavalava* that was tied around my waist. Immediately I heard people shouting, "*E Bero . . . E Bero* . . . [an uncircumcised boy (similar to *Bubeeroo e kanimomi tabona* but spoken in a different way)]." Everyone laughed mockingly at me. I could not do anything but remain standing, naked and dumfounded. Then I felt myself being lifted up, and I heard the sound of footsteps slowly moving away from the hall. I could hear a faint sound of people talking and laughing but could not figure out who they were. The last thing I remember was an injection; I then lapsed into unconsciousness.

I was still sleeping when I heard a cock crow, "*Ten tereekoo* [sound made by crowing cock]" followed by another, then another; the morning was filled with this sound. I woke up half asleep, and as I tried to lift myself up from bed, I felt something unusual between my legs. I made another attempt to stand up, but this time I looked down. With a shock I realized that I had been circumcised. It was all over, and from then on I knew what had been done to me that previous evening.

Clumsily I arose from my bed and tried to make my way out of the house. I did not realize until I got outside that the rest of the family members had been watching me. I received a smile from my father and words of congratulation, "You're now no longer a boy," he said. I felt relieved then that I was escaping from childhood. I made my way to the sea to have my bath.

And that was how I got circumcised; otherwise I would have remained *boci* [Fijian word for an uncircumcised boy] as the Fijians called it. Despite my initial disappointment, it was an important step toward growing up.

From Stewart, R.A.C. (Ed.). *Pacific profiles.* Suva, Fiji: University of The South Pacific Extension Services, 1982.

SEXUAL AWARENESS AND SEX INFORMATION

One of the characteristics of society in recent years has been a less restricted approach to sex and sexuality in the mass media. The availability of pictorial and printed material on the topic of sex, the open display of nudity and sexual behavior in films, and the innuendos on television have subjected individuals of all ages to behaviors and suggestions that in the past were treated with more restraint (Miller and Simon, 1980). What effect this exposure has or will have on today's children is open to speculation.

Psychosexual development and awareness

Sexual awareness begins long before puberty. In a general way it may be said that in earliest infancy children are exposed to environmental stimuli that affect the development of sexuality. Babies' bodies are washed, examined, dressed, and caressed. They are picked up, fed, and rocked. Almost all their feelings of pleasure and security come from some form of physical contact. The importance of the quality of physical contact provided by mothers is indicated by the studies of Harlow and Suomi (1970) with infant monkeys. Monkeys exposed to a "hard-surface" surrogate mother made of chicken wire did not develop as healthy a sexuality in adulthood as did the monkeys exposed to a soft mother.

It is when the child enters school that he or she learns the true meaning of sex differences and sex roles. The boys tend to belong to one group, and the girls to another. A number of activities and situations, such as separate lavatory facilities, increase the awareness of differences. Feelings of modesty develop in earnest.

The child from 5 to 8 years of age has many questions related to sex. Questions such as "How does a baby get inside the mother?" and "Does the mother's egg ever go into the father?" and "How does the baby breathe inside the mother?" are often asked. Six-year-olds are usually satisfied with a simple explanation, but an 8-year-old may need a more detailed answer. Mild forms of sex play between members of the same sex or with the opposite sex are not unusual because they are curious and interested in each other's bodies. By 8 years of age there is some interest in peeping, provocative giggling, and in writing or whispering words dealing with sex or elimination functions. This interest and activity increases during late childhood.

The late childhood youngster generally socializes with his or her own sex. This is a period when emotional identification is with the peers of one's own sex. Just because there is less connection between the two sexes at this time, it does not mean that they are not aware of each other. It is during the preadolescent years that boys draw the female anatomy, look through mail-order catalogues in the section showing pictures of women modeling lingerie, and try to get their hands on pornographic literature. Girls are not all innocent. Some of them also draw pictures, read and write notes with sexual implications, and engage in double-meaning talk among themselves.

Preadolescent girls show an interest in their new physical developments, not only of their own but also of other girls their age. Many look ahead to the day when they can wear a brassiere. Fortunately, manufacturers have recognized the desire and need for a very small brassiere so that even small-breasted girls can qualify when contemporaries check on which ones are wearing brassieres. Not all girls, however, are pleased or proud of their breast development. Some are embarrassed and hunch their shoulders in an effort to hide their development. For most girls, however, this initial embarrassment will be alleviated by 12 or 13 years of age, and they will exchange their loose blouses for sweaters and T-shirts. By 11 years of age most girls have some knowledge about menstruation, intercourse, and reproduction.

Most preadolescent boys, especially at the age of 9 or 10 years, do not feel free to discuss sex matters with their parents. If they do ask questions, they do so at inopportune times for discussion, indicating their immaturity in such matters. Some 10-year-olds will still think that being married is essential for having babies. They still have to learn about the functions of marriage and the importance of the family for the birth and rearing of a baby. An 11-year-old is starting to realize that marriage involves personal relationships that go beyond mating and that someone does not have to be married to have a baby (Bernstein, 1976). Spontaneous erections occur among some 11-year-old boys, caused by such things as physical movements, conversations, pictures, daydreams, and general excitement of any kind, not necessarily sexual in nature. As at all ages, boys are more likely than girls to tell smutty jokes and write four-letter words in public places. They do not completely understand why these words and jokes are emotionally loaded, but they do know that "it sure gets adults."

Sexuality and sexual learning

Some children experience sex play during or before the preadolescent years. Children are experimentalists and curious. The sex play is incidental and transitory in nature. It is not due to love relationships or to a sex urge, since organic development has not yet begun. It is play and not lovemaking. Whether or not emotional scars or guilt feelings result depends a great deal on how the behavior is handled by the parents if such play has been discovered or if the children view their actions as something wrong in the eyes of their parents or God.

Elias and Gebhard (1969) did a study on sex and ***sexuality*** with a sample population of 305 boys and 127 girls, ages 8 to 12 years, grouped by occupational class of the parents. Part of the research was related to sex play engaged in before reaching puberty. The study reported that sex play before puberty involving more than oneself had been experienced by 52% of the boys with other boys and 34% of the boys with girls. In the sample of girls 35% had sex play with other girls, and 37% had heterosexual experiences. The average age for some sex play among boys was 9.2 years and for heterosexual play was 8.8 years. The same study revealed that although boys and girls from blue-collar homes learn at an earlier age about intercourse, abortions, and prostitution (average age range 8 to 10 years), children from white-collar homes (middle-class socioeconomic status) surpass the others in total knowledge in all categories of sex information surveyed. The girls from the lower-class homes were pathetically lacking about some extremely vital information. For example, more of these girls knew more about coitus than they did about the cause of pregnancy; many were unaware of "where babies come from."

Schofield (1965) cites a study of 934 boys and 939 girls designed to determine when they first found out about the facts of life. The research indicated that 67% of the boys and 76% of the girls had such information by the age of 12 or 13 years. The implication is that the time for giving sex information should be no later than late childhood, since after that age period there would be a need for reeducation because of incomplete facts or misinformation learned previously. Most sex learning during this period comes from the peer group and often brings with it many misconceptions. Eighty-eight percent of the boys in the blue-collar group and 70% of the boys in the middle-class group received their sex knowledge from their peer group (Athanasiou, 1973).

sexuality the characteristics of an individual in relation to sexual attitudes or activity.

COGNITION AND SCHOOL LEARNING

As children grow from the ages of 9 to 12 years, there is major improvement in their ability to do more complicated intellectual tasks. According to Bruner (1964) this cognitive development is illustrated (1) by an increased ability to see significant details in a situation and to detect absurdities, (2) by more sensible answers to questions, (3) by using words more correctly and defining abstract words more precisely, (4) by making generalizations from verbal and mathematical relationships, and (5) by exhibiting a larger fund of general information. They are better able to use information they already know to make judgments or deductions in areas that are only indirectly related to the information. Development of cognitive abilities during the concrete operations stage (ages 7 to 12 years) of Piaget was presented in Chapter 8. The reader is referred to that chapter for a theoretical interpretation of cognitive development for this age level.

Cognitive abilities and schooling

Children of this age are seeking reality in social and physical relationships. Not only are they interested in the immediate but also in matters well removed from them in time and place. Their sense of time and space has developed sufficiently so that their thinking reaches backward into ancient lands and times and forward into the world of tomorrow. They are fascinated by faraway places and distant times. They are collectors of facts as well as of baseball pictures, international dolls, and seashells.

Children's oral or spoken vocabularies are about 3,600 words at the age of 8 years, 5,400 words at 10 years, and 7,200 words at 12 years. By sixth grade their reading vocabulary will average 50,000 words (Wolman and Barker, 1965). Words with special meaning and limited use, such as a science, social studies, or health vocabulary, are learned at this time. Sixth graders should know how to use a dictionary, an encyclopedia, a card catalogue, and an atlas. They should understand the use of footnotes and an index.

Current verbal idioms or slang and swear words become part of the vocabulary, more so for boys than for girls (Dalle, 1976). A new form of language, a secret language, may be developed at this time for use in communication with intimate friends. The language may be in written form using a code, in verbal form using "pig Latin" or clicking tongue sounds, or in kinetic form using fingers or gestures.

Girls as a group are better than boys in word building, sentence completion tests, and rote memory (Maccoby and Jacklin, 1974). They write longer compositions and use longer sentences. Generally, girls make higher marks in language arts. Boys and girls, as a group, like to read books about travel, biography, science, nature, home, and school. There is a great range of reading ability in late childhood. A range of reading achievement of 2 years above and 2 years below the grade level is usual within the class. In a heterogeneous classroom of sixth graders the reading ability can range from third to tenth grade.

Boys excel in abilities involving number manipulation and in arithmetical reasoning (Benbow and Stanley, 1980). A boy's ability to reason in the fourth, fifth, and sixth grades seems to be better than that of girls. Numbers take on new meaning. Schoolwork in math helps this age level to formulate more definite ideas of space and distance. Children can estimate short intervals of time more accurately at the age of 12 than at 6 years; in childhood boys do better than girls in this sort of perception.

Most children show the onset of permanent memory by 4 years of age. For some, however, it comes as late as the eighth year. Memory span for digits increases to six digits between fourth and sixth grade.

Meriem Kaluger

Societies that are not living in a subsistence economy (survival level) but have some free time for other matters always provide some type of education for their children. In Chimbu province of the highlands of New Guinea, history and legends of the tribe are passed on by the elders to children of pubertal age.

Meriem Kaluger

Schooling is formal in China, making use of the abacus instead of calculators.

David Strickler

Refugee children from Viet Nam usually adapt quickly to Western style education.

The Daily Tale

WEATHER

It will rain cats and dogs today.

LOCAL ROBBERY

Tom, the piper's son allegedly stole a pig last night. He was last seen fleeing the scene of the crime.

CAT COMES BACK

Be on the lookout for a strange talking cat who keeps returning to the area. He can be identified by his hat. He always wears the same one. See photo below.

Staff Photo

Wanted

Six inch brass bed. Call T. Thumb at 555-6753.

★ ★ ★

Wanted

Twenty bedroom house with ten bathrooms and very large kitchen. Call old woman tired of shoe.

★ ★ ★

Lost

Three pairs of mittens. Three flealined furries crying at home. If found call 555-6739.

Staff photo

Fourth graders published a newspaper with "news" stories based on incidents from children's stories and fairy tales.

RECENT U F O SIGHTINGS

Witnesses across the state reported several sightings of unidentified flying objects this week.

The first report involved an object that looked like a cow jumping over the moon. Also seen in the area were a cat playing a fiddle and a dish and spoon were seen in nearby skies.

In another part of the state, residents described a boy-shaped object wearing a green hat, green panty hose, and a green suit.

Accident

At 3:30 A.M. today Humpty Dumpty had a great fall. He was rushed to General Hospital. He may need open shell surgery.

Staff Photo

HEALTH DEPARTMENT INSPECTS RESTAURANT

A customer reported that he went into a local restaurant and ordered a piece of pie. When he took a bite, 24 blackbirds flew up in his face. He immediately reported the incident to the County Health Inspector. Investigation will begin this morning.

★ ★ ★

Guinness World Record Broken

The record for having the longest nose has been broken this week. The new record holder explained that his nose grows each time he tells a lie.

Staff Photo

THOUGHT FOR THE DAY:

Don't talk to chickens—they use fowl language!

early maturers preadolescents who reach their physical maturity earlier than average for their sex

late maturers preadolescents who reach their physical maturity later than average for their sex.

Children remember what they see longer than what they hear. Words need to be reinforced by pictures. Memorizing is impeded by boredom, worry, a scolding, or daydreaming. It is not unusual for a boy in this age bracket to remember batting averages, completed passes, or the make, model, and year of most cars on the road, but it is difficult for him to remember how much is eight times nine or that he was to take out the trash.

Power of attention gradually increases. Many of an adult's complaints about children's inability to give attention is a wrong appraisal. Children are probably not interested in the thing they are asked to learn or attend to. They are more interested in learning what they want to know than in what the teacher may want to teach. A boy is curious and loves to manipulate objects. He is a creative thinker. He is a questioner. A girl is more likely to remember the details of such things as a presidential campaign. A boy is more likely to question its purpose (Chapman, 1978). Boys outclass girls in mathematics, science, and creative thinking.

In discussing sex differences in verbal, arithmetical, and spatial abilities, two points should be stressed. First, the differences, although consistent over studies, are small (Hyde, 1981). Second, reference to the differences is in terms of an average score, which means that there will be some girls who are better than boys in math and spatial abilities and some boys who are better than girls in verbal abilities.

There is some evidence that the timing of sexual maturity, in terms of early or late maturity, is related to specific abilities. Waber (1977) found that ***late maturers*** were better at visual-spatial tasks than early maturers, regardless of sex. Another study of 6,000 students (Carlsmith et al., 1983) found that girls who matured late matched or outscored their male age mates in mathematical ability. Also, ***early maturing*** boys had better verbal skills than late maturers. In summary, early maturation appears to favor verbal skills. Late maturation favors spatial and mathematical abilities. Since females, on the average, mature earlier than males, the rate of physical maturation may be a determinant of sex differences in ability. Additional information on early and late maturers is presented in Chapter 10.

Between 7 and 11 years of age children are still not capable of formal logical thought. They try to justify their judgments, yet they are often unable to share the point of view of the person with whom they are conversing. By the age of 12 years this special condition of childhood has faded. Children are now able to see the point of view of the person with whom they are talking. No longer do they ask questions as if answers are always possible and as if unforeseen circumstances never intervene in the course of events.

Descriptive mental characteristics

Most 9-year-olds are fairly responsible and dependable. They understand explanations and try to do things well. They have some original ideas and interests and are capable of carrying them out, although not always. They do have many interests and will often drop a project when their attention wanes. They may go on to another project or activity, never finishing the original project. However, their attention span is somewhat longer than that of 8-year-olds, and they are capable of concentrating on a particular subject for a longer period of time. Girls may spend longer on a task than boys do. At 9 years of age children are becoming critical of their performance and may work hard to perfect a skill. They want and need to be good at physical and mental skills so that they can get the admiration of other children.

In general, 10-year-olds are less enthusiastic about rote learning and drill exercises as compared to 9-year-olds. At 10 years children are developing a growing capacity for abstract thinking. They ask many searching questions and want thoughtful answers. They are now aware that people have many varying opinions and that different adults, even among those they admire, have different standards of right and wrong, good and bad. They are sensitive to lying, cheating, and unfairness and may turn on anyone with indignation if they suspect this kind of behavior. They are becoming aware of differences among people and of social problems. Their ideas are broadening, and their attitudes and prejudices are being formed. They cannot understand why there are hungry people and criminals. Why doesn't somebody do something about

David Strickler

Ten-year-olds generally have an expanding curiosity about the world around them. If you put Japanese beetles in the bottom of a soda bottle, will they remain there or will they fly into the bottle placed on top of the other one? Observing just for the sake of observing and learning.

it? In an elementary way they are interested in discussing social concerns.

Many 11-year-olds are rounding out their childhood years and are alert to what it means to grow up. They often seem to be looking curiously and eagerly, but with some apprehension, to adolescence. They are concerned about their own physical and mental development as they approach puberty. These preadolescents are intensely realistic—even imaginative activites are applied in concrete ways. It is a time for eager absorption of information and accumulation of ideas. They ask many questions. Most of their questions are scientific in nature, dealing with the physical world. Almost half their questions concern social studies, an area into which they are just now beginning to gain some insight. They understand the significance of the natural laws of science, but they are just beginning to feel their way with the social realm.

SOCIAL BEHAVIOR IN LATE CHILDHOOD

By the age of 9 years most children will have made the change from being family oriented in activities and control to being members of their own age group. The group begins to have a tremendous influence on the attitudes, desires, and behavior of the child—an influence that increases as the child grows older and becomes an adolescent. Late childhood is a transitional period, during which the social patterns and behavioral characteristics of childhood change to those that are considered more typical of adolescence. Specifically, the social behavior characteristics of preadolescence stem from three basic attitudes. First, there is strong desire to be with age mates of one's own sex (Asher et al., 1977). Second, there is a loyalty to a gang or group composed of other children similar in age, sex, size, and interests (Hartup, 1970). Third, there is a change in regard to authority, expressed largely by a seeming resistance to adult standards (Bossard and Boll, 1966).

Social structure in preadolescence

Williams and Smith (1980) suggest there are five functions of peer group socialization for middle and late childhood. First, the function of companionship, whereby close friendships are formed and wherein much social give-and-take involving a wide variety of activities occurs. Second, the peer group is basically self-controlling and, as such, provides some independence from adults. Groups of children set up different rules from those desired by adults with respect to acceptable behavior.

A third function of the peer group at this age is to serve as a source of information on a wide variety of topics. Very often the information supplied by the peer group is more strongly believed than that offered by parents or teachers (Berndt, 1979). Fourth, middle and late childhood youngsters become more aware of rules and how they govern behavior. The rules are in terms of "what you are supposed to do" rather than things not to do. Breaking the rules results in some form of punishment. Children learn the importance of conformity to group values. Fifth, a sense of sex identity, based on same-sex neighborhood peer groups, is provided.

Social development and change take place rapidly in late childhood. Children no longer want to play at home alone or do things with members of the family. One or two friends are not enough. They want to be with the "gang," their play group. The gang gives them a feeling of belonging and of being liked. Learning to live in the social world, however, is hard for children, especially if they have not received preparatory training for it at home during their earlier years (Asher et al., 1979). The gang members will work it out and help each other. Unfortunately there is a survival element in the give-and-take of group interaction, and some "hurts" will be encountered. Some children will not make the grade and will have to go into adolescence socially unprepared or as misfits.

During late childhood, boys tend to develop a social structure separate from that of girls (Asher, 1978). Boys are more interested in developing and asserting their masculinity than they are in being friendly with girls. To be a "he-man" means to be tough, strong, and daring. Nicknames may crop up among the boys, such as Rocky, Speedy, or Alligator, although some street names may be used to refer to a physical characteristic, like Fat Albert. Other nicknames may evolve from the way a boy performs in a sport, such as Silky for "smooth as silk." Their toughness and adventurousness are expressed by the television programs they watch, the books they read, and the "I dare you" schemes they concoct.

This period is also the age where boys often seek to have their own hideaway. Their retreat may be a tree house, a garage, an abandoned shack, or an outdoor spot difficult to get to or find. It is their way of saying to others, "I belong here and you belong elsewhere." In spite of all this atmosphere of mystery and intrigue, the gang is rather loosely knit with no strong organizational structure and probably even without a recognized leader, except for special activities. As the boys approach the ages of 11 and 12 years, their relationships take on a more organized appearance and become more activity oriented, such as organizing a sports team or joining the Boy Scouts or the YMCA. Boys have an interest in the gang stage longer than do girls.

In late childhood the boys set the social pace; the girls generally form their own groups. Girls' groups tend to be more tightly knit than are those of boys. They are also more exclusive and formal about who can belong and who cannot. They place more demands on themselves as to how to act toward each other and what to do in certain situations (Hartup, 1978). They keep in touch with each other by writing notes in school; note writing is one of their favorite pastimes. Girls usually congregate in the home of a member of the group where there is a minimum of interference.

Girls and boys tend to travel different social routes during late childhood. Furthermore there is some bickering toward each other. Boys seem to work harder at this with their aloofness and teasing than do girls.

Boys and girls set up differing values and standards, too. The most admired qualities in boys at 11 and 12 years of age are competence in group games, ability to lead or keep a game going, and fearlessness and readiness to take a chance.

In girls, aggressive behavior is usually discouraged, unless it might be in a game against the boys. Some girls, however, do get involved in what used to be exclusively the boys' sex role. They may take part in Little League softball, soccer, and other sports. Disturbances in the classroom are frowned on by girls. For girls, prestige demands such qualities as being friendly, attractive, and more "grownup." They are taught to control aggression, including assertion and extension, while being encouraged to regard the familial world as the proper sphere of their interest (Black, 1973). Differing value patterns for boys and girls can, in part, be attributed to an earlier maturity status in girls during these years of growth.

Friendships in later childhood

In addition to the gang or group phenomenon, personal friendships are important to preadolescents. The number of close friends does not increase, but the intensity of the friendship does (Rubin, 1980). The behavior of "friends" might seem strange to onlookers. The more boys like one another, the more frequently they seem to get into fights (Furman and Childs, 1981). Actually they are developing loyalty and the capacity to stand up for each other. Girls tend to have an on-again off-again relationship. They get angry at each other over little things and then make up again. Both boys and girls have long talks on the telephone, calling each other often. The youngsters are mostly seeking support and security from each other while going through the growing-up process.

Children choose friends who are much like themselves. The reasons given for choosing friends are primarily personal. They choose friends who are cheerful, kind, agreeable, even tempered, and loyal. Girls tend to choose one or two close friends; boys have several friends (Eder and Hallinan, 1978). As children grow older, they show a preference for responsibility in their friends and for children of their own socioeconomic and racial groups (Munsinger, 1975). Frequent associations, such as the same grade in school or the same neighborhood, and similarity of interest, age, and social maturity are other factors frequently found among friends.

A statement should be made concerning boy-girl relationships in fifth and sixth grades. Not all prepubertal boys and girls are unmindful of the opposite sex. In some communities and subcultures there are children of these grades or ages who are interested in the opposite sex because the peer culture encourages it. Some are even dating before entering seventh grade. Cultural and social influences have been stressing boy-girl relationships, albeit on an older age level, through television, movies, comics dealing with romance, and books. Some parents consider boy-girl relationships a sign of growing up.

Emerging social independence and the family

Even though the home and family will continue to be a major emotional focus for some time to come, the preadolescent child is taking increasing interest in people outside the home. Consequently, contacts with family members become fewer, less influential, and less meaningful than contacts with persons outside the family unit.

As early as the age of 6 years, when they enter school, children become more independent than previously by virtue of being on their own and by making more independent decisions. By the age of 8 years they make an important discovery—they suddenly realize that adults can make mistakes, that they do not know everything, and that they can be criticized. They are capable of detecting inconsistencies between what parents say is the right thing to do and what they see adults doing. This knowledge provides a giant step toward self-autonomy.

Because of increasing intellectual development, 9- to 12-year-olds reach a point where they can see more clearly the shortcomings of adults. They may challenge the thinking and decisions of persons in positions of authority. Soon they reject or question many of the standards of their parents and of adults in general. This characteristic does not imply that the children become discipline and behavior problems, but it does mean that they are not as ready to accept rules and standards unquestioningly as they did at an earlier age. Clashes may result, overtly or covertly.

Children from 8 through 11 years tend to be willful, critical, easily discouraged, and rejecting of rules and standards that they previously respected (Bossard and Boll, 1966). They begin to wonder about adult intellectual and behavioral competency. A sixth grader was

Harold Geyer

Becoming a member of an organized group not only leads to an expanded social development and the learning of social skills but is also a step toward social independence.

asked to write an essay for his English lesson on the subject of parents. He commented, "We get our parents when they are so old it is very hard to change their habits or to educate them."

Piaget (1955), in discussing the moral judgment of children, suggests that a change takes place in children's relationship to authority at ages 9 or 10 years. He suggests that at the age of 8 or 9 years children begin to respond to the standards of their peers. It is at that age that Piaget finds children beginning to reject adult standards.

Although friction within family relationships may increase, families are still a most significant part of the children's social life (Hartup, 1976). Members of the family can help or hinder the children in their social adjustment process by the way in which they are treated, respected, trusted, loved, and permitted to grow. Personality and adjustment of the parents, parental expectations, methods of child training used, socioeconomic status, parental occupations, and solidarity of the family are all factors that influence the type of relationship preadolescent children have with different family members. These are critical years in adult-child relationships. If children break away from their families, they will have only the judgment and influence of their gang to guide them. Rejecting attitudes of this period will only become more intensified during the adolescent years.

Children's perspective of their parents may change at this age. Their concept of "mother" is usually still primarily in terms of what she does for them. The concept of "father" depends on how the father has been relating to his children. If he has delegated the job of raising the children to the mother and has been more-or-less an outsider providing for the material needs of the family, the children may never develop a close relationship with him because of the distance between them in past years. In fact he may even be rejected if the children had an image of what the ideal father should be like and their father failed to live up to it. On the other hand, if the father has been responsive to his children during their developing years, he may now assume an even greater role of importance in their eyes (Lynn, 1974).

THOUGHTS ON BASEBALL

A player's thoughts

Woke up this morning feeling pretty good. Should be a good game tonight. Let's see, their record is 0-8. This should be a pushover. My batting average will probably go up to at least .450. What must I do today—cut the grass and go swimming. Coach said I shouldn't tire myself. Will have to watch what I eat before the game. Don't want to eat too much and not feel well.

The grass is finished. Will go for a short swim. Can only stay until 2:30. Have to be home to rest for a while.

Mom is always rushing me and making sure I have the cleanest uniform on the field. Where did Mom put my socks? Oh, here they are in my drawer. Wonder where she put my belt when she washed my pants.

Dog-gone-it! I told her I didn't want to eat too much. Come on, I want to be at the field before everyone else to get a little practice in on batting. Well, I'm late again. Everyone else has their shoes on and are throwing. Darn shoelaces—have to remember to tell Mom to get me new ones.

I start tonight—thought I would. This pitcher looks like a piece of cake. My throws to home are a little off tonight. Will have to remember that. Greg is pitching tonight—probably won't have too many hits and those who do hit will be swinging late.

This pitcher has more than what it looks like. Two strikes, one ball. He will probably waste one, a curve. It is, and what a hit! The coach says to hold up. Bunt signal is on. Good bunt. Both safe. Pitch and go for third. Ha, ha, another stolen base. Jimmy just hit a home run. That will bring three of us across. Good lead to start the game with.

If things go right, I will get up in the second inning. I hope I get the bunt signal. Look where the third baseman is playing.

Dog-gone-it! Mr. Mack is taking us all out and letting the others play. Well, I guess he knows what he is doing, but it sure is disgusting sitting here waiting for these guys to do something.

Well, next week is another game. It will be much tougher so we will probably play the whole game. Have to go over and shake those guys' hands.

A sister's thoughts

Oh, no, we have to go home early again today because of baseball. Why do we always have to go home early because of a dumb baseball game? Guess I'll jump in the pool one more time before it's time to leave.

Okay, I'm coming now. Why do we always have to go home because of baseball! Always when it's nice—we have to go home! Sure will be glad when baseball season is over.

Yes, I'm hurrying to get the table set. The milk is poured. Don't see why we always have to go to the baseball game. It's no fun! Just go and sit there! Can't see why Natalie and I just can't stay at home. Well, better get something to drink and our Barbies. Then we can just sit in the car. . . . Well, might just as well watch the game for a little while. Keith is up to bat. Hope he hits it. He didn't even hit it. Why is he going to the base? Now, what's that kid's name? I think it's Davey. Boy, he hit the ball way out to the fence. Keith can run fast.

Wonder how much longer until this game is over. I'm going to the car.

A father's thoughts (as a coach)

Won't be able to finish this tonight. Keith has a baseball game tonight and I must get home in time to line the field.

Hope dinner is ready on time. I want to get to the field early and rake it out and line it.

Keith will have to leave when I do. I will need some help lining up the foul lines and setting up the batting boxes.

I want to get the boys together before the game and give them a little pep talk. This other team's record is not too good, but they are the type of team that will really put one on you if given half the chance.

George, you take third tonight. I'll go on first. Ray, you warm up with Bob while we are on the field. I want you to be good and warm. Randy hasn't pitched that much this year and he may tire.

These kids just are not watching for the signals tonight. They can steal the catcher anytime—especially when the pitcher looks only once.

George, I don't think you should make these changes with only a three run lead. Bob feels the same. I realize you want to get everyone in the game but let's not do it at the team's expense.

Well, we lucked out on this one. Tomorrow is the big one. Let's get these things packed up and go get them tomorrow.

A mother's thoughts

Guess I'd better get the kids over to the pool for a little bit. Won't have much time because we have a game tonight. Better get the potatoes pared while they're getting their suits on. Really should stay home and run the sweeper, but then I haven't been to the pool with them this week.

Why can't they remember their own towels and pool cards? If only they'd put them away, so they'd know where they are. Someone is always forgetting something!

It hardly seems worthwhile. Seems like we just got here and it's time to go home. The girls are going to be complaining again. It will be nice when baseball season is over, but I sure will miss it.

Hope that meat is about done. It's a good thing I got the potatoes ready before we left.

Keith's suit is washed and hanging in the basement. His belt is in the drawer. Hope he remembers to put on clean socks. Oh, no, I forgot to get some new shoelaces.

It hardly seems worthwhile rushing around cooking. Seems like we just had lunch. With all this hurrying around, no one is even hungry. It sure will be nice getting back on schedule and eating at a decent time instead of the middle of the afternoon.

Only missed the first half of the inning. Our team is up to bat. We should win tonight. The opponents don't have a very good record. Hope Gene doesn't holler too much tonight. Hope the coach didn't tell them the game was a pushover. That's why they lost the last time.

Oh, no, Keith is at bat. This sure makes me nervous. Hope he doesn't strike out. Now why did George tell him to bunt? Well, at least, he got on base. Maybe he'll score a run. Wish he wouldn't take such a long lead off the base. Oh, good! Jim got a home run. That gives us a three run lead. If Ed had only called time before he got off the base, we'd have four runs. Wish Gene hadn't hollered so at him. I know he should have known better but . . .

Thank goodness, they won that game! They almost lost it by putting in the second team. Oh well, it's just another game.

BIRTH ORDER AND CHARACTERISTICS

birth order the order of birth in a family, which often affects the child's personality because of differential parental treatment.

No two children living in the same family, not even twins, have exactly the same environment. Each has a different combination of brothers and sisters as well as a different length of time for being the only or the youngest child. Each develops a unique self-concept and personality. Each has a different position in the family and different roles to play. Generally there is agreement that the order of birth does influence a child's development, although this varies with the nature and the sex of the child, the number, age, and spacing of siblings, and favorable or unfavorable parental attitudes (Trotter, 1976).

Studies that have been made correlating achievement with ***birth order*** reveal some interesting information. The five U.S. presidents at or near the top in virtually every ranking—George Washington, Abraham Lincoln, Thomas Jefferson, Woodrow Wilson, and Franklin D. Roosevelt—were all firstborns. Of the first 23 astronauts to go on U.S. space missions, 21 were either the eldest or only children. Nearly 60% of the finalists for National Merit Scholarships are firstborns. There is no reliable evidence that firstborns have more intellect (McCall and Johnson, 1972). Rather, the way they are raised makes them more achievement oriented (Zajonc, 1976). Let's take a look at how children tend to be treated according to their ordinal position in a family. Keep in mind that these generalizations fit large groups of people, but they do not hold up when applied to individual families (Grotevant et al., 1977).

The firstborn child

It can be generalized that firstborn children are usually much more responsive to their parents than are their brothers and sisters. They try hard to conform to parental expectations and to the adult world. They show more zeal, perseverance, and drive than their siblings. They seem to have a higher achievement motive as well as a higher degree of responsibility (Adams and Phillips, 1972; Zajonc and Markus, 1975).

The studies of Zajonc and others have sought to delineate these effects and to postulate causes for them. They found that firstborn children internalize parental expectations with a resulting sense of stronger moral responsibility. They feel that this sense of responsibility is due primarily to the oldest children's having to fulfill parental surrogate functions for their siblings, thus inculcating a high degree of responsibility in later childhood. This same dilution of parental attention, however, may lessen the sense of responsibility of the younger siblings and heighten their peer orientation.

Many firstborn children are considerably more creative than later-born children. This effect is caused by the parental relationships with their initial children. The parents tend to be anxious and protective. These children receive more verbal and physical stimulation than do successive children (Booth, 1981). Their achievement of each developmental stage in growth is appreciated and reinforced by their parents. When other children are born, they tend to look to the first child as a leader for ideas (Cicirelli, 1975). This factor stimulates the firstborns' creative production and reduces that of their siblings, who learn to rely on others for their creative needs.

With the arrival of the second child, firstborns must make adjustments. Eventually they resolve their feelings of jealousy and become the leaders for their siblings. In a sense they could be called the trailblazers for their brothers and sisters. They tend to have a high level of responsibility, since it is their job to care for their siblings (Breland, 1974). As the eldest they are often held responsible for the actions of their younger followers. These factors all seem to indicate definite trends in the development of firstborn children.

The middle child

Middle children often have a difficult position within the family. Their parents have a different attitude toward their second and subsequent children, since they now feel experienced. They are more relaxed and employ trial-and-error less frequently. Middle children are permanently faced with the problem of comparison with their older sibling. They may receive hand-me-down clothes and toys. Not only must they compete with their older sibling, but there are younger children who steal their status as the babies of the family.

Middle children are allowed more freedom to be themselves and to explore their surroundings with less restrictions. Their displacement is usually not as

Meriem Kaluger

Birth-order studies usually discuss only the firstborn, the middle child, and the last born. What if there are more than three children in a family; what characteristics do they develop? As with* any *child, much depends on the timing of birth and the type of attention given the child by the family.

severe as that of the firstborn when another baby arrives since they have always shared their parents. However, they may still feel a little pushed aside and lacking in their due of affection and attention. Sometimes they may exhibit hostility toward their older and younger siblings, regretting the authority of the firstborn and the helplessness of the baby.

The second-borns tend to be calm and relaxed persons. They make the best out of life and seek pleasure. Conversely, third-borns do not resolve their difficulties as middle children. They tend to be restrained and have difficulty getting along with others.

The last-born child

Last-born children grow up in a complicated family situation, since they must interact with their parents and all their siblings. There is a tendency on the part of some parents to prolong the babyhood of these children (Segal and Yahraes, 1979). The parents are older and usually have a stronger financial position. Thus the parents tend to indulge these children, and discipline may even break down. Their siblings also tend to intercede for these children and make contacts for them. Life is a relatively easy matter for the youngest children. Although these conclusions may be overgeneralized, they do show the basic trend of sibling interactions toward last-born children.

Tomeh (1970) found a tendency for last-born girls to visit with friends more often than for other girls. She concluded that this result shows that last-born children have a greater affinity toward their peers than firstborn children. She attributes this outcome to the fact that parents relax their expectations for their last child.

BIRTH ORDER AND CHARACTERISTICS

FIRSTBORN

- Tend to be highly motivated, ambitious, and successful due to parental expectations.
- Likely to succeed in fields where seriousness, intellectual prowess, and high goals are valued.
- Usually conform and adhere to rules; a carry-over of conformity to parental wishes.
- Have highly developed standards and considerable organizational ability but cautious and usually conservative.
- Behave in a mature fashion because of association with adults; are expected to assume responsibilities in the family.
- May not have self-confidence that might be expected of a successful person because of pressure of parental demands or of being replaced as center of attention by the second child.
- Usually successful in school but not particularly popular.

MIDDLEBORN

- Likely to perceive self as less skillful than the firstborn.
- Usually turn to nonacademic endeavors, such as sports, the arts, or physical and action-oriented activities.
- Tend to pick up unconventional ideas or philosophies, possibly as a means of getting back at an oppressive older person.
- May turn to outsiders for peer companionship; more cooperative with peers and less dependent on elders.
- Usually easygoing, cheerful, gentle, not anxious, and not overly concerned with achievement.

LASTBORN

- May resemble firstborn because of being the center of attention for a long time and being somewhat spoiled; tend to be babyish for longer period.
- Tend to underachieve because of fewer parental expectations and demands.
- Have fewer resentments and a great feeling of security as a result of never being replaced by a younger sibling.
- May be willful and demanding as a result of more relaxed parental treatment and less strict discipline.
- Unlikely to develop feelings of independence if not given responsibilites.
- Often quite popular and experiences good social relationships outside the home; have to learn how to negotiate, accommodate, and tolerate.

ONLY CHILD

- Usually more achievement oriented and more dependent than firstborn because of strong parental demands.
- Likely to become self-centered, viewing themselves as unfairly treated; may refuse to cooperate.
- May have some difficulty in relating to peers; often seek out the company of adults.

Compiled from Booth, 1981; Finley and Cheyne, 1976; Segal and Yahraes, 1979; Snow, 1981; Sutton-Smith and Rosenberg, 1970; Zajonc and Markus, 1975.

While the firstborn is adult oriented, the last child is free to establish contacts outside the family. Thus the youngest children seem to be somewhat other directed in their search for social contacts and approval.

Last-born children, then, have greater freedom than their siblings. They are raised in a more permissive environment and tend to be less oriented to adult expectations than their brothers and sisters. These factors all have significance for the personality development of last-born children.

Evaluation of birth order studies

Although there is a composite picture of children representing sibling positions, a variety of factors such as size of family, its economic, social, and personal characteristics, the number of years between children, and so on, can negate the characteristics presented above and in the box. For example, if the sex of the second child is different or if he or she is born many years after the first child, the second child may be treated as the firstborn. Another point is that many of the studies of birth-order characteristics have been based on questionnaires and self-reports, and in particular on middle-class families; the results must be considered flimsy and weak. Nevertheless, patterns have emerged for each of the major birth-order positions, suggesting that a child's ordinal position within a family could have a significant influence on development. More precise experimental studies may yield firmer insights on the significance of birth order.

Studies on the interaction of siblings provide another insight on the limitations of current findings of birth order influences. Cicirelli (1975) found that older sisters are more likely to help younger siblings solve a problem than older brothers are; mothers were more apt to help younger siblings if they have an older brother rather than an older sister. Children from larger families seek and receive more help from one another than do children from small families. However, older children can serve as attachment figures for their younger siblings (Stewart, 1981). Younger children often imitate their older siblings (Pepler, 1981). According to Lamb (1979), siblings are more likely to interact with one another when only one parent is present in the family.

The only child

One couple out of six, of all married couples who have children, have only one child. One child in eighteen children has no brothers or sisters. The absence of siblings can have an effect on the only child's personality development.

The advantages only children realize are the effects of having parents who, in the absence of other children, have more time to devote to their supervision and to a better economic position in life. Most only children receive better medical care, food, and clothing, have their own playthings and room, and later on receive a good education. As a group, firstborn and only children hold a favored educational position. More are listed in *Who's Who in America,* and research has shown that these two groups are more destined to become good readers than middle or youngest children (Zajonc, 1976). Perhaps the greatest asset of being an only child is the feeling of security in being the sole object of the parents' affection. As a result, only children resemble firstborns in that they are dependent and achievement oriented (Segal and Yahraes, 1979).

On the other hand, only children lack the comradeship and social support of having brothers and sisters who could accustom them to being with others of similar age and interests. All is not lost, however, if parents encourage outside-the-family friendships and open their home to potential playmates. School will provide an automatic opportunity for making friends. In middle and later childhood, dancing classes, camp, and playground activities all provide social situations in which only children can seek out and respond to others and in doing so can profit by the associations. The great majority of only children grow up to become well-adjusted adult members of society.

Sex and spacing of siblings

Most of the evidence concerning the sex of and the spacing between siblings as influences on development are reported by Janis (1969). The studies show that the sex of an older sibling affects the sex-typed behavior of a younger child. Girls with older brothers tend to be more masculine; boys with older sisters seem less masculine. This finding goes along with the assumption that younger children, to some degree, identify with older siblings and imitate their desirable behavior.

The effects of birth order were found to be influenced by both factors of sex and spacing. When siblings were of the same sex and less than 2 years apart in age, few behavioral differences were found. When the spacing in age was increased to 4 years in siblings of opposite sexes, the behavioral differences became greater. The most threatening situation to the older child occurs when the age difference is between 2 and 4 years (Latham et al., 1977). This condition results from the anxiety that 2- to 4-year-old children have over the potential loss of their mothers to new babies.

EMOTIONAL BEHAVIOR IN PREADOLESCENCE

Preadolescents and parents

The emotional development of children is closely integrated with cognitive and social development. Children at this stage are greatly influenced by the way others react to them. They have the basic emotional needs of love, belonging, security, success, new experiences, and independence. Although they may exhibit less open expression of love to their parents, they still are greatly concerned about the amount of love their parents have for them. They want to be independent and express this desire in the form of back talk, disobedience, and discourtesy. Many parents at this stage feel they must have brought their children up the wrong way.

Preadolescents often daydream of wild conquests or adventures they will undertake and often engage in a fantasy life. By contrast they often go through long periods of empty daydreaming or staring into space. When asked what they are thinking about, they reply, "Nothing." And nothing may be actually what they are thinking about. Occasionally a child of this age may revert to an infantile form of behavior such as bedwetting, constant moving of legs, arms, and head, or fingernail biting. It is all too frustrating to adults. Although these types of actions are irritating to parents, what angers and troubles them most is the seeming breakdown of the solid relationship they enjoyed with their child during earlier childhood.

One reason for the resurfacing of regressive or infantile characteristics is that the childhood personality is becoming disorganized and too loose to permit the child to develop a new personality for adolescence and adulthood. It is essential for preadolescents to relinquish many of their childhood attitudes, behaviors, and habits. Internal emotional and personality changes are taking place, resulting in conflict and stress. These emotional factors, in turn, express themselves in fears, suspicion, and a withdrawal from parents and other adults. Peer standards take on significant meaning and importance for preadolescent children.

Descriptive emotional characteristics

The emotional characteristics of late childhood are both pleasant and unpleasant. They are pleasant to the children when they are releasing pent-up spirits by giggling, squirming, and using general body activity. They are unpleasant when they involve tempers, anxiety, and feelings of frustration. The emotions found at about the age of 9 are the same as those found in early childhood. The only difference is in the circumstances that give rise to the emotions and in the form of expression. Experiences and learning are responsible for the changes. Girls cry and have temper outbursts, and boys are sullen and sulky, but they both learn that violent expressions of unpleasant emotions are not acceptable to their contemporaries, so they try to control their outward expression of emotions.

There is an increase in the fear of imaginary, fanciful, or supernatural things. This age group is afraid of being "different" or of being called "chicken" or "fraidy cat." The most common worries are about the family, school, personal and social adjustment, and health. School worries are more common than out-of-school worries (Busch-Rossnagel and Vance, 1982). Girls worry more about school and safety than boys do. Generalized anxiety is more common than any one specific worry. This anxiety is greater in the child who is unpopular and, as a rule, is greater in girls. It increases in intensity for girls as they grow older (Maccoby and Jacklin, 1974). Anxiety can be strong enough in late childhood to handicap a child in learning, especially in reading and arithmetic (Phillips, 1978). Errors tend to increase their feelings of insecurity, and as a result the level of anxiety is increased, causing more errors or else inhibiting responses or attempts to learn.

Most ten-year-olds are easygoing and balanced. They seldom cry and do not anger easily. When they get angry, it is physically and emotionally violent and immediate, but it soon becomes resolved. They may plot revenge, but they seldom remember to carry it out. They seem to enjoy noise—at least they make enough of it. They have fewer worries than they do fears. Their worries center around school, such as homework, grades, and being late. They are scared of blood, ghosts, dead bodies of animals, criminals, wild animals, high places, and the dark. During the fourth and fifth grades, children may have the feeling that no one—teachers, friends, or parents—likes them, and this may result in crying sessions with the mother (Sears, 1970). No matter how much is said to allay these fears, the children remain or pretend to be adamant on the subject. They need their ego nurtured and bolstered.

The age of 11 years is an age of concern for many children. They worry about school, money, their parents' welfare, and their own health (Jersild, 1968). Some children even worry about their father's driving, family relations, and world conditions. Some of these concerns may be due to an advanced level of cognitive development but with no knowledge or insight to back up the interpretations of what is seen or experienced. Strange animals are feared most, although the child still has a great fear of being in the dark and of high places. Anger is aroused more frequently than at the age of 10 years. Physical violence is the most common response, although violent verbal retorts are also common. By this time, however, children have developed enough behavior control so that they can suppress laughter where it is inappropriate, such as in church or on a solemn occasion. Instead of laughing, they express their joviality by a twinkle of the eye, a smile through tightly compressed lips, or a meaningful clearing of the throat. Twelve-year-olds have fewer worries than they did at 11 years. School is still the main source of worries, but social and personal worries are on an increase (Rutter et al., 1976).

STAGEFRIGHT

It seems as if it happened in another lifetime, but it was only about fifteen years ago when an incident occurred that had a profound influence on my life. I was in the fifth grade when this event took place, and I can still remember it vividly. It was certainly one of the most traumatic occurrences of my life, and to this day it affects my behavior.

It was early in the day during my homeroom class. We had just finished our section on current events and were moving on to a new section. Toward the end of this section the teacher asked if anyone had an unusual hobby. I had begun to take guitar lessons, and I felt that this could be considered an unusual hobby. I didn't know many other kids who played the guitar at the age of ten. Raising my hand, I answered that I had an unusual hobby. To my later chagrin, she asked if I might like to demonstrate my musical ability to the class. My music teacher had recently said that I was definitely beginning to learn how to handle the guitar, and I was beginning to feel as if I was becoming rather good. "Why shouldn't I play for the class?" I thought to myself. Without hesitation, I volunteered to play a few songs the next time the class met. I was pretty excited about playing for the group and really felt confident. I had been playing the guitar for six months and didn't feel as if there would be any trouble. If only I had known what was in store! What transpired the next day, I'm sure, had a tremendous effect on my life even till this day.

Arriving at class a few minutes early, I quickly made my way to my seat. I had a big guitar case by my side and felt very proud. Sitting at my seat, I felt somewhat anxious, but I cannot say that I was nervous. After the usual class trivia was done, it was time. The teacher made the announcement, and I simultaneously picked up my case. Proudly I strolled to the front of the room and seated myself on a large stool. Slinging the strap over my shoulder, I faced my audience. I had picked a certain song to play because I had done this particular song many times with my teacher. I knew it so well that I didn't even need to use the music. When I felt the moment was propitious, I started to strum. Everything was okay, and I was doing fine.

Now came the vocal part, and I raised my head to look at the audience. As I looked at the thirty pair of eyes centered on me, I realized for the first time what I was doing. Here I was, at the front of the room, with everybody staring at me. As if hit by a hidden paralysis, my body tensed. I felt a sharp pain run the length of my spine, and a vertigo hit me. I felt as if I were going to topple off the stool. As if these symptoms weren't enough, my mouth felt dry and my heart felt like it was going to pound right through my chest. I wanted to run, but I knew I couldn't. Everyone was expecting a performance, and I had to perform. It seemed like an interminable length of time had lapsed since the point when the vocal part was to begin, but it was only a few seconds. My mouth opened to sing but nothing came out—I couldn't speak! No matter how hard I tried, I couldn't speak. My neck muscles were so tight, and I was so dizzy that I felt sure that I was going to faint.

The expressions on my peers' faces began to change. Everyone was smiling, and soon I was able to detect laughter. There was only one thing left to do, and I did it—I ran like hell out of that room into the hallway. Instead of the applause that I had expected to receive before this debacle started, I heard a loud derisive laughter. The teacher tried to quiet the class and explain that I had tried and shouldn't be laughed at. No matter what happened now, I knew that I was an ignominious fool. How could I face my classmates again? Suddenly I started to cry, which only made matters worse because some of my friends saw this. Now, in addition to being a coward, I was also a crybaby. The teacher tried to comfort me, but all I wanted to do was go home to my room. The teacher had enough empathy to call my father and ask him to take me home.

When I arrived home, my father showered me with platitude after platitude, trying his best to make me feel better. I didn't speak to anyone that night and tried to think of some way for me to stay home from school the next day. For some unknown reason, the next day my father took me to school an hour late. In retrospect, I think the teacher instructed him to bring me to class late so that she could have time to talk with the class. She must have really been emphatic with the class because nobody said a word to me about the incident. I approached the class with the most trepidation I had ever experienced. Somehow I got to my seat, and I was shaking like a bowl of gelatin.

I never did continue with my guitar lessons. Actually a strange hysterical reaction occurred whenever I tried to play the guitar. After a few strummings my hand would become stiff and I couldn't continue. About two weeks after the fiasco in school, I sold my guitar. I was really glad to get rid of the instrument, hoping that time would heal the wounds. It never happened. I never did forget what transpired; and until this day, some fifteen years later, I can still remember the incident vividly.

MORAL DEVELOPMENT

Children in late childhood make substantial gains in their understanding of and feelings toward right and wrong. They do have conflicts, however, between the morality of adult authority, including the home, and that of the gang. Although preteen children may assert themselves against authority, this is a period when conscience develops more fully. The home will have the most influence in religion, racial attitudes, and general ideology. The gang will have the most influence in manners, speech, and general behavior. They will make all kinds of rules of conduct for themselves, for what to wear, for the way to talk and act, and for playing games.

Children of 11 and 12 years commonly believe in justice and fair play (Crain, 1980). To this point in age the key to moral development in individuals has been their interaction with others in their environment. Intellectual speculation about right and wrong has been minimal up to now due to an inability to do much abstract reasoning. Now children are on the verge of being able to do formal logic and reasoning, and the next few years will bring about some pointed questions concerning morality.

Selman: Social role-taking skills

An area of study in cognitive development that relates to moral understanding through social reasoning is that of *social cognition*. Social cognition refers to intellectual endeavors in which the aim is to think or learn about the social processes in the self, in another person, or in groups (Flavell, 1983). Selman and Byrne (1974) have taken the role-taking aspect of social cognition and have linked it with the changes in moral judgment. ***Role taking,*** also called perspective taking, refers to the ability to emphathize with or to understand the feelings of others; to have the perspective of the other person.

perspective-taking skills the understanding, by a child, that others have perspectives that are different from his own.

role taking the ability to take the role or point of view of another person; a requirement in cognitive and other forms of development.

Selman (1976a) suggests that as a child approaches adolescence, he or she learns to reason in an increasingly complex manner so that he or she is now better able to put together such complicated thoughts as "I think that you think I think . . . ," implying a perspective of the other's point of view. The preadolescent can more readily identify the different views of others than he or she could in earlier years. Upon reaching early adolescence, the child is beginning to coordinate various thoughts about others into a cohesive "societal perspective" of people in general. The development of a perspective-taking view increases moral understanding.

Selman relates moral development to perspective or role-taking ability. ***Perspective-taking skill*** is the mature understanding of another person's capabilities,

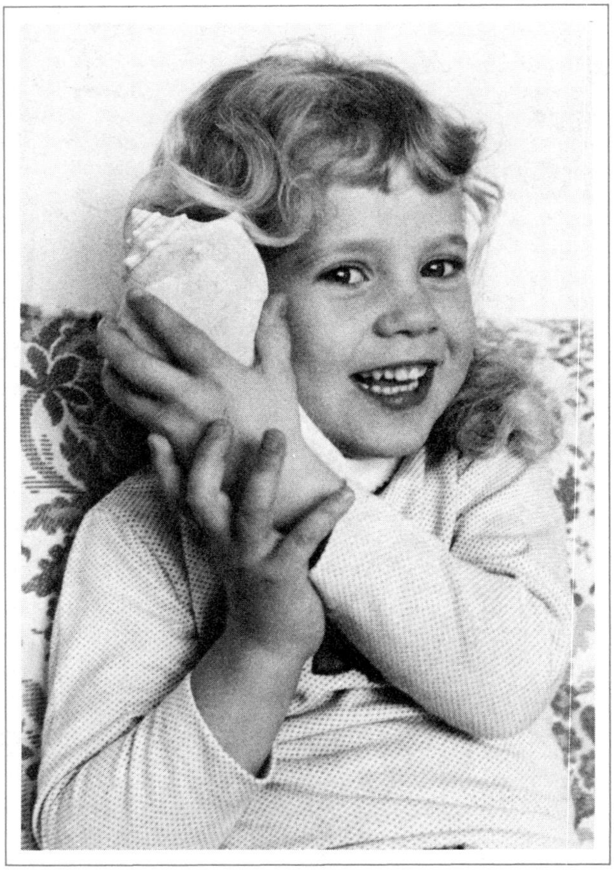

Harold Geyer

I have seen
A curious child, who dwelt upon a tract
Of inland ground, applying to his ear
The convolutions of a smooth-lipped shell,
To which, in silence hushed, his very soul
Listened intensely; and his countenance soon
Brightened with joy, for from within were heard
Murmurings, whereby the monitor expressed
Mysterious union with its native sea.

William Wordsworth
The Excursion

expectations, feelings, motives, and social judgments as a social being. Selman (1971) found a significant relationship between the ability to take the role of another and the attainment of conventional moral reasoning among 8-, 9-, and 10-year-olds. However, some childen appear to attain conventional reasoning without having to develop proficiency in role taking (Kurdek, 1978).

Selman has classified the cognitive development of perspective-taking ability into stages. Table 9–2 shows a comparison of the parallel stages of Piaget's cognitive development and Selman's perspective-taking development. The relationship of the two areas is interesting.

Between the ages of 4 and 6, children are at an egocentric, role-taking level where they do not yet distinguish between their own perspectives or ways of thinking and those of others. Some writers refer to this as stage 0. Children at this age level think that their way of viewing a moral situation is the only alternative or way of thinking. At stage 1, about ages 6 to 8, children reach the subjective role-taking level. Children have the social information to realize that others may have different ways of interpreting a situation. However, they are not aware that other people may also recognize this possibility. The subjectivity of others is understood but not that people can consider each other as subjects.

At the ages of 8 to 10, children are in stage 2, a self-reflective role-taking level. Children become aware that people think or feel differently, not just because they have different information but because they have

TABLE 9-2 Parallel stages in cognitive and perspective-taking development

*Cognitive stage (Piaget)**	*Perspective-taking stage (Selman)†*
Preoperations The "symbolic function" appears but thinking is marked by centration and irreversibility.	**Stage 1 (subjectivity)** There is an understanding of the subjectivity of persons but no realization that persons can consider each other as subjects.
Concrete operations The salient characteristics of an object are separated from action relating to it; and classification, seriation, and conservation skills develop.	**Stage 2 (self-reflection)** There is a sequential understanding that the other can view the self as a subject just as the self can view the other as a subject.
Beginning formal operations There is development of the coordination of reciprocity with inversion; and propositional logic can be handled.	**Stage 3 (mutual perspectives)** It is realized that the self and the other can view each other as perspective-taking subjects (a generalized perspective).
Early basic formal operations The hypothetico-deductive approach emerges, involving abilities to develop possible relations among variables and to organize experimental analyses.	**Stage 4 (social and conventional system)** There is a realization that each self can consider the shared point of view of the generalized other (the social system).
Consolidated basic formal operations Operations abilities are now complete and systematic.	**Stage 5 (symbolic interactions)** A social system perspective can be understood from a beyond-society point of view.

Modified from Walker, L.J. Cognitive and perspective-taking prerequisite for moral development. *Child Development,* 1980, *51,* 131-139.
*Compiled from Colby & Kohlberg. (1975).
†Compiled from Selman & Byrne (1974) and Selman (1976a).

their own particular values and interests. They can put themselves in the other person's shoes and recognize that the other person can do the same thing. Reciprocal awareness is understood. Stage 3, ages 10 to 12, is the level of mutual perspectives or mutual role taking. Children recognize that two people can look at each other's points of view and can look at both person's perspectives from the point of view of some third person (another member of the group, other children, or even a grownup). Evaluation of their view points can come from consideration of both sides plus that of an outside observer.

Stage 4, between ages 12 and 15, is the social and conventional system perspective-taking level. At this stage children recognize that mutual perspectives do not always provide the answer. Social conventions are needed so that personal reactions and beliefs can be communicated to others. These conventions will require thinking in terms of social interactions. At stage 5, ages 16 and over, the symbolic interaction level is reached. Thinking goes beyond social levels to a view that is beyond that of the conventions of society. A universal principle may be involved.

In terms of late childhood moral development, Selman suggests that moral insight is on Piaget's early concrete operations level. Children are just learning to do reasoning but are not quite ready to understand an abstract moral point of view. Piaget's moral development theory and the social learning theory were presented in Chapter 8. The social learning theory is not presented in the chart because it is not a stage theory.

CHAPTER REVIEW

1. The developmental tasks of late childhood are for the most part an extension and a refinement of the developmental tasks and the psychosocial crisis of middle childhood.
2. Physical growth is gradual but steady. The permanent teeth appear during late childhood. Physical health is at a peak because of the extraordinary amount of *lymphoid masses* that this age group has with which to fight infections. In motor coordination there are ony negligible differences between boys and girls until the age of 11 when boys improve their coordination more than girls.
3. Late childhood, the *preadolescent* years, is the prelude to puberty. Girls begin *pubertal development* about 2 years before boys. Body shape changes in both boys and girls; some fatty tissue is usually developed.
4. Sexual awareness increases during this age period. The meaning of sex differences and sex roles becomes apparent. There is a desire and a need for sex information before puberty and adolescence is reached.
5. This age level is still in Piaget's stage of concrete operations in cognitive development. However, as *Bruner* indicates, there is increased ability to see significant details, ask better questions, use language more precisely, make generalizations from relationships, and exhibit a larger fund of general information.
6. Descriptive or normative information has its limitations in terms of age-level specificity, but in general, 9-year-olds can understand explanations and have some original ideas. Ten-year-olds do not usually care much for drill activities; they are aware of varying opinions. Eleven-year-olds like to ask many questions about the physical world and are beginning to show an interest in social studies.
7. This is an age level for developing both speaking and understanding vocabularies. Girls are better than boys in verbal and written skills. Boys do better in math computation and reasoning. The edge of differences between the sexes, although consistent in the research studies, is small. Being a late or an early maturer seems to be a variable in learning. Late maturing girls are better in math. Early maturing boys do better in verbal skills.
8. There are five functions of *peer group socialization:* (a) companionship, (b) self-controlling in the setting of rules, (c) source of information, (d) teaching of group values, and (e) providing sex identity.
9. The social structure for groups of boys is loosely knit with no strong organizational structure, becoming more activity oriented with age. The social structure for groups of girls is more tightly knit than for boys, more formal in organization.
10. Friendships become more intense than previously but not necessarily greater in number. Boys tend to have a larger number of close friends than do girls.
11. Contacts with people outside the home increase as children extend their environmental boundaries. A sense of independence gradually comes as children learn that adults can be wrong. Regardless, the family is still the most significant part of the lives of children in late childhood.
12. *Birth order* and the resulting personality characteristics is an interesting topic. Although there is some consistency in the research findings, there are also a number of people who are exceptions. In general, firstborns tend to have high achievement orientations. The middle child tends to be in a difficult positon but often emerges as a calm and relaxed individual. The last-born is frequently easier going and interested in social contacts. The only child often resembles the firstborn.
13. Preadolescents can get along well with their parents if they wish to do so. They are at the peak of childhood and know how to handle the advantages of still being a child. However, since the personality pattern is beginning to change as adolescence approaches, some regression of behavior may occur.
14. *Fears in late childhood* revolve around the imaginary, the supernatural, strange animals, the dark, and schoolwork. As children get older, school will still be a main source of worries, but social and pesonal problems will increase while fear of animals and such decrease.
15. Selman associates moral development with increased cognitive insight and role-taking ability. *Role taking, or perspective taking,* refers to the ability to perceive and understand another person's point of view on moral choices. Social cognition, in terms of social reasoning, is involved. The stages of perspective taking, after the egocentric level, are (a) subjective role taking, (b) self-reflections, (c) mutual perspectives, (d) interactions within the social and conventional system, and (e) symbolic interactions.

REVIEW QUESTIONS

1. Compare the developmental tasks of middle childhood (Chapter 8) with those of late childhood. What similarities and differences do you see?
2. Compare the physical characteristics of a 9-year-old and an 11-year-old.
3. Why is late childhood considered to be such a healthy period?
4. Review Table 9–1 on motor skills of late childhood. What would you conclude to be the main motor development feature or features of this age stage?

5. Briefly describe the prelude to puberty in girls and boys. Why are there age-level differentials?
6. Why do children of this age level have increased sexual awareness? Does that mean they want to be sexually active?
7. Could you, or would you, make a case for providing sex information, and possibly sex education, to children ages 9 to 11?
8. Describe the social structures of groups of boys and groups of girls during late childhood.
9. Who do children of this age pick as friends? Why do you suppose friendship is more intense at this age?
10. Describe the types of social relationships that may exist between preadolescents and their parents.
11. Review the information on birth order and personality characteristics. Do you agree with the findings? What is the evaluation of studies done on birth order?
12. Describe the types of emotional reactions that may exist between preadolescents and their parents.
13. Keep in mind the limitations of descriptive or normative information. Review the emotional characteristics frequently found in 9-, 10-, and 11-year-olds. Do they match your experiences?
14. How does Selman relate the theory of role taking (perspective taking) to cognitive development? What are the five stages in Selman's theory?

THOUGHT QUESTIONS AND ACTIVITIES

1. Why do you suppose 9- to 11-year-olds develop an interest in sex? Is it because of their physical development, their cognitive development, or the influence of their social environment? Does a desire for sexual knowledge inevitably lead to a desire for sexual intimacy?
2. "Preadolescent children of today are different from those of 20 years ago." Do you agree or disagree with that statement? How do you *know* how they were then? Are you using a stereotyped notion, hearsay, or research findings? Are the preadolescents of today different from you and your peers at that age? How grownup is an 11-year-old today?
3. Visit a middle school. Observe the children in the hallways, outside the building, and in the classrooms. How do they appear to you? Perhaps you could do a short survey or poll to learn something about their interests and preferences. Invite some 9- to 11-year-olds to your class for a friendly discussion.
4. Do a study to determine what this age group likes to read. How much do they read? Consult a school librarian to get some insights.
5. Birth order and personality characteristics is an interesting topic. Do an informal survey in class to determine to what degree the concept holds true for your classmates. How do you account for discrepancies? (Please note the research and evaluation on the topic.)
6. Would you mind being 9-, 10-, or 11-years-old again? Why or why not? If you *were* that age again, knowing what you know now, what changes would you make in your life?

FURTHER READINGS

Asher, S., and Mordechai, J. (Eds.). *The development of children's friendships.* New York: Cambridge University Press, 1981. A series of articles provides wide-ranging reports of studies on children's peer relationships and the impact of these relationships on their development.

Bernstein, A.C. *The flight of the stork.* New York: Dell Publishing Co., 1980. The author interviewed children, ages 3 to 12 years, to determine what they want to know about sex. Stages of development in their interest in this topic were indicated.

Cooper, H., Findley, M., & Good, T. Relations between student achievement and various indexes of teacher expectations. *Journal of Educational Psychology,* 1982, *74*(4), 577-579. A teacher's perception of the student's ability and the discrepancy between teacher-perceived ability and student-tested ability were both positively related to relative achievement change.

Day, R.C., & Sadek, S.N. The effect of Benson's relaxation response on the anxiety levels of Lebanese children under stress. *Journal of Experimental Child Psychology,* 1982, *34*(2), 350-356. Can teaching a relaxation technique to fifth graders reduce their anxiety level?

Maccoby, E.E., & Jacklin, C.N. *The psychology of sex differences* (Vol. 1). Stanford, Calif.: Stanford University Press, 1978. Maccoby and Jacklin are widely known for their research on sex differences. This book reviews the research on the factors that affect the development of sex differences in children.

Stevenson, H.W., Stigler, J.W., Lucker, G.W., Les, S., Hsu, C., & Kitahura, S. Reading disabilities: The case of Chinese, Japanese and English. *Child Development,* 1982, *53*(5), 1164-1181. Strong evidence was found that reading disabilities do exist among Chinese and Japanese as well as among American subjects. Orthography may not be as important as originally thought.

CHAPTER 10

PUBERTY AND EARLY ADOLESCENCE

12 TO 14 YEARS OF AGE

A MOTHER'S THOUGHTS

Dear Son,

In a few minutes you will be coming home from your last day in sixth grade. Next month you will be twelve years old and ready to begin junior high school. Do you find it as difficult to believe as I do that you are now half way through your public school days?

You and your bedroom—what bridges from the past to the future you both are! Each is anchored in yesteryear and reaches for a destination planned for, yet not clearly visible. Your bedroom has a firm foundation—sturdy beams in the basement, a solid floor, rising walls, two sparkling windows, and a brightly lit ceiling. Within it are your treasures, your delights, your fears, and your aspirations.

Yes, you are built very much like your bedroom. Dad and I have supplied the foundation by giving you life, guiding, loving, and nourishing you so that you are becoming more firm. Together we have all laid the sturdy floor. A few boards were difficult to nail down, but most seemed to fit easily into place when we all worked together.

Your eyes are your windows—clear, revealing, allowing the light of knowledge to enter, and occasionally needing the sprinkle of tears to be blotted away.

Your body, "growing into your legs," rises as do your bedroom walls. And what a bright light your mind is—perhaps not brilliant, but certainly illuminating your world and ours.

Your room has changed as you have. Where your crib used to be, there is a new full-sized bed. Remember how hard you tried to stretch out to reach from one end to the other? I'm glad you reach out, son, and are eager to be a man.

Your closet no longer contains snowsuits and diapers. Instead I see your Boy Scout and Little League uniforms. Next to them is your old yellow slicker and rain hat. I remember the day I said you looked like a little yellow duckling and off you went, quacking, to kindergarten. Beside that I see a pair of jeans, just like your older brother's. In many ways he has become more of a model for you than Dad. Also on the floor are the socks I told you three times to pick up!

Your rocking horse has been replaced by a drum set. With the former I worried for your safety; with the latter I'm concerned for *my* sanity. Your record collection, here, is a "now" thing, but I think your interest in music will last. How proud I was of you at your band concert, your head barely visible above the others, but your "flam taps" coming through loud and clear.

Your bookcase and desk reflect your whole life. Your very first books are there, including several well-worn ones by Dr. Seuss. How you loved to "read" before you started to school! You have always been a great one for classifying things. Here is your third grade bird scrapbook, and next to it a notebook you kept on states and birds you counted when we went to California four years ago. Baseball cards, again classified by league and position, will soon need a larger box. Beside the books on baseball are a few mysteries you enjoyed. I think you must have every "Happy Hollister" book ever written. You quickly outgrew these, and room was made for history books and encyclopedias. Do you still want to be a historian? With your love of searching for answers, I know you'd be a good one. Maybe your reluctance to part with things from the past reflects your love of history?

On the edge of the unmade bed is your newspaper bag. I never thought anything would get you up that early! I had reservations about your taking a paper route, but I recognize your need to earn some money on your own besides what you earn mowing the lawn for Dad.

On the wall, almost as good as new, is the .410 you got for Christmas. Again, I think this was your brother's influence. Your compassion for animals and love of nature prevent you from enjoying hunting. Grandma was so pleased when I told her how you rescued a bird from the creek and used the first aid methods you learned in school. You checked its breathing, looked for broken bones or bleeding—but how do you give a bird artificial respiration?

Life will always be interesting and challenging to you. You make learning relevant by applying what you have learned to everyday situations. Remember using fractions to make fudge the other night?

You have also learned early in life that you can't excel in everything. Track was a disappointment to you. Because of your size, you weren't able to keep up to the larger boys. So you competed with yourself and were pleased when each day you were able to run a few seconds faster than you could the day before.

Size is only one thing you've had to compensate for. Being left-handed has never seemed to be a drawback because you haven't allowed it to be. You seem to take pride in the accomplishments of other left-handers. Playing the drums was more difficult because the major parts are written for the right hand. But look how that has helped in baseball. You're a switch hitter. You've said you're not a big hitter, but the team can always count on you to steal when you do get on base. This is perhaps the greatest thing I admire about you. You recognize your limitations and your capabilities. You are always able to rechannel your efforts and to think positively.

Some children find it a disadvantage in school if their parents are teachers. You have not reached the point where you are embarrassed or ashamed of them, as some are. You love to learn, and you dislike a situation where no learning takes place. You prefer a strict teacher with high standards. Remember how proud you were that you could spell so well when you were in first grade? We used to take long walks, and you'd spell any word I'd give you. I'm proud of your scholastic record and the fact that you can appreciate learning for its own sake. You have always been so highly self-motivated that we never had to prod you.

Being a younger child can also present problems, but you seem to have taken it in stride. You are naturally envious because your brother is bigger and can do more things that you can. The other day I saw you trying on his old sixth grade gym suit to see if you are as big as he was. You seemed quite disappointed that the suit was too large. But we talked this over, and I think you understand now that all children don't grow at the same rate. You laugh now and seem so disgusted over the fact that he has a girl friend. I hope you will be able to laugh about it when you get to be his age and become interested in girls.

As I turn to leave your room, the last thing I see is the bureau with pictures of your best friends on it. They have become quite an influence on your life, and I'm pleased to see you've made wise choices. I would put some things away, but I know you have a "private drawer," and I wouldn't destroy the trust you have placed in me.

I hear the school bus coming, so I'll close the door. It's almost like closing the door to elementary school and waiting to see what awaits as it again opens—this time to junior high school, puberty, and probably a very, very different boy. You are leaving childhood and beginning your journey to manhood.

IN THIS CHAPTER . . .

You will read about

1. The concept of puberty and the physical changes that take place when a child becomes an adolescent.
2. The age level characteristics of early adolescents from a personality and an emotional viewpoint.
3. The beginning of formal reasoning as it is indicated in Piaget's theory of cognitive development.
4. Adolescence and moral development as suggested by Piaget and Kohlberg; the implication of moral motivation and the influence of social contacts.
5. Peer group conformity and the beginnings of heterosexuality.
6. Interests, fads, and fashions in the teen culture.

adolescence the developmental period beginning with the onset of major pubertal changes and continuing until adult maturity.

Early adolescence is a time of growing, learning, adventuring, and dreaming. It can be a time of anxieties and problems, but these are outweighed by joy, innocence, excitement, and gladness. The term ***adolescence*** comes from the Latin verb *adolescere,* meaning "to grow into maturity." As such it is a transitional period—a time of physical, social, and emotional metamorphosis. As someone has said, it is a time when the individual is "neither man nor child, nor fish nor fowl." In some ways adolescents are like squirming, wiggling caterpillars engaged in the agonizing fight to escape childhood's cocoon and enter into adulthood's full flight. The world will soon be full of beautiful butterflies. They cannot wait to break out and fly.

Early adolescents are no longer children, yet they are not adults. They are at an in-between stage. What should be recognized is that adolescence is more than a period, or stage, of human development. It is a way of life with its own culture, values, characteristics, activities, demands, situations, and problems. In a complex society, adults must not be too quick to make the child a man or woman. In a primitive society in a less intricate world it might be possible to move from childhood to adulthood with a minimum of complications.

Today's world with its computerized systems approach to the business of life requires more cognitive, communicative, and collective competencies on the part of individuals before they can become independent, self-supporting adults. A longer period of time is required to learn the skills needed for competent adult living. This extended length of time makes it possible for the adolescents of today to reveal their uniqueness and to develop and demonstrate characteristics that are typically adolescent in nature but that in another day and age would not have had the time to be expressed (Baumrind, 1975). In a less complex society youth went about doing the work of an adult world soon after they left the period of childhood. Youth of today need the time to be adolescents.

No sharp age lines separate the stages of growth at any level. Especially is this statement true when one works with narrow developmental divisions, as in this text. As long as we talk about the descriptive characteristics of the group, we are reasonably accurate. If we think in terms of an individual, then we must definitely keep in mind the broad range of normal differences that exist within the group. The reader must make allowances for these individual differences when making application of characteristics mentioned in this book to a specific person. In addition, one must recognize and accept the fact that there will always be an overlapping of characteristics of successive developmental stages in individuals.

During the total span of adolescence the individual is working harder than ever before on two primary developmental tasks: (1) to move in the direction of independence from adults, parents in particular, in terms of self-identity and emotional independence and (2) to develop the social, intellectual, language, and motor skills essential for individual and group participation in heterosexual activities. Other developmental tasks include (1) accepting changes taking place in one's body and physical appearance and learning good grooming practices, (2) achieving appropriate relationships with age-mates of both sexes, (3) accepting a masculine or feminine role that is appropriate for the age level, and (4) acquiring moral concepts, values, and attitudes that contribute something to life in family, school, church, and peer group activities (Havighurst, 1979). Adolescents generally enjoy themselves as they make their way to adulthood.

PUBERTAL AND PHYSICAL DEVELOPMENT

Early adolescence is a time of physical growth and change. Many physiological changes occur without warning and are frequently a striking contrast to characteristics that existed earlier. Physical changes, as at any age, mean that the fairly well-formulated body image of late childhood must now be changed. The new bodily form at least must be reconciled to the existing self-concept. Some individuals find that adjusting to the realities of their new physical selves is a difficult thing to do. This is an adjustment that must be made by the teenager, the middle-aged person, and the individual in senescence. The teenager is confronted with the problem more quickly because changes occur in such a short span of time, almost "overnight."

Puberty is when you're fixing to kiss a girl for the first time and don't know who's supposed to make the smacking noise

Puberty is when you kiss a girl for the first time and neither one of you makes the smacking noise

Puberty is when all the other girls in class have bras whether they need them or not but *your* mom says you're going to wait until you have a reason

Puberty is when you write a love letter to the girl you're crazy about and she starts passing it around

Puberty is when the boy you're crazy about calls and your mom gets to the phone first and starts asking questions

Puberty is . . .

From Allen, W.; reprinted with permission from the January 1968 Reader's Digest.

Onset of puberty

menarche the first occurrence of menstruation.

The early stage of adolescent development is referred to as the pubertal period. The term *puberty* is derived from the Latin word *pubertos,* which means "the age of manhood." The implication is that a person who has gone through the pubertal period has matured physically and is now able to participate in the reproduction of the human species. Manhood or womanhood is not achieved suddenly or completely at puberty. The changes taking place at this stage are part of a developing process that began early in the life of the individual and that will continue to be active for some years to come (Petersen and Taylor, 1980).

The pubertal stage consists of three periods of development: *prepuberty,* puberty, and postpubescence. The entire stage usually lasts about 4 years. Prepuberty or *preadolescence,* refers to the period of about 2 years in late childhood before puberty when the child is developing preliminary characteristics of sexual maturity. It is characterized by the growth of fine, soft hair on the body, a spurt in physical growth, changes in body proportion, and the beginning of primary and secondary sex characteristics (Siegel, 1982).

The peak, or climax, of the pubertal stage is called *puberty,* the period during which the generative (reproductive) organs become capable of functioning and the secondary sex characteristics become highly evident. The initial appearance of these characteristics does not mean that the boy or girl is immediately capable of reproduction, however. There will be a 1- to 2-year period of adolescent reproductive sterility (Katchadourian, 1977; Steen and Price, 1977).

In *postpubescence,* most of the skeletal growth is completed and the new biological functions become fairly well established. The age of nubility or fertility then arrives. It should be noted that in England the term *puberty* is sometimes used in a legal rather than a biological sense. In the eyes of British law, girls reach puberty at the age of 12 years and boys at 14 years. The pubertal sequence of events for girls and boys is presented in Fig. 10-1.

Puberty in girls. Several criteria are used to determine the climax of puberty. ***Menarche*** (pronounced "men-AR-kee"), which is the occurrence of the first menstruation, is usually a valid sign of puberty in girls. At the same time, the secondary sex characteristics appear. The average age at which most North American girls experience their first menses is 12.5 years old. The age range is considered to be 10 to 16 years (Tanner, 1978). About 3% to 4% of all girls have menarche before the age of 10 years. Some school nurses report an increase in this percentage in their districts (Communications, 1978). A few girls begin menses after the age of 16½ years (MacMahon, 1974).

Evidence from many parts of the world indicates that the average age of menarche has dropped by at least 2 years and perhaps by as many as 5 years in the last century. In 1820 working girls in Manchester, England, reached menarche on the average at 15.7 years. Studies done in the late sixties in England and in many other parts of the world show averages at about

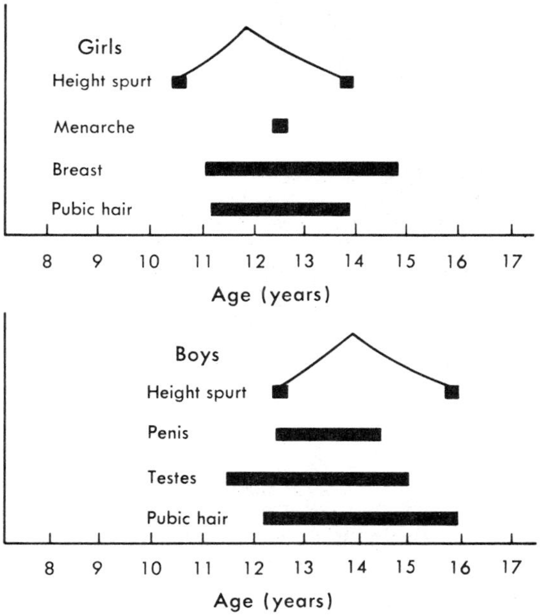

FIG. 10-1 ***Sequence of events of puberty for girls and boys and predictable patterns of development of the secondary sex characteristics.***
Modified from Marshall, W.A., and Tanner, J.M. Archives of Disease in Childhood, *1970, 45, 13-23. Also from Chumlea, W.C. Physical growth in adolescence. In B.B. Wolman (Ed.),* Handbook of developmental psychology. *Englewood Cliffs, N.J.: Prentice-Hall, 1982.*

THE ANOINTED ONE

As a young girl growing up on the island of Kiribati in the South Pacific, I didn't realize how significant it is when a girl reaches the stage of having her first period. I was to learn, however, when a friend of mine began to menstruate.

I was surprised when, for quite a few days, I had not seen my friend around. Then someone told me why, so I decided to go and visit her. To my disappointment, I was only allowed to watch from outside the house.

I saw her sitting clad only in a grass skirt, her skin shining with oil. I could see that a white palm-tree leaf was tied around her waist. No one was allowed to talk to her. She, too, was not allowed to speak or to walk about. She had to sit down and work at making string. She sat facing the south. Her only companion was her grandmother who was carrying out the ritual. I found out that she was not allowed to eat anything besides a piece of dried coconut, with water to drink. She bathed only once a day, when the sun was just setting, and sat from early morning before the sunrise until the late afternoon. The water she bathed with was especially prepared by the grandmother, and from what I saw, there were leaves and oil being put in the tub, turning the water a greenish color.

This went on for three days, but on the third day it was different. This time a lot of her relatives came because a feast was to be held. She could now speak a little but was not allowed to walk about. A special new mat was brought out for her to sit on. Now she faced a young boy, whom I noticed was the firstborn child of the girl's relative. Outside the house the ground was dug very deep, and all the local foods that could be found were cooked in this hole. This ground oven was to be hers; no one was allowed to eat from it before she had taken her food. On the same day she took a bath and was dressed in a reddish colored dress. Her skin was oiled.

On her fourth day she was dressed in another new dress and was now allowed to go out. Most of the relatives had gone back to their homes. I had been keeping an eye on her; when she was on her way to fetch some water from the well, I ran to her. I begged her to tell me the purpose of all those things she was doing. I found out from her that sitting facing the south would indicate that her future husband would be from the southern islands. The coconut leaf around her waist was to prevent her from getting hungry too easily. The fact that on her third day she sat facing the firstborn child would indicate that she herself would marry a firstborn child. She was not allowed to speak because she might spoil the ritual. She ate very little, I noticed; she said this would contribute to the idea of not getting hungry too easily. As she finished her story, I found myself smiling because I was imagining what would happen if it was done to me. I doubted if I would survive with so little food and drinking water.

Later I asked my mother why it was so important that such rituals and a feast have to be held when a young girl has her first period. Her answer to me was that it is the way our society marks the onset of womanhood.

From Stewart, R.A.C. (Ed.). *Pacific profiles*. Suva, Fiji: University of The South Pacific Extension Services, 1982.

midway between 12 and 13 years (Tanner, 1978). In New York City in 1934 the average age of menarche was 13.5 years; in 1978 it was 12.5 years. Better nutrition and better living conditions are generally cited as the reasons for the lowering age of first menses (Muuss, 1975). There is some indication, however, that the drop in the age of menarche may be leveling off in the more affluent populations (Malina, 1979, Zacharias et al., 1976).

The classic view that menarche occurs earlier in hot, humid climates has been largely discredited. The mean age of menarche for girls in warm Nigeria has been found to be 14.22 years, and for Alaskan Eskimos it is 14.42 years. Tanner reports that Chinese girls in Hong Kong and Cuban girls experience menarche as early as European girls on the highest living standard (Tanner, 1973). Girls who are city dwellers, live in low altitudes, or are totally blind appear to reach menarche earlier than their counterparts. An interesting effect of altitude on menarche has been found in the high Andes of Peru by Jean McClung of the Harvard Medical School. Menarche is reported so delayed there that it is difficult to find a girl in the high Andes who has borne children before the age of 18 years (McClung, 1969).

Puberty in boys. In boys there is no striking change to indicate puberty. One of the more reliable indicators of puberty in boys is the presence of live sperm in their urine. The presence of the gonadotropic hormone, or androgen, in the urine is also an indication of puberty. An overt sign in boys is the beginning of nocturnal emissions. When the boy is sleeping, the penis becomes erect, and semen, which is fluid with sperms, spurts out or is released.

Spontaneous nocturnal emissions will persist into adulthood and will occur whenever the reproductive organ has an excess of semen. After puberty this action is frequently accompanied by a dream of short duration whose content usually has sexual connotations. The average age at which boys reach puberty is 14.0 years. Two thirds of all boys attain puberty between 12.5 and 16.5 years of age (Tanner, 1978).

Sex characteristics. At this point it would be well to define the terms. The ***primary sex characteristics*** pertain to the development of the external and internal organs, such as the vagina, the uterus, the penis, and the testes, that carry on the reproductive functions. During infancy and childhood the sex organs are small and do not produce cells for reproduction. The pubescent stage, when functional maturity takes place in these organs, is the dividing line between the sexually immature and the sexually mature person. The primary sex organs were discussed in Chapter 3 on prenatal development.

primary sex characteristics the external and internal sex organs.

secondary sex characteristics physical characteristics that appear in humans around the age of puberty and that are sex differentiated but not necessary for sexual reproduction. Such characteristics include breast development and the appearance of pubic hair in girls and the appearance of facial and pubic hair, enlargement of the penis, and deepening of the voice in boys.

The ***secondary sex characteristics*** are those that distinguish the sexes from each other but play no direct part in reproduction. Secondary sex characteristics in girls include an increase in the width and roundness of the hips; more shapely legs and arms; menarche; thicker, coarser skin with enlarged glands; the

TABLE 10-1 Average maturation sequence in girls

Phase	*Appearance of sexual characteristics*	*Usual age*	*Age range**
Childhood to late childhood	No pubic hair, breasts are flat; growth in height is constant		
Pubescence	Rounding of hips; breasts and nipples are elevated to form bud stage; no true pubic hair	10 to 11 years	9 to 14 years
Puberty and early adolescence	Appearance of pubic hair; increment in height to 18 months before menarche; with menarche, labia become enlarged, vaginal secretions become acid, areola and nipple elevate to form "primary breast"	11 to 14 years	10 to 16 years
Middle adolescence	Pubic hair fully developed; breast fills out to adult form; menstruation is well established; growth in height decelerates between 16¼ and 17¼ years	14 to 16 years	13 to 18 years
Late to post-adolescence	Breasts fully developed; height increases stop	16 to 18 years	15 to 19 years

Compiled from Chumlea (1982); Schonfeld (1969); Siegel (1982).
*The age range is considered to consist of 80% of the cases.

appearance of facial hair on the upper lip and cheeks; and the development of breasts. Other secondary sex characteristics in females are the appearance of pubic hair, first as straight, then as kinky hair (pubic hair appears in a large amount only after the breasts develop); and changes of voice from a high-pitched tone to a more mature tone because of a slight growth of the larynx.

Breast development proceeds through four stages: (1) the *papilla stage* (nipple of early childhood), (1) the *bud stage* about 10 or 11 years of age when there is an elevation of the nipple and surrounding areola, (3) the *primary breast stage* where fatty tissue develops under and around nipple and areola, and (4) the *secondary breast stage* of maturity (Tanner, 1978). Table 10-1 presents the usual maturational sequence of sexual characteristics in girls.

The secondary sex characteristics in boys include pubic hair, which becomes curly, darker, and coarser with adolescent age; facial hair, first above the upper lip, then on other parts of the face; and body hair on the arms, chest, legs, and armpits. Other characteristics are coarser skin with enlarged pores; changes in voice; increased length of the shoulders, depth of the chest, and size of the neck; and slight enlargements or breast knots around the mammary glands, lasting only a few weeks (Tanner, 1978).

At pubescence and puberty the male gonadal hormones also stimulate the growth of the male sexual apparatus, including the penis, the prostate gland, seminal vesicles, and scrotum. These hormones bring about the development of male secondary sexual characteristics. Table 10-2 presents the average maturation sequence in boys.

Physical changes at puberty

Growth spurt. Among the earliest physical signs of puberty are obvious gains in weight and height. The ***growth spurt*** begins 1 to 2 years before the child

TABLE 10-2 Average maturation sequence in boys

Phase	*Appearance of sexual characteristics*	*Usual age*	*Age range**
Childhood to late childhood	No pubic hair; no growth in testes and penis since infancy; growth in height constant		
Pubescence	Testes increase in size; scrotum grows; penis follows with growth in length and circumference; no true pubic hair	12 to 13 years	10 to 15 years
Puberty and early adolescence	Pubic hair becomes apparent; penis, testes, and scrotum continue growing and become larger; significant spurt of growth in height; prostate seminal vesicles mature; spontaneous or induced emissions occur; voice begins to change as larynx thickens	13 to 16 years	11 to 18 years
Middle adolescence	Facial and body hair appear and spread; pubic hair becomes denser; voice deepens; testes and penis continue to grow; growth in height decreases; 98% of mature stature between 17¾ and 18½ years; indentation of frontal hair line	16 to 18 years	14 to 20 years
Late to post-adolescence	Mature and full development of primary and secondary sex characteristics; muscles may continue increasing	Onset 18 to 21 years	Onset 16 to 21 years

Compiled from Chumlea (1982); Schonfeld (1969); Siegel (1982).
*The age range is considered to consist of 80% of the cases.

becomes sexually mature and continues for 6 months to a year afterward. The growth spurt in girls begins at between 7.5 and 11.5 years of age and reaches a peak between 11 and 13 years of age (Tanner, 1970). As indicated in the last chapter, girls will grow 5 to 10 cm (2 to 4 in.) in 1 year during the growth spurt and gain 3.5 to 4.5 kg (8 to 10 lb.) or so. Gains of 12.5 or 15 cm (5 or 6 in.) are not unusual. Boys begin the accelerated growth pattern between 10.5 and 16.0 years of age and reach a peak between 13.0 and 15.5 years (Marshall, 1978). On the average, boys gain 5.5 to 6.5 kg (12 to 14 lb.) and grow 10 to 12.5 cm (4 to 5 in.) in the peak year.

As a teacher of ninth graders, whose average age was 14 years, I (G.K.) had a homeroom group of 38 pupils mark their height on a wallboard during their first week of school in September and again during the last week in May at the end of school. Every youngster in that room grew at least 5 cm (2 in.) during the school year; most grew 7.5 to 10 cm (3 to 4 in.). One boy grew 17.5 cm (7 in.) in 9 months! Increases in height and weight in either sex generally result in a greater intake of food. Appetite becomes ravenous and will be so for 3 or 4 years, necessitating frequent and more costly trips to the supermarket.

Statistical studies show a worldwide tendency in the last century toward an increase of stature (Muuss, 1975). The average 14-year-old boy in the United States is 12.5 cm (5 in.) taller than a boy of the same age in 1880. This increase is proportional for most other countries in the world. American adults weigh more than those of 25 years ago. Women weigh, on the average, 2.5 kg (6 lb.) more and men 4.5 kg (10 lb.) more than the preceding generation (Tanner, 1973).

Body changes. There are sex differences in the distribution of fat during puberty due to hormonal changes and an increase in appetite. About half of all boys and girls go through a fat period. The thickness of the skin in the neck, thorax, and abdomen increases more in boys than in girls. Just before puberty in boys there is an increase in fat around the nipples and over the stomach, hips, and thighs. Fatty tissue in boys decreases after puberty.

With the beginning of puberty girls develop fat over the abdomen and hips. The adolescent fat in girls will be present for about 2 years or so until their bodies gain some physical stability (Faust, 1977). The way girls react to their chubby appearance varies according to their past experiences of behaving under stress. Some girls withdraw to their room, away from people. Other girls resort to wearing loose-fitting clothing. Some girls go on "crash" or starvation diets, often encouraged by well-meaning mothers, whereas other girls go to a "fat camp," where a prescribed routine for losing weight is followed. Some accept their weight gain as being normal.

asynchrony the maturation of different body parts at different rates. This disproportion becomes most pronounced during puberty.

growth spurt physiological change ushering in adolescence, caused by an increased output of growth hormones and gonadotropic hormones controlled by the pituitary gland.

Significant changes in body proportions and contours are characteristic of this age group. The early adolescent boy's form usually is characterized by straight leg lines, slender hips, wide shoulders, broadened chest, and accentuated muscle development in shoulders, arms, and thighs (Forbes, 1976). The girl's leg lines become curved, her breasts fill, and her hips become wider. There is a deposit of fat in the buttocks, thighs, and upper arms.

Disproportionate facial features are noticeable in either sex when the face lengthens. The forehead becomes higher and wider. The nose looks large because it grows before puberty and is nearly completed at puberty. Later the mouth and lips become fuller. The jaw is the last part to reach adult size. A high waistline develops in early adolescence as the trunk lengthens, but it drops as adult proportions are reached.

Just before puberty the legs become longer than the trunk, and the arms increase in length. Hands and feet look disproportionate because they reach their mature size before the arms and legs. Most children will have some obvious, uneven features during these years. ***Asynchrony*** is the term used to describe the different rates of growth for various parts of the body. Fig. 10-2 illustrates changes in body proportions.

Motor awkwardness in early adolescence is often partly caused by uneven growth of muscles and bones. If the bones grow faster than the muscles, the muscles become taut on the bones, making them respond with a quick, jerky motion. If the muscles grow faster than the bones, the muscles become loose and sluggish. The brain has been programmed during late

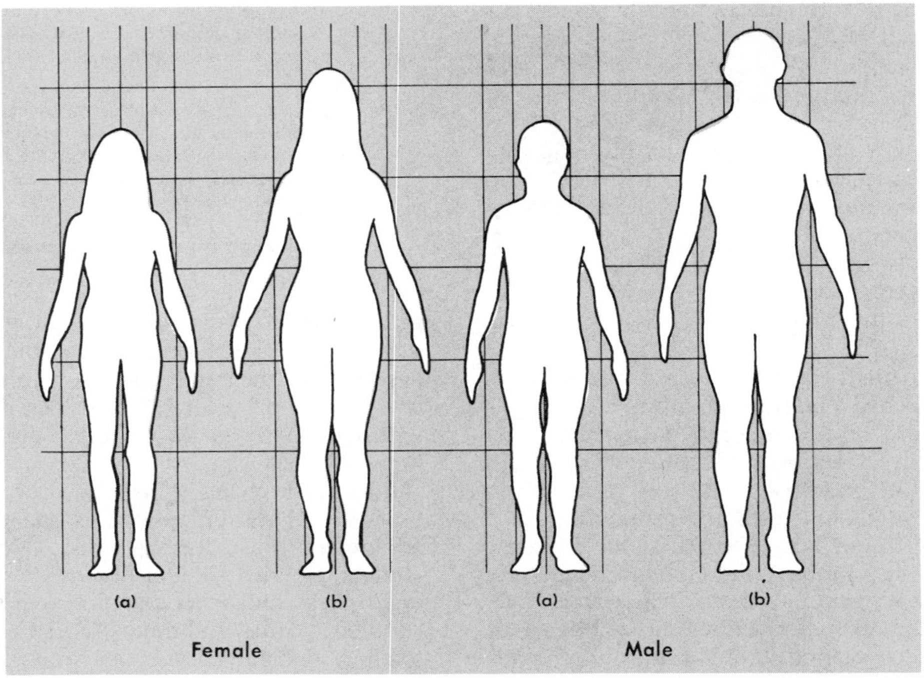

FIG. 10-2 ***Changes in body proportions of boys and girls*** **(a)** ***before and*** **(b)** ***after puberty changes have been completed.***
Modified from Tanner, J.M. Growing up. Scientific American, *1973, 229(3), 35-43. Copyright © 1973 by Scientific American, Inc.*

childhood to provide the muscles with a certain amount of energy to move the limbs of the body to a certain position in space. In early adolescence the ratio of the bones and muscles changes, but the brain still operates on the programming pattern of an earlier age; it will continue to do so until it has been reprogrammed. As a result, when a certain movement is needed, such as reaching out with the arm and hand to catch a ball, the brain sends the same amount of energy to the muscles as it did for the bone-muscle ratio of the younger age. The energy applied now to taut muscles causes the arm to move too fast to catch the ball; applied to loose muscles, the energy is not enough to get the hand up in time to catch the ball. A clumsy-appearing performance results. This awkwardness in arm and leg movements will continue until the growth of bones and muscles reaches a stable condition and the brain can be reprogrammed for the new bone-muscle ratio.

Reactions to physical changes. Considering the magnitude of the physical changes that take place at and after puberty, some impact on the attitudes and personality of the adolescent can be expected. Petersen and Taylor (1980) suggest that three factors appear to affect adolescents' concern about their developing bodies. First, adolescents wonder about the reactions of parents and others to these physical changes. Second, the way adolescents feel about themselves and these changes will have a significant effect on their self-image. Third, how adolescents view cultural standards of attractiveness will affect their image of themselves.

The body ideal or the body type defined by the culture as attractive and sex appropriate is an important influence. ***Body image*** appears to affect the way adolescents feel about themselves (Hamburg, 1974). Adolescents of both sexes are especially sensitive to any body characteristic that might be interpreted as sex inappropriate. Nevertheless adolescents who have a low self-esteem may become anxious about their body image, even though their development is well within normal range (Petersen and Taylor, 1980).

Boys who are awkward in motor skills necessary to play sports or games of their peers tend to believe that they are not acceptable. Embarrassment among boys is often caused by their changing, uncontrollable voices. Boys may be concerned about the size of their genitalia and may be upset about having to shower and change clothes for gym class (Offer et al., 1981). Skin eruptions, clogged pores, perspiration, and body odors bother most teenagers. Learning good grooming habits becomes a major task.

Psychological reactions to being too tall or too short are prevalent among early adolescents. It is no problem for the boy if he is taller than his classmates and is coordinated enough to use the height to his advantage, especially in sports (Clausen, 1975). Shortness in boys, however, is incompatible with their ideal of maleness.

Being tall may be a problem for the early adolescent girl, however, because she dreads being different from the other girls (Jersild et al., 1978). Furthermore few boys want to date or go with a girl who is much taller than themselves. Many women vividly recall the embarrassment they felt as shy teenagers as they towered over their partner's head on the dance floor at a school party. Many postures have suffered as a consequence.

body image the concept or mental representation one has of his/her own body.

Siegel (1982) reviewed studies on the psychological impact of puberty and concluded that over the years they all point to the same conclusions. (1) There is an increased awareness of matters relating to the body (Clifford, 1971); (2) early adolescents are more concerned about their physical appearance than any other aspect of self (Simmons and Rosenberg, 1975); (3) about one third of early adolescent boys and one half of early adolescent girls report dissatisfaction with their physical appearance (Rosenbaum, 1979); and (4) there is a positive relationship between social attractiveness and social acceptance during adolescence (Kleck et al., 1974).

The extent and depth of psychological responses to puberty are predicated partly on the adequacy of the preparations for these changes that the early adolescent has received. If youngsters have been adequately prepared or if the changes occur slowly, the transition

I COULD CRY!

In this sexist society much emphasis is placed upon the appearance of the female. A female must be pretty and have a stunning figure. Fashions are designed for the woman who has the hip size of a teenage boy. Television and motion picture screens emphasize physical beauty. The mass media rarely suggest that the "Plain Jane" exists, and if they do suggest such existence, they never picture a successful one.

This paper is about a girl named Cindy who is between twelve and thirteen years of age. She has a problem suffered by many people in America; she is overweight. She is not the beautiful woman shown on the television screen. She has nondescript, ordinary brown hair. Her eyes are hazel and are functional. They do not, however, glow in the dark or seduce helpless men. As a matter of fact, she resembles her father, who definitely does not resemble Brooke Shields.

We'll let the real Cindy describe her feelings—in her own words—from her diary.

• • •

Dear Diary,

I'm glad you cannot see me when I write in you. Otherwise you would probably lose your key so I couldn't open you. I would understand, though. I looked into the mirror and saw that horror my parents say they love. How can they? I've disappointed them. My sister is so pretty, and my parents can be proud of her, but me! Just look at me. Why do *I* have to look this way? I do not have a waist. I think if I could be about eight inches taller I'd be fine. Then all the fat would stretch out.

The school nurse said not to eat bread and potatoes for a while. She measured and weighed us yesterday. I am four feet, eight inches tall and weigh 142 pounds. At least I'm not like my friends Carol and Nancy. Carol weighs 175, and Nancy weighs 190. What does that nurse know anyway? I have starved myself, and still nothing happened.

• • •

Dear Diary,

Tonight at the school dance the kids started to call me the "vitamin pill." At least that's not as bad as "the ugly dumpling." I'll never go to a school dance again. I was so insulted that I cried. I might go see a doctor without my Mom knowing about it. But how would I pay?

• • •

Dear Diary,

I don't know if you feel this way, but every time I go out I feel like everyone is saying something about me or looking at me and laughing. I don't know why I can't be accepted for myself rather than the way I look. That's what we talked about in class today. I really like my teacher. I really cannot understand why people don't like me. I can't help it if I'm fat. The boys can't stand me. They don't like other girls, either, but they hate me. I could cry!

Dear Diary,

I've started a new hobby after school. I'm reading all the books I can. I love Nancy Drew, but my favorite is Trixie Belden. Trixie is just who I want to be. She's pretty and skinny, but she is nice. If I read after school, then I do not have to go out with the rest of the kids and play games.

may take place without psychological disturbance. One way or another teenagers will have to accept the changes that have occurred in their bodies. Their parents can do much to help them develop pride in their new status.

Early and late physical maturing

Children show enormous variation in growth and sexual maturation. There are early maturers and late maturers. Zacharias and colleagues (1976) found in a study of 781 girls in a middle-class Boston suburb that the age at menarche ranged from 9.1 to 17.7. Since schools tend to keep students in age-level steps, early adolescent boys and girls will vary in physical maturity within any given classroom.

Boys who mature early in adolescence perceive themselves more positively and are more successful in peer relationships than their late-maturing counterparts. Both peers and adults rated the early-maturing boys as physically more attractive, more composed, and more socially sophisticated than late-maturing boys (Weatherley, 1964). The Berkeley longitudinal study found that characteristics of early-maturing boys, such as dominance, independence, and self-control, were still apparent when the individuals were in their thirties (Jones et al., 1971). Late maturers tended to be more eager, talkative, and self-assertive.

Early maturation generally seems to have positive psychological benefits for girls, but the results are not as clear-cut as they are for boys. Peterson (1979) found that girls who are developmentally advanced have less prestige among their age-mates in elementary school but have an advantage in the junior high school years. Some findings show that the early-maturing girls exhibit greater sociability, leadership, poise, and expressiveness than late-maturing girls. Late physical maturation appears to have adverse effects in the personality adjustment of girls.

It is possible that the view of the early-maturing boy and girl as being psychologically healthier than the late maturer may be an oversimplification based upon equating social adjustment with psychological adjustment. The early maturer pays a price for his or her social advantages in terms of emotional constraint, while the late maturer seems somewhat more tolerant of his or her own impulses and inner life (Siegel, 1982). Early maturation may force premature identity formation, pushing early maturers into decisions about their identity too early (Peskin, 1967). By contrast, those adolescents who mature late may have more time to handle their physical changes and may be more flexible in identity formation.

PERSONAL CHARACTERISTICS

The change in physical appearance brought on by puberty is accomplished by a change in emotional control and response. In late childhood youngsters were rather stable individuals. They had reached the peak of childhood development. They knew and understood what their bodies could do. They were generally satisfied with their peer and family relationships. Their pattern of behavior was acceptable to them; they knew what they could get away with and how to manipulate situations to their advantage. In short, they were in control of their life pattern.

All of a sudden puberty comes along and upsets

David Strickler

These girls are in the same grade and of approximately the same age. In adolescence, the characteristics of early and late maturing can be readily noted.

their well-structured approach to the world. Their bodies change rapidly. They no longer look like children, but they usually are not ready for adulthood and its demands. Their former emotional approach to handling frustrating or conflicting situations is no longer appropriate. They are uncertain as to how to act, what to do, or what to think. It looks like they are going to have to start all over again, building new self-images, adapting to new social patterns, and developing new mental health mechanisms.

New mental defense mechanisms must be developed. In the meanwhile the mechanisms used may be taken to extremes. Daydreaming may be so intense that adolescents may not hear a person talking to them (withdrawal mechanism), or they become hostile and ready to fight, complain, or resist everything (aggressive mechanisms). And when an adult seeks to be compassionate, they may get the reply, "Just because I'm a teenager you don't have to be so understanding!"

Descriptive age characteristics

Most 12-year-olds are happy much of the time because the majority are not well into the puberty period. They can still use their preadolescent behavior in acceptable ways. They are becoming more interesting from an adult point of view, but their humor is biting, and they use it to criticize actions of their parents and to insult their friends. "If I couldn't do better than that, I'd go hide my head in the sand." "Oh yeah, you think you're smart—how about the time you . . ." And so it goes. Twelve-year-olds try to keep moods and feelings

I think I could turn and live with animals, they're so placid and self-contain'd. . . .

Walt Whitman
Song of Myself

a secret. However, when their feelings are hurt, they will react with talking back, name calling, or saying something mean rather than leaving the scene.

Although 13-year-olds are moderately calm, occasionally they will sulk and cry and make faces at people. Generally they will simply ignore the situation or the person who hurt their feelings. They will confide in certain friends while hiding their hurts from others.

Generally, 14-year-olds are more adept at controlling their anger in front of people. They may lock themselves in their room and occasionally slam doors or make harsh verbal responses later on to show their discontent. Humor, mostly of the teasing variety, is often used. They are practical jokers, which can make them rather irritating at times. On the average they are more happy than not. They do not cry much, and when they do, it is usually caused by anger.

Need for tender, loving care

Early adolescents need to develop ego strength and to experience acceptance and love. They need to be able to give as well as to receive these qualities. It is important that they be able to display tenderness, admiration, and appreciation. Emotional deprivation only leads to resistive behavior. The following excerpt is from a nun who was a student in one of our classes in human development.

> The lack of love and the inability to express love can lead to the saddest of consequences. This I have observed while working in a protectory, a home for boys staffed by our sisters. The need to be deeply and uniquely loved and accepted was of paramount importance to these boys. The lack of these responses worked havoc with most of them. Yet, more detrimental to them was the fact that they were not able to display any beautiful emotions. They had already experienced deep rejection at home and did not want to be rejected by the boys with whom they were now living. In order to be accepted, they had to conform to the standards set by the other boys.
>
> The first standard was to refuse to be emotional, appreciative, or affectionate toward anyone. They developed an almost hostile reaction toward adults when they were in the presence of the other boys. However, when they were in their own cubicle at bedtime, and I went to say good night to them, they responded beautifully to a pat on the head or a touch on their shoulder. On occasion they would try to display their affection by saying small simple phrases, such as "You're O.K." or "You really understand." It hurt to see the boys looking in all four directions to make sure that no one could see them saying "thanks."
>
> Even more painful was the experience of watching the difficulty these boys had trying to understand how anyone could really care for them. How often have I heard them say, "How can you really love me when even my own parents don't?" Sad to say, they were convinced that this rejection by their parents was due not to parental neglect or indifference, but rather to their own imagined unlovableness.

Even under the best of family conditions there is some anxiety, uneasiness, and uncertainty in early adolescents. There is a great discrepancy between what they are and what they know they have to become. But how do you get there? "There is so much to learn, and

I don't even know where or how to begin." Becoming an adolescent does not alleviate personal concerns and fears, many of which were started in childhood.

AWAKENING OF REASONING

Approximately one year after the beginning of puberty individuals begin to feel confident in their intellectual abilities. There is a growing insistence on submitting all things to the test of one's own reason. They are beginning to show interest in thinking, experimenting, and generalizing. Often these interests are directed to science. The act of formulating a hypothesis and actually testing it gives them great satisfaction. Prior to this time they have used the method of trial and error to reach their learning goals. They will now spend some of their time thinking of a solution rather than immediately acting and then having to make corrections.

formal operational stage according to Jean Piaget, the fourth stage of thought, which begins at about 12 years of age, is the time the individual begins to engage in thinking that is characterized by the ability to consider what is possible, as well as what is. It is the period during which logical thinking begins and is the final step toward abstract thinking and conceptualization. See also **concrete operational stage; preoperational stage; sensorimotor stage.**

metacognition cognition that takes as its object other cognition; for example, thinking about thinking or regulating cognitive activity.

Piaget: Formal operations

Piaget described four major stages in the process of cognitive development. During the sensorimotor stage (0 to 2 years) infants are constructing a cognitive world of permanent *objects* (see Chapter 5). During the preoperational stage (2 to 6 years) young children are involved in constructing a cognitive world of *symbols* that can be manipulated (see Chapter 7). During the concrete operational stage (7 to 11 or 12) children are engaged in constructing a cognitive world of *rules* and *quantities* (see Chapter 8). Finally, during the formal operations stage (11 or 12 to 15 and older) adolescents attain logic operations and begin to construct a cognitive world that involves *thought, ideals,* and *possibilities.*

The stage of ***formal operations*** usually begins at the ages of 11 or 12, although it may begin much later for some children under certain circumstances. During this period, adolescents become capable of learning to do deductive logic or "if-then" reasoning. ("If this hypothesis is true, then I ought to be able to observe. . . .") Children in the concrete operational stage can begin from observations and figure out a theory or a system. But it is only after 11 or 12 years of age that they can reverse the process and go from the theory to hypothesize something that can be implied beyond their own specific, concrete observations. In Piaget's view the formal operations of intelligence are parallel to systems of logic. Systems of formal operations are to concrete operations what algebra is to arithmetic: a formalization of content (Elkind, 1980).

Characteristics of formal reasoning. There appear to be five characteristics or major differences in cognitive competence between children and adolescents or adults (Keating, 1980).

The *first* difference is the ability to think about possibilities versus empirical reality. A concrete reasoner deals in reality, being limited to thinking in terms of actual objects and experiences. At the formal level there seems to be a capacity or inclination to consider and examine possibilities not immediately present. Reality is now secondary to possibility.

A *second* characteristic is that of *thinking about* thoughts, or interpropositional thinking. The concrete reasoner thinks *with* operations (intrapropositional), whereas the formal reasoner thinks *about* the operations he or she is using (interpropositional). The individual is aware of the cognitive activity involved and is thinking about it and how it can be used differently. The term *meta* is used to indicate that the individual is focusing on a cognitive activity. Types of ***metacognition*** are metamemory, metacommunication, and metattention (Flavell, 1977). The adolescent shows metacognitive sophistication and an increased use of introspection, the probing of inner states or thoughts.

The *third* characteristic of formal reasoning is thinking through hypotheses or using hypothetical-deductive reasoning. Concrete reasoners are pretty much restricted to the facts. Formal reasoners are not necessarily tied to testing the facts; they can think about the impossible, the opposite, or the "contrary-to-fact." The implication is that the formal reasoner, by the use of logic, can deal with elements that are entirely abstract.

A *fourth* characteristic difference is the ability to think ahead, or to do combinational reasoning. The concrete thinker can integrate two variables or dimensions of a situation. The formal thinker, on the other hand, may be capable of envisioning situations including many variables. The implication is that planning ahead is possible in problem-solving situations. A variety of activities may be included in the planning process (Siegler and Liebert, 1975). Planning is done more spontaneously by adolescents than by children, and by older adolescents and adults than by younger adolescents.

The *fifth* characteristic or difference between the reasoning of children and adolescents is the ability to think beyond old limits or to extend formal reasoning. Adolescents can use reasoning to make sense of all aspects of experience. They can broaden their horizons on all dimensions, with topics and issues taking on enlarged significance and meaning because the cognitive skills that can be applied to the task are much sharper than they were in childhood.

Memory, reasoning, imagination, and interpreting ability develop to a high peak during late adolescence. Mental growth curves show an increase in mental development from childhood through early adolescence to a gradual increase in late adolescence. Social interaction gives adolescents many experiences and opportunities to help develop their cognitive functions fully while in the adolescent stage of life.

Research on formal thought. There has been much research done on Piaget's theory of cognitive development. Only a few studies will be cited. The early research of Lovell (1961) tested 200 subjects ranging from age 8 to 18 years, using 10 of Piaget's formal tasks. In general the results appeared to corroborate the stages set forth by Inhelder and Piaget (1964). Younger children were rarely able to solve the tasks at the formal-reasoning level; the older subjects were much more successful. The implication is that formal-reasoning tasks are highly related to age. A more effective problem-solving strategy is present during the adolescent period, with older adolescents doing better than younger ones. However, some variations did exist. Some younger children could do some of the formal tasks; not all the adolescents could do all the tasks.

Piaget (1972) offers three explanations as to why variations may exist in the areas where formal operations are applied. First, Piaget states that although most individuals have the potential to reach the stage of formal reasoning, the social environment can influence the time that it takes to reach that level. A socially and culturally disadvantaged environment will hinder the rate of cognitive development. Second, Piaget speculates that the formal operations stage may not be as universal as he once thought. He now recognizes that formal reasoning involves a special aptitude that not all individuals may possess. Variations due to individual differences may exist. Third, the one Piaget considers most plausible, is that although all individuals will eventually develop formal operations (by early adulthood at least), the type of formal reasoning developed may not be capable of being used in solving all types of problems or situations. A selective use of formal reasoning, to suit the occasion, may be needed. Not everyone will be able to do formal reasoning in all situations.

A growing body of research suggests that formal thought is neither inevitable nor as universal a step in development as is the concrete thought of childhood (Keating and Clark, 1980; Super, 1980). Studies in other countries, such as Turkey, indicate that the development of abstract reasoning may be a result of growing up in a highly urban or technological society or of having formal education. Being a resident of a primitive society may restrict the development of formal thought (Cole, 1978; Kohlberg and Gilligan, 1971). Although there are other theories of formal operations, Piaget still holds a strong position in the field (Moshman and Neimark, 1982; Neimark, 1982).

Socioeconomic influence on intelligence

Functional intelligence is traditionally measured by an "intelligence" test. Items on such tests generally include measurements of general information, vocabulary or word usage, the ability to reason, arithmetical reasoning, memory, common sense judgment, and aspects of visual-motor performance. Many of these items are related to or influenced by life-space culture.

Social class has been found to be related to mental ability. Dielman and associates (1974) have found positive correlations between family socioeconomic variables and mental test scores of children and adolescents. At the adolescent level the mental test scores of boys showed a higher correlation with the father's occupation than with any other socioeconomic variable. Girls' test scores showed the highest correlation with the mother's and father's education. It has been noted by Hansen (1975) that a global environmental variable, such as social class, should not be used in studying the relationship between the environment and the adolescent's performance. Variables such as emphasis on school achievement, freedom to engage in verbal expression, and parental involvement with the child were significantly related to the youngster's IQ.

Socioeconomic relationships play an important part in the mental development of the early adolescent. On intelligence tests Billy, who comes from a middle-class white home, as an example, often outscores Harvey, who comes from an economically deprived home. We dare not conclude that Harvey is less intelligent than Billy, however. Billy perhaps has had more verbal and sensory experiences than Harvey. Also important in this situation is the adolescent's relationship with his parents and the motivating atmosphere of the home environment. Harvey has learned to put value on immediate, extrinsic results that he can partake of today rather than on something of an elusive, intellectual nature because the latter is not tangible to him. Billy, on the other hand, thinks about his future, his learning, and further education because he has been guided by parents and siblings and has been influenced by the accepted thinking of his immediate environment, which stresses the future.

AGE OF MORAL TRANSITION

Early adolescents' moral development depends on their parents, their peer group, and their own experiences of resolving right from wrong. They usually adopt the accepted behavior of the group that is most significant to them. They must feel a relatedness to someone or some group to feel free to accept and develop a strong moral code. Right and wrong must be presented in tangible terms.

Groups set norms for their members, and enforcement of the norms results in conforming behavior (Newman, P.R., 1982). Groups also relate to other groups. As a result, group behavior can be influenced in directions that involve status-earning achievements. The influence may be positive, as in the case of a group seeking to excel in sports or some other form of healthy competition, or it may be negative, as in the case of aggressive behavior, gang wars, or disruptive activities.

Children entering adolescence have no difficulty in being able to identify the truth. They have developed the power to reason and easily recognize the truthful manner. However, they are also governed by their peers, and this calls for ability to know when to and when not to be flexible in preservation of the self (Gerson and Damon, 1978; Haan, 1978).

Adolescents also soon discover that what people say and what they do may be two entirely different things in certain situations. This inconsistency results in misunderstanding and questioning in their minds. At this stage in life teenagers are highly idealistic, and when these ideals are shattered by adult hypocrisy, detrimental effects may result if they are not capable enough to accept the fact of fallacy.

Much of the following is based on the work of Martin L. Hoffman, as presented in the *Handbook of Adolescent Psychology* (Adelson, 1980).

cognitive dissonance the condition in which one has beliefs or knowledge that disagree with each other or with behavioral tendencies. When such cognitive dissonance arises, the subject is motivated to reduce the dissonance through changes in behavior or cognition (Festinger).

Cognitive disequilibrium of moral beliefs

Cognitive disequilibrium, also called ***cognitive dissonance,*** refers to a condition in which one has beliefs or bits of knowledge that disagree with each other or with the behavioral tendencies the person has. When such cognitive disequilibrium arises, the subject is motivated to reduce the dissonance (incompatibility of thoughts and actions) through changes in behavior or thinking (Festinger, 1957). This concept of Festinger's is an older view of cognitive operations based on the balance theory of homeostasis. Early adolescence is a period when cognitive disequilibrium can occur because of differences that the individual notes between what he or she has learned to believe is true or good and what is experienced in interaction with the peers or the environment. Piaget and Kohlberg, both cognitive disequilibrium theorists, view moral development as a series of stages of moral reasoning strategies or conceptual frameworks that must build up, reorganize, and encompass the preceding stage. The new stage is more comprehensive, providing new perspectives and criteria for making moral evaluations.

Robert Maust

Early adolescents have so much to learn about themselves and about heterosexual behavior. Many will read magazines for teens, such as* Seventeen*, to learn what others say or do. Moral questions may arise when interest is drawn to "true confession" kinds of magazines.

Cognitive dissonance is lessened or eliminated for the moment.

Piaget's model. Piaget believes that both cognitive development and peer interaction play a role in the transformation from one stage to another. His theory is that on the first level of moral development, young children feel an obligation to comply with rules because rules are rigid and unalterable. This first stage is one of moral realism, the morality of constraint, or heteronomous morality. *Heteronomous morality* means that the concept of morality arises from sources outside the child and is due to the unequal social interaction relationship that exists between children and adults. Young children have moral immaturity because of three limitations: (1) their egocentric nature, their assumption that others view events the same way they do; (2) their sense of realism, their consideration of their subjective experiences as being objective experiences; and (3) their heteronomous respect for the authority of adults, which in turn produces feelings of obligation to comply with adult commands because adult rules are seen as sacred and unchangeable. (See

Chapter 8 for an introduction to Piaget's theory of moral development.)

Moral growth requires that children give up their sense of egocentrism and develop a sense of self that is distinct from others who may have their own (but not the child's) perspective about rules and events. This shift occurs in interaction with peers, beginning in late childhood and extending into adolescence (Hoffman, 1980). As they grow older, children attain more equality with adults and older children, which lessens the heteronomous respect for them. This change, referred to as *autonomous morality,* gives the early adolescent confidence to participate with peers in decisions about applying and changing rules on the basis of ***reciprocity*** (a mutual or cooperative interchange of ideas or privileges). The rules are increasingly products of cooperation and agreement based on the goals they serve; they are also amenable to change by mutual consent.

reciprocity corresponding, complementary, inverse relationships.

When there is interaction with peers, the early adolescent becomes *sensitized* to the inner feelings and thoughts behind the behavior of others. This awareness contributes to the tendency to take the other's intentions for the behavior into account. At the same time, the adolescent recognizes that others are also aware of the fact that events seem different when viewed from different perspectives. Peer interaction stimulates and challenges the individual to cognitive action because interaction results in a contradiction of his or her expectations (cognitive disequilibrium). As a result the individual must use cognitive capability to resolve the conflict. Through this effort, patterns of moral thought are reorganized on a higher level of moral insight.

Kohlberg's model. Kohlberg's theory of moral development has more direct relevance to adolescent moral thought. (See Chapter 12 for Kohlberg's six stages of moral development.) Kohlberg considers that the average adolescent is on stage 3 or 4. Stage 3 is a moral behavior, the goal of which is to gain approval, to please others, and to help others. Intentions are considered in judging actions. Stage 4 is the level of doing one's duty, showing respect for authority, and maintaining social order for its own sake. It is the morality of self-accepted moral principles. It is conformity to shared standards, rights, and duties. If conflicts between two socially acceptable standards exist, attempts will be made to arrive at a rational decision.

Moral growth results from exposure to levels of moral reasoning that are moderately higher than one's current level (Turiel, 1974). The resulting discrepancy is tension producing, resulting in the person's wanting to resolve the conflict. As the adolescent becomes aware of the view of others or of the disequilibrium of views, role taking may occur, taking on the perspective of the others (Selman, 1976b). An individual's progress through the stage is, in part, based on the ability to be involved in cognitive role taking. The role-taking experiences provide the individual with different perspectives and thus help resolve one's own cognitive conflict; this in turn brings about a modification of the existing moral structure.

Brief critique. The theories of Piaget and Kohlberg both depend on the elaboration and modification of moral thought patterns through the use of cognitive processes. According to a review by Hoffman (1980) a limitation exists in these models because they do not take into account desire or motivation to change. They neglect the phenomenon of the "conscience." Concepts are needed to connect moral thoughts to feelings and actions. It is possible that a discrepancy between how one feels about his or her moral beliefs and one's actions could bring about a disequilibrium. Maybe feelings can have something to do with wanting to change one's level of moral thought. Perhaps the motivational side of the moral phenomenon needs to be explored in discussing the nature of moral thought.

Moral motivation

Psychoanalytic theory stresses anxiety and repression as having to do with changes in behavior and thought (Blos, 1976). Anxiety is a strong motivator of behavior, especially if fear or retribution is associated with it. Anxiety-based motivation may account for a good deal of moral behavior by people of all ages. Often the anxiety is over a concern of retribution from God.

Another theory of moral motivation focuses on the role of empathy and its developmental transformations. *Empathy* is defined as a vicarious response to another person. *Hoffman's model of empathy* (Hoffman, 1980) suggests that empathy has three components: an affect arousal component, a cognitive com-

empathy the emotional linkage that characterizes relationships between individuals; the ability to sense the feelings of others.

ponent, and a motivational component. The focus is on the empathic response to another's distress. This response, says Hoffman, is relevant to the moral domain. According to the empathy-based model, young children's feelings for other persons are limited to simple emotions experienced in the immediate specific situation or event; cognitive limitations do not permit deeper insights. Young adolescents, however, can integrate their capacity for empathic arousal ***(empathy)*** with their newly emerging cognitive awareness that others have their own identity, life circumstances, and inner states. This perceived awareness of another's level of well-being, as well as one's own level, is seen as producing a potential force toward moral growth and action, especially if it is linked to religion.

Socialization and moral development

There is research on the effects of child-rearing practices on moral development. Because of the difficulty of obtaining moral data from young children, most of the studies have been done on adolescents.

Parental discipline and moral growth. Most of the socialization research on moral development pertains to discipline. The rationale is that discipline provides an incentive to learn and to internalize a behavioral (moral) standard. The child must decide whether to behave in accordance with his or her wishes or desires or to subordinate those desires and act in keeping with perceived moral standards. Some types of discipline—and some situations—are more effective than others.

A review of *discipline research by Hoffman* (1977) organized types of discipline into three categories: (1) *power assertion,* including the use of force, threat, or deprivation of privileges or objects, (2) *love withdrawal,* usually a nonphysical expression of anger or disapproval, and (3) *induction,* the giving of an explanation or reason for requiring children to change their behavior. A summary of the research by Hoffman reveals that power assertion and love withdrawal comprise a motive-arousal component, which is often necessary to get children to stop what they were doing and to attend. Once attention is gained, induction, the presenting of information, could often influence the children to reduce their desires and demands, especially if the communication implied that harm was being done to someone else. If too little motive arousal was initiated by the discipline, the children would usually ignore the parent. Too much arousal resulted in fear or resentment that prevented an effective use of the inductive or reasoning process. Over a period of time children tended to remember the ideas communicated in induction, as well as the associated empathy or guilt.

Apparently the type of discipline used by the mother has a greater effect on moral internalization than does the type of discipline used by the father (Hoffman, 1980). Fathers do, however, play an important role in moral socialization. Apparently father's behavior toward the mother is often one of the factors that determine what type of discipline the mother will use. Also, in a study of father absence, adolescent boys without fathers scored significantly lower on three out of four indices of moral internalization than a group of boys with fathers (Hoffman, 1971). No differences were found for girls.

Influence of peers. The influence of peers is generally assumed to reach a peak in adolescence. The peer group appears to play an increasingly important role as parental controls gradually change when children grow into adolescents. The research is not consistent in its findings on peer group influence. It is important to recognize that peer groups do not necessarily exert an influence that is apart from that of the parents (Hoffman, 1980). The content of peer-group values and directives, in some instances, has shown broad areas of agreement with adult values and directions. However, where a strong, specific peer culture exists, some differences in emphasis and priorities can exist (Keniston, 1965).

Piaget and Kohlberg emphasize the importance of peer interaction in moral development. Informal play fosters spontaneous, flexible rule making and rule enforcing that are necessary for the development of a mature moral orientation. A resulting disequilibrium between peer and adult norms may compel adolescents to think through and question earlier beliefs, resulting in moral growth that is more discriminating. Bronfenbrenner (1970) disagrees, however, stating that the culturally established patterns of cooperation and mutual concern in society cannot be learned by contact with age-mates alone.

It appears that peer-group influence in moral views

is frequently tempered by the influence and views of the parents—if the parents are accepting individuals and are present in the home. Parents frequently employ inductive reasoning. This approach by the parent may serve as the model for the development of a role-taking perspective in the peer group. It must be recognized, however, that ultimately adolescent moral development does build on childhood morality, but in different ways for different people.

SOCIAL DEVELOPMENT IN EARLY ADOLESCENCE

Just as physical changes at puberty have an effect on emotions, so do they have an effect on social development and relationships. The changes in physical characteristics are great enough to create attitudes and concerns regarding social relationships. Early-maturing children feel different from the others and may want to withdraw. However, younger children may look to early-maturing individuals for leadership and direction. Late maturers have social problems because they seem to be "too far behind" everybody else and are not "grown-up" enough.

On another point the appearance of adult physical characteristics often brings a demand from adults for the teenager to be more responsible and to act more "grown-up." Early teenagers do not possess the social and cognitive skills necessary to be competent as adults. Their physical maturity belies their social maturity. Finally the physical discrepancies in weight and height between girls and boys, especially at the age of 12 or 13 years, is enough to make some boys cringe. There is a gap to be bridged. Can the girls wait for the boys to catch up?

Peer group conformity

Although early adolescents are struggling for independence, strong dependency needs arise as they attempt to find themselves and identify their role in society. ***Peer groups*** play a major part in the gratification of these needs. Through frequent contacts with their peers plus an increasing absence of parents from the home—or at least fewer hours of contact with parents—the peer group becomes the important socializing agent. Fig. 10-3 illustrates the percentage of conformity for various age-level peer groups. Group conformity is beginning to have tremendous effects on behavior. Values and attitudes are being created and reinforced by the group phenomena. Conformity demanded by the group may discourage individualism and self-assertion. However, as adolescents mature, they tend to regain their individual characteristics (Wagner, 1971).

peer group the group of persons who constitute one's associates, usually of the same age and social status.

Adolescents measure much of their whole being by the reaction of their peers. It is they who accept them and encourage them to keep on behaving as they are. If they are ignored or criticized by their peers, they may develop feelings of inferiority, inadequacy, and incompetency. The peer group is responsible for much of the modification of behavior and for providing a forum by which teenagers see themselves for better or for worse.

Teaching how to get along with others is a socializing value of the peer group. Within the group they must learn to be considerate of the feelings of others and must be able to listen to their views. The first groups in early adolescence are usually made up of one sex. This situation is merely a continuation of the group makeup in late childhood. Girls congregate in the intimacy of someone's bedroom to talk about boys, clothes, and makeup. The activities of boys revolve around sports, hobby activities, and rough games. There is some comfort and advantage in being with one's own kind at this time. Give and take are more

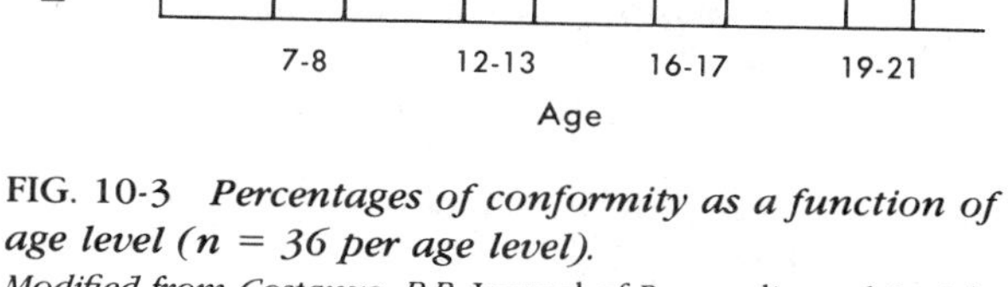

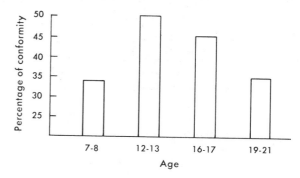

FIG. 10-3 ***Percentages of conformity as a function of age level (n = 36 per age level).***
Modified from Costanzo, P.R. Journal of Personality and Social Psychology, *1970, 14, 366-374. Copyright (1970) by the* American Psychological Association. *Adapted by permission of the publisher and author.*

David Strickler

Organized sports have many advantages because they provide supervised play with peer groups. However, a disadvantage results when emphasis is placed on winning at all costs or when the adolescent does not possess the necessary skills to play the game acceptably.

acceptable. There is more freedom to discuss any and all subjects. They can give each other support in learning about themselves and, eventually, about the opposite sex. Ego development, increased self-reliance, and establishing self-esteem through contributions made to the group are all possible by group association.

By the age of 13 years many girls have begun to form groups based on personal likes, dislikes, interests, similarities in socioeconomic background, and proximity of residence. The peer group may begin to shift from one sex to both, often in imitation of older teens. It must be kept in mind that early adolescents are less concerned with expressing heterosexual feelings than with the questions of growing up, their social status in the group, and their comparative standing with others of their own sex (Jersild, 1978). Here is an opportunity to associate with others having similar growing problems.

Although early adolescence is a gregarious, social stage, it is also one in which youngsters tend to select a

TABLE 10-3 Parental happiness, child-rearing practices, and adolescent rebellion (Figures indicate percent who are rebellious.)

		Child-rearing practices			*Authority*	
Parental happiness	*Total sample*	*Very restrictive or very permissive*	*Slightly restrictive or slightly permissive*	*Average*	*Nonpatriarchal*	*Patriarchal*
Unhappy	29	49	23	22	23	31
Happy	19	23	21	10	22	17

Modified from Balswick, J.O., & Macrides, C. *Adolescence,* 1975, *10,* 256. Used by permission.

"best" friend of the same sex with whom confidences are exchanged (Maccoby and Jacklin, 1974). Some parents become concerned when they note such a strong relationship between their child and another. Parents wonder if good heterosexual relationships with others will ever develop. Parents need not worry about this type of association. As children grow older, they tend to widen their circle of acquaintances and may eventually drift apart from earlier friends. People often talk about this happening by saying, "When they were in junior high school, they were as close as two peas in a pod. No one ever thought that anything could separate them. Now they hardly ever see each other, although they are still friends."

Parent-teenager relationships

A major developmental task in early adolescence is the attempt to achieve emancipation from the home. As a result early adolescence may emerge as a period of ambivalence toward adults. This reaction is not consistent, however, because it varies from mood to mood of the teenager. Sometimes young people feel highly competent and demand their "rights." At other times, after they have been hurt in their battles with the world, they become compliant and accept parental guidance. Adolescents issue their "declaration of independence," but the problem is that they need to be independent in a dependent type of way.

Children who come from families in which the mother and father have helped the child in the growing-up process by providing opportunities to learn responsibility, self-reliance, necessary skills, and self-respect make a much smoother transition from childhood dependency to adulthood competency. Parents who have been liberal, overly permissive, or uninterested about their children's behavior may have more difficulty with their children because they lack a structure or system of standards or values by which they can determine whether their behavior is suitable and their decisions appropriate (Scheck, 1973). Overprotective parents seldom give their child an opportunity to learn how to make important decisions and how to assume responsibilities. Table 10-3 presents an interesting research on the relationship of parental happiness, the type of child-rearing practices, and the degree of parental authority.

Many parents have disquieting feelings about their growing children. Some parents are among the last to accept the fact that their child is growing up. It is alarming, to some fathers in particular, to learn that their "little girl" is going out on her first date with a boy. When teenagers assert their right to be more grown-up, they often create tensions within the home. They may question family control; they resent being treated like a child. This is the age of "You don't understand me" and "You always treat me like a baby." If really pressed, the child may think, if not say, "It's not my fault I was born. You have to put up with me."

Parents sometimes feel hurt at this lack of gratitude or appreciation. "This is the kind of thanks I get for staying up late at night with you when you were sick?

heterosexual emotionally and sexually centered on the opposite sex; seeking and finding erotic gratification with a person of the other sex.

This is the way you treat me after all I have sacrificed for you so that you could have nice things to wear and good food to eat?" It is necessary to recognize that it is difficult for some parents to change as quickly as the child is changing at puberty. For the past 12 or 13 years the parents have been making decisions for their child; the child was dependent on them. How can parents change these relationships overnight, especially when they are struggling with their own problems and life?

The most important thing for parents to keep in mind, at any time or any age of the child, is not to do or say anything that will break down or cut off the lines of communication between parent and child. All teenagers need help, even if they do not recognize this need or seem grateful for it. They must feel free to seek that help from their parents or loved ones. If teenagers cannot talk to their parents or to other acceptable adults, they have only their peers and friends to turn to. How much good advice and information on serious matters can one 13-year-old or 15-year-old give to another?

Conflict areas between parents and children include use of time, homework, performing chores, hours for coming in from activities, choice of friends, readiness for adult responsibilities, use of the telephone, money, grooming habits, and dress. The teenager's room and its cleanliness can be a source of friction. Table 10-4 presents a list of parent and youth conflicts found in one major study.

Concerning good grooming and dress, conflict in these areas is high before the age of 14 years. More likely, parental objections to dress and behavior are related to tradition, status quo, or the sin of disobedience toward one who has their best interest at heart. Adolescence is a period of experimentation during which identity is sought. Since manner of dress usually means conformity to the peer group, some adolescents are willing to defy parental authority, sometimes in a nice way and sometimes more violently, to be acceptable to their group (Weimberger, 1970).

Teenagers want to talk about schools, but they do not want their parents to fight their battles for them, to visit the school, or to attend the parent-teacher organization (secondary level). In fact, some teenagers are embarrassed by being seen with their parents, especially by their friends. Some humorists say that when children become adolescents, they no longer want to sit with their parents in church or go to the movies with them. When they return to sit voluntarily with their parents, they have outgrown their early adolescent stage.

TABLE 10-4 Summary of conflicts between Mormon parents and youths

Sources of conflict	*Frequency mentioned*
Performing home chores	134
Use of time	104
Attitude toward studies	76
Expenditures of money	72
Morals and manners	48
Choice of friends	43
Selection of clothes	42
Use of phone	36
Dating practices	33
Use of car	27
Total	615

Modified from Schvaneveldt, J.D. *Adolescence,* 1973, *8,* 171. Used by permission.

Developing heterosexuality: Descriptive view

Early adolescence begins with gangs or groups made up of members of the same sex and ends with a coming together of the two sexes in crowd activities and possibly with some dating. Fig. 10-4 is the classic illustration of Dunphy, suggesting the stages of group development from early to late adolescence. There is a gradual mixing together of the sexes, starting with parties in sixth and seventh grades. By the ninth grade most boys are willing to relate to girls just for the fun they get from being around them.

As social development takes place in early adolescence, teenagers begin to reconstruct their value systems and interest patterns regarding the opposite sex. They change according to their interpretation of what are considered by their peers, parents, and community to be accepted ***heterosexual*** practices and activities.

THREE VIEWS OF KIM

How Kim's mother thinks Kim sees herself

My name is Kim and I'm thirteen years old. I'll try to describe myself and tell what I like and what I don't like. It will be hard to do, but I'll also try to explain how I feel about things. I guess I should tell something about my family, too.

I'll start with my family. I live in a red brick ranch house with my mother and grandmother. My dad died when I was only five years old. I remember him, and I still miss him. Sometimes I cry when I'm lonely for him but Mom doesn't know that. Mom says he was sick and died. I don't ask her about it much. I don't think she likes to talk about it.

We have a small family, even if you count my dog and cat. We had seven gerbils at one time. I'm glad I have lots of aunts and uncles and cousins. I wish my mother would get married again. I'd like to have a father. Mostly I want brothers and sisters.

I think I'm kind of homely. One time I asked Mother to look at me but not as a mother. When I asked if she didn't think I was ugly, she smiled and said I'm cute. She just wanted to make me feel good.

I'm about four feet, ten inches tall, and my brown hair is long and straight. My eyes are blue, but I wish they were brown. I have to wear braces and I need to wear glasses.

For my birthday Mom let me get contacts. I was surprised because it wasn't even time for my glasses to be changed! I lost the contacts one time. Mom sure was upset and so was I. We got them replaced. Last week I lost my right lens. I sure hated to tell Mom about losing it. Mom didn't fuss much, but she says I have to call the eye doctor and pay for the replacement myself. I didn't call yet. I'm embarrassed to have the doctor know.

I'm kind of thin, but I'm proud that finally I'm starting to get a figure. I like to wear real short shorts and skirts and tight tops. Mom makes me change when we go anyplace. She doesn't understand.

I wish I'd start my periods. All my friends started a year ago. I feel like a little kid.

There are lots of things I like. I really like boys. I think about them more than Mom knows. Alan liked me for a long time. I felt great about that. Lots of girls like Alan, but he liked me best. Sometimes he'd call me on the phone. Then one day he started liking another girl. I don't know why. I pretend I can't stand him. Really I still like him. Mom says it's okay for me to like boys, but she won't even consider letting me date until I'm sixteen. I think that's really dumb. She keeps telling me she understands how I feel about boys and things, but I know she really doesn't! Sometimes I wish my mother were young like our neighbor. She's twenty-five and seems just like me.

I like to mess around in the kitchen. I make real good brownies. But I don't like to clean up afterward. In fact I don't like to do *any* work anymore. I always feel tired if I have to clean my room. It's funny, but I'm not tired when I ride bikes!

Mom says I should be an actress because I can show lots of emotion. She's only kidding, but I really do fool her sometimes. I can cry or get insulted or be mad if I just *want* to. Sometimes people do what I want when I act a certain way.

I really would like to be an actress. I'd like to have lots of people looking at me. That's another funny thing. Sometimes I think people are staring at me at the pool and places like that. I don't like that at all. Mom says they really aren't staring. She thinks I have an overactive imagination. There's a lot she doesn't understand about me.

I like school. Mostly I get good grades but I'm not so good in math. I don't like math. It never makes sense to me.

Thirteen is a good age to be because I'm allowed to baby-sit. I have lots of regular customers. They all tell Mom how dependable I am. I really like little kids. I like being thirteen because I'm a teenager, but I can't do things some teenagers do. I wish I could go to see rock groups when they come to town. I can't get Mom to change her mind. Being thirteen is strange in a way. I'm not a little kid anymore, so I can't do some things I'd really like to do. I'd feel silly. And there are things I'm not old enough to do. I think it will be neat to be grown-up and be my own boss.

I like men, I guess, like the fathers of my friends. But I never know how to act around them. I'm a little afraid of them. I'm not sure when they are kidding or when they're serious.

Since it's summer, I can usually stay up until I want to go to bed. That's something I really like. Once in a while Mom and Grandma go to bed before me. When that happens, I pretend I am the grown-up in the house. I fix myself tea and drink it as I watch TV. Mom gets up long before I do because she goes to work.

I like to wear eye makeup like my friends. Mom lets me wear it around the house and when I play, but she won't let me wear it away from home. She doesn't understand that all the kids are allowed. I bet she won't let me wear makeup because she never wears it. I don't think that's fair. She keeps telling me if she wanted a seventeen-year-old she'd adopt one. I think that's a dumb thing to say!

I take piano lessons. I don't like to practice my lessons very much, but I do like to play songs for people. I'm pretty good. I like to read, ride bikes, listen to tapes, talk on the phone, swim, watch TV, go on trips, and have family reunions. I eat all the time. I laugh every time Mom says my stomach is a bottomless pit.

There are things I don't like. I get mad if I have to come in at night when other kids are still out. I tell my mother she isn't fair, and I go in my room by myself to show her! But usually I come out before long. I don't want Mom to know this, but I am glad she makes me do some things when I say I don't want to do them. I act grumpy to fool her.

I don't like to be lectured because Mom lectures too long. She keeps talking even after she makes her point. You'd think she'd know I'm not a little kid.

I forgot something I really like to do. I like to have friends sleep at my house, and I like to sleep at their houses. I feel popular if I get invited to slumber parties. For my thirteenth birthday, I had twelve friends spend the night with me. Mom tells everyone we went through food like a cloud of locusts!

I'm happy when people talk to me like a grown-up. When they do, I can tell them how I feel about drugs, the Middle East, and the death penalty. Lots of people think kids my age don't have opinions about serious problems.

That's about all I can tell you about myself. I hope it helps you to know me.

• • •

This, then, is how I believe my daughter sees herself and would express her feelings.

I recognize that many of Kim's ideas refer to me. That's natural, considering our situation. While I'm neither overly protective nor overly permissive, her behavior and attitudes are considerably attuned to my approval and disapproval.

From the reading I've been doing I realize Kim is, for the most part, a "typical" thirteen-year-old. She has always been a child to push for limits, but never to the extent she does now! Her thoughts are very much preoccupied with boys and being grown-up.

I'm sure Kim feels I don't understand her, but she does talk things over with me.

Kim writes about Kim

Dear Dr. Kaluger,

I'm thirteen years old and my name is Kim. I am five feet tall and weigh eighty-three pounds. I have blue eyes and light brown hair. I have contacts and braces.

I like boys. I also like to travel. Traveling around the U.S. is lots of fun. I also like all winter sports and swimming in the summer. I really like listening to my eight-track tapes. I like to sketch houses, too.

But I absolutely *hate* to clean my room. My Mom bugs me about it a lot. I don't blame her though; it *is* a wreck! I also hate to go to the dentist. I haven't liked it since I was a little kid. I hate to get nagged!

There's not a whole lot that I'm good at. I'm pretty good at baby-sitting, though (that's coz' I love little kids). I've been taking piano lessons for four years, so I'm getting good at that.

What I most need to improve in is math and history. It seems to go in one ear and out the other. I need to improve in handwriting (guess you can tell). I also put a lot of things off till the last minute. I guess everyone needs a little improvement in personality. No one is completely perfect.

There are so many things I would like to do. So many I couldn't put them all down on paper. For one, I'd like to come to one of *your* classes and see what they're like. My Mom talks about them a lot. She says you make them so interesting. I'd like to attend one of your classes. I'd also like to go somewhere this summer. With my Mom going to school every day, we can't go anywhere this summer. I would also like to be sixteen; then I could drive and date. Boy, I can hardly wait! But I guess my wildest dream is to become an actress in Broadway plays. I'd like to have a southern accent (my neighbor does). Well, that's about it.

Kim

Kim as her mother sees her

Kim is a peppy, cute thirteen-year-old girl. She's about four feet, ten inches tall and weighs about eighty pounds. Kim's brown hair is long and straight. She looks nicest when she wears it in two ponytails. Kim has big blue eyes. She is wearing braces now, and they are really helping to straighten her teeth.

There are so many things Kim likes that I can only put part of them in a list. The list has no particular order of preference! Kim likes baby-sitting, listening to stereo tapes, swimming, boys, riding bikes, and talking on the phone. She also likes baking "goodies," slumber parties, pets, taking trips, reading, telling jokes, shopping, talking to grown-ups, eating, having her picture taken, and getting mail.

Among the things that Kim doesn't like are being told what to do, being lectured, cleaning her room, going to bed early, practicing piano, doing homework, and having people stare at her.

Kim is very good in many activities. She is a good piano player and a very good baby-sitter. She has talent in drawing, singing, and writing creative stories and poems. She will be a good actress for school plays. Kim is very good in her school work. Two of Kim's strongest traits are reliability and honesty.

Like everyone, Kim has areas that need improvement. She needs to develop patience and better math skills. She needs to be a more willing worker. Kim should wear the headgear for her braces more hours each day.

I believe Kim would like to have brothers and sisters, to learn to sew, to be popular, to have a great figure, to wear makeup, to be grown-up, and to be an actress or a teacher.

The age at which heterosexual interests begin is largely determined by these forces. If there is a conflict of thinking among these forces, teenagers respond to the force that has the greatest meaning and influence on them personally.

In some cities heterosexual activities begin on a noticeable scale among 11- and 12-year-olds. In other communities heterosexual involvements are not widely noted until the ages of 14 or 15 years. Two points relevant to our statements concerning age level heterosexual interests and practices will be emphasized. First, there are age level differences in social practices in various communities, social groups, and subcultures. Children in different communal areas are exposed to differences in accepted mores, customs, roles, and degrees of permissiveness in social relationships. In some communities it is proper for a 13-year-old girl to go out on a single date. In other communities this action is deeply frowned upon, especially if it is a "car date," and all kinds of social restrictions are imposed to hinder such dating. Second, regardless of the community, there will always be individuals who do not follow the generally accepted practices. People do not fit neat, rigid categories, and some persons will not abide by the customs. The statements in this section on developing heterosexuality are intended to refer to "commonly observed practices" and not to "the exception to the rule" or to the few who are the forerunners of a change in social behavior.

Early adolescent years usually provide opportunities for a considerable number of heterosexual contacts, most of which are related to school affairs or to com-

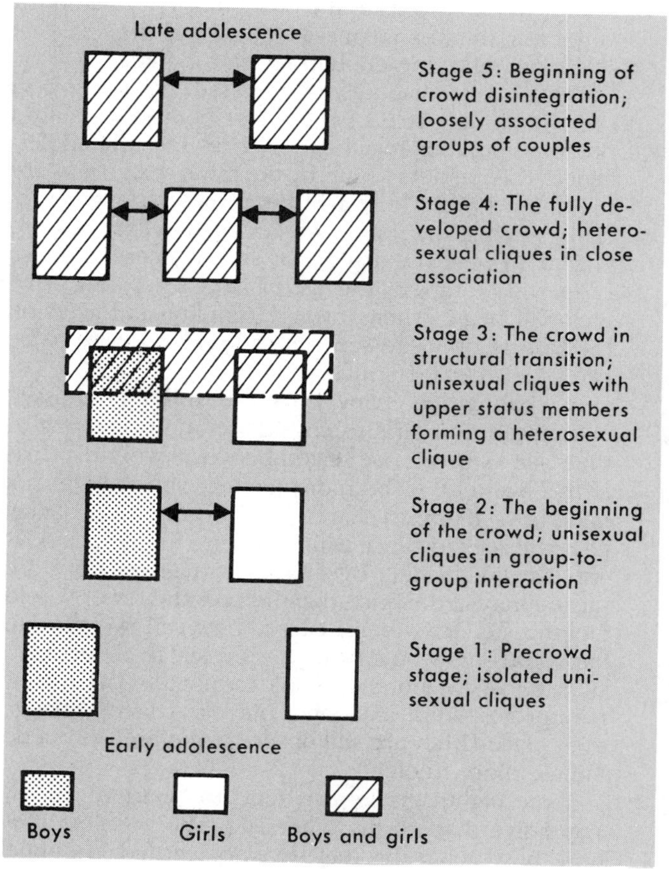

FIG. 10-4 *Stages of group development in adolescence.*
From Dunphy, D.C. Sociometry, *1963, 26, 230-240.*

munity activities provided for young people. Group contacts are desirable because they give opportunities to practice social skills, such as conversation, courtesy, and cooperation.

Usually the first heterosexual activities are "group" or "crowd" affairs. Pairing off by couples is not the usual relationship. A group or the "crowd" is invited to a party. The girls may dance together while the boys watch. Some special activity, such as a mixer game, will be needed to bring the two sexes together. However, at a party in a home, it would not be unusual for the group to play kissing games such as post-office, truth-or-dare, or spin-the-bottle (Kantner and Zelnick, 1974). Boys go along with such games because the products of the games are "daring"—something like "forbidden fruit." Boys get a feeling of pleasant amazement "to think that someone likes me well enough to call *my* number to go to the post office for a stamp!" It is not that the kiss means so much; it is the idea that "someone likes me enough to ask for a kiss."

There is less antagonism toward the opposite sex, an ever-widening circle of friends of both sexes, and a broader range of social experiences in early adolescence. The barriers set up by the same sex groups are tumbling down. There will be a few holdouts, especially among the boys. As far as unwillingness to engage in heterosexual activities is concerned, these cases will be rare by the age of 14 years. Dating activities will begin when shyness, timidity, and aversion toward the opposite sex decrease and a desire to be like older teenagers increases.

In sixth grade many boys are still embarrassed enough around girls to consider it a major threat to their self-esteem to be seated between two girls. Girls at this age tend to be more mature, and they do not mind boys. If given a chance at a party or school dance, girls will seek to dance with boys even though the boys are usually shorter. By the seventh grade boys are more interested in girls than before, and fewer would feel threatened by being placed between two girls. In fact some boys would be highly pleased to be forced to sit next to a girl, but they would try not to show it. They may protest loud and long, but don't try to change their places! They are still unsure of themselves but do mingle more freely.

Some eighth grade girls tend to be more openly aggressive than at any other age. The problem they have, however, is that they have not learned the subtle, social skills necessary to know how to show an interest in boys without appearing too eager, too forward, or too bold. One eighth grade girl was asked by a teasing adult, "Jack McDonald says he likes you, do you like him?" "Yes," replied the girl. "Who is he?" "You mean you don't know him and you say you like him?" "Sure," replied the quick-thinking girl, "if he likes me, he has good taste, and that's all that matters!"

The summer between the eighth and ninth grades seems to bring about unbelievable changes in heterosexual development as a number of boy-girl relationships blossom and begin to be longer lasting. Many boys are now taller than their girl classmates. They are more sure of themselves and less embarrassed about seeking female companionship. Many ninth grade girls are interested in male companions. The more mature girls may be dating fellows who are several years older than themselves.

Sexual awareness

The typical youngster in late childhood appears to be relatively unconfused about sexuality. However, with the onset of puberty and adolescence, even the most well-adjusted child will have some uncertainties and questions. Even when children have received most of their sex education at home in an anxiety-free atmosphere, they may still be perplexed. They are at an age when adult wisdom is not accepted as readily as it once was. The parents of 12-year-olds may find their children far more inclined to believe in the teaching of their peers. As noted in Table 10-5, the common source of adolescent sex information is from peers rather than parents. Discrepancies between what the peers say and what the parents say add to the uncertainty. If the peers provide a more extensive, in-depth discussion concerning sex, children may wonder why their parents are so hesitant or uncomfortable concerning the topic of sex. They begin to look for answers of their own. The parents applaud their desire to look for information relating to a history project but may show no enthusiasm when they seek answers to sex questions. The youngsters are further confused by this inconsistency. Females are generally more knowledgeable about facts of maturation and reproduction. Females also receive more information from their parents than do males (Davis and Harris, 1982).

Adolescents show some concern about their secondary sex characteristics. Boys are conscious of the formation of their sex structure and concerned if they believe there are any deviations. They are troubled by nocturnal emissions and wonder if anyone, especially

TABLE 10-5 Adolescent sex information sources

Source	*Male N–392 (%)*	*Female N–568 (%)*	*Total N–958 (%)*
Peers	45.7	32.4	38.7
Literature	16.7	23.8	20.9
School	18.3	20.4	19.5
Mother	5.6	18.7	13.4
Father	4.1	.7	2.1
Experiences	8.0	2.8	5.0
Minister	1.0	.6	.7
Physician	.6	.6	.6
	100.0	100.0	100.0

From Thomberg, H.D. *Contemporary adolescence: Readings* (2nd ed.). Copyright 1975 by Wadsworth Publishing Co. Reprinted by permission of the publisher, Brooks/Cole Publishing Co., Monterey, California.

their mother who usually washes the pajamas and bedsheets, might find out. Girls are concerned mostly with breast development and whether or not anyone can tell when they are having their monthly periods.

Some adolescents of this age level experience masturbation, boys more so than girls. There are questions such as why is there an erection, what causes it, why does it feel different to masturbate, will it hurt anything, is it sinful or bad, does it mean that I'm oversexed, and does anyone else do this too? Most adolescents probably engage in self-stimulation because of sexual responses that are stirred and the emotional tone experience that is felt (Mondy and Ehrhardt, 1972).

Petting, attachments to others of the opposite sex, and masturbation are the most frequent methods of sexual release during this period. Our counseling work with young teenagers has indicated that there is more sexual involvement taking place among girls of this age than most adults realize. The involvement is generally of the initial necking and petting variety. Almost always this activity involves an older boy. Our counseling experiences indicate that whenever a 13- or 14-year-old girl goes steady for at least 3 months with a boy who is 2 or 3 years older, there is invariably some extensive petting taking place (not necessarily the sex act). Petting takes place sooner if an automobile is used extensively by the couple. Statistics on pregnancies and related matters will be provided in Chapter 11.

TEEN CULTURE AND INTERESTS

The development of interests during early adolescence can offer many positive rewards. Interests open gateways to the mind and usually make a person more receptive and eager to learn. Interests help to establish channels of communication with others. Sharing ideas on the professional football players and exchanging records provide a bond of mutuality among teenagers. Intimacy of friendships increases dramatically in early adolescence. Friends tend to have similar attitudes toward school and peer culture such as rock music and fashion (Berndt, 1982). The development of interests can lead to constructive use of leisure time and may help to crystallize a vocational pattern for later years.

Interests of early adolescents

Boys like to spend a great deal of time in active outdoor sports and just "going out with the guys." They also spend time on hobbies of a mechanical nature. Watching television comprises a good bit of their time. Being with girls does not constitute a large part of their leisure activity, although it does occupy more time as they enter the freshman year of high school.

Girls' leisure activities show a sharp contrast. Their activities include fewer outdoor pursuits than those of boys. More time is spent in "just being with the girls," listening to records, and experimenting with makeup. Due to their increased awareness of the feminine role, they now are highly conscious of their personal appearance. Exploration of the female world seems to be a natural inclination. Lipstick and makeup may appear on girls as early as the age of 9 years. Clothing of the latest style is tempting to them. They like to go shopping for clothes, but some seldom agree with their mothers on fads and colors.

Other interests include listening to new records and loud music. Being able to recite the most popular hit records is part of this pattern. Watching movies or television programs is another pastime. Also typical for this stage is keeping a diary. Daydreams, events, and emotions that cannot be shared with real people are confessed to a diary. The diary affords role playing and fantasy without involving action in reality.

Harold Geyer

Early adolescents are the largest consumers of records, tapes, and pop music items. Music serves as an outlet for physical energy, provides for freedom of movement, and allows for the harmless (sublimated?) expression of emotions.

The preadolescent and young adolescent may become an active community participant as a member of Girl Scouts, Boy Scouts, Boys' Clubs, or Campfire Girls because it is at this time that the young person is greatly interested in forming groups and joining social clubs. For boys, gangs are a spontaneous effort to create a society for themselves and get the thrill of participating in common interests. Girls may be even more organizationally oriented than boys. They are more mature in seeking friendships with others and are more interested in social activities. Girls' club activities include more participation on an organized team than formerly.

Young adolescents may watch television because it is something they can do together. Reading may satisfy their demands for adventure, boys preferring stories about animals, adventure, and sports of all kinds, girls enjoying biographies about women, mysteries, stories of home life, and love stories. In early adolescence there is usually a great interest in movies for the same reason adolescents have an interest in television—because they can go together. Movies catering to youth draw many junior high students on weekends. Girls prefer movies over athletics, whereas boys do not. Boys who go to the movies would prefer to see a sports, mystery, or adventure story or a movie with excitement, realism, humor, or violence.

Whereas a movie is not something a junior high student can enjoy all the time, a radio is. Many young adolescents carry around stereo transistor radios and combine the music with studying, walking, and many other activities. In study halls it is not uncommon to see a boy or girl with a transistor radio hidden in his or her lap and a listener's plug in his or her ear. Rock and roll or popular music is preferred at all grade levels. Girls at early adolescence prefer music on television or the radio to a greater degree than boys do. Rock and roll is one of the surest ways to the heart and wallet of the adolescent, creating a ritualized world of dances, slang, the charts, and fan magazines. However, during the early 1980s the sales of record and cassette tape companies have suffered to a great degree.

When young adolescents are not going to the movies, reading, or listening to music, they are probably talking. They find it easy and desirable to talk to their friends in "rap sessions," which is their main out-of-school activity. Boys may spend hours talking about sports figures, athletics, and cars; girls talk about parties, dates, clothes, and social happenings at school. These conversations may take place on the telephone, exasperating parents and others on the party line alike. However, this conversation with friends is helpful to the young adolescent, building up his or her self-confidence and ability to converse with others.

Fads and fashion

A form of interest that seems most characteristic of early adolescence is the "fad." A *fad* is a short-term fashion or practice pursued with exaggerated zeal. It is usually temporary and unpredictable. Young adolescents are extremely concerned with being accepted by their peers. This intense desire for acceptance is part of the reason why fads catch on so quickly during adolescent years. They help to give each individual a feeling of belonging. It seems that junior high schools can expect at least one major fad to hit the school each year. Teachers often wonder, "What will they think of next!" A perennial fad in some areas is the use of water pistols by the boys.

One junior high school teacher writes concerning her experiences with fads in her school:

> One group of our junior high girls went around for days braless in T-shirts and jeans. The fellows all wore headbands. Girls used curling irons so their hair was in ringlets. (Several years ago I spent hours trying to straighten mine.) When I was in junior high we wore sneakers in the spring to be "in." When my sister reached her junior high school years, a dime in each loafer was the thing to do. I also spent hours making a chain with gum wrappers as tall as my boyfriend at the time, then burning it; if it burned all the way to the end, our "love" would last. Strange as it may seem, none of mine ever made it to the end. Fads, of course, can change overnight as do the interests of early adolescents; but they allow the adolescent to feel he is truly like his peer group.

Other fads include the wearing of certain clothing or certain colors. Stockings and socks have gone the route from white ankle socks, to ribbed white socks half-way up the calf and knee socks, to flesh-colored nylon hose, to colored hose, to textured or patterned hose, to hose and long-line girdles, to colored panty hose and leotards. Hair styles among boys have included crew cuts, skin heads, Mohawk Indian cuts, flat tops, duck style, brush cuts, shaggy hair, and no cuts. Girls would bleach streaks of their hair, use food dye to color their hair green, blue, or red, or let their hair grow stringy and long, giving them an "intellectual, unwashed look." In some schools students would speak in an imitation "Chinese language" by beginning the words with the "y" sound. Can you recall what fads were popular in your crowd when you were 13 to 15 years old?

Various attempts have been made to explain the reason why adolescents' fads take hold. The strongest motive appears to be a combination of the desire to receive attention, the desire to reflect independence from adults, and the desire to be one of the gang. Adolescents receive comfort from being like others their age. Apparently the most important factor in understanding teen fads is recognizing the "herd" instinct to look alike, to feel part of a group by wearing the same clothes, using the same language, or developing the same mannerisms.

At the same time, fads permit adolescents to express their individuality by wearing more of what is in style or by being the first to hear and use a new slang

David Strickler

Some fads make it possible to combine the idealistic expressions of adolescence and the unique characteristics that identify adolescents. T-shirts convey many messages.

phrase. Fads may compensate for a lack of grooming skills and social "know-how"—especially for the adolescents who are patiently waiting for the time until they have developed more confidence in their ability to select clothes and styles that are appropriate for their body build and their personality. They can represent a pioneer spirit and a yearning for freedom from regimentation. In fact, food fads and idiosyncrasies in language, manner, and clothes may be subtle expressions of the desire to hurry the growing-up process.

Another related and familiar phenomenon is simply fashion—the very latest in dressing, writing, behaving, and so on. *Fashion* usually involves a socially approved variation of dress, furniture, music, art, speech, and other areas of culture. Each age-group has its own varieties of fashion, reflecting certain characteristics of that age. Compared to older adolescents, younger adolescents are motivated more by the excitement factor than by thoughts of economy. Younger adolescents also lean toward style considerations rather than quality, they are more influenced by mass media, and they are less sensitive to status symbols (Horowitz, 1982). At times, being in fashion is a question of keeping tabs on changing sizes; knowing, for example, that sunglasses are growing larger, hair lengths are changing, and the width of neckties is different. Whatever their cause or result, fads and fashions are a part of modern society.

PERSONAL PROBLEMS AND CONCERNS

The personal problems of adolescents are fairly well documented. At this point we merely wish to present some personal statements written in a free-response, permissive situation by junior high school pupils. The intent of personalizing the problems of teenagers is to show the degree of intensification these young people have concerning their problems and the implications of these problems for a need on the part of the adolescent to reconstruct and reorganize his or her personality from what it was in childhood. The child of 9, 10, or 11 years was a fairly stable individual. With the coming of puberty every single avenue of growth and development undergoes extensive changes, making the personality of many a younger child inadequate for the emerging new individual.

Problems of adolescents can be grouped under the following categories: (1) physical problems, such as facial problems, uneven growth, late maturing, early maturing, and sex problems; (2) personal problems involving self-identity, self-concept, and personality; (3) social problems relating to home and family, peer group, and social status; (4) scholastic problems of the school, including study, tests, homework, and teachers; (5) religion, moral values, and development of a personal philosophy; and (6) future problems concerning vocations and alienation from society. Categories of student problems in 1979 are indicated in Table 10-6.

The following personal concerns were written by seventh, eighth, and ninth graders in response to the query "What problems or difficulties do you have for which you would like help? In other words, what is bothering you in relation to people, your family,

TABLE 10-6 Percentage of free-response problems stated by 231 junior high school students in an eastern town, population 18,000 (Kaluger and Kaluger, 1979).

	7th grade	*8th grade*	*9th grade*	*Total*
Problems related to school	18	39	36	31
Parents and home	23	18	21	21
Personal; self-concern	11	11	10	11
Peer relationships	10	6	14	10
Sibling relationships	8	6	4	6
Boy-girl relationships	5	8	3	5
No response or inadequate	25	12	12	16

money, friends, or any other part of your life? (Your name is not needed.)" The problems are presented as they were written. They are some of the more common problems and concerns.

It was difficult to pick out representative problems as they were written by early adolescents because there were so many good ones from which to choose. We have conducted this study over a 5-year period in a variety of communities and have over a thousand papers. The first time I (G.K.) collected papers from the students I could not wait to read what they had written. So I read a number of the papers before I left their school to go home. I will never forget the depressed, heavy feeling that overcame me. My shoulders and head actually felt the weight of the burden of their problems. I thought that they were such happy-go-lucky kids, but instead they were immersed in deep, often unresolvable problems. Here were children worrying about their mothers and fathers separating, about when they would get something decent to eat, or how to avoid the clutches of criminal elements and drugs, and we teachers were trying to teach them something about ancient Rome, binomial theorems, and dangling participles!

Girl, 12 years, seventh grade

I don't have any problems other than not getting enough allowance and having pimples. My pimples are getting better, thank goodness.

Girl, 12 years, seventh grade

Do you think I am old enough to let a boy kiss me? He tried to do it a few times, but I covered my face. He asked me to go to the football game, but my mother would not let me go; she said I was too young. I know he will ask me to go some place else. How can I get my mother to let me go? The trouble is I want to go but I would rather pay my own way.

Boy, 12 years, seventh grade

How will I know what to say to a girl so I won't get my head knocked off?

Boy, 13 years, eighth grade

My father left my mother, my sister, and me when I was 12 years old. If I were younger, it wouldn't have meant much to me, but I wasn't and I have felt strong resentment toward him. It bothers me in school and in other places. If I could overcome my resentment toward him, I could get along better with other people.

Boy, 13 years, eighth grade

I don't know when I have time to study, since I work to help support the family because my father is sick. I do not get very much sleep in the evenings. So, when I don't have any written work in class, I sort of doze off.

Girl, 13 years, eighth grade

I have learned to be happy most of the time, and I am very contented with my life. But, when I act happy, people think I am nuts.

Boy, 13 years, eighth grade

Parents are pests. They're always nagging me and will not let me outside past 8 o'clock.

Girl, 13 years, eighth grade

How old do you think I should be before I should be allowed to date? Some of the girls my age are already dating. Do you think this is the right age or should I wait till I'm older?

Girl, 13 years, eighth grade

Last week in geography class I had to collect the homework papers. As I went to collect one of the girl's papers, she told me not to tell the teacher because she didn't have her homework finished. As I went up to tell the teacher I just couldn't figure out whether to tell the teacher or leave it go because I was afraid the girl would be mad at me. Would you please tell me if I should have told the teacher?

Boy, 13 years, eighth grade

What should you do when your parents always seem to be arguing and you don't even want to go home? It seems I'm always trying to figure out a different excuse for going somewhere. The family seems to be growing further apart.

Girl, 14 years, eighth grade

I am worried about someone grabbing me in a car coming home after dark.

Girl, 14 years, ninth grade

My father is under the impression that no boys are good enough for me, and therefore I'm not permitted to associate with them. But this is not true. It's just that I may not be good enough for the boys and they do not seem interested in me.

Boy, 14 years, ninth grade

The school—it stinks! I hate school. I like young teachers, not old, grouchy teachers. School is all right if you don't have too many lessons.

Girl, 14 years, ninth grade

I don't know what course to take in high school. It is hard for me to make up my mind as to what I want to do and what subjects to take.

Boy, 14 years, ninth grade

The main question in my mind is sex education. I wouldn't want anybody to think I am immoral or indecent but rather just trying to receive a good education. When you receive any advice on this matter from another guy, you never get it straight. It is always told to you the wrong way. I have gathered that sex is a thing to be hidden and whispered about. The movies and magazines play it up but that is not sex information. I cannot help but think that educated people should take this open-mindedly and straightforwardly. I would like some advice or help on this question. Maybe I'm too young; I don't know. But if I am, I wish someone that is qualified to say would tell me.

Boy, 14 years, ninth grade

My father and I aren't together enough. I would like to get better acquainted with him and have more activities together when he is not working.

Girl, 14 years, ninth grade

I would like to get along with my sisters and brothers, but they don't seem to like me for some reason.

Boy, 15 years, ninth grade

I live 13 miles from high school. I have to get up at 5 o'clock in the morning so I can do my barn work. Then I leave for school at 7:30 to catch a bus. I don't get home until 5:30 in the evening. After I get my barn work done and eat supper it is time to go to bed. And the teachers want us to work at least two hours at home on our lessons. We should have shorter school days or fewer unimportant subjects.

Girl, 15 years, ninth grade

How can I learn to study at home with a lot of kids playing in the hallways, television sets blaring out all over the apartment house, and people yelling at the top of their voices?

Girl, 16 years, special education class

I don't have much interest in school. But my parents want me to go to school. I try to get my work but can't get it too well. I would like to know of something that might interest me in school. I feel so self-conscious because I am only in eighth grade (special education). I was thinking about quitting school, but then I took the second thought about it. What can you do without an education? My parents don't want me to quit, but I don't seem to have any interest in school.

CHAPTER REVIEW

1. The term *adolescence* comes from the Latin verb *adolescere*, meaning "to grow into maturity." In complex societies the period of adolescence is extended because it takes additional time to prepare for the tasks of modern adulthood.
2. The *developmental tasks* of early adolescence emphasize the transitional state occurring between childhood and adulthood. This transition involves physical changes, heterosexual interests, sex role, appropriate values and morals, a sense of independence, and adaptive skills.
3. *Prepuberty* is the preadolescence period before puberty. *Puberty* is the period when the primary and secondary sex characteristics grow and become obvious. In *postpubescence* the skeletal growth becomes nearly complete, and the new biological functions are fairly well established. There is a one- to two-year period of sterility immediately following puberty.
4. The average age of the first *menses* for North American girls is 12.5 years of age. The average age range is 10 to 16. The average age of menarche has dropped by 5 years in the last century.
5. The indicators of puberty in boys are the presence of live sperm in the urine and nocturnal emissions. The average age of puberty for boys in North America is 14.0 years, with two thirds reaching puberty between 12.5 and 16.5 years of age.
6. *Primary sex characteristics* involve the development of internal and external sex organs. *Secondary sex characteristics* are the physical features, other than the reproductive organs, that distinguish the mature male and the mature female from each other and from children of the same sexes.
7. The *growth spurt* for girls in puberty reaches its peak between the ages of 11 and 13 years. Girls will grow 5 to 10 cm (2 to 4 in.) a year during the growth spurt and will gain 3.5 to 4.5 kg (8 to 10 lb.). The peak of the growth spurt for boys is between 13 and 15½ years of age. The average boy will gain 10 to 12.5 cm (4 to 5 in.) in height and 5.5 to 6.5 kg (12 to 14 lb.) in weight.
8. *Asynchrony*, an uneven rate of growth for various parts of the body, occurs in early adolescence.
9. Body ideal or *body image* affects the way adolescents feel about themselves. Concern with body image may be greater in societies where body build and appearance are emphasized. About one third of the boys and one half of the girls are dissatisfied with some aspect of their physical appearance.
10. *Early maturing boys* perceive themselves as more positive and are more successful in peer relationships than late maturers. *Late maturers* tend to be more eager, talkative, and self-assertive.
11. *Early maturing girls* have positive psychological benefits *after* elementary school age. They have greater sociability, leadership, poise, and expressiveness than late-maturing girls. *Late maturing* in girls seems to have an adverse effect on their personality.
12. Descriptively, most 12-year-olds are happy and in good humor. Thirteen-year-olds are moderately calm but will sulk and cry. Fourteen-year-olds try to control their anger but will retreat to their rooms to be alone.
13. Piaget's *formal operations stage* (11 or 12 to 15 and older) is a period when logic in terms of hypotheses, strategies, propositional thoughts, ideals, and possibilities develops. The research indicates that formal reasoning is highly related to age, but not all adolescents achieve this ability automatically.
14. There are positive correlations between family socioeconomic variables and intelligence scores. Mental test scores are highly correlated with father's occupation, mother's and father's education, and the type of verbal and educational stimulation received.
15. A *moral transition* takes place in early adolescence as the peer group makes its influence known and the youngster responds to conformity. However, *cognitive disequilibrium* causes the early adolescent to restructure the moral reasoning framework. Piaget states that the individual must move from a *heteronomous morality*, where others are the authority and decide the rules, to an *autonomous morality*, where rules are based on commonly agreed goals and cooperation.
16. According to *Kohlberg*, moral growth results from the level of moral reasoning possessed by an individual at the moment. Adolescents usually operate at stages 3 or 4, which is conventional morality designed to gain approval or to show respect for authority. Neither Kohlberg nor Piaget appear to take into account desire or motivation to change. *Moral motivation* may be based on anxiety, fear, or empathy for another person.
17. According to Hoffman, *parental discipline* may be (a) power assertion, (b) love withdrawal, or (c) induction and explanation. Power assertion and withdrawal of love are used to get attention and stop a behavior. Induction reasoning and explanation must be used if communicated ideas are to be remembered.
18. *Peer influence* reaches a peak in adolescence, but peer groups do not appear to exert a widespread influence on values and directions different from those of the parents if the parents are accepting individuals and are present in the home. Parents are the ones who are more apt to employ inductive reasoning.

19. Peer influence through *group conformity* provides some gratification of group dependency needs in terms of a role in society. Peer groups in early adolescence usually make a transition from same-sex groups to mixed groups. Within the group there may still be one or two best friends.
20. *Parent-teen relationships* in early adolescence may be disquieting as both sides are attempting to get used to the changes occurring. The relationship need not be one of strain or stress if the parents offer the proper guidance in providing opportunities, experiences, and responsibilities leading to the development of adult competencies.
21. Conflict areas between parents and early adolescents often involve homework, the performance of chores, the use of time, and the readiness for adult responsibilities. Money, the telephone, the teenager's room, and grooming habits may also be a source of irritation.
22. *Heterosexual social development* usually evolves according to the social and dating patterns of the community or subculture. Typically the movement is from same-sex group activities, to mixed group or crowd activities, to sporadic or scattered dating within groups. Twelve- to 14-year-olds are just learning the social skills for the most part. By the age of 14 most girls are interested in male companions.
23. Development of sexuality often revolves around emerging secondary sexual characteristics. Frequently there are perplexing questions that go unanswered by adults; answers given by other peers often have limitations.
24. The interests of boys center around sports, going out with the guys, and hobbies. Girls are interested in being with the girls, listening to music, and learning about facial makeup and fashions. Both sexes often engage in organized group activities.
25. Fads, or short-term fashions, are prevalent among early adolescents. Fads permit a combination of conformity to an age-level activity unique to the group and an expression of some individuality within the group activity.
26. Personal problems of early adolescents center around self, school, and social needs.

REVIEW QUESTIONS

1. Review developmental tasks of early adolescence. Under what headings might you group them?
2. Define prepuberty, puberty, and postpubescence.
3. What are the criteria for puberty in girls? What is the average age range and the average age of puberty in girls?
4. What are the criteria for puberty in boys? What is the average age range and the average age of puberty in boys?
5. Review Fig. 10-2 and Tables 10-1 and 10-2. How would you summarize the physical maturation of boys and girls of this age level?
6. What is the growth spurt? When does it take place, on the average, in girls and in boys?
7. Besides changes in sexual characteristics, what other bodily changes take place? How do early adolescents generally react to their physical changes? (Review Siegel's conclusions.)
8. What are the characteristics of early maturing boys and girls? Of late maturing boys and girls?
9. Personal characteristics are presented in a descriptive, normative fashion. What thread or threads do you see running through this age level?
10. Define and describe Piaget's concept of formal operations for adolescence. What are the five characteristics involved?
11. What does the research have to say about Piaget's formal operations stage? How does Piaget answer the critics?
12. How do socioeconomic factors affect the development of the intellectual potential?
13. Why is the term *age of moral transition* used as a major heading? What is its implication for early adolescence?
14. Define cognitive disequilibrium. Why does anyone have to do anything about it?
15. Define heteronomous morality and autonomous morality. What moral growth takes place?
16. Kohlberg also has a cognitive disequilibrium model of moral development. How does it differ from that of Piaget?
17. What is moral motivation? How do anxiety and empathy fit into moral motivation?
18. What conclusion can be drawn from the research on parental discipline and moral growth? (Remember the meaning of the three types of parental discipline.)
19. Who has more influence on early adolescent morality, the parents or the peers? What support can you give for your position?
20. As you see it, how are the terms peer pressure, peer influence, and peer conformity different in their meaning? How are they the same?
21. List some of the conflicts between parents and teens. Review Table 10-4.
22. In heterosexual development, why have the sexes been apart up to early adolescence? Why do they come together at that point? How do boys and girls differ in their heterosexual interests and activities in early adolescence?
23. Review the observation theory on early heterosexuality. Do you agree or disagree with it? Why or why not?
24. How much heterosexual awareness is there in early adolescence? Review Figure 10-4.

25. What are the main interests of boys and girls in early adolescence? Did these interest patterns fit you?
26. What fads or short-term fashions can you recall from your early adolescent days?
27. Read the personal concerns. Do they sound familiar? Which ones could you add?

THOUGHT QUESTIONS AND ACTIVITIES

1. What is the transition, as you see it, that takes place in physical development between the child in late childhood and the early adolescent past puberty? Does it seem to you like a three-stage process? Why do some go through the process faster than others? Do you suppose that the girl who goes through puberty when she is 10 years old is different from the girl who goes through puberty when she is 12 years old? Does it really make a difference?
2. In spite of an occasional readjustment period or need, the average teenager really has few problems making the transition from childhood to adolescence. Thinking back to the days when you were about the ages of 12, 13, and 14, did you find it to be a pleasant time, in terms of becoming a teenager? Would you want to relive that period again?
3. Piaget states that abstract reasoning capabilities of the formal operations period start about the age of 12 years. Have you found this to be your experience and that of your friends? Talk about it.
4. The meaning of the "Age of moral transition" is a little nebulous. How would you state what it means? Does the concept of a cognitive disequilibrium in moral judgment seem plausible? Why or why not?
5. Is there such a thing as "peer pressure"? Define it and describe it. Now take a look at the meaning of "peer conformity." Is there a difference between the two terms? To what degree are early adolescents subjected to peer pressure and peer conformity on matters that are really important? Is the influence of the group overexaggerated in the popular media? What does the research say?
6. What were some of the fads or fashions common when you were in the sixth to ninth grades? Why do early adolescents follow fads? Do adults follow fads or do they merely follow fashions? Can there be fads of thoughts, beliefs, and views as well as of clothing and material things?
7. Do a survey of questions, concerns, or problems of sixth to ninth graders to determine what kind of information or help they would like to have.
8. Debate whether boys and girls are maturing earlier today than 20 years ago.

FURTHER READINGS

Everhart, R.B. The nature of "goofing off" among junior high school adolescents. *Adolescence,* 1982, *17*(65), 177-188. Descriptions of "goofing off" behavior lead to the conclusion that it is relegated to a passive role within the school organization. The implication is that the activity could be used in a positive manner.

Kaluger, G., and Kaluger, M. *Profiles of human development.* St. Louis: The C.V. Mosby Co., 1976. This paperback is a collection of vignettes or profiles of real life happenings. Although it covers the life span, prenatal to old age, the sections on adolescence and emerging adulthood are especially relevant to the average reader of this textbook. The reading is easy and enjoyable.

Krosnick, J.A., and Judd, C.M. Transactions in social influence at adolescence: Who induces cigarette smoking? *Developmental Psychology,* 1982, *18*(3), 359-368. The influence of parents and peers on preadolescents and early adolescents concerning smoking behavior is examined. It is concluded that peer influence increases during adolescence.

Muuss, R.E. Social cognition: David Elkind's theory of adolescent egocentrism. *Adolescence,* 1982, *17*(66), 249-265. According to Elkind, as cognitive development progresses through the stages identified by Piaget, the nature of egocentrism changes, and each stage has its characteristics.

Shavelson, R.J., and Bolus, R. Self-concept: The integrity of theory and methods. *Journal of Educational Psychology,* 1982, *74*(3), 3-17. Self-concept apparently does not become increasingly stable toward the apex of a hierarchical construct. However, self-concept appeared to be distinguished from achievement.

Stubbs, M.L. Period piece. *Adolescence,* 1982, *17*(65), 45-55. This article discusses the psychological and social implications of menarche, as experienced by the author and one of her students.

Wenger, C. The suitcase story: A therapeutic technique for children in out-of-home placement. *American Journal of Orthopsychiatry,* 1982, *52*(2), 353-355. A story developed as a vehicle for the expression of many of the feelings experienced by children in out-of-home placement is presented.

CHAPTER 11

MIDDLE AND LATER ADOLESCENCE

15 TO 18 YEARS OF AGE

GOING ON SIXTEEN

Lynn will be sixteen on Saturday. After the turmoil of the junior high years, the picture of the adult Lynn will someday be is starting to emerge. After a growth spurt of four inches and seventeen pounds in one year (sixth grade) and a gradual growth thereafter, Lynn's sixteenth year has seen mostly a rounding out of her boyish figure. Standing five feet, six inches in height and weighing 115 pounds, Lynn is slim and athletic in build, leggy, and well coordinated. She has long, straight brown hair, pretty, dark brown eyes (which she insists are too small), braces on her teeth (which she accepts in good humor), and sporadic bouts with a less than perfect complexion (which she does not accept in good humor).

Lynn's mental abilities have placed her in the honors program in her school, where she maintains A and B grades with an average amount of effort. In the past year, as a result of being involved in activities at school, she has learned to budget her time more wisely; consequently, she accomplishes more in less time than before.

Her moods vary—when she is up, she is euphoric; when she is down, her chin is scraping the pavement. Woe be to the mother who chirps cheerfully at her when she is down or to the household that does not buzz happily when she is up. She is, however, becoming a little easier to live with. She seems less intense—or perhaps more self-controlled. Even her relationship with her ten-year-old sister has improved. There are moments in which she seems almost maternal and tender; most times, though, she is more likely to complain: "Mother, you've got to do something about that child!" Understandably, she is most affectionate to her sibling when she is most angry with her mother—a joining of forces, perhaps, to face the adversary.

Lynn's parents were divorced when she was thirteen, and she has made what seems to be a very good adjustment to a major upheaval in these important years. Remaining in the same home with no change in school or friends may have helped. Because her relationship with her father had been a warm and close one, Lynn has always been at ease with boys; she is on her way to establishing a good rapport with adolescent boys. Although she was interested in boys in junior high, she did not date; this year, as a sophomore in the senior high school, she has been dating occasionally—mostly as part of a group—and enjoying her social life very much. Lately her dates have been limited to one boy who shares her interest in dramatics.

Lynn has become more outgoing and poised this year. In junior high she spent more time on studies than on extracurricular activities; this year the reverse seems true. After an inauspicious beginning in which she announced after the first day of school: "I hate that school—I don't know anybody in my classes—you can't move in the halls—and the food is lousy!" this has turned out to be her best year yet. Making an early decision to get involved in things, she tried out for the school play, became one of the few sophomores to get a part, and her year was underway. In the middle of the year, sports took over, and she made a place on the girls' JV basketball team. Playing every game with unbounded enthusiasm, she earned her letter, an accomplishment that further bolstered her self-confidence. The spring activity was a tossup between the school musical and softball. The musical won by a slight edge; and although she had only two speaking lines in the entire production, she managed to find herself minor dancing and singing parts in about five scenes.

Lynn has made sporadic attempts at keeping a diary, but she possibly expressed herself best when her class was asked by the English teacher to keep a journal of their day-to-day thoughts and activities. This literary effort ranged from the silly to the serious. Most of it was a casual interpretation of the day's activities—the basketball game to be played, freezing on the corner waiting for the school bus, the orthodontist's "implements of destruction" with which he hammered and pounded on her teeth (Are beautiful teeth really worth it? she mused). Occasionally she sounded serious—she reflected on the meaning and worth of a second in time, concluding her writing with the importance of how we spend all those seconds in our lives. Then occasionally a silly unwinding at the end of the day: "I'm so glad, I'm so glad, I'm glad, I'm glad. Today is Thursday. Friday is tomorrow—how do you like that? Anyway, I don't have any philosophical thoughts in my head—I usually don't. I feel like talking. I want to talk. Why can't I talk? Because I'm supposed to be writing."

For the most part Lynn's thoughts are not terribly profound, for she is still at a very self-centered stage. She is mildly concerned that she doesn't know what she wants to be, and she is beginning to question the relevancy of much that she studies. Being an inveterate griper, she complains loudly: "Chemistry tomorrow—a double period, and Mr. B. will lecture for two solid hours. He's driving me up the walls. Why should I care about nitrobenzine?" How much is griping and how much searching? She seemed to sum up her feelings in writing the following poem:

POEM OF THE STUFFY CLASSROOM

Through time I sit here pondering,
every second passing, ticking away
with my life. I grow older, but no wiser.
Education teaches us that the Egyptians
invented toilet paper. I know this, but
I still sit here and become no wiser.
I am cramped and squeezed, my mind
is filled with insignificant data that
I will never use. But sit;
everyday I sit here, hoping
that I may learn something valuable
—like how to live life.

IN THIS CHAPTER . . .

You will read about

1 A historical perspective of adolescence as a stage and the nature of adolescence in different societies.
2 A short physical description of the middle- to late-adolescent.
3 The developmental task of achieving independence from home, including parenting styles and adolescent behavior.
4 The important area of establishing heterosexual relationships, including peer acceptance, dating and social patterns, and love relationships.
5 Childbearing in adolescence: contributing factors, deliverers and aborters, and related topics.
6 The unwed mother and the unwed father.
7 Maturing cognitive mental operations in late adolescence.
8 A description of various emotional characteristics as experienced by adolescents.
9 The concept of values in adolescents.
10 Chemical substance use and abuse: drugs and alcohol.
11 Adolescent aggression: determinants and sex differences.
12 Psychopathology in adolescence, especially suicidal behavior and anorexia nervosa.
13 Adolescents in culturally different environments.

It is more appropriate to title this chapter "middle adolescence" rather than "late adolescence" because the ages it intends to cover do not extend to the ages of 20 or 21 years, usually cited as the ages at which full maturity and development are attained.

In recent years it has seemed unrealistic to speak of a 19- or 20-year-old as an adolescent, even though there is still some "growing up" to be done. The level of worldly sophistication of 18- to 21-year-olds is so much higher than that of the same age-group of recent generations. Their behavior patterns are more adult-like. To further negate the label of *adolescent* for this older age-group, the age at which an individual is legally considered an adult has been changed in most states from the age of 21 to 18 years. Voting privileges in federal elections have been granted to 18-year-olds. However, there are still disquieting questions that ask, "Is an individual matured, in all ways, as an adult, before the age of 21?" "Does a change in laws or in social thinking necessarily produce a change in developmental characteristics?"

People recognize that 18- to 21-year-olds of today are different in many social ways from individuals of the same ages of two or three decades ago. But are they different physically, emotionally, or even intellectually? Do they make better value judgments? There is no common consensus on these points. Therefore we consider "middle adolescence" in this chapter as dealing with high school youth. Chapter 12 will discuss post–high school youth, or emerging adulthood. There is an overlapping of characteristics of these two groups, even though some behavior patterns may differ. We want to stress the need to consider both chapters as discussing final adolescence.

The developmental tasks of this age-group are basically an extension of the tasks of early adolescence. Although the physical changes brought about by puberty are now fairly well established, there is still a

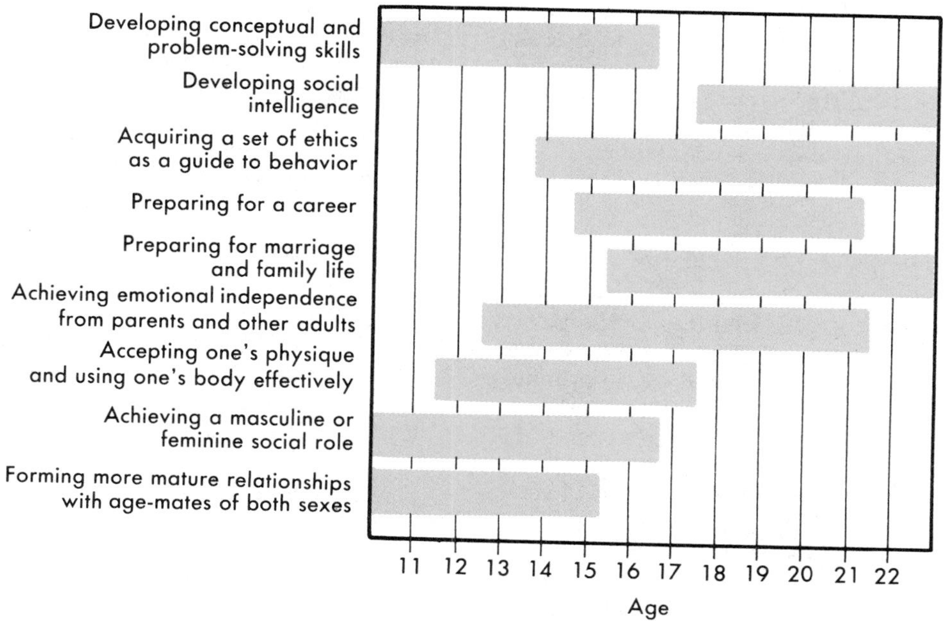

FIG. 11-1 ***Havighurst's developmental tasks and the age range at which they are generally resolved.***

From Development in adolescence *2nd edition by H.D. Thornburg. Copyright © 1982, 1975 by Wadsworth, Inc. Reprinted by permission of Brooks/Cole Publishing Company, Monterey, California.*

need to develop a feeling of physical adequacy and acceptability. A greater degree of social and emotional independence must be attained. Heterosexuality must be established on a higher level than previously, and a regard and respect for others in general must become part of one's attitudinal pattern. Progressive growth in the development of a value judgment system is important for middle adolescents, as is the development of ego identity in personality and character structures. The initial skills, interests, and information related to such matters as civic competency, choice of a vocation, post–high school living, and preparation for marriage and family life must be garnered at this time. A summary of Havighurst's developmental tasks and the age range in which they are generally resolved is presented in Fig. 11-1.

Usually teenagers handle many relationships at one time by keeping the roles isolated and separate. However, in terms of personality development, at some point in time the adolescent will need to integrate the various concepts and assessments of self into a meaningful identity, one that can answer the questions, "Who am I?" and "Who am I to be?" *Identity* is a persisting sense of being the same person whereby the individual orients himself or herself to the external world. It is a sense of unity of personality over a substantial period of time. The ultimate goal is to see oneself as a unique and an integrated person while sustaining appropriate relationships with others.

ADOLESCENCE AND THE COMING OF AGE

In simple, less complex societies a young person had no difficulty in knowing when he or she passed from childhood to adulthood. There was an event or ceremony that marked the coming of age. In primitive tribal societies the transition was and still is marked by initiation or puberty rites. In ancient Rome this changeover was signaled by the wearing of a toga; in medieval times it occurred when the boy of 14 years, who was not a serf, became a squire and began his apprenticeship for knighthood.

Puberty rites refer to rituals or events by which young people are inducted into manhood or womanhood. All of the ceremonies and status symbols stress the passing from the carefree behavior of childhood to the serious accountability of adulthood.

Puberty rites still exist among people such as the Mende of Sierra Leone in Africa, the Hopi Indians of Arizona, the aborigines of Australia, and the Sevaray tribe in the Sahara. The Duna tribe, the Porgaiga tribe, the Arapesh tribe from the Highlands, and the "mudmen" from the Asaro Valley, all from Papua New Guinea, as well as the Amaaiura Indians, also practice puberty rites. The ceremonies of these groups are all different, but a common theme underlies the rites in whatever society they may occur. The theme is that, having learned the traditions and the behavior patterns of the tribe and having passed the tests of adulthood, young people now leave their childhood behind them forever and are accepted as adults by the other tribal members (Muuss, 1970b).

Western societies do not provide a symbolic event, signal, or custom by which young people definitely know that they have entered adulthood and are accepted by adults as such. There are ceremonies such as Confirmation, the first Communion, and the celebration of Bar Mitzvah that give a youngster a sense of identity with "growing up," but these events do not signal a general acceptance into the social world of adults. Western societies of today have increased the amount of knowledge and preparation needed before an individual can be considered ready for adulthood. More education and training are required before that person is ready for an advanced, technological society. Young people no longer go into the job market at the ages of 14 or 16 years. They are not ready for it. The result has been to extend the period between childhood and adulthood, giving the adolescent stage greater visibility (Mead, 1970).

Adolescence, as a stage of development, has received an identity of its own within our society only in the last forty years or so. The term *teenager* has gained wide usage in that same time span. It was after World War II that adolescence was recognized and treated by adults as a separate developmental period with needs and characteristics of its own. Times were changing. For the first time these young people did not drop out of school in large numbers at the end of ninth grade to enter the adult job market.

An identifiable group of young people began to emerge as a significant element of society. First were the bobby-soxers of the prewar and wartime era who were popularized by the news media. No doubt the "zoot suits" of the late forties gave the boys a sense of "being different" from younger children and the more conservative adults. Manufacturers of women's clothing found a ready market for "clothes for teens." Terms such as *junior miss, debutante, teens, preteens,* and others appeared on clothing for girls. Department stores added a "teen" or "juniors" section of clothing

Rivers flow.
The sea sings.
Oceans roar.
Tides rise.
Who am I?
A small pebble
On a giant shore;
Who am I
To ask who I am?
Isn't it enough to be?

American Indian

in addition to their traditional misses and children's sections. The news media of the 1950s popularized the term *teenager*. Unfortunately, it did so in connection with the term *juvenile delinquency*.

The late 1950s saw an emphasis in the news media on the "beat generation" with its beatniks; the 1960s had their hippies; the 1970s had their yippies; and Pepsi-Cola created a whole new emphasis on youth with its "generation" advertising campaign. Today adolescence is accepted as a stage of growth with an identity of its own. A recognition of young adults or the 18- to 21-year-old group has also been achieved (Kett, 1977). The lines between the various groups never have been clear-cut, but there are enough characteristics particular to each developmental group—childhood, adolescence, young adult, adulthood—to permit separate categories and classifications of each.

The primary growth patterns of adolescence, however, are universal and timeless. Adolescents the world over exhibit the same type of needs. The ways in which these needs are expressed differ, but their implications are the same (Boocock, 1974). Teenagers have to accomplish the developmental tasks that will prepare them for adulthood in their society. Societies differ on the criterion of adult maturity. Time alone is not the major factor. The demands of the particular society set the standards. If the requirements are meager, such as in primitive societies, there are few problems. If the criteria of maturity are substantial and require more years to accomplish, such as in more complex societies, youth will have time to assert itself by revealing its level of development and probably exhibiting inexperienced, and often unwarranted behavior, as compared to adult expectations. In some societies the transition runs smoothly; in others, with more effort.

Here are three quotations of interest. "I see no hope for the future of our people if they are dependent on the frivolous youth of today, for certainly all youth are reckless beyond words. . . . When I was a boy, we were taught to be discreet and respectful of elders, but the present youth are exceedingly wise and impatient of restraint." A second quotation is as follows: "Our youth now love luxury. They have bad manners, contempt for authority, disrespect for older people. Children nowadays are tyrants. They no longer rise when their elders enter the room. They contradict their parents, chatter before company, gobble their food, and tyrannize their teachers."

A third quotation: "Could you but take a view of this part of town on a Sunday, you would be shocked indeed, for then the streets are filled with multitudes of these wretches who spend their time in riot and noise, cursing and swearing in a manner so horrid as to convey to any serious mind an idea of hell rather than of any other place. Their parents have no idea of instilling into the minds of their children principles to which they themselves are entire strangers."

The first quotation was written by Hesiod in the eighth century BC; the second quotation is from Socrates, written 2,300 years ago in Plato's *Republic;* and the third quotation is by Robert Raikes of Gloucester, England, founder of the Sunday School movement in 1783. The least that can be said is that adolescence appears to be consistent throughout the years in the sense that "this generation is going to the dogs."

Adolescence bridges the gap between dependency and adulthood. This is a time of trials, experimentation, and learning. Three major types of changes are taking place—physical, social, and psychological changes. To survive, every society must train its young for responsible adult roles.

PHYSICAL GROWTH AND DEVELOPMENT

Increase in height and weight during middle and later adolescence gradually lessens. This slowdown permits the older adolescent to stabilize the organization and functions of the different muscular patterns. As a result, the awkwardness that was characteristic of early adolescence gradually corrects itself.

The ultimate weight and height of adolescents when their growth is completed will depend on such factors as hereditary endowment, prenatal and postnatal feeding and health, race, environmental conditions, exercise during infancy and childhood, and general health. The age at which pubertal maturing occurs influences the ultimate size of the individual, with late maturers tending to be somewhat taller than early maturers. According to national averages the average American male is 177 cm (69½ in.) tall and weighs 75 kg (165 lb.), whereas the average woman is 168 cm (66 in.) tall and weighs 61 kg (135 lb.) (Katchadourian, 1977). Girls reach mature physical development, especially in height, around the age of 18 years, although a few girls continue to grow until about 21 years of age. Growth in height for boys continues until about the age of 21, with a few boys continuing to grow until age 25 (Katchadourian, 1977). Differences in height are less noticeable than are differences in weight. No predictable evidence has been discovered which would show

David Strickler

The world of women in sports is developing rapidly. Physical growth means a readiness for training programs to develop agility, speed, and accuracy.

that the age of maturing has any permanent effect on weight. The increases in weight during late adolescence are usually found in areas of the body that did not fill out during early adolescence.

The problem of a disproportioned body, which causes great anxiety in the young adolescent, slowly changes as the youngster's body takes on the form of an adult. The oversized nose of early adolescence now assumes a correct adult proportion. The lower jaw grows larger in late adolescence, and the lips become fuller (Sinclair, 1978). The trunk elongates and the chest broadens. The "gawky" look of the early adolescent disappears. The breasts and hips of a girl are developed by late adolescence so that her body now has the smooth curves of an adult female. Studies show that late-maturing individuals, girls and boys, tend to have thin legs, whereas early-maturing individuals have stocky legs. Bone measurements show that the skeleton, on the average, stops growing at the age of 18 years for girls and 21 for boys (Chumlea, 1982). The wisdom teeth usually do not emerge until late adolescence.

The oiliness of hair and skin, characteristic of early adolescence, gradually stops, and skin problems like acne usually subside with the onset of late adolescence. The growth of the digestive system also slows, and girls and boys tend to eat less during this growth period than during early adolescence. However, they may have unwise appetites and erratic habits of food consumption (Ingalls and Salerno, 1979).

Secondary sex characteristics are usually mature in development and are functioning late in adolescence. Primary sex organs usually mature a year or two after puberty (Harlan et al., 1979). Menstruation during late adolescence is usually much less uncomfortable than during the previous stage of adolescence. Girls have generally adjusted to the menstrual cycle and can continue with their active daily routines.

ACHIEVING INDEPENDENCE FROM HOME

By the age of 16 years most teenagers will have learned to accept adults in their lives (Coleman, 1980). Parents, if they had been relegated to a minor social role during the previous 2 years, are usually reinstated to their position of prominence within the thinking of the adolescent. If adolescents are treated with respect and positive regard and if they have been permitted to grow responsibly without undue restraint, they will begin to assume their adult roles and to be comfortable with them (Baumrind, 1978). They will think it less necessary to assert their independence with exaggerated, extravagant behavior. Understandings between parent and child still have to be "hammered out," however, but these can be accomplished with less conflict and fewer hurt feelings than previously. Arguments with adolescents should not be interpreted as an indication of an unhappy home. Usually there are few serious disagreements between adolescents and parents (Smith, 1976). Rather, they are indications that the children are growing up naturally. The time to be concerned is when the adolescent is unusually acquiescent or amenable and does not seek to achieve a status outside the family.

Seeking independence

The need for a sense of independence from family domination is a requirement for adolescents if they are to achieve full maturity (Coleman, 1980). There are barriers to be overcome, and there are skills to be attained. Reasons for parent-child conflicts during adolescence tend to fall into two main categories: (1) issues involving greater demands for independence by the adolescent than the parents are willing to grant and (2) issues involving dependent or childish behavior on the part of the adolescent that is more than the parents are able to tolerate.

One cause of conflict is the need for experiences by adolescents to prepare for adulthood but refusal by the parents to grant the adolescents ample experimental opportunity. The young people may feel psychologically ready to declare themselves as grown-ups, but their efforts may be thwarted by a lack of experience or money to carry out their plans or by the parents ignoring their attempts or ideas. Depriving adolescents of their effort to enter adult society may frustrate them into retaliatory action. Dejected, the adolescents

TABLE 11-1 Comparison of adolescent and middle-aged adult personalities

Adolescent personalities	*Middle-aged adult personalities*
1. Daring, willing to try new things, but lack judgment based on experience	1. Cautious, based on experience
2. Present is only reality; past is irrelevant, future is dim, uncertain	2. Oriented to past, compare present with way things used to be
3. Idealistic, optimistic	3. Realistic, sometimes cynical about life, people
4. Liberal, challenge traditional codes, ethics, experiment with new ideas, life-styles	4. Conservative in manners, morals, mores
5. Critical, restless, unhappy with things as they are	5. Generally contented, satisfied, resigned to status quo
6. Want to be grown-up, but never want to become old; contempt for aged	6. Want to keep young, do not want to show aging

Modified from Andersen, W.J. *Design for family living.* Minneapolis: T.S. Dennison & Co., 1964, p. 256. Used by permission.

may restrict communications with their parents and set out on their own to prove they are independent individuals (Blood and D'Angelo, 1974).

Frequently adolescents will aggressively demand adult prerogatives but strenuously resist the efforts of parents or other adults to control or limit their use of them. The fact that some adolescents appear to be uncompromising in their determination to impose their terms on the adult culture leaves their parents in a quandary. A conflict of interests or wishes between the parents and the youth leads to an unfortunate struggle for domination (Conger, 1977).

It is difficult for parents to know when they are overprotective or overrestrictive with their children. Table 11-1 presents some personality characteristics that differ between adolescents and middle-aged adults. Adolescents have different limits of tolerance because of differences in their personalities. They also have different degrees of need for security. Independence does not come overnight for any individual. It is a gradual process, taking place over a number of years. Wise parents and teachers will provide opportunities for children to learn responsibilities at a rate that can be tolerated by the adolescent and will not be too demanding, too restrictive, or too permissive during the learning process (Elkind, 1978). Some semblance

David Strickler

Achieving independence from the home involves both emotional and social growth. By interacting with others on an economic and social basis, young people learn skills that lead to maturity and significant personal judgment.

of direction, structure, and limits is needed. Communication channels must also be kept open at all costs.

Parent-adolescent disagreements

Rice (1981) lists five areas of disagreements with parents: social life and customs, responsibility, school, family relationships, and values and morals.

Some parents demand to know the thoughts and activities of their teenagers. They want to know where they are going, where they have been, whom they are with, and why they are late. Parents have great concern about the use of drugs, alcohol, and sex (Campbell and Cooper, 1975). Some parents may also go through their child's possessions and then justify this action by saying that they were only trying to find out what their son or daughter was doing, since they never talk about their activities. Parents will establish trust only when they show an honest and sincere interest in what the adolescent believes and feels. In their quest for privacy adolescents may ask for their own bedroom and telephone.

Conflicts between parents and adolescents over the young persons' social activities reach a peak in middle adolescence. Disagreements are usually centered around dating and choice of friends (Floyd and South, 1972). Some parents are guilty of fostering a superficial "popularity status" in which they involve their children. This status is measured not only in terms of the number of friends the youngster has but also of the social status they hold in the community and the type of prominent social activities in which they engage. A popular son or daughter is often a source of social prestige for some parents—something to talk about over the telephone or to brag about over the bridge table. Adolescents in this situation will question their own value as well as the true meaning of friendship. In addition, they may see themselves as objects being used by their parents for their own gratification and not as persons of intrinsic worth.

The use of the telephone may be a source of irritation between some parents and adolescents in the home. However, it does not appear to be the problem it once was. Teenagers do spend time talking to friends on the telephone, discussing dates, experiences, school—just about anything. Since their social relationships have greatly increased with adolescence, it is understandable why so much time is consumed conversing on the telephone. Parents, unfortunately, do not always view the problem sympathetically.

Another sensitive but not major area of disagreement centers around use of the family automobile. This is primarily a problem at the age of 16 years, when adolescents have received their driver's license. Arguments often result over the amount of time teenagers use the car, where they plan to go, when they will return, and why they need a car in the first place! A car is a sign of security and independence to adolescents; it may also serve as a status element among their peers. A deeper understanding of adolescents' needs, a concern for them as individuals, and a sense of sharing the family items can do much to eliminate such stress.

Parenting styles and adolescence

A study by Baumrind (1978) on the topic of parental variations in child-rearing techniques revealed several parental structures along a continuum of authority and control as opposed to freedom and autonomy. These parental types, including variations, are as follows: (1) *autocratic*—youths are not permitted to express their views on decisions related to themselves, (2) *authoritarian*—youth may express views, but parents make decisions based on their judgment, (3) *democratic*—youth contributes freely and may make a decision, but parents reserve the right to approve the decision or change it; or *equalitarian*—parents and child are involved to an equal degree in decision making, (4) *permissive*—adolescent is more active and influential than parents in making decisions; or *laissez-faire*—youth is in a position to either accept or reject parental wishes in making decisions, and (5) ignoring—parents do not involve themselves at all in directing the adolescent's behavior or decision making; or *erratic*—parents who are inconsistent in their approach to their children.

Results of a study by Elder (1968) indicate that autocratic parents tend to suppress the orderly development in the adolescent of independence from the domination of the parents. Laissez-faire, ignoring, and permissive parents may fail to encourage the development of responsibility. The parents who retain an interest in and some responsibility for adolescents' decisions, encouraging autonomy as they grow, are likely to develop both responsibility and independence in youths.

The study, involving 7,400 adolescents, also revealed that (1) children exposed to democratic practices consider their parents more fair (85%) as compared to autocratic parents (50%), (2) fathers are more likely to be considered autocratic (35%) than are mothers (22%), (3) parents of larger families tend to be more autocratic regardless of social class, (4) fathers are considered more fair if they at least listen, even though they make all the final decisions, (5) permissiveness is considered a more acceptable role for mothers than for fathers, and (6) by far, the largest percentage of adolescents who felt unwanted were those with autocratic (40%) or laissez-faire or ignoring parents (58%), as compared to democratic parents (8%).

It appears that a feeling of independence occurs more frequently among adolescents whose parents listen, who frequently explain their reasons for decisions and expectations, and who are less autocratic in their exercise of parental powers (Baumrind, 1978).

ESTABLISHING HETEROSEXUAL RELATIONSHIPS

Fifteen- to 18-years-olds have developed rather specific perceptions of their sex roles. Now they are seeking opportunities to play out their roles in adult ways (Keniston, 1975). Boys become more interested in social activities, although sports remain a close second in their interests. Girls continue their interest in social activities and appear to be more exercise- or sports-conscious. A gathering place, possibly a school setting, usually becomes a focal point where young people gather to practice their social skills and to engage in heterosexual activities. Adolescents are sensitive to social approval, acceptance, and demands. No other problem seems to them as important as the establishment of themselves in their own society. Adolescents report that they are happier and more relaxed with their friends than with adults (Newman, 1978).

Peer acceptance

Adolescents have a need to be recognized and accepted by someone. This is most readily done through friends and acquaintances who are their peer mates. Being of the same age, they share their feelings, experiences, goals, and doubts in a way that their parents cannot do (Josselson, 1980). In a peer group situation adolescents can find belonging, affiliation, acceptance, and status as the independent persons that they so strongly desire to be.

Many adolescents are not sufficiently secure or confident enough to tolerate differences between themselves and their colleagues. As a result, sameness becomes a rule within the primary group of friends. This conformity extends to appearance, dress, fads, hair style, makeup, activities, and attitudes. As a result, adolescents often find that their personal values clash with those of their friends in such matters, for example, as drugs, starting to smoke, drink, or engage in questionable behavior. Threatened by a possible loss of friends, adolescents often give in rather than stand by their beliefs (Bixenstine et al., 1976). The fear of losing friends is a powerful threat. This action, in turn, may cause mental anxieties and concerns, since the youngsters are not being true to themselves. This is one conflict that can only be resolved by adopting the behavior of their group or else by leaving these friends and seeking new ones. Group conformity is hard to overcome, especially in early and middle adolescence (Coleman, 1980).

There are several reasons for lack of acceptance by a group. (1) *Being retiring* is one of the causes of not finding social acceptance. If individuals do not have confidence in themselves, the group has none in them. (2) *Social ineptness* may be a stumbling block, since the social skills that provide access to the group have never been learned. (3) A person who seems *emotionally unstable* is actively rejected by the group because the members cannot afford to have such a person identified with their group. (4) *Social distance,* the degree of intimacy to which an individual is willing to accept a certain person, is a relative matter for many individuals. However, in certain localities ethnic, racial, and social differences are magnified and are causes for exclusion, rejection, or ignoring.

Dating and social patterns

The progression by which the dating pattern emerges is fairly certain; the time and rapidity with which it emerges are dependent on many cultural variables. The general attitude and philosophy of the community (or locale), the general wishes of the parents of the children involved, the customs, traditions, and folkways of the area, and the thinking of the young people themselves have a great influence on the age at which different levels of the dating sequence take place (Dornbusch et al., 1981). Some communities may be 2 or 3 years ahead of others in the time at which girls and boys begin to date. In some communities, steps within the dating sequential pattern are

MIRROR IMAGE: TRUE OR FALSE

I know I'll never forget my senior prom if I live to be 100! It will always be one of my happiest memories. That night—and the events leading up to it—had more meaning for me than you could imagine.

It was just two weeks before the prom, and I still didn't have a date. I can remember my girlfriend and I talking about the prom at the beginning of the year. We rambled on about how we'd be absolutely crushed if we didn't have a date. We agreed that if that happened we'd have a good cry, then head for New York City to party all night. We thought getting drunk would be an easy way to forget our problems.

If I would have had a boyfriend, things would have been so much easier. But, I didn't have a boyfriend, nor even any other guy that I felt free to talk to. Up to this point in my life, I had been sort of a loner. Oh, sure, I had a few girlfriends, but as far as guys went, I just shied away. My shyness had always been a hindrance to me socially. A certain amount of shyness is all right, I suppose. I think some guys like girls who are a little more quiet and reserved. I didn't realize until recently that I was really overly reserved. I was always reluctant to become involved in social activities.

Was I ashamed of myself? Did I think that people were continually looking at me and laughing? Maybe I did. In elementary school, I can remember being picked on and teased by some of the boys. The subject was usually my appearance. Kids can be really mean; guess I was just extra sensitive to such criticism. I couldn't understand why anyone would make fun of me when I had never done anything to hurt them. Even during my high school years, every now and then I would hear some crude or nasty remarks about me. I knew that the boys who were saying them were just troublemakers, but still I didn't know how to handle it. It bothered me so much at times that I'd go home and cry for hours, making sure my parents didn't find out for they'd think I was acting silly. I wasn't silly! So, up to and including my senior year, I had developed strong feelings of inferiority about my looks.

All of the "pretty" girls had dates for the prom for weeks or months ahead of time. Even the girls whom I considered to be less attractive than me had found somebody to take them. What was wrong with me? For me, getting a date for the prom became ten times more important than actually going to the prom. If the truth be known, I'd never even gone out on a real date before. Besides, if I had a date, how would I act? I had never been a dancer—I was too self-conscious. Then, there's always been a sort of stigma that, if you couldn't get a date for the prom, you were a nobody—an ugly duckling. I *had* to get a date, but who? Every guy in my class was taken.

As it so happened, I had been working at a supermarket for about four months with several guys of my age. I never took a special interest in any of them except as co-workers. Then one day my girlfriend mentioned that one of these guys wasn't bad looking and that he had a nice Camaro. Suddenly, I went berserk and on the offensive! I'm sorry to say this, but I had an instant crush on Mike Taylor. As friends and co-workers, we were quite comfortable with each other. Now that I had it in my head that I really liked him, I became nervous around him.

About ten days before the prom, my girlfriend at school convinced me that I should ask Mike to the prom. No guy had ever asked me out. How was I supposed to ask him? I felt like a fool. Nevertheless, that night I made certain that Mike and I took our break at the same time. Lorraine, another friend and co-worker, also took her break. While the three of us sat in the employees' lounge talking, the subject of the prom came up. I got butterflies in my stomach. As we talked I found out that Mike, who went to a different high school than I did, already had a date for his prom. That, I figured, ended the whole quest. He had a girlfriend, so why on earth would he want to do anything with me? I was positive that his girlfriend was gorgeous in every respect.

Lorraine, being the sly matchmaker that she was, asked me if I had a date for my prom. I said that I didn't. She suggested that it would really be nice if Mike would take me. In front of him, she said, "Ask him." I replied, "Don't push it, Lorraine. He's got a girlfriend and he doesn't want to go with me." Mike said, "Yeah, Lorraine, don't push it." That hurt because instantly I concluded that he really didn't want anything to do with me. Lorraine said, "Repeat after me: Mike, would you like to go to the senior prom with me?" I struggled, feeling like a scared rabbit, and somehow the words came out. I'll never forget his first reply. He said that he would tell me tomorrow at work; he had to think about it. I could have died! At first I was honored that he would even consider it, but then I was hurt. Just what exactly did he have to think about? Wasn't I his "type"? Was he ashamed to be seen with me? However, later that night as we were leaving work, Mike said that he would be "glad" to take me to the prom. I was so ecstatic! I couldn't believe that someone like Mike Taylor would actually want to go out with me—a nobody.

Well, I had a date for the prom. It seemed as if all my problems were solved, but it wasn't all that simple. Once again my deep-rooted feelings of inferiority stepped in. I remember mentioning to one of the girls at work that I didn't think Mike really wanted to go with me, that he was just doing it out of pity. The word got back to Mike; he confronted me, saying that he wanted to go to the prom with me because he liked me and thought we could have fun, not because he pitied me. That made me feel better.

Prom night came extremely fast. I bought a nice dress, but somehow it looked better on the rack. I was uncomfortable in such formal attire. I remember how nervous I was when we arrived at the prom. But the worst part was dancing. With my high heels I was taller than Mike, so I took my shoes off. For the first dance, I tried to hold his hands and dance the way my Mom had shown me. Talk about old-fashioned!!! I was so embarrassed! Later we danced like everyone else. We left the prom somewhat early and went to Lorraine's house to talk and party for a while. When he dropped me off at home, there was the question of the "goodnight kiss." He walked me to my door, we looked at each other, he smiled and said, "Good night. It was fun." Then he drove off in his shiny white Camaro.

Several days later I began thinking. I was being silly letting myself be shy. It took my experience with Mike to make me realize that I didn't have to be a loner. It seemed as if all my life I believed that I wasn't as good as everyone else. I was self-conscious and pitied myself. It took me many years to learn that not everyone was going to be interested in me. It was ridiculous to even think that they should be.

The summer following the prom was better for me in a lot of ways. I was happier; I even went out on dates with several guys. What was different? Well, one day, shortly after the prom, I just looked at myself in the mirror and said, "There I am. That's the true me. I'm not gorgeous, but I'm not as bad as I've been led to believe by those elementary school boys." Then I looked inside of me. I thought about it and decided that I was a fairly good person. I had limitations, but I always tried to do the best I could. If people would only give me half a chance, I could be great.

Somehow, the experience of my senior prom made me realize that all of us are pretty much the same here on earth. Nobody is really better than anyone else. This means that I'm just as important as the next person. I don't need to worry about what people think of me. It's all right not to be liked by some people. Deep inside I had always had this need to belong to somebody—everybody. I wanted people to approve of me. When they didn't respond, I shied away. I put a barrier around myself and didn't get involved so that I couldn't get hurt. It had taken me this long to realize that such a barrier was foolish and unnecessary. I have become more accepted by others, but first I had to learn to accept myself.

compressed within a short time span, whereas in other places the steps extend over a long period. There are differences in dating practices. The studies of dating practices were done in smaller communities as well as metropolitan areas (Kaluger, 1983). The time sequence presented here is somewhat typical of different sized communities. Large cosmopolitan areas usually have an earlier beginning of the sequential pattern.

Dating sequence. The first typical dating activities are "crowd" dates, usually at organized school functions in the seventh grade. A group of girls just happens to be around a certain group of boys at a football or basketball game. What is interesting is that the same group of girls seems to be around the same group of boys at most of the activities. Pairing off within the groups usually does not occur until the eighth grade. By the ninth grade, crowd dates are still popular, but now there is a noticeable pairing off of couples.

It is not unusual in the seventh grade to notice a few boys and girls who are seeing each other frequently on a paired-off basis. It will be obvious that some eighth grade couples are "going together," but as was stated earlier, this is not the norm of the majority of the seventh and eighth graders. Steady couples are more common in the ninth grade than in earlier grades. In most places, going steady takes a big jump in tenth grade (Kaluger, 1983).

In the tenth grade there will be a number of single dates for special social functions. However, some boys and girls will come to the activity as a couple and then join their crowd. Four, five, or more couples will make up the crowd. There may still be some unattached friends within the group. It is not uncommon in larger cities for single dating to start in eighth or ninth grade and increase in popularity. In some areas double dating is common in eleventh grade and twelfth grade because one of the couples may be able to provide a car for transportation.

By the end of the freshman year about half of the

Dating interests and dating patterns vary from one locale to another, but the result is the same—boy and girl get together, sometimes in a very meaningful relationship.

freshmen boys in socially oriented urban or suburban areas will have dated a girl. By the end of the junior year about three fourths will have dated, and by their senior year 95% have dated to some degree (Cox, 1974). Might there be some single dates in seventh or even sixth grade? Yes, but it probably would not be the common practice. Each community and social group has its own features.

The median age at which young people begin dating has decreased by about 3 years since 1920. The age for girls beginning to date in 1924 was 16 years, in 1958 it was 13.3 years, and in 1968 it was 13.2 years of age (Cox, 1974). Our recent study indicated that in 1982 the age was slightly below 13 years. A study by Place (1975) indicates that the median age for the first date for whites remained relatively stable over a 10-year period, but the median age for blacks decreased from 14.9 years in 1964 to 13.9 in 1974. Fig. 11-2 shows the distribution. In that study, 4% of the whites and 5% of the blacks never had a date.

Dating differs in types and degrees of seriousness. The first stage of dating, during early adolescence, is of a noncommittal nature. It is extremely mobile in style in that there are few if any lasting romantic attachments. The nervous excitement of a novel experience is sufficient to interest a person in another. Playing the field does not produce lasting relationships, and there is a minimum of emotional stress involved. The amount of time spent in this type of dating varies from individual to individual. Interests in courtship and marriage do not reach a peak until late adolescence.

Although dating is still a traditional social pattern, an interesting, more informal social phenomenon has become a norm in many places, a social event that might be termed casual group dating. As described by Reiss (1976), casual group dating occurs when a group of several males and females socialize at a gathering spot, such as a school event, a party, a bowling alley, an eating place, or a "kegger," just to be together but not as couples. It may be just a matter of "going out" and "hanging around together." As the evening wears on, some of the males and females may pair off. An informal, casual type of dating takes place. Sometimes the call to "let's party" is all that is needed to get a group together. From such activities, however, a couple may reach the "going with each other" stage and a more formal type of dating may take place.

Dating, whatever its form, serves a variety of functions. Winch (1971) suggests that dating (1) is a form of recreation, (2) is a means of achieving status, (3) provides opportunities to learn about the opposite sex, (4) provides a means to learn about one's own personality and needs, (5) allows one to evaluate which types of relationships are satisfying and which are not, (6) clarifies values about life-style, sexuality, and marriage, and (7) provides a context for experiencing heterosexual behavior. Within these relationships, young people learn how to handle their feelings of vulnerability and their fear of physical contact, how to cope with difficulties related to sexual demands, and how to provide and receive physical pleasure without upsetting each other (Estep et al., 1977).

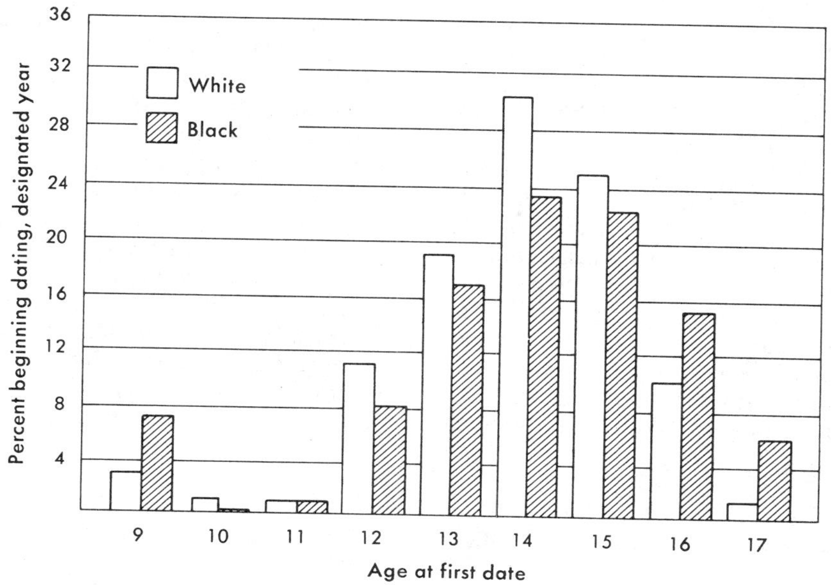

FIG. 11-2 ***Frequency distribution (in percentages) of age at first date in 1974, by race.***

Modified from Dickinson, G.E. Journal of Marriage and the Family, *1975, 37, 604. Copyrighted (1975) by the National Council on Family Relations, 1219 University Avenue Southeast, Minneapolis, Minnesota 55414. Reprinted by permission.*

Personal comment. We would like to illustrate boy-girl relationships from our experiences. We had the extraordinary opportunity of being with the same group of boys from the time they were in seventh grade until they graduated from high school. Of 29 boys who started with us in a seventh grade Junior Hi-Y, 24 boys were still with us when they graduated. This was a most unusual group of boys—service minded and extremely active. They adopted an 84-year-old man and kept him in food, tobacco, and company for over 3 years. While in eighth grade they collected two panel truck loads of comic books and gave them to a nearby veterans' hospital.

In ninth grade these boys sponsored a "Have-a-Heart Week" during the week of St. Valentine's Day as a campaign to improve courtesy within the school. Any young persons seen by a teacher or club member doing a courteous act or a good deed had their name turned in to a central point that evening. The next morning when the pupils returned to school, they found a small paper heart on their desk for each time their names were turned in. The students proudly wore these hearts. At the end of the week a prize was given to the boy and girl with the biggest (most) heart, the homeroom with the biggest heart, and several other prizes for "hearts." No one ever saw a group of 12- to 14-year-olds in a school of 900 pupils who were so courteous, not only for that week but for the rest of the year.

Every boy in the club went on to some type of post–high school education (not all to college). From that group there are now six engineers, four electronics specialists, three lawyers, several merchants, one physician, one teacher, one YMCA secretary, a Roman Catholic priest who studied at the Vatican for 4 years, a boy who studied for the Lutheran ministry, a Greek Orthodox priest, and a Jewish rabbi, who among other things, was arrested in one of the early civil rights marches in the South.

Now for the development of the dating pattern. In seventh grade the boys decided they would like to have a hayride. For 6 weeks they planned whom to contact for the wagons, how to get there, and what to eat. They went on the hayride and had a marvelous time. Nobody mentioned girls, and no one brought a girl. In eighth grade they voted to have another hayride. Someone said, "Let's bring girls." Everyone laughed, but no one brought a girl. In ninth grade they again decided on a hayride. Someone said, "Let's bring girls." Someone else said, "Let's not." They voted, and the girls lost out by two votes. That same night, in early October, they voted to bring girls to their Christmas party. Anyone who did not want to bring a girl could be on the refreshment and clean-up committee. Three boys ended up on that committee, two of whom were the first of the group to get married later on. The hayride was a "so-so" affair that year. Everyone was looking forward to the Christmas party.

While in tenth grade they agreed to have another hayride. The topic of girls was brought up again. Someone said, "Let's vote." The girls won out by a good margin. In the junior year they decided on a hayride. Someone asked, "Are we bringing girls?" Someone replied, "What else?" To continue the tradition of hayrides in twelfth grade they decided to have a final hayride. All the plans for the activity were completed within a half hour. No one mentioned girls, but everyone brought a girl. That was the most eerie hayride by moonlight my wife and I ever went on. For much of the ride we were the only ones who could be seen on the wagons. Laughter, giggling, and singing seemed to be coming from underneath the straw on the wagons. After the hayride we had the biggest problem ever getting the couples off the wagons and out of the hay-

TABLE 11-2 Personality traits liked or disliked

Liked	*Disliked*
Personal appearance	**Personal appearance**
Good-looking	Homely, unattractive
Feminine, nice figure (girls)	Boyish figure or too fat or skinny (girls)
Masculine, good build (boys)	Sissy, skinny, fat (boys)
Neat, clean, well groomed	Sloppy, dirty, unkempt
Appropriate clothes	Clothes out of style, don't fit, not appropriate, dirty
	Greaser (boys)
	Physical handicap
Social behavior	**Social behavior**
Outgoing, friendly	Shy, timid, withdrawn, quiet
Active, energetic	Lethargic, listless, passive
Participant in activities	Nonjoiner, recluse
Social skills: good manners, conversationalist, courteous, poised, natural, tactful, can dance, play many games, sports	Loud, boisterous, ill-mannered, disrespectful, braggart, show-off, not "cool," giggles, rude, crude, tongue-tied, doesn't know how to do or play anything
Lots of fun, good sport	Real drip, poor sport
Acts age, mature	Childish, immature
Good reputation	Bad reputation
Personal qualities of character	**Personal qualities of character**
Kind, sympathetic, understanding	Cruel, hostile, disinterested
Cooperative, gets along well, even-tempered, stable	Quarrelsome, bully, bad-tempered, domineering, sorehead
Unselfish, generous, helpful	Inconsiderate, selfish, stingy
Cheerful, optimistic, happy	Pessimistic, complaining person
Responsible, dependable	Irresponsible, not reliable
Honest, truthful, fair	Liar, cheat, unfair
Good sense of humor	Can't take a joke, no sense of humor
High ideals	Dirty minded
Self-confident, self-accepting but modest	Conceited, vain

Composite from Rice, F.P. *The adolescent* (3rd ed.). Boston: Allyn & Bacon, 1981, p. 291.

stacks on the farm so they could get back to town by midnight!

Traits of dating partners. Within Western culture it has usually been the responsibility of the male to select the dating partner although for certain affairs some girls now feel free to ask a fellow. Girls generally make sure that they are interesting enough to be asked for a date. There are various ways of doing this. External attributes that many girls consider essential for entry into the dating game are looking good and being dressed appropriately, whether it be sweaters and skirts or blue jeans. The point of view of many of today's youth is slowly lessening the emphasis on money, clothes, and social prestige.

What a boy seeks in a date are personality, concern for others, looks, and dependability (Place, 1975). Girls seem to want good personality, manners, and looks; acceptable social behavior and dress; neatness; and an ability to carry on a conversation. Table 11-2 indicates those personality traits that are liked and disliked (Rice, 1981).

These are not the only qualifications, but they provide some idea of what a later adolescent looks for in a dating partner. Similarity in characteristics is also an important factor in date selection. The tendency is to choose someone with similar rather than opposite interests, needs, and appearance. What might be noted is that the qualities being sought are of the type needed for a good life mate (Hansen, 1977). This could indicate the seriousness of dating during this period.

Parental concerns. Early dating and steady dating of adolescents are chief concerns of parents. Parents

Meriem Kaluger

The telephone is a central part of the social lives of many adolescents. They call their friends to keep in touch, they call the opposite sex just to talk or to find out what's going on, and they even call home to let Mom and Dad know that everything is OK. The adolescent's use of the telephone does not seem to be as much of an irritant in the family as it once was. Most parents and children have learned how to live with the telephone in their lives.

TABLE 11-3 Premarital intercourse among teenage females

Study and year	*Percentage reporting sexual intercourse*
Kinsey and others (1938-1949)	18
Sorensen (1973)	45
Zelnik and Kantner (1976)	55
Zelnick and Kantner (1980)	67

The table gives the percentage of 19-year-old, unmarried females who reported having experienced sexual intercourse. This and other evidence indicate a marked increase in premarital sexual experience over the past 50 years—much of it a result of increased sexual activity among white teenage women; for black teenage women it remained virtually unchanged.

fear that pairing off on a steady basis leads young adolescents into sexual and emotional intimacies long before they are ready for marriage. Adolescents, on the other hand, believe that steady dating, even as early as 12 or 13 years of age, provides security and acceptance by the group. They find it difficult to understand their parents' reasoning (Conger, 1975; Sorenson, 1973). Many a household is filled with turmoil resulting from conflicting views on dating. The teenager who is denied dating privileges may feel rejected, resentful, and deceived. Family friction may increase because of youngsters sneaking out on dates; some will exceed sexual behavioral limits simply to spite their parents.

Dating problems. Problems related to dating are of two types: namely, "I can't get a date" or else "Now that I'm dating, how far should I go?" (Elkind, 1980). Individuals who have not had the opportunity to develop social skills will have trouble knowing what to do to get to know the opposite sex better. This may also leave them isolated in other group activities. Concerning the second problem, girls are upset by the aggressive behavior of boys who try to see how far they can go. However, boys tend to dislike the way girls flaunt their sexuality. Even a nice girl can give the wrong impression. As to "How far should I go in kissing, necking, and petting?" usually the boy tries to get as much as possible, and the girl yields as little as possible. The girl is expected to set the limits, and the boy is expected to conform. Girls may be the aggressors, but traditionally that has not been considered to be their role. These questions cause considerable anxiety and tension for adolescents. There are a number of girls who are questioning and resisting the implications of a "double standard" system (Miller and Simon, 1980). Table 11-3 indicates the increase in premarital sex for girls.

Love relationships

Early adolescence, marked by the advent of heterosexual relationships, is a critical period in the life of 13-, 14-, or 15-year-olds (Feinstein and Ardon, 1973). These youngsters are placed in closer social contact with the opposite sex, thus offering them more opportunity to establish feelings of affection for particular members of the opposite sex. They might very well consider themselves in love with a person, yet their strong feelings are too often dismissed by adults as "puppy love," nonsense, or simply a game teenagers play. Closer observation reveals this stage to be a trying one for adolescents, since they have never before felt this way about the opposite sex. In later adolescence the relationships become more involved, hence the problems become more complicated.

Strong feelings of attachment by an adolescent are usually interpreted as love. Initial intense love reactions seem to occur most between 15 and 19 years of age in boys and between 13 and 18 years in girls (Feinstein and Ardon, 1973). Most of them last from 1 to 6 months, some longer. Boys base the attraction on physical and/or mental abilities, whereas girls concentrate mainly on mental and personality qualities.

The first blush of love itself is common and not a problem. The difficulty arises, however, when adolescents become too involved emotionally with the "love object," perhaps to the point where sex interests are implicit in their affection. If the love object fails to recognize or accept the amorous intentions of the other person, deeper frustrations resulting in more extreme behavior may set in (Lasswell and Lubsenz, 1980). It is at this point that many youngsters are torn between their "love" for the individual and their "hatred" at his or her failure to see it and respond to it effectively. Such tensions may cause erratic behavior in school and at home. Often boys and girls with such problems are embarrassed to discuss them at home, fearing faultfinding. Adolescent love relationships, crushes and otherwise, do take place. They necessitate careful consideration and understanding to avoid severe emotional harm to the adolescents involved (Lee, 1977).

A problem arising from being in love and going steady is early marriage. Some adolescents get married within a couple of years after graduation from high school. Marriage between college students or persons living together is increasing at a surprising rate (Glick and Norton, 1977). Prolonged association with one person leads to sexual exploration. Sex "with a commitment" or "for love" is usually considered by young people to be justification for having sex (McKenry et al., 1979). A number of couples who are going steady either end up getting married so that their child will have a father in the traditional sense or making arrangements for the girl to have an abortion (Chilman, 1979). Marriages on this basis are not solid and are a major cause for divorce among those who married during the adolescent years (Furstenberg, 1977).

CHILDBEARING IN ADOLESCENCE

Contributing factors

Speaking to a Symposium on Childbearing in Adolescence, Frederick Green, M.D. (1974) identified factors contributing to the high risk of pregnancy for some adolescents. These include the collective preoccupation with sexuality in our society, familial patterns of adolescent parenthood, membership in a dysfunctional family, and the inadequate knowledge of or an inaccessibility to contraceptive measures. He noted exclusion from peers, unhappy teenage marriages, inescapable dependency on parents, unresolved sexual conflicts, increased medical risk, and limited parental competence in caring for the child as a few of the consequences of teenage parenthood. The effect of the termination of a pregnancy on the ability of adolescents to accomplish many of the developmental tasks is of increasing interest to researchers since many teenagers are using abortion as a method of birth control.

Virginia Abernethy (1974) identifies psychological factors that underlie the predisposition to risk unwanted pregnancy. Factors such as self-esteem, feelings about each parent, and the parents' marriage appear to be related to the variables of sexual and contraceptive behavior. The absence of a feminine identification with a well-regarded mother is associated with low self-esteem. In keeping with her alienation from her mother, the high-risk individual is unlikely to have satisfying friendships with other women. A marriage in which parents are affectionate and close appears to facilitate the daughter's making a satisfactory identification with the mother, probably because the latter is seen as loved and loving and can thus be esteemed. An exceptionally disastrous parental marriage also appears to decrease the daughter's risk of unwanted pregnancy.

Percentage of premarital sex and pregnancy

Research by Zelnick and Kantner (1977) indicates that the percentage of white teenage girls having premarital intercourse and getting pregnant has increased by one third over a 5-year period. The figures indicate that 37.2% of white teenage girls between 15 and 19 years of age in 1976 had engaged in premarital sex and about 10% of them became pregnant. In 1971 only 26.3% of the girls in this category had premarital sex and a little over 6% got pregnant. The increase in pregnancy was in spite of impressive improvement in contraceptive use. The percentage of black teenage girls between 15 and 19 having premarital intercourse was 64.3% in 1976 compared to 54.1% in 1971. The percentage of pregnancy remained rather stable at 25.4%.

The percentage of white girls who had abortions rose from 33% to 45%. For black girls it rose from 5% to 8%. The study also revealed that four out of five pregnancies among teenagers were conceived out of wedlock. All but 7% of the babies born to these girls lived with their teenage mothers despite increasing pressure to put them up for adoption or foster placement (Baldwin, 1976). If they had the baby, they kept it.

Overall, by 1979 premarital sex had been experienced by 56% of the boys and 44% of the girls in high school (18-year-olds or younger). Nonvirgin college men and women were both at the 74% level (Dreyer, 1982).

Use of contraceptives

The majority of pregnant unmarried teenagers use no method of contraception to prevent pregnancy. In a study of 502 patients aged 17 years or younger, unwed, never pregnant, and seeking birth control for the first time, Settlage and associates (1970) indicated that most of the girls became sexually active by 15 or 16 years of age and three out of five had been having intercourse for more than a year. The decision to have intercourse was unrelated to contraception. A majority of teenagers in the study never used even those methods of birth control obtainable without medical assistance.

The data suggest that contraceptive information and educational programs directed at minors will not be a significant factor in the decision to become sexually active. When a teenage girl requests contraception, she is in great need of it, both in terms of prior onset of coital activity and the length of time she has been exposed to the risk of pregnancy.

Teenagers' knowledge of sex and reproduction is generally inadequate. Only 40% of Kantner and Zelnick's sample of sexually active teenage girls had a correct notion of the period of greatest rate of pregnancy in their monthly cycle. The majority thought that the risk of becoming pregnant was greatest during the menstrual period (Kantner and Zelnick, 1972). Of the group, 28% of the white girls and 55% of the black girls thought they could not become pregnant easily. Male-controlled contraceptive techniques were the most popular. The most frequently reported contraceptive methods were the condom, 70%, and withdrawal, 50% to 60% (Bauman and Wilson, 1974). There is an increased use of the contraceptive pill by women (Chilman, 1979). Table 11-4 presents reasons for failure of adolescent women to use contraceptives.

Oskamp and Mindick (1981) conducted a review of personality and attitudinal characteristics related to the nonuse or failure of contraceptives. They found the following reasons why contraceptives failed or were not used at all: (1) viewing oneself as not being sexually active, (2) being deviant or irresponsible, (3) feeling incompetent or passive or expressing learned helplessness, (4) having little knowledge of birth control and reproduction, (5) not being in control of one's impulses, (6) having poor social adjustment or not being able to express oneself well, and (7) having negative attitudes and intentions about contraception.

TABLE 11-4 Reasons revealed by research for failure of adolescent women to use contraceptives or to use effective ones consistently

Demographic variables
Age less than 18
Single status
Lower socioeconomic status
Minority group member
Not going to college
Being a fundamentalist Protestant
Situational variables
Not being in a steady, committed relationship
Not having experienced a pregnancy
Having intercourse sporadically and without prior planning
Being in a high-stress situation
Not having ready access to a free, confidential family-planning service that does not require parental consent
Lack of communication with parents regarding all aspects of life, including sexual behavior and contraceptive use
Psychological variables
Desiring a pregnancy; high fertility values
Ignorance of pregnancy risks, of family-planning services
Attitudes of fatalism, powerlessness, alienation, incompetence, trusting to luck
Passive, dependent, traditional female role attitudes
High levels of anxiety; low ego strength
Lack of acceptance of the reality of one's own sex behavior; thinking coitus won't occur
Risk-taking, pleasure-oriented attitudes
Fear of contraceptive side effects and possible infertility
Wrong assumptions about the "safe times" of the menstrual cycle

From Chilman, C. Adolescent childbearing in the United States: Causes and consequences. In T.H. Field, A. Huston, H.C. Quay, L. Troll & G.E. Finley (Eds.), *Review of human development*. New York: John Wiley & Sons, 1982.

Deliverers and aborters

Dr. Susan H. Fischman (1974) states that an increasing number of teenagers in the United States are ignoring the availability of contraceptive services and legal abortion and are instead choosing to bear their children. In the city of Baltimore, a study was undertaken to determine what characteristics distinguished teenage girls who chose to deliver from those who elected to abort. Of the 229 black unwed adolescents in the Baltimore study group, 66% chose to have their baby. All were experiencing their first pregnancy.

The differences found between the deliverers and aborters challenged many generalizations that have been made in the past about girls pregnant out of wedlock. Contrary to expectations, the majority of the delivery group claimed to have satisfactory relationships with their mother and father and revealed a high or medium self-esteem. The girl who had an abortion was more likely to reveal interpersonal difficulties with family members and to score low on the self-esteem scale. Whereas many studies have frequently linked the absent father with the teenage childbearer, this study showed that half of both groups of girls reported their father out of the home. The deliverer's father, however, tended to be alive and living nearby, while the aborter claimed that her father was dead.

Distinct differences were noted between the two groups in schooling and relationships with boyfriends. In general, the deliverers had either discontinued school or were not on the appropriate grade level for their age, whereas the aborters were apt to be attending school and on grade level. The deliverers' boyfriends, who on the average were older than the boyfriends of the aborters, tended to be school dropouts, currently employed full-time or seeking work, while the aborters' boyfriends were attending school either full- or part-time. In addition, most of the deliverers had longer, more stable relationships with their boyfriend and indicated that he would help to support the baby. The deliverers reported a significantly lower socioeconomic status, in that nearly half of the deliverers were supported by welfare compared to one out of four aborters. The mothers of the deliverers had completed less schooling than the aborters' mothers and, if employed, held a lower-paying job.

In summary, compared to the aborter, the deliverer emerged as one with higher self-esteem, satisfactory family and boyfriend relationships, a poorer school record, and a lower socioeconomic household. These facts suggest that, within the milieu of poverty and inadequate education, childbearing may be deliberately sought by some girls as one of the few acceptable roles available to them. The findings of this study, although not generalizable to diverse populations, suggest that the prevention of adolescent pregnancy and childbearing requires a variety of health, educational, and social services. Foremost, however, it appears that keeping young girls and boys in school could effect a reduction in nonmarital births to teenagers.

Childbearing and adolescence

Childbearing in adolescence has a great effect on the teenage girl's ability to achieve the developmental tasks of the period. A similar effect could be postulated for teenage boys, particularly those who assume responsibility for their part in the pregnancy. An adolescent father must work to support his growing family, necessitating absence from school. This results in the acceptance of unskilled jobs with little opportunity for development intellectually, economically, or socially. The necessity of parental financial and emotional assistance may be devastating for the teenager desiring independence. Childbearing and parenting in adolescence can be considered a maturing experience.

Preventing the crisis of childbearing in adolescence and dealing with the situation when it arises are interwoven processes. The latter may require changing the life-styles of individuals in certain groups—a monumental task not undertaken lightly. Adolescent parents have a great need for adequate health care. There is no typical childbearing adolescent. Adolescence is such a rapid period of transition that the individual maturity of each teenager must be considered. All persons requiring health services need understandable answers to their concerns and questions. They need to be educated so they can become full-fledged members of a team effort to assist them through their illness or crisis. They need to be treated with concern and respect. This is particularly true of the childbearing adolescent.

Sexually transmitted diseases

One of the most serious consequences of the rise in the rate of premarital sexual intercourse is that gonorrhea, syphilis, and herpes have become serious health hazards for the young (Dreyer, 1982). Gonorrhea is the most frequently reported communicable disease recorded by the U.S. Public Health Service (Center for Disease Control, 1977). In 1978 the rate was 978 per 100,000 for males and 1,482 for females. It was less for syphilis. Herpes genitalis, an incurable infection as yet, is quickly becoming widespread. The incidence of gonorrhea among 20- to 24-year-olds is the highest of that for all age-groups, with the incidence for 15- to 19-year-olds being second highest.

UNWED PARENTS

Although legalized abortion and the widespread use of contraceptives are bringing down the national birth rate (at least until 1977 when it went up 5%), the percentage of nonmarital births has gone up 24% since 1965. In 1979 about one half of all babies born out of wedlock were born to teenage mothers. Earlier puberty, liberalized social interaction, mass exposure to sex in the media, permissive attitudes concerning sex, and a general uncertainty concerning moral values, self-restraint, and the consequences of sex before marriage have contributed to this increase. Unfortunately, it is the unborn child who is punished because of the trauma, perhaps the lack of care, that is involved. However, there are also teenagers who are found to be adequate parents, committed to their offspring (Chilman, 1979).

The unwed mother

Juhasz (1974) indicates that the largest number of nonmarital births occur in the 15- to 19-year-old group. Since the birth control pill has become available, it is reasonable to assume that most girls would take some type of precaution in sexual involvements, but Zelnick and Kantner (1978) report that only a relatively small percentage, approximately 50% of white and 20% of black unmarried girls having intercourse have ever used the contraceptive pill to prevent pregnancy. A disturbingly high percentage, between 55% and 75%, have used no contraceptive device whatsoever, at least in their first experience, and only a minority consistently use such a device thereafter. Interestingly, there was only a small difference in percentage of contraceptive use between poor and nonpoor adolescents or between ethnic groups. Approximately 29% of all nonvirgin girls report that they have had at least one premarital pregnancy (Sorenson, 1973).

A number of factors are related to the incidence of early marriage or nonmarital births. These factors frequently involve family conflicts, willingness to get pregnant to get away from home or out of school, social and economic problems, individual psychological hang-ups, lack of knowledge concerning sexual matters, and/or poor understanding of the responsibilities of sexuality in the family and society (Dreyer, 1982).

Communities are becoming increasingly aware of the needs of the young unwed parent. In many places the pregnant girl's formal education is permitted to continue. Programs have been initiated for supervised prenatal care; preparations are made for the experiences of pregnancy, labor, and delivery; instruction in mothering skills is given; and assistance with personal and vocational planning is provided. Physicians and nurses, as well as social workers, are learning more about the needs of the teenage obstetrical patient, both in and out of the hospital or agency setting.

The medical profession recognizes that the incidence of toxemia of pregnancy is higher in this age group, especially for girls in their early teens from lower socioeconomic backgrounds (Ingalls and Salerno, 1979). This increased incidence may be related to the poor diets of many young girls. Some overeat because of anxiety and stress; others feel guilty about the pregnancy and use starvation for self-punishment. These patients always have an especially large number of low-weight babies; the incidence of major defects is from two to four times as high for premature as for full-term infants. Black women at the poverty level have a starkly high percentage of premature births (Menken, 1975).

The unwed father

Unwed fathers are also expectant parents. Consideration of both partners is essential for their growth in maturity and self-esteem. Including the father in discussions often provides better planning for the child (Parke et al., 1980). It improves the father's behavior and his future relationships. Unwed fathers have about as many problems or concerns as unwed mothers. Pannor and associates (1971) have demonstrated that a good counseling relationship must be established and discussions held on attitudes toward sex, mature love, responsibilities of parenthood, and the need for security through family living. In some hospitals, the father is shown the baby to complete the reality of the experience. Both parents are involved in sharing the responsibilities for medical care and living arrangments. Parent participation is usually therapeutic. Pannor learned that (1) most women were willing and able to name the father, (2) the partners were usually close in age and social class, (3) most were from the middle class and had at least completed high school, and (4) ignorance of contraceptive methods was not a factor.

What is interesting is that many unwed fathers want to be involved. The Family Service Association of America conducted a study of unwed fathers (Robinson, 1969). A detailed profile of 149 unwed fathers emerged as follows:

1. The men involved were not irresponsible.
2. Usually they were deeply involved with the unwed mothers, the pregnancy, and the child. Sixty-one percent *wanted, and not because of*

obligation, to marry the woman. It was the woman who usually rejected the idea.

3. Over 60% of the men visited their babies in the hospital and showed strong paternal feelings.

Recognizing the needs, concerns, and identities of both the unwed mother and the unwed father suggests that there are potentials for growth in unwed parenthood (Russell, 1980). Marriage is not always the answer. Age, immaturity, personality and social incompatibilities, financial inadequacies, the need for job or career development, or emotional trauma associated with the event may rule out marriage for some couples. More girls are choosing to keep their babies, yet it must be recognized that adoption is an option to be considered. What can be gained is a process of support and development for the unwed couple that can increase self-esteem and decrease feelings of guilt. Being able to share the responsibility of deciding about this pregnancy and this infant can be therapeutic. The lives of three people, mother, father, and infant, should be considered. There is a lifetime of living that lies ahead. Making them "pay" for their indiscretion is of dubious value to either society or the individuals involved—and especially to the infant.

MATURING COGNITIVE OPERATIONS

Mental operations

Adolescence is a period of steady development in learning how to use the various intellectual functions.

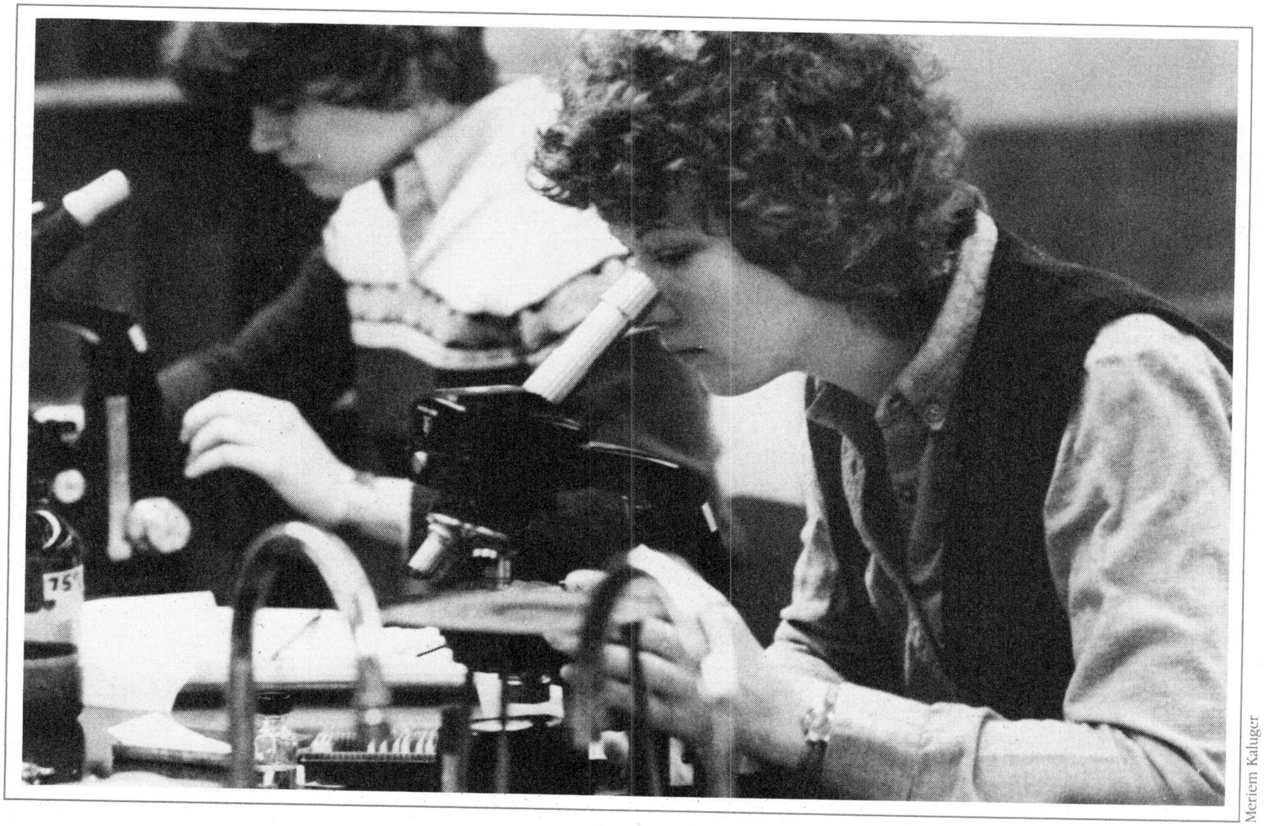

Meriem Kaluger

The development of formal operational skills permits the late adolescent to delve into the abstract world of the universe, doing scientific reasoning or formal logic in verbal activities. Furthermore, this age-group can become quite capable at assessing the quality of their conclusions.

These include mental operations such as (1) *cognitive thinking,* involving discovery, recognition, or awareness of knowledge, (2) *memory* or the retention of what was cognized, (3) *divergent thinking,* the ability to produce a large variety of responses by moving apart from the usual opinions, attitudes, and thinking and to come up with new ideas, (4) *convergent thinking,* the ability to reason or use logic to arrive at the one best answer, and (5) *evaluation,* or assessment, of how adequate one's reasoning or conclusion is at that moment (Guilford, 1967).

The capability to use abstract reasoning is present in some youngsters about the age of 11 or 12 years. Early adolescence is a time when this capability emerges to a functional level. Middle adolescence is the period when this capability matures to a higher potential. One hopes that the late adolescent learns how to use this potential.

Typical 15-year-olds can think rationally and realistically about themselves. They are mainly interested in the present, but they begin to think more about their future. After this age they become increasingly open-minded and liberal in their attitudes. They are largely responsible for determining their own behavior and are willing to assume responsibility for their actions. When necessary, they are able to compromise their intellectual behavior according to the challenges and demands of their life situation. However, their collective cognitive ability to make good judgments and to have deep intellectual insights is limited by an inexperienced, underdeveloped background of knowledge from which they can establish an adequate perspective concerning the problem they are seeking to solve. Their idealistic and pseudo-optimistic nature also distorts their perspective.

Mental characteristics

In any large group of adolescents there will be a wide distribution of mental ages. Among the general population of 15-year-olds, for example, almost 23% are likely to have a mental age between 14-6 and 15-11 years; 23%, a mental age between 13-8 and 14-6 years; 18%, a mental age between 16-0 and 17-6 years. About 2% would have a mental age under 10 years (an IQ of 71 or less), and a little over 4%, a mental age above 19 years (an IQ of 129 or more), with the rest of the group being distributed between these extremes (Terman, 1960).

Intellectual differences increase during adolescence as the experiences and environments of individuals become more diversified. Individual differences *within* any group of late adolescents—boys, girls, blacks, whites, Spanish-speaking, high or low socioeconomic level—are much greater than differences *between* groups.

At one time it was believed that young people stopped growing mentally at about 16 years of age. Now many authorities believe that individuals grow in certain aspects of intelligence beyond the age of 16 years. Intellectual growth after the age of 16 is more a horizontal growth of potential ability than a vertical growth (Siegler, 1976). Some kinds of mental ability increase more than others during the late adolescent years. For example, both boys and girls may be expected to increase in vocabulary. Boys generally show a greater increase in arithmetical scores than do girls. Both sexes show little or no increase in scores on items that primarily involve memory (Anastasi, 1976).

It is during this period of development that young people become capable of scientific reasoning and of formal logic in verbal argument; moreover, they reflect about, evaluate, and criticize the logic and quality of their own thinking (Newman, 1975). They do not need to center their attention on the immediate situation. They can imagine what might be possible and can consider hypotheses that may or may not be true; they can consider also what would follow if they were true (Neimark, 1975). As they approach 15 years of age, they are able to learn how to use formal logic in an adult manner, and when this is possible, Piaget asserts that they have reached the critical stage of intellectual development. From now on learning how to use the tools of logic and frequent practice in their usage will be necessary to enable individuals to function well within their level of potentiality. Use of the tool provides horizontal growth of intellect.

EMOTIONALITY

If children received abundant love and patient understanding during infancy and early childhood, if the imposition of societal demands reflected an understanding by parents of individual patterns of readiness, and if occasional regressions were accepted as merely a part of growing up and as inevitable, at adolescence there is usually a minimal amount of difficulty and strain in coping with the problems and conflicts of this stage. On the other hand, children who have been the object of parental rejection, overdominance, or overindulgence are likely to experience an unusually stormy adolescence. Achievement of independence and emotional maturity is hampered by excesses in parental domination, friction between the parents, sibling rivalry, and an unwillingness on the part of the parents to allow adolescents to share in decisions that affect the family (Balswick and Macrides, 1975). However, we must remember the potential relationship between emotions and cognitive operation. The individual who is reality directed in outlook rather than emotionally dominated will overcome some of the debilitating influences of the environment.

Emotional characteristics

The older adolescent experiences similar emotions as the child and early adolescent. The differences deal with the amount, intensity, types of responses, and types of stimuli that create the emotions of the late adolescent.

Anger. Anger is the major disruptive emotion found in later adolescence. Moodiness is the most common nondisruptive emotion (Blos, 1979). The most common causes of anger are restraints on the adolescent's desire to do something and interruption of activities that have become routine for the adolescent. Environment is the major stimulus for anger. If the environment of later adolescents thwarts their desires, anger will usually result. Girls respond more often and more violently to social situations than do boys. The childish responses to anger of hurting, biting, and throwing objects are no longer found. Name calling and verbal responses are the most common manifestations of anger in later adolescence (Miller, 1974). The duration of anger is longer because older adolescents attempt to conceal their anger, thus making it last longer.

Jealousy. Jealousy displays itself in heterosexual situations in later adolescence more than in any other way. Toward the end of adolescence, interests change from a general regard for members of the opposite sex to one specific person of the opposite sex. In this situation jealousy arises when one member, or both, feels that the other is cheating in their relationship.

Envy. Material possessions and social status have a strong appeal to the later adolescent. Leadership and social status are closely related, and the older adolescent is envious of persons who possess these two items. Adolescents usually seek jobs to acquire material goods, but some resort to shoplifting and stealing as their means of achieving social equality with others. The cause of some juvenile delinquency is envy of the possessions of others more fortunate than the delinquent.

Happiness. Happiness comes from four situations. If the adolescent is able to feel at ease in a situation, contentment will usually follow. The adolescent must also be able to understand the comic parts, the humorous aspects of a situation. When the later adolescent has achieved a sense of superiority over others, happiness and pride are the result. Finally, situations are needed where the adolescent can release stored-up emotional energy (Hurlock, 1973).

Affection. Later adolescence is a period of intense affection because the individuals are concentrating their affection on one member of the opposite sex or on a small group of friends. Generally, if the individuals are well adjusted, this display of affection will be directed toward a member of the opposite sex.

Fear and worry. Fear is less recognizable in later adolescence than it was in the previous period. Fear of social situations, environment, or people is no longer as great a problem as it once was. Adolescents are capable of avoiding embarrassing situations by planning activities that will enable them to avoid these situations.

In later adolescence worries take the form of imaginary fears. Feelings of inadequacy are a common occurrence (Rutter et al., 1976). Problems related to money, jobs, the use of the automobile, physical appearance, social acceptability, sex, and marriage are also causes of worry.

Emotional maturity. Individuals have achieved emotional maturity when they are capable of controlling their emotions until a socially proper time and place are available for them to "let off" their feelings. Emotionally mature individuals are capable of ignoring stimuli that as children they would have reacted to emotionally. Heightened emotionality, when expressed, reflects itself through feelings of insecurity, tension, indecision, and exaggerated or sometimes irrational behavior.

Self-concept

Early in the adolescent period, growing children begin to realize that they are individuals and not simply extensions of their parents. It is at this point that they want to know "Who am I?" This drive for self-

David Strickler

Being "number one" is a popular ambition nowadays. The emotions of adolescents can be very responsive to certain events and circumstances. Generally, older adolescents are more in control of their emotions—and recover from intense emotions more quickly—than younger adolescents.

assertion becomes one of the prime motivating forces during this period (Siegel, 1982). It is a struggle against "getting lost" and feeling like a stranger to oneself. By the time individuals are ready to leave later adolescence, they have probably developed their sense of personal identity and now know who they are. The struggle to find this identity can be a difficult one.

Adolescents achieve their self-identity through their self-concept. The self-concept is developed as youngsters confront the world and gain an impression of it. They must relate the world to themselves and themselves to it. At this time they are greatly concerned with their own personal worth. In their struggle to find themselves they are afraid that they cannot live up to their own expectations. They may ask "Am I good enough, smart enough, or popular enough?"

ERIKSON: IDENTITY FORMATION

Erikson's theory of personality development emphasizes an important goal for adolescence, that of identity formation (Erikson, 1968b). The psychosocial crisis of adolescence that must be resolved is that of ***identity versus role confusion.*** The question to be answered is "Do I know who I am, or am I confused about who I should be?" During this stage of development, the adolescent needs to establish a stable sense of personality, one that is centered around the integration of the various roles the adolescent has to play. This individual, just confronted with major physical changes and increased heterosexual interests, must also deal with changing roles in his or her life.

Think of the roles that a person of this age has: that of a child to parents; a student to teachers; a friend to a group of age-mates; possibly a girlfriend or a boyfriend to someone; maybe a teenage worker; likely a member of a club, a team, a musical group or some other extracurricular activity; and, perhaps, a participant in a scouting group, a church program, a community activity, or another social or civic activity. Each role has its own demands, values, relationships, rewards or aversions, or reasons for being. The various roles have input in terms of feelings, social meaning, and the regard of significant others, all of which contribute to the development of self-esteem and self-definition.

Usually teenagers handle many relationships at one time by keeping the roles isolated and separate. However, in terms of personality development, at some point in time the adolescent will need to integrate the various concepts and assessments of self into a meaningful identity, one that can answer the questions, "Who am I?" and "Who am I to be?" ***Identity*** is a persisting sense of being the same person whereby the individual orients himself or herself to the external world. It is a sense of unity of personality over a substantial period of time. The ultimate goal is to see oneself as a unique and an integrated person while sustaining appropriate relationships with others.

Erikson (1968b) emphasizes that adolescence is a phase, characterized by a fluctuation of ego strength. To establish identity requires individual effort in evaluating personal assets and liabilities and learning how to use them to achieve a clearer concept of who he or she is and what the individual wants to be and to become. There are converging identity elements at this point that can be divided into seven major parts.

1. *Temporal perspective versus time confusion:* Erikson is referring to gaining a sense of time and the continuity of life so that some concept of how long it will take to achieve one's life plans can be gained.
2. *Self-certainty versus self-consciousness:* adolescents go through a period of increasing self-awareness, but self-confidence must be developed so that there is a reasonable chance of accomplishing future aims.
3. *Role experimentation versus role fixation:* adolescents have an opportunity to try out different roles and identities with different personality characteristics, with different ways of talking and ideas, and with different philosophies and goals.
4. *Apprenticeship versus work paralysis:* there is also an opportunity to try out different occupations and career studies before deciding on a vocation.
5. *Sexual polarization versus bisexual confusion:* Erikson feels it is important that adolescents develop a clear identification with one sex or the other as a basis for future heterosexual intimacy and identity.
6. *Leadership and fellowship versus authority confusion:* as social contacts and horizons are expanded, adolescents begin to learn to take leadership responsibilities as well as to follow others. There may be some authority confusion develop as the adolescent wonders whom to listen to, what to believe, and whom to follow.
7. *Ideological commitment versus confusion of values:* this conflict is closely related to a resolution of the other six areas. This struggle as the "search for fidelity" ceases when the adolescent no longer has to question his or her own identity and when childhood identity has been changed into a new self-identification.

identity a sense of one's self; sense of sameness despite growth, aging, and environmental change.

identity versus role confusion Erikson's fifth crisis of psychological development; the adolescent may become confident and purposeful, or may develop an ill-defined identity.

VALUES IN ADOLESCENCE

Changing times bring changes in attitudes and in people's beliefs as to what is and what is not important. This change is illustrated by the "cohort effect." An activity or a point of view acceptable to one generation may not be equally acceptable to another. It is some-

locus of value a personality trait involving a generalized expectancy that people hold regarding the degree to which they control their fate. People with an internal locus of control feel they have a reasonable amount of control over their outcomes. People with an external locus of control feel their fate is largely beyond their control.

value the worth or excellence found in a qualitative appraisal of an object, idea, or behavior by reliance on emotional and rational standards of the individual or of selected reference groups.

times difficult for one generation to appreciate the point of view of another generation. It is important for young people to know the effect of given attitudes or values on themselves and on others. It is also important to know ways and means of developing "good" attitudes and of discouraging "bad" ones. The development of a value judgment system is basic not only because of its moral and behavioral implications but also because of its influence on the decision-making process.

Value judgment system

A *value judgment system* consists of individuals' beliefs, values, and attitudes that reflect their views and opinions of what is good or bad, desirable or undesirable, important or unimportant, right or wrong, valuable or not valuable, and that influence their emotional and rational thought processes in the making of decisions and choices. The development of a value judgment system begins when children learn to inhibit or to stop conducting their behavior according to the wishes of others. It does not become mature until, as adults, they have overcome external domination of their behavioral and judgmental processes.

Environmental factors such as the peer group, parents, institutions, vicarious experiences, and prevailing social attitudes as revealed by communications media are important in shaping an adolescent's attitudes. Of these, peer group and parental influences and dominant social beliefs are the most significant (McKinney and Moore, 1982). In general, adolescents will tend to be readily influenced by those individuals they like or love and by those who possess some attributes or skills that they admire.

Concept of values

Values and attitudes serve as internal decision-making guides for an individual. Although values are more global in meaning than attitudes, both function to make behavioral choices more predictable and consistent. The importance of value and attitude development in adolescence takes on major significance when it is realized that such development plays an important role in the maintenance of identity and continuity at a time when the adolescent is undergoing many personal changes. Along with a dramatic change in cognitive functioning, adolescents experience an increase in the rate of developmental change, physically, emotionally, sexually, and socially.

The term ***value,*** in general, refers to the worth or excellence of something. Psychologists generally think in terms of behavioral values or object values. *Behavioral values* are the prescriptive guides of an "ought to" nature, which serve to direct behavior to a goal that is considered desirable or worthy of achievement. *Object values* are related to values that objects are said to have within themselves (McKinney and Moore, 1982). Money, cars, or clothes have object value; a search for health or financial security is a behavioral value.

The ***locus of value,*** the source of it, is the important factor to be considered: Does value reside within the person—or is value inherent within the object? Many psychologists side with the "person" variable: "A study of a person's values is likely to be much more useful for social analyses than a study of values that objects are said to have" (Rokeach, 1973, p. 5). However, Feather (1980) prefers to assume that values are influenced both by the characteristics of the person who is engaged in valuing and by the characteristics of the object being valued.

Stated values of adolescents

Values can be considered terminal or instrumental in nature. *Terminal values* are those that are goal-oriented and are ends in themselves, such as a comfortable life, freedom, peace in the world. *Instrumental values* are values that are a means of achieving a goal, such as ambition, forgiveness, or love. Beech and Schoeppe (1974), using the Rokeach Value Survey, found a good amount of similarity across the ages and sexes in a high preference for values such as *freedom, honesty,* and a *world at peace.* Values given lower ratings were *salvation, logic,* and *imagination. Family security* was rated higher by young adolescents and preadolescents while older adolescents rated *equality* and *social recognition* higher.

The instrumental values of *cheerfulness, helpfulness,* and *obedience* and the terminal values of a *world of beauty* and *true friendship* tended to decline in importance by the eleventh grade. There were signs that both sexes were valuing achievement, open-mindedness, responsibility, and self-respect increasingly as they grew older and were downgrading modes of behavior connoting conformity to convention and authority.

A point to be recognized is that stated values can be influenced by secular trends and events and by the impact of history and tradition. Changes in social and political institutions, economic crises, wars, and other external influences have lasting effects on developmental outcomes. In addition there are the internal influences that are part of the life course of adolescents. These include coping with biological changes and emerging sexuality, seeking to define identities, developing independence and autonomy, making plans for the future, and taking on new roles and responsibilities. In addition, changes occur in the development of intellectual capacities, ego or personality processes, moral reasoning, sex roles, and social relationships. In other words there are internal life-cycle effects, cohort or generalization effects, and historical period effects (Jennings and Niemi, 1975) that can influence value selection. It is surprising, in view of the variety of factors that can affect value development, that there is as much similarity as there is. An important factor is to note that the family is a significant force in the socialization of adolescent values (Kohn, 1977). Most young people have close and friendly relationships with their parents and regard them as an important reference source (Curtis, 1975). Apparently, influential adults provide enough input to maintain a semblance of agreement on significant values.

Personal concerns reflecting values

The following statements are taken from unpublished research conducted by the authors in which over 1,000 adolescents between 15 and 18 years were sampled.

Male, 15 years, ninth grade

I have trouble with algebra. I don't see why anyone has to take algebra unless they want to be a doctor or an engineer. It's just silly junk. My mother took algebra and it didn't help her. I think I should learn more about how to write a check, how to use interest, and other useful studies.

Female, 15 years, tenth grade

My home is my problem, especially my father. I had to leave my home last year because he beat me and was always threatening me. He has always abused me.

Female, 15 years, eleventh grade

I'm in love! It's real, too! The boy I'm in love with loves me just as much. He's in the service. Every once in a while he gets a weekend pass and comes home. We don't see each other very often and that's really hard when you're in love. We always try to squeeze so much into one evening that things start to happen. We're neither one that kind of person. We just can't help ourselves. So far we've been able to stop before it goes too far. What can we do to keep even this little bit from taking place? It's not what we want, it just happens.

Male, 16 years, eleventh grade

My trouble is money. I have a job and work five nights a week, 4 to 12 o'clock. My parents have very little money so I don't like to ask them for any. But my parents don't want me to work so long. They'd rather I spend more time on my schoolwork.

Male, 16 years, eleventh grade

I seem to find it very hard to get my parents to understand that I have somewhat of a life of my own. They can't understand that I have also grown in age and maturity. They still want me to abide by the privileges they granted me at age 13.

Female, 16 years, eleventh grade

My problem is that I have a very bad inferiority complex. I feel that people are talking about me. When I'm with a group, I hardly know what to say. When I leave the group I get the feeling that they talk about me and don't want me.

Male, 16 years, eleventh grade
I have a slight amount of trouble with my mother. It bothers me because I don't want to make her unhappy. I realize she has done many things for me and I want to repay her.

Male, 17 years, twelfth grade
Although my parents treat me exceptionally well as far as material things are concerned, I would sooner have a little less of these things and a little more understanding.

Female, 17 years, twelfth grade
My parents object to my marriage to a boy of a different race. Why should they object when the boy and girl are willing to give up certain things for each other and are sure they can make it work?

Female, 17 years, twelfth grade
Right now I have the problem that I have applied for admission to a very fine college to further my education. However, I wonder sometimes if I really want to go to college. My parents say it is up to me.

Female, 17 years, twelfth grade
I have gone with a fellow for about two years but we have just recently broken up. I can see him going deeper and deeper on drugs and he won't stop. I still want him, but not that way.

Female, 17 years, twelfth grade
I have been planning to be married in July but the boy is of a different religion than me and is quite a few years older. He is in the Army. My parents don't think it would be good to marry him. I don't agree because he can be depended upon; he is thoughtful and kind and loves me a lot. I'm looking forward to marriage. But there's going to be some trouble because a boy I haven't seen for two years who has been in Germany is coming back. He knows I'm to be married but he says he still loves me.

Female, 18 years, twelfth grade
I have a problem. My mother and father are separated and getting a divorce. I don't know who to go with if I were asked to pick my home.

Male, 18 years, twelfth grade
Do you think it is right to always ask Mom or Dad for some cash to spend if you never stay at home in evenings to be with them? I usually come in at all hours of the night and a word has never been said. Do you think that your parents should worry?

Male, 18 years, twelfth grade
With my senior year drawing to a close it won't be long until I will be going away to college. It bothers me to realize that I will be leaving my family and that I will have to depend upon myself.

CHEMICAL SUBSTANCE USE AND ABUSE

Middle and later adolescents are still in the process of establishing an identity and a pattern of personal adjustment. They are also learning new basic skills and knowledge related to their current phase of life. Some problems, concerns, or delays in development are possible. Because many new situations and challenges are encountered by an adolescent who is still in the process of "putting it all together," this period of growth for some individuals will be one of trial and error, ups and downs, ambivalence, and some experimentation. The demands to adjust to new life circumstances may be more than some adolescents can handle. Their adjustment mechanisms may not be ready to cope with the new set of inner and external pressures and, as a result, maladjustive behavior patterns will emerge.

If a person's adjustive demands are greater than his or her adjustive resources can manage, a psychological disturbance will occur. The resulting behavior may become aggressive, withdrawing, or, perhaps, compromising in nature. The type and degree of deviancy of behavior may be related to one or more of the following factors: (1) not knowing what to do so that following the examples or behaviors of others provides a clue or a direction, (2) not being able to reconcile the problem or demand by one's usual behavior, so a "fight or flight" reaction mechanism is used, or (3) not being able to control the emotional intensity one has in response to a frustrating situation, with the result that cognitive processes become disorganized and confused to the point that one cannot reason logically (Coleman, 1979).

Chemical substance abuse

Drugs and alcohol are chemicals. Chemical ***substance abuse*** refers to the taking in of drugs or alcohol to the point that the body and mind are adversely affected. There are users and abusers of chemical substances. Often it is difficult for the individuals involved to know which they are.

substance abuse drug or alcohol abuse characterized by a minimum of 1 month's physiological dependence, difficulty in social functioning, with or without withdrawal symptoms.

Prevalence of drug and alcohol usage

The adolescent use of drugs or alcohol has been widely publicized. Yet it may be significant to look at some of the statistics on the use of chemical substances by teenagers. There is a concensus of the studies that alcohol, cigarettes, and marijuana are the drugs most frequently used or abused (Sutker, 1982).

Adolescents consume alcohol—preferring beer and wine—more regularly than other drugs. Johnston and associates (1979) report that 72% of high school seniors admitted use of alcohol in the previous month, 7% declared daily use, and 93% had at least tasted an alcoholic beverage.

David Strickler

The use of drugs and alcohol by adolescents, as well as by younger children and adults, has become a national concern. Several states have raised the legal drinking age. An effective educational program concerning chemical substance abuse apparently still has to be generated.

Donovan and Jessor (1978) report that close to 5% of seventh-grade boys and girls admitted problem drinking (by definition in the study) and that, among twelfth-grade boys and girls, nearly 40% and 21%, respectively, were so classified. Greatest increases in drinking occurred between grades 7 and 8 for boys and 8 and 9 for girls.

Fishburne and colleagues (1980) cite marijuana usage at about 31% for 12- to 17-year-olds, with 56% of high school seniors claiming to have used the drug. Smart and Blair (1980) indicate marijuana use by 69% of the students in college. Experimentation with amphetamines, hallucinogens, barbiturates, cocaine, and opiates is relatively widespread, but the regular use of illicit drugs is more limited (Green, 1979). Johnston and associates (1979) report that less than 1% of high school seniors admitted daily illicit use of drugs other than marijuana. Even so, 15 million youths are regular marijuana users or smoke at least once a week (Beschner and Friedman, 1979). Following marijuana in frequency of use are stimulants (23%), tranquilizers (18%), sedatives (17%), hallucinogens (14%), cocaine (14%), and heroin (2%) (Johnston et al., 1979).

Individual reactions to drugs and alcohol

Individuals react in four different ways to mood- and/or mind-altering drugs (including alcohol) (Bejerot, 1972). First, a small percentage have a definite adverse reaction to the effects of chemical substances. These individuals develop disagreeable upsetting symptoms. They may find the loss of mental and physical efficiency very unpleasant; it makes them ill. Second, others who ingest chemical substances experience no particular pleasure or euphoria nor any significant sedative or relaxing effect. They may use chemicals occasionally under social pressure.

Third, by far the largest group consists of the social participants. These individuals experience some euphoria or pleasure and a degree of tranquilization or relaxation that is enjoyable. Social participants enjoy the symbolic meaning of being part of the group. However, when confronted with a possible danger in any area of life, they are able to control and to relinquish the use of chemical substances with reasonable ease. Fourth, a dependent user is one who begins where the social participant's usage terminates. The positive pleasure of getting "high" is observed to be qualitatively and quantitatively different in the dependent user.

The reasons for the difference in reaction are not completely known. Abnormal metabolism, a physiological preference for the chemical, heredity, prenatal influences, and ethnic susceptibility to chemical dependency have all been studied and suggested as possibilities for individual variations. The disease concept as a source of dependency is receiving strong endorsement in preference to the idea of a psychological source of dependency (Mann, 1973). Any theory of drug dependency must begin with the premise that the individual who is dependent on a chemical substance experiences a different response than does the average person (David and Walsh, 1970).

Chemical substance dependency

Huberty and Malmquist (1978) state that adolescent abuse of mood-altering chemicals progresses rapidly to a primary disease entity that deserves the psychiatric or medical diagnostic label of "adolescent chemical dependency." The central issue is one of preoccupation with a welcomed and anticipated mood swing that can be produced reliably by the chemical substances. The euphoric substances help the adolescent to cope, alleviating stresses rather quickly and perhaps providing the individual with improved status and a feeling of belonging in a chemical-using peer group or culture. Increasing chemical-substance involvement follows a steplike, but not necessarily inevitable, progression to extended usage (Kandel et al., 1978). Recurrent preoccupation with the next time "to get high" is the first symptom and the hallmark of chemical substance dependency and abuse.

Heilman (1975) outlines four characteristics of chemical substance dependency.

1. There is a recurrent, overwhelming urge to repeat the experience of "getting high" or of intoxication. The urge to do so usually goes beyond the strength of one's will to make a choice to do otherwise.

2. The strength of this urge is so great that it transcends innate or learned needs. It is so strong that it achieves primacy as a need that requires recurrent, frequent fulfillment.

3. The urge to repeat the experience of "getting high" or intoxicated becomes independent of any other aspect of one's life; the urge is automatic, not symptomatic of tension, stress, or anxiety.

4. Once a person becomes "hooked" or psychologically dependent on a chemical substance, this experience becomes indelibly etched within the mind and

remains a most intense personal experience that cannot be consciously or unconsciously forgotten. With longer periods of sobriety or "staying clean," the intensity of the urge is reduced and the urge does not recur as often, but it does return.

The "Diagnostic and Statistical Manual of Mental Disorders" of the American Psychiatric Association considers the diagnostic criterion for a substance use disorder to be either a pathological usage or an impairment in social or occupational functioning because of the substance use (Spitzer, 1980).

Addiction, according to Bejerot (1972), has the characteristic of a natural drive. It may be considered an artificially induced drive developed through chemical stimulation of the pleasure center. David and Walsh (1970) theorize that chemical substances alter the dopamine pathways, resulting in the formation of morphine-like alkaloids, which, in turn, produce an alcoholic- or drug-responsive metabolism resulting in dependency.

The following profile, Fazed, Dazed, and Burned Out, speaks to the point of the disastrous effect of drugs, alcohol, and driving. Accidents are the number one killer of adolescents. Alcohol and/or drugs are responsible for most of the accidents. The profile may say more than anything we could have written. It is a true story—frequently repeated in one form or another.

FAZED, DAZED, AND BURNED OUT

Debbie is now nineteen years old. She is an alcoholic. Since she has been in junior high school, she has been corrupted by her peers. It was then that she started taking drugs, anything from pot to LSD. She started taking them out of curiosity but continued because it was the "in" thing to do. She kept taking them because she liked the "high." She didn't use them every day but often enough so that her personality changed, maybe because of the drugs or maybe because of the kids she began to run around with.

It was in ninth grade that Debbie and I met. We sat across from each other in history class. She responded well to me and, although we never ran around together, we became friends, the kind that you become close to because of a special liking rather than constant association. Debbie's grades were average, even though she was more into drugs than schoolwork. Debbie became a hell raiser; she was tough, even though she was barely five feet tall and weighed only ninety pounds. Most of our classmates were actually afraid of her, but she was always kind and considerate with me.

When we entered high school, Debbie got into the "freak" crowd. She began to socialize with them and she also got into drinking. In tenth grade, when Debbie was sixteen, she started to date a guy named Steve; eventually, they became very close. Little did she know the problems that were to come!

Across the state line in Maryland there was a bar where teenagers from southern Pennsylvania could go and drink—and get drunk. They couldn't get served at a bar in Pennsylvania unless they had an ID proving they were twenty-one. The legal age limit for drinking was much lower in Maryland at that time. One night Debbie, Steve and three other guys were supposed to drive down to the Maryland line. At the last minute Debbie decided not to go. Steve and the other three guys went anyway and got drunk. On the way home they stopped by the side of the road to empty their bladders because there were no rest stops. Steve and another guy stayed in the car while the other two got out. Just at that moment, another car full of drunk people went out of control for some reason and smashed into the car where Steve and Mike were sitting. They were trapped in the car as it burst into flames. The other two guys tried frantically to get their friends out, but every time they got near the car, they were burned badly. No matter how hard they tried, it was futile. Steve and Mike burned to death in the car.

The news was electrifying. Debbie became hysterical. She took the news very hard. It was at this time that she began drinking heavily. She would not listen to anyone who tried to help her. She started bringing alcohol to school every day, and the smell of alcohol was on her breath constantly. Not only was she into heavy drinking, but she also began to abuse such drugs as pot, hashish, speed, Quāāludes, acid, cocaine, and Valium. Psychologically and physically, Debbie got progressively worse. She tried to commit suicide by slitting her wrists. To this day she has scars that stand out clearly.

It was a year after the accident that Debbie and I became really close. I would listen to her and try to help her without being judgmental. She needed help, not a lecture. She would talk about her drinking and the accident. She kept saying, "I should be dead right now. I was supposed to be with them that night. I should have burned in that car." Once I asked her about her wrists, thinking that she might get that out into the open and release some of her anxieties. But she just abruptly changed the subject.

When Debbie would talk to me about the accident, she used to strike her fists against the wall. One day in school someone had the newspaper article about the accident and showed it to Debbie. That was absolutely the wrong thing to do. She became extremely upset, began sobbing and hitting her fists against the locker door until she dented it. Then she got real quiet and just stood there, looking at her wrists. I'll never forget the expression on her face; I knew what she was thinking about.

Another year had passed when Debbie started to go out with a guy named Arnie. He was worse than bad for her. He constantly gave her alcohol and drugs. Once he gave her Quaaludes, and she took them all! What's worse, she had been drinking that night. When I found that out, I was really upset. I despised Arnie for what he was doing to her. But no one could get Debbie to listen to reason; she just didn't care.

Debbie started gaining a lot of weight and getting into a really bad physical condition. At times when I looked at her face, she looked like a little lost puppy. She began to move into a dream world of illusions. It was getting too late for anyone to help her. Once she started to Alcoholics Anonymous, but that only lasted two weeks. Arnie was absolutely no help at that time. He gave her drinks when he knew she wasn't supposed to have anything to drink. He took her to parties where drinks and drugs were offered to her.

In the middle of our senior year, Debbie's parents finally talked her into going to a rehabilitation center for two months. While she was living at the center, Debbie wrote me a most depressing letter. She told me she had hit rock bottom and the only thing left—besides death—was to go back up and get better.

When she returned from her stay at the center, she was fine for a short time. She even returned to Alcoholics Anonymous, but for some reason she could not stick to her commitment. Debbie graduated from high school but never had any interest in getting a job. Her mind, while still functioning, seems to be burned out. She has no incentive in life—except to drink.

ADOLESCENT AGGRESSION

Incidence of delinquency and aggression

To view the problem of adolescent delinquency in its proper perspective one must keep in mind that only a small percentage, perhaps less than 5% of all adolescents, ever are legally classified as delinquents. Yet almost 23% of all reported arrests are of persons under the age of 18 (Federal Bureau of Investigation, 1979). Not all aggressive or destructive acts result in apprehension, formal arrest, and prosecution. Some forms of antisocial behavior violate no existing statutes. The actual amount of delinquency among adolescents may never be completely known. Over 80% of American adolescents admit to committing one or more minor delinquent acts (Gold and Petronio, 1980).

Aggressive, destructive, and antisocial behavior is characteristically a behavior of youth rather than adulthood. The incidence of delinquency rises during the early teens. It gathers momentum and peaks at the age of 15 years. During the ages of 16 to 18 the rate of delinquency declines, only to rise again at age 19. The level of delinquent and criminal incidence then declines to the age of 23 (O'Malley et al., 1977).

Determinants of delinquent behavior

The probability of delinquency occurring during adolescence is much greater if there is a childhood history of antisocial behavior. In fact, approximately two thirds of adolescent delinquents begin their delinquent careers in preadolescence (Olweus, 1979). Greater freedom of movement and less adult supervision during adolescence also make delinquent behavior more possible.

More important perhaps than greater opportunity and capacity for executing delinquent acts are the familial determinants, antiauthority responses, aggressive attitudes, and peer group sanctions that exist during adolescence (Olweus, 1980). Prolonged status deprivation superimposed on other psychosocial and psychobiological problems increases emotional instability and lowers the threshold for aggressive behavior.

Sex differences in aggressive actions

Important differences exist between boys and girls in the incidence, age of onset, etiology, and kind of delinquency practiced. Four to seven times as many boys as girls become delinquent, but the ratio of boys to girls has shown a steady decline over the past 50 years (Quay, 1982). Boys also become involved in delinquency at an earlier age than girls. This difference results partly from the greater supervision to which younger adolescent girls are subjected and partly from that fact that sex offenses, which constitute the most frequent category of delinquency among girls, do not occur until an older age. However, if these differences between boys and girls are environmentally determined and reflect cultural attitudes toward male and female sex roles, the difference in age of onset of delinquency can be expected to become increasingly less pronounced in the future.

Sex differences in the kinds of offenses committed are striking. Stealing, mischief, traffic violations, truancy, auto thefts, and running away from home are the major misdemeanors of adolescent boys. Delinquent girls, on the other hand, are most frequently charged with ungovernability, sex offenses, and leaving home (Gold and Reimer, 1975).

PSYCHOPATHOLOGY IN ADOLESCENCE

Psychopathology is the study of psychological and behavioral dysfunctions occurring in mental disorder, usually manifested by egocentric and antisocial behavior. Among adolescents, the typical pathologies incurred are personality disorders (31.4%), situation-specific disorders (27.1%), neuroses (13.3%), schizophrenia (8.5%), and suicide attempts (2.8%). Other psychopathologies, such as alcoholism, behavior disorders, anorexia nervosa, and psychophysiological reactions, make up the other 16.9% (Weiner and Del Gaudio, 1976). Selected psychopathologies will be discussed here.

Personality disorders

Personality disorders are long-standing patterns of maladaptive behavior. When personality traits become inflexible and maladaptive to the point that they significantly impair the individual's ability to function, they are personality disorders. They are usually evident by early adolescence and may continue throughout adult life. Usually there is no anxiety or marked disorganization of behavior associated with the disorder. Persons with personality disorders are generally not upset and have little motivation to change their behavior.

According to the American Psychiatric Association (Spitzer, 1980), there are twelve categories of mental disorders. Several relate to personalities with neurotic or psychotic tendencies. The antisocial personality and the passive-aggressive personality disorders are most relevant to adolescents.

Individuals with antisocial personalities seem to have little sense of responsibility, morality, or concern for others. Their behavior is determined almost entirely by their own needs or wishes. They have no conscience. During adolescence such an individual might evidence three or more of the following behaviors: truancy of at least 5 days, expulsion from school, conduct leading to referral to juvenile court, running away from home at least twice (overnight), persistent lying, repeated casual intercourse, substance use, thefts, vandalism, or grades below measured expectations.

The term *antisocial personality* is somewhat misleading because not all persons who commit antisocial acts, such as refusing to abide by commonly accepted social norms or beliefs, have a personality disorder. The individual with an antisocial personality is unable to experience empathy or loyalty to another person. There is also an inability to feel any guilt or remorse, no matter how reprehensible the act committed. The sociopathic type of antisocial personality may be a "good-time Charlie" or a "party girl"—lots of fun, daring anything, with no inhibitions. Such individuals are not necessarily mean or harmful, but they do lack impulse control. Some of them can of course be ruthless and uncaring about whom they hurt.

Those with a *passive–aggressive personality* disorder have a long-standing resistance to demands for adequate performance in school or social functioning. They fight by resisting. The resistance is shown by at

personality disorders ingrained, habitual, and rigid patterns of behavior or character that severely limit the individual's adaptive potential; often society sees the behavior as maladaptive while the individual does not (syn. *character disorders*).

psychopathology psychological and behavioral dysfunctions occurring in mental disorders.

least two of the following: procrastination, dawdling, stubbornness, intentional inefficiency, or "forgetfulness." The behavior continues even under circumstances in which more self-assertive and effective behavior is possible. Now before you begin to diagnose others, please note that this presentation of antisocial personalities is very minimal. All behaviors can be assessed on a continuum, with qualifications of normal, mild, moderate, or severe. Some behavior characteristics that seem to be those of personality disorders may be within the normal range of accepted behavior—and not a disorder.

Suicidal behavior

Suicide rates in the United States increase dramatically after the age of 25. People under the age of 20 account for only 6% of known suicides a year (U. S. Department of Health, Education and Welfare, 1975). However, suicide is the fourth leading cause of death among 15- to 19-year-olds, following accidents, homicide, and cancer. Although adolescents are much less likely to kill themselves than adults, they are about equally likely to make suicide attempts. Among adults there is one death for every 6 to 10 attempts. Among adolescents the ratio of attempted suicides to completed ones is about 1 in 50 (Hudgens, 1974). Completed suicides are three times higher among males than females, since males are more likely to use drastic means, such as shooting or hanging, while females use more passive means, such as taking poison or drugs. Females are three times more likely to make suicide attempts (Weiner, 1980).

The psychological state that poses the greatest risk of suicide is depression. *Depression* is usually characterized by prolonged feelings of gloom, despair, futility, and pessimism. Often there is a feeling of excessive guilt and self-reproach. Depression is considered a major cause of students dropping out of school. Depression is noteworthy among adolescents because of the frequency with which it is expressed through other than typical depressive symptoms—the so-called masked depression or depression equivalents (Malmquist, 1975).

In a comprehensive study of adolescent suicide, Jacobs (1971) concluded that these youngsters typically became increasingly cut off from sympathetic, warm, and secure contacts with others. Communication ties were gradually being severed. The progression of isolation appears to be (1) a long-standing history of problems, (2) a period during which the incidence of problems increased dramatically, (3) a progressive failure of the individual's adjustive mechanisms to cope with frustrations and a consequent withdrawal from others because of social interaction instability, and (4) a chain reaction breakdown of any remaining meaningful social relationships in the period preceding the suicide attempt. For these reasons, communication is a key aspect of adolescent suicidal behavior. The adolescent who has suicidal thoughts or tendencies must be reached and a genuine effort made to help him or her resolve the difficulties that brought matters to such a point. Anger, scorn, or lack of interest only intensify a suicidal tendency (Weiner, 1977). Suicide is a permanent solution to a temporary condition. The condition must not be permitted to "get out of hand."

Aaron Beck, a psychiatrist at the University of Pennsylvania School of Medicine, has developed a "suicidal ideational scale" (Beck et al., 1979). The scale serves as a guideline for an interview. The items are rated in terms of degree of seriousness. The main sections of the scale are (1) characteristics of attitude toward living or dying and the desire to make a suicide attempt, (2) characteristics of the suicide idea or wish in terms of frequency, duration, and attitude toward the wish, (3) characteristics of the contemplated attempt—how, when, and degree of anticipation, (4) actualization of contemplated attempt, in terms of preparation: a note, final acts in anticipation of death, or attempts to conceal the attempt, and (5) background factors relative to previous attempts.

Treatment of adolescents with suicidal tendencies usually involves psychotherapy and, if needed, antidepressant medications such as Elavil and Tofranil. Since many of the victims have experienced hostility, indifference, and rejection by their parents, family therapy is generally in order (Brody, 1976). The therapist seeks to help the teenager develop a better perspective of the problems and of life, learn better coping techniques, and acquire a more confident sense of self. The family also learns of the problems involved and how to provide psychological support.

Anorexia nervosa

Anorexia nervosa is defined as a psychosomatic disease that entails dramatic weight loss caused by self-induced starvation. Untreated, the illness can become very detrimental to the health of the individual and can ultimately cause death by the collapse of the circulatory system, usually involving the heart.

Characteristics. It is usually adolescent girls who suffer from this illness, although there are known cases among males. The underlying reasons given for this self-induced starvation are (1) a panicky concern with gaining weight or becoming fat, (2) a sense of pride, power, and accomplishment that comes from being able to control the intake of food, and (3) an intense fear of hunger (Bruch, 1978). Individuals with anorexia claim that they have no feelings of hunger. If they do experience hunger pangs, they say they enjoy them because "the feeling of hunger makes me feel thinner." In being able to withstand the pangs, they take much pride in seeing themselves become thinner and thinner (Meuller, 1981)

The roots of the problem may be any number of things. However, it seems that most anorexic individuals feel they lack sufficient control of their own lives. They fear they are not going to be able to live up to what is expected of them and therefore will be failures. This dramatic dissatisfaction is a core issue in anorexia nervosa (Lanford and Hutton, 1973).

The feeling of imprisonment and failure seems to be in direct contrast to the fact that most of the girls who become anorexic are from what seem to be happy, well-adjusted homes. However, it is most likely the family situation that has produced feelings of low self-esteem in these girls. The home environment might also be responsible for the inability of the girl to cope with and adjust to the new and, one would hope, enjoyable experiences of adolescence and adulthood. One anorexic individual talks about being born into a financially successful family: "If you are given much, much is expected of you" (Bruch, 1978, p. 14).

Behavior patterns. Together with dramatically reduced food intake, those with anorexia will exercise with intense determination to achieve their goal of thinness. Despite the weakness experienced with such rapid weight losses, they drive themselves relentlessly and usually reduce the number of sleeping hours. Some will exercise continually—jogging, doing sit-ups or push-ups, or exercising in a weight room. They claim they feel fine, are not upset with the way they look, and would feel guilty if they weighed more. The inability to see themselves as they truly are is a common characteristic of anorexia nervosa (Bruch, 1978). These individuals do not see how thin they are and deny the existence of even the most severe weight loss; they take extreme pride in the reduced weight and consider it a major accomplishment.

anorexia nervosa chronic failure to eat for fear of gaining weight; characterized by an extreme loss of appetite that results in severe malnutrition, semistarvation, and sometimes death.

Individuals with anorexia will attempt to achieve weight loss through many methods. In an effort to remove unwanted food from the body, they resort to self-induced vomiting, enemas, or excessive use of laxatives or diuretics. These means of removing food may result in a serious disturbance in the electrolyte balance which, in turn, may play a role in the cases with fatal outcomes (Bruch, 1978). Somatic reactions to such dramatic weight loss include skeleton-like appearance, anemia, dryness of the skin, soft, fine, body-hair growth, loss of menstrual cycle, low body temperature, and low basal metabolism. Any of these conditions carried to an extreme will ultimately be fatal.

Treatment. Treatment techniques for anorexia nervosa are still in a developmental state. A commonly used approach is behavior modification. Frequently, hospitalization is required because the priority is for the patient to gain weight. In severe cases, the patient is fed intravenously. Even before the patient is admitted, she or he must agree on a contract with the psychologist and family members. The contract provides certain privileges contingent on the patient steadily gaining a small amount of weight. These privileges include being able to get out of bed, go to the bathroom instead of having to use a bedpan, watching television, listening to music, or having visits from family and friends.

Once the patient approaches normal weight, she or he is asked to lose 2 or 3 pounds, then regain them. This procedure is used to demonstrate to the patient that she or he is in control. The patient must also participate in individual as well as family therapy. This is an important part of the program since its goal is to encourage self-confidence and a sense of control over one's life (Bruch, 1973). It is important that the patient continue therapy after leaving the hospital. Long-term results show that at least two thirds of the patients do gain the necessary pounds. Most authorities recognize that anorexia nervosa usually has multiple causes and may require a combination of treatment strategies (Bemis, 1978).

ANOREXIA NERVOSA AND ME

My own personal experience began in high school. I was a quiet and rather shy person. I had quite a few girlfriends, mostly ones I had met through running on the cross-country and track teams. I didn't have any boyfriends; in fact, I wasn't really friendly with any guys. For years I had felt very inadequate as a person, even though I did very well in my schoolwork, ranging between a 3.5 and 3.9 grade average. In ninth grade I weighed 110 pounds and was 5 feet, 4 inches tall. As a result of the running, I lost a few pounds and began to develop muscles. People began to notice me and comment on how good I was looking

I started to realize I had something special over the more popular girls; they admired my thinness! I just felt I had to lose more—maybe even to make them jealous—for I had always been jealous of them. By the time two years had gone by, I was down to 80 pounds. My parents were beginning to suspect something was wrong because I wrote down everything I ate, allowing myself only 700 calories a day, exercising constantly, and soaking in a hot tub for hours. My friends also became concerned; this seemed to make me happy because now "I" was being noticed. As is normal with this disorder, I stopped menstruating. I always felt cold, soaking in hot tubs for hours; my skin began to turn yellow, my hair was falling out, and my bones and muscles ached constantly. I was still losing weight, reaching a low of 73 pounds.

The breaking point came on my father's birthday. After having a very small piece of cake, I began crying and became hysterical. I was disappointed in myself for losing control and eating something that was always forbidden. My parents insisted that I have medical treatment. At this point I was passing out if I attempted to do anything strenuous. I remember lying in bed one night, my whole body feeling sore, wishing I wasn't so thin.

I started therapy very reluctantly, to say the least. My mother was very upset by my appearance; she spent most of the day in her room so she didn't have to look at me. My brothers and sister took a slightly different approach. My younger sister became very angry with me because I was upsetting Mother so much. My brothers showed a lot of concern for me; they were afraid I was going to get very sick. My father took the most level-headed, calm approach about the whole thing; he was the one who made my meals and weighed me every day.

The treatment used on me was behavior modification, which, in my opinion, was not the best decision in my case. After signing the "contract," I felt that all the control I had worked so hard for was ripped away from me. It seemed that I couldn't do anything unless I ate. This caused deep-seated anger and resentment toward my father, which I still feel today.

I saw two psychologists on a regular basis. The session usually consisted of me sitting in the chair refusing to say anything and the doctor blaming my mother for my condition. I feel that part of the program failed, for I felt that my privacy was being violated. Finally, it reached a point where I just refused to go to the sessions.

I finally regained weight but was unhappy about it. It didn't feel like me. Even today I'm still not satisfied with myself; I'm constantly trying to find that control again. I still run and exercise every day to stay in shape, hoping to maybe "lose a few pounds."

CULTURALLY DIFFERENT ENVIRONMENTS

Economically poor

Between 15% and 20% of the population of the United States is classified, by federal definition, as living on the poverty level. Often these individuals are members of a minority group or immigrants who have recently migrated to large northern metropolitan areas. The majority of the urban poor live in highly concentrated depressed areas within large cities. However, there is a large segment of economically and socially disadvantaged families who live in rural areas, in geographically isolated parts of the country, such as mountain land, or on reservations. For the most part the disadvantaged comprise the economic underworld of American life, including the unemployed, the underemployed, the blue-collar workers, the minorities, and the aged. This is the segment of the American population that has been isolated and removed from the mainstream of American life by various processes, not the least of which is the mass exodus of the middle class to the sanctity of suburbia, leaving the poor in the cities. Although not as obvious as in previous decades, this hidden portion of American society still suffers the ravages of poor housing, inadequate nutrition, overcrowding, lack of sanitation, and other forms of social and cultural deprivation.

Because the large majority of the disadvantaged class is made up of sporadic laborers, crop followers, and people on relief, there is a tendency for the mainstream of society to look down on these people. Parents in this group are likely to be passive and fatalistic about their status. In general, they work sporadically, move frequently, and live in the poorest dwellings. Because of the meager and often nonexistent earnings of the fathers, the mothers usually work as domestics to supplement the family income. Although there is an average of five children per mother, more than half of the homes are broken by separation, desertion, or death. Because of the instability of marriage, common-law marriages and cohabitation by mutual agreement are increasing in number; the poor cannot afford the cost of a divorce.

Disrupted family structure

Perhaps an extreme but realistic study of the lower class social structure is characterized by the disruption of the family. The statistical data surrounding the family structure of black families reveal that nearly one third of the black women living in large metropolitan areas who have ever been married are divorced, separated, or living apart from their husbands (Wilson, 1976). An offshoot of this disproportionately high divorce, separation, and desertion rate is the fact that only a minority of black children reach the age of 18 years having lived all their lives with both parents.

In general terms the poor nonwhite family has the largest number of children and the lowest net income; consequently, many nonwhite fathers cannot support their families. The only solutions rest in either the mother going to work or the family applying for welfare assistance. Should the mother choose to work, the dependence on her income tends to undermine the position of the father and deprives the children of maternal attention and care. Should the family apply for welfare assistance, in most cases the father will undergo serious feelings of inadequacy. Also, in view of current welfare rulings in some states, the family can obtain increased aid if the father is not in the home but is receiving separate aid. Thus, in some homes the family structure is torn apart in order for the family to seek out a meager subsistence.

Perhaps the individual who suffers the most severe consequences of this disorganization of the basic family structure is the child. Since the discipline and authority of the father figure is lacking in over one third of the families of the lower echelon of society, the process of young males identifying with their fathers as strong figures so necessary in sex typing is forestalled. Often the mother, who heads the family, is forced to neglect the children, since she must earn their living (Wilson, 1976).

Growing up in a family lacking strong traditions and consistent discipline will often produce a child who lacks strong goals and may be characterized as aimless and unambitious. Often the child who has not learned consistent standards of behavior in the home will turn to the streets to find a meaning that appears to be consistent and obviously related to his or her way of life. Since disorganized families tend to be concentrated in the least desirable sections of any city, the codes of conduct that are offered to the child by the street-corner gang are likely to be at best socially disapproved and at worst blatantly antisocial.

Gang membership

During adolescence, social groups such as cliques, crowds, or gangs will be formed. *Cliques* are small, closely knit groups based on clannishness and exclusion. *Crowds* are looser, somewhat less personal groups. *Gangs,* however, have a membership that is highly organized, and they usually arise out of conflict and outside pressures that bring the members together for mutual assistance and support. They are most frequently found among immigrant groups and in neighborhoods where there are racial or ethnic tensions.

Although some gangs are benign, a number appear to be breeding grounds for juvenile delinquency. The male gang member, for example, finds the gang a proving ground, a need-fulfilling but fear-inspiring stage on which to strut his nascent manhood and prove his emancipation. The gang sets tasks and standards he must meet, and there is always the fear that he may not meet these standards, that he may fail the test of gang membership and acceptance. This is especially significant with the disadvantaged adolescent. The motivation to pursue the delinquent act is bolstered by pressure to achieve those things that are of greatest value to the peer or reference groups of the delinquent, rather than by rebellious elements within his personality organization. The compelling elements of gang motivation appear to be adherence to group standards of excitement, toughness, and smartness.

School dropouts

Another segment of culturally different adolescents is the school dropout or, as the case may be, the "shove out." But who are the dropouts? They are more frequently males than females. They are young people who have usually endured environmental, social, and personal liabilities that affected their chances to compete equally with others in most phases of life. Most dropouts quit in the tenth grade because this is the transition grade from junior high school to senior high school, and they generally have reached the age whereby they can legally separate from school. Some of the major factors involved in the dropout problem are reading retardation, grade retention, low intelligence, negative self-images, and poor family attitudes. It should be emphasized that the dropout is not synonymous with the juvenile delinquent.

Several generalizations may be made concerning disadvantaged adolescents. In general they have received inadequate nurturing during early childhood. They are likely to lack ego strength, to have an extremely poor self-image, and to see the world as a pervasively hostile, inconsistent environment. Although disadvantaged individuals share many of the dominant or conventional values of society, they also show more acceptance of certain unconventional or different values. The value structure of the lower class differs in many ways from that of the middle class, and the youngster will be affected by these differences. Immediate, extrinsic values such as a big car or flashy clothes are frequently more sought after than are delayed, intrinsic values such as those that are brought about by schooling or long effort.

CHAPTER REVIEW

1. The *developmental tasks* of middle to late adolescence are an extension of the tasks of early adolescence. The ultimate goal of the adolescent is that of identity as an adult. Erikson's psychosocial crisis for this age level is *identity versus role confusion*.
2. Historically, societies have usually had a ceremony, the puberty rites, or a sign indicating initiation into adulthood. Complex industrial societies require a longer readiness period to prepare for the work and life of an adult. That transitional period from childhood to adulthood is called adolescence.
3. Physical growth and development is fairly well completed by the end of adolescence. *Asynchrony* is reduced or eliminated.
4. By late adolescence, teenagers will have come to accept adults in their lives. Conflicts that may be present will generally center around social life, responsibilities, school, family relationships and values.
5. *Parenting styles* have been classified as (a) autocratic, (b) authoritative, (c) democratic or equalitarian, (d) permissive or laissez-faire, or (e) ignoring or erratic. Each style usually produces a special set of characteristics in the adolescents in that family.
6. The need for *peer acceptance* is still strong, but the pressure of conformity is not as great as it was in early adolescence.
7. Communities vary on the *pattern of dating*, its time of onset and its style. Generally, the sequence is one of crowd dates (all singles), crowd dates with couples, single dates (sometimes joining a crowd), single dating, double dating or crowd dating for convenience or "get-togethers." Average age of a first date is about age 13. Social contacts are important for developing social and communication skills, as well as for learning how to handle feelings.
8. Traits looked for in a dating partner are personality, appearance, and social regard for the other person.
9. Strong feelings of attachment are generally interpreted by the adolescent as love. Difficulties arise when emotions become too strong and the feelings are not returned or when the feelings are returned and rational thought and behavior become distorted.
10. Factors contributing to a *high risk of pregnancy* in adolescence are (a) preoccupation with sexuality, (b) family history of adolescent parenthood, (c) disruptive or dysfunctional family environment, and (d) inappropriate use or lack of use of contraceptives. High-risk psychological factors include (a) low self-esteem, (b) alienated feelings about parents, and (c) an unhappy family situation. The decision to have intercourse is unrelated to use or nonuse of contraceptives.
11. Knowledge of sex and reproduction is generally inadequate among sexually active teenage girls. *Contraceptives* are not used by some adolescent women because they (a) do not consider themselves sexually active, (b) are irresponsible, (c) have a feeling of helplessness in the situation, (d) have little knowledge of birth control, (e) are not in control of their impulses, or (g) have negative attitudes about contraceptives.
12. Pregnant teenagers who *choose to deliver* generally make adequate mothers if they have fair to good self-esteem and a satisfactory family relationship. *Aborters* usually have interpersonal difficulties with family members, tend to stay in school, and often come from a higher socioeconomic level than deliverers.

13. The largest number of *nonmarital births* in adolescents occurs in the 15- to 19-year-old group. Most couples did not use a contraceptive. Babies born to these mothers tend to be at high risk. A study of unwed fathers indicated that over 60% wanted to marry the woman.
14. Late adolescence is a period during which the use of various *intellectual functions* such as discovery, divergent thinking, convergent thinking, memory, and assessment of one's conclusions should be learned and improved. Attitudes involved in thought processing may change, but the use of formal operations does not develop automatically.
15. Development of *emotional control and stability* depends on the quality of understanding, care, and discipline provided by the family. Excesses in domination, parental friction, sibling rivalry, and lack of participation in family decisions hamper emotional growth.
16. *Erikson* relates seven steps in the *establishment of identity:* (a) gaining a sense of time for development, (b) increasing self-awareness, (c) trying new roles, (d) trying out new occupations, (e) developing a clear identification with one of the sexes, (f) learning to take leadership roles, and (g) accepting an ideological commitment.
17. A *value judgment system* consists of an individual's beliefs, values, and attitudes about matters in which decisions must be made. There are *behavioral values* which are person oriented, and *object values,* which are objects with inherent values. The *locus of value* is deemed by some psychologists to reside within the individual.
18. Adolescents generally seek the *values* of freedom, honesty, and a world of peace. Values considered important tend to change as a youngster grows into late adolescence. Value choices can also be influenced by historical factors, political or economic situations, and internal life cycles.
19. Uneven, unsettled, and uncertain development in adolescence may lead to trial and error behavior, ambivalence about decisions and control, and a willingness to experiment along with the crowd. The use of *chemical substances,* referring to drugs and alcohol, provides a form of outlet for experimentation. Alcohol, cigarettes, and marijuana are the most frequently abused chemical substances. Drinking and driving is an irresponsible action; it is the leading cause of automobile accidents.
20. Individuals do not respond in the same way to chemical substances. Some get sick or allergic and thus tend to avoid them. Others do not experience mood swing and see no incentive (other than social) to take them. Most users are social drinkers or users who do get a pleasant effect but who can also control their use to the point of avoiding them when it is not sensible. Others become dependent users who, for a variety of reasons, recurrently seek the use of the chemical substances for the "high" they produce. When the urge to participate is greater than the power to control or avoid their use, this person is "hooked."
21. In some teenagers *adolescent aggression* starts in preadolescence or early teens, peaks at about age 15, declines slightly to age 18, and then, at 19, begins a climb in incidence to about the age of 23.
22. *Psychopathology* is the study of psychological and behavioral dysfunction in mental disorder. Among adolescents, the most common pathologies are personality or antisocial disorders, situation-specific disturbances, neuroses, psychoses, and suicide attempts.
23. *Suicidal behavior* is the fourth leading cause of death among 15- to 19-year-olds. Males are more likely to complete suicide than females. Females are more likely to attempt suicides than males. Psychological states in high-risk suicidal cases are depression and personal attitude.
24. *Anorexia nervosa* is a psychosomatic disease that results in dramatic weight loss caused by self-induced starvation. It can result in the disruption of basic bodily functions and death. Females are more likely than males to become anorexic. Treatment is not well-formulated, although behavior modification in a hospital setting is commonly used as a therapeutic approach.
25. Culturally different environments can result from (a) poverty-level socioeconomic circumstances, (b) disruptive family structures, (c) gang memberships, and (d) dropping out of school.

REVIEW QUESTIONS

1. What is the difference between "coming of age" in a complex, industrial society and in a simple, primitive society? Is the problem a recent one?
2. Describe the overall physical growth of the late adolescent.
3. What are some of the problems encountered by adolescents in seeking personal independence from family direction and control? Does the seeking of independence, with its accompanying problems, have to be a period of "crisis" for the adolescent?
4. According to Baumrind, what are the four types of parenting styles and what personality characteristics do they tend to produce?
5. What conditions or factors may hamper peer acceptance in later adolescence?
6. Compare the dating sequence presented in the chapter with your observation of dating patterns when you were in high school.

7. What functions do dating or heterosexual activities perform? Is it necessary for everyone to date?
8. What traits do guys look for in girls they like to date? What traits do girls look for in guys?
9. Should parents have a concern about whom their youngster dates? Why or why not?
10. What are some of the problems of adolescent love?
11. List some of the high-risk factors leading to teenage pregnancy. Does the percentage of pregnancies surprise you?
12. Why aren't contraceptives used more sensibly to prevent pregnancies?
13. Compare the characteristics of deliverers and aborters.
14. What are some of the conditions that an unwed mother faces? What about the unwed father?
15. What are some of the types of intellectual growth that take place after the age of 16?
16. List seven emotional characteristics of later adolescence, and briefly describe each one.
17. Erikson presents a conceptual approach to the personal need of identity formation. Carefully summarize, in your own words, the seven major elements related to identity development.
18. What is meant by a value judgment system? Why should each person have one?
19. Define the following: behavioral values, object values, terminal values, instrumental values. Which stated values are rated high by adolescents and which ones are rated lower?
20. Define chemical substance abuse. What are the more commonly used chemical substances? Why are drugs and alcohol usage grouped together?
21. What individual differences are there in reactions to the ingestion (taking in) of chemical substances? Do the reasons for developing dependency make sense to you?
22. List—and explain—the four characteristics of chemical substance dependency.
23. How aggressive (delinquent) are adolescents as a group?
24. Define and give some examples of psychopathology.
25. Discuss suicidal behavior among adolescents. Why do they do it? How can you identify suicidal tendencies?
26. Define and explain anorexia nervosa. How can individuals do that to themselves? Read the profile on anorexia nervosa. It is a case with which the authors were familiar.
27. What is the distribution of the poor and economically disadvantaged? Is the distribution limited to minority groups? Do they make up the great percentage?
28. Disrupted family structures can be detrimental in any social group. What are some of the outcomes of such broken family units?
29. Why can gangs become disruptive? Why are they listed as a subgroup under "culturally different"?
30. What are the disadvantages of being a school dropout? What are the advantages?

THOUGHT QUESTIONS AND ACTIVITIES

1. Discussion: Do all adolescents between the ages of 15 to 18 go through a period of "stress and storm," a period when so many things are happening at one time (for which they have few answers) that they don't know if they are "coming or going"?
2. Who or what helped you the most in making the transition from relative dependency to some semblance of independence: your parents, your friends, your relatives, your teachers or coaches, some other adults, books you read, your experiences, or your own characteristics?
3. Think of someone who did something especially important or valuable for you at a time when you needed help or were seeking to find yourself. Perhaps this individual did something that helped you grow as a person. Why not give that person a telephone call, just to inquire how he or she is? Better yet, why not write a nice, short note of appreciation?
4. Is delinquency or chemical substance abuse prevalent in your area? Could it be that the aggressive individual or chemical abuser of today is the target for future psychological problems? Is there any solution?
5. Attend a high school athletic contest, play, or some other activity. Notice the crowd and individual behavior. Did you and your friends act that way when you were in high school?
6. Dating patterns—age of beginning dating, where to go on dates, what is done on dates—appear to differ in various parts of the country. Survey your group for dating practices, keeping in mind the criterion of "When did *most* of the age-group do this practice?" How does it match with what is in this chapter? Do your findings vary by more than 2 years?
7. Some people like to talk about values and morality. Is this an issue in which adolescents should be interested? Are they ready to deal with values and what all that means for behavior direction and control? Why not just "live and let live"?
8. Drugs and alcohol: what do you make of the topic? Is it true that most social partakers have the idea "I can see what they do to others, but I don't think that will happen to me. And if it does—so what! It's my body (and my mind)." Does a drug abuser "owe" anything to anyone else, such as a friend or a parent?
9. Anorexia nervosa is not a common occurrence, but people like Karen Carpenter, the singer, died from it, and Pat Boone's daughter, Cherry, had to struggle to overcome it. Why or how do you suppose a person gets started on the starvation kick? What's the payoff or reinforcement?
10. The United States has always been a nation of immigrants. Different nationalities have arrived in different periods. Some people are minorities because of low family income, broken homes, alienation from society, or lack of schooling. Is racism, ethnicity, or sexism ever

justified? Defend your answer—even if it is "no." It is important to distinguish between stereotyping, prejudice, and bigotry.

FURTHER READINGS

Broughton, J.M. The divided self in adolescence. *Human Development,* 1981, *24,* 13-32. A study of adolescents indicates that many have one view of their inner self and another view of their outer self. The outer self is usually a false one.

Cogle, F.C., Tasker, G.E., & Morton, D. Adolescent time use in household work. *Adolescence,* 1982, *17*(66), 451-455. Findings indicate that sex-role stereotyping in the type of household activities that adolescents pursue at home is still evident.

Ford, M. Social cognition and social competence in adolescence. *Developmental Psychology,* 1982, *18*(3), 323-340. Factor analysis results suggested that social competence represents a domain of human functioning that is at least partly distinguishable from a cognitive or general competence domain.

Langone, J. Too weary to go on. *Discover,* 1981, *2*(11), 54-56. Suggestions are given for interpreting the warning signs of attempted suicide.

Roosa, M.W., Fitzgerald, H.E., & Carlson, N.A. What do we know about teenagers as mothers? *Journal of Home Economics,* Winter 1981, *73,* 38-40. The issues related to research on teenage mothers are reviewed. The results of a short-term study of teen and nonteen mothers are presented.

Rutter, M. *Changing youth in a changing society: Patterns of adolescent development and disorder.* Cambridge, Mass.: Harvard University Press, 1980. This book presents an excellent discussion of problems and disturbances in adolescence as affected by adolescent development and changing society.

Schneider, S. Helping adolescents deal with pregnancy: A psychiatric approach. *Adolescence,* 1982, *17*(66), 285-292. The author examines why the adolescent girl becomes pregnant and how it affects her emotional process. The conclusion is that the adolescent must learn about "the self" and "the other" to foster more meaningful relationships.

Strober, M. Locus of control, psychopathology, and weight gain in juvenile anorexia nervosa. *Journal of Abnormal Child Psychology,* 1982, *10*(1), 97-105. This study is based on 30 female adolescents with anorexia nervosa. Findings are discussed in terms of the psychopathology of anorexia and the relationship of locus of control to personality functioning.

Wilkerson, J., Protinsky, H.O., Maxwell, J.W., & Lentner, M. Alienation and ego identity in adolescents. *Adolescence,* 1982, *17*(65), 133-139. The data indicate that, as ego identity increases, there tends to be a moderate decrease in alienation. All "significant others" share a responsibility in forming the social personality of the adolescent.

CHAPTER 12

EMERGING ADULTHOOD

THE AWAKENING YEARS

JOE COLLEGE TO MANHOOD

Recently I have been noticing the changes that have been taking place in my life as my status changed from college student to husband and provider. In the past, changes in my thoughts and actions have been gradual, occurring over a period of several years. They had to be pointed out by my parents or a friend for me to even notice them. But this time the changes were so rapid and to such an extent that I noticed them as soon as they occurred.

There are two things that have changed in my life: I am no longer a college student but an employed engineer, and I am no longer single but have a wife to support. What I did as a carefree college student last year I can no longer even consider doing.

Even though most college students won't admit it, they live the most protected, cared for, carefree life they ever will have. If a person goes to work after high school, he is usually set free by his parents and considered as being old enough to look after himself and take care of his own responsibilities. But if the person goes on to college, he gets a four-year (or more) extension on his time under parental wings. In college he is responsible to himself and himself only. He is free from direct parental supervision for the first time in his life and will do some pretty crazy things with some of his new friends just to prove that he really can do whatever he wants. If he gets into trouble of any kind, his parents are still there waiting to run to his aid.

I know I did a lot of things in college I could never do now. Those frequent all-night pinochle games are hard to take when one has to get up for work the next day. And those parties where we could let some of our inhibitions hang loose without worrying about our dates are gone too. Now that date is my wife, who can't get a ride back with anyone else because she has to go back with me. And if I do "hang loose," she probably won't talk to me for several days! I can honestly say that the four years I spent at college were the most fun years of my life, even though I am now happily married.

At the ripe old age of twenty-three, only five years older than when I first entered college as a freshman, my life has totally changed from the way it was. I am now officially out of my parents' nest and on my own.

Probably the main thing that has changed my world is not getting out of college but getting into marriage. While I did work summers before I was married, I lived at home, had plenty of money for just myself, and lived fairly well. Right now, only a year later but married, I am making $12,500 more a year, but I am living just above the brink of poverty, not knowing if we can make it week by week. I have more bills coming in than I ever imagined! Because of the unfortunate economic situation, I am forced to get a part-time job. That extra money really does make a difference, but who wants to be limited to a total of about three and one half hours a day with your wife so soon after getting married? It kind of makes both of us suffer. I also have many things I'd like to do and people I'd like to see, but I simply can't because of the lack of time. I feel that the little time I do have should be spent with my wife.

Imagine, one day I was a college playboy with all the wild parties et cetera, and the next day I was a married man with many responsibilities. Under these conditions the little boy must become a true man in every sense of the word.

IN THIS CHAPTER . . .

You will read about

1. The transition into adulthood as viewed by attitudes, generational differences, and theories of young adulthood.
2. The developmental tasks and age level conflicts of emerging adulthood.
3. The physical, intellectual, and social characteristics of young adulthood and the pursuit of identity.
4. The launching of a career through a career development program, a job search, and the first job.
5. The Erikson psychosocial task of intimacy versus isolation.
6. The moral development theory of Kohlberg.
7. Abraham Maslow's theory of maturity and self-actualization.
8. The Levinson and Gould theories of phases of adulthood.

Society in America changed its concept of "when a person becomes an adult" when legislation was passed granting 18-year-olds the right to vote. Before that time the age of 21 years was considered to be the time when a person "legally" became an adult (Goldstein, 1976). Laws, however, cannot dictate or change developmental patterns decreed by nature. The question still remains, "Developmentally, when does a person become an adult?"

THE AGE LEVEL

The terms *late adolescence, postadolescence,* and *young adulthood* are used by developmental psychologists to indicate the age range of 18 to 21 or 22 years of age (Keniston, 1970). The term *emerging adulthood,* as we use it, is a descriptive term referring to the transitional period between adolescence and adulthood. It is similar to the postadolescent and young adulthood stage of life. Labels (terms) as they are applied to human beings are seldom satisfactory categorical descriptive devices because there are so many exceptions to the rule. In adulthood, in particular, it is better to describe developmental stages by a criterion rather than by a label, phrase, or certain age.

Transition into adulthood

In many less complex societies, sometimes referred to as primitive societies, the status differentiating youth and adult is more clearly defined than it is in industrial societies. In a sense the adolescent period in these societies is missing or of no consequence, socially speaking. The individual is not an adult until inducted into adulthood by a special rites-of-passage ceremony. This moment may be when physical maturity is attained and the puberty rites are performed, or it may be a series of ceremonies at different ages ending about the age of 16 or 18 when there are both physical maturity and an assimilation, social understanding, and appreciation of that culture's heritage. We witnessed a "skin-cutting" ceremony performed on two 10-year-old boys in a village on the Karawari River in the jungles of Papua New Guinea. This ritual was but one of eight steps leading to "manhood." With the final stage in these rites of passage came the status of being an adult—"with all the rights and privileges thereof."

The emerging adult is in the final stages of making the transition from being an adolescent to being an adult. This individual will have some adultlike characteristics but not all of them. There will also be some characteristics that are distinctive to the 18- to 22-year age level. A general criterion for suggesting when an individual is more of an adult than an adolescent would be that time when an individual assumes the role of an adult by taking on the responsibilities, obligations, and characteristics of adulthood.

Specifically, adulthood is attained when an individual achieves a competent level of emotional, social, and economic independence, establishes a career or family pattern, and maintains a degree of personal, behavioral, and conceptual maturity that enables that person to live with some measure of satisfaction within a social milieu (Bockneck, 1980). Emerging adulthood is a stage of transition wherein the individual is approaching the attainment of several developmental goals related to adulthood but has not yet completed them.

Attitudes of emerging adults

Attitudinal and behavioral characteristics common in emerging adulthood generally result from (1) an idealistic view of the world, its people, and the means by which progress is accomplished, (2) a recently developed ability to do abstract reasoning about ways of human beings, the course of things, and life in general, and (3) a tendency to intensify on a problem or issue to a degree beyond its worth (Bockneck, 1980).

Since this postadolescent period generally provides some time free from the all-encompassing responsibility of making one's living and providing for one's family, individuals at this stage of growth will focus on topics interesting and important to them. They may be swept up in the current issues and social fads of the times. If so, they generally bring their idealism and power of reasoning and self-answering to bear on these issues. They are influenced by statements or clichés that to them seem so obviously true.

What is not recognized or fully realized by this age group is that their capacity to make good, valid judgments is restricted because they are limited in the effective use of their reasoning powers. They have limited experiences, shallow depth and breadth of knowledge, and inadequately developed problem-solving skills. Their idealism also influences their decision-making processes. As a result their perspective concerning reality is restricted and sometimes even distorted. There is no question that they do have a glimpse of the truth of reality, but often they are unprepared to see the whole picture. There is an old proverb that says, "He who has seen little, amazes much." One might add, "Don't make major pronouncements based on the little that one has experienced."

There is a universal timeless characteristic typical of those who are at the stage of emerging adulthood. Young adults seek to let others know that they are of age and that they possess an intellectual potential. From time to time youth of this age the world over show agitation and even rebellion. In America the "establishment" was attacked. In Japan, where there was a national commitment to antimilitarism, the students pursuing peace were among the most determined of all young radicals. French students had none of the American causes to protest against and none of the Japanese causes, yet as recently as 1983 protests occurred. Even in Venezuela student behavior followed the same pattern, and their protests and actions were perhaps the most violent of all. There appears to be a universal tendency for young people to resist or to challenge the life-style imposed on them by their elders. They want to "improve things." Some cohort

David Strickler

Emerging adulthood is the period during which the individual is achieving a competent level of personal, behavioral, and conceptual maturity. Self-direction becomes more characteristic of the person than does group domination.

groups are aggressive in their pursuit; other cohort groups are passive. Table 12-1 indicates some of the differences of opinions that the cohorts of the early seventies had with their parents.

alienation a feeling of estrangement from and hostility toward society or familiar persons, based in part on a discrepancy between expectations and promises and in part on the actual experience of the role one is playing.

Generational differences

Three basic hypotheses have been proposed to account for different points of view between the generations, especially in terms of social and political alienation. ***Social alienation*** refers to an estrangement, a psychological separation, or a disaffection that has developed between two persons, two groups, or two generations, such as between youth and adults, or between the aged and other age levels.

The first hypothesis states that adultism factors are responsible for alienation. *Adultism* refers to authoritative adults using their power over younger ones

TABLE 12-1 Selected contemporary topics questionnaire (CTQ) items and mean responses for two generational groups. (Members of each group were asked (1) to rate themselves on an attitude scale of 1-7* and (2) to estimate how members of the other group would rate themselves on the same issue.)

CTQ item	*Mean adolescent ratings*		*Mean parent ratings*	
	Self	*Parents*	*Self*	*Children*
1. Premarital intercourse is acceptable for men but not for women.	5.7	4.7	5.9	5.0
2. In respect to youth, shoplifting is of greater moral concern than is premarital sex.	3.7	4.8	4.4	3.5
3. Racial equality deserves more attention in America than does curtailing obscenity.	1.6	3.7	2.9	2.3
4. A home setting for healthy adolescent development is best described as having consistent restrictions.	3.3	2.4	2.1	2.3
5. A person's appearance is his own concern, and others should tolerate whatever that person wears.	2.2	5.5	4.1	2.0
6. Disappointment or concern would overshadow approval if a close friend admitted smoking marijuana.	5.0	2.0	2.2	3.4
7. Suspension from high school for smoking should be enforced, rather than allowing this behavior to exist.	5.5	2.9	4.1	5.5
8. Birth-control devices and information should be made available to all who desire them.	1.5	3.8	1.9	1.7
9. The Church is playing an active role in shaping people's moral character.	5.5	3.4	3.5	4.4
10. Black revolutionaries are harmful to the advancement of their race.	4.1	2.1	2.1	2.8
11. Antiabortion laws are absurd; the woman, and not the government, should have control over her reproductive functions.	2.0	3.9	2.6	2.4
12. Premarital sexual activities have no place in our present society.	6.3	3.2	4.0	4.7
13. I would not hesitate to experiment with marijuana.	3.4	6.6	6.5	4.7
14. Premarital sexual activities are and always should be considered immoral.	6.1	3.4	3.7	4.6
15. Those who use drugs are usually careless about their personal appearance.	5.3	2.2	2.6	3.6
16. A home setting for healthy adolescent development should be highly permissive.	4.6	5.1	6.1	5.5

Modified from Lerner, R. In H.D. Thornburg (Ed.) *Contemporary adolescence: Readings* (2nd ed.). Monterey, Calif., Brooks/Cole Publishing Co., 1975.

*1, Strongly agree; 2, moderately agree; 3, slightly agree; 4, neutral; 5, slightly disagree; 6, moderately disagree; and 7, strongly disagree.

Meriem Kaluger

According to Whitehead, the task of the college or the university is to weld the imagination of young adults with the experience and knowledge of their professors.

because of the special status they hold in society (Flasher, 1978). Youth perceives a sense of powerlessness against adults. They think that they are not readily accepted by older adults. Even some of the retired elderly are alienated because they sense a loss of status, abilities, and resources (Martin et al., 1973). A second approach refers to the existence of cultural and social differences of the same age group from generation to generation, suggesting that discontinuity exists. That is to say, not all generations of 18- to 24-year-olds have the same attitudes, values, or characteristics. Successive generations seldom perceive life quite the same as preceding ones (Gottlieb and Chafetz, 1977). Sometimes groups are given identity media labels such as the "beat generation," the "lost generation," and the "me generation." It is the generation, and not youth per se, that is different in alienation. A *cultural lag* will often exist between a younger generation and their parents in recognizing the latest trends, language, music, and ideas important to youth (Sebald, 1977). Communication may deteriorate, if not break down.

A third hypothesis states that historical or political periods account for the behavior and attitudes of youth. One generation faced an affluent, growing economy; another, an era of political assassinations, the Vietnam War, and Watergate. Another generation has concerns with inflation, unemployment, and an uncertain occupational future. Adelson (1979) concluded that the historical or period effect was the most viable approach for explaining generational differences.

Alfred North Whitehead (1957) made an interesting observation relative to the need of the generations to get together. He writes to the effect that youth is imaginative, and if this imagination can be strengthened by discipline, this energy of imagination can be preserved for life. The tragedy of the world, as Whitehead sees it, is that those who are imaginative have slight experience and those who are experienced have feeble imaginations. Fools act on imagination without knowledge; strong feelings act on knowledge without imagination. The task of the university, says Whitehead, is to weld together imagination and experience. One must go to those older to learn the past; but one must go to youth to learn the future because they are the only ones native to the new technological age.

In every age, every generation, youth takes bold steps toward adulthood. The style and the clamor of those steps change from period to period. No one knows what the future holds, but the underlying universal principles pertaining to the movement of emerging adulthood state that youth will make itself known.

Consider the statement, "Youth is disintegrating. The youngsters of the land have a disrespect for authority of every form. Vandalism is rife, and crime of all kinds is rampant among our youth. The nation is in peril!" This quotation was not written by an adult of this generation. It was written by an Egyptian priest about 4,000 years ago when his country was undergoing one of its periodic transitions.

Anticipation of adulthood

As has been observed, developmental age periods are not dependent entirely upon chronological age. They are also affected by personal experiences, social conditions, psychological perception of age, and the political periods or life events through which the individual lives. Neugarten and Datan (1973) describe age-relatedness as having (1) a *life line,* which is the biological chronological time, (2) a *social line,* which is culture's way of indicating when and how the rites of passage from one stage to another occur, and (3) a *historical role line,* the time when particular periods of life, such as young adulthood, gain general recognition. Each "line" impacts on the developing individual.

According to Coleman and associates (1977), emerging adults have two concepts of themselves: who they are and who they will be. Their concept of who they are remains relatively stable once they have established their identity in adolescence, but their concept of their future selves may change. The majority accept the fact, perhaps unconsciously, that they will soon become adults and must prepare themselves accordingly.

Although their choices reflect the times, many youth enter adulthood preferring somewhat traditional life lines. A survey, Youth's Attitudes (1975), of 14- to 25-year-olds revealed that 82% approved of marriage, that nearly half would delay childbearing at least for 3 years after marriage, and that although 90% accepted the idea of a planned childless marriage, only 5% expected to remain childless. Bachman and Johnson (1979) found that 79% of college students and 76% of noncollege youth ranked a good marriage and family life as their primary goal in adulthood. Young men were attaching importance to their future role in the family; all but a few college women ranked motherhood and marriage first among their future priorities (Mash, 1978). Most, however, expected to combine marriage and a career. The women wanted flexibility in their career plans, with brief interruptions for motherhood. How they resolve the question of their "future selves" is a matter of theoretical debate.

intimacy versus isolation **Erikson's sixth crisis of psychosocial development; the young adult may achieve a capacity for honest, close relationships, or be unable to form these ties.**

Theories of emerging adulthood

Emerging adulthood is not an age level that has been researched extensively as a stage. However, there are theorists who have recognized emerging adulthood as a stage in the life-span perspective and have provided valuable insights into the period. Among these theorists are Erik Erikson, Robert Havighurst, Robert White, and Rudolph Wittenberg. The terms *emerging adult* and *young adult* are used interchangeably in this section and in this chapter.

Erikson. Erikson was one of the first writers to use the term *young adult* (1963b). Erikson's psychosocial crises or stages are based on the assumption "that society, in principle, tends to be so constituted as to meet . . . this succession of potentialities for interaction and attempts to . . . encourage the proper rate and the proper sequencing of their unfolding" (1963a, p. 270). The critical developmental issue of adolescence is identity versus role confusion. The end of adolescence and the entry into young adulthood is marked when identity formation is achieved (Erikson, 1968b).

The core issue of young adulthood is the conflict of ***intimacy versus isolation.*** *Intimacy* covers a variety

David Strickler

A growth trend in emerging adulthood, says White, is the identification of clear, stable interests that are tied to both competence and commitment. The field of mass media attracts many young people because of its potential for creativity and personal growth.

of experiences, all involving a willingness to be close to someone or to at least be accepted. *Isolation* implies a tendency to see others as outsiders and dangerous. *Identity* implies an intrapsychic structural integrity, not simply a group of ideas and attitudes about the self. Intimacy implies a sense of security about one's ego boundaries, so much so that an involvement with another person would not risk the loss of one's identity (Bockneck, 1980). The identity evolves in a sociocultural context, but it should become adaptable as it progresses from one psychosocial issue to another. Erikson therefore sees emerging adulthood as a period taking place after an identity structure is established that is secure enough for the individual to feel comfortable in developing an intimate (close) relationship with others. Erikson's concept of intimacy will be presented in depth later in this chapter.

Havighurst. Havighurst (1973) evolved the concept of developmental tasks: "those things that constitute healthy and satisfactory growth in our society." According to Havighurst, development is the result of a social and psychological learning experience. Since the values and behaviors of a society change, the mores or attitudes of one era may have little in common with another era. There are some unchanging developmental tasks, such as learning to live an independent, competent life, but sex-role expectations can radically alter the social behavior involved.

The listing of specific tasks for a specific, stable culture has some meaning because they can be readily identified as common social expectations. The developmental tasks for emerging adults, therefore, have some meaning, but mostly in a social system that does not change too rapidly. The alternative to stability is to change the list of the developmental tasks as the social expectations change. This type of insight would be difficult to keep updated.

White. White has done extensive clinical and theoretical research with young adults. He draws on social, familial, biological, and developmental sources in formulating his theories. White (1975) has identified five growth trends in emerging adulthood. The *first* is the stabilizing of ego identity, which includes a sense of self, of being a distinct individual within a social framework, and of having self-determined attitudes and preferences. *Second* is a freeing of personal relationships, thus providing a greater sensitivity to others because there is a more realistic assessment of personal relationships.

The *third* growth trend is an identification of clear, stable interests that shape the enjoyment of life—interests that are tied to both competence and commitment. *Fourth* is a humanizing of human and social values whereby young adults can translate these values into terms that can be understood and affirmed in their lives (in a sense this is a transfer from the abstract morality of adolescence to the functional morality of young adulthood). *Fifth* is an expanding of caring for others, the development of a social consciousness concerned with the welfare of those in need within the world community.

Wittenberg. Wittenberg (1968) states that emerging adulthood represents a specific phase of growth in the life cycle. He identifies several metapsychological characteristics and socioeconomic factors that are found in young adults. ***Metapsychology*** refers to the ability of the individual to deal critically with one's own psychological attributes. Among the metapsychological characteristics are (1) a self-image conflict between demands of the conscience (superego) and ego autonomy, (2) brief states during which there is loss of a sense of identity, (3) the end of role playing and the emergence of reality-based awareness, (4) awareness of the passage of time and the need to develop a structure to deal with it, and (5) the search for a partner or love object.

metapsychology philosophical speculation on the origin, structure, and function of the mind and on the relationship between the mind and objective reality.

The socioeconomic factors include (1) the economic bind of wanting to be on their own but being kept out of the labor force, (2) becoming a member of a social, political, or religious group in keeping with their self-perceived roles and self-definition, and (3) evolving a philosophy of life, a *weltanschauung,* that provides an interalized hierarchy of values and priorities. According to Wittenberg these characteristics and factors occur in the transition from adolescence to young adulthood.

Summary. The theorists all speak of qualitative changes that need to be made during emerging adulthood. The transition is not always smooth, not at the same rate, nor in the same format for all persons. Individual differences occur because of a variety of internal and external extenuating factors, but changes must take place sooner or later. Perhaps some people remain "adolescents" all their lives, but this state is not the norm. We all become adults in one way or another. The themes of caring, commitment, attachment, and mastery are important throughout all of adult life.

DEVELOPMENTAL TASKS

The gradual emergence of adolescents' independence from the family and the confrontation with new responsibilities, new abilities, new values, and new freedoms make it necessary for emerging adults to restructure their images of self and their potential and worth for the world. There are new things to be learned at this stage of life; there are new dimensions to be added to one's personality and value judgment system.

Age-level conflicts

Primarily, adolescents define their values in terms of relationships with age-mates. Together they display a high degree of conformity to the norms of that particular peer group. In spite of some degree of conformity to peer norms, post-adolescents have become aware of the adult world and its demands. Most realize that they are expected to "settle down" and make decisions about the future. Such decisions as choice of vocation, choice of post–high school education, and personal code of conduct must be made. The adolescent responds to societal demands by conforming, withdrawing, or challenging (Etkind, 1979).

The idealism that characterizes this period results in a closer evaluation of principles in terms of observable behavior—their own and others. Often the result is disillusionment for those who fail to live up to their perceived ideals. Negative reactions to this feeling result in maladaptive behavior, at times, and are reflected in such ways as social or political unrest, withdrawal from the social order, or in the drug-laden or alcohol-saturated culture.

Positive reactions might be expressed in a desire to change the culture by becoming involved in pursuits that serve humankind, such services as a volunteer in Vista, the Peace Corps, or social agencies. At worst an inability to correlate ideals with life tasks may result in a feeling of meaninglessness, which is expressed in apathy or in extreme manifestations of exaggerated behavior. Such attitudes appear to be characteristic of times of great social and technological change, when the culture fails to provide definitive models for identification (Michener, 1973, p. 48). Moreover, lacking models to emulate, young people may require a longer period of examination to consolidate an adult system of values. The nature of the task demands that it be resolved by the individuals themselves. Theologians suggest that a mature acceptance of spiritual values may provide an organizing principle for this whole process, since it identifies the goals and relationships of the individual during the present life and relates them to a life of happiness hereafter (Special Section on Religion, 1977).

Developmental tasks of emerging adulthood

According to Havighurst (1979) the developmental tasks of emerging adulthood are (1) selecting and preparing for an initial occupation or career pattern, (2) desiring and achieving socially responsible behavior, (3) developing concepts for civic competency in terms of moral, ethical, social, economic, and political aspects of life, (4) building sound personality traits, social and communications skills, and healthy attitudes in preparation for marriage and family life, and (5) acquiring a set of values by the formation of an identity and a concept of one's place in the world as a human being. These tasks of Havighurst are defined as prescriptions, obligations, and responsibilities that produce healthy growth in our society.

White (1975) suggests the developmental tasks or growth trends of (1) a *stabilization of identity* and judgment based on experience, (2) the *humanization of values* by being aware of their relationship to social purposes and by giving human meaning to values, and (3) an *expansion of caring* and the extension of the sense of self in a growing dedication to the welfare of others. White emphasizes activity and the progressive mastery of knowledge and skills in developing mature relationships that allow for warmth, respect, criticism, and tolerance.

Erikson (1974) adds the psychosocial task of *intimacy,* a focusing of identity that transcends the self and reaches out in companionship and communion with others. Erikson places strong emphasis on commitment and fidelity to someone in order to develop a sense of choice, to experience loyalty, and to learn how to take care of those to whom one becomes committed.

Levinson (1978b) states that the emerging adult faces the tasks of (1) exploring alternative possibilities for adult living, keeping options open, and avoiding strong commitments and (2) creating a stable life structure by becoming responsible and "making something" of oneself. Levinson notes that these tasks are antithetical, opposite in many respects, but he believes that a balance must be found between being too changeable with one's life values and activities and becoming prematurely committed to a life structure before the options have been explored. The life events of the structure that are crucial during emerging adulthood include occupational choice, first job, and marriage and the birth of children or making the choice to remain single or childless.

Scanlon (1979) indicates that identifying values to live by is a major developmental task for the emerging adult. The behavioral guidelines followed in childhood and early adolescence are no longer acceptable as standards of behavior or belief. Neither is a value system simplistically structured on a concept of rewards or punishment adequate. Nor is a moral code based on a youthful list of "do's and don'ts" or on "either this or that" criteria substantial enough to serve as a guide for adult behavior.

DEVELOPMENTAL CHARACTERISTICS OF THE EMERGING ADULT

Social development during the youth stage is transitional. However, physical and intellectual growth are essentially coming to a state of completion.

Physical characteristics

The height of the emerging adult has reached its peak for adult life and will remain stable until a person reaches old age. The weight spurts of the adolescent years level off near the end of the second decade of life, increasing gradually until the middle fifties, much to the dismay of many individuals. By the age of 17 years muscle growth has reached adult proportions, but muscular strength continues to grow, reaching its peak in the late twenties.

The brain has reached full size by the age of 16 years, but the adolescent has not developed sufficiently neurologically to use all brain parts adequately. Brain waves reach adult patterns in all cortical areas around the ages of 19 or 20 years, although this range of maturity may extend to 30 years of age (Ornstein, 1977).

Most of the glandular development in the youth stage has reached its peak. The glandular processes level off for adulthood, although certain glands continue to develop. From puberty to the age of 17 to 18 years the heart size doubles, primarily because of the increase in muscular development around the heart. Blood pressure reaches a normal level for adults. The heartbeat stabilizes at about 72 beats per minute. At about the age of 17 years the lung capacity of girls has reached adult proportions; male lung capacity is reached several years later.

Bone growth ends when bone fusion takes place. The growth of bone parts slows down at the age of 18 years for girls and 20 years for boys (Chumlea, 1982). Continual bone fusion takes place over the next few years. In general there is modification of body proportions between the ages of 18 and 22 years, changing the appearance of the oversized limbs and facial features of earlier adolescence (Sinclair, 1978).

Intellectual characteristics

The development of intellectual *potential* is also reaching its peak when a person is 18 to 22 years old. As was noted previously, full brain development occurs around the age of 19 to 20 years. Adults, at least those who are active and have above-average intelligence, can improve their abilities until later adulthood, but those of average or below average intelligence may experience a decline in some abilities. Baltes and Schaie (1974) maintain that young adults are capable of improving four dimensions of intelligence. First, *crystallized intelligence,* which includes verbal comprehension, inductive reasoning, and numerical reasoning, can be improved because it is acquired through education and experience. Mentally active adults will continue to broaden their intellectual insights. Second, the ability to shift from one way of thinking to another, *cognitive flexibility,* also continues to grow if the person does not assume a rigid intellectual stance. Third, the coordination of visual and motor abilities—*visuomotor flexibility,* involving a capacity to shift from the performance of one form of visuomotor operation to another kind—can also continue to develop, but not as readily as the other three dimensions of intellectual abilities. Fourth, *visualization*—the ability to organize and process visual materials, such as finding embedded figures or being alert to visual details—can also continue to be improved.

Parry (1973) supports these observations by indicating that aptitude development will reach a peak between the ages of 18 and 30, making it possible for learning to take place more quickly than at any other age level. However, he adds that success of development depends on the appropriate selection of aptitudes that can be improved and the pursuit of them with patience, persistence, and courage. By appropriate selection Parry means choosing those aptitudes for which an individual has the potential of development to a reasonable degree. It would be hopeless to try to develop a skill for which the individual has no aptitude whatsoever.

Individuals of this age have approximately 85% of their logical reasoning abilities developed. Individuals between 15 and 25 years of age tend to draw logical deductions based strictly on the statements as given in the test. Older adults seek to introduce supplementary premises based on their broader backgrounds or to confine themselves to comments on statements. Younger persons confine their logical reasoning to the question and knowledge at hand, whereas older persons operate from a broader perspective. On the other hand, young subjects can easily shift their thinking processes if they have additional problems to solve,

Meriem Kaluger

Meriem Kaluger

Physical maturity is coming to a state of completion during young adulthood. Although muscular strength and the quality of physical performance may continue to improve during early adulthood, young adults can exhibit a high level of efficient performance.

Meriem Kaluger

Aptitudes can be improved during emerging adulthood if the individual can identify and train in an area in which he or she has the capability to succeed. There is not much sense selecting a career-development program based on job opportunities rather than on aptitude and achievement potentials.

whereas the older group has difficulty with mental flexibility (Baltes and Schaie, 1974).

Social and emotional characteristics

The prolonged task of achieving social and emotional independence actually begins many years before adolescence when children enter school, expand their contacts with peers, and widen their sphere of autonomous activities. Unless the importance and difficulty of the task are realized by parents, some postadolescents will be facing problems of achieving social and emotional independence from parents. The task of achieving emotional independence is made particularly difficult in American society by prolonged education, which forces young people to be financially dependent on their parents for many years, by delay in work opportunities brought about by child labor laws, by mechanization and automation, and by continuous family contacts, which render it difficult for parents to perceive the growth changes that are slowly but steadily pushing the young person toward maturity.

The social growth and development of the adolescent are accompanied by glandular changes that are closely related to emotional control. The heightened emotional states during this period of life have been recognized as a part of the nature of adolescents. There is also an expansion of the emotions into the social realm. Fears and angers related to social situations become important. Self-conscious feelings about one's own inadequacy appear. This type of fear is observed in connection with college classroom situations. Fear of reciting in class, fear of failure, and fear of ridicule are still common, although less common than at 14 to 16 years of age.

One of the most noticeable characteristics of emerging adulthood is an increase in stability and control. Interests, friendships, career choices, and relations with parents are all more stable and predictable than they were in early adolescence. Opinions tend to be based on fact and are less liable to be affected by the generalities of propaganda than they were during the more "impressionable" period of adolescence. Their opinions can and do change under planned study and from the impact of interpersonal relationships. Current experiences still have an impact on the responses of the late adolescent, however.

"I HURT ALL OVER"

He came into my life when, as the axiom states, I least expected it. I was happily going about my own business, just having a good time; then he walked into my life and took over completely. I didn't know I could be so happy. I had somebody besides my family to share with. Every day when we talked, he'd ask me how my day had gone. If I had a problem, he'd listen and advise. I seldom took his advice, but it was comforting knowing that he cared

Then, on Valentine's Day, we had our first and, as a matter of fact, our only major argument. This happened on Friday. That weekend was miserable. He didn't call to break our date on Saturday; when I called him and realized that I was being "stood up," I was quite upset. I cried. Sunday was just as bad. Monday was worse! I could hardly wait to get home from the office so I could let myself "feel." I sobbed.

That night I went to a movie. Really, I only went to get out of the house. Brian called after I got home. I don't remember the conversation, but I do know that he apologized and that we talked it out. He asked me how I felt and I said: "I felt like you dropped me from the third floor, watched me splatter, and laughed." He said, "I wasn't laughing." Everything, I thought, was back to normal.

From that time on, however, we saw each other less and less.

I began to question myself and my situation. I tried to talk it out with him, but all he managed to do was to criticize me. I wanted to say, "Okay, don't bother me anymore." But I couldn't do it. I didn't want to lose him.

One time when we'd had a minor disagreement, I coolly stated our problem as I saw it. We happened "to like each other" in spite of everything. This should be a problem? It was for us because neither of us wanted to hurt the other—or ourselves.

Through April and May, Brian called less and less frequently. By the end of May he wasn't calling at all. How did I feel? I hurt all over. It was especially bad, too, because I'd moved into my own apartment on May 19, and I was not yet used to living alone. I felt absolutely empty. I was lonely, unsure, bereft. All I had to do with my time was to fill it with thinking. Finally he called. He made a date for the next day, and I was elated. He never came. From the heights of ecstasy to the depths of despair in twenty-four hours—that was me! There it was, all over again. All the fresh, new hurt. He called later that week and acted as if nothing at all had happened. He asked about every member of my family, about everything that I was doing. But no date!

So now I'm concentrating on falling out of love. But I find myself daydreaming about him constantly. I have long, involved, imaginary conversations with him that are filled with questions and explanations. Sometimes I quarrel with him. I remember our good times, and I become depressed. When I'm shopping and I see a cute greeting card, I have to remind myself that I can't send it to him. I catch myself thinking, "I'll have to remember to tell Brian that joke . . . or this story . . . or that comment." When I buy a dress, I wonder if he will like it—then I remember that it doesn't really matter any more. I find his name creeping into conversations that shouldn't relate to him at all. I jump when the phone rings, and I'm sad when it doesn't. Until very recently I've had no desire to see other people socially, and I've turned down more dates than I've accepted. I have so much energy that I don't know what to do with it all—and yet I have no ambition to do anything. I get violently jealous when I see couples our age having a good time with each other. I get angry with myself for feeling this way. Knowing that others have had the same experience is no consolation at all. Even the realization that I am better off without him doesn't help. Logic has absolutely nothing to do with my feelings.

So what is it like to fall out of love? It is hard. It is lonely. it is depressing. It is necessary. I keep telling myself that it gets easier every day, and most days it does. I just hope that I never have to do it again.

Pursuit of identity

The question of identity has two aspects. On one hand it is a question of self-concept, "Who am I?" while on the other hand it is a plea, "Don't lose my individuality in the mass of technology and overpopulation." Until the end of formal schooling, individuals have been "role playing" the image of adolescents. They are not sure how they should act or what they should be, so they act out their role as they perceive it from watching their peers. Postadolescents realize that role playing is no longer adequate. They must accept the fact that they are making some decisions that will affect their lives for years to come. They are also taking on some characteristics that will identify them with certain values and life-styles. Self-concept conflicts are common during the transition between adolescence

David Strickler

In a complex, technically oriented society, there is a great need for some form of post–high school education to meet career requirements. However, a college or a university setting may delay development of a personal identity because of the artificial nature of the campus community.

and adulthood and seldom permit the individual to be at rest emotionally.

Postadolescents must have a positive self-concept it they are to function properly. This is a large part of their search during emerging adulthood. They are looking for a stable, balanced self-concept, a reliable view of themselves that remains more or less steady throughout life. This image may come about through the values of community or family or from conflicting groups among their contemporaries.

The struggle for an identity is like a struggle against getting lost. Often it is a feeling of depersonalization, frequently brought on by some distinct change in the life of the postadolescent from a known, familiar environment to an unknown, impersonal world. It may be starting a job, entering college and living in a residence hall, or joining the armed forces (Stein, 1976a). There is an uncertainty as to how one fits into the new world. Then there is a fear that the new world might not recognize and appreciate the individual's uniqueness and competencies. There may be serious questions raised as to whether the individual is as capable or as ready as once thought. "What am I doing here?" "Is this really what I want?" "Save me from getting lost in this maze of life!" Much of young adults' uncertainty results from frustrations encountered in defining goals and in being accepted for what they can produce (Ohlsen, 1971).

Identities are easily questioned by students at big universities, where they may be impersonalized to the extent that they begin to think of themselves as numbers on a class card or anonymous units in a statistics population. At a large university, for example, students often feel used when they pick up the undergraduate catalogue and read the impressive list of outstanding professors assigned to teach their courses and then report to class to find it being taught by a succession of underqualified graduate students, filling in for the Big Name. At smaller schools the feeling of not being part of the "real" world may reinforce the postadolescent's uncertainty of what reality is. "Am I experiencing life as it really is out in the world, or is my college environment just an artificial, structured community that runs my life?"

LAUNCHING A CAREER

Major shifts in the labor force appear to be in the making as population changes, accelerated increases in technology and knowledge, and changing adult roles are taking place. Among the changes cited by Shertzer and Stone (1976) are (1) a diminishing need for unskilled workers, (2) geographical shifts of industry, (3) job obsolescence due to new technological development, (4) a decline in goods-producing industries, (5) a decline in agricultural occupations, (6) an increase in health and service occupations, (7) an increase in jobs that require more education and training, (8) a continued rise of youth unemployment, especially in minority groups, (9) an increase in the number of youths entering the labor force, and (10) a trend toward making a career change in midlife and beginning a second career. These changes have important implications for the educational and vocational plans of emerging and early adults. Education, training, and possibly retraining are a must. No major career or occupation field has lowered its educational or job-entry requirements. Horizontal movement from one job area to another (same level of work, responsibility, and pay) may be possible without further education, but vertical movement to higher positions may involve more or new educational background and training. Emerging adulthood, with its early potential for post–high school education, is an important period

Meriem Kaluger

An external phase of career development is an exploration period during which individuals examine, and perhaps study, a job field that has some attraction for them. It may or may not be their final career choice.

for making educational and career decisions that may have long-term implications.

Career development in emerging and early adulthood includes post-high-school educational decisions, job selection, and establishment, maintenance, and adjustments within the career field. Successful establishment and adult vocational identity usually involve mobility and movement within career fields and work organizations, although the moves could be within the same organization (Flaste, 1976). During one's working life there may be as many as six or seven major changes, usually before age 30 or 35 (Bernard and Fullmer, 1977).

Career development

Van Maanen and Schein (1977) presume the existence of four stages of career development over the adult life span. They acknowledge that individual differences and variations will exist, but they believe that their stage model, as presented in Table 12-2, provides a useful framework for the study of vocational development.

The four stages in the Van Maanen and Schein scheme include (1) the exploration stage, during which a search for a career or job direction is made, (2) the establishment stage, which includes the tasks of job search, job entry, competency development, and gaining status, (3) the maintenance or midcareer stage, at which time a high level of productivity and acceptance is attained, and (4) the later career stage, when the individual's expertise is used to offer judgment and to teach others. The interesting aspect of the Van Maanen and Schein scheme is that it includes an external career path as well as an internal career path.

The *external career path* outlines the stages as they are normally encountered in a job. It describes the way in which an individual proceeds on the occupational path or paths (a person may have more than one external career at a time, such as being a teacher during part of the year and a construction worker during the summer months). The route followed is through the external experiences involved in career exploration, establishment of a career, midcareer maintenance, and the career later in life.

The *internal career path* consists of the individual's expectations and perceptions. It is the career sequence or plan that an individual has in mind. Since the inner career is subjected to the personal life design and events of the individual, the career path of one person may vary sharply from that of another. A person may project an inner career plan that includes job changes, breaks from working in a job field, or continued education. An individual may plan to work for so many years, go back to school (or have a child), or relocate in another part of the country or world. Upward mobility, such as a better job, better pay, or more authority, is generally anticipated. A mental timetable of events and moves is usually part of both an internal career and an external career plan. The timetable, however, generally interacts with other life events, such as getting settled in a home, having children in school, or entry of the spouse into the job market.

Job search and entry

Where are jobs to be found? Year after year we have watched our graduates seek jobs and find them. Who hires them? About 90% of all workers in Western societies are employed by business or industrial organizations and institutions (Van Maanen and Schein, 1977). Quite often, however, circumstances or timing is the most prominent determinant of a job placement or entry into a vocational field (Manaster, 1977). The companies or institutions that have job openings at the moment, the kinds of positions available, and the job candidates who hear about the jobs and are able to make the right contacts to get interviewed are factors in determining where a person works and what kind of work they do. The openings may or may not be in the specific field of educational or vocational training.

The employment or unemployment picture of the moment will also determine what job offers are available and accepted. We remember the unusual, affluent economic picture of the 1960s when so many teaching jobs were available. Some candidates would say, "I want to teach in such-and-such a city, in this particular building, in this specific grade." And they would get that job! The recession of the early 1980s eliminated those kinds of choices. The comment often heard then was, "I just want a job —any job—anywhere. I hope it will be in teaching." The phenomenon of a job by choice or by chance contributes to the so-called first-job dilemma.

First-job dilemma

Young adults frequently experience disappointment on their first job. The individual is usually happy to have a job, but then a disquieting dilemma sets in.

TABLE 12-2 Stages of adult life-span career development

External career	*Internal career*
Exploration	**Exploration**
a. Occupational images b. Advice. c. Success/failure in school tests, sports d. Economic and historical constraints e. Educational choices f. Counseling, letters of recommendation g. Test results	a. Self-image of what's fun b. Self-assessment c. Development of goals, ambitions, tentative choices d. Enlarged self-image based on growing experience e. Need for real test of ability to work f. Anticipatory socialization based on models and images
Establishment	**Establishment**
a. Mutual recruitment b. Acceptance and job entry (1) Orientation (2) Training (3) Informal initiation c. First job assignment (1) Meeting boss and co-workers (2) Learning period (3) Period of full performance (4) Leveling off and/or becoming obsolete (5) Preparing for new assignment d. Leveling off transfer or promotion (1) Feedback on meaning of move, performance review (2) Repeat from *c* if transfer or promotion e. Granting tenure or seniority	a. Reality shock, insecurity, fear of rejection b. Develop image of organization c. First commitment to job versus taking on a task d. Readjustment of self-image based on acceptance/rejection e. Expect first real test of ability (1) Feelings of playing for keeps (2) Learning ropes (3) Testing commitment (4) Feelings of success/failure f. Reassessment of self-image and match to career (1) Sorting out family/work issues and achieving fit (2) Forming career strategy; how to make it? (3) Leave organization if necessary (4) Adjust to failure, revise career aim (5) Turn to unions or other sources if threatened g. Period of maximum insecurity pursuant to tenure review (1) Crisis of full acceptance versus crisis of reassessment (2) Finding a new career versus new learning about self and organization
Maintenance (midcareer)	**Maintenance (midcareer)**
a. Expect maximum productivity b. Occupational and organizational secrets shared c. Assume teacher/mentor role d. Deal with plateauing through remotivation	a. New sense of growth, realistic assessment of ambition and potential b. Settling in, feeling security, danger of stagnation c. Threat of younger, ambitious recruits d. Thoughts of new pastures, second career, midlife adjustment
Later career	**Later career**
a. Assign jobs that draw on wisdom, perspective, judgment b. More community and society-oriented jobs c. More jobs teaching others versus being on the firing line	a. Concern for teaching others b. Psychological preparation for retirement c. Finding new sources of self-improvement d. Deceleration

Modified from Van Maanen, J., & Schein, E.H., Career development. In J.R. Hackman and J.L. Suttle (Eds.), *Improving life at work.* Santa Monica, Calif.: Goodyear Publishing Co., 1977, pp. 55-59.

Schein (1970) reports that many college graduates encounter the dilemma of having successfully completed the educational requirements for graduation but of being unable to find what they consider to be a suitable position, one where they can use their personal creativity and talents. They do not attain personal job satisfaction (Institute for Social Research, 1976). Schein's study indicates that within 5 years many large companies lose more than half the college graduates hired. That is a major loss to the company when the time, money, and effort spent in training or breaking-in a new worker is considered. The reason for job changes appears to be more than a desire for a higher salary.

According to Schein (1970) the reasons given by the graduates for making a job change usually relate to internal career expectations and anticipation of being recognized, being challenged, and being able to make worthwhile contributions. Among the complaints mentioned were (1) not being able to present or promote their own "good ideas," (2) not being able to accept or understand the reality of the company's organization system and politics, (3) not having adequate supervisory feedback on job performance, (4) inability to cope with the frustrations associated with making the change from a collegiate life-style to building a life around the demands of learning and living in a full-time work situation, and (5) having a supervisor who is considered to have less education or training than they themselves. Schein suggests that young adults who aspire to higher positions must recognize their own immaturity and inexperience to begin with and must learn to cope with the circumstances of the organization.

Managers, says Schein, often have a stereotyped image of college graduates as being immature and unrealistic in their expectations, wanting too much money and responsibility too soon. Some managers, who are less educated than their new subordinates, may resent the far higher starting salaries that the graduates receive. They may also be threatened by the "new ideas" and "management theories" that they assume the graduates are bringing with them. Management should recognize that the graduate's first supervisor exerts a strong influence in shaping the attitude of the young adult toward the organization. Supervisors should be mature, secure in their knowledge and understanding of the characteristics and expectations of young adults.

Basically, occupational satisfaction results when there is a good fit between the interests, abilities, and expectations of the individual and the characteristics and demands of the job and the company. However, the basis of job satisfaction differs. Some individuals

TABLE 12-3 Satisfied workers as percent of total workers: 1962 to 1980 (Survey questions asked were variants of "How satisfied are you with your job (or your work)?" Figures for "satisfied" combined responses such as "very satisfied," "somewhat satisfied," and "fairly satisfied.")

Worker characteristic	*1962*	*1972*	*1975*	*1978*	*1980*
Male	84	86	90	89	85
Female	81	86	87	88	83
18-29 years	(NA)*	73	83	83	76
21-29 years	74	76	82	84	78
30-39 years	82	88	88	88	82
40-49 years	84	89	92	92	88
50-59 years	(NA)	91	92	92	86
60 and over	(NA)	95	94	96	90

Worker characteristic	*1962*	*1972*	*1975*	*1978*	*1980*
White	84	87	89	90	84
Black and other	76†	78	85	76	81
Education					
Grade school	83	86	87	88	87
High school	81	86	91	87	81
Some college	86	83	90	90	82
College degree	90	85	85	91	88
Graduate work	84	95	87	91	90

From National Opinion Research Center, *General social surveys,* 1972-1980; *Cumulative codebook.* Chicago, Ill.: National Opinion Research Center. In *Statistical abstracts,* no. 649, 1981.

*Not available.

†Black only.

derive their job satisfaction from wages and the money-related status and benefits that the job presents. These individuals work to purchase material possessions or to be able to engage in activities they want to pursue. A second group of individuals gain their satisfaction from the work itself. Their major source of satisfaction comes from the process of work and its related accomplishments. Through work they feel useful, they have a sense of self-esteem and accomplishment, and they enjoy the companionship of co-workers (Terkel, 1982).

There is a higher proportion of work-oriented individuals among white-collar and professional workers. Blue-collar workers tend to be more dissatisfied with their jobs than white-collar workers are because they have fewer opportunities for interesting and varied tasks; their working conditions are often poorer, Table 12-3 indicates the percentage of satisfied workers by age, race, and education. Fewer young adults were satisfied with their jobs in 1980 as compared to 1975. More older workers than younger workers were satisfied (National Opinion Research Center, 1981).

Skilled and professional workers, after spending several years of searching, tend to settle into a particular occupation and remain until retirement. In contrast the less skilled workers continue to switch employment and employers for most of their working years. Truck drivers and construction workers sometimes show employment in 10 to 20 different jobs before retirement.

Professionals, such as chemists, nurses, accountants, teachers, occupational therapists, and others, rate the nature of their work as the single greatest source of satisfaction (Bird, 1975). Industrial workers with less schooling indicate that working in an area of genuine interest is an important factor in job satisfaction. However, they also emphasize job security and pay rates as conditions that play the most important part in job satisfaction.

Women and careers

Many women pursue dual careers of homemaker and of an occupational role outside the home. Few would quarrel with the observation that women have a fundamental biological difference from men, manifested in the ability to conceive, bear, and nurse offspring. Woman's role has been traditionally organized around the children and the support of the effort of the family's breadwinner. However, neither the biological nor social role of the homemaker is as static as some advocates would have us believe (Wilson and Wise, 1975). Women now have an option in childbearing. Fathers are much more involved in child rearing than previously.

The feminist-suffragette movement of the nineteenth century and the acceptance of women into the work force in World War II have set in motion challenges to the sterotyped social role for women that, paired with the changes in social expectations for men, may ultimately dispel the sterotype roles. Women, free from social pressures, can decide to remain single and to devote themselves to careers of their choosing. Some women prefer to be part of a dual-career family—married, husband and wife both involved in their careers and, perhaps, also having children.

About half of all women between 18 and 64 are in the work force: 90% of all women will work outside the home at some time in their lives. In 1980 the female labor force consisted of 60% married women, 25% single women (age 16 or older), and 15% widowed or divorced (U.S. Bureau of Labor Statistics, 1981). These statistics, however, do not suggest the pay and status differential that exists in many areas between working men and women. Income figures consistently show lower figures for female college graduates than for male graduates in the same field. Women are underrepresented in the ranks of the professions (Ritzer, 1977). Fully 75% of working women in the United States are classified as secretaries, stenographers, household workers, bookkeepers, elementary teachers, and waitresses; 25% have other occupations (Blau, 1975).

Not all women want to work or to have careers. Homemaking can be a full-time occupation. But, if the full-time homemaker has aspirations for a job or career beyond the home, dissatisfaction with her life can become a problem (Pearlin, 1975). Working women who feel the effects of job responsibilities plus those of rearing a family and maintaining a home are subject to depressive reactions. Many professional women believe that family-work conflicts are more significant career obstacles than either professional and social stereotyping or explicit job discrimination (Hackman, 1977).

It is possible that some women erect barriers for themselves, based on a lack of early socialization experiences that would prepare them for success-oriented career roles. This observation was reflected in the findings of a study conducted by Matina Horner (1970).

David Strickler

Women are entering many fields that have previously been the primary domain of men. This young woman may be interested in road and building construction, but her entry-level job may not be what she desires. Job satisfaction depends on many factors, including patience.

Horner asked both male and female subjects to write a story based on the sentence, "After first-term finals, John (Anne, for the women) finds himself (herself) at the top of his (her) medical school class." Ninety percent of the men's stories reflected pride in John's accomplishment. Of the women, however, 65% wrote stories that expressed fear of social rejection, loss of femininity, or denial that a woman could be successful.

Horner's findings were widely publicized, and the trait she labeled as "the motive to avoid success" became known as the "fear of success." Such fears are attributed in part to the conflict between desires for achievement and conditioned sex-role stereotypes. These reactions are a result of learning and not an inherent part of the female personality (Shapiro, 1977). Presumably, as women become more accustomed to taking an active part in the world of work, they may lose some of their fear and anxiety about succeeding in nontraditional female activities.

Minority workers

Statistics on the number of black professionals and white-collar workers suggest that the situation for blacks has improved in some areas since 1960. Although there are fewer blacks in unskilled and agricultural jobs, unemployment has stayed about the same for blacks relative to whites since 1950 (Ritzer, 1977). Many blacks are underemployed because their jobs do not adequately utilize or reward their abilities. However, the percentage of black males who are college bound is substantially above what it was in 1973, and opportunities are improving for employment in skilled jobs and in the professions.

Little information is available about Americans of Hispanic origin. Yet this is the largest minority in the United States, comprising up to 20% of the population of states in the Southwest and West. Even in the Amish area of Lancaster County, Pennsylvania, there are over 30,000 Spanish-speaking persons. The employment status of Hispanics is perhaps even worse than that of the blacks. The problems experienced by this group include low income, high unemployment, migration, low occupational status, and discrimination (Stevens-Long, 1979).

But, as the late Harry Golden wrote in one of his columns, the Spanish-speaking children are readers and learners. They go to the library and devour books. They are building a foundation for their future. The U.S. Commission on Civil Rights (1978) indicated that between 1970 and 1976 the percentage of male Puerto Ricans who graduated from high school increased from 44% to 68%; female Puerto Ricans who graduated increased from 42% to 60%. For the same period, male blacks graduating increased from 59% to 74%, and female blacks from 62% to 74%.

Little to nothing of substance has been reported in the research literature about American Indians or Alaskan natives. The U.S. Commission on Civil Rights (1978) did report that there was an increase of 58% to 70% in males of these groups who graduated from high school between 1970 and 1976. However, the increase for native American females graduating was only from 56% to 58%.

ERIKSON: DEVELOPMENT OF INTIMACY

Erikson (1968b) proposes that psychosocial development occurs in a series of stages, each of which has a psychosocial crisis or task that must be resolved. (See Chapter 2 for Erikson's life-span perspective.) Failure to achieve the positive aspect of the psychosocial crisis makes it difficult for the individual to come to a satisfactory mastery of the psychosocial crisis of the next stage of life.

The challenge of the adolescent period is to develop an identity through the successful resolution of the *identity versus role confusion* crisis. Erikson believes that healthy personality development in adolescence rests on a role adoption in keeping with one's biological, psychological, and social orientations, suggesting a female orientation or a male orientation. The postadolescent needs to integrate the ideas and skills acquired during the previous stage with the social opportunities and roles available during emerging adulthood. If role confusion occurs, the individual feels lost, alienated, or unable or unmotivated to invest the self in anything. The young adult who has developed a sense of identity during adolescence is now ready to care about whom to be with at work and in private life, not only exchanging intimacies, but sharing intimacy (Erikson, 1974).

It is impossible to share yourself on a committed interpersonal level with another if you do not know who or what you are. To share a deep commitment of intimacy involves a strong sense of self (identity) to eliminate the dangers of a threat of ego loss when relating to another person. Many interpersonal decisions have to be made at this age about whom to date, whom to go steady with, and whether or not engagement, marriage, or cohabitation is in the offing. The reason most often given for the failure to develop a strong identity and a good interpersonal commitment is that numerous demands are placed on an individual for fulfilling the needs of the other person, especially if the other person has a weak sense of self and needs much praise, psychological support, and reassurance. However, in the emerging adulthood period, individuals with a fair-to-good sense of identity are willing to risk temporary ego loss in such emotionally demanding situations as a commitment that allows for sexual involvement or for personal sacrifices and compromises.

Erikson (1963b) acknowledges that during young adulthood an individual is supposed to help contribute to the perpetuation of society by establishing a close, stable interpersonal relationship. It is not until this stage that "true genitality" occurs. Up until now sex lives are dominated by the search for identity, which includes seeking for a stabilized sexual identity. Erikson's emphasis on heterosexuality is one of the problems of the theory because it suggests that mature sexual development includes the wish for sharing with a loved person and the desire to have children. Reigel (1975) points out that this assumption reflects traditional middle-class values and does not allow for changes in social values and priorities over succeeding generations.

While the research on adult development underscores the search for intimacy in young adulthood, confirming this Eriksonian stage, it does not confirm the contention that the typical young adult has found an identity during adolescence and is ready for intimacy, as defined by Erikson. The major portion of young adulthood seems to be a continuation of the search for identity. Constantinople (1969) devised a longitudinal study, using more than 900 four-year male and female college students, to see whether supporting data for Erikson's stage of young adulthood development could be found. Constantinople found that stage resolution for intimacy versus isolation was not evident for younger college students such as freshmen. Follow-up studies indicated that there were consistent increases in the scores showing a successful resolution of the adolescent crisis between identity and role diffusion from the freshman to the senior year. There was more successful resolution of the stage crisis among senior males and females who had higher college grade averages than among freshmen and other students. Apparently college provides a socialization experience that helps develop the ability to make an interpersonal commitment. But it also implies that many college-age students are only in a transitional period where they are just beginning to deal with intimacy issues (Hultsch and Deutsch, 1981).

IDENTITY CRISIS

A teenager who rebels against his parents and the establishment and ventures out to find his own values is a familiar story. That is, it seems familiar and run-of-the-mill until it happens to someone you know well. Then all at once the little pat answers and simple solutions that should work fall apart.

When I first met Paul, he was a typical fifteen-year-old high school student. He was popular with both boys and girls; he was interested in sports and was an active participant. He didn't particularly enjoy school. Thinking back, I believe he was about the same as I was when I was in school. But I was to see differences occur only two years later.

As they mature, most adolescents begin to think about their future. But this is where Paul differed. He did nothing to prepare for his future. He was not thinking of an occupation, considering colleges, or doing any of those things that one normally expects of a high school senior. He also refused to assume any responsibilities at home. He made little contribution to the family and took for granted everything that was done or given to him. He did not try very hard to find a job to help earn spending money. His grades, instead of improving, became steadily worse.

He assumed that he would get to go to college, although he didn't know what his major would be. He could decide that later. As for getting accepted, there was no problem. He was quite good in track—he had even gone to the state championships. Paul figured this would be enough to have a college grab him.

To his dismay, Paul soon learned that more was needed for college than to be good in track and have a recommendation from the coach. He did not get accepted to the schools he had wanted. This unexpected rejection disturbed him and affected his behavior. During his last semester in high school he began to display an open, defiant "I don't care" attitude. He gave up many of his interests and values at this time, even to the extent of quitting the track team. Because the establishment had hurt Paul by saying, in effect, that he wasn't good enough, he took refuge in deviant behavior and ideas. He let his hair grow longer, wore wild clothes, and subscribed to the philosophy of "peace, love, and brotherhood." He began to associate with like-minded individuals.

As his new friends became all-important, his family became increasingly less so. Although he was extremely concerned with showing love for his fellow man, the sincerity of this belief was not apparent from his actions toward his family. He treated them with actions that ranged from indifference to contempt.

Paul claimed to be finding himself as an "individual"; instead, he was becoming more like his friends. He was still too confused and insecure to be actually on his own. He needed others who were like himself to give him a feeling of security and acceptance. So, although he was different from the "establishment," he was just conforming to the ways of his friends.

But even as confused and dejected as he was, the summer after he graduated from high school he decided that he would go to college. Apparently he still had the desire to do something and to succeed. He also got a summer job, a sports car, and seemed to be becoming a working member of the establishment. Soon, however, he began thinking of working and going to school every day as a "real drag." He changed his mind about attending college. He also thought of his living at home as being unbearable to his independence, although few restrictions were forced upon him. He made plans to move in with some of his friends.

Also showing his confusion were the many contradictions to his "back-to-nature" philosophy. He kept saying he wanted to do away with luxuries and go back to the simple things. But, on the other hand, he bought a little yellow Triumph sports car, electric guitars and amplifiers, and a good stereo system. When he decided to go to a dance, he bought a flashy knit jump suit.

I don't believe Paul is intentionally being different or difficult, but he is confused. This confusion is manifested in many young people. Most of them have been brought up on traditional values, concepts, and goals, but they cannot see how they can work in today's world. So they claim to disown them while still trying to attain them, although in a different way and under different titles. This, I believe, is what has happened in Paul's case. He has not found himself or a value system he can accept. To keep from having to face this identity problem, he has taken shelter in a new look that seemingly rejects the values of the past while claiming to expound the true "basics" of life.

Paul is still lost.

KOHLBERG: MORAL DEVELOPMENT

A look at the various developmental stages of moral judgment in individuals may give some insight into the levels of moral judgment pursued by societies. Kohlberg (1976) has formulated and validated a conception of moral development based on the core assumptions of the "cognitive-developmental" theory of moral education. Table 12-4, the stages of moral development, suggests the thinking and reasoning that are involved. A key assumption of this theory is that the moral development rests on the stimulation of thinking and problem solving by the individual. It is reasoning that leads to a particular moral response. The theory claims that morality represents a set of rational principles of judgment concerning human welfare and justice that are valid for every culture. Individuals acquire and refine the sense of justice through a sequence of invariant developmental stages. However, even though cognitive development may take place, a person may hit a moral plateau, and no additional progress in moral development takes place.

An individual's level of cognitive development determines the potential of a person's moral reasoning and moral development. Movement from one moral stage to another comes whenever the results of an individual's cognitive reasoning are in conflict with the present stage of his or her moral reasoning. The conflict is between what the person has been thinking was the right moral action to perform and what his or her cognitive reasoning level indicates is the better behavior. Individuals, theoretically, will then upgrade their level of moral reasoning so it will be consistent with their cognitive thinking. Higher levels of cognitive development are needed for more sophisticated concepts of morality. If an individual sees no cognitive reason for upgrading the level of moral reasoning and behavior, no further development occurs.

Kohlberg's theory of moral development will be discussed as it appears in Table 12-4. Level I, the ***preconventional level,*** is a premoral level where moral reasoning is not part of the behavior decision-making process. The behavior to be initiated is based on self-interest because the individual has an *externalized,* egocentric orientation. The motivation for behavior on *stage 1* is to do good in order to avoid punishment by others or to gain the rewards of physical or material power "You told me to do it—I had to do it"; "I did what I had to do to get what I wanted." At *stage 2* the motivation is to gain rewards from others. Behavior is based on a naive, instrumental (means to a goal), hedonistic (self-seeking) orientation. "I wanted to be nice to you so you would be nice to me (reciprocity)"; "I did what I was paid to do"; "I did what satisfies my needs."

preconventional level a stage of moral development in which the child responds to cultural rules and labels of good and bad only in terms of the physical or hedonistic consequences of obeying or disobeying the rules. See also **conventional level; postconventional level.**

TABLE 12-4 Stages of moral development according to Kohlberg

I. Preconventional level: externalized and selfish orientation	Behavior abides by cultural rules because of punishment or reward consequences.
Stage 1: The punishment and obedience orientation	Good and bad and right and wrong are thought of in terms of consequences of action. Avoidance of punishment.
Stage 2: The instrumental and hedonistic orientation	Right action is whatever satisfies one's own needs and occasionally the needs of others. Exchange of favors. "Do for me and I do for you."
II. Conventional level: internalized and social conformity orientation	Behavior is self-controlled due to expectations of others and desire to conform and accept social expectations.
Stage 3: Interpersonal acceptance of "good boy, nice girl" social concept	Good behavior is what pleases and is approved by others. Response to stereotype; social units are loose and flexible.
Stage 4: The "law and order" orientation	Right behavior accepts and shows respect for authority. Doing one's duty for the good of the social order: laws are permanent and not likely to change.
III. Postconventional level: self-chosen principled orientation	Effort to define moral values and principles that are valid beyond the authority of the group and even beyond the self.
Stage 5: The social contract, utilitarian orientation	Adherence to legal rights commonly agreed upon by society but with laws subject to interpretation and change in terms of rational consideration for the rights of the individual while maintaining respect of self and others.
Stage 6: The universal ethical principle orientation (stage 6 has been dropped in Kohlberg's new classification)	Right behavior is defined in terms of ethical principles based on logical comprehensiveness, universality, and consistency; it respects the inherent dignity of human beings as individuals.

Based on data from Kohlberg, L. In T. Lickona (Ed.), *Moral development and behavior.* New York: Holt, Rinehart & Winston, 1976.

conventional level a stage of moral development in which the individual strives to maintain the expectations of the family, group, or nation, regardless of the consequences. See also **postconventional level; preconventional level.**

postconventional level a stage of moral development in which the individual defines moral values and principles in relation to their validity and application rather than in relation to the dictates of society or of any particular group. It is characterized by self-chosen ethical principles that are comprehensive, universal, and consistent. See also **conventional stage; preconventional stage.**

principled level the level of moral reasoning in which value resides in self-chosen principles and standards that have a universal logical validity and can therefore be shared.

Level II, the ***conventional level,*** is more sociocentric, with an *internalized* social conformity orientation. *Stage 3* is one of conformity to social conventions in order to avoid the disapproval of others. Moral behavior is that which is approved by others. It is behavior designed to please and to maintain good relations. "I did it because I want to be accepted"; "I wanted to do the right things so others would like me." *Stage 4* is one of respect for social order and fixed rules as sanctioned by a higher group. It is a law-and-order orientation. It is morality that is demanded by a social or religious authority. The motivation of this behavior is to avoid censure by legitimate authorities. "I did my duty; I followed the orders of my superior"; "My duty is to follow orders."

Level III, the ***postconventional,*** *autonomous,* or ***principled level,*** is a morality based on *self-accepted* moral principles. It has a self-chosen, principled orientation. On this level individuals believe in principles or truths. *Stage 5* stresses the necessity of following the legal standards of society because they are based on democratically accepted laws: a social contract of equality and mutuality is implied. "I did what I had to do because it was the law, and everyone should obey the laws upon which our society is predicated." *Stage 6* is self-directed moral judgment and behavior based on abstract universal principles and ethical standards. A personal, ethical sense and conscience is involved. Principles such as individual rights, human dignity, and equality are the bases for behavior. "I believe each person is a child of the universe and thus deserving of dignity, respect, and attention." This stage has the highest level of cognitive organization and moral reasoning development.

The stages are not defined by opinions or judgments but by ways of reasoning about moral matters and bases of choice. Stages 1 and 2, which are typical of children and delinquents, are described as "premoral," since their moral decisions are based on self-interest and material considerations. The group-oriented stages 3 and 4 are the conventional ones at which most of the adult population operates. Stages 5 and 6 are "principles" stages, with only 5% to 10% of the population ever reaching stage 6.

Why do some people reach higher levels of moral development than others? Much depends on the value judgment system and philosophy developed by the individual. That development depends on the type of reasoning and problem-solving experience individuals have had and the types of knowledge and information they use in their thinking. Development requires personal, social, and moral experience, usually with a strong emotional component on which to base that reasoning. Individuals who receive little or no information develop moral uncertainty because they have to work out so many answers for themselves.

Status of Kohlberg's theory

Considerable research has taken place on Kohlberg's theory of moral development. Based on their longitudinal studies, Colby, Kohlberg, and Gibbs (1980) have moderately altered the definitions of the first five stages of the theory and have deleted the sixth. The data of their study show that change from one stage to the next is gradual in all persons; no subjects skipped any stage (Kohlberg, 1979). In some individuals there was often more than one level of reasoning taking place at a time, but there were specific types of judgment typical for each age level. For example, although adolescence may have some stage-5 moral reasoning, this type of judgment does not show a substantial increase until the mid-twenties. This moral change suggests that the development of higher levels of moral reasoning is an adult phenomenon. Fig. 12-1 presents the scores of moral maturity for each age group as determined by the Kohlberg revised scoring manual of his tests. Moral maturity scores increased to

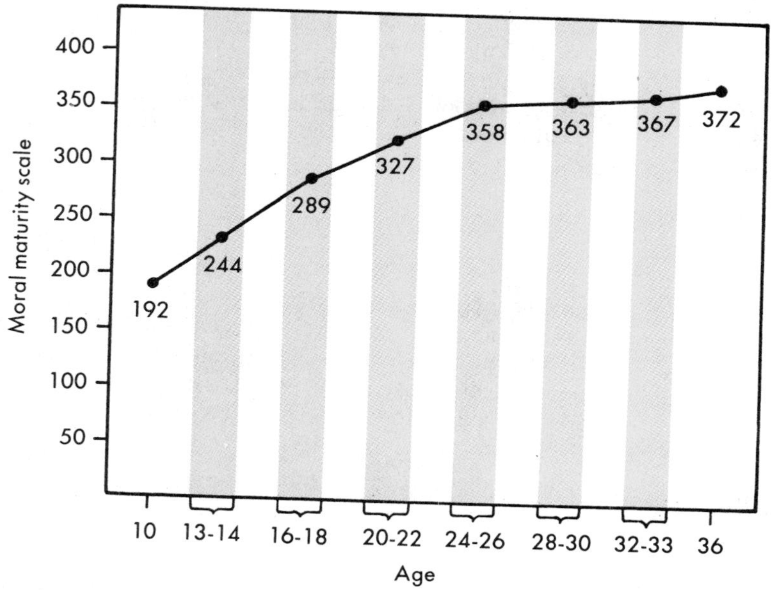

FIG. 12-1 ***Mean moral maturity score for each age group.***
Modified from Colby, A., Gibbs, J., & Kohlberg, L. Standard form scoring manual. *Cambridge, Mass.: Center for Moral Education, 1980.*

age 36. Kohlberg and his associates dropped stage 6 from their revised scoring manual because (1) it seemed to be culturally based, (2) none of his longitudinal subjects had achieved it by 1976, and (3) partly because stage 6 was widely criticized as being elitist and merely a scientific justification for libertarian values (Muson, 1979).

Cross-cultural review of Kohlberg

A review by Edwards (1977) reports on the cross-cultural research done with Kohlberg's test in Mexico, Taiwan, Kenya, the Bahamas, Honduran Carib, India, Nigeria, Israel, Thailand, Turkey, Britain, Canada, New Zealand, and the Yucatan (Mexico). The Kohlberg scoring system seems to be useful in other cultures. The older subjects tend to score at higher stages. Although only stages 1 through 4 appear in the non-Western traditional cultures, there is some support for the claim of universality (Carroll and Rest, 1982).

Moral perspective of the adult woman

Kohlberg's initial research was done only with male subjects. The possibility existed that Kohlberg's scheme contained a sex bias because of a failure to consider that the development of moral thinking in women could develop in a different sequence because of their unique concerns and perspectives. Gilligan (1977) did a study of 29 women to determine how women reason in areas of their lives in which they have a choice, areas such as control of fertility, abortion, and pregnancy. For these women, Gilligan identified a sequence of moral development that consisted of three levels and two transitional periods. Level 1 was oriented to personal survival, or what was practical and best for her. The first transitional period was one of movement from selfishness to responsibility, wherein the woman considered what would be a responsible choice in terms of other people (unborn or born) as well as herself.

Level 2 considers that goodness is sacrificing one's own wishes to do what other people want. It is a period of conflict between considering oneself responsible for others while holding others responsible for influencing her choices. The second transitional period occurs when she bases her decisions not on how others will react to her but on her judgment of what is best for all concerned. Level 3 is the morality of nonviolence responsibility, where she seeks moral equality between herself and others. At this level she uses moral judgment and action designed to hurt no one, including herself, when making decisions involving a moral dilemma.

The woman's perspective is often situation specific, "What do I do in this particular situation that involves me to a very great degree?" We need to appreciate the universal need for compassion and care for others and for ourselves. Gilligan's work challenges the notion that the moral reasoning theories of Piaget and Kohlberg can be related specifically to the theory of cognitive development. It appears that moral motivation and situation specifics may have something to do with moral behavior.

CONCEPT OF ADULT MATURITY

When does an individual become a mature adult? The timing is certainly more than a matter of age because it seems as if some people never become completely mature. On the other hand, some young people seem quite mature in their poise, behavior, and thinking. Considering that individuals develop physically, mentally, socially, emotionally, and morally, it is easy to understand that although some persons are physically developed, they may not be socially or psychologically mature.

Premises of adult maturity

In a general way it can be said that an individual *begins* to achieve adult maturity when he or she assumes the age-related roles and behaviors of an adult and the responsibilities of adulthood. However, achieving adult status involves not only an integration of abilities, skills, and knowledge into a practical func-

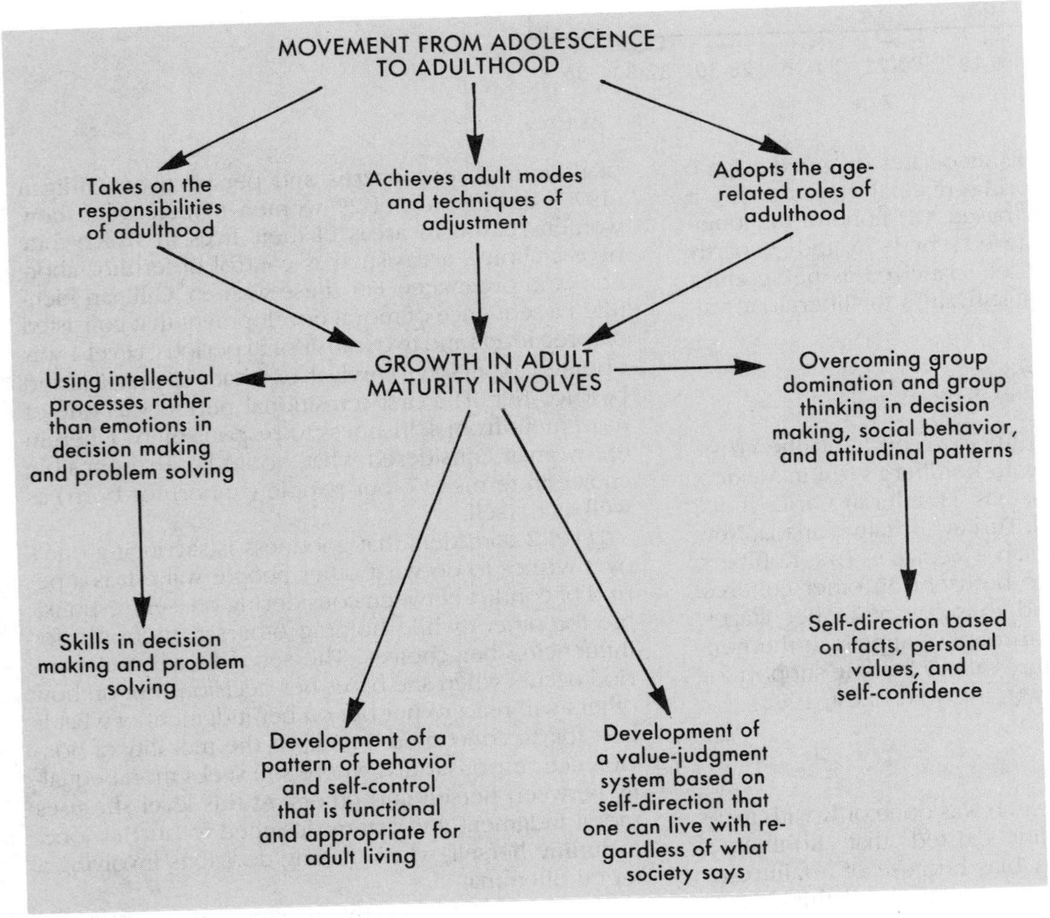

FIG. 12-2 ***Elements of growth in adult maturity.***

tional system but also the acquisition of modes and techniques of adjustment that can be used to cope with conflict situations. An individual may have the required knowledge and skills of adulthood, but if he or she does not know when or how to apply them or cannot function on an adult level of performance because of uncertainties and anxieties, maturity has not been attained. There is a difference between being sophisticated about life and being mature. Maturity has a perspective and judgment capability not found in sophisticates whose verbal ability and social poise are their main claim to competency.

To understand what adult maturity is, it is better to think in terms of elements or premises that reflect the nature of maturity rather than to consider a list of specific forms of behavior. The concept of maturity presented here is more Western than universal in its delineation. Fig. 12-2 summarizes the developmental elements of adult maturity.

The first premise is that mature adults will have learned how to use intellectual processes and to control emotional involvements when it is necessary to make important decisions or when there is a need to do problem solving. To do this, it is necessary to learn decision-making and problem-solving skills. Intellectual competency involves more than mental potential. It includes the learning of cognitive skills and how to use them.

The second premise related to the development of adult maturity is that mature adults have developed a system of internal and external patterns of behavior controls that are functional on and appropriate to the level of adult living. Temper tantrums, impulsive behavior, insensitive behavioral responses, and unreasonable self-seeking behavior are considered inappropriate by most adults. In the life-span perspective, individuals have sought to learn to control their emotions and behavior so they would be acceptable to others ever since they were early adolescents. As adults they should have reached this goal. There are societal age-related expectations in behavior patterns.

The third premise is that mature individuals can make social decisions and choices based on a value-judgment system that will enable them to live acceptably within a chosen social group. This value-judgment system is a personal philosophy of what is important or unimportant, good or bad, desirable or undesirable. It should enable individuals to be self-directed in making choices and decisions that are in keeping with their individuality. They need not choose to be or to live like the others in their social network. However, if they choose to be different, they should be able to live with that choice even if others reject them.

The final premise that relates to personal maturity involves overcoming group domination and groupthink in social behavior patterns and decision-making processes. To be one's own person requires the emotional freedom to be self-directed. The individual who is influenced by what the peer group, media body, or current social fashions say or do is not self-directed. It is one thing to be aware of what others think or believe; it is another thing to let those thoughts be the prime movers in your choice of action. Mature thinkers make their decisions based on what they believe and desire rather than on the notions and actions of others.

Traits of maturity

Mature individuals have perspective regarding their human potential. Their behavior is based on a good balance of intellectual insights and some emotions and imagination. They learn to live with problems they recognize as unsolvable and work to find a solution for those that can be solved. They are open to suggestion but are not overly influenced by others. They learn to profit not only by their own experience but also from the experience of others.

They have some knowledge of social life, love and marriage, and the requirements for living in a society. They take responsibility for their own welfare, do not expect others to make decisions for them, and are willing to work for what they want. Mature adults live partly by intelligent compromise, but at the same time they respect their own individuality. Along with this they accept authority to a point; they know that the first attempt to improve a situation should be through rational discussion.

Mature individuals also take responsibility for their own behavior. They do not blame their background for mistakes they make or use it as an excuse for a shortcoming. They do not evade responsibility or put the blame on someone else.

Mature adults realize the relation of personal gain to personal effort. They are able to endure present discomfort for future gain and satisfaction. Their behavior is based on principles. They do things because they consider them as values and not because someone forces them to do so. Maturity refers to a person's ability and motivation to accept adult rights and obliga-

Free to be, to be me,
Not you, not like, not them.
Free to know, to be known,
Without facade, without demand.
Free to hear, to be heard,
Not to gainsay, not to demean.
Free to have, to behave,
To seek, to search, to find.
Free to love, to be loved,
To touch, to taste, to feel.
Free to be, to become,
To think, to trust, to do.
Free to accept, to be accepted.
Because you are, because I am.

Wallace D. LaBenne
Free

tions in a variety of adult role relationships. Adult responsibility entails attempting to deal with all contingencies as sincerely as possible.

Individuals in this age group, because of the recency of their exposure to the demands and expectations of a formalized learning environment, are probably more receptive to learning than any other age group. However, young adults, especially those who are married, are plagued by numerous distractions that may constitute barriers to the learning process. Some of these are adjusting to marriage, getting ahead on the job, rearing a family, buying a home, and the like. The degree to which these tasks constitute barriers in the educational process depends on the maturity of the learner.

Heath (1965) did a study on maturity that compared definitions of maturity as written by experts and by nonexperts. Definitions of maturity from the writings of 35 expert psychologists were collected. These definitions were based on rich and intimate experiences with a wide range of persons and on the results of general empirical observations. Forty-three nonexpert college male youths were asked to select the most mature person they knew and in 5 to 10 minutes describe that person's most central characteristics. A content analysis was made of both sets of definitions.

Without any pretension of having exhausted available expert definitions or of having used the most rigorous of empirical procedures, the most striking result of the study was the essential similarity of the traits selected both by nonexperts (in 5 to 10 minutes of reflection) and by experts (after years of reflection). Both groups of judges agreed on 8 of the 13 trait categories. In both cases the mature persons emerge as judiciously realistic individuals with a reflective sense of values and an underlying meaning to their life that they maintain with integrity. However, they are not closed to new experience but are open to continued growth. Such persons can adapt to others and can tolerate and control most of the tensions of living. They have a basic human warmth or compassion and respect for their fellow human beings. The experts add that they are integrated, basically accepting of themselves, self-reliant, capable of tender, loving relationships, and creative. The nonexperts say mature persons have wide interests, are happily married, have close family ties, are generous, empathic, and sensitive to others.

MASLOW: HUMAN MOTIVATORS

Abraham Maslow, a leader in the development of humanistic psychology, proposed an interesting way of classifying human motives. Maslow constructed a hierarchy of needs (hierarchy means a graded or ranked series) that ascend from the basic physiological needs required for survival to the most complex psychological motives available to humans. Maslow spoke of deficiency motivation, growth motivation, and human potential. *Human potential* refers to the fundamental tendencies and capacities possessed by human beings that are capable of being maximized and developed into actuality. The potentialities of life are so much greater for humans than for animals. As the Psalmist states, "What is man that Thou art mindful of him? . . . For Thou has made him a little lower than the angels." As human beings approach and achieve their human potential, they become self-actualizers—individuals who are self-motivators in seeking and achieving their own level of capabilities and potentials.

hierarchy of needs Maslow's concept of a series of motivational needs that must be satisfied one by one in the process of development before the adult can achieve self-actualization.

Not all individuals seek to become all that they can be as human beings. People who are motivated only by maintenance or physiological needs possess a *deficiency motivation,* one that does not seek to do much more than strive for survival and safety needs. On the other hand, individuals possessing *growth motivation* are dominated by behavior that strives for higher actualization needs. Emerging adulthood is a crucial time in the life of individuals because it is the time when they consciously or unconsciously make decisions that will influence the direction of their lives for a long period of time to come. If they choose to operate merely on a deficiency motivation level, they just exist. If they strive for growth motivation, they grow!

Hierarchy of needs and values

Human beings have values. They try to reach their total human potential. Animals pretty much have a "horizontal development." Once they have established their systems for survival and response, they seem to be limited in growth of value insight. Some animals, such as our pet cat Paddy, do seem to have some humanlike qualities, but on examination their value system is greatly restricted in scope and depth. Human beings, however, are capable of "vertical development." They learn not only survival values but social values and moral values as well.

Maslow's ***hierarchy of needs*** (1962, 1971) can be translated readily into a hierarchy of values. Table 12-5 combines the hierarchy of Maslow's needs with their values. Together they represent factors that can motivate behavior to higher levels of the human potential.

The level of values and needs closest to survival are the *physiological needs* of food, water, sex, and other biological needs. *Security or safety needs* represent a step-up in values, as manifested in the economic needs of people to make money and collect material possessions. Money-hungry individuals may live most of their lives on this level. Some animals also collect materials, in terms of food, to last them over the winter months. To have some fun and to partake in leisure-time activ-

self-actualization according to Abraham Maslow, the need to develop one's true nature and fulfill one's human potentialities; the human tendency to realize one's full potential in work and love. It develops after the basic needs of food, security, and esteem are met.

ities are also important. It is necessary to re-create the body and spirit.

It is more fun to play with someone, however, so people move up to a category more closely resembling social needs. Belonging to a group, having friends, and being part of an organization have *association values.* Some individuals stress these values more than any others. But people also talk about reputation and "being well thought of" so that on a higher level there are *character values,* which go beyond the individual's need to just be part of a group. An individual could live a whole lifetime on the character value level, and when he or she died, people could say, "There was a good person." Yet that individual may not have made the most of his or her potential as a human being. There is a higher category of values on the intrinsic, cognitive level.

This same person could have made more use of the intellect in a search for truth, *intellectual values,* curiosity, or seeking just for the sake of learning. Even beyond that are the *values of creativity and beauty.* Things that have been created by the hands and minds of human beings are precious, but so are the things of nature that have been created by wondrous ways. The highest intrinsic level to which an individual can aspire is the total being—the level of *universal values* or ***self-actualization*** wherein a person gives of himself or herself in devotion to an ideal beyond the self. On this level personal material needs are transcended for the common welfare.

TABLE 12-5 Maslow: Hierarchy of needs and values

Levels	*Needs and values**	*Characteristics*
Cognitive level "Beyond the self": most advanced	Universal self-actualization needs and values	Devotion to ideals beyond the self; realization of one's potentials
	Aesthetic needs and values	Beauty, creativeness, order and symmetry in nature
	Intellectual needs and values	Cognitive understanding, knowledge, curiosity
Social level "We"	Character and esteem needs and values	Respect, recognition, competency, achievement, worthwhileness
	Association and love needs and values	Friends, belongingness, acceptance, experience of sharing
Biological level "I": most basic	Safety and security needs and values	Shelter, sense of security, material possessions, comfort, leisure time, stimulation, physical well-being
	Physiological needs and values	Food, drink, sex, rest, physical survival

Based on data from Maslow, A.H. *Toward a psychology of being.* (2nd ed.). New York: Van Nostrand Reinhold Co., 1968.
*Needs are motivators because they create a demand for fulfillment. Values are motivators in the sense that they represent a learned incentive and, as such, are deemed important by the individual.

The self-actualized individual, the mature person, according to Maslow, has a realistic orientation, is accepting of self, has spontaneity, is task oriented, has a sense of privacy, independence, appreciativeness, and spirituality, has a sense of identity with humankind, a feeling of intimacy with loved ones, democratic values, philosophical humor, creativeness, and some nonconformity. The box below presents some specifics of the characteristics and behaviors of individuals who attain self-actualization.

All the needs and values on the hierarchy are important; at times some are more important than others. Certainly if people are starving, their physiological needs must be met. What is crucial, however, is which category or which values does an individual tend to emphasize as the person's prime motivator of behavior? Does he or she emphasize the survival values, the social values, or the intrinsic values? What individuals stress will determine their basic philosophy of life and their level of maturity in terms of potential as human beings.

Discussion: Agree or disagree

To keep a proper perspective on life there are five things that people ought to do at least once a year. They should *visit a museum* to see what the creative minds of human beings have been able to produce throughout the years and to note that modern man does not have a claim to an intellect superior to that of ancient man. Cro-Magnon man was also an intellectual giant. Modern individuals should use their creative powers just as the cavemen did. Second, they should *attend a wedding* to see and feel the excitement of a couple saying their vows, sincerely, in anticipation of creating a home and a family unit.

Third, they should *go to a hospital to visit some sick friends* to see the frailty of human beings and their bodies—to be reminded that the physical housing of humans is perishable and destructible and that the individual must take care of it.

Fourth, they should *visit a retirement center or a nursing home* to see more vividly the physical, social, psychological, and economic needs of the elderly and

CHARACTERISTICS OF SELF-ACTUALIZERS

1. Accept themselves and others for what they are
2. Spontaneous and self-directed in thought and behavior
3. Perceive reality efficiently and are able to tolerate uncertainty
4. Problem-centered toward tasks and goals, not ego-centered
5. Have a good sense of humor about self and life in general
6. Able to look at life from an objective viewpoint, but able to be subjective if they have to be
7. Resistant to group influence and domination
8. Capable of deep appreciation of the basic experiences of life and nature
9. Establish deep, satisfying social relations with a few, rather than many, people
10. Concerned for the welfare of humanity
11. Highly creative with fresh thoughts, actions, and ideas

BEHAVIORS LEADING TO SELF-ACTUALIZATION

1. Experience life as a child does, full of wonder, absorption, and concentration
2. Assume responsibility for self and for others if need is there
3. Work hard at whatever you decide to do
4. Try something new rather than sticking to secure and traditional ways
5. Try to identify your defenses and eliminate nonfunctional ones
6. Listen to your own feelings and logic in evaluating experiences rather than to tradition, authority, or the majority
7. Be honest; avoid "game playing"
8. Be prepared to be considered different if your views are not those of most people.

Modified from Maslow, A.H. *Toward a psychology of being* (2nd ed.). New York: Van Nostrand Reinhold Co., 1968.

to become aware of the fact that this age is also part of the life span. What can be done to get ready for that part of life? In the meanwhile, what can we do to help that age group?

Finally, they should *attend a funeral,* at least once a year, to be reminded that this life is limited, that there is an end. This will reinforce a person's awareness that physical things die but that intrinsic values continue to live even after physical death. A proper perspective on life and humanity is needed to encourage human beings to seek the better parts of this earthly existence.

PHASES OF ADULTHOOD

The most commonly designated phases of adulthood are early adulthood, middle adulthood (middle age), and later adulthood. These age levels are rather general and do not present the total picture. For example, a person does not automatically move from early adulthood to middle age on a particular birthday. Even casual observation suggests that people do not age at the same rate. We can also be different ages at the same time, biologically, psychologically, socially, and chronologically. Some writers suggest that there are transitional periods in the life span wherein an individual

Meriem Kaluger

Each individual, in his or her own way, moves in the direction of adulthood. Frequently in emerging adulthood, the prime activity is but a temporary one, although it may be a very searching one. An individual does not stop being an adolescent one day and become an adult the next. The phases of adulthood—as for the life span—allow for transitional stages where the present life-style is examined and either supported, modified, or changed into a different structure.

gradually leaves one phase and moves into the next. Sheehy (1976), in her book *Passages,* makes this transitional phase of adulthood dramatically clear. The reasons for transition and change are sociological, psychological, or physiological in nature. As such, individual differences are definitely involved.

The life course involves many changes. There may be an *inner physical clock* that determines when changes in the structure and functions of the human organism will occur. The term *functional age* is used to refer to aging at different rates in the various physiological functions. In addition to an organic basis for change there may be a cognitive basis for change. Neugarten (1968a) refers to an *inner social clock* that suggests to the individual when age-related milestones are to occur during the adult years. The individual will have a mental expectation of their appearance. This clock also suggests personality characteristics and behavior patterns that can be exhibited at different ages. People tend to set their personal clocks by society's implied age norms and role expectations (Kimmel, 1974). However, at times their expectations may be just vague notions, myths, or stereotypes about what is too young, too old, or just right for the age level (Riley et al., 1972). *Personal age* refers to how an individual relates his or her own experiences to the aging process and to society's age norms.

Factors such as life events and assigned age-role

Robert Maust

developmental trajectories a theoretical progression or line of development over an extended period of time. Some see the development as a hierarchical structure, others as stage or episodes in time.

identities do influence changes in the life course. *Life events* are milestones or occurrences in life that have a major impact on the individual. These include such events as the first major job, marriage, the birth of a child, the purchase of a house, the death of some one close, a career change, and retirement. Cultural and historical events that we live through also leave their mark on us.

Age-role identity is assigned by society. It has the effect of indicating which age group has what responsibilities, prestige, and resources. These age or generation norms have a strong positive or negative influence on the behavior of individuals (Neugarten, 1968b). For example, persons in their fifties and sixties often hesitate to pursue the activities and fashions of those in their twenties and thirties. They have misgivings. They need to know when and if it is proper to act or dress like young adults (Cath, 1975). On the other hand, an older individual is more readily accepted by society in a leadership or management role than a young person. This particular age-role identity has been assigned to older people.

Functional age, personal age, chronological age, life events, age-role identity, and individual differences all suggest the feasibility of transitional periods in the adult life cycle. Levinson (1978) and Gould (1978) provide research and theory to support such a contention.

Levinson: Adult male development

Daniel Levinson and a group of researchers at Yale (1978) have constructed a format to illustrate and define the phases of development in adult males. They did an in-depth interview and analysis of 40 men, ages 35 to 45. Each man was seen 5 to 10 times over a period of 10 to 20 months. The thrust of the analysis was to determine how a life structure evolved for each individual. They also wanted to identify the interrelationships that existed between each person and the environment. Levinson and his associates propose a sequence of five eras, with related periods, that span the male adult life cycle. Each era has its own typical life-style and psychological, physical, and social aspects. While women may follow similar patterns of development, Levinson only focused on the study of men. Four of the five eras are presented in Table 12-6. The fifth era is late late adulthood, ages 80 and over. As can be noted in the table, Levinson, at the time of this study, did not have specific data on the ages over 50.

The major task of adulthood at each phase is to create a stable life structure. This task involves making certain crucial choices and striving to attain particular goals. Periodically it becomes necessary to restructure one's life pattern and style because life events, the growth process, and the aging process demand that changes be made. When a change is in the making, a transition period occurs. The transition periods tend to appear at the significant decade birthdays of 20, 30, 40, 50, and 60 years of age. During each *transition period* there is a need to reappraise the previous life structure and to refine, modify, or create a new structure. More crucial choices, exploration of new possibilities for change, and goal setting are involved. If the appropriate choices and changes are not made, then stagnation instead of renewal will result. The transition period generally lasts 4 to 5 years. During *stable periods* people shape and build their life structures based on the choices they have made. Stable periods generally last 6 to 8 years.

A critique of Levinson's theory would suggest caution in applying the findings too broadly. The theory is based on the initial study of 40 men from four occupational groups: hourly workers, executives, academic biologists, and novelists. This sample does not represent the average man on the street. Levinson did examine the lives of approximately 100 other men by reading their autobiographies. However, this still leaves the population sample suspect. The critics of stage theories in general would also point out such factors as the difficulty in replicating the study, the need to relate adulthood as a process rather than a stage, the observation that relationships between adulthood and environment can vary from time to time because environments also change, and the contention that ***developmental trajectories*** (the paths of growth and development) are modified considerably by the effects of race, sex, generation, and social class (Hall, 1980; Lacy and Hendricks, 1980; Rosenmayr, 1980).

TABLE 12-6 Sequential periods of male adult development

Sequence period	*Characteristics*	*Tasks*
I. Preadulthood		
A. Childhood and adolescence (to ages 17 or 18) B. Emerging adult transition (ages 17-22)	Moving out of preadulthood into adulthood Some financial and emotional independence	1. Terminate adolescent life structure 2. Take the preliminary steps into the adult world 3. Leaving the family
II. Early adulthood		
A. Entering the adult world (ages 22-28)	Novice adult; dealing with career, family, and personal growth needs	1. Explore alternative adult life-styles 2. Establish a temporary, but responsible, stable life structure 3. Launching a career
B. Age 30 transition (ages 28-33)	Crucial stage for providing a strong foundation for future life structure	1. Opportunity to modify the provisional adult life structure created earlier 2. Focus on adjustment and enrichment
C. Settling down (ages 33-40)	Full-fledged adult; deeper commitments to career and family Evolving a dream	1. Pursuit of personal enterprises; "making it" 2. Achieving a measure of independence and authority; becoming one's own person
D. Mid-life transition (ages 40-45)	Period of self reevaluation and redirection or strengthening of "dream"	1. Rediscovery of self, choices, and priorities 2. Resolve the discrepancy between what is and what might be 3. Development of new life constructs
III. Middle adulthood		
A. Entering middle adulthood (ages 45-50) B. Age 50 transition (ages 50-55)	Restructured life pattern provides for restabilization Slight changes in life structure to fit age level	1. Last period for which Levinson has specific data 2. Stability with slight alterations of the life structure from now to retirement
C. Culmination of middle adulthood (ages 55-60) D. Late adult transition (ages 60-65)	A stable period Provides a personal basis for living in late adulthood	
IV. Late adulthood		
Ages 65 and over	(Extension of Levinson) Modification of life structure to meet the demands of retirement and aging	(Extension of Levinson) 1. Adjustment of life in retirement 2. Personal and social adjustment to the aging process

Based on data from Levinson, D.J. *The seasons of a man's life.* New York: Alfred A. Knopf, 1978.

Gould: Studies of men and women

Another major study of adult development is that of Roger Gould (1972, 1978), a psychiatrist who attempted to identify phases of adult life on the basis of a study of attitudes and life histories of 524 patients and nonpatients ages 16 to 60. Gould was primarily concerned with changes and stages in an individual's subjective sense of self or the posturing of self over a period of time. The responses of his seven homogeneous age groups seem to relate to the findings of Levinson.

In the *16 to 18* age group the typical, but somewhat vague, theme that is verbalized is, "We have to get away from our parents." The feeling of being independent at this age is fragile and unsure. As a result the behavior of this group is sometimes characterized by negativism toward parents. Yet the need and desire for a firm footing and acceptance within the family group is still there.

Between *19 and 22* the young people are in a transitional stage between still being dependent on their family and being on their own. They do not feel totally independent yet, but they are getting away from home to some extent. They may be away at college, working at a full-time job, purchasing their own car, or thinking of getting married.

Between the ages of *23 and 28,* individuals are engaged in the work of being adults; they feel like adults. They have established a life-style, have to a large degree become independent of their parents, and are about the business of building for the future. They feel in command of themselves.

The age group of *29 to 34* begins to have some uncertainties and questionings about who they are and where they are going. Some inner sense of identity and direction seems unresolved. They usually feel comfortable and committed to their present lives, but there is an uneasy feeling that things are not all that they want them to be.

The period of *35 to 43* is somewhat of a transitional period. Self-scrutiny and questioning of goals, values, and their lives continue, but now there is an awareness that their time is limited. A sense of time urgency develops. They look back and wonder if they have made the right choices. They look at the present and wonder how to best deal with their growing children. They look ahead and wonder if there is still time to "make it big."

During the *45 to 50* age period, adults become resigned to the reality of limited time and level of accomplishment. Many feel that if they can maintain the status quo of their lives and livelihood, they will be satisfied. These adults appear to be adjusting to the realities and facts of life.

Between *51 and 60* people often undergo a softening and warming of personality style. They become more accepting of themselves and of others. They are more relaxed and contented. As they recognize that life is bound by time and that they too will die, they become less concerned about the past or the future. Many times they reflect on the worthwhileness of the lives they have lived and contemplate their accomplishments.

Gould's study on age-related changes is limited by the nature of his sample and the critique that is made of stage theories in general. However, even the limited findings of Gould and Levinson strongly suggest that personality and life structure continue to change and evolve throughout adulthood. Life changes do not end at adolescence but rather continue indefinitely until old age.

Adult female development

Significant studies of adult female development have not been completed. Yet the changes that have been occurring in the lives of adult women in the decades of the sixties, seventies, and eighties strongly suggest that knowledge of these women is urgent and essential (Targ, 1979). Changing life-styles and patterns from homemaker to working mother or a single career woman, increasing educational, professional, and executive attainments, and a longer life span have outdated much of the previous research and theory.

Levinson's phases for men may not be appropriate for women, especially those who enter the job market or educational studies only after their children have grown. Becoming one's own person may occur at a later age. The timing of Gould's "sense of self" may be different for the women who are in their thirties and who feel the urgency to have a child "before it is too late," as compared to men who begin to take stock of their life status mainly when they are in their forties (Mogul, 1979). The adult experience could, indeed, be quite different for women that it is for men.

MY EXPECTATIONS OF ADULTHOOD

An adult, oh how blissful it will be,
To live life's end in love and harmony.
Forsaking childish selfishness, untruth;
Forgetting the rebelliousness of youth.
Rememb'ring only sweet companionship,
Which stengthened with each hour of fellowship.
And living now for those who mean so much—
Husband, wife, and children, friends and such.
Maturing daily with each new event,
Although it may bring grief and discontent.
And striving to be good in word and deed,
So through life's efforts others might succeed.
Just seeking future happiness each day,
'Til death shall come and snatch this life away.

Sue Manchey

CHAPTER REVIEW

1. *Emerging adulthood* is a transitional period between the development of 17- or 18-year-olds and the individual who has achieved a competent level of emotional, social, and economic independence. This period is characterized by a sense of idealism regarding the nature of adult society that distorts the time reality of the adult world. The *cohort effect* is noted in generational differences.
2. Theories concerning young (emerging) adulthood are few in number. *Erikson* indicates that the adolescent issue of identity versus role confusion must be overcome before adult intimacy can be achieved. *Navighurst* speaks of the developmental tasks that emerging adults must attain. *White* has identified five growth trends of young adults that are related to personal growth, permitting the individual to expand social consciousness and caring. *Wittenberg* suggests metapsychological and socioeconomic factors that distinguish the postadolescent from other age groups.
3. *Developmental tasks* are suggested by Havighurst, White, Erikson, and Levinson. Behavioral guidelines followed in childhood and developing adolescence are not long suitable to guide the judgments of post-adolescents.
4. The physical self is fairly well developed. The intellectual self is ready for formal operations; however, room for improvement is suggested. There are differences between the sexes and other age levels as to the types of mental abilities developed. Social development tends to be characterized by a need to gain emotional independence, but there is more stability and control than in the past. The pursuit of identity continues as the emerging adults find themselves in different, more demanding environments.
5. *Career development* and *career launching* become a major task. The job world of the near future is experiencing many major shifts. *Van Maanen and Schein* present a theory of career development that has an adult life-span perspective and includes an *internal career path* and an *external career path*. Job search, entry into the job field, and first-job dilemmas are experienced as young adults seek to get started in meaningful occupational endeavors. *Career satisfaction* appears to depend on a good fit between the abilities of the individual and the skill demands on the job. About half of all women of employable age are in the work force.
6. The importance of developing *intimacy* as an adult is discussed by Erikson. Ability to have a good interpersonal commitment depends upon having achieved a sense of identity.
7. *Moral development*, as presented by *Kohlberg*, is a development process that places great emphasis on cognitive development in the early stages and increased interaction with social and environmental forces as the individual emerges into adulthood. Cross-cultural studies support the universality of Kohlberg's theory of moral development.
8. *Achieving maturity* in adulthood is a matter of (a) taking on the responsibilities of adulthood, (b) assuming the age-related roles of adulthood, and (c) achieving adult modes and techniques of adjustment. Elements involved in achieving maturity are (a) using intellectual processes and skills in decision making and problem solving, (b) achieving a functional pattern of behavior and impulse control, (c) developing a value judgment system based on self-direction, and (d) overcoming group domination and group think.
9. *Heath* determined that experts and nonexperts agree with each other's *definitions of maturity*. The specific traits of maturity mentioned by both groups relate closely to Maslow's characteristics of self-actualizers. These characteristics include, but are not limited to, being realistic about self and reality, accepting self and others, being open to suggestions and experiences but not influenced by others, taking responsibility for one's behavior, recognizing the relationship between effort and personal gain, establishing satisfying relations with at least a few other people, and having a warm compassion and respect for others.

10. *Maslow* developed a *hierarchy of needs* that serve as *motivators* to behavior in humans. The *basic level* is one of satisfying physiological needs. The *middle level* is one that involves social interactions. The *highest level* is one that makes use of the human qualities of intellect, creativeness, and ability to recognize universal ideals and standards. A commitment to and seeking of these higher levels of behavior suggest that the individual is making use of the human potential and is reaching a high level of *self-actualization*.
11. According to Neugarten there is an *inner social clock* in each of us that influences the timing of structural and functional changes and gives an inner sense of expectation when certain social life events are to occur.
12. Growth in adulthood is uneven, but its level of development can be related to *functional age, personal age, chronological age,* and *age-role identity* and *norms*.
13. *Levinson* and his associates propose a sequence of five eras in adult development. Each era has its unique life-style and aspects. The major task in each era is to create a *stable life structure*. Periodically it becomes necessary to restructure the life pattern and style. At these times a *transitional period* occurs during which a reappraisal of the life structure is conducted and adjustments made. The transition periods tend to appear at decade birthdays.
14. The study by *Gould* of the phases of adulthood is concerned with changes in the individual's subjective sense of self over the adult time span. The adults in the Gould study verbalized many of the actions found in the Levinson study: the seeking of independence from the family; the establishing of a life-style and a career direction; dealing with unresolved directions and sense of identity; looking ahead to the time that is left to "make it big"; the acceptance of reality; and a general acceptance of life as it is.
15. The Levinson study was done on men. Gould's study included men and women. No major research is available on the women of today. Their changing pattern of living has made previous research on women obsolete.

REVIEW QUESTIONS

1. Emerging or young adulthood is a transitional period between adolescence and mature adulthood. What are some of the attitudinal and behavioral characteristics of emerging adults?
2. Look at Table 12–1. Which topics show the greatest difference in attitudes between adolescents and adults? Which topics show the least difference? Which topics indicate that adolescents and adults are mistaken on how they think the other side perceives the problem?
3. What are the three hypotheses that seek to explain generational differences?
4. Make an outline of the four theories of young adulthood. What are the main premises or points of each theorist?
5. Review the developmental tasks of emerging adulthood. There are 11 of them.
6. Consider the developmental self of young adulthood. How close to complete physical maturity is the young adult? What differences are there in intellectual development between this age group and older adults? What are the distinguishing characteristics of social and emotional development? To what degree has identity been developed?
7. Launching a career is a major task for emerging adults. Review the major shifts of the future, the stages of career development, the nature of job search and entry, and the first-job dilemma. What are the special problems of women in the work force? What does the research say about minority workers?
8. Explain Erikson's concept of intimacy. Why is it important?
9. Kohlberg's theory of moral development has three levels and six stages. Review Table 12-4 with the objective of defining or explaining each stage.
10. List the four premises related to defining adult maturity. Discuss each one briefly.
11. What are the steps in Maslow's hierarchy of needs? Why are they considered motivators?
12. Review Maslow's characteristics of self-actualizing people. What do they say to you?
13. Explain Levinson's concept of the phases of adulthood. What happens during transitional periods? What is a period of stability?
14. Take each of Gould's adult stages and give a brief description of the main characteristics of each stage.
15. Do you agree or disagree with the concept that adult female development is different from that of males and that Levinson's studies are not appropriate for women?

THOUGHT QUESTIONS AND ACTIVITIES

1. Conduct a study to determine the kinds of problems and concerns that post-high-school youth have. Where can they turn for information and help?
2. How do you see the future of today's 18- to 21-year-olds as they approach the year 2000? How old will they be? What part will they play in society, technology, information processing, and government? Can we plan for and direct our future somewhat or are we helpless pawns in the chess game of life?
3. What do you want from your job? Do you perceive having more than one career in your life time?

4. Take a good look at the theories of adulthood. You may have to learn more about them. Which theory has the most to offer?
5. Explore career development. Recall the information on cognitive styles presented in Chapter 8. Should college students change their majors to better match their personal styles to college programs and to career settings? How do you "match" the self and the career?
6. Kohlberg's theory of moral development has much to say about cognitive morality in adulthood. Where do you fit on the scale? Surely there must be more to moral consciousness than what Kohlberg says—but what? See Gilligan, C. In a different voice: Women's conceptions of self and of morality, *Harvard Review,* 1977, *47,* 481-517.
7. Maslow's hierarchy of basic needs and values makes interesting reading to most people, as does the concept of maturity. But what exactly does self-actualization mean? Put it into your own words and give some examples of characteristics. What would a behaviorist say about the self-actualization motivation concept?
8. Compare the phases of adulthood as presented by Levinson and Gould. Are there more similarities or differences? What weaknesses would you see? Does Gail Sheehy's *Passages* fit into these conceptual frameworks? Where did she get her data?

FURTHER READINGS

Bolles, R.N. *What color is your parachute? A practical manual for job-hunters and career changers.* Berkeley, Calif.: Ten Speed Press, 1980. A practical and entertaining step-by-step guide to deciding on life goals and finding the work that will help implement them.

Donahue, T.J., & Costar, J.W. Counselor discrimination against young women in career selection. *Journal of Counseling Psychology,* 1977, *24,* 481-486. This title is self-explanatory.

Elkind, D. Growing up faster. *Psychology Today,* 1979, *12*(9), 38; 41-42; 45. According to Elkind there is more pressure today to achieve to a greater degree at an earlier age than was true a generation ago.

Englund, C.L. Using Kohlberg's moral developmental framework in family life education. *Family Relations,* 1980, *29*(1), 7-13. Two strategies are presented for adapting Kohlberg's principles of moral development to marriage and family life courses.

Gilligan, C. New maps of development: New visions of maturity. *American Journal of Orthopsychiatry,* 1982, *52*(2), 199-212. Two modes of moral reasoning are distinguished in male and female children's discussions of moral dilemmas. The representation of these two lines of development yields a new map of moral development that may present an alternative to Kohlberg's theory.

The health consequences of smoking for women: A report of the Surgeon General. Washington, D.C.: U. S. Department of Health, Education and Welfare, 1980. This report includes information on the effects of smoking (citing problems before, during, and after childbirth) and women's increased lung cancer rates, as well as other effects.

Reykowski, J. Social motivation. In M.R. Rosenzweig and L.W. Porter, *Annual Review of Psychology* (Vol. 33), 1982. Palo Alto, Calif.: Annual Reviews, 1982. This article, written by a visiting professor from Poland, reviews the instrumental value of an object (person) and the autonomous value of a social object. Moderate reading difficulty.

CHAPTER 13

EARLY ADULTHOOD

THE DEVELOPING YEARS

MY WEDDING DAY

The hour was late, but falling asleep seemed to be an impossible task. Although my body desperately wished for sleep, my mind refused to submit to this condition. My thoughts seemed to run the entire spectrum of emotions. An anxious thought would be followed by a happy one, which in turn would be followed by one of fear. The reason for this turmoil was that in seven more hours I was to be married!

Since sleep still seemed to be impossible, I began to dwell on these thoughts. First, I attempted to speculate as to what marriage was really like. I tried to imagine what the honeymoon would be like; how it would be to come home from work to a wife; whether we would be able to have children. These were only a few of my thoughts as I mentally tried to encompass the life span of a marriage.

Next my thoughts turned to ones of anxiety. "Was I really ready to get married?" was the foremost one. I began to question myself in relation to this thought. Would I be able to make the transition from being a bachelor to being a married man; could I cope with the responsibilities inherent in marriage; would I resent the loss of my so-called "freedom" that I had heard other married men speak about so often? These were some of the thoughts that raced through my troubled mind. It was with these thoughts that I finally fell asleep.

Again I was awakened. Although I felt as if I had slept only for a few minutes, a glance at my watch showed that three hours had passed. My first thought was "Only four more hours until I'm married!"

I decided to go with my brother and eat breakfast. I thought that having something to do and having someone to talk with would ease the tension that I was starting to feel. However, this proved to be an erroneous assumption on my part. I had little appetite for food and all conversation invariably returned to the subject of my marriage. My brother's attempts to assure me that all men had these last-minute thoughts did little toward alleviating the nervousness that I was feeling. There seemed to be a direct relationship between the passage of time and the intensity of this feeling of nervousness. The closer it came to the hour of eleven, the more nervous I felt!

We returned to my apartment and I started to dress. As I put on my tux, my thoughts took a new and somewhat strange twist. I began to wonder why I had selected this particular woman to be my mate for life. I had dated other girls but had never really considered marriage with any of them. What quality or qualities did this woman possess that made her so different from other women I had known? What was so special about her that I was wanting to change my entire life pattern? She certainly was physically attractive, was interesting to talk with, had a pleasant personality, and was fun to be with. However, I had known other girls who had these same qualities, and I didn't marry any of them. I continued to think along these lines but, try as I did, I couldn't arrive at a concrete solution. My thought process was interrupted by the sound of my brother's voice as he announced it was almost time to leave for the church.

Now I was standing in the sacristy of the chapel. It was now ten minutes before eleven o'clock and the nervousness which began at breakfast had reached a new height. The best man's attempts to ease my tension with some humorous remarks about marriage met with no success. I was again dwelling on the same thoughts that had plagued me since early this morning.

The music started. We left the sacristy and I walked to the center of the chapel. My bride-to-be was walking down the aisle with her father. As I watched her approach, I felt as if a great weight had been lifted from my shoulders. All of the doubts, fears, tensions, and nervousness disappeared. They were replaced by a feeling of happiness and confidence. She arrived at the place where I was standing. I looked at her and she took my arm; as we approached the altar, I had one thought in my mind. I now knew why I had selected this woman to be my wife. I loved her.

IN THIS CHAPTER . . .

You will read about

1 The developmental characteristics of individuals of early adulthood age, with special emphasis on physical and cognitive characteristics and on friendships.
2 The prelude to getting married, why some people do and others don't, what love is, accepting a marriage partner, and how to predict the success of a marriage.
3 Various aspects of being married, such as the personal adjustment needed, sex in marriage, marital problems and crises in marriage, divorce, and the impact of stress on health.
4 The different types of parenting format found in early adulthood, including mothering, fathering, one-parent families, working mothers, and stepparents.
5 The choice to remain single and its implications for adults.

After the transition period of emerging adulthood the developing individual is faced with yet another major task—that of competent, satisfactory integration into adult society and culture. The challenges and responsibilities that must be met and accepted are varied, and the possible hindrance to satisfactory adjustment and development are many. The time has come to be independent, as well as interdependent. The point in time when people become adults cannot be designated in years, but rather as that point when they begin to assume the responsibilities of adulthood and take on the role of adults. For most people this time will be in the early twenties.

One fourth of an individual's life is spent growing up. Three fourths of a person's life is spent in adulthood, growing older. Should we not have more concern than we do with the nature of adulthood and how to enter it, as well as leave it, gracefully and with hope?

Early adulthood, or the period from approximately 20 to 35 or 40 years of age, is a busy and exciting time for most people. In the more complex societies of the world, it is the *expansion* or *growing phase* of adulthood. It is that time of life when adults invest enormous amounts of energy in their work, striving for promotions, positions, and raises. They are also extending their social contacts, widening their circle of friends, and seeking to become part of organized social entities. Most marry, establish homes, and have children. There is forward movement in watching and helping the children grow. A home, a car, a color television set, and a stereo layout become part of the dimensions of a higher standard of living. For the individuals who are striving to get ahead, the road stretches into an indefinite future, a goal beyond dreams. The developing period of adulthood is an ever-growing, ever-expanding time of life. It is beautiful, exciting, and challenging!

DEVELOPMENTAL CHARACTERISTICS

Individuals in early adulthood find themselves confronted with various roles, which include those of workers, consumers, social beings, citizens, taxpayers, and either family persons with children or single persons who choose to pursue a career. They are the ones who must now and for the rest of their lives make decisions, rather than having them made for them.

They are confronted with a number of life-style changes and new experiences. It is in the course of coping with these experiences that people are likely to undergo changes in their personalities. No longer children, men and women of early adulthood must learn to tolerate some frustration and aggravation. They are expected to use logical reasoning and insight in making decisions. The requirements of the adult role not only contribute to changes of personality and modes of adjustment but also to the need for a more mature value-judgment system. Up to the age of 30 years it is not unusual for both men and women to be underdeveloped in some areas of behavior and judgment and, at the same time, show considerable maturity in other areas. With new experiences and new expectations by others, however, development on a more mature level begins to take place.

Developmental tasks of early adulthood

The developmental tasks of early adulthood are varied and many. The social and economic roles of this age-stage are so familiar and so clearly defined that few individuals in early adulthood have any doubt as to the age-related expectations of society. The most common list of developmental tasks and expectations in industrial societies is that indicated by Havighurst (1979). They include the following: (1) courting and selecting a mate, (2) learning to adjust to, and live harmoniously with, a partner (usually in a stable marriage), (3) starting a family and assuming the role of a parent, (4) rearing children and meeting their individual needs, (5) choosing a type and place of residence, learning to manage a home, and assuming household responsibilities, (6) getting started on a career, job, or continuing education, (7) assuming some type of community participation and civic responsibility, and (8) finding a congenial social group and establishing a supportive social network of friends. The developmental tasks will vary for some individuals. Some men and women choose to pursue a career rather than a marriage. Others choose to do both, but on a time schedule which differs from that of most people.

Other tasks that have been suggested are (1) replacing adolescent friendships with more mature relationships that respect individual differences (Vaillant, 1977a), (2) establishing an independent, stable lifestyle (Frenkel-Brunswick, 1970), (3) learning how to combine a marriage and a career if there is a decision

David Strickler

A developmental task of early adulthood is making a firm vocational choice, adapting to the meaningfulness of the work world, and attaining mastery.

to do both (Roper, 1974), (4) making a firm vocational choice, adapting to the meaningfulness of the work world, and attaining mastery (Lowenthal, 1977), (5) establishing priorities in money management (Rogers, 1982), (6) preserving and improving health status (Goleman, 1980), (7) attaining autonomy and a personal identity by establishing oneself as a person distinct from the natal family, especially if the individual is single (Stein, 1976a), (8) redefining values, priorities, and goals in order to modify and improve the life structure (Levinson, 1978b), (9) developing a sense of intimacy and commitment to a few significant others, friends, or a spouse (Erikson, 1970a). White (1975) suggests that the three growth trends in early adulthood are stabilization of identity, humanization of values to social purposes, and the expansion and extension of self in caring for others.

Successful achievement of these tasks will do much to bring about a more satisfying life, not only during early adulthood but in middle and late adulthood as well. It may be that the distant future is not in clear focus for individuals of early adulthood age. Nevertheless, they are planting the seeds that will bear the crops for harvest in their later years.

Personal independence

"To me, independence and responsibility for a person just out of college or just turning 21 means getting out from under parental control and influence and moving into the world of freedom and self-reliance." This opinion typifies the early adult's view of independence and responsibility. Independence is usually demonstrated by early adults moving out of the parents' home and into an apartment to live on their own. They hope to prove to their parents and to themselves that they can accept and handle the responsibilities of living away from home. As our friend said, "I'm supporting myself and, in a sense, going through a dry run for the later responsibilities of marriage and a family." Individuals in early adulthood are formulating goals and probing new areas. This is different from their earlier years of waiting until they "grew up" to achieve any goals in life. Now it is time for them to be what they are to be.

The task of becoming independent and responsible entails attaining emotional independence, social independence, and economic independence. *Emotional independence* is the most important and the most difficult to achieve. The need is to progress from emotional dependence on parents, or others, to relative autonomy while still being able to maintain close emotional ties. The need is to reach a point where, although individuals have strong personal feelings for those close to themselves, they are still able to be emotionally independent enough so that they are not unduly influenced by the emotional responses of despair, displeasure, or disappointment of others around them (Casady, 1976).

There are self-reliant, self-sufficient, and emotionally insufficient people. To be self-reliant rather than the other two is the answer. *Self-sufficient* people draw a circle around themselves and say, "I don't need anybody else—I can take care of my needs." Actually, they are often afraid to let anyone into their bubble for fear of being hurt. *Emotionally insufficient* people say, "I need everybody's love, attention, and support." These people need all kinds of help. *Self-reliant* people say, "I can stand on my own two feet, emotionally, but I'm willing to share my feelings with others and let them become part of me."

The key to emotional independence is the ability to receive, share, and give love, to be interdependent, without becoming overwhelmed and emotionally dominated. The capacity to love someone other than oneself is an integral factor in adult emotional independence. The self-reliant person is such an individual.

Social independence comes more readily because young adults have been working in this direction ever since they were young adolescents. Of course, social independence carries with it responsibilities in civic, political, occupational, educational, religious, social, and community affairs. The essence of social independence is not a "cop-out" or denial of social responsibilities; it is not a matter of "doing my own thing"; rather, it is an assumption of social trust and of self-direction in social thought and decision.

The element of *social trust* entails the extent to which members of a society can count on the individual to make an effort to contribute to the well-being of others by being socially responsible. As someone in our group of young adults said, "I should be able to count on you to drive on your side of the road, to stop at stop signs when I have the right of way, to pay your share of the taxes for our common welfare, and to trust you to control those primitive impulses of yours that would permit you to strike out at me and to steal and to cheat. In return, you should be able to trust me to do my best to act in accordance to those principles that would enable us to live together amicably."

Self-direction implies being free from group domination in establishing or determining a social pattern of living and of thought. Adolescence is a time when the desire for social acceptance is so great that much of what the group says is what the adolescents do or think. At some point individuals must separate themselves from the social and emotional domination of others: "to be my own person." Individuals may subscribe to the views of a group—political, religious, or social in nature—but within that allegiance they should still be able to be selective in the social views, ideals, values, and behaviors they will follow.

Economic independence demands an acceptance of financial responsibility, self-support, and support of family. Knowing the value of money and how to spend it wisely and learning to limit desires to ability to pay are equally important. To be constantly in debt shows poor management and economic immaturity.

Economic independence involves several measures to ensure financial success. *First,* individuals in early adulthood should have at least one marketable or saleable vocational skill they can offer an employer in return for a job that will pay enough to provide for basic needs. *Second,* there should be some type of career plan involving specific training, apprenticeship, or schooling that can lay a foundation for future training and experience. *Third,* some money management knowledge is needed in terms of budget making, clothing management, household expenditures, and repair costs. *Fourth,* some knowledge of credit buying, interest rates, and life insurance would be desirable. Economic independence is more than having a job and being on one's own—it includes the whole concept of economics and money management. It begins with decisions that adolescents make when they decide what courses or programs they want to take in school, what interest areas they develop, and what attitudes they adopt toward work (Scanlon, 1979).

BEING THIRTY IS NOT ALL THAT BAD!

"So you're thirty! Better be careful or you'll start falling apart." "Never trust anyone over thirty." I've heard these comments and many more like them since my thirtieth birthday recently. In fact, in today's youth-oriented society so much ridicule and negative statements seem to be directed toward the thirties that I began to wonder if anything was good about being thirty. While my life-style and personality may not be particularly stimulating to a younger person, I think they offer some definite advantages.

Probably the most advantageous characteristic at this point in my life is a developing sense of autonomy. The recent impact of social and technological changes had imposed such great changes on all of us that it is sometimes difficult to think of oneself as self-governing. However, I feel it's crucial to realize that what one says and does can still make a difference. For me, the years spent in school helped me to develop a sense of competence that, in turn, has helped develop within me a positive self-image.

My personal relationships have been particularly affected by this feeling of autonomy. My older friends reflect my own type of life-style and interests; my newer friends are not always so much like myself. No longer do I feel the need to join the "in" crowd and do the "in" thing. Relationships are now built on more honest levels than on society's current idea of being "with it." I feel more free to be me.

Recently, I find myself in that peculiar position of sometimes being the oldest member of a group. I think, by virtue of my "advanced years," I'm often asked personal opinions and advice regarding all sorts of things. My younger friends' confidence in my viewpoints has actually given me greater self-confidence in decision-making. At one time I would have welcomed someone making difficult decisions for me, but now I usually try to approach problems more maturely: gathering all pertinent information, digesting it, consulting knowledgeable people, and making a decision that seems best for all concerned.

Perhaps decision-making is less difficult because I feel I've gained a clearer sense of myself through the development and awareness of values. When a person has a strong sense of values, the task of choosing from the vast range of alternatives offered today is lighter.

Setting one's values can be a very complicated process since changing times appear to bring about changes in values. I suppose those values taught in early life from parental and religious teaching still affect me; however, I feel more knowledgeable in deciding what's relevant for me today.

Perhaps I can illustrate how changing times and life experiences have affected my position concerning abortion. I was always taught, both at home and in school, that abortion under any circumstance was wrong. This was the unwavering view I held until I recognized the problems of overpopulation, poor quality of life, new permissiveness in sexual attitudes, and so on. Abortion may or may not be the answer to some very complex problems. However, I've also come to realize that abortion and the high regard I place upon human life are incompatible. After attending conferences and meetings regarding the pros and cons of abortion and reading about human development, I've decided that, for me, abortion is still wrong. Nevertheless, I can be understanding of the views of others.

I've mentioned that autonomy and an awareness of values are an important part of my life today. Goals are also very relevant to my daily routine. Life seems more meaningful when arranged around goals—not only long-term goals but simple, everyday goals, such as stating: "Today I'm going to wash windows."

Ideally, the mature individual constantly sets sights on new aims and achievements. This is important since one must be flexible, willing, and able to change in order to exist in our world. Very often change is a refreshing challenge for me. But not always. More than I would like, I opt for the secure in the conflict of stability versus change. Stability and predictability offer a less frustrating, safer way of life. In time I hope to become "vulnerable" to change, as explained by Fromm in *The Revolution of Hope*.

On the whole, my broad goals haven't changed much since first established some time ago. Fortunately, many of them—marriage, family, career—have been realized, and I have confidence to hope for the achievement of the others. It's comforting to dream; it's even more so when I believe I have the abilities and support of others to see dreams become reality.

Along with becoming more sure of my inner self, I've begun to concentrate on maintaining my outer self as well. When friends told me I'd start falling apart at thirty, they were only partially correct. I have noticed some body changes and, consequently, try to take better care of myself through exercise and diet. I'm afraid it's taken thirty years to realize the importance of this!

While I don't always enjoy exercising, I am enjoying other things lately since I've stopped feeling guilty about my inadequacies. Having been raised in a very competitive environment with material rewards the ultimate accomplishment, I constantly strived to compete on the highest level, in sports, in school, and in my work. I've carried this thought with me for a very long time, but, suddenly, last summer, I learned the knack of priorities and self-competition. Having to do two important things adequately always seemed like an impossibility to me until I finally decided that usually one task was more important than the other to my family and me. I did my best work in my first choice and only fulfilled what was necessary for the other. What a relief to let down a little once in a while without feeling I had shortchanged someone!

Just being thirty doesn't automatically make all indecisiveness and insecurities disappear, as this profile might suggest. There are two worries or anxieties which concern me from time to time. They pertain mainly to my family. Our life together is good—so good that I sometimes worry about whether I will be able to cope with difficulty if and when something might go wrong. Besides this, I constantly wonder whether I am doing everything I can to bring greater fulfillment to all of us. I would hope that by trying to move away from my egocentricity and toward a keener perception of my family's feelings, I can be of more help.

I'd be less than honest if I said thirty was the perfect age for me, since I still sometimes reflect and say: "I wish I would have done that." But my concern is really not for the past but for the future. At the moment I am experiencing a great impatience to "get on with things." I'm very anxious to resume my career and, perhaps, start a new phase of my life. However, I also realize giving my small son a good start in life is very much more important. In the meantime I'll use my time to spread the word: "Being thirty is not all that bad!"

Physical characteristics

According to Baltes and Willis (1979), it is important to note several basic themes regarding adult development. First, significant developmental changes do not stop after growth in the adolescent period but continue throughout adulthood. The changes may be either quantitative (change in size, role, or degree) or qualitative (change in characteristic, attribute, or capacity). Second, there is an increasing range of differences among individuals across the life span. In many developmental areas this range is greater in adulthood than in childhood. These differences result, in part, from a wider range of influential life events and a greater diversity of influential environmental factors. Individual differences become progressively greater as individuals age from early adulthood, into midlife, and into the later stages of life.

In early adulthood, men and women are usually excellent physical specimens. They have strength, energy, and endurance. After the middle twenties, when their body growth and functions are fully developed, decline in physical endurance and strength is so gradual to the age of about 50 that changes are barely noticed (Troll, 1977). The changes more readily noted by age 40 are in gross motor speed (such as running), physical prowess, and energy exchange and recovery. Peak physical strength in the striated muscles is achieved between the ages of 23 and 27 (Hershey, 1974). There is a 10% loss of strength between 30 and 60 years of age. Most of the loss occurs in the back and leg muscles. Overall, physical status of early adulthood is best characterized as relatively stable.

Most males reach their full adult height between the ages of 21 and 24. Most women reach their full height between 17 and 21 (Roche and Davila, 1972). The early adults of today tend to be taller than their parents because of better standards of living and health care. Between the ages of 30 and 45, height remains the same; then, it decreases slightly (Tanner, 1978). Weight loss or gain is unpredictable in early adulthood. Much depends on eating and working habits and life-style. Many men, however, do put on weight during the

Meriem Kaluger

Maximum cardiac output reaches a peak between the ages of 20 and 30. Agility, speed, and energy exchange and recovery are high during early adulthood.

5-year period following graduation from college because of lack of attention to food intake.

Maximum cardiac output—the quantity of blood ejected by the heart each minute—reaches a peak between the ages of 20 and 30 and then declines (Hershey, 1974). Hershey also estimates that, for every 10 years or so of adult life, there is an 8% loss in breathing capacity. Fortunately, cardiovascular exercises can help slow down the decline in cardiac output and in the ability of the lungs to allow air to pass into the membranes. Thus sustained moderate exercise is extremely healthful (Scanlon, 1979).

Ninety percent of the people aged 17 to 44 view their health as good or excellent (U. S. Department of Health, Education and Welfare, 1975). Many young adults are never seriously sick or incapacitated. They have far fewer colds and respiratory infections than they did as children. Most have outgrown childhood allergies. Very few have chronic conditions. About half of all acute conditions are respiratory and another 20% are injuries. Women see doctors more frequently than men, usually because of routine checks on the reproductive system. Women also seem to be more sensitive to their bodies than are men (Duffy, 1979).

Good health often reflects the way we live. Smokers are more likely to contract lung cancer and to suffer from heart ailments (Walker, 1977). Drinkers are subject to hepatitis and cirrhosis of the liver (Lieber, 1976). Women who are sexually active and engage in sex frequently with different partners are more susceptible to developing cancer of the cervix (Meisels et al., 1977).

A study by Belloc and Breslow (1972) of 7,000 people, ages 20 to 70, found the following seven health habits to be directly related to their health: (1) eating breakfast, (2) eating regular meals and not snacking, (3) eating moderately and maintaining normal weight, (4) not smoking, (5) drinking alcohol moderately or not at all, (6) exercising moderately, and (7) sleeping 7 to 8 hours a night regularly. The health habits established in adolescence and early adulthood lay the foundation for health in old age.

Cognitive characteristics

Piaget's theory of cognitive development states that the last stage, formal operations, is attained by the age of 16. Some developmental psychologists ask "What happens after the age of 16?"; "What is the nature of adult cognitive development?" According to Piaget (1972), fully mature reasoning is reached with the emergence of formal reasoning. *Formal operations* includes such cognitive processes as the ability (1) to organize and plan an attack on a problem before beginning to work on it, (2) to speculate and differentiate between real and possible options and circumstances, (3) to hypothesize about the explanation for a phenomenon, and (4) to develop a plan of logic for solving a problem and be able to test the plan in an orderly fashion.

Some researchers question if all of these abilities are attained by most individuals before adulthood. Piaget (1972) does imply that the stage of formal operations may not be reached by some individuals until they are closer to age 20. Much depends on the development of an individual's special aptitudes and specific areas of cognitive specialization. Piaget indicates that further studies are needed to determine if special training, such as vocational training or further educational studies, may continue the development of specific cognitive abilities.

Commons and Richards (1978) propose a stage beyond Piaget's formal operations stage of cognitive development to explain what can happen in adulthood. They refer to an additional fifth stage as the Structural Analytic Stage of cognitive development. In the *Structural Analytic Stage* not only are thinkers able to figure out the relationship between initial planning and the end results but they can also make statements about ideational connections between relationships. *Ideation* refers to the process of forming ideas. This ability reflects a much higher level of cognitive functioning because it involves the use of larger sets of elements or concepts.

Arlin (1975) calls this fifth level *the problem-solving stage* of cognitive development, one that focuses on the ability to generate new problematic ideas and to identify errors in approaches to solving problems. This ability emphasizes the generation of questions, issues, conflicts, and problems; it is the most mature stage of adult thought.

The point to be made here is that researchers are strongly suggesting that the development of cognitive ability does not need to stop with Piaget's formal operations. Rather, the ability to do abstract reasoning can be developed to more mature, functional levels of cognitive processing in adulthood. On the other hand, it is also true that some individuals do not attain higher levels of cognitive development because they do not learn the necessary mental skills and processes to do better reasoning; they may choose not to operate on higher levels of mental functioning. Our own work (Kaluger, 1972) with college seniors suggested that many young adults of age 20 could not do formal operations on a high level simply because they had never learned the basic mechanics and skills of formal logic, as taught through the use of syllogisms and fallacies in philosophy classes. Learning these skills made a remarkable difference in improving the students' problem-solving ability.

Lehman (1966) provided information regarding the sciences, medicine, philosophy, arts, practical invention, and other areas. He found that within fields of endeavor the maximum production rate for quality work occurred during the age decade of 35 to 45 years. The rate of creative production did not decline rapidly after the peak years, however. It was gradual at most ages—more gradual for lesser quality products than for higher quality products. Lehman's study showed that creativity varied within different fields of endeavor. For instance, in the study of philosophy the peak age of quality production was from age 60 to 64 years; the highest quality productions in science occurred from 35 to 40 years; for athletes it was 29 years; for soldiers and explorers it was 47 years; for historians, judges, and naturalists it was 54 years; and the overall peak was at 38 years of age. The use of fine motor coordination improves gradually to the early fifties, and mental and spiritual insights increase to about the age of 65 years. However, top speed is at about the age of 30 years, and top energy usage is at about the age of 35 to 38 years. Fig. 13-1 illustrates the development of

self-disclosure the voluntary disclosure of our deeper thoughts or feelings to others.

cognitive growth and achievement according to ages. The bottom line indicates that performance does not always match the potential.

Friendships in early adulthood

We are aware of others and would like others in some way to be aware of us. We need to reach out to others in friendship and have them reach out to us. People are important to most of us. A relationship that reflects *friendship* is one characterized by positive attitudes of each person toward the other and a tendency to interact freely. Liking can turn casual, impersonal encounters into friendships. Adolescents frequently want many friends as an index of popularity. With the maturity of early adulthood, individuals become more selective, narrowing the number of friendships by preferring quality of friendship over quantity. Once formed, close friendships in adulthood can endure for a lifetime even when friends live far apart and only rarely have direct contact (Hess, 1972). Friendships can survive on warm thoughts and pleasant memories.

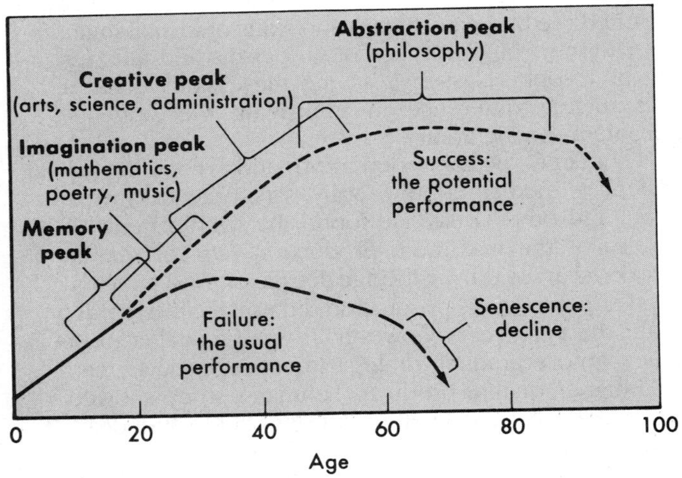

FIG. 13-1 ***Cognitive growth and ages of achievement. Potential and actual performance. The upper lines indicate the psychological potentials of normal people with peak periods for various activities; the lower lines indicate how most people fail to measure up.***

Modified from Still, J.W. Man's potential and his performance. *Copyright 1957 by the New York Times Co. Printed by permission. Also from Lehman, H.C.* Journal of Genetic Psychology, *1966,* 108, *263-277.*

Levinger and Snock (1972) suggest three stages of involvement in the development of close friendships. *First,* there is unilateral awareness, where one person becomes aware of another and makes a social value judgment based on an impression. In the *second* stage there is surface contact, an interaction that is in keeping with the social norms and standards of meeting and greeting other people. Proximity of work space or living area is an important factor in surface contact because it usually results in invitations and social sharing of activities. Similarity of attitudes, socioeconomic class, race, ethnic group, and age are also strong factors in the development of friendship patterns (Schneider, 1976).

The *third* stage, according to Levinger and Snock, is one of mutuality. At this level, a sense of commitment develops and private norms for the regulation of the relationship emerge. ***Self-disclosure,*** the revelation of personal information, takes place and helps to develop an intimate relationship. Proximity and similarity provide the opportunity for a relationship to develop, but personal attributes of sincerity, honesty, and sympathy are necessary for the relationship to proceed to the emergence of self-disclosure in stage three.

Self-disclosure is critical to the development of close ties. Women tend to be more self-disclosing than men (Troll and Smith, 1976). However, there is an optimal level of self-disclosure and intimacy for any responsive interaction. A person who never discloses will not be able to have a close, meaningful relationship. A person who overdoes it by disclosing everything to anyone who will listen is viewed as excessively self-centered or too open. Ideally, one should disclose only a moderate amount of personal information to most acquaintances and reveal a lot to only a very few close friends. Women tend to develop more close friendships than men (Troll and Smith, 1976). By the late thirties or early forties, most adults report that they have three or four friends to whom they feel very close (Haan and Day, 1974). The number of close friends may decrease as they get older.

GETTING MARRIED

Vast social changes have been taking place in American and Western society. The change from rural to urban society, the economic emancipation of women, the increased secularization of social life, the resulting decline in religious sanctions, the individual approach to mate selection and marital expectations have all had their impact on the nature of family life. It is axiomatic that whenever social systems of any type go through change, instability of some type will result. Many professionals see the current status of family life as one phase in the process of social change. The alleged changes in family and marriage are viewed as stemming from the fact that whereas the traditional basis of family has apparently been weakened, a new basis for family living has not yet fully emerged. In the meanwhile, young couples will continue to fall in love, some will marry and some will not, and children will be conceived in either case. Some couples will be happy with their situation; others will not.

The why and wherefore of marriage

Mating is an inborn drive in man, but marriage is a formal institution. Every historical period had its share of common-law marriages, trial marriages, cohabitation or people just living together because "there's no hard, fast commitment that way." Yet the interesting observation is that throughout recorded history, regardless of the sophistication or the simplicity of the society, the family has always been the basic biological and social unit with some aspect of the institution of marriage (Glick, 1979a).

Society can absorb a goodly number of couples who live together without the benefit of "a piece of paper indicating marriage." However, when the number of marriageless couples reaches a saturation point, the social fabric of society's structure will alter. Not only will the elements of social stability deteriorate but so will the pattern of record keeping, on which complex societies depend heavily. Obtaining a marriage license is a systematic method by which a government can keep track of the status of its adults and give legal sanction to the union.

One of the considerations in instituting the custom of marriage was probably the desire to enjoy the sex drive as fully as possible with a minimum of hazards and anxieties. The natural sexual impulses of men and women and the aim of procreation needed to be satisfied, and yet some responsible control over it was also necessary. The man and the woman involved had to be protected, and security needed to be provided (Clayton, 1975). Historically, general promiscuity has been discredited in all types of societies in favor of the stability and security of family life.

More important, family living provides for the nurture and care of the young child. Two parents are important for the proper rearing of the human infant. The child remains helpless for a much longer period than do the offspring of animals. Experience indicates that the emotional needs for growth and development of the child, as well as the physical needs, are best fulfilled by two parents through the stability afforded by the institution of marriage.

Erikson (1963b) considers the establishment of intimacy to be a basic task of early adulthood. This is usually accomplished by adults who create an interpersonal relationship, who socially sanction this relationship with marriage, and who allow reproduction to occur (Hultsch and Deutsch, 1981). There is often social pressure for individuals of early adulthood age to form a close, stable interpersonal relationship.

Doherty and Jacobson (1982) summarize the trends in the marriage and the family as follows:

1. The contemporary family is characterized by a greater emphasis on intimacy, emotional support, companionship, and personal satisfaction than has been found in the traditional institutional form of marriage (Gadlin, 1977).
2. Cohabitation, despite a noticeable increase in the under-25 category since 1970, typically serves as a temporary arrangement, ending within a couple of years either in marriage or in a breakup; marriage continues to be a nearly universal custom (Macklin, 1978).
3. The marriage rate is close to 92% in spite of an increase in life-long singleness among adults (Glick, 1979a).
4. Of the married couples, over 90% will bear children, although there are signs of a small increase in voluntary childlessness (U.S. Bureau of Census, 1979b).
5. A lower fertility rate coupled with a higher life expectancy has extended by 14 years the period of time that a couple will spend without children at home (Glick, 1979b).
6. Divorce rates have been on the increase since 1970, with the greatest incidence in the under-25 age-group but with a great percentage increase in the 25- to 39-year age-group; single parenthood

Meriem Kaluger

Meriem Kaluger

Marriage customs differ around the world. We came across this scene in the highlands of New Guinea. The man with the feathers walked 18 miles to a neighboring community to bargain for a bride for his son. The cost of the bride was 12 birds of paradise tail feathers (highly prized), 17 pigs (pigs are wealth), and 1,000 Kina (about 1300 American dollars) shown on the round money tree. If after a year the bride (wife) is satisfactory, some of the pigs are returned to the man. Later, we saw the bridal party. The bride wore a white cap.

roles, especially for females, is increasingly common (U.S. Bureau of Census, 1979a).
7. The dual-earner couple is becoming an increasingly typical marital pattern (U.S. Bureau of Census, 1979b).

Reasons for marriage. Over 92% of all Americans will be married at least once before they die. The reasons why people marry are many—love, economic security, desire for a home and children, emotional security, parents' wishes, escape from loneliness or from a parental home situation, money, companionship, sexual attraction, protection, notoriety, social position and prestige, gratitude, pity, spite, adventure, and common interests (Bowman, 1970). The law indirectly plays a part in marriage. The individual is not forced by law to marry, but in order to enjoy certain advantages and privileges the person must do so.

A socially induced reason for marriage is conformity. Single persons find themselves different because the majority are married (Spence and Lonner, 1978). A married couple may tend to play matchmaker for the individual still single by arranging dates or even inviting two "singles" for dinner.

The individual may marry for satisfaction of ego needs (Goldin, 1977). To be wanted more than anyone else and to be of value to the other person are important needs for some people. Ego satisfaction plays an important role throughout the individual's entire life, and marriage is one way of achieving this. In general, marriage provides for security, recognition, response, and new experiences. These factors are basic to the emotional needs of human beings.

Marriage and college. Until World War II marriage was generally delayed until education was completed. Before World War II many colleges and universities actually reacted negatively toward students who married while in school, but with the return in the late 1940s of tens of thousands of veterans who attended schools all over the United States on the GI Bill, the married student ceased to be a statistical rarity. Indeed low-rent housing units for the veteran and his family were quickly provided by the hundreds on campuses. The schools also tried to provide part-time jobs for student husbands and wives. Today one in five undergraduates attending American colleges is married and living with a spouse (U.S. Bureau of the Census, 1972), and more than half of the graduate students are married.

Perhaps the central reason for this large percentage of student marriage is the increasing stress associated with the contemporary American mass society. Among the present generation of young people (more than one half of the population is under 25 years) the need to belong which translated means the need for emotional support and security, for companionship, for love, and for a paired relation, has become more pressing and significant in the context of an impersonal and materialist society. Marriage is the primary institution in our society that can reliably and satisfactorily fulfill this need.

cohabitation living together and maintaining a sexual relationship without being legally married.

Cohabitation, however, appears to be practiced in increasing numbers in college communities (Stinnett and Walters, 1977). There are some disadvantages to marrying while attending school. The husband, for example, who both works and attends classes knows that if he falls behind on his job, he may be fired: if he does not keep up his grades, he may flunk out for the rest of his life. On the other hand, if his wife works to support him and any children they may have, he may feel guilty or ashamed at not fulfilling what he considers to be the traditional breadwinning role of the husband. At the same time the working wife may resent the time her student husband devotes in the evenings and on weekends to his studies and may regret that she, too, cannot experience the social and intellectual stimulation of student life.

Cohabitation practices also have their limitations. The impact in this case is not so much economic inasmuch as both members generally contribute to their mutual support. The sting comes in social and emotional matters. Regardless of the rationale given by the couple for living together—such as a sense of personal freedom, honesty and openness in a relationship, rejection of marriage for the time being, and sexual equality—strong emotional attachments usually develop and the couples move into a deep level of intimacy on all fronts, not just the sexual front (Thoman, 1974). The need for personal commitments frequently appears and, if not honored, jealousy and possessiveness may enter the picture. Marriage at some future time is usually planned, but in many cases it never materializes (Macklin, 1973).

Meaning of love

Love is more than just an emotional, physical, or sexual expression of intimacy, yet a definitive meaning

"THE TWO OF US"

Donna and I had been engaged about half a year when we decided to live together for a week. We left for college a week early during the summer before my senior year.

We moved into my apartment on a Saturday morning, so we actually had nine days until classes started. The first day was set aside to get everything in some sort of order and to do general cleaning. Our thoughts seemed to be centered on the idea of how wonderful it would be if we were married and this was our first apartment together.

The freedom we had enjoyed the three previous years at college seemed so much sweeter after a summer of being at home under "parental guidance." We were filled with the excitement of returning to this freedom, and especially so because we returned with each other.

During our stay together, we realized how much we didn't know about each other—spiritually, emotionally, physically, and socially. For example, we quickly learned that each other's early morning grumpiness was short-lived and, in a way, humorous. I began to understand why a girl has to start getting ready for a date an hour before her date. Donna in turn was amazed at how I could get ready in the span of five minutes.

Helping each other with everyday routine such as vacuuming and cooking was so much more enjoyable than ever before. Washing the car and shopping also took on added meaning since it was for and by us.

We found our ideas on sex, and the human body in general, to be different. We both felt sex was an expression of love and should be given and received as such. This view had not been Donna's original outlook, but through sincere talks and openness she gradually took on my viewpoint. I come from an extremely uninhibited family. My parents had literature for us children on birth and conception and would answer any of our questions honestly. We were taught that there was nothing sinful about the human body. It was not an uncommon event to see one another nude while dressing or going to or from the bathroom. We would often skinny-dip in the pool before going to bed.

Donna's background was very inhibited, and her sexual knowledge came entirely from a sex education class and her peers. Her parents viewed sex as dirty and sinful and they never talked to her about it.

Our first sexual relations was enjoyable even though she was scared. She thought it was wonderful because we viewed sex as a shared expression of love. We now feel that the best and only way to deal with sex is openly and honestly.

Through our experiences we learned many things, but perhaps the most important thing was that love is sharing—total sharing of mind, body, and soul into a beautiful relationship.

of love is a difficult item to come by, since each source that speaks of love has its own definition. However, one definition which seems to have widespread appeal is that taken from the New Testament of the Bible, I Corinthians 13:4-8, which reads, "Love is patient, it is kind; love does not envy, it is not pretentious nor puffed up; love is not ambitious, nor is it self-seeking; love is not provoked; thinks no evil and does not rejoice over wickedness, but rejoices with the truth; it bears with all things, believes all things, hopes all things, and endures all things. Love never fails, whereas prophecies will disappear, and tongues will cease, and knowledge will be destroyed." From this definition comes the meaning of love that lasts through times of frustration and achievement, sadness and joy, youth and maturity.

Love, then, is a quality that may defy exact definition, but it can mend strained relationships and reestablish lines of communication between partners when they have been cut off. In her study of 52 married couples over a 10-year period beginning in undergraduate years, Rachel Cox (1970) found that, except for a very few, the strength and satisfaction of the marriage tie increased as the years went by. She asked her subjects to grade various aspects of love as listed on a rating scale. In analyzing the answers, she found that a hopeful, supportive, and essentially uncritical love characterized 33 of the 52 marriages. In 18 marriages love was such that the spouses were objective about the flaws in the other spouse and in their marriage. Love was found to be a needed element in exploring the reaches of another personality and redefining one's own emerging self in relation to the expectations and needs of that other personality.

David Strickler

When your cup is full,
Spill some wine into the wind;
For in a thousand songs,
It will return to you.

And when your cup is empty,
Just lift it up and sing;
And it will fill itself slowly
With the wine that someone spills,
Into the wind.

Author Unknown

Neiswender and colleagues (1975) looked at the quality of love in adulthood and made the following observations. First, men and women do not experience love differently. Men are not more physical in their feelings and women are not more emotional. Second, married love is not necessarily more realistic, less idealistic, or more mature than unmarried love. It can change its degree of responsiveness. Third, while people of different ages do experience love somewhat differently, older people love just as much, and as deeply, as younger ones do. These same researchers identified six types of love: (1) affective—an emotional response, (2) cognitive—intellectual admiration, (3) physical—sexuality, (4) verbal—communication, (5) behavioral—enjoyment of working/living together, and (6) fantasy—a perceived relationship for the future.

People "fall in love" for different reasons. Some fall in love for physical reasons—for physical attraction and sexual response. Others fall in love for social rea-

propinquity theory the tendency for people who live near each other to become acquainted with, and attracted to, each other.

sons—"It is the thing to do." Among some adolescents, "You're nobody unless you've got a boyfriend (girlfriend) and going steady." An older man, having completed an enlistment term in the Armed Forces or returning to college from a job, often finds himself quickly married simply because he publicly expressed the idea that "Well, I'm older now; it's time for me to settle down." Some people fall in love for emotional reasons. It is a tremendous feeling to have "someone who understands me" or to think "she (he) needs me." To want and to be wanted, and to have emotional needs satisfied is truly a good feeling but hardly enough of a basis for a lifetime relationship.

There is infatuation, artificial love, romantic love, and mature love. *Infatuation* is exciting and tingling, but it is shallow because the individual is responding to what he or she is getting out of the relationship. "It's real love—she (he) loves *me*!" *Artificial love* stems from motives, often not even associated with love. Some individuals marry to escape from an unhappy parental relationship or home or from intense feelings of loneliness. Some marry so that they can find meaning in life by living through the accomplishments of their marital partner. Others marry for possessions, a change of scenery, the opportunity to travel to a distant place, or for money. These reasons for marrying are often based on artificial love.

Romantic love is storybook love: "Love means never having to say you're sorry." This kind of love carries with it immature beliefs such as the idea of the one and only, love at first sight, and the thought that love can solve all problems. Romantic love has its place. Some people experience this type of love several times in their lives before marrying. It can serve as a binding or cementing force to help a young couple through their first months, when adjustments are being made toward a more mature outlook on married life (Kephart, 1977).

Mature love emerges out of human interaction. It comes about through the process of adjustment and readjustment of the personalities of two people who have a great regard for each other as total personalities and have a desire to do all that they can to make the other person's life meaningful and happy. An individual who is ready for marriage (1) likes the one who is loved, (2) is not merely in love with the idea of love, and (3) is emotionally mature to the point of surviving an adjustment period while still maintaining a high regard for the other person.

Love, like a diamond, has many sides or facets to it to make it sparkle. If you experience only one or two facets of the diamond, you may miss a serious flaw in one of its other sides. You could be purchasing a worthless diamond. The same is true with love. You must look at all the different aspects of love before you can be sure you have a solid love. Unlike a diamond, however, love can grow if it does not have any serious defects.

Accepting a marriage partner

Studies of marriage for the past generation have tended to emphasize reasons for mate selection as the principal basis for explaining happy or unhappy outcomes. However, explaining what John sees in Mary or why they chose to marry each other can be complex indeed. Their reasons for selecting their mate will vary greatly. In any society, however, there are factors that generally affect and partially explain who marries whom. Certainly laws, religion, age, class, and race are factors that influence the choice of mates.

There are several influential reasons and theories why certain people come together. *First,* considerable study has centered around the ***propinquity theory*** as a major factor in mate choice. Propinquity means nearness or in close proximity. People who usually meet each other in some form of close association such as at work, school, neighborhood, church, or leisure-time activity tend to gravitate together because of familiarity (Rubin, 1973). A positive reaction to this association can become very meaningful. A *second* theory is related to the *"ideal mate" concept,* with traits and characteristics an individual would like to see in a marriage partner. "She's everything I've ever wanted." A person with this approach can usually make a list of desirable qualities in a husband or wife. This theory is close to the value theory, which holds that each person possesses a value system that consciously or unconsciously guides the mate selection (Grush and Yehl, 1979).

Third, the theory of *complementary needs* states that people are attracted to others who have the characteristics they have always wished they had themselves or who can help them to be the person that they need and want to be. Wish fulfillment is the motive for marriage. In people with deep psychological needs opposites do tend to attract, thus complementing the self. Research, however, does not support this theory (Centers, 1975).

Fourth, a widely recognized theory of why certain persons are chosen as marriage partners is the ***homogamy theory.*** In general, couples respond readily to each other if they have similar economic, racial, and social characteristics. Even the divorced and widowed tend to marry their kind (Melville, 1977).

homogamy theory the tendency for people who are similar in attitudes, social class, and other dimensions to marry each other; marriage between people who have similar personal characteristics.

The *last theory* is that of *compatibility,* which in all of its forms does much to bring couples together. Couples who can enjoy a variety of activities together and can communicate, understand, and accept each other because they share a common feeling or philosophy respond to each other deeply. They are compatible. It might be desirable to have complementary emotional needs patterns so that a couple can support and strengthen each other, but it would be just as important to have a supplementary or a common interest pattern in some aspects of their lives so that they can share wonderful experiences together (Murstein, 1973).

Love is a useful criterion in choosing a marriage partner. However, a more thorough, mutual understanding of the individuals involved is needed to discover the cause-and-effect relationships of why they chose each other.

Predictors of marital success

Although love is needed in marriage, it is not the sole requirement. Studies have been made to determine the ingredients of a successful marriage. The studies take on a specific pertinence in view of the increased divorce rate in society today. Unfortunately, there are so many variables involved and the personalities of individuals are so varied that it is difficult to make predictions for individual couples. However, suggestions related to success can be made for the group as a whole. Table 13-1 is a composite of factors in marital happiness with data supported by several studies.

A classical comprehensive study in the field of marriage was conducted by Stanford psychologist L. M. Terman and his associates (Sears, 1977). In their project they tested and interviewed several thousand subjects and followed their progress. From the analysis of their data some surprising conclusions were drawn. It was found that the most important predictor of a happy marriage was the happiness of the parents in their marriage. Other factors were happiness during childhood and firm and consistent discipline during childhood.

In another area Terman found that adequacy of sex instruction, the amount of "petting" before marriage, the use of contraceptives, varieties and types of sexual techniques, and differences between how often intercourse is desired and the actual number of times it occurs had little or no relationship to marital happiness. Terman determined that marital happiness was more dependent as a whole on family background than on sexual factors. He concluded that a large proportion of incompatible marriages are caused by a predisposition to unhappiness in one or the other spouse. The key is the type of attitude toward life and marriage that each partner has (Goodrich, et al., 1973). An embittered pessimistic one has a poor prognosis.

Barry (1970) did a review on factors related to a successful marriage. Some of the predictors of happiness in marriage that he found were (1) possession of positive personality traits such as an optimistic temperament, emotional balance, and sympathetic attitude, (2) similarity of cultural backgrounds, (3) a socially responsive personality, (4) a harmonious family environment, (5) compatible religious observations, (6) satisfying occupation and working conditions, (7) a love relationship growing out of companionship rather than infatuation, and (8) a wholesome growth of attitudes toward sex relations. In general, the most important factors are the social environment within the marriage, the personality factors of the people involved, and the patterns and processes of family interaction. The success factors are always relative to the values held by the individuals and the society to which they respond.

Ultimately, the success of a marriage depends on the capacity of the man and woman to make it successful. This capacity involves personal values, personality traits, social characteristics, and ability to adapt, adjust, and change (Stinnett and Walters, 1977). The key factors are self-insight, self-acceptance, awareness of the needs of one's partner, and the ability to cope, understand, and accept. Expectations are also crucial, since they give the individuals a point of view that will affect their behavior. In addition, consider these detrimental factors to happiness: intense personal problems, incongruity of main personality traits, inability to meet growing obligations, and poor outlook on life. They all reflect some inadequacy in personality maturity.

It is important that the couple learn communicative as well as interpersonal social skills. How do you get along with others, living in a highly personal, close, intimate relationship? The skills required for prolonged, close living are somewhat different from those required for neighborly, occasional social contacts. The success of a marriage will depend largely on the psychological, emotional, and social readiness of the couple, individually and as a pair, to meet the demands of married living.

Age is an important predictor of the success of a marriage. Most individuals under the age of 20 are not experienced or mature enough to handle the additional adjustment demands of a teenage marriage. For one thing most late adolescents have not had enough time to grow in the ways of the world outside the family home or in an educational setting (Otto, 1979). Their contacts with people of different ages—employers, coworkers, authority figures, and strangers—in the arena of life have been limited. Young people have not had enough time simply to live and learn about themselves. Time is needed before a solid self-identity can be put together. An identity is needed before a long-term satisfying intimacy can be established. A crucial note: half of all divorces occur in couples who were married before the age of 20 (Kieren et al., 1975).

In addition, covert as well as overt personality and social characteristics are important. A predisposition to unhappiness or pessimism in one or both spouses can

TABLE 13-1 Factors in marital happiness

	Favorable	*Unfavorable*
Premarital factors		
1. Happiness of parents' marriage (high)	X	
a. Parents divorced		X
b. Parent or parents deceased		X
2. Personal happiness in childhood	X	
3. Ease of premarital contact with the opposite sex	X	
4. Mild but firm discipline by parents	X	
5. Lack of conflict with parents	X	
6. Courtship		
a. Acquainted under 1 year		X
b. Acquainted over 1 year	X	
c. Approval of parents	X	
d. Similarity of age	X	
e. Satisfaction with affection of other	X	

	Favorable	*Unfavorable*
7. Reason for marriage		
a. Love	X	
b. Loneliness		X
c. Escape from one's own family		X
d. Common interests	X	
Postmarital factors		
1. Attitudes		
a. Husband more dominant		X
b. Pair equalitarian	X	
c. Wife more dominant		X
d. Jealous of spouse		X
e. Feels superior to spouse		X
f. Feels more intelligent than spouse		X
2. Good relationships with in-laws	X	
3. Not living with in-laws	X	
4. Community of interest	X	
5. Desire for children	X	

Based on data from Kirkpatrick, 1955; Campbell, 1975; Sears, 1977; Snyder, 1979; Schultz, 1980; Markman, 1981.

lead to unhappiness. No one appreciates or likes to live with a "Gloomy Gus." An optimistic point of view on life in general is desirable. It is interesting to know that all couples, happy and unhappy, have about the same number of grievances and problems in daily living. It turns out that the unhappy couples are the ones who are bothered by them more; they complain longer and more bitterly.

As Tavris and Jayaratne (1976) express it: "Couples who have the best relationships do admit to hacking over problems and worries and disagreeing with one another—but they disagree more or less agreeably" (p. 92). They also conclude that a large majority of wives in their study felt that responsible love, respect, and friendship were the most important elements in their relationship (78%, 74%, and 61%). Sexual compatibility was rated fourth at 34%; however, 2% said sexual compatibility was desirable but not essential.

It would also be helpful socially if the couple enjoy some leisure-time activities together and hold some values in common. It is important for the husband and wife to be friends and companions to each other as well as lovers. Companionship has been singled out as being the primary basis for marital satisfaction (Hawkins, 1970). It encompasses love, esteem, acceptance, insight, and enjoyment of the other individual, receiving as well as giving. It focuses primarily on the affectional relationship of a man and woman, a husband and a wife.

BEING MARRIED

Getting married may seem like a major task, especially to the person who has not found a marriage partner as yet. However, being comfortable in a marriage also requires an effort. There is an adjustment period

Meriem Kaluger

In most cultures, women take the lead in food preparation. The woman in the jungles of New Guinea is preparing a gruel made from the battered pulp of the sago tree.

Meriem Kaluger

Because of a lack of refrigeration, vegetables and other foods are bought daily in the northern territories above Kowloon.

to go through in which two people learn to live as a couple. Then there is the never-ending task of working with the problems, decisions, and unexpected circumstances that always seem to occur. Do not despair. Life is made up of changes, challenges, and choices. That is what it is all about. Meeting these situations as an individual and as a couple is what makes life interesting and exciting, if you let yourself see it that way.

Developmental tasks of newlyweds

Marriage is a developmental process. The conditions of the marriage become modified as people change and adjust to life's situations. A marriage keeps changing as each partner changes; a successful marriage comes about where a potential exists for continued development and adaptation. Adjustment and attainment of the developmental tasks in early married life will do much to bring about desirable adult development and to lay the groundwork for success and happiness in marriage.

Very early in marriage the couple will need to (1) learn to live as a couple instead of singles, (2) work toward integrating their personality traits and styles of living, (3) achieve a satisfying sexual relationship and understanding, (4) become aware of acceptance of the realities of married life, and (5) evolve a marriage development plan that will bring to the couple their desired short-term and long-term goals in life (Kenkel, 1977). Some of the developmental strivings to be accomplished before the first child is born are (1) developing competency in decision making, (2) getting and spending the family income, (3) learning to accept and communicate each other's feelings, (4) developing an attitudinal, as well as material, readiness

This Indonesian housewife prepares a meal on an earthen oven in a two-room straw hut.

for parenthood, (5) learning social skills and increasing socialization as a couple instead of singles, (6) developing a pattern of cooperation and understanding that permits them to overcome adjustment problems with less friction, and (7) working out routine schedules and chore tasks around the house (Kenkel, 1977).

To get along with one's mate it is sometimes necessary to change pet habits and develop new ways of doing things. Although people should not expect to be made to change after marriage, both partners should be reasonable and considerate. Certainly no expectations of major change should be anticipated. The girl who says, "But I know he will not want to do that after we're married" may well be fooling herself and doing wishful thinking. Even simple behavior patterns and habits can be problems that require adjustment—how late one is used to staying up at night, whether one likes to shower in the morning or evening, being accustomed to eating at 5:30 instead of 6:30 PM, sleeping with a window open, finding it hard to give up the personal privacy of a bathroom, learning how to accept relatives who are overwhelming.

Middlebrook (1974) offers some interesting guidelines—elaborated on here—for maintaining good personal adjustment and for building a happy marriage:

1. Be as concerned about the happiness, growth, and well-being of your spouse as you are about your own.
2. Keep the lines of communication open. Discuss grievances and matters that are important to you, but do it in such a way that you do not attack or threaten the self-esteem of the other person. Be honest but not brutal.
3. Be accepting and tolerant of trivial annoyances

and imperfections. Decide if the issue is important enough to really matter. If it hurts, discuss it.

4. Don't try to make your partner into a carbon copy of yourself, of your likes and dislikes, or of your preferences and your opinions.
5. Be aware that we all have our ups and downs and our mood swings. Be sensitive and considerate enough not to take irritating actions too seriously during a down cycle.
6. If you get into an argument—and you will—keep the discussion limited to the issue at hand. Keep personality traits and past events and circumstances out of it. Find ways to cool off an escalating argument that may get out of hand.
7. Be a listener, be a friend, share pleasant events, and show your love.

Personal adjustment

The marriage relationship may have either a positive or a destructive influence on the psychological well-being of the husband or wife. It involves many of the most crucial adjustments a person will ever have to make. Each partner brings to marriage motives, attitudes, and preferred modes of coping, which have been learned through previous experiences.

The two personalities are brought into an intimate and pervasive contact with unique potentialities for working out emotional responses. Some adjustment problems, such as those of school or employment, can be relieved temporarily by evading or ignoring them, but the adjustments of marriage are less escapable. For a successful outcome the personalities of the partners in marriage must be supportive and harmonious at the outset or sufficiently flexible to make new adjustments without undue anxiety or hostility.

If a couple can make the following adjustments, their marriage can be happy, successful, and fun. First, marriage requires a continuous process of adjustment by both members. Second, the couple must have an understanding and acceptance of each other as persons. Third, the couple must be aware of problems and solve them together. Fourth, the couple must learn to accept the fact that not all problems can be completely solved. Fifth, the couple must have a desire for success in marriage. Sixth, marriage is not a fifty-fifty situation but, rather, a situation where the one member may give more in a certain aspect than the other. Seventh, it is the successful interaction of psychological, interpersonal, social, sexual, and financial aspects that makes the marriage a success.

The constructive influence of marriage includes factors other than stable home life and sexual adjustment, although the importance of these primary satisfactions must not be minimized. The well-adjusted husband and wife provide a kind of continuous psychotherapy for one another. This close and confidential relationship aids each partner to gain insight into his or her attitudes and to feel the strength of a united effort against difficulties.

Research is limited on topics related to changes that occur in personal growth and personality in early adulthood after marriage. The Vincent study (1964) and the one by Bachman et al., (1978), although different in methodology and quality of statistical data, present surprisingly similar findings. They both conclude that marriage may be a vehicle used by many young people to gain personal maturity in adult society. The study by Bachman and co-workers found that many young men who were married and parents before the age of 23 had changed from being aggressive in interpersonal relationships to more prosocial behavior. These individuals were drug or alcohol users while in high school but at this point used less drugs and alcohol than those who remained single. Bachman also found that marriage had a positive effect on ambitious job attitudes. Vincent found a higher degree of self-esteem among married couples. Both studies, incidently, refer only to marriages during the period of young adulthood.

Sex in marriage

The function of sex in marriage is an integral part of the concept of marital oneness. It is so defined by society and culture. Religion and customs can influence the sexual attitudes and activities of married couples. In recent years, however, psychologists, marriage experts, and other social scientists have broadened the definition of normal sexual intercourse to include acts that the couple themselves freely and willingly perform in the love-making ritual. One husband and wife may believe foreplay and particular precopulatory tactile, visual, oral, or other activity a vital prelude to sex. Another pair may regard undesirable anything but direct intromission (Hass, 1970).

The specific drives, attitudes, and outlooks of the married couple determine the nature, frequency, and attitude toward their particular sexual activities. Gen-

Meriem Kaluger

According to the latest census reports and articles in the mass media, belief in marriage and in a traditional wedding ceremony are as strong as they ever were—perhaps more so. The pronouncements of a decade ago predicting the decline of marriage and the family as a social institution are believed to have been greatly exaggerated. The divorce rate stabilized or decreased in 1981 and 1982, while the marriage rate and the more traditional, fashionable weddings increased.

erally, it is important that the marriage partners understand each other's levels of sexual arousal, length of orgasm, sensitivity to tactile stimuli, and other facets leading up to and following intercourse.

The problem of sexual adjustment usually occurs during the early months of marriage. During this time, sexual relations will need to be followed with considerable care if the couple is to arrive at a fully satisfactory relationship. One should recognize that sexual satisfaction does not necessarily have to include consistently reaching orgasm. Intercourse does not have to take place each time there is sexual play. The point of view of both partners will determine the nature of sexual satisfaction for themselves.

Hunt (1974) attempted to replicate the famous Kinsey reports (1948, 1953). Hunt's study indicates a widespread improvement in the satisfaction married couples reported with regard to their sexuality. The conclusion is that sex in marriage has become more acceptable, more pleasurable, more free, and more egalitarian over the years since the Kinsey reports. People today, especially the adults who form the younger

FIG. 13-2 ***Average monthly frequency of sexual intercourse by duration of marriage.***
Modified from Westoff, L.A., & Westoff, C.F., From now to zero. *Boston: Little, Brown & Co., 1971.*

cohort group, come to marriage with greater sexual experience (Levin and Levin, 1975). Women show more assertive and experimental attitudes. There are more practical sources of information and stimulation available, as well as accessible contraceptives and sexual therapy (Masters and Johnson, 1970). People of every age and circumstance feel more free to discuss sexual matters and to obtain appropriate information from professionals. The rigid Victorian morality of the late 1800s and early to middle 1900s is generally being replaced by a more liberal perspective. It could be that the media pendulum depicting presumed public sexual attitudes may have swung too far to the opposite end of the spectrum and that a more moderate position is closer to the truth. There are indications of a more moderate approach to sexual activities. The herpes scare may have had something to do with the moderation in outlook and sexual activity. Nevertheless, cultural changes regarding this topic are in a transitional state, with the end result yet to be identified.

A number of studies have reported on sexual morale in the general married population. In the Tavris and Sadd (1977) study of 100,000 readers of *Redbook* magazine, two thirds of the sample reported that the sexual aspect of their marriage was either very good or good. The remaining third were divided between those who rated it as only fair (21%) and those who said it was poor or very poor (12%).

It seems that intercourse makes up 85% to 90% of all sexual activity among married adults of every age (Martin, 1977). Intercourse occurs most frequently in the early months of marriage and then decreases over the length of the marriage. The findings of Westoff and Westoff (1971) are summarized in Fig. 13-2 regarding the average monthly frequency of sexual intercourse by length of marriage.

The biggest drop-off in sexual activity is in the first 3 years, from a monthly frequency average of 13 to about 7. Two factors may be involved in the drop-off. There may be more marital unhappiness during the third and fourth years, when the divorce rate reaches a peak. Second, this is also the period when the first pregnancy usually occurs. What is interesting is that the frequency of sexual intercourse is not reestablished to its prepregnancy level. It is important to also recognize the statistical maneuvering of the term "average." Westoff and Westoff found that in some four-week periods, 6% reported no sexual activity at all. At the other end of the range of scores, 8% reported 19 or more coital encounters.

Sex in marriage provides a sense of mutual gratification between marriage partners. In fact it has been shown that far from becoming bored with the same sexual partner, in the great majority of marriages that have endured, the couple discovered that the exclusive mutuality of their married love was accompanied by increasing capacity to give and receive (Melville, 1977). Sex is a form of communication, probably the most intimate, in which two people express a oneness of mind and feeling.

Marital problems

Marital conflicts are not necessarily undesirable or harmful to a marriage if they do not involve attacks on the self-worth of the marriage partner. Conflicts can be healthy in exposing areas of dissatisfaction and can lead to their eventual resolution. An overriding need to make the marriage work is essential when a conflict occurs. If there is no attempt at making a marriage function successfully under some stress or anxiety, any conflict, however mild, will only serve to drive apart the partners of an already shaky marriage relationship.

The dynamics of conflict need to be understood. How does a person react under stress or frustration? Things being equal, people are likely to externalize their feelings by finding fault with others when the

JOY ON OUR WEDDING DAY

Finally the day of our planned marriage had arrived. It was Thursday morning and we were all ready. A lot of people were gathering at home. Some were preparing a feast. Others were working busily at making fine mats and *tapa* [patterned barkcloth]. Most of the men were having a kava party. People were noisy with preparations for the wedding rituals.

At about 10 o'clock in the morning, cars came from the bridegroom's place. We all went down to the registration office and proceeded with other rituals of the day. My heart was full of joy; the big day that I hoped for had arrived at last! I did not feel too upset about being away from my parents and the rest of the family. I looked forward to the planning and running of my new family.

It was Thursday evening and most people had returned to their own homes, except a few old ladies who still sat around talking in the house. I knew what they were up to. That gave me mixed feelings, happy on one hand and frightened on the other. I felt happy for gaining a husband, but in the Tongan tradition there had to be evidence to show that I was still a virgin. I was frightened because I was not sure of it.

Traditionally, on the first night of marriage, the new couple have their first intercourse. If the girl is proved a virgin, it is celebrated. I was scared that, if I was not proved a virgin, it would be a great humiliation and my happiest day would be spoiled.

We were in bed together at last. I loved my husband but felt shy to make love with him. However, I gained confidence and we both found ourselves enjoying it. Soon we were in heaven. We will never forget the joyous feeling we had for each other. I was even happier at the end when the ladies took all the "holy sheets" (as they called them). They sang songs and shouted that they had proof. This went on outside whilst we lay in bed, enjoying ourselves some more and planning our future.

The happiness of our wedding day has remained with our young family since then. This has helped greatly in the upbringing of our children, and I am certain gave a firm foundation to our marriage.

From Stewart, R.A.C. (Ed.). *Pacific profiles*. Suva, Fiji: University of The South Pacific Extension Services, 1982.

stresses and tensions that they normally carry become too burdensome. This reaction is frequent among men who work in competitive jobs where there is an emphasis to produce. When the husband returns home, he is irritable and anxious. The family suffers a great deal until the stress is relieved. As far as the wife is concerned, the social and career roles, as well as the husband's expectations of her, may create stress and result in externalization in the form of exaggerated behavior.

Another dynamic of conflict takes the form of concealed discord. In this case the partners suppress their true feelings toward each other; they express them by frustrating the other partner or by dropping subtle remarks designed to hurt the other person. If the conflict is not resolved, tension can build up over a period of time and suddenly explode when one of the partners can no longer contain it. Unresolved conflicts usually have a chronic effect on the marriage and may emerge as sexual unresponsiveness (Edwards and Booth, 1976).

Conflict between two people may also be expressed by forms of resistance that make it difficult for the couple to resolve their differences. One form of resistance is a reluctance to admit that a marital problem exists; another form is a lack of communication between partners. Without communication all types of distortions and imagined grievances can occur. Occasionally, a partner will not communicate to avoid hostility and argument or perhaps will hold communication in abeyance to be used strategically at the opportune time. Other dimensions of conflict include (1) dealing with symptoms rather than causes, (2) substituting superficial problems for the real problems, (3) generalizing a problem so that only the surface but none of the nitty-gritty details are recognized, and (4) intellectualizing the problem on a cognitive level to the point that the underlying feelings, which are highly important in conflicts, are ignored.

The sources of marital problems are numerous, and the problems themselves are complex, as noted in Table 13-2. The most often used term to describe an inability to get along is *incompatibility,* but it is only a general term that does not specify the conditions under which marital conflicts arise. Incompatibility, for example, may arise because the ethnic, religious,

TABLE 13-2 Analysis of 1,412 help-request letters addressed to the American Association of Marriage Counselors

Category	*Husband* (%)	*Wife* (%)	*Total* (%)
Affectional relations	11.5	31.0	27.6
Spouse cold, unaffectionate			
Spouse is in love with another			
Has no love feelings for spouse			
Spouse attracted to others, flirts			
Excessive, "insane" jealousy			
Sexual relations	42.1	20.6	24.4
Sexual relations "unsatisfactory"			
Orgasm inability, frigidity, impotence			
Sex deprivation, insufficient coitus			
Spouse wants "unnatural" sex relations			
Personality relations	23.4	17.2	18.3
Spouse domineering, selfish			
Own "poor" personality, instability			
Clash of personalities; incompatible			
Spouse's violent temper tantrums			
Spouse withdrawn, moody, "neurotic"			
Spouse quarrelsome, bickering, nagging			
Spouse irresponsible, undependable			
Intercultural relations	11.5	11.4	11.4
In-law relations troublesome			
Religion or religious behavior			
Deviant behavior	7.5	8.7	8.5
Heavy drinking, alcoholism of mate			
Own heavy drinking or alcoholism			
Spouse's "loose" sex behavior			
Own illicit sex behavior			
Compulsive gambling			
Role tasks-responsibilities	0.0	6.0	4.9
Disagreement over "who should do what"			
Spouse's failure to meet material needs			
Situational conditions	4.0	3.4	3.5
Financial difficulties, income lack			
Physical illness, spouse or self			
Parental-role relations	0.0	1.7	1.4
Conflict on child discipline			
Parent-child conflict			

From De Burger, J.E. Marital problems, helpseeking, and emotional orientation as revealed in help-seeking letters. *Journal of Marriage and the Family,* 1967, **29,** 712-721. © 1967 by the National Council on Family Relations, 1219 University Avenue Southeast, Minneapolis, Minnesota 55414. Reprinted by permission.

or cultural backgrounds of the couple are different; thus there may be differences with respect to attitudes, values, and what each partner may wish to achieve in life and marriage. Some conflicts arise simply because people do not know how to handle stress. Sometimes conflicts are intensified because neither partner has learned skills for dealing with conflicts. As a result, it is usually "the problem" that gets the blame and not the individual's personality that is inadequately prepared for dealing with problems.

What do most married couples quarrel about? What problems lead to separations and divorce? A University of Pennsylvania research team interviewed 300 couples, 200 of whom had once sought marital advice (Problems of marriage, 1966). Husbands and wives, questioned separately, reported that the following problems bothered them most frequently: (1) money, (2) household management, (3) personality clashes, (4) sex, (5) sharing household jobs, (6) children, (7) leisure-time activities, (8) the husband's mother, (9) personal habits, (10) jealousy, (11) husband's occupation, and (12) the wife's mother. Infidelity ranked seventeenth on the list.

Many persons come to physicians with marital problems, even though they are not marital counselors. Herndon and Nash (1962) reported the following problems mentioned in physicians' offices. Men ranked their marital problems as follows: (1) sex, (2) money, (3) too much or too little affection, (4) inability to discuss problems with wife, (5) in-laws, (6) failure of wife to express appreciation, (7) inability of wife to conceive, and (8) wife's fear of pregnancy. Women brought up problems related to (1) sex, (2) fear of pregnancy, (3) too much or too little affection, (4) money, (5) inability to discuss problems with husband, (6) failure of the husband to express appreciation, (7) inability to conceive, and (8) in-laws. For both men and women half of the first six most-mentioned problems had to do with appreciation and communication.

How important is sex in a marriage? It all depends on whether you are male or female. Clifford Adams (Sense of values, 1969) at Pennsylvania State University ranks the importance of sex second with men and sixth with women. After studying 6,000 couples Adams reports that men rank the various ingredients of marriage in the following order: (1) companionship, (2) sex, (3) love-affection, (4) home and family, (5) encouraging helpmate, and (6) security. Women listed (1) love-affection, (2) security, (3) companionship, (4) home and family, (5) community acceptance, and (6) sex. Tavris and Jayaratne (1976) found that, among women, sex ranked fourth behind love, respect, and friendship as the most important element in a marriage. Again social and emotional responses ranked high. Marriages founded on sexual attraction usually have a flimsy foundation on which to build.

We would like to make one last point concerning marital problems. Numerous studies will show that sex and money are most frequently mentioned by couples as their major problems. Counselors have long known that these factors may simply be the outer manifestations of more crucial, deeper, underlying conflicts. There is a real need to "get to the root of the problem." Money problems are easy to pick on because so many people simply do not have enough money for everything they want to do. And how can two people feel free to have sexual intercourse with each other when underneath they are heartsick about the problems they are having with their marriage? It is difficult to have a satisfactory sexual relationship with someone who is causing you to have personal problems.

Crises in marriage

A crisis exists when the family faces a complicated state of affairs for which there is no available solution; for example, loss of income, extramarital affairs, death in the family, and divorce. These crises may permanently disable the family involved, especially if the less affected members are incapable of absorbing the duties of the individuals traumatized by the crisis. On the other hand, the family may be drawn closer together by the threat to their cohesion and may emerge from the crisis stronger than ever.

Unemployment. After the depression of 1929-1936, research found that many afflicted families surprisingly absorbed the shock of poverty without demoralization or great personal disorganization. The disorganization that did occur ended when the family accepted the fact that it could not function by its old buying and living pattern and made the necessary changes. A period of emotional stress followed the loss of income, but it usually terminated with an adjustment to the situation. Otherwise, evidence of pathological reactions resulted (Elder, 1974).

A recession or depression crisis, because it sweeps away the customary ways of living, tends to expose the strengths or deficiencies of the family. The families studied who had refused to face issues in earlier family

Meriem Kaluger

Loss of income can present a crisis in a marriage. According to Powell and Driscoll, the period of concerted effort to find a job does not begin until after a phase of relaxation.

crises were found to be the ones who evaded facing the changes in family life brought about by sudden poverty. This crisis did not always cause new reactions, but it did seem to exaggerate family traits previously exhibited. For example, the occasional drinker began to drink excessively; the happy family became more unified and loyal (Covan and Ranck, 1958).

One of the first studies on the effects of unemployment on middle-class men was made by Powell and Driscoll (1973). These investigators found that when unemployment was prolonged, their subjects progressed through four well-defined phases.

Phase I. The period of relaxation and relief. Since most of the men in this study had anticipated a layoff, unemployment came as no surprise. For the first few weeks they were confident that they would find a new job readily. Their mood following the layoff was one of relaxation, viewing the time as sort of a vacation. Family relationships remained relatively normal. They postponed job hunting and took time to read, catch up on hobbies, or just putter around the house.

Phase II. The period of concerted effort. After 3 or 4 weeks of relaxing, most men became edgy and started to make systematic attempts to find work. This was a period of concerted effort, using job-finding strategies such as telephoning friends, sending out resumés, contacting placement services, and reading the want ads. They were still optimistic and did not get anxious when they received letters of rejection. They did, however, avoid the company of other unemployed men.

Phase III. The period of vacillation and doubt. During this period, the men realized that they had been unemployed for a long time and that their job efforts were not succeeding. Job-hunting became sporadic—

sometimes intense and other times negligible. Moodiness, self-doubt, anxiety, and anger set in, then changed to resignation, hopelessness, and cynicism. Family and other interpersonal relationships began to deteriorate. After 3 to 9 weeks in this phase, the men stopped trying, and job-hunting came to a virtual halt. Marital roles sometimes shifted as many wives returned to work to make ends meet.

Phase IV. The period of malaise and cynicism. The feelings of despair and hopelessness made it more difficult for the men to look for jobs. Those who did look used job-searching strategies that were oriented more to maintaining self-esteem than to obtaining employment. The job had to match their training and experience; they would not search for a lesser position.

Curiously, marital relations often improved as the wives discontinued prodding their husbands to maintain an active search. However, the men did tend to avoid friends and extended families since their own lives were so different. Derr (1977), who did a study on unemployment among women, found considerable evidence to indicate that the loss of employment is equally or more trying for women; often the loss of income becomes a family crisis as well as an individual crisis.

Extramarital affairs. It is difficult to know if infidelity (deceitful, clandestine adultery) is a cause or an effect in a crisis. One study of 800 persons found that many men and women turn to another person when they have been deeply hurt by their partner (Athanasiou and Sarkin, 1974). The Hunt (1974) report states that one fourth of the married wives and one half of the husbands studied had at least one extramarital affair during their marriage. For women the incidence between the ages of 18 and 24 years was three times higher than a generation previously. The percentage of women over 30 involved in extramarital affairs also increased sharply.

In the Kinsey study (1953) of 221 cases of infidelity by wives in which the husbands knew of the affair, only 42% created any serious difficulty in the marriage; 58% of the husbands seemed able to tolerate and forgive their wives' infidelity, and wives were even more tolerant of their husbands' infidelity. Men are more likely to stray from the marital bed in the first 5 years, while for women it is more common after 15 to 20 years of marriage (Levin, 1975).

The husband's infidelity may be an attempt to demonstrate his manliness; it may be a revolt against his conscience; or it may be a method of solving misunderstood impulses originating during childhood. The "other" woman may be a sanctuary from an overbearing, nagging wife or a means of "getting back" at his wife. A wife's infidelity may result from some of the same types of reasons, such as to enjoy, explore, or exploit her womanhood (as a man does his manhood). It also indicates the possibility of resentment and dissatisfaction with the marriage itself. For both men and women, the more sexual partners they had before the marriage, the more likely it is that they will be extramaritally active (Bukstel et al., 1978).

It may be that the double standard that existed in sexual culture is diminishing, that female behavior and attitudes are converging with male behavior and attitudes, and that male attitudes are becoming the norm (Wolman and Money, 1980). Comarital adultery (consensual adultery) seems to exist in small numbers, appearing in such activities as group marriage, open-ended marriage, and recreational adultery (swinging) (Clanton, 1977). Research on group marriage and open-ended marriage is minimal. The research on recreational adultery suggests that, despite elaborate attempts to preserve the integrity of their marriage, couples who agree to swing take substantial risks (Edwards and Booth, 1976).

Death in the family. Prolonged illness and/or death of a member of a family creates both financial and emotional difficulties. At these times a closely knit family will have more security on which to lean; they will be more readily able to overcome the crises than the family without close ties.

Two things happen to a member of the family when another member dies: (1) a person senses that the circle is broken and that the family is threatened and (2) the individual senses that a part of the self as a person has been lost. The first reaction is a sense of disbelief and then numbness. The numbness usually helps to ease the shock.

The routines of the funeral help the family to accept the idea of death, but afterward there is no built-in help. This is the most difficult period. Expectations are that families are better off if they adjust quickly and then carry on in a normal manner. However, it may well be a while before reality and its implications set in. Our personal experiences are that children generally do not manifest a change in their school work patterns until about the third month after the death. Then there is a lowering of grades and sometimes a start of behavior problems.

DIVORCE

The impression created by the mass media, and professionals as well, is that divorce rates are astronomical and that the family unit, as it was traditionally known, is deteriorating rapidly. It is very important to put these matters into a clear perspective. Some quick answers: Yes, the divorce rate is higher than it used to be; no-fault divorce laws do make it easier to get divorces. No, the family unit is not deteriorating because of the divorce rate or because of alternative styles of living (Libby, 1977).

The statistics

The divorce figures generally given are those that compare the number of divorces in 1 year with the number of marriages in the year. That's like mixing oranges and apples to get an average. We're dealing with two different sets of people. It's a misleading way to use statistics. In the first place, the comparison is between people getting divorces who may have been married 3 months, 3 years, or 30 years or more and the number of individuals getting married during 1 year's time.

A better approach is to look at what happens to marriages over a period of time. Glick (1973) did such a study on the lifetime marriage and divorce experience in 50,000 homes. Of the married women now in their late 20s or early 30s, the study showed that 71% to 75% of these married women *stayed* married (a big difference from the idea that one in two or three marriages ends in divorce).

A second factor to consider is that four out of every five divorced persons get married again (Glick and Norton, 1977). Of these, only 2% will be divorced twice and married three times. Of those with three or more divorces, there is less than one fourth of 1% divorcing and remarrying. By far the highest incidence of divorce is found in the below 25 age-group—three times the overall average. Wives under 20 are involved in almost half of all the divorces recorded yearly.

Kieren and associates (1975) found that girls who marry before they are 18 years old are nearly three times more likely to be divorced than women who marry when they are 22 to 24 years old. Why are early marriages generally less stable than later marriages? No one knows for certain, but there are several possible interpretations. Chronologically immature people are likely to be emotionally immature and, in consequence, make unsound mate selections. Early marriages may simply reflect the socioeconomic pressure

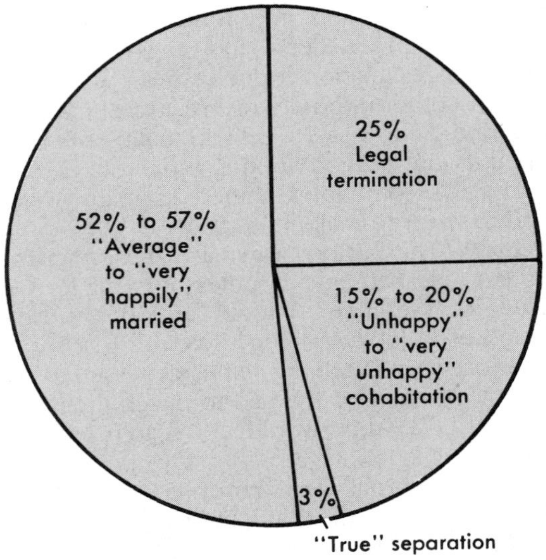

FIG. 13-3 ***Total incidence of marriage failure.***
From Saxton, L. The individual, marriage, and the family *(2nd ed.). Copyright 1972, by Wadsworth Publishing Co., Inc. Belmont, Calif. Reprinted by permission of the publisher.*

of this group. Often early marriage curtails the husband's education; thus there would be greater economic pressures in early marriages than in later marriages. If the husband does continue his education while his wife works, he may "outgrow" her. Finally, in many young marriages the wife was pregnant before marriage; premarital pregnancy is correlated with a relatively high divorce rate.

The current estimates based on numbers of marriages and divorces reported by the various states indicate that about one out of every three marriages is terminated by divorce or annulment compared to one out of seven marriages in 1920 and one out of twelve in 1900.

In addition to this high rate of divorce 3% of all marriages are terminated by "true separation," that is, those couples with legal decrees of separation, those living apart with the intention of obtaining a divorce, and those permanently or temporarily separated because of marital discord. Finally, numerous studies agree that about 15% to 20% of all married couples can be classified as unhappy cohabitants—those whose marriage is considerd extremely unhappy, both by the couple themselves and by their friends. Fig. 13-3 presents a diagram indicating the total incidence of marriage failure. The positive finding is that more than half the married couples consider themselves to be happily to very happily married.

Nature of marital complaints

Most of the writings on divorce quote statistics while ignoring specifics on the nature of marital complaints leading to divorce. The reason for this approach is that it has been very difficult to differentiate all the variables involved in a personal relationship that is in difficulty. For example, significant sex differences have been found in the extent of dissatisfaction with the marriage failure. Women describe their marriages in more negative tones than men do, women voice more complaints about their marriages, and women are more negative in their criticism of their husbands (Wallerstein and Kelly, 1980). Forty-three percent of the women said that three quarters, if not all, of their married life was unhappy, as compared to 27% of the men who describe their married life that way. In the California Divorce Study reported by Wallerstein and Kelly (1980), women precipitated the divorce in a ratio of three to one.

The nature of marital complaints varied according to the kind of studies done, the methodology involved, and the time period (cohort effect) in which the study was completed. Kelly (1982) summarized a number of the complaints indicated in the studies. She noted the cohort differences of complaints presented in the comparative studies of Goode (1969). Thirty years earlier the Goode women of Cleveland reported such complaints as nonsupport, authoritative husbands, drinking, and staying out with the boys. The recent group (1982) of Cleveland women focused more on affective or emotional failings related to the husband's personality, the quality of home life, the authority of the husband, and his values. They stressed contentedness and marriages that were emotionally and sexually satisfying. A lack of communication or understanding was also suggested in the later study.

In the 1981 Cleveland study, the men complained mostly about joint conflict and disagreement over the roles of the husband and the wife; authoritarian stance of the wife was also mentioned. Men frequently were not sure what had happened; women's complaints were specific, such as extramarital affairs, drinking, and immaturity of the spouse. Men and women of higher social status who had been married more years complained more often of a lack of emotional support and deficiencies in the interpersonal relationships. Respondants of lower social status and those married fewer years complained of the spouse's failings and lack of performance of tasks. Parents complained more than nonparents about communication difficulties, verbal abuse, infidelity, and feeling unloved.

The California Divorce Study (Wallerstein and Kelly, 1980) was conducted more by interview than by a restricted choice-of-answers method. Two thirds of the women complained of feeling unloved (ranked first by the women and third by the men). A corresponding feeling of emptiness led many to initiate divorce. The first-ranked complaint for the men (55%) was of the wife being inattentive or neglecting what husbands saw as their needs and wishes. The second complaint for the men was a major incompatibility in interests, values, and goals, especially if there were recent changes in interests and goals. The second and third most frequent complaints of the women in the California Divorce Study were being belittled by their husbands in regard to their competency and their intelligence. One third of the wives reported that their husbands were hypercritical of everything about them. Fourth for both men and women (about 34%) was sexual deprivation. About one third of the men and one fourth of the women complained that their spouses were chronically "bitchy" or extremely angry.

Stress of divorce

Bohannan (1972) has analyzed the enormously complex experiences involved in the divorce process. He terms them the "six stations of divorce." They are (1) *the emotional divorce*, the growing antagonism and grief, (2) *the legal divorce*, the anxiety-provoking grounds for divorce, (3) *the economic divorce*, the settling of property and assets, (4) *the coparent divorce*, centered around custody and violation rights with the children, (5) *the community divorce*, the loss of community ties and social network built on the marriage, and (6) the *psychic divorce*, the psychological separation from the past and the development of a new autonomy.

Divorce has been identified as a stress factor second only to the death of a spouse in terms of the demands made on the adult's need to reorganize life in a major way (Kitson et al., 1980). The marital separation is frequently more traumatic to women than the final decree or the period after the final decree. The period before the decision to divorce may also be traumatic, especially for women. Men appear to have more stress in the postseparation period (Chiriboga and Cutter, 1977). Adjustment to separation and postdivorce did

life crisis unit (LCU) the average mean score assigned by Holmes and Rahe to various life events.

come more easily to the woman or the man who initiated the proceedings. The psychosocial readjustment process, however, was always more difficult for older men and women who had been married for longer periods of time.

Relatively few divorced people stay single. The present increase in divorce is not a sign that people do not want to be married. It means that they want to be reasonably happy in their marriage and to have the comforting, loving response of someone who cares about and respects them.

LIFE CRISIS AND STRESS

Holmes and Rahe (1967) empirically determined that certain changes in a person's daily life pattern could make that individual more susceptible to disease and illness. They developed the Social Readjustment Rating Scale (SRRS), presented in Table 13-3, for the purpose of evaluating the impact of life changes in bringing about a disease. Their scale consists of 43 items of pleasant and unpleasant life events of varying negative or positive consequences ranging from minor traffic violations, to marriage, to the death of spouse. Each life change has a score based on its impact and severity. The total score is called the ***life crisis unit (LCU).*** The higher the LCU score, the higher the likelihood of developing an illness (Holmes and Masuda, 1973).

Holmes and his colleagues predict that people who have been exposed to stress events that add up to an LCU score of 200 to 299 within recent months have a risk factor of about 50% of developing a major illness in the next 2 years. For those with an LCU total score of above 300, the risk is much higher, approximately 80%. In addition, those who usually remained well during flu epidemics were more likely to have flu after a major life change (Rahe and Holmes, 1966). When an

TABLE 13-3 Life stress and life change units (LCU)

Events	*Scale of impact (LCU)*	*Events*	*Scale of impact (LCU)*
Death of spouse	100	Son or daughter leaving home	29
Divorce	73	Trouble with in-laws	29
Marital separation	65	Outstanding personal achievement	28
Jail term	63	Spouse begins or stops work	26
Death of close family member	63	Begin or end school	26
Personal injury or illness	53	Change in living conditions	25
Marriage	50	Revision of personal habits	24
Fired from work	47	Trouble with boss	23
Marital reconciliation	45	Change in work hours or conditions	20
Retirement	45	Change in residence	20
Change in health of family member	44	Change in schools	20
Pregnancy	40	Change in recreation	19
Sex difficulties	39	Change in church activities	19
Gain in new family member	39	Change in social activities	18
Business readjustment	39	Mortgage or loan less than $10,000	17
Change in financial state	38	Change in sleeping habits	16
Death of close friend	37	Change in number of family get-togethers	15
Change to different line of work	36	Change in eating habits	15
Change in number of arguments with spouse	35	Vacation	13
Mortgage over $10,000	31	Christmas	12
Foreclosure of mortgage or loan	30	Minor violations of the law	11
Change in responsibilities at work	29		

Modified from Holmes, T.H., and Rahe, R.H. Published with permission from *Journal of Psychosomatic Research, 11,* The social readjustment rating scale, © 1967, Pergamon Press, Ltd.

individual's life is in a relatively steady state of psychosocial adjustment with few recent life changes, little or no illness tends to be reported.

You can, if you like, calculate your personal LCU score to determine if you should be doing something special to prevent a physical or mental disorder. Make certain you look at the whole life pattern. For example, getting married would rate 50 LCUs, but its impact may be greater because marriage usually involves a change in living conditions (25 LCUs), a change in personal habits (24 LCUs), and a change in residence (20 LCUs), for a total of 119 LCUs.

Lowenthal and co-workers (1975) did a study pertaining to age-stage related perceptions of stress. Individuals in young and early adulthood perceived from two to three times as many stresses in their lives as did the middle-aged adults. This finding may be a result of the transitional state in which many young adults find themselves, such as changing from an educational setting to a work setting or from being single to being married. Fortunately, their ability to cope with the increased amount of stress, real or unreal, is aided by the fact that they are at their prime in physical, mental, and social resources.

Underlying most critical life events is a separation from other people. Even a positive event, such as a marriage, involves a separation from an established social network of friends and family. Berkman (1977) computed a social network index for 7,000 adults. The findings of the study revealed a positive significant correlation between the index of social disconnection and overall mortality (death) rates for every age-group and sex group. More people with minimal social contacts die than those with many social contacts. Society and community ties may be powerful determinants of consequent health status.

Thoits (1978) classified the life change events into (1) isolating events, such as deaths, separation, children leaving home, (2) integrating events, such as marriage, reconciliation, beginning employment, and (3) events that increase or decrease one's prestige. She determined that isolation events and those that decrease personal prestige *raise* the distress levels in all groups studied. Integrating events, even though they had a high LCU score, *reduced* distress levels in married males but had no effect on married females. The impact of each isolating event on the distress level is greater for isolated males than for those who are part of a social network. The research on effects for females was not clear. The idea that people need people—that they need their warmth—is given solid empirical evidence.

PARENTING

Traditionally, the study of parenting was concerned primarily with the effects of parenting on the child. It was only in the last decade that any extensive research began to consider the needs of the parents. Earlier studies were directed toward the identification of parental behaviors as they affected the functioning of children (Clarke-Stewart, 1978). Changes in family structure and roles, such as increased employment of mothers outside the home, the use of day care for children, single parenthood, and the increased role of the father in the care of children have extended the meaning of parenting.

Parenthood

Any discussion of parenting should include the concept of the family in its psychological and sociological dimensions. Changes in the ages of the individuals in the family bring about developmental growth that reflects itself in different forms of interaction among the family group. The timing of events in the family, such as the birth and spacing of the children, also have important consequences for the development of individuals in the family. These factors imply a developmental or life-cycle approach to family analysis and parenthood by considering internal and external factors that influence family development, changing role expectations and behaviors, and achievement of the developmental tasks necessary for the survival of the family (Nock, 1982).

Duvall (1971) defines these developmental strivings of the family as (1) physical maintenance, (2) allocation of resources, (3) division of labor, (4) socialization of family members, (5) reproduction, recruitment, and release of family members, (6) maintenance of order, (7) placement of members in the larger society, and (8) maintenance of motivation and morale.

As far as parenting is concerned, Alpert and Richardson (1980) present a family-stage model based on the age of the older child in the family life cycle. The five stages they consider are (1) the childless period before becoming parents, (2) childbirth and postpartum, (3) parenting of infants and children, (4) parenting with adolescent children, and (5) parenting with adult children. Some of these stages can be experienced simultaneously if the births are widely spaced. Aldous (1978) provides an example of stages based on the age and school placement of the oldest child. These categories include the family with an infant, with a preschool child, with a school-aged child, with an adoles-

Meriem Kaluger

Parenting includes psychological and sociological—as well as economical and physical—dimensions. A life-cycle approach to family analysis considers the changing role expectations, family interactions, and behavior as well as internal and external factors of development.

cent, and with a young adult (to the leaving of the home by this child). Obviously, life cycles differ for families as to time, structure, and role. Parenting will also differ in the same ways.

Pregnancy and the family

Having a baby is a family affair. We should really think of a pregnant family rather than of a pregnant woman. The woman has the physical responsibility of pregnancy and labor, but the entire family faces many changes in its way of life.

From the very beginning the support and encouragement given to a woman during her pregnancy are very important to her. The father should attend the clinic or meet the doctor during early pregnancy so both he and the mother can hear what the doctor has to say about the pregnancy and any problems that may be connected with it. Prospective fathers should learn how to help their wives during labor and how to care for newborn babies. Both mother and father are likely to be equally clumsy at changing that first diaper unless they have attended a "new parents" class (Apgar, 1973).

Pregnancy is rehearsal for family life. The physical change in the mother is related to a baby being created. The psychological change involved in this event actually creates a family. The first trimester is frequently a period of developmental crisis or transition. The coming birth is recognized as a cause of major changes; the wife becomes more dependent and the husband gives support "as a father" (Peterson et al., 1979). The second trimester is more peaceful. The most important event is the "quickening"; feeling the movements strengthens the realization that "the baby is human." During the third trimester, there are two themes. First, the couple becomes increasingly aware of obvious sexual differences. It heightens their feelings of femininity and masculinity. Second, there is some worry over the delivery. This concern disappears quickly after the birth and is followed by joy, a feeling of triumph, and a sense of having been creative. (The source of this idea on the influence of pregnancy on parents is unknown. It was taken from notes in our file.)

The pregnancy

Among the basic instincts of humans is the procreation of the species. Starting a family is one of the developmental tasks of early adulthood. The nature of the task is to have a first child successfully. As for the psychological task of starting a family, Havighurst (1979) states that questions are raised, such as acceptance or rejection of the pregnancy on the part of the woman, confidence in the physician, worry over possible failure to have a normal baby, desire for sexual relations during pregnancy, the uncertainty of breast feeding, and the matter of the reactions of relatives and friends to the pregnancy.

Probably the most crucial task is that of acceptance or rejection of the pregnancy on the part of the mother. If she is frightened or disgusted at the thought of pregnancy, the task will be difficult for her. The husband's attitude toward the baby must also be considered. An attitude of rejection of the pregnancy on his part can have almost as serious an effect on the woman and the family as if the woman has rejected the pregnancy.

Next in order of importance is confidence in the physician who, to some extent, will have both lives in his or her hands during the period of birth. The woman's confidence in her physician can cure many lingering doubts she may have about her pregnancy.

Some women experience little desire for sexual intercourse during pregnancy, whereas others have increased sexual desire. The adjustment of the husband's sexual behavior is important.

There can be a deep sense of pride in being pregnant since the mother "makes" the baby. The sense of pride, however, also fills her with concern about the many possible "things that could go wrong." While fathers are waiting for the baby to be born, the mother is afraid of miscarriage, neonatal death, or a deformed baby.

The question of breast-feeding can be answered with a sterilized bottle and enriched milk. Many women in the past several decades preferred not to nurse the child. Now there seems to be a general trend back toward breast-feeding.

Finally, the reaction of friends and relatives should be considered. The in-laws especially may express adverse opinions about the entire idea of having a baby, especially if they consider the timing inappropriate. This seems to be the least tenuous task.

Once the child is born, the family life revolves around the newborn child for some time. During this period the parents have to adjust to new demands placed on their time and energy. One young couple said, "The baby can be quite demanding of attention and help; often at times it is a real sacrifice to stop whatever you're doing and tend to his (her) needs." The early years of childhood are day-to-day happenings in which the child slowly develops physically, psychologically, socially, morally, and mentally.

Mothering

In most traditional societies, maternal and paternal roles are sharply defined. Women are supposed to accept most of the responsibility for meeting the daily survival and supportive needs of children. Women are usually regarded as the primary influence on childhood development. However, in contemporary American society, the distinction between maternal and paternal roles, at least in influencing and controlling the children, is rapidly disappearing (Bell, 1975). Society has recognized the idea that fathers, as well as mothers, can parent. In fact, some women may not want to have children or may not want to be the sole caregiver. Lott (1973) showed that college women who expressed positive attitudes toward feminism considered homemaking noncreative and monotonous and were less eager to bear and rear children than were antiliberationist women.

Motherhood as an instinctive behavior has come to be questioned (Field and Widmayer, 1982). History presents many accounts of the dangers that surround infants and children of every era. Pressures placed on

David Strickler

Motherhood appears to be experienced by stages. Mothers seem to grow and develop with their children. Some researchers and writers question the assumption that motherhood is an instinctive behavior.

society by economic, subsistence, demographic, and role patterns have made it necessary for some societies to formulate laws in order to protect offspring from physical and psychological abuse. Infanticide, child abuse, and abandonment were, and still are, common in many parts of the world. Field and Widmayer (1982) conclude that " . . . it is a misconception to view motherhood as an 'instinctive' behavior. . . . It is more likely learned behavior which is subject to numerous environmental pressures" (p. 683).

Motherhood is experienced by stages; mothers appear to grow and develop with their children. As Peter DeVries implies, the value of motherhood may not be that women (mothers) produce children but that children produce mothers. The stages of motherhood include pregnancy and delivery, the neonatal period, infancy, preschool and early childhood, and middle childhood and adolescence; each stage places special tasks and demands on the mother. The ***mothering*** process will often have its share of disturbances and aberrations, usually based on interactions of the mother and father or of the child and the parent (Field and Widmayer, 1982). Nevertheless, disturbed interactions can be modified by coaching or parent training (Field 1978b), usually involving the matching of mother's pace of activity to that of the infant *(rhythm),* using a variety of behaviors in interacting with the child *(repertoire of behaviors),* and making certain that the child perceives a response of reaction from the mother *(responsivity).* Mothers (and fathers) can learn to be effective teachers and effective behavior-change agents. Instinctive responses may not be enough.

mothering taking the maternal responsibilities for protecting and raising one's offspring or adopted children.

Fathering

Recent literature on parenting suggests that, while fathers may differ somewhat from mothers, there is nothing in behavior that is particularly innate or exclusive to the biological mother. Field (1978b) has collected data which suggest that during the first 2 years at least (1) fathers are no less preferred as attachment objects (Lamb, 1977a, 1977b), (2) fathers are more playful than mothers with their infants (Yogman, 1979), (3) fathers use more "baby talk" with their infants than mothers (Golinkoff and Ames, 1977), and (4) when fathers are the primary caregivers of infants, they are more like mothers than like fathers in vocalization and imitative behaviors (Field, 1978a). Greenberg and Morris (1974) found that fathers of newborns were observed to be "engrossed" in their infants and stated that they were bonded, absorbed, and preoccupied with their child in a way that did not differ from mothers. Infants can and do form active, close relationships with their fathers during the first 2 years of life.

Children enjoy being with their fathers. Studies of both males and females suggest that parental influence may be critical in the sex-role development of both boys and girls (Biller, 1981). Boys who have strong relationships with their fathers appear to be more emotionally stable and well adjusted than those who do not. Women who achieve great success in the career world often report special relationships with their fathers. They describe their fathers as especially attentive and supportive of their ambitions (Sheehy, 1977). Longitudinal research has indicated that the quality of a father's relationship with his children can have a significant impact on the father's overall life satisfaction (Levinson, 1978b).

Biller (1982) did an extensive review of the research on fatherhood. His reviews suggest that the primary effects of father-absent families are manifested in terms of deficits and/or abnormalities in the boy's sex-role development. There also seems to be an association between inadequate father-son relationships and academic difficulties among boys. Although antisocial behavior among children and adolescents can have many causes, parental deprivation is a frequent contributing factor. Early father-absence has a particularly strong association with delinquency among males; yet the degree of family cohesiveness and supervision appears to be almost as significant. For example, boys in father-absent families who have a positive relationship with their mothers seem less likely to become delinquent than do boys in father-present families who have inadequate fathers (Biller, 1974).

In addition to sharing the responsibilities of parenthood, the new father must also accept the change in his pattern of daily relationship with his wife. At this stage of the family life cycle, when the first child arrives, the father must learn that his wife's affection must be shared with the baby. Normally, both parents are filled with affection for each other and for the new arrival. Strong emotional attachments are made with the newborn child; however, these feelings are usually more intense for the mother. As a result, the mother may make the child, rather than the father, the emotional center of her life (Kelly, 1974). Some husbands may feel neglected or rejected, especially if this change in emotional focus continues as the infant grows older. It is a task for both husband and wife to understand the meaning of parental love and of marital love and to strive for a harmonious balance.

The one-parent family

Because of desertion, separation, divorce, and death or because the mother never married, 20% of the children in the United States are growing up in a home with only one parent. In some low-income black neighborhoods, the percentage often jumps to one child out of every two (Glick and Norton, 1977). In 90% of the cases the absent parent is the father. Much of this absence of the father may result from the fact that in nine out of ten divorce cases the mother gets custody of the children (Espenshade, 1979). Many mothers, however, manage to provide adequate models of sex-role behavior through relatives and friends.

Children growing up in one-parent homes are usually at the higher risk of having problems and having to make adjustments than children growing up in homes where there are two parents to share responsibilities and to provide security. Many single-parent families are relatively poor; they represent 25% of the families whose incomes are below the government's official definition of poverty level (Stinnet and Walters, 1977). Even single-parent families with sufficient economic resources may have special social and psychological problems. For example, the single parent with young children to care for may become a victim of social isolation and loneliness, unable to take advantage of what limited social opportunities might be available. Schlesinger (1977) reports that single parents consistently relate feelings of loneliness and alienation. They also express frustration about the need to forego satisfying sexual gratification or social contacts with the opposite sex.

It should be noted that the two-parent home is not always ideal and the one-parent home is not necessarily unwholesome. Homes of either type that demonstrate serious conflicts, tension, anger, strife, or unhappiness can be disruptive to the development of a child. Rutter (1979) reports that antisocial behavior of children, as a result of a divorce, appears to result more from the discord in the home that caused the divorce than from the separation. Rutter found that children from intact homes where there is much parental strife are also likely to get into trouble. Whether the single-parent home is good or bad for the child appears to depend on the stability, the absence of strife and malcontent, and the presence of love and security that is experienced by the child.

Working mothers

In a day and age when so many mothers are working, it is only natural that there would be some concern about the effects of mothers who work outside the home on the care and development of their children. The research findings, thus far, are incomplete. There are many variables involved.

Hoffman (1974) did a review on maternal employment and its effects. In general, she concluded that (1) working mothers provide different role models than do nonworking mothers, (2) the way in which employment affects the mother emotionally influences the quality of the mother-child interaction, (3) situational demands (such as working nights or odd hours) affect child-rearing practices, (4) working mothers provide less adequate supervision, (5) school-aged children do not appear to suffer any deprivations just because the mother worked, and (6) children of working mothers tend to be more open in their sex-role views and have higher educational and career aspirations.

Howell (1973) did find that the timing of a mother's entry or reentry into the job market could have an adverse affect on infants. There are times in the child's development when it would be important for the mother (or the principal caretaker) to avoid going to work for the first time. Such times include the seventh to ninth months after birth when close attachments are being made secure, the period around the twenty-fourth month when language development is crucial, and any time the child faces a major adjustment in the family structure or life cycle. However, the children of working mothers do not differ from other children with respect to peer relationships, school performance, IQ, emotional problems, or degree of dependence or independence (Howell, 1973).

A key factor in how a mother affects child development appears to be the degree of satisfaction that the mother has in her role, either as a homemaker or as a working mother. Whether the mother works outside the home or not is less important than whether she enjoys and is satisfied with what she is doing. Working mothers who express satisfaction with their occupational role do not differ from satisfied full-time homemakers on measures of maternal behavior including control, emotional satisfaction, or adequacy of mothering (Yarrow et al., 1962). Women who enjoy their lives are more likely to communicate that sense of joy to their children.

Stepparents

Since the divorce rate is so high and so many divorced parents remarry, there is the problem of integrating a new adult member into the family. According to Einstein (1979) the inability to resolve this change in the family life cycle leads to divorce in 40% of these families within the first 5 years of the remarriage.

A comprehensive review of the literature on stepparenthood (Walters and Stinnet, 1971) indicates that (1) stepparents are more easily accepted by young children and by adult children than by adolescents, (2) integration appears to be easier in families that have been split by divorce rather than by death, (3) male children accept a stepparent more readily, especially if the new parent is also a male, (4) children of both sexes tend to see a stepparent of the opposite sex as playing favorites with their own children, (5) most children continue to admire their absent biological parent, and (6) stepparents and stepchildren often come to the reconstituted or "blended" family with unrealistic expectations for their relationships (Stinnet and Walters, 1977). Instant love and togetherness are not automatic. Time is needed for the development of trust and affection.

The area of greatest stress for stepparents is that of child rearing (Kompara, 1980). Certainly the more that the parents and stepparents can agree on the approach to childrearing, the less will be the amount of strife. In some cases the stepparent takes a "hands-off" policy and does not interfere with the rearing or behavior direction of the child. This situation can raise unpleasantness, especially when the stepparent has a different perspective and harbors strong feelings about what is going on. According to Kompara (1980), becoming a stepparent is more difficult for a woman because children are usually closer to their biological mothers and have spent more time with them than with the father. This condition makes it more difficult for the stepmother to step into the role of the biological mother.

THE CINDERELLA STEPMOTHER SYNDROME

I never would have believed that Cinderella's stepmother could have been a basically nice person. But now that I am a stepmother, I can start to empathize with that wicked old woman (and even begin to understand the origins of such fairy tales).

About two years ago, I began to see a man who was undergoing a separation and divorce. Ken had two children—Billy, aged 6, and Mary, aged 3. I remember thinking that the children were "adorable," "cute," and "well-behaved."

As our relationship progressed, I often visited at Ken's house during the weekends when the children were present. After a few weekends of staying around the house, I suggested that we do other things like going for rides, walks, and picnics. Since Ken was more than agreeable to this, the four of us began to enjoy recreational outings almost as a family unit.

During the first few months, whenever we were at Ken's house, he was in charge of most of the household duties. It was his home and I felt little or no responsibility for its maintenance. Ken cleaned the house, did the laundry, and often made dinner for the four of us. During the week, when he visited at my apartment, I did most of the work.

After a while, as I increasingly wanted to become "one of the family," I began to take over some of the chores at his house. This gave me a sense of being part of their lives and gave Ken time to play with the kids. Things went well; I felt that I had a good relationship with the children, although I realized that my further involvement in the household events had also dictated that I become an authority figure with the kids. In that role I found that I was somewhat more strict about manners and rules than Ken.

After Ken and I were married, he moved into my apartment while his house was being sold and we waited for the inevitable division-of-property settlement with his ex-wife. When the children visited with us on weekends, we continued to go on outings together. Certain patterns began to emerge in our relationships.

In the late summer, Ken and I bought "our dream"—a 54-acre farm. It is a beautiful place but a real "handyman's special," needing a lot of work. I also began a new job teaching fourth grade in a different district than the one by which I had previously been employed. So, in addition to commuting 45 minutes twice a day, I often had to stay at school very late to prepare for the next day. The job was very important to me. I had taught in specialized programs before, but this was my first teaching job in a regular classroom and I was determined to be proficient. I had been hired for one year as a maternity substitute and planned to prove my worthiness to the administration in the hope of a more permanent position.

Often I would arrive home around seven, Ken and I would grab a bite to eat, and then we would work on the house until bedtime. We sanded floors, scraped paint, scrubbed, painted, and generally wore ourselves out. On weekends, the kids would visit, but we really didn't have (or make) the same kind of time for recreational activities and playful interaction. Getting the house into shape became a priority over excursions.

About this time I began to realize that most of my interactions with the kids were at critical times: meals, baths, and bedtime. And I noticed that my relationship with them was becoming increasingly negative. Their faults and inadequacies became of paramount importance. I resented their presence and even considered them invaders because weekends meant only that even more work was squeezed into my already overcrowded schedule. Also, my already diminished private-quiet times with Ken were further reduced when the kids were around. I nagged and criticized and seldom had anything nice to say to them. And, of course, I felt guilty about the jealousy that I had of the time Ken devoted to them.

At this point I began to cut myself off from involvement with the three of them. I was always "too busy" to play and "too tired" to initiate interactions. I backed myself into the role of a live-in maid who had to pick up after the three of them and resented every minute of it!

One situation that I remember was becoming the prototype of my interactions with the children. Billy, who was nearing the age of 8 but still a bedwetter, had been reminded to strip his bed and bring the soiled laundry down to the washing machine. After I had washed the load and put it in the dryer, I went upstairs to make Mary's bed and discovered Billy's wet underwear lying in a heap on the floor. In a veritable rage, I called Billy and severely reprimanded him for being so careless (and sloppy, and lazy and . . .). I was exhausted and shaking when I was through and felt guilty because I had become so verbally violent. Situations like this, coupled with my nagging and general intolerance, certainly did not make for a happy household.

Of course the children must have resented my attitude. Billy, who was somewhat withdrawn already, pulled further from me. Mary, being younger and more resilient, would add to my guilt by continuing in her overt affection for me. I was torn between wanting to be accepted, loved, and needed by them and my desire to stay away from them altogether.

My wicked stepmother image haunts me. Every weekend I privately vow to be more understanding, to take time to enjoy the kids outside of the critical times, to be less judgmental, and to learn how to love them. As the weekend approaches, I become more tense and have knots in my stomach, fearing failure. Too often my fears are realized.

However, women whose natural children live in the same home as the stepchildren generally have more positive stepparenting experiences.

Childfree families

The cohort effect appears to be operating in regard to the question of whether or not a married couple should have children and, if so, how many. During the 1950s many couples opted for three to five children. It seemed as if that was the thing to do. Then, in the sixties and seventies came the emphasis on "zero population growth"—the era of "don't increase the population level by having more children than are needed to replace the number of people who die." Currently, the fashion in United States appears to be none to two children at the most. Above 5% of American married women are choosing not to have children. In the People's Republic of China, posters expound the virtue, "One child is enough."

The minority of couples who expect to remain childfree choose to do so for a number of reasons. First, the younger generation has accepted the childfree marriage as a viable option. Second, some couples

CHOOSING TO BE CHILDFREE

At the age of twenty-six, with several years of teaching behind me and my impending marriage only several months ahead of me, I find myself having gone through several equally adamant conclusions concerning the available choice of motherhood. At present I seem once again to have made a lasting decision. I've surpassed the high school—"Oh, yes, but of course I will have a child"—and have transcended various college stages from "Yes, most likely" to "What do I care at this point in my life?" "Who knows?" "Well, maybe, but mine won't act like that!" "Absolutely not" and so on, repeat chorus, and so on, respectively. By this time the indecisiveness, the apathy, and the vehemence no longer tinge my reply. Time, experience, and the maturity which follows, in combination with inner inquiry and dialogue, have enabled me to conclude that "I don't feel that motherhood would provide me with an appropriate avenue for growth and development."

Why, though, as I write, do I feel as if I must actively defend my decision? Basic personal assertiveness would tell me that an inherent right is that which states, "You have the right to offer no reasons or excuses for justifying your behavior." Ellis would tell me that I'm reacting on the irrational belief that "It is a dire necessity for an adult to be loved by everyone for everything he or she does." I could go on, but I can, with common sense, tell myself that even though I experienced the backlash of the sixties and have reaped the benefits of women's awareness, individual personal awareness, the importance of fulfilling, and the actualizing of one's own needs or potential, I must admit that a bit of "parent" modeling or societal expectation unconsciously brandishes its taped dialogue. Furthermore, when I launch my justification, I fear that what I would willingly term a "Positive selfishness" (sound judgment based on the awareness of my own and my partner's needs and aspirations), others may refer to as just plain selfishness, which has a bad connotation.

At any rate, let me deal with several reasons, all of which would be outgrowths of this "positive selfishness." Financially, on the salaries of two teachers, the life we would be able to provide for our children and ourselves would be more limited than I would like to see for any of us. I say children, by the way, because I would want my child to have the experience of having a sibling to grow with, play with, fight with, compromise with, and grow old with. I would hope to have the ability to provide my children with educational opportunities and many "experiential" opportunities which I do not feel our budget would permit. At the same time, I would also say that Joe and I would appreciate rewards other than the vicarious reward persons receive through sacrificing for those they love.

Freedom versus responsibility is another consideration in my decision against motherhood. I am twenty-six, as I mentioned, and Joe is thirty-one. Both of us have developed quite independent life-styles, out of necessity and desire. We enjoy the freedom of the potentiality for spontaneity. The responsibility we feel toward our careers, students, each other, and our individual selves is responsibility which we willingly assume. At this time, we do not feel that we'll choose to assume more responsibility in the form of another life.

In relation to the concern for freedom is my concern for the early years of my child's life in respect to my career. I am devoted to my career; I enjoy it. My thoughts concerning the early years of a child are that I should be with him/her at home. As I don't foresee my belief system changing, I would either be leaving my career and feeling stunted or I would be returning to teaching after a year and feeling guilty about not only being away from my baby but also the lessened amount of time I would be devoting to my career. In addition, I am pursuing a graduate degree which has me absolutely energized. I assume the next large area of growth for me, after marriage, may very well involve a career change to counseling rather than motherhood. So once again I have prioritized—I know myself and I do not quickly adapt to change. I will want my energies available for this career change.

Since I've touched on personality, I need also to note that I am a fairly hearty example of a perfectionistic personality. I am aware of the self-induced tension increases which motivate me. I am proud of my high standards and the achievements I reach, but I am also struggling to become more aware of and intolerant of the self-punishing compromise inherent in this system. Joe is not unlike me in this respect. Imagine the poor child of such a match!!! Seriously, I fear our expectations of ourselves as parents as well as our plausible expectations for our child.

I would not negate a certain unwillingness to experience the pain of watching a child, one's own child, grow. As teachers who care very much about our junior high students, Joe and I vicariously experience the pain of watching youngsters hurt, struggle, question, fail, and so on. This vicarious experiencing also works in reverse. We are privileged to share energies, hopes, successes, and joys of children. To imagine being the actual parent of one of these children is overwhelming. We are in the unique position of being able to emotionally experience children from a safer vantage point. It is enough for us.

As I consider my justification, I realize that each support can be countered—the inevitable result of stating reasons. I suppose the bottom line is that, after weighing the situation, I don't want children and neither does Joe. Very soon we will begin a journey together, one which we want to see flourish. Change is the product of growth. The needs and aspirations of each of us can be expected to change, and therefore, thankfully, we can be expected to grow. Integral to our commitment is that we will nourish each other's growth and, at the least, not hinder it. A time may come when one of us may feel a need or desire to grow into the area of parenthood. If this should occur, the alternative to choose to have children is available to us.

The key word in my mind is *choice*, which suggests "the opportunity or privilege of choosing freely." What I intend to intimate, I guess, is that one should decide only for oneself whether becoming a parent is the step to take. My additional feelings are that such a choice deserves a great amount of inner searching. The very least one can do for a child is to actively desire and choose to conceive and parent the child.

believe that population growth is a problem and that they should do their part to slow down the pace of growth. Third, the great expense of child rearing has become a major factor for many couples. Fourth, some couples express a concern and a fear of raising children "in today's world" with all of its problems of violence and threat of war. Fifth, other couples prefer to remain childfree because of the greater freedom available to them to pursue careers and not be hemmed in with family responsibilities (Veevers, 1974).

Houseknecht (1979) did a study of 50 mothers and 50 voluntarily childfree wives. She found a very small difference in overall marital adjustment. Both groups appeared to be about equally well adjusted; both groups reported similar levels of agreement and expression of affection. The childfree women were more likely to engage in outside activities, to work on projects with their husbands, and to discuss things calmly with their husbands. They also tended to agree more on the division of household tasks, leisure-time activities, and career decisions.

Houseknecht (1979) also found that childfree wives were better educated, more likely to be employed, and less religious than mothers. These factors may have some bearing on the marital adjustment level of wives without children, just as did the decision not to have children. It is also true that some couples made their decision not to have children even before they married. Other couples kept postponing conception until it was too late to have or to want children (Veevers, 1974). The fact that a couple has had no children during the first years of marriage is not proof that they never hope to have them. It has become fashionable in some quarters to postpone having children until the woman is 23 to 32 years of age. By then they consider that the marriage should be emotionally and financially stable.

CHOICE TO REMAIN SINGLE

There are adults who never pursued the idea of wanting to be married. For some, it is a deliberate choice not to get married. For others it is a case of "if it happens—it happens; if not, it won't." The demographer, Glick (1977), indicates that the percentage of females who remain single in the United States is on the increase, and he projects that 6% to 7% of these women will never marry. Part of this increase may have been caused by the custom of women marrying men a few years older than themselves. The "baby boom" of the late 1940s and 1950s had produced a "marriage squeeze" because there was a shortage of men 2 or 3 years older than the typical female of that baby boom era (Glick and Carter, 1976). Glick and Carter, however, also point to a reversal of the situation in the 1980s when males of the baby boom era will find a shortage of marriageable women a few years younger. The census report of 1976 reveals that among 20- to 35-year-olds, one in four was single.

The social pressure to get married is not as strong as it used to be. The unmarried young adult has more freedom to leave home, to change jobs, and to travel.

The poor prognosis for teenage marriages and the frightening cries of the divorce rate cause many young people to wait before making a permanent commitment. Career opportunities for women have increased and many are choosing to enter the job market before, or instead of, considering marriage. There is a freedom of choice that did not exist before without questions and pressures to get married.

Marriage is still part of the picture of the future, however. Of the men still unmarried at 30 years of age, 75% will ultimately marry; of the women still unmarried at 30 years, 55% will marry before 50 years of age (Adams, 1971). Of those still unmarried at 35 years, half the men and about one third of the women will marry. By 40 years of age the ratio of men getting married is one in four and for women it is one in six.

Aspects of remaining single

The aspects of remaining single differ somewhat for the sexes. Women who remain single are more likely to be better educated than married women. Female scientists and engineers are six times as likely to be single as their male counterparts (Havens, 1973). According to Kangas (1978) very successful women tend to avoid or terminate intimate commitments that may lead to marriage. Males remain single mostly because they dislike the feeling of being tied down. They also may have easier access to sex.

Stein (1976a) interviewed 60 single men and women between the ages of 22 to 62 to determine what they considered to be the positive and negative aspects of being single. Among the positive aspects were reasons such as career opportunities, self-sufficiency, mobility and freedom to change, sexual availability, and opportunities to have sustaining friendships and a variety of experiences. These options can lead to more varied lives; single people can afford to take chances. Among the negative aspects were psychological factors, such as boredom, unhappiness, anger, being forced to role play, poor communications, sexual frustrations, lack of friends, social restrictions in certain cases because they were single, limited mobility, and lack of available new experiences. Some contradictions can be noted. Apparently, much depends on the personality and social pattern of the individual as to whether or not he or she can have or obtain the "freedoms" that are available to those in singlehood.

Social attitudes and reactions

Some unfortunate attitudes and stereotypes regarding singles persist in society today. Singles, especially women, are sometimes viewed as being lonely and/or running away from deep commitments. It is true that their single status may present them with problems—if they desire to get married—because after age 35 their potential for marriage becomes much less. By contrast, the opportunity for men to get married does not lessen as much (Weaver, 1979). The majority of single women, however, do feel a strong need for independence even though they desire close relationships, especially with men (Stein, 1976b). If there are problems, they usually arise from pressures from parents, relatives, friends, and colleagues to marry.

Those who are single by choice often feel no defensiveness. They just regret being subjected to a kind of discrimination. For example, the older single man is viewed as socially eligible and may date women much younger than himself. For an older women to date a much younger man somehow seems improper to many. The double standard still exists in some respects.

Single women are more active and work through their problems more realistically than men, partly because single women are more likely to become part of warm, supportive networks (Stein, 1976b). Campbell (1975) observes that single women of all ages are happier with their lives than single men. Apparently the network of human relationships developed by women provides the basic satisfactions of intimacy, sharing, and continuity. It seems that women can get along better without men than men can get along without women. However, both men and women do place a high value on enduring, close relationships.

Living arrangements

Singles have a variety of living arrangements. Some live alone, others live with roommates, and still others live in urban communal groups and share space in condominiums or apartment buildings where they find support and friendship (Stein, 1976a).

Living-together–arrangements (LTA) or cohabitation has an appeal for some people because of the simplicity of the arrangement—you just move in together. In the United States unmarried couples living together make up 1% of the population. In Sweden, 12% of couples living together are unwed. The idea is not as new as some mass media would suggest. There have always been "common-law marriages." Communes and multiple marriages were tried in the 1870s. The free-love and trial-marriage movements were well publicized in the 1920s. Sociologists indicate that there is no solid research to support the notion that a significant, meaningful trend toward new marital or nonmarital living arrangements exists. Open marriages, swinging couples or mate swapping, group marriages, and communal living are not common in the United States (Constantine and Constantine, 1973). Nowadays some women do not want to put up with marital situations that they find unsatisfactory and that they cannot remedy.

Of all the new approaches to adulthood, "singlehood," when the individual chooses to remain unmarried and unencumbered, is the one new style of life and living that is most rapidly emerging in Western societies. Happily, the social consciousness of our culture is changing and is making it possible for those who choose not to marry to do so without being stereotyped as much as they were previously.

CHAPTER REVIEW

1. Early adulthood is that period termed the *expansion years* of adulthood when all aspects of adult living are being developed.
2. The *developmental tasks* of early adulthood in more complex societies follow rather traditional social, psychological, and economic age-role expectations. The tasks include becoming part of the adult world, adapting to a career or occupation, establishing a supportive network of friends, possibly getting married and starting a family and home, becoming a contributing member of society, establishing priorities and values, and somehow integrating all of these tasks into a personal identity and a way of living.
3. *Personal independence* is a matter of attaining emotional, social, and economic independence. The implication is for an individual to become detached enough from others so that their moods, emotions, and values do not readily become part of one's own emotions or attitudes.
4. Most early adults view their health as good or excellent. In many physical characteristics, qualitative or quantitative, adults differ to a greater degree from one another than they did when they were adolescents. Decline in strength and endurance is very gradual to about the age of 50. Cardiovascular exercises can slow down the decline in cardiac output.
5. There is a possibility that Piaget's stage of formal operations may continue into early adulthood for many people. Special training may continue to develop specific cognitive abilities. A fifth stage, the *Structural Analytic Stage*, has been proposed to explain the type of cognitive development that takes place in adulthood.
6. *Crystallized intelligence* reflects intentional learning, mostly verbal in nature. *Fluid intelligence* develops from incidental learning and is not based on academically related learning. Fluid intelligence tends to peak in early adulthood. Crystallized intelligence continues to develop as long as there is exposure to verbal learning and the culture. Fig. 13-1 illustrates the capabilities of crystallized intelligence in adulthood.
7. Levinger and Snock have suggested three stages in the development of close friendships: (a) unilateral awareness, (b) surface contact, and (c) mutuality. *Self-disclosure* is critical to the development of close ties because it contributes to close, meaningful relationships.
8. Marriage as a formal institution is found in every society. The family has always been the basic biological and social unit in every culture.

9. *Trends in marriage* and the family include the following: (a) greater emphasis is placed on the emotional and social aspects of marriage, (b) cohabitation is generally a short, temporary arrangement, (c) more than 90% of adults get married, (d) of those who get married, 90% will have children, (e) a longer life expectancy means that couples have more years to spend without children at home, (f) divorce rates as well as single-parent families are on an increase, and (g) two-earner families are an increasingly typical marital pattern.
10. People fall in *love* for social, emotional, physical, and, possibly, economic reasons. There are varying degrees of maturity in love, ranging from infatuation to mature, responsible love, which continues to grow. Responsible love, respect, and friendship are rated higher than sexual compatibility by a large majority of women.
11. Theories of the reason marriage partners are chosen include: (a) the *propinquity theory*, (b) the *ideal mate concept* theory, (c) the *theory of complementary needs*, (d) the *homogamy theory*, and (e) the *theory of compatibility*.
12. In the Terman and Sears study of *predictors of marital happiness*, the most important predictor of happiness was the happiness of the parents in their marriage. The key is the type of attitude the young couple has toward life and marriage and their capacity to make it work.
13. The *developmental tasks and newlyweds* center around learning to live as a couple by integrating personality traits, styles of living, and attitudes relating to marriage, home, and family. Communication skills, social skills, and readiness for marriage are important factors in marital adjustment.
14. *Sexual adjustment* is usually accomplished during the early months of marriage. The *Hunt Study* reports a widespread improvement regarding sexuality among married couples. Apparently, changing social attitudes regarding the acceptability of sex for pleasure in a marriage as well as for conception are making a difference.
15. *Marital problems* frequently result from conflicts, often involving dynamics of behavior that do not resolve the conflicts but contribute to dissatisfaction. The dynamics of behavior take many forms, and the partners do not always recognize the source of a problem.
16. Although money and sexual problems are cited most frequently as heading the lists of marital problems, it appears that these are surface factors and that *lack of appreciation* and *poor communication* are the major factors contributing to the problems.
17. Among the more serious crises in marriage are a sudden loss of income, death in the family, extramarital affairs, and divorce. How a couple responds to these crises depends greatly on the degree of phsychological strength each individual has and the nature of psychological support the individuals provide for each other.
18. The divorce process has been described by Bohannan as encompassing *six stations:* (a) the emotional divorce, (b) the legal divorce, (c) the economic divorce, (d) the coparent divorce, (e) the community divorce, and (f) the psychic divorce.
19. Early adults perceive two to three times more stress in their lives than do middle-aged adults. Early adulthood is less stable, is more expansive, and has more mobility than is found in midlife, thereby permitting more life changes to take place.
20. *Parenthood* has many dimensions including pregnancy, mothering, fathering, stepparenting, and the one-parent family. The working mother is another factor in parenthood.
21. The *choice to remain single* is a viable option today compared to the traditional past. The positive aspects of remaining single include career opportunities, mobility, freedom to change, opportunities for sustaining friendships, and having a greater variety of experiences. The negative aspects of remaining single are boredom, unhappiness, being forced to play a role, sexual frustration, and social restrictions.

REVIEW QUESTIONS

1. Why is early adulthood called the "expansion" phase of adulthood?
2. Make two lists of developmental tasks for early adulthood. One list should be based on Havighurst and the other list on ideas of other writers.
3. What is meant by personal independence and why is it important in early adulthood? Define emotional independence, social independence, and economic independence.
4. Why are there more individual differences in physical characteristics among adults than among adolescents?
5. Describe the physical characteristics of early adults in (a) strength and endurance, (b) height and weight, (c) cardiac output, and (d) health satisfaction.
6. What is Piaget's stage of formal operations? What do the researchers have to say about adult cognitive development "beyond Piaget"? Do they agree with Piaget that development of formal operations is completed by age 16?
7. Review Fig. 13-1 on the cognitive growth and levels of accomplishment in adulthood.

8. What are the three stages in the development of a close friendship? Briefly describe each stage. What is self-disclosure? Who does more of it, men or women?
9. Why does the government require people to get a license in order to be married?
10. What are the advantages of marriage and the family in any society?
11. Summarize the trends in marriage and the family.
12. List at least ten reasons why people get married. In your judgment, which four or five are the most valid reasons for getting married?
13. Do marriage and college go together? Give your reasons.
14. Indicate the different kinds of love and briefly define each one. Which one or two kinds lead to more successful marriage? Give your reasons.
15. List and define the five theories of why marriage partners are chosen. Which theories seem most valid?
16. Make a list of predictors of marital happiness. What do you consider to be the ultimate factor contributing to marital happiness?
17. Review the developmental tasks of newlyweds both in terms of adjustment needs and preparations for the first child.
18. What are some of the personal or psychological adjustments that must be made in a new marriage?
19. Discuss sex in marriage in terms of the research since Kinsey.
20. Marital problems involve the dynamics of conflict. Identify some of the dynamics. What forms of behavior do they take?
21. Look at the types of marital problems mentioned by the studies cited. What psychological needs seem to appear? Are money and sexual problems primary sources of conflict or, basically, secondary sources?.
22. Divorce is a complex, emotionally involved topic. Beyond the statistics that are usually presented, what are the specifics on the nature of marital complaints leading to divorce? Summarize the California Divorce Study and the Cleveland Study on divorce.
23. What do Bohannan's "six stations of divorce" mean (say) to you?
24. What effect do stress and life crises have on health? Why is stress more prevelant in early adulthood than in later adulthood?
25. Make a table on parenting. List pregnancy, mothering, fathering, one-parent family, working mothers, and stepparents. Then briefly state some research findings for each group.
26. What are some of the characteristics of men and women who choose to remain, or who are, single?

THOUGHT QUESTIONS AND ACTIVITIES

1. Personal independence implies emotional independence, social independence, and economic independence. How are these forms of independence interrelated? How do they aid and abet, or possibly interfere with, career development?
2. Is love necessary for a happy marriage? Survey a number of married and unmarried people. Ask them the question: "What does it take to make a happy marriage?" See how many mention love. How do they seem to rank love on their list of what is considered to be important?
3. Does an individual have to be married in order to live a fulfilling, satisfying adult life (until death)? How do you (and your class) view unmarried adults in today's society? How do you see these persons ten years from now? Twenty years from now? Thirty years from now? Does it matter that unmarried adults constitute a minority?
4. What would it be like to be an adult 25 to 35 years of age? What are the sociological, psychological, and physiological factors involved? Are there major differences between these two ages? What would one of these persons be like if he or she decided to go (or to return) to college?
5. What qualities, characteristics, or attributes do you consider important in someone you would consider marrying?
6. What qualities, characteristics, or attributes do you consider important in parenting? Is maternal love stronger than paternal love?
7. Marital problems are often adjustment problems. Different kinds of adjustment need to be made at different stages of marriage. Can you think of changes in life-style or life patterns that may necessitate a change in the thinking and behavior of the couple toward each other and a consequent adjustment?

FURTHER READINGS

Hultsch, D.F., & Deutsch, F. *Adult development and aging.* New York: McGraw-Hill, 1981. This textbook is a gold mine of recent research on all phases of adulthood. The information is detailed enough to have depth and concise enough to be to the point. Moderate reading level.

Huston-Stein, A., & Higgens-Treuk, A. Development of females from childhood through adulthood: Career and feminine role orientations. In P. Baltes (Ed.), *Lifespan development and behavior* (Vol. 1). New York: Academic Press, 1978. An excellent presentation of the socializing influences that have led to different achievement and career orientation of young female adults. Easy to moderate reading.

Kirkley-Best, E., & Keelner, K.R. The forgotten grief: A review of the psychology of stillbirth. *American Journal of Orthopsychiatry,* 1982, *52*(3), 420-429. The authors discuss the psychological effects of a perinatal loss. Studies have found that holding the dead baby and arranging a funeral as well as having an autopsy performed may help parents allay guilt and cope with the death.

Levinson, D. *The seasons of a man's life.* New York: Ballantine Books, 1978. Levinson's study of the phases or eras of adulthood is presented in an interesting, readable fashion. Extensive biographical material is presented.

Miller, R.S., & Lefcourt, H.M. The assessment of social intimacy. *Journal of Personality Assessment,* 1982, *46*(5), 514-518. Married couples scored highest on intimacy, followed by unmarried couples and couples seeking therapy.

Sibisi, Y.T., & Yule, W. Parent training in a small group: A pilot study. *Child Care, Health and Development,* 1982, *8*(3), 141-150. Sibisi and Yule describe a study in which three mothers in their twenties were given a course in behavior management of preschool children. Results showed that the mothers employed the new skills to good effect outside the sessions.

Yankelovich, D. New rules in American life: Searching for self-fulfillment in a world turned upside down. *Psychology Today,* April 1981, pp. 35-91. Yankelovich did this research on young adults and their views. He presents interesting data on how the views of young adults have changed in the period of a decade.

CHAPTER 14

MIDDLE ADULTHOOD

THE YEARS OF CONTINUITY

ON THE OTHER SIDE OF FORTY

Some years ago during my undergraduate years in college I read a book entitled *The Best Is Yet to Come*. I don't recall the author or much that was written other than, as each stage of life was described, the author developed the theme that when an individual was in a certain stage in life, even though he was contented and happy, the best was yet to come. I remember that in the later stages of life the author believed that then and then only did the individual realize real contentment as he evaluated his life and looked toward death, believing that the best was yet to come. Young at the time, in my early twenties, I remember thinking, "Well, that's his opinion."

Today, on the other side of forty, I am inclined to think that perhaps the author knew what he was talking about. Does life begin at forty? Well, it depends on what you mean concerning "life."

If you mean that physical life begins at forty years, we all know that isn't so. By that age, after having lived over 45 years—days and nights—physical being is definitely not beginning. Oh, no, physical suffering would be more like it! If you have had a healthy body, prepare for some aches and pains of a general nature to creep into your being. Chronic illnesses may emerge at this time so that yearly checkups begin to make sense. Believe me, even the faithful eyes that have always seen everything and never failed begin to sting, water, and even blur everything together. Needles can no longer be threaded. Help is obviously needed.

On the other hand, when you are on the other side of forty, you have begun to accept your limitations. A certain amount of rest is needed so you see that you get it—not because some health book tells you but because you know you have to have it. You also follow a sensible diet because you now know that you alone will suffer the consequences if you don't. It is easier to do the right thing after you are forty years old. You accept and understand what must be and go on from there.

You don't become so upset over the trivial things of life. By the age of forty years you have experienced enough really important incidents of life so that energy is not wasted on the unimportant. What once seemed likely to be "the end of the world" is no longer viewed disproportionately. Little things are left to take care of themselves, and activities and problems are kept in their proper place.

When you are young, you have so many dreams and ideals. When you are over 40 years old, you now know that some of these dreams will never come true. Rich? Probably you will never be rich in material things, only in the things that make your life what you want it to be. You no longer plan to conquer or improve the world. You no longer expect the impossible from yourself or from those you love. What a relief! Now you can settle down to do the kind of thing you can do well and be satisfied with the doing of it. Gone is frustration. Now you can be satisfied. Now you can realize self-fulfillment in many facets of life.

If you are a parent, by this time your children are well on their way to adulthood. How nice it is not to wash diapers, observe schedules, and pick up after messy children! How proud you can be of your children and their accomplishments. How great it is to discuss interesting affairs of the world with them. If you are so fortunate as to be the mother of sons, how delightful it is to be "spoiled" by these fast-growing men. I love every minute of it!

Married couples who are over forty years old have found the person they most want to be married to. Long ago they gave up trying to change the other member in their marriage. They accept him, limitations, behavior lackings, and all, and are thankful for them. So what if your husband is not the greatest lover of the century! After all, you are no prize package yourself. Positive attributes are appreciated, and negative aspects are either forgotten or overlooked. It is nice to love and be loved just as one is. Gone are the role playing, games, and lack of communication that characterize a new marriage. Understanding and insight have taken over, and it is marvelous!

The sad part of being on the other side of forty years is that you begin losing some of your loved ones, especially those parents whom you have loved for so long. Sitting through my own dear mother's funeral and listening to the preacher expound on some of the familiar and beautiful passages from the Bible, "I am the Way and the Life . . . The Lord is my Shepherd," I was suddenly overwhelmed with the feeling that this is what life is all about. Life does go on! Life does have meaning! Wonderful!

When you are over forty, you don't have to keep up with the Joneses any more. In fact, who cares about the Joneses? Let them have or do what pleases them, and we'll find our own satisfaction. How free it is to relax with those of your choosing, those you really enjoy being with, and to no longer worry what others will think.

Being on the other side of forty is nice careerwise too. By now you hope that you have developed some common sense and learned some valuable lessons from experience that will enable you to do a better job. Some of us have reached our goals or see them in sight. Some of our dreams have been fulfilled.

Intellectually it is pleasant to know a little bit about a lot of things. It is also good to realize that even though you can't know everything—ever—you can know where to find out what you don't know. This calms down nervous feelings of inferiority. By forty years of age you know that others are just like you. No one is ever perfect. There is a lot of congenial give-and-take and little pretense at this time.

At forty, or on the other side, you can look at the world, love it; look at yourself, accept it; and feel that it's a great thing to be alive after all. Life is meaningful and fulfilling, and the best is yet to come!

Forty?
Contented, fulfilled,
Facing the future confidently,
  Enjoying the present.
The other side is best.

IN THIS CHAPTER . . .

You will read about

1. The developmental tasks of middle adulthood. They reveal a different type of tasks than have generally been presented for younger age groups.
2. The physical characteristics and health problems of individuals who are middle-aged.
3. The symptoms, complexities, and implications of menopause, the so-called change of life.
4. Personality changes and midlife crises.
5. Cognition and achievement in middle age.
6. The family at midlife, social roles and status, and life satisfaction.
7. Midlife career status and career satisfaction.

The developmental trend has come to that point in time known as middle age or as our Pennsylvania Dutch friends say, "Ve get too soon oldt, und too late schmart." They also say, "Throw the horse over the fence some hay," which does not make sense. But, then, to many people middle age does not make much sense, yet somehow the message gets across. However, we are not here to condemn middle age. We wish to present it in its proper perspective and place in the total life span. It can be a beautiful time of life because it ushers in the years of stability and freedom. The age of anxiety is over.

Early adulthood comprises the "developing years"—that period when all growth movement is vertical, upward and forward. The expansion phase of adulthood is a fast-moving period in which the young adult strives to achieve mastery over the external world, seeking material gain and approval of others. Sooner or later in each life there comes a time when the expansion phase tapers off. When and how this time occurs varies. It may come when people find themselves looking over their life situation and saying, "You know, if I can just maintain what I now have and am for the rest of my working days, I would be happy." To maintain the status quo, to just keep pace, to live and let live because life is satisfying at that point is to have arrived at the years of stability, where life will be on a more even keel. Now is the time when a person can turn his interests inward to achieve self-satisfaction and self-mastery. Activities that offer personal satisfaction can now be most important. The children are out of school, many of them are married, and the mother and father now have more time for each other and their own interests.

THE AGE LEVEL

As with most age levels, it is difficult to cite an age at which middle adulthood begins and ends. When one reads the literature, it is interesting to note that as the life span of men and women lengthens into the upper seventies, the ages cited for different adult levels are shifted upward (Newman, B.M., 1982). Three and four decades ago middle adulthood, or midlife, was indicated as starting at the age of 35 years, and in some cases at 30 years, and extending to 45 and 50 years of age. More recently some United States Census reports define midlife as covering ages 45 to 64.

There is more agreement on the circumstances that surround these years than on the actual age range itself. Middle age is generalized as the period between the time when the traditional roles of child rearing and becoming established as a provider have been completed and full retirement. The intervening period is one of more personal freedom, less economic stress, greater availability of leisure time, and fewer demands for material growth.

There are two major points of view of midlife in the literature. One model views middle adulthood primarily as a period of transition from one age stage to another; it is not inevitably a period of midlife crisis. Neugarten and Datan (1974) believe that a crisis may occur, but only when developmental processes are disrupted. Costa and McCrae (1980) interpret the so-called midlife crises, if they do occur, as mostly a continuation of earlier adjustment problems.

The other model of midlife views life as both a period of transition and crisis. Perun and Bielby (1979) make the assumption that crisis is a critical element in intrapsychic development of every individual. Crises are thought to occur throughout development and are viewed as mechanisms for change within individuals.

Perhaps the most valid conclusion that can be drawn about midlife is that, as with all periods of the life cycle, this period is also characterized by changes and transition. Not all adolescents undergo a period of "storm and stress"; not all middle-aged adults have a "midlife crisis." Much depends on the adjustive capabilities of the individual and the set of events or circumstances encountered.

Developmental tasks of middle adulthood

The connotation of the years of stability and freedom can be grasped more clearly by examining the developmental tasks of middle adulthood. The tasks are more intrinsic in nature; they relate to interpersonal roles as well as intrapersonal development, and for the first time many of them stress the "comforts" of life (Havighurst, 1979).

Relating to spouse. This is a time for the renewal and full development of the wife-husband relationship. It is a time of cutting through the thick overlay of habits of child-centered days and of nurturing a deep and abiding intimacy as a couple. This renewed awareness of the initial relationship in the marriage partnership will lead to rich and satisfying interaction between husband and wife. The couple will find encourage-

Harold Geyer

These are the thankful things in our lives:
. . . things that make memories of yesterday
. . . things that make life worth living today
. . . things that make for peace and love and hope in each tomorrow.

Meriem Kaluger

ment, support, and reassurance from each other. There will be the time and desire to do things as a couple again and to find each other after years of struggling with the physical, financial, and emotional strain of parenthood.

The joint responsibility that seems to be most difficult for couples at this time is the finding of each other as individuals again and of redefining or modifying their roles as husband and wife. The ability to meet each other's needs emotionally and sexually at this time is a goal to which the middle-aged couple must address itself if this drawing together is to become a reality. The man and woman need to reassure each other and fully accept one another as they are at this moment if their individual identity is to be recognized and, with that, their identity as a couple. Learning to share feelings and satisfactions and to recognize and appreciate each other as individuals who have desires,

As leisure time becomes available in midlife after the children are grown or have left home, the development of talents and skills provides a source of contentment and brings new feelings of self-worth.

aspirations, and disappointments will lead to a fuller life for both partners.

Grown children. The "mature" mother and father respond to the tasks of middle adulthood with the serenity born of a knowledge of "selfhood" that has been nurtured over the years. Their children are free to develop as persons without their being emotionally dependent on them. They feel no threat in sharing the affection of their offspring as their circle of social contacts grows. Standing by to assist their children practically or in an emotionally supportive way is a positive task of the mother and father at this stage in life.

At this time in life the task of intergenerational adjustment comes to the fore as well. The new in-law and grandparent roles are now part of the middle-aged adult's emotional scope (Duvall, 1971). The way in which each member accepts these new roles, whether enthusiastically or reluctantly, will determine in some measure his or her contentment at this time. Fragmentation of the whole family unit may result, with its ensuing loneliness and heartache, if this task is not successfully met. Middle-aged couples must rise to the occasion and realize the enrichment that these relationships can bring to their lives.

Leisure time. Development of creativity that has perhaps lain dormant during the child-rearing phase can be a highly satisfying task of the woman or man at this point in life. This may take the form of career pursual or resumption, of an active part in civic, social, or religious organizations, or of exploring new hobbies and areas of talent and skill. The satisfactory use of leisure will be a source of contentment and bring feelings of self-worth to the woman of this age group who needs something to replace the task of raising children (Spence and Lonner, 1978). The use of leisure time is the task that befuddles the male born and brought up in the work-oriented framework of American culture. This task is a "natural" for those who have learned the art of the "minivacation" and the joy of the long weekend, but to many serious, competitive business and professional men this poses a great challenge.

Social responsibility. Mature social and civic responsibility is a goal toward which the middle-aged adult must grow. This includes the understanding of one's civic responsibilities and how one can fit into the broad scheme of civic and social betterment of the world. As a rule, at this time the man and the woman have the time and vision to make their mature judgment a source of community, national, and international contribution.

Aging parents. The middle-aged adult also faces the task of developing a wholesome relationship with aging parents. Being aware of their interests and needs without allowing dominance or undue dependence to creep in requires much maturity and compassion. The adult of this age must stand as a bridge between the younger generation and the aging parent, allowing each to understand and value the other.

Physical changes. The middle-aged man and woman must come to terms with the changes in their physical being. Distress at signs of changes in hair, skin, and energy output tends to rob a person of the ability to face the task at hand—that of "relishing the bloom and peace of maturity." The climacteric phase must be viewed as a normal functional change rather than a threat to youth and desirability.

Some of the biological events of middle adulthood that require unique adaptation include menopause, deteriorating visual and hearing acuity, and the illnesses of heart disease, diabetes, and arthritis. An adapting self-image and a change in life-style may be required.

Economic standards. Creation and maintenance of a pleasant home occupies the adult at this stage, meaning the enrichment of the existing home to meet the needs and long unrealized desires of the couple. For a small percentage of couples this may mean moving to an apartment and giving up what is considered a burdensome house and yard.

Learning to strike a balance between spending money for personal gratification and putting aside funds for future security is another challenge for the family unit. Many couples find great joy in "living it up" without neglecting their future security needs now that their children have been successfully launched. Conversely, some cannot free themselves of their former frugal habits and cannot strike a healthy balance between having some fun and salting away every available cent for the proverbial rainy day.

There is an important lesson to be learned in middle age—that all that any of us really has is the moment we are now living. The time has come to be prudent about how much stress should continue to be placed on "saving for a rainy day." The world of economics is different today. Life is also short, and there are no guarantees. Now is the time to enjoy, the time to fulfill dreams.

Reappraisal and commitment. Levinson (1978a) says it is important to examine one's accomplishments, relationships, abilities, values, and goods to determine if the perspectives and commitments made in early adulthood are still valid in terms of a new life structure. If they are valid, they are to be continued; if not valid, then they should be changed. A basic point is that it is not possible during early adulthood to identify all the aspects of self that are important and necessary for development as life is lived. The natural outcome of the reorientation process is commitment to new directions or recommitment to old choices, but within a new framework. Involved in the reappraisal process are (1) recognition of biological limitations and health risks, (2) acceptance of death and mortality, (3) restructuring of sexual identity and self-concept, (4) reorientation to work, career, creativity, and achievement, and (5) reassessment of primary relationships (Cytrynbaum et al., 1980).

Productive contributor. According to Erikson (1968a) the psychosocial crisis of midlife is *generativity versus stagnation*. Generativity is an "expansion of ego interests and a sense of having contributed to the future" (1968, p. 85). The generative person has a deep concern for the development and nurturance of the next generation. It is being a producing, contributing member of society by assuming a responsibility of providing for the well-being of future generations. If output is perceived as being below expectations or if the role requirements are not fulfilled, a sense of stagnation can result. Stagnation leads to a feeling of not growing, of being bogged down in life, and of lacking in self-fulfillment.

Midlife developmental patterns. Peck (1968) introduces four sets of considerations in terms of midlife developmental patterns. *First,* he says that the individual must come to value wisdom and the ability to make effective choices over physical strength, stamina, and physical attractiveness. *Second,* an emphasis on socializing based on friendship and companionship must become the focus of human relationships rather than the sexuality or sex object emphasis as is found in youth. *Third,* the individual must have the flexibility necessary to shift one's affective attachments to new people, activities, and roles when old ones lose their potential for satisfaction. *Fourth,* mental flexibility is needed in order to use personal experience and understanding as a guideline for thought and behavior rather than rigid, automatic roles.

Sense of timing of events. According to Neugarten (1970) a *sense of timing of events in the life course* is needed. There will be challenges or periods of crisis during the middle years. The more that these periods can be viewed as times of transition and readjustment, the less likely is the event to have a disruptive effect. An inner "social clock," a sense of timing of the rhythm of the life cycle, is needed in order for the individual to be oriented to whatever happens in that part of the life cycle. When an event is viewed as a crisis, it is because the individual did not anticipate interruptions of the course of life.

"Youth is better" syndrome: A commentary

For some not entirely clear reason the United States has developed a thought form that places great stress on the desirability of being young, looking young, and feeling young. As a result the middle-age group seems to feel, or has felt, a need for a prestige role in American society. The age group of 40 to 60 years comprises only one fifth of the population, yet it is this group that occupies the seats of power, foots the bills, and makes decisions that affect the other four fifths of the people (Newman, B.M., 1982). It is the "in-charge generation."

The self-concept of the middle-aged person is frequently fragmented by the humorists, who enjoy capitalizing on a reluctance of many people to release their hold on youth and its often-glorified advantages. We saw a cartoon recently in which a man is saying to his wife, who is hiding under the bed, "But, Ethel, everyone has to become 40 some day!" Most oldsters forget how they dreaded becoming 30 years old. And how many people refer to middle age as "15 years older than I am"? Humorist Peg Bracken (1969) notes the period as "not quite twilight, and certainly not bedtime! Call it the cocktail hour, the happy hour, or high tea if you prefer." She refers to contemporaries who resist the aging process as victims of the "Peter Pan syndrome: everyone else is supposed to grow older but me."

Age needs to be put into its proper perspective without the undue distortions caused by the beating advertising drums from Madison Avenue. It is not that 40 years is so awfully old, it is just that being 20 years old is so awfully young! How much has a 20-year-old really lived and experienced of life? If we are speaking of people who went to college, they actually have spent almost all their life "going to school." Is this living? Think of what people do in the second 20 years of their life as compared to the first 20 years. It is in that second 20-year period that life is lived, loved, lost, laughed at, regained, reconstituted, enhanced! Change is an inevitable aspect of life. The person of 40 years is different in many ways from the youth of 20. The 40-year-old individual anticipates change and knows how to bring about desired changes. By this age life has meaning based on having been lived, not on the expectations of what will be. The forties are the old age of youth; the fifties are the youth of old age.

Probably most people associate getting older with a loss of the physical attractiveness of youth. But ask the question, "At what age does a woman reach her highest peak of physical attractiveness?" Pick an age, any age from one to a hundred. Would you believe that the majority of people are their most attractive in their thirties and early forties? It is at the age of 38 years that average adults reach their peak of total development (Marshall, 1973). That could be hard to believe if you are in your early twenties. There is an essence of beauty and attractiveness that can only come with age. Call it a mellowness, if you wish. It is an inner glow that manifests itself outwardly in beauty. It takes time to mature.

For physical beauty we would choose individuals in their late thirties; for excitement and exuberance in living, the twenties; for volatileness, the teens; for simplicity of life and faith, the little child; for charm, graciousness, and sincerity, old age. On the college campus it is always interesting to visit the various 5-year reunion classes on alumni day. Invariably the most attractive women and men are in the twentieth year reunion class. They know how to dress, how to communicate, and how to be attractive. Each class, however, has its own aura of attractiveness about it, each in its own way.

A final word on attractiveness. Each age level has its own criteria for attractiveness. The important thing for the individual is to learn how to be attractive to people of his or her own age level, not to those who are 20 years younger (or older) than themselves. It is important for adults, women especially, to keep up with changing fashions for their age levels, particularly hair styles. What looked good on the individual in college may continue to be attractive for another 5 years or so, but at some point a change in clothing or hair style may be needed.

It may well be that the "youth-cult threat" is diminishing as values are being reconsidered. Demographers have discovered that the 44.5 million people between the ages of 45 and 64 are fairly well off compared to the rest of the population. The U.S. Bureau of Census Report (1981a) indicates middle-aged people are less likely to be victims of crime than are other people. Less than 2% were victims of crime in 1978 as compared to 6% of the 20-to-24 age group. Middle-aged people are usually employed. In 1979 their unemployment rate was 3% versus an average of 6.8% for all others. Only 8% were below the poverty line in 1978 versus 12% for other age groups. Middle-aged people were responsive to civic duty. In the 1980 election 69% of their age group voted, compared to only 55% of the rest of the voting age population.

The demographers suggested that this age group was *not* a problem. They noted that middle age is a time of increasing personal and financial freedom, a time for travel, and a time to catch up on activities that have been postponed or denied altogether. It is a period of midlife noncrisis. Youngsters, oldsters, and those in between seem to agree that the middle years represent the prime of life (Taylor, 1976).

Physical characteristics

Developmental changes during the middle adult years occur slowly, since this period represents a long plateau in the life span. Furthermore there is an overlapping of ages at both ends of middle adulthood when some adults are manifesting the changes and characteristics of an earlier or later developmental stage. The point is that changes will take place—sooner in some people and later in others. We must discuss these changes, but some judgment must be used in applying the characteristics too rigidly to ages. It is important to consider the characteristics and changes in the total developmental perspective of the individual. Seen in that manner, changes that seem pessimistic when viewed in isolation lose some of their harshness when seen in the total framework of developmental age.

Generally speaking the human body is still functioning at almost peak efficiency as a person enters the phase of life that has been labeled the middle years. There are few characteristics to distinguish the middle adult from the young adult at the onset of this developmental stage. However, as this phase progresses, gradual changes can be identified as being peculiar to this time of life. Fig. 14-1 illustrates the potential and actual performance of physical capabilities throughout adulthood.

The implication of Fig. 14-1 is that there is a difference between what a person actually does in performance (the usual performance as shown by the bottom line) and what a person has the capability of doing (the potential as shown by the top line). Physical and psychological potential increase dramatically between the ages of 20 and 40. Actually the potential for improvement in cognitive development increases until past the

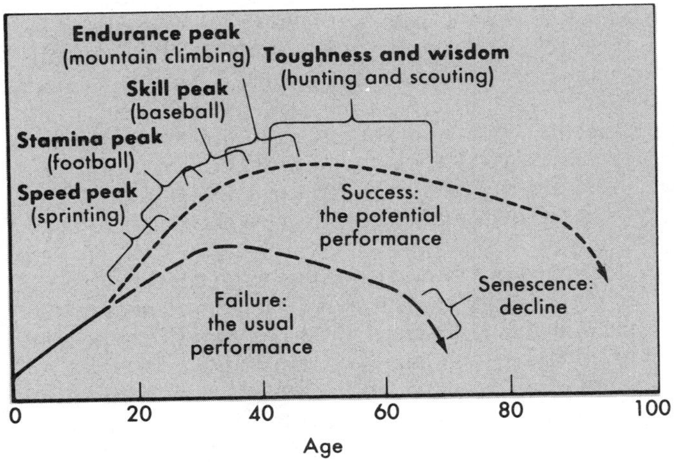

FIG. 14-1 ***Physical growth and ages of peak performance. Potential and actual performance. The upper lines indicate the physical potentials of normal people with peak periods for various activities; the lower lines indicate how most people fail to measure up.***

Modified from Still, J.W. Man's potential and his performance. *Copyright 1957 by the New York Times Co. Printed by permission. Also from Lehman, H.C.* Journal of Genetic Psychology, *1966,* 108, *263-277.*

age of 60. Physical potential changes according to the type of performance. The peak in speed and agility is achieved during the ages of 18 through 30 (Marshall, 1973). This is the age of most Olympic athletics.

During the decade of 30 to 40 there is some loss of speed but not of skill and endurance. By promoting and practicing physical fitness, an individual can maintain a high level of conditioning until the fifties. The discouraging note in Fig. 14-1 is to realize how most people fail to measure up to their physical and cognitive potentials by failing to remain active in these areas after the ages of 35 to 40. It can be stated, however, that barring disease, physical vigor and mental alertness can be expected to be retained during the middle adult years. All it takes is a little time and effort. You are now in the process of manufacturing a little old man or a little old lady. What kind of fitness foundations are you building? Most of the characteristics in the next paragraphs pertain to the individual who is closer to 50 or 55 than to 40 years of age.

Appearance. Most readily identifiable are the slight and gradual changes beginning to take place in physical appearance that have a tendency to "sneak up" on the individual. One day the "fortyish" adult becomes aware of a few gray hairs beginning to appear. The all-discerning mirror reflects an image of small creases or lines (optimistically referred to as laugh lines rather than wrinkles!). Skin may become dry and begin to show signs of loss of elasticity. There is a redistribution of fatty tissue in both males and females at this time, regardless of lack of change in diet or exercise patterns (Timiras, 1972).

Physical attractiveness does appear to convey an image. Bush (1976) showed slides of men and women to a group of students and asked them to speculate about personal characteristics portrayed by their physical images. They judged the physically attractive persons to be richer, smarter, and more successful in their careers and social lives. However, a study by Berscheid and Walster (1975) determined that women who had been attractive during college days tended to be less happy, less satisfied with their lives, and less well adjusted than women who were more ordinary or typical looking. The study did not actually say why this was so. Men's happiness appeared to be unrelated to attractiveness. Does physical attractiveness make a difference in how it affects one's life? Maybe. It can help promote an image that may be considered more desirable, but overall attractiveness can also be found in individuals who have a pleasing disposition, who are engaging conversationalists, or who are friendly, caring persons. Image is only an appearance. Personal characteristics have impact when they are revealed.

Motor and energy. Energy is no longer something that can be expended endlessly. There is a longer period needed to recoup strength after strenuous and extended activity. Few middle-aged adults can work long hours and pursue a taxing and unabated social life without feeling the need of slowing down (Welford, 1977). Minor illnesses such as the common cold seem to hang on longer, and there is a decided increase in the length of time necessary to recover from more serious ailments.

Physical fitness has become an adult obsession. There are more and more individuals of this group jogging, running, and working out in gymnasiums. Medical science approves of their physical activities. Some middle-aged men go to great lengths to convince themselves and others that their bodies are still in good condition. However, they find that after a day of hard physical exercise it takes longer to get the weariness out of their joints and muscles. Activities that improve cardiovascular function are more healthful than muscle-building ones (De Vries, 1977). Middle-aged women are also more conscious of health and fitness, but they show more concern with the physical well-being of their husbands than with their own (Neugarten and Datan, 1974). Women are involved in jogging, stretching exercises, and aerobic dancing.

A person employed as a laborer will realize soon after his fiftieth birthday that he does not have the vigor that he had formerly. However, his muscles are still strong. When a person reaches middle age, he or she is best at tasks that require endurance rather than quick bursts of energy (Welford, 1977). The middle-aged person must learn new limitations.

It is a fact that bodies do undergo changes at about the time of middle age. The skeletal muscles increase in bulk until the age of 50 years, but they stay on a plateau until they begin to degenerate at about the age of 60 years (Garn, 1975). Gross motor coordination depends on these muscles, and therefore the peak is at an earlier age. It has been found that the smooth muscles change little with age. Therefore the vital organs can, in reality, be kept healthy until death.

Sense organs. The sense organs of middle-aged people undergo change at an amazing rate of uniformity among individuals. The sense organs are the means by which people keep in contact with the external world. Thus any change in the functional efficiency of the senses affects people not only in physical but also in psychological ways.

George Kaluger

Meriem Kaluger

Physical fitness through exercise is available to anyone of any age. **Top,** *Aerobic dancing aids these women, ages 38 to 75.* **Bottom,** *In Shanghai and elsewhere, the practice of Tai Chi helps middle-aged and older individuals keep physically and mentally fit.*

One of the most noticeable changes is in vision. Many people feel the shock of realizing that they have hit middle age when they are required to wear bifocals or reading glasses. One of the most common occurrences at approximately 45 years of age is ***presbyopia,*** a condition characterized by the reduction in the elasticity of the crystalline lens of the eye that has progressed to the point where the lens can no longer change its curvature sufficiently to allow accommodation for near points of vision (Fozard et al., 1977). This is the reason why older people start to hold their reading material at arm's length until they are fitted for glasses with convex lenses. Many ophthalmologists are now finding this condition initially at the age of 50 years instead of 45 years. A second kind of visual structure change concerns the deterioration of the retina and the function of the nervous system related to vision. Fozard and associates (1977) state that this change begins to be important between 55 and 65 years of age.

Hearing acuity also undergoes change during middle life. This sensory change especially brings a need for emotional adjustment to the individual, since it is this change, more than any other, that can affect the individual's relations with others. Beginning with middle age there is a gradual deterioration and hardening of the auditory nerve cells. Almost everyone experiences some degree of loss of auditory acuity. The most common hearing difficulty is identified with age and is not pathological in origin (Corso, 1977). This is ***presbycusis,*** which is the loss of hearing for tones of higher frequency. This decline may begin in early adulthood and becomes greater as age increases. There are significant sex differences in auditory sensitivity between men and women of all ages. There are no differences between the sexes up to the middle ranges of frequency, 2,048 cycles, but above this point women of all ages are able to hear much better than men (Timiras and Vernadakis, 1972). Hearing loss for voice-range tones or lower usually does not occur until about the age of 60 years. Most individuals can adjust to these changes unconsciously, but when hearing loss interferes with work or participation in normal activities, a hearing aid of some type is needed.

Although the literature on *taste, touch,* and *smell* in adulthood has increased substantially during the last decade, there is not yet enough information to make generalizations that may be of practical value (Engen, 1977). These senses appear to decline in sensitivity as adult age advances, but the evidence is too general.

presbycusis progressive loss of hearing for high-frequency tones; associated with degenerative changes in the auditory system.

presbyopia physiological changes in accommodation power in the eyes in advancing age.

Taste sensitivity appears to be relatively stable except for changes due to disease, smoking, and sex differences (Engen, 1977).

State of physical changes. It is pragmatic to consider that most problems peculiar to aging start at about 40 to 45 years of age, the approximate median of life. There is a general slowing down of metabolism in the early forties, causing a weight gain and its undesirable effects on the other systems of the body. There may be signs of diabetes, and the incidence of kidney and gall stones increases (Lindeman, 1975). General decrease in the elasticity of the lungs is evident around 45 years of age; chronic bronchitis may develop slowly (Rockstein, 1975). The loss of elasticity and changes in appearance and structure of the lining coats of the arteries that can lead to many cardiovascular conditions is an acknowledged fact for people past the age of 45 years (Harris, 1975). The body systems should be periodically checked as the middle years begin so that physiological vigor can be maintained throughout the middle adult years. It is completely possible for a person to remain in a condition of sound health throughout this time period, despite the general slowing down process. Table 14-1 presents the functional capacities of different age levels as compared to those of a 30-year-old man.

It is of interest to note that scientists working with the space program consider the age of 38 years to be the peak year of adult development. The adult of this age can be more mentally alert, physically sound, and emotionally stable than at any other age. Neil Armstrong, first man to step on the moon, was 38 years old. The ages of the moon astronauts ranged from 36 years to Alan Shepard's 45 years. The look of youth may not be present, but the stamp of maturity is indelible.

Health problems and concerns

People are concerned about the sort of physical and mental health that increases their probability of living a full life, not necessarily in terms of length of life but

TABLE 14-1 Functional capacity of men at various age levels compared to 100% capacity of an average 30-year-old man

	Age					
Physiological characteristic	*30*	*40*	*50*	*60*	*70*	*80*
Nerve conduction velocity	100%	100%	95%	93%	91%	87%
Basic metabolic rate	100	98	95	92	86	83
Body water content	100	98	94	90	87	81
Work rate	100	94	87	80	74	
Cardiac output (at rest)	100	93	83	70	58	
Filtration rate of kidney	100	98	90	82	77	59
Maximum breathing capacity (voluntary)	100	92	78	61	50	41

Modified from Shock, N.W. *The psychology of aging.* Copyright 1962 by Scientific American, Inc.

particularly in terms of quality of life. The "fitness boom," the emphasis on nutritional diets and health care, and the admonitions of the Surgeon General's report on the health damaging effects of smoking have made many people, especially the middle-aged, conscious of wellness and good health habits. Not only is physical health stressed but mental health as well. Formerly, middle-aged patients seeking clinical counseling generally emphasized psychosomatic complaints, such as feeling tired, lacking energy, and being nervous. Today they are concerned about personal fulfillment, self-realization, and their quality of living (Lionells and Mann, 1974).

To die at 45 is to die prematurely. Heart disease and malignant neoplasm (cancer) are the major causes of these premature deaths. In general the health of both young and middle-aged adults has been improving; the death rates have been steadily declining. Between the years 1900 and 1975 the death rate for ages 45 to 54 declined from 15.5 to 7.8 persons per 1,000; for the ages 55 to 64 the decline was from 28.5 to 20 persons per 1,000. For the younger ages of 35 to 44 the decline was a dramatic 10.6 to 3 per 1,000 (Golenpaul, 1977). It is important to recognize the cohort effect for the 55 to 64 age group. This group was the World War II cohort group, which means a number of these cohorts may have been in the armed forces and possibly in combat, prisoner of war camps, or concentration camps. According to Schenck (1963) 1 year in war ages a person as much as 2 years, and 1 year in a concentration camp as much as 4 years. Survivors of concentration camps were reported to appear about 10 years older than their age, with deterioration in physical and mental efficiency.

Although females report higher rates of illness than men do, they have a longer life span. There is some evidence that women may live longer because their bodies offer better protection against disease (Shock, 1977). However, as women are becoming increasingly involved in domains formerly populated mainly by men, women are experiencing more conditions believed to reduce longevity (Friedman and Rosenman, 1974). Women who smoke, drink, do not exercise, and experience job stress do not live as long as women who do the opposite. Interestingly enough, employed women report less illness than do unemployed ones (Gove and Hughes, 1979). The leading chronic conditions for middle-aged males are diseases of the heart, lower-extremity impairments, back and spine impairments, visual impairments, and asthma. For middle-aged women the leading chronic conditions are arthritis and rheumatism, mental and nervous conditions, and hypertension without heart involvement (Verbrugge, 1975).

THE CHANGE OF LIFE

In the middle years a change occurs for men and women. Climacteric (andropause), the change of life in men, and menopause, the change of life in women, are the cause of much uncertainty in the minds of both sexes. The concerns and fears of the change of life are without scientific reason. Every period of life, from childhood to old age, has its joys and trials. This stage of life is no different; it has its compensations and can become an era of great fulfillment leading to years of happiness and serenity.

climacteric the period marking the end of the time at which women can conceive, and for men the time at which there is a significant decline in sexual virility. The term *menopause* is generally used for women instead of *climacteric*.

What is it?

At a certain time in middle adulthood the body will undergo certain physical changes associated with the gradual inability of certain glands to secrete the hormones they provided earlier. The word *menopause,* used to designate the change-of-life period in women, comes from the Greek words meaning "month" and "cessation." It refers to that time in a woman's life when there is a pause in the menses, a cessation of the monthly reproductive function. The word ***climacteric*** comes from two Greek words meaning "rung of a ladder" and "a critical time." In popular usage it is applied to a change in men, although the word *andropause* would be more appropriate to indicate the change in men. The term *change of life* for both men and women denotes the leaving of one phase of life and the beginning of a new one.

Symptoms of menopause begin with major hormonal shifts that take place in the woman between the ages of 36 and 55 years. Out of 903 cases reported the average age at which there was a complete cessation of menses was 49.2 years (McKinley et al., 1972). Only 3.5% of the cases occurred before the age of 40 years; 20% occurred between 40 and 44 years; 44% occurred between 45 and 49 years; 30% occurred between 50 and 54 years; and only 1.5% occurred at the ages of 55, 56, or 57 years. It usually takes 2 to 5 years for menopause to be completed (McKinley and Jeffreys, 1974). There is some indication of a hereditary pattern for the onset of menopause. All things being equal, daughters generally begin and end menopause in the same manner and at the same age as their mothers.

Symptoms of menopause

During menopause there is a reduction of action of the ovaries, affecting other glands and producing symptoms that may be disturbing to a woman. In about 75% of women menopausal disturbances are either absent or minor (Goodman et al., 1978). Only about 25% of women need some type of medical therapy (Kirby, 1973).

Menopause starts with a change in a woman's menstrual pattern. One of the following four things will happen: (1) there will be a general slowing down of flow of blood without irregularity; (2) there will be an irregularity of timing with skipped periods; (3) there will be an irregularity of timing and an irregularity in the amount of flow; or (4) there will be an abrupt cessation of menstruation. The usual pattern is skipped periods, with the periods coming farther apart until there may be only one period in 6 months.

Inside the woman's body certain changes take place. The ovaries become smaller, no longer do they secrete ova regularly as before. The fallopian tubes, having no more eggs to transport, also become smaller and shorter. The uterus hardens and shrinks. The vagina shortens and loses some of its elasticity. The urine is even different in its hormonal content (Sherman, 1971). The internal changes all concern the reproductive system because there is no longer a need for this function.

There are other internal physical symptoms that have nothing to do with the reproductive system. The spleen and lymphatic glands decrease in size. There is an increased tendency to constipation due to the changes in the wall of the intestine. There may be urinary incontinence—an inability to retain urine.

The symptoms noticed most by women are the external physical ones. There are many symptoms, however, and not all will occur in every woman. Women experience only one or two symptoms. Some women will experience the symptoms for several years, some for several months, and some not at all.

One of the most common and most talked-about symptoms is the *hot flushes,* sometimes called hot flashes. Most symptoms, including the hot flush, involve the nervous system and the blood. During a hot flush, the body becomes warm and there is excessive perspiration followed by chilliness. These hot flushes may involve only the face and neck, or they may extend over the whole body. Frequently they occur during the months when periods are missed but usually cease after the menses stop completely. They are probably the most annoying of all the symptoms, usually lasting only a minute or so; they can be controlled by medication.

There are many other symptoms. The breasts eventually become smaller and lose some of their firmness. The body contour may change, and there is often a tendency to gain weight. This may be checked by a careful diet. However, some women get progressively thinner. The hair on scalp and external genitalia becomes thinner. The labia may lose their firmness and become flabby. Muscles, especially of the upper arms and legs, may lose their elasticity and strength. Itchiness, particularly after bathing, may occur. Insomnia sometimes occurs, headaches may increase. Certain male characteristics may appear, such as hair growth at the corners of the mouth or the upper lip. This can be helped by prescribed hormones. These symptoms are the ones that occur most frequently.

Hormonal deficiency, causing many of the physical and psychological symptoms of menopause, has been greatly reduced in the past several years by the use of estrogen replacement therapy. However, hormonal therapy helps only those complaints that are related directly or indirectly to hormonal deficiency (Bardwick, 1971). A woman who has reached menopause may have other reasons to feel the depression and general psychological upset that can be part of her life at this time. Bart (1971) identified the source of depression in a sample of women between the ages of 40 and 49 as the result of overinvolvement with their children and overidentification with the role of motherhood. For some women the overinvolvement was with themselves as individuals.

Psychological factors

In addition to the various physical symptoms there are also psychological ones, but, again, not every woman experiences psychological symptoms. Usually if a woman is well adjusted mentally and emotionally before menopause, she will have no problems (Flint, 1976). However, if a woman has been poorly adjusted or unhappy, she may have mental problems during menopause. Table 14-2 presents a number of attitudes concerning menopause and middle age reported by women. Notice that only 4% mentioned menopause as their worst problem.

Psychologically the cessation of menstruation for some women is a state of anxiety that is related to the woman's concept of herself as a human being (Bart and Grossman, 1978). Some women believe that with the menopause comes the end of their attractiveness, thus the end of their sex life. Their children are grown and married. They no longer feel needed. They no longer use their leisure time advantageously. They just worry. What happens to these women who cannot adjust? Some women drink to solve their problems. Some seek out "loving" men. Some avoid a social life of any kind—they isolate themselves. Some women cry all the time and are usually depressed.

The degree of anxiety about menopause depends on the individual woman's feelings about not being able to bear children and growing old, as well as the kind of information she has about the symptoms that accompany menopause. Postmenopausal women have more positive attitudes about menopause than do premenopausal women (Neugarten et al., 1963). Having gone through the event, the older women realized that the symptoms were temporary, an upsurge in sexual impulses and activity could occur, the childbearing years were over and energies could be redirected into other areas of skill development, and the new-found freedom had the potential for gains in feelings of well-being and vigor.

The larger majority of women do not have these psychological problems because their lives have been filled with usefulness, happiness, charm, self-appreciation, and accomplishment (Newman, B.M., 1982). They have been emphasizing values and interests in life that can be pursued with vigor at any age.

When is menopause over? No one knows exactly when ovulation will end for any woman. She may not have a period for 5 or 6 months, and then another may occur. Most authorities agree that menopause has been completed if there has been no menstrual period for 1 year. With the end of ovulation also usually comes the end of the physical symptoms. If they do not end, they are caused by something other than menopause.

Middle-aged pregnancy is uncommon as women approach menopause. The "change-of-life" baby is a possibility but not the usual occurrence for the woman who begins noticing changes in the menstrual cycle. One study indicated that, in general, pregnancy after 47 years of age is highly unlikely; another study stated that pregnancy in women over 50 years of age is "extremely rare" (Bardwick, 1971). During the time of irregular periods it is difficult to know when ovulation takes place. Conception would be possible, but the correct combination of events would be unexpected

TABLE 14-2 Women's attitudes and views toward menopause

	Percent		Percent
The worst thing about middle age		**The worst thing about menopause**	
Losing your husband	52	Not knowing what to expect	26
Getting older	18	The discomfort and pain	19
Cancer	16	Sign of getting older	17
Children leaving home	9	Loss of enjoyment in sexual relations	4
Menopause	4	Not being able to have more children	4
Change in sexual feelings and behavior	1	None of these	30
What I dislike most about being middle-aged		**How menopause affects a woman's appearance**	
Getting older	35	Negative changes	50
Lack of energy	21	No effect	43
Poor health or illness	15	Positive changes	1
Feeling useless	2	No response	6
None of these	27		
The best thing about the menopause		**How menopause affects a woman's physical and emotional health**	
Not having to worry about getting pregnant	30	Negative changes	32
Not having to bother with menstruation	44	No effect	58
Better relationship with husband	11	Positive change or improvement	10
Greater enjoyment of sex life	3	**How menopause affects a woman's sexual relations**	
None of these	12	Sexual relations become more important	18
		No effect	65
		Sexual relations become less important	17

Modified from Neugarten, B. *Vita Humana,* 1963, *6,* 140-151.

and unlikely. When middle-aged pregnancy becomes a reality, particularly if the child is the first conceived, there is a greater tendency for longer labor due to the loss of elasticity of the cervix and vagina. There is a higher risk of the over 40-year-old mother producing a child with some defect. The rate of Down's syndrome in the offspring of younger mothers is one in 600, whereas the rate of Down's syndrome in the offspring of older mothers rises to 1 in every 50 births. Spontaneous abortions are not unusual in women who become pregnant after the age of 40 years. Some doctors who believe that menopause is over when there is no menstrual period for 12 months still suggest that some type of birth control be continued for another 12 months.

What about men?

There is really no such thing as a "male change" in the literal sense of the word. There is no physical change in the male comparable to the change in the female. Some emotional changes occur in men around middle age, but these can be attributed to progressive aging or to diminishing sexual desire (Beard, 1975). The main change is in the man's thinking patterns and self-image. This is not the result of hormonal deficiency—androgen levels decline slowly. The reproductive function does not end, and sperm manufacture continues with no sudden change until old age. Fertility is not interfered with even when sperm production slows (Weg, 1978). However, the quality of the sperm cell may deteriorate. Fatherhood is possible until extremely late in life. Possible loss of sex drive and potency is more a matter of the mind than a set of physical facts.

There is a gradual decline in the production of testosterone, resulting in some changes in the sex organs and sexual activity. The testicular tubes become narrower, and there is less seminal fluid. Ejaculation occurs with less force. Older men may take longer to achieve an erection, but once the penis is erect, erection can be maintained for some time (Cleveland, 1976). However, older men must have a longer period of time (the refractory or recovery period) before erection can be regained after an orgasm (Hyde, 1979).

Psychologically there are two facts that may suggest a kind of male climacteric. First, some men have almost neurotic reactions to middle age. They do not want to be old; they try to look and act very young. Some even divorce their wives and marry women 10 or 20 years younger. Second, some men have depressive reactions, but they occur about 10 or 15 years later in men than in women, around the ages of 55 to 65 years (Notman, 1978). These are probably a result of fatigue, retirement, boredom, financial problems, or fear of sexual impotency. According to Pfeiffer and Davis (1972) health status, life satisfaction, and social class are the determinants that relate most positively to sexual functions. For both men and women, good health, good attitudes, and a good life mean much in terms of being able to be sexually active.

In about 1 of every 100 men there is a period during which reproductive powers suddenly end. When this happens, it is due to primary testicular failure. The discomforts of this disease are similar to the symptoms of menopause in women. The cure is slow and expensive because it is an illness. This problem does not occur naturally like menopause (Kimmel, 1974).

Sex in middle age

The years between the ages of 20 and 30 are ones in which sexual capacity and drives are strong. However, with the aging process and physiological changes the male usually experiences some decline in sexual behavior at about the ages of 55 to 60. Hunt (1974) reports that at 60 years of age only 5% of males in his study were inactive sexually. By the age of 70 years nearly 30% were inactive, but the others were active. There is usually little decrease in sexual interest, but there may be a decrease in sexual activities due to

TABLE 14-3 Current frequency of sexual intercourse (percentage)

Age group	*Number*	*None*	*Once a month*	*Once a week*	*2-3 times a week*	*More than 3 times a week*
Men						
46-50	43	0	5	62	26	7
51-55	41	5	29	49	17	0
56-60	61	7	38	44	11	0
61-65	54	20	43	30	7	0
66-71	62	24	48	26	2	0
Total	261	12	34	41	12	1
Women						
46-50	43	14	26	39	21	0
51-55	41	20	41	32	5	2
56-60	48	42	27	25	4	2
61-65	44	61	29	5	5	0
66-71	55	73	16	11	0	0
Total	231	44	27	22	6	1

From Pfeiffer, E., Verwoerdt, A., & Davis, G.C. Sexual behavior in middle life. In E. Palmore (Ed.), *Normal aging II: Reports from the Duke longitudinal studies 1970-1973*. Copyright 1974 by Duke University Press, Durham, N.C.

pressures or psychological attitudes. Table 14-3 indicates the frequency of sexual intercourse at different age levels for men and women. The higher percentages of "none" for women aged 61 and over is due in part to the lack (death) of a spouse.

Psychologically, midlife men and women frequently undergo changes in sexuality that reflect changes in the activity/passivity dimensions of personality (Norman and Scaramella, 1980). Women in the middle years tend to shift from a dependent stance to one that emphasizes development of their own abilities in a more active sense. Women tend to become considerably more sexually active and responsive than before the midlife period (Gadpaille, 1975). Men tend to emphasize more gentle aspects of self, such as expressed tenderness, a need for security, and an awareness of the feelings of others (Lowenthal et al., 1975). If men and women in their midlife years are not responding sexually as they would want to, their sexual relationships can become a focus of concern and disturbance (Kaplan, 1974). Levinson and his associates (1978) did find that some midlife men have anxieties about sexuality. They have concerns about the possibility of waning virility and worries about physical attractiveness.

During the midlife is a good time for a husband and wife to take stock of their sexual selves and to ascertain if they have really reached the pinnacle of marital bliss with each other. Individuals who have always enjoyed intimate relations to the fullest may expect to continue to do so; those who have never achieved sexual fulfillment now have an opportunity to "try again."

There is one condition that will prevent a woman from having sexual pleasure during or after menopause; it may even cause severe pain. This is *dyspareunia,* or painful intercourse. During and after menopause (and in some women approaching this time of life) an insufficient quantity of female sex hormone (estrogen) causes the lining of the vagina to thin out and become sensitive and painful to the touch. The administration of estrogen by injection, by mouth, or by suppositories in the vagina will thicken the epithelium lining the vagina and repair the damage (Goldstein, B., 1976).

The extent and degree of waning sex energy in middle-aged men and women vary with the individual's state of mind and physical fitness. The so-called change of life tends to intensify existing body disorders and permit others to occur. More often than not a woman's mental and emotional disturbance over menopause does more harm than the process itself. Anxiety has been proved to be the prime danger to the well-being of a man or woman during this period.

personality an individual's characteristic pattern of behavior and thought, including an accordant self-concept and a set of traits consistent over time.

PERSONALITY CHANGE IN MIDLIFE

Midlife would be the ideal stage of life to study the question "How stable are personality traits over the span of a lifetime?" The growth and developmental influences of childhood and adolescence have made their impact, and the settling, reconciling forces of early adulthood have taken place. By middle age the development of one's personality should be rather firm. Thus it would appear to be a time when it would be possible to examine characteristics and compare them with traits of the past in order to determine if personality factors are basically stable or changeable. It appears that the question is so complex that research design and methodology have not been developed to the point that validity can be established.

Personality organization consists of a relatively consistent set of thoughts, feelings, and behavior patterns that guides action, provides meaning to experiences, and gives individual direction to life (Newman, B.M., 1982). The adult personality is a product of the interaction of biological forces, life space, and the individual's own ego organization or structure. It represents the integration of four major psychosocial factors: role expectations, traits and abilities, motive patterns, and coping styles. Changes in any of these factors could bring about a change in personality. The adult, however, has been involved in the learning of role behavior over a long period of time, with the result that role behavior becomes rather set and the attitudes accompanying that behavior are difficult to modify. Most people persist in their habits, opinions, attitudes, and behavior. As a rule they will resist any change that tends to threaten their patterns of behavior and beliefs (Neugarten, 1977).

Theories of personality in midlife

Troll (1975) suggests that there are three alternative views of adult personality development. *One approach* contends that the self is stabilized early in life, sometime before adulthood is reached. As such, personality development has a consistent identity that can minimize the disturbing effects of environmental influences. A *second alternative* interprets personality as a response to environmental situations. As environments change, so do aspects of the personality. The *third view* is that the self-system (personality) deals with both external and internal changes; it incorporates change into the existing self-system, and as it does, it develops a new and different personality characteristic. Troll (1975) suggests that some personality characteristics remain unaltered throughout adult life but others change as a consequence of environmental influences. However, people cannot and do not change their personalities automatically. Change may come about because of a learning experience. Old patterns and habits have to be unlearned. Being involved in a counseling relationship, a traumatic situation or series of events, a prolonged, deep emotional experience, or thoughtful contemplation are inducements to accomplish change. Even then the experience has to be meaningful and internalized before discernible change results.

Theories of personality vary in terms of the relative emphasis placed on these three alternative views of personality development. Traditional psychoanalytic theory emphasizes the role of internal factors and a stabilized development of personality soon after childhood is completed. Freud (1949) hypothesized that life and behavior are governed by the libido, a psychic energy that reflects erotic desire or pleasure. The quality of one's personality development depends on how satisfying psychosexual development was at the five stages of libido expression in earlier life. According to Freud, personality development can be arrested or fixated at one of the stages by a traumatic disruption of the gratification need. As a result, personality development will remain immature, even into adulthood. During adulthood personality remains relatively stable. The only change that takes place is when an individual is confronted with difficult stress situations and events to the level where personality development was fixated. Psychoanalytic theory of personality was discussed in depth in Chapter 6.

The role of external factors, the environment, is emphasized by social learning theories. These theories suggest that personality characteristics are learned as a response to, or in interaction with, the environmental context (Mischel, 1973). The individual learns by observing the behavior of others (models) and recognizing the appropriateness of the behavior. New responses are acquired by appreciating the reward, payoff, or reinforcement involved or by the vicarious, cognitive acknowledgement of the correctness of the behavior as indicated by the consequences of the action. Personality is learned by social interaction. In adulthood the implication is that there is a possibility of personality change if the individual internalizes the meaningfulness of an observed behavior or its conse-

George Kaluger

Both internal and external factors determine how well a person can relate to a constantly changing personal and environmental reality. A person who feels good about herself or himself can usually cope with changes because the personality structure can adapt in a variety of ways to new motivations and demands instead of clinging to the behavior patterns of the past.

quence and seeks to adopt that behavior so the same results can be obtained. Changes in adulthood often center around changing social situations. The behavioral theory of personality was also presented in Chapter 6.

A group of neopsychoanalytic theories emphasize the role of both external and internal factors in personality development. *Neopsychoanalytic* refers to contemporary psychoanalysts who consider their position to be a major modification of the traditional Freudian position (Bühler, 1968, Erikson, 1963). Sometimes called *ego theories,* these views have their roots in the orthodox psychoanalytic perspective of Freud. However, rather than stressing the dominant role of the id and its internal process, ego theorists emphasize the role of the ego. They consider the function of the ego to be that of adapting to reality by organizing processes such as perception, cognition, and interpersonal behavior. This approach has meaning for change in adult personality because reality is constantly changing, and adaptations must be made.

Bühler (1968) suggests that personality changes over the life span take place because of motivation changes. She believes that the motivation pattern of an individual affects the ways in which goals are reached and new goals structured. Some personality development takes place in the years of 45 to about 65. Healthy people evaluate their past and revise their plans for the future. Immature people avoid assessing themselves and fail to make effective decisions.

According to Erikson (1963a) personality is determined by the interaction of an inner, biologically based maturational plan and the external demands of society. In adulthood, Erikson indicates that there are three psychosocial capabilities of the ego that must be developed. In early adulthood the development of intimacy must be attained; in middle adulthood the capability of generativity is required; and in late adulthood a sense of ego integrity must be reached.

The implication of these three views of personality development is that there are some aspects of personality that appear to continue throughout adulthood, while other aspects are subject to change. Middle adulthood at least holds the potential for personality development.

Continuity and change of personality

Research examining the issue of continuity versus change in adult personality has produced mixed results. Evidence for both continuity and change exists (Hultsch and Deutsch, 1981). The evidence for age-related continuity appears to be stronger than the evidence for age-related change. Some research suggests that sex and cohort differences are more significant than age stages. An introductory statement on the continuity versus discontinuity issue is presented in Chapter 1.

transcendence extending or lying beyond the limits of ordinary experience.

Cross-sectional studies. A series of large-scale investigations of the social and psychological aspects of middle age and aging was carried out over a ten-year period under the sponsorship of the Committee on Human Development of the University of Chicago (Neugarten and Datan, 1974). Cross-sectional data gathered on more than 700 men and women, ages 40 to 70 years, revealed seven psychological attributes or *characteristics related to overall adjustment* and mental health of the middle-aged person. These characteristics include the following:

1. *Cathectic or emotional flexibility,* the capacity to shift emotional outlay from one person to another and from one activity to another.
2. *Mental flexibility,* the capacity to use experience and prior mental sets as provisional guides rather than as fixed, inflexible rules in the solution of new problems.
3. *Ego differentiation,* the thought capacity to pursue and to enjoy a varied set of major activities in life and not to rely entirely on one or two life roles.
4. *Body* ***transcendence***, the capacity to feel whole and happy because of one's social and mental powers and to avoid preoccupation with health, physique, and bodily comfort.
5. *Ego transcendence,* the capacity to engage in a direct, gratifying manner with the people and events of daily life with a strong concern for the well-being of others and not with self-centered desires.
6. *Body satisfaction,* the degree of satisfaction one subjectively feels with one's body.
7. *Sexual integration,* the capacity to mesh one's sexual desires with other aspects of life, among them affection for the sex partner and an integration of sexual and other motivations in social relationships.

extroversion an attitude in which a person directs his or her interest to outside phenomena rather than to feelings within.

midlife crisis turmoil precipitated by the review and reevaluation of one's past, typically occurring in the early to middle 40s.

neuroticism state of being partially disorganized due to anxieties.

Personality adjustment in the middle years appears to be related to the individual's capacity to properly utilize these seven characteristics. *Emotional flexibility* is needed because middle age is a period when parents die, children leave home, and the individual's circle of friends begins to be broken by death. Middle adults need to be able to reinvest their emotions in others and to redefine existing relationships. *Mental flexibility* is needed in middle age to be able to work out a set of answers to life. The impact of retirement can be lessened by a good capacity for *ego differentiation,* permitting the individual to take up new roles. *Body transcendence, ego transcendence,* and *body satisfaction* are needed to be able to move beyond the self so that one's interest can lie in others rather than self. *Sexual integration* becomes necessary because of the demand for personal growth that occurs in middle age. There is no question that the transition from early adulthood to middle adulthood is equal in difficulty to any other period of transition in the growth and development of people.

Neugarten and her group found evidence for both continuity and discontinuity. On the one hand, personality structure was stable as were *socioadaptational aspects* of personality, such as goal-directed behavior, coping styles, and life satisfaction. These characteristics were not age related. On the other hand, marked age differences in the *intrapsychic dimensions* of personality, including active-versus-passive mastery and inner-versus-outer orientation, were found. Forty-year-olds felt in charge of their world and saw themselves as a source of energy. Sixty-year-olds, however, found the environment threatening and the self as passive and accommodating (Neugarten and Datan, 1973). There also appeared to be increased self-reflection and preoccupation with inner life among older adults.

Longitudinal studies. The Berkeley longitudinal studies covered a 40-year time span. A summary of the results presents some evidence for both continuity and change. Personality characteristics reflecting information processing and interpersonal relations tend to change, while those reflecting socialization and self-presentation tend to remain stable (Haan, 1976). During the life span there seems to be movement toward greater comfort, candor, and an objective sense of self. Researcher Livson (1973) suggests that the age 50 rather than the age 40 is the real beginning of life for some people because of the time needed to make necessary changes.

Costa and McCrae (1980) propose that personality may be described by three broad clusters of traits centered around the characteristics of ***neuroticism*** (anxiety, depression, impulsiveness), ***extroversion*** (attachment, gregariousness, activity), and *openness to experience* (openness to aesthetics, feelings, ideas, values). These clusters are generalized dispositions to think, feel, and behave in certain ways. A longitudinal, normative analysis of these traits suggests that adult personality is characterized by continuity rather than change. The traits remained stable.

Findings. The findings and studies cited above suggest the complexity of research in adult personality and the difficulty in drawing conclusions. Perhaps the question of continuity versus change is not an adequate one. A better question may be, "How much change can be expected and what prompts this change?" People differ in how and when they experience great changes in personality. Different consequences emerge from change in one period of life as compared to another. Sex-role expectations and how they are followed may add another dimension to personality development. It appears that growth may depend on the person's capacity for further development (Newman, P.R., 1982). Openness to new ideas, willingness to take risks, and interpersonal responsiveness are all qualities that predispose the individual to continued personal growth in adulthood.

Midlife crisis: True or false

Middle age has frequently been compared to the age of adolescence, as being one of dramatic change and transition (Gould, 1978). The term *crisis* has often been used to describe the period of stress during which the transition is experienced. However, the concept of crisis seems to have lost scientific meaning as it has become widely used, and misused, in the popular media (Perun and Bielby, 1979). In addition, there seem to be some conceptual problems differentiating between a developmental task and a "crisis." Every stage of life contains tasks that must be learned. Learning them is a challenge. The challenge may be termed a crisis.

According to Erikson (1963a) the crisis is the vehicle through which the challenge is met and the transition accomplished. The term *crisis* is sometimes defined as a "transition vehicle" and other times as a "stressful, disruptive condition." Both definitions represent a turning point for better or worse. Because of the ambiguity of the use of the term crisis, it is inaccurate to ask the question, "Is there a midlife crisis or not?" It is more correct to ask, "How do events affect an individual in a transitional period?" Some individuals could truly have a crisis; others may have only a momentary readjustment period. Either way, most researchers agree that middle age is marked by reflective introspection (Rappaport, 1976).

Midlife as crisis. The statistics of middle-age health factors and disruptive life events are revealing. Peptic ulcers, hypertension, and heart disease are most often first diagnosed in middle-aged patients (Rosenberg and Farrell, 1976). The suicide rate for males between the ages of 40 and 60 is approximately three times the rate for males 15 to 24. Infidelity and desertion, by both men and women, were major problems in the marriages of the middle-aged in the mid-1970s (Bradbury, 1975). Higher rates of first admissions for alcoholism are found among middle-aged individuals than among younger or older adults. Do these statistics suggest a midlife crisis or just the intervention of other variables that simply emerge at this stage of life?

Levinson and colleagues (1978) believe that the midlife transition period spans 4 to 6 years, reaching its culmination when a person is in the early forties. About 80% of the Levinson subjects deemed midlife transition as a time of moderate or severe crisis. Some of the major crisis experiences of this period are (1) bodily decline and a vivid recognition of one's mortality, (2) the sense of aging, (3) the emergence and integration of the more feminine aspects of self, (4) a reappraisal of past life structures, and (5) a need to make choices that will modify earlier structures and provide a basis for living in middle adulthood. An important part of the reappraisal process is what Levinson labels *de-illusionment.* In early adulthood an individual creates illusions of what the future will be like. In midlife these illusions must be examined if effective reappraisal and change are to take place. An outcome of the reappraisal process should be a commitment to new choices or recommitment to old choices within a new framework. Levinson (1977) observes that those who have formerly worked very hard at their jobs and supported the values of their culture came to question both the meaning of their work and their values.

Gould (1978) saw a corresponding transitional period for both men and women between the ages of 35 and 43. The early forties mark a period of personal discomfort, a feeling that life will not change much from year to year. People in the later forties tend to feel that the "die is cast." They become resigned to their past experiences and present personalities. There is some negativism accompanied by anxiety over the children, dependency on their spouses, perhaps some bitterness toward their parents, and a general negative feeling toward life in general. In the fifties the shadow of negativism diminishes. The awareness that time is running out tends to help make people mellow. They want their children to be happy regardless of what they achieve; they see their spouses as companions; and they accept their parents as they are. Questionnaire results of points of view at different age levels are summarized in Fig. 14-2. Note items 1, 4, 5, 8, 12, 13, and 17. The phases of adulthood as developed by Levinson and Gould were presented in detail in Chapter 12.

The 40-year longitudinal Grant Study of Harvard graduates, conducted in part by Vaillant and McArthur (1972), suggests that more overt depression was experienced in their forties than when they were in young adulthood. They often felt disenchanted with life and went through difficult periods of self-appraisal. Between 25 and 35 these young men had worked hard at their careers. They were following the rules, good at performing tasks, anxious to be promoted, and dedicated to the system. By age 30 they had given over to conformity, but they were poor at self-reflection. By the time they were 35, they could not wait to take charge. However, at 40 most of them had a sense of anxiety and turmoil; the 40 to 50 age span was a difficult decade for many. Yet they proceeded with self-appraisal and came out with their lives restructured. They looked back on the years 35 to 49 as the happiest of their lives. According to Vaillant (1977b), individuals who had been organized, integrated, and practical in adolescence were best adapted at age 50, while those who were asocial in adolescence were least likely to achieve the best outcomes.

Midlife as transition. The researchers subscribing to this view suggest that midlife is a period of transition but not necessarily of crisis. If an individual develops an inner sense of the life cycle and the notion of usually expectable life events, then midlife is not doomed to a crisis entity. Periods of crisis may occur, but they

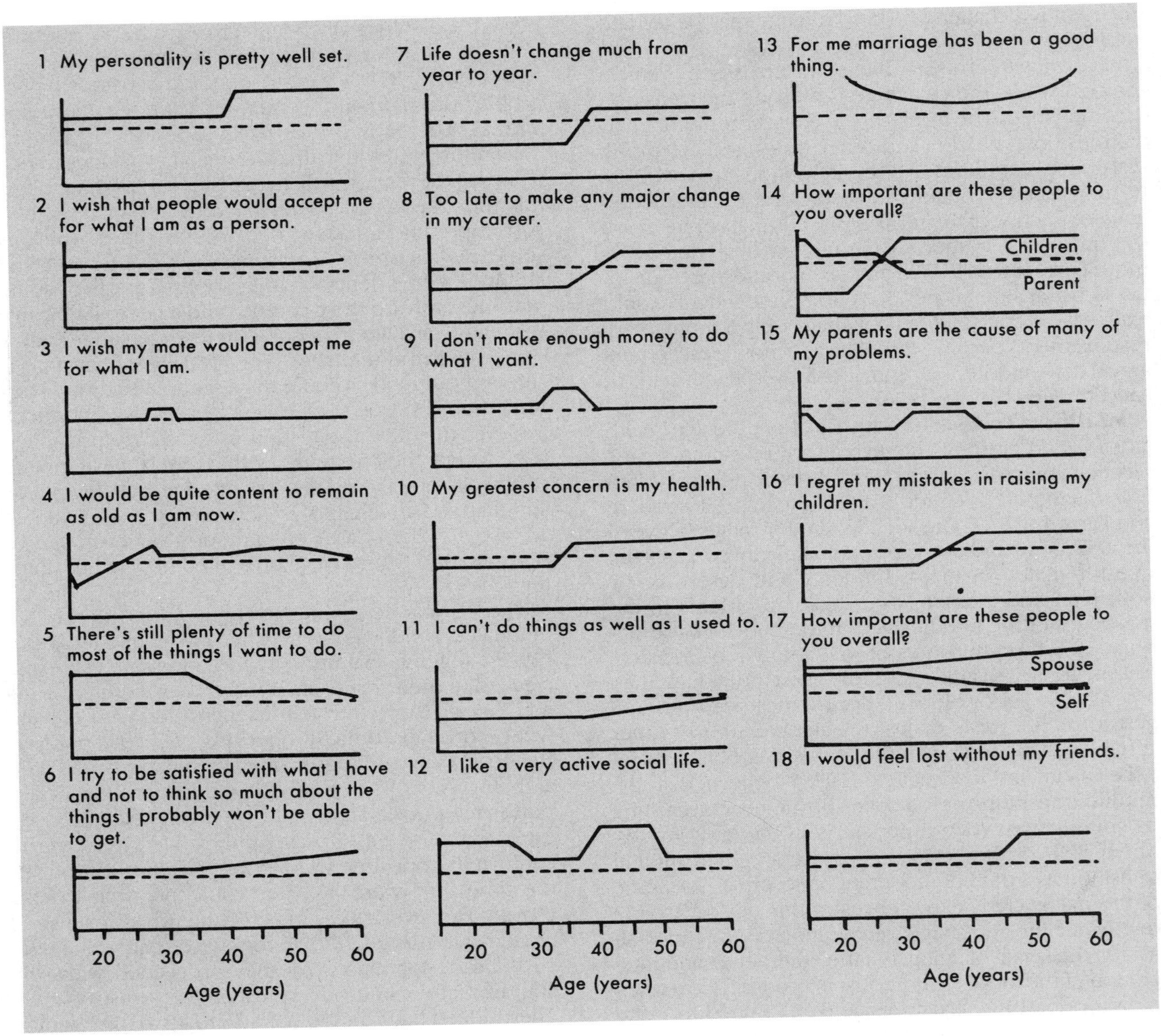

FIG. 14-2 ***Sample curves associated with the time boundaries of the adult life span.***
From Gould R., American Journal of Psychiatry, *1972. 129. 521-531. Copyright 1972 the American Psychiatric Association. Reprinted by permission.*

do not dramatically alter an individual's sense of self or sense of the life course (Neugarten, 1970).

The female climacteric may be taken as an example of normal life events. Menopause has been traditionally considered by psychiatrists to be a critical psychological event of middle age. Yet behavioral and attitudinal studies of normal populations do not support the contentions of psychiatrists (Neugarten et al., 1963). Older women report some climacteric symptoms as disagreeable, but most never require medical or psychological treatment. The climacteric changes in men are far too gradual to account for any abrupt or critical

	DENIAL OF STRESS	OPEN CONFRONTATION WITH STRESS
Dissatisfied	I. ANTIHERO 1. High alienation 2. Active identity struggle 3. Ego oriented 4. Uninvolved interpersonally 5. Low authoritarianism	III. PSEUDODEVELOPED 1. Overtly satisfied 2. Attitudinally rigid 3. Denies feelings 4. High authoritarianism 5. High on covert depression and anxiety 6. High in symptom formation
Satisfied	II. TRANSCENDENT-GENERATIVE 1. Assesses past and present with conscious sense of satisfaction 2. Few symptoms of distress 3. Open to feelings 4. Accepts out-groups 5. Feels in control of fate	IV. PUNITIVE-DISENCHANTED 1. Highest in authoritarianism 2. Dissatisfaction associated with environmental factors 3. Conflict with children

FIG. 14-3 ***Typology of responses to middle age stresses.***
Modified from Farrell, M.P., & Rosenberg, S.D. Men at midlife. *Boston: Auburn House Publishing, 1981. Reprinted by permission of the publisher.*

stages in adjustment or emotional state.

The transition from parenthood with the launching of children—the so-called empty-nest syndrome—does not appear to have a negative emotional impact on most women and men. Women often report strongly positive feelings to the "graduating" of their children. They often experience a new sense of freedom and delight in having time to use talents and abilities in ways that were impossible with a household of children (Neugarten, 1968b). The empty nest is not usually a focus of unhappiness. Most women seem to anticipate the departure of the youngest child positively (Lowenthal and Chiriboga, 1972).

The Oakland Guidance Studies (Clausen, 1976), a series of longitudinal studies, found occupational satisfaction among the male subjects to be high during middle age. Only one fourth expressed dissatisfaction with the course of their careers. The Oakland research group found no indications of a midlife crisis for either the men or the women in their sample. At 40 the more traditional subjects had moved smoothly into middle age with little change in life-style. They appeared emotionally happy. However, those individuals who had been "sex-role rebels" in adolescence experienced some conflict and depression at age 40. But even these individuals had come to appreciate and respect their inner natures by age 50.

Costa and McCrae (1980) designed a Mid-life Crisis Scale to reflect the stresses of midlife. They did not find age differences on this scale in their sample of men 33 to 79 years. The scale did find a positive correlation over a 10-year period on the personality variable of neuroticism. These findings led them to suggest that men who seem to be crisis prone at midlife may have exhibited problems of adjustment for a long time. Thus midlife crises may be the result of unadjusted adolescents and young adults who grow up to be unadjusted middle-aged adults rather than the result of a universal crisis confined to midlife.

Conclusions and interpretations. Perhaps the most valid conclusion that can be drawn about midlife is that this period, like other periods of the life cycle, is characterized by changes and transition. For some individuals this transition appears to precipitate a crisis; for others it does not (Hultsch and Deutsch, 1981). It may be that a tendency to being crisis prone is a matter of personality type. Farrell and Rosenberg (1981) characterized the types of middle-aged men according to how they responded to middle-age stresses. The four types are (1) the *anti-hero* or dissenter, self-reflective and overly dissatisfied with life and work, (2) the *transcendent-generative,* those able to assess the past and present and relate them to inner feelings with a positive sense of satisfaction, (3) the *pseudodeveloped* man who presents a false front of masculine potency and self-competence, and (4) the *punitive-disenchanted* or authoritarian type who combines denial of inner feelings with projection and the turning of anger and self-hatred toward "outsiders." Fig. 14-3 presents the four types and the manner of response.

Sheehy (1976) believes that women enter midlife and maybe have their "midlife" problems earlier than men do. Making use of the research of Vaillant (1977a) and Gould (1978), which was available before they published it in book form, Sheehy suggested that women enter the midlife adjustment period about the age of 35, especially if they have a sense of urgency to do some things in life "before it is too late." At least six statistical facts related to female life patterns combine to bring a sense of "my last chance" to the surface at this age.

According to Sheehy the following factors all converge at about the age of 35 for women as a group. Thirty-five is the average age when (1) mothers send their last child off to school, (2) married women in America reenter the job market, (3) divorced women remarry, (4) most wives run away, (5) some women begin the dangerous age of infidelity, and (6) women become aware of the approaching end of the child-bearing period. As these factors become relevant, many women begin to feel a need to change their perspectives concerning life, what it means to them, and what they should do about it.

Sources of stress

Holmes and Rahe (1967) developed the Social Readjustment Rating Scale to determine the degree to which events and life changes influence the onset of illness. Their scale has been widely used and shown to have some relevancy to the relationship between life stress caused by changes in circumstances of daily living and an ensuing illness. The scale was reported in detail in Chapter 13. A question raised about the use of the scale concerns the frequency at which different age groups experience life events. It appears that young persons, such as high school seniors and newlyweds,

TABLE 14-4 Sources of stress over a 10-year period

	Younger (high school seniors and newlyweds)			*Older (middle age and up)*		
Source of stress	*Men*	*Women*	*Total*	*Men*	*Women*	*Total*
Education	71*	80	76	2	9	6
Residential	33	40	36	9	4	6
Dating and marriage	33	50	40	2	12	8
Friends	27	44	35	13	5	9
Family	24	36	30	13	26	20
Marriage	18	28	23	9	12	11
Health	10	22	16	13	38	27
Work	22	14	18	45	21	32
Leisure activities	35	12	23	6	2	4
Military	27	2	14	0	4	2
Death	14	12	13	18	19	19
Finances	6	4	5	18	11	14

Modified from Lowenthal, H.F., Thurnher, M., & Chiriboga, D. *Four stages of life: A comparative study of women and men facing transitions.* San Francisco: Jossey-Bass, Inc., Publishers, 1975.

*Percentage of respondents indicating area as a source of stress.

report more exposure to life events than older persons who are middle-aged parents or adults about to retire (Lowenthal et al., 1975). The two younger groups reported more positive stress, while the two older groups reported more negative stress. Age and sex differences were noted. It also appears that the death of a child may have more impact on the parents than was previously determined. The degree of stress depends upon the length of time since the occurrence.

Table 14-4 indicates that the major cause of stress in the younger group was education; stresses related to dating, marriage, and residence were next. Young women had more stress events related to dating, marriage, friends, residential arrangements, and family

AFTEREFFECTS OF A DEATH

My husband was killed in an automobile accident at the age of forty-three years, six months, no days. His death was instantaneous.

At 1:30 AM, when I was notified by a local policeman of my husband's death, my physical reaction was externally placid. I did not faint, cry, or show any hysteria, yet I felt trancelike and couldn't think of anything to say. No pain, headache, or other discomfort was experienced except for a numbness and inability to talk. After that night the emotional outlet that most women seem to savor—crying—became possible and offered a welcome relief. There was a temporary loss of appetite. My silence was temporary also. In fact, I talked incessantly, beginning that day and continuing for the next few days.

Emotionally I was able to laugh and felt the need to cheer everyone else up. Before this time I had no conscious awareness of any ability to use laughter as a defense mechanism. Laughter had evidently become habituated and integrated into my personality. Thus it served as an outlet for which people rewarded me with their approval.

Spiritually I suffered no loss of faith. In fact, I felt more a dependence and need to go to church. While I remain inactive in any church groups, I need the contemplation provided by a Sunday trip to church and a nightly prayer. It is as though I have a reason for going to church not spelled h-a-b-i-t. Call it belief in God or call it rationalization. I believe I had the best years of married life and that I am now experiencing an independence of life never previously tested. Was this God's reason that I had no children? Well, the best years of marriage, plus a lack of children, combined with the apparent independence of spirit I now feel, give me reason to accept the need for, and belief in, a higher Being.

The experiencing of independence was not evident for at least two years after the event. The time period—two years—brings me to another phase of adjustment, prefaced by a Johnny Carson joke: "What is a widow's peak?" Answer: "About two years." Perhaps my feelings concerning sex should be mentioned in a paragraph dealing with physical reactions. Yet I am unable to separate sex from the emotional and the spiritual. I feel no sexual needs, but I think this may be the result of attitudes ingrained in my personality from premarital days. Unmarried sex is a no-no. I can make this much of a statement: What seemed to be repression of an urge during adolescence doesn't take half as much effort in one's forties!

Socially, in the months after the event, I went anywhere my friends and relatives invited me. After about six months the need for forced socialization seemed to subside, and I was able to become more selective and enjoy a social event on my own rather than going because duty called. Today I am fortunate in having a friend to escort me, and I feel the need for his companionship. I am relieved to know I still have the capacity to care for someone as part of my personality.

What psychological changes have taken place within me? Before my husband's death I never experienced sudden and permanent forgetting. When the policeman asked me to call my brother, I walked to the telephone and, still not wanting to acknowledge that anything had happened, I forgot his telephone number. For two years thereafter, until he and his family moved and changed their number, I was unable to recall it at will. Today I still find it hard to believe that I could forget this commonly called number.

Another reaction has been that of not feeling that I have to please a husband's friends and family. I cultivate a friendship on the basis of my own likes without that nagging compulsion that I must be nice to everybody and that everyone must like me. This idea of a smaller circle of friends may be an aspect of age also.

Adjustment to the death of my husband has been like going through adolescence all over again. My acne of the heart is clearing up, and the remaining scars can be covered.

crystallized intelligence the class of mental abilities acquired and developed through cultural contact, such as language and social knowledge.

fluid intelligence ability to adapt, and to perceive and integrate things mentally; separate from experience or organized education.

relationships than did young men. Compared to the women, the men had more stresses related to leisure activities, the military, and work.

There was no overall major source of stress for the middle-aged group. The most significant source of stress for men was work, while the salient sources of stress for women were health and the family. The other sources of stress were relatively comparable for both men and women. Longitudinal data obtained by Chiriboga (1978) suggested that middle age is a time of change, reflecting both positive and negative components of stress. Later life (nearer retirement) tends to be associated with an increasing amount of negative stress.

COGNITION AND ACHIEVEMENT

Professional opinion concerning cognitive ability at midlife has changed in recent years because researchers have become more aware of the shortcomings of various research designs. Cross-sectional studies have problems because they do not allow for cohort differences. Longitudinal studies have difficulties because over the span of years some subjects die or drop out of the studies, making the sample more selective. As a result, cross-sectional studies of intellectual performance generally suggest declines, beginning sometime in early adulthood. Longitudinal studies, on the other hand, demonstrate little or no decline throughout adult life. The newer research designs that use sequential data-collection strategies find that cohort and historical event factors do contribute to age differences in intellectual performance. Therefore the most reasonable conclusion is that most of early adulthood, middle age, and old age is characterized by stability or increases in intellectual performance. However, decline in intellectual ability does occur late in life (Hultsch and Deutsch, 1981).

Cognition in midlife

The work of Horn and Donaldson (1980) adds a new dimension to the theoretical study of adult cognitive development. They make use of the concepts of fluid intelligence and crystallized intelligence. Both types of intelligence involve perceiving relationships, making abstractions, reasoning, forming concepts, and solving problems. The difference is that ***fluid intelligence*** develops these abilities from *incidental learning*. As a result the abilities are not developed from culturally based (verbal) content. That means they are not based on academically related learning. It would be like developing the ability to do abstract reasoning in nonverbal ways through abilities like inductive reasoning and visualization.

Crystallized intelligence, however, reflects *intentional learning* processes that suggest the degree to which individuals have incorporated conceptual verbal knowledge and skills of the culture into their thinking and actions. Examples of this type of abstract reasoning would include the use of verbal meaning, knowledge, and other learned information in problem-solving situations. This learning is best achieved during "teachable moments," of which there are many in early adulthood (Havighurst, 1979).

Psychometric approaches, those that use tests to measure intelligence, suggest that there is an age difference in the functional use of fluid intelligence and crystallized intelligence. *Fluid intelligence* is believed to reflect "innate general cognitive capacity" (Bromley, 1974); it is dependent upon a physiological base instead of culturally based content. Its development comes through incidental learning. It is reflected in performance on tests, mostly nonverbal, that require productive relational thinking but little cultural knowledge or experience. *Crystallized intelligence* is the general cognitive capacity that reflects the degree to which the individual has incorporated the knowledge and skills of the culture into thinking and actions. Its development comes through intentional learning of cultural content. Measures such as vocabulary, general information, similarities, and judgment are thought to be important in the assessment of crystallized intelligence (Horn, 1978).

Fluid intelligence tends to peak in early adulthood because incidental learning processes are strongly influenced by physiological and neurological functioning. (Horn and Donaldson, 1980). These biological functions are at a high point during adulthood, then

Meriem Kaluger

The quality of crystallized intelligence depends on verbal knowledge and skills. Chinese culture has a wide array of stories, legends, and songs that are passed on from generation to generation, providing verbal input and memory stimulation. Most of these people probably know all of the words and actions in a Chinese opera or play.

decrease in capacity of performance as a person gets older. As a result, there is a decline in fluid intellectual ability. On the other hand, *crystallized intelligence* is intentional learning derived from exposure to verbal learning and the culture. As long as knowledge is used or can be added to the information-processing system, crystallized intelligence can continue to operate on a high functional level. This potential for exposure to intentional verbal learning is available throughout the adult life. Therefore crystallized intelligence is thought to continue to grow in adulthood. Fig. 14-4 illustrates how fluid intelligence ability decreases during adulthood because the physiological components related to this type of incidental learning decrease in functional capacity. Crystallized intelligence continues to develop because its function is based on the accumulation of verbal information, which is more dependent on cultural input than on physiological involvement. Omnibus refers to the combination of measures of both kinds of factors. Omnibus shows a level of stability, and even a slight rise, in adulthood up to the age of 61 (Horn, 1978).

Does intelligence decline, remain stable, or improve during middle age? The answer requires that

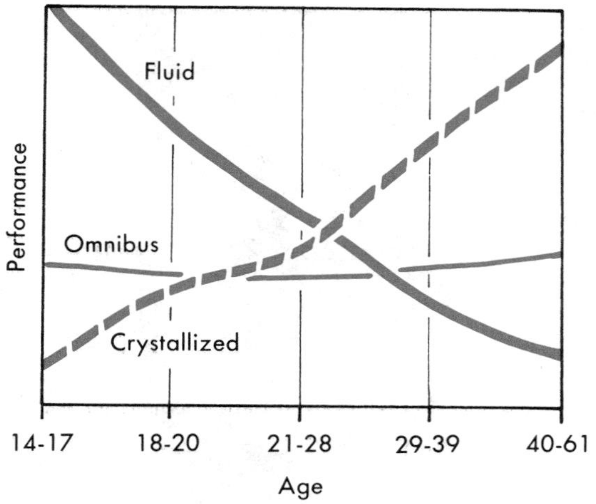

FIG. 14-4 ***Life span changes of fluid and crystallized intelligence.***

Based on Horn, J.L., & Donaldson, G. Cognitive Development II: Adulthood Development of Human Abilities, In O.G. Brim & J. Kagan (eds.), Constancy and change in human development: A volume of review essays. *Cambridge: Harvard University Press, 1980.*

many variables be examined. These variables relate to the type of intelligence being measured, whether the performance is timed or not, physical and mental health factors, intellectual and educational level to begin with, and even occupational status. Learning and cognitive development can take place, but it requires involvement, effort, capacity, and opportunity.

Achievement in middle age

Mental functions, if used, are at a peak in middle age. Cerebral capacities deteriorate slowly and only begin to weaken at the age of 70 years (Schaie and Parham, 1977). Many cultures, in fact, look to their middle-aged population for wisdom and judgment. Studies now reveal that a person's general intellectual capacity is as great in middle age as it was when the person was younger (Botwinick, 1977).

Adults who have used their minds actively and productively throughout their years will have a highly refined ability to use these powers through the middle years and later perhaps (Blum and Jarvik, 1974). Adults who have "completed" their education with the last formal class attended will be subject to a more rapid rate of deterioration of these powers. Since the growth of the mind is a product of many outside factors, it is possible for the adult to grow intellectually through involvement in verbal activities (Giambra and Arenberg, 1980).

However, many middle-aged people do not make full use of their intellectual power; they cling to the old cliché that You can't teach an old dog new tricks. To some it is a convenient excuse to not make use of their capabilities. Many older people find that they do have trouble learning new ideas and techniques, but these individuals have not lost their recall or their ability to learn. They have merely become "rusty," or they refuse to change their life patterns to allow for study time and learning.

When adults enroll in a class, it often takes a few weeks to adjust to the demands of learning; they have trouble remembering what they have heard or read. Unfortunately, many people get discouraged or quit at this time, but those who stay with it soon reach a high level of proficiency. People at the age of 45 years learn at nearly the same rate and in the same manner as they did at 25 years. The only difference is that they emphasize accuracy rather than speed as they get older (Hoyer et al., 1979).

In summary, Botwinick (1977) makes the following observations concerning the maintenance or decline of various mental abilities: (1) a gradual decline in all types of measurable ability sets in after the age of 30 years but does not become significant until well after 50 years; (2) sensory and perceptual abilities decline most and earliest—about the age of 50; (3) motor abilities hold up well until late middle age, but there is a change in the methods by which the tasks are done; (4) decline in learning ability varies with the type of material to be learned; verbal abilities last longer than perceptual abilities; and (5) there are wide individual differences so that in any age group some persons are superior to the average for groups much younger.

SOCIAL LIFE IN MIDDLE ADULTHOOD

With rapid technology and social changes many of today's middle-aged adults are faced with the question of their social position in society. Many are in a period of internal and external anxiety. Some become uncertain of values; some feel bored, restless, dissatisfied, self-involved, and hemmed in by society. Middle age is marked by reflective thinking (Rappaport, 1976).

The ways of handling this psychosocial situation are

as varied as the individuals themselves. Some indulge in hypochondria; others try to act like their college children; many find new interests and hobbies; and still others find a change in jobs, careers, or houses. A poll of this age group reveals that middle-aged adults do not really want to be young again and have to suffer through the struggling of the young. They believe that they have done their work and now deserve the freedom to enjoy it.

When people reach this age, they enjoy the freedom of expressing themselves unselfconsciously (Nye and Berado, 1973). They do not depend on peer acceptance. Most adults realize that they will not impress their peers or their juniors by being false, so they are usually honest. They can indulge in their whims and be a little eccentric without offending anyone. Possibly the greatest pleasure of middle age is the acceptance of one's limitations without surrender, the right to relax without giving in. Life *can* begin at 40 years for the one who has learned to give up inhibitions brought on by false social and personal values.

There are three major social considerations for middle age: the family, social role and status, and life satisfaction.

Family at midlife

Parents are usually between the ages of 30 to 55 years when their first child reaches adolescence. Several important developmental tasks must be faced at this time (Havighurst, 1979). First, parent and teenager must learn to communicate effectively; the parent-adolescent communication network must, of course, work in both directions. There is a responsibility for all concerned to develop meaningful interaction skills. Frequently success in parent-child communication depends upon the degree of successful parenting exhibited when the children were younger.

Another task for the parents is to provide support and direction to their teenagers in their search for identity and their place within their peer group (Erikson, 1963b). Adolescence can be a period of intense peer identification. Parents often feel as if they have to combat the prevailing peer culture and attitudes in order to present an alternative view of values and behavior to their teenagers. Many parents stress morality and sexual restraints (Landis, 1975). Some want to exercise control over the ways in which friends are chosen and behavioral limits set (Brannen, 1975). Frequently parents come to believe that their sons and daughters resent their help (Perry and Perry, 1977).

A third developmental task for midlife parents is to nurture independence, autonomy, and responsibility on the part of their adolescents (Havighurst, 1979). The pursuit of this task may result in friction, resentment, and even hostility between parent and teenager. Many parents have not developed skills or attitudes that enable them to talk with their children without arousing resistance. Some parents assume an authoritarian stance of control, creating a stressful situation and defeating their own purpose of encouraging responsibility. It is difficult for parents to know how to deal with adolescents because it is so complex a period of life. Sometimes teenagers appear to be so capable; other times they seem to have no insights at all. The fact is that adolescents often lack the experiences, learning, and skills necessary to follow through on what they know they should be doing. Wise parenting should start early in the child's life to anticipate events and tasks. It is important to build a foundation of knowledge and habits that can help provide a smooth transition from early dependence to semidependence and then to independence.

Elkind (1979) proposes that there should be three basic controls between parents and teenagers. *First,* a mutually accepted contract that structures the nature and limits of freedom and responsibility. Certain freedoms can be taken without parental consent. In other areas, such as dating and the use of the car, parents could still set limits. Duties and chores should be identified and pursued. A *second* type of parent-adolescent contract pertains to achievement and support. Some type of achievement in academic, extracurricular, and social activities may be expected. In return for this expectation, parents should provide approval and support. Parents should make provisions for lessons, equipment, uniforms, transportation, and the like. The *third* type of contract involves loyalty and commitment to values and beliefs, including respect and understanding. Just as the parent may expect these of the child, so can the child expect the parents to be visibly committed to the ideals expressed.

Children leaving the home. One of the major events in a person's life, which brings the realization that an individual is in middle age, is the time when the children leave the home (Hagestad, 1979). Most children become fully independent on graduation from college or on their marriage. This can be a time of happiness and reward, or it can be a time of heartbreak and disillusionment. To keep the facts in proper perspective, it should be noted that the majority of women actually look forward to the time when their youngest child will leave home (Lowenthal and Chiriboga, 1973). In fact, some families experience stress when adult children return home for a while to refill the "empty nest" (Foote, 1978).

Too often during parenthood the adult, especially the mother, will focus all her attention on the children, sometimes at the expense of depriving her spouse of her company. Many adults do not even realize that they are doing this, and thus it is a traumatic occasion when the last child leaves the home. The husband and wife will really see each other for the first time in 20 or 25 years. All too often they are shocked by what they see. They have changed gradually, but the change is not noticed until this time. The only bond between them, the children, is no longer there (Perry and Perry, 1977). Some people at this stage believe that their life is over; there is nothing more to be done but to wait for old age. Some parents take a different approach by encouraging continued dependency of their children by making mother's house too readily available and father's pocketbook too easily opened.

The couples who manage this period gracefully are those who have kept their interest and love for each other alive and also have common interests and hobbies (Kelley, 1974). Therefore, when they find themselves alone again, they can enjoy each other and often view it as a second honeymoon. Many find that at this time they can afford to travel and take up activities that they missed when they were young and struggling. These are the people who believe that the spouse's needs take precedence over those of the children. This not only leads to a happier middle age for the parents but can help to prevent the development of self-centered children.

Grandparenting. Recognizing that the average age at which men and women get married is in the early twenties it is reasonable to assume that many individuals will first become grandparents while they are in their forties. They will be in their fifties and early sixties when they will be the grandparents of adolescents. The typical grandparent, therefore, is not likely to be the kindly, white-haired, bespectacled older person so frequently pictured in the visual media. Instead the grandparent is usually still very active outside the home. Many are working at full-time jobs. Nevertheless the role of grandparenting is readily accepted—unless the person is upset at the idea of being old enough to be a grandparent! Over 80% of the grandmothers in the Robertson (1977) study expressed satisfaction, comfort, and pleasure over their role as grandparents. The younger grandmothers tend to emphasize a social orientation, while the older ones emphasize a personal orientation (Robertson, 1977).

The classic research of Neugarten and Weinstein (1968) also investigated the meaning of grandparenthood to the grandparents. Most of the grandmothers and grandfathers spoke of grandparenthood as a source of biological renewal or continuity with the future. For many there was a sense of emotional self-fulfillment, an opportunity to be better grandparents than they were parents. A third meaning was to serve as a teacher or resource person to the grandchild, contributing either through financial aid or unique life experiences. A few saw grandparenthood as an exten-

ROLES PLAYED BY GRANDPARENTS

THE FORMAL ROLE

The grandparents follow a "hands-off" policy as far as care and discipline are concerned, although they may enjoy providing treats for special occasions.

THE FUN-SEEKING ROLE

The grandparents enjoy an informal, playful relationship with their grandchildren but do not want to assume any responsibility for them.

THE SURROGATE-PARENT ROLE

The grandparents assume responsibility for the care of grandchildren in the event of divorce or the death of a parent, if the mother must work outside the home, or when the parents want to take a short vacation from the children. Usually the grandmother is more active in this role.

THE "RESERVOIR OF FAMILY WISDOM" ROLE

The grandparents dispense special knowledge to the grandchildren or teach them certain skills. The grandfather is usually more active in this role.

THE DISTANT-FIGURE ROLE

The grandparents appear only on special occasions and have fleeting and infrequent contacts with their grandchildren. This role is especially common when grandparents are geographically or socially remote.

Based on Neugarten, B.L., & Weinstein, K.K., *Journal of Marriage and the Family,* 1964, *26,* 199-204. Copyrighted 1972 by the National Council on Family Relations, 1219 University Avenue Southeast, Minneapolis, Minnesota 55414. Reprinted by permission.

sion of the self and an opportunity to live or accomplish vicariously through the grandchild. Finally, about one fifth of the group reported that grandparenthood had no effect on their lives; a sense of remoteness or psychological distance from the kin was implied. Sometimes strained relationships were involved; others spoke of being "too busy with my own life"; and some were simply not ready to be grandparents.

Neugarten and Weinstein (1968) examined variations in styles of grandparenting. They found age differences. Young grandparents had more diverse styles of grandparenting than older. Most younger grandparents were fun seekers, although some were distant figures. Older grandparents were almost always formal and distant. At the beginning, grandmothers assume a more active role. Grandfathers appear to become more actively involved with their grandchildren after retirement (Leslie, 1973).

Some styles of grandparenting as well as the significance of the grandparent role are listed in the box on p. 548. About one third of the grandparents were formal in their style of grandparenting. They followed a "hands-off" policy as far as details of care and discipline were concerned, but they often enjoyed providing treats for special occasions. About one fourth, with more grandmothers than grandfathers, enjoyed the fun-seeking role. They enjoyed an informal, playful relationship but did not want to assume any responsibility for the grandchildren. None of the grandfathers but 14% of the grandmothers assumed a surrogate-parent role. Often this was done because the mother was working, divorced, or dead. The "reservoir of family wisdom" role occurred rarely, and then usually only in the grandfather. This role was one of teaching special skills or knowledge to the children. The distant-figure role was fairly common when the grandpar-

Meriem Kaluger

Middle-aged adults are often the children of elderly parents. In some ways the role relationship changes in that the child becomes the prime giver of assistance and support. Taking older parents to events they enjoy can be pleasurable for all persons.

ents were geographically or socially remote from the children. The grandparents appeared only on special occasions and usually had but fleeting contacts with their grandchildren. This role was indicated by many more grandfathers than grandmothers.

Adult children and elderly parents. Middle-aged parents raise their children and often see them become married or settled. There comes a time when the parents become elderly and the children are middle-aged. Now we have adult children who have elderly parents. In some ways the role relationship changes. The middle-aged couple becomes the prime giver of assistance and emotional support to the older generation. The helping behavior provided is not necessarily financial. It may be one of visitation, securing information, or providing transportation.

Most elderly people perfer to remain independent and take care of their own needs as long as possible (Cicirelli, 1981). This finding seems typical for the majority of elderly people who still live in the community in contrast to the approximately 5% who live in nursing homes or other institutions. When elderly people do feel they need help, they prefer to receive it from their adult children. As the world changes and friends die, their own children become the mediating link to the outside world. In return, 85% to 88% of the adult children indicate a commitment to help their elderly parents in the future (Cicirelli, 1981).

The adult children who were interviewed in the Cicirelli (1981) study for the Andrus Foundation of the American Association of Retired Persons (AARP) showed considerable attachment behavior (visiting, telephoning) in their relationships with their elderly parents. Most lived in the same city. The adult children, however, expressed only a moderate sense of filial (son or daughter) responsibility toward their parents, with the strongest feeling of responsibility directed toward caring for parents when they were sick. Clearly the family helped when help was needed. Overall there was not a great deal of conflict between adult children and their elderly parents, but some increase in conflict was expected if the parents were to live with them. There was slightly more conflict with mothers than with fathers. Daughters felt more strain than sons (Troll, 1971). There was also the experience of filial anxiety when anticipating the possibility of providing help to the elderly parent. Table 14-5 indicates some areas of conflict between elderly fathers and mothers and their adult children.

As an elderly parent becomes progressively less able

TABLE 14-5 Areas of conflict of adult children with 81 elderly fathers and 148 elderly mothers

	Percentage reporting conflict with	
Area of conflict	*Fathers*	*Mothers*
Parent's temperament	21	17
Parent's health, taking care of self	20	23
Things child thinks parent should do	19	20
The way parent treats child's mother or father	14	7
Parent tells child how to live life	11	18
Parent's criticism of child's bad habits	7	14
Parent demands too much of child	7	12
Parent's criticism of adult child's children	5	14
Parent's handling of money	5	6
Parent's living arrangements	2	6
Parent's criticism of child's friends	2	5
Parent's criticism of child's spouse	1	6
Other area (e.g., parent's ideas and opinions, relations with other family members and nonfamily)	10	7

Modified from Cicirelli, V.G. *Helping elderly parents: The role of adult children.* Boston: Auburn House Publishing Co., 1981.

to care for himself or herself, role reversal occurs and the adult child is forced to take on additional responsibilities (Sussman, 1977). The biggest problem in caring for the physically debilitated older person is the delivery of personal health care services. Adult children may easily misdiagnose physical complaints or symptoms. Some children label the first signs of forgetting as senility; some confuse poor hearing with lack of mental concentration; some interpret the first signs of physical slowing as an indication that the parents should give up participation in activities; some may interpret complaints as a sign of contrariness when all the parent may want is someone to show that he or she cares.

Commentary. Caring for an elderly parent can result in much stress for the adult child. A procedure we recommend is to follow the principle, "Always show interest and concern but do not take away any more of the parent's sense of independence than is needed." Consider a step-by-step procedure for personal and health care. The first step is to permit the parents to live in their own home or apartment as long as they can reasonably take care of themselves. Provide transportation, daily contacts, and help with the paper work that comes with health insurance and medical services.

If more direct care is needed, provide for a day person to come in for home and health care. It may eventually be necessary to provide for a live-in person. The idea of an elderly parent and adult child living together in the child's home is feasible only if the two have a good living and loving relationship, one of mutual respect, help, and understanding, and if the parent has mobility. If total care is needed for the elderly parent, the adult child's home may not be the best solution. There is much effort, time, and responsibility involved. As one physician said, "If you're not careful, the wear, tear, and frustration could kill you." A good nursing home has many services that can provide care and comfort for the patient and peace of mind and rest for the adult child. If an elderly person expresses a desire to enter a nursing home or a retirement home, that wish should be respectfully considered and honored.

Marital adjustment. In recent years there has been a sharp rise in divorces between middle-aged couples (Hunt and Hunt, 1974). Many people are shocked to find friends who have been married for 25 or 30 years and who seemed to have had a good marriage suddenly get divorced.

Much of this drifting apart is because the partners have lost touch with each other during parenthood and no longer have a common bond. They have not "grown" in the same direction or to the same degree during the expansion stage of adulthood. In a true sense, they have grown apart. Separation or divorce may take place. According to Hunt and Hunt (1974), however, only about 12% of divorcing males are 40 or over, and about 14% of divorcing females are 45 or older. Proportionately there is no divorce boom in midlife; almost half of all divorces occur in the first 7 years of marriage.

Some middle-aged adults suddenly find themselves trapped by their lives and their marriage. They try to recapture some of their youth and experience the "good life" before they are too far over the hill. Some people in middle age suffer through an identity crisis, and sometimes they lose sight of their values temporarily by engaging in extramarital affairs. These affairs often do not depend on what the husband or wife is like—in fact, many of these people still love their spouse deeply. Yet they jeopardize their marriage, their business prestige, and their relations with friends by seeking "the romance of a bygone era."

Social roles and status

Socially speaking, it can be said that middle age is the time when there is an expansion of horizons through friendships, business contacts, and acquaintances made in the community. This is the stage of development in which the individual enjoys the highest social status in adult society.

Active club and organization membership is at its peak during these years. Adults who never before had time become productive and enthusiastic members of the groups that have goals akin to their own. Some aspects of the social contacts of adults will be business or professionally related because career advancement still plays a role in their social life. However, there is now time to become involved socially in things that really matter to them as individuals. There is a drop in formal social participation in the early twenties, especially among hard-pressed married couples; there is a climb to a peak in the middle years, a slight drop off, and then a sag in the sixties.

The family-centered woman will now find that her social life can be "other directed" and can take on a more creative aspect rather than simply being an extension of her mother role. Cultivation of new

"REJECTION—AND DEJECTION"

Two people have been married for fourteen and a half years. As half of that marriage, I had expected to be a part of the relationship until one of us died. We shared many things—numerous friends, the creation of two children, the stillborn birth of another, the adoption of a third, many and varied sexual experiences, camping vacations in many areas, three different homes, ideas, books, and many other things. Now I wonder if maybe there wasn't a lack of inner sharing and feeling of these things that I thought were so meaningful to both of us; otherwise why would a split occur and a parting of the ways seem necessary?

There was a feeling of utter desolation within me when I realized that someone I still loved had rejected me. I can't sleep at night, and in my nightmares I continually ask, Why? How could I have avoided this? What is wrong with me that I am rejected so? I examine and look at things that have happened during recent years, and many of them I see in a different light. I wonder why I was so naive about some things so obvious now. Or maybe I now understand words that were spoken long ago in a new way. For example, I asked, "Do you love me?" and got the answer, "I'm committed to you." Why didn't I see through that half-hearted reply?

First and foremost, I realize how little I knew and understood about him, even though I supposedly lived very close to him. I know, even more now, how we are all truly islands unto ourselves when it comes to knowing what goes on within our minds. Some people apparently seem to prefer to maintain more of that "islandness" than others. Why do some people not want to share what is going on inside? Are they afraid of what other people will see and know about them or don't they know how to share themselves? Who can understand and comprehend the mind?

I know that more than anything else I dread the aloneness that is at hand. I wonder about my attractiveness and whether I have the courage to try to build a new relationship. Am I even capable of a satisfying relationship with another human being, especially if that being is male? I know that I don't want to go to bed alone for the next twenty, thirty, or forty years that I might have yet to live. I know that I want to have someone with whom to share ideas, love, laughter, sex, problems, and all that makes up life. Can I ever trust myself to someone again? I ask, "Will someone want me or does my having been rejected mean that I'm not much to be desired?" If someone else never comes along, can I live alone happily? Looking at my marriage through new eyes, I realize that in its present state it could never be very fulfilling, and as much as it pains me to see it end, I somehow know that it may very well be for the good. No matter how I look at it, the pain is excruciating; unless one has experienced it, I doubt that another can understand.

I can't quite put the puzzle together, but somehow I know that some of what is being said in the women's liberation movement has some logic. Women should have their own identity. What they are should not depend completely on their husbands. Women should not be raised to all fit into one mold type—that of wife and mother. New ways of dealing with marriage have to be tried. What and where are the answers?

He is gone, and he has even refused to communicate with me, so I am completely in the dark and very much alone. My heart aches, my stomach churns, and I wonder each day how I can ever continue to live without falling apart. I watch people around me laugh and carry on life's simplest tasks with contentment, and I wonder if ever again I will be able to live as happily.

friends and enjoyment of friends of long standing are often a pleasant aspect of life now. Visiting friends without an eye on the clock can be a rewarding social aspect for the woman whose family is now fairly independent.

Church-related social life with its often-attendant social service aspect may become more significant. Pressures of time and finances that did not allow for this activity previously are possibly the reason for this increased involvement. The way in which people adjust to changes in their social life depends on the way in which they have adjusted to the physical and emotional changes that are occurring.

Middle-aged individuals find themselves with more freedom from responsibility and the job; this in turn leaves them often with more money to spend and more leisure time. Some people use this leisure time as an extension of interests, broadening their scope with enrichment and fulfillment in new activities. But many people engage in activities that do not offer a worthwhile return, and others drift into boredom and dissatisfaction. The manner in which people conduct themselves in middle age depends on the way they have conducted their whole life. Table 14-6 indicates opinions concerning characteristics and social behavior.

Many middle-aged adults find the time to engage in regular social activities with friends. Social contacts are usually well established and interaction comes easily.

There is some importance in developing good interpersonal relationships throughout life. Making friends by being thoughtful, kind, and generous is the kind of status that cannot be taken away during middle life. The college athlete who helped and respected his teammates will be remembered long after he made the winning touchdown. The people from the big house with the swimming pool who were kind and helpful to their neighbors will be remembered even after the big house and pool are gone. The best insurance for an emotionally rich and satisfying old age is to build a vast store of interests that are varied and not dependent on the conditions that old age automatically removes and to work with people in such a way that the individual keeps their respect and his or her own self-respect.

Life satisfaction

According to Lowenthal and Chiriboga (1972) men and women at midlife reported more high than low points of happiness throughout their lives. The ratio was higher for men than for women. The women's lowest point of life satisfaction was early middle age, while the men's most unhappy time was young adulthood. When men spoke of current frustration, they were most likely to bring up money or jobs. Women mentioned frustrations centered around problems with their husbands or their children. Both sexes referred to their marriages and children as things of which they were proud.

A cross-sectional "happiness" study reported by Sheehy (1979) was based on a survey of 52,000 women who read *Redbook Magazine* and 2,000 male readers of *Esquire*. Both groups were overwhelmingly white, young, and well educated, so the findings do have a bias. Nevertheless it was interesting to note that after reaching the low point in the 45 to 50 range, both sexes indicated a rapidly increasing degree of life satisfaction. Fig. 14-5 presents the span of happiness from late adolescence to young old age. The women placed

TABLE 14-6 Consensus among middle-class, middle-aged people regarding the appropriate time for various characteristics and behavior

Characteristics or behavior	*Age range designated as appropriate or expected*	*Percent who agree on the age range*	
		Men (N = 30)	*Women (N = 43)*
Best age for a man to marry	20-25	80	90
Best age for a woman to marry	19-24	85	90
When most people should become grandparents	45-50	84	70
Best age for most people to finish school and go to work	20-22	86	82
When most men should be settled on a career	24-26	74	64
When most men hold their top jobs	45-50	71	58
When most people should be ready to retire	60-65	83	86
A young man	18-22	84	83
A middle-aged man	40-50	86	75
An old man	65-75	75	57
A young woman	18-24	89	88
A middle-aged woman	40-50	87	77
An old woman	60-75	83	87
When a man has the most responsibilities	35-50	79	75
When a man accomplishes most	40-50	82	71
The prime of life for a man	35-50	86	80
When a woman has the most responsibilities	25-40	93	91
When a woman accomplishes most	30-45	94	92
A good-looking woman	20-35	92	82

Modified from Neugarten, B., Moore, J.W., & Lowe, J.C. Age norms, age constraints and adult socializations, Table 1, p. 712. Reprinted by permission of The University of Chicago, © 1965.

top value on the goals of family security, mature love, and inner harmony. The men valued a sense of accomplishment, a comfortable life, and mature love.

VOCATIONAL STATUS

The economic functions of work are obvious—people work to support themselves and their families. As important as this function is, however, there are also enormously significant personal and social functions of work, especially in midlife. To a large extent, people become what they do. Personal identity is frequently tied in with the work an individual does. Closely related to personal identity is the significance of work for self-evaluation. To the degree that one may take pride in the quality or significance of one's work, self-esteem may be enhanced. One of the major determinants of status in our society is occupation. The work that an individual does relates to social status. Not only does work become a key focus of the individual's life, but the entire family typically takes on the status of the job held by the head of the household. In middle age, vocational status takes on a special meaning because the individual is no longer just out of school but is a seasoned worker.

Midlife career satisfaction

The peak of vocational success for men comes during middle age, in the forties and early fifties. After the age of 35 years men are more stable in their jobs and are skilled enough to avoid acts that cause accidents. There are fewer accidents by the older worker than by the younger worker, and the older worker has less absenteeism from work.

Many people reach their peak of income in the 40-

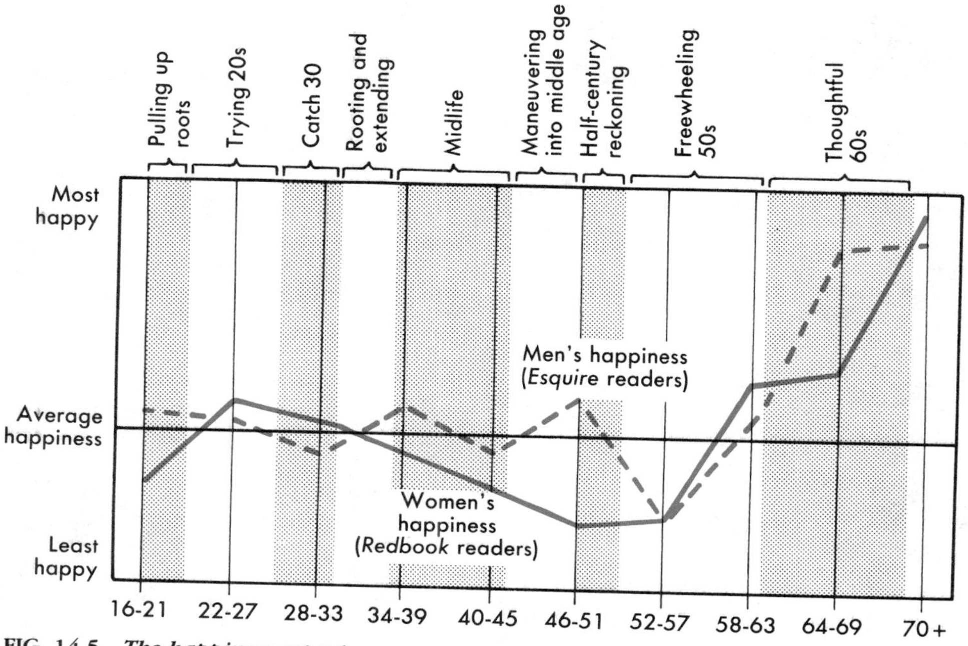

FIG. 14-5 ***The happiness report.***
© 1981 by Gail Sheehy. Adapted by permission of William Morrow & Co.

to 45-year age bracket. It is at this time that men attain their greatest power and prestige in the business world (Hunt and Hunt, 1974). For both men and women it can be a time of great accomplishments in their lives.

It would seem that vocational adjustment problems are over for the midlife individual, but for some people middle age brings new complications. Dissatisfaction with the present job, instability, restlessness, and loss of child-rearing responsibilities prompt some people to make a vocational change at this time of life.

People work for different reasons beyond the need to provide for daily living. Some work to make a lot of money, others work for status, companionship, service, prestige, or satisfaction (Terkel, 1982). Occupational satisfaction or dissatisfaction often depends on the relationship between a person's reasons for working and the characteristics of the work situation. For some individuals a major source of satisfaction comes from the process of work and the related accomplishments. For others, satisfaction is derived from the things that their salary can buy, such as a home, an automobile, clothes, travel, and so forth. Both orientations—work satisfaction related or money related—exist across all fields of work, although there is a higher proportion of work-oriented white-collar workers than blue-collar workers in this category. Older workers consistently indicate that they are more satisfied with their jobs than younger workers do (Wright and Hamilton, 1978).

Midlife career change

Traditionally, career choice and direction was considered to be a one-time decision, made during early adulthood after a brief exploratory period. That view appears to be changing to one that considers work in terms of career cycles, with change, including very abrupt ones, in career direction as a distinct possibility and option. The personality characteristics that allow for career shifts are risk taking, willingness to assume new roles, and a feeling of control over one's destiny (Heath, 1976).

Meriem Kaluger

Harold Geyer

David Strickler

Occupation satisfaction or dissatisfaction often depends on the relationship between the person's reasons for working at a certain occupation and the characteristics of the work situation. The scientist, the farmer, the steel-worker can all have one thing in common: they can all be happy with their jobs.

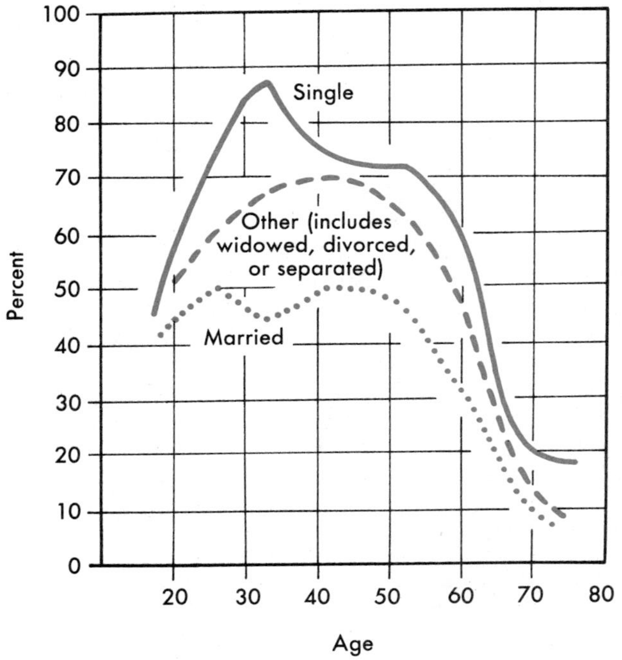

FIG. 14-6 ***Rates of working as a function of age for single, married, and other women.***
From U.S. Department of Labor. U.S. working women: A chartbook (Bureau of Labor statistics bulletin 1880). *Washington, D.C.: U.S. Department of Labor, 1975.*

Thomas (1977) looked at the relationship between change in career and change in "life structure," made up of one's goals, roles in life, and personal values and dreams. Thomas found that people in midlife could be classified as (1) *changers,* people who experienced both a major change in life structure and a change in career, (2) *pseudochangers,* those who made a switch in careers but retained the same life structure, (3) *cryptochangers,* individuals who changed their life structure but not their careers, and (4) *persisters,* those who adhered to the same goals, values, life-style, and careers without making any changes. According to Thomas (1977), career change by itself is only a rough indicator of what is going on in a individual's life during the midlife period.

What factors propel an individual to change careers in midlife? Heald (1977) presents the following events: *first,* the "emptying of the nest"—one of the most important events—as it permits a reorientation from concerns about the family to one that evaluates career directions; *second,* events that arouse anxiety or restlessness because of technological advancements that make present career skills obsolete, social or historical conditions, or personal factors; *third,* changes in job circumstances, status quo, or value orientation, making the individual feel unwanted pressure or guilt; and *fourth,* financial concerns, usually related to retirement preparation, which often renew energies to accumulate a nest egg while capable of substantial earnings.

Midlife career development for women

The vocational adjustment problem of middle age is as serious for women today as for men, if not more so. At present more than one half the women between the ages of 35 and 55 years are in the labor force (Sheppard, 1976).

Many reasons can be cited for the overflow of middle-aged women desiring work outside the home. The various labor-saving devices permit them to care for their home in much less time than in the past. Earlier marriages, earlier childbearing, and smaller families ready the middle-aged woman for employment outside the home. The increase in cost of living and the desire for a better standard of living demand more money than the husband can bring home; thus the wife is willing to take a job to have some of the finer things in life (Kreps, 1976).

Fig. 14-6 shows the rate of working by age category for single, married, and other women, including widowed, divorced, and separated. Single women consistently lead in the percentage of women who work at any age level. Over 70% of the single women in their middle years work. That percentage is approached by women who are widowed, divorced, or separated. Half the women work shortly after they get married; then there is a slight drop-off, apparently while raising young children. They are back into the job market by age 40.

Without question the opportunity for women to earn money outside the home is security in itself. If the time were to arise that she would need to be self-supporting (through divorce or death of the husband), she could carry on with much less frustration.

As the later years of middle age bring retirement into focus, it is conceivable that retirement benefits from both husband's and wife's company retirement plan, in addition to Social Security benefits, will make the "golden years" most enjoyable.

According to Vriend (1977), many of the individuals who experience midcareer changes are women who feel trapped in low-paying jobs with no job satisfaction. Fewer than 2% of the directorships of top American corporations, fewer than 1% of top management posts, and only about 5% or 6% of all middle-management positions are held by women (Crittenden, 1977).

Middle-aged women who do change careers most often move into a different but related field (Dullea, 1977). A social worker may become a nurse. A few women who are highly motivated may seek to make a complete change, selecting an entirely new profession. An example would be an office worker who decides to become a clinical psychologist. Sometimes new possibilities are introduced or discovered while in an education program, and a career direction change is made.

Are working women more satisfied than those who choose to be full-time housewives? Many studies find little difference in overall satisfaction between the two roles (Wright, 1978). Baruch and Barnett (1980) found that the sources of satisfaction and self-esteem varied for employed and unemployed women. The well-being of the full-time housewife was highly dependent on the husband's approval of her activities. In contrast, the satisfaction of the working woman was affected by her view of her job and career, as well as her interaction with her husband.

Black workers at midlife

The social and civil rights movements have brought about a major change in the economic circumstances of at least part of the black community. There is a definite emerging black middle class that is larger than ever before. The national effort to give blacks a more equitable share of the nation's goods and benefits has had results—uneven, but undeniable. Increasingly blacks are seen in offices of corporations and banks, in classrooms of colleges, in officers clubs, in affluent suburbs, and in tourist areas. As middle-class blacks have prospered, a gap has opened between them and the black underclass that remains fixed in poverty and despair.

Statistics are an inadequate way to demonstrate middle-class status. After all, to be middle class is a matter of income, education, life-style, attitude, and that indefinable sense of well-being—being a useful functioning part of society. For some individuals—black, white, or brown—a different level of income would bring about this condition. Some would live comfortably on $10,000 to $12,000 a year. Others would not make it on $30,000 to $40,000 a year (America's rising, 1974).

The rise of the black middle class is suggested by a variety of statistics. Comparing 1965 to 1974, there are 30% more blacks making over $10,000 a year and 12% more making over $15,000. In the North and West, in 1971, a black husband and wife unit earned 93% of comparable white income. College enrollment of blacks doubled between 1967 and 1972; 18% of blacks, compared to 26% of whites, attend college. Professional and technical positions for blacks have increased by 128%. The number of black managers, officials, and proprietors has doubled. The implications are that as this trend continues, the socioeconomic composition of the middle-aged, middle-class population of the near future will change to more egalitarian levels.

CHAPTER REVIEW

1. Middle adulthood is the *maintenance or status quo phase* of adulthood, the years of continuity. If the status quo of life can be maintained, the individual is content.
2. Midlife may be viewed as a period of transition from one age stage to another or as a period of both transition and crisis. Individual differences exist.
3. The *developmental tasks* relate to (a) family circumstances involving grown children, aging parents, and the renewal of the husband and wife relationship, (b) the restructuring of personal commitments and obligations, (c) social outreach and responsibilities, and (d) physical and psychological changes.
4. Midlife changes in *physical characteristics* begin on a plateau, then change slowly but gradually. There is a rather steady decline in the latter part of middle age. Facial appearance changes, strength and energy decrease, sensory organs lose some acuity, and body systems begin to lose their vigor. On the positive side, physical decline can be slowed down by good nutrition and fitness activities.
5. *Menopause*, also known as *climacteric*, occurs in most women between the ages of 40 and 55. In spite of the major hormonal changes taking place, three out of every four women have no menopausal disturbances that require medical therapy. The phase of menopause is considered complete when a woman has not had a menstrual period for 12 months.
6. Sexual activity generally continues during middle age but at a reduced frequency. Psychological factors affect some midlife men and women because of changes in personality traits or because of anxieties associated with the idea of being middle aged. Sexual energy is related to an individual's state of mind and physical fitness.
7. There are three *views of personality development* in midlife: first, that the self and personality are stabilized early in life (Freud's concept); second, that personality continues to respond to environmental situations (social learning theory); and third, that personality deals with external and internal changes, incorporating changes into the existing personality system (neopsychoanalytic). Research findings exist for both continuity and change.
8. The concept of a midlife crisis has ambiguous meanings. Some theorists, such as Erikson and Neugarten, use the term *crisis*, but they are referring to a "transitional vehicle." Other theorists, such as Levinson and Gould, consider a crisis as a "stressful, disruptive condition," even though a transitional state is implied. Apparently midlife, like other periods of the life cycle, is characterized by change and transition. Some individuals can handle the changes better than others. It also appears that the research on changes in midlife of men is not appropriate, on an age-related basis, for changes in the midlife of women.
9. The most significant *source of stress* in middle-aged men is work, while for women it is health and the family. Younger adults are exposed to more life events that can be stressful than are middle-aged adults.
10. In midlife cognitive development, *fluid intelligence* declines because the physiological and neurological functions on which it depends also decline. *Crystallized intelligence* continues to increase with exposure to cultural and verbal learning activities. Older adults solve everyday practical problems more easily than they can solve the type of assessment questions or tasks given on tests.
11. Concerning achievement in midlife, the maximum production rate for quality work generally occurred during the ages of 35 to 45 years. Creative production does not decline rapidly after those peak years.
12. Developmental *tasks for parents* with adolescent children include (a) building an effective two-way communication channel, (b) providing support and direction to teenagers seeking identity and a place in a peer group, and (c) nurturing independence, autonomy, and responsibility.
13. The *empty-nest syndrome*—when all the children have gone from the home—may not be as traumatic as it may seem. The majority of women actually look forward to the time when the youngest child leaves home. There is a need at that time, however, for the husband and wife to relate to each other more and to establish a strong relationship built on each other rather than around the children.

14. Many adults become grandparents during middle age. There are five *styles of grandparenting:* first, a formal, "hands-off" approach, second, a "fun-seeking" role, third, a surrogate-parent role, fourth, the role of the teacher of wisdom, and fifth, the distant-grandparent figure role.
15. Adult *children with elderly parents* frequently assume a helping behavior role by visitation, securing information, or providing transportation for their parents. Most elderly parents prefer to remain independent and to take care of their needs as long as possible. However, 85% to 88% of the adult children express a commitment to help their elderly parents.
16. Middle age is the time when most adults enjoy the highest social status in adult society. Club and organization membership is at a peak. Social life often becomes "other directed." Life satisfaction increases rapidly after the ages of 45 or 50.
17. The peak of vocational success, power, and prestige frequently comes during middle age. However, *career satisfaction* often depends on the relationship between a person's reasons for working and the characteristics of the work situation. Older workers consistently indicate more satisfaction with their jobs than younger workers. Because of a rapidly changing technology that makes some occupations obsolete while creating new fields, many middle-aged individuals feel free to make major midlife career changes.
18. For many women midlife career development is slightly different than it is for men. Women experience different life events, such as pregnancy and rearing children. After working a few years, some drop out of the job market, only to return after the children are older. Many women feel trapped in low-paying jobs with no career satisfaction. Job satisfaction for a woman is affected by her view of her work and her interaction with her husband. Satisfaction of full-time housewives was highly dependent on the husband's approval of her activities.
19. Although some progress has been made in equalizing job status and pay between whites and nonwhites, there remains a major discrepancy between the two groups, just as exists between men and women. A nonwhite middle class is emerging, but slowly.

REVIEW QUESTIONS

1. Why is middle adulthood considered to be the years of continuity or maintenance of the status quo?
2. List the developmental tasks of middle adulthood. Briefly indicate what each task entails.
3. What findings do the demographers present to suggest that middle-aged people are "alive and well" and not necessarily in a period of crisis?
4. Study Fig. 14-1. What differences exist between the usual performance and the potential performance of physical skills in midlife? Why the difference?
5. Physical appearance is altered in midlife. What impact do physical changes have on personal characteristics, as viewed by the individual and as viewed by younger adults?
6. Review the material on physical characteristics. What characteristics change? Do all changes have negative connotations? Can physical changes be slowed down? If so, how?
7. What are the major health problems and concerns of middle-aged men? Of middle-aged women?
8. What is menopause? What are its symptoms? When does it take place? Do most women suffer distress during menopause? Is there a similar hormonal change in men?
9. Discuss the nature of sexual activity during middle age. What are the key factors related to frequency of sexual involvement?
10. Describe personality organization in the adult. Is change implied or not?
11. List and describe the three alternative views of adult personality development.
12. Discuss the concept of continuity and change in adult personality. Remember the nature and limitations of cross-sectional studies and longitudinal studies.
13. What is the concept of midlife crisis? What are the pros and cons of the existence of a midlife crisis? Cite the research and the various views. These views include (a) midlife as crisis and (b) midlife as transition.
14. What are the major causes of stress in middle age?
15. What happens to fluid intelligence and crystallized intelligence development during middle adulthood?
16. How does Piaget's theory of cognitive development relate to cognition in midlife?
17. Compared to other age groups, how does middle age rank in terms of achievement levels?

18. List the developmental tasks of parents with adolescent children.
19. How are parents affected by the empty-nest syndrome, the time when the youngest child has left home? Don't guess. Look at the research.
20. There are several different roles that grandparents can play. What are they? What are the age differences as they relate to grandparenting?
21. Consider the topic of adult children and their elderly parents. What conflicts did the elderly parents have with their adult children?
22. What marital adjustments may need to be made in midlife? What aspects of the marital relationship are most rewarding?
23. What are some of the characteristic social roles and status of middle-aged individuals?
24. What is the level of life satisfaction in midlife?
25. What is the level of midlife career or job satisfaction?
26. What are midlife career changes? Who makes them? Why?
27. Discuss midlife career development for women.
28. What is the status of black workers at midlife?

THOUGHT QUESTIONS AND ACTIVITIES

1. What is it like to be an adult 40 to 50 years of age? What are the sociological, psychological, and physiological factors involved? In what ways is such an adult different from a 30-year-old or a 20-year-old?
2. What's so bad about becoming 40 years old? What's so great about it?
3. Are adults of middle age capable of doing good reasoning and thinking? Are they beginning to deteriorate in mental abilities?
4. What is it like to be an adult 50 to 60 years of age? What are the sociological, psychological, and physiological factors involved?
5. Should the frequency and type of sexual activities decrease or decline after the age of 50 or 55 years because a couple may no longer be capable of reproducing? What seems to be the key to continued sexual activity?
6. Let's take a look at your future. Take your present age and quickly review your family circumstances, your career or educational status, your social life, and your life in general. Add 10 years to your life and to the lives of those in your family circle, including parents, brothers, sisters, grandparents, friends, husband or wife, and children, if any. What might life be like in 10 years? How do you see yourself and your circumstances? Add 10 more years to your life and the lives of those around you. What will your family, home, and vocational circumstances likely be? Add another 10 or 20 years. How do you see you and your life now? Are your efforts, resources, goals, and planning of today sufficient to meet the changes and challenges of tomorrow and to get you where you want to be?
7. Survey or interview a number of people between the ages of 40 and 60 to determine what they like about their age group—and what they don't like about it. Would they suggest an age level that they would like better? If so, ask what makes the suggested age level better than the present one?
8. Ask your parents, if they are in this age bracket, what lessons they have learned from their past lives that have been of some help to them. Ask what they know now that they wish they would have known when they were much younger. Any surprises? Any ideas for you?
9. Mastectomy is a concern for many women. What personal knowledge do you have of women who have had this operation? Have you ever heard of a man having this operation?
10. The term *midlife crisis* has been a popular media term. What does the research say about the idea? Look for the latest literature in professional journals.

FURTHER READINGS

Ahrons, C.R. Divorce: A crisis of family transition and change. *Family Relations,* 1980, *29*(4), 533-540. This research presents normative crises of family transitions that occur in cases of divorce. Both the stresses and the coping strategies relevant to the transitions are cited.

Block, M.R., Davidson, J.L., & Grambs, J.D. Women over forty. New York: Springer Publishing Co., 1981. This book is an excellent source of information about the physical development of women in middle and late adulthood.

Burstein, B., Bank, L., & Jarvick, L.F. Sex differences in cognitive functioning: Evidence, determinants, implications. *Human Development,* 1980, *23,* 289-313. This article reviews the evidence of sex differences in cognitive functioning. It examines hormonal, genetic, neuroanatomical, and cultural determinants. There are some inadequacies in the evidence.

Farrell, M.P., & Rosenberg, S.D. *Men at mid-life.* Boston: Auburn House Publishing Co., 1981. A survey and interview study done by the authors reveals the developmental pattern of middle-aged men. Relationships with wives, children, and extended family are also presented. The appendix contains The Mid-life Crisis Scale: Physical Health Question.

Francoeur, R.T. The sexual revolution: Will hard times turn back the clock? *The Futurist,* 1980, *14*(2), 3-12. Historically, sexual attitudes appear to vary with prosperity levels. When economic times are good, attitudes favor sexual freedom; when times are poor, sexual attitudes are more conservative. New life styles and sex roles have emerged. Will there be a break in the historical pattern?

National Institute of Mental Health. Families today: A research sampler on families and children. *Science Monographs,* 1979, *1* and *2.* These two volumes report 30 projects that summarize recent research on families. Look at the table of contents and choose a topic for further reading.

Norman, W.H., & Scaramella, T.J. *Mid-life: Developmental and clinical issues.* New York: Brunner/Mazel, 1980. This book is a collection of chapters written by different authors on the issues and problems of midlife. An interesting chapter is "Changing Roles for Women at Mid-Life."

Santrock, J.W., Warshak, R., Lindbergh, C., & Meadows, J.L. Children's and parent's observed social behavior in stepfather families. *Child Development,* 1982, *53*(2), 472-480. The effects of remarriage on the parents' and the child's social behavior were studied. Parenting behavior, sex of the child, and marital conflict were factors in explaining the social behavior of the children.

CHAPTER 15

LATER ADULTHOOD

THE AGED AND AGING

MY OLD AGE IS GETTING TO ME

Old age can become very frustrating and depressing when one increasingly realizes a growing dependence on others accompanied by a feeling of failure in oneself. I am eighty-five years old, and I have observed a gradual decline in my physical and mental alertness over the past few years. This age reminds me greatly of the young child who needs someone to guide his actions and make his decisions. To me it seems like a sad and difficult period of life.

At the age of eighty, just five short years ago, I lived a very full, patterned, and contented life. My wife and I were both in good health, owned our home, and were able to care for ourselves. I enjoyed gardening in my double lot of ground while my wife busied herself cooking delicious foods and cleaning house. We passed the evenings watching television and reading the newspaper. We had daily visits from our three children and their families who lived in the same community. Yes, life was pleasant then, with few upsets in the routine.

Two years later my beloved wife died suddenly, and that pleasant way of living came to an abrupt end. Henceforth, life was rather lonely in that big house, even though friends and family visited regularly and tried to brighten each day. Oh, there were still things to do: garden to tend, furnace to fire, and house to clean; but somehow life was empty. The children bought me a little house dog, and he became my main concern and constant companion. Here was someone who needed me and shared my day from sunrise to sunset. Summer days became enjoyable with gardening in the morning, a nice nap with my pup curled at my feet through the afternoon, and a relaxing evening on the back porch under the stars. Winter days found me more restless since I could not get outside. The children were wonderful to me, always visiting, cooking my meals, doing my laundry, and helping in countless other ways. I had life better than many at my age. Then, one by one, my old friends died off, leaving me more and more alone. But my dog and I carried on.

Gradually, almost unnoticed by me, I became a little less responsible. A few times I forgot to turn down the furnace thermostat before retiring for the night, and then I misplaced my phone bill once or twice. My memory grew shorter and I misplaced things continually. They tell me I asked the same questions five or six times within an hour, and still I couldn't recall the answer. Yes, I was going downhill, but never would I leave my home; it was my life.

Then one day I did a foolish thing but it was very important at the time. I was eighty-four and, as always, the spring housecleaning had to be done. There was a hired lady to help, but washing windows was no job for a woman. That had always been my department, and this year was no exception. We began upstairs and although I had been warned not to do the windows this year, I positively could not surrender my duties! Well, you can picture the rest. I climbed out on the porch roof and two minutes later was on the cement floor below, unable to move. It was a miracle that my injuries were light—a few broken ribs and a concussion. A few weeks in the hospital and I would be as good as new, or so I thought.

I demanded to go back home, but the family seemed to have full say now and I soon found myself in a nursing home. I've been here now for several months and I suppose you'd say I've adjusted well. I can't walk on my own any more, but I have a walker and a wheelchair to help me get around. The aches and pains are more prominent these days, and I get so bored with myself. Neither television nor the newspaper is of any interest to me. People keep trying to interest me in something, but my mind can't concentrate on any one thing for longer than a few minutes. That is, unless it is something that worries me. For instance, some days all I want to talk about is getting new pants or needing socks. About every five minutes I bring it up again, even though others keep trying to change the subject.

The other people at this home are so irritating. I declare they're always stealing my clothes, although my family insists I just misplace them. But they can't fool me; they're stealing them! When I get new things, I hide them under my pillow or behind the dresser. You just can't trust these folks at their old age.

My family is rather disgusting these days. They never agree with me and always try to change my mind. They tell me my bedroom is on the first floor, but I've gone upstairs to bed all my life, and I want to go upstairs to my room. Why can't they understand these facts?

I guess I can put up with this kind of life until spring, but then I'm going to get a trailer and live alone again. I could do everything I used to do if I were in my own home. I'll get my dog back from the farm where he is now, and we'll have a good life together again. I'll put the trailer on my son's lot, have a little garden to tend, and have a back porch to sit on during those nice summer evenings. All those friends will come to visit again and life will be nice.

IN THIS CHAPTER . . .

You will read about

1 The meaning of gerontology, geriatrics, and levels of oldness. Stereotyping, life changes, and personal losses will be discussed.

2 Physical characteristics of old age as they occur in twelve physiological systems, structures, or processes. Factors influencing the aging process are also presented.

3 The concept of wellness and factors that contribute to health maintenance.

4 A variety of educational pursuits by the elderly that help keep the mind and body alert.

5 The diseases and causes of death in the later years.

senescence the period of old age and the changes that occur.

senility significant loss of physical and cognitive functions in old age or preceding it, due to some brain disorder.

Early adulthood is a period of growth in every direction, a time when expansion is taking place in all phases of life. At some point in time enough growth, development, and accumulation has taken place so that individuals become content to just maintain their position and status in life, not pushing for any further major gain. The years of stability and status quo are ushered in. There comes another time, however, when major changes take place physically, socially, and psychologically so that individuals find themselves in a drastically different role and status of life, as compared to that of younger generations. This stage usually occurs at retirement.

From the time of retirement on, individuals are in the age of recompense, the bitter-sweet years. It is a period when the major tasks of adulthood have either been completed or set aside, and a new role, that of older members of society, is assumed. How gracefully, how happily, how effectively the new role is lived will depend on the capability of the individuals to be graceful, happy, and effective. Their past life and their adjustment to it will determine how smoothly or awkwardly they move into this new stage and how well they can adapt to it (Neugarten, 1971). Recompense means a return for something given or done. It is a compensation, in kind, for past efforts and services rendered. The age of recompense is the time when people reap the rewards of the kind of life they lived in earlier years. Bitter-sweet implies that some moments will be pleasant and others will be displeasing.

THE AGE LEVEL OF LATER ADULTHOOD

Old age is the last major segment of the life span. Within it there exists a variety of patterns of well-being and aging. Individual differences are probably greater at this time than at any other age. Not all elderly people are "old," and certainly they are not all senile. Most will continue to be highly capable for many years (Zarit, 1977). Yet a characteristic of the age level is that as age increases, there comes a regression, a decrease in effective functioning of the various bodily systems.

Levels of oldness

Although physical decline and psychological decline occur at varying rates, the ages of 60 to 65 are usually cited as the dividing line between middle age and old age (Hareven, 1976). These years are chosen because retirement usually occurs at that time. However, Neugarten (1974) says that most people 65 and under consider themselves (in terms of activities and life-style) to resemble the middle aged rather than the elderly. The ages after 65 do not conveniently fit into one stage because of major differences in the degree of physical and psychological decline that occurs as age advances. Gerontologists have attempted to deal with this aspect of "oldness" by dividing old age into two groups: "young-old," ages 65 to 74 years, and "old-old," ages 75 years or more (Hall, 1980). Physiological, sociological, and psychological ages are poor measures of determining the beginning of old age because of the major differences as to the onset of debilitating effects. Most men and women living in Western societies today do not show appreciable physical and mental characteristics of decline until the late sixties or the early seventies. Better living conditions and better medical and health care are factors in prolonging good health into later life.

As people grow older, they may have less strength, vigor, and speed of reaction, but they learn to compensate for this change (Botwinick, 1978). For example, the reaction time of older individuals is not as quick as before, causing them to be more accident prone when driving. They compensate for this by driving more slowly and not driving when road conditions are dangerous. This period of old age, when decline is taking place gradually and when compensation is made for the decline, is known as ***senescence.*** Senescence means to have grown old and to show the characteristics of old age. Depending on the degree of mental and physical decline, a person may become senescent as early as the late fifties; however, senescence does not usually occur until the late sixties or early seventies. ***Senility*** occurs when a person has a major physical breakdown, personality disorganization, and/or loss of mental faculties because of a brain disorder. Behaviors associated with senility are loss of memory, anger over inability to carry out various tasks, night waking, sus-

David Strickler

Recipe For Contentment
Health enough to make work a pleasure.
Wealth enough to support your needs.
Strength to battle with difficulties and overcome them.
Grace enough to confess your sins and forsake them.
Patience enough to toil until some good is accomplished.
Charity enough to see some good in your neighbor.
Faith enough to make real the things of God.
Hope enough to remove all anxious fear concerning the future.

Goethe

piciousness, and difficulty communicating. Family members often suffer from anger and depression as a result of their loved one's senility and from fatigue from having to care for them. Most senile patients are cared for by family members, not by institutions (Rabin, 1982). An elderly person who is in a deep depression will act in a way that may be considered senile. However, the depression problem is functional (psychological) and not organic. A differential diagnosis has to be made. Senility may occur early in life if there is an organic disease present. Usually it does not occur at all. Most people become senescent; few become senile.

A variety of factors that can produce individual differences in regard to the length of the life span are shown in the box on life expectancy. Some of these factors are reversible and can be changed to enhance or worsen the chances of extended life. Other factors are permanent and cannot be changed. For example, the condition of being overweight is reversible. It is possible to lose weight and increase the number of years of life.

HOW LONG WILL YOU LIVE?

This is a rough guide for calculating your personal longevity. The basic life expectancy for males is age 67 and for females it is age 75. Write down your basic life expectancy. If you are in your fifties or sixties, you should add 10 years to the basic figure because you have already proven yourself to be quite durable. If you are over age 60 and active, add another 2 years.

BASIC LIFE EXPECTANCY _____

Decide how each item below applies to you and add or subtract the appropriate number of years from your basic life expectancy.

1. Family history
   Add 5 years if two or more of your grandparents lived to 80 or beyond. _____
   Subtract 4 years if any parent, grandparent, sister, or brother died of heart attack or stroke before 50. Subtract 2 years if anyone died from these diseases before 60. _____
   Subtract 3 years for each case of diabetes, thyroid disorders, breast cancer, cancer of the digestive system, asthma, or chronic bronchitis among parents or grandparents. _____
2. Marital status
   If you are married, add 4 years. _____
   If you are over 25 and not married, subtract 1 year for every unwedded decade. _____
3. Economic status
   Subtract 2 years if your family income is over $40,000 per year. _____
   Subtract 3 years if you have been poor for greater part of life. _____
4. Physique
   Subtract 1 year for every 10 pounds you are overweight. _____
   For each inch your girth measurement exceeds your chest measurement deduct 2 years. _____
   Add 3 years if you are over 40 and not overweight. _____
5. Exercise
   Regular and moderate (jogging 3 times a week), add 3 years. _____
   Regular and vigorous (long-distance running three times a week), add 5 years. _____
   Subtract 3 years if your job is sedentary. _____
   Add 3 years if it is active. _____
6. Alcohol
   Add 2 years if you are a light drinker (1-3 drinks a day). _____
   Subtract 5 to 10 years if you are a heavy drinker (more than 4 drinks per day). _____
   Subtract 1 year if you are a teetotaler. _____
7. Smoking
   Two or more packs of cigarettes per day, subtract 8 years. _____
   One to two packs per day, subtract 4 years. _____
   Less than one pack, subtract 2 years. _____
   Subtract 2 years if you regularly smoke a pipe or cigars. _____
8. Disposition
   Add 2 years if you are a reasoned, practical person. _____
   Subtract 2 years if you are aggressive, intense, and competitive. _____
   Add 1-5 years if you are basically happy and content with life. _____
   Subtract 1-5 years if you are often unhappy, worried, and often feel guilty. _____

From Richard Schulz, *The psychology of death, dying and bereavement.* © 1978, Addison-Wesley Publishing Co., Inc. Reading, Mass. Page 97-98, table 5.1. Reprinted with permission.

Continued.

BASIC LIFE EXPECTANCY—cont'd

9. Education
   Less than high school, subtract 2 years. ____
   Four years of school beyond high school, add 1 year. ____
   Five or more years beyond high school, add 3 years. ____
10. Environment
   If you have lived most of your life in a rural environment, add 4 years. ____
   Subtract 2 years if you have lived most of your life in an urban environment. ____
11. Sleep
   More than 9 hours a day, subtract 5 years. ____
12. Temperature
   Add 2 years if your home's thermostat is set at no more than 68°F. ____
13. Health care
   Regular medical checkups and regular dental care, add 3 years. ____
   Frequently ill, subtract 2 years. ____

geriatrics the medical study and care of aging persons.

gerontology the study of the improvement of the life habits of aging persons; the psychology and sociology of aging.

Gerontology and geriatrics

The word ***gerontology*** refers to the scientific study of the aging process of life from a physiological, pathological, psychological, sociological, and economic point of view.

Geriatric, in the singular form, pertains to the aged or their characteristic tribulations (geriatric problems). For example, the "tea and toast geriatric" is an aged person who is too enfeebled or unable to shop adequately for food or to cook a meal. As a result, this person subsists on a diet of tea and toast or milk and cereal.

Geriatrics, in plural form, is the medical specialty of gerontology in which physiological and pathological changes of the aging human system are studied and treated. Much study and attention are also paid to "the aging process," that is, how aging takes place. The problems of the aged are one thing, the process of aging is another.

There are several factors that account for most of the interest and development of gerontology and geriatrics in recent years. A major factor is the decline of the death rate in Western societies. In 1860 only 2.7% (860,000 people) of the American people were over 65 years of age. By 1950 the percentage had risen to 7.6%, and by 1980 there were 12.1% (22 million people) in that age-group. Since the life expectancy of people 65 years of age and over is now nearly 13 additional years, the problems of older people can be of major consequence for both sexes, but for women especially. The ratio of women to men changes from 120 women per 100 men for ages 65 to 69 years to more than 160 women for every 100 men at the age of 85 years and over (Cranston, 1980). Women should be taught how to be widows.

A second underlying factor for recent interest in gerontology is the vast array of problems that confront the aged. Many problems are brought on by a new adult role, problems of living and living arrangements, and changes that affect the well-being and life-style of the individual.

A third factor for increased interest is that many individuals are not prepared or educated for old age. Oftentimes retirement is unplanned. People who have worked hard all their lives suddenly reach retirement age and find nothing but a void in their lives. They are unable to cope with their unscheduled time.

A fourth factor in the growth of interest in gerontology and geriatrics has been the enactment of legislation on behalf of older people, including the Social

The large increase in the number of elderly persons has given special impetus to the field of gerontology to study problems of housing, nursing care, social activities, and political and economic status.

Security Act, old age assistance. Medicare, and laws passed to prohibit discrimination against older workers.

A fifth factor is the long-festering dissatisfaction with institutional forms of rehabilitation and terminal care for the aged. Newer forms, such as outpatient geriatric clinics, have been created. Seeing the state mental hospitals overcrowded with geriatric patients who no longer needed institutional care but who did require some form of rehabilitation and motivation therapy before being placed in the community, the legislature of Pennsylvania established the South Mountain Geriatric Center to provide this service. The center seeks to rehabilitate the elderly to independent self-help care and then to place them in foster homes.

The impressive increase in the number and variety of clubs and fraternal organizations by and for the aged is a sixth factor for new interest in geriatrics. Golden Age Clubs, American Association of Retired Persons, and similar "senior citizens" organizations are principally social and seek to overcome the detrimental byproducts of isolation in old age. The Gray Panthers and other political pressure groups seek to influence legislative action. All of these groups provide a measure of group therapy that helps to meet some of the needs of the aged.

The seventh factor is the evolving awareness of the traditional professions that have an interest in the problems of the elderly. More and more professional organizations of medicine, psychology, social science, occupational therapy, nursing, and housing have formed committees and divisions to deal with the problems and needs of the aged.

Finally, the fields of gerontology and geriatrics have increased their activities in research. Systematic exploration into the aging process and its problems is now being conducted in every conceivable discipline. Two of the major areas of current research are aging and the diseases of old age. There are still a great many unanswered questions in this area, however. For example, some of the pressing questions include: What are the factors that influence the rate of aging? What potentials and capacities do older people possess? What methods are most appropriate in the care of the senile aged person?

Stereotyping and negativism

The aged were not always, as they are today, a significant proportion of the population. Wars, famines, injuries, diseases, and inadequate health knowledge and care contributed to a relatively brief life span up to the twentieth century. Life expectancy in 1900 was only 48 years (Eisdorfer and Lawton, 1973). However, since the time of recorded Biblical history, there have been expressions of interest and efforts on behalf of the elderly in the community. Gold and Kaufman (1970) traced the development of institutional care for the elderly. They cite the Talmud and the Old Testament (Ruth IV, v. 5) as stressing the obligation "to provide for the support and comfort of the old." The earliest shelters for the aged were tents, but they did reflect one of the ideals of mankind: to care for those who cannot care for themselves. There is concern for the aged today, but along with that concern have emerged some stereotypes of old age that are mainly negative in nature.

As Butler and Lewis (1977) state: "Few people in the United States can think of old age as a time of potential health and growth." In a way, the negative view of old age is an aspect of Western civilization; it is not found in Oriental thinking. The difference appears to be based on how life is viewed. Oriental philosophy emphasizes ancestral worship and places death within the process of human experience. Death is part of the full spectrum of life. Older persons see themselves as approaching a point in time where they are to be revered. As a man India said to us when we commented on frailties that age brings to a person, "But, old is gold!" We remember the aggressiveness, almost to the point of rudeness, of a young Japanese woman at a buffet dinner in a restaurant in Osaka as she gathered food on a plate. Our friend said, "Don't be upset or shocked by her behavior. The food is not for her; it is for her aged mother." In Beijing, China, it was heartening to see young men and women showing their elderly parents or grandparents the sights of the Forbidden City. We remember a sing-sing in a village on the Sepik River in Papua New Guinea being held in honor of an older man. His people wanted a party for him while he was still alive; they said it would please him immensely if we took his picture. We like the concept of the Abkhasians in the Soviet Union who simply describe older persons as the "long-living," which is an emphasis on life rather than on being just a step from death's doorway.

In Western societies there is much emphasis on youth, on individuality, and on productivity. Death is considered beyond the living self and not acceptable. Death is something to be avoided rather than a logical and necessary aspect of life. As such, anything that implies "getting old" or "beginning to fail" is an affront to the individual and rejected because of the inference that the self is no longer in control. It is the worst thing that could happen to a person. We even joke and halfheartedly rationalize about it when we say: "Well, getting old isn't too bad when you consider the only alternative." Expressions such as "being over the hill"; "They say life begins at 40—but nobody says what it begins . . ."; and that subduing realization, "They're saying I have to retire," are common.

Scientific studies and medical science contribute to negative stereotyping by reporting debilitating characteristics of the elderly—neglecting to mention that most studies are done on institutionalized persons whose physical and mental decline was primarily responsible for their being there in the first place. Literature written about the "age of decline," "the failing years," and "the waning time of life" does nothing to dispel the negative view of old age. Even physicians contribute to this idea when they say "Well, you'd better face it, you're getting older. Your problem is one of age." The truth of the matter is that nobody dies of "old age." They die of a heart condition, a disorder of the circulatory system, a cancerous development, or some other cause. They do not die because they are 69, 75, or 82 years of age.

Recent observations and studies by Kahana (1982) suggest that some of the negative stereotypes of aging among young people seem to be breaking down. Kahana compares studies from 1959 with research in 1973 and 1975 and concludes that there are more positive than negative attitudes toward the aged in recent years. Kahana states that one reason for changes toward more positive attitudes may be the new tolerance that now exists toward minority groups in society, including the aged. There may also be an increased awareness of the positive potentials of the aged in our society, as well as of their plight.

Life changes and attitudes

The essential ingredient for having a happy old age is not the desire for longevity or the avoidance of change but the determination of how to improve the quality of life at that point in time, regardless of the physical condition of that phase of life. The quality of life emanates from within the self; it cannot be imposed from the outside by someone else. Outside factors and forces can make it easier for an individual to evolve a better quality of life through attitudes, thoughts, and feelings, but "it's what's inside" that counts. We have seen very miserable, mean, unhappy persons living in the finest of homes and receiving the best of care and love; we have seen accepting, gracious, loving, believing individuals living in the most unfortunate of circumstances.

Consider these statements made to us at different times by residents of a nursing care unit. An 85-year-old said, "I want to die. I'll never again be able to do what I used to do." A 92-year-old said, "I'm grateful for these extra years, even though I have some suffering. They give me more time to spend with my loved ones."

What makes the difference between the complainer and the accepting individual? Their attitudes, faith, and consideration for others make the difference. Lest you get the wrong idea, this task is easier said than done. It is simplistic to say: "Change your attitudes and you change everything." Circumstances can be very overwhelming and detrimental, making coping behavior difficult to attain. In some cases, the older person may simply not know how to deal with frustration and change. It is not easy to change patterns of thoughts, values, and dispositions.

It is important not to place undue stress on changes that occur in an aged person. Changes occur at all stages of life. It is true that, because of some changes, older persons cannot do what they could do at an earlier age, but should this fact be the controlling element in determining how life should be considered and lived?

What is important is for others not to be too hard on older persons when they act cranky and hard-to-live-with. After all, change works both ways. Life circumstances are changed for the elderly, but they are also changed for those taking care of them. Why should the old be the only persons who are expected to readjust so they can better cope with circumstances? Should not the same principle apply to the younger persons who are taking care of them?

It is important to consult research studies to see what they might contribute to an understanding of attitudes of the aged toward aging and toward life in general.

Attitudes of the aged toward themselves differ according to age, sex, geographic location, and other factors. Youmans (1977) found that the urban "old-old" aged were more satisfied and had a more positive self-image than did the same age-group in rural areas. Ninety percent of the older persons in a Florida retirement community identified with an image of "young-old" and expressed optimism about their changing status (Kahana et al., 1980). Within this group there were a number of adventurous aged who adopted new careers, residences, and life-styles. As people age, they do not "naturally" become disengaged, rigid, or senile (Kahana, 1982). The elderly who suffer the most from old age are those who see themselves as very old, in poor health, a burden to others, and who are socially isolated.

Cameron (1971) found that when ranking age decades for happiness, freedom from worry, and ambition, all age-groups (including the old) put adulthood first, followed by childhood, middle age, and lastly, old age. There was general agreement that old age was the least desired period of life. In spite of these findings, research in the area of self-image showed about as many studies indicating that old people had positive views of themselves as there were studies indicating the opposite. Research of self-image, attitudes toward life in general, and morale seem to indicate that these attitudes were less affected by age than by some concomitant of aging, such as ill health, low socioeconomic status, isolation, inactivity, and institutionalization. It is possible that improvement in the life conditions of the elderly would lead to a reduction of negative views held by the aged concerning themselves. Butler (1975) observes that "to extend the quantity [of life], but not its quality, is a macabre joke" (p. 356).

Changes and personal losses

Consider some of the changes and personal losses that are age-related. Pastalan and Carson (1970) trace age-level changes. When individuals are between the ages of 50 and 65, grown children leave the household, if they have not already done so, and the parents begin to consider retirement and its implications. At 65 to 75 years of age, there is a decline in income because of retirement from a job, a loss of friends, possibly of a spouse, and some changes in body image. During the period of 75 to 85 years there is an increased loss of sensory activity, health, strength, and independence. At 85 years plus, there is serious loss of health and independence. Table 15-1, adapted from the National Center for Housing Management resource book (1977), gives a more detailed presentation of age-related evironmental changes and personal loss.

Conditions responsible for changes in old age include health status, social status, economic status, marital status, living conditions, educational level, and the sex of the individual. Changes in health and energy

Dear John and Ellen,

It certainly was wonderful to see you again. I only wish you hadn't moved to sunny California so that we could get together more often. I do hope that you enjoyed the visit as much as we did. It has done wonders for Dad to see you two and his first grandson again.

Actually, I've been meaning to write to you about Dad for some time. I'm sure you have noticed the changes since you have been separated from him for several years. Little things go unnoticed around here until all at once something happens, and we become aware of still another change.

It all started, I think, when Dad was forced to retire from the bank a little more than a year ago. And it's no wonder. After all, he has been working for almost fifty years. During the war he worked an evening shift at the steel mill in addition to his position at the bank. As a child, I cannot remember seeing him much, even after the war, because he was also working as a salesman at the garage at night for a number of years. It's no wonder that retirement poses some problems for him!

The bank put him down a number of times. I especially remember, as I'm sure you do, John, that time he should have become the head of his department but instead some college graduate received the promotion. It's not surprising that Dad was disturbed, particularly when he had to spend the next month showing the younger man how to keep the records, how to handle the clients, and most of the other things about which the college graduate had no idea. The guy did, of course, have a degree and that makes one an expert, right?

Dad saw this same put-down happening to many of his friends as well, and I'm sure these were some of the things that started his deterioration. Perhaps deterioration is too strong a word. Maybe it is simply a personality change. Even when Dad was working, there were pressures—particularly about money. His job was demanding and the pay not exactly adequate, as you know. With the Women's Lib movement swelling, the idea of working mothers is not often questioned. I think, though, that Dad has always blamed himself that Mother had to work all these years. Certainly you and I would not be where we are, John, if they hadn't both been working. Even with our scholarships and loans, we would not have made it without them. And I never heard Dad toss it up to us.

Anyway, about a month before his retirement, Dad started elaborating on all the things he was going to do, places he was going to visit. He really *seemed* quite happy about retirement. However, I do remember how we remarked among ourselves that he seemed "frightened" and was trying to keep us from worrying. Of course, he had the two perfect examples of retired men enjoying their leisure in Uncle Bob and Uncle Lee. It's really difficult to understand how they can do so little and still be alive. But that's another story!

After the party they had for Dad at the bank, the changes started to take place. That was about a year ago. Instead of using the tools he had been talking about and building that workshop in the basement, he sat in the living room or on the back porch. Occasionally he played with the new puppy. You remember how he said he would help Mother with the housework (like doing the dishes, running the sweeper, and so on)—well, he could think up some beautiful excuses! One day he said he just had to sit because every time he went to use the vacuum, Skipper barked and carried on. So, he sat! When Skipper went to sleep, Dad started the sweeper but Skipper would wake up and begin his antics. Of course, he never thought to put Skipper outside or even to shut him in the kitchen!

Another time, Dad had been complaining about the dog's nails needing to be clipped. Dad's skin is delicate and a simple scatch from the dog tore it open. One day, the dog got sick, and Dad took him to the veterinarian. Mother had written a note, about the dog's actions and symptoms. When they got home, I asked Dad if he had Skipper's nails clipped while they were there. He really blew his stack. He said it wasn't on the note and he couldn't read minds. I had only asked for his sake, since the nails really didn't bother anyone else. He often takes harmless remarks and treats them as personal attacks.

I thought I could kill two birds with one stone, so I asked Dad to paint my room. You remember how he has always loved to paint. (And what a perfectionist!) Well, it took him almost three weeks to paint my ten-by-twelve room. I don't know what he was doing. At least it kept him busy, and he really did seem in better spirits.

You mentioned that his hearing seemed worse, but actually he just doesn't pay as much attention as he used to. He often accuses us of not telling him anything only minutes after we have. I think maybe he "tunes" us out because many times we are talking about work and activities in which he cannot participate. Before his retirement he listened to everything we said.

I guess it bothered him that you two and the baby moved so far away. I really don't like to think how he will feel when I leave next summer. . . .

All in all, Dad is less active, more quickly irritated, often confused, and worried about money. We try to reassure him without his knowing, but I don't know if it helps. I love having him home all day and not seeing him frustrated by problems at work. I guess, though, that he feels frustrated by a whole new set of problems. I hope he can adjust and shake that feeling of inadequacy that seems to be at the root of all this. We all love him and that's all that counts. It has helped me to get all of this off my chest; I certainly hope it hasn't caused you to worry needlessly. I guess many men go through a period like this. Pray that the period ends quickly and that he can be happy with his new freedom.

Love,

Cindy

TABLE 15-1 Age-related environmental changes and personal losses

50-65	*65-75*	*75-85*	*85+*
Loss of relationship to acquaintances of children; loss of neighborhood role to schools and youth; home too large, but mortgage payments are low and equity high	Loss in relation to work environment; loss of mobility due to lessened income; dissolving of professional work associations and friendships; move to apartment, smaller home, or struggle with increased maintenance costs of larger home	Loss of ability to drive independently, must rely on bus or relatives and friends; connections with community, church associations slowly severed; move to more supportive housing, such as apartments with meals and care service; maintenance costs for single-family house unmanageable	Loss of ability to navigate in the environment, loss of strong connection with outside neighborhood; dependence on supportive services; move to supportive environment necessary, such as nursing home, home for the aged, or home of grown children

Modified from *Managing housing and services for the elderly*. Washington: The National Center for Housing Management, Inc., 1977.

bring about an increased interest in sedentary pursuits and a decrease in activities requiring strength. As physical limitations such as poor eyesight or physical frailty develop, the individual tends to prefer activities that can be enjoyed in the home rather than going out into crowds and public places that requires more effort and care.

Social status usually reflects the range of interests that a person has developed. Generally, the higher the socioeconomic level of the social group with which an individual has associated, the wider the range of interests. Some of these interests, such as playing bridge or attending concerts and lectures, can carry over into old age.

Reduced income after retirement may force an individual to give up many interests that were appealing and force a concentration on ones that can be afforded. This is especially true of older people in low socioeconomic groups. Occasionally, we hear some individuals complain of people living in poor economic circumstances who have a large colored television set or some other so-called luxury item that is much better than they have in their own homes. They point to this circumstance and say that the money could have been better spent. Yet they fail to realize that the TV set (or whatever) may be the only means of commercial entertainment that poor families, young and old, have. Other people may go to the movies, go golfing or bowling, or go on trips, but the elderly and poor cannot afford such luxuries in abundance.

Marital status also determines what a person can do. When both spouses are living, their life-style and living arrangements are usually determined by their interests, economic status, and health. Single men and women find that frequently they have to make some changes in their pattern of living because one person cannot do, or does not enjoy doing, what two persons could do, such as being invited to activities and gatherings that are usually frequented by couples.

Living conditions also are responsible for changes in life. A home for the aged frequently has planned activities; living by oneself or in the home of a married child can limit opportunities for recreation. Poor or failing health or transportation problems can prevent participation in community-sponsored events. Usually, however, the more educational interests a person has, the better he or she can enjoy intellectual activities, such as reading, working crossword puzzles, or watching game shows on television. Women tend to have more interests in old age than men because they usually have broader interests throughout adulthood (Havighurst, 1975). Men, by contrast, tend to limit their interests to sports or puttering around the house. Both of these activities must be curtailed to the spectator level as energy and strength diminish. Men who are retired often find it difficult to develop new interests to occupy their time.

Changes abound. The best remedy is to cultivate interests earlier in life that can be pursued in old age in

A developmental task of old age is to adjust to the changes that occur in life and in living conditions. Companionship and something to look forward to each day are essential to personal well-being.

a more sedentary setting. In addition, it is important to develop an attitude that not only recognizes and accepts change but also encourages the individual to find positive, adaptable ways to deal with changes—and even to bring about desired changes. Since an individual is confronted with changes throughout life, it seems important to learn how to confront, control, and adapt to changes in living and in physical being rather early in life.

Developmental tasks of later adulthood

Old age is no different from other age levels when it comes to having special adaptations that need to be made and special tasks to be achieved if the individual wishes to live effectively, happily, and confidently on that age level. The only difference is that the developmental tasks of old age are the final or ultimate ones in life and relate to the conditions of life in that time period.

The box on p. 577 summarizing developmental tasks for old age is compiled from several sources: Havighurst (1979), Peck (1968), Frenkel-Brunswick (1970), and Erikson (1968a). Task numbers 8, 9, and 13 are from Peck, number 10 is from Erikson, and number 11 is from Frenkel-Brunswick. In some respects, the items suggested by Erikson and Frenkel-Brunswick overlap; they are extensions of each other.

DEVELOPMENTAL TASKS OF OLD AGE

1. Adjusting to the fact of retirement and to a lower income.
2. Learning how to live with one's spouse in retirement.
3. Affiliating with individuals of one's own age-group or with associations for the aged.
4. Maintaining interest in friends and in family ties.
5. Continuing to meet social and civic responsibilities.
6. Adapting to social roles, which will now change more frequently.
7. Finding satisfactory living arrangements at the different stages of old age.
8. Adjusting to changing physical strength and health as age progresses and overcoming bodily preoccupation.
9. Reappraising self-concept, personal values, and personal worth in light of new life circumstances.
10. Resolving the psychosocial crisis of integrity versus despair in old age.
11. Reviewing life's accomplishments and failures and coming to terms with one's worth.
12. Coping with bereavement and loss of spouse and/or friends.
13. Accepting the prospect of death, not by morbid resignation, but by recognition of having made life better for cultural descendants.

Compiled from Havighurst, 1979; Peck, 1968; Frenkel-Brunswick, 1970; Erikson, 1968a.

Havighurst. The older person must accept the concept and the fact of retirement. Furthermore, an adjustment must be made to living on Social Security and/or small retirement income. Both of these tasks involve a change in personal attitudes and concepts. Learning how to live in retirement and how to occupy leisure time so that life is pleasant will require some thought. Some people manage this problem by establishing contact with organizations for retirees and sharing with others of the same age-group whatever benefits the organizations can offer. The elderly couple will also have to become closer companions to each other and learn how to intermesh their lives without getting on each other's nerves.

It will be necessary for the individual to reevaluate self-concept and personal identity in light of one's new role in life. A workable, personal philosophy of life, including a view about death and eternity, will probably be evolved. A major task will be to accept physical changes and their limitations by learning to conserve strength and resources when necessary. Other specific developmental tasks include finding satisfactory housing on retirement income, maintaining interest in people outside the family, maintaining some degree of family ties with children and grandchildren, taking care of elderly relatives, being able to cope with bereavement and widowhood, and continuing to meet social and civic responsibilities by being involved in society and its affairs.

Perhaps three of the most significant adjustive tasks in later life are adaptation to loss, identity or life review, and remaining active in order to retain function. The *first* adjustive task is adaptation to loss. Common losses include loss of spouse; loss of social relationship, especially of work associates and others still active in economic and community activities; decline in income; decrease in mobility; decline in physical vigor; and loss of opportunities for recognition and achievement. The task is to replace the losses with new relationships, new roles, or the retraining of lost capacities (Pfeiffer, 1977).

The *second* adaptation task is to conduct an evaluative life review. Clinicians have long recognized that most older persons engage in such a review, reflecting on their accomplishments and failures, their satisfactions and disappointments, seeking to integrate or evaluate the diverse elements of their lives so that they can come to a reasonably positive or acceptable view of their life's worth. According to Butler and Lewis (1977), failure to accomplish this task may result in overt psychopathology in the age.

The *third* task—remaining active in order to retain function—is concerned with maintenance of physical activity, of social interaction, of intellectual and emotional stimulation, and of self-care capacity. Studies of successfully aging individuals by Pfeiffer (1974b) at the Duke University Center for the Aging indicate that such persons characteristically maintain regular, vigorous, and stimulating activities.

Peck. Robert Peck (1968) suggests that there are three primary *psychological adjustments* that must be resolved during later adulthood. These adjustments all have to do with a preoccupation of some kind, an excessive concern about something. The first issue is that of *self-differentiation versus work-role preoccupa-*

body transcendence versus body preoccupation according to Peck, the need in later adulthood to equate well-being with satisfying relationships and experiences rather than dwelling on physical health.

integrity versus despair in Erikson, the stage of personality development corresponding to old age, in which acceptance of one's life leads to a sense of integrity.

life review a looking back at one's life; may be characterized by reminiscence, anxiety, or by extreme preoccupation with the past. The process, according to Robert Butler, is set in motion by looking forward to death.

tion. Retirement represents a crucial shift in one's life. A new role must be acquired. The individual has to emphasize new interests and dimensions of the self that extend beyond a long-time specific role as a worker. The question of personal worth enters the picture. "Am I a worthwhile person only insofar as I can do a full-time job or can I be worthwhile in other, different ways . . .?" (p. 90). A second issue is that of ***body transcendence versus body preoccupation***. Physical aches and pains and illnesses increase with age. Recuperative powers decline. Many older people become preoccupied with their state of health. Others seem to enjoy life in spite of declining health. Peck suggests that bodily concerns are not related to age per se but rather reflect special life circumstances. People who have learned to define happiness and comfort in terms of satisfying social relationships or creative mental activities can overlook all but the most serious of physical debilitations.

The third issue is one of *self-transcendence versus self-preoccupation*. The realization of the inevitability of death must be dealt with. According to Peck, it is possible to make a positive adaptation to this most unwelcome prospect. It can be done by having a vital, gratifying interest in making life more meaningful, secure, or happier for those who go on living after one dies. The main concern should not be with "poor me" but rather with "What can I do to make life better for those who will survive me?"

Erikson. The final crisis in Erikson's theory of psychosocial development (1963a) is that of ***integrity versus despair***. Ego integrity implies a feeling of having achieved a respected character during one's lifetime. Integrity is characterized by an inner sense of completion brought on by the wisdom of accrued knowledge, understanding, and mature judgment. It is a perceived acceptance of human dignity and love. Despair is characterized by regrets, frustration, discouragement, and the thought that somehow things should have been— or might have been—different. In despair, it is difficult to deal effectively with the concept of the inevitability of death. For people in despair, death may, at best, be considered a way of escaping from a dismal life. The essence of meaningful personal development in the later years of life is to be able to be comfortable with the thought that "I am what survives me."

Frenkel-Brunswick. A review of the literature on developmental tasks of old age leaves the impression that many elderly persons undergo an important search for meaning and integrity in old age. Older people frequently reflect on their past life and consider the future in terms of the meaning of the death experience. It is as if they were seeking to put together the final pieces of the puzzle of life so it would make some kind of sense. Robert Butler (1963) calls this reminiscence a ***life review***. Frenkel-Brunswick (1970) refers to it as "drawing up the balance sheet of life." It approximates the writing of memoirs and autobiographies. Frenkel-Brunswick considers this retrospection as evidence of a "tying together of loose ends" and a final reevaluation of one's life.

PHYSIOLOGICAL AGING

As with all age levels, later adulthood has characteristics that are peculiar to it. Many changes take place in old age. If the types and numbers of these changes are carefully considered, they will be found to be no greater or more drastic than those of other age levels.

Factors influencing aging

Everyone ages. Genetic and prenatal influences set the stage for the aging sequence. Postnatal environmental factors, such as economic, social, and demographic conditions, act to modify this biological sequence. According to Wilson (1974), the rate of psychological aging is directly related to how well an individual will accept change. The acceptance or rejection of aging is an ingredient in psychological aging.

Most theories of aging are presented from a biological point of view; however, some do come from a sociological, environmental, or psychological perspective (Shock, 1977). An increasingly popular view is that of *interactionism,* which seeks to combine the various theoretical approaches and permits the consideration of multiple-causation factors of aging (Baltes and Willis, 1977).

The state of the art so far as theories of physiological aging is concerned is that, although attention has been given to this topic, there are very few theories that are considered viable from a research point of view (Shock, 1977). Aging is a very complex puzzle to unravel. There seem to be many variables involved. Creating the appropriate research design is a very difficult task. The information in the box summarizing

PHYSIOLOGICAL THEORIES OF AGING

I. GENETIC THEORIES

Genetic theories suggest that aging results from change or damage to the *genetic information* involved in the formation of cellular proteins.

A. Cellular genetic theories of DNA damage

Damage or changes to DNA molecules alter the message and result in the inability of the cell to manufacture essential enzymes. Death of the cell occurs because of damage to the cellular DNA. This concept is too general for specific differentiation in research.

B. Somatic mutation by radiation

Abnormal chromosomes develop after exposure to radiation. However, recent research makes it doubtful that this type of damage results in cellular senescence.

C. Error theory of aging

Aging is the result of errors involved in the transmission of information from the DNA to the final protein product. Accumulation of errors would result in "error catastrophe" and cell death. The hypothesis is considered viable.

II. NONGENETIC CELLULAR THEORIES

Nongenetic theories of aging assume that changes take place in the *cellular proteins* after they have been formed.

A. Wear and tear theory

"Wear and tear" of the cellular structure occurs after long use and exposure to stressful elements during the process of living. No adequate research design has been devised that can rule out other variables or that can show a cause and effect relationship in this approach.

B. Deprivation theories

These theories assume that aging is caused by deprivation of essential nutrients and oxygen to cells of the body because of vascular changes. Research has not been able to support this hypothesis as far as aging is concerned.

C. Accumulation theories

Aging results from the accumulation of harmful substances, such as lipofuscin, in the cells of an organism. If this theory is to be considered seriously, the toxic substances must be isolated and identified.

D. Free radical theory

Free radicals are chemicals that contain oxygen in a highly activated state and that react with other molecules in their vicinity. It is theorized that this condition has damaging effects on these cells. Experiments, so far, have many limitations and the theory is unproven.

E. Cross-linkage theory

Bonds or "cross-linkages" develop between molecules or components of the same molecules. These cross-links change the physical and chemical properties of the cells, affecting their proper functions. The protein's elastin and collagen are especially studied. Research thus far makes this theory a viable one for further study.

Compiled from Shock, N.W. Biological theories of aging. In J.E. Birren & K.W. Schaie (Eds.), *Handbook of the psychology of aging*. New York: Van Nostrand Reinhold Co., 1977, pp. 103-112.

Continued.

PHYSIOLOGICAL THEORIES OF AGING—cont'd

III. **PHYSIOLOGICAL THEORIES**

Physiological theories attempt to explain aging on the basis of a breakdown of an organ system or impairment in *physiological control mechanisms.*

A. **Single organ system theories**

These theories include the study of the cardiovascular system (blood flow and oxygen), thyroid gland (metabolism), sex glands (hormone secretions), and the pituitary gland (regulatory functions). In spite of their importance to life, it is questionable if these organs are primary causes of aging.

B. **Stress theory**

Aging is the result of the accumulation of the effects of the stresses of living. Adaptation to these stresses leaves a residual of impairment and accumulants. The experimental data question the basic assumption of accrued impairment.

C. **Immunological theories**

The immune system protects the body from invading micro-organisms and atypical mutant cells that may form. After adolescence the production of antibodies by the immune system diminishes and protection ability decreases. Sometimes normal cells are engulfed and digested. Evidence is meager but the hypothesis is reasonable and can be researched.

D. **Endocrine control system theory**

Considerable evidence shows that the functions of the endocrine system decline with age. It is suggested that aging may be administered on the hormonal level just as puberty and menopause are. Endocrine research is being continued on the cellular level.

E. **Nervous control mechanisms**

Research demonstrates a reduction in the effectiveness of a physiological control mechanism with increasing age; the rate of adjustment or performance diminishes. A slower response may be caused by impaired integrative functions at the neural and endocrine levels. Increased emphasis is being placed on the role of the central nervous system in aging and in regulating important biological processes.

categories of theories of physiological aging is adapted from Birren and Schaie's *Handbook of the Psychology of Aging* (1977). As far as sociopsychological and psychological theories of aging are concerned, there are very few integrative theories. The research problem is extremely complex.

Although the aging process is gradual, it is sometimes speeded up by the advent of disease (Makinodan, 1974). A person with a severe handicap will often age much faster and earlier than a person who is not handicapped. Even with the so-called "normal" person there is always a difference in the rate of aging because of the combined forces of biological, psychological, and sociological factors.

Many people do not realize that environmental factors play a large part in aging. Environmental factors include the people and attitudes that surround the individual. Activity tends to slow down the aging process, but insecurity, lack of someone to talk to, and a strange environment may speed up the aging process (Rosenmayr, 1980).

Throughout life the body is exposed to a procession of accidents, illnesses, and stress, such as a bout of pneumonia, a broken leg, a severe burn, or a period of great psychological stress. The cumulative effect of such "biological insults" may well hasten aging (Bierman and Hazzard, 1973). In some people the connective tissue becomes increasingly hard and impervious, and this may interfere with the distribution of nutrients and the disposal of wastes.

Malnutrition is a major contributor to physical deterioration. Older persons oftentimes lose their appetite and will not eat much. Their diet may not be adequate, since they may not be eating the proper foods or not be eating enough of them. Poor eating habits may accelerate aging (Kent, 1980).

Genetic inheritance definitely plays a role. People with long-lived parents have a somewhat greater life expectancy than people with short-lived parents. The general genetic theory supports the view that there is a certain length of time, genetically determined, in which the body has to function. A timing device within the organism causes tissues and organ systems to break down at specific times (Shock, 1977).

Functional activity of the cells seems to be all-important to the aging process. The cellular error theory of aging states that cells sometimes make errors when they reproduce. This leads to an accumulation of mutant cells that are unable to survive or to cells that may become malignant (Cutler, 1972). Occasionally, aberrations in cells activate the immune mechanism, which in turn reacts against these cells and seeks to destroy them. Ordinarily, the immune mechanism reacts only against bacteria and viruses.

Nature apparently has a built-in mechanism or factors that promote aging. Growing old is part of the natural developmental process. Biological aging is marked by a lowering metabolic rate, which slows down energy exchange. This in turn makes general health more precarious. Almost all bodily systems deteriorate in both their functional and structural efficiency. Structural decline occurs in the blood vessels, heart, and circulatory system in general (Rothbaum et al., 1974). The capacity of the lungs at the age of 60 years is only half of that at 30 years. Therefore less oxygen gets into the system and fewer nutrients and fluids are circulated throughout the body, permitting the occurrence of degenerative diseases and illnesses, with a diminished capacity of bodily resources to overcome them.

In summary, the physical condition of the aging person depends on (1) psychological temperament, (2) manner of living, (3) hereditary constitution, and (4) factors in the environment. Hereditary constitution plays the major role as a cause of physical change. Within a family group, the rate of aging shows a high correlation for the different family members. Secondary causes that have significant influences on the rate of physical decline include a life-style related to faulty diet, malnutrition, gluttony, emotional stresses, overwork, passivity, infections, drug or alcohol intoxications, traumas, and endocrine disorders. Environmental conditions such as heat and cold also influence the rate of aging (Shock, 1977). Positive factors to deter the effects of aging would be the psychological support and care of the family and the attitudes and coping style of the individual.

Physical characteristics in old age

It is true that physical changes do occur with aging and that they are generally in the direction of degeneration. Individual differences are so great, however, that no two individuals of the same age are necessarily at the same state of deterioration. Within the same person there are also variations in the rates of aging of different structures. Different parts of the body resist aging more than others, and the various abilities fade at different rates.

Perhaps the most significant change in the older person is slowness of behavior (Birren et al., 1980). Slowness is not limited to motor responses or to peripheral sensory phenomena but is also evident in more complex behaviors such as cognition, learning and information processing, speed factors in intelligence, and judgment responses that are influenced by a sense of cautiousness. As Botwinick (1978) states, "Older people do not tend to risk being wrong for the sake of being right or fast" (p. 125).

Appearance. Some age changes such as wrinkles, graying hair, stooping shoulders, reduced agility and speed of motion, decrease in strength, decrease in the steadiness of the hands and legs, and increased difficulty in moving about are obvious in the aging individual. Some changes such as thinning hair and varicose veins can be upsetting to those who find it difficult to adjust to changes in physical appearance.

Wrinkling of the skin is caused by the loss of elastic tissue and the fatty layer (Rossman, 1977). The skin does not snap back as readily when stretched. If you pinch the skin on the back of an older person's hand, you will see how it has lost much of its elasticity. The skin also has increased sensitivity to changes in temperature. Since automatic regulation of bodily functions no longer takes place as promptly as previously, older persons often "feel the cold more." The sense of touch also declines with age because there is a general drying, wrinkling, and toughening of the skin.

Sensory acuity. During the period of senescence, the sensory functions seem to be one of the first areas of the body to deteriorate. However, writers in the *Handbook of the Psychology of Aging* (Birren and Schaie, 1977) (Chapters 20 to 23) cite a number of research studies questioning the common belief, as suggested by earlier research, that individuals automatically lose some sensory acuity, especially in touch, smell, and taste, as they get older. It appears that the state of health, previous living style, and sex differences influence the degree and type of deterioration that takes place.

Hearing begins to decline about the age of 65 years. First affected in hearing is the ability to hear very high tones; as time goes on, the level of auditory acuity becomes progressively lower. Approximately 13% of the people over 65 show advanced signs of *presbycusis,* an impairment of hearing in older people. Hearing impairment is five times as common in persons aged 65 to 79 as it is in individuals between the ages of 45 and 64 years (Fig. 15-1). Women appear to retain more of their hearing capacity than do men. For men over 70 years, sound frequencies over 2,000 hertz (the frequency at which whispers are spoken) are heard at a 30-decibel loss or more (Lebo and Reddell, 1972). Normal hearing is considered to be at 25 decibels or less.

As the individual grows older, there is also a decline in *vision*; few people over 60 years of age see well without glasses. This decline is usually caused by deterioration of the cornea, lens, iris, retina, and optic nerve (Botwinick, 1970). Color perception and the power of the eye to adjust to different levels of light and dark are reduced. There is a gradual loss of orbital fat so that eventually the eyes appear sunken, the blink reflex is slower, and the eyelids hang loosely because of poorer muscle tone.

Fig. 15-2 shows the corrected visual acuity for different age-groups. While 57% of those aged 60 to 69 have optimal visual acuity, only 27% of those 70 to 79 and only 14% of those aged 80 and over function at that level. Visual acuity of 20/50 or worse (with correction) in the better eye indicates impairment sufficient to limit activities such as reading, watching TV, or driving.

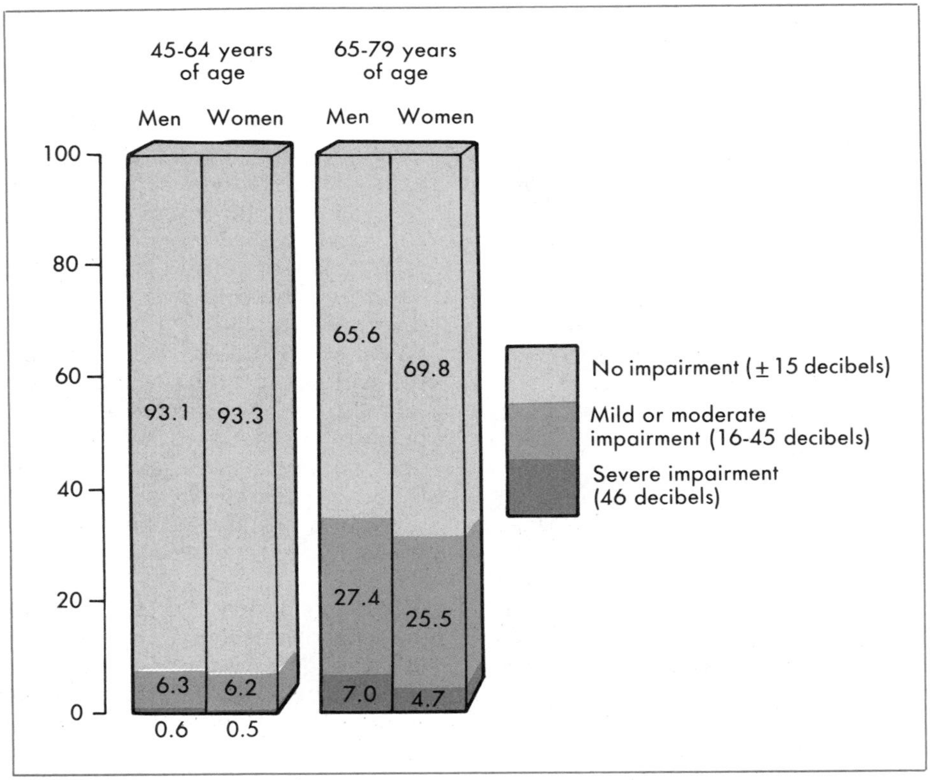

FIG. 15-1 ***Hearing impairment at ages 45 to 64 and 65 to 79, by sex. (Impairment is limited to frequencies essential for speech—500, 1000, and 2000 hertz.)***
From Health in the later years of life: Selected data from the National Center for Health Statistics. *Washington, D.C.: U.S. Government Printing Office, 1971.*

Cataracts are generally a concern to older persons. However, the Duke University study by Anderson and Palmore (1974) shows that the incidence of senescent cataracts in persons over 65 is not high. The initial incidence was 9%, 18%, and 36%, respectively, for participants in their 60s, 70s, and 80s. After 10 years, the incidence increased by only 3% in the group initially in their 70s and not at all in the youngest group.

A ***cataract*** is an opacity of the lens that impairs vision. The consequences of a cataract for visual functioning depend on its location. The most common cataract is associated with excessive nuclear sclerosis, a hardening of cell tissues in the nucleus of the lens. Before any onset of cataracts, the hardening of the lens may increase the refractive power of the eye, improving myopia and making people believe that their near-point vision has improved. If the cataract is located in the anterior cortex, the front or outer layer of the lens, then acquired hyperopia, or far-point vision, may occur. Double vision may result if the degrees of opacity between the cortex and the nucleus are sufficiently large. Generally, cataracts are surgically removed and a substitute lens supplied. The use of contact lenses is then desirable (Paton and Craig, no date).

The level of illumination required for various tasks differs according to the type of task and details involved. Special consideration must be given to planning a visual environment for the elderly so that sufficient light is available for the different activities in which they engage. As Fozard and Popkin (1978) have shown, the level of illumination required for various tasks is greater for the elderly than for younger persons. They recommend that greater freedom for individual control of lighting be available in areas where various tasks are performed. It is suggested that visual environments be designed for the average older eye rather than for the average young eye.

cataract a loss of transparency of the crystalline lens of the eye or of its capsule.

The senses of *taste* and *smell* are said to be reduced in functional capability during advancing years. However, studies by Hermel et al., (1970) on taste, and by Rovee et al., (1975) on smell report, as do a number of other studies, that reduced sensitivity to taste and smell are related more to health, illness, and sex differences than to age. It was also thought at one time that because there is a decrease of 36% in the number of taste buds in an older person as compared to younger individuals, these buds would not be as keen as they were at a younger age. Research by Beidler (1965) indicates that taste buds are seldom damaged permanently and have the power of regeneration. Moulton (1974) suggests that replacement and regeneration may also be possible in the case of the sense of smell. The older person who becomes easily upset about certain things associated with the senses, such as the taste of food, may be reflecting a poor health condition rather than a deterioration of sense organs caused by

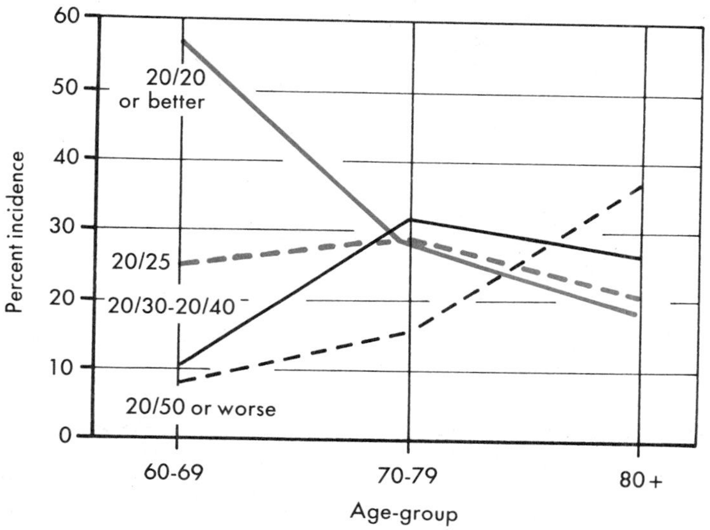

FIG. 15-2 ***Corrected best distance vision in the better eye.***

Modified from Anderson, B., Jr., & Palmore, E. In E.B. Palmore (Ed.). Normal aging II: Reports from the Duke longitudinal studies, 1970-73. *Copyright 1974 by Duke University Press, Durham, N.C.*

aging. Older people dislike bitter tastes more than young adults, although they do not appear to be more sensitive to bitter tastes. Children prefer the odor of flowers. Adults prefer fruits and more sophisticated floral scents like lavender oil and hyacinth (Engen, 1977).

Voice. Vocal changes are partly caused by the hardening and decreasing elasticity of the laryngeal cartilages. The voice becomes more highly pitched, and in advanced old age it becomes less powerful and is restricted in range. Singing and public speaking show deterioration earlier than do normal speaking voices in younger individuals. Speech becomes slower, and pauses become longer and more frequent; slurring often occurs because of pathological changes in the brain.

Vocal strain and vocal fatigue, the so-called "tired voice," are frequently encountered. Vocal misuse may interfere with the communication process and may lead to the development of nodes, polyps, and contact ulcers on the vocal folds (Cooper, 1970).

Teeth. In adult life teeth may cause pain and discomfort; the gums recede, and the teeth become yellowish. Loss of teeth or changes in their appearance may bring home the fact that the individual is aging physically. Having to resort to dentures often means that, at least temporarily, the person cannot eat or sleep as well, which may cause dismay and embarrassment. A person's disposition can be affected greatly. Changes in the jaws and face associated with old age are primarily consequences of reduction in size, and many of the facial evidences of old age may be prevented by proper care or dentures.

Homeostasis. There is some evidence that homeostasis is less efficient in older people (Frolkis, 1977). If stabilizing mechanisms become sluggish, the physiological adaptability of the individual is reduced. Wounds heal more slowly. It takes longer for the breathing and heart rate to return to normal. Heat losses are less quickly restored. Sleep habits may undergo a change. The thyroid gland is smaller, resulting in a lower rate of basal metabolism. The pancreas loses some of its ability to produce the enzymes that are used in sugar and protein metabolism. Most glands function at close to normal rates all through life.

Nervous system. There are some structural changes in the nervous system and brain that occur as the person ages. Although there is little functional change in the nerves, the nerve tissue will be gradually replaced by fibrous cells. There will be a slower reaction and reflex time. The folds of the brain become less prominent, possibly resulting in decreased circulation of blood within the brain. There might be a decrease in the total number of cells, but the brain functions normally unless its blood supply is blocked, even briefly. The cortical area of the brain responsible for organizing the total perceptual processes often experiences degenerative changes. A person afflicted with cerebral arteriosclerosis will show some atrophy of brain tissue (Bondareff, 1977).

Skeletal changes. The skeleton gives shape and firmness to the body, provides attachments for the muscles, protects important organs such as the brain, heart, and lungs, and together with the striated muscles provides man with a leverage system for pushing and lifting. Full stature is reached by the late teens or early twenties. Afterward there is little or no change in the length of the individual bones, although there may be a slight loss in overall height in old age, brought about by atrophy of the discs between the spinal vertebrae (Garn, 1975). As age progresses, the chemical composition of the bone changes; the bones become less dense and more brittle. This increases the risk of breakage late in life. Movement of the joints becomes stiffer and more restricted, the incidence of diseases affecting these parts of the body increases with age, and the skeleton may suffer from cumulative effects of damage and disease.

In our contacts with the aged we have noticed an increase in this stiffness as the individuals begin to withdraw from activity. It therefore seems reasonable to follow the advice so often given—for families to be aware of activities that older people can do for themselves so that they will be forced to exercise their joints and keep them functioning for a longer time. As soon as someone begins to assist some elderly persons, they stop doing things for themselves and become dependent on others.

Muscular changes. The functional capacities of a 30-year-old man and a 75-year-old man are compared in Table 15-2. After the age of 30 years there is a gradual and small reduction in the speed and power of muscular contractions and a decreased capacity for sustained muscular effort caused by biochemical changes in the protein molecules of the fibers. Muscles begin to lose their strength in the middle years. After about the age of 50 years the number of active muscle fibers steadily decreases, and eventually the typical diminished appearance of the older person occurs (Gutmann, 1977). The involuntary smooth muscles that operate under the autonomic nervous system are affected only slightly, as compared to the other struc-

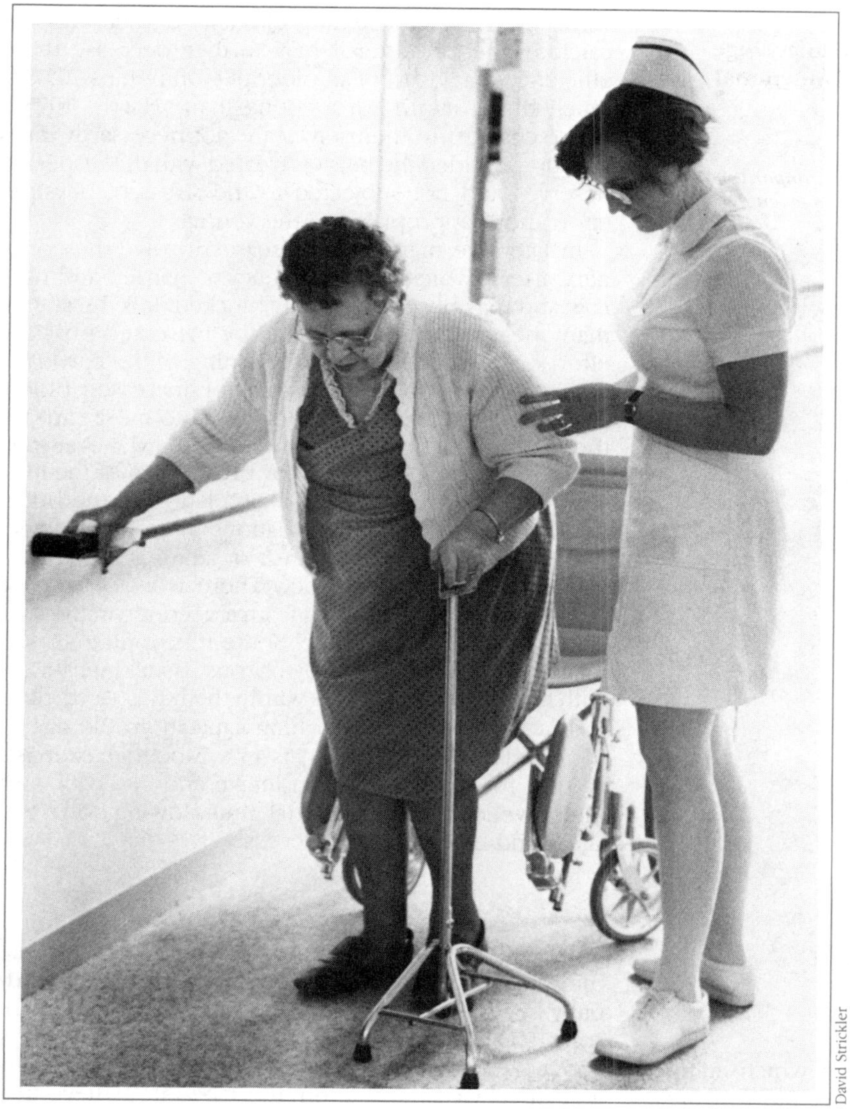

There are major individual differences in the rate at which physical aging and muscular changes take place. The chemical composition of the bones change, especially in women, and the ligaments tend to contract, causing the back to hump.

tures. They appear to function without difficulty even until late senescence. The ligaments, however, do tend to contract and harden, causing the familiar hunched-over body position.

Digestive changes. The digestive system also seems to alter with age; in fact, complaints about the digestive system are among the most common of all the complaints of the aged. There is a reduction in the amount of saliva, gastric juices, and enzyme action, thus upsetting the digestion process (Rockstein, 1975). Because the digestive system is highly sensitive to emotional disturbances, anxieties and worries that accompany old age will play an important part in bringing about stomach deterioration. The regularity of bowel movements will also be affected, resulting in diarrhea or, more frequently, in constipation. Laxatives become an integral part of the daily habits of many elderly individuals, frequently resulting in a "laxative habit."

Heart. Of all the organs in man's body, the heart

TABLE 15-2 Functional capacity of an average 75-year-old man compared to 100% functional capacity of a 30-year-old man

Physical characteristic	*Comparative percentage*
Nerve conduction velocity	90
Body weight for males	88
Basal metabolic rate	84
Body water content	82
Blood flow to brain	80
Maximum work rate	70
Glomerular filtration rate	69
Number of nerve trunk fibers	63
Brain weight	56
Number of glomeruli in kidney	56
Vital capacity	56
Hand grip	55
Cardiac output (at rest)	54
Maximum ventilation volume (during exercise)	53
Kidney plasma flow	50
Maximum breathing capacity (voluntary)	43
Maximum oxygen uptake (during exercise)	40
Number of taste buds	36
Speed of return to equilibrium of blood acidity	17
Also:	
Less adrenal and gonadal activity	
Slower speed of response	
Some memory loss	

From Shock, N.W. *The physiology of aging.*

and the blood vessels are the ones in which aging produces the most detrimental changes. Most of the other organs, such as the lungs, kidneys, and brain, would probably last for 150 years if they were ensured an adequate blood supply. The heart and arteries are the weakest link in the chain of life (Harris, 1975).

Aging affects the heart in several ways. The muscles in the heart tend to become stringy and dried out with the passage of time. Deposits of a brown pigment within the cells of the heart tend to restrict the passage of blood and impede the absorption of oxygen through its walls. The heart shrinks in size during the normal course of aging, and the fat in the heart increases. The valves of the heart lose their elasticity, and deposits of calcium and cholesterol may further decrease their efficiency. The heart of an older person pumps 70% as much blood as that of a young man (Harris, 1975). These changes in themselves are not necessarily dangerous, provided the heart is treated with the respect it deserves and not subjected to the stress of physical effort more appropriate to the young.

In later life many heart diseases involve the coronary artery, which has a tendency to harden and narrow and may become partially blocked. It is the site of many heart attacks brought on by increased physical effort or emotional stress. Hardening of the coronary artery may also be responsible for increased blood pressure, reducing the flow of blood to most parts of the body. Poor circulation of blood, whatever the cause, may result in trouble or breakdown of the kidneys and other organs. Poor circulation to the brain causes many personality deviations in older persons.

Respiration. Another effect of aging is the reduction of respiratory efficiency. There is a decrease of oxygen utilization resulting from a decrease in the size of the lungs in senescence. Some functioning air sac membranes are replaced by fibrous tissue, interfering with the exchange of gases within the lungs. According to Leaf (1973), maximum lung capacity in old age is 56%, and breathing capacity is 43%. Moderate exercise is ideal for keeping oxygen intake and blood flow at their level of highest potential, thus slowing down the aging and deterioration process.

Sexuality

There is a substantial body of research literature that indicates that both sexual interest and behavior gradually decline among healthy aging individuals (Jacobson, 1974). However, there are many misconceptions about the nature and extent of the decline in interest and in activity. In addition, most people believe that biological aging is basically responsible for diminishing interest and activity. To a degree, this belief is true, but it is not true to the magnitude that this idea has been expressed. It is becoming increasingly apparent in the research that a significant proportion of this decline is not caused by physical incapacities but is attributed to social, cultural, and psychological factors that adversely affect the expression of sexual drives and desires (Young, 1975). Specifically, some of these factors are related to the powerful influence of attitudes and misconceptions regarding sex in the later

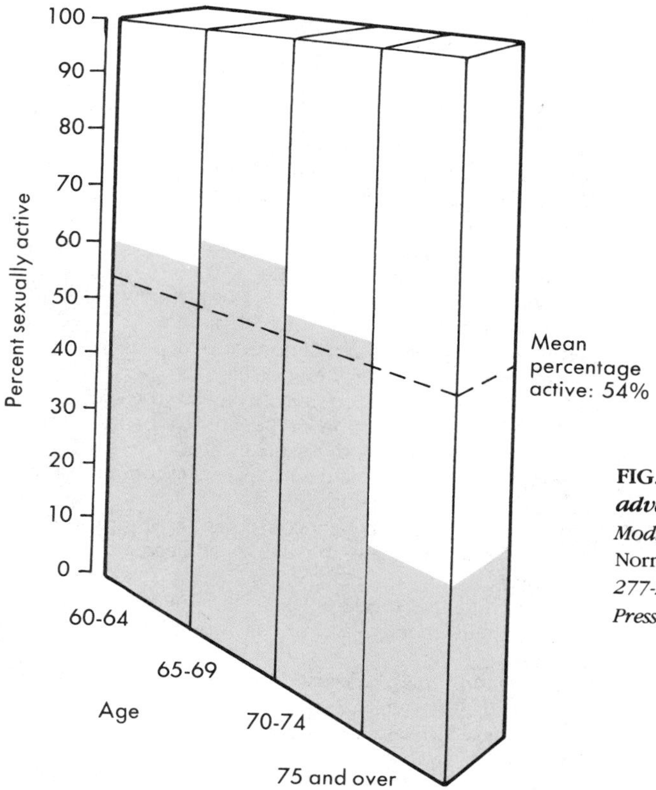

FIG. 15-3 ***There is a decline in sexual activity with advancing age.***

Modified from Newman, G., & Nichols, C.R. In E.B. Palmore (Ed.). Normal aging. *Durham, N.C.: Duke University Press, 1970, pp. 277-281. Used by permission. Copyright 1974 by Duke University Press, Durham, N.C.*

years of life; the lack of privacy in many living arrangements that the elderly have to share; the loss of a spouse, thus the loss of a sexual partner; feelings of guilt or moral transgressions for any number of unwarranted reasons; and feelings of anxiety, depression, or hostility. According to Butler and Lewis (1977), the fear of death because of a heart attack or stroke deters some individuals from engaging in excitable sexual activity. Studies show that there is a greater interest and desire for sexual activity in old age than is generally assumed by both oldsters and younger people. It must also be stated, however, that because of some of the reasons listed above, there is usually more interest than there is sexual activity. Feigenbaum (1977) found that both healthy males and females are capable of sexual activity, including intercourse, well into the seventh decade.

Elderly men are more sexually active than elderly women. Approximately 60% of the men are still sexually active at age 70 and 40% are still active at age 75. Although it is reported that older women are less sexually active than men, this may be the result of factors other then differences in sex drive. Remember that a large percentage of women are widows (Aiken, 1978). Fig. 15-3 indicates levels of current sexual activity by age levels.

According to a major study by Newman and Nichols (1970) 54% of persons between the ages of 60 and 75 indicated some degree of sexual involvement. After the age of 75, the percentage who were sexually active declined sharply to 27% (Newman and Nichols, 1970).

The three most significant studies of geriatric sexual behavior have been made by Kinsey et al. (1948), Duke's Center for the Study of the Aging (Pfeiffer, 1974a), and Masters and Johnson (1966, 1968, 1970). In each, the findings clearly show that men and women in general good health are physiologically able to have a satisfying sex life well into their 70s and beyond. The studies also indicate that those who were most active

wellness the practice of preventative physical and mental care.

sexually during youth and middle age usually retain their vigor and interest longer into old age. The Duke studies, which have been conducted on a continuing basis for 20 years or more, are particularly interesting because they present evidence that 15% of the men and women studied showed a steady rising rate of sexual interest and activity as they got older. The nature of the sexual activity involved either participation with a partner or self-stimulation.

In regard to the needs of older persons, one matter that is all too frequently overlooked is the need for privacy. This is true in congregate living arrangements, such as homes for the aged, nursing homes, family care homes, or living-in with relatives or children. The right to privacy is an important social right that should not be curtailed just because care facilities did not consider the matter of privacy when the plans were made for construction (Butler and Lewis, 1976).

By the same token, the right to private behavior should not be abrogated, whether that behavior is related to expressions of sexual interest or not. Sexuality is reflected in many forms and has several purposes. The primary function of sex is the creation of new life so that the species may be propagated. Beyond that, another significant function of sex is the expression of love, by means of intimate communication, between two people who are very fond of each other. Sexuality need not involve coitus in order to provide an intimate relationship of love. There is a rewarding, emotional exchange of shared joy in the comforting warmth of physical nearness, the positive response to being touched by someone who cares, and the stimulating pleasure of close companionship. Do not those who are older need an expression of love as much as anyone else? Older people should not be denied the opportunity to find, to experience, and to express the closeness that says, "I care about you."

HEALTH MAINTENANCE

Physical and psychological well-being are matters of great social and personal concern. Health and illness affect an individual's performance of basic personal tasks of daily living and of expected economic and social roles. As Shanas and Maddox (1976) state it, health is a key personal resource for any individual because performance of social roles in economic, family, and community organizations requires individuals who can function competently.

SYMPTOMS AND COMPLAINTS OF THE ELDERLY

Breathlessness: common; may reflect heart failure, disease of the lungs, or anemia
Constipation: irregular function of bowel movements
Difficulty in swallowing: common; may indicate need for a change in diet to soft, minced, or liquid foods
Dizziness (vertigo): innumerable causes; may result in falls and consequent injuries
Fainting: may result from anemia or a variety of blood vessel, neurological, or surgical causes
Fatigue: may be symptom of boredom, depression, anemia, malnutrition, or heart disease
Headaches: less common in later life; may be caused by muscle strain, infection of the sinuses, or inflammation of walls of blood vessels in head
Impaired hearing: some degree of loss is common; may lead to social isolation
Inability to sleep: may be a consequence of various discomforts, poor sleeping habits, anxiety, or depression
Lack of appetite: sudden change in appetite should be examined; may be a result of a physical or mental difficulty
Loss of vision: may be caused by loss of elasticity in the lens

Modified from You and Your Aging Parent: The Modern Family's Emotional, Physical, and Financial Problems, by Barbara Silverstone and Helen Kandel Hyman. Copyright © 1976 by Barbara Silverstone and Helen Kandel Hyman. Reprinted by permission of Pantheon Books, a division of Random House, Inc., pp. 345-347.

Wellness

Traditionally, the health profession has focused on treatment of the disease rather than on the prevention of disease. It is interesting that the Chinese approach the medical problem from the point of view of ***wellness;*** it is assumed that the physician's obligation is to help a person maintain good health. The holistic concept of the "treatment of the whole person" is gaining ground in America and Canada. There is more emphasis on wellness, prevention, and treatment of the patient psychologically and socially as well as physically than there has been in the past (Rosen and Wiens, 1979).

TABLE 15-3 Perceived health status by ethnicity

	Percent who consider their health to be poor or very poor (ethnicity)		
	Black (n: 413)	Mexican-American (n: 449)	Anglo (n: 407)
Ages: 45-54	13.8	16.9	1.7
55-64	15.2	20.8	9.1
65-75	27.0	23.2	4.0

From Bengston. V.L., Kasschau, P.L., & Ragan, P.K. The impact of social structure on aging individuals. In J.E. Birren & K.W. Schaie (Eds.), *Handbook of the psychology of aging.* New York: Van Nostrand Reinhold Co., 1977.

TABLE 15-4 Average remaining years of life at ages 40, 50, and 65, by sex and race: United States, 1975

	Average remaining years of life		
Sex and race	At age 40	At age 50	At age 65
White			
Men	33.0	24.3	13.7
Women	39.4	30.3	18.1
All others			
Men	29.8	22.4	13.7
Women	36.2	27.5	17.5

From U.S. National Center for Health Statistics Life tables and actuarial tables; and vital statistics of the United States Annual. In *Statistical Abstracts,* 1977.

One thing that has made a difference in health care has been the observation that some declines in cognitive abilities, memory, and psychomotor speed are linked to remediable diseases. Certain risk factors have been identified, such as the finding that dietary habits and the use of tobacco influence the incidence of atherosclerotic disease (LaRue and Jarvik, 1982). It is possible that the 20% decline in coronary heart disease mortality during the past decade may be attributed to public awareness of and response to these risk factors (Havlick and Feinlieb, 1979). Society's awareness of the importance of physical exercise is also increasing. There are data suggesting that continued exercise as people grow older might well reduce the degree of slowness so common in old age (Botwinick, 1977). The box on p. 588 indicates physical symptoms of the elderly. Generally, the symptoms are not serious, but they should be medically checked to make certain there are no hidden diseases.

Perceived health status and aging

In a Southern California study of 1,269 black, Mexican-American, and Anglo respondents, Bengtson and associates (1977) asked about self-perceived and functional health status of the participants. Table 15-3 indicates the perceived health status by ethnicity and age. At age 45 to 54, almost 17% of the Mexican-Americans considered their health to be poor, almost 14% of the blacks considered their health poor, but only about 2% of the Anglos considered that they had poor health. The figures jumped to 23% Chicano, 27% black, and 4% Anglo by 65 to 75 years of age.

The percent that considered themselves elderly also varied widely. Before age 57 to 59, none of the individuals who considered themselves as being "old" exceeded 15% of their respective groups. At 63 to 65, about 48% of the Mexican-Americans, 33% of the blacks, but only 8% of the Anglos thought of themselves as being elderly. Between the ages of 69 to 71, the figures changed respectively to 61%, 55%, and 39%. Of the three groups, however, at the age of 69 to 71, blacks had the greatest expectation of living 10 or more years (62%). Only 28% of the Mexican-Americans and the Anglos had the same expectation.

According to the National Center for Health Statistics (1983), the life expectancy for men in the United States is 69.9 years, and for women it is 77.6 years. The average life expectancy for Japanese men is 74.23 years, highest in the world, and that of Japanese women is 79.66 years, second only to Icelandic women, for whom life expectancy is 79.7. Table 15-4 presents the average remaining years of life in the United States at ages 40, 50, and 65 by sex and race. Up to age 75, whites have a longer life expectancy than any other race, and women have a longer life expectancy than men. Of interest are the age categories used by the U.S.

National Health Survey reports. They speak of the *young old* as being 65-74 and the *old old* as 75 and over.

There appears to be an upper age limit for human beings. The age of 120 is frequently cited as the probable absolute maximum limit. People are not living that long, in spite of medical advances. Scientists have pretty much given up the idea of increasing life span in older age and are now concentrating on making the latter years of life a time of less debilitating disease and a higher quality of enjoyment and comfort. The quality of life is being emphasized rather than longevity.

Stress and health changes

There is a convincing link between stress and both physical and mental health. Holmes and Rahe (1967) have shown that any major change in daily living, in either a pleasant or unpleasant way, produces a greater susceptibility to disease and illness. Their research instrument, the Schedule of Recent Events (SRE) (presented in detail in Chapter 13 on early adulthood), is based on the premise that stress, negative or positive, is descriptive of homeostasis, which in turn affects bodily conditions. Life events have varying degrees of stress caused by changes. They have been given psychometrically derived weights to assess degree of stress in the change. These weights are known as Life Crisis Units (LCU). For persons exposed to stress events adding up to an LCU score of 300 or more within recent months, Holmes and Rahe found that the risk of developing a major illness in the next 2 years was 80%. This readiness is especially true if the life change is accompanied by depression and much anxiety.

Six of the most stressful life changes characteristic of later life are death of a spouse, death of a close family member, personal injury or illness, retirement, change in the health of a family member, and sex difficulties. How much these life changes affect the elderly is being researched to learn if older people are affected as much as are younger adults. One conclusion thus far is that there is a general decrease in the experiencing of life events later in life (Masuda and Holmes, 1978). A second conclusion is that the degree of stress reaction to various life events is rated by older persons as being lower than it is for younger adults (Masuda and Holmes, 1978). In other words, not only are major life events less frequent, but, in a sense, the older person puts more distance between the self and the events that do intrude; at least the older person perceives this to be the case (Chiriboga and Cutler, 1980). However, researchers in gerontology also speculate that in old age fewer conditions would be required to produce health changes, particularly if the physiological state is already weakened by disease.

Diet and nutrition

Any advice to the elderly concerning the maintenance of good health consistently includes suggestions for an adequate diet. Increasingly, evidence points to the necessity for the aged to be vitally concerned about their eating habits. The report of the White House Conference on Aging indicates that individuals in 53% of the households containing people over 60 years of age had generally inadequate diets. Pepper (1980) reports that 83% of deaths caused by malnutrition involve people over age 65.

Of concern, especially in recent years, has been diet and its relationship to cardiac problems. As a result, physicians have almost always put their older patients on low-fat, high-protein diets. An interesting observation is made by volunteers of the Meals on Wheels program that brings at least one warm meal per day to elderly persons. The volunteers often note a distinct improvement in the physical appearance and health of the individuals who receive a regular, balanced meal (Norton, 1981).

Older people have the tendency to neglect their diets for a variety of reasons. Sadly, this neglect can frequently be traced to inadequate incomes. As a consequence, these people eat inexpensive foods that invariably are of the high-calorie, low-protein variety. Many times food is packaged in too large a quantity for one or two persons to use in a reasonable amount of time. Another common reason why people often do not receive adequate food is the preparation necessary for a nourishing, well-balanced meal. Often the person sees no real reason to go to a lot of "fuss" for just one or two persons. As a result, shortcuts are taken and an inadequate diet results.

Another danger concerning the diet is that often elderly people have a tendency to overeat. They do not seem to realize that their caloric requirements are probably decreasing as the years pass, and the excess calories they consume simply turn into fat. This, then, becomes one more factor in the eventual deterioration of health. Physicians will frequently prescribe light exercise for their elderly patients. The exercise or activity is beneficial physically and also mentally because it helps the older person to avoid the "illness of idleness."

Many elderly people have difficulty chewing food that has to be cut with a knife. As a result much of their food is ground or made soft so eating can be enjoyed.

Sleep

Many elderly persons complain of a variety of sleep disturbances. These include difficulty in falling asleep, insomnia, early awakening, falling asleep while watching television, restless sleep, not enough sleep, frequent awakening during the night, and feeling tired or exhausted after having had a good night's sleep. Relatives worry about the older person sleeping too much, falling asleep while company is present, or taking catnaps too often during the day, resulting in an inability to sleep at night. What is a normal sleep pattern for the elderly?

It is important to be aware of stereotypical fallacies concerning sleep in old age and to differentiate between changes in sleep patterns that are part of normal aging and those sleep disturbances that indicate physical or emotional distress. How much sleep does an older person need? It is doubtful that any elderly person in reasonably good health requires any more sleep than was required in middle adulthood.

Although some researchers say that people need less sleep as they grow older, it is probably more correct to say that sleep patterns tend to change as a result of illness, anxiety, depression, or simply the need for more exercise and activity during the day. Early morning awakenings are common among those who are inactive and go to bed early, those who catnap too much, and those who have physical discomfort, such as arthritic pains or poor circulation, that builds up during long periods of rest. Older people who suffer from illnesses and degenerative diseases may need more sleep, not less.

Some important changes in patterns of sleep do take place in elderly persons. Kales (1975) has found that deep sleep (stage 4 of sleep) virtually disappears. The elderly require a somewhat longer period to fall asleep, their sleep is lighter, and they have more frequent awakenings. Of greater importance is the fact that normal aging persons distribute their sleep somewhat differently during the 24-hour cycle. They generally have several catnaps of 15 to 60 minutes during the daylight hours (Pfeiffer, 1974b). Since this pattern is normal, caution should be exercised when considering regular use of sleeping medication to keep the person asleep for 8 hours throughout the night or in some other way disturbing the normal pattern of sleep developed in old age. People develop their own individual patterns of sleep according to their conditions and their needs.

Exercise and aging

Much has been written in recent years about the value of exercise in maintaining good health and in slowing down aging. An interesting study has been conducted on this topic by Herbert de Vries (1975) of the University of Southern California's Gerontology Center. He and his team took a mobile laboratory designed for research in the physiology of exercise and aging to a retirement community in Laguna Hills, California. Over 125 older men volunteered to work out in his program. Statistics indicated dramatic improvement in physical conditioning of the subjects who followed a program of modified Royal Canadian Air Force calisthenics, jogging, walking, a static stretching routine, and swimming. For the group, maximum oxygen increased 9.2% and oxygen pulse (a measure of cardiovascular function) improved 8.4%. Oxygen intake appears to be the key to endurance fitness.

De Vries found that age-related losses in functional capacity of the individual were a result of (1) the true aging process, (2) a functional decline resulting from loss in physical fitness, and (3) incipient, undiagnosed degenerative disease processes. The loss in vigor by older people is the result of well-documented losses in aerobic (intake of oxygen) capacity, which, in turn, lessens physical working strength. The significance of aerobic capacity and lessened working performance is suggested by "bedrest" studies where, in a matter of weeks, young, well-conditioned individuals approximate long-term aging effects. With proper exercise programs, these young people could regain their func-

Meriem Kaluger

The Senior Olympics for the aged have demonstrated that men and women in their sixties, seventies, and eighties can still participate vigorously in physical activities. This woman, in the age 70-and-over category for women, won gold medals in four events. The small medal was won 50 years earlier in a national event for throwing a baseball the greatest distance.

tional working capacities. De Vries learned that both middle-aged and older healthy men and women are relatively as trainable as are young people. The training effect on older people is demonstrable in the cardiovascular and respiratory systems, in the musculature, and in decreased percentage of body fat, lowered blood pressure, and the ability to achieve neuromuscular relaxation.

In general, improvement from training varies directly with the type of exercise involved, the intensity of the exercise, and inversely with the pretraining aerobic capacity. Brief walking may suffice for poorly conditioned elderly males (age 60 to 79). Later, a jog-walk regimen can be initiated under proper medical supervision. Exercises for older people should maximize the rhythmic activity of large muscle masses and minimize isometric (static) contraction and extensive use of small muscle masses. The natural activities of walking, jogging, running, and swimming are best suited to this purpose.

Accidents and safety

Older people have a disproportionate share of accidents that cause bodily injury or death. This is especially true for accidents that occur in the home. They also have an extremely high accident rate on the highway when the total number of miles driven is taken into consideration. Persons 65 years of age and older make up 12% of the total population but account for 28% of all accidental deaths and 20% of all accidents causing bodily injury.

An analysis of accidents by young and old persons found that those that increased in frequency with age could be explained by slowness in getting out of the way of hazards or recovering balance, whereas those that became less frequent with age were attributable to carelessness and taking undue risks. Automobile accidents among older drivers seem to be a result of slowness and a tendency to confusion, whereas those characteristic of younger drivers are caused by various kinds of recklessness. Similar causes seem to lie behind the traffic violations characteristic of older and younger drivers (Road Traffic Board, 1972).

It has been found that safety devices, especially those that help older persons maintain balance, such as hand rails, have contributed significantly to their physical and mental well-being. In addition, care should be taken to remove all accident "traps" that may cause elderly to fall, such as loose carpets. A small amount of concern on the part of family and neighbors may save the elderly persons from dangers they do not realize exist and to which they are therefore extremely susceptible.

EDUCATIONAL PURSUITS

Just as physical exercise helps to maintain the level of physiological functions, mental exercise helps to maintain good cognitive functioning. Denny (1982) concludes that there are age-related declines in cognitive abilities but that the declines in abilities that are

David Strickler

The adult education movement has made it possible for many older folks to maintain a keen interest in the world around them. The study of genealogy has wide appeal. At a nearby retirement village, a class in the writing of personal autobiographies proved very popular. One paper was 110 pages long!

used frequently appear to begin at a later age and to be less drastic than are the declines in abilities that are exercised less frequently. Denny states that the performance of elderly adults can be facilitated by various training techniques, although younger adults are likely to benefit more from training than are older adults. The educational intervention strategies for older adults involve a structured, concrete, step-by-step, and relevant approach. Actually, these teaching techniques can be recommended for any age level from childhood through adulthood.

The adult education movement has gained wide acceptance in the 1970s. The continuing education programs, the proliferation of minicourse offerings, and the Elderhostel programs have become widespread (Hartford, 1980). Older persons have responded well to these courses. Some pursue educational programs for the purpose of enriching their lives, others want to update earlier studies, while some simply want to acquire basic learning skills or possibly a high school diploma. In spite of the reason for further schooling, the interpersonal and group experiences are as vital for the participants as the course content.

The Elderhostel programs are held at a large number of colleges and universities during the summer months. The courses are usually of 2 or 3 weeks' duration, but since there is usually a series of such courses, it is possible to spend 6 weeks on a campus. The Elderhostel programs are held in almost every state, in Canada, and in many European countries. Elderhostel participants frequently plan their programs by deciding which state or country they would like to visit. The endeavor becomes a pleasant travel as well as an educational experience. A related travel opportunity is the large number of tours, sponsored by the American

OLD PETELO

Petelo is a very old man, but his age seems to fade away and his weary eyes lighten when he shares a joke or when he talks of his younger days.

He lives with his relatives in Western Samoa and is always moving around, as he is needed by his family to look after his grandchildren.

One thing that touches me is Petelo's childish simplicity. To a stranger's eye he is just a quiet old man but to those who have been with him for a while, he is different.

It was during one sunny afternoon that I met him walking along a road. He was carrying a heavy load of coconuts and firewood balanced on a stick over his shoulder. He was not wearing any shirt, only a dirty, shaggy *lavalava.* His wrinkled dark skin was sweaty and shiny against the hot afternoon sun. I did not want to take much of his time because I knew that he would keep on talking. I only asked him why he was carrying such a load on this particular afternoon. He replied in his usual soft voice that one of his grandchildren would have to leave school as they could not afford the school fees. The load he was carrying was to make an *umu* [earth oven used for cooking large amounts of food] so that they could sell some *dalo* [taro] and *palusami* [dish made with taro leaves] to get some money.

His voice still had that serene and calm tone but something told me that he was very sad. I felt like giving him everything I had, but I knew he was not the type to take things for pity's sake. He had once told me that, when he was young, his father did not feed him for one whole day because he did not do what his father had told him to do. So he was used to hardship.

As we parted I thought of old Petelo—a man who was content and who did things without complaining. My thoughts began to turn to my own parents and how much they loved me. I thought of how I argued with them when I did not like things. I did not know the real meaning of hardship. Petelo did; he had experienced it most of his life, even in his old age. Yet he was still able to smile, be content, and most of all happy. I was just too used to taking everything for granted—love, security, shelter, food and money.

I looked back and saw his tiny figure ambling along far away, blurred by the heat waves rising from the tar-sealed road. One could not help having respect for this calm old man. It was then that I recalled Petelo's words to us whenever we got a bit mischievous and disrespectful.

"Tupulaga i nei ona po, tia tele le pia malolosi." Translated word by word into English, it would read:

"Today's generation is too much wanting to have power!"

From Stewart, R.A.C. (Ed.). *Pacific Profiles.* Suva, Fiji: University of The South Pacific Extension Services, 1982.

Association of Retired Persons (AARP), that offer travel within the States as well as to all parts of the world. These experiences are enlightening, educational, and enjoyable.

The appearance of adults, including the aged, on college campuses is a more common sight than in the past. Some institutions appear to be "three-tiered," serving traditional students, middle-aged students, and retirees. Many retirement villages and home settings are providing minicourses for their residents. The authors of this text participated in an unforgettable experience of teaching a minicourse on stress management to residents of one such retirement settlement. There were 24 participants, ages 71 to 92, in the class. They took notes, asked questions, and made many astute observations based on their life experiences. They were keeping themselves both mentally and physically active. That year they were "walking to San Francisco from Pennsylvania." Each day they would walk 3 to 5 miles around the retirement village. They then plotted the distance on a large map. They expected to "be in San Francisco" by October.

DISEASES AND CAUSES OF DEATH

Since more people within the total population are living to older ages, health problems associated with the degenerative diseases have become a major concern. Progress in finding early diagnostic methods and effective treatments for degenerative diseases has been

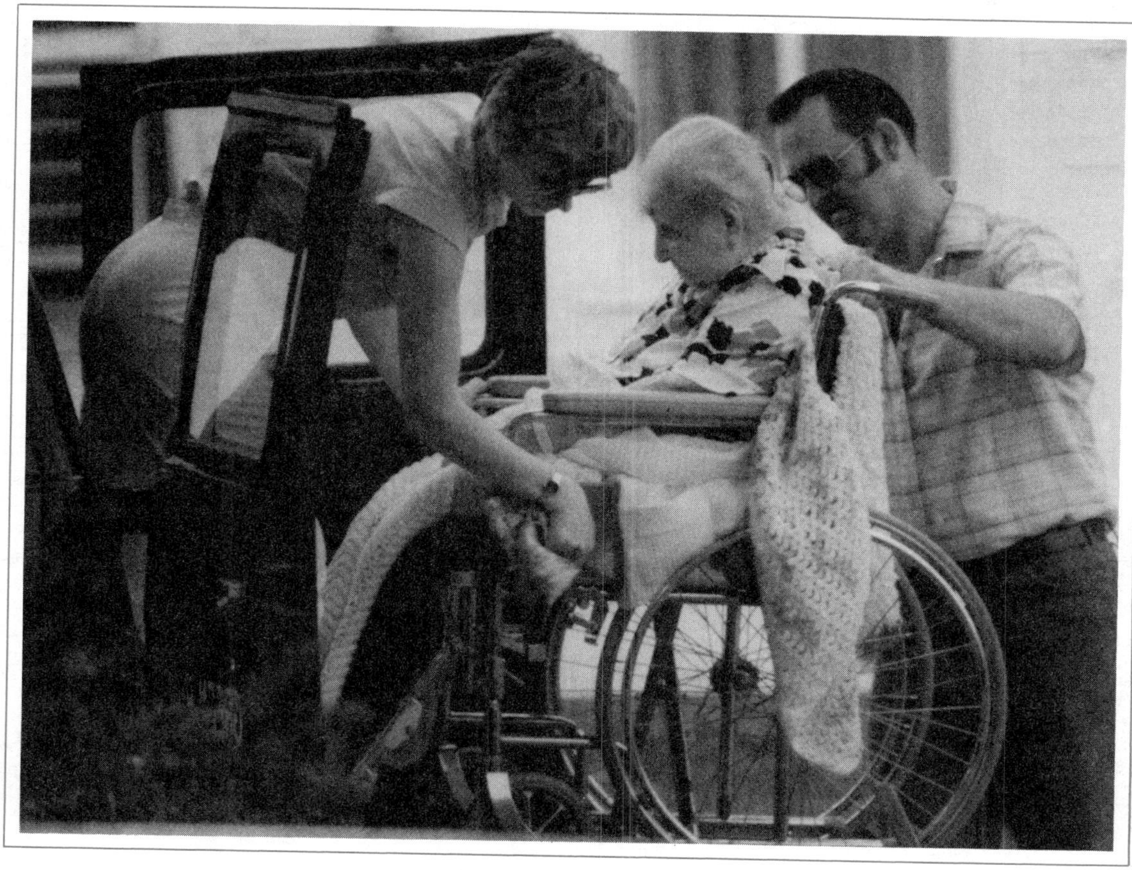

David Strickler

As the average life span has increased and people are living to older ages, health problems associated with degenerative diseases have become more common. Geriatric medicine has a real challenge in learning how to provide comfort or curative treatment.

organic brain syndrome (OBS) degenerative effects of brain pathology on a variety of functions, including memory, judgment, perception, social behavior, and motor coordination.

slow. But research in geriatric medicine is progressing, and one hopes that a "comfort level" of maintenance can be attained if not an outright curative solution.

Diseases and illnesses

Because of lower resistance to disease and of diminished organic and systemic functional capacities, 86% of very old people have chronic health problems of one kind or another. They visit the doctor more frequently than the young do, go to the hospital more often and stay there longer, and spend more days each year sick at home. Older people complain chiefly of ill-defined discomfort, rheumatism, some form of arthritis, and digestive problems. Despite these complaints, 81% of older adults move around on their own

TABLE 15-5 Common diseases of the elderly

Disease	*Organic factors*	*Symptoms/signs*	*Treatment*
Alzheimer's disease	Neurological illness affecting cortex	Severe intellectual impairment; loss of memory for recent events; inability to store new memories	No cure as yet; physician's care; supportive measures
Arteriosclerosis (atherosclerosis)	Narrowing and closing of the arteries supplying blood to the brain	Silent until complications intervene; disturbances in behavior, cognition and, possibly, language	Lower blood fats by diet; drug regime; physical activity; possible surgery
Arthritis	Osteoarthritis—wear and tear on weight-bearing joints Osteoporosis—thinning of the bones Rheumatoid—inflammation of multiple joints Gout—severe pain in the joints due to metabolic disease	Chronic degeneration or inflammation of the joints; tenderness in "active" joints; deformities may develop; stiffness on arising	Treatment varies with cause; physiotherapy; anti-inflammatory medication; orthopedic devices; replacement of joints
Bronchitis and emphysema	Inflammation of cells in the bronchial air tubes and lungs	Shortness of breath; cough; wheezing; recurrent respiratory infections; spitting up sputum	Antibiotics; drugs; cessation of smoking; devices that help patient breathe; exercises
Cancer: malignant neoplasm; tumor	Uncontrolled growth of a tissue or portion of an organ; it may spread (mestastasize)	Usually detected by examination; some loss of organic function	Surgery; radiotherapy; chemotherapy; combination of all three
Congestive heart failure	Weakened heart muscle so it cannot provide sufficient circulation	Fast heart beat; fatigue with exertion; labored breathing with mild activity; intolerance to cold; coughing at night	Improvement of heart's pumping efficiency; eliminating excessive fluids; digitalis and diuretics; treatment of precipitating disease

Modified from You and Your Aging Parent: The Modern Family's Emotional, Physical, and Financial Problems, by Barbara Silverstone and Helen Kandel Hyman. Copyright © 1976 by Barbara Silverstone and Helen Kandel Hyman. Reprinted by permission of Pantheon Books, a division of Random House, Inc., pp. 340-344.

and only 5% live in institutions (Weg. 1973a).

Table 15-5 is a compilation of diseases and illnesses frequently found in the elderly. The list is presented in alphabetical order and is not a ranking of prevelancy. In fact, Alzheimer's disease is found in less than 3% of the population. Note the Symptoms/signs and Treatment columns.

Of special consideration is ***organic brain syndrome*** (OBS)—disorders that involve mental conditions caused by or associated with impairment of brain tissue function. Many people inaccurately refer to OBS conditions as "senility." The distinctive features of OBS are (1) disturbance and impairment of memory functions, (2) impairment of intellectual function or comprehension, (3) impairment of judgment, (4) impairment of orientation, and (5) shallow or unstable affect (Butler and Lewis, 1977). These mental signs may not all be present at the same time or to the same degree. The signs may be reversible (acute brain syndrome) or irreversible (chronic brain syndrome), with gradual or rapid decline of mental abilities. A sign of reversible brain syndrome is a fluctuating level of awareness.

TABLE 15-5 Common diseases of the elderly—cont'd

Disease	*Organic factors*	*Symptoms/signs*	*Treatment*
Coronary artery heart disease	Some atherosclerosis; general decrease in muscle-cell size and efficiency; blood supply is cut off	Myocardial infarction—heart attack; may have intense and prolonged pain; in the elderly, usually a shortness of breath and dizziness or fainting instead of crushing pain	Drugs; oxygen; electrical equipment; bed rest; then rehabilitation
		Angina pectoris—severe but vague or brief pain over midchest that may radiate to arms, neck, jaws or back; strangling sensation	Administration of nitroglycerin; rest
Diabetes mellitus (Type II diabetes)	Deficiency of insulin or a disturbance in the action of insulin	May have few clinical signs; complications involving larger blood vessels; elevated blood glucose; thirst, hunger, weight loss	Control of diet; loss of weight; possible insulin injection; foot care
Diseases of the ear	Problems in the external, middle or inner ear	Hearing loss due to impacted ear wax; swelling of tissues; infection and fluid accumulation	Physician's care; surgery for correctable middle ear loss; hearing aids
Diseases of the eye	Cataracts—opaque spots in lens	Blurring and dimming of vision	Surgery for removal; special glasses; lens implants
	Glaucoma—increased pressure in eyeball	Marginal vision; intraocular tension	Eyedrops; drugs; possible surgery
	Macular disease—degeneration of parts of the retina	Poor perception of fine details and print	Use of low-vision aids
Hypertension	High blood pressure; may lead to arterial disease	Frequently no signs until complications develop; retinal changes	Salt restriction; milder drugs; prudent exercise
Neuritis	Inflammation and degeneration of nerve fibers	Loss of conduction of nerve impulses; loss of feeling; loss of reflexes	Neurological work-up; treatment of specific causes

Alzheimer's disease a presenile dementia involving rapid intellectual deterioration, speech impairment, loss of body control, and death, usually within 5 years of onset.

Pick's disease a rare but fatal presenile psychosis in which the frontal and temporal lobes of the brain gradually atrophy, causing impairment of memory and cognitive, emotional, and motor functions.

Diseases of the irreversible chronic brain syndrome type are senile psychosis (senile dementia) and psychosis associated with cerebral atherosclerosis. ***Alzheimer's disease*** and ***Pick's disease*** are common forms of presenile dementia; they occur at an earlier age than senile dementia. The average survival after onset of senile dementia is about 5 years, although some individuals have lived 10 years more (Butler and Lewis, 1977).

TABLE 15-6 Order of 11 leading causes of death, by death rate* for 7 age-groups, 1976

Total	*25-34*	*35-44*	*45-54*	*55-64*	*65-74*	*75-84*	*85+*
Diseases of the heart (337.2)	Accidents	Malignant neoplasm	Diseases of the heart	Diseases of the heart	Diseases of the heart	Diseases of the heart	Diseases of the heart
Malignant neoplasm (175.8)	Suicide	Diseases of the heart	Malignant neoplasms	Malignant neoplasms	Malignant neoplasms	Malignant neoplasms	Malignant neoplasms
Cerebrovascular disease (87.9)	Malignant neoplasm	Accidents	Accidents	Cerebrovascular disease	Cerebrovascular disease	Cerebrovascular disease	Cerebrovascular disease
Accidents (46.9)	Diseases of the heart	Cirrhosis	Cirrhosis	Accidents	Influenza and pneumonia	Influenza and pneumonia	Influenza and pneumonia
Influenza and pneumonia (28.8)	Cirrhosis	Suicide	Cerebrovascular disease	Cirrhosis	Diabetes	Diabetes	Arteriosclerosis
Diabetes (16.1)	Cerebrovascular disease	Cerebrovascular disease	Suicide	Diabetes	Accidents	Arteriosclerosis	Accidents
Cirrhosis (14.7)	Influenza and pneumonia	Influenza and pneumonia	Influenza and pneumonia	Influenza and pneumonia	Bronchitis, emphysema and asthma	Accidents	Diabetes
Arteriosclerosis (13.7)	Diabetes	Diabetes	Diabetes	Bronchitis, emphysema, and asthma	Cirrhosis	Bronchitis, emphysema, and asthma	Bronchitis, emphysema, and asthma
Suicide (12.5)	Bronchitis, emphysema, and asthma	Bronchitis, emphysema, and asthma	Bronchitis, emphysema, and asthma	Suicide	Arteriosclerosis	Cirrhosis	Suicide
Bronchitis, emphysema, and asthma (11.4)	Arteriosclerosis	Arteriosclerosis	Arteriosclerosis	Arteriosclerosis	Suicide	Suicide	Cirrhosis

From U.S. Department of Health, Education, and Welfare, *Monthly vital statistics report, final mortality statistics,* 1976. Washington, D.C.: U.S. Government Printing Office, March 30, 1978, pp. 20-21.

*Death rate per 100,000 estimated population per age-group.

Causes of death

Diseases of the cardiovascular system represent the major causes of death in the United States. The U.S. Department of Health, Education and Welfare report of mortality statistics (1978b) shows that diseases of the heart were the leading cause of death, accounting for 37.8% of all deaths. These figures are for all age-groups. When cerebrovascular and arteriosclerotic diseases are included, almost 50% of all deaths are related to the cardiovascular system. Malignant neoplasm (cancer) accounts for 20.4% while accidents, ranked fourth, account for 5.4% of the deaths.

Table 15-6 is an interesting one in that it presents the order of leading causes of death by death rate for seven age-groups. Accidents are the leading cause of death in the 25-34 age-group, and suicide is second. After that age level, diseases of the heart and malignant neoplasm consistently rank first and second. Cerebrovascular disease, influenza and pneumonia, diabetes and arteriosclerosis make substantial gains in ranking after age 54. Of the white males who commit suicide, 39.4% are aged 65 or over, as compared to 8.5% for white females, 11.8% for nonwhite males, and 3.0% for nonwhite females. The suicide rate among the *elderly white males* showed a steady increase in percentage for succeeding age-groups (U.S. Public Health Service, 1977).

Rowland (1977) reviewed the literature concerned with life events that predict death in the elderly. The only items deemed significant were losses of a spouse and environmental relocation. Death following loss of spouse appeared to occur mostly for males who were themselves ill and who lost their source of care with their spouses. The relocation studies generally involved a move to a nursing care facility. A move of this kind implies that the individual is at greater health risk. As a result, it is not surprising to note that many patients moved to this type of a facility die in 3 or 4 months.

CHAPTER REVIEW

1. There are considerable individual differences and variations in aging. Chronological age is not a prime consideration for determining the beginning of old age. Table 15-1 presents a number of variables, some reversible and some permanent, that affect longevity.
2. *Gerontology* is the scientific study of the aging process. *Geriatrics* is the medical specialty of gerontology. As the number of people living beyond the age of 65 increases, the problems and the study of the aging become major concerns of society.
3. The image of the aged in Western societies has been stereotyped as a negative one. Older people tend to view themselves differently than do younger adults. However, a newer image is beginning to emerge as retired individuals demonstrate their ability to remain active participants in society. The *American Association of Retired Persons* (AARP) has been a major force in directing the affairs of the elderly in very positive ways.
4. *Life circumstances* do change for older persons. Physical, psychological, and social conditions are not the same as they were in the earlier years of adulthood. Positive attitudes toward life take on special significance in terms of personal adjustment. Environmental changes, personal losses, and physical declines place special demands on the mental health and well-being of the aged.
5. The *developmental tasks* of the elderly cover an age span that includes the young-old (65-74) and the old-old (75 and over). As such, the tasks are not emphasized to the same degree throughout this stage of life. *Havighurst* stresses adjustment to psychosocial competencies, *Peck* focuses in on psychological adjustments, *Erikson* emphasizes integrity and meaningfulness of life, and *Frenkel-Brunswick* speaks of drawing up "the balance sheet of life." There is some overlapping of ideas. The box on p. 577 gives a summary of the various developmental tasks.
6. Although *physiological theories of aging* abound, not very many have been verifiable through reliable research. *Genetic theories* are based on the assumption that aging results from change or damage to genetic information (DNA, RNA) in the formation of cellular proteins. *Nongenetic cellular theories* assume that changes take place in the cellular proteins after they are formed. A group of *physiological theories* of aging suggests that impairment of an organ system or physiological control mechanism causes aging. Each of the categories has one or more viable hypotheses that can be researched if the proper design can be determined and if equipment and instrumentation can be developed. *Psy-*

chological and sociological theories of aging are still in the early stages of development. The box on p. 579-580 gives a summary of the theories.

7. Among the *factors influencing aging* are genetic and prenatal influences, environmental factors related to social interaction and activities, lifetime illnesses, diseases and stress, poor nutrition and eating habits, deterioration of functional activity of the organs because of metabolic changes affecting energy exchange, and physical environmental factors. The *multiple-causation concept of interactionism* is an increasingly acceptable view; more than one thing affects the rate at which aging takes place in an individual.
8. *Physical characteristics* of old age take on many dimensions:
   a. The slower behavior and thought result in increased cautiousness.
   b. The skin becomes drier and thinner and loses its elasticity.
   c. Sensory acuity diminishes in hearing, vision, and sensitivity of touch. Taste and smell may not be affected as much as was once believed.
   d. The voice becomes restricted in range, and vocal fatigue is frequently encountered. Loss of teeth may change facial appearance, cause changes in eating habits, and affect speech.
   e. Homeostatic changes affect energy exchange and influence the functioning of the organic systems.
   f. The nervous system, skeletal structure, and muscle capabilities change gradually with age.
   g. The digestive system, circulatory system, and respiratory system no longer function as they did at an earlier age.
   h. Sexual interest and activity remain rather steady between the ages of 60 and 74 but decline by 50% after that age.
9. Elderly whites perceive their health status to be fairly good. About a fourth of elderly blacks and Mexican-Americans consider their health to be poor.
10. A current emphasis on *wellness* and a *holistic* approach to health maintenance appears to be making a change in the health habits of people in Western societies. There are courses on stress management, information on good diets, and a general surge of interest in exercise for health's sake. Research shows that exercise delays the effects of aging. Educational pursuits keep mental factors alert.
11. Diseases of the heart, malignant neoplasm, cerebrovascular disease, and influenza and pneumonia are the *leading causes of death* among the elderly. The most prevelant diseases are arthritis, hypertension, heart disease, and diabetes. The box on p. 588 gives the more common symptoms and complaints of the elderly. Table 15-5 lists common diseases and Table 15-6 presents the leading causes of death.

REVIEW QUESTIONS

1. Look at the box on pp. 569-570. Compare the factors that are reversible and those that are irreversible (permanent) in influencing longevity. Which ones are the most crucial in lengthening life? What are the top three conditions that you can do something about?
2. Define gerontology, geriatric, and geriatrics. Briefly list seven factors responsible for society's increased interest in old age. Can you think of some other factors?
3. Review the concept of stereotyping and negativism about old age. Do you agree with the existence of the concept? What changes do you see taking place?
4. How can attitudes help a person adjust to changes in life? A student once said, "Aging seems to be a loss of bodily processes. Attitudes can't help much if the body falls apart." Do you agree or disagree?
5. What are the more common changes and personal losses that occur over the span of old age?
6. Review the developmental tasks of old age and give an example or opinion of each task.
7. There are many factors considered to contribute to the aging process. List these factors and indicate how they affect aging.
8. Look at the boxed material on pp. 579-580 that presents physiological theories of aging. Don't try to memorize them. Instead, write a brief paragraph describing the basic characteristics that identify and separate each of the major categories from one another. Which theory seems to be the most logical?
9. Make a table of physical characteristics of the aged. In one column list, by heading, the characteristics to be described. In the second column, write a few major elements of that characteristic.
10. Why do you suppose whites have a better perception of health in middle and late adulthood than do blacks and Mexican-Americans?
11. Indicate ways in which stress, diet, sleep, exercise, and educational pursuits can affect health. Cite some of the findings of research to back up your observations.
12. What are some of the common symptoms and complaints of the elderly? What are some of the common diseases and illnesses? What are the most common causes of death? What relationships do you detect among these three groups?

THOUGHT QUESTIONS AND ACTIVITIES

1. Think about the appearance of grandparents as they are portrayed on television and in the movies. Are they shown as retirees with white or gray hair, a wrinkled look of the skin, and an older body that seems lacking in

strength? Is that a true picture, or are the visual media perpetuating a stereotype? Can a person become a grandparent between the ages of 40 and 50? How old are your grandparents now? How old were they when you were 6 years of age and in first grade?

2. It is so easy to attach a negative label to the lives of the elderly because we "see" them as being old. Think how old you consider a person to be who retires at the age of 65. Now imagine that person being 80 years old and recognizing that 15 years have passed since retirement. Are *you* the same now as you were 15 years ago? What changes have taken place in your life in 15 years? Why not allow for changes to take place in that number of years in the life of a retired person? What is aging—at any age?
3. What would it be like to be an adult 60 or 70 years of age? What are the sociological, psychological, and physiological factors involved? Consider the same for an adult who is 70 to 80 and one who is 80 to 90. What major differences do you perceive? Now go out and interview several people in these different age brackets and note how correct your personal perceptions are.
4. Think of elderly white persons. Think of elderly black persons. Think of elderly Spanish-speaking persons. Think of elderly Europeans. Think of elderly Orientals. Think of all the different elderly ethnic groups that you can recall. How do they differ? How are they the same? Are they more alike or more different? How do their cultures treat them?
5. Who would you enjoy being with more—a young old person, an old young person, or an old old person? What differences would there be?
6. Wellness and holistic medicine are interesting concepts. Find out all you can about them. What meaning do they have for people of your age? For the elderly?
7. What can you do now to slow down the aging process that is already at work in your body?
8. Do you want to live a long life? How long? Why? Do you have any mental reservations, such as "Only if. . ."?
9. Check into the Senior Olympics that has age categories for men and women 60 to 69, 70 to 79, and 80 and over. What types of physical activities or events are sponsored? Does it surprise you to learn that jogging and long-distance running are not only for the young? Did you know that the Wham-O Corporation has been sponsoring a World Senior Flying Disc Championship Event every year for people over 50 and 60?
10. Have you ever heard anyone say about an older person: "She (he) is a young 85-year-old"? Why does it have to be "better" to be a "young" 85-year-old than to just be one's age? Is there a hint of ageism or stereotyping involved?

FURTHER READINGS

Birren, J.E., Cunningham, W.R., & Yamamoto, K. Psychology of adult development and aging. In M.R. Rosenzweig & L.W. Porter (Eds.), *Annual review of psychology* (Vol. 34). Palo Alto, Calif.: Annual Review, 1983. A review of current research and literature on adult development and aging is presented in this chapter. The current research status of 30 topics is presented.

Koger, L.J. Nursing home life satisfaction and activity participation. *Research on Aging,* 1980, *2*(1), 61-72. This is a study of two groups of nursing home residents. One group was involved in an 8-week writing workshop and the other was not. There was a significant increase in life satisfaction for those who attended the workshop.

Labouvie-Vief, G. Growth and aging in life-span perspective. *Human Development,* 1982, *25*(1), 65-79. This paper questions the usual notion that aging and development are opposing processes. The author contends that life-span development can be seen as a single, spiral-like progression in which individual aging is part of systematic development.

Lawton, M.P., & Yaffe, S. Victimization and fear of crime in elderly public housing tenants. *Journal of Gerontology,* 1980, *35*(5), 768-79. Crime rate, fear of crime, and personal victimization were studied in relation to measures of well-being in 53 public housing sites. The data indicated that fear of crime had made strong impact on the psychological well-being of the residents.

Poon, L.W. (Ed.). *Aging in the 1980's.* Washington, D.C.: American Psychological Association, 1980. A number of articles about biological views on aging are presented. There is much information on the aging of the brain, the nervous system, cells, and organs. Reading level: moderately difficult.

Wiswell, R.A. Relaxation, exercise and aging. In J.E. Birren & R.B. Sloane (Eds.), *Handbook of mental health and aging.* Englewood Cliffs, N.J.: Prentice-Hall, 1980. This chapter discusses the role of exercise and relaxation in late adulthood. Suggestions and implications for advancing physical and mental health are given. Reading level: moderately difficult.

Yearnick, E.S., Wang, M.L., & Pisias, S.J. Nutritional status of the elderly: Dietary and biochemical findings. *Journal of Gerontology,* 1980, *35*(5), 663-671. The dietary nutrient intake and certain biochemical measurements were made of 100 elderly persons. It was determined that, in general, their diet was deficient in certain dietary nutrients. It was determined that 27 persons taking nutrient supplements either took excessive amounts or took supplements that were inappropriate for them.

CHAPTER 16

LATER ADULTHOOD

SOCIAL AND PERSONAL

NINETY-FIVE AND ALL'S WELL

I am of the opinion that many people in our society today consider an individual in the later phases of life as a person who has lived life fully, grown old gracefully, and is now biding time here on earth. They feel these individuals should be content with being given a comfortable place in which to live, food to eat, and their monthly retirement or welfare checks to buy their necessities. Many people fail to see the tremendous adjustment these older individuals have to make and how totally alone they are in a world that offers so much to the younger generations.

Aunt Byrd was ninety-five on June 13 of this year, which definitely places her in a later phase of life. Upon meeting her, everyone will invariably say: "Isn't she marvelous for her age?" and I agree. Just to be ninety-five is an accomplishment in itself!

Aging, in the physical or biological aspect, can be seen quite readily, but Aunt Byrd still possesses many characteristics that enable her to get along in this world. She is almost deaf but, through the use of a hearing aid, she can function quite adequately. Her eyesight is very good; she reads two newspapers daily and *Time* and *Newsweek* each week. She has difficulty walking and must constantly use a cane to aid her. This presents a mobility problem; therefore, she can never go far from home. Her sense of taste is deficient, because she complains of never being able to tell whether things are too salty or too sweet.

Her biological or physical aging is not as great as it would be for most ninety-five-year-old individuals, due to the fact that her diet has always been and still is quite adequate and substantial. She eats everything, even at this age. Also, she has not suffered from any major illnesses for the past thirty years; she has always led a very healthy life. She was a nurse at one time.

Since her ability to move about is curtailed but she still has the desire to get about, she has taken quite a number of spills in her adventures. She has bruised herself quite badly at times but still has not learned her lesson. She feels she is being a burden by asking others to get things for her and wants to get these things for herself. It is difficult for her to accept the fact that she must now depend on others to do even simple things for her.

In memory ability, Aunt Byrd has declined greatly in some aspects. She can vividly remember days of long ago and can relate them in detail, but she can't remember such things as where she placed her pocketbook or what happened to her the previous day. I think she realizes that she is declining in cognitive ability because she admits her memory isn't as good as it used to be. This must be a difficult adjustment to make as she was always very alert and interested in world events and affairs.

She is interested in politics and is staunch, even stubborn, in her beliefs. She follows the role: "I have always been a ________ and I will always remain so." Her stubborn trait shows in other aspects of her personality as well as in her politics. Of course, in her younger days, she was remarkably well known in her family for stubbornness. This aspect of her personality has remained even where others have declined.

Social adjustment has probably been the most difficult for Aunt Byrd. Her husband passed away thirty years ago, and she has no children of her own. She lives with her nephew and his family. All her friends have passed away, and she really has no one to communicate with or reminisce about old times. Every chance she gets, she likes to talk about how things used to be when she was young. She wants desperately to talk with someone but only about her time. She can't communicate about the "now" or present age.

Her chief source of interest is television. She sits for hours watching the television and enjoys this medium thoroughly. The only other interest she has is reading.

As I think about the social aspect of adjustment in old age, I can't help but feel sorry for people at this stage of life. They are so very much alone because of their lack of communication with the younger generation. Aunt Byrd is content, though, to be considered a part of the family with whom she lives. They help reduce some of her needs for companionship. It would be of such great help to elderly people if others could realize this difficult adjustment to loneliness and the desire to relate to someone.

Perhaps Aunt Byrd's greatest strength is in her spiritual and religious commitments. She has much faith and her beliefs are strong. It very well may be that her life has been so full and rewarding because of her beliefs and her tenacity in following them. No doubt her faith has helped her through her period of adjustment.

I have always wondered how she compares life of now to life as it was during her childhood. She has seen so many changes in her lifetime that it must be both rewarding and yet bewildering. I envy her the fact that she has seen and experienced so much in her lifetime. Imagine living in an age that started before the invention of the automobile and eventually saw man walking on the moon. It is no wonder she regrets that we all couldn't have lived "back then." Perhaps if I had lived back then, I would feel the same way.

IN THIS CHAPTER . . .

You will read about

1 The statistical population distribution (demography) of older men and women.
2 Reaching the age of retirement: its stages, adjustment, and enjoyment.
3 The psychological variations that may take place in the personality style and role status.
4 Individual differences and cognition changes in the elderly, with some abilities remaining steady while others do not.
5 Social contacts among the aged; the interaction of the elderly with their grown children and family.
6 Those who grow old but have never married.
7 Housing and living arrangements of the retired and the elderly.
8 Bereavement and adjustment when a spouse dies.
9 Concerns with death and the experience of dying.

The process of aging and old age itself have become major topics of discussion, research, and speculation in recent years. One of the reasons for such activity is that more and more people are reaching old age. Approximately 4,000 Americans have their sixty-fifth birthday every day, and almost 12% of the population is over the age of 65 years. Western society has never experienced such a large percentage of its population living in retirement. The social, economic, and medical implications of this increased aged population are tremendous. Problems never before encountered are now facing a society that must not only learn how to live with a sizable number of its members in retirement but also how to incorporate this older segment of the population into the mainstream of life. For the most part the aged are people who still have vigor and vitality for life. To isolate and segregate them will only serve to force them into becoming "old" before their time.

demography the statistical study of human populations, especially with reference to size and density, distribution, and vital statistics.

DEMOGRAPHY OF OLD AGE

Who are the elderly, how many are there, and where do they live? ***Demography*** is the statistical study of human populations. The answers to these questions have all sorts of social, political, and economic ramifications. For example, Ragan and Dowd (1974) point out that the growth in the number of older persons—in conjunction with such matters as inflation, increases in health care costs, and decreased value of pension dollars—has caused the elderly to identify themselves as a group, seeking to promote political actions favorable to their needs and status. Prominent among these groups are the American Association of Retired Persons (AARP) and the Gray Panthers, an aggressive political action group. Another area of concern is the skyrocketing cost of old age insurance payments to Social Security recipients. The number of people eligible for payments has far exceeded the estimate envisioned when the Social Security Act was passed in 1937. There is concern, not only in the United States of America but in most countries of the world that have some form of old-age pension, that the system may become bankrupt and not be able to pay those who are eligible for Social Security allotments.

According to United Nations calculations, of the total of 4.4 billion persons on the globe in 1980, approximately 227 million were 65 years of age or older. The rate of increase of this age-group will average about 2.5% per year until the year 2000. By that year the number of persons over 65 in the world is expected to double. Table 16-1 shows the estimated changes in population between 1970 and 2000. Note that developing regions of the world are expected to have a higher percentage of older people as the years go on. It is reasoned that their earlier higher fertility rate and a rapidly declining mortality rate for persons of all ages as a result of better health care will account for the increased number of older people in these regions.

In the United States of America the older population has grown from 3.1 million in 1900 to about 22.6 million in 1980. Of the total older population in 1980, 14.6 million or 73% lived in urban areas, the majority in the heavily populated areas in central cities. Only 4.3 million old people lived in the suburbs. This disproportionate distribution of older people in the center of cities makes problems of congestion, transportation, housing, crime, and living costs of paramount importance to those interested in the health and well-being of older persons (Cutler and Harootyan, 1975).

More people are living longer. In 1900 only 3.1% of the population were over age 65. In 1940 it was 9.0%, and in 1980, 11.3% of the population in the United States were aged 65 or over (U.S. Bureau of Census, 1981c). Of those 65 years and over, 62% are "young-old" (65-74) and 38% are "old-old" (75 and over). People over age 65 will make up at least 17% of the United States' population by the year 2000.

A representation of the ratio of females to males is seen in Table 16-2. In the United States in 1976 there were 105.2 females per 100 males in the total population. More boy babies were born than girls. But by age 25 males outnumbered females by only 1.5 persons. After that age, the number of females exceeded the number of males. After the age of 65, there were 131.8 females for every 100 males.

The distribution of older people by marital status shows a reason for the difference in the percentage of the sexes. In 1980, 40.3% of the women between 65 and 74 were widowed; 68% of women 75 and older were widowed. For men, only 8.5% of the age-group

To be old need not mean to be alone or to not enjoy life. Facilities, such as this home unit, must be provided where the elderly can live, visit, read, and in general enjoy a variation on family life. Twelve women live in this house with a caretaker.

65 to 74 and 24% of the age-group 75 and over were widowed. Women outlive men. Related marital-status figures indicate that 77.6% of the men over 65 were married, as were 38.7% of the women. It is interesting to note that 3.7% of the men over 65 and 3.4% of the women over 65 were divorced. Only 5.1% of men and 5.9% of the women over 65 never married (U.S. Bureau of Census, 1981b). One in seven men and almost a third of all women over age 65 live alone (U.S. Department of Health, Education and Welfare, 1978a).

Black people in the United States have a shorter life expectancy than whites. Although blacks comprise more than 11% of the total population, they make up only 7.9% of the older age-group. The number of black elderly has risen from 1.2 million in 1960 to 2.1 million in 1980 (U.S. Bureau of Census, 1981a). Black elderly women outlive black men. Black females make up 56.7% of the total black aged population. In 1980 there were 131 black females over 65 for every 100 black males.

THE TIME OF RETIREMENT

Few issues in recent years have raised the ire and interest of old persons more than have issues relating to retirement, except that of reducing Social Security

TABLE 16-1 Demographic characteristics of various countries

Country	*1975 population (millions)*	*Percentage 65 and over*	*Life expectancy at birth*		*Percentage urban*
			Male	*Female*	
Austria	8	15	67	75	52
Canada	23	8	69	76	76
Chile	10	6	60	66	76
Denmark	5	12	71	76	67
Federal Republic of Germany	62	14	68	74	NA*
Finland	5	10	67	75	58
France	53	13	69	76	70
German Democratic Republic	17	16	69	74	75
Greece	9	11	70	74	65
Hungary	11	11	67	73	50
Ireland	3	11	69	73	52
Israel	3	9	70	73	82
Italy	56	11	69	75	NA
Japan	111	7	71	76	72
Mexico	60	4	63	67	63
Netherlands	14	10	71	77	77
New Zealand	3	9	69	75	81
Norway	4	14	71	78	45
Poland	34	9	68	75	54
Rumania	21	9	67	71	43
South Africa	25	4	50	53	48
Switzerland	6	12	70	76	55
Union of Soviet Socialist Republics	256	8	65	74	61
United Kingdom	56	13	68	74	78
United States of America	214	10	68	76	74
Uruguay	3	NA	66	72	NA
Venezuela	12	2	66		74
Yugoslavia	21	8	66	70	34

Modified from United Nations *1976 Demographic Yearbook.* New York: United Nations, 1977.
*Not available.

payment (Kalish, 1977). There are those who want early retirement so they may spend some leisure years in relatively good health, still capable of getting around. They would reject plans to force continued work. There are those who vigorously oppose compulsory retirement on the grounds that they are not ready to retire and feel that they are being discriminated against just because of their age. A federal law now prohibits most mandatory retirement provisions. There is a third group known as the "double-dippers" who get involved in several retirement systems. They work long enough under one system to qualify for a pension, then leave that job and go to work elsewhere under a different retirement plan, thus qualifying for two or maybe three pension plans before they retire. For example, a person may retire with a state and/or federal pension, a military retirement, a railroad or industrial pension, and, in addition, still receive Social Security payments. Needless to say, double-dippers receiving more than one pension from funds paid for

TABLE 16-2 Number of females per 100 males by age in 1976

Age in years	*Females per 100 males*
Under 14	96.2
14 to 24	98.5
25 to 44	103.4
45 to 64	108.2
65 and over	131.8
Total U.S.	105.2

Data from U.S. Bureau of the Census. Current Population Reports (Series P-25, No 643). In *Statistical abstracts,* Washington, D.C.: United States Government Printing Office, 1977.

by taxpayers are being criticized, but what they are doing is currently legal.

The age of 65 years has been established in American society as the usual retirement age. This age was chosen by the United States Congress on the basis of actuarial charts and concepts of longevity of the mid 1930s. Little did the planners realize that longevity would increase so much in the next 40 years. The age 65 is no longer the harbinger of old age. Table 16-3 presents retirement age and other related data for countries of the Organization for Economic Cooperation and Development (OECD) (1971).

TABLE 16-3 Pension systems in OECD countries by normal age of retirement, qualifications for early retirement, reduced payments for early retirement, by requirement for retirement, and by increments paid for deferment of normal retirement

	Normal age for retirement		*Early retirement qualifications*						
Country	*Male*	*Female*	*Work 35-40 years*	*Unemp. 1 year*	*Tiring work*	*Long illness*	*Early retirement less pay*	*Substantial requirement to retire*	*Increments if retirement deferred*
Austria	65	60	x	x		x		x	
Belgium	65	60					5 yr	x	
Canada	65	65						*	
Denmark	67	62				x			
France	60	60							x
West Germany	65	65		x					
Greece	62	57			x		2 yr	x	
Iceland	67	67							x
Ireland	70	70							
Italy	60	55	x		x				x
Japan	60	55						x	
Luxembourg	65	65	x						
Netherlands	65	65							
Norway	70	70							
Portugal	65	65						x	
Spain	65	65			x			x	
Sweden	67	67					4 yr		x
Switzerland	65	63							
Turkey	60	55				x		x	x
United Kingdom	65	60						x	x
United States	65	65					3 yr	x	x

Modified from Hyden, S. *Flexible retirement provisions in public pension systems in Organization for Economic Cooperation and Development flexibility in retirement age.* Paris: Organization for Economic Cooperation and Development, 1971, pp. 21-37.

*In Canada the universal pension program does not require retirement, but the social insurance program does require substantial retirement.

"TO RETIRE GRACEFULLY"

My Dad had been employed by a communications company as an electronic engineer, a well-paying position that he held for his entire working career until his retirement. He found his work a constant challenge and was very happy at it.

He was always a great perfectionist and would not settle for anything unless it was correctly done. He was creative and spent much of his leisure time working out problems, making things for his work, and seeing if he could improve anything and everything in any way possible. Actually, it might be said that he did not permit himself to have any leisure time to relax.

To quote him, "Television was the biggest piece of trash ever invented." He thought that it kept people from expanding their knowledge to a useful degree. He also had little use for anyone who wasted his time and money "boozing it up" in the local tavern or puffing away on a cigarette. As he once said, "There is not enough time in life to throw it around carelessly." He was definitely a man geared to work—almost like a machine that never wanted to quit. But, he was 64 years of age.

As retirement time grew nearer, Dad became uneasy. He started to wonder what he would do with himself. He wrote down a list of his many hobbies and interests that might occupy his time after retirement. He also started making lists of engineering companies that would hire an "old man" to work for them. He discussed moving to a farm for the sole purpose of raising hogs and experimenting with breeding. There were other ideas that passed through his mind, but they all seemed to be in hopes of finding a way out of being forced into retirement.

An outsider looking at Dad would most likely think that he was a calm man—a man who would have no difficulty adjusting to his retirement. It appeared that his financial standing would enable him to maintain his family and home, and his interests would enable him to occupy his mind successfully. All of these things were true; however, it did not seem quite so easy to Dad at this time.

The expected day of retirement arrived. To quote him, "One minute I am a useful working citizen, contributing to the welfare of my country, and the next minute I am no longer of any use to anyone." It was a discouraging thought for a man of his nature.

During the first couple of weeks in retirement, he found himself sitting around watching television, the "trash box" that he despised so much, and taking the dogs for their morning walk. He would trail around after mother, watching every move she made, seeing if he could be of help. However, he found that he was only getting in the way of her daily household chores. He started taking naps in the afternoon just as if he had become an old man at the precise time that his retirement went into effect. It was sad to see all of his talent and enthusiasm for life being wasted.

He had grown accustomed to feeling sorry for himself until months after his retirement, when he received a phone call from an engineering associate. He wanted to employ him on a part-time basis. Of course, Dad accepted immediately. He had received his chance to become useful again. This new job required him to work for a period of ninety days, with the option of continuing in another area at the end of that period.

The first job that he completed for his new company was acceptable. However, during the ninety days he found that there were many young men who were working successfully in engineering and could soon be doing the identical job that he had been doing. He also found that he was not used to keeping up with the fast pace that was common in such a company. He realized that he was not as young as he wished. He also found that he enjoyed having leisure time when he desired it, and consequently he decided that it was not so bad to be retired after all. After realizing all of this he turned the second job offer down. He had finally made his own choice to accept retirement gracefully and, I might add, graciously.

At this point in life he was a changed man, but actually he had not changed at all. It seems likely that he would have made his adjustment to retirement sooner or later without the assistance of his acquaintance and the part-time job; however, I do believe that this opportunity helped to speed him on his way to successful adjustment. He now had a feeling of self-worth that had been temporarily discarded but was fortunately restored.

Phases of retirement

Retirement is not something that happens suddenly to a person, except in very drastic or unusual circumstances. The idea of retirement is acknowledged from an early age on, perhaps from the time a person has the first Social Security deduction taken from the paycheck. For others the idea may start with their first career position when there is discussion about a pension or retirement plan as part of the fringe benefits of employment. Retirement is still far away, but the groundwork for that time has begun.

Atchley (1976) views retirement not only as a process but also as a social role that unfolds. He believes that various adjustments must be made as different stages in the retirement process emerge. Basically, there are three major divisions: the preretirement period, the retirement event and retirement, and the end of the retirement role. There are phases in these divisions, as can be noted in the box on phases of retirement.

The *preretirement phase* is one of recognizing that the moment of retirement is a milestone in life that is available to anyone living long enough. For the young worker a major concern may be to make certain that some type of retirement plan is being developed. For many people this plan is based almost entirely on the Social Security System. For others there may be an additional pension plan involved or possibly an annuity program that individuals can establish on their own. Older workers become more aware of retirement as the years go by. Thoughts about "when" and "how" and "what's it like" enter their minds. Adjustments

PHASES OF RETIREMENT

I. PRERETIREMENT

A. Remote phase

Retirement is distant event. Phase begins about time of first job.

B. Near phase

Realization that retirement is near. Adjustments must be made for successful transition.

II. RETIREMENT EVENT AND RETIREMENT

C. Honeymoon phase

Occurs immediately after retirement. There is a sense of euphoria; time is filled with activities. This may be a short or long period, depending on resources available.

D. Disenchantment phase

As life pace settles, an emotional letdown sets in. Some activities lose appeal. Unrealistic anticipations about retirement are recognized.

E. Reorientation phase

A more realistic view of life alternatives in retirement is developed. New avenues of involvement are explored.

F. Stability phase

A routine and criteria for dealing with change are established. Life is dealt with in a fairly comfortable and orderly fashion. The retirement role is mastered.

III. END OF RETIREMENT ROLE

G. Termination phase

Retirement role is cancelled out by loss of able-bodied status and autonomy, by a return to employment, or by death.

Modified from Atchley, R.C. *The sociology of retirement*. Cambridge, Mass.: Schenkman Publishing Co., 1976.

need to be made to arrange for a smooth transition from one phase to the other.

The *retirement event and the retirement phase* require a readjustment and reestablishment of one's role in society. Chosen or accepted retirement usually moves smoothly. Forced retirement often has its bad moments. The initial phase of retirement for most people is a pleasant one (Terkel, 1982). There is usually a sense of euphoria that is partly the result of newfound freedom. There are no imposed work schedules and time allotments to interfere with what the individual wants to do.

When the full impact of what it is really like to be retired—when what it means hits home—then some reassessment and readjustment of attitudes and values must take place. One hopes that after some reorientation of thoughts, a period of stability and acceptance will take place. At last there is contentment, or at least acquiescence, in living the retired life. The *end of retirement role phase* occurs when the individual is no longer capable of maintaining competent, independent living or when the person decides that the world of work is preferred to the life of a retiree and becomes employed again.

Retirement concerns

For some people one of the results of retirement is what some have chosen to call "retirement shock." The word "shock," in this instance, is similar to the concept of "cultural shock." It refers to the uncertainty of what retirement life might be like or to unexpected differences in living style and circumstances. This condition may be identified as a period of great personal uncertainty, not unlike that which individuals face during late adolescence or early adulthood when they are confronted with the responsibility of finding a meaningful field of endeavor (Kimmell, 1974). More frequently, it is the prospect of retirement rather than retirement itself that leads to an unsettled state of mind. This feeling of estrangement manifests itself in many ways. Doubts about future usefulness, financial worries because of reduced income, and the emptiness felt because of the lack of social intercourse are only a few ramifications of the retirement shock phenomenon (Atchey, 1980).

Anyone who is forced to retire must have some feeling of apprehension concerning future usefulness to society. Satisfactions once derived from a job well done are now removed from the immediate experience and can now only be used as the material for reflection. This would seem to be especially true for persons engaged in helping or service occupations, where much or all of the person's time was spent helping other people. Occupations such as teaching, the ministry, medicine, and social work fall into this category. On the other hand, a factory-type occupation, where workers are a small part of an assembly-line process, gives little opportunity to see the results of labor and therefore affords little personal satisfaction. In this respect perhaps the question of retirement is not as great for the person who is engaged in blue-collar occupation.

Financial matters preoccupy many people of postretirement age. It is possible that this is the most realistic concern of old age. After being financially independent for 45 or 50 years, many elderly people dread the possibility of not being able to support themselves. As a result, they have a tendency to become rather frugal and cautious with their financial resources. We know of several persons who went into great depth trying to figure out how they were going to live on their retirement income. Every penny was counted. Fixed expenditures were figured out. Often the person would say things like "I have to stop subscribing to the newspaper" or "I'll have to drop out of the club." It should be recognized, however, that for a number of old people retirement incomes are inadequate for current prices, and becoming miserly is an economic necessity. On the other hand, it is also true that less income is needed in retirement. Income needs decrease by 40% to 60% because of the decrease in employment-related activities, social activities, and even clothing and eating needs (Irelan and Bond, 1976).

The theory of disengagement, presented later in the chapter, states that one of the elements of aging is a decreased amount of social interaction between the elderly and their former social contacts. In this regard, retirement represents perhaps the most important occurrence in the process of disengagement (Lowenthal, 1972). Often the workers' associates constitute the bulk of their social acquaintances. The severance of the associations with the people with whom they work may also mean a corresponding loss in more general social activity. Here, then, is another concern to which retirees need to adjust.

To keep concepts in the proper perspective, it is important to note that not everyone who retires experiences retirement shock. With proper planning, realistic understanding, or even eager anticipation, it is

compulsory retirement a designated age at which a person must retire from working at his or her place of employment; mandatory retirement.

discretionary retirement the age and timing of retirement is the choice of the individual; voluntary retirement.

possible to make the transition to retirement with no discomfort. A study of persons over the age of 55 by the American Association of Retired Persons indicated that half of those who had retired had done so by choice. Sixty-four percent were glad they had retired (Stevens, 1979). This finding is not to say they did not experience some retirement concern, but it can be assumed that they were at least willing to encounter it.

Compulsory versus discretionary retirement

As more and more is being learned about the specific problems of retirement, increased attention is being focused on the problem of forced retirement, although it is no longer a legal issue. Researchers are finding that many of the problems associated with retirement are the results of individual differences and the state of "readiness" for the transition (Streib and Schneider, 1971). Some of the country's largest employers are split down the middle on whether or not retirement should be compulsory at the age of 65 years.

Those who support ***compulsory retirement*** argue their position with the following point of view: (1) It is the fairest way. (2) It avoids giving workers the stigma of being "washed up." (3) It is a painless way of getting rid of those who have outlived their usefulness. (4) Finally, compulsory retirement opens promotion opportunities for younger people (Litras, 1979).

Those who are opposed to compulsory retirement but are in favor of ***discretionary retirement*** cite the following factors: (1) Most workers at age 65 still have several years ahead during which they are very capable of effective performance. (2) It is necessary, in some cases, to keep people beyond the age of 65 who are making important contributions to the company. (3) Hiring and promotion policies could be more readily established on the basis of merit and ability if flexible retirement policies were in force. (4) Employees with significant knowledge could fall into the hands of competitors if released. (5) Many who are forced to retire lack adequate income and would have to subsist below the official poverty level. (6) Finally, since work is the main substance in the lives of some people, it would be psychologically healthier for them to continue to work (Palmore, 1977).

Welford (1980) maintains that within the over-65 age-group there is an immense source of knowledge, skill, and experience. It would be the ultimate in wastefulness to require that all persons retire at the age of 65 just because of their age.

When people retire voluntarily, presumably they do so because they believe that they will be happier in retirement than continuing as a member of the labor force. Granted they may be dissatisfied with their job or may have some motive other than the primary motive of entering into a better way of life with retirement. In any case, if the decision to retire is theirs, the chances are that they enter retirement without the feeling of having outlived their usefulness to society that so often accompanies compulsory retirement (Leslie and Leslie, 1977).

Early retirement

Retirement before age 65 has become more prevalent in our society (Barfield and Morgan, 1978). Many of these early retirees are civil servants and military personnel, but the early-retirement phenomenon is becoming widespread in a diversity of industries and occupations. A study of college and university professors who retired early revealed that they did so because of increased annuities or a substantial lump-sum payment available from their retirement plan. It seems that if individuals can retire early and still be financially secure, they will exercise the option (Kell and Patton, 1978).

Bischof (1976) presents the following reasons for early retirement: (1) positive and high-status image of an early retiree, (2) anticipation of a comfortable income, (3) pressures generated by a lack of skills to keep up with the requirements of a rapidly advancing technology, (4) relocation of firms to other parts of the country, (5) encouragement from family, friends, and fellow workers to retire, and (6) a desire for early retirement because of declining health, preference for a lighter work load, inability to keep up with the demands of the job, wish for fewer responsibilities, or an awareness of "time left to live." Occasionally, attendance at a program focusing on preretirement preparation is enough to convince a person that it is all right to retire early.

Some individuals have the choice of discretionary retirement and may not want to take advantage of it. So long as a person can perform chores, why insist that he or she stop? Older persons will usually stop an activity when they believe it may be harmful to them.

Preretirement planning

Whether or not a person wishes to retire, the time does eventually come. Ideally, retirement should come gradually, with a tapering off of job activity. Some company executives, if they happen to be owners or part owners of the company, are able to do this. Professional people are often able to slow down and move out gradually. But most people cannot do this; therefore, it would seem advisable to begin making retirement plans long before the time actually arrives—to anticipate and overcome as many of the problems of retirement as possible.

Individuals should prepare themselves for retirement in the same way that they would prepare themselves for any other undertaking. Planning should start in a practical and positive way while workers are still on the job. They should cultivate a wholesome attitude toward retirement. It is vitally important that they look at retirement from the forward-looking position of "retiring to" rather than "retiring from." In this way retirees will possess the optimism and adaptability necessary to cope with the various problems they will almost certainly have to face.

Preretirement presentations have become part of the personnel policies of new companies. The purpose of these programs is to facilitate the financial, social, and psychological adjustments associated with a transition from regular working hours to a life of retirement (Manion, 1976). Atchley (1976) indicates the positive effects that frequently emerge from preretirement planning. First, uncertainties about retirement are reduced because of the information provided. Second, the individual begins to look ahead with more confidence, so the tendency to miss the job is lessened. Third, there is less dissatisfaction with retirement because of myths or negative stereotypes that an individual may have believed. Fourth, worries about postretirement health are reduced. Since retirement is a different experience for the spouse, it is important to include this person in retirement preparations. Attitudes of each partner will influence the level of satisfaction derived during the retirement years (Heyman and Polansky, 1977).

In preparing for retirement, it should be remembered that security in retirement is a balance of three things: *physical security*—reasonably good health to be able to do the things the individual really wants to do, *activity security*—a program and the opportunity for satisfying and rewarding accomplishments, and *financial security*—having sufficient money to make it possible to achieve these goals. Of the three, activity security usually receives the least consideration during the planning, yet it is extremely important.

Ewald W. Busse (1969), Director of The Center for the Study of Aging and Human Development at Duke University Medical Center, Durham, North Carolina, urges a "social career" for the retired person. Young persons have student careers, adults have economic careers, and if older persons have social careers, it will provide them with an orderly work pattern as well as personal recognition and respect in their community. This corresponds with the point of view that health in old age is improved through mental and physical activity. The elderly can and should make valuable contributions to society.

SOCIAL LIFE CHANGES

One of the most important things an older person must do is to keep active. An old proverb says: "It is difficult to remain at peace in idleness." A life of doing nothing will only lead to increased emptiness. Work, to some degree, should continue.

George Burns, the noted comedian, appearing on a TV talk show at the age of 86, gave this advice, "Get up every morning about 8:00 or so and do something. Plan any kind of activity that will get you out of bed. Go some place, if you can. If you can't, have someone come to your house to play bridge, talk, or relax." At this age, Burns was making films after having been on the sidelines for a while.

Men and women should start some of the projects that they have put off for so long. Reading, travel, visits to art museums, and developing new talents are excellent activities. Although it is important for people to keep active and alert, they must also know when to stop, even if they are just taking a walk.

Social contacts among the elderly

As people develop, they become part of a social network. They are members of a family, and they have friends who add satisfaction and joy to their life. The social life of old people is narrowed increasingly by the loss of work associates; the death of relatives, friends, and spouse; and poor health, which restricts their participation in social activities. There are three types of social relationships that are affected by aging: (1) close personal friendships, such as husband and wife, siblings, and friends from childhood days, (2) friendship cliques made up of couples banded together in a social crowd when they were younger, and (3) formal groups or clubs. Once broken, these social relationships are rarely replaced in old age. Married people are socially more active in old age than are those who are single or widowed, and those from upper socioeconomic groups are more socially active than those from lower socioeconomic groups.

Larson (1978) has reviewed the last 30 years of research on life satisfaction. He revealed a consistent body of findings. Subjective well-being is most strongly related to health, socioeconomic factors, and the degree of social interaction in older populations. The results indicate that for both sexes activity was strongly related to life satisfaction. Income was found to be only indirectly significant in terms of activity. According to Conner and associates (1979), it is the *quality* of social interactions rather than the quantity that is the important determinant of life satisfaction.

Many communities are trying to meet the social needs of the aged by starting social clubs with activities planned to fit into their interests and capacities. Older people feel more comfortable with those of their own age. They get along better with persons who have shared the same period of early socializaton and historical times. They share recollections of the same movies, automobiles, politicians, and ball players; they remember dancing the same dances, using the same slang, fighting the same wars, and wearing the same clothing styles (Kalish, 1975).

Those who take advantage of opportunities for social participation and who make an effort to retain

MARTHA LEAVES HOME FOR GOOD

Martha was now approaching her eighty-fourth birthday. Most of her time, after the death of her husband fifteen years ago, was spent with her children. She loved her children equally but her son, Paul, was the apple of her eye. She used to visit her two daughters but could not stay there for more than two weeks. However, now that she was very old, the two daughters decided when she was to go back to Tonga.

Martha now knew that there was nothing which could convince her daughter to let her go back to her son. Her only request was—"May I be taken to my home island when I die and be buried there together with my husband." Her daughter, Fifita, who is my aunt, reassured her that her wish would be carried out.

After this request, Martha hardly moved around. She spent most of her time in bed meditating, singing and praying. She was cheerful at times, although sometimes she preferred to be left alone. She had a very good appetite and ate well.

On a Friday afternoon of the same week, she wanted her daughter to run a warm bath for her. After having her bath, she dressed and then joined the grandchildren outside, watching their play. She even strolled around the place, examining the flower garden, and talked to some of the ladies in the neighbourhood. When evening came, she returned to the house.

Unlike the other evenings, Martha joined the rest of the family for dinner. She was very attentive to the conversation and never yawned for a single moment. She was cheerful, lively and enjoyed her food to the end of the dinner.

After dinner that evening she retired to the sitting room with the grandchildren, waiting there for the others to join them in their family evening prayers.

Her son-in-law gave the words of a hymn and they all sang, including Martha. She was also asked to pray, which she did very well.

On Saturday she returned to her usual self. She spent the whole day in bed and hardly opened her eyes. Her food was not touched, and she refused to talk much. Fifita, her daughter, noticed and asked whether she was feeling unwell. Fifita left after being assured that she was not sick. Sunday came and Martha was still behaving as she had the day before.

Fifita felt that there might only be a few hours left before Martha passed away. She decided to stay with Martha in case things changed for the worse. Fifita started to panic when she realized how weak her mother was. However, she gained control of herself and kept calm for the rest of the afternoon. About six o'clock on that Sunday night Martha opened her eys and asked Fifita whether she was still up. She then told Fifita—"You are the eldest; look after your brother and your sister, and love one another." Then she took Fifita's right hand and placed it on her chest. She closed her eyes. Finally she gave a deep breath, and everything was still.

Fifita knew that her mother had passed away. She was so overwhelmed with what she had just witnessed that she did not know what to do. She just sat there in the darkness staring at her mother, too numb to move or to think. The children had gone to bed, and everything was lulled to stillness in the house. The rustle of the wind among the trees outside was no longer heard. Suddenly in the midst of this silence came the shrill sound of an owl. This lingering echo brought Fifita back to reality and she found tears rolling down her cheeks.

Sione, her husband, came to inquire about Martha and was surprised when told that—Martha had already left home for good.

From Stewart, R.A.C. (Ed.). *Pacific profiles*. Suva, Fiji: University of The South Pacific Extension Services, 1982.

old friendships or establish new ones not only make a better adjustment to old age than do those who are socially inactive but find old age a far happier period of life than they had anticipated when they were younger. As is true at every age, the social needs of individuals at that period of their life must be met to their satisfaction if they want to be happy.

Frequently, a retired couple will decide that their present home is too large to take care of, so they decide to sell their home and move to a more convenient-size dwelling. Sometimes a home is sold to enable a move from a neighborhood that has deteriorated with time. The neighborhood has changed so much that the couple no longer feels comfortable or at ease in it. The choice of where to move is usually made in terms of (1) moving near one of the children, (2) moving to the "sun belt" area or to a better climate, or (3) moving to a retirement village or home.

Moving always requires adjustments. If the move is to the sun belt area or a retirement village, it may entail the purchase or rental of a house, a condominium, an apartment, or a mobile home, often in an area inhabited primarily by older people. New adjustments to living quarters and social contacts are required (Brand and Smith, 1974). The couple must learn to live in a new town (or neighborhood), in a new climate, and among new people. They are usually far from old friends, children, and grandchildren.

Some people can make the adjustments without any problems. Others yearn for "back home" and often feel they made a mistake in moving. Still others find it depressing or nonstimulating to be cut off from younger people. Occasionally, some are disappointed at the class or caliber of people who live in their new location: "They're not the kind of people I feel comfortable with; our values are so different." However, the fact that so many people do adjust to such a change in life-style indicates that changes can be made and that they can be happy. The best advice is not to make decisions too quickly nor without a thorough investigation of the new dwelling site. The social, climatic, housing, medical, cultural, political, and taxation situations should be studied.

Elderly parents and adult children

For elderly persons their family makes up the nucleus of their social life. The older they become, the more they tend to rely on their family for companionship. Their friends have either died or are physically unable to do things with them. They cannot keep pace with younger friends and, as a result, no longer consider themselves welcome members of a younger group. Thus older persons must limit their social contacts to family members or to individuals their own age. This means, generally, a group of intimate friends, some of whom have been friends since childhood or young adulthood days. One advantage of living in a social institution or a retirement home or village is that it provides the great advantage of opportunities for social contacts with contemporaries. Elderly persons' contemporaries have interests, problems, and physical traits in common with theirs. However, many elderly people resist making this adjustment and, as a result, cut themselves off from social contacts.

Several studies (e.g., Mancini, 1979; Medley, 1976) underscore the importance of family-life satisfaction for life satisfaction as a whole. Mancini especially stresses the role of quality of family interaction in influencing well-being. It is suggested that the helping professions begin to see the aged as having the potential for more productive interactions and work to strengthen the family relationships of the elderly.

Parent-child relationships. The aged often have definite opinions concerning their relationships with their children. In a study by Streib (1977) 84% of the parents of adult children believed that the children should visit often; 82% wanted the children to write often. Many of the feelings that older individuals experience are vicarious ones. Because of this, they feel a deep need to keep in close touch with their children and to continue to share their experiences. At the same time the parents do not want to interfere in their children's lives.

The aged think that their children should be expected to "help some" in financial assistance but "not a great deal." Many of the children, however, want the parents to apply for old-age assistance, even though the children themselves could help. Kalish (1975) found that elderly parents do not take their chidren's assistance for granted. Aging individuals try to maintain themselves without seeking help. While relationships with kin persist, fewer older people reside with them. Arling's research (1976) suggests that, while parents and children are concerned about each other, they may be unable to share experiences or to empathize with each other because adult children have their own household affairs and jobs to attend to. Older parents who live in a son's or daughter's home often experience a role reversal as they become dependent on their children. An older person's autonomy can be maintained by providing financial assistance, helping him or her to cope with physical disabilities, and teaching young people to respect the elderly as individuals (Rogers, 1982).

Most aging parents consider their relationship with their children to be satisfactory. They have reached some kind of mutual agreement and know how each stands. They have a list of acceptable responses from their children that are usually met. Many elderly individuals, when surveyed, present a picture entirely different from that usually thought of in connection with the elderly. Instead of a lonely person sitting around in a rocking chair, Streib (1977) found a group of people who were useful both to themselves and society with a wide range of interests that many younger people do not have.

The degree of satisfaction that elderly persons find in their relationships with their sons and daughters depends, to a large degree, on the extent to which both parents and children can communicate in a pleasant, friendly way with each other. The ease and clarity of communication depends, in part, on the attitudes that both groups have toward each other and toward

TABLE 16-4 Importance of twelve services to elderly and to middle-aged adult children

Elderly group: Ranking type of service	*Middle-aged group: Ranking type of service*
1. Protection	1. Transportation
2. Transportation	2. Personal care
3. Bureaucratic mediation	3. Home health care
4. Reading materials	4. Psychological support
5. Psychological support	5. Protection
6. Social and recreation	6. Social and recreation
7. Enrichment	7. Bureaucratic mediation
8. Spiritual	8. Spiritual
9. Home health care	9. Reading materials
10. Personal care	10. Enrichment
11. Employment	11. Employment
12. Career education	12. Career education

From Cicirelli, V.G. *Helping elderly parents: the role of adult children.* Boston: Auburn House Publishing Co., 1981. Reprinted by permission of publisher.

their age levels in general. It also depends somewhat on the willingness of the son-in-law or daughter-in-law to be respectful and responsive.

Some parents cannot shift their attitudes or perspectives toward their adult children to match their adult age (usually in middle adulthood or later), their needs, and their family groups. Some elderly have to remain as the dominant authority figure until their dying day, no matter how totally dependent they are on their children and regardless of how competent the children may be. On the other hand, the children may resent the lack of recognition of their competency by their parent(s). This same disregard for changing levels of development, changing values, and changing life-styles may also filter down to the grandchildren and great-grandchildren. Fortunate is the family that can respect each other's individuality and values and accept differences as they exist for the different age levels.

Family support and care. Traditionally, women were the mainstay of family support systems for the elderly (Bengtson and Treas, 1980). They would run errands for widowed mothers, provide custodial care, and take them into their households. Today more women are in the work world, which occupies their time and energy, leaving little time to take care of elderly parents. Perhaps adult children should adopt a more preventive approach to their elderly parents' needs by helping their parents find ways of learning and growing to meet their own needs. By doing so they may be forestalling decline. Adult children place too much emphasis on "support" strategies of helping, in which they try to provide whatever the elderly parents need (Kazuza and Firestone, 1980). This approach may lead to learned helplessness and dependency, whereas timing and motivation strategies may be more helpful in prolonging independence and self-sufficiency.

Cicirelli (1981) conducted a study for the NRTA [National Retired Teachers' Association] - AARP [American Association of Retired Persons] Andrus Foundation on the role of adult children in helping their elderly parents. Cicirelli measured views, feelings, and provisions of services to parents. He found that most elderly people prefer to remain independent and take care of their own needs as long as possible. Only 5% of the parents lived in nursing homes or other institutions. When elderly people do feel they need help, they prefer to receive it from their adult children above all others.

Table 16-4 contains twelve services and their ranking of importance as viewed by the elderly parents and their adult children. The elderly see their own most important needs as involving protection, transportation, bureaucratic mediation, reading materials, and psychological support. In contrast, the adult children see their parents' most important needs as involving transportation, personal care, home health care, psychological support, and protection. These same areas were the ones in which adult children provided the most help.

Most adult children perceived their elderly parents as only slightly to moderately dependent. They saw their parents as having low need for services or help. Most adult children reported relatively strong feelings of attachment to their parents. Although there was not a great deal of conflict between adult children and their elderly parents, most expected an increase in conflict if their parents were to live with them (Cicirelli, 1981).

Adult-child adjustment. Probably the time of greatest conflict between aged parents and their children is at retirement. One should remember that retirement at the age of 65 years means that the "children" are probably about 45, 40, or 35 years old—at the peak of adulthood. The retiring couple are having their problems adjusting their thoughts and attitudes to the idea of retirement. They are uncertain and indecisive. They worry out loud about their concerns and try to reason out their problems from all angles. They may come up with "logical" answers, but they never seem to do anything about them. They are on a merry-go-round with their concerns and do not know how to get off.

The children always seem to see things more clearly, "It's so obvious," and they are quick to give them opinions." You should move out of this big house into a smaller place, maybe an apartment, where you won't have as much housekeeping to do." "You should move here (or there) . . ." for any number of reasons that make sense to the children. Yet the retiring couple is reluctant to act. It becomes most exasperating to the children.

This would be the moment for the children to step back and examine what is happening. Their parents are at a point in life where they are contemplating major changes and moves. On the one hand the move seems so sensible, yet on the other hand the "feel" is not quite right, thus the hesitancy. It should be recognized that not all good decisions can be based on cold, hard facts alone. People are not machines. They are warm-blooded human beings with feelings, sentimental attachments, and maybe even fears. Children must keep in mind that just because their parents of retirement age find it hard to make decisions about where to live and what to do, this is no indication that their parents have become enfeebled and have lost their powers of intellectual reasoning and judgment. The parents should be allowed to move at their own pace. It is surprising how, in spite of all the concerns, they work things out. Children should not interfere unless asked specifically to do so. Even then, they should not be upset if their advice is not taken. The final decision should rest with the parents.

William T. Swaim, Jr. (no date), a former administrator of Presbyterian Homes of Central Pennsylvania, has written much on the aged and their lives. He gives some tips in *What Shall We Do With Granny?*

1. Let Granny do what she wants to do, even if it kills her. She is not as vulnerable as you think.
2. Do not expect perfection.
3. Make due allowance for any words or actions that may be caused by cerebral changes.
4. Treat Granny as a person. Let her make her own decisions. Respect her interests and needs.
5. Be demonstrative. Shake hands, hug her, kiss her.
6. Learn to listen long and smile even if you've heard it all before.
7. Do everything possible to build up her ego.
8. Impart information; tell her why, if you must change her mind or wishes.
9. Do not ruin your own health and happiness to minister to her nursing needs if they are beyond your capabilities.
10. Encourage Granny to remain employed as long as possible.
11. If Granny desires to remarry, remember "It is not good that man should be alone."
12. Move heaven and earth to keep Granny living with her own furniture and amid familiar scenes and faces as long as possible.
13. Do not force three-generation living which may deny Granny privacy, quiet and independence.
14. Make it easy and delightful for Granny to share chores.
15. Let her go to a home for the aging if that is her desire.
16. Welcome old age. Let your study of Granny's personality remind you to grow older graciously.
17. Have respect for Granny's age. Nurses should not call elderly patients by their first names.

Burr (1970) did an interesting study showing the degree of satisfaction that parents had with their children at different stages of married life. The findings are indicated in Fig. 16-1. Not surprisingly, there is much parental satisfaction with young children. But, as the children get into school and become teenagers, there is decreasing satisfaction. Satisfaction with their children as adults is quite good, only to diminish some-

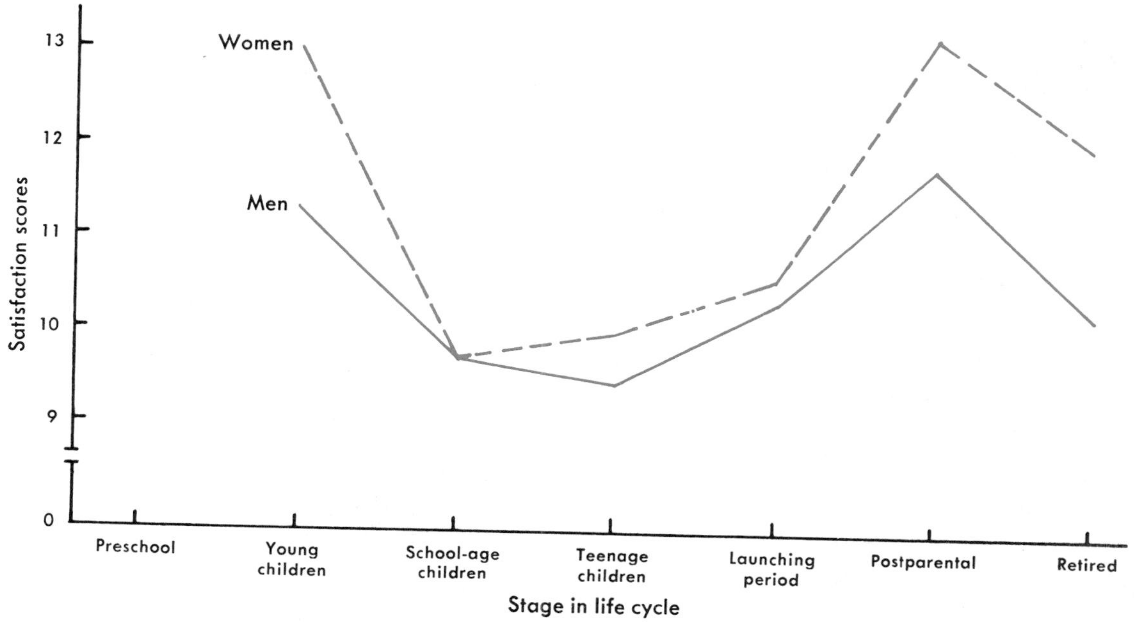

FIG. 16-1 ***Parents' satisfaction with their children at different stages of their married life.***
Modified from Burr, W. R. Journal of Marriage and the Family, *1970, 32, 29-37. Copyrighted 1970 by the National Council on Family Relations, 1219 University Avenue Southeast, Minneapolis, Minnesota 55414. Reprinted by permission.*

what after retirement. Women tend to show more interest and are more absorbed in the lives of their children and grandchildren than men.

Marital satisfaction of the elderly. According to the research of Stinnett and co-workers most older people feel that their marriages have been very satisfactory, that their lives are calmer now that their children are grown, and that they have a new freedom to do as they please. This is as true for husbands as for wives. There may be worries about how fast the money is going, disagreements about moving, disagreements over relationships with children, and health problems, but, all-in-all, a married couple who have reached the later adulthood years together will probably be able to handle the stress engendered. Often the most significant transition point in later marital life is the husband's retirement. With thoughtful consideration and planning, the stress of this time can also be minimized.

Wives look forward with less enthusiasm than husbands to marital togetherness following the husband's retirement (Lowenthal et al., 1975). After husbands have retired, wives enjoy togetherness less than husbands do. Keating and Cole (1980) found that three fourths of the women but almost no men reported a disadvantage of retirement that was related to the marital relationship. Wives complained of loss of personal freedom, too much togetherness, and too many demands on their time. Few wives discussed these issues with their husbands. Most wives were compensated by the increased centrality of the marital relationship or by a sense of being needed; a minority simply suffered in silence.

Table 16-5 shows the most rewarding and the most troublesome aspects of marriage as reported by older married people. Stinnett and co-workers (1972) conducted this cross-sectional study. It is difficult to know whether these interpersonal factors were perceived as critically important throughout the marriage or whether they are characteristic of the relationship after the children were launched and one spouse had retired. What is interesting to note is that 36% of the couples reported "nothing troublesome."

Generally, marriages that were good to begin with will continue to be good (Nye and Berardo, 1973). But marriages that were unhappy in their earlier years do

TABLE 16-5 Perceptions of older husbands and wives concerning the most troublesome and most rewarding aspects of marriage relationships during the later years

	Percent
Rewarding aspects	
Companionship	18.4
Mutual expression of true feelings	17.8
Economic security	16.2
Being needed by mate	12.0
Affectionate relationship with mate	11.2
Sharing of common interests	9.3
Having physical needs cared for	7.6
Standing in the community	7.0
Troublesome aspects	
Different values and life philosophies	13.8
Lack of mutual interests	12.5
Mutual inability to express true feelings	8.6
Unsatisfactory affectional relationships	8.5
Frequent disagreements	8.5
Lack of companionship	7.7
Other	8.5
Nothing troublesome	36.2

From Stinnett, N., Carter, L.H., & Montgomery, J.E. *Journal of Marriage And The Family,* 1972, *34,* 665-670. Copyrighted 1972 by the National Council on Family Relations, 1219 University Avenue Southeast, Minneapolis, Minnesota 55414. Reprinted by permission.

not seem to get better unless major improvements are made in attitudes, respect, and acceptance of one another. It appears that the more the relationship meets each other's needs for love, fulfillment, respect, recognition, communication, and meaning in life, while downplaying negative or weak aspects of an individual's personality or behavior, the happier the marriage is in later years (Keating-Groen, 1977). Happy older people generally say that companionship and being able to express true feelings to each other are the most rewarding aspects of their relationship. With time, mutual leisure-time interests can or should be developed, drawing the partners closer together. Problems and crises also have the potential of bonding a couple to face an adversity.

In very old age when both spouses find the tasks of household maintenance beyond their strength, they may shift to what has been called a *symbiotic relationship* (Troll, 1971), in which each contributes the best he or she can. The fact that people who have been married many years tend to die within a short time of each other suggests that they are holding each other up in the form of an arch, which collapses when either side falls (Turner, 1982). The death rate increases during the first 4 to 6 months and does not return to the normal rate for a year (Klerman, 1979).

GROWING OLD AND NEVER MARRIED

Some individuals grow old and have been single for all or most of their lives. Sometimes the choice to be single was deliberately made, and in other instances the decision was one of happenstance or circumstances. The reason for remaining single is not the issue. The question is how these people do as elderly individuals. It is true that single elderly individuals do not live as long as married individuals, but that statistical bit of information does nothing to indicate the level of life satisfaction.

Approximately 5.1% of the men and 5.9% of the women over 65 years of age in the United States have never married (U.S. Bureau of Census, 1981b). The never-married often live alone and are generally better adjusted than widows of that age (Gubrium, 1975). In general, the elderly never-married believe their future would simply be an extension of the past. They did not worry about it; they looked on death as simply one more event in the life cycle. With regard to social relationships, they often associate more with friends than with relatives. They would admit to missing someone, but they usually would not say they were lonely. Compared to older married persons, however, they engage in more solitary activities and say that they are satisfied with them. Those who have been isolates tend to remain isolates (Mass and Kuypers, 1974).

The research concerning being single and old is meager. The results of observational studies done in clinical and institutional settings suggest that single men and women who have reached a stage of competent, independent living in younger years develop attitudes, interests, and involvement in activities that tend to decrease their need for close family relationships (Lowenthal and Robinson, 1977). Such persons sometimes develop a vicarious response of closeness to others through the families of their relatives, close friends, or even pets. Doing work with social agencies or volunteer work in group or individual care services sometimes provides satisfaction. Others find precious contentment in moments of solitude, in worship, or in church activity.

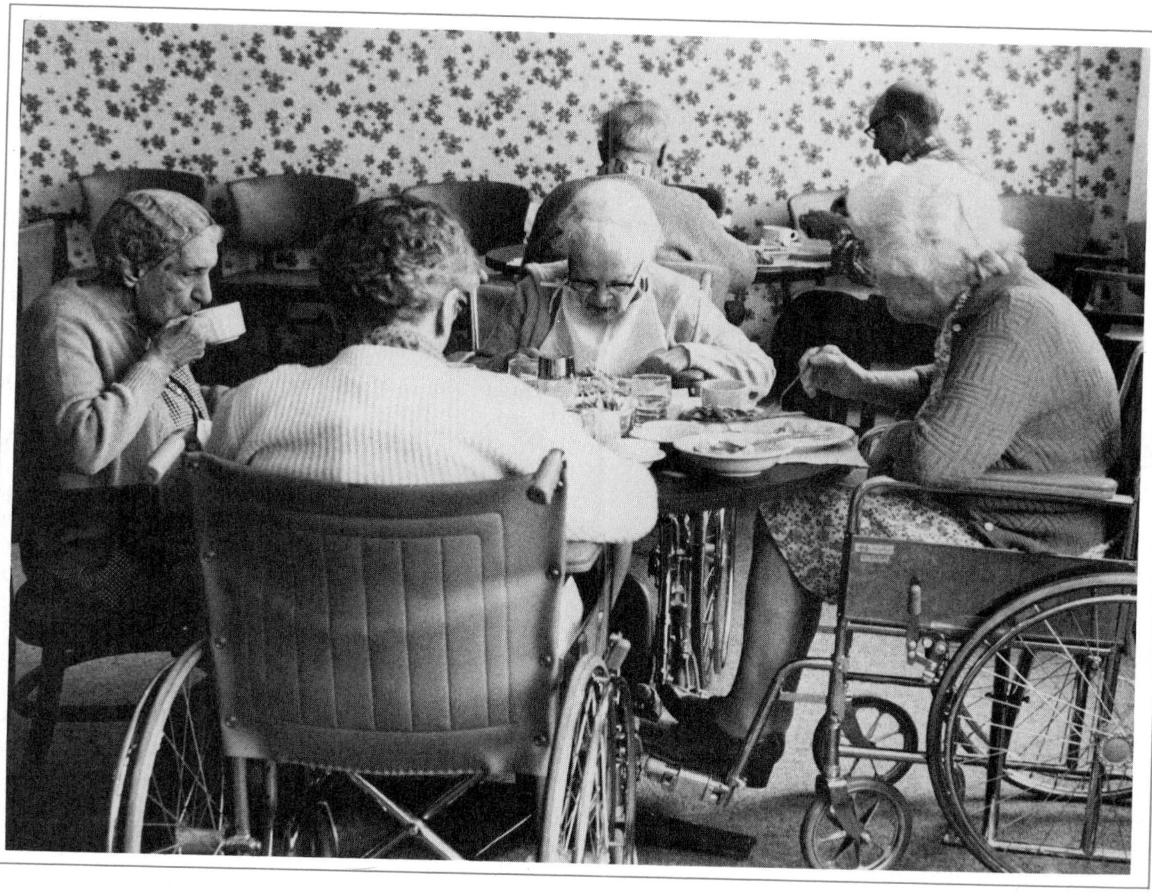

Homes for the elderly provide different amounts of care and facilities—some with only living accommodations but no nursing care. Others, such as this one, provide minimum care for those who are not bedridden and who can feed themselves. Special-skills facilities are needed for those requiring total care. It is not uncommon for the elderly in nursing homes to be in wheelchairs, reducing the chance of falling and breaking a bone.

To grow to be a happy, nice little old woman or a nice old man, you must start early in life to give, to share, and to respond to the needs and the well-being of others. Happiness can only be had if it is shared with others; sorrow is something that can be engaged in by yourself. Married or single, the principle is the same.

HOUSING AND LIVING ARRANGEMENTS

The proceeding of the White House Conference on Aging (White House Conference, 1973) raised the question, "What does housing mean to the elderly?" The answer was, "Aside from his [or her] spouse, housing is probably the single most important element in the life of an older person." There is clear documentation that housing can have a decisive impact on the life-style and well-being of older persons (Carp, 1976).

Housing and the elderly

There are a few main prerequisites of good housing for older people. Housing should provide as much independence and privacy as possible, while still being near other older people and proper medical facilities. Older people need greater warmth and freedom from drafts and often other types of controls such as air pollution and humidity controls. Proper illumination is also important because the eyes of older people are slower to adjust to changes in light; therefore each room they use should have the same intensity of light (Lawton and Nahemow, 1973).

Noise level is a factor that many people do not consider. Older people, especially those with a vision problem, become most annoyed and tense when there is too much silence because they depend on their hearing for sensory input. As older people gradually lose their hearing, they must adjust sound volume to a higher level.

The tendency is for the old to maintain independent households. Only 5% live in an institutional setting. The types of housing are home-owned; apartments, usually in older buildings; rooms, boarding houses, and hotels, generally used by old men; mobile home parks; vacant dormitories, usually on college campuses, for housing the elderly; intermediate housing such as nursing homes for those not requiring institutional care; institutions for the aged; and residential villages or large building units especially developed for retired people (Carp, 1976).

Group housing units tend to be either relatively affluent retirement communities designed for people who can afford more luxurious living environments or low-cost public-supported facilities for the elderly. Since 60% of the elderly live in metropolitan areas, most public-supported housing units are found in larger cities. The inner city is apt to house predominantly ethnic minority groups and the frailest of the old from the ethnic majority (Carp, 1976).

However, the rural old, especially if black, have the worst housing and living arrangements. The rural poor are among the most impoverished segment of the oldest population and are among the least healthy of the elderly groups. Other groups at special risk are the black elderly, about 70% of whom live in poverty (Jackson, 1971); Mexican-American and Spanish-speaking (mostly Puerto Rican) elderly; Asian-American, especially elderly residents of America's Chinatowns; Jewish inner-city dwellers, who tend to be less mobile and less socially active; widows; and the poorly educated and multiply deprived (Carp, 1976). A great deal of study must be conducted before a satisfactory solution can be found for adequately housing the elderly of all geographic, economic, and ethnic groups.

Living arrangements

Most older people prefer to live in their own dwellings. The next acceptable arrangement would be to live with someone of the same sex. Most widows think that it would not be wise to live with married sons or daughters. Living with relatives often causes overcrowding, annoying situations caused by small children, and tense situations with the children. In today's society, however, family belongingness in many cases is being replaced by community belongingness, which is making individuals less dependent on their families.

The box from Hurlock (1982) very nicely summarizes the physical and psychological needs in living arrangements. The older an individual gets, the more frail the body strength becomes. Equilibrium and balance also deteriorate and, as a result, everything possible should be done in living accommodations to prevent accidents that involve falling. In many cases the mind of the individual is still very alert even though the body is weak. The story is told of Oliver Wendell Holmes, the famous jurist, who, although in his 80s, was out taking a walk. An acquaintance met him and asked, "How is Oliver Wendell Holmes today?" The reply was, "Oliver Wendell Homes is very well, thank you, but the housing of his body is slowly deteriorating and falling apart." The mind was clear but the physical organism was not what it used to be.

The late Faith Baldwin, the writer, when she was 80, said something to the effect that she wished people would stop telling her how well she looked for her age and that she should not complain about her age but be glad that she got to live so long. Her response was that those comments didn't make her feel any better because, although she was in her right mind, she was not enjoying life simply because "I hurt" (Baldwin, F., 1976). The point is that in living arrangements it is important to consider psychological needs as well as physical needs, as indicated in the box on p. 623.

The usual types of living arrangements are a married couple living alone; a person living alone in his or her own home; two or more members of the same generation living together in a nonmarital relationship (brothers, sisters, friends of the same sex, friends of different sexes); a widow or widower living with children, grandchildren, or relatives; and an elderly person living in a home for the aged, a nursing home, a club or hotel, or an institution.

PHYSICAL AND PSYCHOLOGICAL NEEDS IN LIVING ARRANGEMENTS

PHYSICAL NEEDS

The house temperature should be comparatively even from floor to ceiling because poor circulation makes the elderly person especially sensitive to chilling.

The elderly person needs large windows to ensure plenty of light because of the gradual impairment of his vision.

Provisions should be made for the safety of the elderly person. He should have to climb few steps and floors should be unwaxed.

There should be adequate space for indoor and outdoor recreation, a condition best met in multiple housing developments or homes for the aged.

Noise should be controlled, especially during the night. This can be done by locating the elderly person's sleeping quarters in a quiet part of the house.

The elderly person should have laborsaving devices, especially for cooking and cleaning.

The living quarters should be on one floor to avoid possible falls on steps.

PSYCHOLOGICAL NEEDS

The elderly person should have at least one small room of his own so that he can have an opportunity for privacy. The living arrangements should include space for sedentary recreations, such as reading and television watching.

There should be provision for storage of cherished possessions.

The elderly person should live close to stores and community organizations so that he can be independent in his activities, and he should also be near relatives and friends so that frequent contacts are possible.

From Hurlock, E.B. Developmental psychology (5th ed.). New York: McGraw-Hill Book Co., 1982.

Mobility and the retired

The idea that retired people generally move to warmer climates, to more convenient locations, or to places near their children may be a myth. The U.S. Bureau of Census (1979a) reported that approximately four out of every five Americans 65 years or older remain in the same residence. Most older couples have positive feelings toward their neighborhoods and like their homes a great deal. They also have an unwillingness to face adjustment problems associated with moving. If relocation does take place, it is based on the pull of the new environment rather than on dissatisfaction with previous living arrangements (Kahana, 1982). Retired people generally move to mobile homes estates, senior citizen hotels, or retirement communities.

PSYCHOLOGICAL VARIATIONS IN OLD AGE

The study of psychological and personality changes in the retired and the aged is both perplexing and difficult. The state of the art is such that very little is known about how to measure psychological characteristics and changes. Even less is known about the dimensions, attributes, and variances that make up personality dynamics and traits. So it is a matter of groping in the dark, coming up with a tidbit here and a tidbit there, but not being certain of what you really have or are dealing with. Nevertheless, it is important to make a start and, inconclusive and unsubstantiated as it may be, it is a beginning at evolving a scientific concept of the parameters of personality. In reference to the aged, it is important to know about the psychological changes that are taking place because, for most, it is a period of uncertainty and change, and the strength and adaptability of the entire personality structure and its well-being are being tested.

Role changes and needs

Older people frequently need tangible relationships and experiences that will bolster their waning ego and provide them with evidence that will help them to sustain their identity. Changes in ego, as the result of aging, lead some older people to seek new sources of gratification to shore up their declining self-esteem. They are essentially seeking the love, respect, and recognition that they often have difficulty receiving from other people. These needs become intensified at a time when their availability is diminished. Older people face a variety of challenges in their struggle to maintain a positive self-identity. They usually receive little psychological support from society in this struggle because society, as a whole, knows little about the needs of the elderly and even less about what to do about them.

As the person changes intellectually and physically, so does personality change. Elderly people who are in contact with reality can easily see that younger people are taking the place in the world that their generation formerly occupied. They also realize that they are now dependent on the younger person, whereas the younger person was once dependent on them. As their sensory acuity deteriorates, their effective contacts with the outside world are reduced. Many of their friends are suffering with debilitating diseases or are dead, and thus the older persons find themselves lonely, isolated, and often preoccupied with themselves and with small matters that are of no consequence.

Neugarten and Gutmann (1968) found that, regardless of social class, older men and women see themselves as reversing their roles in family authority. Many individuals over 65 years of age *think* of an older man as being submissive, whereas they *think* of the older woman as being dominant and an authority figure.

Substantial evidence suggests that men come to recognize and accept more of their affiliative and emotional needs later in life, while women exhibit more instrumental, aggressive behaviors. Sex roles crossover appears to be taking place. Longitudinal and cross-cultural studies support this observation (Gutmann, D.L., 1977). Of course, the degree to which these changes occur depends on the characteristics of the individuals. Often there is simply a matter of sharing more in decision making, with the woman in a couple taking the initiative in carrying out the decision. There are some cases where the wife, in a quiet, subtle way, is the acknowledged authority figure and decision maker. The husband will not take the initiative or make a decision unless "Mother" approves the action. "What do you think, Mother, shall we buy this one?"

In terms of perceived goals and self-concept, there are differences between the generations. Ahammer and Baltes (1972) found that middle-aged adults were more concerned about achievement than were young adults and the elderly. Both the early and late adult groups were more concerned with affiliation. All three groups wanted to be providing for themselves and to be autonomous. The early and middle-aged adult groups, however, saw the elderly as being more nurturing and less independent than the older adults actually wanted to be. Also, the self-concept of older people differed between (1) what they desired for themselves and (2) the self-concept they actually had of themselves, as changes in health and social roles made them less independent. Older people also tend to cling to views they have had of themselves when they were younger. As Atchley (1972) points out, older people continue to think of themselves as the skilled workers or the professionals they had been, or as someone who always "walked five blocks downtown, twice a day," with the assumption they should still be able to do as they did before.

The essential psychological task of the ego is to aid the individual in adapting to new roles in life; it also strives to cope with progressive losses caused by aging, such as loss of physical capabilities, loss of modes by which basic drives are satisfied, loss of status in a culture oriented to the future and to youth, and some loss of social attractiveness.

Changes in personality

For many years the Committee on Human Development at the University of Chicago (also known as the Chicago group) studied questions related to personality changes associated with chronological age in the latter part of life. These studies were known as the Kansas City Studies of Adult Life because the field work was carried out in Kansas City. A series of investigations of the social and psychological aspects of middle age and aging, involving over 700 men and women, were carried out for over 15 years. This work has resulted in a sociopsychological theory of aging (the disengagement theory) and has laid the groundwork for a number of studies regarding personality changes by other investigators.

Bernice L. Neugarten (1972), one of the Chicago group, did a series of studies related to inner-life processes. She focused on the individual's perception of and styles of coping with the inner world of experiences. The *inner world of experiences* refers to what individuals think about themselves, their lives, their work. It is a matter of "what's on my mind—what I am experiencing inside of me." Neugarten found that 40-year-olds saw the environment as a place of rewarding boldness and risk-taking and saw themselves as being capable of meeting the opportunities of the outer world. Sixty-year olds saw the environment as complex and dangerous and the self as conforming to outer-world demands. As a person grew older, different modes of dealing with impulse life became obvious.

Older individuals became increasingly self-occupied by focusing many of their thoughts on themselves and their needs. Preoccupation with the inner life became greater; the directing of emotional energy toward persons and objects in the outer world seemed to decrease; the readiness to attribute activity and affect to persons in the environment was reduced; and, in general, there was a movement away from outer-world to inner-world orientation (Neugarten, 1977). These decreases began in the late 40s and 50s.

Differences between the sexes appear with age. Aging men seem to move from active involvement with the world to more introversive, passive, and self-centered positions. Women, however, move in the opposite direction, from passive mastery to active involvement, and they become more domineering. Thus these characteristics verify the sexual role reversal mentioned earlier. Men become more ***nurturant*** (wanting to provide care to the young and to the weak and incapable), and women grow more aggressive and egocentric. In both sexes, however, older people move toward more eccentric, self-preoccupied behavior. They want to be more in charge of controlling and satisfying their personal needs.

nurturant **supportive—involving warmth and involvement (personal love and compassion).**

There is no general decrease in competency of performance of adult social skills nor any decline of social interaction until the mid 60s or early 70s. It is true that as people get older they may give up various role responsibilities with relative ease and remain highly content with life. Some show a drop in life satisfaction as they experience a drop in social interaction, but others who had been content with a low level of activity in younger years tend to remain content in later years with a small amount of social participation.

TABLE 16-6 Personality types, activity, and life satisfaction

Personality type	*Life-style*	*Activity*	*Degree of life satisfaction*
Integrated	Reorganizers	Competent, engaged, and involved; substitutes new activities for old	High
	Focused	Integrated personality, moderately active, centered in one or two role areas	High
	Disengaged	Low levels of activity and role involvement, reduced role commitment, high self-esteem	High
Armored-defended	Holding on	Holds on to midlife roles and activities; when successful, maintains adequate levels of life satisfaction	High
	Constricted	Low to medium involvement in a few role areas; preoccupied with losses and deficits	High to medium
Passive-dependent	Succor-seeking	Medium to high activity levels; if successful at gaining attention from others, maintains adequate levels of life satisfaction	Medium
	Apathetic	Low role activity; does not expect much from or give much to life; passive	Medium to low
Unintegrated	Disorganized	Deteriorated cognitive processes, poor emotional control	Low

Modified from Neugarten, B.L., Havighurst, R.J., & Tobin, S.S. Personality and patterns of aging. In B.L. Neugarten (Ed.), Middle age and aging. Chicago: The University of Chicago Press, 1968.

activity theory an aging theory which indicates that older individuals who remain active and involved are less likely to age than their withdrawn counterparts.

disengagement theory a social theory of aging which suggests that the older person disengages from society and society also moves from the individual. This break is thought to be necessary to maintain satisfaction in late adulthood.

Neugarten, Havighurst, and Tobin (1968) refer to eight different patterns of aging that they observed emerging in a group of 70- to 79-year-olds. They named these categories of behavior patterns the Reorganizers, the Focused, the Disengaged, the Holding-on, the Constricted, the Succorance-seeking, the Apathetic, and the Disorganized. These life-style behavior patterns are described in Table 16-6.

The implication of all of these studies on personality changes is that individual differences do abound in old age, even though there are some general characteristics or patterns of old age that are different from those exhibited at a younger age.

Disengagement theory versus activity

Two theories have speculated on the reasons why people curtail their activities as they get old. One view is called the ***activity theory*** or social needs theory (Maddox, 1968). This point of view implies that older people have essentially the same psychological and social needs as do middle-aged people, except for needs brought on by changes in physiological makeup and health. As a person gets older, society withdraws or pulls away from that person, causing decreased social interaction. Although the older person does not want this to happen, society backs off.

In the past the activity theory received limited empirical support and has been criticized as an oversimplification of the question (Hendricks, and Hendricks, 1977). However, Palmore (1979), using data from the Duke Longitudinal Study of Aging, presents findings supporting the activity theory. He defined successful aging as "survival to age 75 with good health and happiness." Palmore found that two of the strongest predictors of successful aging for both men and women were group activity and physical activity.

The ***disengagement theory*** states that there is decreased social interaction but that *both* society and the aging person withdraw. There is a mutual involvement in lessening the degree of interaction. Older people no longer desire the deeper emotional involvement in activities and relationships that they had in middle age. Cumming and Henry (1961), who first set forth the disengagement theory, also believed that as older persons disengaged themselves from outer world social interaction, they developed a better sense of psychological well-being. The studies of the Chicago group found that this last assumption was not necessarily so and that great diversity in individual differences existed.

Neugarten and co-workers (1968) concluded that personality organization or personality type was the crucial factor in predicting which individuals would age successfully. They also found that the ability to adapt to biological and social changes was paramount in determining the degree of life satisfaction. Aging is not a leveler of individual differences. Psychological disengagement seems to precede social disengagement.

If an individual has been active, involved, and satisfied throughout life and if the environment continues to provide opportunities for similar involvement, then there is life satisfaction in old age (Neugarten and Hagestad, 1976). Older people choose to pursue activities that are of importance to them and drop those that have lost significance. It is not the quantity of activities or the number of roles that determines satisfaction but the quality of participation. The most important problems arise not when older people decline to participate in some activities but when social conditions and circumstances make it impossible for them to pursue the kind of life they want (Lowenthal et al., 1975). In terms of morale, readiness for disengagement is more significant than age, sex, or current social interaction.

Loneliness and depression

The older person is often a lonely person. Most people 70 years or older are widowed, single, or divorced. Individuals who have been single throughout life will not experience as much loneliness because they have been accustomed to being alone, but people who were married early in life and enjoyed love, devotion, and constant companionship will have a different reaction. If a loved one has died, this results in a sense of loneliness that seems unbearable; the years ahead seem full of nothing but emptiness, unless of course the person can grasp reality and adjust to it. In later years, even in

Depression and loneliness are fairly common complaints among older adults. Depression is sometimes misdiagnosed as senility because the person makes no responses. Loneliness is a problem often caused by isolation in living arrangements.

cases when both spouses are alive, an elderly person will show a certain amount of depression and moodiness.

The psychological aspect of depression is, sadly, a part of the life of many elderly people. Concerned with themselves, depressed people lack suitable judgment of their own self-worth. *Depression* in old age may be evident by feelings of uselessness, of loneliness, of being a burden, of hopelessness, and too often, of being unneeded. Depression is often accompanied by regressive behavior; it also shows somatic symptoms of fatigue, loss of appetite and weight, constipation, insomnia, and dryness of the mouth. This is an extremely important point to remember because many so-called losses of health could be a result of the individual's state of depression rather than an organic disorder.

Symptoms of depression are probably the most common psychiatric complaint among older adults (Butler and Lewis, 1977). The importance of attending to depressive symptoms among the elderly is underscored by the high rate of suicides among older adults,

reactive depression a state of depression that has presumably come about because of changes in the environment, sometimes known as exogenous depression.

especially white males. The suicide rate (per 100,000) is 39.4 for white males, the highest for any age level for males (Vital Statistics of the United States, 1977). The rate is 11.8 for nonwhite males, 8.5 for white females, and 3.0 for nonwhite females. The depressed person tends to be morose, dependent, and demanding, thereby discouraging the very people who might be supportive. Family and friends do not enjoy being around a depressed person. Medications may be of some help in enabling an individual to overcome depressive behavior but, on the other hand, there are some medications, such as the antihypertensives, that contribute to depression (Salzman and Shader, 1979).

The elderly frequently suffer from ***reactive depression*** following the death of significant others or following a series of losses. Reactive depression is caused by some external situation. It is often diminished when the situation is resolved or when met with adjustment behavior. *Chronic depression,* in general, appears to be more prevelant than reactive depression (Epstein, 1976). Chronic depression is a persistent state of depression. There is also a *"masked" depression* commonly found in the elderly. In masked depression the elderly individual has somatic complaints, apathy, withdrawal, and functional slowness. Reluctance to respond to questions is frequently attributed to the "contrariness" of old age when this lack of communication is really a sign of significant depression (Levy et al., 1980).

AGING AND COGNITIVE ABILITIES

As Arenberg and Robertson-Tchabo (1977) state in their chapter in the book, *Handbook of the Psychology of Aging,* "If the adage, 'You can't teach an old dog new tricks,' was not buried in the previous handbook by Birren, the research reported since then should complete the interment." Researchers in the field are beginning to recognize the inadequacy of past research studies and are designing better research instruments.

Many earlier studies were done with institutionalized elderly, which could hardly be considered a typical or normal sample of the aged population. Current studies are finding that individual differences in learning and cognitive abilities are substantially influenced by such factors as intellectual level, educational status, physical condition, stimulating environment, and possibly, even the number of years left before death. The research in the area has narrowed from the use of gross variables, which covered too much territory, to more judicious specifics (Denney, 1982; Schaie et al., 1973). It is important to note that mental decline associated with old age may not be as great as was previously supposed.

Individual differences and cognition

It has been observed by lay people as well as researchers that, in general, the more that individuals involve themselves in stimulating learning and thinking situations and the more they use their minds and memories, the better and longer they will be able to learn, think, and remember (Denney, 1982). This notion has been substantiated by Eisdorfer and Lawton (1973) who concluded, after a review of studies made of intellectual changes in the aged, that those who continue to work or to interact with intellectually stimulating environments as they reach old age have more normal brain functioning and do better on intelligence tests than those who are inactive or unoccupied.

We have noticed this intellectual enhancement in elderly persons who, when in their late 70s and 80s, composed well-written papers for presentation to our Historical Society and to the Tuesday Club. Old people who watch and enjoy television game programs that involve some form of cognitive or informative involvement also appear to be mentally alert and interested in community and national affairs.

The amount of formal education (and in some cases, informal education) also appears to be instrumental in reducing the amount of decline in intellectual functional ability in the elderly. Selzer and Denney (1980) did a study of cognitive performance of the elderly on the Piagetian task of conservation. They tested the variables of age, sex, education, and residence (institutional versus community). They found that education was the only significant predictor of sustained intellectual ability among the middle-aged and elderly adults. The same type of emphasis has been given to the role of education by other researchers, including Granick and Friedman (1973), who found that performance in a

David Strickler

Normal brain functions in the elderly appear to deteriorate when the individuals are inactive and unoccupied for long periods of time. An active person usually remains an alert person until some extenuating factor enters the picture.

variety of intellectual tasks was modified by the level of education of the individuals in these studies. The age variable accounts for only about 25% of the variance in IQ test scores.

It would be misleading to say that there is no decline in intellectual functioning as age progresses. A survey of the literature by Denney (1982) revealed that both cross-sectional and longitudinal studies indicate that cognitive abilities exhibit age differences that are related to age changes. Cross-sectional and longitudinal studies differ in the age at which decline begins and the extent of the decline. Cross-sectional studies suggest that decline begins at an earlier age and is more extensive than is found in longitudinal studies. Some individuals show a great deal of change while others show little or no change.

Owens (1973) found that individuals with higher intellectual levels experienced relatively less decline in mental efficiency than those of lower levels. Studies of the gifted also reveal that for these individuals men-

sensory register the first stage in a three-process model of memory; in this stage information is registered automatically as an exact copy of the environment.

tal decline sets in much later than is generally surmised.

Mental changes in learning and memory

If intelligence is considered in terms of performances that require the use of long-term memory and the use of acquired verbal skills, there appears to be little decline in intellectual ability until after the age of 60 or 65 in healthy persons. In fact, acquired verbal skills (those that involve language skills and the use of long-established habits) reveal some increase in performance, a late peak, and high stability or slow decline. Often, the value of experience and knowledge are ignored when the intellectual competence of older persons is being evaluated.

If one defines intelligence in terms of a set of behaviors that reflect rapid responding and competency with problem-solving ability with an emphasis on visual-motor skills, older persons do not do as well as younger ones (Elias et al., 1977). It may be that these skills are not as important to the elderly adult as they are to the younger person. However, when time constraints are relaxed, elderly adults improve in performance. It is wise to remember, nevertheless, that older adults must still function in a world where rapid response and problem-solving ability are important.

Learning. Studies indicate that the ability to learn is approximately the same at the age of 80 years as it is at 12 years (Denny et al., 1979). If the aged want to learn, they can. Learning may be slower, but it can be accomplished. The Duke University Center for Study of Aging and Human Development (Wilkie and Eisdorfer, 1973) has exhaustively tested the learning ability of the aged. The researchers conclude that the aged can learn, but more slowly than the young. They state that the older person's goal is more to avoid failure than to gain success. However, certain changes in the brain can make a difference in thinking along the "flexibility-rigidity" continuum. The person becomes more rigid and less capable of doing the problem-solving reasoning that requires a broad dimension of thought.

An elderly person attacks a problem differently than a younger person, tending to refer back to previous personal experience in an attempt to solve problems. If this approach is appropriate, a person can cope effectively with the situation; but if it is inappropriate, the older person often misunderstands the problem and makes frequent mistakes because of misconceptions and misinterpretations. An older person adopts a literal instead of a hypothetical approach to solving problems with logical implications.

In training situations the older person seems to be more involved and shows more care and greater concentration than a younger person. In working to minimize the risk of error, the older person usually sacrifices speed to stress accuracy. There is a slowing down of mental action and sensorimotor speed because of delay within the central nervous system. The slower performance of the elderly on many tasks is not necessarily a result of loss of capacity for the task but, rather, of insufficient time for the slowed cognitive processes to be completed (Spirduso, 1975).

Memory. Lack of mental alertness is common in many older people. "I just can't remember anything. I am becoming so forgetful," say many elderly persons. There are two major reasons for this forgetfulness. First, it may be organically caused by a deterioration of the arteries, commonly called hardening of the arteries. When blood flow is impaired, the brain ceases to receive the nourishment necessary for effective functioning of cognitive processes. The other reason is an apparent loss of interest in current events. Also, older people take refuge in their memories of previous undertakings in which they were successful.

Consider the fact that older persons often have less to do in their everyday living. There are few major events or changes that take place in their world and, as a result, there is a great deal of "sameness" to each day. Consequently, one day flows into the next one without anything significant to differentiate them. There is very little worth remembering. Reminiscence of the past is more attractive. It is remembered. The immediate, dull affairs of the present time are not. It is no wonder that the most noticeable symptoms of mental decline in old age are the deterioration of memory for recent events and the gradual loss of power of attention.

Loss of memory ability in later life appears to be related to the input-output sequence (information processing) rather than to sensory registry or to primary memory. ***Sensory register*** refers to how well the sensory systems of vision, hearing, touch, taste, and smell can pick up related stimuli. Even though these systems

"Hi, Ralph, how's Peg?"

"Oh . . . about the same, I guess."

This dialogue has been rerun so many times that Ralph just answers automatically. The last time we repeated our lines, however, an additional comment was attached.

"Oh . . . about the same, I guess. But you know, I guess I'm going to have to give it all some more thought. She's really *not* the same. I don't know but what I should retire from my work to keep an eye on her."

Since I had already decided to write a profile about Peg, the discussion was pursued. "You're afraid to leave her alone for long periods of time?"

"Well, she's having a harder time caring for herself all day along. I'm concerned for her safety at this point."

It now becomes necessary to backtrack and consider the events leading to this conversation. The couple mentioned are in their late sixties. Seven years ago a very close and rich relationship began to change dimensions. At that time Peg was an amateur artist who painted landscapes in oil. A gift of her love and talent hangs in all the homes of her close friends. This was a talent that had emerged after years of being mother, church choir member, Sunday Church School teacher—always giving of herself—and once again doing this through her paintings.

One of Peg's greatest loves was the piano. She still plays well—anything from church hymns to honky-tonk or simple jazz. If she didn't have the music before her, she would play by ear or, better still, compose her own tunes. Many hours of singing around the piano fill Ralph's treasury of memories.

To put this all in perspective, seven years ago Peg's good health began to deteriorate. For years she had sought medical help from both an internal specialist and a general practitioner. She often took medicine from both doctors at the same time. However, at the time in question, Peg began to seek help from a third doctor and again took additional medicine. No one really knows what this combination of drugs or the effects of these self-administered dosages were, but a condition of hyperthyroidism developed. Soon after this, there appeared to be some brain damage occurring, so the thyroid medication was stopped.

The effects of the damage were gradual in appearance. At first Peg appeared to just be forgetful. She then began to overreact with emotional overlay in any group situation. She wept first with joy and then in despair on Sunday mornings during the worship services. Soon she had to stop attending.

Her daily life at home also began to change. No longer did she spend her days painting or doing the homemaking tasks which had occupied so much of her weekly routine. Instead, Ralph began to receive reports that Peg had been spotted driving all around the rural area of the county during the hours that he was at work. This continued up until the time that Peg had an accident at an intersection. Her injury was sufficient for Ralph to realize that she could no longer drive a car safely. Now, without a car, her days were to be filled with monotonous repetitious walking around the four rooms of the downstairs—counting each time she passed the hurricane lamp in the dining room. When she reached one thousand, she stopped to rest and sleep on the sofa.

Even this routine became boring to Peg, so she began to take outside walks. She didn't know how far to walk so she would count on her fingers when she had reached the end of a block. When she had counted five fingers, she knew it was time to turn around and return home.

Each day Peg stands at the window, waiting for Ralph to arrive and take her for their afternoon drive. This is a daily ritual which Ralph performs unselfishly in the late afternoon. In his words, "She looks forward to our ride through the mountains each day."

There aren't many visitors in the home these days. Peg is unaware of this. Ralph is lonely. Even the sons and grandchildren are becoming strangers in Peg's mind. She mutters, "I love all of you, but I just *can't* say your names." A church directory with pictures of the congregation is the only way she can match names and faces. A conversation during the visit is almost impossible, so Peg is usually asked to play some of her old favorites on the piano. Her fingers just fly over the familiar notes; one almost forgets that there has been any brain damage.

Ralph's concern with what he faces now involves Peg's inability to care for her daily needs during the hours that he is working. Although Ralph is past retirement age, he still chooses to maintain contact with his peers through his work at a local lumberyard. Each morning he faithfully does his exercises, keeping in good physical condition. Each day, adversely, Peg eats and continues to gain weight. Although Ralph attempts to regulate her diet, an older brother of Peg's brings her food which she hides from Ralph and eats during the day when she is alone.

The current medical diagnosis is now "hardening of the arteries." Peg is like a small child with an unpredictable next move. She can still make a bed and dust a table top, but gone are the skills of cooking, baking, and ironing. These are now the tasks to which Ralph must come home. His big question is "*When* must I begin to stay home?" At that point also begins the slow death of joy and contact in his own life.

primary memory conscious awareness of recently perceived events; identified by psychologist William James.

secondary memory recall of events that have left the consciousness, identified by psychologist William James.

may be less effective with age, they do not appear to affect memory loss (Botwinick, 1978). ***Primary memory*** is immediate or short-term recall, a response given without effort. It is a temporary maintenance system for conscious processing. A task of primary memory would be to repeat a series of digits or a set of words. Botwinick (1978) indicates that primary memory shows only slight differences between young and old subjects. ***Secondary memory,*** however, which involves the processing, storage, and retrieval of new information, does show a loss. Secondary memory is related to the permanent, long-term memory storage system. It has a semantic (language) content. The three-process model of memory, including the sensory register, primary memory, and secondary memory, is indicated in Fig. 16-2.

Performance on tests

In spite of the fact that an older person may score lower on intelligence tests than before, the ability to learn declines slowly in senescence. Age changes in the ability to learn are small under most circumstances. When differences do appear, they do not seem to be readily attributed to a change in the capacity to learn but rather to a change in the processes of perception, set, attention, motivation, and physiological condition of the individual, including disease states (Botwinick, 1977). As Botwinick indicates, "even slight alterations of optimum health of the elderly can adversely affect their intellectual functioning" (p. 194). Depression can also have a major impact on cognitive functioning.

Perceptual accuracy shows a decline in the older person and results from the decline of the peripheral sense organs. The motor skills deteriorate next, followed by intellectual functions. The elderly person is not as efficient intellectually as in earlier years.

During senescence, however, not all aspects of intellectual functioning decline at the same rate. In most cases the person's intelligent use of vocabulary and the recall of general information are not affected until the later years of senile decline. Verbal skills seem to dete-

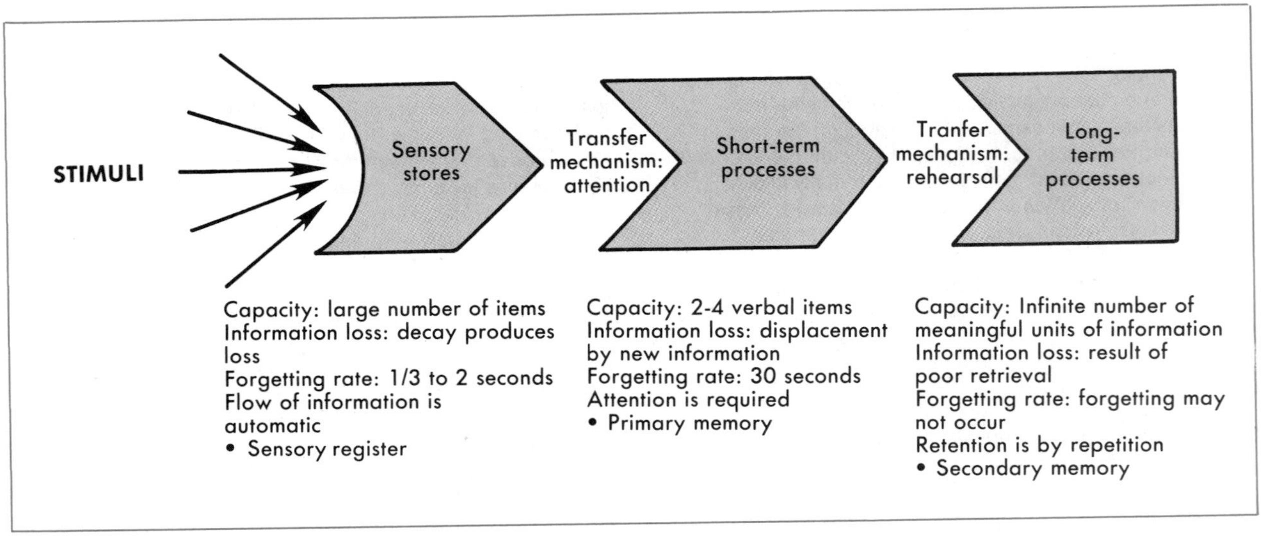

FIG. 16-2 ***Three-process model of memory and the way information is stored and retrieved.***
Compiled from Craik, 1977; Elias et al., 1977; Stevens-Long, 1979; Walsh, 1975.

riorate more slowly than mathematical skills. Judgment and imagination generally do not decline as rapidly as memory and attention. Little is known about the difference between men and women in the way the intelligence is affected by aging. Existing evidence suggests that the age changes are the same for both sexes (Turner, 1982).

In a 12-year study conducted by the National Institute of Health and the Philadelphia Geriatric Center (Birren et al., 1968) with regard to the correlation between intelligence and longevity, it was found that the subjects who lived longest functioned at a higher intellectual level than those who died before the study was completed. Of the original 47 volunteers, 23 survived until the end of the study with an average age of 81 years at that time. Intelligence tests used were the Wechsler Adult Intelligence Scale (WAIS) and the Raven Progressive Matrices Test. The researchers found "no significant decline" on the test performances and actually saw "significant increases in ability" for the vocabulary and picture arrangement subtests of the WAIS. Therefore, for these 47 men, survival seemed to be correlated with retention of intellectual vigor and capabilities.

Keeping active apparently is of vital importance not only for one's physiological well-being but also for helping to retain intellectual capabilities. The word *active* applies both to mental activity and to physical activity through a regular fitness routine.

Terminal drop

Retrospective analyses of test results suggest that certain test performance levels and changes in these levels over a period of time may be related to the closeness to death of the aged individual. The implication is that those elderly subjects who succumb to death before the others tend to be the ones who had the lowest test scores. This phenomenon is called terminal drop. The concept of ***terminal drop*** is defined as a decline in test performance some few years before death, a result perhaps of physiological deterioration or damage. In other words, age decline in test results is generally to be found in those test takers who are in the process of dying. The others, with longer lives to live, show little or no age decline. At the moment, these observations are still speculative.

The 12-year study conducted by Birren and associates (1968) is often cited in survival discussions because the elderly subjects who were involved in the study had extraordinarily good health. Five years after the initial testing, the survivors showed better scores in verbal information skills than those who subsequently died. The subjects were tested a third time and again there was a difference in the results.

terminal drop a significant decline in intellectual abilities that often precedes death.

Blum and co-workers (1973) found a correlation between the decline on three tests of cognitive functioning and mortality, although they were careful to say that the decline was not a predictor of mortality. These three tests are Digit Symbol, Similarities, and Vocabulary from the Wechsler Adult Intelligence Scale. Over a period of 10 years, an annual decrement rate of at least 2% on Digit Symbol, 10% on Similarities, or any decline on the Vocabulary test was associated with the subjects' death during the following 5 years. Further studies are needed to confirm these results.

WHEN A SPOUSE DIES

According to the U.S. Bureau of Census (1972), 25% of the women aged 60 to 64 are currently widows but only 6% of the men are widowers. Half of the women aged 70 to 74 are widows, while 85% of the women aged 85 and older are widows. Of the men 85 years of age and over only half are widowers.

Adjustment and change

Adjustment to the death of a spouse is especially difficult in old age because at this age all adjustments are increasingly difficult to make. The widow usually has a decreased income, necessitating giving up interests and certain social contacts, possibly moving to smaller quarters, or going to live with a child or in an institution. The widower may not have as serious an economic problem, but he will miss the care of a wife who provided him with companionship, cared for his needs, and managed the home. Men tend to be more reluctant to enter a home for the aged or move in with their children, so they frequently remarry in order to overcome loneliness and dependency problems. A number of older people find it impossible to deal with widowhood. It is not uncommon for an older widowed person to die soon after the spouse's death. Some commit suicide.

bereavement the state or fact of suffering because of the loss of a loved one by death.

It appears that women who are widowed do not experience the death of a spouse in the same way that men do. A study by Barrett (1978) of 403 community residents aged 62 and over found that widowers experienced lower morale, felt more lonely and more dissatisfied with life, needed more help with household chores, had greater difficulty getting medical appointments, ate more poorly, and had stronger negative attitudes about continued learning than widows. Widowers were also more reluctant to talk about widowhood and death than widows were. An analysis of national survey data by Arens (1979) indicated that among men the negative impact of widowhood was interpreted by low levels of social participation; among women, adverse effects of widowhood were interpreted by their low economic resources. Widows have far lower incomes than do widowers, especially in the working class (Atchley, 1980).

Bereavement and recovery process

The Harvard Bereavement Study (Glick et al., 1974), although dealing with middle-aged individuals who lost their spouses, gives some indication of the bereavement and recovery process after a death. The *initial phase* is one of shock and numbness. The immediate impact of ***bereavement*** was somewhat the same for both men and women in the sense of being overwhelmed, experiencing shock and anguish, and feeling that there were no limits to their suffering. The newly bereaved woman felt numb and seemed as if she could not move or she cried as if she could never stop. She reported a sense of abandonment, of being left alone. The husband who became a widower had the same feelings, but he reported a sense of dismemberment, as if "both my arms were cut off."

There were some differences encountered if the death was anticipated rather than sudden. One in five experienced a completely unexpected bereavement, by accident or a sudden coronary thrombosis, for example. Another 20% knew their husband was not in good health but did not expect death. The other 60% had known for some time that their spouses were seriously ill. Only in a few cases, however, did the women use this information as the basis for making plans for life as a widow. The women who anticipated the death felt pained and desolate when the death did come, but they also were better able to pull themselves together and to more quickly regain a relatively normal level of functioning.

The *second phase* is one of coping with anxiety and fear. Bewilderment and despair often continued after the first impact of death was experienced. Many physical symptoms appeared and lingered for weeks. Sleep disturbances were common and distressful. The widowers were more likely to be uncomfortable with direct emotional expression of their distress. They seemed to require more rational justification for their thoughts and feelings. Although less troubled by anger, as were the women, they did have difficulty with guilt about not doing as much as they could have to show their love or help their wives. Leave-taking ceremonies, as the funeral and memorial service, served the purpose of establishing the fact of death as an emotional reality for both the widowed person and the community. However, for widows the funeral was more of a milestone, whereas for many widowers it was a necessary involvement. The men were more concerned with how to manage in the months to come (Kastenbaum, 1981).

The *third phase,* the intermediate phase, is one of understanding death and seeking the presence of the deceased one. The type of emotional and social recovery from the impact of bereavement appeared to be related to the suddenness of the death, to the preparation for death, and to the quality of the marital relationship. Men seemed to make a quicker adjustment. Actually, their recovery was more social in nature than it was emotional. The widower who had not sought out female companionship a year after his wife's death was much more likely than the widow to feel lonely and depressed.

Parkes (1972) found that poor recovery by both men and women occurred if the death was sudden, as in cases of accidents or heart attacks. Poor recovery usually means being socially withdrawn or still preoccupied with the details of the death slightly more than a year after a death. Those who were most disturbed a few weeks after the death usually were the ones who continued to be disturbed a year or so later. The quality of the marital relationship also seemed related to the rapidity of recovery. Recovery was more difficult where there were mixed or ill feelings toward one another or where there was a clinging, dependency relationship.

The *fourth phase,* the recovery phase, usually occurs during the second year. In recovery, the widowed person must develop a new social identity and learn to relate to other people differently, especially people of the opposite sex (Kimmell, 1974). It is a time of learning to live alone. Friends and relatives mean well but they can only do so much. After a while they drift back into their life patterns and find it difficult to be as attentive to the bereaved as they would like to be. There is a need for social adjustment for both the bereaved and his or her friends and family. In the final analysis, sooner or later, the widowed person will have to reach out to others for social interaction. If it is offensive to their sense of values to be with the opposite sex, then at least they should reach out to contact members of their own sex.

Remarriage

According to Butler and Lewis (1973), despite the fact that women over 65 years of age outnumber men by 3 million, there are more than twice the number of men remarrying as there are women of that age-group who remarry. Several factors are part of this phenomenon. To begin with, if every elderly single man were to remarry or even marry for the first time, there would still not be enough men for all the available women. Second, there seems to be an unfortunate cultural bias against elderly widows getting remarried, especially if they remarry "too soon" after their spouses die (Black, 1977). The bias seems to rationalize itself around the idea that "I have too much respect for my late husband to ever let anyone replace him in my love life." Right or wrong, for better or for worse,

David Strickler

Companionship is considered one of the most rewarding aspects of a marriage relationship. It is no wonder that a number of older individuals decide to remarry after their spouses have died. Men are more likely to remarry than women.

such ideas do keep some individuals, both men and women, from getting remarried. Occasionally the individual involved does not hold too strongly to the idea, but the important (significant) people left in the widowed person's life have that view and the widowed individual is hesitant to go against the bias of the group.

The third factor restricting or inhibiting the remarriage of the elderly is, again, a cultural bias in terms of how long a person should wait before getting remarried. It appears that it is socially more acceptable for a widower than it is for a widow to remarry after about a year's time. Widowers rarely wait more than a year or so before remarrying. McKain (1972) found that widows are more likely to take their time, usually about 7 years. McKain also found that over half of the older people who remarry have known their new spouses for a long time before being widowed. In many cases they have known these individuals for most of their lives, were already related by marriage, were childhood sweethearts, or were simply old friends and neighbors. Considering the companionship, joy, and comfort that two people can bring to each other when they share a common life space or home, and considering the relatively short number of surviving years that remain, it seems somewhat cruel to have a criterion based on "what others think" to prohibit, postpone, or delay a marriage of two elderly persons capable of contributing to a meaningful relationship. McKain (1972) found that most couples who marry late in life have highly successful marriages. The decision of remarriage or not should be left primarily to the couple rather than to the consent and approval of others, such as the children. However, it is true that each group of concerned and involved individuals must work out their own decisions.

There is an emergence of alternatives to marriage on the part of some of the elderly. The usual alternative is simply living together without the benefit of a legal recording of the marriage (Glick, 1975). We do not know to what an extent such a living arrangement would, under the differing laws of the various states, eventually constitute a "common law" marriage, with all the legal rights pertaining thereto. The major reason for this type of a living-in arrangement is mostly financial. That is, one of the individuals would lose a source of income, such as income from a trust, a pension fund of the deceased spouse, or Social Security benefits. The reduction in income for the couple could make it difficult to live comfortably or adequately on the income of just one person.

Another alternative life-style is a form of communal living where several older people, sometimes including married couples, group together to share living expenses and living quarters. We are not aware of any research done on these living arrangements. These groups do not exist in sufficiently large numbers to provide adequate research data. We do believe that eventually some type of acceptable arrangements should be made to care for the lonely, the impoverished, and the ailing elderly.

DEATH AND DYING

In considering death and dying, the matter of individual differences once again is important. Some people truly seem to be unconcerned. They "trust in the Lord" and have faith that, no matter how they die, after death (in Heaven) they will not only be reunited with loved ones who have "gone before" but will see God "face to face." Others regard this view as scientifically and intellectually unrealistic, and they matter-of-factly (and without fear) insist that the only life human beings have is here on earth. Some individuals, usually those who have seen loved ones suffer in their last days, state that they are not afraid of death itself but are afraid of the event of dying. Still others, who may not fear the act of dying, have a fear of the cessation of life. They dread the thought of nothingness, of ceasing to exist, of being in everlasting, dreamless sleep.

Death and dying is a universal phenomenon. Yet it is described in many ways. As Kalish (1976) states, "Death is a biological event, a rite of passage, an inevitability, a natural occurrence, a punishment, an extinction, the enforcement of God's will . . . separation, reunion and a time for judgment. It is disruption of the social fabric by removing a significant person from the scene . . ." (p. 483).

Concerns with death

Death is a difficult concept for young adults to comprehend. They think of death occasionally but do not linger on the thought. They can appreciate traumatic deaths, brought on by accidents, but deaths caused by illness or organic failures seem to be something that happens only to "older people." In middle adulthood the notion of death comes closer to home. Few adults in their forties or fifties will not have experienced the death of at least one of their parents. Forty-year-old people frequently read in the papers about someone not many years older than themselves who died; at 50 years they are surprised at how many people their age and younger have died.

Men and women appear to respond differently to the issue of death. Men tend to react with hostility and anger when they realize that illness, decline, and death are realities in their personal lives; women feel less conflict about accepting their own ultimate destiny (Mann, 1980). In late adulthood the elderly are concerned to realize how many friends and associates are dying; for some, this notion may become phobic.

The first thing many older adults read in the newspaper is the obituary column. We recall an elderly person telling us, "You know, of all the charter members of the church, there are only five of us left"; later, "Now there are only two of us left"; finally, "I am the only surviving member that helped found this church." This kind of a realization must have some emotional impact on the individual. The interesting thing is that, in spite of these thoughts, most older people continue to make the most of their days as best they can.

Lieberman (1967) found that death as a salient theme only occurs frequently when the aged individual is within close proximity to death, not throughout all of old age. Elderly people living in a stable environment approach death as if they had made peace with many issues, including death. These people do not have a denial or avoidance attitude toward death. On the other hand, persons living in unstable settings regard death as a disruption. They view the approach of death more anxiously and have not formulated any personal philosophy to deal with it. Death is not a prime issue of the very aged.

Weisman and Kastenbaum (1968), reporting on the psychological autopsies of 100 cases, indicated that the commonly held assumption that old people lose contact with reality when they are dying is a fallacy. The behavior and conversation of most of these persons seemed to be influenced by the recognition of impending death and by an attitude of acceptance or readiness.

Hospice care

In our travels in the Orient, we recall seeing "homes for the dying," places where the terminally ill were taken to spend their last days. Members of the family could be in attendance; frequently, it was the family members who provided the necessary care as they could. Our first reaction was one of "how different," but it soon turned into "how considerate" for everyone involved. The dying person was treated well in the last moments. The burden and concern of care in the home was lessened. People who were dying knew their condition and wanted to die with dignity.

hospice care lodging or care for the dying and the family, providing for psychological as well as physical needs.

The ***hospice care*** program as it is conducted in Europe, the United States, and Canada, seeks to turn the experience of death, still a tragedy, into a positive experience. The hospice program attempts to help families with the physical and emotional demands of taking care of a dying family member at home. With the assistance of visiting nurses and other caretakers, family members are taught how to administer drugs and physical therapy and how to do simple medical procedures. The object is not to cure (although there certainly is no rejection of or objection to a cure). The objective is to make the terminally ill individual as comfortable as possible while helping the family members.

The open acceptance of death as a natural occurrence and the belief that a person's last days can still be "quality time" apparently has an enormous appeal. The hospice movement was begun in England. The first hospice in America was started in 1974; by 1983 there were 800 (Cunningham, 1983). The growth of the movement is partly a result of the realization that a hospice is not a place "to which you transfer a person to die." Hospice care is directed at meeting the emotional, as well as the physical, needs of both the patient and the family. This care and direction can be attended to in the home. In many cases the contact person with the family is a trained volunteer who can provide answers and information as well as supportive care. In a hospice program, the caregiver who was present at the time of diagnosis usually continues as the family support person. When the family members feel totally helpless, they have someone to turn to for direction and help. Often it is the dying person who simply wants to talk with a sympathetic person. Many dying individuals have a sense of helplessness, a feeling of unrelatedness, a lack of control, and an overwhelming sense of loss (Nash, 1977). Volunteer hospice workers may employ relaxation techniques to reduce anxiety and pain, or they may encourage discussion of the individual's fear of death. At times the volunteers work in helping an entire family to cope with the fact that one of them is about to die.

What makes hospice care far more significant than

comprehensive home care is its attempt to meet the emotional, spiritual, and economic needs of the family (Saunders, 1976). The family, not just the dying member, is viewed as the unit of care. More than two thirds of the people in the United States die outside the home, in contrast with about 50% only 30 years ago. Yet patients often prefer to spend their last days at home in a familiar environment. For those who must spend their last days away from the home, the hospice center can still provide special care. Hospice care is not so much a place as it is an attitude. It can be provided in nursing homes and hospitals by giving support, comfort, and dignity to the dying individual (Butler, 1978-1979).

Several authorities have found that the dying elderly are not afraid of dying and death. Cicely Saunders (1976) of St. Joseph's Hospice in London (a lodging for the terminally ill), although acknowledging the fact that every case is different, insists that most deaths come quietly and peacefully. When other terminally ill patients see this occurring to those about them, they become relieved of their own anxieties and are able to discuss death openly and without fear. Saunders believes that (1) the patient should not be in pain—it should always be controlled, (2) the physician and others should be ready to discuss dying and death when the patient wishes it, (3) the patient must always be aware of "personal, caring contact," and (4) when death comes, it should be with dignity, and the patient should not be alone.

Kübler-Ross: The dying experience

Undoubtedly, as more and more people live longer lives, researchers will continue to try to learn more about death and dying and what can be done to make the final phase of life less fearsome and more natural. Elisabeth Kübler-Ross (1969), whose seminars on death at the University of Chicago have attracted much attention, expresses the view that the terminally ill can teach people much about the anxieties, fears, and hopes in the last stages of life. In her seminars dying patients are interviewed, and their responses and needs are noted and evaluated.

Kübler-Ross (1974) states unequivocally that patients who are terminally ill should be told that they are seriously ill. They should then be given hope immediately by being told of all the treatment possibilities. Patients are given straightforward answers if they ask for specifics. However, they are not told that they are dying or that they are terminally ill; they are told that everything humanly possible will be done to help them. No judgment is given as to the length of time until death.

According to Kübler-Ross, patients go through five stages or ways of responding to the prospects of death and the miseries of dying. Individuals vary as to the rate at which they go through these stages. Some people may skip some of the stages, some do not make it through all of the stages, and others move back and forth through the stages. The five "stages" should not be thought of as a sequential phenomenon but rather as coping mechanisms that people use when confronted with the shocking, unexpected news of their own death and dying. These coping mechanisms deal with feelings and behaviors of patients who made the best adjustment in finally accepting their own death.

Denial is the first stage. For most patients, the initial reaction to news of their terminal condition is one of shock and disbelief. It is a denial, a saying "No!" to the thought of death. Many feel a mistake has been made. Some seek a second opinion or continue their medical searching until they receive a more favorable diagnosis. Others turn to religion for help and reassurance. Some look for "miracle cures." Once the idea of death is accepted as a definite possibility, anxiety, distress, and anger are usually expressed.

Anger is the second stage. This stage is one of anger, resentment, and envy. During this time the patient is saying, "Why me?" or "Why am I to die?" Rage and hostility may be directed at members of the medical team, friends, family, anything or anyone, even God. Frustration is expressed at not being able to complete plans or goals. Once the anger subsides, the person seeks to make a bargain with fate.

Bargaining is the third stage. The patient seems to be looking for a way to gain more time. "Just let me live long enough to see my daughter get married" or "I will be a better person. I will devote my life to helping others." The person may try to make a deal with God or the medical staff. Kübler-Ross indicates that such bargains are seldom kept; the person who outlives a bargain (such as living long enough to see a daughter married) seeks to make a new bargain.

Depression is the fourth stage. This stage is characterized by grief. The person experiences a feeling of hopelessness, increasing weakness, or physical deterioration. The symptoms are too obvious to ignore. Feelings of guilt (about letting family members down) or shame (at not being able to accept impending death) are frequently experienced. Kübler-Ross suggests that by permitting patients to express their grief and communicate it to others, they eventually come to accept the coming of death and develop a sense of calmness about it.

Acceptance is the last stage. Acceptance represents the end of the struggle to overcome or by-pass death. It is not necessarily a blissful or happy state, but it is a recognition of the end and is accepted without anger, despair, or remorse. It is not resignation; it is quiet expectation.

Critique. Kastenbaum (1981) has some friendly reservations about the Kübler-Ross stage theory of dying. He points out that knowing the five stages is not the equivalent of knowing what the dying process is all about. More significantly, the stage theory is just a theory, he says, and it must not be used as objective truth to determine what should or should not be done with a dying patient. Kastenbaum believes that more evidence is needed to demonstrate the existence of the stages and of movement through the stages. He does praise Kübler-Ross for her work and believes it is a good basis on which to build a more comprehensive understanding of the nature of death and dying. He believes that Kübler-Ross's work has helped to bring the topic of death out of the "conspiracy of silence" and into the open, to the benefit of all concerned—especially to students of medicine, theology, sociology, psychology, and therapy.

Pattison (1977) suggests a phase theory as an alternative approach to the Kübler-Ross concept of stages of dying. He states that there are three phases in the dying process. First, there is the *acute crisis phase.* This phase is a crisis event when the individual becomes aware of impending death. There are high levels of anxiety, denial, and anger. The individual may even seek to bargain.

As the individual adjusts to the idea of being gravely ill, there is a reduction in anxiety and the second phase, the *chronic living-dying phase,* begins. In this phase a variety of feelings are usually experienced. There may be fear of the unknown, fear of loneliness, and anticipatory grief over the loss of friends, of identity, of body, and of self-control (Pattison, 1977). The dominating feeling is grief. Levels of anxiety and sorrow may alternate, or they may coexist with hope, determination, and acceptance (Shneidman, 1973).

The third phase, the *terminal phase,* begins when the individual starts to withdraw from people, objects, and events in the world. This phase is the shortest. It is ended by death.

Living will. There is no one best way to die. Each person is different. What is desired is an appropriate death and a death with dignity. The expectations of the patient should receive major consideration (Weisman, 1972). The ethical question of sustaining life by "heroic measures" (at all costs, in all ways) or simply providing "comfort measures" until nature works its course toward death has not been, and may never be, resolved for society at large. Some individuals are making their own requests as to how they want to be treated should desperate medical measures be needed to prolong a life that would otherwise be terminal. They express their wishes by the use of a ***living will*** (Fig. 16-3).

life after death the experience of clinical death and then a return to life; descriptive accounts of this interim are very similar.

living will a legal document, signed while a person is healthy, which states that the individual does not wish to be kept alive by artificial means.

What is it like to die?

There is increasing interest in the phenomenon referred to as ***life after death*** or a "personal glimpse at the other side." Raymond A. Moody, Jr., M.D. (1975), in his medical experience observed over 150 cases of survival after "bodily death": people who were resuscitated after being pronounced clinically dead; people who came very close to physical death in the course of accidents, severe injury, or illness; and people who, as they died, told of their experience to others. Moody noted that the experiences of dying of these individuals had a striking similarity in their accounts.

There were a number of elements that recurred again and again, not in the same words or form but at least the same in principle. In general, the most common element in the near death experience was (1) language difficulty in describing what happened to them. Words were inadequate to describe what was experienced. Other elements were (2) the effect of hearing the news of being pronounced dead, or nearly so, when the others did not know the person could hear, (3) a pleasant feeling of peace and quiet during the early stages of their near-death experience, often reported by people saved at the last moment from drowning, (4) in many cases, various auditory sensations, such as buzzing noises or music were noted, (5)

TO MY FAMILY, MY PHYSICIAN, MY LAWYER, MY CLERGYMAN
TO ANY MEDICAL FACILITY IN WHOSE CARE I HAPPEN TO BE
TO ANY INDIVIDUAL WHO MAY BECOME RESPONSIBLE FOR MY HEALTH, WELFARE, OR AFFAIRS

Death is as much a reality as birth, growth, maturity and old age—it is the one certainty of life. If the time comes when I, ______________________________, can no longer take part in decisions for my own future, let this statement stand as an expression of my wishes, while I am still of sound mind.

If the situation should arise in which there is no reasonable expectation of my recovery from physical or mental disability, I request that I be allowed to die and not be kept alive by artificial means or "heroic measures." I do not fear death itself as much as the indignities of deterioration, dependence, and hopeless pain. I, therefore, ask that medication be mercifully administered to me to alleviate suffering even though this may hasten the moment of death.

This request is made after careful consideration. I hope you who care for me will feel morally bound to follow its mandate. I recognize that this appears to place a heavy responsibility upon you, but it is with the intention of relieving you of such responsibility and of placing it upon myself in accordance with my strong convictions that this statement is made.

Signed ______________________________

Date ______________________________

Witness ______________________________

Witness ______________________________

Copies of this request have been given to ______________________________

____

____

FIG. 16-3 *Courtesy Euthanasia Educational Council, 250 West 57th St., New York, NY 10019; 1980.*

often in concurrence with the noise was a sensation of being pulled very rapidly through a dark space of some kind, such as a dark tunnel, a void, or an enclosure.

Another element was (6) an out-of-body experience, wherein the person, looking down at his or her own physical body, saw those who were trying to help. This phenomenon was reported by many individuals. Quite a few told of (7) becoming aware of the presence of spiritual beings trying to help them or, in the case of a few, telling them that their time had not come to die yet and to go back. One of the most incredible com-

Harold Geyer

"The day will bring some lovely thing,"
I say it over each new dawn:
"Some gay, adventurous thing to hold
Against my heart when it is gone."
And so I rise and go to meet
The day with wings upon my feet.

I come upon it unaware—
Some sudden beauty without name:
A snatch of song—a breath of pine—
A poem lit with golden flame;
High tangled bird notes—keenly thinned—
Like flying color on the wind.

No day has ever failed me quite—
Before the grayest day is done,
I come upon some misty bloom
Or a late line of crimson sun.
Each night I pause—remembering
Some gay, adventurous lovely thing.

Author Unknown

mon elements, certainly one that had a profound effect on the individual, was (8) an encounter with a white or clear light that became very bright. Not one person who experienced this phenomenon expressed any doubt that it was a personal being of light. Often with the light there was a nonjudgmental probing effect that resulted in (9) a panoramic review of one's life. The review frequently occurred after the presence of the light.

A few persons described (10) a border or a limit of some kind, a line beyond which there would be no return to life. After encountering this depth in the near-death experience, (11) the person did come back, although a number said "I never wanted to leave" or "I am not ready to cross over." After the return there was (12) no doubt of the reality of the experience and its importance, (13) an effect on the lives involved, usually a change that took a subtle, quiet form, and (14) new views of death, usually containing no fear of death. There were a number of (15) corroborations of the feelings experienced by those who had near-death experiences. These corroborations were usually of the sort experienced in elements 2 and 6, where people were involved in "telling the news" or "working on the patient" while the patient was having an out-of-body experience.

Is this what dying is like? Of course it is difficult to say. But people involved in near-death experiences seldom, if ever, are skeptical of the existence of life after death. They also seem to have less fear of death.

Coming to terms with death

Not everyone can come to terms with death as did Abraham Maslow. He had just finished an important piece of work when he suffered a near-fatal heart attack, and in discussing it afterward he stated that since he had really "spent" himself and had done the best he could do, it would have been a good time to die— a "good ending." He believed that his life after that was a bonus, and everything—flowers, babies, friendships, the very act of living—became more beautiful; he had a "much-intensified sense of miracles." Maslow (1969), who was President of the American Psychological Association in 1968, stated in the last tape recording that he made just before his death: "If you're reconciled with death or even if you are pretty well assured that you will have a good death, a dignified one, then every single moment of every single day is transformed because the pervasive undercurrent—the fear of death—is removed."

Through understanding, growth, and participation the healthy aging person can attain a stature, intellectually and spiritually, that can bring fulfillment in the evening of life. Research shows that elderly persons increase in favorable attitudes toward religion as they grow older. As a person's age increases past 65 years, the time spent listening to church services or watching religious programs on television increases. More blacks attend church and participate in church-related activities than do the white elderly (Hirsch et al., 1968). Attending church and reading the Bible weekly increases up to the age of 80 years, declining somewhat thereafter. This decline is not a result of lack of interest but of the decline of physical powers, which limit mobility and amount of reading. As a person grows older, there is an increase in the feelings of security afforded by religion, especially among women (Britton and Britton, 1972). Death can be considered the final stage of growth or the beginning stage of a new life, depending on your view.

CHAPTER REVIEW

1. The *demography* (study of characteristics of the population) of old age indicates that 11.3% of the people in the United States are 65 years of age and over. The percentage is increasing. Of this group almost two thirds are "young-old" (ages 65 to 74) and over one third are "old-old" (ages 75 and over).
2. The majority of the aged live in urban areas, mostly in the heavily populated areas of center cities. There are 131.8 females over 65 for every 100 males over that age. Forty percent of women between ages 65-74 are widowed; over age 74, 68% are widowed. Only 8.5% of men 65-74 and 24% over age 74 are widowed.
3. The seven *phases of retirement* are (1) remote phase, (2) near phase, (3) honeymoon phase, (4) disenchantment phase, (5) reorientation phase, (6) stability phase, and (7) termination phase. Note the box on p. 610.
4. Retirement concern is a matter of meeting unexpected changes or differences in retirement from those one had anticipated. *Discretionary retirement* tends to reduce the "shock" of retirement because of the willingness of the individual to assume the change in life. *Compulsory retirement* is viewed as discrimination against a person because of age. Early retirement, however, is still preferred by many workers. So, for them, the question of mandatory retirement is moot.
5. *Sociological aging* occurs as the social life of old people is curtailed. Well-being for the elderly is related to health, socioeconomic factors, and social interaction. Quality of social activity is more significant than quantity.
6. Elderly parents generally seek to remain independent as long as possible. The degree of *family satisfaction* found between elderly parents and adult children is related to the degree to which they can communicate with and respect each other.
7. Most older people feel that their marriages have been very satisfactory. Companionship and being able to express true feelings are rewarding aspects of their relationship. A *symbiotic relationship* usually develops in performing household tasks and maintenance.
8. *Housing* for the elderly should include special considerations for mobility, sensory, safety, and psychological needs. Most elderly own their own homes and live with a spouse or family member. Only 4% live in an institutional setting. Most elderly do not move from their homes or relocate in another part of the country.
9. *Psychological aging* involves a need to adjust to modifying or changing social and personal roles that

affect older people. Sex-role crossovers appear to take place in men and women. Ego strength needs to be supported; emotional needs are frequently intensified. Self-concepts must adjust to changing physical capabilities and to a different level of autonomy.

10. Loneliness and *depression* become a part of the lives of older people as they lose their spouses, their friends, and their contacts with society. Depression can affect the state of one's physiological well-being. The suicide rate for the elderly is among the highest for all age-groups; it is especially high for white elderly males.
11. *Personality changes* occur because of changes in perception and styles of coping with inner images and outer-world demands. Older people become more preoccupied with their needs. Men tend to move toward a more introverted, passive position; women move to more active involvement. In the young old years, there is no general decrease in social skills or competencies.
12. The *activity theory* implies that, as a person gets older, society pulls away and decreases social interaction. The *disengagement theory* states that both society and the aging person withdraw. The research is not strongly supportive of either position but does indicate that successful aging for both men and women requires both group activity and physical activity. The ability to adapt psychologically is related to life satisfaction.
13. Although individual differences vary widely in *cognitive abilities* of the aged, a general principle is that the more an individual is involved in stimulating learning and thinking activities, the longer mental capacity will function at a sound level. The amount of formal education appears to be a significant predictor of cognitive performance.
14. There appears to be less decline in long-term memory and acquired verbal skills than in rapid responding and problem-solving ability involving visual-motor skills. The elderly can continue to learn effectively, but they approach problem solving differently than those who are younger.
15. *Memory functions* remain strong for long-term memory but deteriorate for short-term memory capability. Loss of memory ability in the elderly appears to be related to the input-output sequence of the perceptual-conceptual process.
16. The normal *bereavement and recovery process* at the loss of a spouse involves (a) the initial response of shock, disbelief, and/or numbness, (b) coping with anxiety and fear, usually about a month, (c) the intermediate phase of seeking for an understanding of death, and searching for the presence of the deceased one, (d) and, in the second year, the recovery phase, as evidenced by a positive attitude toward life.
17. Death is a concern, but not particularly a major one, for the elderly. Those living in a stable setting appear to approach the thought of death as a reality with more calmness and peace than do the elderly in more unstable environments.
18. The *stages of dying* according to Kübler-Ross are (a) denial, (b) anger, (c) bargaining, (d) depression, and (e) acceptance. Pattison indicates the phases of dying as (a) the acute phase, (b) the chronic living-dying phase, and (c) the terminal phase.
19. *Life-after-life experiences* show a remarkable similarity of perceived phenomena. The elements include (a) an awareness of a loud sound, (b) the sensation of moving rapidly through an opening toward an intense light, (c) the out-of-body experience of "seeing" people working on the body, (d) the feeling of previously deceased individuals helping with the transition from life, (e) bright light or a power that did not cast judgment, (f) seeing life pass in review, and (g) an awareness that the individual's time has not arrived for departure from this life.

REVIEW QUESTIONS

1. Review the statistics on the elderly. How many are there? Where do they live? What is the ratio of females to males over 65? What is their marital status?
2. Describe the stages of retirement.
3. What is retirement concern? Is it universal? What are some of the problems encountered?
4. Discuss compulsory retirement versus discretionary retirement. What are the advantages and disadvantages?
5. What is the nature and impact of early retirement?
6. Adjustment to retirement is helped by preretirement planning. Describe what is needed in good preretirement planning.
7. What are the major contributors to life satisfaction in the elderly? Why are social contacts important?
8. Make a list of factors indicating positive and negative relationships between elderly parents and adult children.
9. What are the signs of a good marital relationship in elderly couples?
10. What are the phases and characteristics of the grief and bereavement process? Does it make a difference if the death was anticipated rather than sudden? How?
11. What factors inhibit the remarriage of the elderly? Are remarriages of the elderly usually successful?
12. How do "never-married" elderly differ from the others in their social contacts in old age? How are they the same?
13. What are the main physical and psychological prerequisites for good housing for the elderly?

14. What are typical living arrangements for the elderly? Describe each one.
15. Psychological changes occur in the elderly.
    a. What role changes take place? Why?
    b. What is meant by sex-role crossover? What is its implication for the elderly?
    c. What causes loneliness and depression in the elderly? What are the effects?
    d. Review the eight personality patterns of aging listed in the second column of Table 16-6.
16. Define and compare the activity theory and the disengagement theory. Does either one have the research evidence needed to substantiate it?
17. Which intellectual traits hold and do not deteriorate in older persons? Which ones do not hold?
18. Why do older people tend to forget? What kind of memory is especially affected?
19. What is terminal drop? What is the relationship between test performance and terminal drop?
20. How much of a concern is death to the elderly? What suggestions are made by Saunders (St. Joseph's Hospice) for the care of the terminally ill?
21. Kübler-Ross presents five stages of dying. List each one and present its characteristics.
22. According to Pattison, what are the three phases of dying?
23. What is it like to die? Describe the life-after-life phenomenon.
24. What did Maslow have to say about coming to terms with death?

THOUGHT QUESTIONS AND ACTIVITIES

1. Is there an identity problem in old age? Is there ever an age when some changes are not needed in one's identity?
2. The advent of retirement can be a traumatic experience for some people. How or what can be done to help the person approaching retirement get ready for the transition to a new life pattern? Is the age of 20 too early to do some planning for retirement? At what age would you begin—25, 30, 40, 45, 50 years? Interview some people about to retire and some who have retired. Do they share a common view on retirement?
3. Ageism is discrimination against the elderly. Is ageism as bad as sexism, racism, or any other kind of "ism"?
4. What social changes can be anticipated for those over the age of 78 years of age? What kind of family relationship can an 80-year-old mother or father have with a child who is 55 to 60 years of age?
5. A discussion concerning death is uncomfortable for some people, yet death touches everyone in one way or another. How do you handle the realities of death? Visit a hospice and learn about their caring treatment of a coming death. You may want to visit a funeral home and let the director tell you about preparations for a funeral—buying a casket, a burial plot, and so on.
6. What do you suppose it would be like to be over 80 years of age? What are the sociological, psychological, and physiological factors involved? Visit an older person in his or her home, another in a retirement village or housing unit, and another in a nursing home. What perspectives did you get?
7. How would you teach a spouse to be a widow or a widower? What should each one learn and know?

FURTHER READING

Bryer, K.B. The Amish way of death: A study of family support systems. *American Psychologist,* 1979, *34*(3), 255-261. Amish families provide support systems to help individuals cope with the death of a loved one. The attitudes of the Amish toward death are also examined. Their way of dealing with death provides a contrast to the usual customs of American society.

Kahana, E., Liang, J., & Felton, B.J. Alternative models of person-environment fit: Prediction of morale in three homes for the aged. *Journal of Gerontology,* 1980, *35*(34), 584-95. This study reviews the impact of a fit between a person and his or her environment at three homes for the aged. There was a difference in matters of impulse control, congregation, and segregation.

Kastenbaum, R. (Ed.). *Old age on the new scene*. New York: Springer Publishing Co., 1981. This book consists of a series of articles on a wide variety of topics dealing with late adulthood. Some of the topics included are learning and age, motivation, educational opportunities for the elderly, and creativity.

Lawton, M.P. Housing the elderly: Residential quality and residential satisfaction. *Research on Aging,* 1980, *2*(3), 309-338. Over 12,000 households were assessed. It was determined that an individual's satisfaction with the residence depended on a variety of factors but that no specific factor stood out more than another. It was a matter of personal taste.

Ragan, P.K. (Ed.). *Work and retirement: Policy issues*. Los Angeles: University of Southern California Press, 1980. This book contains papers on aging, work, and retirement, which were given at a conference.

Siegel, R.K. The psychology of life after death. *American Psychologist,* 1980, *35*(10), 911-931. This article critically reviews the historical and current cross-cultural evidence regarding life after death.

Williamson, J.B., Munley, A., & Evans, L. *Aging and society: An introduction to social gerontology*. New York: Holt, Rinehart & Winston, 1980. This introductory book on social gerontology contains a series of essays on topics such as work, retirement, leisure activities, sexuality, and nursing homes.

BIBLIOGRAPHY

Abernethy, V. Illegitimate conception among teenagers. *American Journal of Public Health,* 1974, *64*(7), 662-665.

Abroms, K., & Bennett, T.J. *Paternal contributions to Down's syndrome dispel maternal myths.* ERIC, 1979.

Acredolo, L.P., & Hake, J.L. Infant perception. In B.B. Wolman (Ed.), *Handbook of developmental psychology.* Englewood Cliffs, N.J.: Prentice-Hall, 1982.

Adams, C. Sense of values. *Parade,* Nov. 2, 1969, 12.

Adams, M. The single woman in today's society: A reappraisal. *American Journal of Orthopsychiatry,* 1971, *41*(5), 776-786.

Adams, R.L., & Phillips, B.N. Motivational and achievement differences among children of various ordinal birth positions. *Child Development,* 1972, *43,* 155-164.

Adelson, J. Adolescence and the generation gap. *Psychology Today,* 1979, *12*(9), 33-37.

Adelson, J. (Ed.). *Handbook of adolescent psychology.* New York: John Wiley & Sons, 1980.

Ahammer, I.M., & Baltes, P.B. Objective versus perceived age differences in personality: how do adolescents, adults, and older people view themselves and each other? *Journal of Gerontology,* 1972. *27,* 46-51.

Aiken, L.R. *The psychology of later life.* Philadelphia: W.B. Saunders Co., 1978.

Ainsworth, M.D.S. *Infancy in Uganda: Infant care and the growth of attachment.* Baltimore: Johns Hopkins University Press, 1967.

Ainsworth, M.D.S. The development of infant-mother attachment. In B.M. Caldwell & H.N. Ricciutti (Eds.), *Review of child development research* (Vol. 3). Chicago: The University of Chicago Press, 1973.

Ainsworth, M.D.S. Infant-mother attachment. *American Psychologist, 1979, 34*(10), 932-937.

Ainsworth, M.D.S., & Bell, S.M.V. Attachment, exploration and separation: Illustrated by the behavior of one-year-olds in strange settings. *Child Development,* 1970, *41,* 49-67.

Akchin, D. Revising the rules of the dating game. *Nutshell: The Magazine for the College Community,* 1978/1979.

Aldous, J. *Family careers: Developmental change in families.* New York: John Wiley & Sons, 1978.

Aldrich, R. The watermelon theory: A concept of human life-span development. *Saturday Review,* 1977, *13*(1), 32-33.

Almy, M., Chittenden, E., & Miller, P. *Young children's thinking: Studies of some aspects of Piaget's thinking.* New York: Teachers College Press, 1966.

Alpert, J.L., & Richardson, M.S. Parenting. In L.W. Poon (Ed.), *Aging in the 1980s: Psychological issues.* Washington, D.C.: American Psychological Association, 1980.

Als, H., Tronick, E., Lester, B.M., & Brazelton, T.B. Specific neonatal measures: The Brazelton Neonate Behavioral Assessment Scale. In J.D. Osofsky (Ed.), *Handbook of infant development.* New York: John Wiley & Sons, 1979.

American Academy of Pediatrics, Committee on Nutrition. Encouraging breast-feeding. *Pediatrics,* 1980, *65*(3), 657-658.

America's rising black middle class. *Time,* June 17, 1974, 19-28.

Anastasi, A. Heredity, environment and the question "how"? *Psychological Review,* 1958, *65*(4), 197-208.

Anastasi, A. *Psychological testing* (2nd ed.). New York: Macmillan Publishing Co., 1976.

Anders, T., Emde, R., & Parmelee, A. *A manual of standardized terminology, techniques and criteria for scoring of states of sleep and wakefulness in newborn infants.* Los Angeles: UCLA Brain Information Service, 1971.

Anderson, B., & Palmore, E. Longitudinal evaluation of ocular function. In E. Palmore (Ed.), *Normal aging.* Durham, N.C.: Duke University, 1974, pp. 24-32.

Antonioli, D., Burke, L., & Friedman, E. Natural history of diethylstilbestrol-associated genital tract lesion: Cervical ectopy and cervicovaginal hood. *American Journal of Obstetrics and Gynecology,* 1980, *137*(7), 847-853.

Apgar, V. The Apgar scoring chart. *Journal of the American Medical Association, 168,* 1958.

Apgar, V. Perinatal problems and the central nervous system. In U.S. Department of HEW, *The child with central nervous system deficit,* Washington, D.C.: U.S. Government Printing Office, 1967, pp. 75-76.

Apgar, V. *Be good to your baby before it is born.* New York: The National Foundation—March of Dimes. 1973.

Apgar, V., & Beck, J. *Is my baby all right?* New York: Simon & Schuster, 1972.

Apgar, V., & James, L.S. Further observations on the newborn scoring system. *American Journal of Diseases of Children,* 1962, *104,* 419-428.

Arenberg, E.A., & Robertson-Tchabo, E.A. Learning and aging. In J.E. Birren & K.W. Schaie (Eds.), *Handbook of the Psychology of Aging.* New York: Van Nostrand Reinhold Co., 1977, chap. 18.

Arens, D.A. *Well-being and widowhood: Interpreting sex differences.* Paper presented at the 32nd Annual Scientific Meeting of the Gerontological Society, Washington, D.C., November 1979.

Arlin, P.K. Cognitive development in adulthood: A fifth stage? *Developmental Psychology,* 1975, *11,* 602-606.

Arlin, P.K. *Adolescent and adult thought: A search for structures.* Paper presented at meetings of the Piaget Society, Philadelphia, June 1980.

Arling, G. The elderly widow and her family, neighbors and friends. *Journal of Marriage and Family,* 1976, *38*(4), 757-768.

Asher, S., Renshaw, P., Geraci, K., & Dor, A. *Peer acceptance and social skill training: The selection of program content.* Paper presented at the biennial meeting of the Society for Research in Child Development, San Francisco, March 1979.

Asher, S.R. Children's peer relations. In M.E. Lamb (Ed.), *Social and personality development.* New York: Holt, Rinehart & Winston, 1978.

Asher, S.T., Oden, S.L., & Gottman, J.M. Children's friendships in school settings. In L.G. Katz (Ed.), *Current topics in early childhood education* (Vol. 1). Norwood, N.J.: Ablex Publishing Corp., 1977.

Atchley, R.C. *The sociology of retirement.* Cambridge, Mass.: Schenkman Publishing Co., 1976.

Atchley, R.C. *The social forces in later life: An introduction to social gerontology* (3rd ed.). Belmont, Calif.: Wadsworth Publishing Co., 1980.

Athanasiou, R. A review of public attitudes on sexual issues. In J. Zubic & J. Money (Eds.), *Contemporary sexual behavior; Critical issues in the 1970's.* Baltimore: Johns Hopkins University Press, 1973.

Athanasiou, R., & Sarkin, R. Premarital sexual behavior and postmarital adjustment. *Archives of Sexual Behavior,* 1974, *3*(3), 207-224.

Ausubel, D.P., & Sullivan, E.V. *Theory and problems of child development* (3rd ed.). New York: Grune & Stratton, 1980.

Azren, N., & Fox, R. *Toilet training in less than a day.* New York: Pocket Books, 1976.

Babson, S.G., Pernoll, M.L., Benda, G.I., & Simpson, K. *Diagnosis and management of the fetus and neonate at risk: A guide for team care* (4th ed.). St. Louis: The C.V. Mosby Co., 1980.

Bachman, J.G., and Johnson, L.D. The freshmen. *Psychology Today,* 1979, *13*(4), 78-87.

Bachman, J.G., O'Malley, P.M., & Johnston, J. *Youth in transition* (Vol. 6). Ann Arbor, Mich.: Institute for Social Research, 1978.

Baldwin, F. My crabbed age. *Today's Health,* 1976, *53*(3), 18.

Baldwin, W.H. Adolescent pregnancy and childbearing: Growing concerns for Americans. *Population Bulletin,* 1976, *31,* 1-34.

Balswick, J.O., & Macrides, C. Parental stimulus for adolescent rebellion. *Adolescence,* 1975, *10,* 253-266.

Baltes, P.B., Reese, H.W., & Lipsitt, L.P. Life-span developmental psychology. *Annual Review of Psychology,* 1980, *31,* 65-110.

Baltes, P.B., & Schaie, K.W. Aging and the IQ: The myth of the twilight years. *Psychology Today,* 1974, *7,* 35-40.

Baltes, P.B., & Willis, S.L. Toward psychological theories of aging and development. In J.E. Birren & K.W. Schaie (Eds.), *Handbook of the psychology of aging.* New York: Van Nostrand Reinhold Co., 1977, chap. 7.

Baltes, P.B., & Willis, S.L. Life span development psychology: Cognition and social policy. In M.W. Riley (Ed.), *Aging from birth to death.* Boulder, Colo.: Westview Press, 1979.

Bandura, A. *Aggression: A social learning analysis.* Englewood Cliffs, N.J.: Prentice-Hall, 1973.

Bandura, A. *Social learning theory.* Englewood Cliffs, N.J.: Prentice-Hall, 1977.

Bandura, A. The psychology of chance encounters and life paths. *American Psychologist,* 1982, *37,*(7), 747-755.

Bandura, A., & McDonald, F.J. The influences of social reinforcement and the behavior of models in shaping children's moral judgment. *Journal of Abnormal Psychology,* 1963, *67,* 274-281.

Banks, M.S., & Salapatek, P. Infant pattern vision: A new approach based on the contrast sensitivity functions. *Journal of Experimental Child Psychology,* 1981, *31,* 1-45.

Baratz, J. Teaching reading in an urban negro school system. In F. Williams (Ed.), *Language and poverty.* Chicago: Markham, 1973.

Bardwick, J.M. *Psychology of women.* New York: Harper & Row, Publishers, 1971.

Barfield, R.E., & Morgan, J.N. Trends in satisfaction with retirement. *The Gerontologist,* 1978, *18,* 19-23.

Barnes, A., Colton, T., Gunderson, J., Noller, K., Tilley, B., Strama, T., Townsend, D., Hatab, P., & O'Brien, P. Fertility and outcome of pregnancy in women exposed in utero to diethylstilbestrol. *New England Journal of Medicine,* 1980, *301*(11), 609-613.

Barrett, C.J. Effectiveness of widows' groups in facilitating change. *Journal of Consulting and Clinical Psychology,* 1978, *46,* 20-31.

Barry, W.A. Marriage research and conflict: An integrative review. *Psychological Bulletin.* 1970. *73*(1), 41-45.

Bart, P.B. Mother Portnoy's complaints. *Trans-Action,* Nov.-Dec. 1970, *8,* 69-74.

Bart, P.B. Depression in middle-aged women. In V. Gornick and B.K. Moran (Eds.), *Woman in sexist society.* New York: Basic Books, Inc., Publishers, 1971.

Bart, P.B., & Grossman, M. Menopause. In M. Notman & C. Nadelson (Eds.), *The woman patient.* New York: Plenum Press, 1978.

Bartoshuk, A.K. Human neonatal cardiac acceleration to sound: Habituation and dishabituation. *Perceptual and Motor Skills,* 1962, *15,* 15-27.

Baruch, G.K., & Barnett, R.C. On the well-being of adult women. In L.A. Bond & J.C. Rosen (Eds.), *Competence and coping during adulthood,* Hanover, N.H.: University Press of New England, 1980.

Bauer, D. An exploratory study of developmental changes in children's fears. *Journal of Child Psychology and Psychiatry,* 1976, *17,* 69-74.

Bauman, K.E., & Wilson, R. Contraceptive practices of white unmarried university students: The significance of four years at one university. *American Journal of Obstetrics and Gynecology,* 1974, *118,* 190-194.

Baumrind, D. Child-care practices anteceding three patterns of preschool behavior. *Genetic Psychology Monographs,* 1967, *75,* 43-88.

Baumrind, D. Socialization and instrumental competence in young children. In W.W. Hartup (Ed.), *The young child* (Vol. 2). Washington, D.C.: National Association for the Education of Young Children, 1972.

Baumrind, D. Early socialization and adolescent competence. In S.E. Dragastin & G.H. Elder, Jr. (Eds.), *Adolescence in the life cycle: Psychological change and social context.* New York: John Wiley & Sons, 1975.

Baumrind, D. Parental disciplinary patterns and social competence in children. *Youth and Society,* 1978, *9*(3), 239-276.

Bayley, N. *Bayley Scales of Infant Development.* New York: The Psychological Corporation, 1969.

Beard, R.J. The menopause. *British Journal of Hospital Medicine,* 1975. *12,* 631-637.

Beck, A.T., Kovacs, M., & Weissman, A. Assessment of suicidal intentions: The scale for suicide ideation. *Journal of Consulting and Clinical Psychology,* 1979, *47,* 343-352.

Beckwith, L. Prediction of emotional and social behavior. In J.D. Osofsky (Ed.), *Handbook of infant development.* New York: John Wiley & Sons, 1979.

Beech, R.P., & Schoeppe, A. Development of value systems in adolescents. *Developmental Psychology,* 1974, *10,* 644-656.

Behrman. R.E. (Ed.). *Neonatology: Disease of the fetus and the infant* (2nd ed.). St. Louis: The C.V. Mosby Co., 1977.

Beidler, L.M. Comparison of gustatory receptors, olfactory receptors, and free nerve endings. *Cold Spring Harbor Symposia on Quantitative Biology.* 1965. *30,* 191-200.

Bejerot, N. A theory of addiction as an artificially induced drive. *American Journal of Psychiatry,* 1972, *128,* 842.

Bell, R.R. *Marriage and family interaction* (3rd ed.). Homewood, Ill.: Dorsey Press, 1975.

Beller, E.K. Early intervention programs. In J.D. Osofsky (Ed.) *Handbook of infant development.* New York: John Wiley & Sons, 1979.

Bellingham, F.R. Syphilis in pregnancy: Transplacental infection. *Medical Journal of Australia.* 1973, *2,* 647.

Belloc, N.B., & Breslow, L. Relationship of physical health status and health practices. *Preventive Medicine,* 1972, *1*(3), 409-421.

Bemis, K.M. Current approaches to the etiology and treatment of anorexia nervosa. *Psychological Bulletin,* 1978, *85,* 593-617.

Benbow, C., & Stanley, J. Math talent search. *Science,* December 12, 1980, 1262.

Bench, J. The auditory response. In V. Stave (Ed.), *Perinatal physiology.* New York: Plenum Press, 1978.

Bender, S. Problems of prematurity. *Practitioner,* 1970, *204,* 366.

Benedict, R. Continuities and discontinuities in cultural conditioning. In W. Martin & C. Stendler (Eds.), *Readings in child development.* New York: Harcourt Brace Jovanovich, 1954, pp. 142-148.

Benedict, H. *The role of repetition in early language comprehension.* Paper presented at the annual meeting of the Society for Research in Child Development. Denver, 1975.

Bengtson, V.L., Cuellar, J.B., & Ragan, P.K. Contrasts and similarities in attitudes toward death by race, age, social class and sex. *Journal of Gerontology,* 1977, *32,* 204-216.

Bengtson, V.L., & Treas, J. The changing family context of mental health and aging. In. J.E. Birren & R.B. Sloane (Eds.), *Handbook of mental health and aging.* Englewood Cliffs, N.J.: Prentice-Hall, 1980.

Berg, W.K., Adkinson, C.D., & Strock, B.D. Duration and frequency of periods of alertness in neonates. *Developmental Psychology,* 1973, *9,* 434.

Berkman, L.F. *Psychosocial resources, health behavior and mortality: A nine year follow-up study.* Paper presented at the American Public Health Association Annual Meeting, Washington, D.C., October 1977.

Bernard, H.W. & Fullmer, D.W. *Principles of guidance* (2nd ed.). New York: Thomas Y. Crowell Co., 1977.

Bernardo, F. Widowhood status in the United States: Perspective on a neglected aspect of the family life-cycle. In M.E. Lasswell & T.E. Lasswell (Eds.), *Love, marriage, family: A developmental approach.* Glenview, Ill.: Scott, Foresman & Co., 1973, pp. 458-464.

Berndt, T.J. Developmental changes in conformity to peers and parents. *Developmental Psychology,* 1979, *15,* 608-616.

Berdnt, T.J. The features and effects of friendship in early adolescence. *Child Development,* 1982, *53*(6), 1447-1460.

Bernstein, A.C. Six stages of understanding: How children learn about sex and birth. *Psychology Today,* 1976, *9*(8), 31-35; 66.

Berscheid, E., & Walster, E.H. Physical attractiveness. In L. Berkowitz (Ed.), Experimental social psychology. New York: Academic Press, 1975.

Beschner, G.M., & Friedman, A.S. (Eds.). *Youth drug abuse: Problems, issues and treatment.* Lexington, Mass.: D.C. Heath & Co., 1979.

Bibbo, M., Gill, W., & Azizi, F. Follow-up study of male and female offspring of DES-exposed mothers. *Obstetrics and Gynecology,* 1977, *49,* 1.

Bierman, E., & Hazzard, W. Biology of aging. In D. Smith & E. Bierman (Eds.), *The biologic ages of man.* Philadelphia: W.B. Saunders Co., 1973.

Bigner, J.J. *Parent-child relations.* New York: Macmillan Publishing Co., 1979.

Biller, H.B. *Paternal deprivation.* Lexington, Mass.: Lexington Books, 1974.

Biller, H.B. The father and sex role development. In M.E. Lamb (Ed.), *The role of the father in child development* (2nd ed.). New York: John Wiley & Sons, 1981.

Biller, H.B. Fatherhood: Implications for child and adult development. In B.B. Wolman (Ed.), *Handbook of developmental psychology.* Englewood Cliffs, N.J.: Prentice-Hall, 1982.

Biomedicine. Eyeball to eyeball with the human fetus. *Science News,* 1982, *120,* 142.

Bird, D. *The case against college.* New York: David McKay Co., 1975.

Birren, J.E., Butler, R.N., Greenhouse, S.W., Sokoloff, L., & Yarrow, M.R. *Human aging.* Public Health Pub. No. 986. Washington, D.C.: U.S. Government Printing Office, 1968.

Birren, J.E., & Morrison, D.F. Analysis of the WAIS subtests in relation to age and education. *Journal of Gerontology.* 1961. *16,* 363-369.

Birren, J.E., & Schaie, K.W. (Eds.). *Handbook of the psychology of aging.* New York: Van Nostrand Reinhold Co., 1977, chap. 20-23.

Birren, J.E., Woods, A.M., & Williams, M.V. Behavioral slowing with age: Causes, organization, and consequences. In Poon, L.W. (Ed.), *Aging in the 1980s.* Washington, D.C.: American Psychological Association, 1980.

Bischof, L.J. *Adult psychology* (2nd ed.). New York: Harper & Row, Publishers, 1976.

Bixenstine, V.E., DeCorte, M.S., & Bixenstine, R.A. Conformity to peer-sponsored misconduct at four grade levels. *Developmental Psychology,* 1976, *12,* 226-236.

Black, D. The older person and the family. In S.H. Zarit (Ed.), *Readings in aging and death: Contemporary perspectives.* New York: Harper & Row, Publishers, 1977.

Black, J.H. Conceptions of sex roles: Some cross-cultural and longitudinal perspectives. *American Psychologist.* 1973, *25,* 512-526.

Blau, F.D. Women in the labor force: An overview. In J. Freeman (Ed.), *Women: A feminist perspective.* Palo Alto, Calif.: Mayfield Publishing Co., 1975.

Blazer, D.G. The OARS Durham surveys: Description and application. In *Multidimensional functional assessment: The OARS methodology.* Durham, N.C.: Duke University, Center for the Study of Aging and Human Development, 1978.

Block, J.H. Another look at sex differentiation in the socialization behaviors of mothers and fathers. In J. Sherman & F. Denmark (Eds.), *Psychology of women: Future directions for research.* New York: Psychological Dimensions, 1978.

Blood, L., & D'Angelo, R. A progress report on value issues in conflict between runaways and their parents. *Journal of Marriage and the Family,* 1974, *36,* 486-491.

Blos, P. *The adolescent passage.* New York: International Universities Press, 1979.

Blos, P. The split parental image in adolescent social relations. *Psychoanalytic Study of the Child,* 1976, *31,* 7-33.

Blum, J.E., Clark, E.T., & Jarvick, L.F. The New York State Psychiatric Institute study of aging twins. In L.F. Jarvick, C. Eisdorfer, & J.E. Blum (Eds.). *Intellectual functioning in adults.* New York: Springer Publishing Co., 1973, pp. 13-19.

Blum, J.E., & Jarvik, L.F. Intellectual performance of octogenarians as a function of education and initial ability. *Human Development,* 1974, *17,* 364-375.

Bockneck, G. *The young adult: Development after adolescence.* Monterey, Calif.: Brooks/Cole Publishing Co., 1980.

Bohannan, P. The six stations of divorce. In J. Bardwick (Ed.), *Readings on the psychology of women.* New York: Harper & Row, Publishers, 1972.
Bondareff, W. The neural basis of aging. In J.E. Birren & K.W. Schaie (Eds.), *Handbook of the psychology of aging.* New York: Van Nostrand Reinhold Co., 1977.
Boocock, S.S. Youth in three cultures. *School Review,* 1974, *83,* 93-111.
Booth, C.L. *Contingent responsiveness and mutuality in mother-infant interaction: Birth-order and sex differences?* Paper presented at the Society for Research in Child Development, Boston, 1981.
Bornstein, M.H. Chromatic vision in infancy. In H.W. Reese & L. Lipsitt (Eds.), *Advances in child development and behavior* (Vol. 12). New York: Academic Press, 1978.
Bossard, J.H. & Boll, E.S. *The sociology of child development* (4th ed.). New York: Harper & Row, Publishers. 1966.
Botwinick, J. Geropsychology. *Annual Review of Psychology,* 1970, *21,* 239-272.
Botwinick, J. Intellectual abilities. In J.E. Birren & K.W. Schaie (Eds.), *Handbook of the psychology of aging.* New York: Van Nostrand Reinhold Co., 1977, Chap. 24.
Botwinick, J. *Aging and behavior* (2nd ed.). New York: Springer Publishing Co., 1978.
Bouchard, T.J., Jr., & McGue, M. Familial studies of intelligence: A review. *Science,* 1981, *212,* 1055-1059.
Bower, T.G.R. *Development in infancy.* San Francisco: W.H. Freeman & Co., Publishers, 1974.
Bower, T.G.R. Repetitive processes in child development. *Scientific American,* 1976, *235*(5), 38-47.
Bowman, H.A. *Marriage for moderns* (6th ed.). New York: McGraw-Hill Book Co., 1970.
Brackbill, Y., & Broman, S.H. *Obstetrical medication and development in the first year of life.* Unpublished manuscript, January 15, 1979.
Bracken, M., Holford, T., White, C., & Kelsey, J. Role of oral contraception in congenital malformations of offspring. *International Journal of Epidemiology,* 1978, *7*(4), 309-317.
Bracken, P.: Middle age: for adults only. *Reader's Digest,* 1969, *95,* 86.
Bradbury, W. (Ed.). *The adult years.* New York: Time-Life Books, 1975.
Bradley, R.A. *Husband-coached childbirth.* (3rd ed.). New York: Harper & Row, Publishers, 1981.
Brand, F., & Smith, R. Life adjustment and relocation of the elderly, *Journal of Gerontology,* 1974, *29,* 336-340.
Brannen, P. (Ed.). *Entering the world of work: Some sociological perspectives.* London: Her Majesty's Stationery Office, 1975.
Braungart, R.G. Youth movements. In J. Adelson (Ed.), *Handbook of adolescent psychology.* New York: John Wiley & Sons, 1980.
Brazelton, T.B. Effects of prenatal drugs on the behavior of the neonate. *American Journal of Psychiatry,* 1970, *126*(9), 95-100.
Brazelton, T.B. Neonatal behavioral assessment scale. *Clinics in Developmental Medicine,* No. 50. Philadelphia: J.B. Lippincott Co., 1973.
Breland, H.M. Birth order, family configuration, and verbal achievement. *Child Development,* 1974, *45,* 1011-1019.
Brenner, H. *Estimating the social costs of national economic policy: Implications for mental and physical health and criminal aggression* (Paper No. 5). Washington, D.C.: U.S. Government Printing Office, 1976.
Bridges, K.M.B. Emotional development in early infancy. *Child Development,* 1932, *3,* 324-341.
Britton, J.H., & Britton, J.O. *Personality changes in aging.* New York: Springer Publishing Co., 1972.
Brody, J.E. How mother affects her unborn child. *Womans Day,* 1970, *12,* 114-115.
Brody, J.E. Personal health. *New York Times,* May 16, 1976, C1; 12.
Brody, J.E. Fetal health: A new view emerges. *New York Times,* Science Times, May 16, 1982, C1-2.
Bromley, D.B. *The psychology of human aging.* Baltimore: Penguin Books, 1974.
Bronfenbrenner, U. *Two worlds of childhood: U.S. and USSR.* New York: Russell Sage Foundation, 1970.
Bronson, G.W. Infant's reactions to an unfamiliar person. In L.J. Stone, H.T. Smith, & L.B. Murphy (Eds.), *The complete infant.* New York: Basic Books, Inc., Publishers, 1973.
Brown, G.S. *Laws of form.* New York: Crown Publishers, 1973.
Brown, R. *A first language: The early stages.* Cambridge, Mass.: Harvard University Press, 1973.
Brown, R., & Hanlon, C. Deprivation complexity and order of acquisition in child speech. In J.R. Hoyes (Ed.), *Cognition and the development of language.* New York: John Wiley & Sons, 1970.
Bruch, H. *Eating disorders, obesity, anorexia nervosa, and the young person within.* New York: Basic Books, Inc., Publishers, 1973.
Bruch, H. *The golden cage: The enigma of anorexia nervosa.* Cambridge, Mass.: Harvard University Press, 1978.
Bruner, J.S. Course of cognitive development. *American Psychologist,* 1964, *19,* 8.
Bruner, J.S. Nature and uses of immaturity. *American Psychologist,* 1972, *27,* 687-708.
Bruner, J.S., Oliver, R.R., & Greenfield, P.M. *Studies in cognitive growth.* New York: John Wiley & Sons, 1966.
Bryden, M.P. Evidence for sex-related difference in cerebral organization. In M.A. Wittig & A.C. Petersen (Eds.), *Sex related differences in cognitive functioning: Developmental issues.* New York: Academic Press, 1979.
Bühler, C. The course of human life as a psychological problem. *Human Development,* 1968, *11,* 184-200.
Bukstel, L.H., Roeder, G.D., Kilmann, R., Laughlin, J., & Sotile, W.M. Projected extramarital sexual involvement in community college students. *Journal of Marriage and the Family,* 1978, *40,* 337-340.
Burr, W.R. Satisfaction with various aspects of marriage over the life cycle: A random middle-class sample. *Journal of Marriage and the Family.* 1970. *32,* 29-37.
Busch-Rossnagel, N.A., & Vance, A.K. The impact of the schools on social and emotional development. In B.B. Wolman (Ed.), *Handbook of developmental psychology.* Englewood Cliffs, N.J.: Prentice-Hall, 1982.
Bush, S. Beauty makes the beast look better. *Psychology Today,* 1976, *10*(3), 15-16.
Busse, E.W. Viewpoint. *Geriatrics,* 1969, *24,* 42-44.
Butler, N.R., & Goldstein, H. Smoking in pregnancy and subsequent child development. *British Medical Journal,* 1973, *4,* 573-575.
Butler, R.N. The life review: An interpretation of reminiscence in the aged. *Psychiatry,* 1963, *26,* 65-76.
Butler, R.N. *Why survive? Being old in America.* New York: Harper & Row, Publishers, 1975.
Butler, R.N. Public Interest Report No. 26: Compassion and relief from pain. *International Journal of Aging and Human Development,* 1978-79, *9*(2), 193-195.
Butler, R.N., & Lewis, M.J. *Sex after sixty. A guide for men and women for their later years.* New York: Harper & Row, Publishers, 1976.
Butler, R.N., & Lewis, M.J. *Aging and mental health* (2nd ed.). St. Louis: The C.V. Mosby Co., 1977.
Butterfield, E., & Siperstein, G. Influence of contingent auditory stimulation upon non-nutritional suckle. In J. Bosma (Ed.), *Oral sensation and perception: The mouth of the infant.* Springfield, Ill.: Charles C Thomas, Publisher, 1972.

Cairns, R.B. Attachment and dependency: A psychobiological and social learning synthesis. In J. Gewirty (Ed.), *Attachment and dependency.* Washington, D.C.: V.H. Winston & Sons, 1972.
Calderone, M. How parents should teach their children about sex. *Today's Health.* December 1973, 68-70.
Cameron, P. The generation gap: Beliefs about stability of life. *Journal of Gerontology,* 1971, *26,* 81.
Campbell, A. The American way of mating: Marriage si, children only maybe. *Psychology Today,* 1975, *8*(12), 37-42.
Campbell, M.M., & Cooper, K. Parents' perception of adolescent behavior problems. *Journal of Youth and Adolescence,* 1975, *4,* 309-320.
Campos, J.J., Emde, R.N., Gaensbauer, T., & Henderson, C. Cardiac and behavioral interrelationships in the reactions of infants to strangers. *Developmental Psychology,* 1975, *11,* 589-601.
Cantor, J.H., & Spiker, C.C. The effects of introtacts on hypothesis testing in kindergarten and first-grade children. *Child Development,* 1979, *50*(4), 1110-1120.
Caplan, F. (Ed.). *The first twelve months of life.* New York: Grosset & Dunlap, 1981.
Capon, N., & Kuhn, D. Logical reasoning in the supermarket: Adult females' use of proportional reasoning strategy in an everyday event. *Developmental Psychology,* 1979, *15,* 450-452.
Carey, S. Cognitive competence. In K. Connolly & J. Bruner (Eds.), *The growth of competence.* New York: Academic Press, 1974.
Carlsmith, J.M., Dornbusch, S.M., & Gross, R.T. Paper in preparation. Stanford University, 1983.
Carp, F.M. Housing and living environments of older people. In R.H. Binstock & E. Shanas (Eds.), *Handbook of aging and the social sciences.* New York: Van Nostrand Reinhold Co., 1976. chap. 10.
Carroll, J.L., & Rest, J.R. Moral development. In B.B. Wolman (Ed.), *Handbook of developmental psychology.* Englewood Cliffs, N.J.: Prentice-Hall, 1982.
Casady, M. The pinch of stepping out of stereotype. *Psychology Today,* 1976, *9*(9), 102-103.
Cath, S.H. The orchestration of disengagement. *Journal of Aging and Human Development,* 1975, *6*(3), 199-213.
Center for Disease Control. *VD fact sheet, 1976* (33rd ed.). Atlanta: The Center, 1977.
Centers, R. *Sexual attraction and love: An instrumental theory.* Springfield, Ill.: Charles C, Thomas, Publisher, 1975.
Chapman, R.B. Academic and behavioral problems of boys in elementary school. *Counseling Psychologist,* 1978, *7*(4), 37-40.
Chilman, C. *Adolescent sexuality in a changing American society: Social and psychological perspectives.* Washington, D.C.: U.S. Government Printing Office, 1979.
Chiriboga, D.A. *Life events and metamodels: A life span study.* Paper presented at the meeting of the Gerontological Society, Dallas, November 1978.
Chiriboga, D.A., & Cutler, L. Stress responses among divorcing men and women. *Journal of Divorce,* 1977, *1,* 95-106.

Chiriboga, D.A., & Cutler, L. Stress and adaptation: Life span perspectives. In L.W. Poon (Ed.), Aging in the 1980s. Washington, D.C.: American Psychological Association, 1980.

Chiriboga, D.A., & Lowenthal, M.F. Psychological correlates of perceived well-being. *Proceedings of the 79th Annual Convention of the American Psychological Association,* 1971, *6,* 603-604.

Chomsky, N. *Syntactic structures.* The Hague: Mouton, 1957.

Chomsky, N. *Aspects of a theory of syntax.* Cambridge, Mass.: The MIT Press, 1965.

Chomsky, N. *Language and mind* (Enl. Ed.). New York: Harcourt Brace Jovanovich, 1972.

Chomsky, N. *Reflections on language.* New York: Pantheon Books, 1975.

Chown, S.M. Morale, careers, and personal potentials. In J.E. Birren & K.W. Schaie (Eds.), *Handbook of the psychology of aging.* New York: Van Nostrand Reinhold Co., 1977.

Chumlea, W.C. Physical growth in adolescence. In B.B. Wolman (Ed.), *Handbook of developmental psychology.* Englewood Cliffs, N.J.: Prentice-Hall, 1982.

Cicirelli, V.G. Effects of mother and older siblings on the problem solving behavior of the younger child. *Developmental Psychology,* 1975, *11,* 749-756.

Cicirelli, V.G. Categorization behavior in aging subjects. *Journal of Gerontology,* 1976, *31,* 676-680.

Cicirelli, V.G. *Helping elderly parents: The role of adult children.* Boston: Auburn House Publishing Co., 1981.

Clanton, G. The contemporary experience of adultery: Bob and Carol and Updike and Rimmer. In R.W. Libby & R.N. Whitehurst (Eds.), *Marriage and alternatives: Exploring intimate relationships.* Glenview, Ill.: Scott, Foresman & Co., 1977.

Clark, E.V. Strategies for communicating. *Child Development,* 1978, *49*(4), 953-959.

Clarke-Stewart, K.A. Popular primers for parents. *American Psychologist,* 1978, *33,* 359-369.

Clausen, J.A. The social meaning of differential physical and sexual maturation. In S.E. Dragastin & G.H. Elder, Jr. (Eds.), *Adolescence in the life cycle: Psychological change and social context.* New York: Halsted Press, 1975.

Clausen, J.A. Glimpses into the social world of middle age. *International Journal of Aging and Human Development,* 1976, *7,* 99-106.

Clayton, R.R. *The family, marriage, and social change.* Lexington, Mass.: D.C. Heath & Co., 1975.

Cleveland, M. Sex in marriage: At 40 and beyond. *Family Coordinator,* 1976, *25*(3), 233-240.

Clifford, E. Body ratification in adolescence. *Perceptual and Motor Skills,* 1971, *33,* 119-125.

Clifton, R.K., & Nelson, M.N. Developmental study of habituation in infants: The importance of paradigm, response system and state. In T.J. Tighe & R.N. Leaton (Eds.), *Habituation: Perspective from child development, animal behavior, and neurophysiology.* Hillsdale, N.J.: Lawrence Erlbaum Associates, 1976.

Clinical Pediatrics, NIH Consensus Development Conference. *Clinical Pediatrics,* 1979, *18*(9), 535-538.

Colby, A., Kohlberg, L. *The relation between logical and moral development.* Unpublished manuscript, Harvard University, 1975.

Colby, A., Kohlberg, L., & Gibbs, J. *A longitudinal study of moral judgment.* Unpublished manuscript, Harvard University, 1980.

Cole, M. How education affects the mind. *Human Nature,* 1978, *1*(4), 50-58.

Coleman, J.C. *Contemporary psychology and effective behavior* (4th ed.). Glenview, Ill.: Scott, Foresman & Co., 1979.

Coleman, J.C. Friendship and the peer group in adolescence. In J. Adelson (Ed.), *Handbook of adolescent psychology.* New York: John Wiley & Sons, 1980.

Coleman, J.S. *The adolescent society.* New York: The Free Press, 1971.

Coleman, J.S., Hersberg, J., & Morris, M. Identity in adolescence: Present and future self-concepts. *Journal of Youth and Adolescence,* 1977, *6*(1), 63-75.

Comer, J.P., & Poussaint, A.F. *Black child care: How to bring up a healthy black child in America.* New York: Simon & Schuster, 1975.

Commons, M.L., & Richards, F.A. *The structural analytic state of development: A Piagetian post-formal operational stage.* Paper presented at the meeting of the Western Psychological Association, San Francisco, April 1978.

Communications from public school nurses to the authors. Class discussion, fall, 1978.

Conger, J.J. (Ed.). *Contemporary issues in adolescent development.* New York: Harper & Row, Publishers, 1975.

Conger, J.J. *Adolescence and youth: Psychological development in a changing world* (2nd ed.). New York: Harper & Row, Publishers, 1977.

Conger, J.J., & Miller, W.E. *Personality, social class and delinquency.* New York: John Wiley & Sons, 1966, p. 4.

Conner, K.S., Powers, E.A., & Bultena, G.L. Social interaction and life-satisfaction: An empirical assessment of late life patterns. *Journal of Gerontology,* 1979, *34,* 116-121.

Constantine, L., & Constantine, J.M. The group marriage. In M.E. Losswell & T.E. Losswell (Eds.), *Love, marriage and family. A developmental approach.* Glenview, Ill.: Scott, Foresman & Co., 1973.

Constantinople, A. An Eriksonian measure of personality development in college students. *Developmental Psychology,* 1969, *1,* 357-372.

Constanza, P.R., & Shaw, M.E. Conformity as a function of age level. *Child Development,* 1966, *37,* 967-975.

Cooper, M. Voice problems of the geriatric patient. *Geriatrics,* 1970, *25,* 107-110.

Corsale, K., & Ornstein, P.A. Developmental changes in children's use of semantic information in recall. *Journal of Experimental Child Psychology,* 1980, *30,* 231-245.

Corso, J.F. Auditory perception and communication. In J.E. Birren & K.W. Schaie (Eds.), *Handbook of the psychology of aging.* New York: Van Nostrand Reinhold Co., 1977.

Costa, P.T., Jr., & McCrae, R.R. Still stable after all these years: Personality as a key to some issues in aging. In P.B. Baltes & O.G. Brin, Jr. (Eds.), *Life-span development and behavior* (Vol. 3). New York: Academic Press, 1980.

Covan, R.S., & Ranck, K.H. *The family and the depression.* Chicago: University of Chicago Press, 1958.

Cox, F.D. *Youth, marriage and the seductive society.* Dubuque, Iowa: William C. Brown, 1974.

Cox, R. *Youth into maturity.* New York: Mental Health Materials Center, 1970.

Craik, F.I.M. Age differences in human memory. In J.E. Birren & K.W. Shaier (Eds.), *Handbook of the psychology of aging.* New York: Van Nostrand Reinhold, 1977.

Crain, W.C. *Theories of development: Concepts and application.* Englewood Cliffs, N.J.: Prentice-Hall, 1980.

Cranston, A. Progress in controlling the aging process, *U.S.A. Today,* 1980, *108*(2420), 17-18.

Cratty, B. *Perceptual and motor development in infants and children.* Englewood Cliffs, N.J.: Prentice-Hall, 1979.

Crittenden, A. In the corporate world more talk than progress. *New York Times,* May 1, 1977, p. 1ff.

Cromer, R.F. Reconceptualizing language acquisition and cognitive development. In R.L. Schiefelbusch & D. Bricker (Eds.), *Early language: Acquisition and invention.* Baltimore: University Park Press, 1981.

Cronback, L.J. & Snow, R.E. *Aptitudes and instructional methods.* New York: Irvington Books, 1977.

Crook, C.K. The organization and control of infant sucking. *Advances in Child Development and Behavior,* 1979, *14,* 209-252.

Crouch, J.E. *Functional human anatomy* (2nd ed.). Philadelphia: Lea & Febiger, 1972.

Cumming, E., & Henry, W.E. *Growing old.* New York: Basic Books, Inc., Publishers, 1961.

Cunningham, S. Hospice: a place for children. *APA Monitor,* 1983, *14*(4), 9-10.

Curtis, R.L., Jr. Adolescent orientations toward parents and peers: Variations by sex, age, and socioeconomic status. *Adolescence,* 1975, *10,* 484-494.

Cutler, N.E., & Harootyan, R.A. Demography of the aged. In D.S. Woodruff & J.E. Birren (Eds.), *Aging: Scientific perspectives and social issues.* New York: Van Nostrand Reinhold Co., 1975, pp. 31-69.

Cutler, R.G. Transcription of reiterated DNA sequence classes throughout the life-span of the mouse. In B.L. Strehler (Ed.), *Advances in gerontological research* (Vol. 4). New York: Academic Press, 1972, pp. 219-321.

Cytrynbaum, S., Blum, L., Patrick R., Stein, J., Wadner, D., & Wilk, C. Midlife development: A personality and social systems perspective. In L.W. Poon (Ed.), *Aging in the 1980s.* Washington, D.C.: American Psychological Association, 1980.

Daehler, M.W., & O'Connor, M.P. Recognition memory for objects in very young children: The effect of shape and label similarity on preferences for novel stimuli. *Journal of Experimental Child Psychology,* 1980, *29,* 306-321.

Dale, P.S. *Language development: Structure and function.* New York: Holt, Rinehart & Winston, 1976.

Damon, W. *The social world of a child.* San Francisco: Jossey-Bass, Inc., Publishers, 1977.

Danforth, D.H., & Holly, R.G. Other disorders during pregnancy. In O.H. Danforth (Ed.), *Obstetrics and gynecology* (3rd ed.). New York: Harper & Row, Publishers, 1977.

David, V., & Walsh, M.J. Data link alcoholism and opiate addiction. *Chemical and Endocrinology Journal,* February 1970, 44-45.

Davis, S.M. & Harris, M.B. Sexual knowledge, sexual interests, and sources of sexual information of rural and urban adolescents from three cultures. *Adolescence,* 1982 (Sum) *17*(66), 471-492.

Day, M.C. Developmental trends in visual scanning. In H.W. Reese (Ed.), *Advances in child development and behavior* (Vol. 10). New York: Academic Press, 1975.

Denney, N.W. Classification criteria in middle and old age. *Developmental Psychology,* 1974, *10,* 901-906.

Denney, N.W. Problem solving in later adulthood: Intervention research. In P.B. Baltes and O.G. Brim, Jr. (Eds.), *Life-span development and behavior* (Vol. 2). New York: Academic Press, 1979.

Denney, N.W. Aging and cognitive changes. In B.B. Wolman (Ed.), *Handbook of developmental psychology.* Englewood Cliffs, N.J.: Prentice-Hall, 1982.

Denney, N.W., Jones, F.W., & Krigel, S.W. Modifying the questioning strategies of young children and elderly adults. *Human Development,* 1979, *22,* 23-36.

Derr, M. Unemployment: The family crisis. *Marriage and Family Living,* 1977, *59*(1), 18-20.

deVilliers, J.G., & deVilliers, P.A. *Language acquisition.* Cambridge, Mass.: Harvard University Press, 1978.
DeVries, H.A. Physiology of exercise and aging. In D.S. Woodruff & J.E. Birren (Eds.), *Aging: Scientific perspectives and social issues.* New York: D. Van Nostrand Co., 1975, chap. 12.
DeVries, H.A. Physiology of exercise and aging. In S.H. Zarit (Ed.), *Readings in aging and death: Contemporary perspectives.* New York: Harper & Row, Publishers, 1977.
Dick-Read, G. (Revised and edited by H. Wessel & H.F. Ellis). *Childbirth without fear* (4th ed.). New York: Harper & Row, Publishers, 1972.
Dielman, T.E., Barton, K., & Cattell, R.B. Adolescent personality and intelligence scores as related to family demography. *Journal of Genetic Psychology.* 1974, *124,* 151-154.
Doherty, W.J., & Jacobson, N.S. Marriage and the family. In B.B. Wolman (Ed.), *Handbook of developmental psychology.* Englewood Cliffs, N.J.: Prentice-Hall, 1982.
Dollard, J., & Miller, N.E. *Personality and psychotherapy: An analysis in terms of learning, thinking and culture.* New York: McGraw-Hill Book Co., 1950.
Donaldson, M. *Children's minds.* New York: W.W. Norton & Co., 1979.
Donovan, J.E., & Jessor, R. Adolescent problem drinking: Psychosocial correlates in a national sample survey. *Journal of Studies on Alcohol,* 1978, *39,* 1506-1564.
Dornbusch, S.M., Carlsmith, L., Gross, R.T., Martin, J.A., Jenning, D., Rosenberg, A., & Duke, D. Sexual development, age and dating. A comparison of biological and sociological influences upon the set of behaviors. *Child Development,* 1981, *52,* 179-185.
Doyle, A., Connolly, J., & Rivest, L. The effect of playmate familiarity on the social interactions of children. *Child Development,* 1980, *51,* 217-223.
Drake, C.T., & McDougall, D. Effects of the absence of a father and other male models in the development of boys' sex roles. *Developmental Psychology,* 1977, *13,* 537-538.
Dreyer, P.H. Sexuality during pregnancy. In B.B. Wolman (Ed.), *Handbook of adolescent psychology.* Englewood Cliffs, N.J.: Prentice-Hall, 1982.
Duffy, M. Calling the doctor: Women complain about illness more often than men. *New York Daily News,* Feb. 8, 1979.
Dullea, G. Women change careers in midlife now, too. *New York Times,* 1977.
Dunn, J., & Kendrick, C. The speech of two- and three-year-olds to infant siblings: "Baby talk" and the context of communication. *Journal of Child Language,* 1982, *9*(3), 579-595.
Dunning, J. Women are warned to give up drinking during pregnancies. *New York Times,* June 1, 1977, 30.
Duvall, E.M. *Family development* (5th ed.). Philadelphia: J.B. Lippincott Co., 1971.

Eder, D., & Hallinan, M.T. Sex differences in children's friendships. *American Sociological Review,* 1978, *43,* 237-250.
Edwards, C.P. The comparative study of the development of moral judgment and reasoning. In R.L. Monroe, R.H. Monroe, & B.B. Whiting (Eds.), *Handbook of cross-cultural human development.* New York: Garland Publishing, 1977.
Edwards, J.N., & Booth, A. Sexual behavior in and out of marriage: An assessment of correlates. *Journal of Marriage and the Family,* 1976, *38*(1), 73-81.
Eibl-Eibesfeldt, I. *Ethology: The biology of behavior* (E. Klinghammer, Trans.). New York: Holt, Rinehart & Winston, 1970.
Eichorn, D.H. Physical development: Current foci of research. In J.D. Osofsky (Ed.), *Handbook of infant development.* New York: John Wiley & Sons, 1979.
Eimas, P.D. Developmental aspects of speech perception. In R. Held, H. Leibowitz, & H.L. Teuber (Eds.), *Handbook of sensory physiology* (Vol. 8). New York: Springer-Verlag, 1978.
Einstein, E. Stepfamily lives. *Human Behavior,* April 1979, 63-68.
Eisdorfer, C., & Lawton, M.P. *The psychology of adult development and aging.* Washington, D.C.: American Psychological Association, 1973.
Eisenberg, R.B. The development of hearing in man: An assessment of current status. *Journal of the American Speech and Hearing Association,* 1970, *12,* 119-123.
Eisenberg, R.B. Stimulus significance as a determinant of infant responses to sound. In E.B. Thoman (Ed.), *Origins of the infant's social responsiveness.* Hillsdale, N.J.: Lawrence Erlbaum Associates, 1979.
Elder, G.H., Jr. Parent-youth relations in cross-national perspective. *Social Science Quarterly,* 1968, *49,* 216-228.
Elder, G.H., Jr. *Children of the Great Depression.* Chicago: The University of Chicago Press, 1974.
Elder, G.H., & Bowerman, C.E. Family structure and child-rearing patterns, the effect of family size and sex composition. *American Sociological Review,* 1963, *28,* 891-905.
Elias, J., & Gebhard, P. Sexuality and sexual learning in childhood. *Phi Delta Kappa,* 1969, *50,* 401-405.
Elias, M.F., Elias, P.K., & Elias, J.W. *Basic processes in adult developmental psychology.* St. Louis: The C.V. Mosby Company, 1977, chap. 4.
Elkind, D. *Children and adolescents: Interpretive essays on Jean Piaget.* New York: Oxford University Press, 1970.
Elkind, D. Understanding the young adolescent. *Adolescence,* 1978, *13*(49), 127-134.
Elkind, D. Growing up faster. *Psychology Today,* February 1979, 38-45.
Elkind, D. Strategic interactions in early adolescence. In J. Adelson (Ed.), *Handbook of adolescent psychology.* New York: John Wiley & Sons, 1980.
Engen, T. Taste and smell. In J.E. Berrin & K.W. Schaie (Eds.), *Handbook of the psychology of aging.* New York: Van Nostrand Reinhold Co., 1977.
Epstein, L. Symposium on age differentiation in depressive illness: Depression in the elderly. *Journal of Gerontology,* 1976, *31,* 278-282.
Erikson, E.H. *Childhood and society* (2nd ed.). New York: W.W. Norton & Co., 1963a.
Erikson, E.H. *Youth: Change and challenge.* New York: Basic Books, Inc., Publishers, 1963b.
Erikson, E.H. Generativity and ego integrity. In B.L. Neugarten (Ed.), *Middle age and aging.* Chicago: The University of Chicago Press, 1968a.
Erikson, E.H. *Identity: Youth and crisis.* New York: W.W. Norton & Co., 1968b.
Erikson, E.H. Reflections on contemporary youth. *Daedalus,* 1970a, *99*(1), 144-157.
Erikson, E.H. Reflections on the dissent of contemporary youth. *International Journal of Psychoanalysis,* 1970b, *51,* 11-22.
Erikson, E.H. Eight ages of man. In C.S. Lavatelli & F. Stendler (Eds.), *Readings in child behavior and child development.* New York: Harcourt Brace Jovanovich, 1972.
Erikson, E.H. *Dimensions of a new identity.* New York: W.W. Norton & Co., 1974.
Espenschade, A.S., & Eckert, H.M. *Motor development.* Columbus, Ohio: Charles E. Merrill Publishing Co., 1967.
Espenshade, T.J. The economic consequences of divorce. *Journal of Marriage and the Family,* 1979, *41*(3), 615-625.
Estep, R.E., Burt, M.R., & Mulligan, H.J. The socialization of sexual identity. *Journal of Marriage and the Family,* 1977, *39,* 99-112.
Ethical principles of psychologists. *American Psychologist,* 1981, *36*(6), 633-638.
Etkind, S. *Two patterns of ego identity formation in underachieving "special needs" adolescents.* Unpublished dissertation, Boston University, 1979.
Ewy, D., & Ewy, R. *Preparation for childbirth: A Lamaze guide by Donna and Roger Ewy* (3rd ed.). New York: The New American Library, 1982.
Eysenck, M.W. *Human memory.* Elmsford, N.Y.: Pergamon Press, 1977.

Fagan, J. Infants' delayed recognition memory and forgetting. *Journal of Experimental Child Psychology,* 1973, *16,* 424-450.
Falender, C. & Heber, R. Mother-child interaction and participation in a longitudinal intervention program. *Developmental Psychology,* 1975, *11,* 830-836.
Falender, C. & Heber, R. Conceptual tempo and mother interaction: Results from a longitudinal intervention program. *Psychological Reports,* 1977, *41,* 995-1002.
Fantz, R.L. Complexity and facial resemblance as determinants of response to facelike stimuli by 5 and 10 week old infants. *Journal of Experimental Child Psychology,* 1974. *18,* 480-487.
Farrell, M.P., & Rosenberg, S.D. *Men at midlife.* Boston: Auburn House Publishing Co., 1981.
Faust, M.S. Developmental maturity as determinant in prestige of adolescent girls. *Child Development,* 1960, *31,* 173-184.
Faust, M.S. Somatic development of adolescent girls. *Monographs of the Society for Research in Child Development,* 1977, *42,* 1-88 (Serial No. 169).
Feather, N.T. *Values in education and society.* New York: The Free Press, 1975.
Feather, N.T. Values in adolescence. In J. Adelson (Ed.), *Handbook of adolescence.* New York: John Wiley & Sons, 1980.
Federal Bureau of Investigation. *Uniform crime reports for the United States.* Washington, D.C.: U.S. Government Printing Office, 1979.
Federal Council on Aging. *White House Conference on Aging chart book.* Washington, D.C.: U.S. Government Printing Office, 1961. p. 60.
Feigenbaum, E.M. Sexual behavior in the later years. In R.A. Kalish (Ed.), *The later years: Social application of gerontology.* Monterey, Calif.: Brooks/Cole Publishing Co., 1977.
Feingold, B.F. *Why your child is hyperactive.* New York: Random House, 1974.
Feinstein, S.C., & Ardon, M.S. Trends in dating patterns and adolescent development. *Journal of Youth and Adolescence,* 1973, *212,* 157-166.
Ferris, T. Toxemia and hypertension. In G. Burrow, & T. Ferris (Eds.), *Medical complications during pregnancy.* Philadelphia: W.B. Saunders Co., 1975.
Festinger, L. *A theory of cognitive dissonance.* Stanford, Calif.: Stanford University Press, 1957.
Field, T. Interaction behaviors of primary versus secondary caretaker fathers. *Developmental Psychology,* 1978a, *14,* 183-184.
Field, T. The three R's of infant-adult interactions: Rhythms, repertoires and responsivity. *Journal of Pediatric Psychology,* 1978b, *3,* 131-136.

Field, T.M., & Roopnarine, J.L. Infant-peer interactions. In Field, T.M., Huston, A., Quay, H.C., Troll, L., & Finley, G.E., *Review of human development*. New York: John Wiley & Sons, 1982.

Field, T.M., & Widmayer, S.M. Motherhood. In B.B. Wolman (Ed.), *Handbook of developmental psychology*. Englewood Cliffs, N.J.: Prentice-Hall, 1982.

Finley, G.E., & Cheyne, J.A. Brith order and susceptibility to peer modeling influences in young boys. *Journal of Genetic Psychology*, 1976, *129*, 273-277.

Fischman, S.H. Characteristics associated with pregnancy resolution decisions of unwed adolescents. *Symposium on Childbearing in Adolescence*, Washington, D.C., 1974.

Fischman, S.H. Delivery or abortion in inner-city adolescents. *American Journal of Orthopsychiatry*, 1977, *47*(1).

Fishburne, P.M., Abelson, H.I., & Cisin, I. *National survey on drug abuse: Main findings, 1979*. Rockville, Md.: National Institute of Drug Abuse, 1980.

Fisher, K.W. A theory of cognitive development: The control and construction of hierarchies of skills. *Psychological Review*, 1980, *87*, 477-531.

Fitzgerald, N., & Brackbill, Y. Classical conditioning in infancy: Development and constraints. *Psychological Bulletin*, 1976, *83*(3), 353-376.

Flasher, J. Adultism. *Adolescence*, 1978, *13*(51), 517-523.

Flaste, R. Career ambitions: Keeping the options open. *The New York Times*. February 27, 1976, p. 15.

Flavell, J.H. The development of inferences about others. In T. Misebel (Ed.), *Understanding other persons*. Oxford, England: Blackwell & Mott, 1973.

Flavell, J.H. *Cognitive development*. Englewood Cliff, N.J.: Prentice-Hall, 1977.

Flavell, J.H. Monitoring social-cognitive enterprises: Something else that may develop in the area of social cognition. In J.H. Flavell & L. Ross (Eds.), *Social cognitive development: Frontiers and possible futures*. New York: Cambridge University Press, 1983.

Flint, M. Cross-cultural factors that affect age of menopause. In P.A. Van Keep, R.B. Greenblatt, and M. Albeaux-Fernet (Eds.), *Consensus on menopause research*. Baltimore: University Park Press, 1976.

Floyd, H.H., Jr., & South, D.R. Dilemma of youth: The choice of parents or peers as a frame of reference for behavior. *Journal of Marriage and the Family*, 1972, *34*, 627-634.

Fodor, J.A. *The language of thought*. New York: Thomas Y. Crowell, 1975.

Foman, S.J., Filer, L.J., Jr., Anderson, T.A., & Ziegler, E.E. Recommendations for feeding normal infants. *Pediatrics*, 1979, *63* (1).

Foote, A. Kids who won't leave home. *The Atlantic*, March 1978, 118.

Forbes, G.B. Biological implications of the adolescent growth process: Body composition. In J.I. McKigney & H.M. Munroe (Eds.), *Nutrient requirements in adolescence*. Cambridge, Mass.: M.I.T. Press, 1976.

Foreman, G., & Sigel, I. *Cognitive development: A life-span view*. Belmont, Calif.: Wadworth Publishing Co., 1979.

Fozard, J.L., & Popkin, S.J. Optimizing adult development: Ends and means of an applied psychology of aging. *American Psychologist*, 1978, *33*, 975-989.

Fozard, J.L., Wolf, E., Bell, B., McFarland, R.A., & Podolsky, S. Visual perception and communication. In J.E. Birren & K.W. Schaie (Eds.), *Handbook of the psychology of aging*. New York: Van Nostrand Reinhold Co., 1977.

Frankenburg, W.K., & Dodds, J.B. The Denver Developmental Screening Test, *Journal of Pediatrics*, 1967, *71*, 181-191.

Frenkel-Brunswick, E. Adjustments and reorientation in the course of the life-span. In R.G. Kuhlen & G.G. Thompson (Eds.), *Psychological studies of human development* (3rd ed.). New York: Appleton-Century-Crofts, 1970.

Freud, S. *An outline of psychoanalysis*. New York: W.W. Norton & Co., 1949.

Freud, S. *A general introduction to psychoanalysis* (J. Reviere, Trans.). New York: Permabooks, 1953.

Freuh, T., & McGhee, P.E. Traditional sex role development and amount of time spent watching television. *Developmental Psychology*, 1975, *11*, 109.

Fricker, H., & Segal, S. Narcotic addiction, pregnancy, and the newborn. *American Journal of the Diseases of Children*, 1978, *132*, 360-366.

Friedman, M., & Roseman, R.H. *Type A behavior and your heart*. New York: Alfred A. Knopf, 1974.

Frolkis, V.V. Aging of the autonomic nervous system. In J.E. Birren & K.W. Schaie (Eds.), *Handbook of the psychology of aging*. New York: Van Nostrand Reinhold Co., 1977.

Furman, W., & Childs, M.K. *A temporal perspective on children's friendship*. Paper presented at meetings of the Society for Research in Child Development, Boston, 1981.

Furstenberg, F.F. *Unplanned parenthood: The social consequences of teenage bearing*. Riverside, N.J.: The Free Press, 1977.

Gabert, H.A., & Stanchever, M.A. Electronic fetal monitoring as a routine practice in an obstetric service: A progress report. *American Journal of Obstetrics and Gynecology*, 1974, *118*, 534.

Gadlin, H. Private lives and private order: A critical review of the history of intimate relationships in the U.S. In G. Levinger & H. Raush (Eds.), *Close relationships*. Amherst: University of Massachusetts Press, 1977.

Gadpaille, W.J. *The cycles of sex*. New York: Charles Scribner's Sons, 1975.

Galton, L. *Your child in sports*. New York: Franklin Watts, 1980.

Gardner, H. *Developmental psychology: An introduction* (2nd ed.). Boston: Little, Brown & Co., 1982.

Garn, S.M. Bone loss and aging. In R. Goldman & M. Rockstein (Eds.), *The physiology and pathology of human aging*. New York: Academic Press, 1975.

Garnica, O.K. Some prosodic and paralinguistic features of speech directed to young children. In C.E. Snow & C.A. Ferguson (Eds.), *Talking to children: Language input and acquisition*. Cambridge, England: Cambridge University Press, 1977.

Garvey, C. *Play*. Cambridge, Mass.: Harvard University Press, 1977.

Gazzaniga, M.S. *The bisected brain*. New York: Appleton-Century-Crofts, 1970.

Gelman, R. Cognitive development. *Annual Review of Psychology*, 1978, *29*, 297-332.

Gergen, K.J. *Toward transformation in social knowledge*. New York: Springer-Verlag, 1982.

Gergen, K.J., & Gergen, M.M. *Social psychology*. New York: Harcourt Brace Jovanovich, 1981.

Gerson, R.P., & Damon, W. Moral understanding and children's conduct. *New Directions for Child Development*, 1978, *2* 41-59.

Gesell, A. *The first five years of life*. New York: Macmillan Publishing Co., 1940.

Gesell, A., & Ilg, F.L. *Child development: An introduction to the study of human development*. New York: Harper & Row, Publishers, 1949.

Gesell, A., Ilg, F.L., & Ames, L.B. *Youth: The years from 10 to 16*. New York: Harper & Row, Publishers, 1956.

Gesell, A.L., Ilg, F.L., Ames, L.B., & Rodell, J.L. *Infant and child in the culture of today: The guidance of development in home and nursery school* (Rev. ed.). New York: Harper & Row, Publishers, 1974.

Gholson, B. *The cognitive-development basis of human learning: Studies in hypothesis testing*. New York: Academic Press, 1980.

Giambra, L.M., & Arenberg, D. Problem solving, concept learning, and aging. In L.W. Poon (Ed.), *Aging in the 1980s*. Washington, D.C.: American Psychological Association, 1980.

Gibson, E.J. *Principles of perceptual learning and development*. New York: Appleton-Century-Crofts, 1969.

Gibson, E.J. Trends in perceptual development: Implications for the reading process. In A.D. Pick (Ed.), *Minnesota symposia on child psychology* (Vol 8). Minneapolis: University of Minnesota Press, 1974.

Gibson, E.J., & Walk, R.D. The "visual cliff." *Scientific American*, 1960, *202* (April), 64-71.

Gibson, J.L. *The senses considered as perceptual systems*. Boston: Houghton Mifflin Co., 1966.

Gilbert, J.H. Babbling and the deaf child: A commentary on Lenneberg et al. (1965) and Lenneberg (1967). *Journal of Child Language*, 1982, *9*(2), 511-515.

Gilligan, C. In a different voice: Women's conceptions of self and of morality. *Harvard Educational Review*, 1977, *47*(4), 481-517.

Glaser, D. Social disorganization and delinquent subcultures. In H.C. Quay (Ed.), *Juvenile delinquency*. New York: D. Van Nostrand Co., 1965, pp. 30-36.

Gleason, J. *Fathers and other strangers: Men's speech to young children*. Paper presented at the 26th Georgetown Round Table, Georgetown University, Washington, D.C., 1975.

Glick, I.O., Weiss, R.S., & Parkes, C.M. *The first year of bereavement*. New York: Wiley-Interscience, 1974.

Glick, P.C. (quoting census figures). In Velie, L., The myth of the vanishing family. *Reader's Digest*, February, 1973.

Glick, P.C. A demographic look at American families. *Journal of Marriage and the Family*, 1975, *37*, 15-26.

Glick, P.C. Updating the life cycle of the family. *Journal of Marriage and the Family*, 1977, *39*, 5-13.

Glick, P.C. The future of the American family. *Current Population Reports* (Special Studies Series P-23, No. 78), Washington, D.C.: U.S. Government Printing Office, 1979a.

Glick, P.C. *Who are the children in one-parent households?* Paper presented at Wayne State University, Detroit, 1979b.

Glick, P.C., & Carter, H. *Marriage and divorce: A social and economic study* (2nd ed.). Cambridge, Mass.: Harvard University Press, 1976.

Glick, P.C., & Norton, A.J. Marrying, divorcing and living together in the U.S. today. *Population Bulletin*, 1977, *32*(5), 1-41.

Golbus, M., Loughman, W., Epstein, C., Halbasch, G., Stephens, J., & Hall, B. Prenatal genetic diagnosis in 3,000 amniocenteses. *New England Journal of Medicine*, 1979, *300*(4), 157-163.

Gold, J.G., & Kaufman, S.M. Development of care of elderly: Tracing the history of institutional facilities. *Gerontologist*, 1970, *10*, 262-274.

Gold, M., & Petronio, R.J. Delinquent behavior in adolescence. In J. Adelson (Ed.), *Handbook of adolescent psychology*. New York: John Wiley & Sons, 1980.

Gold, M., & Reimer, D.J. Changing patterns of delinquent behavior among Americans 13 through 16 years old: 1967-72. *Crime and Delinquency Literature*, 1975, *7*, 483-517.

Goldberg, S. Social competence in infancy: A model of parent-child interaction. *Merrill-Palmer Quarterly,* 1977, *23,* 163-177.

Goldin, R. *Therapy as education.* Unpublished dissertation, Boston University, 1977.

Goldstein, B. *Human sexuality.* New York: McGraw-Hill Book Co., 1976.

Goldstein, J. On being adult and being an adult in secular law. *Daedalus,* 1976, *105*(4), 69-87.

Goleman, D. 1,528 little geniuses and how they grew. *Psychology Today,* 1980, *13*(9), 28-43.

Golenpaul, A. (Ed.). *Information Please Almanac, 1977.* New York: Simon & Schuster, 1977.

Golinkoff, R.M., & Ames, G.J. *Do fathers use "motherese"?* Paper presented at Society for Research in Child Development, New Orleans, March 1977.

Goode, W.J. *Women in divorce (1956).* Republished as *Divorce and after.* New York: The Free Press, 1969.

Goodman, M.J., Grove, J.S., & Gilbert, F., Jr. Age at menopause in relation to reproductive history in Japanese, Caucasian, Chinese and Hawaiian women living in Hawaii. *Journal of Gerontology,* 1978, *33,* 688-694.

Goodrich, W., Ryder, R.G., & Rausch, H.L. Patterns of newlyweds. In M.E. Losswell & T.E. Losswell (Eds.), *Love, marriage and family: A developmental approach.* Glenview, Ill.: Scott, Foresman & Co., 1973.

Gorbach, A., & Feinbloom, R.I. Diseases and conditions that complicate pregnancy. In R.I. Feinbloom (Ed.), *Pregnancy, birth and the newborn baby.* New York: Delta, 1979.

Gordon, J. Nutritional individuality. *American Journal of Diseases of Children,* 1975, *129*(4), 422-424.

Gottlieb, D., and Chafetz, J.S. Dynamics of familial, generational conflict and reconciliation: A research note. *Youth and Society,* 1977, *9*(2), 213-224.

Gould, R.L. The phases of adult life: A study in developmental psychology. *American Journal of Psychiatry,* 1972, *129*,(5), 521-531.

Gould, R.L. *Transformations: Growth and change in adult life.* New York: Simon & Schuster, 1978.

Gove, W.R., & Hughes, M. Possible cause of the apparent sex differences in physical health: An empirical investigation. *American Sociological Review,* 1979, *44,* 126-46.

Graham, F.K., Strock, B.D., & Zeigler, B.L. Excitatory and inhibitory influences on reflex responsiveness. In W.A. Collins (Ed.), *Minnesota symposium on child psychology* (Vol. 14). Hillsdale, N.J.: Lawrence Erlbaum Associates, 1980.

Granick, S., & Friedman, A.S. Educational experience and maintenance of intellectual functioning by the aged: An overview. In L.F. Jarvick, C. Eisdorfer, & J.E. Blum (Eds.), *Intellectual functioning in adults.* New York: Springer Publishing Co., 1973, pp. 59-64.

Green, F. Factors contributing to the high risk of pregnancy for adolescents. *Symposium on Childbearing in Adolescence.* Washington, D.C., 1974.

Green, J. Overview of adolescent drug use. In G.M. Beschner & A.S. Friedman (Eds.), *Youth drug abuse: Problems, issues and treatment.* Lexington, Mass.: D.C. Heath & Co., 1979.

Greenberg, M., & Morris, N. Engrossment: The newborn's impact upon the father. *American Journal of Orthopsychiatry,* 1974, *44,* 520-531.

Grotevant, H., Scarr, S., & Weinberg, R. Intellectual Development in family constellations with adopted and natural children: A test of the Zajonc and Markus model. *Child Development,* 1977, *48,* 1699-1703.

Gruber, H.E. Courage and cognitive growth in children and scientists. In M. Schwebel and J. Raph (Eds.), *Piaget in the classroom.* New York: Basic Books, Inc., Publishers, 1973.

Grush, J.E., & Yehl, J.G. Marital roles, sex differences and interpersonal attraction. *Journal of Personality and Social Psychology,* 1979, *37,* 116-123.

Gubrium, J.F. Being single in old age. *International Journal of Aging and Human Development,* 1975, *6,* 29-41.

Guilford, J.P. *The nature of intelligence.* New York: McGraw-Hill Book Co., 1967.

Gunter, B.G, & Moore, H.A. Youth, leisure and post-industrial society: Implications for the family. *Family Coordinator,* 1975, *24*(2), 199-207.

Gutmann, D.L. The cross-cultural perspective: Notes toward a comparative psychology of aging. In J.E. Birren & K.W. Schaie (Eds.), *Handbook of the psychology of aging.* New York: Van Nostrand Reinhold Co., 1977.

Gutmann, E. Muscles. In C.E. Finch & L. Hayflick (Eds.), *Handbook of the biology of aging.* New York: Van Nostrand Reinhold Co., 1977.

Haan, N. Change and sameness: Reconsidered. *International Journal of Aging and Human Development,* 1976, *7,* 59-65.

Haan, N. Two moralities in action contexts. Relationships to thought, ego regulation and development. *Journal of Personality and Social Psychology,* 1978, *36,* 286-305.

Haan, N. Can research on morality be "scientific"? *American Psychologist,* 1982, *37*,(10), 1096-1104.

Haan, N., & Day, D. A longitudinal study of change and sameness in personality development: Adolescence to later adulthood. *International Journal of Aging and Human Development,* 1974, *5,* 11-39.

Hackman, J.R. Work Design. In J.R. Hackman & J. Lloyd Suttle (Eds.), *Improving life at work.* Santa Monica, Calif.: Goodyear Publishing Co., 1977.

Hadfield, J.A. *Childhood and adolescence.* Baltimore: Penguin Books, 1962.

Hagestad, G.O. Life transitions and adult family roles. *Generations,* 1979, *4,* 16-17.

Haith, M.H., & Campos, J.J. Human infancy. In M.R. Rosenzweig & L.W. Porter (Eds.), *Annual review of psychology* (Vol. 28). Palo Alto, Calif.: Annual Reviews, 1977.

Hall, E., Acting one's age: New rules for old. *Psychology Today,* 1980, *13*(11), 66-80.

Hamburg, B. Early adolescence: A specific and stressful stage of the life cycle. In G. Coelho, D.A. Hamburg, & J.E. Adams (Eds.), *Coping and adaptation.* New York: Basic Books, Inc., Publishers, 1974.

Hansen, R.A. Consistency and stability of home environmental measures related to IQ. *Child Development Quarterly,* 1975. *46,* 470-480.

Hansen, S.L. Dating choices of high school students. *Family Coordinator,* 1977, *26,* 133-138.

Hanson, J., Streissguth, A., & Smith, D. The effects of moderate fetal alcohol consumption during pregnancy on fetal growth and morphogenesis. *Journal of Pediatrics,* 1978, *92*(3), 457-460.

Hareven, T.K. The last stage: Historical adulthood and old age. *Daedalus,* 1976, *105*(4), 13-27.

Harlan, W.R., Grilld, G.P., Coroni-Huntley, J., & Leaverton, P.E. Secondary sex characteristics of boys 12 to 17 years of age: The U.S. Health Examination Survey. *Journal of Pediatrics,* 1979, *95,* 292-297.

Harlap, S., & Shiono, P. Alcohol, smoking and incidence of spontaneous abortions in the first and second trimester. *Lancet,* July 26, 1980, 173-176.

Harlow, H.F. *Learning to love.* San Francisco: Albion Publishing Co., 1971.

Harlow, H.F., & Suomi, S.J. The nature of love—simplified. *American Psychologist,* 1970, *25,* 161-168.

Harris, R. Cardiac changes with age. In R. Goldman & M. Rockstein (Eds.), *The physiology and pathology of human aging.* New York: Academic Press, 1975.

Harter, S. Developmental perspectives on the self-system. In E.M. Hetherington (Eds.), *Carmichael's manual of child psychology* (4th ed.). New York: John Wiley & Sons, 1982.

Hartford, M.E. The use of group methods for work with the aged. In J.E. Birren & R.B. Sloane (Eds.), *Handbook of mental health and aging.* Englewood Cliffs, N.J.: Prentice-Hall, 1980.

Hartup, W.W. Peer interaction and social organization. In P.H. Mussen (Ed.), *Manual of child psychology.* New York: John Wiley & Sons, 1970.

Hartup, W.W. Aggression in childhood: Developmental perspectives. *American Psychologist,* 1974, *29,* 336-341.

Hartup, W.W. Peer interaction and the behavioral development of the individual child. In E. Schopler & R.J. Reichler (Eds.), *Psychopathology and child development.* New York: Plenum Press, 1976.

Hartup, W.W. Children and their friends. In H. McGurk (Ed.), *Issues in childhood social development.* London: Methuen & Co., 1978.

Hass, K. *Understanding adjustment and behavior.* Englewood Cliffs, N.J.: Prentice-Hall, 1970.

Havens, E.M. Women, work, and wedlock: A note on female marital patterns in the United States. *American Journal of Sociology,* 1973, *78,* 975-981.

Havighurst, R.J. Human development (2nd ed.). New York: David McKay Co., 1972.

Havighurst, R.J. Social roles, work, leisure, and education. In C. Eisdorfer & M.P. Lawton (Eds.), *The psychology of adult development and aging.* Washington, D.C.: American Psychological Association, 1973.

Havighurst, R.J. The future aged: The use of time and money. *Gerontologist,* 1975, *15,* 10-15.

Havighurst, R.J. *Developmental tasks and education* (4th ed.). New York: David McKay Co., 1979.

Havighurst, R.J. The world of work. In B.B. Wolman, (Ed.), *Handbook of developmental psychology.* Englewood Cliffs, N.J.: Prentice-Hall, 1982.

Havlik, R.J., & Feinleib, M. (Eds.). *Proceedings of the Conference on the Decline in Coronary Heart Disease Mortality* (NIH Publication No. 79-1610). Washington, D.C.: U.S. Department of HEW, 1979.

Hawkins, J.L. Associations between companionship, hostility, and marital satisfaction. *Journal of Marriage and the Family,* 1970, *17,* 282.

Heald, J. Mid-life career influences. *Vocational Guidance Quarterly,* 1977, *25*(4), 309-312.

Heath, D.H. *Explorations of maturity.* New York: Appleton-Century-Crofts, 1965.

Heath, D.H. Adolescent and adult predictors of vocational adaptation. *Journal of Vocational Behavior,* 1976, *9,* 1-19.

Hebb, D.O. The possibility of a dual type mechanism. In T.D. Landauer (Ed.), *Readings in physiological psychology: The bodily basis of behavior.* New York: McGraw-Hill Book Co., 1967.

Heber, R. The Milwaukee project: Early intervention as a technique to prevent mental retardation. Report of second annual Vermont Conference on the Primary Prevention of Psychopathology. *APA Monitor,* September/October, 1976.

Heilman, R.O. *Early recognition of alcohol and other drug dependence.* Center City, Minn.: Hazelden, 1975.

Heinonen, O.P., Slone, D., Monson, R.R., Hook, E.B., & Shapiro, S. Cardiovascular birth defects and antenatal exposure to female sex hormones. *New England Journal of Medicine,* 1977, *296,* 67-70.

Heinonen, O.P., Slone, D., & Shapiro, S. *Birth defects and drugs in pregnancy.* Littleton, Mass.: Publishing Sciences Group, 1977.

Hellman, L.M., & Pritchard, J.A. *Williams obstetrics* (15th ed.). New York: Appleton-Century-Crofts, 1976.

Henderson, R.W., & Bergan, J.R. *The cultural context of childhood.* Columbus, Ohio: Charles E. Merrill Publishing Co., 1976.

Hendricks, J., & Hendricks, C.D. *Aging in mass society: Myths and realities.* Cambridge, Mass.: Winthrop Publishers, 1977.

Herbst, A.L., Scully, R.E., Robboy, S.J., & Welch, W.R. Complications of prenatal therapy with diethylstilbestrol. *Pediatrics,* 1978, *62,* 1151-1159.

Herbst, A.L., Ulfelder, H., & Poskanzer, D.C. Adenocarcinoma of the vagina. *New England Journal of Medicine,* 1971, *284*(16), 878-881.

Hermel, J., Schönwetter, S., & Samueloff, S. Taste sensation identification and age in man. *Journal of Oral Medicine,* 1970, *25,* 39-42.

Herndon, C.N., Nash, E.M. Premarriage and marriage counseling: A study of North Carolina physicians. *Journal of American Medical Association,* 1962, *180,* 395-401.

Hershey, D. *Life span and factors affecting it.* Springfield, Ill.: Charles C Thomas, Publisher, 1974.

Herzog, E., & Leurs, H. Children in poor families: Myths and realities. In S. Chess & A. Thomas (Eds.), *Annual progress in child psychiatry and child development,* New York: Brunner/Mazel, 1971.

Hess, B. Friendship. In M.W. Riley, M. Johnson, & A. Foner (Eds.), *Aging and society: A socialization of age stratification* (Vol. 3). New York: Russell Sage Foundation, 1972.

Hetherington, E.M., Cox, M., & Cox, R. Family interaction and the social, emotional and cognitive development of children following divorce. In V. Vaughn & T.B. Brazelton (Eds.), *The family: Setting priorities.* New York: Harcourt Brace Jovanovich Legal & Professional Publications, 1979.

Heyman, D.K., & Polansky, G.H. Social services in the community. In R.A. Kalish (Ed.), *The later years: Social applications of gerontology.* Monterey, Calif.: Brooks/Cole Publishing Co., 1977.

Hildebrand, V. *Introduction to early childhood education* (2nd ed.). New York: Macmillan Publishing Co., 1976.

Hirsch, G., Kent, D.P., & Silverman, S.L. *Homogeneity and heterogeneity among low income Negro and white aged.* Paper presented at the Annual Gerontological Society Meetings, Denver, 1968.

Hirschman, R., Melamed, L.E., & Oliver, C.M. The psychophysiology of infancy. In B.B. Wolman (Ed.), *Handbook of developmental psychology.* Englewood Cliffs, N.J.: Prentice-Hall, 1982.

Hodapp, R.M., & Mueller, E. Early social development. In B.B. Wolman (Ed.), *Handbook of developmental psychology.* Englewood Cliffs, N.J.: Prentice-Hall, 1982.

Hoffman, L.W. Effects of maternal employment on the child: A review of the research. *Developmental Psychology,* 1974, *10*(2), 204-228.

Hoffman, M.L. Father absence and conscience development. *Developmental Psychology,* 1971, *4,* 400-406.

Hoffman, M.L. Moral internalization: Current theory and research. In L. Berkowitz (Ed.), *Advances in experimental social psychology* (Vol. 10). New York: Academic Press, 1977.

Hoffman, M.L. Moral development in adolescence. In J. Adelson (Ed.), *Handbook of adolescent psychology.* New York: John Wiley & Sons, 1980.

Hogan, E.O., & Green, R.L. Can teachers modify children's self-concepts? *Teacher's College Record.* 1971, *62,* 423-426.

Hogan, R. Dialectical aspects of moral development. *Human Development,* 1974, *17,* 107-117.

Holmes, T.H., & Masuda, M. Life changes and illness susceptibility. In J.P. Scott & E.C. Seray (Eds.), *Symposium on separation and depression* (Publication No. 94), Washington, D.C.: American Association for the Advancement of Science, 1973.

Holmes, T.H., & Rahe, R.H. The social readjustment rating scale. *Journal of Psychosomatic Research,* 1967, *11,* 213-218.

Holtzman, N.A., Meck, A.G., & Mellits, E.D. Neonatal screening for phenylketonuria. I. Effectiveness. *Journal of the American Medical Association,* 1974, *229,* 667.

Horn, J. Easing a baby's way into the world. *Psychology Today,* 1977, *10*(10), 314.

Horn, J.L. Organization of data on life-span development of human abilities. In L.R. Goulet & P.B. Baltes (Eds.), *Life-span developmental psychology: Research and theory.* New York: Academic Press, 1970.

Horn, J.L. Human ability systems. In P.B. Baltes (Ed.), *Life-span development and behavior* (Vol. 1). New York: Academic Press, 1978.

Horn, J.L., & Donaldson, G. Cognitive development II: Adulthood development in human abilities. In O.G. Brim, Jr., & J. Kagan (Eds.), *Constancy and change in human development: A volume of review essays.* Cambridge, Mass.: Harvard University Press, 1980.

Hornblum, J.M., & Overton, W.F. Area and volume conservation among the elderly: Assessment and training. *Developmental Psychology,* 1976, *12,* 68-74.

Horner, M. Femininity and successful achievement: A basic inconsistency. In J. Bardwick, E. Dorivan, M. Horner, & D. Guttman (Eds.), *Feminine personality and conflict.* Belmont, Calif.: Wadsworth Publishing Co., 1970.

Horowitz, T. Excitement vs. economy: Fashion and youth culture in Britain. *Adolescence,* 1982 (Fall), *17*(67), 627-636.

Houseknecht, S.K. Childlessness and marital adjustment. *Journal of Marriage and the Family,* 1979, *41,*(2), 259-266.

Howell, M.C. Effects of maternal employment on the child. *Pediatrics,* 1973, *52*(3), 327-343.

Hoyer, W.J., Rebok, G.W., & Sved, S.M. Effects of varying irrelevant information on adult age differences in problem solving. *Journal of Gerontology,* 1979, *14,* 553-560.

Huberty, D.J., & Malmquist, J.D. Adolescent chemical dependency. In A.R. Clark, *Perspectives in psychiatric care* (Vol. 16). Hillsdale, N.J.: Nursing Publications, 1978.

Hudec, T., Thean, J., Kuehl, D., & Dougherty, R. Tris (dichloropropyl) phosphate, a mutagenic flame retardant: Frequent occurrence in human seminal plasma. *Science,* 1981, *211*(27), 951-952.

Hudgens, R.W. *Psychiatric disorders in adolescence.* Baltimore: The Williams & Wilkins Co., 1974.

Hultsch, D.F., & Deutsch, F. *Adult development and aging: A life-span perspective.* New York: McGraw-Hill Book Co., 1981.

Hunt, B., & Hunt, M. *Prime time.* New York: Stein & Day, Publishers, 1974.

Hunt, E. Varieties of cognitive power. In L.B. Resnick (Ed.), *The nature of intelligence.* Hillsdale, N.J.: Lawrence Erlbaum Associates, 1976.

Hunt, M. *Sexual behavior in the 70's.* New York: Dell Books, 1974.

Hurlock, E.B. *Adolescent development* (3rd ed.). New York: McGraw-Hill Book Co., 1973.

Hurlock, E.B. *Development psychology* (5th ed.). New York: McGraw-Hill Book Co., 1982.

Huston, A.C. Sex typing. In E.M. Hetherington (Ed.), *Carmichael's manual of child psychology* (4th ed.). New York: John Wiley & Sons, 1982.

Hyde, J.S. *Understanding human sexuality.* New York: McGraw-Hill Book Co., 1979.

Hyde, J.S. How large are cognitive gender differences? *American Psychologist,* 1981, *36,* 382-901.

Hyden, S. Flexible retirement provisions in public pension systems. In Organization for Economic Cooperation and Development, *Flexibility in retirement age.* Paris: The Organization, 1971, pp. 21-37.

Hymes, D. On communicative competence. In J.G. Pride & J. Holmes (Eds.), *Sociolinguistics.* Harmondsworth, England: Penguin Books, 1972.

Ilg, F., & Ames, L. *Parents ask.* New York: Harper & Row, Publishers, 1962.

Illingworth, R.S. *The development of the infant and young child: Normal and abnormal.* Baltimore: The Williams & Wilkins Co., 1971.

Ingalls, A.J., & Salerno, M.C. *Maternal and child health nursing* (4th ed.). St. Louis: The C.V. Mosby Co., 1979.

Inhelder, B., & Piaget, J. *The early growth of logic in a child.* New York: Harper & Row, Publishers, 1964.

Institute for Social Research. Education and job satisfaction. Reported in *Science News,* May 8, 1976, p. 267.

Iorio, J. *Childbirth: Family-centered nursing* (3rd ed.). St. Louis: The C.V. Mosby Co., 1975.

Irelan, L.M., & Bond, K. Retirees of the 1970s. In C.S. Kart & B.B. Manard (Eds.), *Aging in America: Readings in gerontology.* New York: Alfred Publishing Co., 1976, 231-251.

Jackson, H.C. National caucus on the black aged: A progress report. *Aging and Human Development,* 1971, *3,* 226-231.

Jacobs, J. *Adolescent suicide.* New York: John Wiley & Sons, 1971.

Jacobson, S.B. The challenge of aging for marriage partners. In W.C. Bier (Ed.), *Aging: Its challenge to the individual and to society.* New York: Fordham University Press, 1974.

Janis, I.L. (Ed.). *Personality: Dynamics, development and assessment.* New York: Harcourt Brace Jovanovich, 1969.

Jennings, M.K., & Niemi, R.A. Continuity and change in political orientations: A longitudinal study of two generations. *American Political Science Review,* 1975, *69,* 1316-1335.

Jensen, M.D., Benson, R.C., & Bobak, I.M. *Maternity care: The nurse and the family* (ed. 2). St. Louis: The C.V. Mosby Co., 1981.

Jersild, A.T. *Child psychology* (6th ed.). Englewood Cliffs, N.J.: Prentice-Hall, 1968.

Jersild, A.T., Brook, J.S., & Brook, D.W. *The psychology of adolescence* (3rd ed.). New York: Macmillan Publishing Co., 1978.

Johnson, L.D., Driscoll, S.G., Hertig, A.T., Cole, P.T., & Nickerson, R.J. Vaginal adenosis in stillborns and neonates exposed to diethylstilbestrol and steroidal estrogens and progestins. *Obstetrics and Gynecology,* 1979, *53,* 671-679.

Johnston, L.D., Bachman, J.G., & O'Malley, P.M. *1979 highlights: Drugs and the nation's high school students: Five year national trends.* Rockville, Md.: National Institute on Drug Abuse, 1979.

Jones, M.C., Bayley, N., Macfarlane, J.W., & Honzik, M.P. *The course of human development.* Waltham, Mass.: Xerox, 1971.

Jones, N.B. (Ed.). *Ethological studies of child behavior.* London: Cambridge University Press, 1972.

Josselson, R.L. Ego development in adolescence. In J. Adelson (Ed.), *Handbook of adolescent psychology.* New York: John Wiley & Sons, 1980.

Juhasz, A.M. Unmarried adolescent parent. *Adolescence,* 1974, *9,* 263.

Kagan, J. Acquisition and significance of sex typing and sex-role identity. In M.L. Hoffman & C.W. Hoffman (Eds.), *Review of child development* (Vol. 1). New York: Russell Sage Foundation, 1964.

Kagan, J. The baby's elastic mind. *Human Nature,* 1978, *1,* 1.

Kagan, J. Overview: Perspectives on human infancy. In J.D. Osofsky (Ed.), *Handbook of infant development.* New York: John Wiley & Sons, 1979.

Kagan, J., Kearsley, R.B., & Zelazo, P.R. *Infancy: Its place in human development.* Cambridge, Mass.: Harvard University Press, 1978.

Kagan, J., & Moss, H.A. *Birth to maturity: A study in psychological development.* New York: John Wiley & Sons, 1962.

Kahana, B. Social behavior and aging. In B.B. Wolman, (Ed.), *Handbook of developmental psychology.* Englewood Cliffs, N.J.: Prentice-Hall, 1982.

Kahana, B., Kahana, E., & McLenigan, P. *The adventurous aged: Voluntary relocation in the later years.* Paper presented at the 33rd Annual Scientific Meeting of the Gerontological Society, San Diego, November 1980.

Kaiser, J.H. Fertilization and the physiology of fetus and placenta. In D.N. Danforth (Ed.), *Obstetrics and gynecology* (3rd ed.). New York: Harper & Row, Publishers, 1977.

Kales, J.D. Aging and sleep. In R. Goldman & M. Rockstein (Eds.), *The psychology and pathology of human aging.* New York: Academic Press, 1975.

Kalish, R.A. *Late adulthood: Perspectives in human development.* Monterey, Calif.: Brooks/Cole Publishing Co., 1975.

Kalish, R.A. Death and dying in a social context. In R.H. Binstock & E. Shanas (Eds.), *Handbook of aging and the social sciences.* New York: Van Nostrand Reinhold Co., 1976.

Kalish, R.A. After work: Then what? In R.A. Kalish (Ed.), *The later years: Social applications of gerontology.* Monterey, Calif.: Brooks/Cole Publishing Co., 1977.

Kaluger, G. *Knowledge of use of syllogisms and logic by college seniors.* Unpublished paper, Shippensburg State College, 1972.

Kaluger, G. *Dating practices of 152 adolescents from communities of varying populations.* Shippensburg, Pa.: Unpublished research, April, 1979.

Kaluger, G. *Age and type of dating practice in various size communities in Eastern United States as reported by college students 1979-1982.* Unpublished report, Shippensburg University, 1983.

Kaluger, G., & Heil, C.L. Basic symmetry and balance: Their relationship to perceptual-motor development. *Progress in Physical Therapy,* 1970, *1,* 132-137.

Kaluger, G., & Kaluger, M.F. *Profiles of human development.* St. Louis: The C.V. Mosby Co., 1976.

Kaluger, G., & Kaluger, M.F. Study of characteristics of LD children. In G. Kaluger & C.J. Kolson, *Reading and learning disabilities* (2nd ed.). Columbus, Ohio: Charles E. Merrill Publishing Co., 1978, pp. 93-95.

Kaluger, G., & Kaluger, M.F. *Human development: The span of life* (2nd ed.). St. Louis: The C.V. Mosby Co., 1979.

Kaluger, G. & Kaluger, M.F. *Free-response statements of problems of 231 junior high school students.* Unpublished research, Shippensburg State College, 1979.

Kaluger, G., & Kolson, C.J. *Reading and learning disabilities* (2nd ed.). Columbus, Ohio: Charles E. Merrill Publishing Co., 1978.

Kandel, D.B., Kessler, R.C., & Margulies, R.Z. Antecedents of adolescent initiation into stages of drug use: A developmental analysis. *Journal of Youth and Adolescence,* 1978, *7,* 13-40.

Kangas, P.E. The single professional woman: A phenomenological study. *Dissertation Abstracts International,* February 1978, *38*(8-B), 3888.

Kantner, J.F., & Zelnick, M. Sexual experience of young unmarried women in the U.S. *Family Planning Perspectives,* 1972, *4,* 9-17.

Kantner, J.F., & Zelnick, M. Contraception and pregnancy: Experience of young unmarried women in the United States. *Family Planning Perspectives,* 1973, *5,* 21-35.

Kantner, J.F., & Zelnick, M. Three-fourths of teenage first pregnancies are premaritally conceived. *Family Planning Digest,* 1974, *3*(4), 14-15.

Kaplan, H.S. *The new sex therapy.* New York: Brunner/Mazel, 1974.

Kastenbaum, R.J. *Death, society and human experience* (ed. 2). St. Louis: The C.V. Mosby Co., 1981.

Katchadourian, H. The biology of adolescence. San Francisco: W.H. Freeman, 1977.

Kaye, K. Imitation over a series of trials without feedback: Age six months. *Infant Behavior and Development,* 1978, *1,* 141-155.

Kazuza, J., & Firestone, I.J. *Cross-generational helping. Preference for alternative helping strategies.* Paper presented at the 33rd Annual Scientific Meeting of the Gerontological Society, San Diego, November 1980.

Keating, D.P. Toward a multivariate life-span theory of intelligence. In D. Kuhn (Ed.), Intellectual development beyond childhood. *New Directions for Child Development,* 1979, *5,* 69-84.

Keating, D.P. Thinking processes in adolescence. In J. Adelson (Ed.), *Handbook of adolescent psychology.* New York: John Wiley & Sons, 1980.

Keating, N.C., & Clark, L.V. Development of physical and social reasoning in adolescents. *Developmental Psychology,* 1980, *16,* 23-30.

Keating, N.C., & Cole, P. What do I do with him 24 hours a day? Changes in the housewife role after retirement. *Gerontologist,* 1980, *20,* 84-89.

Keating-Groen, N. *Marital satisfaction and retirement.* Unpublished doctoral dissertation, Syracuse University, 1977.

Kell, D., & Patton, C.V. Reaction to induced early retirement. *Gerontologist,* 1978, *18,* 173-179.

Kelley, R.K. *Courtship, marriage and the family* (2nd ed.). New York: Harcourt Brace Jovanovich, 1974.

Kelly, J.B. Divorce: The adult perspective. In B.B. Wolman (Ed.), *Handbook of developmental psychology.* Englewood Cliffs, N.J.: Prentice-Hall, 1982.

Kendall, T.S. The development of discrimination learning: A levels-of-functioning explanation. In H.W. Reese & L.P. Lipsitt (Eds.), *Advances in child behavior and development* (Vol. 13). New York: Academic Press, 1979.

Kendrick, C., & Dunn, J. Caring for a second baby: Effects on interaction between mother and firstborn. *Developmental Psychology,* 1980, *16,* 303-311.

Keniston, K. *The uncommitted.* New York: Harcourt Brace Jovanovich, 1965.

Keniston, K. Youth as a stage of life. *American Scholarship,* 1970, *39,* 631-654.

Keniston, K. *Youth and dissent.* Harcourt Brace Jovanovich, 1971.

Keniston, K. Prologue: Youth as a stage of life. In R.J. Havighurst & P.H. Dreyer (Eds.), *Youth.* Chicago: The University of Chicago Press, 1975.

Kenkel, W.F. *The family in perspective* (4th ed.). Santa Monica, Calif.: Goodyear Publishing Co., 1977.

Kennell, J.H., Jerauld, R., Wolfe, H., Chesler, D., Kreger, N.C., McAlpine, W., Steffa, N., & Klaus, M.H. Maternal behavior one year after early and extended post-partum contact. *Development Medicine and Child Neurology,* 1974, *16,* 172-179.

Kennell, J.H., Voos, D.K., & Klaus, M.H. Parent-infant bonding. In Osofsky, J.D. *Handbook of infant development.* New York: John Wiley & Sons, 1979.

Kent, S. *The life-extension revolution.* New York: William Morrow & Co., 1980.

Kephart, N.C. *The slow learner in the classroom* (2nd ed.). Columbus, Ohio: Charles E. Merrill Publishing Co., 1970.

Kephart, W.M. *The family, society and the individual* (4th ed.). Boston: Houghton Mifflin Co., 1977.

Kett, J.F. *Rites of passage.* New York: Basic Books, Inc., Publishers, 1977.

Kieren, D., Henton, J., & Marotz, R. *Hers and his.* Hinsdale, Ill.: Dryden Press, 1975.

Kimmell, D. *Adulthood and aging.* New York: John Wiley & Sons, 1974.

Kinsey, A.C., Pomeroy, W.B., & Martin, C.R. *Sexual behavior in the human male.* Philadelphia: W.B. Saunders Co., 1948.

Kinsey, A.C., Pomeroy, W.B., Martin, C.E., & Gebhard, P.H. *Sexual behavior in the human female.* Phildelphia: W.B. Saunders Co., 1953.

Kirby, I.J. Hormone replacement therapy for postmenopausal symptoms, *Lancet,* 1973, *2,* 103.

Kirkpatrick, C. *The family as process and institution.* New York: The Ronald Press, 1955.

Kitson, G.C., Lopata, H.Z., Holmes, W.M., & Mayerling, S.H. Divorces and widows: Similarities and differences. *American Journal of Orthopsychiatry,* 1980, *50,* 291-301.

Klaus, M.H., & Kennell, J.H. *Maternal-infant bonding* (ed. 2). St. Louis: The C.V. Mosby Co., 1981.

Kleck, R.E., Richardson, S.A., & Ronald, L. Physical appearance cues and interpersonal attraction in children. *Child Development,* 1974, *45,* 305-310.

Klemme, H.L., as reported in Rausberger, B. Three phases of adulthood: Transitions termed as difficult as adolescences. *The New York Times,* July 11, 1971, p. 32.

Klerman, G.L. The age of melancholy, *Psychology Today,* 1979, *12*(11), 37-42, 88.

Kline, J., Shrout, P., Stern, Z., Susser, M., & Warburton, D. Drinking during pregnancy and spontaneous abortions. *Lancet,* July 26, 1980, 176-180.

Knobloch, H., & Pasamanick, B. *Predicting from assessment of neuromotor and intellectual status in infancy.* Paper presented at the American Psychopathological Association meeting, 1966. In H.T. Thomas, Psychological assessment instruments for use with human infants. *Merrill-Palmer Quarterly, 16,* 1970.

Koch, S. The nature and limits of psychological knowledge: Lessons of a century qua "science." *American Psychologist,* 1981, *36*(3), 257-269.

Kogan, N. Cognitive styles in older adults. In Fields, T.M., Huston, A., Quay, H.C., Troll, L., & Finley, G.E. *Review of human development.* New York: John Wiley & Sons, 1982.

Kohlberg, L. Moral stages and moralization: The cognitive-developmental approach. In T. Lickona (Ed.), *Moral development and behavior: Theory, research and social issues.* New York: Holt, Rinehart & Winston, 1976.

Kohlberg, L. *The meaning and measurement of moral development.* Clark Lectures, Clark University, 1979.

Kohlberg, L., & Gilligan, C. The adolescent as a philosopher: The discovery of self in a postconventional world. *Daedalus,* 1971, *100,* 1051-1086.

Kohn, M.L. *Class and conformity: A study in values* (2nd ed.). Chicago: The University of Chicago Press, 1977.

Kohn, R.R., *Principles of mammalian aging.* Englewood Cliffs, N.J.: Prentice-Hall, 1971.

Kolata, G.B. Infertility: Promising new treatments. *Science,* 1977, *202,* 200-203.

Kompara, D. Difficulties in the socialization on process of step parenting. *Family Relations,* 1980, *29*(1), 69-73.

Kopp, C.B., & Parmelee, A.H. Prenatal and perinatal influences on infant behavior. In J.D. Osofsky (Ed.), *Handbook of infant development.* New York: John Wiley & Sons, 1979.

Korones, S.B. High-risk newborn infants—the basis for intensive nursing care (3rd ed.). St. Louis: The C.V. Mosby Co., 1981.

Kravitz, H., & Scherz, K.G. Preventing crib deaths. *Journal of the American Medical Association.* *149*(5), 444-447, 1976.

Kreps, J.M. (Ed.). *Women and the American economy.* Englewood Cliffs, N.J.: Prentice-Hall, 1976.

Kreutzer, M.A., & Charlesworth, W.R. *Infant recognition of emotions.* Paper presented at meetings of the Society for Research in Child Development, 1973.

Kubler-Ross, E. *On death and dying.* New York: Macmillan Publishing Co., 1969.

Kubler-Ross, E. *Questions and answers on death and dying.* New York: Macmillan Publishing Co., 1974.

Kurdek, L.A. Perspective taking as the cognitive basis of children's moral development: A review of the literature. *Merrill-Palmer Quarterly,* 1978, *24,* 3-28.

Kvaraceus, W.C. *Anxious youth: Dynamics of delinquency.* Columbus, Ohio: Charles E. Merrill Publishing Co., 1966.

Labouvie, E.W. Issues in life-span development. In B.B. Wolman (Ed.), *Handbook of developmental psychology.* Englewood Cliffs, N.J.: Prentice-Hall, 1982.

Lacy, W.B., & Hendricks, J. Developmental models of adult life: Myth or reality? *International Journal of Aging and Human Development,* 1980, *11*(2), 89-110.

Lamaze, F. Natural childbirth. Explained in D. Tanzer & J.L. Block. *Why natural childbirth?* Garden City, N.Y.: Doubleday & Co., 1972.

Lamb, M.E. The development of mother-infant and father-infant attachments in the second year of life. *Developmental Psychology,* 1977a, *13*(6), 637-648.

Lamb, M.E. Father-infant and mother-infant interactions in the first year of life. *Child Development,* 1977b, *48,* 167-181.

Lamb, M.E. Parental influences and the father's role: A personal perspective. *American Psychologist,* 1979, *34,* 938-944.

Lamb, M.E., and Baumrind, D. Socialization and personality development in the preschool years. In M.E. Lamb (Ed.), *Social and personality development.* New York: Holt, Rinehart & Winston, 1978.

Landis, P.H. *Making the most of marriage* (5th ed.). Englewood Cliffs, N.J.: Prentice-Hall, 1975.

Lanford, W.S., & Hutton, H.D. *Psychodynamic study of a pubescent girl with anorexia nervosa.* New York: Basic Books, Inc., Publishers, 1973.

Langman, L. *Economic practices and socialization in three societies.* Paper presented at the American Sociological Association meeting. New York, 1973.

Larson, R. Thirty years of research on the subjective well-being of older Americans. *Journal of Gerontology,* 1978, *33,* 109-125.

LaRue, A., & Jarvik, L.F. Old age and biobehavioral changes. In B.B. Wolman (Ed.), *Handbook of developmental psychology.* Englewood Cliffs, N.J.: Prentice-Hall, 1982.

Lasswell, M., & Lubsenz, N.M. *Styles of loving.* New York: Doubleday & Co., 1980.

Latham, H.C., Heckel, R.V., Herbert, L.J., & Bennett, E. *Pediatric nursing* (3rd ed.). St. Louis: The C.V. Mosby Co., 1977.

Laupres, W. Feeding of infants. In V.C. Vaughan III & R.J. McKay, *Nelson's textbook of pediatrics* (10th ed.). Philadelphia: W.B. Saunders Co., 1975.

Lawton, M.P., and Nahemow, L. Ecology and the aging process. In C. Eisdorfer & M.P. Lawton (Eds.), *The psychology of adult development and aging.* Washington, D.C.: American Psychological Association, 1973.

Leaf, A. Getting old. *Scientific American.* 1973. *229,* 45-52.

Lebo, C.P., & Reddell, R.C., Spoor's composite presbycusis curves for men and women, modified to conform to ANSI-1969 standard. *Laryngoscope,* 1972, *82,* 1403.

Leboyer, F. *Birth without violence.* New York: Alfred A. Knopf. 1975.

Lee, J.A. A typology of styles of loving. *Personality and Social Psychological Bulletin,* 1977, *3,* 173-182.

Lee, P.C., & Wolinsky, A.L. Male teachers of young children. *Young Children,* 1973, *28,* 342-353.

Lefrancois, G.R. *Of children.* Belmont, Calif.: Wadsworth Publishing Co., 1973.

Lehman, H.C. The most creative years of engineers and other technologists. *Journal of Genetic Psychology,* 1966, *108,* 263-277.

Leifer A.D., Leiderman, D.H., Barnett, C.R., & Williams, J.A. Effects of a mother-infant separation on maternal attachment behavior. *Child Development,* 1972, *43,* 1203-1218.

Lenneberg, E.H. *Biological functions of language.* New York: John Wiley & Sons, 1967.

Lerner, R.M., & Spanier, G.B. *Adolescent development: A life-span perspective.* New York: McGraw-Hill Book Co., 1980.

Leslie, G.R. The family in social context (2nd ed.). New York: Oxford University Press, 1973.

Leslie, G.R., & Leslie, E.M. *Marriage in a changing world.* New York: John Wiley & Sons, 1977.

Lessing, E.E. Racial prejudice: Doing what comes naturally? *Contemporary Psychology,* 1977, *22,* 680-682.

Leukel, F. *Introduction to physiological psychology* (3rd ed.). St. Louis: The C.V. Mosby Co., 1976.

Levin, R.J. The Redbook report on premarital and extramarital sex. *Redbook,* October 1975.

Levin, R.J., & Levin, A. The Redbook report: A study of female sexuality. *Redbook,* September 1975.

LeVine, R.A. Cross-cultural study in child psychology. In P.H. Mussen (Ed.), *Carmichael's manual of child psychology* (3rd ed.). New York: John Wiley & Sons, 1970.

LeVine, R.A. Parental goals: A cross-cultural view. *Teachers College Record,* 1974, *76,* 226-289.

Levinger, G., & Snock, D. *Attraction in relationships: A new look at interpersonal attraction.* Morristown, N.J.: General Learning Press, 1972.

Levinson, D.J. The midlife transition: A period in adult psychosocial development. *Psychiatry,* 1977, *40,* 99-112.

Levinson, D.J. Growing up with the dream. *Psychology Today,* 1978a, *11*(8), 20-31.

Levinson, D.J. *The seasons of a man's life.* New York: Alfred A. Knopf, 1978b.

Levinson, D.J., Darrow, C.N., Klein, E.B., Levinson, M.H., & McKee, B. *The seasons of a man's life.* New York: Alfred A. Knopf. 1978.

Levy, S.M., Derogatis, L.R., Gallagher, D., & Gatz, M. Intervention with older adults and the evaluation of outcome. In L.W. Poon (Ed.), *Aging in the 1980s,* Washington, D.C.: American Psychological Association, 1980.

Lewin, K. *Dynamic theory of personality* (D.K. Adams & K. Zener, Trans.). New York: McGraw-Hill Book Co., 1935.

Lewis, M., & Brooks, J. Self, other, and fear: Infants' reactions to people. In M. Lewis & L.A. Rosenblum (Eds.), *The origin of fear.* New York: John Wiley & Sons, 1974.

Lewis, M., & Brooks, J. Self-knowledge and emotional development. In M. Lewis & L.A. Rosenblum (Eds.), *The development of affect.* New York: Plenum Press, 1978.

Lewis, M., & Brooks-Gunn, J. *Social cognition and the acquisition of self.* New York: Plenum Press, 1979.

Lewis, M., & Starr, M.D. Developmental continuity. In J.D. Osofsky (Ed.), *Handbook of infant development.* New York: John Wiley & Sons, 1979.

Libby, R.W. Extramarital and comarital sex: A critique of the literature. In R.W. Libby & R.N. Whitehurst (Eds.), *Marriage and alternatives: Exploring intimate relationships.* Glenview, Ill.: Scott, Foresman & Co., 1977.

Lickona, T. (Ed.). *Moral development and behavior.* New York: Holt, Rinehart & Winston, 1976.

Lieber, C.S. Alcoholic fatty liver: Its pathogenesis and precursor role for hepatitis and cirrhosis. *Panminerva Medica,* 1976, *18*(9-10), 346-358.

Lieberman, I. Social setting determines attitudes of aged to death. *Geriatric Focus,* 1967 *6*(1), 1-6.

Liebert, R.M., Poulos, R.W., & Marmor, G.S. *Developmental psychology.* Englewood Cliffs, N.J.: Prentice-Hall, 1977.

Lind, J., Vuorenkoski, V., & Wasz-Höckert, O. Paternal-infant bonding. In N. Morris (Ed.), *Psychosomatic Medicine in Obstetrics and Gynaecology.* Basel: S. Karger, 1973.

Lindberg, M.A. Is knowledge base development a necessary and sufficient condition for memory development? *Journal of Experimental Child Psychology,* 1980, *30,* 401-410.

Lindeman, R.D. Changes in renal function. In R. Goldman & M. Rockstein (Eds.), *The physiology and pathology of human aging.* New York: Academic Press, 1975.

Lionells, M., & Mann, C.H. *Patterns of midlife in transition.* New York: William Alanson White Institute, 1974.

Litras, T.S. The battle over retirement policies and practices. *Personnel Journal,* 1979, *58*(2), 102-110.

Livson, N. Developmental dimensions of personality: A life-span formulation. In P.B. Baltes & K.W. Schaie (Eds.), *Life-span developmental psychology: Personality and socialization.* New York: Academic Press, 1973.

Lorenz, K. *On aggression.* New York: Harcourt Brace Jovanovich, 1966.

Lott, B. Who wants the children? Some relationships among attitudes toward children, parents and the liberation of women. *American Psychologist,* July 1973, 573-582.

Lovell, K. A follow-up of Inhelder and Piaget's "The growth of logical reasoning." *British Journal of Psychology,* 1961, *52,* 143-153.

Lowenthal, M.F. Some potentialities of a life-cycle approach to the study of retirement. In F.M. Carp (Ed.), *Retirement.* New York: Behavioral Publications, 1972.

Lowenthal, M.F. Toward a sociopsychological theory of change in adulthood and old age. In J.E. Birren & K.W. Schaie (Eds.), *Handbook of the psychology of aging.* New York: Van Nostrand Reinhold Co., 1977.

Lowenthal, M.F., & Boler, D. Voluntary vs. involuntary social withdrawal. *Journal of Gerontology,* 1975, *20,* 363-371.

Lowenthal, M.F., & Chiriboga, D. Transition to the empty nest: Crisis, change, or relief? *Archives of General Psychiatry,* 1972, *26,* 8-14.

Lowenthal, M.F., & Chiriboga, D. Social stress and adaptation: Toward a life-course perspective. In C. Eisdorfer & M.P. Lawton (Eds.), *The psychology of adult development and aging.* Washington, D.C.: American Psychological Association, 1973.

Lowenthal, M.F., & Robinson, B. Social networks and isolation. In R.H. Binstock & E. Shanas, *Handbook of aging and the social sciences.* New York: Van Nostrand Reinhold Co., 1977.

Lowenthal, M.F., Thurnher, M., & Chiriboga, D. *Four stages of life: A comparative study of women and men facing transitions.* San Francisco: Jossey-Bass, Inc., Publishers, 1975.

Lynn, D.B. *The father: His role in child development.* Monterey, Calif.: Brooks/Cole Publishing Co., 1974.

Maas, H.S., & Kuypers, J.A. *From thirty to seventy.* San Francisco: Jossey-Bass, Inc., Publishers, 1974.

Maccoby, E.E. Sex differentiation during childhood development. In *Master Lecture Series.* Washington, D.C.: American Psychological Association, 1976.

Maccoby, E.E. *Social development: Psychological growth and the parent-child relationship.* New York: Harcourt Brace Jovanovich, 1980.

Maccoby, E.E., & Feldman, S.S. Mother-attachment and stranger-reactions in the third year of life. *Monographs of the Society for Research in Child Development,* 1972, *37*(1), No. 146.

Maccoby, E.E., & Jacklin, C.M. *The psychology of sex differences.* Stanford, Calif.: Stanford University Press, 1974.

Macfarlane, J.A. Olfaction in the development of social preferences in the human neonate. Parent-infant interaction. *CIBA Foundation Symposium No. 33,* New series, ASP, 1975.

Macfarlane, J.A. *The psychology of childbirth.* Cambridge, Mass.: Harvard University Press, 1977.

Macfarlane, J.A. What a baby knows. *Human Nature,* 1978, *1*(2), 74-81.

Macklin, E.D. A third cohabit at Cornell. *The New York Times,* December 23, 1973.

Macklin, E.D. Review of research on nonmarital cohabitation in the United States. In B.I. Murstein (Ed.), *Exploring intimate life styles.* New York: Springer Publishing Co., 1978.

MacMahon, B. Age at menarche: United States, vital health statistics. *Science II,* 133. Washington, D.C.: U.S. Department of HEW, 1974.

Maddox, G.L. Persistence of life style among the elderly: A longitudinal study of patterns of social activity in relation to life satisfaction. In B.L. Neugarten (Ed.), *Middle age and aging.* Chicago: The University of Chicago Press, 1968.

Mahler, M.S. *Separation-individuation* (Vol. 2). London: Jason Aronson, 1979.

Makinodan, T. Cellular basis of immunosenescence. In *Molecular and cellular mechanisms of aging.* Paris: INSERM, Coll. Inst. Nat. Sante Rec. Med., 1974, Vol. *27,* pp. 153-166.

Malina, R.M. Secular changes in growth, maturation, and physiological performance. *Exercise and Sport Science Reviews,* 1979, *6,* 203-255.

Malmquist, C.P. Depression in childhood. In F.F. Flack & S.C. Draghi (Eds.), *The nature and treatment of depression.* New York: John Wiley & Sons, 1975.

Manaster, G.J. *Adolescent development and the life tasks.* Boston: Allyn & Bacon, 1977.

Mancini, J. Family relationships and morale among people 65 years of age and older. *American Journal of Orthopsychiatry,* 1979, *49,* 292-300.

Manion, U.V. Pre-retirement counseling: The need for a new approach. *Personnel and Guidance Journal,* 1976, *55*(3), 112-115.

Mann, C.H. Midlife and the family: Strains, challenges, and options of the middle years. In W.H. Norman & T.J. Scaramella (Eds.), *Midlife: Developmental and clinical issues.* New York: Brunner/Mazel, 1980.

Mann, G.A. The disease concept of chemical dependency. *Hospital Progress,* 1973, *54,* 100-102.

Manosevitz, M., Prentice, N.M., & Wilson, F. Individual and family correlates of imaginary companions in preschool children. *Developmental Psychology,* 1973, *8*(1), 72-79.

Marcia, J.E. Identity in adolescence. In J. Adelson (Ed.), *Handbook of adolescent psychology.* New York: John Wiley & Sons, 1980.

Markman, H.J. Prediction of marital distress: A 5-year follow-up. *Journal of Consulting and Clinical Psychology,* 1981, *49,* 760-762.

Marshall, W.A. The body. In R.R. Seas & S.S. Feldman (Eds.), *The seven ages of man.* Los Altos, Calif.: William Kaufmann, 1973.

Marshall, W.A. Puberty. In F. Falkner & J.M. Tanner (Eds.), *Human growth* (Vol. 2: Postnatal growth). New York: Plenum Press, 1978.

Martin, C.E. Sexual activity in the aging male. In J. Money & H. Musaph (Eds.), *Handbook of sexuality* (Vol. 4), New York: Elsevier North-Holland, 1977.

Martin, W., Bengtson, V.L., & Acock, A. Alienation and age: A context-specific approach. *Social Forces,* 1973, *54,* 67-84.

Mash, D.J. The development of life-style preferences of college women. *Journal of National Association of Women Deans and Counselors,* Winter, 1978, 72-76.

Maslow, A.H. *Toward a psychology of being* (2nd ed.). New York: D. Van Nostrand Co., 1968.

Maslow, A.H. Editorial. *Psychology Today,* 1969, *24,* 26-34.

Maslow, A.H. Motivation and personality (2nd ed.). New York: Harper & Row, Publishers, 1970.

Maslow, A.H. *Farther reaches of human nature.* Esalen Institute Book-Publishing Program. New York: Viking Press, 1971.

Masters, W.H., & Johnson, V.E. *Human sexual response.* Boston: Little, Brown & Co., 1966.

Masters, W.H., & Johnson, V.E. Human sexual response: The aging female and the aging male. In B.L. Neugarten (Ed.), *Middle age and aging: A reader in social psychology.* Chicago: The University of Chicago Press, 1968, pp. 269-279.

Masters, W.H., and Johnson, V.E. *Human sexual inadequacy.* Boston: Little, Brown & Co., 1970.

Masuda, M., & Holmes, T.H. Life events: Perceptions and frequencies. *Psychosomatic Medicine,* 1978, *40,* 236-261.

Maternal alcoholism and birth defects seen related. *Nursing Care,* 1974, *7,* 34.

McCall, J.N., & Johnson, O.G. The independence of intelligence from family size and birth orders. *Journal of Genetic Psychology,* 1972, *121,* 207-213.

McCall, R.B., Parke, R.D., & Kavanaugh, R.D. Imitation of live and televised models in the first three years of life. *Monographs of the Society for Research in Child Development.* 1977, *42* (5, Whole No. 173).

McClearn, G.E., & DeFries, J.C. *Introduction to behavioral genetics.* San Francisco: W.H. Freeman & Co., Publishers, 1973.

McClinton, B.S., & Meier, B.G. *Beginnings: Psychology of early childhood.* St. Louis: The C.V. Mosby Co., 1978.

McClung, J. (quoted in Alexander, W.M.) *The emergent middle school.* New York: Holt, Rinehart & Winston, 1969, p. 76.

McKain, W. A new look at older marriages. *The Family Coordinator,* 1972, *21,* 61-69.

McKay, J., Sinisterra, L., McKay, A., Gomez, H., & Lloreda, P. Improving cognitive ability in chronically deprived children. *Science,* 1978, *200,* 270-278.

McKenry, P.C., Walters, L.H., & Johnson, C. Adolescent pregnancy. A review of the literature. *Family Coordinator,* 1979, *28,* 17-28.

McKinley, S.M., & Jeffreys, M. The menopausal syndrome. *British Journal of Preventative and Social Medicine,* 1974, *28,* 108-115.

McKinley, S.M., Jeffreys, M., & Thompson, B. An investigation of the age at menopause. *Journal of Biosocial Science,* 1972, *4,* 161-173.

McKinney, J.P., & Moore, D. Attitudes and values during adolescence. In B.B. Wolman (Ed.), *Handbook of developmental psychology.* Englewood Cliffs, N.J.: Prentice-Hall, 1982.

McLennan, C.E., & Sandberg, E.C. *Synopsis of obstetrics* (9th ed.). St. Louis: The C.V. Mosby Co., 1974.

McNeil, E.B. *Human socialization.* Belmont, Calif.: Brooks/Cole Publishing Co., 1969.

McNeill, D. *The acquisition of language: The study of developmental psycholinguistics.* New York: Harper & Row, Publishers, 1970.

Mead, M. *Culture and commitment: A study of the generation gap.* New York: Doubleday & Co., 1970.

Medley, M.L. Satisfaction with life among persons sixty-five years and older: A causal model. *Journal of Gerontology,* 1976, *31,* 448-455.

Meisels, A., Begin, R., & Schneider, V. Dysplasias of uterine cervix. Epidemiological aspects: Role of age at first coitus and use of oral contraceptives. *Cancer,* 1977, *40*(6), 3076-3081.

Meltzoff, A.N., & Moore, M.K. Imitation of facial gestures by human neonates. *Science,* 1977, *198,* 75-78.

Melville, K. *Marriage and family today.* New York: Random House, 1977.

Mendelson, M.J., & Haith, M.M. The relation between audition and vision in the human newborn. *Monographs of the Society for Research in Child Development,* 1976, *41*(4), Serial No. 167.

Menken, T. *Health consequences of early childbearing.* Paper presented at Conference on Consequences of Adolescent Pregnancy, Washington, D.C., October 1975.

Messer, S.B. Reflection-impulsivity: A review. *Psychological Bulletin,* 1976, *83,* 1026-1052.

Meuller, K.J. Clinical nutrition newsletter: Anorexia nervosa. Philadelphia: University of Pennsylvania, December 1981.

Michel, G.F. Right-handedness: A consequence of infant supine head-orientation preference? *Science,* 1981, *212,* 685-687.

Michener, J.A. An interview: What's good about today's youth. *U.S. News and World Report,* Dec. 10, 1973.

Middlebrook, P.N. *Social psychology and modern life.* New York: Alfred A. Knopf, 1974.

Milgram, S. The experience of living in cities. *Science,* 1970, *167,* 1461-1466.

Miller, 1983(g 16)

Miller, D. *Adolescence.* New York: Jason Aronson, 1974.

Miller, G.A. The acquisition of word meaning. *Child Development,* 1978, *49,* 999-1004.

Miller, P.Y., & Simon, W. The development of sexuality in adolescence. In J. Adelson (Ed.), *Handbook of adolescent psychology.* New York: John Wiley & Sons, 1980.

Milunsky, A. *How dangerous is amniocentesis?* Paper presented at Annual Meeting, American Academy of Pediatrics, October 1975.

Minton, C., Kagan, J., & Levine, J.A. Maternal control and obedience in the two-year-old. *Child Development,* 1971, *42,* 1873-1894.

Mischel, W. Sex-typing and socialization. In P. Hussen (Ed.), *Carmichael's manual of child psychology.* New York: John Wiley & Sons, 1970.

Mischel, W. Toward a cognitive social learning reconceptualization of personality. *Psychological Review,* 1973, *80,* 252-283.

Mogul, K.M. Women in midlife: Decisions, rewards and conflicts related to work and careers. *American Journal of Psychiatry,* 1979, *136,* 1139-1143.

Molfese, D.L., Molfese, V.J., & Carrell, P.L. Early language development. In B.B. Wolman (Ed.), *Handbook of developmental psychology.* Englewood Cliffs, N.J.: Prentice-Hall, 1982.

Mondy, J., & Ehrhardt, A.A. *Man and woman, boy and girl: The differentiation and dimorphism of gender identity from conception to maturity.* Baltimore: Johns Hopkins University Press, 1972.

Montagu, A. *The direction of human development* (Rev. ed.). New York: Hawthorn Books, 1970.

Moody, R.A., Jr. *Life after life: The investigation of survival of bodily death.* New York: Bantam Books, 1975.

Moore, K. *Before we are born.* Philadelphia: W.B. Saunders Co., 1974.

Moore, W.M., Silverberg, M.M., & Read, M.S. (Eds.). *Nutrition, growth, and development of North American Indian Children.* Washington, D.C.: U.S. Department of HEW, Publication No. (NIH) 72-26, 1972.

Morgan, G.A., & Riciuti, H.N. Infants' responses to strangers during the first year. In L.J. Stone, H.T. Smith, & L.B. Murphy (Eds.), *The competent infant, research and commentary.* New York: Basic Books, Inc., Publishers, 1973.

Moshman, D., & Neimark, E. Four aspects of adolescent cognitive development. In T.M. Field, A. Huston, H.C. Quay, L. Troll & G.E. Finley, *Review of Human Development.* New York: John Wiley & Sons, 1982.

Moulton, D.G. Cell renewal in the olfactory epithelium of the mouse. *Annals of the New York Academy of Science,* 1974, *237,* 52-61.

Munsinger, H. *Fundamentals of child development* (2nd ed.). New York: Holt, Rinehart & Winston, 1975.

Murray, A.D. Infant crying as an elicitor of parental behavior: An examination of two models. *Psychological Bulletin,* 1979, *85,* 191-215.

Murstein, B. Self-ideal-self-discrepancy and the choice of marital partner. In M.E. Lasswell & T.E. Loswell (Eds.), *Love, marriage and family: A developmental approach.* Glenview, Ill.: Scott, Foresman & Co., 1973.

Muson, H. Moral thinking: Can it be taught? *Psychology Today,* 1979, *12*(9), 48-58, 67-68, 92.

Mussen, P.H. Early sex-role development. In D.A. Goslin (Ed.), *Handbook of socialization theory and research.* Skokie, Ill.: Rand McNally, 1969.

Muuss, R.E. Adolescent development and the secular trend. *Adolescence,* 1970a, *5,* 267-284.

Muuss, R.E. Puberty rites in primitive and modern societies. *Adolescence,* 1970b, *5,* 109-128.

Muuss, R.E. Adolescent development and the secular trend. In R.E. Muus (Ed.), *Adolescent behavior and society: A book of readings.* New York: Random House, 1975.

Naeye, R.L. Pregnancy weight gain. *American Journal of Obstetrics and Gynecology,* 1981, *135,* 3.

Nagle, J.J. *Heredity and human affairs* (ed. 2). St. Louis: The C.V. Mosby Co., 1979.

Nash, M.L. Dignity of person in the final phase of life: An exploratory study. *Omega,* 1977, *8,* 71-80.

National Center for Health Statistics. *World-wide longevity statistics for men and women.* Washington, D.C.: National Center for Health Statistics, 1983.

National Center for Housing Management. *The one-site housing managers resource book: Housing for elderly.* Washington, D.C.: The National Center for Housing Management, 1974.

National Center for Housing Management. *Managing housing and services for the elderly.* Washington, D.C.: The National Center for Housing Management, 1977.

National Institutes of Health. *The health consequence of smoking.* Washington, D.C.: U.S. Department of HEW, 1973.

National Institutes of Health. Caesarean childbirth. *In Consensus Development Conference Summary* (Vol. 3, No. 6). Bethesda, Md.: U.S. Government Printing Office, 1981, NIH No. 1981-0-341-132/3553.

National Opinion Research Center. *General social surveys, 1972-1980: Cumulative codebook.* Chicago: The Center, 1981.

Neeson, J.D. Herpesvirus genitalis: A nursing perspective. *Nursing Clinics of North America,* 1975, *10,* 599.

Neimark, E.D. Intellectual development during adolescence. In F.D. Horowitz (Ed.), *Review of child development research* (Vol. 4). Chicago: The University of Chicago Press, 1975.

Neimark, E.D. Adolescent thought: Transition to formal operations. In B.B. Wolman (Ed.), *Handbook of development psychology.* Englewood Cliffs, N.J.: Prentice-Hall, 1982.

Neimark, E.D. Cognitive development in adulthood. In T.M. Field, A. Huston, H.C. Quay, L. Troll, & G.E. Finley, *Review of human development.* New York: John Wiley & Sons, 1982.

Neiswender, M., Birren, J., & Schaie, K.W. *Age and the experience of love in adulthood.* Paper presented at the annual meeting of the American Psychological Association, Chicago, 1975.

Nelson, K. Structure and strategy in learning to talk. *Monographs of the Society for Research in Child Development,* 1973, *38*(1 & 2).

Nelson, K., Rescorla, L., Gruendel, J., & Benedict, N. Early lexicons: What do they mean? *Child development,* 1978, *49,* 960-968.

Nelson, N., Enkin, M., Saigal, S., Bennett, K., Milner, R., & Sackett, D. A randomized clinical trial of the Leboyer approach to childbirth. *New England Journal of Medicine,* 1980, *302*(12), 655-660.

Neugarten, B.L. The awareness of middle age. In B.L. Neugarten, *Middle age and aging.* Chicago: The University of Chicago Press, 1968b.

Neugarten, B.L. Adult personality: Toward a psychology of the life cycle. In E. Vinacke (Ed.), *Readings in general psychology.* New York: American Book Co., 1968a.

Neugarten, B.L. Dynamics of transition of middle age to old age. *Journal of Geriatric Psychiatry,* 1970, *4,* 71-78.

Neugarten, B.L. Grow old with me! The best is yet to be *Psychology Today,* 1971, *5*(7), 45-48.

Neugarten, B.L. Personality and the aging process. *Gerontologist,* 1972, *12*(1), 9-15.

Neugarten, B.L. Personality changes in late life: A developmental perspective. In C. Eisdorfer & M.P. Lawton (Eds.), *The psychology of adult development and aging.* Washington, D.C.: American Psychological Association, 1973, 319-321.

Neugarten, B.L. Age groups in American society and the rise of the young old. *Annals of the American Academy,* September 1974, 187-198.

Neugarten, B.L. Personality and aging. In J.E. Birren & K.W. Schaie (Eds.), *Handbook of the psychology of aging.* New York: Van Nostrand Reinhold Co., 1977, chap. 26.

Neugarten, B.L., and Datan, N. Sociological perspectives on the life cycle. In P.B. Baltes and K.W. Schaie (Eds.), *Life-span developmental psychology: Personality and socialization.* New York: Academic Press, 1973.

Neugarten, B.L., & Datan, N. The middle years. In S. Arieti (Ed.), *American handbook of psychiatry* (Vol. 1). New York: Basic Books, Inc., Publishers, 1974.

Neugarten, B.L. & Gutmann, D.L. Age-sex roles and personality in middle age: A thematic apperception study. In B.L. Neugarten (Ed.), *Middle age and aging: A reader in social psychology.* Chicago: The University of Chicago Press, 1968, pp. 58-71.

Neugarten, B.L., & Hagestad, G.O. Age and the life course. In R.H. Binstock & E. Shanas (Eds.), *Handbook of aging and the social sciences.* New York: Van Nostrand Reinhold Co., 1976.

Neugarten, B.L., Havighurst, R.J., & Tobin, S.S. Personality and patterns of aging. In B.L. Neugarten (Ed.), *Middle age and aging.* Chicago: The University of Chicago Press, 1968, pp. 173-177.

Neugarten, B.L., & Weinstein, K. The changing American grandparent. *Journal of Marriage and the Family,* 1964, *26,* 199-204.

Neugarten, B.L., and Weinstein, K. The changing American grandparent. In B.L. Neugarten (Ed.), *Middle age and aging: A reader in social psychology.* Chicago: The University of Chicago Press, 1968.

Neugarten, B.L. Wood, V., Kraines, R.J., & Loomis, B. Women's attitudes toward the menopause. *Vita Humana,* 1963, *6,* 140-151.

New light on adult life cycles. Time. In White, S., *Human development in today's world.* Boston: Educational Associates of Little, Brown & Co., 1976.

Newman, B.M. Characteristics of interpersonal behavior among adolescent boys. *Journal of Youth and Adolescence,* 1975, *4,* 145-153.

Newman, B.M. The study of interpersonal behavior in adolescence. *Adolescence,* 1978, *13,* 157-166.

Newman, B.M. Mid-life development. In R.B. Wolman (Ed.), *Handbook of developmental psychology.* Englewood Cliffs, N.J.: Prentice-Hall, 1982.

Newman, G., & Nichols, C.R. Sexual activities and attitudes in older persons. In E.B. Palmore (Ed.), *Normal aging.* Durham, N.C.: Duke University Press, 1970.

Newman, P.R. The peer group. In B.B. Wolman (Ed.), *Handbook of developmental psychology.* Englewood Cliffs, N.J.: Prentice-Hall, 1982.

NIH Consensus Development Conference. *Clinical Pediatrics,* 1979, *18*(9), 535-538.

Nock, S.L. The life-cycle approach to family analysis. In B.B. Wolman (Ed.), *Handbook of developmental psychology.* Englewood Cliffs, N.J.: Prentice-Hall, 1982.

Norman, W.H., & Scaramella, T.J. *Mid-life: Developmental and clinical issues.* New York: Brunner/Mazel, 1980.

Norton, N. Personal correspondence. Shippensburg, Pa., 1981.

Notman, M. Is there a male menopause? In L. Rose (Ed.), *The menopause book.* New York: Hawthorn Books, 1978.

Nye, F.I., & Berado, F.M. *The family: Its structure and interaction.* New York: Macmillan Publishing Co., 1973.

O'Brien, P., Noller, K., Robboy, S., Barnes, A., Kauffman, R., Tilley, B., & Townsend, D. Vaginal epithelial changes in young women enrolled in the National Cooperative Diethylstilbestrol Adenosis (DESAD) Project. *Obstetrics and Gynecology,* 1979, *53*(3), 300-308.

Offer, D.E., & Offer, J.L. *The psychological world of the teen-ager.* New York: Basic Books, Inc., Publishers, 1969.

Offer, D.E., Ostrov, E., & Aoward, K.I. *The adolescent: A psychological self-portrait.* New York: Basic Books, Inc., Publishers, 1981.

Ohlsen, M.M. Dissident students. *Contemporary Education,* 1971, *42,* 157.

Olweus, D. Stability of aggressive reaction patterns in males: A review. *Psychological Bulletin,* 1979, *86,* 852-875.

Olweus, D. Familial and tempermental determinants of aggressive behavior in adolescent boys: A causal analysis. *Developmental Psychology,* 1980, *16,* 644-660.

O'Malley, P.M., Bachman, J.G., & Johnston, J. *Youth in transition. Final report: Five years beyond high school: Causes and consequences of educational attainment.* Ann Arbor, Mich.: Institute for Social Research, 1977.

Opie, P., & Opie, I. *Children's games in street and playground.* New York: Oxford University Press, 1969.

Oppel, W.C., Harper, P.A., & Rider, R.V. The age of attaining bladder control. *Pediatrics,* 1968, *42*(4), 614-626.

Ornstein, P.A., & Corsale, K. Process and structure in children's memory. In G.J. Whitehurst & B. Zimmerman (Eds.), *The functions of language and cognition.* New York: Academic Press, 1979.

Ornstein, R.E. *The psychology of consciousness* (2nd ed.). New York: Harcourt Brace Jovanovich, 1977.

Oskamp, S., & Mindick, B. Personality and attitudinal barriers to contraception. In D. Byrne & W.A. Fisher (Eds.), *Adolescents, sex, and contraception.* New York: McGraw-Hill Book Co., 1981.

Oster, H.S. *Color perception in ten-week-infants.* Paper presented at the biennial meeting of the Society for Research in Child Development, Denver, 1975.

Otto, L.B. Antecedents and consequences of marital timing. In W.R. Burr, R. Hill, F.I. Nye, & I.L. Reiss (Eds.), *Contemporary theories about the family* (Vol. 1). New York: The Free Press, 1979.

Owens, W.A. Age and mental abilities: A longitudinal study. In D.C. Charles & W.R. Looft (Eds.), *Readings in psychological development through life.* New york: Holt, Rinehart & Winston, 1973, pp. 243-254.

Palazzoli, M.S. *Paradox and counterparadox.* New York: Jason Aronson, 1978.

Palmore, E.B. Compulsory versus flexible retirement: Issues and facts. In S.H. Zant (Ed.), *Readings in aging and death: Contemporary perspectives.* New York: Harper & Row, Publishers, 1977.

Palmore, E.B. Predictors of successful aging. *Gerontologist,* 1979, *19,* 427-431.

Pannor, R., Massarck, F., & Evans, B. *The unmarried father: New approaches for helping unmarried young parents.* New York: Springer Publishing Co., 1971.

Papalia, D.E. The status of several conservation abilities across the life-span. *Human Development,* 1972, *15,* 229-243.

Parfitt, R.R. *The birth primer.* Philadelphia: Running Press, 1977.

Parke, R.D. Perspectives on father-infant interaction. In J.D. Osofsky (Ed.), *Handbook of infant development.* New York: John Wiley & Sons, 1979.

Parke, R.D., Power, T.G., & Fisher, T. The adolescent father's impact on mother and child. *Journal of Social Issues,* 1980, *36,* 88-106.

Parkes, C.M. *Bereavement.* New York: International Universities Press, 1972.

Parry, J. Abilities. In R.R. Sears & S.S. Feldman (Eds.), *The seven ages of man.* Los Altos, Calif.: William Kaufmann, 1973.

Pascual-Leone, A. *Cognitive development and cognitive style.* Lexington, Mass.: D.C. Heath & Co., 1973.

Pascual-Leone, J. Constructive problems for constructive theories. In H. Spada & R. Kluwe (Eds.), *Developmental models of thinking.* New York: Academic Press, 1980.

Pastalan, L., & Carson, D. *Spatial behavior of older people.* Ann Arbor, Mich.: University of Michigan Press, 1970, p. 98.

Paton, D., & Craig, J.A. Cataracts: Development, diagnosis, management. *CIBA Clinical Symposia, 26*(3), 1-32 (no date).

Pattison, E.M. The dying experience—retrospective analysis. In E.M. Pattison (Ed.), *The experience of dying.* Englewood Cliffs, N.J.: Prentice-Hall, 1977.

Paull, J. Laws of behavior: Fact or artifact? *American Psychologist,* 1980, *35*(12), 1081-1083.

Pearlin, L. Sex roles and depression. In N. Datan & L. Ginsburg (Eds.), *Life-span developmental psychology: Normative life crises.* New York: Academic Press, 1975.

Peck, R.C. Psychological development in the second half of life. In B.L. Neugarten (Ed.), *Middle age and aging.* Chicago: The University of Chicago Press, 1968.

Peeples, D., & Teller, D. Color vision and brightness discrimination in two-month-old infants. *Science,* 1975, *189,* 1102-1103.

Penfield, W. & Roberts, C. *Speech and brain mechanisms.* Princeton, N.J.: Princeton University Press, 1958.

Pepler, D.J. *Naturalistic observations of teaching and modeling between siblings.* Paper presented at the Society for Research in Child Development, Boston, April 1981.

Pepper, C. Will there be a brighter tomorrow for the nation's elderly. *USA Today,* 1980, *108*(2420), 14-16.

Perry, J., & Perry, E. *Pairing and parenthood: An introduction to marriage.* San Francisco: Canfield Press, 1977.

Perry, T., Hechtman, P., & Chow, J. Diagnosis of Tay-Sachs disease on blood obtained at fetoscopy. *Lancet,* May 5, 1979, 972-973.

Perun, P.J., & Bielby, D.D.V. Mid-life: A discussion of competing models. *Research on Aging,* 1979, *1,* 275-300.

Peskin, H. Pubertal onset and ego functioning. *Journal of Abnormal Psychology,* 1967, *72,* 1-15.

Petersen, A.C. Female pubertal development. In M. Sugar (Ed.), *Female adolescent development.* New York: Brunner/Mazel, 1979.

Petersen, A.C. Hormones and cognitive functioning in normal development. In M.A. Wittig & A.C. Petersen (Eds.), *Sex related differences in cognitive functioning: Developmental issues.* New York: Academic Press, 1979.

Petersen, A.C., & Taylor, B. The biological approach to adolescence: Biological change and psychological adaptation. In J. Adelson (Ed.), *Handbook of adolescent psychology.* New York: John Wiley & Sons, 1980.

Peterson, G., Mehl, L., & Leiderman, P. The role of some birth related variables in father attachment. *American Journal of Orthopsychiatry,* 1979, *49,* 330-338.

Pfeiffer, E. *Sexuality in the aging individual.* Paper presented as part of the Symposium on Sexuality in the Aging Individual at the 31st Annual Meeting of the American Geriatric Society, Toronto, Canada. 1974.

Pfeiffer, E. *Successful aging.* Durham, N.C.: Duke University Center for the Study of Aging and Human Development, 1974.

Pfeiffer, E. Psychopathology and social pathology. In J.E. Birren & K.W. Schaie (Eds.), *Handbook of the psychology of aging.* New York: Van Nostrand Reinhold Co., 1977, chap. 27.

Pffeiffer, E., & Davis, G.C. Determinants of sexual behavior in middle and old age. *Journal of the American Geriatrics Society,* April 1972, p. 157.

Phillips, B. *School stress and anxiety: Theory, research and intervention.* New York: Human Sciences, 1978.

Phillips, J.L., Jr. *The origins of intellect: Piaget's theory* (2nd ed.). San Francisco: W.H. Freeman & Co., Publishers, 1975.

Piaget, J. *The origins of intelligence in children.* New York: International Universities Press, 1952b.

Piaget, J. *The moral judgment of the child.* New York: Macmillan Publishing Co., 1955.

Piaget, J. *The language and thought of the child.* New York: The Humanities Press, 1959.

Piaget, J. *The child's conception of number.* New York: W.W. Norton & Co., 1965.

Piaget, J. *The child's conception of physical causality.* London: Routledge & Kegan Paul, 1966.

Piaget, J. Piaget's theory. In P.H. Mussen (Ed.), *Carmichael's manual of child psychology* (Vol. 1) (3rd ed.). New York: John Wiley & Sons, 1970.

Piaget, J. Intellectual development from adolescence to adulthood. *Human Development,* 1972, *15,* 1-12.

Piaget, J., & Inhelder, B. *The psychology of the child.* New York: Basic Books, Inc., Publishers, 1969.

Piaget, J., & Inhelder, B. *Memory and intelligence.* New York: Basic Books, Inc., Publishers, 1973.

Pickard, P.M. *The activity of children.* London: Longmans. Green & Co., 1965.

Place, D.M. The dating experience for adolescent girls. *Adolescence, 1975, 10,* 157-174.

Posner, M.I., & McLeod, P. Information processing models: In search of elementary operations. In M.R. Rosenzweig & L.W. Porter, *Annual review of psychology.* Palo Alto, Calif.: Annual Reviews, 1982.

Powell, D.H., & Driscoll, P.F. Middle class professionals face unemployment. *Society,* 1973, *10*(2), 18-26.

Pressley, M., & Levin, J.R. The development of mental imagery retrieval. *Child Development,* 1980, *51,* 558-560.

Problems of marriage. *Parade,* November 6, 1966, p. 28.

Proceedings of the 1971 White House conference on aging. *Toward a national policy on aging.* November 28-December 2, 1971. Washington, D.C.: U.S. Government Printing Office, 1973.

Purpura, D. *Symposium on fetal brain life.* New York: Rose Fitzgerald Kennedy Center, Albert Einstein College of Medicine, 1975.

Quay, H.C. Adolescent aggression. In T.M. Field, A. Huston, H.C. Quay, L. Troll, & G.E. Finley, *Review of human development*. New York: John Wiley & Sons, 1982.

Quinn, R., Staines, G., & McCullough, M. Job satisfaction: Is there a trend? *Manpower Research Monograph No. 30*. Washington, D.C.: U.S. Department of Labor, 1974.

Rabin, P.V. *Journal of the American Medical Association*, July 16, 1982.

Ragan, P.K., & Dowd, J.J. The emerging political consciousness of the aged: A generation interpretation. *Journal of Social Issues*, 1974, *30*, 137-158.

Rahe, R.H., & Holmes, T.H. Life crisis and major health changes. *Psychosomatic Medicine*, 1966, *28*, 744.

Rains, S., & Morris, R. The role of the primary teacher in character education. *Young Children*, 1969, *25*, 105.

Rappaport, L. Adult development: Faster houses . . . and more money. *Personnel and Guidance Journal*, 1976, *55*(3), 106-108.

Rebelsky, F., & Hanks, C. Fathers' verbal interaction with infants in the first three months of life. *Child Development*, 1971, *42*, 63-68.

Reese, H.W. Imagery and associative memory. In R.V. Kail, Jr., & J.W. Hagen (Eds.), *Perspectives on the development of memory and cognition*. Hillsdale, N.J.: Lawrence Erlbaum Associates, 1977.

Reigel, K.F. Adult life crisis: A dialectic interpretation of development. In N. Datan & L.H. Ginsburg (Eds.), *Life-span developmental psychology: Normative life crisis*. New York: Academic Press, 1975.

Reiss, I.L. Family systems in America (2nd ed.). Hinsdale, Ill.: Dryden Press, 1976.

Rheingold, H.L., & Cook, K.V. The contrasts of boys and girls room as an index of parents' behavior. *Child Development*, 1975, *46*, 459-463.

Rice, F.P. *The adolescent: Development, relationships, culture* (3rd ed.). Boston: Allyn & Bacon, 1981.

Rice, M.L. Child language: What children know and how. In T.M. Field, A. Huston, H.C. Quay, L. Troll, & G.E. Finley, *Review of human development*. New York: John Wiley & Sons, 1982.

Riley, M.W., Johnson, M., & Foner, A. *Aging and society: A sociology of age stratification* (Vol. 3). New York: Russell Sage Foundation, 1972.

Ritzer, G. *Working: Conflict and change* (2nd ed.). Englewood Cliffs, N.J.: Prentice-Hall, 1977.

Road Traffic Board of South Australia. *The points demerit scheme as an indication of declining skill with age*, 1972.

Robertson, J.F. Grandmotherhood: A study of role conceptions. *Journal of Marriage and the Family*, 1977, *39*, 165-174.

Robertson, M., & Halverson, L. The developing child: His changing movements. In B.I. Logsdon et al. (Ed.), *Physical education for children: A focus on the teaching process*. Philadelphia: Lea & Febiger, 1977.

Robinson, D. Our surprising moral unwed fathers. *Ladies Home Journal*, August 1969, 49-50.

Roche, A.F. & Davila, G.H. Late adolescent growth in stature. *Pediatrics*, 1972, *50*(6), 874-880.

Rockstein, M. The biology of aging in humans: An overview. In R. Goldman & M. Rockstein (Eds.), *The physiology and pathology of human aging*. New York: Academic Press, 1975.

Rogers, C.R. *On becoming a person*. Boston: Houghton-Mifflin Co., 1961.

Rogers, C.R. The concept of the fully functioning person. *Psychotherapy*, 1963, *1*, 17-26.

Rogers, D. *The adult years: An introduction to aging*. Englewood Cliffs, N.J.: Prentice-Hall, 1982.

Rokeach, M. *The nature of human values*. New York: The Free Press, 1973.

Root, A.W. Endocrinology of puberty. I. Normal sexual maturation. *Journal of Pediatrics*, 1973, *83*, 1-19.

Roovik, D.M. & Shettles, L.B. *Your baby's sex—now you can choose*. New York: Dodd, Mead & Co., 1970.

Roper Organization Poll, Ruder and Finn, 110 E. 59th Street, New York, N.Y. 1974.

Rosen, J., & Wiens, A. Changes in medical problems and use of medical services following psychological intervention. *American Psychologist*, 1979, *34*, 420-431.

Rosenbaum, M.B. The changing body image of the adolescent girl. In M. Sugar (Ed.), *Female adolescent development*. New York: Brunner/Mazel, 1979.

Rosenberg, S.D., and Farrell, M.P. Identity and crisis in middle-aged men. *International Journal of Aging and Human Development*, 1976, *7*, 153-170.

Rosenfeld, A. The "elastic mind" movement: Rationalizing child neglect? *Saturday Review*, 1978, *5*, 26-28.

Rosenmayr, L. Achievements, doubts and prospects of the sociology of aging. *Human Development*, 1980, *23*, 46-62.

Rosenthal, M. Attachment and mother-infant interaction. Some research impasse and a suggested change in orientation. *Journal of Child Psychology, Psychiatry and Allied Disciplines*, 1973, *14*, 201-207.

Rosenthal, T.L., & Zimmerman, B.J. *Social learning and cognition*. New York: Academic Press, 1978.

Rosett, H.L., & Sander, L.W. Effects of maternal drinking on neonatal morphology and state regulation. In J.D. Osofsky (Ed.), *Handbook of infant development*. New York: John Wiley & Sons, 1979.

Rossman, J. Anatomic and body composition changes with aging. In C.E. Finch & L. Hayflicks (Eds.), *Handbook of the biology of aging*. New York: Van Nostrand Reinhold Co., 1977.

Rothbaum, D.A., Shaw, D.J., Angell, C.S., & Shock, M.W. Age differences in the baroreceptor response of rats. *Journal of Gerontology*, 1974, *29*, 488-402.

Rotter, J.B. Generalized expectancies for internal versus external control of reinforcement. *Psychological Monographs*, 1966. *80* (1, whole No. 609).

Rovee, C.K., Cohen, R.Y., & Shlapack, W. Life span stability in olfactory sensitivity. *Developmental Psychology*, 1975, *11*, 311-318.

Rowland, K. Environmental events predicting death for the elderly. *Psychological Bulletin*, 1977, *84*, 349-372.

Royce, J.R. Philosophic issues, Division 24, and the future. *American Psychologist*, 1982, *37*(3), 258-266.

Rubin, J.Z., Provenzano, F.J., & Luria, Z. The eye of the beholder: Parent's views on sex of newborns. *American journal of Orthopsychiatry*, 1974, *43*, 720-731.

Rubin, Z. *Liking and loving*. New York: Holt, Rinehart & Winston, 1973.

Rubin, Z. *Children's friendships*. Cambridge, Mass.: Harvard University Press, 1980.

Russell, C.S. Unscheduled parenthood: Transition to "parent" for the teenager. *Journal of Social Issues*, 1980, *36*, 45-63.

Rutter, M. Separation experiences: A new look at an old topic. *Pediatrics*, 1979, *95*(1), 147-154.

Rutter, M. Attachment and the development of social relationships. In M. Rutter (Ed.), *Scientific foundations of developmental psychiatry*. Baltimore: University Park Press, 1981.

Rutter, M. The city and the child. *American Journal of Orthopsychiatry*, 1981, *51*(4), 610-625.

Rutter, M., Graham, P., Chadwick, O., & Yule, W. Adolescent turmoil: Fact or fiction. *Journal of Child Psychology and Psychiatry*, 1976, *17*, 35-36.

Rutter, M., Yule, W., & Graham, P. Enuresis and behavioral deviance: Some epidemiological consideration. In I. Kolvin, R.C. MacKeith, & S.R. Meadows (Eds.), *Bladder control and enuresis. Clinics in Developmental Medicine*, No. 48/49. London: Heinemann/S.I.M.P., 1973.

Sachs, J.S. Development of speech. In E.C. Cartevette & M.P. Friedman (Eds.), *Handbook of reception* (Vol. 8). New York: Academic Press, 1976.

Salamy, A., & McKean, C.M. Postnatal development of human brainstem potentials during the first year of life. *Electroencephalography and Clinical Neurophysiology*, 1976, *40*, 418-426.

Salzman, C., & Shader, R.I. Clinical evaluation of depression in the elderly. In A. Paskin & L.F. Jarvik (Eds.), *Psychiatric symptoms and cognitive loss in the elderly*. Washington, D.C.: Hemisphere Publishing Corp., 1979.

Sampson, E.E. Cognitive psychology as ideology. *American Psychologist*, 1981, *36*(7), 730-743.

Sandberg, E.C. *Synopsis of obstetrics* (10th ed.). St. Louis: The C.V. Mosby Co., 1978.

Sarnat, H.B. Olfactory reflexes in the newborn infant. *Journal of Pediatrics*, 1978, *92*, 624-626.

Saunders, C. St. Christopher's Hospice. In E.S. Shneidman (Ed.), *Death: Current perspectives*. Palo Alto, Calif.: Mayfield Publishing Co., 1976.

Scanlon, J. *Young adulthood*. New York: Academy for Educational Development, 1979.

Schaefer, E.S. Converging models for maternal behavior and child behavior. In J. Gildewell (Ed.), *Parental attitudes and child behavior*. Springfield, Ill.: Charles C Thomas, Publisher, 1961.

Schaffer, H.R., & Emerson, P. The development of social attachments in infancy. *Monographs of the Society for Research in Child Development*, 1964, *29*(3).

Schaie, K.W. Cross-sectional methods in the study of psychological aspects of aging. *Journal of Gerontology*, 1959, *14*, 208-215.

Schaie, K.W. A general model for the study of developmental problems. *Psychological Bulletin*, 1965, *64*, 92-107.

Schaie, K.W., & Hertzog, C. Longitudinal methods. In B.B. Wolman (Ed.), *Handbook of developmental psychology*. Englewood Cliffs, N.J.: Prentice-Hall, 1982.

Schaie, K.W., Labouvie, G.V., & Buech, B.V. Generational and cohort-specific differences in adult cognitive functioning: A fourteen-year study of independent samples. *Developmental Psychology*, 1973, *9*, 151-161.

Schaie, K.W., and Parham, I.A. Cohort-sequential analysis of adult intellectual development. *Developmental Psychology*, 1977, *13*, 649-653.

Scheck, D.C., Emerick, R., & El-Assal, M.M. Adolescents' perceptions of parent-child relations and the development of internal-external control operation. *Journal of Marriage and the Family*, 1973, *35*, 643-654.

Schein, E.H. The first job dilemma. In J. DeCello (Ed.), *Readings in educational psychology today*. Del Mar, Calif.: CRM Books, 1970.

Schenck, E.G. The problems of premature senescence after a life under extremely difficult conditions. In *Pathology of the captivity of the prisoners of World War II*. Paris: International Confederation of Ex-Prisoners of War, 1963.

Schlesinger, B. One-parent families in Great Britain. *Family Coordinator*, 1977, *26*, 139-141.

Schneider, D.J. *Social psychology*. Reading, Mass.: Addison-Wesley, 1976.

Schofield, M. *The sexual behavior of young people.* Boston: Little, Brown, & Co., 1965.

Schonfeld, W.A. The body and the body image in adolescence. In G. Caplan & S. Lebovici (Eds.), *Adolescence: Psychosocial perspectives.* New York: Basic Books, Inc., Publishers.

Schulte, F.J., Busse, C., & Eichhorn, W. Rapid eye movement sleep, motoneurone inhibition, and apneic spells in preterm infants. *Pediatric Research,* 1977, *11*(6), 709-713.

Schultz, T. Does marriage give today's women what they want? *Ladies Home Journal,* June 1980, 89-91, 146-155.

Schwantes, F.M. Cognitive scanning processes in children. *Child Development,* 1979, *50,* 1136-1143.

Scrimshaw, N.S. Infant malnutrition and adult learning. *Saturday Review,* 1968, *50,* 64 ff.

Sears, R.R. Relations of early socialization experiences to self-concept and gender roles in middle childhood. *Child Development,* 1970, *41,* 267-289.

Sears, R.R. Sources of life satisfaction of the Terman gifted men. *American Psychologist,* 1977, *32,* 119-128.

Sears, R.R., Maccoby, E.E., & Levin, N. *Patterns of child rearing.* New York: Harper & Row, Publishers, 1957.

Sebald, H. *Adolescence: A social psychological analysis* (2nd ed.). Englewood Cliffs, N.J.: Prentice-Hall, 1977.

Segal, J., & Yahraes, H.A. *A child's journey: Forces that shape the lives of our young.* New York: McGraw-Hill Book Co., 1979.

Self, P.A., & Horowitz, F.D. The behavioral assessment of the neonate. In J.D. Osofsky (Ed.), *The handbook of infant development.* New York: John Wiley & Sons, 1980.

Selim, R. *The futurist.* Washington, D.C.: World Future Society, February 1979.

Selman, R.L. The relation of role taking to the development of moral judgment in children. *Child Development,* 1971, *42,* 79-91.

Selman, R.L. The development of social-cognitive understanding: A guide to educational and clinical practice. In T. Lickona (Ed.), *Morality: Theory, research and social issues.* New York: Holt, Rinehart & Winston, 1976a.

Selman, R.L. Toward a structural analysis of developing interpersonal relations concepts: Research with normal and disturbed preadolescent boys. In A.D. Pick (Ed.), *Minnesota symposia on child psychology* (Vol. 10). Minneapolis: University of Minnesota Press, 1976b.

Selman, R.L., & Byrne, D. A structural-developmental analysis of levels of role-taking in middle childhood. *Child Development,* 1974, *45,* 803-806.

Selye, H. The evolution of the stress concept. *American Scientist,* 1973, *61,* 692-699.

Selye, H. Stress. *Intellectual Digest,* 1974, *4*(10), 43-46.

Selzer, S.C., & Denney, N.W. Conservation abilities among middle-aged and elderly adults. *Aging and Human Development,* 1980, *11,* 135-146.

Sense of values. *Parade,* November 2, 1969, p. 12.

Serunian, S., & Broman, S. Relationship of Apgar scores and Bayley mental and motor scores. *Child Development,* 1975, *46,* 696-700.

Settlage, C.F., Baroff, R., & Cooper, A. Adolescence and social change. *Journal of the American Academy of Child Psychiatry,* 1970, *9,* 205-215.

Shaffer, D. The development of bladder control. In M. Rutter, *Scientific foundations of developmental psychiatry.* Baltimore: University Park Press, 1981.

Shanas, E., & Maddox, G. Aging, health and the organization of health resources. In R.H. Binstock & E. Shanas (Eds.), *Handbook of aging and the social sciences.* New York: Van Nostrand Reinhold Co., 1976, chap. 33.

Shapiro, L. Did "fear of success" lie? *Ms.,* July 1977, 19.

Shatz, M., & Gelman, R. Beyond syntax: The influences of conversational constraints on speech modification. In C.E. Snow and C.A. Ferguson (Eds.), *Talking to children: Language input and acquisition.* Cambridge, England: Cam-Bridge University Press, 1977.

Sheehy, G. *Passages: Predictable crises of adult life.* New York: E.P. Dutton & Co., 1976.

Sheehy, G. The mentor connection. In D. Elkind & D.C. Hetzel (Eds.), *Readings in human development: Contemporary perspectives.* New York: Harper & Row, Publishers, 1977.

Sheehy, G. The happiness report. *Redbook,* 1979, *153*(3), 29; 64 ff.

Shepherd-Look, D.L. Sex differentiation and the development of sex roles. In B.B. Wolman (Ed.), *Handbook of developmental psychology.* Englewood Cliffs, N.J.: Prentice-Hall, 1982.

Sheppard, H.L. Work and retirement. In R.H. Binstock & E. Shanos, *Handbook of aging and the social sciences.* New York: Van Nostrand Reinhold Co., 1976.

Sherman, J.A. *On the psychology of women: A survey of empirical studies.* Springfield, Ill.: Charles C Thomas, Publisher, 1971.

Shertzer, B., & Stone, S. *Fundamentals of guidance* (3rd ed.). Boston: Houghton Mifflin Co., 1976.

Shettles, L.B., & Vande Weile, R.L. Can parents choose the sex of their baby? *Birth and Family,* 1974, *1,* 3-5.

Shneidman, E.S. Psychological death and resurrection. In E.S. Scheidman (Ed.), *Death and the college student.* New York: Behavioral Publications, 1972.

Shneidman, E.S. *Deaths of Man.* New York: New York Times Book Co., 1973.

Shock, N.W. Biological theories of aging. In J.E. Birren & K.W. Schaie (Eds.), *Handbook of the psychology of aging.* New York: Van Nostrand Reinhold Co., 1977.

Siegel, D. Personality development in adolescence. In B.B. Wolman (Ed.), *Handbook of developmental psychology.* Englewood Cliffs, N.J.: Prentice-Hall, 1982.

Siegler, I.C. Nowlin, J.B., & Blumenthal, J.A. Health and behavior: Methodological considerations for adult development and aging. In L.W. Poon (Ed.), *Aging in the 1980s.* Washington, D.C.: American Psychological Association, 1980.

Siegler, R.S. Three aspects of cognitive development. *Cognitive Psychology,* 1976, *8,* 481-510.

Siegler, R.S., & Liebert, R.M. Acquisition of formal scientific reasoning by 10- and 13-year-olds: Designing a factoral experiment. *Developmental Psychology,* 1975, *11,* 401-402.

Silvian, L. *Understanding diabetes.* New York: Monarch Press, 1977.

Simmons, R.G., & Rosenberg, F. Sex, sex roles, and self-image. *Journal of Youth and Adolescence,* 1975, *4,* 225-258.

Simon, N.A. Information processing models of cognition. In M.R. Rosenzweig & L.W. Porter *Annual review of psychology.* Palo Alto, Calif.: Annual Reviews, 1981.

Sinclair, D. *Human growth after birth.* London: Oxford University Press, 1978.

Sinclair, H. Sensorimotor action patterns as a condition for the acquisition of syntax. In R. Huxley & D. Ingram (Eds.), *Language acquisition: Models and methods.* New York: Academic Press, 1971.

Singer, J.L., & Singer, D.G. The values of imagination. In B. Sutton-Smith (Ed.), *Studies in play and games.* New York: Gardner Press, 1979.

Singer, J.L., & Singer, D.G. *Television, imagination, and aggression: A study of preschoolers.* Hillsdale, N.J.: Lawrence Erlbaum Associates, 1981.

Sinnott, J.D., & Guttman, D. Piagetian logical abilities and older adults abilities to solve everyday problems. *Human Development,* 1978, *21,* 327-333.

Skinner, B.F. *Science and human behavior,* New York: The Free Press, 1953.

Skinner, B.F. *Verbal behavior.* New York: Appleton-Century-Crofts, 1957.

Skinner, B.F. *Beyond freedom and dignity.* New York: Alfred A. Knopf, 1971.

Skinner, B.F. *About behaviorism,* New York: Alfred A. Knopf, 1974.

Slobin, D.I. They learn the same way all around the world. *Psychology Today,* 1972, *6,* 71-82.

Smart, M.S., & Russell, C. *Children: Development and relationships.* New York: Macmillan Publishing Co., 1972.

Smart, R.G., & Blair, N.L. Drug use and drug problems among teenagers in a household sample. *Drug and Alcohol Dependence,* 1980, *5,* 171-179.

Smith, C.V., & Henry, J.P. Cybernetic foundations of rehabilitation. *American Journal of Physical Medicine,* 1967, *46,* 379-467.

Smith, D.R. *General urology.* Los Altos, Calif.: Lange Medical Publications, 1975.

Smith, P. A longitudinal study of social participation in preschool children: Solitary and parallel play re-examined. *Developmental Psychology,* 1978, *14,* 517-523.

Smith, T.H. Push versus pull: Intra-family versus peer-group variables as possible determinants of adolescent orientation towards parents. *Youth and Society,* 1976, *8,* 5-26.

Snow, C.E. Mother's speech research: From input to interaction. In C.E. Snow & C.A. Ferguson (Eds.), *Talking to children: Language input and acquisition.* Cambridge, England: Cambridge University Press, 1977.

Snow, C.E. The conversational context of language acquisition. In R.N. Campbell & P.T. Smith (Eds.), *Recent advances in the psychology of language* (Vol. 4a: Language development and mother-child interaction). New York: Plenum Press, 1978.

Snow, M.E. *Birth and differences in young children's intentions with mother, father, and peer.* Paper presented at the Society for Research in Child Development, Boston, April 1981.

Sommer, R. & Sommer, B.A. Mystery in Milwaukee: Early intervention, IQ, and psychology textbooks. *American Psychologist,* 1983 *38*(9), 982-985.

Sorenson, R.C. *Adolescent sexuality in contemporary America: Personal values and sexual behaviors, ages 13-19.* New York: Harry N. Abrams, 1973.

Snyder, D. Multidimensional assessment of marital satisfaction. *Journal of Marriage and the Family,* 1979, *41,* 813-823.

Special Section on Religion. A portrait of religious America, *U.S. News and World Report,* April 11, 1977.

Spence, D.L., & Lonner, T.D. Career set: A resource through transitions and crises. *International Journal of Aging and Human Development,* 1978, *9*(1), 51-65.

Sperry, R.W. Hemisphere deconnection and unity in conscious awareness. *American Psychologist,* 1968, *23,* 723-733.

Sperry, R.W. Perception in the absence of neocortical commissures. In *Perception and its disorders* (Research publication, A.R.N.M.D. Vol. 48). New York: The Association for Research in Nervous and Mental Disease. 1970.

Sperry, R.W. Some effects of disconnecting the cerebral hemispheres. *Science,* 1982, *217,* 1223-1226.

Spirduso, W.W. Reaction and movement time as a function of age and physical activity level. *Journal of Gerontology,* 1975, *30,* 435-440.

Spitzer, R.L. (chairperson). *Diagnostic and statistical manual of mental disorders* (3rd ed.). Washington, D.C.: American Psychiatric Association, 1980.

Spock, B. *Baby and child care.* New York: Pocket Books, 1976.

Sroufe, L.A. Socioemotional development. In J. Osofsky (Ed.), *Handbook of infant development.* New York: John Wiley & Sons, 1979.

Sroufe, L.A., & Walters, E. Attachment as an organizational construct. *Child Development,* 1977, *48,* 1184-1199.

Steen, E.B., & Price, J.H. Human sex and sexuality. New York: John Wiley & Sons, 1977.

Stein, P.J. *Being single: Backing the cultural imperative.* Paper presented at the 71st annual meeting of the American Sociological Society, Sept. 3, 1976a.

Stein, P.J. *Single.* Englewood Cliffs, N.J.: Prentice-Hall, 1976b.

Stein, Z., & Susser, M. Prenatal nutrition and mental competence. In J. Lloyd-Still (Ed.), *Malnutrition and intellectual development.* London: M.T.P. Press, 1976.

Steiner, J.E. Human facial expressions in response to taste and smell stimulation. In H. Reese & L. Lipsitt (Eds.), *Advances in child development and behavior* (Vol. 13). New York: Academic Press, 1979.

Stevens, C.W. Aging Americans: Many delay retiring or resume jobs to beat inflation and the blues. *Wall Street Journal,* November 15, 1979, 1, 22.

Stevens-Long, J. *Adult life: Developmental processes.* Palo Alto, Calif.: Mayfield Publishing Co., 1979.

Stevenson, H.W. *Children's learning.* New York: Appleton-Century-Crofts, 1979.

Stewart, R.B. *Sibling attachment relationships: An observation of child-infant interaction in the stranger-situation.* Paper presented at the Society for Research in Child Development, Boston, April 1981.

Stinnett, N., Carter, L.M., & Montgomery, J.E. Older persons' perceptions of their marriage. *Journal of Marriage and the Family,* 1972, *34,* 665-670.

Stinnet, N., & Walters, J. *Relationships in marriage and family.* New York: Macmillan Publishing Co., 1977.

Strain, B., & Vietze, P. *Early dialogues: The structure of reciprocal infant-mothers vocalization.* Paper presented at the annual meeting of the Society for Research in Child Development, Denver, 1975.

Streib, G.F. Older people in a family context. In R.A. Kalish (Ed.), *The later years: Social applications of gerontology.* Monterey, Calif.: Brooks/Cole Publishing Co., 1977.

Streib, G.F., & Schneider, C.J. *Retirement in American society: Impact and process.* Ithaca, N.Y.: Cornell University Press, 1971.

Streissguth, A.P., Landesman-Dwyer, S., Martin, J.C., & Smith, D.W. Teratogenic effects of alcohol in humans and laboratory animals. *Science,* 1980, *209,* 353-361.

Super, C.M. Cognitive development: Looking across at growing up. In C.M. Super & S. Harkness (Eds.), *New directions for child development* (No. 8: Anthropological perspectives on child development). San Francisco: Jossey-Bass, Inc., Publishers, 1980.

Sussman, M.B. Family life of old people. In R.H. Binstock & E. Shanas (Eds.), *Handbook of aging and the social sciences.* New York: Van Nostrand Reinhold Co., 1977.

Sutker, P.B. Alolescent drug and alcohol behavior. In T.M. Field, A. Huston, H.C. Quay, L. Troll, & G.E. Finley, *Review of human development.* New York: John Wiley & Sons, 1982.

Sutton-Smith, B. *The folkgames of children.* Austin, Tex.: The American Folklore Society, 1972.

Sutton-Smith, B., and Rosenberg, P. *The sibling.* New York: Holt, Rinehart & Winston, 1970.

Suyur, C.M. Environmental effects on motor development. *Developmental Medicine and Child Neurology,* 1976, *18,* 561-567.

Swaim, W.T., Jr. *What shall we do with Granny?* Dillsburg, Pa.: Presbyterian Homes of Central Pennsylvania, undated.

Tanner, J.M. Earlier maturation in man. *Scientific American,* 1968, *218,* 21-27.

Tanner, J.M. Physical growth. In P.H. Mussen (Ed.), *Carmichael's manual of child psychology* (3rd ed.) (Vol. 1). New York: John Wiley & Sons, 1970.

Tanner, J.M. Growing up. *Scientific American,* 1973, *229*(3), 35-43.

Tanner, J.M. Sequence and tempo in the somatic changes in puberty. In M.M. Crumbach, G.D. Grave, & F.E. Mayer (Eds.), *Control of the onset of puberty.* New York: John Wiley & Sons, 1974.

Tanner, J.M. *Fetus into man: Physical growth from conception to maturity.* Cambridge, Mass.: Harvard University Press, 1978.

Targ, D.B. Toward a reassessment of women's experience at middle age. *Family Coordinator,* 1979, *28,* 377-382.

Taub, H.B., Goldstein, K.M., & Caputo, D.V. Indices of neonatal prematurity as discriminators of development in middle childhood. *Child Development,* 1977, *48,* 797-805.

Tauber, M. Parental socialization techniques and sex differences in children's play. *Child Development,* 1979, *50,* 225-234.

Tavris, C., & Jayaratne, T.E. How happy is your marriage? What 75,000 wives say about their most intimate relationship. *Redbook,* June 1976, 90-92; 132; 134.

Tavris, C., & Sadd, S. *The Redbook report on female sexuality.* New York: Delacorte Press, 1977.

Taylor, R. *Welcome to the middle years.* Washington, D.C.: Acropolis Books, 1976.

Terkel, C. *Working.* New York: Avon Books, 1982.

Terman, L.M., & Merrill, M.A. *Standford-Binet Intelligence Scale: Manual* (3rd ed.). Boston: Houghton Mifflin Co., 1960.

Thoits, P. *Life events, social isolation and psychological distress.* Unpublished doctoral dissertation. Stanford University, 1978.

Thoman, G. Living together unmarried. A study of thirty couples at the University of Texas. *The Humanity,* March/April 1974, 15-18.

Thomas, A., & Chess, S. *Temperament and development.* New York: Brunner/Mazel, 1977.

Thomas, L. Mid-life career changes: Self-selected or externally mandated? *Vocational Guidance Quarterly,* 1977, *25*(4), 320-328.

Thomes, M.M. Children with absent fathers. *Journal of Marriage and the Family,* 1968, 30(1), 89-96.

Timiras, P.S. *Developmental phsyiology and aging.* New York: Macmillan Publishing Co., 1972.

Timiras, P.S., & Vernadakis, A. Structural, biochemical, and functional aging of the nervous system. In P.S. Timiras, *Developmental physiology and aging.* New York: Macmillan Publishing Co., 1972.

Tomeh, A.K. Birth order and friendship associations, *Journal of Marriage and the Family,* 1970, *32,* 361-362.

Toth, A., & Lesser, M.L. Ureaplasma urealyticum and infertility: The effect of different antibiotic regimens on the semen quality. *Journal of Urology,* 1982, *128*(4), 705-707.

Towbin, A. Cerebral dysfunction related to prenatal organic damage: Clinical-neuropathologic correlations. *Journal of Abnormal Psychology,* 1978, *87,* 617-635.

Travis, C., & Offir, C. The longest war: Sex differences in perspective. New York: Harcourt Brace Jovanovich, 1977.

Troll, L.E. The family of later life: A decade review. *Journal of Marriage and the Family,* 1971, *33,* 263-290.

Troll, L.E. *Early and middle adulthood.* Monterey, Calif.: Brooks/Cole Publishing Co., 1975.

Troll, L.E. Poor, dumb and ugly. In L.E. Troll & K. Israel (Eds.), *Looking ahead: A woman's guide to the problems and joys of growing old.* Englewood Cliffs, N.J.: Prentice-Hall, 1977.

Troll, L.E., & Smith, J. Attachments through the life span: Some questions about dyadic bonds among adults. *Human Development,* 1976, *19,* 135-182.

Tronick, E., & Brazelton, T.B. Clinical uses of the Brazelton Neonatal Behavioral Assessment. In B.Z. Friedcander and L. Rosenblum (Eds.), *Exceptional infant* (Vol. 3). New York: Brunner/Mazel, 1975.

Trotter, S. Zajonc defuses IQ debate: Birth order wins prize. *American Psychological Association Monitor,* 1976, *7,* 1.

Tulkin, S., & Kagan, J. Mother-child interaction in the first year of life. *Child Development,* 1972, *43,* 31-41.

Tumblin, A.B., Gholson, T.L., Rosenthal, T.L., & Kelley, J.E. The effects of gestural demonstration, verbal narration, and their combination on the acquisition of hypothesis-testing behavior by first-grade children. *Child Development,* 1979, *50,* 254-256.

Turiel, E. Conflict and transition in adolescent moral development. *Child Development,* 1974, *45,* 14-79.

Turner, B.F. Sex-related differences in aging. In B.B. Wolman (Ed.), *Handbook of developmental psychology.* Englewood Cliffs, N.J.: Prentice-Hall, 1982.

United Nations, Demographic Yearbook 1972. New York: United Nations, 1973.

U.S. Bureau of Census. 1970 Census of Population. *Subject reports: marital status.* Washington, D.C.: U.S. Government Printing Office, 1972.

U.S. Bureau of Census. *Increase in the older population of the United States,* 1900-2000. Current Population Reports (Series P-25, No. 390). Washington, D.C.: U.S. Government Printing Office, 1974.

U.S. Bureau of Census. *Social and economic characteristics of students, October 1975.* Current Population Reports (Series P-20, No. 303). Washington, D.C.: U.S. Government Printing Office, 1976.

U.S. Bureau of Census. *Marital status and living arrangements, March 1978.* Current Population Reports (Series P-20, No. 388). Washington, D.C.: U.S. Government Printing Office, 1979a.

U.S. Bureau of Census. *Population characteristics.* Current Population Reports (Series P-20, No. 341). Washington, D.C.: U.S. Government Printing Office, 1979b.

U.S. Bureau of Census. Current Population Reports (Series P-20, No. 365). Washington, D.C.: The Bureau, 1981a.

U.S. Bureau of Census. Current Population Reports (Series P-25). Washington, D.C.: The Bureau, 1981b.

U.S. Bureau of Census. Current Population Reports, (Series P-60, No. 129). Washington, D.C.: The Bureau, 1981c.

U.S. Bureau of Labor Statistics, Special Labor Force Reports. Washington, D.C.: The Bureau, 1981.

U.S. Commission on Civil Rights. *Social indicators of equality for minorities and women.* Washington, D.C.: U.S. Government Printing Office, 1978.

U.S. Department of Health and Human Services. Healthy people: *The Surgeon General's report on health promoted and disease prevented.* Washington, D.C.: U.S. Government Printing Office, 1981.

U.S. Department of Health, Education, and Welfare. *Vital statistics of the United States, 1971* (Vol. 2: Mortality). Rockville, Md.: The Department, 1975.

U.S. Department of Health, Education, and Welfare. *Monthly vital statistics report: Provisional statistics.* Rockville, Md.: National Center for Health Statistics, April 18, 1978a.

U.S. Department of Health, Education and Welfare. *Statistical Reports on older Americans: Some prospects for the future elderly population.* DHEW Publication No. (OHOS) 78-20288, 1978b.

U.S. Department of Health, Education, and Welfare. *Monthly vital statistics report: Advance report, final mortality statistics, 1977.* Hyattsville, Md.: National Center for Health Statistics, 1979a.

U.S. Department of Health, Education, and Welfare. *Smoking and health.* Washington, D.C.: U.S. Government Printing Office, 1979b.

U.S. Public Health Service. *Vital statistics of the United States, 1975* (Vol. 11: Mortality, part A). Rockville, Md.: The Service, 1977.

Uzgiris, I.C. *Patterns of cognitive development in infancy.* Paper presented at Merrill-Palmer Institute Conference on Infant Development, Detroit, February 9-12, 1972.

Uzgiris, I.C., & Hunt, J. *Assessment in infancy.* Urbana: University of Illinois, 1975.

Vaillant, G.E. *Adaptations to life.* Boston: Little, Brown & Co., 1977a.

Vaillant, G.E. The climb to maturity: How the best and the brightest come of age. *Psychology Today,* 1977b, *11* (4), 34-38.

Vaillant, G.E., & McArthur, C.C. Natural History of male psychological health: The adult cycle from eighteen to fifty. *Seminars in Psychiatry,* 1972, *4,* 415-427.

Van Maanen, J., & Schein, E.H. Career development. In J.R. Hackman & J.L. Suttle (Eds.), *Improving life at work.* Santa Monica, Calif.: Goodyear Publishing Co., 1977.

Vaughan, V.C., III, McKay, R.J., & Behrman, R. Nelson's textbook of pediatrics (11th ed.). Philadelphia: W.B. Saunders Co., 1979.

Veevers, J.E. Voluntary childlessness and social policy: An alternative view. *Family Coordinator,* 1974, *23*(4), 397-406.

Venn, J.R., & Short, J.G. Vicarious classical conditioning of emotional responses in nursery school children. *Journal of Personality and Social Psychology,* 1973, *38,* 249-255.

Verbrugge, L. *Sex differences in morbidity and mortality in the United States.* Paper presented at the Annual Meeting of the Population Association of America, 1975.

Vincent, C.E. Sociological data in research on young marrieds. *Acta Sociologica,* 1964, *8,* 118-127.

Vital statistics of the United States, 1975 (Vol. 2: Mortality, Part A). Rockville, Md.: U.S. Public Health Service, 1977.

Vlietstra, A.G., & Wright, J.C. *Sensory modality and transmodal stimulus properties in children's discrimination learning and transfer.* Annual Report, Kansas Center for Research in Early Childhood Education. Lawrence: University of Kansas, 1971.

Vogel, S.R., Masters, M.M., & Merrill, G.S. Shaping cooperative behavior in young children. *Journal of Psychology,* 1970, *74,* 181-186.

Vriend, T.J. The case for women. *Vocational Guidance Quarterly,* 1977, *25*(4), 329-331.

Vygotsky, L. *Thought and language.* Cambridge, Mass.: The MIT Press, 1962.

Waber, D.P. Sex difference in mental abililities, hemispheric lateralization, and rate of physical growth at adolescence. *Developmental Psychology,* 1977, *13,* 29-38.

Wachs, T. Relation of infants' performance on Piaget's scales between 12 and 24 months and their Stanford Binet performance at 31 months. *Child Development,* 1975, *46,* 929-935.

Wadsworth, B.J. *Piaget's theory of cognitive development,* New York: David McKay Co., 1971.

Wagner, H. Increasing impact of the peer group during adolescence. *Adolescence,* 1971. *2,* 52-53.

Walker, L.J. Cognitive and perspective-taking prerequisites for moral development. *Child Development,* 1980, *51,* 131-139.

Walker, W.J. Changing United States life-style and declining vascular mortality: Cause or coincidence. *New England Journal of Medicine,* 1977, *297*(3), 163-165.

Wallerstein, J.S., & Kelly, J.B. *Surviving the breakup: How children and parents cope with divorce.* New York: Basic Books, Inc., Publishers, 1980.

Walsh, D. Age differences in learning and memory. In Woodruff, D.S., & Birren, J.E. (Eds.), *Aging: Scientic perspectives and social issues.* New York: D. Van Nostrand, 1975.

Walters, J.; & Stinnet, N. Parent-child relationships: A decade of research. *Journal of Marriage and the Family,* 1971, *33,* 70-118.

Waters, H.S. Memory development in adolescence: Relationship between metamemory, strategy use, and performance. *Journal of Experimental Child Psychology,* 1982, *33,* 183-195.

Watson, J.S., & Ramey, C. Reaction to response contingent stimulation in infancy. *Merrill-Palmer Quarterly of Behavior and Development,* 1972, *18*(3), 219-227.

Watzlawick, P., Fisch, R., & Weakland, J.H. *Change: Principles of problem formation and problem resolution.* New York: W.W. Norton & Co., 1974.

Weatherley, D. Self-perceived rate of physical maturation and personality in late adolescene. *Child Development,* 1964, *35,* 1197-1210.

Weaver, M.J. Single blessedness? *Commonwealth,* October 12, 1979, 588-591.

Weg, R.B. The aging and the aged in contemporary society. *Journal of Physical Therapy,* 1973a, *53,* 749-756.

Weg, R.B. The changing physiology of aging. *American Journal of Occupational Therapy,* 1973b, *27,* 213-217.

Weg, R.B. The physiology of sexuality in aging. In R.L. Solneck (Ed.), *Sexuality and aging* (Rev. ed.). Los Angeles: The Ethel Percy Andrews Gerontology Center/University of Southern California Press, 1978.

Weimberger, M.J. Dress codes—we forget our own advice, *Clearing House,* 1970, *44,* 471-475.

Weimer, W.B. *Notes on the methodology of scientific research.* Hillsdale, N.J.: Lawrence Erlbaum Associates, 1979.

Weiner, I.B. Adjustment to adolescence. In B.B. Wolman (Ed.), *International encyclopedia of neurology, psychiatry, psychoanalysis, and psychology.* New York: Van Nostrand Reinhold Co., 1977.

Weiner, I.B. Psychopathology in adolescence. In J. Adelson (Ed.), *Handbook of adolescent psychology.* New York: John Wiley & Sons, 1980.

Weiner, I.B., & Del Gaudio, A.C. Psychopathology in adolescence: An epidemiological study. *Archives of General Psychiatry,* 1976, *33,* 187-193.

Weisman, A.D. *On dying and denying: A psychiatric study of terminality.* New York: Behavioral Publications, 1972.

Weisman, A.D., & Kastenbaum, R. The psychological autopsy: A study of the terminal phase of life. *Community Mental Health Journal Monograph,* New York: Behavioral Publications, 1968.

Welford, A.T. Motor performance. In J.E. Birrren & K.W. Schaie (Eds.), *Handbook of the psychology of aging.* New York: Van Nostrand Reinhold Co., 1977.

Welford, A.T. Sensory, perceptual, and motor processes in older adults. In J.E. Birren & R.B. Sloane (Eds.), *Handbook of mental health and aging.* Englewood Cliffs, N.J.: Prentice-Hall, 1980.

Wellman, H.M., Collins, J., & Glieberman, J. Understanding the combination of memory variables: Developing conceptions of memory limitations. *Child Development,* 1981, *52,* 1313-1317.

Werner, E. Cross-cultural child development. Monterey, Calif.: Brooks/Cole Publishing Co., 1979.

Westoff, L.A., & Westoff, C.F. *From now to zero.* Boston: Little, Brown & Co., 1971.

White, R. *Lives in progress: A study of the natural growth of personality* (3rd ed.). New York: Holt, Rinehart & Winston, 1975.

Whitehead, A.N. *Aims of education.* New York: Macmillan Publishing Co., 1957.

Whitehurst, G.J. Language development. In B.B. Wolman (Ed.), *Handbook of developmental psychology.* Englewood Cliffs, N.J.: Prentice-Hall, 1982.

Whitehurst, G.J., & Vastra, R. Is language acquired through imitation? *Journal of Psycholinguistic Research,* 1975, *4,* 37-59.

Wilkie, F., & Eisdorfer, C. *Intellectual changes: A 15-year follow-up of the Duke sample.* Unpublished manuscript read at the 26th Annual Meeting of the Gerontological Society, Miami, Fla., 1973.

Willensen, E. *Understanding infancy.* San Francisco: W.H. Freeman & Co., Publishers, 1979.

Williams, J., & Smith, M. *Middle childhood: Behavior and development* (2nd ed.). New York: Macmillan Publishing Co., 1980.

Williams, J.E., & Morland, J.K. *Race, color, and the young child.* Chapel Hill, N.C.: University of North Carolina Press, 1976.

Williams, J.R., & Gold, M. From delinquent behavior to official delinquency. *Social Problems,* 1972, *20,* 209-229.

Willson, J.R., & Carrington, E.R. *Obstetrics and Gynecology* (16th ed.). St. Louis: The C.V. Mosby Co., 1979.

Wilson, A.N. *The developmental psychology of the black child.* New York: Africana Research Publications, 1978.

Wilson, D.L. The programmed theory of aging. In M. Rockstein (Ed.), *Theoretical aspects of aging.* New York: Academic Press, 1974, pp. 11-22.

Wilson, S.R., & Wise, L. *The American citizen: 11 years after high school.* Palo Alto, Calif.: American Institutes for Research, 1975.

Winch, R.F. The function of dating. In R.F. Winch, *The modern family* (Rev. ed.). New York: Holt, Rinehart & Winston, 1971.

Winick, M. Food and the fetus. *Natural History,* 1981, *90*(1), 76-81.

Winick, M. *Malnutrition and brain development.* New York: Oxford University Press, 1976.

Witkin, H.A., Moore, C.A., Oltman, P.K., Goodenough, D.R., Friedman, F., Owen, D.R., & Raskin, E. Role of the field-dependent and field-independent cognitive styles in academic evolution: A longitudinal study. *Journal of Educational Psychology,* 1977, *69,* 197-211.

Wittels, I., & Bornstein, P. A note on stress and sex determination. *Journal of Genetic Psychology,* 1974, *124,* 333-334.

Wittenberg, R.M. Post-adolescence. New York: Grune & Stratton, 1968.

Wolff, P.H. Observation on newborn infants. In L.J. Stone, H.T. Smith, & L.B. Murphy (Eds.), *The competent infant, research and commentary.* New York: Basic Books, Inc., Publishers, 1973, pp. 257-268.

Wolman, B.B., & Money, J. (Eds.). *Handbook of human sexuality.* Englewood Cliffs, N.J.: Prentice-Hall, 1980.

Wolman, R.D., & Barker, E.N. A developmental study of word definitions. *Journal of Genetic Psychology,* 1965, *107,* 119-166.

Wright, J.C., & Vlietstra, A.G. The development of selective attention: From perceptual exploration to logical search. In H.W. Reese (Ed.), *Advances in child development and behavior* (Vol. 10). New York: Academic Press, 1975.

Wright, J.D. Are working women *really* more satisfied? Evidence from several national surveys. *Journal of Marriage and the Family,* 1978, *40,* 301-313.

Wright, J.D., & Hamilton, R.F. Work satisfaction and age: Some evidence of the "job change" hypothesis. *Social Forces,* 1978, *56,* 1140-1158.

Yang, R.K. Early infant assessment: An overview. In J.D. Osofsky (Ed.), *Handbook of infant development.* New York: John Wiley & Sons, 1979.

Yang, R.K., & Douthitt, T.C. Newborn responses to threshold tactile stimulation. Child Development, 1974, *45,* 237-242.

Yankelovich, D., & Clark, R. College and noncollege youth values, *Change,* 1974, *6*(7), 45-46.

Yarrow, L. Attachment and dependency: A developmental perspective. In J. Gerwitz (Ed.), *Attachment and dependency.* Washington, D.C.: V.H. Winston & Sons, 1972.

Yarrow, L.J., Rubenstein, J.L., & Pedersen, F.A. *Dimensions of early stimulation: Differential effects of infant development.* Paper presented at the meeting of the Society for Research in Child Development, 1971.

Yarrow, M.R., Scott, P., de Leewe, L., & Heinig, C. Child-rearing in families of working and nonworking mothers. *Sociometry,* 1962, *25,* 122-140.

Yarrow, Y. Emotional development. *American Psychologist,* 1979, *34*(10), 951-957.

Yogman, M.W. *The goals and structure of face-to-face interaction between infants and fathers.* Paper presented at biennial meeting of the Society for Research in Child Development, San Francisco, March 1979.

Youmans, E.G. Attitudes: Young-old and old-old. *Gerontologist,* 1977, *17,* 175-178.

Young, P. For a zestier life . . . Rx sex over sixty. *The National Observer,* February 1, 1975, pp. 1, 1B.

Youth's attitudes. *Children Today,* 1975, *4*(6), 14-15.

Zacharias, L., Rand, W.M., & Wurtman, R.J. A prospective study of sexual development and growth in American girls: The statistics of menarche. *Obstetrical and Gynecological Survey,* 1976, *31*(4), 323-337.

Zajonc, R.B. Family configuration and intelligence. *Science,* 1976, *197*(4236), 227-236.

Zajonc, R.B., & Markus, G.B. Birth order and intellectual development. *Psychological Review,* 1975, *82,* 74-88.

Zarit, S.H. Gerontology: Getting better all the time. In S.H. Zarit (Ed.), *Readings in aging and death: Contemporary perspectives.* New York: Harper & Row, Publishers, 1977.

Zelnick, M., & Kantner, J.F. Teenage sex and pregnancy, *Family Planning Perspectives,* 1977, *9,* 102-116.

Zelnick, M., & Kantner, J.F. Contraceptive patterns and premarital pregnancy among women aged 15-19 in 1976. *Family Planning,* 1978, *10,* 135-142.

Zelnick, M. & Kantner, J.F. Sexual activity, contraceptive use, and pregnancy among metropolitan-area teenagers: 1971-1979. *Family Planning Perspectives,* 1980, *12*(5), 231.

Zelniker, T., & Jeffrey, W.E. Reflective and impulsive children: Strategies for information processing underlying differences in problem solving. *Monographs of the Society for Research in Child Development,* 1976, *41.*

Zelniker, T., & Oppenheimer, L. Effects of different training methods on perceptual learning in impulsive children. *Child Development,* 1976, *47,* 492-497.

Zorgniotti, A.W., Sealfon, A.I., & Toth, A. Further clinical experience with testis hypothermia for infertility due to poor semen. *Urology,* 1982, *9*(6), 636-640.

GLOSSARY

A

aberration a general term for any deviation from the normal or typical.

accommodation the tendency to change one's schema or operations or to make new ones to include new objects or experiences enabling a higher level of thinking. Term is used by Piaget in his theory on cognitive development. See also **assimilation.**

achievement quotient (AQ) the ratio between a person's scores in scholastic performance and the standard.

ACTH adrenocorticotropic hormone produced by the pituitary gland to stimulate corticoid production in stress situations.

action-instrument in the two-word stage of language development, the indication of knowledge of the use of instruments, as in "cut knife."

action-location in the two-word stage of language development, the expression of the location of an action, as in "sit chair."

action-recipient in the two-word stage of language development, the indication of who is to benefit from an action, as in "cookie me."

activity theory an aging theory which indicates that older individuals who remain active and involved are less likely to age than their withdrawn counterparts.

actualization-fulfillment theory the version of the fulfillment theory of personality holding that the personality force is in the form of an inherited blueprint determining the person's special abilities. Term *self-actualization* was used by Maslow.

actualizing tendency the potential for the fullest development that, under appropriate circumstances, will occur.

acuity the ability to see objects clearly and to resolve detail.

adaptation a key principle in ethological theories referring to the way that behavior changes or develops to meet environmental demands and to ensure survival and reproduction.

addition according to Flavell, a sequence in intellectual development in which the later-emerging skill is added to the earlier one and supplements but does not replace it. An example is the addition of counting ability to one's knowledge of number concepts.

adjustment processes and behaviors that satisfy a person's internal needs and enable the person to cope effectively with environmental, social, and cultural demands.

adjustment, emotional a state of emotional maturity proper to the age of a person and marked by a relatively stable and moderate emotional reactivity to affect- and mood-eliciting stimuli.

adjustment, social reaction patterns toward others conducive to harmonious relationships within family and other reference groups.

adolescence the developmental period beginning with the onset of major pubertal changes and continuing until adult maturity.

adrenalin (epinephrine) the chief hormone of the normal adrenal medulla, which stimulates the sympathetic nervous system.

adrenals a pair of ductless or internal secretion glands attached to the kidneys and secreting epinephrine and cortin, important in emergency and stress situations.

adult a postadolescent person whose growth is completed in most aspects of development and who is capable of satisfactory reality testing and adjustment to self and environment.

adulthood the stage of the human life cycle that begins when the individual achieves biological and psychological maturity and ends with the gradual onset of old age.

aerobic exercise exercise such as running, swimming, or cycling that increases heart and lung capacity, slows muscle and joint deterioration, and reduces body fat. Especially important during middle age.

affect a vital feeling, mood, or emotion characterized by specific physiological (psychophysical) changes and states.

afterbirth the placenta, its attached membranes, and the rest of the umbilical cord, delivered in the final stages of labor.

age, mental (MA) the level of development in intelligence, particularly the age level at which the child has attained the capacity to function intellectually. The term should be obtained from the results of a mental test.

age norm the average for a given age as revealed by sample group performances at this age.

ageism prejudice against older people.

agent, action, and object in the two-word stage of language development, the expression of an agent's action on an object, using only two of the components of the thought, as in "Daddy ball" for "Daddy throw ball."

aggression feeling and behavior of anger or hostility.

aggressiveness verbal or physical behavior that is inappropriate or harms someone.

aging the continuous developmental process beginning with conception and ending with death during which organic structures and functions of an immature organism first grow and mature, then decline and deteriorate.

alienation a feeling of estrangement from and hostility toward society or familiar persons, based in part on a discrepancy between expectations and promises and in part on the actual experience of the role one is playing.

alleles pairs of genes on corresponding chromosomes that affect the same traits. When the two alleles are identical, a person is said to be homozygous for that trait. When the alleles carry differing instructions, he or she is said to be heterozygous for that trait.

allergy heightened sensitivity to pollen or any other foreign substance, causing respiratory, skin, or gastrointestinal irritation, including swelling. Hay fever and hives are frequent allergic conditions.

altruism deep unselfish concern for others, often expressed in helping them or in charitable activities.

Alzheimer's disease a presenile dementia involving rapid intellectual deterioration, speech impairment, loss of body control, and death, usually within 5 years of onset.

ambivalence internal tendency to be pulled (usually psychologically) in opposite directions, for example, acceptance-rejection, love-hate, participation-withdrawal.

amenorrhea abnormal absence or suppression of menstrual discharge.

amnesia defensive forgetting caused by a strong conflict or inability to face a certain event or experience, with subsequent repression.

amniocentesis a means of detecting fetal abnormality by the insertion of a hollow needle through the maternal abdomen and the drawing out of a sample of amniotic fluid on which chromosomal analyses can be performed.

amnion the translucent sac in which the developing prenatal organism lies.

amniotic interchangeable with **amnioic.**

amniotic fluid the fluid in the amnion in which the developing prenatal organism is suspended; it protects the organism from external pressure.

amniotic sac fluid-filled membrane encasing the embryo/fetus.

anal stage in psychoanalytic theory the second stage of psychosexual development, during which the child's interest centers on anal activities such as those related to toilet training. See also **genital stage; oral stage; phallic stage.**

androgens male sex hormones, produced primarily by the testes.

androgynous the capability of expressing both masculine and feminine behaviors and attitudes, depending on their appropriateness to the particular situation.

anencephaly the lack of a brain at birth.

anesthesia lack of psychophysical response to sensory stimuli; unawareness of pain.

animism a characteristic of preoperational thought in which human qualities are inappropriately attributed to inanimate objects.

anlage an original basis for or a disposition toward a specific developmental trend or factor.

anorexia nervosa chronic failure to eat for fear of gaining weight; characterized by an extreme loss of appetite that results in severe malnutrition, semistarvation, and sometimes death.

anoxia a severe deficiency in the supply of oxygen to the tissues, especially the brain, causing damage to their structural integrity.

anterior pituitary gland the front part of the pituitary gland, an endocrine gland situated at the base of the brain. The anterior pituitary produces hormones that regulate growth and other hormones that regulate the functions of the other endocrine glands.

anxiety a feeling of uneasiness or distress that arises when a person is torn by inner conflict because of incompatible motives, or when he feels apprehension over a possible threat to himself or herself.

anxiety neurosis distress and helplessness due to ego damage or weakness, accompanied by an expectation of danger or misfortune.

Apgar scale developed by Apgar and James in 1962, a much-used and practical scoring system for assessing, on a scale from 0 to 2, color, heart rate, reflex irritability, muscle tone, and respiratory effort in newborns. The totaled score may vary from 0 to 10 (10 being best).

aphasia the loss or impairment of the ability to use speech resulting from lesions in the brain.

apperception a mental process of interpreting and assimilating a new experience or behavior in the experiential background (apperceptive schema).

aptitude the potential ability to perform certain tasks or functions effectively in certain situations if given proper training or opportunity to develop skill or learning.

arthritis inflammation or deformation of one or several joints, accompanied by pain, stiffness, and swelling, often chronic.

aspiration, level of the intensity of striving for achievement, or the standard by which a person judges his own activity in reference to expected end results.

assertiveness verbal or physical behavior that is appropriate and that injures no one.

assimilation the incorporation of new objects and experiences into a structure or schema in the mind to be used later in problem-solving situations. See also **accommodation.**

asymmetrical one side of the physique, object, or figure lacks similarity or correspondence with the other side.

asynchrony the maturation of different body parts at different rates. This disproportion becomes most pronounced during puberty.

atrophy progressive decline of a part, its decrease in size, or possible degeneration.

attachment the primary social bond that develops between an infant and its caretaker.

attention the focusing of perception on a certain stimulus while ignoring others; needed for learning to take place.

attentional deficit disorder a childhood disorder characterized by an inability to focus attention.

attitude an acquired persistent tendency to feel, think, or act in a certain way.

attribution in the two-word stage of language development, the modifying of nouns with attributes, as in "red truck."

auditory perception ability to hear sounds accurately and to be able to organize them into meaningful units.

authoritarian parenting a style of childrearing that focuses on parental power and strict obedience to rules.

authoritative parenting a childrearing pattern that places moderate restrictions on the range of acceptable behaviors but also incorporates nurturance and sensitivity to the child's needs.

autism a schizophrenic syndrome characterized by absorption in fantasy to the exclusion of interest in reality and in others.

autistic self-centered; with perception, feeling, and thinking unduly controlled by personal needs, desires, and preferences at the expense of sensitivity to others or to situational demands.

autogenous self-originated, as distinguished from what is initiated by outside stimuli and learning.

autonomic nervous system the division of the peripheral nervous system that regulates smooth muscle; i.e., organ and glandular activities. It is divided into the sympathetic and parasympathetic divisions.

autonomous morality in Piaget, the moral thinking of children 11 or older; rules are flexible and considered to be mutual agreements among equals; intentions are considered in evaluating guilt.

autonomy a feeling of self-control and self-determination. According to Erikson's theory of psychosocial development, this feeling develops around the ages of 2 to 4 and manifests itself in the child's increasing demands to determine his own behavior.

autonomy versus shame and doubt according to Eriksonian theory, the second nuclear conflict of personality development.

autosomes the chromosomes of a cell, excluding those that determine sex.

axillary hair underarm hair.

B

babbling speech patterns found in infants, comprising repetitious sequences of alternating consonants and vowels, such as "ba ba ba ba." They may be a form of motor practice that facilitates later speech development.

basal metabolism the rate of energy required to maintain the body's functioning while resting.

behavior any kind of reaction, including complex patterns of feeling, perceiving, thinking, and willing, in response to internal or external, tangible or intangible stimuli.

behavior modification an approach to changing behavior that involves a wide variety of techniques based on learning principles such as conditioning and reinforcement.

behavioral sciences those disciplines that study the various aspects of human living. Psychology, sociology, and social anthropology are considered to be the major behavioral sciences. However, the evolution of the interdisciplinary approach to the study of behavior has introduced certain aspects of history, economics, political science, physiology, zoology, and physics into the field of the behavioral sciences.

behaviorism the school of psychology holding that the proper object of study in psychology is behavior alone, without reference to consciousness. Behavior theorists are particularly interested in learning mechanisms.

bereavement the state or fact of suffering because of the loss of a loved one by death.

binocular disparity the incongruent views the two eyes receive because of their different positions in space.

binocular fusion the integration of the two different views of the eyes.

birth injury temporary or possibly permanent injury to the infant that occurs during the birth process. Many disabilities are attributed to brain damage occurring as a result of birth injury.

birth order the order of birth in a family, which often affects the child's personality because of differential parental treatment.

birth order effects any behaviors believed to be brought about by birth position in the family relative to siblings (first born, middle child, and so on). These effects are seen in children of the same birth order across a majority of families and are therefore felt to be a result of birth position.

blastocyst the cluster of cells that begins to differentiate itself into distinct parts during the germinal period of prenatal development.

blastula the cluster of cells that make up the prenatal organism in the first few days after conception.

body ideal the body type defined by one's culture as ideally attractive and sex appropriate.

body image the concept or mental representation one has of his/her own body.

body stalk during the germinal period of prenatal development, the structure that differentiates to become the embryonic disc and the umbilical cord.

body transcendence versus body preoccupation according to Peck, the need in later adulthood to equate well-being with satisfying relationships and experiences rather than dwelling on physical health.

Brazelton scale scale used to assess neurological integrity and behaviors of neonates.

breech delivery a birth in which the baby's buttocks appear first, then the legs, and finally the head.

Brodmann's areas Brodmann made a map of the cerebral cortex of the brain and identified each small area by number. Neurologists have a common basis for identifying the locations in the brain.

bulimia excessive overeating or uncontrolled binge eating.

C

canalization the temporary deviation from and subsequent return to a child's normal growth curve.

carcinogenic capable of eliciting cancer.

cataract a loss of transparency of the crystalline lens of the eye or of its capsule.

catharsis the relief of feelings, particularly negative ones, through talking, playing, drawing, or painting; it is a technique used in psychology and psychiatry.

cathexis attachment of affects and drives to their goal objects; direction of psychic energy into a particular outlet.

cause-and-effect relationships between factors in an experiment suggest a correlation; association between elements in an experiment in which one factor leads to the other.

central nervous system (CNS) the brain and spinal cord.

central tendency a statistical term that represents the central point on a scale of scores. The mean, median, and mode are such measures.

centration tendency to focus on one aspect of a situation and to neglect the importance of other aspects; characteristic of preoperational thought in Piaget's theory.

cephalocaudal sequence the progression of physical and motor development from head to foot. For example, a baby's head develops and grows before the torso, arms, and legs.

cerebral dominance refers to the fact that one cerebral hemisphere is dominant over the other in the control of body movements, as in handedness.

cerebral thrombosis formation of a blood clot in a blood vessel leading to the brain.

cerebrovascular accident also called *cerebral vascular accident, apoplexy,* or *stroke*. An impeded blood supply to some part of the brain.

cervix the narrow canal connecting the vagina and the uterus.

cesarean section a surgical operation through the walls of the abdomen and uterus for the purpose of delivering a child.

character the acquired ability to act and conduct oneself in accordance with a personal code of principles based on a scale of values, and facility in doing so.

chemical substance abuse the use of drugs or alcohol to the point that the brain and the thought processes are adversely affected.

child a person between infancy and puberty.

childhood the period of development between infancy and puberty (or adolescence).

chorion the protective and nutrient cover of the amnion, which contains the developing organism in the womb.

chorionic villi capillaries that link the developing umbilical veins and arteries of an embryo with the uterine wall; they eventually become part of the placenta along with the surrounding maternal tissues.

chromosomal aberration a typical development or growth caused by extra chromosomal material or insufficient chromosomal material on one of the chromosome pairs.

chromosome the minute, threadlike body within the nucleus of the cell that carries many DNAs, RNAs, proteins, and genes and transmits hereditary traits.

chronological age (CA) age in calendar years.

chunks bits of information organized into larger single units.

cirrhosis replacement of regular tissue, especially of the liver, by fibrous tissue—a frequent liver disease of alcoholics.

classical conditioning an experimental method in which a conditioned stimulus is paired with an unconditioned stimulus to condition a particular response.

classification ability to sort stimuli into categories according to characteristics (for example, color or shape); occurs in Piaget's concrete operations stage.

climacteric the period marking the end of the time at which women can conceive, and for men the time at which there is a significant decline in sexual virility. The term *menopause* is generally used for women instead of *climacteric*.

clinical study a study consisting of in-depth interviews and observations. It can be controlled or can be varied for each subject.

coefficient of correlation a numerical index used to indicate the degree of correspondence between two sets of paired measurements. The most common kind is the product-moment coefficient designated by Pearson.

cognition the process of gaining knowledge about the world through sensing, perceiving, using symbols, and reasoning; the actual knowledge that an individual has about the world. Knowing the world through the use of one's perceptual and conceptual abilities.

cognitive development the development of a logical method of looking at the world, utilizing one's perceptual and conceptual powers.

cognitive dissonance the condition in which one has beliefs or knowledge that disagree with each other or with behavioral tendencies. When such cognitive dissonance arises, the subject is motivated to reduce the dissonance through changes in behavior or cognition (Festinger).

cognitive processes the operations or routines that the mind performs including the encoding of information, the storage and retrieval of information in memory, the generation of hypotheses, their evaluation according to criteria, and inductive and deductive reasoning.

cognitive style an individual's characteristic style of processing information. For example, some people are deliberate, reflective, and analytical; others are impulsive, inflexible, and intolerant of ambiguity.

cognitive theorists theorists such as Jean Piaget and Jerome Bruner who describe intellectual development and Roger Brown who describes early language behavior. They see children's thinking as different but no less effective than that of adults.

cohabitation living together and maintaining a sexual relationship without being legally married.

cohort perspective emphasizes the similarities of individuals in the same age strata; notes generational differences.

cohorts the members of a certain age group; a group of people of the same age.

coitus sexual intercourse.

compensation a defense mechanism in which the individual works especially hard to avoid defeat or failure (direct compensation) or turns to another area of endeavor to allay anxiety (indirect compensation).

compensatory education special school programs for children in poverty areas, designed to raise their level of educational readiness.

compulsory retirement a designated age at which a person must retire from working at his or her place of employment; mandatory retirement.

concept a type of symbol that represents a set of common attributes among a group of other symbols or images.

conception the merging of the sperm and ovum in human fertilization, which signals the beginning of life.

conceptualization the process of concept formation in which various items are grouped into units on the basis of commensurable characteristics.

concrete operational stage the stage of cognitive development that occurs from about 7 to 12 years of age and during which the child develops the operations of conservation, class inclusion, and serialization. This stage begins when children understand new kinds of logical operations involving reversible transformations of concrete objects and events.

conditioned reflex in classical conditioning, one of two kinds of reflexes in which the reflex is one that comes to be elicited by a previously neutral stimulus.

conditioning a mode of training whereby reinforcement (reward or punishment) is used to elicit desired (rewarded) responses.

conduct that part of a person's behavior, including insufficiencies and reverses, which is guided by ethical, moral, or ideological standards.

confabulation an attempt to fill in the gaps of memory without awareness of the falsification involved.

conflict an intrapsychic state of tension or indecision due to contrary desires, ungratified needs, or incompatible plans of action; such tension may also exist between conscious and unconscious choices.

congenital referring to characteristics and defects acquired during the period of gestation and persisting after birth as distinguished from heredity.

connective tissue. fibers that lie between cells of the body.

consciousness cognizance of the immediate environment plus the ability to utilize encoding, memory, and logic at will.

conservation the realization that one aspect of something (for example, quantity) remains the same, while another aspect is changed (for example, shape, position). Used by Piaget. For example, rearranging a row of objects does not affect their number.

constitution the organization of organic, functional, and psychosocial elements within the developing person that largely determines his or her condition.

contact comfort cuddling and other forms of warm physical caressing that bring consolation, relaxation, or ease.

continuity/discontinuity a concept in developmental psychology referring to the way in which changes in growth and development occur. Continuity states that the changes take place in a gradual, continuous, methodical manner. Discontinuity states that changes emerge in a series of distinct, quantitative changes reflecting structural or functional reorganization.

continuous reinforcement in operant conditioning, a schedule in which each correct response is reinforced.

contraception the prevention of pregnancy by artificial means.

control the intentional modification of any condition of an investigation. These modifications may include the selection of subjects for study, the experiences they have in the study, and the possible responses that they can give to that experience.

control group a group used for comparison with an experimental group with the exception that the independent variable is not applied to the control group.

conventional level a stage of moral development in which the individual strives to maintain the expectations of the family, group, or nation, regardless of the consequences. See also **postconventional level; preconventional level.**

convergence the mechanism by which the slightly different images of an object seen by each eye come together to form a single image.

convergent thinking a type of thought wherein attention is directed toward finding a single solution from a given set of circumstances. See also **divergent thinking.**

conversion as used in the present work, transformation of anxiety and energies elicited by a conflict into somatic symptoms.

cooing vowel-like sounds; after crying, this sound is among the first made by an infant.

cooperative (reciprocal) play play in which the children begin to adjust their behavior to the activities and desires of their peers.

coordination of secondary schemes Piaget's fourth substage in the period of sensorimotor development.

correlation the relationship between two variables as measured by the correlation coefficient.

correlation coefficient a statistical index for measuring correspondence in changes occurring in two variables. Perfect correspondence is $+1.00$; no correspondence is 0.00; perfect correspondence in opposite direction is -1.00.

critical periods specific times in development during which a child is best able to learn a specific lesson; also, in fetal development, crucial times at which various specific physical features and organs develop; detrimental environmental influences during those periods can adversely affect organic development.

cross-sectional research studies that compare different age groups at some specific point in time.

crystallized intelligence the class of mental abilities acquired and developed through cultural contact, such as language and social knowledge.

culture the man-made aspects of human environment—customs, beliefs, institutions, modes of living—including the attitudes and beliefs held, and acted on, by a specific group of people about aspects of living that they consider important.

culture-fair tests IQ tests developed as alternatives to the standard IQ tests; used to test children who speak another language or who have not had an equal exposure to the kinds of information found on the standard IQ tests.

D

daydreaming a form of withdrawal from unpleasant or frustrating reality into the realm of fantasy and reverie, frequently of a pleasant, wish-gratifying type.

DDT acutely poisonous pesticide. If ingested by humans, it produces heightened excitability, muscle tremors, and motor seizures; deadly in larger amounts.

decay a process by which information is lost from sensory stores simply as a function of time.

defense mechanism any habitual response pattern that is spontaneously used to protect oneself from threats, conflicts, anxiety, frustration, and other conditions that a person cannot tolerate or cope with directly.

demography the statistical study of human populations, especially with reference to size and density, distribution, and vital statistics.

dependence the desire or need for supporting relationships with other persons. See also **independence.**

dependent variable some facet of a child's functioning that is measured in an experiment and presumed to be under the control of one or more manipulated factors. See also **independent variable.**

descriptive psychology the study of human and animal behavior that describes patterns of behavior.

descriptive data numerical statistics assembled, classified, and tabulated to describe and summarize the characteristics of the data.

descriptive study a research method, such as a case study or survey, that describes a phenomenon as it exists or occurs in nature.

detachment the infant's desire to try out new experiences and to expand his competence. Developing in the second year, it coexists and interacts with the attachment system.

determinism a philosophical doctrine stating that all decisions of the mind or acts of the will, all social and psychological phenomena, and all acts of nature are determined by prior causes.

development, level of a period in a person's life marked by specific clusters of traits, interests, and attitudes and by a similarity in interests and concerns to other persons in that period of life.

developmental-level approach in psychology, the approach in which the total personality of the person is considered at each phase of life.

developmental psychology a division of psychology that investigates the growth, maturation, and aging processes of the human organism and personality, as well as cognitive, social, and other functions, throughout the span of life.

developmental study research methods, such as cross-sectional, longitudinal, and retrospective studies, used to investigate changes in behavior over time.

developmental task a specific learning problem that arises at a particular stage of life and that individuals must accomplish to meet the demands of their culture. Developmental tasks vary with one's age and persist as objectives throughout life. The nature of the developmental task is such that one learning is related to, merges into, and forms the basis for the next learning.

developmental trajectories a theoretical progression or line of development over an extended period of time. Some see the development as a hierarchical structure, others as stages or episodes in time.

diabetes mellitus a chronic disorder of carbohydrate metabolism due to insulin deficiency or a disturbance of the normal tissue responsiveness to insulin.

differentiation the process by means of which structure, function, or forms of behavior become more complex or specialized; the change from homogeneity to heterogeneity.

dilation enlargement of an opening, blood vessel, canal, or cavity.

dimension a coherent group of processes having a particular denominator—for example, intelligence, emotion, and language dimensions of personality.

dimensional approach in psychology, the approach in which a specific aspect or area of personality is considered throughout various phases of life.

directionality an inner sense of left and right, or directions, that can be projected into the external environment.

discretionary retirement the age and timing of retirement is the choice of the individual; voluntary retirement.

disengagement theory a social theory of aging which suggests that the older person disengages from society and society also moves from the individual. This break is thought to be necessary to maintain satisfaction in late adulthood.

disequilibrium according to Piaget, disequilibrium exists whenever the mind is confronted with inconsistencies or gaps in knowledge and a change is needed from one level of understanding to another to attain a more clearly delineated structure of knowledge; for example, movement is toward a state of relative equilibrium of cognitive structures.

disjunctive concept a concept in which a member of a category may possess some, but need not possess all, of several different attributes to be included in the category.

displacement the ability to communicate information about objects, people, and events in another place or another time; one of three formal properties of language.

divergent thinking a kind of creative thought process exercised when a person's imagination provides many different answers to a single question. See also **convergent thinking.**

dizygotic (DZ) twins twins who develop from two separate eggs; fraternal twins. See also **monozygotic (MZ) twins.**

DNA deoxyribonucleic acid molecule, containing the genetic code—"the molecule of life." Each cell in its nucleus contains DNAs arranged in the form of a double helix.

dominant gene a gene whose hereditary characteristics always prevail.

Down's syndrome a congenital physical condition associated with mental retardation, characterized by thick, fissured tongue, flat face, and slanted eyes. Formerly called mongolism.

drive the tension and arousal produced by an ungratified need and directed toward a chosen object or end.

dyadic as used in the present work, pertaining to active relationships between two persons, for example, mother and child, father and son.

dynamic refers to forces and potent influences that are capable of producing changes within the organism or personality.

dysfunction disturbance or impairment of the functional capacity of an organ or system, including mental abilities.

dyslexia partial impairment of reading ability.

E

early intervention programs programs for lower-class, educationally deprived mothers, designed to improve their child-rearing skills and enhance the cognitive and personality development of their children.

early maturers preadolescents who reach their physical maturity earlier than average for their sex

echolalia a speech pattern in which the child repeats rather than responds to spoken communications; characteristic of autistic children.

eclecticism method or system of thought in which one chooses various sources and selects materials from many doctrines.

ecological the approach to studying development that takes into account the limiting and determining effects of the physical and social environment.

ectoderm the outermost cell layer in the embryo from which structures of the nervous system and skin are developed.

EEG (Electroencephalogram or electroencephalograph) a graphic record of the electric activity of the brain obtained by placing electrodes on the skull.

egg cell the female reproductive cell; also called the **ovum.**

ego the conscious core of personality that exercises control demanded by the superego and directs drives and impulses of the id in accordance with the demands of reality; guides a person's realistic coping behavior and mediates the eternal conflicts between what one wants to do (id) and what one must or must not do (superego).

ego differentiation versus work-role preoccupation according to Robert Peck, an issue to be dealt with in old age; at this point the person should concentrate on extending his perception of self beyond his work role.

ego identity according to Erik Erikson, a clear and continuing sense of who one is and what one's goals are.

ego integrity versus despair the final conflict in Erickson's theory of development. This stage involves retrospective glances at and evaluations of life.

ego transcendence versus ego preoccupation the issue in later adulthood, according to Peck, at which point the individual must recognize that death is inevitable. Accepting this realization should lead to a more satisfying life.

egocentric speech speech that fails to take into consideration the needs of the listener and thus is not appropriate for communication.

egocentrism failure to appreciate that another person's perceptions of a situation may differ from one's own; a characteristic of preoperational thought.

Electra complex a Freudian conflict involving young girls, parallel to the Oedipus conflict in boys. There is sexual desire of the girl for her father accompanied by hostility toward her mother.

embryo the form of prenatal life from the second to the eighth week. The period of the embryo follows the germinal period and is succeeded by that of the fetus.

embryology the study of the development of the individual from conception to birth.

embryonic disc during the germinal period, the part of the prenatal organism that will eventually become the embryo.

embryonic period the period of prenatal growth that follows the germinal period, lasting from the second to the eighth week after conception; marked by development of a primitive human form and life-support system.

emotion a conscious state of experience, characterized by feeling or excitement that is accompanied and frequently preceded by specific physiological changes and frequently resulting in excitation of the organism to action. Emotions are the physiological forms that result from one's estimate of the harmful or beneficial effects of stimuli.

emotional dependence dependence on others, which has as its aim the obtaining of their comfort and nurturance.

empathy the emotional linkage that characterizes relationships between individuals; the ability to sense the feelings of others.

empirical pertaining to, or founded upon, experience.

empty nest syndrome the experience of parents when their children leave home. The mother who has devoted her entire life to nurturing the children is more likely to feel "empty" than the parent who has developed wider interests and realistic attitudes about parental responsibility.

enactive a Bruner term meaning that the mode of thinking is one that responds through motor actions, as is done in infancy.

encoding the transformation of external stimuli into internal signals that stimulate behavior appropriate to them. In the perceptual process it is the point wherein the message or meaning is translated into behavior that is deemed an appropriate response to the stimuli.

endocrine glands the ductless glands of internal secretion, such as the pituitary, thyroid, and adrenals, that secrete hormones into the bloodstream or lymph system.

endoderm the innermost of the three cell layers of the embryo from which most of the visceral organs and the digestive tract are developed.

endogenous developing from within; originating internally.

endometrium the mucous membrane lining the uterus.

endorphins opiates produced in the brain that act as natural pain suppressants.

endowment capacity for development, physical or mental, conditioned by heredity and constitution.

envy a distressful feeling aroused by the observation that another person possesses what one desires to have.

epigenesis appearance of new phenomena not present at previous stages in an organism's development from fertilized egg to adult maturity.

episiotomy surgical incision of the vulva for obstetrical purposes to prevent uneven laceration during delivery.

epistemology the branch of philosophy that is concerned with discovering the nature of knowledge and knowing.

equilibration the most general development principle in Piaget's theory, which states that an organism always tends toward biological and psychological balance and that development is a progressive approximation to an ideal state of equilibrium that it never fully achieves.

estrogens female sex hormones, produced primarily in the ovaries.

estrous cycle the periodic waxing and waning of sexual desire and receptivity, with accompanying physiological changes, in the female animal.

ethical relativity the doctrine stating that different cultures or groups hold different fundamental moral values and that these values cannot themselves be judged as more or less adequate or more or less moral.

ethics moral values and ideals. See also **morality.**
ethnic designating any of the basic groups of humankind as distinguished by customs, characteristics, or language.
etiology the investigation of origins, causes, and factors contributing to a trait, attitude, or disease.
euphoria an intense, subjective sensation of vigor, well-being, and happiness that may exist despite some problem or disability.
existentialism the philosophy that man forms his own nature in the course of his life, with man's situation in the universe seen as purposeless or irrational.
exogenous originating from or resulting from external causes.
expectancy anticipation of a given stimulus determined by one's previous experiences with related stimuli. Deviation from expectancy is a factor in selective attention.
experiential freedom according to Carl Rogers, the subjective sense that one is free to choose among alternative courses of action in defining one's life.
experimental method the method of investigation of natural events that seeks to control the variables involved so as to more precisely define cause and effect relationships. Most frequently done in a laboratory, but need not be.
experimentation a type of study designed to control the arrangement and manipulation of conditions in order to systematically observe particular phenomena.
expression the second component of a baby's sucking, during which the nipple is pressed against the roof of the mouth with the tongue applying heavy pressure at the front of the mouth and then progressively moving toward the rear.
expressive jargon type of prelinguistic speech that develops during the second year; characterized by a string of meaningless gibberish that contains pauses, inflections, and sentence-like rhythms.
expressive language the ability to produce meaningful utterances.
extended family the family that consists of three generations—children, parents, grandparents, and even aunts and uncles—under the same roof. See also **nuclear family.**
extinction a process in which a conditioned response is reduced to its preconditioned level. Previously reinforced responses are no longer reinforced.
extinguish to gradually eliminate a response by withholding reinforcement.
extroversion an attitude in which a person directs his or her interest to outside phenomena rather than to feelings within.
extrovert a type of personality whose thoughts, feelings, and interests are directed chiefly toward persons, social affairs, and other external phenomena.
eye-hand coordination the ability to coordinate vision with motor activities so that one can accurately reach for and grasp objects.

F

fallopian tube either of the tubes that carries the ovum from the ovaries to the uterus.
fantasy a function of imagination marked by engagement in vicarious experiences and hallucinatory actions; reveries, daydreaming.
fertilization the union of an egg cell with a sperm.
fetal period the period of prenatal growth lasting from about the eighth week until birth.
fetoscopy method used with ultrasound to visually inspect part of the fetus while it is still in the uterus.
fetus the prenatal human organism from approximately 8 weeks after conception to birth. See also **embryo.**
field study a study of naturally occurring behavior in which the researcher controls only some aspects of the situation.
fixation the persistence of infantile, childish, pubertal, or adolescent response patterns, habits, and modes of adjustment throughout successive phases of development.
fluid intelligence ability to adapt, and to perceive and integrate things mentally; separate from experience or organized education.
formal operational stage according to Jean Piaget, the fourth stage of thought, which begins at about 12 years of age, is the time the individual begins to engage in thinking that is characterized by the ability to consider what is possible, as well as what is. It is the period during which logical thinking begins and is the final step toward abstract thinking and conceptualization. See also **concrete operational stage; preoperational stage; sensorimotor stage.**
formal rules statements of relations between units or classes that are always true and specifiable, such as the rules of mathematics.
fraternal (dizygotic) twins twins resulting from the fertilization of two separate ova by two separate sperm.
free will the ability to choose between alternatives so that the choice or the behavior is freely determined by the individual.
frustration the experience of distress induced by failures and by thwarting of attempts to gratify one's needs or ambitions.
fully functioning person Carl Roger's term for an individual characterized by openness to experience, existential living, organismic trusting, experiential freedom, and creativity.

G

G-factor the common root of intellectual behavior that runs through the functioning of those specific subabilities identified by various authorities. G-factor is not general intelligence but the pervasive element in all types of intelligence.
galvanic skin response (GSR) a change in the electrical resistance of the skin.
gamete a mature reproductive cell; an egg or a sperm.
gender identity an individual's sense of being a boy or a girl, a male or a female.
generalization (1) in concept formation, problem solving, and transfer of learning, the detection by the learner of a characteristic or principle common to a class of objects, events, or problems; (2) in conditioning, the principle that once a conditioned response has been established to a given stimulus, similar stimuli will also evoke that response.
genes the microscopic elements carried by the chromosomes. They contain the codes that produce inherited physical traits and behavioral dispositions.
genetic counseling analysis and communication of a couple's chances of producing a child with birth defects.
genetic epistemology the developmental study of what is known and how it comes to be known; most closely associated with Piaget's theory.
genetic error theories a biological theory of aging which suggests that aging is caused by a breakdown or error in the cell's DNA-RNA structure.
genetic psychology the branch of psychology that studies the human organism and its functions in terms of their origin and early course of development.
genetics the branch of biology concerned with the transmission of hereditary characteristics.
genital organs the male and female sex organs.

genital stage in psychoanalytic theory the final stage of psychosexual development, during which heterosexual interests are dominant. This stage begins in adolescence and lasts throughout adulthood. See also **anal stage; oral stage; phallic stage.**

genome all the genes found in a haploid set of chromosomes.

genotype the characteristics of an organism that are inherited and that can be transmitted to offspring; also, the traits or characteristics common to a biological group. See also **phenotype.**

geriatrics the medical study and care of aging persons.

germ cell a sex cell that has the capability of being fertilized.

germinal period the first stage of prenatal development. It is roughly the first 2 weeks after conception, during which time the developing individual is primarily engaged in cell division. See also **embryo; fetus.**

gerontology the study of the improvement of the life habits of aging persons; the psychology and sociology of aging.

gestation period the amount of time the prenatal organism spends in the uterus; the total period of prenatal development calculated from the beginning of the mother's last menstruation (280 days, 40 weeks, or 9 calendar months).

gestational age the age of the fetus calculated from the date of conception.

gonadotropic hormones secretions of the anterior pituitary that stimulate activity in the gonads.

gonads the sex glands; the ovaries in females and the testes in males.

gonococcus the bacterium that produces gonorrhea.

gonorrhea a venereal disease.

grammar the structural principles of a language; syntax.

grasping reflex the tendency during the first few weeks of life for an infant to clutch any small object placed in his or her hand.

grief work the sequence of phases to recovery from the loss of a loved one. This "work" is aimed at freeing oneself from the ties to the deceased, adjusting to the new situation, and forming new relationships.

group, reference the group a person belongs to or is interested in belonging to, for example, peer groups, usually with a molding influence on the individual.

growth strictly speaking, the addition of height and weight through simple physical accretion; sometimes used interchangeably with development, which includes the foregoing but also embraces the improvement of function.

growth spurt physiological change ushering in adolescence, caused by an increased output of growth hormones and gonadotropic hormones controlled by the pituitary gland.

growth trajectory the curved path that a normal individual follows in terms of growth and development; for children, the growth pertaining to height and weight.

guidance refers to a variety of methods, such as advising, counseling, testing, and use of special instruction and corrective teaching, by means of which a person may be helped to find and engage in activities that will yield satisfaction and further adjustment.

guilt a negative feeling that stems from deviation from one's own internalized moral standards.

H

habit an acquired or learned pattern of behavior, relatively simple and regularly used with facility, which leads to a tendency to use such acts rather than other behavior.

habituation the process of becoming accustomed to a particular set of circumstances or to a particular stimulus, resulting in decreased awareness.

handedness the tendency to use either the right or the left hand predominantly.

hedonism a psychological or philosophical system of motivation explaining all behavior and conduct in terms of seeking pleasure and avoiding pain.

heredity the totality of characteristics biologically transmitted from parents and ancestors to the offspring at conception.

heritability an estimate, based on a sample of individuals, of the relative contribution of genetics to a given trait or behavior.

heterogeneous a term used to describe any group of individuals or items that show great differences in reference to some significant criterion or standard.

heteronomous morality in Piaget, the moral thinking of children up to age 10, in which rules are sacred and consequences of an act determine guilt regardless of a person's intentions.

heterosexual emotionally and sexually centered on the opposite sex; seeking and finding erotic gratification with a person of the other sex.

heterosexuality attraction or interest toward members of the opposite sex.

heterozygous the condition in which cells contain different genes for the same trait. The dominant gene will determine the appearance of the trait.

hierarchy of needs Maslow's concept of a series of motivational needs that must be satisfied one by one in the process of development before the adult can achieve self-actualization.

high-risk infant term used to describe babies whose histories contain factors related to psychological or educational handicaps; for example, problems related to the parents' genetic makeup, the mother's pregnancy, or the birth process.

holistic emphasizing the need to study people as a whole, as opposed to looking at fragments of their behavior; stressing the unified, integrated organization of behavior.

holistic medicine treatment of the whole person; removal or alleviation of any sources of stress as well as pharmaceutical and physical treatment of symptoms of illness.

holophrase the single-word utterance of a child who is just learning to talk; from the child's point of view, the single word may be an entire phrase or message.

homeostasis the tendency to preserve a stable or constant internal state, despite fluctuations of bodily conditions and external stimulations. Cannon's term for the relative constancy—for example, in temperature, blood pressure, and pulse rate—that the body must maintain to function properly.

hominids members of several extinct species of the primate order from which man is descended.

homogamy theory the tendency for people who are similar in attitudes, social class, and other dimensions to marry each other; marriage between people who have similar personal characteristics.

homogeneous a term used to describe any group of individuals or items that show great similarity or low variability in the qualities or traits considered.

homosexual centered on the same sex; marked by a tendency to find sexual and erotic gratification with a person of the same sex.

homozygous the condition in which cells have matching genes for a trait.

hormonal theory the concept that aging is the result of the decline of the efficiency of the body's hormonal system. Aging is suggested to be a result of a hormonal imbalance, or of a series of brain-stimulated hormonal changes.

hormone a specific chemical substance produced by an endocrine gland, which brings about certain somatic and functional changes within the organism.

hospice care lodging or care for the dying and the family, providing for psychological as well as physical needs.

hostile aggression behavior that aims at hurting another person.

humanism the philosophical view that humans have free will and both the right and capacity for self-determination based on purpose and values (in contrast to Freud's emphasis on unconscious forces).

humanistic psychology a psychological approach that emphasizes the uniqueness of human beings; it is concerned with subjective experience and human values. Often referred to as a third force in psychology in contrast to behaviorism and psychoanalysis.

hypothesis a tentative interpretation of a complex set of phenomena or data on the basis of supportive facts or findings.

I

iconic a sensory image.

id according to Freud, that part of the personality consisting of primitive instincts toward sexuality and aggression; an aspect of personality in which all unconscious impulses reside. The id seeks immediate gratification regardless of the consequences but is held in check by the superego. See also **ego; superego.**

ideal a standard approaching some level of perfection, usually unattainable in practice.

identical twins twins who develop from the same fertilized ovum; **monozygotic twins.**

identification the process by which a person takes over the features of another person whom he admires and incorporates them into his own personality.

identification (language) in the two-word stage of language development, the verbal extension of a simple pointing response, as in "See doggy."

identity a sense of one's self; sense of sameness despite growth, aging, and environmental change.

identity versus role confusion Erikson's fifth crisis of psychological development; the adolescent may become confident and purposeful, or may develop an ill-defined identity.

imitation the principle and the process by which an individual copies or reproduces what has been observed.

implanted attached; after floating freely for several days, the fertilized ovum becomes implanted in the uterine wall.

imprinting the alteration of an apparently instinctive behavior that occurs at a certain, extremely early critical period of development; for example, ducklings from an incubator will follow a man or dog as though they were following a mother duck and form a strong, long-lasting social attachment to the surrogate.

impulsivity uncontrolled action; acting without first thinking.

inclusion according to Flavell, a sequence in intellectual development in which the earlier item becomes incorporated as an integral part of the later item. An example is the inclusion of children's early naming skills into all later language development.

incubation a period in assimilation and the problem-solving process during which certain presented ideas gain in motivational strength and begin to condition a part of behavior, especially during childhood.

independence self-reliance.

independent variable the variable that is controlled by the experimenter to determine its effect on the dependent variable.

individuation differentiation of behavior into more distinct and less dependent parts or features.

induced abortion the premature removal of the fetus by deliberate interference.

industry versus inferiority Erikson's fourth crisis of psychological development; the school-aged child may develop a capacity for work and task-directedness, or he may view himself as inadequate.

infancy the stage of human development lasting from birth until the organism is able to exist independently of its mother, capable of feeding itself, of walking, and of talking, usually until the age of 2 years.

infantile pertaining to the lowest level of postnatal maturity; mode of behavior or adjustment resembling the infant level.

inferiority Adlerian term used to describe the feelings of inadequacy that characterize some people.

inferiority attitude or complex an emotionally conditioned and frequently unconscious attitude with reference to one's organism, self, or personality, characterized by serious lack of self-reliance and notions of inadequacy in many situations.

infertility the state of being unable to reproduce offspring.

informal rules statements of imperfect relations between two or more units or classes. See also **formal rules.**

information processing approach a theoretical view of cognition that analyzes cognitive activity in terms of successive stages of information processing such as attention, perception, memory, thinking, and problem solving.

inhibition prevention of the starting of a process or behavior by inner control despite the presence of the eliciting stimulus.

initiation rite a symbolic event or ritual to mark life transitions, such as the one from childhood to adulthood.

initiative versus guilt Erikson's third crisis of psychological development, occurring during the preschool years; the child may develop a desire for achievement, or he may be held back by self-criticism.

innate existing before birth and accounting for a particular trait or characteristic.

inner speech Vygotsky's term denoting the language of the mind, the private speech we use only for our own thinking and reasoning.

insecurely attached—avoidance according to Ainsworth, a mother-infant bond that is insecure and distinguished by the child's avoiding the mother and failing to seek closeness.

insecurely attached—resistant an insecure mother-infant bond marked by the child's reaching for the mother, but then showing ambivalence or hitting and pushing.

instinct unlearned, biologically based behavior.

instrumental aggression behavior that aims at retrieving or acquiring an object, territory, or privilege.

instrumental conditioning a type of conditioning in which an organism's responses change as a result of reinforcement; **operant conditioning.**

instrumental dependence dependence that involves seeking assistance as a means of accomplishing some task or activity.

integration (hierarchic) the developmental trend of combining simple, differentiated skills into more complex skills.

integrity versus despair in Erikson, the stage of personality development corresponding to old age, in which acceptance of one's life leads to a sense of integrity.

intelligence the ability to conceptualize effectively and to grasp relationships; also, according to Jean Piaget, the coordination of operations.

intelligence quotient the index or rate of mental development. The ratio of mental to chronological age as expressed in the formula: Mental age divided by chronological age, times 100, equals IQ. IQ must be regarded as an indication rather than a measure, since different tests yield different results and performance fluctuates.

internalization the incorporation of beliefs, attitudes, and ideas into the personality so that they become part of one's makeup.

interval reinforcement in operant conditioning, the schedule of the partial reinforcement in which a person is reinforced for his first correct response after a specified period of time has passed.

intimacy versus isolation Erikson's sixth crisis of psychosocial development; the young adult may achieve a capacity for honest, close relationships, or be unable to form these ties.

intimate an individual who has been able to form a deep, long-lasting love relationship.

introjection a basal (crude) form of identification in which a person assimilates simple behavior patterns of other persons.

introvert orientation inward toward the self rather than toward association with others.

invention of new means an infant's discovery and first use of new combinations of mental thoughts to initiate intentional means-to-an-end behavior in order to achieve a goal; early intentional accommodation.

in vitro fertilization fertilization of an ovum in a laboratory setting, outside the woman's body. The egg is later implanted in the woman's uterus. Commonly referred to as "test-tube" fertilization.

irreversibility the inability to undo or reverse an action or an imagined action in thought.

J

juvenile pertaining to an older child or adolescent.

K

karyotype picture of the chromosomes, in a tiny photograph, created with a high-powered microscope and a stain.

kibbutz an Israeli collective farm or settlement.

kinesthesis the muscle, tendon, and joint senses, yielding discrimination of position and movement of parts of the body.

kinship blood relationship between two or more persons; usually includes marriage and adoption ties.

Klinefelter's syndrome a congenital physical condition in men that occurs when the individual has two X chromosomes and one Y chromosome. The symptoms include sterility, small testes, small femalelike breasts, and usually mental retardation.

knee-jerk reflex the involuntary response that occurs when the patellar tendon is tapped; **patellar reflex.**

Korsakoff's psychosis an irreversible nutritional deficiency due either to alcohol poisoning or to vitamin B deficiency associated with alcoholism; characterized by anterograde amnesia and confabulation.

Kübler-Ross's stages of dying denial, anger, bargaining, depression, and acceptance.

kwashiorkor the severe, often fatal, disease caused by prolonged protein deficiency.

L

lability in psychology the tendency to shift erratically from one emotional state to another.

language an abstract system of word meanings and syntactic structures that facilitates communication.

language acquisition device (LAD) inborn mental structure that enables children to build a system of language rules.

lanugo a fine, wooly fuzz that appears briefly on the fetus in the later months of development; the fine hair appearing on parts of some newborns' bodies that may remain several weeks before disappearing.

late maturers preadolescents who reach their physical maturity later than average for their sex.

latency period in psychoanalytic theory a stage in psychosexual development that appears between the phallic and genital stages and during which sexual drives become temporarily dormant; usually begins about the age of 4 or 5 years and lasts until adolescence.

laterality the developmental process in which one side of the body is preferred.

learning a relatively permanent modification of behavior resulting from experience.

Leboyer method a method of childbirth proposed by a French physician, Leboyer. The newborn is not spanked or held by the feet after birth but is placed on the abdomen of the mother, and a peaceful and calm postdelivery environment is maintained to minimize the shock of childbirth for the infant.

left hemisphere the left cerebral hemisphere. Controls the right side of the body and, for most people, speech and other logical, sequential activities (syn. *major hemisphere*).

level of significance in the T test expression of the confidence with which a null hypothesis can be rejected, usually expressed as a decimal fraction. If the desired result could occur by chance 1 in 20 times, the level of significance is .05.

libido according to Freud, a basic psychological energy inherent in every individual; this energy supplies the sexual drive, whose goal is to obtain pleasure.

life after death the experience of clinical death and then a return to life; descriptive accounts of this interim are very similar.

life change units (LCU) the average mean values assigned to various life events by Holmes and Rahe.

life cycle the total time from birth to death, divided into a number of stages and phases and emphasizing recurrence of certain important events.

life expectancy the number of years, based on a statistical average, that a person is expected to live in a given culture.

life review a looking back at one's life; may be characterized by reminiscence, anxiety, or by extreme preoccupation with the past. The process, according to Robert Butler, is set in motion by looking forward to death.

life-style the particular and unique pattern of living that characterizes the individual. It is a product of one's capacities, abilities, social milieu, family experiences, and the values one holds.

living will a legal document, signed while a person is healthy, which states that the individual does not wish to be kept alive by artificial means.

location in the two-word stage of language development, the signaling of the location of an object with such words as "here" and "there."

locus of control the perceived location of the control over an individual's life. It can be internal, as when one believes he controls his own life, or it can be external, as when one believes his life is controlled by forces outside himself.

locus of value a personality trait involving a generalized expectancy that people hold regarding the degree to which they control their fate. People with an internal locus of control feel they have a reasonable amount of control over their outcomes. People with an external locus of control feel their fate is largely beyond their control.

longitudinal research a study technique in which the same individual is examined over a long period or over a complete developmental stage.

long-term memory type of memory that involves long-term storage of material; appears to hold up well with advanced age.

love in the general sense an intense emotional response involving a feeling of affection toward a person or persons. According to John B. Watson, it, along with fear and rage, is one of the inherent or primary emotions.

love withdrawal discipline method of discipline that predominantly uses a loss of affection and approval as a consequence of misbehaving.

low birth weight any neonate weighing less than 2500 g (5½ lb.) with limited fat deposits, poor temperature and muscle control, and other frailties.

M

marijuana (also spelled **marihuana**) a product derived from *Cannabis sativa* containing tetrahydrocannabinol (THC), which has sedative-hypnotic effects and induces the experience of a "high" and some release of tension.

maternal deprivation disturbances of the mother-infant relationship in which the infant is rejected or abandoned, thus disrupting the usual physical and emotional mother-infant bonds.

matrix a framework or enclosure that gives form, meaning, or perspective to what lies within it.

maturation developmental changes manifested in physiological functioning primarily due to heredity and constitution; organismic developments leading to further behavioral differentiation.

maturational lag a delay in the normal or usual rate of development of the central nervous system structure and its perceptual functions.

maturity the state of maximal function and integration of a single factor or a total person; also applied to age-related adequacy of development and performance.

median the measure of central tendency that has half of the cases above it and half below it; the fiftieth percentile.

mediating mechanisms mechanisms assumed to intervene between a stimulus situation and a response and to explain the resulting behavior.

mediation according to Flavell, a sequence of intellectual development in which an earlier-developed item serves as a bridge to a later one. An example is the necessity of knowing how to count before one can understand that five coins remain the same no matter how they are arranged.

meiosis the process of cell division in which the daughter cells receive half the normal number of chromosomes, thus becoming gametes.

memory the mental activity of reliving past events. It can be considered as having two functions: the storage of experience for a period of time and the revival of that information at a later time.

menarche the first occurrence of menstruation.

mendelian ratio the proportion of dominant to recessive phenotypes.

menopause the stage in a woman's life when menstruation ceases, usually in the late forties or early fifties.

menstrual age the age of a prenatal organism calculated from the first day of its mother's last menstrual period.

menstruation the cyclic discharge of blood and discarded uterine material that occurs in sexually mature females monthly from puberty to menopause, except during pregnancy.

mental age the knowledge of concepts or the ability to perform tasks appropriate to a certain chronological age as determined by specific tests. Mental age is thus a unit of mental measurement that, like IQ, is a relative measure. A child of any age whose tested performance equals that of an average 8-year-old is said to have a mental age of 96 months (8 × 12 months).

mental conflict an intrapsychic state of tension or indecision caused by contrary desires or incompatible plans of action.

mental hygiene the art and science of mental health; application of the principles and measures necessary for its prevention and promotion.

mental operations model an approach to the information processing model that studies the specific elements of processing, such as attention, memory, and problem solving.

mental retardation a condition of mental deficiency, usually defined as being below 75 in IQ.

mentifact the ideas, customs, values, cultural heritage, and knowledge of a society.

mesoderm the middle of the three fundamental layers of the embryo that forms a basis for the development of bone, muscle structure, alimentary canal, and various digestive glands.

metabolism the physiochemical changes within the body for supplying, repairing, and building up (anabolism) and for breaking down and removing (catabolism).

metacognition cognition that takes as its object other cognition; for example, thinking about thinking or regulating cognitive activity.

metamemory conscious or intuitive knowledge about memory.

metaphysics the system of principles underlying a particular study or subject; the nature of first principles and the problems of ultimate reality.

metapsychology philosophical speculation on the origin, structure, and function of the mind and on the relationship between the mind and objective reality.

method a logical and systematic way of studying a subject.

midlife crisis turmoil precipitated by the review and reevaluation of one's past, typically occurring in the early to middle 40s. Reason for the review is, most likely, the awareness of one's own mortality, which occurs in midlife; this is followed by a period of stabilization.

miscarriage the spontaneous expulsion from the uterus of a fetus less than 28 weeks old.

mitosis the process of ordinary cell division that results in two cells identical to the parent cell.

modeling a principle and a process by which an individual learns by observing the behavior of others.

modification according to Flavell, a sequence in intellectual development in which the later-emerging behavior represents a differentiation or a generalization of a more stable form of an earlier skill. An example is children's coming to realize that quantities do not change if only certain perceptual properties do.

mongolism see **Down's syndrome.**

monozygotic (MZ) twins twins who develop from the same fertilized ovum; identical twins. See also **dizygotic (DZ) twins.**

moral conduct a form of complex behavior involving three aspects: reasoning, feeling, and action.

moral development the nature and course of development of an individual's moral thoughts, feelings, and actions.

moral judgments judgments as to the rightness or wrongness of actions.

morality a sense of what is right and wrong.

mores social norms of behavior invested with great moral importance. They involve matters of health, sex, religion, property, and other activities that are deemed important.
Moro's reflex the newborn infant's involuntary response to having the head fall backward—arms are stretched outward and brought together over the chest in a grasp gesture. A reflex that is most easily elicited during the infant's first 3 months of life.
morpheme a combination of phonemes that makes up a meaningful unit of a language.
mother fixation deep identification with the mother to the virtual exclusion of other females as models or idols.
motherese the speech and language interaction between the mother and the infant.
mothering taking the maternal responsibilities for protecting and raising one's offspring or adopted children.
motivation a general term referring to factors within an organism that arouse and maintain behaviors directed toward satisfying some need or drive or toward accomplishing a goal.
motive any factor that stimulates or contributes to a conscious effort toward a goal.
motor skill any skill, such as walking or riding a bicycle, that requires muscular coordination.
multisensory relating to or involving several physiological senses.
mutagenic altering the genetic structure of cells, which results in the production of new forms.
mutation any change of a gene, usually from one allele to another.
myelin sheath a white fatty covering on many neural fibers that serves to channel impulses along fibers and to reduce the random spread of impulses across neurons.
myelinization the process by which neural fibers acquire a sheath of myelin.

N

naturalistic observation a form of study in which there is observation of behavior without any interference from the investigator.
nature the genetic-biological determinants used to explain developmental changes.
need any physiochemical imbalance within the organism due to a lack of particular nutrients that arouses tension and drives. By analogy, psychological and personality needs are recognized. Primary or genetically determined needs and derived needs (generated by the operation of primary needs) are usually distinguished.
negation in the two-word stage of language development, the use of a negative construction to contradict or to avoid a misunderstanding.
negative pressure the first component of a baby's sucking. A vacuum is produced by closing the oral cavity in the back of the mouth, sealing the lips around the object to be sucked, and lowering the jaws.
negative reinforcement in operant conditioning, the termination of an aversive stimulus as the result of a response. See also **positive reinforcement.**
negativism a primary mode of expressing one's own will by persistent refusal to respond to suggestions from parental and authority figures.
neonate a newborn infant.
neuromuscular pertaining to both nerve and muscle, their structure and functions.
neuropsychology the study of the organic and the perceptual-conceptual processes involved in cognition.
neurosis a mental disorder that prevents the victim from dealing effectively with reality; it is characterized by anxiety and partial impairment of functioning.
neurotic mentally and emotionally disturbed; characterized by recurrent symptoms often caused by unconscious conflicts.
neuroticism state of being partially disorganized due to anxieties.
neurotransmitters a group of chemicals that facilitate the transmission of electrical impulses between nerve endings in the brain.
nonexistence in the two-word stage of language development, the expression of object disappearance or cessation of activity, as in "all-gone ball."
norm an outline that describes the development of an important attribute or skill and the approximate ages at which it appears in the average child.
normative data based on averages, standards, values, or norms.
novelty a possible factor in selective attention, involving a different or unique aspect of a stimulus.
nuclear family the family, rather typical in the United States, that consists of only parents and children. See also **extended family.**
nurturant supportive—involving warmth and involvement (personal love and compassion).
nurture the impact of environmental factors on child growth and development. Nurture is usually contrasted with nature in describing development.

O

object identity in cognitive development, the understanding that an object remains the same even though it may undergo various transformations.
object permanence in cognitive development, the ability to recognize the continuing existence of an object that is no longer visible or audible. It is achieved at about 11 months by the majority of infants.
observational method studying events as they occur in nature, without experimental control of variables; for example, studying the nest building of birds or observing children's behavior in a play situation.
oedipal conflict according to Freud, a conflict that appears during the phallic stage. It consists of sexual attraction to the parent of the opposite sex and hostility toward the parent of the same sex.
ontogenesis origin and development of an individual organism and its functions from conception to death. See also **phylogenesis.**
openness to experience according to Carl Rogers, the state in which every stimulus from the organism or the external environment is freely relayed through the individual without distortion by defenses.
operant conditioning a type of conditioning in which an organism's responses change as a result of the application of reinforcement or reward. It is based on the principle that organisms tend to engage in behavior that succeeds in producing desirable outcomes. Associated with B. F. Skinner, it is also called instrumental conditioning.
operation according to Jean Piaget, the mental action one performs in adapting to the environment.
optimal weight gain the most desirable or satisfactory weight gain in pregnancy.
oral stage in psychoanalytic theory, the first stage of psychosexual development. In this stage gratification centers around the mouth and oral activities. See also **anal stage; genital stage; phallic stage.**
ordinal scale a ranking device that indicates the order of development in a series.
organic brain syndrome (OBS) degenerative effects of brain pathology on a variety of functions, including memory, judgment, perception, social behavior, and motor coordination.
organismic age the average of all basic measures of a person's development at a particular time, such as carpal development, dental development, height, weight, and lung capacity. Often it includes achievement and educational, mental, and social age.

orgasm a period of intense physical and emotional sensation usually resulting from stimulation of the sexual organs, as in sexual intercourse, and generally followed in the male by the ejaculation of semen.

orienting reflex (OR) the initial response to any novel situation, maximizing its stimulus value.

orthogenesis theory that the germ plasm is gradually modified by its own internal conditions and that the organism (and personality) has a sequential and specific, species-related course of development unless blocked.

ovaries the female reproductive organs in which egg cells or ova are produced.

overextension a generalization in the apparent meaning of a word so that it includes a number of dissimilar objects or events.

overregularization a kind of temporary error in language development in which the apparent attempt is to simplify or to make language more regular than it actually is. In English, this is likely to be shown when a child overregularizes the past tense of verbs ("breaked") and the plural forms of nouns ("foots").

ovulation expulsion of an ovum from the ovary, which occurs once about every 28 days from puberty to menopause.

ovum the female reproductive cell, sometimes called the egg; produced by one of two ovaries; the plural of ovum is ova.

P

parallel play the side-by-side play of two or more children with some independence of action yet heightened interest because of each other's presence.

parasocial speech in a young child, talking to one's self. This behavior, thought to be social in origin, occurs most frequently when others are listening or when the child encounters difficulties.

parasympathetic nervous system a division of the autonomic nervous system.

parent-infant bonding an attachment between neonate and parent that occurs in the first few hours after birth under conditions of close physical contact.

Parkinson's disease a presenile psychosis involving degenerative lesions of midbrain nerve tracts responsible for relaying motor impulses. Symptoms include tremors, a mask-like countenance, stiff gait, and withdrawal.

partial reinforcement in operant conditioning, the reinforcement of a selected response on an interval or ratio schedule.

parturition the act of bringing forth the young; delivery of the baby.

passive-dependent personalities Neugarten's description for persons who are dissatisfied with their lives and apathetic and who lean on others for succor and support.

patellar reflex the involuntary response that occurs when the patellar tendon is tapped, commonly known as the knee-jerk reflex.

patterns of behavior organized ways of behaving in certain situations.

peak experiences Maslow's term for a momentary state of ecstasy and a sense of unity with the whole world.

peer any individual of about one's same level of development and therefore equal for play or any other mode of association.

peer group the group of persons who constitute one's associates, usually of the same age and social status.

penis the male copulatory organ.

percentile the rank of a given measure in a theoretical group of 100. High rank is indicated by 99, meaning that the individual exceeds 99 out of 100 subjects in the measure concerned; middle average would be 50.

percept the unit of immediate knowledge of what one perceives.

perception the awareness of one's environment obtained through interpreting sensory data.

perceptual pertains to the process or the data of perception.

perceptual constancy the tendency for perceptions of objects, symbols, and sounds to remain relatively unchanged in spite of changes in the way the stimuli are received.

perceptual-motor match the process of comparing and combining the information received through the motor system and the input data received through perception.

perfection-fulfillment theory the version of the fulfillment theory of personality maintaining that the personality force takes the form of internalized but culturally universal ideals of what is good and meaningful in life. See also **personality, fulfillment theory of.**

perfectionism the tendency to demand frequently of oneself or others a maximal quality of achievement without proper consideration of limiting factors.

peripheral nervous system (PNS) that part of the nervous system outside the brain and spinal cord; it includes the autonomic nervous system and the somatic nervous system.

permissive parenting parenting with few demands about rules and regulations and lax control.

personality an individual's characteristic pattern of behavior and thought, including an accordant self-concept and a set of traits consistent over time.

personality disorders ingrained, habitual, and rigid patterns of behavior or character that severely limit the individual's adaptive potential; often society sees the behavior as maladaptive while the individual does not (syn. *character disorders*).

personality, fulfillment theory of the theory maintaining that maturity lies in the full expression of one psychological force, lying within the individual. See also **actualization-fulfillment theory; perfection-fulfillment theory.**

perspective-taking skills the understanding, by a child, that others have perspectives that are different from his own.

phallic stage in psychoanalytic theory, the third stage of psychosexual development, during which gratification centers on the sex organs. The oedipal conflict also manifests itself during this stage. See also **anal stage; genital stage; oral stage.**

phase (in development) a concept which indicates that development is continuous across the life span; the divisions are culturally determined.

phenomenological approach a therapeutic procedure in which the therapist attempts to see the patient's world from the vantage point of the patient's own internal frame of reference.

phenotype the observable features of a person, including genetic traits and characteristics. See also **genotype.**

phenylketonuria (PKU) an error of metabolism caused by a recessive gene that gives rise to a deficiency in a certain enzyme. It can cause mental retardation if it is not caught in time. The inherited inability to metabolize phenylalanine, a component of some foods. It occurs when the two recessive genes for PKU are paired.

phyletic pertaining to species.

phyletic scale a line of descent from the lowest to the highest living species.

phylogenesis evolution of traits and features common to a species or race; rehearsal of the prehistory of man. See also **ontogenesis.**

Pick's disease a rare but fatal presenile psychosis in which the frontal and temporal lobes of the brain gradually atrophy, causing impairment of memory and cognitive, emotional, and motor functions.

placebo an inert preparation often used as a control in experiments.

placenta the organ that forms in the uterine lining and through which the developing prenatal organism receives nourishment and discharges waste.

placing a reflex movement, which is most easily elicited during the first 3 months of an infant's life, consisting of a baby's lifting his foot onto a surface.

plasticity the capability to be shaped or formed; in particular, the ability to learn from the external environment.

polygenic indicates that several genes have an equal and cumulative effect in producing a trait.

positive reinforcement in operant conditioning, the presentation of a rewarding consequence contingent on the desired response. See also **negative reinforcement.**

possession in the two-word stage of language development, the expression of ownership, as in "Daddy coat."

postconventional level a stage of moral development in which the individual defines moral values and principles in relation to their validity and application rather than in relation to the dictates of society or of any particular group. It is characterized by self-chosen ethical principles that are comprehensive, universal, and consistent. See also **conventional stage; preconventional stage.**

postpartum immediately after birth; the first week of life.

practice play play in which the infant finds pleasure and satisfaction in repeating what he already knows.

pragmatics rules concerned with the appropriate use of language in social contexts.

preadolescence the period of human development just preceding adolescence, usually between the ages of 9 and 12 years.

precausal a kind of thinking in which a child maintains that some events are either completely or partly caused by psychological, subjective factors. An example is a child's idea about the origin of dreams.

preconventional level a stage of moral development in which the child responds to cultural rules and labels of good and bad only in terms of the physical or hedonistic consequences of obeying or disobeying the rules. See also **conventional level; postconventional level.**

prehension the ability to pick up a small object using thumb and index finger.

premature, or preterm baby baby born before the 37th week of pregnancy, dated from the mother's last menstrual period.

premoral level the level of moral reasoning in which value is placed in physical acts and needs, not in persons or social standards.

prenatal before birth; the stage of human development lasting from conception to birth.

preoperational stage according to Jean Piaget, the stage in a child's development occurring from 18 months to 7 years of age, during which he begins to encounter reality on the representational level. A subperiod of the representational period, which begins when children start to record experiences symbolically; involves the use of language to record experiences, and involves the appearance of the ability to think in terms of classes, numbers, and relationships. See also **concrete operational stage; formal operational stage; sensorimotor stage.**

prepared childbirth method of childbirth in which the woman is prepared for delivery by knowledge about the physiological processes involved and by learning a series of exercises that make the delivery easier.

presbycusis progressive loss of hearing for high-frequency tones; associated with degenerative changes in the auditory system.

presbyopia physiological changes in accommodation power in the eyes in advancing age.

presenile degenerative disorders deterioration of intellectual, emotional, and motor functioning prior to age 60; they include Huntington's chorea, Pick's disease, and Alzheimer's disease.

primary circular reactions a reaction, generally occurring between 1 and 4 months of age, in which the infant attempts to repeat a pleasurable event that first happened by chance; for example, sucking the fingers when they accidentally come close to the mouth.

primary memory conscious awareness of recently perceived events; identified by psychologist William James.

primary sex characteristics the external and internal sex organs.

principled level the level of moral reasoning in which value resides in self-chosen principles and standards that have a universal logical validity and can therefore be shared.

problem solving thinking directed toward the goal of solving a problem.

processing deficit an inadequacy in the capacity needed for memory processing; it may be that older people are less capable than other individuals of the processes that aid memory work.

productivity the ability to combine individual words into an unlimited number of sentences; one of the three formal properties of language.

progesterone a female sex hormone produced by the ovaries; it helps prepare the uterus for pregnancy and the breasts for lactation.

projection a type of defense mechanism characterized by the tendency to blame others or external circumstances for one's own shortcomings or failures. May attribute to others his own qualities and traits, usually undesirable ones, such as hostility or dishonesty.

propinquity theory the tendency for people who live near each other to become acquainted with, and attracted to, each other.

proximodistal sequence the progressive growth of the body parts in a center-to-periphery direction. See also **cephalocaudal development.** For example, a baby learns to control the movements of the shoulders before the direction of arms or fingers.

psychoanalysis a method of psychotherapy developed by Sigmund Freud. Psychoanalysis has been subsequently extended to include the theoretical foundations of Jung, Adler, Rank, Sullivan, Horney, and their followers. It emphasizes the techniques of free association and transference and seeks to give the patient insight into his unconscious conflicts and motives.

psychoanalytic theory the basis of the school of psychology that emphasizes the development of emotions and their influence on behavior. It postulates a theory of the development and the structure of personality.

psychological growth personality change; the increasing of inner differentiation and integration, the acquisition of autonomy and flexibility, and the development of new capacities for self-determination.

psychopathology psychological and behavioral dysfunctions occurring in mental disorders.

psychosexual development in Freudian theory, the sequence of stages through which the child passes, each characterized by the different erogenous zones from which the primary pleasure of the stage is derived. See also **anal stage; genital stage; oral stage; phallic stage.**

psychosis severe mental disorder.

psychosomatic pertaining to the effects of psychological and emotional stress on health and pathology; indicating that a phenomenon is both psychic and bodily (somatic).

psychotherapy the various techniques for the systematic application of psychological principles in the treatment of mental or emotional disturbance or disorder.

pubertal pertaining to anything related to the developmental period of puberty.

puberty the period of life during which an individual's reproductive organs become functional and secondary sexual characteristics appear; the period characterized by rapid somatic growth and the assumption of adult traits or features.

pubescence time of life span characterized by rapid physiological growth, maturation of reproductive functioning, and appearance of primary and secondary sex characteristics.

pubescent pertaining to an individual in the early part of puberty or to anyone who exhibits significant characteristics of that period of maturation.

pubic hair hair that appears in the genital area during adolescence.

Q

questions in the two-word stage of language development, the transformation of all sentence types into questions by the use of rising intonation or question words, as in "Where ball?"

quickening the first fetal movements that a mother can readily perceive.

R

race an aggregate of persons who share a set of genetically transmitted and physically identifiable characteristics.

rage an emotional response involving intense anger and feelings of hostility. According to John B. Watson, it, along with fear and love, is one of the inherent or primary emotions.

random sample a method of selecting research subjects that allows all members of the population under study an equal chance of being selected, with the expected result that the selection will be representative of the population.

rapid eye movement (REM) a type of eye movement that occurs during a certain period of sleep and that is accompanied by changes in respiratory, muscle, and brain-wave activity.

ratio reinforcement in operant conditioning, the partial reinforcement schedule in which a person is reinforced only after he has responded correctly a certain number of times.

rationalization to rationalize: a dynamism of self-defense whereby a person justifies his activities or conduct by giving rational and acceptable, but usually untrue, reasons; the opposite of rational thought.

reaction formation a defense mechanism involving the replacement in consciousness of an anxiety-inducing impulse or feeling by its opposite.

reaction range the limits on an individual's possible behavior set by genetic conditions.

reaction time the interval of time that elapses between the instant a stimulus is presented and the individual's reaction to it.

reactive depression a state of depression that has presumably come about because of changes in the environment, sometimes known as exogenous depression.

readiness the combination of growth development and experience that prepares an individual to acquire a skill or understanding with facility.

readiness, principle of refers to the neurological and psychological disposition to attend to and assimilate a category of stimuli to which sensitivity and learning responses were previously lacking.

recall the form of remembering in which previously learned material is reproduced with a minimum of cues. See also **recognition.**

receptive language the ability to understand the spoken word.

recessive gene a gene whose hereditary characteristics will not prevail when paired with a dominant gene.

reciprocity corresponding, complementary, inverse relationships.

recognition the form of remembering in which the previously learned material is merely recognized as such without actually being recalled. See also **recall.**

recurrence in the two-word stage of language development, the indication of the presence, absence, or repetition of things and actions, as in "book again."

reductionism a general point of view which holds that complex phenomena can be understood and explained by breaking them into simpler components.

reference groups the groups that affect in substantial measure the individual's personal goals and behavior. The groups to which he belongs and wants to belong.

reflex an unlearned or naturally occurring reaction to a stimulus.

regression returning, because of frustrating experiences, to an earlier and less mature level of behavior and personality functioning than that previously achieved.

rehearsal to recycle information in short-term memory. The process facilitates the short-term recall of information and its transfer to long-term memory.

reinforcement in operant conditioning, the presentation or withdrawal of an event following a response, which increases or decreases the likelihood of that response occurring again.

reinforcement schedule a well-defined procedure for reinforcing a given response.

releasing stimuli those events that regularly evoke certain behavior in all members of a species; a key concept in ethological theories.

reliability the dependability and consistency of a measure, observation, or finding.

replication in studies, the attempt to repeat the essential features of an investigation and its findings.

representational level the level of cognitive development at which the child begins to use symbols as well as images.

representational skills those cognitive skills or ways in which an individual represents and constructs an understanding of his world and the people, objects, and events in it.

representational stage a stage in Piaget's theory of cognitive development that begins with the preoperational and ends with the concrete-operational period.

repression in psychoanalytic theory, the defense mechanism of forcefully rejecting unpleasant memories or impulses from conscious awareness.

resistance opposition offered by a child or adolescent to the suggestions, orders, or regulations of the parents.

respiratory distress syndrome the lung condition (formerly called hyaline disease of the lungs) in which the fetus is unable to maintain necessary surfactin levels and dies.

retrolental fibroplasia condition in which an opaque fibrous membrane develops on the posterior surface of the lens; occurs chiefly in premature infants subjected to high oxygen concentration.

reversibility the mental operation or understanding, according to Piaget's theory of cognitive development, in which one can think of a transformation that would reverse a sequence of events or restore the original condition.

Rh factor an agglutinizing factor present in the blood of most humans; when introduced into blood lacking the factor, antibodies form. Such a situation occurs when an organism with Rh-positive blood inherited from its father resides within a mother whose blood is Rh negative. A first-born child is rarely affected, but subsequent children may require transfusions.

RhoGAM: specially prepared gamma globulin that prevents the RH-negative mother from producing anti-RH antibodies after the miscarriage or birth of an RH-positive child.

ribonucleic acid (RNA) RNA molecules playing the role of a messenger or transfer agent for vital DNA functions by lining up amino acids in ribosomes to form proteins according to a particular sequence.

rickets the condition caused by a calcium deficiency during infancy and childhood and characterized by the softening and malformation of the bones.

right hemisphere the right cerebral hemisphere. Controls the left side of the body and, for most people, spatial and patterned activities (syn. *minor hemisphere*). See also **left hemisphere.**

role a socially expected behavior pattern or character that is assigned or assumed; see **sex roles; social role.**

role conflict the situation in which a person is expected to play two or more roles that he cannot integrate into his self-system.

role taking the ability to take the role or point of view of another person; a requirement in cognitive and other forms of development.

rooting reflex a reflex that is most easily elicited during the baby's first 2 weeks of life, consisting of the baby turning the head in the direction of any object that gently stimulates the corner of the mouth; the newborn infant's involuntary movement of the mouth toward any source of stimulation in the mouth area.

rote learning memorization in which the task is to commit the various components of the material to memory with little or no understanding, requiring only the ability to later reproduce what has been learned in the exact form in which it was presented.

rubella German measles. Rubella in a pregnant woman can cause damage to the developing child if she contracts it during the first 3 months of pregnancy.

S

saccadic rapid movements of the eye from one fixation point to another during the course of reading or visual scanning.

schedules of reinforcement in operant conditioning, the timetables for reinforcing behavior; they have different effects on the rate of responding.

schema or schemes Piaget's term for action patterns that are built up and coordinated throughout the course of cognitive development. In the infant, they are like concepts without words. Throughout development, such schemes are presumed to be involved in the acquisition and structuring of knowledge.

schizophrenia a form of psychosis in which the patient becomes withdrawn and apathetic. Hallucinations and delusions are common.

sebaceous fatty, oily; sebaceous glands secrete oily matter for lubricating hair and skin.

secondary circular reactions between 4 and 8 months of age, actions that the infant attempts for more than personal need satisfaction; for example, shaking a rattle or imitating baby talk or physical gestures.

secondary memory recall of events that have left the consciousness, identified by psychologist William James.

secondary sex characteristics physical characteristics that appear in humans around the age of puberty and that are sex differentiated but not necessary for sexual reproduction. Such characteristics include breast development and the appearance of pubic hair in girls and the appearance of facial and pubic hair, enlargement of the penis, and deepening of the voice in boys.

self-actualization according to Abraham Maslow, the need to develop one's true nature and fulfill one's human potentialities; the human tendency to realize one's full potential in work and love. It develops after the basic needs of food, security, and esteem are met.

self-concept the individual's awareness of and identification with his or her organism, cognitive powers, and modes of conduct and performance, accompanied by specific attitudes toward them.

self-demand feeding a feeding schedule in which a baby is fed according to when he is hungry, not according to a schedule designed by others.

self-direction independent selection of goals and of the proper means and actions to attain them.

self-disclosure the voluntary disclosure of our deeper thoughts or feelings to others.

self-esteem the amount and quality of the regard that a person has toward himself.

self-realization the lifelong process of unhampered development marked by self-direction and responses in terms of one's capabilities or potentialities.

self-regulation the regulation of one's own conduct.

semanticity the learning of the meaning of words, and the process of communicating meaning. One of the three formal properties of language.

semantics the study of meaning conveyed in language.

semen the fluid produced by the male testes that contains the sperm.

senescence the period of old age and the changes that occur.

senility significant loss of physical and cognitive functions in old age or preceding it, due to some brain disorder.

sensation a necessary aspect for cognitive development involving the reception, through the various sense organs, of stimulation from the external world.

sensitive periods periods of development during which an organism is most likely to be susceptible to a particular influence.

sensorimotor reflexes the basic reflex repertoire with which the infant is born—the Moro reflex, rooting reflex, patellar reflex, and so on.

sensorimotor stage according to Jean Piaget, the stage in cognitive development during which the child is essentially involved in perfecting contact with the objects that surround him or her. It generally occurs from birth to 2 years of age. It is characterized by the development of sensory and motor functions and by the infant's coming to know the world as a result of interacting with and affecting it. See also **concrete operational stage; formal operational stage; preoperational stage.**

sensory register the first stage in a three-process model of memory; in this stage information is registered automatically as an exact copy of the environment.

sentiment an affective and cognitive disposition to react in a certain way toward a particular value, object, or person.

separation anxiety the distinctly negative reaction of an infant to separation and his attempts to regain contact with his attachment figure.

sequence (in development) a concept used to explain the relationship among developmental changes in behavior, indicating that some behaviors precede others in a meaningfully related way.

sequential strategies complex descriptive research designs that permit the separation of within- and between-cohort changes and differences.

seriation ability to sort stimuli into categories according to characteristics (for example, color or shape).

sex-linked diseases any of the diseases carried by the X chromosome as a genetic recessive that occur predominantly in men because the smaller Y chromosome has no homologous gene to cancel out the deleterious one.

sex-linked inheritance pattern of inheritance in which characteristics are carried in the X chromosome.

sex roles patterns of behavior deemed appropriate to each sex by society.

sex-role stereotypes simplified fixed concepts about the behaviors and traits typical of each sex.

sex typing the learning of behavior patterns appropriate to the sex of the person; for example, acquisition of masculine behavior traits for a boy.

sexuality the characteristics of an individual in relation to sexual attitudes or activity.

shame a negative feeling response that is a reaction to the disapproval of others.

shaping behavior applying reinforcement to every increment of behavior that approximates one's goal or target behavior.

short-term memory (STM) the assumption that certain components of the memory system have limited capacity and will maintain information for only a brief period of time. The definition varies somewhat from theory to theory.

sibling one of two or more offspring of the same parents; a brother or sister.

sickle cell anemia a form of anemia (a blood condition) in which abnormal red blood corpuscles of crescent shape are present.

skeletal age a measure of the maturity of the skeleton, determined by the degree of ossification of bone structures.

skelic index the index that measures the ratio of lower limb length to sitting height.

small-for-dates the condition in which a baby is underweight for his gestational age.

social age age measured in terms of an individual's social habits relative to society's expectations.

social class a social stratum or category differentiated from other such strata on the basis of such economic considerations as wealth, occupation, and property ownership. See also **socioeconomic class.**

social deprivation the lack of economic, educational, and cultural opportunities.

social role a set of expectations or evaluative standards associated with an individual or a position.

social-learning theory a set of concepts and principles from behavior learning theory, frequently used in describing and explaining personality characteristics and social behavior.

socialization a progressive development in relating and integrating oneself with others, especially parents, peers, and groups; the process of psychologically growing into a society, in which an individual acquires the behaviors, attitudes, values, and roles expected of him.

socialized speech speech intended to communicate.

socioeconomic class a grouping of people on a predetermined scale of prestige according to their social and economic status. Such status is based on many factors, including nature of occupation, kind of income, moral values, family genealogy, social relationships, area of residence, and education. See also **social class.**

sociogram a graphic representation of social preferences within a group; a mapping of preferences and rejections in social behavior.

sociometric analysis a method for charting how often a child is chosen by his peers as a preferred friend or companion.

sociometry the graphical or columnar representation of interpersonal attractions or avoidances in group situations. The study of reactions and avoidances between individual members of a social group. The study of interpersonal relationships—person to person, person to group, and group to group—pursued through tabulations or the plotting of lines of attraction, indifference, or dislike.

somatic pertaining to the body or organism.

somatic cells the cells of the body that compose the tissues, organs, and other parts of the individual, other than the germ cells.

sperm the male germ cell, containing chromosomes, DNA, RNA, protein, and other substances.

spermatozoon a single sperm cell.

spontaneous abortion the expulsion from the uterus of a fetus older than 28 weeks.

stage (in development) a concept used to explain the orderly relationship among developmental changes in behavior and indicating that the organization of behavior is qualitatively different from one stage to the next.

standard deviation a statistical technique for expressing the extent of variation of a group of scores from the mean. It is a distance on a curve of probability, of which the first unit in both directions from the mean includes 68.3% of the total group of scores. About 99.7% of the scores are within three standard deviations in each direction from the mean.

startle response a reaction to stimuli in infants outwardly characterized by eye widening, jaw dropping, cooing, squealing, or crying and inwardly characterized by changes in heart rate, respiration, and galvanic skin potential.

stepping a reflex movement, which is most easily elicited during the infant's first 2 weeks of life, that consists of straightening the legs out at the knees and hip, as if to stand, when the infant is held with his feet touching a surface.

stereotype an overgeneralized, often false, belief about a group of people that lets one assume that every member of the group possesses a particular trait; for example, the false stereotyped belief that all male homosexuals are effeminate.

stimulus any form of environmental energy capable of affecting the organism

stimulus generalization a process or phenomenon in which a response learned in reaction to one stimulus can be elicited by separate but similar stimuli.

strain the condition within a system or organ exposed to stress, for example, overactivity or deprivation.

stranger anxiety the negative response and withdrawal that occurs in reaction to strangers, usually developing a month or two after specific attachments begin.

subjectivity state or quality of imposing personal prejudices, thoughts, and feelings into one's work.

sublimation a dynamism of self-defense whereby the energies of a basic, socially unacceptable drive are redirected into a higher and socially more acceptable plane of expression. The altering, in socially acceptable ways, of forbidden impulses. According to Freud, it is one of the processes important in the development of rational behavior.

substance abuse drug or alcohol abuse characterized by a minimum of 1 month's physiological dependence and difficulty in social functioning, with or without withdrawal symptoms.

substitution according to Flavell, a sequence in intellectual development in which the later-emerging item replaces the earlier one completely or almost completely. An example is children's recognition of the true nature of their dreams.

successive approximations in operant conditioning, a procedure in which behaviors that resemble more and more closely the final desired response are reinforced.

sudden infant death syndrome (SIDS) major cause of death for American infants between 1 week and 1 year of age. The cause of SIDS is unknown. Also called "crib death."

superego a psychoanalytic term that refers to the part of the personality structure that is built up by early parent-child relationships and helps the ego to enforce the control of primitive instinctual urges of the id; later functions as a moral force; analogous to an early form of conscience. An aspect of personality, in Freud's theory, defined as the conscience.

surfactin the liquid that coats the air sacs of the lungs and permits them to transmit oxygen from the air to the blood.

surrogate mother someone or something that takes the place of a mother in an organism's life.

symbolic play play that becomes more symbolic and complex as the ability to imagine and pretend develops.

symbolic representation a Bruner term referring to the use of abstract and logical thought to employ symbols as the representation of things or ideas.

sympathetic nervous division the part of the nervous system that regulates vital body functions in response to emergency.

syntax the rules for combining morphemes to form words and sentences.

syphilis a venereal disease due to systemic infection with *Treponema pallidum.*

T

Tay-Sachs disease a genetic disorder of lipid metabolism.

telegraphic speech early speech that uses salient words (nouns and verbs) and omits auxiliary parts of speech.

temperament the general nature, behavioral style, or characteristic mood of the individual; usually thought to have a physical or constitutional basis.

tension a state of acute need, deprivation, fear, apprehension, and so on that keeps an organism or certain organs in a state of intensified activity, for example, adrenal glands.

teratogen any agent that causes birth defects.

teratogenic capable of causing organic malformation.

term (prenatal development) the gestational age of 266 days from conception. Formerly, babies born before term were considered premature.

terminal drop a significant decline in intellectual abilities that often precedes death.

terminal illness a disease that results in death.

tertiary circular reactions schemes in which the infant (between ages 12 to 18 months) explores new possibilities with the same object, changing what is done and examining the results. This is the first reaction that is not imitation; marking the beginnings of curiosity.

testes the male reproductive organs in which sperm are manufactured; testicles.

thalidomide a drug once used by women during pregnancy to assuage morning sickness; it caused birth defects in the limbs of children.

theory (developmental) a set of logically related statements about the nature of development that help psychologists understand, predict, and explain human behavior.

thinking the active process of conceptualization, involving integrating percepts, grasping relationships, and asking further questions.

thumb opposition the ability to oppose the thumb to the fingers and to bring the fingertips in contact with the ball of the thumb.

thyroxine a hormone produced by the thyroid gland; it regulates metabolism.

toddler the child between the ages of about 15 and 30 months.

tonic neck reflex an infant's reaction to having his or her head turned sharply to one side. An infant will extend the arm and leg on the same side and flex the arm and leg on the opposite side.

totalism defined by Erikson as an organization of one's self-concept that has rigid, absolute, and arbitrary boundaries.

toxemia blood poisoning; the presence of poisonous or infective matters in the bloodstream.

tracking the act of following an object with one's eye.

trait a distinctive and enduring characteristic of a person or his behavior.

transcendence extending or lying beyond the limits of ordinary experience.

transfer a process or phenomenon in which the learning of one task results in improvement of learning or performance in another related, but different, task.

transformation a Piagetian term referring to the ability to tell how one state or appearance of a substance is changed into another state or appearance.

transformations syntactical rules that explain how a common deep structure can assume alternative surface forms, such as active and passive, positive and negative, statement and question.

transitivity a concept that requires the joining together of two or more instances of an abstract relation; for example, if A is larger than B and B is larger than C, then A is larger than C.

trauma any somatic or psychological damage to the individual, including stressful and terrifying experiences.

trimester a period of approximately 3 months; often used in discussing pregnancy.

trust versus mistrust the first stage in Erikson's eight-stage theory of development, in which the infant develops either the comfortable feeling that those around him care for his needs or the worry that his needs will not be taken care of.

Turner's syndrome a congenital physical condition resulting from the individual's having only one X chromosome and no Y chromosomes. The afflicted individual looks like an immature female and is characterized by a lack of reproductive organs, abnormal shortness, and mental retardation.

U

ultrasound method of scanning the womb for detection of fetal outline to determine whether the pregnancy is progressing normally.

umbilical cord the cord that connects the prenatal organism with the placenta. The embryo receives nourishment from the blood that is supplied by the arteries within the cord that connects the placenta and the fetus.

unconditioned reflex in classical conditioning, one of two kinds of reflexes; it is inborn and occurs naturally to a stimulus.

unconscious the area of motivational structure and thought process of which the person is not directly aware.

unconscious impulses in Freud's theory, those irrational impulses that reside in the id and that the individual is unaware of.

uniformism a concept indicating immersion into the peer group and the acceptance of its norms as infallible and regulatory.

universal principles moral propositions that are the end point of an unchanging ethical developmental sequence. They are of an absolute nature as opposed to beliefs or standards developed or determined by a reasoning approach to morality.

uterus the female organ in which the prenatal organism develops and is nourished prior to birth.

V

vagina the female genital canal (passage) extending from the uterus to the vulva. It is a copulatory organ.

valence in Gestalt psychology, a term referring to the subjective appraisal of an object or situation in the life space, by virtue of which the object is sought (positive valence) or avoided (negative valence). The term was introduced by K. Lewin.

value the worth or excellence found in a qualitative appraisal of an object, idea, or behavior by reliance on emotional and rational standards of the individual or of selected reference groups.

variability variations due to individual differences as well as other sources of influence.

variables those factors in an investigation that can vary in quantity or magnitude, or in some qualitative aspect, and that may or may not affect the results of the investigation.

vernix the white greasy material that covers and lubricates the newborn for passage through the birth canal.

vernix caseosa a sebaceous deposit covering the fetus due to secretions of skin glands.

vertex presentation the birth of a baby in which the head appears first.

viability capability for maintaining life. A fetus is viable after 28 weeks, since it can then usually be kept alive if born prematurely.

vicarious learning the strengthening of a behavior in a person through his observation of someone else's being rewarded for that behavior; learning that occurs through modeling or imitation.

visual accommodation the ability to alternate focus for objects at different distances.

visual discrimination the ability to discern similarities and differences visually.

vital capacity the air-holding capacity of the lungs.

vital capacity age (VA) relationship between lung capacity and age.

W

warmth-hostility a dimension along which parents can be discriminated in how they interact with their children. At one extreme (warmth), parents exhibit considerable affection, love, and reinforcement toward their children. At the other extreme (hostility), the child is treated harshly, is the subject of repeated anger, and may be punished but not reinforced very often.

Wechsler Adult Intelligence Scale a widely used individual intelligence test.

Wechsler Intelligence Scale for Children-Revised (WISC-R) an intelligence test for school-age children that yields separate subtest scores in individual areas, as well as overall verbal and performance scores and an intelligence quotient.

wellness the practice of preventative physical and mental care.

weltanschauung a configuration of attitudes and views toward all dimensions of reality, both material and metaphysical; key tenets of a philosophy of life.

Wetzel grid a graphical representation of the longitudinal development of an individual in height and weight, devised by N. C. Wetzel. Rather than making interpersonal comparisons, as on height-weight charts, the grid takes into account variations in basic body build.

womb the female organ in which the prenatal organism develops and is nourished before birth; **uterus.**

X

X chromosome a chromosome that, when paired with another X chromosome, programs a gamete to develop as a female.

Y

Y chromosome a chromosome that determines an individual will be male.

yolk sac a nonfunctional sac that forms during the germinal period of human prenatal development.

youth a stage of the human life cycle experienced by persons who are psychologically and physically mature but who are not sociologically mature, in that they have not made any commitments to career or family. This stage intervenes between adolescence and adulthood.

Z

zygote a new individual formed by the union of male and female gametes; the resultant globule of cells during the first phase of prenatal development after conception and lasting approximately 2 weeks.

TYPES OF BIRTH DEFECTS, ESTIMATES, DESCRIPTION, AND TREATMENT

Type of defect	*Numbers affected annually*	*Description*	*Causes and treatment*
Birthmarks	Very common	There are many unimportant birthmarks. The disfiguring ones are reddish or wine-colored patches consisting of numerous small dilated blood vessels. True blood vessel tumors are more rare. These are elevated and may occur on any part of the body.	Cause unknown. Skilled plastic surgeons can remove many marks. Skin grafts are often used. A new technique for large marks is to tattoo normal skin colors right over the purple area.
Cleft lip (harelip)	About 1 in every 1,000 babies in white populations is born with a cleft lip. Seventy percent of these also have cleft palates. The frequency appears higher in Japanese and lower in black populations.	When the embryo is about 6 weeks, swellings that will become the upper lip have not yet met. If they do not fuse at the proper time, the gap will remain and the baby will have a cleft lip.	These conditions are sometimes related to genetic defects. In experiments with animals it appears that the environment in the uterus, such as the position of the embryo or the blood supply, may be a factor, and some drugs given during pregnancy are also under suspicion. There are now many new operative techniques for repairing the defects. Harelip can be repaired in the first few weeks after birth, and cleft palate before the child is 14 months old in most cases.
Cleft palate	About 1 in every 2,500 babies has a cleft palate without a cleft lip. The two conditions are not genetically related.	A cleft palate is a hole in the roof of the mouth. More boys than girls have a harelip, and more girls have a cleft palate.	
Clubfoot	1 in 250	The foot turns inward (usually) or outward and is fixed in a tiptoe position.	Possibly due to the position of the child in the uterus, although maldevelopment of the limb bud may also be the cause. Mild deformities respond well to shoe splints worn at night. Simple braces and corrective shoes may be needed. More serious clubfoot often will be associated with other defects as well. Treatment must begin early and is prolonged because the condition tends to recur. The muscles and ligaments must be stretched and the bones realigned. Plaster casts can often correct the condition. Surgery is sometimes necessary.

From Apgar, V. *With best wishes for a happy birthday*. New York: The National Foundation—March of Dimes, 1963, pp. 4-8.

Continued

Type of defect	Numbers affected annually	Description	Causes and treatment
Congenital heart disease	1 in 160	There are many known types of congenital heart defects. Some are so slight as to cause little strain on the heart; others are fatal. In some of the abnormalities, the baby appears blue.	Few causes are known, but German measles during pregnancy is one An ever-increasing number of heart conditions can be repaired by surgery, saving lives and preventing invalidism.
Congenital urinary tract defects	1 in 250	There are many different types, involving the kidneys, ureters, bladder, and genitalia. Organs may be absent, fused, or obstructed.	Some causes are known, such as certain hormones given during pregnancy. There is some hereditary tendency. Most conditions can be corrected by surgery.
Diabetes	Very common. About 1 in 4 carries the trait. Clinical diabetes, or actual cases, seen in about 1 in 2,500 persons between ages 1 and 20; in 1 in 50 persons over 60 years of age.	Metabolic disorder in which there is a shortage of insulin hormone. Glucose, which comes from carbohydrates, accumulates in the blood and is excreted through the kidneys instead of being stored in the body as glycogen. Possibility of manifestation increases with age. Patient may be susceptible to infection of cuts and bruises. Among older persons serious involvement could lead to hardening of the arteries, gangrene in legs, and blindness.	Cause unknown; possible enzyme defect. Marked hereditary tendency. Persons with family history of diabetes should seek periodic checkups. Physicians can recognize symptoms, make positive diagnosis, and prescribe specific treatment. Special diets, oral medication, and injections of insulin are measures that will usually keep condition under control and permit normal activity.
Erythroblastosis	About 10% of the babies born to Rh-negative mothers married to Rh-positive fathers have this condition. One in seven of total American population has Rh-negative blood. Among Orientals the figure is 1 in 20.	The baby is often yellow in color soon after birth. Anemia is another symptom. Mental retardation may be severe. Erythroblastosis is a common cause of stillbirth.	Rh blood factor is inherited. Physicians should know Rh factor of both parents. Rh problem exists only if father is Rh positive (baby inherits Rh-positive gene from the father) and mother is Rh negative. Red blood cells of fetus reach mother's blood, causing her blood to form antibodies that pass back through the placenta to the baby and destroy the red cells in varying degrees. First pregnancy is usually uneventful. Cure can now be effected if condition is detected early. Infant mortality used to be 45% but is now 5%. Exchange transfusion, replacing baby's blood with compatible blood right after birth, is the cure. Several transfusions are sometimes necessary.
Extra fingers and toes (polydactyly)	Extra digits are twice as frequent as fused digits. The incidence is 1 in 100 among the black population; 1 in 600 in the white population.	Extra fingers or toes.	Cause unknown; frequently hereditary. Cure is simple amputation of the extra digits. This can often be done at birth or at about 3 years of age.
Fused fingers and toes (syndactyly)	Fused digits do not have such racial variation.	Too few digits.	In syndactyly surgery can improve the function and appearance of the hand or foot. Occasionally artificial limbs are necessary.

Type of defect	*Numbers affected annually*	*Description*	*Causes and treatment*
Fibrocystic disease (cystic fibrosis)	About 1 in 1,000 births. Rare among black populations; found very infrequently in Orientals.	A recently identified disease, now separated from a vast group of conditions producing a sickly, malnourished child with persistent intestinal difficulties. Victims have chronic respiratory problems, and death is usually due to pneumonia or other lung complications. One clue to disease is perspiration with high salt content.	Hereditary. Due to a metabolic error. Manifests self soon after birth. Mucous material blocks the exit of the digestive juices from the pancreas into the intestinal tract. Excess mucus is also secreted by lungs. Formerly death was expected before age 2. Now antibiotics, chemical substitutions for enzymes, and other treatments have extended life expectancy. Increasing numbers of adults are found to have a mild form of the disease.
Galactosemia	Somewhat more rare than phenylketonuria	A disorder causing eye cataracts and severe damage to the liver and the brain, resulting in mental retardation.	Hereditary. Caused by the absence of an enzyme required to convert galactose to glucose, important in digestion of milk sugar. Formerly led to many early deaths, but experiments now show that early recognition and dietary treatment can arrest the disease. Diagnosis can be made at birth.
Hydrocephaly (water on brain)	1 in 500	Enlargement of the head due to excessive fluid within the brain. Most cases result from obstruction to circulation of cerebrospinal fluid. In others fluid is produced in excess or is not absorbed fast enough. Pressure from fluid often causes compression of the brain with resulting mental retardation.	Obstruction to flow may result from prenatal infection or abnormality in development. Cause of excess fluid not known. Treatment is "shunt" operation to relieve pressure on the brain. A tube with a one-way valve is inserted surgically to lead fluid from the brain directly into the bloodstream or into some other body cavity. Condition frequently fatal if not treated.
Missing limbs	Very rare	Congenital amputees are born with one to four limbs missing or seriously deformed.	Cause unknown. Recently an international outbreak of this defect was traced to the drug thalidomide used by pregnant women. Great strides have been made in prosthetic, or artificial, devices. Emotional problems of the affected parents and children are great but are being overcome to a large extent in many families.
Mongolism	1 in 600. Women 25 years of age have about 1 chance in 2,000 of producing a mongoloid child. For women of 45 the average expectation is about 1 in 50.	Mongolism, mongoloid idiocy, or the Langdon-Down syndrome is characterized by short stature, slightly slanted eyes, and varying degrees of mental retardation.	All patients have chromosomal error. Causes can be hereditary or environmental. Whereas the normal human cell has 46 chromosomes, cells of those afflicted by this defect have 47 or the equivalent. No known cure, although IQ can be improved by special training.
Open spine (spina bifida)	Approximately 1 in every 500 births. It is more common among white children than among black. About half the patients are also victims of hydrocephaly.	Failure of the spine to close permits the protrusion of spinal cord or nerves. This often leads to total dysfunction of the legs, bladder, and rectum. Often the child has other serious defects.	Cause unknown. In some cases surgery in the first 3 months of child's life can either correct or arrest the condition so that other complications do not occur. In the more serious cases, several new surgical techniques are being used on the bladder, rectum, and spinal cord.

Continued

Type of defect	*Numbers affected annually*	*Description*	*Causes and treatment*
Phenylketonuria (PKU)	Approximately 1 in 10,000	Chemical imbalance, resulting in a form of mental deficiency, inherited from apparently normal parents, each of whom has one defective gene. The child appears normal at birth, but his mind stops developing during the first year of life. Retardation is severe. One-third never learn to walk, and two-thirds never learn to talk. The pigment of skin and hair is decreased.	Caused by a hereditary defect in an enzyme of the liver. In normal metabolism, phenylalanine, a compound making up one twentieth of the weight of proteins in the diet, is changed to tyrosine. In PKU the enzyme responsible for this step is inactive or absent, and phenylalanine accumulates. PKU can be detected between the fifth and seventh days of life. Treatment is dietary; specifically manufactured food with low-phenylalanine content is fed to the infant. The treatment does not cure retardation already present but can prevent it from developing. Therefore treatment should begin soon after birth. Some experiments show that after a few years PKU children can be fed normal diets.
Sickle cell trait	Low among white populations. Very high (about 40%) in black populations in Africa and high (10%) among American blacks.	When red blood cells of people with the sickle-cell trait are exposed to low-oxygen atmosphere, the cells lose normal form and become crescent or sickle shaped. When accompanied by severe anemia, the condition is usually fatal. The sickle-cell trait carries some immunity to malaria.	Hereditary condition. Severe anemia results if the child receives the abnormal trait from both parents.

AUTHOR INDEX

SUBJECT INDEX

D